Why Do You Need This New Edition?

If you're wondering why you should buy this new edition of *Living Democracy*, here are 10 good reasons!

1. **Key Objectives** included at the start of each chapter and repeated throughout each section help prepare you for learning and also reinforce the essential concepts covered in the chapter.

2. **"Participate and Prepare"** activities at the end of the book provide you with critical study tools for final exams. This section uses active learning techniques and other proven pedagogical apparatus to reinforce the learning objectives and provide multiple avenues for critical thinking. For each national edition chapter the following exercises are included: *Capture the Focus, Map the Story, Match the Concepts, Role Play,* and *What You Can Do.*

3. **Myth Exposed** feature in each chapter takes concepts commonly misunderstood by all Americans and reframes them to dispel myths or misconceptions. This feature encourages you to think critically about your role as a citizen and a voter, making you a more effective participant in the classroom, the community, and in politics.

4. **Key Concept Maps** at the end of each chapter help you to visualize disparate elements, think critically, and more fully understand the major concepts covered in each chapter.

5. **Exclusion Brainstorming** activities (*Identify the Concept That Doesn't Belong*) at the end of each section are based on active learning techniques used by the authors in their courses to promote student success.

6. **Timelines** now appear within selected chapters to prompt you to consider the interrelated forces that affect the democratic process at logical points in the text.

7. **Extensive updates** in each chapter help you understand how recent political changes are affecting your lives.

8. **The Judiciary chapter** has been moved to the end of Part Two to more closely reflect the way this course is generally taught and to provide you with the appropriate context for understanding the role of the courts in American government.

9. **New design** makes the "chunking" of material around the key learning objectives more visible to help you navigate the book more efficiently and to better process and retain information.

10. **MyPoliSciLab,** Pearson's streamlined and interactive Web site, offers an array of new multimedia activities that are integrated with this edition to make learning more effective.

S0-AGA-851

PEARSON

LIVING
DEMOCRACY

BRIEF CALIFORNIA EDITION

ELECTORAL COLLEGE VOTES IN THE 2008 ELECTION

THE UNITED STATES
A political map showing the number of electoral votes per state

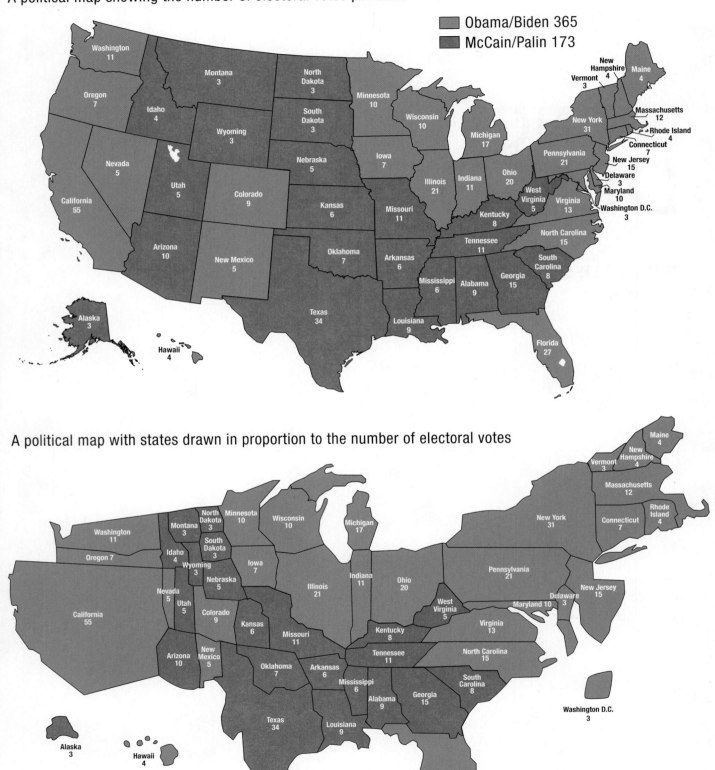

Obama/Biden 365
McCain/Palin 173

A political map with states drawn in proportion to the number of electoral votes

Obama victory
McCain victory

THIRD EDITION

LIVING
DEMOCRACY

BRIEF CALIFORNIA EDITION

Daniel M. Shea
Allegheny College

Joanne Connor Green
Texas Christian University

Christopher E. Smith
Michigan State University

Milton Clarke
Los Medanos College

Longman

Boston   Columbus   Indianapolis   New York   San Francisco   Upper Saddle River
Amsterdam   Cape Town   Dubai   London   Madrid   Milan   Munich   Paris   Montreal   Toronto   Delhi
Mexico City   Sao Paulo   Sydney   Hong Kong   Seoul   Singapore   Taipei   Tokyo

Executive Editor: Reid Hester
Editorial Assistant: Elizabeth Alimena
Director of Development: Meg Botteon
Development Editor: Lisa Sussman
Associate Development Editor: Donna Garnier
Marketing Manager: Lindsey Prudhomme
Production Manager: Eric Jorgensen
Project Coordination, Text Design, and Electronic Page Makeup: PreMedia Global, Inc.
Cover Design Manager: Wendy Ann Fredericks
Cover Photo: Bill Fredericks
Photo Researcher: Jody Potter
Senior Manufacturing Buyer: Dennis J. Para
Printer and Binder: Courier Kendallville
Cover Printer: Phoenix Color Corporation

For permission to use copyrighted material, grateful acknowledgment is made to the copyright holders on pages C–1—C–2, which are hereby made part of this copyright page.

Library of Congress Cataloging-in-Publication Data

Living democracy: brief California edition / Daniel M. Shea ... [et al.].—3rd ed.
  p. cm.
ISBN 978-0-205-82766-4
1. United States—Politics and government—Textbooks. 2. California—Politics and government—Textbooks. I. Shea, Daniel M. II. Title.
JK276.S34 2011e
320.473—dc22

2010046448

Copyright © 2011, © 2009, © 2007 by Pearson Education, Inc.

All rights reserved. No part of this publication may be reproduced, stored in a retrieval system, or transmitted, in any form or by any means, electronic, mechanical, photocopying, recording, or otherwise, without the prior written permission of the publisher. Printed in the United States.

To obtain permission to use material from this work, please submit a written request to Pearson Education, Inc., Permissions Department, 1900 E. Lake Ave., Glenview, IL 60025 or fax to (847) 486–3938 or e-mail glenview.permissions@pearsoned.com. For information regarding permissions, call (847) 486–2635.

3 4 5 6 7 8 9 10—CKV— 13 12

National Edition ISBN-13: 978-0-205-80671-3
National Edition ISBN-10:   0-205-80671-6
Texas Edition ISBN-13: 978-0-205-82593-6
Texas Edition ISBN-10:   0-205-82593-1
Alternate Edition ISBN-13: 978-0-205-82586-8
Alternate Edition ISBN-10:   0-205-82586-9
Brief National Edition ISBN-13: 978-0-205-80672-0
Brief National Edition ISBN-10:   0-205-80672-4
Brief Texas Edition ISBN-13: 978-0-205-82767-1
Brief Texas Edition ISBN-10:   0-205-82767-5
Brief California Edition ISBN-13: 978-0-205-82766-4
Brief California Edition ISBN-10:   0-205-82766-7

Longman
is an imprint of

PEARSON

www.pearsonhighered.com

To all first-time voters and newly active campaign
volunteers who helped to reinvigorate our democracy
by their participation in the 2008 and 2010 national elections

Contents

CHAPTER **8**
Bureaucracy 227

CHAPTER **9**
The Judiciary 259

CHAPTER **10**
Political Socialization and Public Opinion 295

CHAPTER **11**
The Politics of the Media   327

CHAPTER **12**
Interest Groups and Civic and Political Engagement   363

CHAPTER **13**
Elections and Political Parties in America   391

CHAPTER 17
Democracy, California Style
527

CHAPTER 18
The California State Legislature   559

CHAPTER 19
The California Executive and Bureaucracy   591

Appendices

Participate . . .

LIVING DEMOCRACY, Third Edition, fulfills an important need in today's classroom: It inspires students to want to learn about American government. With a passionate emphasis on political **participation,** the text provides students with a clear, engaging overview of the dynamics of the American political system and with knowledge they can use long after they leave the classroom.

Written with the belief that the American Government course is critically important for students—as well as for the long-term stability of the democratic process—*Living Democracy* helps students draw connections between course topics and current events and find a role for themselves in politics and government. The text's innovative approach to American government presents the dynamic nature of our country's democratic process while offering all the material found in a comprehensive, traditionally organized text.

Now in its third edition, *Living Democracy* builds on its message of participation with new features, each designed to deepen long-term comprehension. An **innovative pedagogical system** designed around **Key Objectives** and based on cognitive psychology provides an easy-to-follow chapter organization that breaks content into more manageable and self-contained "chunks." **Myth Exposed** takes concepts commonly misunderstood by students and reframes them, dispelling myths or misconceptions. This feature is based on the premise that students must be accurately informed to participate effectively. Novel **self-assessment opportunities,** also based on proven learning techniques, help students participate more fully in their own learning process. **Key Concept Maps** in the conclusion of each chapter help all students to visually pull together disparate elements, think critically, and more fully understand the major concepts covered in each chapter. Finally, a new **Participate and Prepare** section at the end of the book provides students with a critical study tool for final exams. This section uses active learning techniques and other pedagogical apparatus to reinforce the learning objectives, provide multiple avenues for critical thinking, and prepare students to participate outside of the classroom.

Living Democracy is the American government text that engages students, enriches their understanding of government, and inspires them to be active participants in their daily lives.

New to the Third Edition

Living Democracy has been substantially updated and revised throughout. What follows are just some of the changes that are new to the third edition.

CHAPTER **1** (American Government: Democracy in Action) opens with a new vignette examining the important role played by young citizens in the 2008 presidential election and the ramifications of signs from 2009 and 2010 that young adults are again moving to the political sidelines. This chapter also includes a new Pathways of Action on Powershift '09, and an updated Timeline that deals with the issue of immigration. This chapter ends with an examination of how average citizens can shape the course of government in a democracy.

CHAPTER **2** (Early Governance and the Constitutional Framework) includes a new vignette dealing with a surprising and impactful decision made by Lewis and Clark on their expedition to America. This chapter also includes a new Pathways of Change from Around the World dealing with a democratic uprising in Indonesia, and it ends with a close look at how early events led to the creation of a democracy in the United States.

CHAPTER **3** (Federalism) begins with a look at how federalism impacted the government's response to the swine flu (H1N1) health emergency. This chapter also includes a new Student Profile on the revitalization of a 1960s organization (Students for a Democratic Society), a streamlined discussion of cooperative and creative federalism, and a look at how the passage of recent laws related to the economy, finance, and healthcare have impacted federalism. This chapter concludes with a close examination of Hurricane Katrina, and how federalism affected the government's response.

CHAPTER **4** (Civil Liberties) opens with a new vignette on a controversial decision by the Supreme Court that the due process clause does not provide a right to retest scientific evidence, even when newer testing methods might prove an individual's innocence. The chapter also includes new information on controversial civil liberties issues decided by the Supreme Court in its 2009-2010 term, a new Pathways of Action on the right to own guns, and a revised Timeline dealing with capital punishment and the courts. This chapter concludes with a look at how judges' interpretations of the Constitution limit the power of government.

CHAPTER **5** (Civil Rights) This chapter includes a new Pathways of Action dealing with a female high school student's challenge to an all-male military institute in Virginia, a new Student Profile on a group of college students' challenge to voting registration rules, and a revised Timeline on same-sex marriage. This chapter ends with an exploration of how the pathways of action shaped the civil rights movement.

CHAPTER **6** (Congress) open with a new vignette comparing the congressional midterm elections of 2010 with those of 2004. The chapter also includes a streamlined and updated discussion of how a bill becomes a law, the results and ramifications of the 2010 congressional contests, a new Pathways of Action on the ousting of committee chair John Dingell, a new student profile on young members of Congress, and a new Pathways of Change from Around the World on a British Parliament corruption scandal. The chapter concludes with a look at how the organization of Congress both enhances and inhibits the legislative process.

CHAPTER **7** (The Presidency) examines the first two years of Obama's presidency. The chapter also includes a new Student Profile on working at the White House, a new Timeline dealing with the battle over healthcare reform, a new Pathways of Change from Around the World on Liberia's first elected female head of state, and a deeper look at key scholarly perspectives on executive powers. The chapter concludes with an examination of how presidential powers have evolved since the adoption of the Constitution.

CHAPTER **8** (Bureaucracy) opens with a new vignette on the BP oil spill and the expectations that Americans

have of federal agencies. The chapter also includes updated data on federal agencies throughout, and an in-depth look at the structure of the Department of Homeland Security. This chapter ends with an exploration of how the elements of the bureaucracy both strengthen and weaken its effectiveness.

CHAPTER **9** (The Judiciary) includes coverage of the nomination and confirmation of both Sonia Sotomayor and Elena Kagan to the nation's highest court, as well as information on the Supreme Court's 2009-2010 term. This chapter opens with a look at the 2009 case of *Safford Unified School District* v. *Redding* and what it shows about the power of judges to interpret the U.S. Constitution. The chapter also includes a new Student Profile on how student editors of a college newspaper fought their administration on First Amendment grounds. The chapter concludes with an examination of how politics affects the selection of Supreme Court Justices.

CHAPTER **10** (Political Socialization and Public Opinion) opens with a new vignette on the appointment of a transgendered person to a high-profile position in the Commerce Department and whether this and the election of openly homosexual members of Congress signals a change in the public's opinion regarding sexuality, or whether these are isolated events. This chapter also includes updated data on trends in political ideology, the percentage of Americans favoring particular public policies, and a new Pathways of Action on celebrities and global activism. The chapter ends with a look at how the way people acquire and maintain their political values and beliefs has changed.

CHAPTER **11** (The Politics of the Media) includes a new section on citizen journalism and an updated discussion of the strategic use of leaks, including the controversy surrounding the Web site WikiLeaks in their efforts to expose governmental actions and promote transparency. This chapter ends with an examination of how the media impact our political system.

CHAPTER **12** (Interest Groups and Civic and Political Engagement) presents a streamlined organization and discussion of interest groups and civic and political engagement. The chapter opens with a new vignette on the roots of the Tea Party Movement and also includes a new Student Profile on Tim Tebow's relationship with the Christian organization Focus on the Family. The chapter concludes with a look at how interest groups mobilize the masses.

CHAPTER **13** (Elections and Political Parties in America) offers a new vignette on Republican Scott Brown's surprising win in a Massachusetts special election. The chapter also includes a new Pathways of Action on close elections, a new Pathways of Change from Around the World on the subject of Iran's contentious 2009 election, and an updated discussion of the role of money in elections, including the Supreme Court's controversial 2010 decision in *Citizens United* v. *Federal Elections Commission*. The chapter concludes with an examination of how aspects of the electoral process influence the democratic character of our political system.

CHAPTER **14** (The Policy Process and Economic Policy) features a revised and updated Timeline on the environmental movement, a new Pathways of Action on FocusDriven, a new Student Profile on one student's efforts to establish an organization that promotes social entrepreneurship by young people, and a discussion of President Obama's proposed 2011 budget. This chapter concludes with an exploration of how individuals can influence the policy-making process.

CHAPTER **15** (Foreign and National Security Policy) begins with an updated and reorganized section on the competing principles of American foreign policy and the conflicting evaluations of the wars in Iraq and Afghanistan. The chapter also features a new Pathways of Action on U2's Bono and his organization ONE, and coverage of the removal of General Stanley McChrystal as head of operations in Afghanistan. The chapter concludes with an examination of how foreign policy and domestic policy are linked.

CHAPTER **16** (California: Historical Perspective) opens with a new vignette on the relationship between California state government and the federal government. The chapter concludes with an examina-

tion of how key events in California's past have shaped its politics.

CHAPTER **17** (Democracy, California Style) begins with a new vignette on the outcome of the 2010 elections including the election of Jerry Brown as governor and Propositions 22 and 25, which affect the use of funds earmarked for local governments and passage of the state's budget. The chapter also features a new Pathways of Action on California's controversial campaign finance reform law and a revised and updated section on unconventional political participation. The chapter ends with a look at how the avenues of direct democracy have impacted California state government.

CHAPTER **18** (The California State Legislature) opens with a new vignette on California's Global Warming Solutions Act. The chapter also includes a new Pathways of Action on how lobbying and the confirmation process collide in the state senate and updated information on the importance of legislative staff in the legislative committee system. The chapter concludes with an examination of how historic events have impacted the professional growth of the state legislature.

CHAPTER **19** (The California Executive and Bureaucracy) begins with a new vignette dealing with California's rating by the *Government Performance Project*. The chapter also features a new Pathways of Action on racial profiling and the California Highway Patrol and an updated discussion of the role of the state treasurer. The chapter ends with an exploration of how the powers of the California governor compare with those of the president of the United States.

CHAPTER **20** (The California Judiciary) opens with a new vignette on the subject of *Perry et al* v. *Schwarzenegger*, the controversial same-sex marriage case filed in response to the passage of Proposition 8. This chapter also includes a revised Pathways of Action on exonerations in California and an updated section on trends in the California judicial system. The chapter concludes with a look at how California laws and official guidelines empower most residents of the state.

CHAPTER **21** (Local Government in California) includes new information on planning commissions, a new Pathways of Action on California citizens' successful efforts to vote down Proposition 16, which would have placed restrictions on public power, and new information on California's unsuccessful bid for the federal government's Race to the Top funding awards. The chapter ends with an examination of how local governments maintain standard levels of services amid budgetary reductions.

CHAPTER **22** (California Fiscal Policy) begins with a new vignette on CalWORKs, California's version of the Temporary Assistance to Needy Families Act. The chapter also discusses the changes to the state's budgetary process as a result of the passage of Proposition 25 in the 2010 elections, and it includes a new Pathways of Action on the efforts of consumer groups and state officials to reverse a health insurance rate hike. The chapter concludes with a look at how the policies and actions of the state government affect the California economy.

Innovative Pedagogy . . .

Informed by cognitive psychology and proven learning concepts, *Living Democracy*, Third Edition, is breaking new ground in American Government texts. The "chunking" of content in each chapter promotes easier retention and recall of information. The design presents the material in an organized way and in discrete, self-contained spreads to help you absorb and process information on each topic. With learning objectives and review pedagogy for each section of each chapter, this edition provides an excellent and unique set of tools for learning.

American Government: Democracy in Action

CHAPTER 1

KEY OBJECTIVES

After completing this chapter, you should be prepared to:

1.1 Illustrate how citizens participate in a democracy and why this is important.

1.2 Relate the themes of this book to American politics today.

1.3 Outline the various "pathways" of involvement in our political system.

1.4 Analyze the forces of stability in American politics.

Each chapter begins with a list of **Key Objectives** that enumerate the main concepts that will be covered in each section. These key objectives serve as a key navigational device to help prime you for learning and also reinforce the key concepts covered in the chapter.

It obviously can't be argued that young voters alone elected Barack Obama president in 2008, but it seems rather clear that young Americans played a pivotal role. Obama netted a whopping 68 percent of the vote from those under 30—likely the largest vote share of an age group that any candidate has ever received. In addition, some 43 percent of 18- to 29-year-olds were first-time voters in 2008. This compares to just 11 percent for all voters. Whatever the cause of the participation, 2008 demonstrated that young Americans, long civically involved, can channel their interests into *political* action, if they are motivated to do so.

However, there is disturbing evidence that young people may once again be tuning out. One of the frustrations of the Obama administration during the first year was the lackluster response of young Americans to the ongoing policy debates—especially over health care reform. A 2009 study by the Pew

Can average citizens play a meaningful role in American politics?

2008 to 10 percent in 2009. That trend continued in the 2010 midterm election, which witnessed very meager young voter turnout.

Why are young Americans moving to the sidelines? Don't they understand their power and their potential to shape the outcome of elections and policy? For those unaccustomed to the difficulties of policymaking in a highly polarized political climate, the value of an electoral win might seem trivial. Great! We won . . . now where's all that change? Discussion of our nation's history of incremental change or the theoretical values of constitutional obstruction would likely fall on deaf ears.

We know young Americans are attracted to volunteer service out of compassion and a desire to make a difference in their communities and other people's lives. By lending a hand at soup kitchens, literacy programs, youth projects, elderly homes, as well as with untold other community endeavors, these committed individuals strive to make their world a better place. They are turned off by conflict, ego, and gridlock. Should we care about a generation that turns its back on politics—that leaves the heavy lifting of policy development to others? Perhaps by the end of this book you will agree that our nation cannot live up to its potential as a democracy when an entire generation sits on the sidelines. Politics is not for the faint of heart, but it is also not for "others."

---

4 CHAPTER 1 AMERICAN GOVERNMENT: DEMOCRACY IN ACTION

Resource Center
• Glossary
• Vocabulary Example
• Connect the Link

■ **Politics:** The process by which the actions of government are determined.

EXAMPLE: *By appealing to members of the city council to change the new housing ordinance, several students decided to roll up their sleeves and become engaged in local politics.*

It's Your Government

1.1 Illustrate how citizens participate in a democracy and why this is important.

(pages 4–7)

On some level, everyone knows that government affects our lives. We must obey laws created by government. We pay taxes to support the government. We make use of government services, ranging from police protection to student loans. It is easy, however, to see government as a distant entity that imposes its will on us. It provides benefits and protections, such as schools, roads, and fire departments. But it also limits our choices by telling us how fast we can drive and how old we must be to get married, purchase alcoholic beverages, and vote.

Would your view of government change if a new law dramatically affected your choices, plans, or expectations? Imagine that you and your four best friends decide to rent a house together for the next academic year. You find a five-bedroom, furnished house near campus that is owned by a friendly landlord. Then, you sign a lease and put down your deposit. During the summer, however, the landlord sends you a letter informing you that two of your friends will need to find someplace else to live. The city council has passed a new ordinance—the kind of law produced by local governments—declaring that not more than three unrelated people may live

councils. These activities, *voting* and *elections,* are the most familiar forms of citizen participation in a democracy.

• You could organize your friends to contact members of the city council asking them to change the restrictive new law. You could also go to city council meetings and voice your opposition to the law. We often characterize these activities as *lobbying* lawmakers in order to pressure or persuade them to make specific decisions.

• You could talk to the local landlords' association about whether it might file a lawsuit challenging the ordinance on the grounds that it improperly interferes with the landlords' right to decide how to use their private property. You might talk to an attorney yourself about whether, under the laws of your state, a new ordinance can override the rental lease agreement that you and your friends had already signed. If the new ordinance violates other existing laws, then taking the issue to court by filing lawsuits—a process known as *litigation*—may provide the means for a lawyer to persuade a judge to invalidate the city council's action.

• You could write articles in the college newspaper or blog about the new ordinance to inform other students about the effect of the law on their off-campus housing choices. You could publicize and sponsor meetings in order to organize *grassroots activities,* such as marches, sit-ins, or other forms of nonviolent protests. These actions would draw news media attention and put pressure on city officials to reconsider their decision.

Each section of a chapter begins on the top of a new left-hand page and includes the **Key Objective** to keep in mind as you read the section. Definitions of important **Key Terms** appear in the top margin, along with an illustrative example or explanation to fully clarify the significance of the term in context.

6 CHAPTER 1 AMERICAN GOVERNMENT: DEMOCRACY IN ACTION

CONNECT THE LINK
(Chapter 2, pages 34–35) How does one classify different types of government?

■ **Democracy:** A political system in w
have a chance to play a role in shaping gov
and are afforded basic rights and liberties.

distant, remote entity; instead, it comprises the rules and structures that shape our lives every day. Second, while dramatic
change might not occur quickly, American history is filled with
examples of how average citizens rolled up their sleeves and
changed the course of government. This book highlights several

ernmer
action.
totalita
hold all
U

Connect the LINK features in the top margin help you to make connections about particular topics from one chapter to another.

It's Your Government

1.1 Illustrate how citizens participate in a democracy and why this is important.

PRACTICE QUIZ: UNDERSTAND AND APPLY

1. According to the Map of Freedom in Figure 1.1, most of the continent of Asia is labeled
   a. free.
   b. partly free.
   c. not free.
   d. failed states.

2. Unlike national politics, when it comes to shaping local public policies there are very few options for involvement.
   a. true
   b. false

3. Much of political action is designed to affect
   a. public policy.
   b. who serves in government.
   c. the powers government has.
   d. all of the above.

ANALYZE

1. What are some of the distinguishing features of a democracy? Can a system be called democratic if it holds fair elections?

2. What are some aspects of democratic government that are unique to the United States?

3. What are some aspects of our system of government that do not seem especially democratic?

IDENTIFY THE CONCEPT THAT DOESN'T BELONG

   a. Knowledge and awareness
   b. Participation
   c. Responsive leaders
   d. Fixed policies
   e. Engaged youth

1.1

CONCLUSION **CHAPTER 1** **25**

KEY CONCEPT MAP   How do average citizens shape the course of government in a democracy?

Self-assessment tools throughout each chapter help you review material as you work through the text. Each section concludes with a **Practice Quiz: Understand and Apply, Analyze** (critical thinking questions), and **Identify the Concept That Doesn't Belong** (an exclusion brainstorming exercise based on active learning techniques).

Elections

Strengths
Elections are generally egalitarian; everyone's vote is counted equally, so the "majority will" can be harnessed to create change.

Weaknesses
Hefty resources shape the outcome; the "majority will" can sometimes stifle democratic change.

Critical Thinking Question
Given the "checks and balances" inherent in the structure of government, how can we expect the election of a particular leader, such as a new president or governor, to shape the outcome of public policy?

Courts

Strengths
Courts are the protectors of rights and liberties for all citizens; decisions can overrule the will of the majority when necessary.

Weaknesses
Change can come about slowly; litigation can be expensive.

Critical Thinking Question
How democratic can the court pathway be when federal judges (and many state judges) are appointed and serve for life?

Lobbying

Strengths
Big change can occur quickly behind the scenes.

Weaknesses
Effective lobbying often entails "connections," which requires big resources.

Critical Thinking Question
Many are critical of "special interest lobbying," but what's wrong with citizens promoting their own interests?

Grassroots Mobilization

Criminals Love Gun Control
Unarmed Citizens are Their Goal

Strengths
Grassroots efforts can be effective at getting decision makers to pay attention to an issue.

Weaknesses
Changes are seldom effective immediately; organizational skill, careful planning, and truly committed activists are necessary.

Critical Thinking Question
Can you think of a time in American history when policy makers turned a deaf ear to massive public demonstrations?

Cultural Change

Strengths
Cultural change can involve a variety of issues, particularly those that are at first opposed by the majority.

Weaknesses
Change takes a long time to be effective and is by no means certain.

Critical Thinking Question
How does popular culture, such as music, television, and sports, ultimately shape public policy?

Many Americans believe they can't play a meaningful role in politics. While it is true that change can sometimes come slowly, and that certain citizens have more resources than others, our history also suggests that steadfast, determined individuals and groups can make a big difference by using the five pathways of change: elections, courts, lobbying, grassroots mobilization, and cultural change. —*Will any of these pathways become more or less influential in the digital age? Why or why not?*

Each chapter includes a **Key Concept Map** within the Conclusion that visually illustrates a "How" question central to the topic of the chapter. Looking at how things actually unfold provides you with the opportunity to think critically about the process and about what would happen if something in the process changed. Each map includes an explanatory caption and critical thinking questions.

A **Review of Key Objectives** section appears at the end of each chapter that recaps the information in each topic section along with **Key Terms** and **Critical Thinking Questions** (to help you consider the material in a more conceptual way) as well as **Internet Resources** and **Additional Reading**.

Review of Key Objectives

It's Your Government

1.1 Illustrate how citizens participate in a democracy and why this is important.

(pages 4–7)

Many Americans, especially young Americans, believe "government" and "politics" are distant, beyond their immediate world. In reality, government is around us; it shapes our lives in important ways every hour of every day. That is why it is particularly important for citizens in a democracy to become involved. Government matters, and you can make a difference.

KEY TERMS

Politics 4
~~Public Policy 4~~

Themes of This Book

1.2 Relate the themes of this book to American politics today.

(pages 8–17)

There are numerous ways to investigate and explore our political system. This book focuses on three essential themes. First, in a democracy, it's essential that citizens become participants and not merely spectators of the political process. Second, while many in the United States believe their options for effective involvement are limited, there are numerous pathways for change. Indeed, throughout American history, different political actors have used different pathways to achieve their goals. Finally, issues of diversity have and will continue to shape the process and outcome of our political system. America's diversity contributes to most political controversies, while at the same time adding complexity to the mix of actors seeking to affect change.

KEY TERMS

Pathways of Action 10
Boycott 13

CRITICAL THINKING QUESTIONS

1. Why do political activists use different pathways for their involvement? What are the factors that shape the choice of which route to use? Which of these factors is most important, in your view?
2. In what ways has diversity shaped the nature of politics in the United States? Do you see additional changes in the years ahead?

INTERNET RESOURCES

To read about one organization's strategies for using various pathways to affect government policy concerning firearms, see the Web site of the National Rifle Association at http://www.nra.org

Another good example of a powerful political action organization is the AARP, a massive, nationwide unit that works to protect the interests of older Americans: http://www.aarp.org/

There are numerous youth and student political action organizations. To read about the Student Environmental Action Coalition, see http://www.seac.org/

ADDITIONAL READING

Frantzich, Stephen F. *Citizen Democracy: Political Activism in a Cyn-*

---

28 CHAPTER 1 AMERICAN GOVERNMENT: DEMOCRACY IN ACTION

Chapter Review   Test Your Knowledge

1. Which of the following best describes the activities of government officials and citizens who intend to affect the structure, authority, and actions of government?
   a. propaganda
   b. discourse
   c. the public's right to know
   d. politics

2. When a government decides what citizens can and cannot do, it is
   a. engaging in public discourse.
   b. making public policy.
   c. influencing public opinion.
   d. bringing public awareness.

3. *Pathways of action* refers to
   a. the organizational channels of government bureaucracy.
   b. the connections among the various branches of government.
   c. the activities, institutions, and decision points that affect public policy.
   d. the confidential relationships between government officials.

4. The selection of leaders by popular vote, and holding those leaders accountable for their deci...

9. Which of the following is an example of the grassroots mobilization pathway?
   a. e-mailing your state legislators to convince them to vote for your position on an upcoming bill
   b. organizing a boycott against dangerous toys
   c. sending a check to a candidate to help secure her election
   d. using desktop publishing to create a political pamphlet

10. Citizens will be most successful in implementing desired change in government if they focus on a single pathway to action.
    a. true
    b. false

11. Litigants in the Supreme Court abortion case *Roe* v. *Wade* successfully used which of the following pathways of action?
    a. court
    b. grassroots mobilization
    c. lobbying
    d. a, b, and c

12. A broadly accepted political and economic framework, powerful political culture, and a variety of ways to seek political change are all measures of a government's

icans are indifferent... have suggested... ...me time, some...those with the... Does this make... ...y the people"... ...engage in the... ...nocracy? Does... ...erence is a sign...

...and other coun-...idual freedom,...http://www...ates and other...he Web site of...

Halperin, Morton, Joseph T. Siegle, and Michael M. Weinstein. *The Democracy Advantage: How Democracies Promote Prosperity*

Each chapter concludes with a **Test Your Knowledge** exam that offers twenty multiple-choice questions (and answer keys in the back of the book) so that you can check your progress.

Participate and Prepare

CHAPTER **1**
American Government: Democracy in Action

CAPTURE THE FOCUS: KEY OBJECTIVES

Review these learning objectives highlighted throughout the introductory chapter:

1.1 Illustrate how citizens participate in a democracy and why this is important.

1.2 Relate the themes of this book to American politics today.

1.3 Outline the various "pathways" of involvement in our political system.

1.4 Analyze the forces of stability in American politics.

1. Write a brief paragraph in response to each of the learning objectives. Use your responses as a study aid for the chapter.

Match the Concepts

Match the statement to the concept with which i... closely related.

1. "When I was first elected to Congress I thought g... would somehow win the day. Boy was I naive!"
2. "You mean to say that I can go to war for my co... I can't have a beer with my pals because I'm not...
3. "The surest way to change the course of governm... change the personnel of government."
4. "Clearly, it is an important department of gover... terms of protecting the individual liberties of the...
5. "As you dig deeper into the national charact... Americans, you see that they have sought the... everything in this world only as it relates to the... this single question: how much money will it bri...
6. "Most realize that if you can win the hearts and... average citizens, policy change will follow."
7. "Four score and seven years ago our fathers brou... upon this continent, a new nation, conceived in Li... dedicated to the proposition that all men are creat...
8. "Give me your tired, your poor, your huddle... yearning to be free."

A **Participate and Prepare** section at the end of the book uses active learning techniques and other pedagogical apparatus to reinforce the **Key Objectives** and provide you with a critical study tool for final exams.

A Theme of Participation . . .

Living Democracy includes a variety of engaging features that foster in-class participation and discussion. Additionally, the book offers activities and features that encourage you to apply key concepts outside the classroom and participate in our political system.

suggesting that the system itself should be changed.

American political culture, as noted by the Swedish social scientist Gunnar Myrdal (GUN-er MEER–dahl) in 1944, is "the most explicitly expressed system of general ideals" of any country in the West[7]—so much so that he saw fit to call our belief system the "American Creed." At least in the abstract, Americans embrace the concepts of "freedom," "equality," "liberty," "majority will," "religious freedom," and "due process under the law." According to Myrdal, "Schools teach the principles of the Creed; the churches preach them; the courts hand down judgment in their terms."[8] According to historian Arthur Schlesinger, Jr., "Myrdal saw the Creed as the bond that links all Americans, including nonwhite minorities, and as the spur forever goading Americans to live up to their principles."[9] Yale University political scientist Robert Dahl echoed this idea a few decades later when he called our set of beliefs the "democratic creed." He wrote, "The common view seems to be that our system is not only democratic but is perhaps the most perfect expression of democracy that exists anywhere. . . . To reject the democratic creed is in effect to refuse to be American."[10]

There are many things that define the American Creed, many of which will be discussed in later chapters. The important point here is to understand that the United States possesses a powerful political culture that is clearly defined and long-lasting. The historical national consensus on political values and democratic institutions helped create stability during times of profound social change. As waves of change transformed the workplace, home life, leisure patterns, and intellectual fabric of

NUMEROUS AVENUES OF CHANGE Two necessary conditions for any country's political stability are broad popular acceptance of its government and economic system and a clearly defined political culture. But they do not guarantee stability. For a democratic system to remain stable, its citizens must believe that they can influence the outcome of government activity. The design and operation of government must permit popular participation. In addition, the political culture and laws must encourage civic involvement and protect activists from being silenced either by the government or by majority opinion. There must also be a variety of ways to achieve desired ends. Severe limitations on citizen participation and influence can lead to frustration, cynicism, and in the end, conflict and potential upheaval. Stated a bit differently, stability in a democratic regime springs from a system that allows participation, a culture that promotes involvement, and a set of options (or, shall we say, "pathways") to help redirect public policy.

STUDENT profile

Like most young Americans, Nick Anderson and Ana Slavin spend a lot of time on social networking sites. Facebook and MySpace are entertaining, a way to make social connections, but can they also be harnessed to do good work?

During a trip to South Africa in 2005, Anderson was horrified by the plight of people in the Darfur region of western Sudan. For nearly a decade, Arab militias backed by the Sudanese government had waged a genocidal war on tribes in the region, killing upward of 300,000 men, women, and

Student Profiles showcase the actions and accomplishments of young people who have become active in American politics or engaged in making changes in public life. This feature promotes awareness of your potential to be part of the process.

TIMELINE The Immigration Debate

● COURTS   ● CULTURAL CHANGE   ● ELECTIONS   ● GRASSROOTS MOBILIZATION   ● LOBBYING DECISION-MAKERS

Before 1882, anyone who wished to live in the United States could. Things have changed dramatically since that time. Some of the more controversial issues facing our government today include who should be allowed to immigrate to our country, what we should do to secure our borders, and what should be done with immigrants illegally residing in the country. People on both sides of this debate have increasingly turned to mass protest to express their positions, and individual states have begun passing their own immigration laws. The Pew Hispanic Center estimates the number of illegal immigrants in the United States to be just under 12 million.

Essay Questions

1. Many proposals for immigration reform have been debated in recent years. Write an essay in which you critically examine the various proposals presented, being certain to indicate which proposal(s) you think would be most effective in addressing illegal immigration.
2. Many states confront the difficult repercussions of illegal immigration, and yet the Constitution stipulates that the federal government is charged with regulating immigration. Should states have the right to adopt their own immigration laws when they believe the federal government is not acting accordingly?

PRO IMMIGRATION

1986 Immigration Reform and Control Act allows illegal aliens living in America continuously since January 1, 1982 to apply for legal status; the act also forbids the hiring of illegal aliens, outlines penalties for lack of compliance, and raises annual immigration ceiling to 540,000.

1990 Immigration Act sets immigration quotas at 700,000 annually for the next 3 years and 675,000 for every year thereafter; eliminates denial of admittance to the U.S. on the basis of individual's beliefs, statements, or associations.

1965 | 1977–78 | 1980–86 | 1990 | 1996

ANTI IMMIGRATION

1965 Immigration Act of 1965 Major reform in immigration policy. Sets overall limit of 170,000 immigrants from the Eastern Hemisphere and 120,000 from the Western Hemisphere.

1977 Immigration and Nationality Act of 1965 Limits immigration to 290,000 worldwide with no more than 20,000 coming from any one country.

1978 John H. Tanton founds the Federation for American Immigration Reform, an anti-immigration group.

1980 Refugees Act distinguishes refugees from other immigrants and limits the worldwide immigration quota to 270,000.

CLOSE THE BORDER

1996 Immigration Act doubles Border Patrol to 10,000 agents over 5 years; also calls for fences to be built at key points on the America-Mexico border; approves a program to check job applicants' immigration status.

1996 President Clinton signs a bill into law cutting numerous social programs for both legal and illegal immigrants in the interest of welfare reform.

Timelines offer in-depth, photographic presentations of core policy issues. These timelines, located in selected chapters, combine photographs and text to present a visually rich treatment of a specific, core policy issue. Provocative essay questions prompt you to consider the interrelated forces that affect the democratic process.

Vietnam War, individuals concerned about restrictive immigration policies, and others have organized protest marches as a means to attract public attention and pressure the government to change laws and policies. These actions are seldom instantly successful, but over time, they may draw more and more supporters until elected officials begin to reconsider past decisions. Successful grassroots mobilization requires organizational skill, publicity, careful planning, and a solid core of committed activists who are willing to take public actions in support of their cause.

CULTURAL CHANGE PATHWAY The cultural change pathway is an indirect approach to influencing government. It is a long-term strategy that requires persistence and patience. Through this approach, individuals and organized groups attempt to change the hearts and minds of their fellow citizens. By educating the public about issues and publicizing important events, the dominant values of society may change over time. This can lead to changes in law and policy as newly elected officials bring the new values into government with them.

14

Living Democracy provides you with the means—and the inspiration—to participate directly in the political process. Recurring *Pathways* features help you to understand the dynamic nature of the American political system—and your ability to make a difference.

Pathways of Change from Around the World sections offer a comparative perspective by spotlighting stories of political action by young persons in different parts of the world.

---

all levels of government—even president and vice president, as demonstrated in the 2008 election. Law and policy changed through the long-term effort to change the culture and values of American society.

Individuals and groups can use the cultural change pathway to try to affect changes in laws and policies related to a variety of issues, including abortion, the death penalty, and environmental protection. For people who seek to change society's values, the ultimate outcome of the cultural change pathway can be quite uncertain. Indeed, for some issues, change may occur long after the passing of the people who initiated the efforts to alter public opinion and social values. And sometimes change never comes.

PATHWAYS of change from around the world

Would you risk your future career defending a television station? In May 2007, Venezuelan President Hugo Chavez moved to shut down one of the country's most popular television stations, Radio Caracas Television International (RCTV). Chavez claimed that the station had played a key role in an effort to overthrow the government. Yet RCTV was Venezuela's most popular station, especially with younger citizens, and many saw the move as an attempt to limit criticism of Chavez and his government.

In response, tens of thousands of Venezuelan students took to the streets. They staged massive demonstrations—marches, rallies, sit-ins, and more. For weeks, university exams were put off, and classes were rescheduled. Political science major Ana Cristina Garanton, who took part in the protests, said the battle was for more than a television station: "We are fighting for the rights we should have as students so that when I graduate I can pursue any career without being discriminated against for political reasons. Our parents will one day leave the country to us. And it is up to us, the young people, to take the reins of the country."

The students understood the dangers of their activism, which included the real possibility of being put on a government bla...

Diversity in American Society

This book's third theme is the impact of diversity on American government and on the laws and policies that government produces. Many of the issues facing American government are products of the country's history, and many policy issues have their roots in America's history of race-based slavery. Slavery and its consequences, including blatant discrimination against African Americans, which persisted until the 1970s, are at the heart of such difficult contemporary problems as chronic poverty, decaying urban neighborhoods, disproportionate minority unemployment rates, and lingering racial and ethnic hostility and mistrust.

Cultural change eventually created a widespread consensus in American society about the need to eliminate overt racial discrimination. Laws and policies, such as the Civil Rights Act of 1964 and the Voting Rights Act of 1965, were enacted in the second half of the twentieth century to prohibit many forms of discrimination that had been endorsed and enforced by various levels of government. However, there is no consensus on how to address other problems arising out of the legacy of slavery and racial discrimination. Attempts to apply specific remedies, such as court-ordered busing to achieve public school desegregation, affirmative action programs to increase minority enrollment in colleges and universities, and programs to diversify government employment and contract opportunities have all caused bitter debate and political conflict.

Immigration is another challenging policy controversy related to the nation's diversity. Contemporary debates about immigration often focus on undocumented workers arriving from Mexico and other countries in violation of American law. Some Americans want stronger measures to prevent illegal immigration, but many businesses hire undocumented workers because they often work for less money than U.S. citizens. At the same time, Latinos in the United States have grown in numbers. In 2004, Latinos became the nation's largest minority group. As noted in Table 1.2, the Hispanic population in the United States is expected to double in the next few decades. Hispanics have also expanded their political power...

ELECTIONS PATHWAY American government is based on representative democracy, in which voters elect leaders and then hold those leaders accountable for the decisions they make about law and public policy. If the voters disagree with the decisions that leaders make, the voters can elect different leaders in the next election. Because government leaders in a democracy are usually concerned about maintaining public support in order to gain reelection, they feel pressured to listen to the public and to please a majority of the voters with their actions. Even officials who do not plan to run for reelection or who have served the maximum number of terms the law permits, such as a president who has been elected to a second, four-year term, demonstrate their concern for voters' preferences, because they want to help the election chances of other members of their political party.

A variety of activities, actors, and institutions are involved in the elections pathway. For example, political parties organize like-minded individuals into groups that can plan strategies for winning elections, raise money, and provide public information, to help elect leaders who share the party's specific values and policy preferences. Activities in the elections pathway include voter registration drives, fundraising, political campaigning, and each individual voter's action in casting a ballot.

LOBBYING PATHWAY Legislatures are the central law-making bodies at the national, state, and local levels of government. At the national level, the federal legislature is Congress. States also have their own legislatures, and local legislatures include city councils, county commissions, and village boards. Legislatures are made up of elected representatives who must regularly face the voters in elections. Unlike the elections pathway (the mechanisms by which candidates are chosen to fill offices), the lobbying pathway involves attempting to influence the activities, actors, and institutions of government by supplying information, persuasion, or political pressure. Lobbying activities target legislatures and executive officials, such as presidents and governors, as well as the bureaucrats who staff government agencies.

In the lobbying pathway, individuals and organized groups present information and persuasive arguments to government officials. The aim is to convince these decision makers either to support specific proposed laws, to...

by financial contributions to the reelection campaigns of legislators or elected executives.

Lobbying, in the form of information and persuasion, can also be directed at permanent employees in government agencies who have the authority to create government regulations, such as rules concerning the environment, business practices, and consumer products. Effective lobbying typically requires money, time, and other resources, such as a large organizational membership to flood officials' offices with letters and e-mails, or personal relationships between lobbyists and government officials, as when interest groups hire former members of Congress to represent them in presenting information and arguments. Under the right circumstances, people who lack resources may effectively influence government by getting the attention of key officials. For example, research has shown that letters, emails and phone calls from ordinary citizens are an important source of ideas for new laws and policies.[1]

PATHWAYS of action

Powershift '09

Nearly 12,000 students at a single conference? Seriously?

In late February 2009, students and young activists from around the nation and Canada convened in Washington D.C. for a three-day conference—an event dubbed *Powershift '09*. Sponsored by the Energy Action Coalition, the event became the largest youth-centered global warming conference ever held. The goals of the event were to share information about the growing threat of climate change, help committed young citizens become effective political advocates, and lobby lawmakers for immediate change.

"We want[ed] to make sure our new president and new Congress pass bold federal energy and climate legislation . . . ," noted Brianna Cayo Cotter, one of the event organizers. "[Leaders] understand that young voters were a key to this 2008 election. We have come of age as a powerful voting constituency."

Dozens of organizers, policy experts, celebrities and public officials addressed the gathering, including House Speaker Nancy Pelosi, who has called young global warming activists the "mag-

---

Pathways of Action explain how an individual or a group has influenced government. These stories help you to understand how average citizens have affected change—and how you might, too.

Myth Exposed feature in each chapter takes concepts commonly misunderstood by all Americans and reframes them to dispel myths or misconceptions. This feature encourages you to think critically about your role as a citizen and a voter, making you a more effective participant in the classroom, the community, and in politics.

---

296 CHAPTER 9 THE JUDICIARY

Resource Center
• Glossary
• Vocabulary Example
• Connect the Link

■ **Senatorial Courtesy:** Traditional deference by U.S. senators to the wishes of their colleagues concerning the appointment of individuals to federal judgeships in that state.

EXAMPLE: *Democratic senators were angry at their Republican colleagues during Bill Clinton's presidency for blocking judicial appointments and thereby violating the tradition of senatorial courtesy for controlling the selection of federal judges in their home states.*

Judicial Selection

9.3 Outline the selection process for federal judges.
(pages 296–297)

Political parties and interest groups view the judicial selection process as an important means to influence the court pathway. By securing judgeships for individuals who share their political values, these groups can enhance their prospects for success when they subsequently use litigation to shape public policy.

MYTH EXPOSED Many Americans believe that our methods for selecting judges ensure that the most qualified lawyers are chosen. In reality, American lawyers do not become judges because they are the wisest, most experienced, or fairest members of the legal profession. Instead, they are selected through political processes that emphasize their affiliations with political parties, their personal relationships with high-ranking officials, and often their ability to raise money for political campaigns. The fact that judges are selected through political processes does not necessarily mean that they are incapable of making fair decisions. Individuals who are involved in partisan politics may prove quite capable of fulfilling a judge's duty to be neutral and open-minded. On the other hand, the use of openly political processes for selecting state judges inevitably means that some people will be placed in judgeships who are not well-suited to the job.

Judicial Selection in the Federal System

The Constitution specifies that federal judges, like ambassadors and cabinet secretaries, must be appointed by the president and confirmed by a majority vote of the U.S. Senate. Thus, both the White House and one chamber of Congress are intimately involved in judicial selection.

selected are usually acquainted personally with the senators, active in the political campaigns of the senators and other party members, or accomplished in raising campaign funds for the party.

The process begins with the submission of an appointee's name to the Senate Judiciary Committee. The committee holds hearings on each nomination, including testimony from supporters and opponents. After the Judiciary Committee completes its hearings, its members vote on whether to recommend the nomination to the full Senate. Typically, upon receiving a nomination, the full Senate votes quickly based on the Judiciary Committee's report and vote. But in controversial cases or when asked to confirm appointments to the Supreme Court, the Senate may spend time debating the nomination. A majority of senators must vote for a candidate in order for that person to be sworn in as a federal judge. However, members of the minority political party in the Senate may block a vote through a **filibuster** (see Chapter 6, pages xxx–xxx), keeping discussion going indefinitely unless three-fifths of the Senate's members—60 senators—vote to end it.

Presidents seek to please favored constituencies and to advance their policy preferences in choosing appointees they believe share their values. Interest groups find avenues through which they seek to influence the president's choices as well as the confirmation votes of senators. Judicial selection processes are a primary reason that American courts are political institutions despite their efforts to appear "nonpolitical."

Judicial Selection in the States

Compare the federal judicial selection process with the various processes used to select judges for state court systems. In general, there are four primary methods that states use for judicial selection: partisan elections, nonpartisan elections, **merit selection**, and gubernatorial or legislative appointment. Table 9.4 shows how judges are selected in each state. Although each of these methods seeks to emphasize different values, they are all closely [tied to] political processes.

[Bot]h partisan and nonpartisan elections emphasize the [importan]ce of popular accountability in a democratic govern[ment.]

[...] more than 20 states have eliminated judicial elections to [reduce t]he role of politics and give greater attention to candi[dates' qu]alifications when selecting judges. These states have [adopted] various forms of merit selection systems, usually involv[ing a com]mittee reviewing candidates' qualifications and making [recomm]endations to the governor about which individuals to [appoint] to judgeships. It is presumed that the committee will [focus on] the individuals' personal qualities and professional [qualifica]tions rather than on political party affiliations. In a few [states, go]vernors or legislatures possess the authority to directly [appoint] individuals of their choice to judgeships.

---

300 CHAPTER 9 THE JUDICIARY

CONNECT THE **LINK**
(Chapter 4, pages 100–102) The First Amendment's wording requires judges to interpret the meaning of "an establishment of religion" and the "free exercise" of religion.

Elena Kagan, shown here at her Senate confirmation hearings, was nominated by President Obama to replace John Paul Stevens on the U.S. Supreme Court in 2010. Because it was widely believed that Kagan might strengthen the Court's liberal wing, conservative Republican senators opposed her confirmation. —*Is it proper for senators to oppose the nomination of a highly experienced nominee simply because they believe he or she will make decisions with which they will disagree on certain constitutional issues?*

Political Science and Judicial Decision-Making

Supreme Court justices may claim they apply "judicial restraint" or a "flexible interpretation" of the Constitution in making their decisions, and they may honestly believe that [these interpretations...]

result that they do not desire. For example, the justices permitted the Nebraska state senate to hire a minister to lead prayers at the start of each legislative session (*Marsh* v. *Chambers*, 1984). If they had applied the usual test that asked whether or not a government activity has a religious purpose, however, they would presumably have been required to prohibit this entanglement of church and state. Instead, perhaps seeking to avoid public controversy by ruling out legislative prayers, the majority of justices ignored the established legal test in this case and simply declared that legislative prayers are acceptable as a historical tradition.

An alternative theory of judicial decision-making, known as the **attitudinal model,** states that Supreme Court justices' opinions are driven by their attitudes and values. Advocates of this model see the justices' discussion of interpretive theories and precedent as merely a means to obscure the actual basis for decisions and to persuade the public that the decisions are, in fact, based on law. Researchers who endorse the attitudinal model do systematic analyses of judicial decisions to identify patterns that indicate the attitudes and values possessed and advanced by individual justices. Put more simply, the attitudinal theorists argue that some justices decide cases as they do because they are conservative (e.g., generally supportive of business interests and expanded power for prosecutors and police) and that others decide cases differently because they are liberal (e.g., generally supportive of broad definitions of criminal defendants' rights, environmental regulation, and civil rights).[6]

Other political scientists see judicial decision-making as influenced by a **strategic voting model.**[7] According to this theory, Supreme Court justices vote strategically in order to advance their preferred goals, even if it means voting contrary to their actual attitudes and values in some cases. For example, a chief justice may vote strategically to end up among the majority of justices and thereby retain the authority to decide which [...]

The text features **compelling photos** with many captions that pose questions about important concepts in the text along with many different types of graphs and charts. The presentation of information in a variety of formats helps you to grasp key concepts.

Resources in Print and Online

Name of Supplement	Print	Online	Available to	Description
MyClassPrep		✔	Instructor	This new resource provides a rich database of figures, photos, videos, simulations, activities, and much more that instructors can use to create their own lecture presentation. For more information visit **www.mypolscilab.com**
Instructor's Manual 020508480X		✔	Instructor	Offers chapter overviews, lecture outlines, teaching ideas, discussion topics, and research activities. All resources hyperlinked for ease of navigation.
Test Bank 0205084648		✔	Instructor	Contains over 100 questions per chapter in multiple-choice, true-false, short answer, and essay format. Questions are tied to text Learning Objectives and have been reviewed for accuracy and effectiveness.
MyTest 0205084702		✔		All questions from the Test Bank can be accessed in this flexible, online test generating software.
PowerPoint 0205109942		✔		Slides include a lecture outline of the text, graphics from the book, and quick check questions for immediate feedback on student comprehension.
Transparencies 0205084621		✔	Instructor	These slides contain all maps, figures, and tables found in the text.
Pearson Political Science Video Program	✔		Instructor	Qualified adopters can peruse our list of videos for the American government classroom. Contact your local Pearson representative for more details.
Classroom Response System (CRS) 0205082289		✔	Instructor	A set of lecture questions, organized by American government topics, for use with "clickers" to garner student opinion and assess comprehension.
American Government Study Site		✔	Instructor	Online package of practice tests, flashcards and more organized by major course topics. Visit **www.pearsonamericangovernment.com**
You Decide! Current Debates in American Politics, 2011 Edition 020511489X	✔		Instructor/ Student	This debate-style reader by John Rourke of the University of Connecticut examines provocative issues in American politics today by presenting contrasting views of key political topics.
Voices of Dissent: Critical Readings in American Politics, Eighth Edition 0205697976	✔		Student	This collection of critical essays assembled by William Grover of St. Michaels College and Joseph Peschek of Hamline University goes beyond the debate between mainstream liberalism and conservatism to fundamentally challenge the status quo.
Diversity in Contemporary American Politics and Government 0205550363	✔		Student	Edited by David Dulio of Oakland University, Erin E. O'Brien of Kent State University, and John Klemanski of Oakland University, this reader examines the significant role that demographic diversity plays in our political outcomes and policy processes, using both academic and popular sources.
Writing in Political Science, Fourth Edition 0205617360	✔		Student	This guide, written by Diane Schmidt of California State University—Chico, takes students through all aspects of writing in political science step-by-step.
Choices: An American Government Database Reader		✔	Student	This customizable reader allows instructors to choose from a database of over 300 readings to create a reader that exactly matches their course needs. For more information go to **www .pearsoncustom.com/database/choices.html**
Ten Things That Every American Government Student Should Read 020528969X	✔		Student	Edited by Karen O'Connor of American University. We asked American government instructors across the country to vote for the ten things beyond the text that they believe every student should read and put them in this brief and useful reader. Available at no additional charge when packaged with the text.
American Government: Readings and Cases, Eighteenth Edition 0205697984	✔		Student	Edited by Peter Woll of Brandeis University, this longtime best-selling reader provides a strong, balanced blend of classic readings and cases that illustrate and amplify important concepts in American government, alongside extremely current selections drawn from today's issues and literature. Available at a discount when ordered packaged with this text.
Penguin-Longman Value Bundles	✔		Student	Longman offers 25 Penguin Putnam titles at more than a 60 percent discount when packaged with any Longman text. Go to **www.pearsonhighered.com/penguin** for more information.
Longman State Politics Series	✔		Student	These primers on state and local government and political issues are available at no extra cost when shrink-wrapped with the text. Available for Texas, California, and Georgia.

Save Time and Improve Results with

PEARSON

mypoliscilab™

The most popular online teaching/learning solution for American government, MyPoliSciLab moves students from studying and applying concepts to participating in politics. Completely redesigned and now organized by the book's chapters and learning objectives, the new MyPoliSciLab is easier to integrate into any course.

✔ STUDY A flexible learning path in every chapter.

Pre-Tests. See the relevance of politics with these diagnostic assessments and get personalized study plans driven by learning objectives.

Pearson eText. Navigate by learning objective, take notes, print key passages, and more. From page numbers to photos, the eText is identical to the print book.

Flashcards. Learn key terms by word, definition, or learning objective.

Post-Tests. Featuring over 50% new questions, the pre-tests produce updated study plans with follow-up reading, video, and multimedia

Chapter Exams. Also featuring over 50% new questions, test mastery of each chapter using the chapter exams.

✔ APPLY Over 150 videos and multimedia activities.

Video. Analyze current events by watching streaming video from the AP and ABC News.

Simulations. Engage the political process by experiencing how political actors make decisions.

Comparative Exercises. Think critically about how American politics compares with the politics of other countries.

Timelines. Get historical context by following issues that have influenced the evolution of American democracy.

Visual Literacy Exercises. Learn how to interpret political data in figures and tables.

MyPoliSciLibrary. Read full-text primary source documents from the nation's founding to the present.

✔ PARTICIPATE Join the political conversation.

PoliSci News Review. Read analysis of—and comment on—major new stories.

AP Newsfeeds. Follow political news in the United States and around the world.

Weekly Quiz. Master the headlines in this review of current events.

Weekly Poll. Take the poll and see how your politics compare.

Voter Registration. Voting is a right—and a responsibility.

Citizenship Test. See what it takes to become an American citizen.

✔ MANAGE Designed for online or traditional courses.

Grade Tracker. Assign and assess nearly everything in MyPoliSciLab.

Instructor Resources. Download supplements at the Instructor Resource Center.

Sample Syllabus. Get ideas for assigning the book and MyPoliSciLab.

MyClassPrep. Download many of the resources in MyPoliSciLab for lectures.

✔ 📖 👁 ✳ The icons in the book and eText point to resources in MyPoliSciLab.

With proven book-specific and course-specific content, MyPoliSciLab is part of a better teaching/learning system only available from Pearson Longman.

✔ To see demos, read case studies, and learn about training, visit www.mypoliscilab.com.

✔ To order this book with MyPoliSciLab at no extra charge, use ISBN 0-205-07315-8.

✔ Questions? Contact a local Pearson Longman representative: www.pearsonhighered.com/replocator.

 Follow MyPoliSciLab on Twitter.

Developing LIVING DEMOCRACY

LIVING DEMOCRACY is the result of an extensive development process involving the contributions of hundreds of instructors and students. More than 400 manuscript reviewers provided invaluable feedback. More than two-dozen focus group participants contributed to decisions about text organization, content coverage, and pedagogical innovation. More than 100 instructors helped shape the design of the text. Over 750 students class-tested the manuscript before publication. Student reviewers evaluated the writing style and visual design, helped to select the text's photos, and provided feedback on the in-text assessment tools. We are grateful to all who participated in shaping the manuscript and design of this text.

We would like to thank the following instructors who offered valuable comments during the development of the third edition of *Living Democracy*:

Andrew Aoki, Augsburg College
Alicia Biagioni, Cisco Junior College
Rachel Bzostek, California State University, Bakersfield
James Calvi, West Texas A&M University
Eric Cox, Texas Christian University
Gary Donato, Bentley University
Douglas Dow, University of Texas at Dallas
Henry Esparza, University of Texas at San Antonio
Charles Gossett, California State Polytechnic University, Pomona
Christopher Hammons, Houston Baptist University
Lori Han, Chapman University
Jeff Harmon, University of Texas at San Antonio
Joseph Jozwiak, Texas A&M, Corpus Christi
Richard Kiefer, Waubonsee Community College
Derek Maxfield, Capital Community College
Adam McGlynn, The University of Texas-Pan American
Vinette Meikle Harris, Houston Community College, Central
Melissa Miller, Bowling Green State University
T. Sophia Mrouri, Lone Star College
Brian Newman, Pepperdine University
Angela Oberbauer, San Diego Mesa College
Daniel Ponder, Drury University
Allen Settle, California Polytechnic State University
Clifton Sherrill, Mississippi College
Robert Sterken, The University of Texas at Tyler
Bruce Stinebrickner, DePauw University
Christy Woodward Kaupert, San Antonio College

We would also like to extend our thanks to the following instructors who offered valuable comments during the development of the first and second editions of *Living Democracy*:

Danny Adkison, Oklahoma State University
William Adler, Hunter College
Victor Aikhionbare, Palm Beach Community College
Victoria Allen, Queens College
Bruce Altschuler, SUNY Oswego
John Ambacher, Framingham State College
Lydia Andrade, University of the Incarnate Word
Kwame Antwi-Boasiako, Stephen F. Austin State University
Andrew Aoki, Augsburg College
Clay Arnold, University of Central Arkansas
John Arnold, Itawamba Community College
Daniel Aseltine, Chaffey College
Yan Bai, Grand Rapids Community College
Evelyn Ballard, Houston Community College
Robert Ballinger, South Texas College
Jodi Balma, Fullerton College
Joseph A. Barder, Robert Morris College
Susan M. Behuniak, Le Moyne College
Paul Benson, Tarrant County College
Demetrius Bereolos, Tulsa Community College
Steven Berizzi, Norwalk Community College
Rory Berke, U.S. Naval Academy
Prosper Bernard, Baruch College
David Birch, Tomball College
Amy Black, Wheaton College
Melanie J. Blumberg, California University of Pennsylvania
Chris Bonneau, University of Pittsburgh
Michael Bordelon, Houston Baptist University
Carol Botsch, USC Aiken
Catherine Bottrell, Tarrant County College

Laura Bourland, University of Alabama
Phil Branyon, Gainesville State College
Ronald Brecke, Park University
Mike Bressler, Long Beach City College
Claudia Bryant, Western Carolina University
Martha Burns, Tidewater Community College
Randi Buslik, Northeastern Illinois University
Stephen Caliendo, North Central College
Jamie Carson, University of Georgia
James Chalmers, Wayne State University
Mark Cichock, University of Texas at Arlington
Allan Cigler, University of Kansas
Daniel Coffey, University of Akron
Scott Comparato, Southern Illinois University
Paul Cooke, Cy-Fair College
Chris Cooper, Western Carolina University
Frank Coppa, Union County College
James Corey, High Point University
Eric Cox, Texas Christian University
Jim Cox, Georgia Perimeter College
Gregory Culver, University of Southern Indiana
John H. Culver, California Polytechnic State University
Carlos Cunha, Dowling College
William Cunion, Mount Union College
Marian Currinder, College of Charleston
Donald Dahlin, University of South Dakota
Mark Daniels, Slippery Rock University
Kwame Dankwa, Albany State University
Kevin Davis, North Central Texas College
Paul Davis, Truckee Meadows Community College
Robert De Luna, St. Philip's College
Michael Deaver, Sierra College
Denise DeGarmo, Southern Illinois University, Edwardsville
Robert Dewhirst, Northeast Missouri State University
Brian Dille, Mesa Community College
Agber Dimah, Chicago State University
Alesha Doan, University of Kansas
Peter Doas, South Texas College
John Domino, Sam Houston State University
Rick Donohoe, Napa Valley College
Douglas Dow, University of Texas at Dallas
William Downs, Georgia State University
Morris Drumm, Texas Christian University
B. M. Dubin, Oakland Community College–Highland Lakes

Dave Dulio, Oakland University
Donna Duncan, Westwood College
Keith Eakins, University of Central Oklahoma
J. Eddy, Monroe Community College
Jodi Empol, Montgomery County Community College
Matthew Eshbaugh-Soha, University of North Texas
Henry Esparza, University of Texas at San Antonio
Karry Evans, Austin Community College
Hyacinth Ezeamii, Albany State University
Russell Farnen, University of Connecticut
John Fielding, Mount Wachusett Community College
Terri Fine, University of Central Florida
John Fliter, Kansas State University
Joseph M. Fonseca, St. Mary's University
Brian Frederick, Northern Illinois University
Heather Frederick, Slippery Rock University
Rodd Freitag, University of Wisconsin–Eau Claire
Scott Frisch, California State University, Channel Islands
Joyce Gelb, City College of New York
Anthony Giarino, Tarrant County College
Sandra Gieseler, Palo Alto College
Barbara Giles, Florida Southern College
Dana Glencross, Oklahoma City Community College
Richard Glenn, Millersville University
Dennis Goldford, Drake University
Fran Goldman, Binghamton University
Charles Gossett, California State Polytechnic University, Pomona
John C. Green, University of Akron
Richard Griffin, Ferris State University
Nathan Griffith, Belmont University
Martin Gruberg, University of Wisconsin–Oshkosh
Baogang Guo, Dalton State College
Hans Hacker, Stephen F. Austin State University
Mel Hailey, Abilene Christian University
Yolanda Hake, South Texas College
Angela Halfacre-Hitchcock, College of Charleston
Willie Hamilton, Mt. San Jacinto College
Roger Handberg, University of Central Florida
Michael Harkins, Harper College
Rebecca Harris, Washington and Lee University
Brian Harward, Allegheny College
Paul Hathaway, Idaho State University
Diane Heith, St. John's University

Christopher Henrichsen, *Brigham Young University*

Frank Hernandez, *Glendale Community College*

Marjorie Hershey, *Indiana University*

Fred R. Hertrich, *Middlesex County College*

Kenneth Hicks, *Rogers State University*

Anne Hildreth, *SUNY Albany*

Bill Hixon, *Lawrence University*

Trey Hood, *University of Georgia*

Donna Hooper, *North Central Texas College*

Jennifer Hora, *Valparaiso University*

Alison Howard, *Dominican University of California*

Nikki Isemann, *Southeastern Iowa Community College*

Charles Jacobs, *Kent State University*

Amy Jasperson, *University of Texas at San Antonio*

Shannon Jenkins, *University of Massachusetts at Dartmouth*

Alana Jeydel, *American River College*

Alana S. Jeydel, *Oregon State University*

Scott P. Johnson, *Frostburg State University*

Susan Johnson, *University of Wisconsin–Whitewater*

Terri Johnson, *University of Wisconsin–Green Bay*

Frank Jones, *Saint Leo University*

Frank Jones, *Del Mar College*

Mark Joslyn, *University of Kansas*

Joseph Jozwiak, *Texas A&M University, Corpus Christi*

Srujana Kanjula, *Community College of Allegheny County, North Campus*

Nina Kasniunas, *Allegheny College*

David Keefe, *SUNY Brockport*

William Kelly, *Auburn University*

Stephen Kerbow, *Southwest Texas Junior College*

Beat Kernen, *Southwest Missouri State University*

Irina Khmelko, *Georgia Southern University*

Richard Kiefer, *Waubonsee Community College*

Bob King, *Georgia Perimeter College*

Dina Krois, *Lansing Community College*

Michael Kryzanek, *Bridgewater State College*

Ashlyn Kuersten, *Western Michigan University*

Ronald Kuykendall, *Greenville Technical College*

Paul Labedz, *Valencia Community College*

Lisa Langenbach, *Middle Tennessee State University*

Christopher Latimer, *SUNY Albany*

Mike Lee, *Western Texas College*

Ron Lee, *Rockford College*

John Linantud, *University of Houston, Downtown*

Robert Locander, *North Harris College*

Brad Lockerbie, *University of Georgia*

Fred Lokken, *Truckee Meadows Community College*

Robert C. Lowry, *University of Texas at Dallas*

Tim Luther, *California Baptist University*

Gay Lyons, *Pellissippi State Technical Community College*

Susan Macfarland, *Gainesville College*

Hamed Madani, *Tarrant County College*

Gary Malecha, *University of Portland*

Maurice Mangum, *Southern Illinois University, Edwardsville*

David Mann, *College of Charleston*

Michael Margolis, *University of Cincinnati*

Steve Marin, *Victor Valley College*

Nancy Marion, *University of Akron*

Asher J. Matathias, *St. John's University*

Derek Maxfield, *Capital Community College*

Madhavi McCall, *San Diego State University*

Richard Medlar, *Dickinson State University*

Vinette Meikle Harris, *Houston Community College, Central*

Mark Milewicz, *Gordon College*

Eric Miller, *Blinn College*

Rhonda Miller, *Eastfield College*

Richard Millsap, *University of Texas at Arlington*

Ken Moffett, *Southern Illinois University, Edwardsville*

Matthew Morgan, *Bentley College*

Wyatt Moulds, *Jones County Junior College*

Stacia Munroe, *Lincoln Land Community College*

William Murin, *University of Wisconsin–Parkside*

Martha Musgrove, *Tarrant County College–SE Campus*

Jason Mycoff, *University of Delaware*

Carolyn Myers, *Southwestern Illinois College*

Napp Nazworth, *Texas A&M University, Corpus Christi*

Steven Nelson, *Northern Michigan University*

Katherine Nelson-Born, *Columbia Southern University*

Brian Newman, *Pepperdine University*

James Newman, *Idaho State University*

Adam Newmark, *Appalachian State University*

Peter Ngwafu, *Albany State University*

Randy Nobles, *Northeast Texas Community College*

Pat O'Connor, *Oakland Community College*

Laura Olson, *Clemson University*

Richard Pacelle, *Georgia Southern University*

Richard M. Pearlstein, *Southeastern Oklahoma State University*

David Penna, *Gallaudet University*

Clarissa Peterson, *DePauw University*

Geoffrey Peterson, *University of Wisconsin–Eau Claire*

J.D. Phaup, *Texas A&M University–Kingsville*

Daniel Ponder, *Drury University*

Greg Rabb, *Jamestown Community College*

Jan Rabin, *Roanoke College*

Lee Rademacher, *Purdue University, Calumet*

Mitzi Ramos, *University of Illinois at Chicago*

Kirk Randazzo, *University of Kentucky*

Christopher Reaves, *School of Social and Behavioral Sciences*

Deanne Repetto, *Folsom Lake College*

Steven Reti, *College of the Canyons*

James Rhodes, *Luther College*

Laurie Rice, *Southern Illinois University, Edwardsville*

Ken Robbins, *U.S. Military Academy at West Point*

John Roche, *Palomar College*

J. Philip Rogers, *San Antonio College*

Bernard Rowan, *Chicago State University*

Donald Roy, *Ferris State University*

Paul Rozycki, *Mott Community College*

Cristina Ruggiero, *Chabot College*

Chris Saladino, *Virginia Commonwealth University*

Erich Saphir, *Pima Community College*

Greg Schaller, *Villanova University*

Calvin Scheidt, *Tidewater Community College*

Adam Schiffer, *Texas Christian University*

Andrew Schlewitz, *Albion College*

Diane Schmidt, *California State University*

Erin Scholnick, *College of San Mateo San Francisco State University*

Ronnee Schreiber, *San Diego State University*

Joseph Scrocca, *U.S. Military Academy at West Point*

T.M. Sell, *Highline College*

Brett Sharp, *University of Central Oklahoma*

James F. Sheffield, *University of Oklahoma*

Charles Shipan, *University of Michigan*

Mark Shomaker, *Blinn College/Bryan Campus*

Steve Shupe, *Sonoma State University*

Tom Simpson, *Missouri Southern State University*

Brian Smith, *St. Edward's University*

Candy Smith, *Texarkana College*

Daniel Smith, *Northwest Missouri State University*

Karen Smith, *Columbia Southern University*

Gary Sokolow, *College of the Redwoods*

Robert Speel, *Penn State, Erie*

John Speer, *Houston Community College, Southwest*

Debra St. John, *Collin County Community College District*

Jim Startin, *University of Texas at San Antonio*

Robert Sterken, *University of Texas at Tyler*

Theresia Stewart, *Elizabethtown Community and Technical College*

Adam Stone, *Georgia Perimeter College*

J. Cherie Strachan, *Central Michigan University*

Pamela Stricker, *Ohio University*

Michael Sullenger, *Texas State Technical College*

Bobby Summers, *Harper College*

Dari Sylvester, *University of the Pacific*

Barry Tadlock, *Ohio University*

Carolyn Taylor, *Rogers State University*

Jeremy Teigen, *Ramapo College*

Kenneth Tillett, *Southwestern Oklahoma State University*

Judy Tobler, *Northwest Arkansas Community College*

Charles Turner, *California State University, Chico*

Chris Turner, *Laredo Community College*

Wilson Ugwu, *Concordia University*

Jamilya Ukudeeva, *Cabrillo College*

Richard Unruh, *Fresno Pacific University*

David Uranga, *Pasadena City College*

James Van Arsdall, *Metropolitan Community College*

Laura van Assendelft, *Mary Baldwin College*

Ronald Vardy, *Wharton County Community College*

Dwight Vick, *University of South Dakota*

Adam Warber, *Clemson University*

Eddie Washington, *Rio Hondo College*

Ruth Ann Watry, *Northern Michigan University*

Wendy Watson, *University of North Texas*

Paul Weizer, *Fitchburg State College*

Mike Lee Western, *Texas College*

Lois Duke Whitaker, *Georgia Southern University*

James Wilson, *Southern Methodist University*

Sean Wilson, *Penn State*

Robert Wood, *University of North Dakota*

Heather Wyatt-Nichol, *Stephen F. Austin State University*

Ann Wyman, *Missouri Southern State University*

Peter Yacobucci, *Walsh University*

Chunmei Yoe, *Southeastern Oklahoma State University*

Acknowledgments

We are extremely grateful to the people at Pearson Longman for building on the success of the first and second editions of *Living Democracy* and helping us find ways to improve it. Although it required the work of numerous people to make this revision possible, several deserve special recognition. Development editor Lisa Sussman provided wonderful suggestions at every stage of the project. Senior Production Editor Doug Bell (of PreMedia Global) deserves thanks for playing an essential role in keeping the authors on track, solving numerous problems, and ensuring the quality and consistency of our presentation. Former Editor-in-Chief for Political Science, Eric Stano, was instrumental in shaping the revision, and he deserves our gratitude for his energy and support. Finally, we would also like to thank Executive Editor, Reid Hester, for his support.

Three scholars were kind enough to make significant contributions to the content of the policy chapters and Texas and California editions: Christopher Borick of Muhlenberg College, Paul Benson of Tarrant County College, and Milton Clarke of Los Medanos College. For their contributions to features in this book, we are grateful to Bradley Dyke, Des Moines Area Community College; Laura Moyer, Louisiana State University; and Holley Tankersley, Coastal Carolina University.

Joanne would like to thank her students in her American Politics classes, who have solidified her love of the subject. They are a continuing source of inspiration and motivation. A special thanks go to her family, Craig, Emma, and Connor—to whom her efforts are devoted—for their continued patience. Chris thanks his wife, Charlotte, and children, Alicia and Eric, for their support and encouragement. Dan would like to thank his colleagues in the Department of Political Science and the Center for Political Participation at Allegheny College for their assistance and encouragement. And, as always, he offers a special thanks to his wonderful family—Christine, Abby, Daniel, and Brian—for their love, guidance, and unwavering support.

About the Authors

Daniel M. Shea is a Professor of Political Science and Director of the Center for Political Participation at Allegheny College. He  earned his Bachelor of Arts degree in Political Science and American Studies from the State University of New York at Oswego, his Master of Arts degree in Campaign Management from the University of West Florida, and his Ph.D. in Political Science from the State University of New York at Albany. Dan has received numerous awards for his teaching and scholarship and has authored or co-authored several books on the American political process. In the fall of 2002, he founded the Center for Political Participation (CPP) to foster a greater appreciation for political engagement and to develop hands-on programs that bring young people into the civic realm. The CPP develops programs for Allegheny students, for community partners, and for scholars nationwide, and several of their recent initiatives have garnered national media attention.

Joanne Connor Green is an Associate Professor and Department Chair of Political Science, and the former Director of Women's Studies at Texas Christian University. She earned  her Bachelor's degree in Political Science from the University of Buffalo in 1990 and her Ph.D. in American Politics from the University of Florida in 1994. Joanne's research and teaching interests include the role of gender in congressional elections and interest group politics. She has published a number of articles in scholarly journals, including *Women & Politics,* as well as other academic outlets.

Christopher E. Smith is a Professor of Criminal Justice at Michigan State University. He previously taught at the  University of Akron and the University of Connecticut at Hartford. He earned his Ph.D. in Political Science at the University of Connecticut at Storrs and also holds degrees from Harvard University, the University of Bristol (U.K.), and the University of Tennessee College of Law. As a specialist on courts and constitutional law, he has written more than 20 books. He has also written more than 100 scholarly articles on law and politics.

LIVING
DEMOCRACY

BRIEF CALIFORNIA EDITION

American Government: Democracy in Action

KEY OBJECTIVES

After completing this chapter, you should be prepared to:

1.1 Illustrate how citizens participate in a democracy and why this is important.

1.2 Relate the themes of this book to American politics today.

1.3 Outline the various "pathways" of involvement in our political system.

1.4 Analyze the forces of stability in American politics.

I t obviously can't be argued that young voters alone elected Barack Obama president in 2008, but it seems rather clear that young Americans played a pivotal role. Obama netted a whopping 68 percent of the vote from those under 30— likely the largest vote share of an age group that any candidate has ever received. In addition, some 43 percent of 18- to 29-year-olds were first-time voters in 2008. This compares to just 11 percent for all voters. Whatever the cause of the participation, 2008 demonstrated that young Americans, long civically involved, can channel their interests into *political* action, if they are motivated to do so.

However, there is disturbing evidence that young people may once again be tuning out. One of the frustrations of the Obama administration during the first year was the lackluster response of young Americans to the ongoing policy debates— especially over health care reform. A 2009 study by the Pew Research Center for the People and the Press found that the proportion of young people getting *no* news on a typical day has actually increased substantially over the past decade. Most discouraging is turnout data from a few states in the 2009 election. For example, those voters under 30 made up 22 percent of the electorate in New Jersey in 2008. This figure dropped to just 8 percent in 2009. In Virginia, turnout went from 21 percent in

> **Can average citizens play a meaningful role in American politics?**

2008 to 10 percent in 2009. That trend continued in the 2010 midterm election, which witnessed very meager young voter turnout.

Why are young Americans moving to the sidelines? Don't they understand their power and their potential to shape the outcome of elections and policy? For those unaccustomed to the difficulties of policymaking in a highly polarized political climate, the value of an electoral win might seem trivial. Great! We won . . . now where's all that change? Discussion of our nation's history of incremental change or the theoretical values of constitutional obstruction would likely fall on deaf ears.

We know young Americans are attracted to volunteer service out of compassion and a desire to make a difference in their communities and other people's lives. By lending a hand at soup kitchens, literacy programs, youth projects, elderly homes, as well as with untold other community endeavors, these committed individuals strive to make their world a better place. They are turned off by conflict, ego, and gridlock. Should we care about a generation that turns its back on politics—that leaves the heavy lifting of policy development to others? Perhaps by the end of this book you will agree that our nation cannot live up to its potential as a democracy when an entire generation sits on the sidelines. Politics is not for the faint of heart, but it is also not for "others."

Resource Center
• Glossary
• Vocabulary Example
• Connect the Link

■ **Politics:** The process by which the actions of government are determined.

EXAMPLE: *By appealing to members of the city council to change the new housing ordinance, several students decided to roll up their sleeves and become engaged in local politics.*

It's Your Government

1.1 Illustrate how citizens participate in a democracy and why this is important.

(pages 4–7)

On some level, everyone knows that government affects our lives. We must obey laws created by government. We pay taxes to support the government. We make use of government services, ranging from police protection to student loans. It is easy, however, to see government as a distant entity that imposes its will on us. It provides benefits and protections, such as schools, roads, and fire departments. But it also limits our choices by telling us how fast we can drive and how old we must be to get married, purchase alcoholic beverages, and vote.

Would your view of government change if a new law dramatically affected your choices, plans, or expectations? Imagine that you and your four best friends decide to rent a house together for the next academic year. You find a five-bedroom, furnished house near campus that is owned by a friendly landlord. Then, you sign a lease and put down your deposit. During the summer, however, the landlord sends you a letter informing you that two of your friends will need to find someplace else to live. The city council has passed a new ordinance—the kind of law produced by local governments—declaring that not more than three unrelated people may live in a house together.

Now what would you think about government? After your initial feelings of anger, you might resign yourself to the disappointment of moving back into a dormitory or finding a different apartment. You might also ask yourself an important question: Is there anything that I can do about this new ordinance?

A distinguishing feature of democracy—the form of government in the United States—is that people have opportunities to influence the decisions of government. One individual cannot realistically expect to control the government's choice of priorities or the laws that are produced. However, in some circumstances, individuals can participate in activities that ultimately change government and lead to the creation of new laws and regulations. Let us take the example of the housing ordinance and consider what you might do to attempt to change that law:

• You could encourage students to register to vote and help with political campaigns for city council candidates who promise to listen to students' concerns and get rid of the housing ordinance. In some college towns, individual students have become so energized by specific political issues that some have actually run for and been elected to city

councils. These activities, *voting* and *elections,* are the most familiar forms of citizen participation in a democracy.

• You could organize your friends to contact members of the city council asking them to change the restrictive new law. You could also go to city council meetings and voice your opposition to the law. We often characterize these activities as *lobbying* lawmakers in order to pressure or persuade them to make specific decisions.

• You could talk to the local landlords' association about whether it might file a lawsuit challenging the ordinance on the grounds that it improperly interferes with the landlords' right to decide how to use their private property. You might talk to an attorney yourself about whether, under the laws of your state, a new ordinance can override the rental lease agreement that you and your friends had already signed. If the new ordinance violates other existing laws, then taking the issue to court by filing lawsuits—a process known as *litigation*—may provide the means for a lawyer to persuade a judge to invalidate the city council's action.

• You could write articles in the college newspaper or blog about the new ordinance to inform other students about the effect of the law on their off-campus housing choices. You could publicize and sponsor meetings in order to organize *grassroots activities,* such as marches, sit-ins, or other forms of nonviolent protests. These actions would draw news media attention and put pressure on city officials to reconsider their decision.

There is no guarantee that any of these approaches would produce the change you desire. But each of these courses of action, depending on the circumstances in the community and the number of people who provide support, presents the possibility of changing the government's decision.

Each one of these approaches is part of **politics**■. You'll find a more complete discussion of this topic in Chapter 2, pages 32–33, but for now, you should understand that politics concerns the activities that seek to affect the composition, power, and actions of government.

American government should *not* be viewed as "distant," "all-powerful," or "unchangeable." Although government buildings are often designed to instill feelings of respect and admiration and to convey permanence, stability, and power, they are much more than awe-inspiring works of architecture. They are *arenas of activity* that determine **public policy**■. The laws and policies produced by government in these arenas affect the lives of everyone in the United States—including students like you, as suggested in Table 1.1. It is essential for you to understand that laws and policies are influenced by the actions of groups and individuals and that *you* can play an important role in the policy process.

MYTH EXPOSED Many Americans believe there isn't much an ordinary citizen can do to change the course of government. That's simply not true. First, "our government" is not a

CONNECT THE LINK
(Chapter 2, pages 32–33) Is there really a
difference between government and politics?

■ **Public Policy:** What government decides to
do or not do; government laws, rules, or expenditures.

EXAMPLE: *It is public policy that you must be
21 years old to purchase alcohol in Pennsylvania.*

TABLE 1.1 | Government Is All Around Us

Do you doubt that government plays a role in your daily life? Consider the following timeline of a typical day in the life of an average college student and the number of times governmental control comes into play. Keep in mind that this is only the tip of the iceberg.

TIME	EVENT	GOVERNMENT AGENCY
6:22 A.M.	You awaken to the sounds of a garbage truck outside. Annoyed, you realize that you forgot to bring the recyclables to the street last night.	Local department of sanitation; local recycling program
6:49 A.M.	Unable to get back to sleep, you take a shower, thinking about the cost of rent for your apartment and wondering if your next place will have a decent shower.	Local water filtration plant; federal Department of Housing and Urban Development
7:22 A.M.	You read the news, noting that interest rates are going up and the war in Afghanistan seems to be getting worse.	Federal Reserve Board; Selective Service; Department of Defense
8:34 A.M.	Driving to class, you notice the airbag—but you don't notice dirty car exhaust. You also note that your inspection sticker is about to expire.	Federal Environmental Protection Agency, state and local environmental agencies; state Motor Vehicle Bureau
8:43 A.M.	You stop at a gas station and wonder why gas prices continue to shoot upward.	Federal government investments in oil exploration and alternative fuels; presidential oversight of the Strategic Oil Reserves; federal trade agreements
9:05 A.M.	You arrive on campus, find a parking space, and walk to class.	State and federal support for higher education; state and federal tuition support and student loan programs
11:00 A.M.	In accounting class, you discuss the CPA exam.	State professional licensing program
12:09 P.M.	At lunch, you discuss the upcoming elections. Your best friend realizes that she won't be able to vote because she missed the registration deadline.	State election commission; Secretary of State Office
3:00 P.M.	You receive a paycheck for your part-time restaurant job. In spite of the low hourly wage you receive, a bunch of money has been deducted for taxes.	Federal and state minimum wage laws; local, state, and federal income tax regulations; federal unemployment program; federal Social Security program
4:15 P.M.	You figure out a customer's bill, carefully adding the sales tax to the total.	Local and state sales taxes
9:47 P.M.	You settle in for some television after studying and wonder why profanity is allowed on some cable shows, but not on network television.	Federal Communications Commission
11:49 P.M.	You collapse into bed and slip into a peaceful sleep, taking for granted that you are safe.	Local police department; state militia; U.S. military

| CONNECT THE **LINK** (Chapter 2, pages 34–35) How does one classify different types of government? | ■ **Democracy:** A political system in which all citizens have a chance to play a role in shaping government action and are afforded basic rights and liberties. | **EXAMPLE:** *Since 1994, South Africa has been considered a democracy, because all citizens have the chance to vote and basic political rights are protected.* |

distant, remote entity; instead, it comprises the rules and structures that shape our lives every day. Second, while dramatic change might not occur quickly, American history is filled with examples of how average citizens rolled up their sleeves and changed the course of government. This book highlights several of these stories.

Our Unique Political System

The United States is different from other countries in the world. Our government and laws reflect our unique history as a group of former British colonies that fought a war for independence, expanded westward across a wilderness through the efforts of pioneers, and survived a bloody civil war that occurred, in large part, over the issue of race-based slavery. While many aspects of American government, such as elections and the right to a fair trial before being convicted of a crime, can be found in other countries, the organization of American elections and the rights possessed by criminal defendants in American courts differ from those found elsewhere in the world. For example, in the United States, defendants are presumed innocent until proven guilty, which forces the government to prove someone's guilt, rather than compelling individuals to prove their own innocence. In addition, judges at the federal level are appointed for life, a scheme designed to remove them from the pressures of public opinion. Compared to judges in other democracies, American judges also possess significant power to invalidate laws and policies created by other government decision makers. Thus, Americans have unique opportunities to use litigation as a means to influence government.

If we look at countries around the world, we can discover a variety of forms of government. By classifying forms of government according to two factors, citizen participation in governmental decisions and freedom for individuals, a number of different types of governments emerge. (We'll also say more about this in Chapter 2, pages 34–35.) Freedom House, a nonprofit, nonpartisan organization, makes just such an assessment. Every year, it issues a rating of countries according to the extent of political rights (for example, voting) and individual liberties (for example, freedom of speech) that their citizens have. Countries are rated on a scale from 1 to 7, with 1 meaning the highest level of political rights. Political rights are evaluated based on a number of factors, including whether the process of candidate selection is free from government approval, whether voters are presented with genuine choices at the ballot box, and whether the elections and governments are free from military involvement. Representative findings are shown in Figure 1.1.

At the top end of the scale are **democracies**■, including the United States, in which citizens enjoy a large measure of personal freedom and have meaningful opportunities to participate in government through voting, organizing protests against gov-

ernment policies, and other forms of free speech and political action. At the other end of the scale are countries with **totalitarian regimes**■, in which the leaders of the government hold all of the power and control all aspects of society.

Unlike residents living in countries with totalitarian regimes, you can actually use your knowledge, critical analysis skills, time, and energy to improve America's laws and policies. Your efforts might be aimed at decisions by local government, as in the example of the controversial housing ordinance, or

FIGURE 1.1 ■ Global Ratings on Political Rights
Do you find anything in this figure surprising, or are the ratings as you expected?

COUNTRY	RATING	CLASSIFICATION
Canada	1	Free
France	1	
Netherlands	1	
United States	1	
South Africa	2	
India	2	
Jamaica	2	
Mexico	2	
Bolivia	3	Partly free
Kenya	4	
Nigeria	5	
Afghanistan	6	Not free
Jordan	6	
Egypt	6	
Russia	6	
China	7	
North Korea	7	
Saudi Arabia	7	

MAP OF FREEDOM, 2010

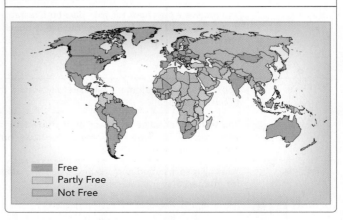

- Free
- Partly Free
- Not Free

SOURCE: Reprinted by permission of Freedom House, Inc.
www.freedomhouse.org

■ **Totalitarian Regime:** A system of government in which the ruling elite holds all power and controls all aspects of society.

EXAMPLE: *Nazi Germany was a totalitarian government in the 1930s and early 1940s.*

you might roll up your sleeves to help an underdog candidate win an election, as some young Americans did for Barack Obama in 2008. There are numerous pathways for your involvement, and you can seek to affect government at the local, state, and national levels. The chapters of this book will help you to see how you can actively participate in processes that influence the decisions and actions of your government.

One of the great myths of our day is that young Americans are apathetic, indifferent, and lazy. In truth, many are deeply concerned about public matters and are civically active. Unfortunately, however, many doubt the effectiveness of politics as a viable avenue for change. This book is designed to help students understand their potential in a democratic political system. —*Why do you think young Americans are committed to community service but generally less interested in politics?*

It's Your Government

1.1 **Illustrate how citizens participate in a democracy and why this is important.**

PRACTICE QUIZ: UNDERSTAND AND APPLY

1. According to the Map of Freedom in Figure 1.1, most of the continent of Asia is labeled
   a. free.
   b. partly free.
   c. not free.
   d. failed states.

2. Unlike national politics, when it comes to shaping local public policies there are very few options for involvement.
   a. true
   b. false

3. Much of political action is designed to affect
   a. public policy.
   b. who serves in government.
   c. the powers government has.
   d. all of the above.

ANALYZE

1. What are some of the distinguishing features of a democracy? Can a system be called democratic if it holds fair elections?

2. What are some aspects of democratic government that are unique to the United States?

3. What are some aspects of our system of government that do not seem especially democratic?

IDENTIFY THE CONCEPT THAT DOESN'T BELONG

a. Knowledge and awareness
b. Participation
c. Responsive leaders
d. Fixed policies
e. Engaged youth

1.1

Resource Center
• Glossary
• Vocabulary Example
• Connect the Link

Themes of This Book

1.2 **Relate the themes of this book to American politics today.**
(pages 8–17)

American government is complex. The functions of government are divided among different institutions and people. While in some countries, a national government creates law and public policy to handle all issues and priorities for its people, in the United States, by contrast, there are multiple governments. In addition to the familiar institutions of the national government, including the president, Congress, and the U.S. Supreme Court, there are parallel institutions and actors in all 50 states, plus additional agencies and actors in cities, counties, and townships within each state.

To illustrate how government works and how you can affect the way it works, this book first shows the opportunities for *citizen participation in democratic government.* Second, the text identifies and analyzes the *pathways of action* through which individuals and groups can seek to influence law and public policy in American government. Third, the text emphasizes the importance of American society's *diversity and the effect that has on government and our participation in it.* Let's take a moment to consider these three themes in greater detail.

Citizen Participation in Democratic Government

As we noted earlier, a distinguishing feature of democracy is that it provides opportunities for citizens to participate in their government. In nondemocratic governing systems, people have few lawful ways, if any, to shape law and policy. For example, *totalitarian governments* swiftly arrest and even kill people who express opposition to the central authority. In some of these countries, the only option available to citizens who want to affect change is an armed revolt—using violence to change the system of government.

In contrast, people in the United States have opportunities to express their viewpoints and take actions to influence the government without resorting to violence. Opportunities for citizen participation can help create and maintain a stable society. The chapters of this book provide many examples of such opportunities.

These opportunities for citizen participation will not be fully effective, however, unless people actually become engaged in public affairs. If large numbers neglect to vote, fail to keep themselves informed about the government's actions, or passively accept all decisions by lawmakers, governing power may come to rest in the hands of a small number of individuals and groups. The quality and effectiveness of laws and policies may

Rallies, protests, and demonstrations have always been effective modes of political participation in our country. —*Have you ever taken part in this type of political action?*

suffer if there is inadequate input from the full range of people who will be affected by them. Without knowledge about carbon dioxide emissions, for example, well-intentioned decisions to address climate change by Congress and the president may be misdirected and fail to get at the actual source of the problem. In the same way, lawmakers might make more effective laws concerning financial aid programs for college students, if students provide information and express their viewpoints about the best courses of action. In other words, the laws and policies of a democracy can reflect the preferences and viewpoints of a diverse country only if citizens from all segments of society make their voices heard.

Now look at the comparison of voting rates in Figure 1.2. Does this raise any concerns about whether Americans are active enough in shaping their government's decisions? Note that some of the countries with the highest voting rates impose fines on citizens who fail to register to vote and cast their ballots. Would such a law violate Americans' notions of freedom?

To many, it seems ironic that the legal opportunities to participate in the electoral process have expanded greatly during the past 50 years, but a bare majority of Americans seem willing to do so. Numerous measures of political engagement suggest a rather disengaged citizenry in the United States. The American National Election Study at the University of Michigan has been surveying the public every two years since the late 1940s. Scholars will often turn to this data to explore all sorts of political behaviors and trends. It suggests that about 7 percent of Americans attend political meetings, 10 percent give money to political candidates, and only 3 percent work for political parties or candidates. Just one-third of us actually try to influence how others vote (in some years, this figure has been below 20 percent).

FIGURE 1.2 ▪ (a) A Comparative Look at Voting Rates Since 1992; (b) Voter Turnout in Six Democracies

Historically, Americans have voted less often than citizens in other countries. However, in the last two elections, the percentage of voters in the United States participating in the election increased. —*Why do you suppose this is true?*

	Average Voter Turnout*	Compulsory Voting
Greece	86.5%	No
Italy	84.9	Yes
Belgium	84.6	No
Australia	82.8	Yes
Denmark	82.7	No
Sweden	79.7	No
Finland	78.6	No
New Zealand	78.1	No
Spain	77.8	Yes
Israel	77.2	No
Norway	75.5	No
Netherlands	75.4	Yes
Austria	74.9	No
Germany	73.3	No
France	73.0	No
United Kingdom	61.7	No
India	60.0	No
Japan	59.3	No
Canada	57.1	No
United States	53.3	No
Ireland	47.7	No
Switzerland	36.9	No (a)

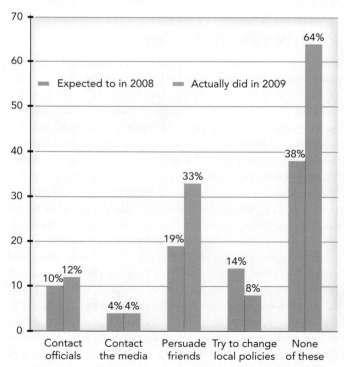

*Percentage of total voting-age population participating in election for highest-level office (president of the United States, for example).
SOURCE: International Institute For Democracy and Electoral Assistance, "Voter Turnout 2008," Accessed at http://www.idea.int/vt/index.cfm, November 1, 2009.

The National Conference on Citizenship, chartered by Congress in 1953, tracks, measures, and promotes civic participation and engagement. Since 2006, they have published yearly reports called *America's Civic Health Index*. In 2009, the report was based on a survey of over 1,500 Americans. In the first wave of the survey, conducted in the spring of 2008, respondents were asked if they intended to undertake a series of political activities. In the second wave, conducted one year later, respondents were asked if they had actually done the activities in the previous year. Figure 1.3 notes the results for

FIGURE 1.3 ▪ Political Engagement Before and After the 2008 Election

The National Conference on Citizenship interviews thousands of Americans each year, with the goal of assessing the public involvement in politics and a host of civic projects. This graph shows data from two polls: one conducted early in 2008, before most of the presidential nomination contests had been held, and another in 2009. As you can see, in some areas the level of engagement was actually higher than expected, but in others it was a bit lower than expected. —*Overall, do you think this graph depicts an engaged public?*

Totals are greater than 100%, because individuals did more than one thing. Respondents are separate, though both nationally representative, groups of individuals from 2008 and 2009.

SOURCE: From "Some Political Engagement Continues After the Election," National Conference on Citizenship, August 27, 2009. http://www.ncoc.net/index.php?tray=content&tid=top31&cid=2gp65. Reprinted by permission of NCOC.

■ **Pathways of Action:** The activities of citizens in American politics that affect the creation, alteration, and preservation of laws and policies.

EXAMPLE: *Average citizens can help change the course of public policy by lobbying legislators.*

four types of engagements. On the one hand, many citizens underestimated what their level of activity would be in the 2008 election. This was likely due to the dramatic nature of that contest—the excitement and energy of a landmark presidential campaign. But on the other hand, these data suggest only modest levels of engagement, especially for a dramatic election year. For example, only one-third of Americans tried to persuade others about who to vote for or what policies to support, and only eight percent tried to change local policies.

As noted, active participation by citizens is necessary in order for a democracy's laws and policies to reflect what people want. Yet, there will always be disagreements and conflicts among an active citizenry, which can prolong decision making and make democracy seem inefficient. Laws and policies in a democracy often represent compromises between the viewpoints and interests of different individuals and groups. On top of this, the framers, the individuals who drafted the U.S. Constitution, worried a great deal about sudden shifts in public policy, and so they sought to create a system that would produce slow, moderate change. What does all of this mean? It means that active citizen participation does not produce smooth, dramatic policy making. Instead, it ensures that a range of viewpoints and interests are presented before compromises are reached.

Pathways of Action

Pathways of action■ are the activities, institutions, and decision points in American politics and government that affect the creation, alteration, and preservation of laws and public policies. In other words, they are the routes of change in our system of government. Certain pathways are open to individual citizens, who can cast their votes, initiate lawsuits, and organize public demonstrations as a means to influence government. The effectiveness of activities within these pathways may depend on the resources, organizational skills, and knowledge possessed by the people making use of them. For example, people who have a lot of money may be able to use litigation more effectively, because they can hire experienced lawyers and carry their lawsuits through all levels of the court system. Resources and organizational skills can also affect people's efforts to conduct petition drives, advertise community meetings, and stage public rallies. Because resources, knowledge, and skill can enhance the effectiveness of citizen participation, powerful organized groups, such as the National Rifle Association, the Chamber of Commerce, and the AARP, are often better positioned than single individuals to achieve their public policy goals through specific pathways.

As you will see, not all pathways of action are equally open to all people. For example, effective lobbying and the use of personal contacts to influence decisions by Congress may require resources and skills possessed only by organized groups

and experienced, well-connected individuals. However, because personal freedom in the United States includes opportunities to publicize ideas and form political organizations, highly motivated individuals may be able to gain the resources and contacts necessary for active participation in these less accessible pathways of action. For example, Mothers Against Drunk Driving (MADD) was started in 1980 by a small group of ordinary people with friends or family members who had been killed by drunk drivers. Over three decades later, MADD has over 3 million members and continues to exert substantial influence over national, state, and local policies concerning alcohol consumption and traffic enforcement.

The existence of several pathways of action to influence American government does not mean that people in the United States always resolve conflicts peaceably. The bloody Civil War of 1861–1865, which resulted in over 600,000 American deaths (more American deaths than in any other war) reflected the nation's inability to use democratic processes to resolve the controversial issues of race-based slavery and federal versus state control of public policy. In addition, if individuals fundamentally object to the nature and existence of the democratic governing system of the United States, they may resort to terrorism. Timothy McVeigh's politically motivated bombing of a federal office building in Oklahoma City in 1995, killed 168 people, and showed that some individuals and groups reject nonviolent pathways of action in a democratic society.

Brief episodes of public disorder and violence also erupt periodically in urban neighborhoods, sometimes fueled by individuals or groups who perceive their opportunities for effective political participation and economic success to be blocked by racial, ethnic, or social-class discrimination. Some may participate, in part, because they do not believe that pathways of action, such as voting, lobbying, and organized protests, provide realistic opportunities to make their viewpoints heard and understood by decision makers in government. Throughout American history, we can identify instances in which people, seeking to express themselves and influence government, used violence instead of the pathways of peaceful action presented in this book. However, the relative stability of American society and the longevity of its governing system are attributable to the existence of nonviolent pathways that provide opportunities for meaningful participation in democratic government.

The chapters of this book are organized to highlight important pathways of action that provide opportunities for participation in and influence over American government. As you consider these opportunities for action, think about how you might contribute to or participate in activities within each pathway. Figure 1.4, on page 11, shows the 10 steps for choosing a pathway of action. As an example, we review the creation of tough drunk driver laws in the past two decades.

FIGURE 1.4 ■ The Ten Steps in Choosing a Pathway of Action *An Illustration: Toughening Drunk Driving Regulations*

In this case, the pathway selected was grassroots mobilization. MADD began with a massive letter-writing campaign, attracted media attention, and changed public opinion. In the end, decision makers had little choice but to respond.

Step 1   Historical Context

It is essential that the activist understand the legal context, the history surrounding the issue, past governmental and political developments, and previous actors. It is especially important to understand the successes and failures of similar movements and the pathways that were used. → Drunk driving and related injuries and deaths are rampant in the United States. In 1980, some 25,000 are killed by drunk drivers.

Step 2   The Trigger

Why did you become involved in an issue? What fueled your motivation? Was it a steady development or a sudden event that motivated you to act? → 13-year-old Cari Lightner is killed by a drunk driver as she walks down a quiet street. Her grieving mother, Candy, sets her sights on tougher drunk driving laws and in 1980 forms Mothers Against Drunk Driving (MADD).

Step 3   Actors That Will Help

Who might you expect to help your efforts and what are their motivations? Who are your potential supporters and what would trigger their action? → Other grieving parents, those in communities that have seen horrific drunk driving accidents, youth advocacy groups such as Students Against Destructive Decisions (SADD).

Step 4   Actors with the Opposition

Who is likely to oppose your efforts and why? How motivated will they be? → Tavern and restaurant owners, liquor industry, civil libertarian groups such as the Center for Consumer Freedom.

Step 5   Timing

When might you best proceed with your efforts? Will there be particular stages or a singular bold stroke? How long will things take? → As new data are revealed on drunk driving accidents, after a high-profile event stirs public emotions.

Step 6   Your Resources

What resources will you bring to the cause? A partial list includes your time, intelligence, passion, financial resources, networks of like-minded activists, ability to garner sympathetic media attention, expertise and experience in similar endeavors, and much else. → Passion, time, media attention, public sympathy.

Step 7   Your Opposition's Resources

What will your opposition bring to the table? Will their resources be similar or different? If they are similar, how can you take best advantage of your resources and minimize the effectiveness of your opponents' resources? → Lobbyists, money, long-standing access to decisionmakers, campaign resources.

Step 8   Pathway Access

Even though your resources might suggest a particular course of action, not all issues fit each of the pathways. For example, there might be no way to pursue a legal course of action. Along similar lines, decision makers might be more receptive to efforts directed down certain pathways. For instance, judges often express indifference to rallies and protests surrounding an issue. → No clear court pathway point of access, yet the cause is ideal for attracting public attention. Graphic stories and visuals are available.

Step 9   Pathway Selected by the Opposition

What pathway has your opposition used, and has it proved successful? If your efforts are successful, which pathway will the opposition likely take? → Lobbying decision makers; elections.

Step 10   How to Measure Success

How will you measure success? How will you sustain your efforts until success is reached? Establishing incremental goals can allow for celebration as they are achieved to create and sustain momentum. → New laws passed, data shows a shrinking number drive while intoxicated, fewer are injured and killed by drunk drivers.

*NOTE: It is critical that the activist understand that the selection of a pathway is not fixed, but rather is dependent upon new developments, successes and failures, and the adjustments of the opposition. Yet, all political action begins with a step down a pathway of action. Also, remember that several pathways often exist to pursue your objectives—if you are not successful using one pathway, look to another. History has proved that diligence is often the key to success.

ELECTIONS PATHWAY American government is based on representative democracy, in which voters elect leaders and then hold those leaders accountable for the decisions they make about law and public policy. If the voters disagree with the decisions that leaders make, the voters can elect different leaders in the next election. Because government leaders in a democracy are usually concerned about maintaining public support in order to gain reelection, they feel pressured to listen to the public and to please a majority of the voters with their actions. Even officials who do not plan to run for reelection or who have served the maximum number of terms the law permits, such as a president who has been elected to a second, four-year term, demonstrate their concern for voters' preferences, because they want to help the election chances of other members of their political party.

A variety of activities, actors, and institutions are involved in the elections pathway. For example, political parties organize like-minded individuals into groups that can plan strategies for winning elections, raise money, and provide public information, to help elect leaders who share the party's specific values and policy preferences. Activities in the elections pathway include voter registration drives, fundraising, political campaigning, and each individual voter's action in casting a ballot.

LOBBYING PATHWAY Legislatures are the central lawmaking bodies at the national, state, and local levels of government. At the national level, the federal legislature is Congress. States also have their own legislatures, and local legislatures include city councils, county commissions, and village boards. Legislatures are made up of elected representatives who must regularly face the voters in elections. Unlike the elections pathway (the mechanisms by which candidates are chosen to fill offices), the lobbying pathway involves attempting to influence the activities, actors, and institutions of government by supplying information, persuasion, or political pressure. Lobbying activities target legislatures and executive officials, such as presidents and governors, as well as the bureaucrats who staff government agencies.

In the lobbying pathway, individuals and organized groups present information and persuasive arguments to government officials. The aim is to convince these decision makers either to support specific proposed laws or to oppose proposed changes in existing laws and policies. Lobbying occurs in the context of the decision-making processes used by each institution. In the legislature, individuals and organized groups can testify before committee hearings attended by legislators. With the president or a governor, the individual or group representative seeks a direct appointment with the decision maker or presents information and arguments to the executive's top aides. Lobbyists also seek meetings with legislators, often buying them meals or taking them on trips that will supposedly educate them about issues. Information and persuasion may well be accompanied

by financial contributions to the reelection campaigns of legislators or elected executives.

Lobbying, in the form of information and persuasion, can also be directed at permanent employees in government agencies who have the authority to create government regulations, such as rules concerning the environment, business practices, and consumer products. Effective lobbying typically requires money, time, and other resources, such as a large organizational membership to flood officials' offices with letters and e-mails, or personal relationships between lobbyists and government officials, as when interest groups hire former members of Congress to represent them in presenting information and arguments. Under the right circumstances, people who lack resources may effectively influence government by getting the attention of key officials. For example, research has shown that letters, emails and phone calls from ordinary citizens are an important source of ideas for new laws and policies.[1]

PATHWAYS of action

Powershift '09

Nearly 12,000 students at a single conference? Seriously?

In late February 2009, students and young activists from around the nation and Canada convened in Washington D.C. for a three-day conference—an event dubbed *Powershift '09*. Sponsored by the Energy Action Coalition, the event became the largest youth-centered global warming conference ever held. The goals of the event were to share information about the growing threat of climate change, help committed young citizens become effective political advocates, and lobby lawmakers for immediate change.

"We want[ed] to make sure our new president and new Congress pass bold federal energy and climate legislation . . . ," noted Brianna Cayo Cotter, one of the event organizers. "[Leaders] understand that young voters were a key to this 2008 election. We have come of age as a powerful voting constituency."

Dozens of organizers, policy experts, celebrities and public officials addressed the gathering, including House Speaker Nancy Pelosi, who has called young global warming activists the "magnificent disrupters of our time"; Environmental Protection Agency Administrator Lisa Jackson; President and Chief Executive Officer of American Progress and Chief of Staff for President Bill Clinton John Podesta; Secretary of the Interior Ken Salazar; and Congressman Ed Markey (D, MA). Numerous break-out sessions, panels, and workshops were held where activists learned how to become effective at organizing and lobbying.

Among those putting these newly acquired lobbying skills to use was Ayesha Siddiqi, of Transylvania University in Lexington, KY. Her foremost concern centered around the effects of strip mining and mountaintop coal removal in her state. "We don't have

Angelina Jolie and George Clooney posing with these devastated mountains . . . We're rising to the challenge of climate change ourselves."

But was anybody listening? Can mobilization efforts of this sort really work? During her keynote address, EPA Administrator Lisa Jackson had the following to say about the potential of *Powershift '09*: "All [significant change] has occurred because of a group of passionate, energetic, informed Americans decided enough was enough, and that they were going to push for change until change came about. . . . You are following a long line of vibrant, robust youth movements that have forever changed their world. There is not a social movement in this country that was not positively impacted by young people."

To watch video clips of the *Powershift '09* speakers, visit: http://itsgettinghotinhere.org/2009/03/02/sights-and-sounds-of-power-shift-2009/

SOURCE: Jonathan Mummolo, "Young People to Swarm Capitol with Green Agenda" *Washington Post Online,* March 1, 2009. Accessed at: http://www.washingtonpost.com/wp-dyn/content/article/2009/02/28/AR2009022801877.html

COURT PATHWAY In the United States, judges have broader authority than in other countries to order the government to take specific actions. Because people in the United States are granted specific legal rights, they can use those rights as a basis for filing lawsuits against the government. For example, if a man was charged under an old state law for the crime of shouting profanity in front of women and children, his lawyer could challenge the validity of the law by asking a judge to declare that it violated the man's legal right to freedom of speech. Such a case actually occurred in Michigan in 1998, where judges eventually ruled that the law violated the man's free speech rights because it was too vague to give him guidance about what words were illegal.[2] Individuals can also file lawsuits asking judges to order the government to follow its own laws. This often happens in cases concerning environmental issues or consumer products when people believe that government officials are failing to enforce the law properly.

Litigation is expensive. People who use this pathway must hire an attorney and pay for gathering and presenting evidence to a court. Organized groups interested in the issue may use their resources to help people carry their cases through the courts. For example, the National Rifle Association (NRA) may provide assistance to individuals who sue to invalidate firearms regulations, or the American Civil Liberties Union (ACLU) may supply attorneys to represent people who believe that their rights to freedom of speech have been violated by the government. Many important policies have been shaped by the actions of individuals and groups who successfully used the court-centered pathway. The U.S.

Supreme Court's decision in *Brown* v. *Board of Education of Topeka* (1954), which prohibited state and local governments from engaging in racial discrimination in public schools, is one of the most famous examples of this pathway in action. The origins of the case can be traced to a lawsuit filed by the father of Linda Brown, an African American girl in Topeka, Kansas, who was not permitted to attend an all-white public school near her home. Lawyers from an interest group, the National Association for the Advancement of Colored People (NAACP), represented the Brown family.

GRASSROOTS MOBILIZATION PATHWAY Highly motivated individuals can seek to attract the attention of government officials and influence the direction of law and policy by mobilizing others to join them in taking strategic actions. Historically, when members of certain groups in society feel that the government is unresponsive to their concerns (as expressed through lobbying and elections activity), they seek other means to educate the public and pressure those officials. Martin Luther King Jr. became a nationally known civil rights figure in the 1950s as a result of his role in organizing and leading a boycott of the public transit system in Montgomery, Alabama, to protest racial segregation on buses. A **boycott** is a coordinated action by many people who agree not to buy a specific product, use a specific service, or shop at a specific store until a policy is changed. Boycotts can place financial pressure on businesses and governments that rely on daily revenue, such as bus fares or the sale of products, in order to stay in business. Advocates of racial equality, opponents of the

There are many ways to draw attention to political concerns. Here, protestors take on ghostly costumes to underscore their concerns and grief about the war in Iraq and the continued loss of lives. —*Have you ever made your views known to decision makers in government? What were the results?*

TIMELINE   The Immigration Debate

● COURTS   ● CULTURAL CHANGE   ● ELECTIONS   ● GRASSROOTS MOBILIZATION   ● LOBBYING DECISION-MAKERS

Before 1882, anyone who wished to live in the United States could. Things have changed dramatically since that time. Some of the more controversial issues facing our government today include who should be allowed to immigrate to our country, what we should do to secure our borders, and what should be done with immigrants illegally residing in the country. People on both sides of this debate have increasingly turned to mass protest to express their positions, and individual states have begun passing their own immigration laws. The Pew Hispanic Center estimates the number of illegal immigrants in the United States to be just under 12 million.

Essay Questions

1. Many proposals for immigration reform have been debated in recent years. Write an essay in which you critically examine the various proposals presented, being certain to indicate which proposal(s) you think would be most effective in addressing illegal immigration.

2. Many states confront the difficult repercussions of illegal immigration, and yet the Constitution stipulates that the federal government is charged with regulating immigration. Should states have the right to adopt their own immigration laws when they believe the federal government is not acting accordingly?

PRO IMMIGRATION

1986
Immigration Reform and **Control Act** allows illegal aliens living in America continuously since January 1, 1982 to apply for legal status; the act also forbids the hiring of illegal aliens, outlines penalties for lack of compliance, and raises annual immigration ceiling to 540,000.

1990
Immigration Act sets immigration quotas at 700,000 annually for the next 3 years and 675,000 for every year thereafter; eliminates denial of admittance to the U.S. on the basis of individual's beliefs, statements, or associations.

| 1965 | 1977–78 | 1980–86 | 1990 | 1996 |

ANTI IMMIGRATION

1965
Immigration Act of 1965
Major reform in immigration policy. Sets overall limit of 170,000 immigrants from the Eastern Hemisphere and 120,000 from the Western Hemisphere.

1977
Immigration and Nationality Act of 1965
Limits immigration to 290,000 worldwide with no more than 20,000 coming from any one country.

1978
John H. Tanton founds the Federation for American Immigration Reform, an anti-immigration group.

1980
Refugees Act distinguishes refugees from other immigrants and limits the worldwide immigration quota to 270,000.

1996
Immigration Act doubles Border Patrol to 10,000 agents over 5 years; also calls for fences to be built at key points on the America-Mexico border; approves a program to check job applicants' immigration status.

1996
President Clinton signs a bill into law cutting numerous social programs for both legal and illegal immigrants in the interest of welfare reform.

Vietnam War, individuals concerned about restrictive immigration policies, and others have organized protest marches as a means to attract public attention and pressure the government to change laws and policies. These actions are seldom instantly successful, but over time, they may draw more and more supporters until elected officials begin to reconsider past decisions. Successful grassroots mobilization requires organizational skill, publicity, careful planning, and a solid core of committed activists who are willing to take public actions in support of their cause.

CULTURAL CHANGE PATHWAY The cultural change pathway is an indirect approach to influencing government. It is a long-term strategy that requires persistence and patience. Through this approach, individuals and organized groups attempt to change the hearts and minds of their fellow citizens. By educating the public about issues and publicizing important events, the dominant values of society may change over time. This can lead to changes in law and policy as newly elected officials bring the new values into government with them.

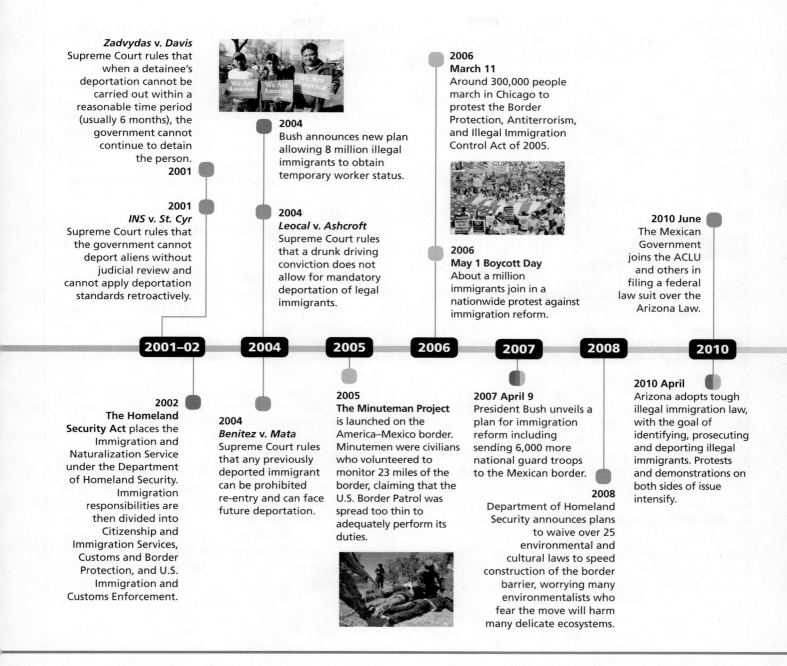

Zadvydas v. Davis
Supreme Court rules that when a detainee's deportation cannot be carried out within a reasonable time period (usually 6 months), the government cannot continue to detain the person.
2001

2001
INS v. St. Cyr
Supreme Court rules that the government cannot deport aliens without judicial review and cannot apply deportation standards retroactively.

2004
Bush announces new plan allowing 8 million illegal immigrants to obtain temporary worker status.

2004
Leocal v. Ashcroft
Supreme Court rules that a drunk driving conviction does not allow for mandatory deportation of legal immigrants.

2006
March 11
Around 300,000 people march in Chicago to protest the Border Protection, Antiterrorism, and Illegal Immigration Control Act of 2005.

2006
May 1 Boycott Day
About a million immigrants join in a nationwide protest against immigration reform.

2010 June
The Mexican Government joins the ACLU and others in filing a federal law suit over the Arizona Law.

2001–02   **2004**   **2005**   **2006**   **2007**   **2008**   **2010**

2002
The Homeland Security Act places the Immigration and Naturalization Service under the Department of Homeland Security. Immigration responsibilities are then divided into Citizenship and Immigration Services, Customs and Border Protection, and U.S. Immigration and Customs Enforcement.

2004
Benitez v. Mata
Supreme Court rules that any previously deported immigrant can be prohibited re-entry and can face future deportation.

2005
The Minuteman Project is launched on the America–Mexico border. Minutemen were civilians who volunteered to monitor 23 miles of the border, claiming that the U.S. Border Patrol was spread too thin to adequately perform its duties.

2007 April 9
President Bush unveils a plan for immigration reform including sending 6,000 more national guard troops to the Mexican border.

2008
Department of Homeland Security announces plans to waive over 25 environmental and cultural laws to speed construction of the border barrier, worrying many environmentalists who fear the move will harm many delicate ecosystems.

2010 April
Arizona adopts tough illegal immigration law, with the goal of identifying, prosecuting and deporting illegal immigrants. Protests and demonstrations on both sides of issue intensify.

Until the twentieth century, for example, many Americans—both men and women alike—believed that women should devote themselves to the roles of wife and mother. Federal, state, and local laws reflected this belief, generally preventing women from voting in elections and working in certain occupations. Over a period of several decades, beginning before the Civil War, activist women and their male supporters used newspaper articles, speeches, and demonstrations to educate the public about women's capabilities and about the need to grant women opportunities to live and work as citizens equal to men.

In the late nineteenth and early twentieth centuries, women finally gained the right to vote, first on a state-by-state basis but eventually through passage of the Nineteenth Amendment (1920), which guaranteed the vote to women nationwide. But discriminatory attitudes toward women remained prevalent through the 1960s, requiring decades of continued educational work. Gradually, laws and policies changed to protect women against gender discrimination. Eventually, most Americans accepted the idea of women becoming doctors, lawyers, police officers, and elected officials at all levels of government—even president and vice president, as demonstrated in the 2008 election. Law and policy changed through the long-term effort to change the culture and values of American society.

Individuals and groups can use the cultural change pathway to try to affect changes in laws and policies related to a variety of issues, including abortion, the death penalty, and environmental protection. For people who seek to change society's values, the ultimate outcome of the cultural change pathway can be quite uncertain. Indeed, for some issues, change may occur long after the passing of the people who initiated the efforts to alter public opinion and social values. And sometimes change never comes.

PATHWAYS of change from around the world

Would you risk your future career defending a television station? In May 2007, Venezuelan President Hugo Chavez moved to shut down one of the country's most popular television stations, Radio Caracas Television International (RCTV). Chavez claimed that the station had played a key role in an effort to overthrow the government. Yet RCTV was Venezuela's most popular station, especially with younger citizens, and many saw the move as an attempt to limit criticism of Chavez and his government.

In response, tens of thousands of Venezuelan students took to the streets. They led massive demonstrations— marches, rallies, sit-ins, and more. For weeks, university exams were put off, and classes were rescheduled. Political science major Ana Cristina Garanton, who took part in the protests, said the battle was for more than a television station: "We are fighting for the rights we should have as students so that when I graduate I can pursue any career without being discriminated against for political reasons. Our parents will one day leave the country to us. And it is up to us, the young people, to take the reins of the country."

The students understood the dangers of their activism, which included the real possibility of being put on a government blacklist that would decrease their chances of finding a good job after graduation. But they protested and spoke out nonetheless. Another student, Carlos Julio Rojas, put it this way: "At the beginning of the year, the government said that, to impose [its program of] '21st Century Socialism,' it would be necessary to control communications . . . That is undemocratic. We believe in debate, freedom of thought."

SOURCE: Michael Bowman, "Venezuelan Students at Forefront of Campaign for Freedom of Expression," Voice of America, VoANews.com, July 2, 2007. Accessed at http://www.voanews.com/english/archive/2007-07/2007-07-02-voa1.cfm? CFID=186364115&CFTOKEN=88761349

Diversity in American Society

This book's third theme is the impact of diversity on American government and on the laws and policies that government produces. Many of the issues facing American government are products of the country's history, and many policy issues have their roots in America's history of race-based slavery. Slavery and its consequences, including blatant discrimination against African Americans, which persisted until the 1970s, are at the heart of such difficult contemporary problems as chronic poverty, decaying urban neighborhoods, disproportionate minority unemployment rates, and lingering racial and ethnic hostility and mistrust.

Cultural change eventually created a widespread consensus in American society about the need to eliminate overt racial discrimination. Laws and policies, such as the Civil Rights Act of 1964 and the Voting Rights Act of 1965, were enacted in the second half of the twentieth century to prohibit many forms of discrimination that had been endorsed and enforced by various levels of government. However, there is no consensus on how to address other problems arising out of the legacy of slavery and racial discrimination. Attempts to apply specific remedies, such as court-ordered busing to achieve public school desegregation, affirmative action programs to increase minority enrollment in colleges and universities, and programs to diversify government employment and contract opportunities have all caused bitter debate and political conflict.

Immigration is another challenging policy controversy related to the nation's diversity. Contemporary debates about immigration often focus on undocumented workers arriving from Mexico and other countries in violation of American law. Some Americans want stronger measures to prevent illegal immigration, but many businesses hire undocumented workers because they often work for less money than U.S. citizens. At the same time, Latinos in the United States have grown in numbers. In 2004, Latinos became the nation's largest minority group. As noted in Table 1.2, the Hispanic population in the United States is expected to double in the next few decades. Hispanics have also expanded their political power by becoming a significant voting presence in many cities and winning an increasing number of important offices. Many native-born and naturalized Latino citizens are wary of certain anti-immigration proposals, fearing that they may contribute to ethnic discrimination against U.S. citizens while treating noncitizens unduly harshly.

The policy debates over immigration show how America's diversity contributes to political controversies at the same time that it adds complexity to the mix of actors seeking to use various pathways of change. Indeed, the Timeline dealing with the immigration debate (see Timeline, pages 14–15) highlights the history and the complexity of the issue, as well as the various approaches used by concerned individuals to shape the outcome of the debate. All these pathways—elections, lobbying, courts,

TABLE 1.2	The Face of a Changing Nation					
	PERCENTAGE OF TOTAL POPULATION					
	2000	**2010**	**2020**	**2030**	**2040**	**2050**
Total	100.0%	100.0%	100.0%	100.0%	100.0%	100.0%
White not Hispanic	69.4	65.1	61.3	57.5	53.7	50.1
Black not Hispanic	12.7	13.1	13.5	13.9	14.3	14.6
Asian	3.8	4.6	5.4	6.2	7.1	8.0
All other races[1]	2.5	3.0	3.5	4.1	4.7	5.3
Hispanic (of any race)	12.6	15.5	17.8	20.1	22.3	24.4

[1]Includes American Indians and Alaska Natives, Native Hawaiians, other Pacific Islanders, and people who belong to two or more racial designations.

SOURCE: U.S. Census Bureau, International Database, Table 094. http://www.census.gov

grassroots mobilization, and cultural change—have been used by a diverse array of Americans, including women, the disabled, homosexuals, and people of color, who have felt excluded from meaningful participation in American government.

Now that we have highlighted the book's important themes, in the next section we'll consider an example that illustrates how citizen participation and pathways for action affect the operations of American government.

Themes of This Book

1.2 Relate the themes of this book to American politics today.

PRACTICE QUIZ: UNDERSTAND AND APPLY

1. Changing the hearts and minds of citizens over the long term is an example of which pathway of action?
   a. elections
   b. courts
   c. grassroots mobilization
   d. cultural change

2. An important trend in American politics has been the growing demographic diversity of citizens.
   a. true
   b. false

3. While Americans tend to vote less often than citizens in other democracies, many find alternative ways of participating actively and meaningfully in politics.
   a. true
   b. false

ANALYZE

1. Can't we interpret modest political participation in the United States as a sign of contentment? That is, do you think people tune out because they see everything as more or less okay?

2. What does this text mean by *pathways of action*? Describe some of the pathways featured in American politics.

3. Do you think certain pathways of change are better suited for particular types of issues and groups?

IDENTIFY THE CONCEPT THAT DOESN'T BELONG

a. Elections
b. Violence
c. Lobbying
d. Culture
e. Courts
f. Grassroots

Resource Center
• Glossary
• Vocabulary Example
• Connect the Link

Citizen Participation and Pathways: The Example of Abortion

1.3 Outline the various "pathways" of involvement in our political system.

(pages 18–19)

Abortion is a divisive, wrenching issue that continues to generate controversy among Americans nationwide. Several major institutional components of American government, including Congress, the president, the U.S. Supreme Court, and state governments, have been involved in defining and changing abortion laws and policies. Thus, the abortion issue helps show how American government operates and how citizens can use pathways of action to influence the results of those operations.

Although women gained the right to vote nationwide in the early twentieth century, advocates using the *lobbying pathway* failed to persuade state legislatures to enact abortion choice laws until the 1960s, and then only in a few states. In the early 1970s, however, two young lawyers in Texas volunteered to help a woman who unsuccessfully sought an abortion after she claimed that she had been raped. The lawyers began a legal case to challenge the Texas law that made it a crime to obtain or perform an abortion. The case worked its way through the levels of the court system until it reached the U.S. Supreme Court. In a landmark decision in *Roe* v. *Wade* (1973), the justices of the Supreme Court voted 7-2 to strike down the Texas law as a violation of women's right to privacy in making personal choices about reproduction. Much more will be said about this case in subsequent chapters. For now, you should understand that the *court pathway* was used to change the law for the entire nation.

Of course, opponents of abortion were anxious to move government in a different direction. In the aftermath of *Roe* v. *Wade*, opponents of abortion mobilized supporters and organized political action groups. They used several pathways in their efforts to reimpose legal prohibitions on abortion. In the *elections pathway*, they sought to recruit and elect candidates who pledged to fight abortion. They used the *lobbying pathway* to pressure and persuade elected officials to pass new laws that would place restrictions on abortion that would be acceptable to the courts. They also used the *grassroots mobilization pathway* to organize protest marches and, especially, demonstrations at abortion clinics intended to discourage women from entering to seek abortions. A few opponents of abortion even rejected democratic processes as a means to seek change, instead engaging in such violent acts as firebombing abortion clinics and assaulting or even killing doctors who performed abortions.

Americans are free to use many methods of expressing their views to public officials. —*Why do activists use various pathways for an issue that was originally defined in the court pathway?*

Abortion opponents who worked within the governing system achieved partial success in many state legislatures and in Congress. New laws were adopted imposing restrictions that could discourage or hinder women's efforts to obtain abortions—for example, blocking the use of government funds to pay for poor women's abortions. During the heated negations over health care reform in 2009, the issue of whether government-assisted insurance plans should include any reimbursement for abortions became a central and hotly debated issue. Laws also limited the ability of teenagers to obtain abortions without informing their parents or obtaining the permission of a judge. States imposed new requirements for counseling women about abortion procedures and, after the counseling session, making them wait 24 hours before making a second trip to the clinic to have the abortion procedure performed by a doctor.

Throughout the three decades in which abortion opponents used these pathways to seek restrictions on abortion, they also focused on the *elections pathway* in an effort to elect Republican presidents who might appoint new Supreme Court justices willing to overturn *Roe* v. *Wade* and to elect senators who would confirm these justices. As a result, the process of obtaining the U.S. Senate's approval of the president's nominees for the Supreme Court became part of the political battles over abortion. Both opponents and supporters of women's abortion rights used the *lobbying pathway* to pressure senators to either endorse or oppose judicial nominees on the basis of their perceived stance on abortion.

The struggle between opponents and defenders of abortion choice moved between *different* pathways. With each legislative success that abortion foes won, advocates of choice returned to the *court pathway* to challenge the laws on the grounds that they improperly clashed with the Supreme Court's declaration in *Roe* v. *Wade* that women had a constitutionally protected right to choose to have an abortion. Although the Supreme Court and lower federal courts struck down some state laws as conflicting with *Roe* v. *Wade,* the courts also upheld many laws that imposed regulations.

In March 2006, shortly after Justices John Roberts and Samuel Alito, both nominated by President George W. Bush, were confirmed by the Senate, state legislators in South Dakota acted quickly to enact a statute that would virtually abolish abortion in their state. Under the law, abortion would be permitted only to save the life of a pregnant woman. Doctors faced criminal prosecution and prison sentences for performing other abortions, including those performed in the aftermath of rape or incest. The purpose of the statute, in large part, was to generate a legal challenge that might ultimately lead the newly constituted Supreme Court to overturn *Roe* v. *Wade.*

A countermove by pro-choice forces might have been a lawsuit, but opponents of the law chose a different strategy instead. They gathered petition signatures to place the measure on the general election ballot for a statewide vote—a process called a *ballot initiative,* which is possible in 23 states. Their

strategy worked: The abortion ban was rejected by 55 percent of South Dakota voters in 2008.

Both sides in the abortion debate have attempted to shape public opinion through the *cultural change pathway.* Supporters of choice seek to persuade the public that control over "reproductive freedom" is a key component of women's equality in American society. They also raise warnings about the risks to women's health if abortion is banned, referring to the time when abortion was illegal and women turned to abortionists who were not doctors, causing many desperate women to die from bleeding and infections. Opponents of abortion insist that abortion is murder and use graphic pictures of both developing and aborted fetuses in their publicity campaigns.

This brief snapshot of the abortion issue illustrates how law and policy develop and change through the complex interaction of the pathways of action and the American government's various institutions. Throughout this continuing battle over abortion, both sides rely on the participation of individual citizens for lobbying, contributing money, campaigning, voting, engaging in public protests, and carrying out the specific activities of each pathway of action.

Citizen Participation and Pathways

1.3   **Outline the various "pathways" of involvement in our political system.**

PRACTICE QUIZ: UNDERSTAND AND APPLY

1. Once the court pathway has been used to change the outcome of a court case, no other pathways can legally be used to make a change.
   a. true
   b. false

2. As a result of *Roe* v. *Wade,* no lower court can make a decision to change any aspect of abortion law.
   a. true
   b. false

3. Pathways of action have been a critical feature of democracy because
   a. they allow different groups of citizens to change government policy.
   b. they promote active participation of citizens from all walks of life.
   c. they prevent discrimination against minorities.
   d. a and b.

ANALYZE

1. How does the issue of abortion reflect diversity in American society?

2. How do changes in the membership of the Supreme Court affect political and legal changes in our society?

3. Is it appropriate for "single issue candidates," such as those opposed to abortion, to run for office?

IDENTIFY THE CONCEPT THAT DOESN'T BELONG

a. Court cases
b. Court nominations
c. Protests
d. Ballot initiatives
e. Local laws

Resource Center
- Glossary
- Vocabulary Example
- Connect the Link

■ **Checks and Balances:** A system in our government where each branch (legislative, executive, judicial) has the power to limit the actions of others.

EXAMPLE: *Even though President Obama announced a decision to send 30,000 additional troops to Afghanistan in December 2009, it did not automatically mean that Congress would appropriate the funds necessary to carry out the plan. Ironically, many of the harshest critics of the plan were members of the President's own party—Democrats.*

Change and Stability in American Government

1.4 Analyze the forces of stability in American politics.

(pages 20–23)

As we have seen, the pathways of action provide opportunities for citizens to take nonviolent actions to make their voices heard by decision makers in American government. The existence of these pathways is also important for the preservation of the American governing system. No form of government is automatically stable. No form of government automatically functions smoothly. If disagreements within the population are great enough, or if a segment of the population does not accept the design and operation of the governing system, then even democracies will experience violence, disorder, instability, and collapse. The American Civil War vividly reminds us of what can happen when pathways fail to resolve controversies. In that example, the divisive issues of slavery and state government authority were inflamed rather than resolved through actions in the elections pathway (the election of Lincoln as the antislavery president) and the court-centered pathway (a Supreme Court decision that helped the spread of slavery to western territories—*Dred Scott* v. *Sandford,* 1857).

To understand American government and its ability to endure, we must examine the factors that contribute to stability as well as those that help Americans change what their government does. This book focuses on pathways of action as a key element for understanding how American government operates. These pathways help explain why the American system of government continues to exist, even after two centuries that included significant social changes and a bloody civil war.

Every nation experiences periods of transformation. These are eras in which new issues, fundamental changes in social and economic conditions, or major events spur adjustments in society and in the priorities and actions of government decision makers. These transformations can also produce changes in a country's system of government. In the 1990s, the world witnessed the emergence of new governing systems in places such as South Africa and the formerly communist countries of Eastern Europe and Russia. In the United States, we have maintained the same Constitution and general blueprint for government through more than 200 years of significant changes in society, politics, and the economy—topics taken up throughout the book.

Sources of Stability

Stability in American government and in the governing systems of other countries cannot be taken for granted. We cannot automatically assume that governing systems will be stable or remain stable for any predictable period. Stability in any political system is the result of three closely related elements:

- A broadly accepted political and economic framework
- A stable, powerful political culture
- A variety of ways for citizens to seek and achieve policy changes

We will discuss each of these elements in turn.

BROADLY ACCEPTED FRAMEWORK: REVERENCE FOR THE CONSTITUTION AND CAPITALISM

Early in his political career, Abraham Lincoln delivered a speech in which he urged that our Constitution be the "political religion of the nation."[3] We have taken his advice to heart. Indeed, one of the interesting and somewhat unique aspects of American politics is our reverence for the structure of our governing system. Some would say that we treat the Constitution as our nonreligious "bible"—the written document that Americans deeply respect and obey.

The authors of the Constitution, the Framers, would likely have found this surprising. The Constitution they developed was a collection of compromises, ambiguities, and generalized grants of authority to the national government. It divided powers between the national government and the states, and it tried to compel the sharing of powers among three branches of government, with an elaborate system of **checks and balances**■ to limit the actions of each branch. However, the Constitution replaced an earlier governmental blueprint, the Articles of Confederation. If the Constitution had been rejected by the American public or had failed to work well, they might have been forced to go back to the drawing board to write a third version. In other words, to the Framers, the Constitution was a practical plan for creating a government. It was not a set of sacred principles. Yet today, Americans express a shared belief in the special wisdom of the Constitution's authors for creating a system of government that would both endure and embody important principles of democracy.

Americans' reverence for the institutional framework of our political system extends to our economic system as well. Indeed, the "American dream" rests mostly on the notion that intelligence, ingenuity, and hard work will lead to economic success. Faith in **capitalism**■ is deeply ingrained in Americans' values and beliefs. Capitalism is the economic system based on free enterprise in which individuals compete with each other for jobs, operate privately owned businesses that may succeed or fail, and focus their efforts on accumulating wealth for themselves and

■ **Capitalism:** An economic system where business and industry are privately owned and there is little governmental interference.

EXAMPLE: *Some have suggested that Hong Kong boasts one of the most open capitalist systems in the world.*

■ **Socialism:** An economic system in which the government owns and controls most factories and much or all of the nation's land.

EXAMPLE: *The Socialist Republic of Vietnam.*

their families. In an alternative economic system, **socialism**■, the government owns and controls key factories and sometimes also the land. It may even use that control to assign individuals to specific jobs. Socialist systems may focus on the ideal of individuals working for the good of society rather than pursuing self-interest. In the United States, by contrast, most people have always believed that society as a whole benefits through the continuous creation of new businesses, new jobs, and increased wealth when all individuals pursue their own interests and have opportunities to use their own private property and businesses to create jobs and generate income.

The American idea that we have ample opportunities to become economically successful through our own hard work is not always fulfilled in practice. Historically, racial and gender discrimination have limited opportunities for many Americans to find good jobs or start their own businesses. The ability of rich people to provide superior education for their children and pass on their wealth to family members provides and perpetuates advantages that most Americans do not share. The significant power wielded by corporations in the United States and vast disparities of individual wealth have led to occasional calls for a change in the American economic system. Various plans for a redistribution of wealth to assist poor people have been proposed—for example, through higher taxes on the rich to fund antipoverty programs. For the most part, however, criticisms are focused on specific aspects of the capitalist system, and in recent decades, people have rarely suggested that the United States switch to a different system. For example, when President Barack Obama pressured Congress to move forward with a health care reform initiative in the spring of 2009, the idea of a "single payer plan" (that is, a government-run health care system) was considered "off the table" from the very beginning. Support for free enterprise and capitalism remains strong even when critics point out that the United States falls short of its ideals of equal economic opportunities for all Americans.

Americans believe strongly in the core elements of our political and economic system. Lincoln's hope that Americans would protect their system through an almost religious reverence has come to pass. James Madison and the other framers of the United States would presumably be pleased—and perhaps surprised—to know that the experimental governing system they designed has survived for more than two centuries. They would be doubly surprised to see how Americans cherish the Constitution—the experimental document full of compromises—as the crown jewel of democracy.

POLITICAL CULTURE: THE "AMERICAN CREED"

Scholars have long recognized the powerful influence of a nation's *political culture*. Much more will be said about this concept in Chapter 10, but for now, simply note that the term refers to the fundamental values and dominant beliefs that are shared throughout society and that shape political behavior and

One of the best illustrations of our nation's reverence for the Constitution *and* capitalism is our currency. On one side of the dollar bill we pay tribute to the hero of the Revolution and the first president, and on the other side we find the Great Seal of the United States (front and back). The pyramid symbolizes strength, and its 13 steps represent the original 13 colonies. The unfinished summit on the pyramid implies a "work in progress." *—Do you think the larger message is that our government's fate is linked to the future of free enterprise in America? Or, as capitalism goes, so goes our system of government?*

government policies. It is the umbrella under which political activities take place, and it defines the arena where political questions are resolved. Political culture incorporates both citizens' personal values—that is, their ideas about what is right and wrong—and their shared ideas about how they should be governed.[4]

A nation's political culture springs from a number of sources, including the origins of the nation (sometimes called the nation's "creation myth"), historical struggles in the nation's history, the deeds and thoughts of past leaders, important documents and texts, economic conditions, and distinct subcultures. Religion may also play a role, depending on a nation's history and culture. To some extent, a nation's popular culture, including its entertainment, fashions, and media, also contribute to its political culture. For instance, the counterculture movement in the 1960s (hippie culture) had a direct impact on the political process—especially on policies

■ **Alexis de Tocqueville:** A French scholar who traveled throughout the United States in the early 1830s. **SIGNIFICANCE:** *His published notes,* Democracy in America, *offer a telling account of our nations formative years—it is a book that is still widely read.*

related to gender equity, civil rights, and the war in Vietnam. And many observers suggest that the portrayal of gay men and women in film and on television in recent years has raised levels of tolerance toward homosexuals throughout society. When some or all of these pieces are missing or are not clearly defined, the nation's political identity becomes less clear. Nations with a strong, clearly defined political culture are generally more stable.[5]

Alexis de Tocqueville■ (uh-lek-see duh TOKE-vil), a French scholar who traveled throughout the United States in the early 1830s, found our nation's emerging political culture to be distinctive and powerful. The essence of American politics, Tocqueville wrote in *Democracy in America,* lies not in the complex maze of political institutions but rather in the shared values of American citizens. In fact, he suggested, along with this powerful political identity comes a downside: "I know of no country in which there is such little independence of mind and real freedom of discussion as in America."[6] The widespread nature of shared values and beliefs among Americans, which was observed by Tocqueville and continues today, has tended to limit the range of discussions about government and public policy. As with the economic system, people tend to focus on fixing specific problems within the current system rather than suggesting that the system itself should be changed.

American political culture, as noted by the Swedish social scientist Gunnar Myrdal (GUN-er MEER-dahl) in 1944, is "the most explicitly expressed system of general ideals" of any country in the West[7]—so much so that he saw fit to call our belief system the "American Creed." At least in the abstract, Americans embrace the concepts of "freedom," "equality," "liberty," "majority will," "religious freedom," and "due process under the law." According to Myrdal, "Schools teach the principles of the Creed; the churches preach them; the courts hand down judgment in their terms."[8] According to historian Arthur Schlesinger, Jr., "Myrdal saw the Creed as the bond that links all Americans, including nonwhite minorities, and as the spur forever goading Americans to live up to their principles."[9] Yale University political scientist Robert Dahl echoed this idea a few decades later when he called our set of beliefs the "democratic creed." He wrote, "The common view seems to be that our system is not only democratic but is perhaps the most perfect expression of democracy that exists anywhere. . . . To reject the democratic creed is in effect to refuse to be American."[10]

There are many things that define the American Creed, many of which will be discussed in later chapters. The important point here is to understand that the United States possesses a powerful political culture that is clearly defined and long-lasting. The historical national consensus on political values and democratic institutions helped create stability during times of profound social change. As waves of change transformed the workplace, home life, leisure patterns, and intellectual fabric of the nation, Americans found strength in the stability of their political system.

Americans have always had a deep sense of patriotism, especially when it comes to honoring those who have defended our country during times of war. *—Is it possible to be truly patriotic while at the same time speaking out against our involvement in a war?*

NUMEROUS AVENUES OF CHANGE Two necessary conditions for any country's political stability are broad popular acceptance of its government and economic system and a clearly defined political culture. But they do not guarantee stability. For a democratic system to remain stable, its citizens must believe that they can influence the outcome of government activity. The design and operation of government must permit popular participation. In addition, the political culture and laws must encourage civic involvement and protect activists from being silenced either by the government or by majority opinion. There must also be a variety of ways to achieve desired ends. Severe limitations on citizen participation and influence can lead to frustration, cynicism, and in the end, conflict and potential upheaval. Stated a bit differently, stability in a democratic regime springs from a system that allows participation, a culture that promotes involvement, and a set of options (or, shall we say, "pathways") to help redirect public policy.

STUDENT profile

Like most young Americans, Nick Anderson and Ana Slavin spend a lot of time on social networking sites. Facebook and MySpace are entertaining, a way to make social connections, but can they also be harnessed to do good work?

During a trip to South Africa in 2005, Anderson was horrified by the plight of people in the Darfur region of western Sudan. For nearly a decade, Arab militias backed by the Sudanese government had waged a genocidal war on tribes in the region, killing upward of 300,000 men, women, and children. Anderson witnessed a crisis of humanity, and it tugged at his heartstrings. Slavin learned about the situation during an internship at Wellesley College's Women's Research Center. It, too, set her aback. How could Americans sit by and do nothing?

Together, Anderson and Slavin created a plan to use MySpace and Facebook to urge their peers to host fundraisers to increase awareness about the violence in Darfur. Eventually they met with the Save Darfur Coalition in Washington, D.C., which agreed to support them. "Things kind of snowballed from there," Anderson said. The Dollars for Darfur National High School Challenge spawned a national movement, with young people showing videos about the conflict and collecting money to support refugees. The program raised awareness of the crisis among young Americans and over $300,000. Anderson and Slavin were named ABC News' "Persons of the Week" in June 2007, and they were called to testify before a congressional committee about the efforts to send aid to Darfur.

If you have ever doubted the power of committed citizens, even young citizens, to make a real difference, read the *Student Profile* about Nick Anderson and Ana Slavin. Here, they are testifying before a congressional committee about the efforts to send aid to Darfur. —*Do you think stories of this sort can help young people understand their potential as citizens in a democracy and motivate them to get involved?*

Change and Stability in American Government

1.4   **Analyze the forces of stability in American politics.**

PRACTICE QUIZ: UNDERSTAND AND APPLY

1. Which of the following are considered a source of stability in any political system?
   a. a stable and powerful political culture
   b. a variety of ways for citizens to seek and achieve policy changes
   c. a broadly accepted political and economic framework
   d. a, b, and c

2. According to this textbook, which of the following are basic features of the U.S. Constitution?
   a. checks and balances
   b. division of power between national and state governments
   c. compromises and ambiguities
   d. a, b, and c

3. In terms of economic prosperity, Americans tend to believe that
   a. the state should place strict limits on the amount of wealth and property any individual may own.
   b. all professions should offer similar pay and benefits.
   c. few governmental restrictions should be placed on individual wealth and ownership of property.
   d. all citizens are entitled to ownership of property, even if the government must help them to pay for it.

4. The social scientist who termed America's system of political beliefs the "American Creed" was
   a. Alexis de Tocqueville   c. George Gallup
   b. Gunnar Myrdal   d. Robert Dahl

ANALYZE

1. Which aspects of American political culture are most dominant? Have they changed over time?

2. Are there elements of our political culture that make our nation less democratic than it should be?

3. How do democracy and capitalism work together to create a society unique to the United States?

IDENTIFY THE CONCEPT THAT DOESN'T BELONG

a. Indifference   d. Small government
b. Individualism   e. Republic
c. Free market

Conclusion

A key feature of all democracies is the opportunity for citizens to participate in public affairs in order to influence the decisions of government. The design and operation of American government provide a variety of opportunities for citizens to make their voices heard at the national, state, and local levels. In the United States, individuals can use the different pathways for action to influence government and public policies. These pathways include opportunities to participate in campaigns and elections, to file lawsuits in the courts, to lobby government officials, and to mobilize large groups of people to pressure officials or seek to change the culture and values of society.

In the debate over health care policy during the summer and fall of 2009, Americans used numerous avenues to shape the final outcome. They held several large protests on Capitol Hill, both for and against reform; they flooded legislative offices with e-mails and letters; and they made phone calls and visits to district offices. Although the debate took place during an off-election year, how members of Congress voted became a central piece of their individual campaigns for office in 2010. Republicans veered from supporting broad changes, for instance, in part because they worried about confronting strong primary challengers. Reform supporters from more Democratic districts touted their votes as examples of their responsiveness to a major societal issue.

The issue of youth engagement also featured prominently in the health care debate. Numerous surveys suggested young Americans were anxious for significant health care reform and that they tended to back the so-called, "public option." Given that young voters made up such a large, relatively unified bloc in the 2008 election—a phenomenon referenced at the start of this chapter—initially, politicians likely paid close attention to the opinions of younger voters. But after lackluster youth voter turnout in the 2009 election, some legislators may have felt comfortable moving in a different direction. After all, astute legislators pay the *closest* attention to constituents who vote.

Citizen participation should not be viewed as just a hobby or something that takes place every two or four years. It is an essential element for maintaining stability in a democratic society. In the United States, stability also depends on shared beliefs in the political and economic systems as well as the shared values that make up what has been called the American Creed. In many other countries, ethnic conflict and social transformations can lead to profound changes in the form of government or public policies. By contrast, despite significant social changes in our diverse society, the United States has maintained a high degree of stability under a founding document, the Constitution, which was written in the eighteenth century. At one point, profound disagreements in society led to the bloody, four-year Civil War. However, after the North's victory started the process of resolving regional disagreements over slavery and states' rights, the United States again became a stable democracy thanks to the opportunities it granted citizens to participate and share in political and economic values.

In the next chapter, we examine the design of American government, beginning with the blueprint developed in the Constitution. Subsequent chapters will discuss key elements in government and politics, such as the news media and public opinion, as well as the specific institutions of government, such as Congress and the U.S. Supreme Court. As you learn about these key elements and institutions, think about which pathways of action are most important for each aspect of American government. You should also consider how you can participate as an engaged citizen when you want to assert influence over the decisions and priorities of your government.

As you think about your daily life, are there laws or government policies that you regard as unfair or misguided? Listen to the people around you. Are they debating issues that affect their lives? Many people disagree about whether motorcyclists should be required to wear helmets. Some think it unjust that one can vote at age 18 but can't drink alcohol until age 21. Other people feel deeply about issues such as abortion or American military actions overseas. Some of your classmates may believe that public universities have raised their tuition and fees to a level that is too high for the average individual to afford. Yet others may feel most strongly about the availability of health insurance for students and other individuals with limited incomes. Throughout the country, Americans debate such issues as gun control and affirmative action. Do you worry about whether Social Security funds will be available when you retire? Or what should be done about immigration? Should dramatic steps be taken to reduce climate change? Unfortunately, many people, including students, appear to feel helpless, and they act as if there is no point in getting involved in contemporary issues. This may explain, in part, why voter participation rates in the United States are low compared to those in many other democracies. As you evaluate your views about government and society, ask yourself: As a college-educated person, do you really want all laws and policies that affect your life and determine what happens in your country to be decided by other people?

KEY CONCEPT MAP

How do average citizens shape the course of government in a democracy?

Elections

Strengths
Elections are generally egalitarian; everyone's vote is counted equally, so the "majority will" can be harnessed to create change.

Weaknesses
Hefty resources shape the outcome; the "majority will" can sometimes stifle democratic change.

Critical Thinking Question
Given the "checks and balances" inherent in the structure of government, how can we expect the election of a particular leader, such as a new president or governor, to shape the outcome of public policy?

Courts

Strengths
Courts are the protectors of rights and liberties for all citizens; decisions can overrule the will of the majority when necessary.

Weaknesses
Change can come about slowly; litigation can be expensive.

Critical Thinking Question
How democratic can the court pathway be when federal judges (and many state judges) are appointed and serve for life?

Lobbying

Strengths
Big change can occur quickly behind the scenes.

Weaknesses
Effective lobbying often entails "connections," which requires big resources.

Critical Thinking Question
Many are critical of "special interest lobbying," but what's wrong with citizens promoting their own interests?

Grassroots Mobilization

Strengths
Grassroots efforts can be effective at getting decision makers to pay attention to an issue.

Weaknesses
Changes are seldom effective immediately; organizational skill, careful planning, and truly committed activists are necessary.

Critical Thinking Question
Can you think of a time in American history when policy makers turned a deaf ear to massive public demonstrations?

Cultural Change

Strengths
Cultural change can involve a variety of issues, particularly those that are at first opposed by the majority.

Weaknesses
Change takes a long time to be effective and is by no means certain.

Critical Thinking Question
How does popular culture, such as music, television, and sports, ultimately shape public policy?

Many Americans believe they can't play a meaningful role in politics. While it is true that change can sometimes come slowly, and that certain citizens have more resources than others, our history also suggests that steadfast, determined individuals and groups can make a big difference by using the five pathways of change: elections, courts, lobbying, grassroots mobilization, and cultural change. —*Will any of these pathways become more or less influential in the digital age? Why or why not?*

Review of Key Objectives

It's Your Government

 1.1 Illustrate how citizens participate in a democracy and why this is important.

(pages 4–7)

Many Americans, especially young Americans, believe "government" and "politics" are distant, beyond their immediate world. In reality, government is around us; it shapes our lives in important ways every hour of every day. That is why it is particularly important for citizens in a democracy to become involved. Government matters, and you can make a difference.

KEY TERMS

Politics 4
Public Policy 4
Democracy 6
Totalitarian Regimes 6

CRITICAL THINKING QUESTIONS

1. Why do you suppose many young Americans are indifferent to their political world? Some have suggested that we pay scant attention to politics because we are doing well (we are affluent), but at the same time, some of the most "turned off" citizens are those with the most to gain from government action. Does this make sense?

2. If democracy implies a government "by the people" but many of our fellow citizens do not engage in the political process, do we really have a democracy? Does engagement really matter? Perhaps indifference is a sign of contentment?

INTERNET RESOURCES

To see comparisons of the United States and other countries in terms of political rights and individual freedom, visit the Freedom House Web site at http:/ /www .freedomhouse.org

To see comparisons of the United States and other countries in terms of voter turnout, see the Web site of International IDEA at http://www.idea.int

ADDITIONAL READING

Almond, Gabriel A., and Sidney Verba. *Civic Culture: Political Attitudes and Democracy in Five Nations.* Princeton, NJ: Princeton University Press, 1963.

Halperin, Morton, Joseph T. Siegle, and Michael M. Weinstein. *The Democracy Advantage: How Democracies Promote Prosperity and Peace,* Revised Edition. New York: Routledge, 2009.

Themes of This Book

 1.2 Relate the themes of this book to American politics today.

(pages 8–17)

There are numerous ways to investigate and explore our political system. This book focuses on three essential themes. First, in a democracy, it's essential that citizens become participants and not merely spectators of the political process. Second, while many in the United States believe their options for effective involvement are limited, there are numerous pathways for change. Indeed, throughout American history, different political actors have used different pathways to achieve their goals. Finally, issues of diversity have and will continue to shape the process and outcome of our political system. America's diversity contributes to most political controversies, while at the same time adding complexity to the mix of actors seeking to affect change.

KEY TERMS

Pathways of Action 10
Boycott 13

CRITICAL THINKING QUESTIONS

1. Why do political activists use different pathways for their involvement? What are the factors that shape the choice of which route to use? Which of these factors is most important, in your view?

2. In what ways has diversity shaped the nature of politics in the United States? Do you see additional changes in the years ahead?

INTERNET RESOURCES

To read about one organization's strategies for using various pathways to affect government policy concerning firearms, see the Web site of the National Rifle Association at http://www.nra.org

Another good example of a powerful political action organization is the AARP, a massive, nationwide unit that works to protect the interests of older Americans: http://www .aarp.org/

There are numerous youth and student political action organizations. To read about the Student Environmental Action Coalition, see http://www.seac.org/

ADDITIONAL READING

Frantzich, Stephen F. *Citizen Democracy: Political Activism in a Cynical Age,* 3rd ed. Boulder, CO: Rowman and Littlefield, 2008.

Wasserman, Gary. *Politics in Action: Cases in Modern American Government.* New York: Cengage Learning, 2006.

Citizen Participation and Pathways: The Example of Abortion

1.3 Outline the various "pathways" of involvement in our political system.

(pages 18–19)

Abortion is one of the most controversial issues of our day, and this long, heated debate has been played out though the five pathways of change: lobbying, courts, elections, grassroots mobilization, and cultural change. As one side has begun to achieve its goals via one pathway, the other side has responded by heading down a different pathway. The story of abortion says a lot about various routes of change in all of American politics.

CRITICAL THINKING QUESTIONS

1. Why do you suppose early defenders of the right to an abortion used the court-centered pathway to achieve their goals?
2. Which of the pathways would likely lead to a longer-lasting victory when it comes to the issue of abortion?

INTERNET RESOURCES

One of the most prominent, well-organized groups to defend abortion rights is Planned Parenthood: http://www.plannedparenthood.org/index.htm

There are many organizations dedicated to ending abortions. One such group is the National Right to Life: http://www.nrlc.org/

ADDITIONAL READING

Hendershott, Anne. *The Politics of Abortion.* New York: Encounter Books, 2006.

Hull, N.E.H., and Peter Charles Hoffer. Roe *v.* Wade: *The Abortion Rights Controversy in American History.* Lawrence: University Press of Kansas, 2001.

Sanger, Alexander. *Beyond Choice: Reproductive Freedom in the 21st Century.* New York: Public Affairs, 2004.

Change and Stability in American Government

1.4 Analyze the forces of stability in American politics.

(pages 20–23)

There is no doubt that our nation has undergone significant change in the last three centuries. At the same time, however, core elements of our political system have remained remarkably stable. This is due to reverence for democracy and free market capitalism, to a well-crafted Constitution, and to numerous pathways for average citizens to voice their concerns and redirect the course of public policy.

KEY TERMS

Checks and Balances 20
Capitalism 20
Socialism 21
Alexis de Tocqueville 22

CRITICAL THINKING QUESTIONS

1. Is there a relationship between the likelihood of violence erupting in a society and the opportunities for citizens to change public policy? Put a bit differently, do you think our political process has been relatively peaceful because citizens can affect the outcome of government?
2. How does reverence for our "creation myth" continue to shape American politics? For example, might there be a relationship between how our nation started and our current reluctance to create a publicly funded health care system?

INTERNET RESOURCES

There are numerous sites to explore events in American history, including this one: http://www.americanheritage.com/

ADDITIONAL READING

Tocqueville, Alexis de. *Democracy in America.* New York: Signet Books, 2001. (Originally published 1835–1840.)

Chapter Review Test Your Knowledge

1. Which of the following best describes the activities of government officials and citizens who intend to affect the structure, authority, and actions of government?
   a. propaganda
   b. discourse
   c. the public's right to know
   d. politics

2. When a government decides what citizens can and cannot do, it is
   a. engaging in public discourse.
   b. making public policy.
   c. influencing public opinion.
   d. bringing public awareness.

3. *Pathways of action* refers to
   a. the organizational channels of government bureaucracy.
   b. the connections among the various branches of government.
   c. the activities, institutions, and decision points that affect public policy.
   d. the confidential relationships between government officials.

4. The selection of leaders by popular vote, and holding those leaders accountable for their decisions, is an example of which pathway of action?
   a. court
   b. grassroots mobilization
   c. cultural change
   d. elections

5. All pathways to action are equally open to all people in the United States.
   a. true
   b. false

6. Democracy can often seem inefficient, because
   a. competition and debate among groups slows down decision making.
   b. the framers wanted a system of change that was slow and moderate.
   c. only a majority can effect change in our system of government.
   d. a and b.

7. Which of these resources can help citizens to use the pathways of action?
   a. money
   b. organizational skills
   c. social status and personal connections
   d. a, b, and c

8. Which pathway of action involves individuals and groups presenting information and persuasive arguments to government officials in order to implement desired change?
   a. lobbying
   b. elections
   c. cultural change
   d. court

9. Which of the following is an example of the grassroots mobilization pathway?
   a. e-mailing your state legislators to convince them to vote for your position on an upcoming bill
   b. organizing a boycott against dangerous toys
   c. sending a check to a candidate to help secure her election
   d. using desktop publishing to create a political pamphlet

10. Citizens will be most successful in implementing desired change in government if they focus on a single pathway to action.
    a. true
    b. false

11. Litigants in the Supreme Court abortion case *Roe* v. *Wade* successfully used which of the following pathways of action?
    a. court
    b. grassroots mobilization
    c. lobbying
    d. a, b, and c

12. A broadly accepted political and economic framework, a powerful political culture, and a variety of ways to seek political change are all measures of a government's
    a. reliability.
    b. elasticity.
    c. stability.
    d. honesty.

13. The authors of the Constitution intended it to be a practical plan for creating a government, not a set of sacred principles.
    a. true
    b. false

14. The economic system that features government ownership of property, individuals working for the greater good of society rather than for personal gain, and government control of jobs and wages is
    a. capitalism.
    b. communism.
    c. socialism.
    d. corporatism.

15. The economic system based on free enterprise, private ownership of property, open competition, and pursuit of individual wealth is
    a. capitalism.
    b. communism.
    c. socialism.
    d. corporatism.

16. Historically, which of the following factors have placed limits on economic opportunities for many Americans?
    a. gender and racial discrimination
    b. wealthy persons' access to superior education
    c. the power of corporations
    d. a, b, and c

17. Political culture refers to
    a. the prominence of a core set of religious principles in a society.
    b. the fundamental values and dominant beliefs shared in a society.
    c. the fundamental principles of fairness and equality in a society.
    d. a and b

18. Which of the following are potential sources of a nation's political culture?
    a. historical origins
    b. important documents and texts
    c. presence or absence of civilized leaders
    d. a and b

19. Alexis de Tocqueville emphasized which aspect of America's political culture?
    a. racial composition of the population
    b. active citizenship
    c. universal suffrage
    d. slavery

20. Disparity of wealth threatens to undermine the popularity of capitalism in our society today.
    a. true
    b. false

PEARSON mypoliscilab **Exercises**

Apply what you learned in this chapter on **MyPoliSciLab.**

Read on **mypoliscilab.com**

    eText: Chapter 1

Study and **Review** on **mypoliscilab.com**

    Pre-Test
    Post-Test
    Chapter Exam
    Flashcards

Watch on **mypoliscilab.com**

    Video: Facebook Privacy Concerns
    Video: The President Addresses School Children
    Video: Who is in the Middle Class?

Explore on **mypoliscilab.com**

    Simulation: What Are American Civic Values?
    Timeline: Major Technological Innovations that Have Changed the Political Landscape
    Visual Literacy: Using the Census to Understand Who Americans Are

Early Governance and the Constitutional Framework

KEY OBJECTIVES

After completing this chapter, you should be prepared to:

2.1 Identify the difference between government and politics.

2.2 Differentiate between different types of governments.

2.3 Describe how forces in Colonial America helped set the stage for the American Revolution.

2.4 Identify the core principles of the American Revolution.

2.5 Determine the reasons for the failure of the Articles of Confederation.

2.6 Assess how compromises at the Constitutional Convention shaped our political system.

2.7 Identify the core principles of the Constitution.

2.8 Analyze how the ratification debate structured the nature of our democracy.

In the summer of 1803, Thomas Jefferson, our third president, commissioned Army Captains Meriwether Lewis and William Clark to explore the American West. The nation was in its infancy, but Jefferson recognized the importance of the western frontier. After two years of unimaginable toil, their *Corps of Discovery* finally reached the Pacific Ocean.

Shortly after arriving on the coast, Lewis and Clark had to decide where to spend the winter. Rather than simply making the decision themselves, the two leaders did something different; they put the matter to a vote. For most soldiers, this was likely their first chance with a ballot, given lingering religious and property qualifications in many states. They also gave Sacagawea, their Shoshone guide and interpreter, a vote, even though women would not have suffrage for another 100 years. And York, Clark's personal slave, was allowed to cast a ballot, too, despite the fact that African Americans would not be fully welcomed at the voting booth for another 160 years.

Why would Lewis and Clark do such a thing? They never explained their decision, but part of their rationale was surely pragmatic. The late historian Stephen Ambrose suggests "maybe they just wanted to involve everyone so that none would have the

> **How does our nation's formative period continue to shape contemporary politics?**

right to complain."[1] Still, it is comforting to imagine that the two leaders may have chatted about the difficulties of their journey and the great land they had crossed. They may even have talked about the future of their government. Liberty, honor, and respect would come to mind, as would equality, dignity and freedom. Maybe it seemed only right to them that every member of their tiny community would have a say.

The moment was fleeting, however. While the Constitution had been ratified some 18 years earlier, insurances of equality and liberty for women and diverse groups lay in the distant future. As the explorers returned to the East the following summer, Sacagawea remained the property of her husband. Clark would keep York as his slave for several more years, despite having promised him his freedom. Even many of the white soldiers would come back to limits on their political opportunities.

For a brief moment the expedition had been transported to a time and place when all were equals, when government was truly of, by, and for *all* citizens. Out west, far from the economic, social, and political establishments of the East, the *Corp of Discovery* stepped into America's future—a future we are still trying to discover.

Resource Center
• Glossary
• Vocabulary Example
• Connect the Link

■ **Power:** The ability to exercise control over others and get them to comply.

EXAMPLE: *The NRA wields power because legislators fear the wrath of its large, active membership.*

The Nature of Government and Politics

2.1 Identify the difference between government and politics.
(pages 32–33)

In real ways, *government* is all around us. Government is the formal structures and institutions through which binding decisions are made for citizens of a particular area. We might also say that it is the organization that has formal jurisdiction over a group of people who live in a certain place. Government is *not* the process by which things take place in a political system; rather, it is the "rules of the game" and the structures (the institutions) that make and enforce these rules. However, the rules of the game can, and do, shape the political process. For example, due in large part to the Supreme Court's view that giving and spending money during elections is akin to speech, and thus protected by the First Amendment of the Constitution (government), money has become a central part of the elections process (politics).

In the United States, institutions include legislatures (city councils, state legislatures, Congress), executives (mayors, governors, the president), the courts, the bureaucracy, and a few independent agencies, such as the Federal Reserve System. Government does not include political parties, interest groups, and public opinion, for example; they are key elements of our political system but not formal parts of the governmental structure.

This definition of government helps clarify the different types and layers of government. The rules and formal structures of a city government apply to the people living in that city. The rules of a school or club government apply only to the students in that school or the members of that club.

What does it mean to be "under the rule of the government"? At the most basic level, this suggests that government has the power to enforce its regulations and collect the resources it needs to operate. Rules can be enforced in many ways. One way, called *civil law*, is for citizens to be required to pay money as a penalty for breaking a rule. *Criminal law*, by contrast, prescribes that citizens who do not follow regulations pay a monetary penalty (a fine), be removed from society for a period of time or even permanently (through a sentence of death or of life imprisonment without parole), or both. Taxation is the most common way to collect revenue to make the government run.

The words *power* and *authority* are related to government's ability to enforce its rules and collect resources. **Power**■, in the political context, is the ability to get individuals, groups, or institutions to do something. Power determines the outcome of conflicts over governmental decisions; it charts the course of public policy. When the ranks of an interest group grow to the point that governmental decision makers are forced to listen, that group is said to have power. If a handful of corporate elites can persuade public officials to steer public policy their way, they have power.

Authority■ is defined as the *recognized* right of a particular individual, group, or institution to make binding decisions. Most Americans believe that Congress has the authority to make laws, impose taxes, or draft people into military service. We may not like the decisions made in Washington, in our state capital, or at city hall, but we recognize that in our system of government, elected officials have the authority to make those decisions. However, many people balk at the idea of *appointed* bureaucrats making regulations, given that they are not elected, which means that they don't have to answer to the people, only to those who appointed them. Thus bureaucrats have *power* but lack *authority*.

Some individuals, groups, and institutions have both power and authority. Congress has the authority to make laws, and federal law enforcement units have the power to enforce those laws. Perhaps the best contemporary example of when power and authority collide might be education reform. In 2002, President Bush signed into law a dramatic effort to improve public education, the No Child Left Behind Act. There is little question that the federal government has the power to enforce this sweeping law. Yet for all of our nation's history, state and local governments have controlled education policy. Many are angered at the notion of "legislators off in Washington telling us how to run our schools," and they may believe that the federal government lacks the authority to regulate education policy.

A final term to consider is *politics*. As noted in Chapter 1, page 4, politics is the *process* by which the character, membership, and actions of a government are determined. It is also the struggle to move government to a preferred course of action. All citizens might agree that a change is needed, but how to reach the desired goal can be hotly disputed. Given that governmental decisions create winners and losers—that is, acts by the government rarely please everyone—politics is a process that causes many to be left frustrated and at times angry. Moreover, politics can prove to be a slow process. The famous German sociologist Max Weber once suggested that politics is the "strong and slow boring of hard boards," and this makes good sense.[2]

The key difference you should keep in mind is that politics is the *process,* whereas government involves the *rules* of the game. An analogy might be helpful: The baseball rulebook is long and complex. It states how runners can arrive at first base safely, how outs are made, and how a team wins. Most rules are clear and have remained the same for generations. But the actual *conduct* of the game is another matter. The rulebook says nothing about split-finger fastballs, change-ups, bunts, intentional walks, double steals, pitching rotations, closers, stoppers, line-up strategy, and other aspects of how the game is played. The rulebook represents government; the way the game is played is politics (see Figure 2.1).

■ **Authority:** The recognized right of an individual, group, or institution to make binding decisions for society.

EXAMPLE: While some might disagree with certain Supreme Court decisions, they recognize the Court's authority.

FIGURE 2.1 ▪ Government and Politics: What's the Difference?

It is important that you understand the difference between government and politics. We suggest government is analogous to the official rules of baseball, and politics is similar to how the game is actually played. —*What is another analogy that might help you and your classmates better understand the difference between governmental institutions and the political process?*

Baseball

Official Rules (Government)	How the Game Is Played (Politics)
1. Pitchers can start from either the windup or the stretch position.	Pitchers grip the ball in different ways to throw fastballs, curveballs, or knuckleballs. Also, pitchers release the ball at different points to change the batter's view of the ball.
2. Batters must keep both feet in the batter's box while hitting.	Batters can "crowd the plate" by standing close to the inside edge of the box.
3. A batter will run to first base after hitting a ball in fair territory.	Batters do not always make a full swing with the bat (for example, bunting).
4. All fielders must be in fair territory when that team's pitcher delivers the ball.	Defense can shift to accommodate for a batter who tends to hit in a certain direction.

American Government

Official Rules (Government)	How the Game Is Played (Politics)
Article I, Section 2 The House of Representatives shall choose their speaker and other officers	The majority party uses their power to elect a speaker and other officers from their party, thus enabling them to push their legislative agenda.
First Amendment Freedom of the Press	Corporate conglomerates own media outlets.
Article I, Section 7 Presidential Veto	Presidents can threaten to veto a bill before it passes through Congress in order to influence the legislation.
Article I, Section 3 Each Senator shall have one vote	Lobbyists can provide information on issues and influence the way a Senator or Representative votes.
Article I, Section 2 The House of Representatives shall be composed of members chosen every second year by the people of the several States	Candidates raise money and campaign before election day to influence the opinions of the voters.

SOURCE: www.usconstitution.net

The Nature of Government and Politics

2.1 Identify the difference between government and politics.

PRACTICE QUIZ: UNDERSTAND AND APPLY

1. Which of the following is an institution of government?
   a. state legislature
   b. governor's office
   c. political parties
   d. a and b

2. Which of the following best describes "politics"?
   a. the process of influencing government decisions— making public policy
   b. the process by which politicians seek to gain a preferred outcome
   c. the process of determining the character and actions of government
   d. a, b, and c

3. Which of the following would be an example of politics shaping government?
   a. Passage of the 1964 Voting Rights Act.
   b. Women being granted the right to vote through the 19th Amendment.
   c. The Supreme Court's ruling that "white primaries" are unconstitutional.
   d. a and b.

ANALYZE

1. What is the relationship between government and politics? That is, how might the structure of government affect the conduct of politics?

2. Which of the following is probably more stable: a government that has power, but little authority, or a government that has authority, but little power?

IDENTIFY THE CONCEPT THAT DOESN'T BELONG

a. Congressional elections every two years
b. Negative campaigning
c. Guaranteeing 18 year-olds the right to vote
d. Allocating House seats based on each state's population
e. Forcing voters to be registered in their state

2.1

Resource Center
• Glossary
• Vocabulary Example
• Connect the Link

■ **Democracy:** A political system in which all citizens have a chance to play a role in shaping government action and are afforded basic rights and liberties.

EXAMPLE: *Since 1994, South Africa has been considered a democracy, because all citizens have the chance to vote and basic political rights are protected.*

Types of Governments

2.2 Differentiate between different types of governments.
(pages 34–35)

Governments come in many forms and modes of operation. Perhaps the best way to think about these differences is to focus on two critical questions: Who is allowed to govern? And how are governmental decisions reached?[3] In terms of *who* is allowed to set the rules and regulations and to enforce them, there are several broad possibilities. **Monarchy** is a system of rule in which one person, such as a king or queen, possesses absolute authority over the government by virtue of being born into a royal family and inheriting the position. Monarchies have been the most common form of rule in world history, and they are still in place in some nations around the globe. For example, Saudi Arabia still relies on a royal family for ultimate authority. In history, few monarchies were truly "absolute"; kings were normally limited by custom and by the need to consult powerful groups. But in theory, the monarch's authority was unlimited. Almost all kings and queens today head **constitutional monarchies** in which they perform ceremonial duties but play little or no role in actually governing their country. Examples include the United Kingdom, Spain, Belgium, the Netherlands, and Japan.

A **dictator** is also a sole ruler, but often this person arrives at the position of power through a violent overthrow of the previous government. Sometimes contemporary dictators, such as North Korea's Kim Jong Il or Syria's Bashar Assad, succeed to power like a king or queen on the death of a parent. Like an absolute king, a dictator theoretically has unlimited control of the government, but again, this power is often limited by the bureaucracy, the military, the ruling party, or even members of the dictator's family.

In some forms of government, a small group, such as military leaders or the economic elite, holds the reins of power. This is known as elitism or **oligarchy** (rule by a few). Decisions in such systems are often made through a council. Some have suggested that Russia has become an oligarchy in recent years due to the growing power of a small group of leaders. **Pluralism** occurs when a number of groups in a system struggle for power. In a pluralist system there are multiple centers of power. Consider the arduous battle over health care reform in the United States. Just a sampling of the concerned groups included the insurance industry lobby, hospitals, health care professionals, labor unions, health reform advocates, conservative groups, liberal organizations, and so forth. On nearly every contentious issue there are multiple groups struggling to shape the outcome.

A **democracy**■ is a political system in which all citizens have a right to play a role in shaping government action—a mechanism often referred to as *popular sovereignty*. Citizens in a democracy are afforded basic rights and liberties, as well as freedom from government interference with private actions (that is, *liberty*). In a *direct or pure democracy,* all citizens make all decisions. Some tiny Swiss cantons (states) operate in this way, and a small number of communities in the United States are governed through town hall meetings, where everyone in the community has a say in making town policy.

Finally, a **republic**■ is a system of government in which a small group of elected representatives acts on behalf of the many. If these representatives closely follow the wishes of their constituents (the people they are sent to represent), and if they are elected through a fair and open process in which everyone has the same opportunity to participate, the system is considered a **representative democracy.** The United States is a republic—as are most of the industrialized nations of the world (though some are constitutional monarchies). Whether or not we are a true representative democracy, however, is a point of dispute.

The second important question to consider is *how* decisions are reached in a government. In a **totalitarian regime,** leaders have no real limits on how they proceed or what they do. Formal constitutions might exist in such regimes, seemingly full of limits on power, but in practice, such limits are meaningless. Totalitarian governments control—or at least try to control—almost every aspect of society.[4] The term *totalitarian* was invented in the 1920s by Benito Mussolini in Italy, although in practice, his government exercised less than total control. Nazi Germany, the Soviet Union under Joseph Stalin, China under Mao Zedong, and present-day North Korea are the clearest examples of truly totalitarian dictatorships. Under a dictatorship, there may be an individual ruler, a small group, or even a number of groups, but none of these acknowledges any formal limitations.

In an **authoritarian regime,** government policies are kept in check by informal limits, such as other political forces (maybe political parties), the military, and social institutions (for example, religious groups). Leaders face real limits, but there are no formal or legal restrictions. A good example would be the president of Egypt, Hosni Mubarak. The Egyptian constitution grants the president exceptional powers, and parliament generally agrees to all of Mubarak's wishes. Yet he does face limits from business leaders and religious groups in his country. For instance, Mubarak himself has seemed inclined to maintain a close relationship with the United States but has been forced to demonstrate greater independence due to these influences. When there are both informal and legal limits, the system is a **constitutional government.** In the United States, for example, government action is controlled by strong social and political forces (including religions, interest groups, political parties, and the media) and by what the laws, the courts, and the Constitution allow (see Table 2.1).

■ **Republic:** A system of government in which members of the general public select agents to represent them in political decision-making.

EXAMPLE: *Most campus student organizations can be considered republics, because elections are held to choose student representatives.*

TABLE 2.1 | Types of Government Systems

GOVERNMENT SYSTEMS	DEFINITION	EXAMPLES
Who Is Allowed to Participate?		
Monarchy	Individual ruler with hereditary authority holds absolute governmental power	Bhutan, Saudi Arabia, Swaziland
Constitutional Monarchy	Monarch figurehead with limited power, actual governing authority belongs to another body	Denmark, Japan, United Kingdom
Dictatorship	Individual ruler with absolute authority, often comes to power through violent uprising	Hussein's Iraq, North Korea
Oligarchy	A small group of the rich or powerful controls most of the governing decisions	Tunisia, 20th-century South Africa, Pakistan
Pluralism	Multiple centers of power vying for authority	Canada, Great Britain, United States
How Are Decisions Reached?		
Pure Democracy	Citizens make all governmental decisions	Some Swiss states, some towns in New England
Representative Democracy	Citizens elect representatives to carry out government functions	United States, Germany, France
Totalitarian Regime	Leaders have no limits on authority	Nazi Germany, 1920s Italy
Authoritarian System	Leaders have no formal legal restraints on authority but are limited by informal forces (i.e., the military, religious forces)	South Korea, Singapore, Taiwan
Constitutional System	Government has both informal and legal restraints on the exercise of power	United States, Germany, France, Mexico

Types of Governments

2.2 Differentiate between different types of governments.

PRACTICE QUIZ: UNDERSTAND AND APPLY

1. A political system in which a number of competing groups struggle for power is termed
   a. pluralism. c. autocracy.
   b. direct democracy. d. communism.

2. This textbook defines *liberty* as
   a. freedom from want and freedom from fear.
   b. freedom from government interference with private actions.
   c. freedom with provisions for minorities.
   d. freedom with imposed limitations.

3. One feature that an authoritarian regime has in common with democratic government is that
   a. government policies are enforced primarily by armed force.
   b. political power is concentrated among a small group of national leaders.
   c. government policies are kept in check by informal limits.
   d. the mass media are controlled by governing elites.

4. In a democracy, the right to participate is much more important than the protection of basic civil liberties.
   a. true b. false

ANALYZE

1. What are three ways in which a democratic government is different from a totalitarian government?

2. What do you suppose is the relationship, if any, between a country's economic system and its government? Can a democracy also boast a socialist economic system, for example?

IDENTIFY THE CONCEPT THAT DOESN'T BELONG

a. Constitutional government d. Liberty
b. Republic e. Oligarchy
c. Pluralism

2.2

Resource Center
• Glossary
• Vocabulary Example
• Connect the Link

Early Governance in America

2.3 Describe how forces in Colonial America helped set the stage for the American Revolution.
(pages 36–37)

Imagine you have arrived with your family, friends, and a group of strangers in a land without any formal rules or regulations. —*What type of government would you seek to establish? Would it make more sense to rely upon a few smart or powerful leaders to get things started, or would you try to establish a system of laws from the very beginning?*

In 1620, a tiny group of English people (41 men and an unknown number of women and children) sailed across the Atlantic to what was called at the time the New World. They were crammed into a leaky old ship called the *Mayflower*. Some members of this band would later be dubbed the **Pilgrims,** because they were coming to America in hopes of finding religious freedom. But other passengers were not part of this religiously motivated group. All of the *Mayflower* passengers were bound for Virginia, where they expected to join an English colony that had been founded a few years earlier, in 1607. Unfortunately, the place where they landed—New England—was outside the recognized boundaries of Virginia, and the captain of the ship refused to go any farther because winter was coming. When spring arrived, the captain took his ship back to England, leaving the passengers on the coast of New England.

Recognizing that they were stuck in this bleak place, the Pilgrim leaders insisted that everyone, Pilgrim and non-Pilgrim alike, sign the **Mayflower Compact,** a document legalizing their position as a "civil body politic" under the sovereignty of King James I. Most important for our concerns is that these people, finding themselves in a place outside the jurisdiction of English rule, sought a system where laws, not a small group or a single person, would rule their society.

From the Mayflower Compact until the American Revolution, a mixed system characterized colonial governance. On the one hand, most of the colonies were established through charters from England. There was no question that these settlements would be governed under English rule. Governors were appointed by the Crown to oversee different colonies and were responsible only to the king. On the other hand, the New World was an ocean away. Settling an untamed wilderness created its own set of problems, and ideas favoring self-governance grew in intellectual circles both in America and in England. The compromise came in the form of colonial assemblies. Here, colonists elected representatives to speak on their behalf and to counsel the governors on the best courses of action. Every colony had an assembly, usually located in the largest city. These bodies had little legal authority. But while the governors did not have to listen to the advice of the assemblies, they often did so in order to win the esteem of citizens. This mix of appointed rule and self-governance seemed to work, at least at first.

Two developments upset this balance. First, many colonists brought with them the political customs and traditions from their homeland, meaning that the debate over the extent of royal authority in the conduct of government came along as well. As in England, those supporting the Crown were often the wealthiest, having received immense land grants and special privileges from the king. Those who were not part of the political in-group were deeply suspicious of the favored elite, and their numbers swelled as the years passed. On top of this, if a local governing authority proved oppressive, colonists had the option of simply packing up and moving. This made opposition to royal and elite control easier.

Second, and more significantly, new financial pressures were thrust on the colonists in the mid-1760s. The **French and Indian War** in North America, which began in 1754 and ended nine years later, pitted Great Britain against France. The war, part of a larger Anglo-French struggle for global power, began over control of the upper Ohio River valley. However, the larger issue was which nation would eventually control the continent. Most of the settlers in this area were British, but the French had entered into trade agreements (and later a military alliance) with many Indian tribes. Through a series of spectacular military engagements over the course of several years, the British defeated the French and took control of North America, with relatively little colonial assistance.

All wars are expensive, but given that this one had been waged an ocean away, the price of protecting Britain's New World empire proved very high. Facing massive debt and grumbling taxpayers, Parliament, with the king's blessing, looked for new ways of raising revenue. Because the war had been fought to protect the colonists, it seemed logical that they should bear much of the responsibility for paying the bill. Thus began a period known as the **Great Squeeze**■, in which Parliament passed one measure after another, including the Sugar Act (1764), the Stamp Act (1765), the Townshend Acts (1767), and the Tea Tax (1773), all designed to wring as much revenue from the colonists as possible. To make matters worse, the Great Squeeze came after more than a generation of what was called "salutary neglect," a policy of casual, loose enforcement of trade laws in the colonies. Parliament had hoped that this freedom would stimulate greater commercial growth, leading to greater profits for British investors. Parliament's

■ **Great Squeeze:** A period prior to the American Revolution when the British Parliament sought to recoup some of the costs associated with the French and Indian War by levying new taxes and fees on colonists.

EXAMPLE: *The Sugar Act and the Stamp Act were measures imposed on the American colonists during the Great Squeeze.*

decision to raise revenue through a number of taxes after a century of trade freedom proved a bitter pill for the Americans.

In truth, the new taxes were not severe, and colonial Americans were probably among the least taxed people in the Euro-American world at the time. But the colonists were in constant fear of the corruption that, in their eyes, a faraway and arbitrary government could impose on them. ("Corruption" to eighteenth-century Americans included the distribution of government favors to what we would today call "special interests.") It seems, then, that the colonists' obsession about corruption and tyranny and their insistence on guaranteeing limited, accountable government became fundamental to Americans' ideas of just governance—surely an explicit theme in the Constitution. The relationship between the royal governors and the colonial assemblies soured. Because it was the duty of the governors to enforce these unpopular revenue-raising acts, they became the targets of colonial outrage.

PATHWAYS of action

The Sons of Liberty

During the uneasy and turbulent times of pre-Revolutionary America, various resistance groups began to organize, often in secret. Several of these early interest groups became collectively

known as the Sons of Liberty, a name closely linked with protests against parliamentary rule over the colonies. Led by powerful, important figures such as John and Samuel Adams, but also enlisting the support of artisans, shopkeepers, and other working people who could be depended on to rebel against abuses like the Tea Tax, the Sons of Liberty organized in one community after another.

They held rallies, sponsored "committees of correspondence" (letter-writing campaigns) to spread their views, and recruited community leaders to their cause. They understood the importance of building organizations, rallying individuals in every community, and shaping public opinion. However, recently, controversy has developed over some of their more violent efforts. For instance, they used intimidation and aggression, including the burning of a property owned by the Distributor of Stamps for Massachusetts, to get stamp collectors to resign their posts.

In the end, the Sons of Liberty proved to be one of our nation's first and most influential interest groups, helping set the stage for a revolution and for the creation of a democratic system of government. But, do you think violence and intimidation of the sort used by the Sons of Liberty could be justified in contemporary politics?

Early Governance in America

2.3 Describe how forces in Colonial America helped set the stage for the American Revolution.

PRACTICE QUIZ: UNDERSTAND AND APPLY

1. Before the Revolution, the colonies were governed by a "mixed system." This meant that
   a. some colonies were ruled democratically while others were more autocratic.
   b. some colonies resented British rule while others were content with the system.
   c. most colonies were governed by a local assembly in addition to the authority of the Crown.
   d. the colonies restricted religious freedom, but favored free trade.

2. The taxes imposed during the "Great Squeeze" crippled the colonial economy, leading to widespread disease and starvation.
   a. true   b. false

3. "Salutary neglect" referred to
   a. the British army's refusal to protect colonial settlements during the French and Indian War.

   b. the Crown's casual enforcement of trade laws, with the expectation of greater economic gains.
   c. the shift in military policy to attack the French and Indians instead of placing garrisons in frontier forts.
   d. Parliament's indifference toward "provincial" affairs in the New World.

ANALYZE

1. How did the governing institutions in America change from the time of the Mayflower Compact to the Revolution?

2. Is there a connection between colonial perceptions of corruption and President Barack Obama's struggle to pass certain initiatives through Congress?

IDENTIFY THE CONCEPT THAT DOESN'T BELONG

a. The French and Indian War   d. Fears of corruption
b. Financial pressures   e. Fears of Tyranny
c. Oppressive taxes

Resource Center
• Glossary
• Vocabulary Example
• Connect the Link

■ **Thomas Paine:** An American revolutionary writer and a democratic philosopher whose pamphlet *Common Sense* (1776) argued for complete independence from Britain.

SIGNIFICANCE: *Paine's writings helped inspire colonists to join the Patriot cause and to bolster support for the Continental Army.*

The American Revolution

2.4 Identify the core principles of the American Revolution.

(pages 38–43)

The causes and meanings of the American Revolution are best broken into two broad categories: financial (pragmatic) and ideological. With regard to the financial concerns, the Great Squeeze made life in the colonies harder and the prospects for a profitable future seem dimmer for all colonists. The Stamp and Sugar acts were viewed as tyrannical, and the backlash against them was fierce. Parliament also passed many measures that placed lands in the western regions under British control. Because land represented profits—from sales of acreage, lumber, or farm products—many colonists saw this move as unbearable. The **Acts for Trade** were an additional series of moves by Parliament to channel money back to the commercial class in Great Britain. King George III (along with Parliament) sought to save money by demanding that each colony pay for the upkeep of the British soldiers occupying its territory. On a practical level, the Revolution was about the money.

At a deeper level was a growing desire among Americans to create a system in which all citizens (at least all white, male, propertied citizens) would have a say in the conduct of government and in which basic freedoms of life and liberty would be protected. Echoing this idea, one of the rallying cries during this period was "No taxation without representation." The essence of self-governance, Americans argued, was the ability to control taxes. After Parliament imposed yet another revenue-raising measure, this time giving the bankrupt but politically powerful East India Company a monopoly on importing tea into the colonies, a band of enraged colonists, disguised as Indians, stormed a merchant ship in Boston Harbor in the dark of night and threw the company's tea overboard. For many colonists, the so-called Boston Tea Party was a galvanizing event that rallied patriotic sentiment. For Parliament and George III, the event reflected growing unrest in the colonies—it was an act of insolence that had to be punished and suppressed. Parliament quickly passed five new measures, which the British called the **Coercive Acts** and the colonists referred to as the **Intolerable Acts.** In short, these were punitive measures, designed to punish the rebellious colonists: One act closed the Port of Boston; another altered the Massachusetts government to bring it under British control; anther made the quartering of soldiers in colonial homes easier; and so forth. Of course, these new measures only stoked the flames of rebellion.

Taxation without representation was not the only ideological issue. The old splits over parliamentary prerogatives were transformed into a debate on the exact nature of self-governance. The colonists had grown accustomed to an unprecedented level of freedom. In Great Britain and throughout Europe, laws and customs limited access to trades and professions, controlled land usage, and compelled people to belong to established churches. The Pilgrims had come to the New World in search of religious freedom, and in large measure, they had found it. The generations that followed began to consider and demand what they saw as their "rights."

During this period, a good deal of attention was paid to the writings of great philosophers on the rights of citizens and the proper conduct of government. The English political theorist **John Locke** (1632–1704), in particular, had written a number of widely read essays on the subject, most notably *Two Treatises of Government,* which first appeared in 1690. Locke argued that all legitimate governing authority is based on the consent of the governed and that all individuals have "natural rights." Later, in the eighteenth century, the Scottish economist **Adam Smith** (1723–1790) wrote about the importance of limiting government in order to protect the economic rights of citizens.

In the colonies, a number of people started to write on liberty, including a young Massachusetts lawyer named **John Adams** (1735–1826), who would later become president of the new nation. In 1765, he began publishing a series of essays in which he offered a fervent defense of patriotism. "Liberty must at all hazards be supported," he argued.[5] The writings struck an immediate chord, noted one historian.[6] That same year, a group of delegates from the colonies gathered to discuss the new Stamp Act and to consider responses to it. The **Stamp Act Congress** produced the Declaration of Rights and Grievances, a powerful statement on the rights of citizens that was widely circulated. A decade later, when Americans found themselves debating the fateful step of seeking independence, **Thomas Paine**■ (1737–1809) wrote a highly influential and persuasive tract, *Common Sense,* promising freedom, equality, and the prospect of democracy.

The Declaration of Independence

By September 1774, in the aftermath of the Coercive Acts and the Boston Tea Party, events seemed to be spinning out of control. Every colony except Georgia sent delegates to the First Continental Congress in Philadelphia. At this point, few openly spoke of breaking ties with Great Britain; most still hoped to find a compromise that would protect the rights of Americans and pull back the harshest tax measures. Still, in the absence of dramatic changes by George III and Parliament, the delegates called on the colonists to boycott all British goods.

This twentieth-century lithograph depicts the Boston Tea Party of 1773. —*What similarities, if any, are there between the modern day Tea Party movement and the Boston Tea Party of 1773?*

Matters did not improve. Within a year, the royal governor of Massachusetts, Thomas Gage, ordered his troops to seize what was believed to be a growing supply of arms from the colonists at Concord. Before the 700 red-coated British troops sent from Boston reached Concord, however, 77 "Minutemen" (militia) met them at the small town of Lexington. Shots were fired, and the Minutemen retreated. The Redcoats pressed forward, but by the time they arrived at Concord, the Patriot forces had swelled to more than 300. After another battle, the royal troops had to retreat and were attacked repeatedly as they marched back to Boston. In the end, some 270 British soldiers and 95 colonists were killed. The event sent shockwaves throughout the colonies and across the Atlantic Ocean. The wheels of war had been set in motion.

Although there was still strong sentiment in America for reconciliation with Great Britain, many of the delegates who attended the Second Continental Congress in 1775 considered compromise impossible. They understood that war had, in fact, begun. But they still had to convince others throughout the colonies that armed rebellion was their only remaining chance. Not all Americans were convinced. British oppression had been real, but a war for independence was an altogether different matter. Many of those who had protested British abuses still remained loyal to England. At the very same time that delegates were arriving at Philadelphia, petitions were circulating in towns and villages throughout the colonies calling

for reconciliation with Great Britain. Something needed to be done to convince more colonists to rebel, to move with force toward a system of self-governance. A committee of five was formed, and the task of writing a clearly written rationale for rebellion was given to a young, rather shy delegate from Virginia by the name of Thomas Jefferson.

Jefferson's Declaration of Independence is today regarded as one of the most lucid statements ever written on the rights of citizens and the proper role of government in a free society. It is one of the world's great democratic documents and has been an inspiration to people yearning for freedom around the globe. As one recent writer noted, even today, "you can still get a rush from those opening paragraphs. 'We hold these truths to be self evident.' The audacity!"[7] The core of the statement can be found in just 83 words:

> We hold these truths to be self-evident, that all men are created equal, that they are endowed by their Creator with certain unalienable Rights, that among these are Life, Liberty and the pursuit of Happiness. That to secure these rights Governments are instituted among Men, deriving their just power from the consent of the governed, That whenever any Form of Government becomes destructive of these ends, it is the Right of the People to alter or abolish it, and to institute new Government. . . .

■ **Natural Rights:** Basic rights that no government can deny.

EXAMPLE: *The right to a fair, impartial trial would be considered a natural right.*

■ **Social Contract Theory:** A political theory that holds individuals give up certain rights in return for securing certain freedoms. If the government breaks the social contract, grounds for revolution exist. This notion was at the core of the Declaration of Independence.

SIGNIFICANCE: *This concept reminds us that just governments spring from the will of citizens.*

This famous picture depicts one of the greatest moments in the history of democratic governance—the signing of the Declaration of Independence. —*Did you know that these men all feared they were signing their own death warrants? Indeed, if the British had won the war, it is highly likely that these men would have been hanged as traitors. Would you have put your life on the line for the "cause of liberty"?*

Rarely has more been said in so few words. Let us examine this passage in detail. (You might also wish to examine the annotated version of the Declaration in Appendix 1, pages A-1 through A-7.)

First, Jefferson presents a notion of **natural rights**■. That is, individuals possess certain privileges—certain guarantees by virtue of being human. Second, these rights are *not* granted by government but instead by God, whom Jefferson calls the Creator. They cannot be given, nor can they be taken away. Third, Jefferson introduces the **social contract theory**■, drawn in large measure from the writings of John Locke. Humans have the option of living alone in what Locke called "the state of nature." According to this theory, humans originally lived without government or laws, enjoying complete personal freedom. Yet the state of nature meant "a war of all against all," in which—in the words of another philosopher, **Thomas Hobbes**—life was "solitary, poor, nasty, brutish, and short." To end this perpetual conflict and insecurity, people created governments, thereby giving up some of their freedoms in order to protect their lives and their property. Fourth, Jefferson agreed with Locke that governments, having been created by the people to protect their rights, are limited; they get their powers from the will of the people and no one else. (In arguing this, Locke was attacking the traditional claim that kings ruled by the will of God.) Finally, said Jefferson (again following Locke), when a government fails to respect the will of the people—that is, when it appears no longer to be limited—it becomes the right, indeed the obligation, of citizens to change the government. This passage is Jefferson's call for revolution.

How effective was the Declaration of Independence in rallying support behind the Revolutionary cause? This is a difficult question to answer because there were no accurate ways to measure public opinion in those days. While we know that many New Yorkers were so inspired on hearing these words that they toppled a statute of King George and had it melted down to make 42,000 bullets for war,[8] many balked at joining the Revolution and even enlisted in the British Army. We also know that public support for the Continental Army, headed by George Washington, lagged considerably throughout the Revolution. Most Americans were deeply suspicious of professional armies, fearing them as a threat to liberty. There were no mechanisms to collect funds to support the Continental Army; state contributions were very stingy, which helps explain the terrible conditions that the troops suffered at Valley Forge in the winter of 1777–1778. And many citizens remained cautious about joining in the bold gamble for independence, especially if it seemed to threaten their economic future. We often point to the valor of soldiers at Valley Forge, but fail to recognize that the very reason for the widespread starvation was because area farmers chose to sell their produce to the British Army—who were willing to pay a higher price.

Either way, war had begun between the most powerful nation in the world—Great Britain—and the American colonies. At first, things looked grim for the Patriot cause, and many Americans feared that all would be lost within a matter of weeks. By December 1776, the end seemed near. But three startling developments seemed to turn the tide.

First, with bold leadership from George Washington, the Continental Army was able to gain a few high-profile victories,

Patriots pulling down a statue of King George III in New York, after hearing the news of the signing of the Declaration of Independence. —*How does this painting symbolically capture the spirit of the American Revolution?*

Statue of Saddam Hussein being pulled down in Baghdad on April 9, 2003. Many assumed that with the toppling of Hussein's regime, a democracy could be created in Iraq. But this goal has proved vastly more difficult than most had expected. —*Can you think of some reasons why this is so? Can a democracy be created by just having elections? What is the relationship between culture and politics?*

which served to assure patriots and foreign governments that the war could, in fact, be won and that financial contributions to the war effort would not be wasted.

Second, from 1776 to 1783, Thomas Paine espoused the virtues of democracy in his sixteen famous "Crisis" papers. Their tone is apparent in the famous opening of "The American Crisis, Number 1," published on December 19, 1776, when Washington's army was on the verge of disintegration:

> These are the times that try men's souls. The summer soldier and the sunshine patriot will, in this crisis, shrink from the service of their country; but he that stands it

now, deserves the love and thanks of man and woman. Tyranny, like hell, is not easily conquered; yet we have this consolation with us, that the harder the conflict, the more glorious the triumph.

This was powerful writing, and Washington ordered the pamphlet read to all of his troops.[9]

Third, the French government decided to support the Revolutionary forces. This decision came, after a prolonged diplomatic effort spearheaded in Paris by Benjamin Franklin, upon news that the Americans had inflicted a serious defeat on the British Army at Saratoga in October 1777.

CONNECT THE **LINK**
(Chapter 1, page 20) Why are avenues for
involvement so important in a democracy?

Financial support, arms and ammunition, and military assistance from the French government proved immensely helpful—particularly on occasions when the prospects for victory still seemed bleak.

STUDENT profile

When most of us think of a soldier in the Revolutionary War, an image comes to mind of a farmer pulling his gun from the mantel, kissing his wife and children goodbye, then jumping in line with other patriots. The story of the "citizen soldier" has some validity, especially in the early years of the conflict. As one historian writes, "At the beginning . . . farmers, artisans, rich and poor, young and old—patriots came forth with uncommon zeal."[10]

But another reality is that the Patriot army soon faded. By late 1776, George Washington wrote to Congress, "The few who act upon principles . . . [are] no more than a drop in the ocean."[11] States resorted to a draft to fill their ranks, but drafts worked differently in those days. A draftee simply had to produce someone, anyone, to fill that position. Those with money often hired a person to fill their spot. Others enlisted because they were without property or jobs. The Continental Army was filled with poor farm boys eager for adventure.

One of these boys was Joseph Plumb Martin. At the age of 15, Martin enlisted as a private in the Connecticut state troops. A year later, in the spring of 1777, he enlisted in Washington's Continental Army—where he served for the duration of the war, seeing action at a number of major battles.

Plumb's experience is recounted in a detailed diary—one of the very few accounts of a teenage soldier in the American Revolution. Of one cold November, Plumb scribbled, "Here I endured hardships sufficient to kill half a dozen horses . . . [W]ithout provisions, without clothing, not a scrap of either shoes or stockings to my feet or legs." Regarding one battle, he wrote, "Our men were cut up like cornstalks. I do not know the exact number of the killed and wounded but can say it was not small." And of a fort after a battle, he noted, "The whole area of the fort was completely ploughed as a field. The buildings of every kind hanging in broken fragments, and the guns all dismounted, and how many of the garrison sent to the world of spirits, I knew not."[12] Several books catalogue Plumb's writings—and what a fascinating tale it is!

The Colonial Experience and the Pathways of Change

Having some gripes with your government is one thing; deciding to break away and form a new government is quite another. A move of this sort would seem especially momentous

given that in 1776 Britain had the world's most powerful army and navy. It has been said that the signers of the Declaration of Independence assumed they were signing their own death warrants. Barbara Ehrenreich writes, "If the rebel American militias were beaten on the battlefield, their ringleaders could expect to be hanged as traitors."[13]

How did things come to this? Ideas of liberty, equality, and self-governance—captured so well by Jefferson's pen—had simmered throughout the colonies for decades. Jefferson's prose captured a sentiment, but he did not bring the idea of democracy to life. Like flowers bursting from the ground after a long winter, liberty and equality were destined to blossom in the American soil. Also, as we noted in Chapter 1, page 20, governments whose citizens yearn for liberty are stable only if those citizens have avenues of change—that is, the means to move public policy in new directions as times and circumstances change. What pathways of change had been available to the colonists? Could they have elected a new government or petitioned the courts for redress? Might average citizens have effectively lobbied members of Parliament, an ocean away? Their protests, such as the Boston Tea Party, were met with additional acts of repression. There seemed no option for change. Their only recourse was to declare independence and prepare for war. In a very real way, the American Revolution underscores the importance of our pathways concept.

Another interesting issue to ponder is what might be the right course for those who *perceive* no viable pathways of change. If you think that your government is no longer listening to your concerns—the concerns of average citizens—and that there is no way to bring the system back in line, must revolution follow? Is not Jefferson clear that under such circumstances revolution is justified? In 1787, Jefferson claimed that "the tree of liberty must be refreshed from time to time with the blood of patriots and tyrants."[14] And have we seen this process played out in American history since the Revolution? Indeed we have.

PATHWAYS of change from around the world

Do democratic revolutions, similar to what occurred in 1776, happen any more? In truth, democratic uprisings occur regularly across the globe. One such uprising and change occurred in Indonesia in 1998.

Three decades earlier, after a violent coup (overthrow) of the Indonesian government, a dictator by the name of Suharto came to power. His first acts were to couple his rule with key military leaders and to nullify most civil liberties. Perhaps realizing that governments lacking in legitimacy are generally short–lived, Suharto cooked up a scheme to hold presidential elections. Yet, the electoral rules rigged the system so that Suharto was reelected time and again. Through the years, groups and individuals pushed for meaningful reform, but the ruling government controlled the media, and the reformers were jailed.

Things came to a head in 1997. In that year, the Asian financial crisis hit, with Indonesia at the center of the storm. Massive debt, high taxes, poor fiscal management, and corruption compounded the problems and soon massive protests erupted, with the aim of pushing Suharto from power. In early May 1998, peaceful campus protests broke out and turned violent when they spilled into the streets. The riot in Jakarta, the nation's capital and largest city, caused massive destruction and over 1,000 deaths. By the end of May, nearly 8,000 homes and businesses had been destroyed, and over 5,000 Indonesians had been killed.

Suharto resigned on May 21. By early fall, nearly 150 million Indonesians went to the polls to pick a new president, and soon after changes were made ensuring fair elections and the protection of core civil liberties, including protections for the media. Indonesia is now considered a democratic government.

The American Revolution

2.4   **Identify the core principles of the American Revolution.**

PRACTICE QUIZ: UNDERSTAND AND APPLY

1. The call for "no taxation without representation"
   a. implied that taxes were too high and that a new government must be formed to reduce them to reasonable levels.
   b. inspired a new ideological movement to create a government based upon the preferences of the citizens.
   c. did not really inspire citizens to join the revolutionary movement.
   d. a and c.

2. According to Jefferson, people created governments
   a. to end perpetual conflict and insecurity.
   b. to give up some personal freedom to gain protection of their lives and property.
   c. only with the consent of the will of the people.
   d. a, b, and c.

3. According to the Declaration of Independence, citizens are endowed by their Creator with
   a. provisions and prospects.
   b. universal truths.
   c. unalienable rights.
   d. divine principles and protections.

4. Jefferson suggested that "just" governments should be "limited"; this means that government must
   a. be limited to no more than three branches.
   b. derive their powers from the consent of the governed.
   c. tax citizens only if average citizens are allowed to vote on the issue.
   d. restrict the number of departments and personnel.

ANALYZE

1. Does the "consent of the governed" imply majority rule at all times? What if a majority wants to trample the rights of a minority?

2. How would Thomas Paine go about expressing his radical ideas using modern technology and the mass media?

IDENTIFY THE CONCEPT THAT DOESN'T BELONG

a. Enlightened rules
b. God-given rights
c. Security
d. Self-rule
e. A duty to rebel

Resource Center
• Glossary
• Vocabulary Example
• Connect the Link

■ **Shays's Rebellion:** An armed uprising in western Massachusetts in 1786 and 1787 by small farmers angered over high debt and tax burdens.

SIGNIFICANCE: *This event helped bring about the Constitutional Convention, as many worried that similar events would happen unless there were changes.*

The Articles of Confederation

2.5 Determine the reasons for the failure of the Articles of Confederation.

(pages 44–45)

Less than a week after the signing of the Declaration of Independence, the Continental Congress set to work drawing up a system of government for the self-declared independent American states. After a year's effort, the model that emerged was called the *Articles of Confederation*. The idea was to draw the 13 states together but, at the same time, to allow each state to remain independent. In this system, the central government could coordinate and recommend policies, but it had no ability to enforce these policies if the states refused. An analogy would be today's United Nations, where each nation has one delegate and one vote and the representative serves at the discretion of the home government. On paper, at least, this Congress had power to conduct foreign affairs, wage war, create a postal service, appoint military officers, control Indian affairs, borrow money, and determine the value of the coinage.[15] But the Articles did not give the national government the power to force its policies on the states, nor did it allow the levying of taxes to support the federal government (see Table 2.2). It was up to the states to contribute to the federal government's support as they saw fit (just as each member nation of the United Nations contributes what it wishes to the UN budget). And the Articles said nothing about judicial matters.

The fact that the Articles guarded state sovereignty is really not surprising. In a very real way, our first system of national government was designed to be the opposite of what colonists had experienced under authoritarian, centralized British rule. It was also widely believed at the time that democracy was possible only when government was local.

TABLE 2.2	Powers of Congress Under the Articles of Confederation
WHAT CONGRESS COULD DO	**WHAT CONGRESS COULD NOT DO**
Borrow money	Regulate commerce
Request money from states	Collect taxes from citizens
Conduct foreign affairs	Prohibit states from conducting foreign affairs
Maintain army and navy	Establish a national commercial system
Appoint military officers	
Establish courts	Force states to comply with laws
Establish a postal system	Establish a draft
Control Indian affairs	Collect money from states for services

Limitations of the Articles of Confederation

The Articles of Confederation failed for several reasons. First, the national government had no way to collect revenue from the states or from the states' citizens. No government can survive without some means of obtaining the resources it needs to operate. Second, the national government had no way of regulating commerce. Third, the national government was unable to conduct foreign affairs—that is, to speak to other nations with a unified voice. Fourth, the mechanism to alter the Articles proved too difficult, as any change required the unanimous consent of all 13 states. So even if adjustments, such as giving the national government the power to collect taxes, could have improved matters, the chances of achieving unanimous agreement to do so were slim.

Yet another shortcoming of the Articles was the lack of leadership and accountability within the national government. There was no one in charge. This issue of accountability came to a head in 1786 with an event that rocked western Massachusetts.

During the mid-1780s, the nation had experienced an economic depression. Particularly hard-hit were farmers, who received much less for their crops than in previous years due to a flood of imports. Desperate for relief, a group of farmers led by Daniel Shays, a veteran Patriot militia captain who had fought against the British at Bunker Hill in 1775, gathered to demand changes. Frustrated that their calls for help seemed to fall on deaf ears at the state legislature, Shays's forces grew to nearly 2,500. Soon violence broke out as the group clashed with state militia forces. The governor and state legislature appealed for assistance in putting down the protest, which they argued had deteriorated into a full-blown riot. But there was no person or group outside Massachusetts to take the call for assistance, and no help was available.

Many of the rebels were captured and sentenced to death for treason, but all were later pardoned. Yet **Shays's Rebellion**■ had a profound impact on the future of our nation, because it suggested that liberty and freedom—that is, an open democratic society—carried risks. A few months after the uprising in Massachusetts, a meeting was organized to revise the Articles. This was the **Constitutional Convention**■.

Shays's Rebellion: An Alternative Look

Why would Shays and his 2,500 followers turn to violent protest? Were there no other pathways for change?

Money, especially specie or "hard money" (silver and gold coin), became very scarce throughout the United States in the 1780s, resulting in a severe depression that lasted nearly a decade. But not everyone was affected the same way. Hardest hit were working-class citizens and small farmers. Because these people had little or no hard money with which to pay their debts, bank foreclosures skyrocketed. By the mid-1780s, demands for action grew louder. Very much in keeping with the structure of government

■ **Constitutional Convention:** A meeting in Philadelphia in 1787 at which delegates from the colonies drew up a new system of government. The finished product was the Constitution of the United States.

SIGNIFICANCE: *A great deal of our current governing system can be traced back to this gathering in the summer of 1787.*

during this period, people's cries for assistance were directed to the state legislatures. "Stay laws" were passed by state legislatures to postpone foreclosures, and "tender laws" allowed farmers to use agricultural products (rather than hard money) to help pay loans. Partly as a result, inflation surged, and as paper money became more widespread, it became easier to use this inflated currency to pay off debts, such as the mortgage on a farm.[16]

However, in Massachusetts, the legislature dragged its feet. What made this state different? For one thing, business interests dominated the state legislature. Instead of helping small farmers, the legislature saw fit to levy heavy taxes in an attempt to pay off the state's wartime debts, with most of the money going to wealthy business owners in Boston. From this vantage point, Shays's Rebellion broke out because the channels of the democratic process were *not* working in Massachusetts. There seemed to be no other viable pathway for change, and so violence erupted.

This perspective also allows us to reconsider the motivations of the delegates to the Constitutional Convention. Today, many believe that the aim of that meeting was to fine-tune the democratic process and create a stronger national government. In some ways, this is true. But the policies of the state governments designed to protect farmers and laborers during the depression of the 1780s created hardship for a different group—the economic elite. As noted earlier, there are always winners and losers in politics, and during this period, much that was given to the farmers was taken from business owners and bankers. Perhaps,

Shays's Rebellion, shown here, was an armed uprising that shocked the nation in 1786 and led to the Constitutional Convention a year later. —*What caused Shays and his followers to vent their frustration at the government in Springfield, Massachusetts? Does the answer say anything about the nature of government in Massachusetts in the 1880s?*

then, some of the rationale for calling delegates to Philadelphia was to revise the Articles in order to make sure that state governments could not limit the "liberty" of the economic elite.

The Articles of Confederation

2.5 Determine the reasons for the failure of the Articles of Confederation.

PRACTICE QUIZ: UNDERSTAND AND APPLY

1. Why did the Articles of Confederation deliberately provide for a weak national government?
   a. The planners made a number of serious mistakes in its construction.
   b. There was residual fear of a strong, centralized government.
   c. There was a widely held belief that democracy could only survive if governments were small and localized.
   d. b and c.

2. Shays's Rebellion was a major event leading to the Constitutional Convention, because
   a. it showed that even one individual could bring down the government.
   b. the federal government proved too weak to respond to the crisis.
   c. state governments were willing to curtail the liberties of individuals if given the opportunity.
   d. Shays was a powerful innovator who was strongly supported by the political elites of the day.

3. One alternative view of Shays's Rebellion is that the framers of the Constitution were powerfully motivated by their own economic interests.
   a. true   b. false

ANALYZE

1. Do the Articles of Confederation continue to influence American politics?

2. How would you respond to the claim that Shays's Rebellion signaled not only a failure of the Articles, but also a failure of limited government in Massachusetts?

IDENTIFY THE CONCEPT THAT DOESN'T BELONG

a. Focus on state governments
b. Strong executive office
c. Legislative-centered government
d. Limited ability to regulate commerce
e. No way to collect taxes from citizens

Resource Center
• Glossary
• Vocabulary Example
• Connect the Link

■ **Virginia Plan:** A plan made by delegates to the Constitutional Convention from several of the larger states, calling for a strong national government with a bicameral legislature, a national executive, a national judiciary, and legislative representation based on population.

SIGNIFICANCE: *Much of this plan found its way into the Constitution, shaping the system we live under today.*

The Constitutional Convention

2.6 Assess how compromises at the Constitutional Convention shaped our political system.

(pages 46–49)

In late May 1787, some 55 delegates from every state except Rhode Island came together at the Pennsylvania State House in Philadelphia for the purpose of proposing changes to the Articles of Confederation. Congress itself had authorized the meeting, but it did not expect that the Articles would be completely replaced by a new system of government. The delegates were not "average" men but rather included many of America's leading political, economic, and social figures of the time. (Thomas Jefferson, then serving as U.S. minister to France, was not present.) George Washington was selected as the convention's presiding officer, and on May 29, the delegates set to work. Interestingly, and perhaps contrary to what you might think, the convention deliberated in total secrecy—even to the extent of nailing the windows shut!

Opening the convention, Governor Edmund Randolph of Virginia offered a series of resolutions that amounted to an assault on the Articles. Rather than attempting to modify them, Randolph argued, the Articles should be dumped altogether. The delegates agreed; something new and vastly different was needed. Small groups were formed, charged with drawing up plans for a new government. In the end, five plans were submitted for consideration, but the delegates quickly narrowed their consideration to two.

The first was the **Virginia Plan**■, named for the home state of its principal author, James Madison. The delegates from the more populous states favored it. Table 2.3 provides an overview of what the new government would look like under this plan.

Most delegates agreed with the core idea of the Virginia Plan—that the central government should be strengthened. Yet big differences in population between the states seemed a problem. The most populous states were Virginia, Pennsylvania, North Carolina, Massachusetts, and New York; the smallest states included (besides absent Rhode Island) Georgia, Delaware, Connecticut, and New Jersey. Delegates from the smaller states realized that this scheme would put them at a real disadvantage in the national government—a smaller state's interests would be overwhelmed by those of the larger states. Opposition to the Virginia Plan grew. William Paterson of New Jersey offered an alternative approach. His **New Jersey Plan**■ was designed to stick closer to the Articles of Confederation and create a system of equal representation among the states:

TABLE 2.3	The Virginia Plan

• Have three branches of government—a national legislature, an executive, and a judiciary.
• Force each of the branches to rely on the others.
• Grant each branch the ability to keep an eye on the other two so that no one segment of the government becomes too powerful.
• Have a legislature with an upper and lower house, with members of the lower house chosen by the people in the various states and the upper chamber made up of legislators chosen by the lower house from a list of nominees put forward by the state legislatures.
• Allow each state a number of seats in the national legislature based on its population (thus the larger states would have more delegates and the smaller states fewer).
• Have an executive, selected by the legislature and serving a single term.
• Have judges who would be appointed to the bench by the legislature for life terms.
• Establish a "council of revision," with members from both the executive branch and the judiciary, which would review all national and state laws; this body would have some control over national legislation and an absolute veto over state legislation.
• Be supreme over the state governments—that is, acts of the new national government would override state law.

Each state would have the same number of national legislators. Table 2.4 is an overview of this plan.

Although it might seem that both models were similar in terms of the supremacy of the national government, this was not the case. A national legislature was at the core of both plans, but under the New Jersey Plan, each *state* would have equal say in the making of public policy. Since a majority of state governors could change the makeup of the executive council, this plan was more state-centered and in keeping with the confederation model that underlay the Articles. In contrast, the Virginia Plan clearly laid out what was called at the time a "consolidated government," one that all but absorbed the states.

TABLE 2.4	The New Jersey Plan

• Have three parts of government—a national legislature, an executive council, and a judiciary.
• Have a legislature consisting of one body, in which each state would have one vote.
• Have a multiperson executive council, chosen by the legislature, with the responsibility of executing national laws; its members could be removed by a vote of a majority of state governors.
• Have a judiciary appointed by the executive council.
• Have a national legislature with the ability to tax the states, proportional to their population.
• Be supreme over the state governments, with the national legislature having the right to override state law.

■ **New Jersey Plan:** A scheme for government advanced at the Constitutional Convention that was supported by delegates from smaller states. It called for equal representation of states in a unicameral legislature.

EXAMPLE: *Under this approach, each state would have the same say in the national legislature, and the president would have modest powers.*

The Great Compromise

All the delegates at the convention knew that the legislative branch was critical, but the argument over the allocation of seats in the legislature nearly ended the proceedings. "Delegates conferred, factions maneuvered, and tempers flared."[17] The dispute was serious, because the delegates believed that if the new national government had real powers (as they all hoped), control of the legislative branch would be critical.

The issue also boiled down to different views of representation: a *state-based approach* versus an *individual-based approach*. It should be remembered that at this time most Americans felt loyalty to their state over any sort of national allegiance. At the time, even Thomas Jefferson considered Virginia, not the United States, "my country." A widespread sense of national citizenship did not emerge until after the Civil War, some 80 years later. So the argument over representation came down to which states would have more sway in the new system, and delegates of the smaller states were not about to join a union that would put their own people at a disadvantage. *States* were the units to be represented, not the citizens within each state. But the large states relied on an individual-based notion of representation. The new national government should speak on behalf of *citizens,* not states. If one state had significantly more citizens than another, it was self-evident that the bigger state would have more national representatives.

On June 30, 1787, Roger Sherman of Connecticut presented a compromise plan: The national legislature would have a House of Representatives, based on proportional representation (as under the Virginia Plan), but a second branch, the Senate, would contain an equal number of representatives from each state (as under New Jersey Plan). This **Great Compromise**■, sometimes called the **Connecticut Compromise,** settled the matter (see Table 2.5). Few of the delegates were completely satisfied. Indeed, some walked out of the proceedings, but most agreed that it was the best possible solution. Several of the states had tried this in their own legislatures, with much success. The plan was accepted, and the convention continued.

This compromise—the creation of a Senate with an equal number of representatives from each state—has proved incredibly significant through our history. Consider that several of President Obama's policy initiatives, such as those dealing with climate change and health care reform, moved quickly through the House of Representatives, but stalled in the Senate. A handful of Senators from sparsely populated states, representing a mere fraction of the overall public, can stop a piece of legislation in its tracks (a topic discussed in greater detail in Chapter 6). Some would argue that the Senate is one of the *least* democratic institutions in our government. Others would argue that it is an institution that reflects state interests and also leads to careful, incremental policy change. As we have tried to highlight throughout this chapter, developments during the formation period continue to shape contemporary politics.

The Three-Fifths Compromise

If one of the chambers of the national legislature was to be based on population (the House of Representatives), and if taxation was to be fixed around each state's population, how would the inhabitants of each state be counted? The delegates quickly agreed that a **census** (a complete count) would be

TABLE 2.5	Differences Between the Virginia Plan, the New Jersey Plan, and the Great Compromise		
ISSUE	**VIRGINIA PLAN**	**NEW JERSEY PLAN**	**COMPROMISE**
Source of Legislative Power	Derived from the people and based on popular representation	Derived from the states and based on equal votes for each state	A mix; from the people for one house, from the states for the other
Legislative Structure	Bicameral	Unicameral	Bicameral; one house of equal representation, and another based on population
Executive	Size undetermined; elected and removable by Congress	More than one person; removable by state majority	Single executive; removed by impeachment
Judiciary	Life tenure, able to veto legislation in council of revision	No power over states	Life tenure, judicial review ambiguous
State Laws	Legislature can override	Government can compel obedience to national laws	National supremacy
Ratification	By the people	By the states	Ratification conventions in each state, thus allowing both the people and the states to be involved

■ **Great Compromise/Connecticut Compromise:** An agreement at the Constitutional Convention that the new national government would have a House of Representatives, in which the number of members would be based on each state's population, and a Senate, in which each state would have the same number of representatives.

SIGNIFICANCE: *This was a compromise between two competing proposals, the Virginia Plan and the New Jersey Plan, without which the Constitutional Convention would likely not have ended with an agreement.*

conducted every 10 years, and this was written into the Constitution. But *who* might be counted as an inhabitant was a vastly more difficult matter. Here we find one of the most distressing parts of the Constitutional Convention. The issue boiled down to slavery. More than 90 percent of the slaves in North America at that time lived in five American states: Georgia, Maryland, North Carolina, South Carolina, and Virginia.[18] The delegates from these states argued that for the purposes of allocating House seats, slaves should be counted. This was quite a twist, given that slaves were considered property and were not given any rights of citizenship in these states—and the delegates from the northern states retorted as much. Yet given the huge slave populations in the southern states (40 percent or more in some states), not counting them would prove significant. If slaves were not counted, the southern states would have just 41 percent of the seats in the House; if slaves were counted, the South would have 50 percent.

Once again, the convention came to a standstill, delegates threatened to bolt, and a compromise was reached. Population would be used to determine each state's delegation to the House of Representatives, and slaves would be counted as three-fifths of a white person. Put a bit differently, five slaves would equal three white persons in the census. Slaves would not be allowed to vote or to have any of the rights that Jefferson had written about in his Declaration, but they would be counted as inhabitants—or rather as three-fifths of an inhabitant—in order to get both sides to agree to the Constitution. Our history is filled with such tragic ironies.

The Sectional Compromise

Still another deal reached at the Constitutional Convention—what James Madison and some historians have called the most important compromise—related to slavery and commerce.[19] Many Northerners hated slavery and pointed out the irony of celebrating the American Revolution and creating a free nation while preserving the institution of slavery. However, southern delegates were not about to join a government that stripped them of their slaves, and even Northerners realized that abolishing slavery would shatter the South's economic base. According to one observer, "The subject haunted the closed-door debates."[20]

Most delegates agreed that the new Congress would have the power to regulate commerce, but many also worried about the potential for abuse. This was a very important power. Southern delegates in particular worried that because the House of Representatives would be based on proportional representation and the power to regulate commerce would reside in the new national government, their states' economic future was at risk. They argued that Congress should require a supermajority (a two-thirds vote, rather than a simple majority) whenever it attempted to regulate commerce. The northern delegates said no, once again worried about giving too much power to less populous states.

This led to another compromise: The Atlantic slave trade would be protected for at least 20 years. Article 1, Section 9, Clause 1 of the Constitution prohibited Congress from stopping

One of the tragic ironies of our nation's formative period is that while notions of freedom and equality warmed the hearts of patriots, slavery was not eliminated in the Constitution. Indeed, it took two centuries, a bloody civil war, and the courageous acts of untold men and women to advance the cause of racial equality. Here, Rosa Parks, who Congress later called the "mother of the modern-day civil rights movement," refuses to sit in the back of the bus. —*Do you think our nation's history of slavery and racism is something that should be continually recounted? Or, is it something that is best relegated to the history books? Why?*

the importation of slaves from overseas until 1808. (Slave trading within and among states was not mentioned.) In exchange, it was agreed that a simple majority of both houses of Congress would be needed to regulate commerce. Sometimes it is difficult to see how the acts of the Framers have a direct bearing on our lives.

Rest assured, congressional regulation of commerce has, and continues, to shape the world in which we live—from the products we buy at the store, to the roads we drive on, to what we watch on television. This is one compromise that has proved extraordinarily important throughout the centuries.

The Constitutional Convention

2.6   **Assess how compromises at the Constitutional Convention shaped our political system.**

PRACTICE QUIZ: UNDERSTAND AND APPLY

1. Which of the following were elements of the Virginia Plan?
   a. a plural executive (an executive branch with several members)
   b. allotting seats in the legislature in proportion to each state's population
   c. lifetime appointment of federal judges
   d. b and c

2. The "Great Compromise" created
   a. three branches of government.
   b. a bicameral legislature.
   c. a branch of the legislature directly elected by the voters.
   d. b and c.

3. The sectional compromise addressed
   a. the legality of slavery.
   b. the control of commerce by the national government.
   c. the counting of slaves as a portion of each state's voting population.
   d. a and b.

4. Which comment best describes the impact of the Articles of Confederation on the contents of the Constitution?
   a. The Constitution merely revised a few of the principles of the Articles.
   b. The Constitution replaced the Articles with a virtually new document.

   c. The Constitution granted more power to the states and less power to the federal government than the Articles.
   d. a and c.

ANALYZE

1. If you could go back in time and make a speech at the Constitutional Convention about governance in the twenty-first century, what would you say?

2. What do you believe to be the relationship between the three-fifths compromise and the history of racial segregation in America?

IDENTIFY THE CONCEPT THAT DOESN'T BELONG

a. Slavery
b. States' rights
c. Commerce
d. Free speech
e. Foreign affairs

Resource Center
• Glossary
• Vocabulary Example
• Connect the Link

■ **Sharing of Powers:** The U.S. Constitution's granting of specific powers to each branch of government while making each branch also partly dependent on the others for carrying out its duties.

EXAMPLE: *The Supreme Court ruled that "separate but equal" educational systems were unconstitutional in 1954, but the task of actually desegregating schools was left to President Eisenhower.*

The U.S. Constitution

2.7 **Identify the core principles of the Constitution.**

(pages 50–53)

On September 17, 1787, following five hot, argumentative months, the delegates to the Constitutional Convention finished their work. After hearing the clerk read the entire document, Ben Franklin rose to the floor to remark that although the form of government they had drafted was not perfect, it was the best that could have been achieved under the circumstances. He then made a motion that each delegate sign the final version. Thirty-nine of the original 55 who had begun the convention did so.

Most Americans believe that our Constitution is one of the greatest schemes of government ever devised—due in no small measure to the overarching structural framework that created a vibrant yet controlled government, a system that is both rigid and flexible. Much more will be said of the provisions in the Constitution in subsequent chapters, but some key points are outlined here. (Review the annotated Constitution in Appendix 2.)

The Constitution breaks down into seven articles:

Article I: The Legislative Branch (Congress)

Article II: The Executive Branch (President)

Article III: The Judicial Branch (Courts)

Article IV: Guidelines for Relations Between States

The Constitutional Convention was one of the great triumphs of our nation's formative years. Facing long odds, a sweltering summer, and a membership that boasted radically diverse interests, these 55 men were somehow able to craft a model for government that has, with only modest adjustments, lasted to this day. —*Do you think these individuals imagined that their "experiment" would someday become the model for scores of other nations seeking to establish viable democratic systems of government?*

Article V: The Amendment Process

Article VI: Federal–State Relations (Supremacy Clause); Oath for Officers

Article VII: How the Constitution Will Be Ratified

Let us consider several core principles embodied in the Constitution:

• **Three Branches of Government.** Understanding both the complexity of governance and the potential for corruption, the framers saw fit to create a system with different branches of government—legislative, executive, and judicial. Simply stated, the legislature would *make* the laws, the president would *enforce* the legislature's will, and the judicial branch would *interpret* the laws and *resolve* disputes according to the law.

• **Separate Institutions Sharing Powers.** One of the greatest challenges the framers faced was creating a system that was neither too weak nor too strong. A weak government would suffer the fate of the Articles of Confederation, but too strong a government might lead to corruption and an excessive concentration of power, minimize the role of the states, infringe on individual rights, and perhaps collapse in civil war. The framers believed that they had found a middle ground through the granting of specific powers for each branch while at the same time making each branch partly dependent on the others for carrying out its powers. This is called the **sharing of powers**■.

We will say a lot more about the powers and duties of each branch and the connections between the branches in the chapters that follow, but a few examples might be helpful here. Although Congress passes laws and appropriates funds, the executive branch enforces these laws and spends the money. The judicial branch can pass judgment on disputes that arise, but it must rely on the executive branch to enforce its rulings. The president can negotiate treaties with other nations, but the Senate must ratify these agreements before they take effect.

• **Checks and Balances.** Just as each branch shares powers with the others, each branch is limited ("checked") by the other two. That is to say, each branch can review, and in some ways restrict, the acts of the other branches. For instance, Congress passes laws, but the president can veto proposed legislation—and if both houses of Congress can put together a two-thirds vote, they can override a presidential veto. The president can be impeached by the House and, if convicted by a two-thirds vote in the Senate, be removed from office. Federal judges can likewise be removed by impeachment and conviction. The judiciary can invalidate acts of Congress or the president when they are considered unconstitutional, but Congress and the states can enact amendments to the Constitution that get around judicial decisions (see Figure 2.2).

■ **Expressed Powers:** The powers explicitly granted to the national government in the U.S. Constitution.

EXAMPLE: *Article I, Section 8 of the Constitution grants Congress the power to regulate commerce.*

■ **Police Powers:** The powers reserved to state governments related to the health, safety, and well-being of citizens.

EXAMPLE: *Many consider the job of educating children to be the concern of local governments; a police power.*

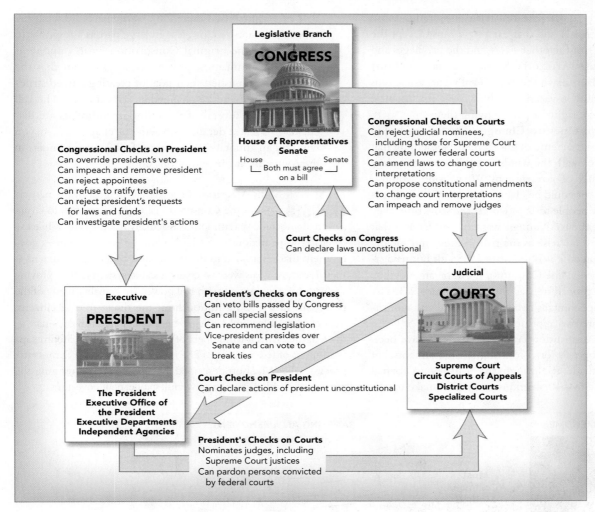

FIGURE 2.2 ■
Shared Powers, Checks and Balances
Many applaud this unique system of government in which each branch is somewhat dependent on the others, and each branch is in some ways checked by the others. Our system's longevity would suggest this model works, but others argue that this model makes change difficult— especially when different political parties control other branches of the government. *—What do you think? Does this system favor pathways for change, or does it stifle the will of the people?*

Within the figure:

Legislative Branch
CONGRESS
House of Representatives
Senate
House — Both must agree on a bill — Senate

Congressional Checks on President
Can override president's veto
Can impeach and remove president
Can reject appointees
Can refuse to ratify treaties
Can reject president's requests for laws and funds
Can investigate president's actions

Congressional Checks on Courts
Can reject judicial nominees, including those for Supreme Court
Can create lower federal courts
Can amend laws to change court interpretations
Can propose constitutional amendments to change court interpretations
Can impeach and remove judges

Court Checks on Congress
Can declare laws unconstitutional

President's Checks on Congress
Can veto bills passed by Congress
Can call special sessions
Can recommend legislation
Vice-president presides over Senate and can vote to break ties

Court Checks on President
Can declare actions of president unconstitutional

Executive
PRESIDENT
The President
Executive Office of the President
Executive Departments
Independent Agencies

Judicial
COURTS
Supreme Court
Circuit Courts of Appeals
District Courts
Specialized Courts

President's Checks on Courts
Nominates judges, including Supreme Court justices
Can pardon persons convicted by federal courts

- **Representative Republicanism.** The framers wanted to create a limited government, a government "by the people," but they worried that the whims of public opinion would lead to an unstable government and perhaps even mob rule or "anarchy." The government, as Madison would later remark, should "enlarge and refine" the public's will. Representative republicanism proved to be the solution. The system would not be a direct democracy, where each person has a say on all public matters, but rather a representative republic, in which a small group of elected leaders speak and act on behalf of the many. Members of the House are elected directly by the voters; under the original Constitution, senators were to be selected by the state legislatures (a provision that changed to direct popular election when the Seventeenth Amendment was adopted in 1913); and the president would be chosen by an electoral college—envisioned in 1787 as a gathering of a small group of notable leaders in each state to select the federal chief executive. The Constitution rests firmly on the representative republican principle.

- **Federalism.** None of the framers intended to create a centralized government; instead, they envisioned a system in which a viable national government would undertake certain responsibilities and state governments would handle others. This is known as *federalism*—a system of government in which powers and functions are divided among different layers of the system. The Constitution clearly defines many of the powers of the national government, which are referred to as the **expressed powers**■. State governments were considered closest to the people and thus best able to look after their health, safety, and well-being. These powers were called **police powers**■. The national government, for its part, would focus on commercial matters, foreign affairs, and national security.

- **Reciprocity Among the States.** Although the Constitution permitted each state a degree of independence, delegates to the convention were concerned that citizens should be treated equally in every state. The framers had in mind, for example, that a marriage in one state would be recognized in other states. Two "comity" clauses

■ **Bill of Rights:** The first 10 amendments to the U.S. Constitution, ratified in 1791, protecting civil liberties.

EXAMPLE: *Freedom of speech is one of our core civil liberties, protected in the First Amendment.*

accomplished this goal. The full faith and credit clause (Article IV, Section 1) said that each state must accept the legal proceedings of the other states, and the privileges and immunities clause (Article IV, Section 2) mandated that out-of-state citizens have the same legal rights as citizens of that state. While on vacation in New York, for instance, you have the same rights as people living there.

• **A Fixed System Open to Change.** The framers had in mind a rather fixed scheme of government, something that would not change with the winds of public opinion or the shifting personnel of government. What good would a constitution be if it could be changed each time new issues emerged or new people took office? At the same time, they recognized that their document was not perfect and that new pressures would arise as the nation grew and society changed. The outcome was to create a difficult but navigable route for change. The Constitution can be amended by a total of four procedures, as noted in Figure 2.3. The amendment process entails two steps: proposal and ratification, and there are two approaches for each step.

Since the Constitution's ratification, there have been thousands of proposals for constitutional amendments, but only 27 have made it through the journey to formal amendment. The first 10 amendments, which make up the

Bill of Rights■ (see Table 2.6), were enacted during the very first session of Congress, in large part as a response to criticisms of the original Constitution by its opponents during the ratification process. It would seem that the framers accomplished their goal of creating a fixed structure that could also be changed at critical times. The Bill of Rights and several of the other amendments are discussed in greater detail in subsequent chapters. Also, you will find an annotated discussion of all 27 amendments in the Appendix at the end of this book.

MYTH EXPOSED Many Americans believe that the goal of the participants at the Constitutional Convention was to create a more democratic system. This was actually not the case. While the delegates were anxious to establish a limited government—a government that responded to the wishes and concerns of citizens—their foremost goals were to create a stable system and to provide the national government with real powers. In actuality, many of the provisions in the Constitution limit the direct role of citizens, including the Electoral College, the indirect election of Senators, the lengthy terms for members of the Senate, and the lifetime appointment of federal judges. The idea was to slow the democratic process, what Madison described as, "enlarging and refining the public will," and to create a powerful, stabile, new government.

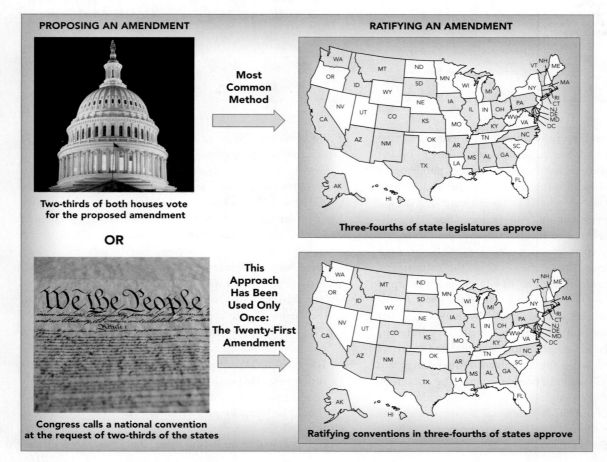

PROPOSING AN AMENDMENT

Two-thirds of both houses vote for the proposed amendment

Most Common Method

OR

This Approach Has Been Used Only Once: The Twenty-First Amendment

Congress calls a national convention at the request of two-thirds of the states

RATIFYING AN AMENDMENT

Three-fourths of state legislatures approve

Ratifying conventions in three-fourths of states approve

FIGURE 2.3 ■
How the Constitution Can Be Amended
The framers wanted to create a fixed system, but at the same time allow for some modifications under certain circumstances. —*With just 27 amendments since 1789, would you say they got things right?*

TABLE 2.6	The First Ten Amendments to the Constitution (The Bill of Rights)

Safeguards of Personal and Political Freedoms
1. Freedom of speech, press, and religion, and right to assemble peaceably and to petition government to redress grievances
2. Right to keep and bear arms

Outmoded Protection Against British Occupation
3. Protection against quartering troops in private homes

Safeguards in the Judicial Process and Against Arbitrary Government Action
4. Protection against "unreasonable" searches and seizures by the government
5. Guarantees of a grand jury for capital crimes, against double jeopardy, against being forced to testify against oneself, against being deprived of life or property without "due process of law," and against the taking of property without just compensation
6. Guarantees of rights in criminal trials, including right to speedy and public trial, to be informed of the nature of the charges, to confront witnesses, to compel witnesses to appear in one's defense, and to the assistance of counsel
7. Guarantee of right of trial by a jury of one's peers
8. Guarantees against excessive bail and the imposition of cruel and unusual punishment

Description of Unenumerated Rights and Reserved Powers
9. Assurance that rights not listed for protection against the power of the central government in the Constitution are still retained by the people
10 Assurance that the powers not delegated to the central government are reserved by the states, or to the people

The U.S. Constitution

2.7	Identify the core principles of the Constitution.

PRACTICE QUIZ: UNDERSTAND AND APPLY

1. Which of the following is a core principle of the Constitution?
   a. Each state has equal representation in the federal government.
   b. One branch of government can check the acts of the other branches.
   c. Power is divided among the layers of government.
   d. b and c.

2. The framers of the Constitution wanted a government by popular consent but also one that would check the "passions of the public."
   a. true   b. false

3. Reciprocity among the states implies that
   a. citizens must be treated equally in every state.
   b. each state must accept the legal proceedings of the other states.
   c. states with larger populations should have a greater say in the federal legislature.
   d. a and b.

4. What are the constitutional intentions of the three branches of government?
   a. The executive will create the laws, the legislature will enforce them, and the courts will administer fines and punishments for violations of the laws.
   b. The legislature will create the laws, the executive will enforce them, and the courts will resolve disputes according to the laws.
   c. The legislature will pass laws, the president will approve them, and the courts will enforce them.
   d. The national government will create laws, the states will cooperate to enforce them, and the courts will resolve disputes according to the laws.

ANALYZE

1. Consider the idea of creating a democracy where the "passions of the people" are checked by the indirect election of Senators (prior to the 17th Amendment), the Electoral College, and lifetime appointment of federal judges, among other things. Do these provisions diminish the democratic character of our "democracy?"

2. Most governments are unitary—that is, they do not separate powers between layers of governments. What might be the relationship between our system of federalism and the roots of the American Revolution?

IDENTIFY THE CONCEPT THAT DOESN'T BELONG

a. Reciprocity   d. Expressed powers
b. Federalism   e. National citizenship
c. Police powers

Resource Center
• Glossary
• Vocabulary Example
• Connect the Link

■ **Federalists:**
Supporters of the
ratification of the
U.S. Constitution.

SIGNIFICANCE: *In the late 1780s, this referred to supporters of ratification of the Constitution. James Madison was one of the leading Federalists during this time. By the late 1790s, it was the name given to one of the first political parties, headed by Alexander Hamilton and John Adams. Many of the early Federalists, such as Madison, later joined the Democratic-Republican Party, in opposition to the Federalist Party.*

The Struggle over Ratification

2.8 Analyze how the ratification debate structured the nature of our democracy.
(pages 54–57)

Reaching agreement at the Constitutional Convention on the framework of government was the first step. But for the Constitution to become the law of the land (replacing the Articles of Confederation), it would have to be ratified by 9 of the 13 states. Most contemporaries also understood that if larger states, such as Virginia, Pennsylvania, and Massachusetts, failed to ratify the document, the chances for the long-term success of the new government were slim. The framers said that nine states were needed, but most hoped that ratification would be unanimous. The document was sent to the states, where special *ratification conventions* would be held.

As soon as the ratification process began, two sides emerged. The Constitution's supporters became known as **Federalists**■, and its opponents were called **Anti-Federalists**■. Both sides took their dispute to state capitals, to city halls, to taverns, and to kitchen tables across the nation. In the end, the matter was settled peacefully, through logic, persuasion, eloquence, and deliberation. It was the first test of our new take on democracy—and we passed.

The Federalists believed that a representative republic was possible and desirable—especially if populated by citizens "who possess [the] most wisdom to discern, and [the] most virtue to pursue, the common good of society."[21] The Anti-Federalists countered with the argument that representatives in any government must truly reflect the people, possessing an intimate knowledge of their circumstances and their needs. This could be achieved, they argued, only through small, relatively homogeneous republics, such as the existing states. A prominent Anti-Federalist put it this way: "Is it practicable for a country so large and so numerous [as the whole United States] . . . to elect a representative that will speak their sentiments? . . . It certainly is not."[22]

The Federalist Papers

Persuading citizens that the Constitution should be approved was no simple matter. Today the battle for public opinion would be fought on cable news programs, through television and radio advertisements, in direct mail, and over the Internet. In the late 1780s, the battle raged in interpersonal settings, such as formal meetings or casual tavern conversations, and in newspapers and pamphlets, which were often read aloud in group settings or passed from hand to hand. Three leading Federalists—James Madison, Alexander Hamilton, and John Jay—teamed up to

write a series of essays, known collectively as *The Federalist Papers*■, on the virtues of the Constitution. These 85 essays were published in a New York City newspaper, because New York State, where Anti-Federalist sentiment ran high, was a key battleground in the campaign for ratification. The three authors adopted the *nom de plume* Publius (Latin for "public man").

Step by step, *The Federalist Papers* worked their way through the most fought-over provisions in the Constitution, laying out in clear logic and powerful prose why each element was necessary. The essays also explained what the framers had been thinking in Philadelphia while hammering out the document. Indeed, in many places, the Constitution is vague, and if you are interested in understanding what the framers had in mind, *The Federalist Papers* are the best place to look. Constitutional lawyers and Supreme Court justices still cite them.

Federalist No. 10, written by James Madison (reprinted in the Appendix) was particularly important. Madison begins with a detailed discussion of the dangers of "factions," groups that form to pursue the interests of their members at the expense of the national interest. "Measures," Madison notes, "are too often decided, not according to the rules of justice and the rights of the minor party, but by the superior force of an interested and overbearing majority." What can be done about factions? Madison takes the reader through different alternatives, suggesting that suppressing them would be a huge mistake: "Liberty is to faction what air is to fire." Instead, he presents a two-part solution. First, if the faction is less than a majority, then the "republican principle" will solve things, meaning that elected officials, representing the wishes of a majority of constituents, will do the right thing. But if the faction constitutes a majority, which often happens in a community or a state, Madison writes:

> Extend the sphere, and you take in a greater variety of parties and interests; you make it less probable that a majority of the whole will have a common motive to invade the rights of other citizens; or if such a common motive exists, it will be more difficult for all who feel it to discover their own strength, and to act in unison with each other.

Using powerful, direct reasoning, Madison explains why one large nation is preferable to many smaller ones—thus challenging the logic of many political theorists who argued that only small democracies could survive. *Federalist No. 10* is a lucid justification for forming the United States of America, and Madison's insistence on this seeming paradox makes him one of the greatest political philosophers of all time.

Another important essay is *Federalist No. 51,* also written by Madison (and also reprinted in Appendix 4). Here he explains the logic behind the sharing of powers and the essence of checks and balances. It is an awkward scheme of government, he admits, but also the best way to give the new government power but not *too much* power. "If men were angels, no government would be necessary," he writes. And "if angels were

■ **Anti-Federalists:**
Opponents of ratification of the
U.S. Constitution in 1787 and 1788.

SIGNIFICANCE: *Those who worried that the new system would give the national government too much power worked against ratification and thus were Anti-Federalists. (Note that those opposed to the Federalist Party in the late 1790s were not Anti-Federalists but rather Democratic-Republicans.)*

to govern men, neither external nor internal controls on government would be necessary." Since neither condition prevails, other precautions are needed. Madison proposes that "ambition must be made to counteract ambition"—a truly innovative idea, since all republican thought for 2,000 years had focused on schemes to make citizens more virtuous. In brief, a system of shared powers and of checks and balances would secure the democratic character of the government. Madison also introduces a "double security": Not only will each branch of the national government be dependent on the others, the federal system itself, in which powers are divided between national and state governments, will help secure the rights of the people. Madison's argument is incredibly innovative when viewed from the standpoint of classical political theory. It had always been assumed that virtue (truly good citizens) could ensure the survival of a republic—a view that stretched back to Plato in ancient Greece. Madison, by arguing that ambition can be harnessed and checked by other ambitions through a layered system of governments, was turning political theory on its head.

The Anti-Federalists' Response

The Anti-Federalists offered clear and thought-provoking counterarguments, many of which also appeared in newspapers. Some of these essays, published under the byline Brutus (the name of the ancient Roman republican leader who had assassinated Julius Caesar to stop him from establishing a monarchy), called attention to the very nature of democracy. Echoing traditional republican ideology, one of the important Brutus essays (reprinted in Appendix 5) insists that large governments could not heed the wishes of average citizens. "If respect is to be paid to the opinion of the greatest and wisest men who have ever thought or wrote on the science of government, we shall be constrained to conclude, that a free republic cannot succeed over a country of such immense extent . . ." What is more, if we want legislators to speak on behalf of citizens, as democracy demands, these leaders must know the interests of their constituents. When districts are large, as they would have to be in the proposed government, the number of constituents per legislator would be excessive. How could a legislature actually know the wishes of 30,000 residents, the number proposed for House districts? (Today there are more than 650,000 residents per House district!) The Anti-Federalists further argued that the president would inevitably build up too much power and dominate the other branches. Indeed, much of their concern centered on Article II of the Constitution, the office of president. Their worries were only slightly eased by the realization that if the Constitution were ratified, George Washington, with his spotless reputation for honesty and patriotism, would be chosen as the first president. One of the arguments against ratification of the Constitution that continues to be used today against the current political system is what appears to be the expanding scope of presidential powers.

Finally, the Anti-Federalists argued that the Constitution did not contain provisions to protect individuals. There were checks on each branch of government but none against the government's infringement on individual rights and liberties. This omission would seem glaring, yet Madison took exception to the criticism, arguing that the national government would be limited exclusively to the powers outlined in the document. It could not infringe on the rights of citizens, because it did not have the power to do so. The absence of such provisions, argued Madison, would be a clear check. But many people found this "protection by omission" worrisome.

In response to these objections, the Federalists gave in: If the states would ratify the Constitution, they agreed that the first matter of business for the new government would be to amend the Constitution to include a list of individual safeguards—a list of individual protections, which became known as the *Bill of Rights.* With this guarantee, the tide of public opinion shifted, and by June of 1788, the necessary nine states had ratified the Constitution (see Figure 2.4). In the end, all the states did so. (North Carolina at first rejected the Constitution but then hastily reconvened a ratification convention after the other states had accepted the document. Rhode Island also at first rejected the Constitution and then waited until 1790, when its convention finally voted to join the Union.) The vote in many of the state conventions was quite close. In New York, the margin was 30 to 27; in Massachusetts, 187 to 168; in New Hampshire, 57 to 47; in Virginia, 89 to 79; and (eventually) in Rhode Island, 34 to 32.

The Federalists kept their word and moved to amend the Constitution with the goals of protecting individuals from government infringements. Numerous changes were offered, and eventually 12 amendments were voted on. Ten of these amendments were successful; all passed in 1791. One additional draft amendment did not receive ratification by three-fourths of all the states until 1992, whereupon it finally became the Twenty-Seventh Amendment. This amendment delays any increase in compensation for members of Congress by at least one election cycle.

A Second Revolution?

We often assume that the war against the British had a singular focus, even though two names for the conflict are often used interchangeably: the War for Independence, and the Revolutionary War. These names suggest different ways of interpreting the same event. To some observers, the war was about breaking away from British control. A distant government had imposed laws and taxes on Americans without the input of Americans. British citizens had rights and liberties that were for some reason not extended to those citizens living in the new lands. After repeated appeals, it seemed only proper that a new nation be established, the better to protect these liberties. After victory had been won,

■ *The Federalist Papers:* A series of 85 essays in support of ratification of the U.S. Constitution that were written by James Madison, Alexander Hamilton, and John Jay and published under the byline Publius in New York City newspapers between October 27, 1787, and May 28, 1788.

SIGNIFICANCE: *We often turn to* The Federalist Papers *to better understand the intent of the framers.*

FIGURE 2.4 ■ The Ratification of the Constitution, 1787–1790

Clearly, support for ratification of the Constitution was more robust in some parts of the country than others. —*Why was this true? Do you think commercial interests might have been an important factor?*

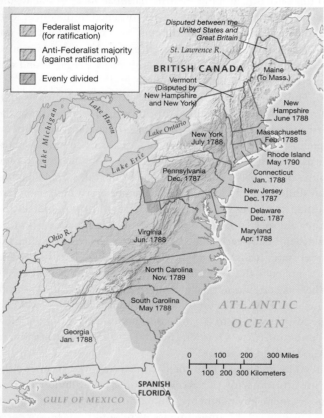

SOURCE: John Mack Faragher, Daniel Czitrom, Mari Jo Buhle, Susan H. Armitage, *Out of Many: A History of the American People*, combined 5th ed. (Chs. 1-31), © 2006. Electronically reproduced by permission of Pearson Education, Inc., Upper Saddle River, NJ.

and opportunities for common men by defying domestic aristocrats as well as British rule."[24]

The distinction between these perspectives was very important during the early years, as we began the difficult process of taking our first steps as a sovereign nation. The matter came to a head in the late 1790s as big issues—namely, a series of economic and foreign policy questions—pulled Americans into a debate about the role of average citizens in governance. Alexander Hamilton, Washington's Secretary of the Treasury, proposed a series of measures that he believed would secure the nation's long-term economic future. But these policies seemed to help the business class at the expense of the poor. As for foreign policy, our allegiance in the war between England and France was fiercely debated. Should we help England, our principal trading partner, or France, our ally in the Revolution? The group in power during this period, led by the second president, John Adams, had adopted the name Federalists (inspired by the leaders who had worked to get the Constitution ratified a few years earlier). The other group, led by Thomas Jefferson and James Madison, had begun referring to itself as the Republicans or the Democratic-Republicans, the distant precursor of today's Democratic Party.

This political cartoon depicts a fight in Congress between Roger Griswold (wielding the cane) and Matthew Lyon (wielding the fire tongs), the most notable victim of the Sedition Act of 1798. Proponents of the Sedition Act, which mandated fines or imprisonment for criticizing the government, argued that the Act was designed to prevent the new government from being weakened from within, especially during a time of impending war. Opponents argued the act was unconstitutional.
—*Are there ever instances when it is acceptable for the government to punish citizens for speaking out in opposition to its policies?*

there would be a return to the established order, much as before. Liberty and equality were wonderful theoretical constructs, but day-to-day rule should be entrusted to enlightened gentlemen, to whom ordinary people should accord great deference. Those holding this perspective argued that "once the state and national constitutions secured the election of rulers, they warranted obedience, rather than suspicion, from the people."[23]

To others, the war was not only about independence but also about a dramatic change in the nature of governance. It was about shifting control from a small group of elites to *all* citizens. It was a revolution in governance and in thinking about the proper nature of government and politics. The "Spirit of '76" was about liberty, equality, and the creation of a limited government. "The Revolution had been a social upheaval," this side argued, "a transformation that had won equal rights, liberties,

The ferocity of the debate and the depth of feelings on each side seemed to threaten the nation in its infancy. Republicans believed that the economic policies of the Federalists and their moves to stifle criticism were an assault on free government. For many people, the issue boiled down to the role of average citizens in society and in the conduct of government. Things came to a head during the election of 1800, which pitted John Adams against Thomas Jefferson. Jefferson narrowly defeated his former friend. Republicans swept into the Congress and state legislatures across the nation.

Beyond policy changes, the election of 1800 marked three critically important events. First, one administration (led by the Federalists) was removed from power peacefully, being replaced by its political rival. A "Second Revolution" had occurred without violence—a rarity in history. This in itself was a stunning success for the new government. Second, efforts to stifle criticism of government leaders, through the Alien and Sedition Acts (measures passed by Adams and the Federalists), backfired. The notion of "legitimate opposition" took hold, meaning that it would be healthy for our system to have an out-of-power group keeping an eye on the in-power group. Third, the election of 1800 seemed to signify that there should be no privileged class in American politics. The process set in motion by the Declaration of Independence was indeed a revolution, not simply a war for independence.

The Struggle over Ratification

2.8 **Analyze how the ratification debate structured the nature of our democracy.**

PRACTICE QUIZ: UNDERSTAND AND APPLY

1. The struggle over ratification of the Constitution was
   a. one of the low points of American history due to the violence that broke out during the process.
   b. quite congenial, because the framers were so widely respected and trusted.
   c. especially contentious, because it pitted slaveholding states against abolitionist states.
   d. a high point of American history, because it resolved a contentious issue by logical and peaceful means.

2. The Anti-Federalists opposed ratification of the Constitution primarily because
   a. they believed that too much power would be concentrated in the national government.
   b. they feared that too much power would be granted to the presidency.
   c. they feared that members of Congress would be isolated from their constituents due to the large size of their districts.
   d. a, b, and c.

3. In *Federalist No. 10*, James Madison extolled the virtues of a large national government as opposed to a number of smaller governments.
   a. true
   b. false

4. The "double security" Madison discussed in *Federalist No. 51* refers to
   a. the virtue of checks and balances.
   b. the separate powers of federal and state courts.
   c. the division of power between the national government and the states as well as checks and balances.
   d. the president's veto power and shared powers between the branches.

ANALYZE

1. Since the Constitution was ratified, we know the Federalists' argument better than the Anti-Federalists'. But is there anything we can learn from the Brutus? Were the Anti-Federalists right about anything?

2. How would the process of ratification fare in the modern mass media environment?

IDENTIFY THE CONCEPT THAT DOESN'T BELONG

a. Vigorous debate
b. Violence
c. Pamphlets
d. Newspaper columns
e. Logic

Conclusion

One of the virtues of our political culture has been the widespread celebration of our formative period. However, a vibrant democracy did not arrive with the signing of the Declaration of Independence, the victory of the Continental Army, the ratification of the Constitution, or any other event. Rather, the American story has been one of triumphs and tragedies, great achievements and monumental setbacks, fits and starts. The early period began the journey of liberty and equality in our country, but most observers would agree that we have not yet arrived at a final destination.

We might also underscore the interplay of political power, authority, and legitimacy. As noted, even though a government might have the power to compel action by citizens, it may not have the authority; the cry of "no taxation without representation" clearly echoed this notion. But after independence was secured, the tables were turned. On paper, the Articles of Confederation seemed to give Congress an avenue for collecting funds, but the scheme contained few provisions to impose the will of the national government on the states. The central government simply lacked power. And of course, the true challenge of the framers was to find a balance between power and legitimacy.

Another theme springing from these pages is the importance of political participation. Citizens stood up, demanded liberty and freedom, and forged their own system of government. We often hear that the framers were an atypical lot—much wealthier and better educated than average citizens. Although this may be true, we still need to remember the role played by average men and women during this period, not the least of which were the patriots who helped fill the ranks of the Continental Army and local militias and also young citizens like Joseph Plumb Martin. Our democracy would have stumbled—indeed, it would not have taken its first step—were it not for

the hard work of citizens fighting for a better life and a better system of government. Widespread political and civic engagement has been one of the many things that has distinguished the American system of government.

Finally, this chapter is also about the importance of pathways of change. As colonists came to believe in individual liberties and their right to participate in the conduct of government, they felt more frustration over British rule. The Revolution was about creating a limited government—a government that would reflect the concerns of the people. Yet the framers had to fashion a system that was *both* responsive to popular will *and* stable. In some very real ways, the Constitution limits the democratic process and harnesses the will of the people, with the goal of creating a powerful, secure system of government. On its face, you might be hard-pressed to label the original Constitution (before the amendments) a plan to enhance democratic principles. But thanks to changes to the original framework (the Bill of Rights in particular) and the toil and sacrifice of countless citizens, numerous pathways have emerged to make the system more democratic.

We opened the chapter with a quick story about Lewis and Clark's decision to allow all members of their force to vote on where to spend the winter in 1805. This took place after Thomas Jefferson defeated John Adams, in what some have called the Second Revolution. But was racial and gender equality ushered in at this moment? Of course not. It would take generations and generations—and some would say we are not yet there. But that tale was a glimpse of what our nation would someday become. Perhaps there is a very distant, but very real, link between York's vote on the edge of the Pacific Ocean and the election of Barack Obama 200 years later. And so goes the evolving true story of our democracy.

KEY CONCEPT MAP **How did early events lead to the creation of a democracy in the United States?**

1620
Signing of the Mayflower Compact

The Pilgrims and others left England in search of a system where laws, not an individual or a small group, would rule society.

Critical Thinking Questions

What if the Pilgrim leaders had not insisted that everyone sign the Compact legalizing their position as a "civil body politic"? What if the Pilgrim leaders had instead tried to set up a monarchial system similar to what they had experienced in England?

1700–1764
Salutary Neglect

Because British elites wanted commercial growth, they maintained a policy of loose enforcement of trade laws with few taxes and regulations placed on early settlers. Early Americans thus became accustomed to liberty and freedom.

What if British elites had imposed stricter trade laws from the start? If early American colonists had not experienced salutary neglect, would they have been as motivated to revolt against the later regulations?

1764–1776
Great Squeeze

In an effort to repay the costs of winning the French and Indian War, Parliament and King George III imposed a series of revenue-raising measures on the colonists. This helped fuel the notion of oppression under monarchial rule.

Why weren't the colonists sympathetic to Parliament's call for them to help pay the debt from the French and Indian War, especially when it had been fought to protect the colonies?

1700s
Writings of Democratic Philosophers

The ideas of Locke, Smith, Paine, and Montesquieu—addressing concepts such as natural rights, limited government, consent of the governed, and rule by the people—spread like wildfire.

Why was the notion of a "limited government" so radical at the time?

1776
Signing of the Declaration of Independence

Thomas Jefferson's lucid prose captured the reasons why it was essential to break from England and the rationale for a democratic government.

What if Jefferson had not been such a skilled writer? Or what if the Declaration had never been written? Would as many colonists have rallied behind the revolutionary cause?

1775–1783
American Revolution

More than just a war for independence, the American Revolution firmly planted the idea that governments must guarantee "life, liberty, and the pursuit of happiness."

If the American Revolution was about freedom and liberty, how do we explain the oppression of blacks, women, Native Americans, and many other groups in the generations that followed?

1791
Bill of Rights

The first ten amendments to the U.S. Constitution laid out core liberties that have been essential for the expansion of democracy in the United States.

What if the Bill of Rights had limited the actions of state governments in addition to the federal government from the start? How would this have impacted later civil rights struggles?

Democracy did not *arrive* with the signing of the Declaration of Independence, the American Revolution, the ratification of the Constitution, or any other singular event. Yet, many events in the formative years planted the seeds of a more just system. Our nation's democratic character continues to blossom and evolve today. —*If it's true that each generation confronts battles over fundamental democratic principles, what are the great issues of our day? How do they compare to the battles fought by previous generations?*

Review of Key Objectives

The Nature of Government and Politics

 2.1 Identify the difference between government and politics.

(pages 32–33)

Before beginning our exploration of American government, it is important to understand the difference between government and politics, power and authority, and legitimacy. Government refers to the official rules and institutions that structure the development and implementation of public policy (what government does). Politics, on the other hand, refers to the various ways individuals and groups seek to influence the final outcome of policy disputes. A governmental entity is said to have authority, if there is a legal foundation for a particular action. Legitimacy means that most citizens *believe* an action taken is proper. Thus, authority is based on institutional elements, but legitimacy is based on perceptions. For example, while the federal government might have the authority to regulate elementary school curricula, many think this should be done at the local level.

KEY TERMS

Power 32
Authority 32

CRITICAL THINKING QUESTIONS

1. Is it possible for the political process to shape the structure of government? If so, can you think of examples in American history when this has occurred?
2. Does the Supreme Court have political power? Does it have authority? Under what conditions does the authority of the Court become threatened?

INTERNET RESOURCES

Many theorists have written about the relationship between power and authority. This Web site offers some thoughts from Montesquieu, an eighteenth-century French philosopher whose writings had a great impact on the framers of our political system: http://www.lonang.com/exlibris/montesquieu/sol-02.htm

ADDITIONAL READING

Pious, Richard. *President, the Congress, and the Constitution: Power and Legitimacy in American Politics.* New York: Free Press, 1984.

Types of Governments

 2.2 Differentiate between different types of governments.

(pages 34–35)

There are many types of governments, the foremost distinguishing characteristics being who is allowed to participate and how decisions are made. Using these two dimensions, systems such as monarchies, oligarchies, and totalitarian regimes are more easily understood. In brief, as the number of participants in a system expands, the system moves more toward a democracy. This section also explores the differences between a *democracy* and a *republic*. In a direct democracy, all citizens participate in all policy questions, but in a republic, citizens ask others, usually elected officials, to make policy decisions.

KEY TERMS

Monarchy 34
Constitutional Monarchy 34
Dictator 34
Oligarchy 34
Pluralism 34
Democracy 34
Republic 34
Representative Democracy 34
Totalitarian Regime 34
Authoritarian Regime 34
Constitutional Government 34

CRITICAL THINKING QUESTIONS

1. What is the difference between a republic and a democracy? Put a bit differently, are all republics also democracies?
2. In January 2005, Iraqi citizens were given the right to vote, leading some to speculate that democracy was taking hold in that country. But violence continued, and the rule of law seemed elusive. Can elections bring democracy to a country? Is it that simple?

INTERNET RESOURCES

Numerous Web sites chart differences between types of governments around the world. Two of interest include http://home.earthlink.net/~kingsidebishop/id2.html and http://www.stutzfamily.com/mrstutz/WorldAffairs/typesofgovt.html

ADDITIONAL READING

Derbyshire, Denis J. and Ian Derbyshire. *Political Systems of the World.* New York: Palgrave Macmillan, 1996.

Early Governance in America

2.3 Describe how forces in Colonial America helped set the stage for the American Revolution.

(pages 36–37)

During the pre-Revolution period, governance was not exactly democratic. Royally appointed governors ruled most colonies with few checks by citizens. Yet, the seeds of a democratic movement were planted. For example, most colonies had assemblies, where delegates came to discuss issues of concern, and to provide reports and suggestions to the governors. We might say that these were budding legislative institutions. Moreover, notions of liberty and equality were increasingly discussed during this time.

KEY TERMS

Pilgrims 36
Mayflower Compact 36
French and Indian War 36
Great Squeeze 36

CRITICAL THINKING QUESTIONS

1. What was so significant about the Mayflower Compact? What did it say about the nature of governance in the New World?
2. This section touches upon the suspicion of elites in colonial politics. Has this been a recurring theme in American politics?

INTERNET RESOURCES

To learn more about the formative years in American history, visit the Library of Congress's America's Story Web site at http://www.americaslibrary.gov/cgi-bin/page.cgi

ADDITIONAL READING

Burns, James MacGregor. *The Vineyard of Liberty.* New York: Knopf, 1982.

Butler, Jon. *Becoming America: The Revolution Before 1776.* Cambridge, MA: Harvard University Press, 2000.

Ellis, Joseph. *Founding Brothers: The Revolutionary Generation.* New York: Vintage Books, 2002.

The American Revolution

2.4 Identify the core principles of the American Revolution.

(pages 38–43)

When Abraham Lincoln spoke of our nation's birth as "Four score and seven years ago," he was referring to the Revolution and to the signing of the Declaration of Independence, not to the ratification of the Constitution in 1789. This is because the core of the "American experiment" in self-governance springs from this revolutionary period. Ideas of liberty, equality, self-governance, and economic advancement set in motion a revolution, and later a new, democratic system of government.

KEY TERMS

Acts for Trade 38	**Stamp Act Congress** 38
Coercive Acts 38	**Thomas Paine** 38
Intolerable Acts 38	**Natural Rights** 40
John Locke 38	**Social Contract Theory** 40
Adam Smith 38	**Thomas Hobbes** 40
John Adams 38	

CRITICAL THINKING QUESTIONS

1. We often hear about the principles that drove the Patriot cause, such as notions of "No taxation without representation!" But is it fair to say that economic issues also compelled action? Was the Revolution also about financial interest—about making and keeping more money?
2. If Thomas Jefferson was right about the duty of citizens to jettison their government when it no longer serves their interests, wouldn't that lead to recurrent revolutions? What would stop "patriots" from starting wars for independence whenever they got really upset with their government?

INTERNET RESOURCES

To better understand some of the developments from the first 100 years of our nation's history, visit From Revolution to Reconstruction: http://odur.let.rug.nl/~usa

ADDITIONAL READING

Bailyn, Bernard. *The Ideological Origins of the American Revolution.* Cambridge, MA: Harvard University Press, 1967.

Wills, Garry. *Inventing America: Jefferson's Declaration of Independence.* New York: Random House, 1978.

Ellis, Joseph J. *American Creation.* New York: Vintage, 2007.

The Articles of Confederation

 2.5 Determine the reasons for the failure of the Articles of Confederation.

(pages 44–45)

Our first stab at self-governance was a flop, because there was no way for the new national government to regulate commerce, raise needed funds, or conduct foreign policy. Most significantly, the system was unstable, ready to collapse at any moment. However, the experience under the Articles of Confederation shaped the motivations of the framers, thus shaping the Constitution and our system of government.

KEY TERMS

Shays's Rebellion 45
Constitutional Convention 45

CRITICAL THINKING QUESTIONS

1. The Articles of Confederation provided for a very weak national government. Why was such a decentralized system created in the first place? Didn't its creators know it would not work?
2. What does the alternative view of Shays's Rebellion say about the core rationale for the Constitutional Convention? Do you agree with this perspective?

INTERNET RESOURCES

For general information on numerous early American documents, try the Avalon Project at Yale University at http://avalon.law.yale.edu

ADDITIONAL READING

Jensen, Merrill. *The Articles of Confederation: An Interpretation of the Social-Constitutional History of the Revolution, 1774–1781.* Madison, WI: University of Wisconsin Press, 1959.

Morgan, Edmund S. *The Meaning of Independence: John Adams, Thomas Jefferson, George Washington.* New York: Norton, 1978.

The Constitutional Convention

 2.6 Assess how compromises at the Constitutional Convention shaped our political system.

(pages 46–49)

We often hear that the framers came to the Constitutional Convention eager to create a stronger national government. But the truth is more complex. Numerous, often conflicting motivations drove this historic event, and from these concerns our Constitution was born. The many compromises, such as dividing power between states and the federal government, and between branches of government, also speak to the interests of the framers and to the nature of our political system. We have a democracy, but also a system of government that seeks to "enlarge and refine" the public will.

KEY TERMS

Virginia Plan 46
New Jersey Plan 46
Great Compromise 47
Connecticut Compromise 47
Census 47

CRITICAL THINKING QUESTIONS

1. Looking back at the Constitutional Convention, we often shake our heads over the compromises that kept things going. What do you think would have happened if these agreements were not reached? Would there ever have been a "United States" without these agreements?
2. Some have noted that while these compromises kept things going, they also diminished the democratic character of our system. Do you agree?

INTERNET RESOURCES

Visit the Annenberg Learning Center: A Biography of America at http://www.learner.org/biographyofamerica

Learn about the periods before, during, and after the Constitutional Convention at the History Place Web site at http://www.historyplace.com

ADDITIONAL READING

Wood, Gordon S. *The Radicalism of the American Revolution.* New York: Vintage Books, 1993.

The U.S. Constitution

 2.7 Identify the core principles of the Constitution.

(pages 50–53)

The Constitution is made up of both broad principles, such as the sharing of powers and the checks and balances, and specifics, such as the enumeration of congressional powers. In order to understand how our government operates, both elements must be acknowledged. For example, while the Constitution affords Congress the duty to create public policy, the bicameral legislature may lead the Senate to have a very different take on a policy question than the House, as was evident in the 2010 debate over health care reform. Added on top of this, the president can veto legislation and is also responsible for implementation of legislation. And, finally, the courts may declare all or parts of legislation unconstitutional.

KEY TERMS

Sharing of Powers 50
Expressed Powers 51
Police Powers 51
Bill of Rights 52

CRITICAL THINKING QUESTIONS

1. The U.S. Constitution has been modeled across the globe. Why? What makes our structure of government so special?
2. How would you respond to the argument that the cost of "checks and balances" and "shared powers" is a slow-moving system? (Note that the framers also did not anticipate political parties, which can slow things down when different parties control different parts of the government.)

INTERNET RESOURCES

To access the Declaration of Independence, the Constitution, and other key documents in our nation's history, see the Library of Congress, Primary Documents in American History at http://memory.loc.gov/ammem/help/constRedir.html

ADDITIONAL READING

Bowen, Catherine Drinker. *Miracle at Philadelphia: The Story of the Constitutional Convention May–September 1787.* Boston: Back Bay Books, 1986.

Collier, Christopher. *Decision in Philadelphia: The Constitutional Convention of 1787.* New York: Ballantine Books, 2007.

The Struggle over Ratification

 2.8 Analyze how the ratification debate structured the nature of our democracy.

(pages 54–57)

While Lincoln might have been right to assert that our nation began in 1776, this does not mean that who we are as a people was defined at that point. There have been numerous transformative events in our history, and this short section takes a look at the election of 1800. Here, political parties, each representing different versions of what they believed was "just" public policy, fought to win the presidency. In the end, the Jeffersonian Republicans won the contest, and John Adams was sent into private life. More importantly, the election of 1800 showed that the new system of government could change leaders and policies peacefully—a rarity in world history at that time. Perhaps political parties were not so bad; they could even play an important role in the new system of government.

KEY TERMS

Federalists 54
Anti-Federalists 54
The Federalists Papers 54

CRITICAL THINKING QUESTIONS

1. What was so special about the ratification of the U.S. Constitution? Why would some suggest this was a proud moment in our nation's history?
2. How does the Election of 1800 continue to shape American politics?

INTERNET RESOURCES

For an online, searchable copy of *The Federalist Papers,* see http://www.law.ou.edu/hist/federalist

For an online look at the Anti-Federalist Papers, see http://www.angelfire.com/pa/sergeman/foundingdocs/antifedpap/main.html

ADDITIONAL READING

Ketcham, Ralph. *The Anti-Federalist Papers and the Constitutional Convention Delegates.* New York: Signet, 2003.

Smith, Page. *The Shaping of America: A People's History of the Young Republic.* New York: McGraw-Hill, 1979.

Chapter Review   Test Your Knowledge

1. Based on the definition in this textbook, which of the following is an example of *authority*?
   a. the federal government imposing and collecting a tax
   b. a judge "legislating from the bench"
   c. a teacher telling students to vote for a certain candidate for public office
   d. a minister telling his congregation to disobey a law

2. What role did the Sons of Liberty play in the independence movement?
   a. They sent diplomatic missions to Parliament in support of economic relief for the colonists.
   b. They sponsored "committees of correspondence."
   c. They held rallies to recruit citizens to protest British policies.
   d. b and c.

3. Since slavery is obviously undemocratic, why didn't the framers abolish it when they drafted the Constitution?
   a. Because the framers all agreed that slavery was legal.
   b. Because slavery was widely practiced and tolerated during the eighteenth century.
   c. Because it was necessary to compromise with the southern delegations on this sensitive issue.
   d. b and c.

4. What drove the colonists toward revolution?
   a. their suspicions about the British monarchy
   b. the "Big Squeeze"
   c. a century of "salutary neglect," which gave colonists a sense of independence from England.
   d. a, b, and c.

5. What was the main difference between the Second Continental Congress and the First Continental Congress?
   a. The Second spoke glowingly of expanding women's rights.
   b. The Second introduced a proposal to outlaw slavery.
   c. The Second advocated armed rebellion against the Crown.
   d. The Second argued for an open trade policy with all nations, not just those allied with Great Britain.

6. Jefferson passionately suggested that "the tree of liberty must be refreshed … with
   a. the sweat of the toiling merchants, the backbone of our colonies."
   b. the blood of patriots and tyrants."
   c. the sweat and blood of our noble citizens, patriots all."
   d. the blood, sweat and tears of our citizens, to free us for all posterity."

7. Social contract theorist John Locke was important to American revolutionary philosophy because
   a. he argued persuasively that legitimate governments must be based upon the consent of the governed.
   b. he argued passionately that government must be limited in order to protect the universal principle of free trade.
   c. he was a co-founder of the Sons of Liberty, and a major contributor to the "committees of correspondence."
   d. a, b, and c.

8. When Thomas Paine wrote in 1776 that "[t]hese are the times that try men's souls," he was
   a. consoling British subjects, because General Washington's army was defeating the British army.
   b. referring to the unfair trading practices of the Navigation Acts.
   c. complaining about the weaknesses of the Articles of Confederation.
   d. None of the above.

9. The Declaration of Independence was supported enthusiastically by the majority of colonists.
   a. true
   b. false

10. In 2009, a group calling themselves the Tea Party Activists began holding a series of protests and rallies against tax increases and what they saw as an expanding and oppressive federal government. How were the actions of this group different from the violent revolt justified by the Declaration of Independence?
    a. The Tea Party Activists had more pathways of action open to them than the colonists, so violence was unnecessary.
    b. The Declaration of Independence does not condone violence under any circumstances.
    c. The Declaration of Independence does not condone protests against one's own country.
    d. The Declaration of Independence suggests that once governments are created, citizens should always support their government.

11. The "Great Compromise" at the Constitutional Convention refers to the decision to
    a. count a slave as equivalent to three-fifths of a vote in determining the number of representatives allocated to each state in the House.
    b. allow congressional representation to both reflect a state's population and represent each state equally (regardless of population).
    c. protect the Atlantic slave trade for at least 20 more years.
    d. grant strong executive powers to the president but limit his tenure in office to two terms.

12. Among numerous other effects, the ratification of the Constitution created an immediate and widespread sense of national citizenship.
    a. true
    b. false

13. Why is it logical to describe our system of government as both rigid and flexible?
    a. It is possible to add amendments to the Constitution, but only through an intricate and challenging process.
    b. Power-sharing by way of checks and balances makes it unlikely that any one branch or individual officeholder could seize control of government.
    c. Rigidity implies stability; flexibility implies the possibility of major change at any time.
    d. a and b.

14. What is the difference between "expressed powers" and "police powers"?
  a. Expressed powers are those asserted through speech and written decree; police powers are those that are physically exerted.
  b. Expressed powers are the prerogative of the national government; police powers are the prerogative of the states.
  c. Expressed powers refer to commercial matters, foreign affairs, and national security; police powers refer to matters of health, safety, and individual well-being.
  d. b and c.

15. In order for an amendment to the Constitution to become ratified, it must supported by three-fourths of the residents of all states, meaning 75 percent of the adult U.S. population.
  a. true
  b. false

16. Why do constitutional lawyers and scholars still make reference to *The Federalist Papers*?
  a. because *The Federalist Papers* are so relevant to issues of federal (versus state) power
  b. because citing *The Federalist Papers* is a requirement of federal judicial procedure
  c. because *The Federalist Papers* offer a comprehensive explanation of Constitutional principles and intentions
  d. none of the above

17. James Madison referred to "the vice of faction" in *Federalist No. 10*. But he did not recommend suppressing such factions, because
  a. if a faction represents less than a majority, its representatives will be outvoted or overruled by those in the majority.
  b. all factions naturally wither over time—"No living thing endures over the long course of human affairs."

  c. in the "extended republic" of the nation as a whole, factions would usually never constitute a majority and thus would not direct government policy.
  d. Suppressing factions would be akin to limiting civil liberties; namely, the right to assemble and petition government to address grievances.

18. Madison asserted that a divided system of government, with checks and balances, would ensure the longevity of the republic, because
  a. such a system would cultivate the virtue of every citizen.
  b. such a system would ensure that ambition would counter ambition among competing factions.
  c. a and b
  d. none of the above

19. One of the core arguments made by the Anti-Federalists was that
  a. the new national government would not place sufficient strength in the presidency.
  b. an extended public would not allow legislators to know the concerns of constituents.
  c. enlightened rules were likely a better safeguard against corruption than "checks and balances."
  d. a legislature composed of "average" citizens was risky because they would often become corrupt.

20. The Bill of Rights
  a. is a list of individual protections of the rights of all citizens.
  b. are those amendments to the Constitution passed in the late eighteenth century.
  c. is one of the key negotiating points that led to unanimous ratification of the Constitution.
  d. all of the above

mypoliscilab Exercises

Apply what you learned in this chapter on **MyPoliSciLab.**

Read on mypoliscilab.com

  eText: Chapter 2

Study and **Review** on mypoliscilab.com

  Pre-Test
  Post-Test
  Chapter Exam
  Flashcards

Watch on mypoliscilab.com

  Video: Mexico Border Security
  Video: The Bailout Hearings
  Video: Vaccines: Mandatory Protection
  Video: Animal Sacrifice and Free Exercise
  Video: Polygamy and the U.S. Constitution

Explore on mypoliscilab.com

  Simulation: You Are James Madison
  Simulation: You Are Proposing a Constitutional Amendment
  Comparative: Comparing Constitutions
  Timeline: The History of Constitutional Amendments
  Visual Literacy: The American System of Checks and Balances

Federalism

CHAPTER 3

KEY OBJECTIVES

After completing this chapter, you should be prepared to:

3.1 Explain why the Framers divided authority between layers of government.

3.2 Characterize dual federalism both before and after the Civil War.

3.3 Compare and contrast cooperative and creative federalism.

3.4 Trace the evolution of federalism in recent decades.

On April 26, 2009, President Barack Obama declared the swine flu (H1N1) a public health emergency, enabling the national government to expedite the shipping of flu-fighting medications from federal stockpiles to states. When President Obama declared the emergency, only 20 cases of the flu had been diagnosed in the United States, with no deaths. Some thought that the declaration of the health emergency was premature, but supporters claimed that it was an important first step to prepare for a possible pandemic. Following the declaration, the Centers for Disease Control took the lead in developing a vaccine. The government initially estimated that 160 million doses of a vaccine would be made available in October 2009; however, by the end of October only 24.8 million doses were on hand, with fewer than 12 million shipped to local health departments, doctors' offices, and health care facilities. Access to the limited vaccine doses became controversial as states grappled with the shortfall.

On October 25, 2009, President Obama identified the outbreak as a threat to national security and declared it a national emergency. The declaration was a preemptive measure, which gave the Health and Human Services Secretary, Kathleen Sebelius,

How has federalism in the United States evolved?

the power to bypass federal rules in order to enable more flexibility in treating outbreaks in localities across the country. By the time the national emergency was declared, more than 1,000 people in the United States, including 100 children, had died of the H1N1 flu, with more than 5,700 deaths worldwide. Nearly every state had widespread flu outbreaks, with experts preparing for the possibility of an epidemic. Under the state of emergency, the federal government allowed states and localities greater flexibility in treating and containing the virus, and they also agreed to assume a larger financial burden for the treatment.

Increasingly we turn to our federal government to address what were traditionally seen as local issues—from environmental cleanups to the treatment of the flu. Many are concerned that we rely too heavily upon Washington and that we need to decrease the authority and budget of the federal government. Others are comfortable with an active federal government, arguing that an energetic and vigorous national government is necessary to respond quickly to health and national security threats and to promote equality. At what point do we hold states and localities liable, and conversely, what responsibility does the federal government have to ensure the health and welfare of its citizens?

Resource Center
• Glossary
• Vocabulary Example
• Connect the Link

■ **Unitary System:** A system of government in which political power and authority are located in one central government that runs the country and that may or may not share power with regional subunits.

EXAMPLE: *Under a unitary system of government, the central government would determine who was eligible to marry whom, at what age, under what conditions, and the process, including the difficulty or ease, by which marriages would be ended.*

Dividing Governmental Authority

3.1 **Explain why the Framers divided authority between layers of government.**

(pages 68–71)

Governmental authority in the United States has been a source of conflict for more than two centuries. Unlike countries such as the United Kingdom and France, which are governed under a **unitary system**■ (that is, a system in which all ruling authority rests in a single national government), the United States divides powers and responsibilities among layers of governments, in a **federal system**■.

The framers included in the Constitution a division of power and responsibility between the national and state governments to create yet another check against potential abuses. Yet, our unique system has created much uncertainty and many practical management problems. At times in our history, it has even led to violence. Indeed, the greatest crisis in our history, the Civil War, was very much about "states' rights" versus the authority of the national government. We can imagine why foreign policy would fall under the scope of the national government, but what about the general welfare of American citizens? Is crime a problem for a local government, a state government, or the national government? Should the national government be able to control the conduct of doctors and regulate what services they can or cannot provide? How about lawyers, electricians, or hairdressers? If a state considers the medical use of marijuana permissible, should the federal government be able to step in and ban it? Can the federal government bar gay couples from getting married under one state's laws, or force other states to recognize that marriage?

Then there is the issue of transportation. Just because the Constitution says that Congress shall regulate commerce, does that mean the federal government is responsible for fixing all roads and bridges? Would we want the federal government telling us how many stop signs to put up on a stretch of road? That may seem an extreme example, yet the issue of speed limits has been controversial for decades. In the mid-1970s, when the nation faced a fuel shortage, one of the measures used to save energy was fixing the national speed limit at 55 mph. Many states, especially those in the West, refused to abide by the federal law. In response, Congress threatened to cut off federal highway aid to any state that did not enforce this law. Some states rejected the money and set the speed limits they wanted. Others simply lowered the fines for speeding tickets. The federally mandated 55 mph limit has since been dropped, but some states still abide by it while others allow up to 75 mph. If you exceed the 75 mph limit in Montana, you might get a $40 fine. In many other states, it could cost you more than $300.

In education, law, medicine, transportation, environmental protection, crime, and many other areas of American life, the line between federal and state control has been controversial and fluid. For example, until more recently, education had been largely the domain of state and local governments. However, No Child Left Behind (enacted under President George W. Bush in 2001 with high levels of bipartisan support) instituted standards-based education reform that required states to develop assessments of basic skills as a condition for receiving additional federal funding for education. Another example of the increased interaction between the state and federal levels comes in the area of cleanup after natural disasters. It used to be that cleanup after a flood or hurricane was entirely the responsibility of state and local governments; today, everyone expects the federal government to take the lead. Indeed, one of the low points in President George W. Bush's administration was the federal government's inept response following Hurricane Katrina in the summer of 2005. Ironically, many of these critics are the same people who argue that the federal government is getting too big and should stay out of the affairs of local governments.

You might be tempted to draw a conclusion that things have moved toward more federal control, but even if this is true in some policy areas, in other spheres the states have been given more control and greater responsibility. Politicians eager to promote local control often suggest that state governments are the "laboratories of democracy," a concept first enunciated by Supreme Court

President Bush addresses Congress to urge the passage of the No Child Left Behind Act of 2001. He pushed the legislation to dramatically alter our federal education policy and signed the act into law on January 8, 2002. —*How well do you think schools have done in leaving "no child behind"?*

CONNECT THE LINK
(Chapter 2, pages 36–37) Why are documents that legalize relationships between people and their government important for stability?

■ **Federal System:** A system of government in which power and authority are divided between a central government and regional subunits.

EXAMPLE: *Under a federal system of government, state governments would determine the conditions of marriage and divorce to allow local or regional norms to influence public policy. Some states have discussed making divorce more difficult to reflect their political culture's belief in the sanctity of marriage.*

Justice Louis Brandeis in 1932, meaning that difficult challenges are more likely to be resolved when 50 entities are working to find innovative solutions rather than just the federal government.

This chapter explores the complex issues surrounding federalism in the United States. As with other elements in our political system, many changes have occurred over the years. Today, the relationship between the states and the federal government is vastly different from what it was at the dawn of our nation's history. Rather than being simply a unique, interesting aspect of our government, the debate over governmental authority has been at the center of most of the trying events in our history, and it is likely to impact future directions in American government.

The goal of this chapter is to help you understand that public policy does not spring simply from "government" but rather from different *layers* of government. It would make little sense, for example, to lobby members of Congress to change the zoning laws in a particular town or to ask a city council to help lower the cost of prescription drugs. Different governments are responsible for different policies in the United States. This chapter explains why we have such a unique system, examines its advantages and disadvantages, and explores changes over the past 200 years. Politics is not simply about pushing government in a given direction; instead, it is about knowing *which* government to push and how.

National Government: Reasons for Federalism

The federal structure of the United States is not unique. But most countries, whether or not they are democratic, have unitary systems (see Table 3.1). In those countries, there may be viable and active local authorities, but the national government has

sovereignty. This means that the national government has the ultimate governing authority (and the final say). In the United Kingdom, for example, Parliament can change city and town government boundaries at any time. It may allow certain regions to create their own government, as has been the case with Scotland and Northern Ireland, but at any point, Parliament can abolish these structures and override any of their policies.

Why, then, would the United States choose to create a federal system in which sovereignty is divided among different levels of government? One explanation is rooted in the history of government in North America. During the period of exploration and discovery, set into motion by Christopher Columbus's voyage in 1492, a number of nations, including England, France, Spain, Portugal, and the Netherlands, sought to establish colonies in the New World. England eventually planted more than 13 colonies on the North American mainland. As settlers eventually moved to these colonies, they set up their own governments.

As we noted in Chapter 2, pages 36–37, before setting foot on American soil in 1620, the Pilgrims drew up the Mayflower Compact, which was essentially an agreement to form a government. In the Virginia colony, a legislative body called the House of Burgesses was established. Eventually, each colony established its own governing structure. These governments were not sovereign, of course, given that the English Parliament and king could dissolve them at any time (and did so on various occasions), but as our nation began to take shape, there were many distinct governing entities. Moreover, there existed a great deal of suspicion and rivalry among the colonies and among the early states. One of the greatest hurdles confronted by those anxious to break ties with Great Britain on the eve of the American Revolution was to get people to consider themselves as citizens of an American nation rather than just citizens of their individual colonies.

TABLE 3.1	Federal, Confederate, and Unitary Systems of Government	
Each type of governmental system uses a different means to enact policies. —*Look at this table carefully; which system do you think works best? Why?*		
Let's consider how each system of government would work to promote water conservation.		
The federal government would pass broad guidelines and provide some financial incentives, but the implementation of the conservation programs would be left to state and local governments.	The central government would pass broad guidelines with the hope that state governments agree to comply.	The central government would pass specific guidelines and ensure that local governments comply with national decrees.
FEDERAL	**CONFEDERATION**	**UNITARY**
Governmental authority is divided between a national government and state governments. United States under the Constitution (1789–present), Australia, Brazil, Germany, Mexico, Nigeria	Ultimate authority comes from the states. United States under the Articles of Confederation (1781–1789), Confederate States of America (1861–1865), Confederation of Independent States (states of the former Soviet Union)	Ultimate governmental authority comes from the national government. France, Spain, Tanzania

CONNECT THE LINK
(Chapter 2, pages 38–40) How important are
the theories presented by these philosophers
to contemporary political thought?

After independence had been won, the central point of dispute over the ratification of the Constitution in 1787 and 1788 was the extent to which the new national government might, at some future time, take over the role of state governments. Many Americans agreed that a stronger national government was needed to regulate commerce and deal with foreign nations, but few envisioned that the national government would be fully sovereign.

One explanation for our federal system lies, then, in the historical roots of the United States. Our nation was born through the fusing of independent states—states that would never have agreed to a merger if giving up their independence had been part of the deal. Federalism was a compromise. We might also point to the writings of philosophers who guided the thinking of the framers of our system. As discussed in Chapter 2, pages 38–40, the framers relied heavily on the writings of John Locke, Adam Smith, and Thomas Hobbes. Another influential philosopher was the Frenchman Baron Montesquieu, who in the early eighteenth century wrote about the virtues of dividing power and authority between different parts of the government. This might be done, he argued, by having different branches of government *and* by creating layers of governmental authority. James Madison echoes Montesquieu's idea in *Federalist No. 51*:

> In the compound republic of America, the power surrendered by the people is first divided between two distinct governments, and then the portion allotted to each subdivided among distinct and separate departments. Hence a double security arises to the right of the people.

In other words, federalism, coupled with the checks and balances and the sharing of powers at the national level, would help guarantee a republican government. Montesquieu also argued that republican institutions were more likely to flourish in smaller political systems, yet such small states were incapable of defending themselves against attack. The problem could be solved by the creation of a system that would permit a consensus for domestic affairs among the separate governing units but provide unified action for the common defense.[1]

Still another significant factor behind federalism is the geographic, cultural, and economic diversity of the United States. The distinctiveness of different American regions has eroded dramatically in recent decades, due in large measure to changes in transportation, entertainment, and the economy. A Wal-Mart in Boise, Idaho, looks exactly the same as a Wal-Mart in Bath, Maine. Kids in Albany, Georgia, watch the same Saturday morning cartoons as kids in Albany, New York. Throughout most of our history, however, culture, language, demographics, economic conditions, and other aspects of life varied in different regions, states, and even communities. And the United States remains one of the most diverse nations in the world, which has contributed to a sense of a localized citizenship.

Finally, federalism made sense in the American setting for practical reasons. Historians agree that if in 1787 the separate states had not been permitted to have significant powers, the Constitution would never have been ratified.

STUDENT profile

In January 2006, two high school students, Jessica Rapchik and Pat Korte, decided to revive a 1960s organization, Students for a Democratic Society (SDS), because they wanted to create a multi-issue student and youth organization to empower and mobilize young people. The original SDS was a highly visible organization that epitomized student activism and the New Right in the 1960s. Rapchik and Korte wanted to reignite the SDS goal of student power by uniting groups from across the country to fight for social justice, an end to bigotry, and the promotion of peace. They sought guidance from leaders of the old SDS to relaunch the organization for today's youth.

SDS emphasizes activism through a variety of mechanisms, including hosting regional and national conferences to train youth to be more efficient leaders and organizers. Many are not attracted to some of the more radical actions advocated by SDS (such as illegal war protests), but they are a committed group of individuals working to promote youth activism across the United States. For more information, see the official SDS Web site at http:// www.studentsforademocraticsociety.org/

State Government: Dillon's Rule Versus Home Rule

When most people think about "the government," they think about the government in Washington, but there is a long-standing tradition in the United States of active and powerful local governments. In the earliest days of colonial America, many colonies were actually federations of local governments. In fact, newly independent states often included stipulations in their first constitutions to guarantee that local governments would retain influence over their own affairs.

Some states, however, did hold to the English tradition of weak local governments. A ruling in 1868 by Judge John Dillon of the Iowa Supreme Court held that local governments could rule only in areas explicitly permitted by the state government, providing a legal framework for this view of state-local relationships. His decision became known as **Dillon's rule.** Legally, state governments create and control local governments. Because of this, state governments have great influence on the nature and character of local municipalities. States that follow Dillon's rule give local governments very narrow and explicit power to fulfill their responsibilities. Consequently, these state governments are very powerful and have a great deal of influence over municipalities

■ **Special Governments:** Local governmental units established for very specific purposes, such as the regulation of water and school districts, airports, and transportation services.

EXAMPLE: *The decisions made by special governments, most notably cities, counties, and school districts, have a very large impact on the daily lives of individuals in many profound ways.*

within the state. Currently, 39 states follow Dillon's rule, though some more stridently than others.[2]

In contrast are states that follow the theory of **home rule,** which holds that city governments can do anything to serve the needs of their residents that is not prohibited by state law. Although city ordinances must comply with state laws and state legislatures can preempt local laws, home rule states give far more authority to the local governments, which are very important for the administration of many governmental services. As you can see in Figure 3.1, there were 89,476 local governments in 2007, the largest of which were special governments. While local governments are multipurpose, **special governments**■ exist to fulfill one or a few special needs, the most numerous of which are natural resource, fire, housing, and community development districts. It is difficult to imagine life without our local governments.

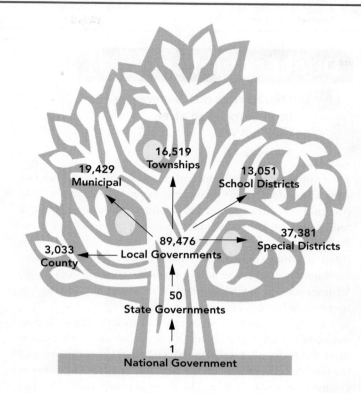

FIGURE 3.1 ■ **Forms of Local and Special Governments**
There are more than 175,000 types of governments in the United States, and the branches of government stretch far and wide, giving residents many points of access to governmental officials and leaders. Thus there are numerous pathways that can be used to initiate change or promote the status quo.

Dividing Governmental Authority

3.1 Explain why the Framers divided authority between layers of government.

PRACTICE QUIZ: UNDERSTAND AND APPLY

1. Federalism, along with a system that includes a separation of power and checks and balances, helps republican governments govern.
   a. true   b. false

2. Which of the following was not a reason for the establishment of a federal system in the United States?
   a. The historic roots of the United States
   b. The writings of philosophers such as Locke, Smith, Hobbes, and Montesquieu
   c. The geographic, cultural, and economic diversity of the United States
   d. The desire of the framers to create a sovereign national government

3. What is the best explanation for the difference between Dillon's rule and home rule?
   a. Dillon's rule asserts the national supremacy over the states, while home rule asserts the opposite.
   b. Dillon's rule grants to state governments significant influence over how cities operate, while

home rule asserts that local government can do anything not prohibited by state law.
   c. Dillon's rule reflects a states' rights position consistent with current Republican Party ideals, while home rule reflects that position consistent with current Democratic Party ideals.
   d. b and c

ANALYZE

1. What are some of the advantages of a federal system of government that we experience in today's society?

2. How do speed limits illustrate the way in which government authority is divided in a federal system?

IDENTIFY THE CONCEPT THAT DOESN'T BELONG

a. Federal system
b. Ease in governing
c. Layers of governmental authority
d. Diversity
e. Checks and balances

3.1

Resource Center
• Glossary
• Vocabulary Example
• Connect the Link

■ **Dual Federalism:** A theory stating that the powers of the federal and state governments are strictly separate, with interaction often marked by tension rather than cooperation.

SIGNIFICANCE: *Under a system of dual federalism, governments have separate spheres of responsibilities and influence and do not cooperate among themselves. As our society becomes more and more complex, it is doubtful that dual federalism can be implemented, as the issues our governments often deal with are too complicated and multifaceted to be addressed exclusively by one level of government without the cooperation of the other levels.*

Dual Federalism

3.2 Characterize dual federalism both before and after the Civil War.
(pages 72–77)

The people who wrote and ratified the Constitution did not share a consistent, clear vision of the meaning of American federalism. Fairly broad agreement about the need for a stronger national government had led to the end of the Articles of Confederation and the drafting of the Constitution, but there remained strong disagreements about exactly how much power the states kept under the new governing document. As a result, arguments about federalism played a central role in shaping the country's political system.

During the 1800s, both before and after the Civil War, the theory of federal-state relations that prevailed was one known as **dual federalism**■. Under this system, state governments and the national government are equally authoritative; the national government is not superior. The national government possesses authority over its powers listed in the Constitution, such as coining money and establishing post offices and military forces, while the Tenth Amendment specifically reserves to the states all other governmental powers not discussed in the Constitution.

Before the Civil War

In the United States, disputes are often resolved through lawsuits that call on federal judges to interpret constitutional provisions defining the extent of federal authority. The judiciary's role in shaping American federalism is not a modern development. Judges have issued rulings on federalism since the first decades after the Constitution's ratification.

In 1816, Congress enacted legislation to charter the Second Bank of the United States. Two years later, the Maryland legislature imposed a tax on all banks within the state that were not chartered by the state legislature. James McCulloch, an official at the Baltimore branch of the federally chartered Bank of the United States, refused to pay the tax. The dispute arrived before the U.S. Supreme Court as the case of *McCulloch* **v.** *Maryland* (1819), and it presented Chief Justice John Marshall with the opportunity to define the respective powers of the state and federal governments.

Marshall's opinion in the case first examined whether the U.S. Constitution granted to Congress the power to charter a bank. Such a power is not explicitly stated anywhere in Article I of the Constitution, which defines the authority of the national legislature. But Marshall focused on the constitutional provision that grants Congress the power to make "all laws which shall be necessary and proper, for carrying into execution the foregoing powers, and all other powers vested by this constitution, in the government of the United States, or in any department thereof." This phrase in the Constitution, known as the **necessary and proper clause,** does not specify what powers, if any, flow from its words. Nevertheless, Marshall relied on the necessary and proper clause to conclude that Congress possessed the power to charter a national bank. The chief justice concluded that the creation of the Bank of the United States was "necessary and proper" as a means to carry out other powers that Article I explicitly granted to Congress, such as the powers to collect taxes, coin money, and regulate commerce. Marshall's opinion rejected Maryland's claim that the word *necessary* granted only powers that were absolutely essential. In this case, Marshall interpreted the Constitution in a way that enhanced the powers of the federal government and empowered Congress to make choices about how it would develop public policy.

After establishing that Congress had properly chartered the bank, Marshall's opinion went on to invalidate Maryland's efforts to impose taxes on the federal government's agencies. "The power to tax," wrote Marshall in a memorable phrase, "is the power to destroy." Realizing that states could use taxation to weaken or destroy federal institutions, the chief justice asserted that the federal government necessarily retained the power to preserve its creations. According to Marshall, the people of the United States grant powers "to a government whose laws, made in pursuance of the constitution, are declared to be supreme. Consequently, the people of a single state cannot confer a sovereignty" on their own government that would extend beyond the borders of the state. By invalidating Maryland's tax on the bank chartered by Congress, Marshall made a strong initial statement about the superior position of the national government in the evolving system of federalism.

Chief Justice Marshall also led the Supreme Court in making other decisions that shaped the law affecting federalism. In *Cohens* v. *Virginia* (1821), for example, brothers who had been convicted under a Virginia law for selling tickets in a lottery approved by Congress appealed to the U.S. Supreme Court. Virginia claimed that the Court had no authority to review decisions by its state courts. Marshall wrote an opinion rejecting that argument and asserting that the U.S. Supreme Court had ultimate authority over judicial matters concerning federal law, whether or not earlier decisions on the matter had been issued by state courts or by lower federal courts.

In *Gibbons* v. *Ogden* (1824), Marshall's Court considered a challenge to a New York law that granted specific steamboat operators the exclusive privilege of providing service between New York and New Jersey. The chief justice announced a broad definition of the power granted to Congress by the

■ **Doctrine of Secession:** The theory that state governments had a right to declare their independence and create their own form of government. Eleven southern states seceded from the Union in 1860–1861, created their own government (the Confederate States of America), and thereby precipitated the Civil War.

EXAMPLE: *The Civil War demonstrated that the doctrine of secession is invalid, but the idea that state governments ought to be very powerful and act in their own self-interest has resurfaced from time to time since that war.*

Chief Justice John Marshall, admistering the oath of office to Andrew Jackson in 1829, played a major role in Supreme Court decisions that helped define the power of the federal government in the early nineteenth century. —*How would history have been different if Marshall had not led the Supreme Court to issue decisions strengthening the federal government's authority?*

Constitution to regulate commerce "among the several states." His opinion concluded that Congress possessed exclusive authority over the regulation of interstate commerce, including navigation, and therefore New York and other states had no power to grant such exclusive licenses to steamboat operators. In short, by these and other key decisions, the early U.S. Supreme Court, under Marshall's leadership, shaped federalism by interpreting the Constitution to give the federal government superior powers in certain matters of public policy, thereby imposing limits on the powers of the states.

Despite these decisions, however, the wording of the Constitution raised many questions about the powers of states and the national government. For example, the Tenth Amendment states that "the powers not delegated to the United States by the Constitution, nor prohibited by it to the States, are reserved to the States respectively, or to the people." Many Americans viewed this amendment as embodying a fundamental premise of the Constitution: Governmental powers not explicitly granted to the federal government continue to reside with the states. This viewpoint supported the theory of dual federalism, which says that governments and the national government are equally authoritative; the national government is not superior.

In practice, in early nineteenth-century America, dual federalism faced criticism from two directions. Advocates of a strong national government believed that where their spheres of activity overlapped, the powers of the federal government must be superior to those of the states. For example, both the states and the federal government sought to regulate certain aspects of business and commerce, and the Marshall Court had ruled in *Gibbons* v. *Ogden* (1824) that Congress has exclusive authority over "interstate commerce." Others saw the states as the central, sovereign governmental entities in the American governing system. These advocates of "states' rights" asserted that the states possessed specific powers superior to those of the national government.

Before the Civil War, many southern leaders and advocates of states' rights relied on a **doctrine of nullification,** which declared that each state had retained its sovereignty upon joining the United States. The doctrine asserted that the government established by the constitution represented a voluntary pact between states and that the federal government had limited powers. If the federal government exceeded the power that had been delegated to it by the Constitution, then a state could declare any laws or actions of the national government "null and void" if they clashed with that state's interests and goals. In the 1830s, the South Carolina legislature voted to nullify federal tariffs that were believed to help northern manufacturing businesses while hurting southern planters and slave owners. The state later cancelled its action after a compromise tariff bill was passed by Congress, and no other states acted on the nullification doctrine. The idea, however, was advocated by many who wanted to protect southern agricultural interests and to prevent Congress from interfering with slavery.

The most extreme expression of dual federalism before the Civil War was the **doctrine of secession**■. By asserting that states retained sovereignty and were not subordinate to the national government, advocates of secession claimed that states could choose to withdraw from the United States if they had profound disagreements with laws and policies produced by the national government. In 1861, when 11 states acted on this theory by leaving the United States and forming the Confederate States of America, a bloody, four-year civil war erupted. The Confederacy's defeat in 1865 ended—presumably forever—the idea that dual sovereignty could be carried to the point of justifying secession.

MYTH EXPOSED Many Americans believe that competing conceptions of federalism were the root cause of the Civil War, however historians have convincingly demostrated that slavery—not federalism—was the key basis for the war. Until the second half of the twentieth century, students in many southern states were taught to call the conflict of 1861–1865 the "War Between the States." This label was

ABOVE: The bloody Civil War reflected the failure of the pathways of political action to solve disagreements about slavery and federalism. The usual democratic mechanisms of lobbying, elections, and litigation could not forge a compromise resolution. —*Are there reasons that make another civil war highly improbable in today's United States? What are they?*

BELOW: Although the Civil War put to rest the most extreme arguments advocating states' rights, such claims lingered for decades afterward, often as a means to justify discrimination against African Americans. In the 1950s, for example, President Dwight Eisenhower sent federal troops to Little Rock, Arkansas, to protect nine brave African American students who were attempting to desegregate Central High School. State and local officials in Arkansas were opposed to desegregation. —*What circumstances today might require the president to use the military in order to force state and local officials to comply with the law?*

based on an understanding of the war as reflecting profound disagreements about the rights of states to manage their own affairs without interference from the federal government, and it coincided with efforts by southern whites to defend state-mandated racial segregation. By contrast, elsewhere in the United States, students learned to call the bloody event the "Civil War" and to interpret it as having been fought over North-South disagreements about the institution of slavery and the southern states' unlawful assertion of a right to secede. As the historian James W. Loewen has noted, "History textbooks now admit that slavery was the primary cause of the Civil War."[3] However, the policy issue of slavery was intertwined with disputes about federalism, because the slave states resisted any move by the federal government to outlaw slavery in new territories and states.

PATHWAYS of action

The Civil War and the Failure of American Politics

Throughout this book, we describe the pathways of American politics that produce public policies and shift the balance of power between different political actors and governing institutions. However, the Civil War represents the best example of a policy dispute that was *not* controlled by one of the pathways of American politics.

The operation of the pathways depends on the American people's shared democratic values, commitment to the preservation of the constitutional governing system, and willingness to accept individual policy outcomes that are contrary to their personal preferences. In the case of slavery, however, no workable compromise balanced the interests of those who sought to abolish or at least prevent the territorial expansion of slavery and those who wanted to preserve the institution. As a result, people turned to violence to advance their interests.

It took many battles and more than a half-million deaths to settle American policy regarding slavery and secession. The bloodshed of the Civil War stands as a reminder about what can happen when Americans fail to use the pathways of action to settle policy disputes.

The doctrines of nullification and secession were put to rest with the Union victory in the Civil War. The war's outcome did not, however, end all attempts to preserve a "states' rights" conception of federalism. Such arguments remained common, for example, by those southerners who during the 1950s and 1960s resisted passing and enforcing federal voting rights legislation and other antidiscrimination laws seeking to prevent the victimization of African Americans. The term *states' rights* is seldom used today because of its discredited association with efforts to preserve slavery and, later, to deny civil rights to African Americans.

After the Civil War

In the aftermath of the Civil War, the Constitution was amended to prevent specific assertions of state authority, particularly with respect to the treatment of newly freed African Americans. The Thirteenth Amendment (1865) banned slavery, thereby eliminating that issue as a source of conflict between states and the national government. The Fourteenth Amendment (1868) sought directly to limit states' authority to interfere with certain rights of individuals. "No State," the Fourteenth Amendment declares, shall deny "due process of law" or "the equal protection of the laws." According to the Fifteenth Amendment (1870), the right to vote shall not be denied "by the United States or by any State on account of race, color, or previous condition of servitude" (that is, slavery). In addition, each of the three post–Civil War amendments contained a statement empowering Congress to enact legislation to enforce them. These amendments specifically limited state authority and enlarged that of the federal government.

For nearly a century after the passage of these amendments, federal institutions—courts, Congress, and presidents alike—failed to vigorously apply the powers granted by these amendments to protect African Americans from discrimination at the hands of state and local authorities. However, in what was called "nationalizing the Bill of Rights," federal courts, in the 1920s and 1930s, slowly began using the Fourteenth Amendment to strike down state laws and state-sanctioned policies that violated the Bill of Rights in such areas as criminal justice, freedom of speech, and the separation of church and state. And as early as the 1940s, presidents began issuing executive orders designed to ensure the equal treatment of racial minorities and enforce antidiscriminatory court decisions and congressional legislation. In the 1960s, the Supreme Court revived nineteenth-century federal antidiscrimination statutes affecting contracts, housing, and other matters by declaring that they were appropriate exercises of congressional power under the Thirteenth Amendment. Congress meanwhile relied on the Fifteenth Amendment to enact important voting rights legislation aimed at preventing discrimination in state elections.

In the decades following the Civil War, American society transformed enormously. Many new technologies developed that helped reshape the economy. The expanded use of railroads, telegraph, and industrial machinery shifted the country away from an agriculture-based economy to one deriving most of its wealth from urban industry. Cities grew with the spread of factories. Industrial demands for energy expanded employment opportunities in coal mines, in shipyards, and on railroads. People left farms and small towns to seek jobs in factories, urban offices, and retail businesses. Increasing numbers of job-seeking immigrants arrived from Europe and East Asia in search

The Tea Party movement began in 2009 with a series of antitax protests that rejected excessive government spending in the stimulus bill, asserting that individual freedom is at risk.
—*Do you agree with the protesters that our government has become fiscally irresponsible?*

of new lives in American cities. In addition, large corporations grew, attempting to consolidate control over entire industries. The changes brought by urbanization and industrialization presented the country with new kinds of economic and social problems. Many government officials believed that new policies were needed to foster economic growth, prevent predatory business practices, protect the interests of workers, and address the growing problems of urban poverty.

In the late nineteenth century, Americans looked first to their states to deal with the effects of industrialization and urbanization. But in most states, corporate interests had significant influence on the state legislatures, which therefore did relatively little to address these issues. Because industries (such as mining companies in West Virginia) could use their substantial resources to influence politics and policy, in only a few states did the legislatures enact economic regulation and social welfare legislation.

At the federal level, Congress enacted statutes intended to address specific concerns that affected the entire nation. For example, the Interstate Commerce Act of 1887 established

Through the first decades of the twentieth century, it was common for American children to work long hours under harsh and dangerous conditions in textile mills, mines, and other industrial settings. Until the late 1930s, the U.S. Supreme Court blocked legislative efforts to enact laws that would protect workers, including children, from danger and exploitation in the workplace. —*What would labor laws be like today if all regulation was controlled by state governments?*

the Interstate Commerce Commission, a regulatory agency responsible for implementing rules for transporting goods by rail and ship. The Sherman Antitrust Act of 1890 sought to prevent individual companies from controlling entire industries and to stop companies from working together to rig prices at artificially high levels. It was thought that **monopolies,** companies that gained control over most or all of a particular industry, could harm the national economy and consumers by raising prices in unjustified ways, because there would be no competition to which consumers could turn. Congress wanted to encourage the existence of a variety of companies in each industry so that market forces, in the form of competition between companies, would keep prices at economically justifiable levels. But such federal legislation did relatively little to curb the excesses of big business.

Many laws passed in response to changing social conditions and problems were tested in the court. But unlike Marshall's Supreme Court a century earlier, which had consistently sought to strengthen and expand the powers of the federal government, the justices of the Supreme Court of the late nineteenth and early twentieth centuries handed down decisions that generally limited governmental authority to regulate commerce and address issues of social welfare. For example, in 1895 the Supreme Court rejected the government's charge that the American Sugar Refining Company had become an illegal monopoly in violation of the Sherman Antitrust Act, even though the company, by buying up competing sugar businesses, had gained control over 98 percent of the country's sugar-refining capacity (*United States v. E. C. Knight Company*). The Court concluded that although the Constitution empowered Congress to regulate interstate commerce, "manufacturing," such as sugar refining, was a separate activity from "commerce." Therefore, the federal government could not regulate the company and other manufacturing enterprises.

In *Hammer* v. *Dagenhart* (1918), the Supreme Court struck down the 1916 federal statute barring the interstate transport of goods produced by child labor. The Court said that because the goods themselves were not harmful, the statute had improperly sought to regulate child labor. It ruled that Congress, in exercising its power over "interstate commerce," possessed only the authority to regulate the *transportation* of goods. Decisions like these temporarily limited the expansion of federal governmental authority during decades when Congress sought to become more active in regulating the economy and advancing social welfare goals.

The Supreme Court's actions in limiting federal power did not necessarily mean that the justices intended to shift federalism's balance of power in favor of the states. The Court also struck down similar laws enacted by state legislatures. In 1905, for example, in *Lochner* v. *New York,* the Supreme Court invalidated a New York State statute that sought to limit the working hours of bakery employees to not more than 10 hours per day or 60 hours per week. Although the New York legislature intended to protect the health and well-being of bakers, the Court found that the statute interfered with the workers' liberty to work as many hours as they wished to work. (Of course, workers typically toiled such long hours because hourly wages were so low that they had no choice.) In effect, the Supreme Court's decisions reflected the justices' views on the limits of legislative power generally, both state and federal.[4] Still, the judicial decisions of this era had the primary effect of preventing the federal government from expanding its authority.

Dual Federalism

3.2   Characterize dual federalism both before and after the Civil War.

PRACTICE QUIZ: UNDERSTAND AND APPLY

1. Which of the following is not true under dual federalism?
   a. State governments and the national government are equally authoritative.
   b. The national government possesses authority over its powers listed in the Constitution.
   c. Interactions between state and federal governments are often marked by tension.
   d. State governments are more powerful than the federal government.

2. In general, Chief Justice John Marshall's opinions regarding federalism before the Civil War tended to
   a. strengthen the power of the national government.
   b. strengthen the power of state governments.
   c. reduce the impact of the federal courts on federalism issues.
   d. b and c.

3. The doctrine of nullification
   a. was never fully exercised by any state.
   b. was a logical extension of Chief Justice Marshall's federalist philosophy.
   c. is implied in the Tenth Amendment.
   d. is now endorsed by most of the states.

4. The Civil War resolved the dispute over the proper balance of power between the federal and state governments.
   a. true   b. false

ANALYZE

1. In what ways could federalism be used to address the problems of our nation in an economic recession?

2. What do you think is the longest lasting impact of the Civil War as it pertains to federalism? Which view of federalism, the one dominant before or after the civil war, would be most effective in dealing with the problems facing our country today?

IDENTIFY THE CONCEPT THAT DOESN'T BELONG

a. Rigid division of authority between layers of government
b. Conflict
c. Cooperation and flexibility
d. Tension
e. Equally authoritative

Resource Center
• Glossary
• Vocabulary Example
• Connect the Link

■ **New Deal:** Programs designed by President Franklin D. Roosevelt to bring economic recovery from the Great Depression by expanding the role of the federal government in providing employment opportunities and social services; advanced social reforms to serve the needs of the people, greatly expanding the budget and activity of the federal government.

SIGNIFICANCE: *The New Deal was a set of initiatives that were designed to stimulate the economy. Their ultimate success helped redefine the very nature of federalism and how Americans viewed their national government.*

Cooperative and Creative Federalism

3.3 Compare and contrast cooperative and creative federalism.

(pages 78–81)

With the advent of the twentieth century and the heightened complexity brought by industrialization and urbanization, the rigid separation mandated by dual federalism no longer allowed the government to address the pressing social, political, and economic problems facing the nation. Responding to increased expectations from citizens, our leaders began to see the need for a more dynamic view of federalism.

The New Deal: Cooperative Federalism

The stock market crash of 1929 signaled the beginning of the Great Depression, which would last through the 1930s. Manufacturing dropped, banks failed, and by early 1933, nearly one-quarter of the American workforce was unemployed. Elected president in 1932, Franklin D. Roosevelt (FDR) was inaugurated in early 1933 at the depth of the economic crisis, and he immediately sought to use the federal government's power to spur economic recovery and revive employment. FDR's domestic policy, known as the **New Deal**■, included programs to regulate farm and industrial production; to provide government jobs in construction, environmental conservation, and other public sector projects; and to give relief to people suffering from economic hardships. It also established the Social Security system.

President Roosevelt used the power of the presidency and his remarkable personal skills to sell his New Deal programs and new vision of federalism to the American people. Under his leadership, the power and influence of the federal government changed dramatically, as did the relationship between the national and state governments. Many of FDR's programs involved unprecedented interactions and cooperation between the states and the national government to deal with complexities of the economic crisis. Political scientists refer to this relationship as **cooperative federalism**■ —the belief that state and national governments should work together to solve problems.

Programs that involved joint involvement were far-ranging, including public works projects, welfare programs, and unemployment assistance. Morton Grozdins, a historian of federalism, aptly contrasted a layer cake and a marble cake in describing the shift from the older, dual federalism to the new, cooperative federalism with its high levels of national-state interaction.[5] In a marble cake, the two types of cake are separate, like state and federal governments, but they exist next to each other rather than resting exclusively in separate layers. The marble cake analogy symbolically portrays state and federal government as coexisting and cooperating in a variety of policy areas.

Many of the New Deal programs that Congress enacted collided with the conservative views of the supreme Court justices on the limits of government authority, and the Court initially struck down several important laws that Roosevelt had sponsored. In 1936, for example, the Court decided that Congress lacked the power to impose minimum wage and maximum work hour regulations on coal mines (*Carter* v. *Carter Coal Co.*). President Roosevelt criticized the Supreme Court for blocking New Deal economic and social welfare laws.

In 1937, after he had been elected to a second term, Roosevelt proposed changing the Supreme Court so that the president could appoint a new justice whenever a sitting justice reached the age of 70. At the time, six justices were older than 70. This proposal became known as Roosevelt's **court-packing plan.** Even though Roosevelt had won reelection by an overwhelming popular margin, the public responded negatively to this proposed change, and Congress rejected the proposal. In the late 1930s, after several elderly conservative justices left the bench, Roosevelt was finally able to reshape the Supreme Court by appointing new justices, whom the Senate confirmed. Their views on congressional commerce power and federalism led them to uphold the constitutionality of the New Deal's expansion of federal power.

A boy uses a drinking fountain on the county courthouse lawn in Halifax, North Carolina. The Civil Rights Act of 1964 barred racial discrimination in "public accommodations." —*What examples of discrimination have you observed in recent years?*

■ **Cooperative Federalism:** A system in which the powers of the federal and state government are intertwined and shared. Each level of government shares overlapping power, authority, and responsibility.	**EXAMPLE:** *We increasingly see cooperative federalism at work in the War on Drugs. Joint operations commonly are conducted between the DEA, ATF, FBI, and local law enforcement agencies to fight the illegal trafficking and selling of illicit drugs.*	■ **Creative Federalism:** A system in which the role of the federal government is expanded by providing financial incentives for states to follow congressional initiatives.	**SIGNIFICANCE:** *Creative federalism establishes programs that are funded and regulated by Congress centralizing congressional authority over the states to provide social services. Many oppose this system because they believe that it usurps the authority of states and makes the national government too powerful.*

For decades thereafter, the Court permitted Congress to justify nearly any kind of social, economic, and civil rights legislation as an exercise of power under its constitutional authority to regulate interstate commerce. Congress used this power to enact a variety of laws, some of which clearly had primary goals other than the regulation of commerce. For example, in 1964 Congress enacted Title II of the Civil Rights Act of 1964, barring racial discrimination in restaurants, hotels, movie theaters, and other "public accommodations" provided by private businesses. Although it was widely recognized that the statute was created to advance civil rights and combat discrimination, the Supreme Court rejected challenges to the law and accepted the federal government's argument that Title II regulated commerce by attacking a major barrier to interstate travel by African Americans. The Court's decisions in this and other cases seemed to indicate that Congress had nearly unlimited authority to make laws under the premise of regulating interstate commerce. The expansion of federal lawmaking affected federalism by simultaneously limiting the scope of the states' authority to control their own affairs in certain areas (see Figure 3.2).

The Great Society: Creative Federalism and Federal Grants

The nature and role of the federal government and of federalism itself changed throughout the twentieth century. The presidency of Lyndon B. Johnson (1963–1969) marked a critical point in the evolution of federalism. Johnson proposed many new social programs

to achieve what he called the *Great Society*. Of crucial importance in his vision was the *War on Poverty*, which channeled federal money to states, local governments, and even citizen groups to combat poverty and racial discrimination. Funds were allocated to a variety of social programs for urban renewal, education, and improving the lives of underprivileged children. The money was used to advance the agenda of President Johnson and liberal Democrats in Congress, the direct result of which was to bypass governors, state legislatures, and local officials. This new view of federalism, coined **creative federalism**■—articulated by Johnson as an expanded partnership between the federal and state governments—began to infiltrate policymaking in the 1960s and early 1970s.

As we see in Figure 3.3, federal departments such as agriculture and commerce, which Democratic leaders did not target, saw only limited growth in the 1960s, while agencies with responsibility for health care, education, and community development saw dramatic growth during Johnson's presidency. These patterns reflected the domestic priorities of Johnson and the liberal wing of the Democratic Party, especially when it came to urban development. Figure 3.4 shows the remarkable increases in federal grants for subsidized housing and in urban renewal grants.

Under President Johnson, the federal government funneled record amounts of money to states to combat discrimination and fight poverty. Many states (especially in the South) were blamed for dragging their feet in carrying out social reforms to promote equal rights. If the federal authorities decided that states and local communities were not cooperating, they withheld funds. By using a reward-and-punishment system to allocate resources, the

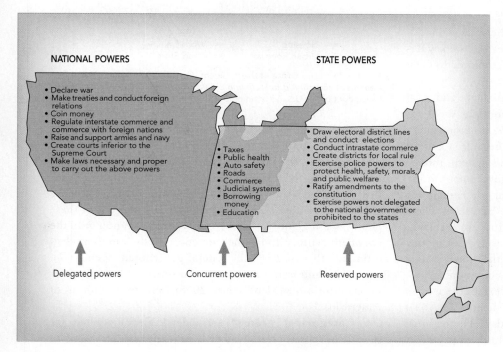

FIGURE 3.2 ■ Distribution of Powers Between National and State Governments

The founders of our government created a system that divided power, authority, and responsibility between the federal and state governments. Some powers are exclusive to one entity (delegated powers represent powers that are given—delegated—to the national government, while reserved powers remain with the states), but many are shared (concurrent powers). Throughout our history, the power of the federal government has grown, but states remain important actors in our political system. Unfortunately, many in our country are overwhelmed with the size of the government and do not correctly understand which level of government is responsible for different issues. —*How do you think we can better explain to individuals how power is divided and shared?*

■ **Grants-in-Aid:** Funds given from one governmental unit to another governmental unit for specific purposes.

SIGNIFICANCE: *Grants-in-aid cover a wide array of programs, from welfare to health care to construction/maintenance of roadways to education. Such grants help equalize services among states and allow the federal government to influence policy making at state and local levels.*

FIGURE 3.3 ■ Grants-in-Aid from the Federal Government to States (1964–1970)

The pattern of distributions of federal grants-in-aid is a good indicator of the priorities of our government and its leaders. During the 1960s, we saw enormous growth in grants for commerce, education, and community development. While there was an increase in grants for agriculture and health care, the rate of growth was substantially less than the other categories, reflecting the policy priorities of Lyndon Johnson and the Democratic leadership in Congress.

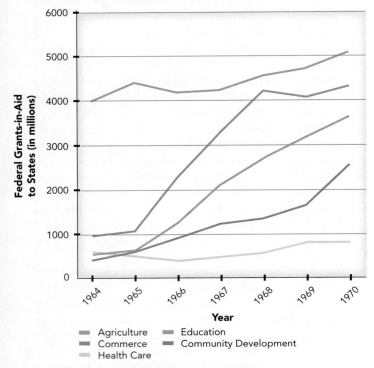

FIGURE 3.4 ■ Grants-in-Aid Selected Programs 1964–1970

Federal grants for subsidized housing and urban renewal grants increased from around $212 million in 1964 to $1.049 billion in 1970. Spending for Head Start and work training increased dramatically over the same time period. During that decade, we saw greater demands for minority voting rights and protection from racial and ethnic discrimination. As a larger number of less affluent people got involved in politics, using the grassroots mobilization and elections pathways, the manner in which we allocated federal grants changed.

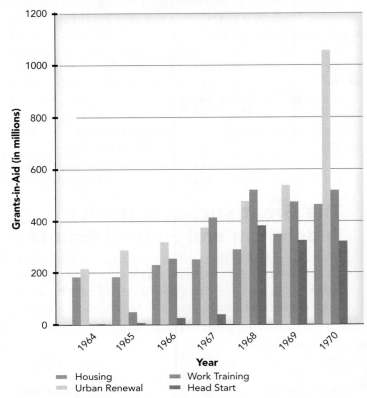

SOURCE: Executive Office of the President, Bureau of the Budget, *Special Analysis of Federal Aid to State and Local Government (2009),* derived from the Budget of the U.S. Government.

federal government was successful in getting the states and localities to comply. This use of financial incentives was the key device Johnson and the Democrats in Congress employed to fulfill their vision for a just society.

Grants-in-aid■—federal funds given to state and local governments on the condition that the money is spent for specified purposes defined by officials in Washington—are a key tool of creative federalism, and they became a crucial means for redistributing income. Under this system, money collected from all citizens by the national government in the form of taxes is then allocated by the federal government for the benefit of certain citizens in specific cities and states. These grants often work to reduce notable inequalities among states, as many are based on economic need. However, grant money always comes with stipulations to ensure that the money is used for the purpose for which it was given; other conditions are designed to evaluate how well the grant is working. Both give rise to complex reporting and accounting requirements.

Grants-in-aid go back to our earliest days. The national government gave money to the states to help them pay debts

from the Revolutionary War. One of the most important early examples of grants-in-aid was the decision of the national government in the mid-nineteenth century to give the states land grants for educational institutions and to build railroads that promoted westward expansion. (Many of today's leading public universities were founded with the proceeds of these grants.) Cash grants-in-aid did not become common until the twentieth century. Today, they are enormously important. It is estimated that in 2009, the federal government spent more than $538 billion in grants-in-aid to state and local governments (up from $461 billion in 2008), benefiting millions of Americans.[6]

Categorical grants■ are federal funds targeted for specific purposes. Typically, they have many restrictions, often

■ **Categorical Grants:** Grants of money from the federal government to state or local governments for very specific purposes. These grants often require that funds be matched by the receiving entity.

EXAMPLE: *Federal assistance to put more police officers on the street is often in the form of categorical grants (which help localities but usually do not leave much discretion).*

■ **Block Grants:** Funds given to states that allow substantial discretion to spend the money with minimal federal restrictions.

EXAMPLE: *State and local governments tend to prefer block grants to other forms of grants-in-aid, as there is more flexibility in how the money is spent.*

leaving little room for discretionary spending. Two types of categorical grants exist: formula grants and project grants.

Formula grants are funds distributed according to a particular formula, which specifies who is eligible and for how much. For example, the number of school-age children living in families below the poverty line is used to allocate federal funds to each state to subsidize school breakfasts and lunches. The states must spend this money on school meals, according to a very specific formula allowing no flexibility. The money at stake under grants of this type is one reason why the state population figures and other demographic data revealed each decade by the national census are so important—and so controversial. Consider what happens when it is proposed to allocate money to states for homeless shelters based on the number of homeless people in each state. States that are better at finding and counting the homeless would receive more money than states that are less successful or less diligent in accounting for their homeless population—a problem compounded by the irregular lives of many homeless people, who often migrate for a variety of reasons (including the weather).

Project grants, the second type of categorical grants, are awarded on the basis of competitive applications rather than a specified formula. Consider homeless shelters: A community could apply for a project grant to develop a new model of a shelter, one that not only houses the homeless but also involves the efforts of other community organizations to provide education, job training, and substance abuse counseling. The community

could receive federal grant money based on the strength of its application and its prospect for innovation.

Typically, state governments must contribute some money of their own, but many times the federal funds support the primary cost of the program. State and local officials have often found these grants frustrating, because they are defined so narrowly and may not fit the needs of the locality. For example, money might be available to hire more public school teachers, but a local school district may actually need money to purchase new textbooks and build new schools. Under most categorical grants, school districts lack discretion: They must either follow Washington's requirements (hire new teachers, for example) or forgo the funds. The lack of flexibility has often meant that local needs are not well served and that money is wasted.

Block grants■ were developed in 1966 as a response to these problems. Block grants are still earmarked for specific programs, but they are far more flexible. To continue our earlier example, a categorical grant for education might specify that the money be used for teacher salaries, even if that is not the greatest need in the school district. A block grant, by contrast, would still be available to improve education, but the school district could decide (within specified parameters) how to spend the money—it might choose to buy textbooks rather than hire more teachers. Because block grants allow greater spending flexibility, many observers feel they are a more efficient and more effective form of federal grants.

Cooperative and Creative Federalism

3.3 Compare and contrast cooperative and creative federalism.

PRACTICE QUIZ: UNDERSTAND AND APPLY

1. The New Deal
   a. was a collection of antitrust legislation instigated by Theodore Roosevelt.
   b. was a collection of domestic policies instituted by Franklin Roosevelt to help the nation recover from the Great Depression.
   c. was implemented by the introduction of federal programs at the state and local level.
   d. b and c.

2. Block grants
   a. are generally more appealing to local officials than categorical grants.
   b. are more flexible than categorical grants.
   c. disburse funds that are allocated at the discretion of state and local managers.
   d. a, b, and c.

3. In which type of federalism does the national government use financial incentives to influence the actions of state governments?
   a. collaborative   c. cooperative
   b. combined   d. creative

ANALYZE

1. Discuss the relative advantages and disadvantages of creative federalism. Do you think the use of grants can be seen as tools to manipulate state governments? Do these financial incentives give the federal government too much power?

2. In what ways could block grants be abused by their recipients and managers?

IDENTIFY THE CONCEPT THAT DOESN'T BELONG

a. Dual federalism   d. Flexibility
b. The Great Society   e. War on Poverty
c. Grants-in-aid

Resource Center
• Glossary
• Vocabulary Example
• Connect the Link

■ **Devolution:** The transfer of jurisdiction and fiscal responsibility for particular programs from the federal government to state or local governments.

SIGNIFICANCE: *State governments like some components of devolution, most notably having more responsibility over decision-making that impacts their residents; however, the fiscal responsibility that comes with devolution is often difficult for states and localities to bear.*

Recent Trends in Federalism

3.4 Trace the evolution of federalism in recent decades.

(pages 82–85)

The power and influence of the federal government expanded dramatically in the twentieth century. Every president since Richard Nixon (1969–1974) has voiced concern over the size and influence of the federal government. In 1976, Georgia Governor Jimmy Carter successfully ran for the White House as an outsider who opposed federal mandates (requirements imposed by the government without funding), which as governor he had disagreed with for a variety of reasons. Although as president Carter did cut back federal grant expenditures, his cuts paled in comparison to those of his successor, Ronald Reagan.

Winning election over Carter in 1980, Reagan pledged to promote a new form of federalism that returned more power and responsibility, including financial responsibility, to the state. Reagan strongly disagreed with the diminishing role of state governments that had developed over the previous decades. He saw states as vital instruments in our governmental apparatus and vowed to increase their presence. His goals were reflected not only in his rhetoric but also in his budgetary policies. In addition to large income tax cuts, Reagan proposed massive cuts in domestic spending that would roll back and even eliminate many programs created by the Democratic administrations from the New Deal to the Great Society. Reagan successfully pressed Congress not only to reduce the amount of federal grant money that it disbursed but also to shift more money into flexible block grants, which fell into four broad categories—income guarantees, education, transportation, and health. He argued that the states knew best how to serve their citizens and that mandates from Washington were wasteful, failing to meet the needs of the people and also taking away legitimate authority from state and local governments.

This idea of state authority is not new; it goes back to a view of states as laboratories for public policy experiments. However, this view of states' independence and control over their own affairs had diminished over the course of the twentieth century. By the 1980s, with the power and the budget of the federal government reaching record levels, the idea of strengthening states and curbing the federal government struck a chord with the American public. As is evident in Figure 3.5, Reagan was successful in fulfilling his pledge to reduce the role of the federal government in funding state and local government budgets.

FIGURE 3.5 ■ Federal Grants-in-Aid as a Percentage of State and Local Government Budgets

In 1980, 40 percent of local government budgets came from the federal government in the form of grants-in-aid. Ronald Reagan campaigned on a platform arguing that the size, scope, and budget of the federal government needed to be limited. As this graph indicates, he was successful in diminishing the reliance of local governments on federal grants. During Bill Clinton's first term in office, federal grants-in-aid increased, but they began to decrease in the mid-1990s. —*Why might it be a mistake for local governments to rely on federal grants?*

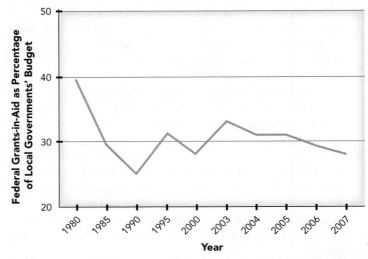

SOURCE: U.S. Office of Management and Budget, based on *Historical Tables and Analytical Perspectives, Budget of the United States Government (2009)*, annual.

Devolution

Americans and elected leaders of both the Republican and Democratic parties continued to voice concerns about the power and influence of the national government after President Reagan left the White House. Republicans objected to the national government asserting such a large role in the federal system. In 1994, the Republican congressional leadership announced its "Contract with America," which called for reducing the size of the federal government and for returning money, responsibility, and power to the states—what has come to be known as **devolution**■, or the transfer of power to political subunits. With Republican majorities elected in the House and Senate in 1994, interest in minimizing the role of the federal government increased. The Republican initiative focused, in part, on returning power to the states and having states complete what had once been federal tasks. One prominent example of this is welfare. Congress passed reforms (which the Democratic President Bill Clinton signed) that returned management of welfare programs to the states. With the aim of moving welfare mothers into the workplace, new rules were enacted to limit the number of years women with dependent children could continue receiving public assistance.

Devolution has been motivated by a number of factors, including an ideological belief that the federal government is less effective than the states and localities in delivering services and solving problems. Many supporters of devolution believe that the state governments are best equipped to solve their own problems and that they only need the power and flexibility to do so. Worry over increasing federal deficits also fuels devolution, with the aim of transferring not only power but also fiscal responsibility to the states. However, many policy advocates are opposed to devolution, fearing a return to the days of great inequality among states and among citizens within states. The weak economies of some states prevent them from keeping pace with other states in education funding, highway construction, and other vital services unless they have financial support from the federal government.

In economic hard times, the number of people in need grows dramatically, while the tax revenues required to satisfy these needs shrink. Thus, at a time of great hardship, states often have little ability to meet their citizens' needs adequately. Moreover, most state and local governments are legally prohibited by their own state constitutions from incurring budget deficits, whereas the federal government can freely cover whatever deficits it incurs by selling bonds. So when their tax revenues fall, states have to make the difficult choice between raising taxes and cutting services. Devolution has complicated state and local politics by forcing states to compete for fewer and fewer federal grants.

A Return to Creative Federalism?

When Barrak Obama was elected president, the country was in the middle of the worst economic crisis since the Great Depression. Hoping to stem the downturn, Obama ushered into effect dramatic changes involving the federal government in businesses and localities in extraordinary ways. Facing a battered stock market, a precarious banking system, decreased exports, a desperate car industry, and a housing crisis, the president made a number of unprecedented proposals. He advocated for direct and immediate aid to individuals around the country in the form of extended unemployment benefits and home-owner relief. He proposed providing automobile and home-buying incentives to jump-start consumer spending. He urged Congress to authorize funds to rescue banking institutions and domestic car companies on the brink of collapse, because their failure would have had a long-term and far-reaching impact on our economy. And on February 17, 2009, President Obama signed the American Recovery and Reinvestment Act, a $787

The federal "cash for clunkers" program—officially the Car Allowance Rebate System—offered people from $3,500 to $4,500 to trade in an old car for a newer, more fuel-efficient vehicle. In addition to helping stimulate the faltering car industry, the stimulus program had the benefit of using a market—based approach to promote an environmentally friendly subsidy. —*Do you think that subsidies to stimulate particular American industries are unfair to international competitors? How free should our market be?*

billion economic stimulus bill dramatically expanding the scope of the federal government for the foreseeable future. Some believe that these changes have overextended the role and responsibilities of the federal government in a dangerous way. Others believe that more needs to be done. Time will tell whether or not this shift marks a dramatic turn in the nature of our federal system.

Although the idea of having more powerful and more independent state governments has been popular under a theory of "new" federalism, we have yet to see it reach fruition, and many observers doubt that this vision will ever become a reality. The very issues that brought about a more active federal government—poverty, economic instability, complex relationships at home and with other global powers—still exist. It is therefore difficult to imagine that the federal government might become substantially less active and less involved in the wide array of policy issues. Consider what would happen if one state did not maintain high educational standards. The economy of the entire region could be harmed as the quality of the workforce deteriorated, encouraging employers to relocate their businesses. If the health care system of one state became significantly substandard, neighboring states would experience

The Violence Against Women Act of 1994 was passed to enhance the investigation and prosecution of violent crimes perpetrated against women. The law provided federal funds to local law enforcement agencies and allowed victims of gender-based violence the right to sue for compensation in federal court. The Supreme Court ruled that the component of the law guaranteeing victims greater power to seek redress in federal court was unconstitutional (*United States* v. *Morrison,* 2000). —*Do you think that domestic violence should be addressed by Congress? Or, should this be left to the states? Do you think enough is being done to end partner violence in the United States?*

a crisis as people flocked to them seeking better services. Population shifts can create new burdens for states. With increased globalization and the resultant international competition for scarce resources, the days of big national government are not likely to end.

The Supreme Court's Shift in Perspective

Over the past 40 years, Republican presidents have selected 13 of the 16 new justices who have served on the Court. Through their judicial opinions, several of these justices have expressed concern about a steady lessening of states' authority to manage their own affairs. By the mid-1990s, justices who were concerned about striking a new balance of power in American federalism gained a slim 5–4 majority. And beginning in 1995, the Supreme Court issued decisions limiting the power of the federal government and consequently opening the way for states to control a greater number of policy issues. In *United States* v. *Lopez* (1995), the Supreme Court struck down the Gun-Free School Zones Act of 1990, which made it a crime to possess a firearm near a school. The Court's majority concluded that

congressional power to regulate interstate commerce did not include the authority to create this particular law. The Court made a similar decision in striking down portions of the Violence Against Women Act of 1994, in which Congress had permitted victims of sexual violence and gender-based attacks to file federal lawsuits against their attackers (*United States* v. *Morrison,* 2000).

The Court also revived the Tenth Amendment, a provision of the Constitution that was generally treated as a powerless slogan by justices from the late 1930s through the mid-1990s. In *Printz* v. *United States* (1997), the Court declared that Congress cannot require state and local officials to conduct background checks on people who seek to buy firearms. The Court's decisions on the Tenth Amendment's protection of state authority and the limits of congressional power to regulate interstate commerce indicated that the Supreme Court would no longer automatically endorse assertions of federal power at the expense of state authority.

While the federal government remains actively involved in a wide array of public policies, including many that do not seem intimately connected with the congressional power to regulate interstate commerce, recent decisions indicate that the

Supreme Court stands ready to selectively reject specific assertions of federal power that it considers excessive under its new vision of the Constitution's framework for federalism.

PATHWAYS of change from around the world

What do farmers and college students have in common? In Thailand they are joining forces to push for sustainable agriculture and social justice. At Mahasarakham University, students have hosted conferences and seminars to revive cooperation between these two diverse groups. Democratic reforms during the last 20 years have done little to help local villagers who are concerned both with economic growth and environmental protection. Young people are a core group in Thailand's Sustainable Agriculture Movement, working with a variety of groups across the globe. Student activists have been pushing for local empowerment and economic development that helps local farmers and communities. In the process, they are proving they can be a force to promote social justice, fight for the rights of slum communities and farmers, and promote conservation.

SOURCE: Surin Farmers Support: Updates from Thailand's Sustainable Agriculture Movement http://www .surinfarmersupport.org/

Recent Trends in Federalism

3.4 **Trace the evolution of federalism in recent decades.**

PRACTICE QUIZ: UNDERSTAND AND APPLY

1. "New" federalism shifts more power and responsibility
   a. to the executive branch.
   b. to the legislative branch.
   c. back to the states.
   d. back to the federal agencies that started the programs.

2. Reducing the size of the federal bureaucracy while transferring the funds, responsibility, and power to the states is termed
   a. evolution.
   b. devolution.
   c. resolution.
   d. dissolution.

3. Although new federalism ideals remain popular, we have yet to see it reach fruition.
   a. true
   b. false

4. Federalism under Barack Obama's administration reminds scholars of which view of federalism?
   a. Creative
   b. Cooperative
   c. Dual
   d. New

ANALYZE

1. What are some of the pitfalls associated with a devolution strategy? What drawbacks do you think might be associated with a return to creative federalism?

2. What is the correct balance between the rights of states and the need for the federal government to equalize opportunity and minimize inequality?

IDENTIFY THE CONCEPT THAT DOESN'T BELONG

a. *Printz* v. *United States* (1997)
b. Unfunded mandates
c. New federalism
d. Increased inequality between states
e. Devolution

Conclusion

We have outlined some practical and theoretical reasons for a federal system—why a democracy such as ours might have layers of governmental authority. The foremost original explanation for federalism in the American setting was the need for compromise. Most Americans understood the necessity of a stronger national government given the failures of the Articles of Confederation, but many also worried about a distant, unresponsive, and potentially tyrannical national government. Why not look to one level of government to regulate commerce, conduct foreign policy, and safeguard national security while another level provided basic services and looked after law and order? Dual federalism seemed natural, even logical, during the early years of our republic. Yet, determining precisely which layer of government is responsible for certain functions—and, when push comes to shove, which layer is superior—has never been simple. The struggle over appropriate governmental authority has been at the heart of nearly all critical periods in American history.

Given that there is no clear or universally agreed upon way to allocate responsibilities among layers of our government, the nature of federalism has been shaped by the individuals who happened to be in charge of government, either as elected officials or as judges, during crucial periods. In effect, the course of federalism is like a pendulum that swings between different approaches to allocating national and state authority, depending on the problems faced by the nation and the viewpoints of the individuals in positions of political and judicial power. From the New Deal until the 1980s, for example, the Democrats controlled the federal government most of the time, and argued that a strong national government offered the best means of helping citizens reach their potential and ridding society of its ills. Their approach called for merging each layer of government into unified action to attack these problems. The use of categorical grants under Lyndon Johnson's Great Society program is a clear example of how officials in Washington have used federal monies to advance their priorities at the state and local levels.

The election of Ronald Reagan in 1980 and of a Republican Congress in 1994 produced a shift to less federal intervention—and less federal money—at the state level. George W. Bush's 2001–2008 budget proposals reflected an even more constrained view of the federal government's role in many domestic policy areas. In direct contrast to this, in February 2009, with the nation facing a severe economic crisis, President Obama signed into law a massive federal economic stimulus package. The package rekindled the debate about the proper role of the federal government and federalism itself. On April 15, 2009, the governor of Texas, Rick Perry, stated at an anti-tax "tea party" that Texans who were frustrated with politicians in Washington might want to secede from the nation. Though he stopped short of advocating secession, his comments received a great deal of national attention. In October 2009, Obama declared the H1N1 flu outbreak a national emergency—further expanding the involvement of the federal government into an area that had been traditionally seen as the state's responsibility. Many see these expansions as evidence of Obama's support of "big government," and these expansions have served to renew debate about our federal system and the vitality of state governments.

Make no mistake, state and local governments will remain vital in the United States no matter which party controls Congress, the White House, or the federal judiciary. But exactly how much federal help (or interference) states and communities will receive is an open question. One thing is certain: Anyone who is interested in playing a role in politics should pay close attention to the federalism debate. The pathways of change are not simply about pushing government in a certain direction but rather about pushing the *correct level* of government in a new direction.

KEY CONCEPT MAP

How did federalism affect the government's response to Hurricane Katrina in 2005?

August 26

State Government

Louisiana Governor Kathleen Blanco declares a state of emergency.

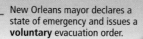

10,000 National Guard troops are dispatched to Gulf Coast.

August 27

Federal and Local Government

National Hurricane Center calls New Orleans Mayor Ray Nagin and advises mandatory evacuation.

New Orleans mayor declares a state of emergency and issues a **voluntary** evacuation order.

August 28

Local Government

Mayor Nagin issues a **mandatory** evacuation order.

Buses pick up people from around the city to take them to shelters, including the Superdome and Convention Center, even though the emergency plan calls for them to be evacuated from the city.

August 29

Hurricane Katrina Makes Landfall

August 30

Federal, State, and Local Government

Water covers 80 percent of New Orleans. An estimated 50,000 to 100,000 people are stranded on roofs.

FEMA delays rescue efforts until the city can be secured by the National Guard (which is not sufficiently staffed); the state and local response is insufficient to protect life and property.

August 31

Federal Government

Buses begin evacuation of Superdome.

The Pentagon sends four Navy ships with emergency supplies and launches search and rescue; military transport planes take seriously ill and injured to Houston; FEMA deploys 39 medical teams and 1,700 trailer trucks.

September 3

Federal Government

President Bush orders 7,200 active duty forces to Gulf Coast.

Active duty forces join 40,000 National Guard troops now on the Gulf Coast.

September 7

Federal Government

New Orleans, a city steeped in history and culture, is left empty and in ruins; leaders vow to rebuild.

President Bush calls for a $52 billion aid package, which Congress approves the next day; supplement funds in the amount of $10.5 billion had previously been approved by Congress on September 2nd for immediate rescue and relief efforts.

Critical Thinking Questions

? Should citizens expect their government to anticipate emergencies? Who should be responsible for anticipating disasters—local, state, or federal authorities?

? What if the mayor had issued a mandatory evacuation order earlier? Could the disaster and human suffering have been minimized?

? What if New Orleans had followed its established evacuation plan? How prepared do you think most cities are for disasters? How can cities be encouraged to develop and follow plans to ensure safety in the event of emergencies?

? At this critical turning point, what steps could have been taken (and by whom) to prevent the crisis from escalating?

? Was FEMA's delayed response an indictment of the federal government's ability to respond to local disasters? Or, was this crisis an isolated event from which much was learned?

? What if more federal troops had been deployed earlier? Public safety is largely seen as a state and local responsibility, but what circumstances warrant federal intervention?

? Should Congress spend such large sums of tax dollars to help one locality? How much of the rebuilding costs should fall to the federal government—and taxpayers across the nation—versus to the state and locality?

The Framers of our Constitution devised a federal system that allows for flexibility in governing our vast and diverse country and that also balances power, authority, and influence among the national and state and local governments. However, during times of crises, such as in the wake of natural disasters, federalism can often make for slow and cumbersome governing.—*Should natural disasters be seen as national problems? Or should we expect states and localities to take responsibility for cleanup and rebuilding? What can federalism tell us about how the government responds to crises such as Hurricane Katrina?*

Review of Key Objectives

Dividing Governmental Authority

 3.1 Explain why the Framers divided authority between layers of government.

(pages 68–71)

Unlike most democracies in the world, which have unitary systems of governance, the United States has a federal system. In this country, power and authority are divided among layers of government. There are many explanations—historical, theoretical, cultural, and pragmatic—for why the United States relies on a federal system. Probably the best explanation is that dividing power between the national government and the state governments was a compromise that kept the Constitutional Convention on track.

KEY TERMS

Unitary System 68
Federal System 68
Sovereignty 69
Dillon's Rule 70
Home Rule 71
Special Governments 71

CRITICAL THINKING QUESTIONS

1. Do you think the people in the United States today are best governed by a federal system? Or would a unitary system be more efficient and appropriate? Why?
2. Do you believe that states are policy "laboratories" and, as such, the sources of innovation? Or do you think resources are wasted by duplication in the absence of coordination?

INTERNET RESOURCES

The Federalism Project: http://www.federalismproject .org
   The Federalist Society: http://www.fed-soc.org/

ADDITIONAL READING

Barbour, Christine, and Gerald C. Wright. *Keeping the Republic: Power and Citizenship in American Politics,* 4th ed. Washington, DC: CQ Press, 2008.

Burgess, Michael. *Comparative Federalism: Theory and Practice.* New York: Routledge, 2006.

Rocher, Francois, and Miriam Catherine Smith. *New Trends in Canadian Federalism,* 2nd ed. Peterborough, Canada: Broadview Press, 2003.

Dual Federalism

 3.2 Characterize dual federalism both before and after the Civil War.

(pages 72–77)

During the early years of our republic, there was much confusion over the division of authority, and this controversy produced crucial Supreme Court cases such as *McCulloch v. Maryland* (1819). Until the Civil War, dual federalism existed, meaning that neither the state nor the federal government was superior, and each had specific duties and obligations. To a large extent, the Civil War was fought over the issue of supremacy—determining which level of government, state or national, should be supreme. In the years after the Civil War, as a consequence of Supreme Court decisions, the power of the federal government was limited until the Great Depression.

KEY TERMS

Dual Federalism 72
McCulloch **v.** *Maryland* 72
Necessary and Proper Clause 72
Doctrine of Nullification 73
Doctrine of Secession 73
Monopolies 76

CRITICAL THINKING QUESTIONS

1. How did the Civil War change our views of federalism? Which issue—federalism or slavery—do you think was more important in causing the war? Why?
2. Do you believe that the system of dual federalism inherently promotes inequality, or are notions of equality so deeply ingrained that states would be leery of allowing inequality to increase within their borders?

INTERNET RESOURCES

The Council of State Governments: http://www.csg.org/
   The history of U.S. federalism: http://www.cas.sc .edu/poli/courses/scgov/History_of_Federalism.htm

ADDITIONAL READING

May, Christopher N., and Allan Ides. *Constitutional Law: National Power and Federalism,* 4th ed. Gaithersburg, MD: Aspen Publishers, 2007.

Norman, Wayne. *Negotiating Nationalism: Nation-Building, Federalism, and Secession in the Multinational State.* Oxford, England: Oxford University Press, 2006.

Cooperative and Creative Federalism

3.3 Compare and contrast cooperative and creative federalism.

(pages 78–81)

The nature of federalism in the United States changed irrevocably during the Great Depression as Franklin Roosevelt's New Deal thrust the federal government into nearly every realm of domestic governance and ushered in an era of cooperative federalism. For the next several decades, the power of the federal government continued to grow. Beginning with Johnson's administration and the Great Society programs, federalism became more creative with the use of federal grants to promote national goals; these grants continue to be controversial today.

KEY TERMS

New Deal 78
Cooperative Federalism 78
Court-Packing Plan 78
Creative Federalism 79
Grants-in-Aid 80
Categorical Grants 80
Formula Grants 81
Project Grants 81
Block Grants 81

CRITICAL THINKING QUESTIONS

1. How did the Great Depression alter the way in which we expect the federal government to act? Do you think we look too much to the federal government to address societal needs? Should the states and localities be held to higher standards for their failure to problem solve?
2. Do you think that the way in which the federal government uses grant money has a corrupting effect on the relationship between federal, state, and local officials?

INTERNET RESOURCES

National Governors Association: http://www.nga.org
    United States Conference of Mayors: http://www.usmayors.org

ADDITIONAL READING

Nagel, Robert F. *The Implosion of American Federalism*. New York: Oxford University Press, 2001.

Rodden, Jonathan A. *Hamilton's Paradox: The Promise and Peril of Fiscal Federalism*. Cambridge, England: Cambridge University Press, 2005.

Recent Trends in Federalism

3.4 Trace the evolution of federalism in recent decades.

(pages 82–85)

As our society continues to change, so too does federalism. Federalism is best viewed as a "pendulum model," whereby power and authority continually shift, reflecting the perspective of the people in power, the social and economic conditions, and the outlook of the courts. Although it may seem that there are fewer and fewer policy areas where the reach of the national government does not extend, a growing concern, especially among conservative politicians, has been to revive local governing authority. *Devolution* is the term used to describe the return of authority from the federal to the state level, and this occurred in some policy areas during the Bush administration. However, in the first year of Obama's presidency, with the national economic crisis and debate surrounding health care reform, it became clear that the trend toward devolution evident under the Bush administration had ended.

KEY TERM

Devolution 82

CRITICAL THINKING QUESTIONS

1. What aspects of recent trends in federalism do you think are positive? Negative? Overall, do you think the changes are a healthy or harmful evolution of federalism?
2. Do you agree with the more recent trend of the Supreme Court to limit some of the authority of the federal government? Why?

INTERNET RESOURCES

Real food challenge: Uniting students for just and sustainable food. http://realfoodchallenge.org/
    The Office of Management and Budget: http://www.whitehouse.gov/omb/
    The Federalism Project: http://www.federalismproject.org/

ADDITIONAL READING

Chemerinsky, Erwin. *Enhancing Government: Federalism for the Twenty-first Century.* Stanford, CA: Stanford University Press, 2008.

Miller, Lisa L. *The Perils of Federalism: Race, Poverty and the Politics of Crime Control.* New York: Oxford University Press, 2008.

Chapter Review Test Your Knowledge

1. In reference to federalism, what is meant by the layers of government?
   a. the legislative, executive, and judicial branches of the federal government
   b. federal government officials and all those who work for them
   c. the federal, state, and local governments
   d. the different federal systems that have succeeded each other over time

2. Federalism developed in response to which of the following factors?
   a. the fusing of independent states
   b. the geographic, cultural, and economic diversity of the nation
   c. significant powers being granted (reserved) to the states
   d. a, b, and c

3. Which of the following is an example of letting states serve as "laboratories of democracy"?
   a. allowing states to individually challenge welfare reform to assess which policy innovations are the most successful.
   b. privatizing Medicaid programs.
   c. developing a national educational assessment program to reward students.
   d. nationalizing health care.

4. The federal structure of the United States is unique among the nations of the world.
   a. true   b. false

5. The Supreme Court case *McCulloch* v. *Maryland*
   a. made ample use of the Bill of Rights.
   b. found it "necessary and proper" that the state tax all banks within its boundaries, even a branch of the Second Bank of the United States.
   c. found that the federal government's power to charter a national bank was consistent with the "necessary and proper" clause in the Constitution.
   d. a and c.

6. Which of the following statements does not describe a component of dual federalism?
   a. The federal and state governments have distinct and separate responsibilities.
   b. The federal and state governments are equally influential and vital.
   c. The relations between the federal and state governments are marked by teamwork.
   d. The relations between the federal and state governments are marked by strain and conflict.

7. What is significant about the southern tradition of referring to the Civil War as the "War Between the States"?
   a. The "states' rights" point of view endures in that region.
   b. Southern resistance to the notion that the Civil War was fought primarily over the issue of slavery continues.
   c. The southern conception of federalism was at odds with President Lincoln's conception.
   d. a, b, and c.

8. To this day, there is widespread acceptance for the theory of nullification and "states' rights" at the national as well as state levels.
   a. true   b. false

9. Which statement best summarizes the shared intent of the Thirteenth, Fourteenth, and Fifteenth Amendments?
   a. All forms of racism are contrary to the goals of American democracy.
   b. No state has the authority to deny full citizenship rights to any citizen.
   c. Dual federalism shall apply to all states.
   d. a, b, and c.

10. From the time of their inception, how long did it take for the Fourteenth and Fifteen Amendments to have a genuine and positive affect on the lives of African Americans?
    a. 10 years   c. 50 years
    b. 30 years   d. 90 years

11. The Sherman Antitrust Act of 1890
    a. represented a backward step in the expansion of federal authority.
    b. represented a forward step in the expansion of federal authority.
    c. is an early example of Congress enacting a law that addressed a national problem (corporate monopolies).
    d. b and c.

12. Congressional legislation around the turn of the century was successful in preventing the abuses of corporate power.
    a. true   b. false

13. Judicial decisions in the late nineteenth century tended to slow the expansion of federal authority.
    a. true   b. false

14. Following President Franklin D. Roosevelt's appointment of several new justices to the Supreme Court, the Court's decisions
    a. tended to preserve states' rights when they conflicted with federal authority.
    b. upheld the constitutionality of most New Deal legislation.
    c. constituted a reliable check against the president's executive powers.
    d. a and c.

15. What specific constitutional authority enhanced the ability of Congress to pass civil rights legislation in the 1960s?
    a. the First Amendment
    b. the Tenth Amendment
    c. the provision to regulate interstate commerce
    d. Article IV

16. How does the issue of federal funding impact federalism in modern America?
    a. Federal funding may act as another form of interstate commerce.
    b. Federal funding may act as a regulatory mechanism at the state and local levels.
    c. The federal government simply has more funds available than the states.
    d. a, b, and c.

17. Examples of cooperative federalism include all of the following except:

    a. joint drug raids between the Drug Enforcement Administration (DEA) and local police.

    b. the FBI's exclusive right to profile serial killers.

    c. federal bailouts of a local credit union.

    d. No Child Left Behind educational reform law.

    e. federal job training programs for welfare recipients.

18. Which of the following statements is false regarding "home rule"?

    a. City governments may do anything to serve their residents that is not specifically prohibited by state law.

    b. Local governments have very narrow power and authority.

    c. Localities in states governed by home rule have more latitude in addressing local problems than those in states governed by Dillon's rule.

    d. All of the above are true of home rule.

19. President Lyndon Johnson's "Great Society" initiatives

    a. allocated federal funds to state and local governments to eradicate poverty and racial discrimination.

    b. advanced the agenda of southern "Dixiecrats" in Congress.

    c. are useful examples of devolution.

    d. a and c

20. Welfare reform in the 1990s demonstrated

    a. our nation's preference to have social programs administered by the states.

    b. the validity of the "laboratories of democracy" concept.

    c. our nation's decreasing support for President Johnson's War on Poverty.

    d. a, b, and c

 **Exercises**

Apply what you learned in this chapter on **MyPoliSciLab.**

Read on **mypoliscilab.com**

    eText: Chapter 3

Study and **Review** on **mypoliscilab.com**

    Pre-Test
    Post-Test
    Chapter Exam
    Flashcards

Watch on **mypoliscilab.com**

    Video: Proposition 8
    Video: The Real ID
    Video: Water Wars

Explore on **mypoliscilab.com**

    Simulation: You Are a Federal Judge
    Simulation: You Are a Restaurant Owner
    Comparative: Comparing Federal and Unitary Systems
    Timeline: Federalism and the Supreme Court
    Visual Literacy: Federalism and Regulations

Civil Liberties

KEY OBJECTIVES

After completing this chapter, you should be prepared to:

4.1 Distinguish between the two dimensions of freedom of religion in the First Amendment.

4.2 Specify the limits on free speech in the United States.

4.3 Assess the test for justifying governmental limitations on written words and images.

4.4 Specify the protections afforded to criminal suspects in the Bill of Rights.

4.5 Evaluate the legal protections that ensure only guilty people receive criminal punishment.

4.6 Explain why the right to privacy is controversial.

On a deserted Alaska road in March 1993, a woman who solicited sex from two men in exchange for a promised payment of $100 was sexually assaulted, beaten, shot in the head, and left for dead. A man confessed to the crime and identified William Osborne as the other participant. The victim, who had pretended to be dead after the bullet grazed her head, thought she recognized Osborne as one of her attackers. A DNA test on semen in the condom used in the crime indicated that Osborne was among the 16 percent of the population who might have produced the biological evidence. Osborne was sentenced to 26 years in prison for the crime.

Years later, after DNA testing had improved to match specific individuals with biological evidence, Osborne sought to retest the preserved evidence at his own expense, so that the newer tests could prove he did not commit the sexual assault. The State of Alaska rejected his request to retest the evidence. Osborne filed a legal action asserting that the state violated his Fourteenth Amendment right to due process by blocking a reexamination of evidence that might prove he had wrongly spent more than a dozen years in prison.

> **Do Americans have too many or too few civil liberties protections?**

By a 5–4 vote in 2009, the U.S. Supreme Court rejected Osborne's claim and announced that the due process clause does not provide a right to retest scientific evidence, even when newer testing methods, unavailable at the time of the defendant's trial, might prove an individual's innocence (*District Attorney* v. *Osborne*, 2009). The Court's highly controversial decision limited the definition of a particular civil liberty and thereby narrowed the meaning of the right to due process for prisoners who claim they have been wrongly convicted.

Judges make decisions that define the civil liberties—individuals' freedoms and legal protections that cannot be denied by actions of government—guaranteed by the Bill of Rights and the Fourteenth Amendment. Judges use their power of interpretation to examine claims about the Constitution's protections. When they decide that a specific legal protection exists, it is available even for individuals whose ideas and actions anger the majority of Americans. The existence of judges' power to interpret the Bill of Rights and other provisions of the Constitution means that the definitions of civil liberties change over time as new judges assume office and as sitting judges change their ideas about values and public policy.

Resource Center
• Glossary
• Vocabulary Example
• Connect the Link

■ **Civil Liberties:** Individual freedoms and legal protections guaranteed by the Bill of Rights that cannot be denied or hindered by government.

EXAMPLE: *The Supreme Court declared that the Fourth Amendment protection against "unreasonable searches and seizures" forbids a city from setting up roadblocks to check all cars and drivers for possession of illegal drugs* (City of Indianapolis v. Edmond, 2000).

First Amendment Rights: Freedom of Religion

4.1 **Distinguish between the two dimensions of freedom of religion in the First Amendment.**

(pages 94–97)

The ten constitutional amendments that make up the Bill of Rights were added to the U.S. Constitution in 1791 to provide **civil liberties**■ for individuals—freedoms and legal protections that cannot be denied or hindered by government. The Bill of Rights spelled out the legal protections that individuals could expect from the federal government. Later, the Fourteenth Amendment added words to declare the existence of legal protections against state governments, such as the right to "due process." The **Due Process Clause**■ and other mere words on paper, however, do not by themselves, provide protections. Those words must be respected by officials, and judges must be willing to interpret and enforce the underlying meanings.

Religious liberty is the very first right protected by the Constitution's First Amendment: "Congress shall make no law respecting an establishment of religion, or prohibiting the free exercise thereof." The amendment's first section, called the **establishment clause**■, concerns the connections between government and religion. The establishment clause can be characterized as providing "freedom *from* religion"—namely, limiting government's ability to favor specific religions or impose religion on the people. The second section, the **free exercise clause**■, focuses on people's ability to practice their religion without governmental interference. This clause provides "freedom *of* religion." Individuals and interest groups have used the court pathway to challenge governmental actions related to both of these aspects of the First Amendment.

Establishment of Religion

Agreement is widespread that the establishment clause forbids the designation by government of a national religion. Many people describe this clause as mandating "the separation of church and state." However, significant disagreements exist about what connections between religion and government are permitted by the First Amendment. Under a strict **separationist** view, government must avoid contacts with religion, especially those that lead to government support or endorsement of religious activities. This perspective argues not only for preventing

government-sponsored religious practices, such as teachers leading prayers in public school classrooms, but also strict limits on government financial support for religion-connected practices. Separationists advocate prohibitions on government financial support for religious schools, religion-based rehabilitation programs in prisons, and the display of religious items in public buildings and parks, such as posters showing the Ten Commandments or Christmas nativity scenes. Advocates of this viewpoint see such actions as improperly implying governmental favoritism or endorsement of one religion over others—or even of religion itself.

By contrast, the **accommodationist** view would permit the government to provide support for religion and associated activities. For strong accommodationists, the Establishment Clause is primarily intended to prevent the creation of an official, national religion. Advocates of this perspective argue that religious displays are permissible on public property and that government can even give financial support to religious schools for the non-religious aspects of education.

During the 1960s, the Supreme Court issued two controversial decisions that tilted toward the strict separationist perspective. In *Engel* v. *Vitale* (1962), the Court found a violation of the establishment clause in the common public school practice of beginning each day with a teacher-led prayer. Parents in New York filed lawsuits to challenge the practice. According to Justice Hugo Black's majority opinion, "When the power, prestige, and financial support of government is placed behind a particular religious belief, the indirect coercive pressure upon religious minorities to conform to the prevailing officially approved religion is plain."[1] A second decision barred public schools from reading the Lord's Prayer and Bible verses over their public address systems (*School District of Abington Township, Pennsylvania* v. *Schempp*, 1963). By declaring that long-standing practices provided improper government endorsement and pressure on behalf of religious beliefs, the Supreme Court generated a storm of controversy that continues today. Although many Americans wonder whether such governmental practices actually cause any harm, the Court has been sensitive to the concern that nonbelievers or members of minority religions, especially children, will feel pressured to participate or will be ostracized by others if they decline to participate.

In the years following these decisions, critics complained that the Supreme Court had "improperly removed God from the schools" and thereby reduced morality and social order in society. Some state legislatures and local officials challenged the Court's decision through various means, such as mandating public display of the Ten Commandments in schools, teaching Bible-based creationism in public school science classes, and conducting student-led school prayers or moments of silence. Such practices

■ **Due Process Clause:** A statement of rights in the Fifth Amendment (aimed at the federal government) and the Fourteenth Amendment (aimed at state and local governments) that protects against arbitrary deprivations of life, liberty, or property. The Fourteenth Amendment phrase is also interpreted by the Supreme Court to expand a variety of rights.

EXAMPLE: *In* Roe *v.* Wade *(1973), establishing a right of choice about abortion, the Supreme Court declared that the right to privacy is based on the concept of personal "liberty" embodied in the Fourteenth Amendment due process clause's protection of "liberty" against arbitrary government interference.*

TABLE 4.1	Two Pillars of Religious Freedom in the First Amendment

"Congress shall make no law respecting an establishment of religion, or prohibiting the free exercise thereof."	
ESTABLISHMENT CLAUSE	**FREE EXERCISE CLAUSE**
Prohibits:	Protects:
1. the establishment of a national religion by Congress	1. the freedom to believe
2. government support for or preference of one religion over another or of religion over nonreligious philosophies in general	2. the freedom to worship and otherwise act in accordance with religious beliefs

were challenged in the court pathway by parents who viewed government-sponsored religious activities as inconsistent with civil liberties under the establishment clause.

In deciding cases concerning establishment clause issues, the Supreme Court has usually instructed judges to follow the so-called **Lemon test** (*Lemon* v. *Kurtzman,* 1971). Under this test, a court is to ask three questions about any governmental practice challenged as a violation of the establishment clause (see Table 4.1):

1. Does the law or practice have a secular (nonreligious) purpose?
2. Does the primary intent or effect of the law either advance or inhibit religion?
3. Does the law or practice create an excessive entanglement of government and religion?

If a law or government practice flunks any of the three questions, the law or practice violates the establishment clause and is unconstitutional. The Supreme Court has used the test to invalidate programs that provided public support for religious schools (*Grand Rapids* v. *Ball,* 1985), school-sponsored benediction prayers at public school graduation ceremonies (*Lee* v. *Weisman,* 1992), and mandatory instruction in "creation science" as an alternative to evolutionary theory in high school science classes (*Edwards* v. *Aguillard,* 1987).

In the past two decades, several justices on the Supreme Court have harshly criticized the *Lemon* test and sought to replace it with an accommodationist perspective. In a case concerning public school graduation prayers (*Lee* v. *Weisman,* 1992), the test may have come close to being eliminated. The justices originally voted 5–4 to permit such prayers, but during the process of drafting opinions, Justice Anthony Kennedy changed his mind. He provided the decisive fifth vote to declare such prayers unconstitutional, because a high school student could have, in his words, "a reasonable perception that she is being forced by the State to pray in a manner her conscience will not allow."[2]

On a single day in 2005, the Court issued two establishment clause decisions that highlighted the difficulties experienced by the justices in attempting to interpret the First Amendment in a clear, consistent manner. In *McCreary County* v.

ACLU (2005), a majority of justices applied the *Lemon* test to rule that copies of the Ten Commandments could not be posted in Kentucky courthouses. A different combination of justices declared that the *Lemon* test need not apply, however, when those justices formed a majority in *Van Orden* v. *Perry* (2005) to permit Texas to keep a Ten Commandments monument on the state capitol grounds amid a variety of other monuments. The justices regarded the two situations as distinctively different, because the Kentucky courthouses displayed only the religious documents whereas Texas mixed the religious monument with other cultural and patriotic symbols. These decisions create uncertainty about how the Court will decide individual cases in the future.

The U.S. Supreme Court is regularly presented with lawsuits alleging excessive government involvement in religion. One such lawsuit concerned the display of a Ten Commandments monument on the grounds of the Texas state capitol. —*If you applied the* Lemon *test to the use of the words "under God" in the Pledge of Allegiance and the words "In God We Trust" on the nation's currency, how would you decide cases challenging these expressions as violations of the establishment clause?*

■ **Establishment Clause:** A clause in the First Amendment guaranteeing freedom from religion by providing a basis for Supreme Court decisions limiting government support for and endorsement of particular religions.

EXAMPLE: *Critics have sought to stop public schools from having children recite the Pledge of Allegiance because they claim that the words "under God" in the Pledge mean that the government is imposing a particular religious concept on children in violation of the establishment clause.*

Free Exercise of Religion

The free exercise clause concerns the right of individuals to engage in religious practices and to follow their beliefs without governmental interference. Several of the important cases that expanded civil liberties in this area were pursued by Jehovah's Witnesses. Just prior to World War II, the Supreme Court ruled that public schools could punish Jehovah's Witness students for refusing to salute the flag and recite the Pledge of Allegiance, even though the students claimed that being required to salute anything other than God violated their religious beliefs (*Minersville School District v. Gobitis,* 1940). Shortly afterward, several justices had second thoughts about the issue, and the Court reversed itself in *West Virginia v. Barnette* (1943). Justice Robert Jackson's opinion contained a lofty statement about the importance of freedom of thought and religious belief:

> If there is any fixed star in our constitutional constellation, it is that no official, high or petty, can prescribe what shall be orthodox in politics, nationalism, religion, or other matters of opinion or force citizens to confess by word or act their faith therein.

This does not mean, however, that the free exercise clause provides an absolute right to do anything in the name of religion. For example, if a person believed that his religion demanded that he engage in human sacrifice or cannibalism, the Supreme Court would permit legislation to outlaw such practices. In 1990, an opinion written by Justice Antonin Scalia declared that the "right to free exercise of religion does not relieve an individual of the obligation to comply with a 'valid and neutral law of general applicability'" (*Employment Division of Oregon v. Smith*).

Many members of Congress want judges to look carefully at laws that would override religious practices. In effect, these legislators want judges to apply an analysis called **strict scrutiny** (or the compelling government interest test), which places the burden on the government to demonstrate the necessity of a specific law in order to outweigh an individual's desire to engage in a religious practice. The Supreme Court already applies the compelling government interest test to analyze whether other fundamental rights have been violated. In 1993, Congress enacted the Religious Freedom Restoration Act, which protects individuals' free exercise of religion against actions by the federal government. This act was used by the Supreme Court in 2006 when it found that the government did not have a compelling justification to prevent a small religious sect from following its traditional religious practices of ingesting tea containing a hallucinogenic, controlled substance from South America (*Gonzales v. O Centro Espirita Benficiente Unaio do Vegetal*). The government believed that it had demonstrated the harms of the

hallucinogenic tea merely by pointing to its status as a controlled substance under federal law, but the justices unanimously decided that the government needed to show specific, significant harms caused by the tea in order to override the free exercise right.

There are often apparent conflicts between civil liberties protected under the establishment clause and those protected under the free exercise clause. For example, some critics argue that the Court's establishment clause decisions barring sponsored prayers in public schools effectively violate the free exercise rights of students who wish to pray. The apparent clash with free exercise of religion, however, is less substantial than it may first appear. Students can pray on their own in school as long as school officials do not organize or lead the prayers. In addition, the Supreme Court has not ruled against student-organized and student-led prayers in public schools except when those prayers are conducted in a manner that implies sponsorship by school officials, such as a student reading a prayer over the stadium public address system before high school football games (*Santa Fe Independent School District v. Doe,* 2000).

In 1962, the Supreme Court decided that teachers could not lead public school students in prayer because such actions violate the First Amendment as an improper "establishment of religion" by government. As a result of the Supreme Court's decision, students in public schools can bow their heads individually in prayer or meet before school for a student-led prayer. However, school officials are not supposed to be involved. —*Why did this Supreme Court decision generate so much controversy?*

■ **Free Exercise Clause:** A clause in the First Amendment guaranteeing freedom to practice one's religion without government interference as long as those practices do not harm other individuals or society.

EXAMPLE: *Some people argue that free exercise of religion should prevent the government from using public safety as a justification to prevent individuals from handling poisonous snakes, taking illegal drugs, sacrificing animals, or engaging in other regulated practices as part of religious ceremonies.*

First Amendment Rights: Freedom of Religion

4.1   **Distinguish between the two dimensions of freedom of religion in the First Amendment.**

PRACTICE QUIZ: UNDERSTAND AND APPLY

1. The establishment clause of the First Amendment
   a. limits Americans' freedom of religion.
   b. requires people of all religions to salute the American flag.
   c. guarantees that churches can design their own religious services.
   d. is relevant to prayer cases involving public schools.

2. Posting the Ten Commandments in courthouses can be construed as a violation of the establishment clause, because
   a. not all citizens follow the Ten Commandments.
   b. the Supreme Court concluded that posting the Ten Commandments advances the beliefs of a particular religious perspective.
   c. Christianity is criticized in Article III of the U.S. Constitution.
   d. most American judges are not Christians.

3. As currently interpreted by the Supreme Court, the free exercise clause grants citizens the right to practice any form of religion
   a. provided that such practices do not "offend [current] community standards."
   b. provided that the participants can prove their practices are a "long-standing component of a genuine religious ceremony."
   c. provided that such practices do not violate "a valid and neutral law of general applicability," such as the crime of murder.
   d. provided it is one of the four religions most commonly practiced by people throughout the world.

4. If a law or government policy would create an "excessive entanglement" between government and religion, that policy would violate
   a. the establishment clause.
   b. the free exercise clause.
   c. everyone's understanding of Christianity.
   d. a, b, c.

ANALYZE

1. Discuss the three components of the *Lemon* test. What issues would likely cause debates and disagreements in interpreting these three components?

2. What kind of justification could the government present to enact a law that the Supreme Court might accept as a "compelling government interest" that could outweigh an individual's free exercise of religion?

IDENTIFY THE CONCEPT THAT DOESN'T BELONG

a. Separationist
b. *Lemon* test
c. Prayer in private schools
d. Strict scrutiny
e. Prayer in public schools

Resource Center
• Glossary
• Vocabulary Example
• Connect the Link

■ **Clear and Present Danger Test:**
A test for permissible speech articulated by Justice Oliver Wendell Holmes in *Schenck v. United States* (1919) that allows government regulation of some expressions.

EXAMPLE: *Imagine the injuries that would occur if, as a practical joke, someone yelled "He's got a gun!" in a crowd of hundreds of people waiting in line for a ride at Disney World. Such false statements likely to cause disorder and injuries are a primary focus of the test developed by Justice Holmes.*

First Amendment Rights: Freedom of Speech

4.2 Specify the limits on free speech in the United States.

(pages 98–99)

The First Amendment protections for speech and press are expressed in absolute terms: "Congress shall make no law . . . abridging the freedom of speech, or of the press; or the right of the people peaceably to assemble, and to petition the Government for redress of grievances." Although the words of the amendment seem to say that the government cannot impose *any* limitations on your ability to speak, write, or participate in peaceful public demonstrations, you can probably think of several kinds of expressions that are limited under American law—for example:

> If you claimed you were exercising your right to freedom of speech when you telephoned the leaders of Iran and told them how to build nuclear weapons

> If you claimed you were using freedom of speech and freedom of the press when you filled bottles with tap water and sold them through advertisements calling them "The Amazing Liquid Cure for Cancer"

These examples raise questions about whether freedom of speech is absolute or whether the government can impose limitations. Judges interpret the First Amendment in ways that seek to strike a balance between individual liberty and important societal interests. In the first example, national security interests may outweigh an individual's desire to transmit a specific communication. And in the second example, the government can regulate product advertisements and medicines in ways that protect society from harm, even when they limit an individual's speech and written expression. Judges typically demand that governmental regulations concerning speech and the press be supported by strong, persuasive justifications before they can be applied to limit individuals' opportunities to express themselves.

Supreme Court Justice Oliver Wendell Holmes argued for a **clear and present danger test**■ that would permit prosecution only for speeches and publications that actually posed a tangible, immediate threat to American society (*Schenck v. United States,* 1919). Holmes illustrated his point with an especially famous descriptive example: "The most stringent protection of free speech would not protect a man in falsely shouting fire in a theater, and causing a panic."

By the 1960s, the Supreme Court had adopted, expanded, and refined Holmes's suggested test so that political protests, whether by civil rights advocates, antiwar activists, or communists, could express critical viewpoints as long as the nature and context of those expressions did not pose an immediate threat (*Brandenburg v. Ohio* [1969]).

Today, it is difficult for people to be prosecuted for **political speech** that expresses their viewpoints about government and public affairs. By contrast, **commercial speech** may be subject to greater regulation because of concerns about protecting the public from misleading advertisements and other harms.

STUDENT profile

In 2003, Bretton Barber, a senior at Dearborn High School in Michigan, was sent home from school for refusing to remove a T-shirt that was harshly critical of President George W. Bush. Bretton Barber filed a lawsuit that led a federal judge to support his right to wear an expressive T-shirt. Cases about students' rights to express themselves rely on a Supreme Court decision concerning a courageous Iowa student in the 1960s.

In 1965, Mary Beth Tinker, a 13-year-old student at Harding Junior High School in Des Moines, Iowa, wore a black armband to school to express her opposition to the Vietnam War. She was suspended from school. Despite receiving numerous death threats, Tinker continued to assert her right to peacefully express her views about a matter of public concern through the use of **symbolic speech**■—an action (such as wearing a black armband) designed to communicate an idea. Tinker's case eventually reached the U.S. Supreme Court. In a 7–2 ruling, the Court decided that the Des Moines school board had violated Tinker's First Amendment rights (*Tinker v. Des Moines Independent Community School District,* 1969).

Judges do not support every form of expression by students. As a joke, Joseph Frederick, a student in Alaska, held up a banner that said "Bong Hits for Jesus" on the sidewalk outside his high school. After he was suspended from school, he pursued a lawsuit all the way to the U.S. Supreme Court. In 2007, a divided Court ruled against him by concluding that the school could prevent expressions that encouraged the use of illegal substances (*Morse v. Frederick*).

How far has the Supreme Court moved in broadening the concept of freedom of speech? In 1989, a five-justice majority on the U.S. Supreme Court declared that burning the flag is symbolic speech, a protected form of political expression that falls within the coverage of the First Amendment (*Texas v. Johnson,* 1989). In the words of Justice William Brennan, who wrote the majority opinion, "If there is a bedrock principle underlying the First Amendment, it is that the Government may not prohibit the expression of an idea simply

■ **Symbolic Speech:** The expression of an idea or viewpoint through an action, such as wearing an armband or burning an object. Symbolic speech can enjoy First Amendment protections.

EXAMPLE: *The U.S. Supreme Court says that the First Amendment protects people's right to express their opposition to government policies by burning American flags, even though such actions make many Americans very angry (Texas v. Johnson, 1989).*

The Ku Klux Klan was founded after the Civil War to terrorize African Americans. As shown in this photo of a 1998 Klan demonstration in Texas, when the Klan holds protests today, the police must often protect their right to free speech by guarding them against attacks. —*Do Klan members have the right to express their ideas, or should they be prohibited from using hate speech? What reasons would you give for prohibiting the use of hate speech?*

because society finds the idea itself offensive or disagreeable." The Court's decision aroused anger in many segments of American society and spurred members of Congress to propose constitutional amendments to protect the flag. Despite the outcry, the Court's decision remains in place and demonstrates that protected speech has been defined broadly, even when it offends or angers many people.

The Court accepts **reasonable time, place, and manner restrictions** on political assemblies. Judges recognize that chaos and disruption might harm society if protesters can freely block roadways, jail entrances, hospital parking lots, and other locations in a community. However, the government must demonstrate that important societal interests justify any restrictions on expression.

First Amendment Rights: Freedom of Speech

4.2   Specify the limits on free speech in the United States.

PRACTICE QUIZ: UNDERSTAND AND APPLY

1. Freedom of speech in the United States is
   a. protected absolutely.
   b. limited because the First Amendment describes specific limitations.
   c. limited because of judges' interpretations about permissible laws to limit speech.
   d. limited because certain words are immoral.

2. The government cannot pass a law to limit political speech unless that law merely
   a. forbids criticism of the American government.
   b. requires people to respect the president.
   c. prohibits any suggestion that Americans switch to some other form of government.
   d. bars words and statements that incite imminent lawless action.

3. Justice Oliver Wendell Holmes developed an initial test for permissible regulation of speech by using the concept of
   a. hate speech   c. obscenity
   b. symbolic speech   d. clear and present danger

ANALYZE

1. What expressive actions, if any, should not be protected as symbolic speech?

2. Should campaign advertisements be defined as political speech or commercial speech? Why or why not?

IDENTIFY THE CONCEPT THAT DOESN'T BELONG

a. First Amendment free exercise rights
b. Clear and present danger
c. Commercial speech
d. Symbolic speech
e. Time, place, and manner restrictions

4.2

Resource Center
• Glossary
• Vocabulary Example
• Connect the Link

First Amendment Rights: Freedom of the Press and Obscenity

4.3 Assess the test for justifying governmental limitations on written words and images.
(pages 100–103)

Freedom of the Press

Like free speech, freedom of the press is guaranteed by the First Amendment's absolutist language, and Americans regard this freedom as an essential element of democracy. Voters need free-flowing, accurate information in order to evaluate their elected leaders. They have little hope of using democratic processes to hold their leaders accountable or to elect new legislators and executive officials unless they have access to information. As illustrated in Figure 4.1, limitations on freedom of the press, like limitations on speech, are based on important government interests such as national security.

The Supreme Court issued a strong statement against **prior restraint** of publications that criticize public officials in *Near* v. *Minnesota* (1931). Prior restraint is the government's attempt to prevent certain information or viewpoints from being published. In the *Near* case, the Supreme Court struck down a state law intended to prevent the publication of articles or editorials that used inflammatory language to criticize government officials. As a result, the government generally cannot prevent articles from being published. However, the principle of no prior restraint does *not* prevent authors and publishers from later being sued for the publication of false or misleading information that harms

FIGURE 4.1 ▪ Freedom of Speech and Press
Civil liberties protections enjoyed by Americans are defined by judges' interpretations of the words in the Bill of Rights. For the First Amendment and several other provisions of the Bill of Rights, judges often seek to strike a balance between protecting the liberty of individuals and acknowledging the need to protect important interests of society. Thus there are limitations on many civil liberties.

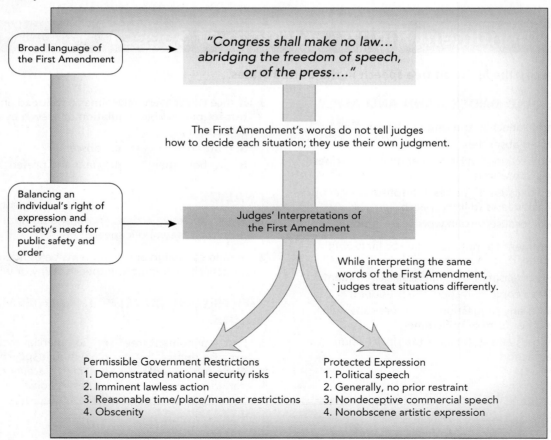

Broad language of the First Amendment

"Congress shall make no law... abridging the freedom of speech, or of the press...."

The First Amendment's words do not tell judges how to decide each situation; they use their own judgment.

Balancing an individual's right of expression and society's need for public safety and order

Judges' Interpretations of the First Amendment

While interpreting the same words of the First Amendment, judges treat situations differently.

Permissible Government Restrictions
1. Demonstrated national security risks
2. Imminent lawless action
3. Reasonable time/place/manner restrictions
4. Obscenity

Protected Expression
1. Political speech
2. Generally, no prior restraint
3. Nondeceptive commercial speech
4. Nonobscene artistic expression

■ **Press Shield Law:** A statute enacted by a legislature establishing a reporter's privilege to protect the confidentiality of sources.

EXAMPLE: *In 2006, the Connecticut legislature enacted a law to permit reporters to protect the identities of their sources unless overriding societal interests lead judges to order them to provide information sought by prosecutors.*

people's reputations. Such civil lawsuits are for **defamation**— false, harmful statements either through spoken words (*slander*) or through written words (*libel*). The Court's decision established the basic presumption that the government will not censor the news media, except perhaps in the most extreme circumstances.

In 1971, the Supreme Court faced a case that raised the issue of prior restraint when the federal government claimed that publication by newspapers of a top-secret internal Defense Department study concerning the Vietnam War would seriously damage national security. The so-called Pentagon Papers had been given to the *New York Times* and the *Washington Post* by Daniel Ellsberg, a Defense Department analyst who had concluded that the public needed more information about what was really happening in the war, even though he was legally forbidden to make the information available. When the newspapers began to publish this book-length document, under the title *History of the U.S. Decision-Making Process on Vietnam Policy,* the government sought a court order to stop the newspapers. The two newspapers in question, arguably the nation's most prominent at that time, had the money and legal expertise to battle the government on equal terms in the court pathway. The Supreme Court majority declared that the newspapers could continue to publish the report (*New York Times Company* v. *United States,* **1971**). Three justices adopted the absolutist position that the First Amendment bars *all* prior restraint by the government, and three additional justices decided that the government had not adequately proved that publication of the report would actually harm national security.[3] The decision demonstrated that many judges would require exceptionally compelling proof of harm to society before permitting government censorship of publications about public affairs.

The interests of the press can clash with governmental priorities when reporters have information sought by the government and refuse to share it with prosecutors and other officials. Reporters claim that a free press can survive only if they can protect the identities of their sources of inside information. Otherwise, people would not be willing to provide reporters with controversial and even potentially incriminating information about governmental activities and issues of public interest. Government officials argue in response that reporters, like other citizens, should be required to cooperate with criminal investigations to ensure that criminal enterprises are thwarted and that guilty people receive appropriate punishment.

Advocates for the news media feel that the First Amendment should be interpreted to recognize a **reporter's privilege**, the right of news agencies to decline to provide information requested by the government. Although some states have enacted **press shield laws**■ to protect reporters in state justice processes, the federal courts have refused to recognize a constitutional privilege to protect reporters nationwide. Thus reporters are occasionally jailed for contempt of court if they refuse to cooperate with criminal investigations. For example, in 2001 Vanessa Leggett, a freelance writer in Houston who was

Vanessa Leggett was jailed when she asserted that reporters possess the right to protect the identities of their sources and withhold information from prosecutors. —*Should freedom of the press be interpreted to include a "reporter's privilege" to withhold information? What would be the costs and benefits for society from such a redefinition of the First Amendment right?*

conducting research for a book on a controversial murder case, spent 168 days in jail for refusing to testify before a federal grand jury about her interviews with criminal suspects. She was released only when the grand jury ended its investigation.[4]

PATHWAYS of change from around the world

If you were the editor of a student newspaper, would you risk your liberty or life to educate people about democracy? Editors of student newspapers often are visible leaders on university campuses. They shape the content of information made available to students and the public. Because newspapers traditionally present opinionated viewpoints in editorials or arouse controversy by choosing to investigate specific issues, student editors risk severe sanctions when they question and criticize government policies in countries that do not enjoy freedom of expression. During 2006 in Iran, a country in which the government's critics can be threatened and arrested, 47 student publications were closed, and 181 students received letters warning them not to become involved in politics.[5] In March 2007, two student editors were arrested at Amirkabir University in Iran and accused of publishing articles that insulted Islam. The editors claimed that they were framed and targeted for arrest because they were known to support student organizations that wanted to reform the government and make it more democratic.[6]

Throughout modern history, newspaper editors, including editors of student newspapers, have stood up for freedom of expression and democracy and, in many cases, endured prison or worse. Can you picture yourself writing for a newspaper in order to educate and arouse the public on matters of justice, ethics, equality, and other elements of democracy? Would you be willing to assume the visible position of editor if you knew that authorities might choose to make an example of you? Student editors in the United States face the prospect of losing their positions or perhaps being suspended from school if school or government authorities believe they have gone "too far" in discussing controversial issues. In some other countries, by contrast, student editors find themselves at far greater risk of losing their liberty or lives by standing up for matters of principle.

Obscenity

Judges face challenges in determining if expressions that offend the sensibilities of some community members fall under the protection of the First Amendment. In particular, legislators have regularly sought to prohibit or regulate material with sexual content, such as books, magazines, live performances, films, and Web sites. The Supreme Court has said anything that is "obscene" falls outside of the First Amendment and is not considered part of free expression. It has been very difficult, however, for the Court to provide a clear definition of *obscene*. This issue can cause major conflicts because images and performances that some people consider artistic expression can be regarded by others as harmful to the morals of society.

In the early twentieth century, people were regularly prosecuted in various communities for possessing or selling written materials or pictures with sexual content. James Joyce's novel *Ulysses,* published in France in 1922 and today regarded as one of the great works of modern literature, could not legally be printed, imported, or sold in the United States because it contained four-letter words and certain sexual allusions. Only in 1933 did a federal judge lift the ban after a leading American publisher brought a lawsuit challenging it.

In the 1950s, the Supreme Court developed a test for obscenity. Its initial efforts focused on whether the work in question was "utterly without redeeming social importance" (*Roth v. United States,* 1957). This test was refined as the Court's composition changed over the next two decades.

In an important case challenging the prosecution of a man who mailed brochures that advertised sexually explicit books, the Supreme Court articulated a new test for obscenity. According to Chief Justice Warren Burger's opinion, materials that met a three-part test for obscenity could be prohibited by legislation and lead to prosecutions. The Court's test was stated as follows in **Miller v. California (1973)**:

The basic guidelines for the trier of fact must be: (a) whether the "average person, applying contemporary community standards" would find that the work, taken as a whole, appeals to the prurient interest; (b) whether the work depicts or describes, in a patently offensive way, sexual conduct specifically defined by the applicable state law; and (c) whether the work, taken as whole, lacks serious literary, artistic, political, or scientific value.

The test for obscenity is thus based on "community standards," and those standards change over time. For example, in the 1960s, actors portraying married couples in movies and on television were often shown sleeping in separate single beds so as not to convey any sexual implications by having a double bed on the set. Today, by contrast, scantily clad performers in sexy

Radio broadcaster Howard Stern moved his show to satellite radio in 2006 in order to avoid government-imposed fines for broadcasting graphic sexual discussions. By moving his program to satellite radio, Stern now entertains only voluntary, paying customers and thereby moved himself outside the Federal Communications Commission's mandate to protect unsuspecting consumers. The Supreme Court has ruled that obscene material is not protected by the First Amendment and thus can be regulated by the government. —*What kinds of verbal expression do you think are outside the protections of the First Amendment?*

embraces and dance routines are everyday fare for music videos shown around the clock on cable. It seems clear that "community standards" regarding acceptable entertainment have changed over the years. Does this mean that "anything goes" in American entertainment media? No. The Federal Communications Commission (FCC) continues to regulate television and radio broadcasts, and it imposes fines for profanity and sexual content that it believes has gone too far. Broadcasting is subject to stricter government control than newspapers, because the government has the power to regulate use of the public airwaves. The uproar over the momentary exposure of singer Janet Jackson's bare breast on television during the halftime show for the 2004 Super Bowl served as a reminder that there are still limits to expression, especially when that expression is broadcast to the televisions and radios of unwitting consumers who assume that certain standards are in place.

Obviously, a different situation exists for consumers who intentionally seek sexually explicit material in specific magazines or specialty stores or online. Generally, pornographic films and magazines that once would have led to prosecution in most communities are now widely available in the United States and without legal repercussions, as long as the sellers and distributors of such materials take steps to keep such items away from children.

Indeed, except for content standards for broadcasts regulated by the FCC, most regulation of obscenity today focuses on the exposure of children to obscene material or their exploitation in its production. Laws impose prison sentences for the creation, dissemination, and possession of child pornography.

First Amendment Rights: Freedom of the Press and Obscenity

4.3   Assess the test for justifying governmental limitations on written words and images.

PRACTICE QUIZ: UNDERSTAND AND APPLY

1. Freedom of the press is often considered
   a. a form of symbolic speech.
   b. essential for the maintenance of a democracy.
   c. less important than the government's need to keep officials from being criticized.
   d. a right that does not need protection when the nation is at war.

2. The mayor of a city learns that a newspaper is about to print an inaccurate story claiming that she has cheated on her husband by having several affairs with staff members. The mayor can
   a. send the police to prevent the newspaper from printing the article.
   b. send the police to seize all copies of the newspaper before they are delivered to the public.
   c. sue the newspaper for defamation after the article is printed and sold.
   d. do nothing.

3. The federal government learns that a newspaper is about to print an article describing secret plans for a raid on a suspected terrorist training camp. The federal government can
   a. send U.S. Marines to take over the newspaper building and printing presses.
   b. seek a court order to prevent publication, if the government can prove that the article will cause a significant harm to national security.

   c. arrest the newspaper editors and reporters.
   d. issue a presidential order barring the newspaper from publishing any articles in the future.

4. What test did the Supreme Court instruct judges to use in order to determine if material is "obscene" and not protected by the First Amendment?
   a. offensive compulsion test
   b. strict scrutiny test
   c. rational basis test
   d. community standards test

ANALYZE

1. Under what circumstances, if any, should the government be able to force a journalist to reveal confidential sources?

2. If we think of everyone in the United States as being part of a national "community," what kinds of things would this community regard as obscene?

IDENTIFY THE CONCEPT THAT DOESN'T BELONG

a. Prior restraint
b. First Amendment establishment by government
c. Press shield laws
d. *New York Times Company* v. *United States*, 1971
e. Defamation

Resource Center
• Glossary
• Vocabulary Example
• Connect the Link

■ **Exclusionary Rule** A general principle stating that evidence obtained illegally cannot be used against a defendant in a criminal prosecution. The Supreme Court has allowed certain exceptions to the rule in particular circumstances.

EXAMPLE: *The Supreme Court ruled that prosecutors could not use blood test results showing traces of cocaine when the blood tests were supplied by a hospital without the consent of the patients and without a warrant issued by a judge.*

Civil Liberties and Criminal Justice

4.4 Specify the protections afforded to criminal suspects in the Bill of Rights.
(pages 104–105)

Several amendments in the Bill of Rights describe protections afforded people who are subject to police investigations, prosecutions, sentencing, and criminal punishment. These amendments are designed to protect everyone in the United States, including innocent people, from excessive actions by overzealous law enforcement officials who are seeking to prevent and solve crimes.

Search and Seizure

The Fourth Amendment protects people against improper searches and seizures. In the words of the amendment:

> The right of the people to be secure in their persons, houses, papers, and effects, against unreasonable searches and seizures, shall not be violated, and no Warrants shall issue, but upon probable cause, supported by Oath or affirmation, and particularly describing the place to be searched, and the persons or things to be seized.

The two key parts of the amendment are the prohibition on "unreasonable searches and seizures" and the requirements for obtaining search and arrest warrants. Like other provisions of the Constitution, the Fourth Amendment contains inherently ambiguous language that must be interpreted by judges. The word *seizure*, for example, includes arrests when people are taken into police custody (that is, seizures of people) as well as situations in which officers seize property that may be evidence of criminal wrongdoing. But how do you know whether a search or seizure is "unreasonable"? Clearly, such a determination is a matter of judgment, and all people will not agree about whether specific actions are "searches" or whether they are "unreasonable."

The U.S. Supreme Court endorsed application of the **exclusionary rule**■ in *Weeks* v. *United States* (1914). Under this rule, evidence obtained improperly by the police cannot be used to prosecute someone accused of a crime. The intent of the rule is to stop police from undertaking illegal searches or improperly questioning suspects and to remedy the violation of suspects' civil liberties. At first, the rule applied only against federal law enforcement officials, such as FBI agents, but the Supreme Court, in the famous case of **Mapp v. Ohio (1961)**, subsequently applied it to all police officers throughout the country.

As Republican presidents appointed new justices in the 1970s and 1980s who interpreted civil liberties under the Bill of Rights in a narrower manner, Chief Justice Warren Burger

New York City police search the bags and packages of subway riders in order to reduce the threat of a terrorist attack. The Supreme Court has interpreted the Fourth Amendment to require a balance between protecting the individual's right against unreasonable searches and the need for government officials to maintain safety and security. —*When your bag is searched at an airport, concert, or stadium, are your privacy rights being violated?*

(1969–1986) was able to lead the changing Court toward creating limitations on and exceptions to the exclusionary rule.

Chief Justice Burger never succeeded in eliminating the exclusionary rule, but law enforcement officers now have greater leeway to make errors in conducting searches and questioning suspects without automatically facing the exclusion of evidence.

With respect to a **warrant**—an order from a judge authorizing a search or an arrest—the Fourth Amendment specifically requires the police and prosecutor to show the judge sufficient reliable information to establish "probable cause" about the location of evidence or a person's criminal behavior.

Other searches conducted without warrants are governed only by the prohibition on "unreasonable searches and seizures." The Supreme Court has identified specific situations in which warrants are not required, because these searches are considered reasonable. Permissible warrantless searches include

- "stop and frisk" searches of a suspect's outer clothing on the streets when officers have a reasonable basis to suspect that person is involved in criminal behavior and potentially poses a danger to the public (*Terry* v. *Ohio,* 1968);
- "exigent circumstances" in which an immediate warrantless search must be undertaken because of danger to the public or the possible loss of evidence (*Cupp* v. *Murphy,* 1973);

Self-Incrimination

The Fifth Amendment describes several rights related to criminal justice, including the concept of **double jeopardy,** which refers to the protection against being tried twice for the same

■ *Miranda* **v.** *Arizona* **(1966):** A U.S. Supreme Court decision that requires police officers, before questioning a suspect in custody, to inform that suspect about the right to remain silent and to have a lawyer present during custodial questioning.

EXAMPLE: *If a police officer arrests you, the officer is not supposed to ask you any questions about what you did until you have been informed of your right to remain silent and your other* Miranda *rights. These warnings are intended to protect you from incriminating yourself without being aware of your rights.*

crime. Many controversial cases arise concerning another protection: the privilege against **compelled self-incrimination.** In the words of the amendment, no person may be "compelled in any criminal case to be a witness against himself."

If an individual is not free to walk away from police questioning, the police must make it clear that the person has a right to remain silent and to have an attorney present during questioning. The latter requirement emerged from the Supreme Court's famous and controversial decision in **Miranda v. Arizona (1966)**■. Police officers read "*Miranda* rights" to people in custody:

> You have the right to remain silent. Anything that you say can and will be used against you in a court of law. You have the right to have an attorney present during questioning. If you cannot afford an attorney, one will be appointed to represent you.

When police question people on the street, or when people come to the police station voluntarily, the police do not have to inform them of their rights. The primary exception to this rule concerns motorists stopped for traffic violations who are not free to drive away; the police can ask them questions without informing them about their *Miranda* rights.

MYTH EXPOSED Many Americans believe that significant numbers of guilty people go free by simply exercising the right to remain silent. In reality, however, police have developed techniques to follow the *Miranda* rules, while still eliciting incriminating information. These techniques include asking questions before making an arrest and pretending to befriend the suspect during questioning.[7] In addition, many suspects make incriminating statements despite being given *Miranda* warnings, because they are seeking a deal, wish to pin the crime on an accomplice, feel frightened or overwhelmed with guilt, or simply do not listen closely to and think about the implications of the warnings.

Civil Liberties and Criminal Justice

4.4 **Specify the protections afforded to criminal suspects in the Bill of Rights.**

PRACTICE QUIZ: UNDERSTAND AND APPLY

1. If a police officer breaks down the door to your house and searches your house without a warrant or other legal justification, the officer's actions
   a. violate the Fourth Amendment prohibition on "entering a house with evil intentions."
   b. violate the Fourth Amendment prohibition on "unreasonable searches and seizures."
   c. satisfy the Fourth Amendment rule that warrants be used "except during a necessary house search."
   d. violate the Fifth Amendment rule against obtaining evidence from a person that will be used against that person.

2. When prosecutors are not permitted to present evidence in court because the police obtained that evidence through an illegal search, we say this evidence has been subjected to
   a. the warrantless search exception.
   b. the probable cause doctrine.
   c. the exclusionary rule.
   d. the good faith exception.

3. *Miranda* rights are intended to protect a person's
   a. right to probable cause.
   b. right against warrantless searches.
   c. right against double jeopardy.
   d. privilege against compelled self-incrimination.

ANALYZE

1. What would be the consequences of a U.S. Supreme Court decision that abolishes the exclusionary rule?

2. What would be the consequences of a U.S. Supreme Court decision that abolishes the requirement of *Miranda* warnings?

IDENTIFY THE CONCEPT THAT DOESN'T BELONG

a. *Cupp* v. *Murphy*, 1973
b. Fourth Amendment
c. First Amendment
d. *Miranda* v. *Arizona*, 1966
e. Exclusionary rule

Resource Center
• Glossary
• Vocabulary Example
• Connect the Link

■ **Trial by Jury:** A right contained in the Sixth Amendment to have criminal guilt decided by a body of citizens drawn from the community.

EXAMPLE: *In 2008, actor Wesley Snipes went to trial in Ocala, Florida, on charges of failing to pay federal income tax. After questioning 60 citizens drawn from the community about their knowledge of the case, the judge and the attorneys selected 12 jurors and four alternate jurors to hear the case.*

Trial Rights and Capital Punishment

4.5 Evaluate the legal protections that ensure only guilty people receive criminal punishment.

(pages 106–107)

Trial Rights

The Sixth Amendment contains a variety of legal protections for people who face criminal trials:

> In all criminal prosecutions, the accused shall enjoy the right to a speedy and public trial, by an impartial jury of the State and district wherein the crime shall have been committed, which district shall have been previously ascertained by law, and to be informed of the nature and cause of the accusation; to be confronted with the witnesses against him; to have compulsory process for obtaining witnesses in his favor; and to have the Assistance of Counsel for his defense.

The right to a **speedy and public trial** ensures that the government cannot hold secret proceedings that prevent citizens from knowing whether evidence exists to prove a defendant's guilt. The right to a speedy trial also prevents the government from ruining a person's life by holding charges over his or her head for an indefinite period of time.

The right to **trial by jury**■ applied only to federal cases, but the Supreme Court incorporated the right in 1968 and applied it to state proceedings (*Duncan* v. *Louisiana*).

Although dramatic scenes from jury trials are a central feature of television shows, in reality only about 10 percent of criminal convictions result from trials, and only half of those are the result of jury trials.[8] The other trials are **bench trials,** in which the verdict is determined by a judge without a jury. Defendants may request bench trials because they are afraid that jurors may be biased and emotional, especially if there are controversial charges involving sex offenses, guns, or drugs. The other 90 percent of criminal convictions are obtained through **plea bargaining,** a process approved by the Supreme Court in which prosecutors and defense attorneys negotiate a guilty plea in exchange for a less severe sentence. Plea bargaining has become an essential way to dispose of the vast number of cases that otherwise would overwhelm the resources of the criminal justice system if they all proceeded to trial.

The Sixth Amendment's exact words—"In all criminal prosecutions, the accused shall enjoy the right to . . . an impartial jury"—have not been enforced by the Supreme Court. According to the Court, the right to a trial by jury applies only in cases concerning "serious offenses" that are punishable by six

months or more in jail or prison (*Lewis* v. *United States*, 1996). For lesser crimes, the accused can be forced to accept a bench trial.

The right to counsel is an especially important part of the Sixth Amendment. As early as 1932, the Supreme Court, in *Powell* v. *Alabama,* recognized the value of this legal protection by requiring Alabama to provide attorneys for nine African American youths who had previously been convicted and sentenced to death. Their brief, attorneyless proceeding was based on rape accusations from two white women, one of whom later admitted that her charges were false.

Later, the Supreme Court required that the government provide attorneys for all indigent defendants facing serious criminal charges in federal court (*Johnson* v. *Zerbst,* 1938) and state courts (*Gideon* v. *Wainwright,* 1963). Indigent defendants are people who do not have enough money to hire their own attorneys. If people have sufficient funds, they are expected to hire an attorney, and the Sixth Amendment right merely means that the government cannot prevent them from seeking legal advice.

The right to counsel for indigents was expanded to all cases in which the potential punishment involves incarceration, even if only a short stay in jail (*Argersinger* v. *Hamlin,* 1972), as well as initial appeals (*Douglas* v. *California,* 1963).

Capital Punishment

The Constitution also provides rights for people who have been convicted of even the very worst crimes. The words of the Eighth Amendment include a prohibition of "cruel and unusual punishments." This clearly implies some limitation on the government's ability to punish. Criminal sanctions must not violate this provision, either by being similar to torture or by being disproportionate to the underlying crime. The Supreme Court has said that the phrase "cruel and unusual punishments" must be defined according to society's contemporary standards, so the meaning of the phrase changes as society's values change (*Trop* v. *Dulles,* 1958).

An important battleground for the meaning of the Eighth Amendment has been cases concerning **capital punishment**■ that are appealed through the court pathway.[9] As you can see in the Timeline on Capital Punishment and the Courts (see pages 108-109), although the courts have produced many major decisions on the issue over the past four decades, supporters and opponents of capital punishment have also used elections and lobbying to influence state laws on the subject. In 1972, the Supreme Court ruled that the death penalty was unconstitutional, as it was then being administered (*Furman* v. *Georgia*). Some justices thought that the death penalty was unconstitutional, because it was "cruel and unusual" according to the values of contemporary civilization. Other justices believed that the punishment was applied too inconsistently and unfairly and thus violated the Fourteenth Amendment right to due process.

■ **Capital Punishment:** A criminal punishment, otherwise known as the *death penalty*, in which a person is subject to execution after conviction. Reserved for the most serious offenses.

EXAMPLE: *In 2001, Timothy McVeigh was executed by lethal injection after being convicted for killing 168 people when he used a truck bomb to destroy the Murrah Federal Office Building in Oklahoma City in 1995.*

The death penalty was reinstated in 1976 after the latter group of justices became persuaded that states had adopted fairer procedures for administering capital punishment cases (*Gregg* v. *Georgia*). The special procedures for death penalty cases include *bifurcated proceedings* (separate trials to determine guilt and to decide on the appropriate sentence). In addition, judges and juries look specifically for *aggravating factors* that make a particular crime or offender worse than others, such as a murder by a repeat offender or a killing in the course of committing another felony. They also weigh *mitigating factors,* such as the offender's age or mental problems, which might make an offender less deserving of the death penalty.

The weight of scholarly evidence suggests that the death penalty does not deter crime.[10] Advocates of the death penalty argue that only the ultimate punishment can satisfy victims and survivors and show how strongly society disapproves of the worst crimes. Yet, many states have discovered significant problems with the accuracy of their legal proceedings. Between 1973 and 2009, a total of 138 people condemned to death in the United States were later released from prison when it was discovered they were actually innocent.[11] Debates therefore continue about whether the American legal system is capable of imposing capital punishment accurately and fairly.

Because the Supreme Court has addressed so many issues concerning capital punishment, the court pathway has significantly shaped public policy. For example, the justices have forbidden states from executing mentally retarded murderers (*Atkins* v. *Virginia*, 2002) as well as individuals who committed murders before having reached the age of 18 (*Roper* v. *Simmons*, 2005). The Court has also banned the use of capital punishment for the crime of rape, including rape of a child (*Kennedy* v. *Louisiana*, 2008).

Trial Rights and Capital Punishment

4.5   **Evaluate the legal protections that ensure only guilty people receive criminal punishment.**

PRACTICE QUIZ: UNDERSTAND AND APPLY

1. The Sixth Amendment right to counsel means that
   a. all criminal defendants have always had attorneys provided for them by the government.
   b. all criminal defendants since 1963 have had attorneys provided for them by the government.
   c. the government must provide attorneys for indigent criminal defendants in all cases.
   d. the government must provide attorneys for indigent criminal defendants only when they face serious charges for which they may be jailed.

2. The Supreme Court's current interpretation of the Sixth Amendment right to trial by jury means
   a. a right to a jury trial "in all criminal prosecutions."
   b. a right to a jury trial only if the prosecutor agrees to also request a jury trial.
   c. a right to a jury trial only in federal court cases, not in state court cases.
   d. a right to a jury trial in cases concerning serious crimes.

3. If a criminal trial uses bifurcated proceedings and focuses on aggravating and mitigating factors, then that trial must
   a. concern the rights of juvenile offenders.
   b. concern a felony rather than a misdemeanor case.
   c. concern capital punishment.
   d. be a jury trial for any serious charge.

ANALYZE

1. Discuss the pros and cons of a trial by jury. Are there circumstances in which a defendant would *not* want a jury trial?

2. How should a judge determine which punishments are "cruel and unusual"?

IDENTIFY THE CONCEPT THAT DOESN'T BELONG

a. Sixth Amendment
b. Bench trials
c. Fourth Amendment
d. Lethal injection
e. Eighth Amendment

COURTS   CULTURAL CHANGE   ELECTIONS   GRASSROOTS MOBILIZATION   LOBBYING DECISION-MAKERS

PRO CAPITAL PUNISHMENT

1976
Gregg* v. *Georgia
The death penalty is reactivated after approving Georgia's revised procedures for trying and sentencing accused murderers. The new procedures include a trial to determine guilt and then a separate hearing to consider the death penalty. Six justices conclude that the new procedures resolve the previous problems with inconsistent and arbitrary application of capital punishment.

1988
Anti-Drug Abuse Act
Congress makes capital punishment a penalty for murders committed as part of drug trafficking.

1987
McCleskey* v. *Kemp
Supreme court rules that statistics cannot be used to prove that the death penalty violates the equal protection clause of the Fourteenth Amendment.

1989
Stanford* v. *Kentucky
Supreme Court upholds capital punishment for juveniles who are 16 or 17 at the time that they commit murders.

1989
Penry* v. *Lynaugh
Supreme Court upholds capital punishment for mentally retarded murderers.

1972   **1976**   **1986–88**   **1989**

ANTI CAPITAL PUNISHMENT

1972
Furman* v. *Georgia
Supreme Court hears three capital punishment cases as a group. These cases are pursued by interest group lawyers for the NAACP Legal Defense Fund. Two cases concern interracial rapes in Georgia and Texas and the other concerns a murder in Georgia. The death penalty is temporarily halted when five of the Court's nine justices agree that the punishment is applied inconsistently and arbitrarily.

1976
Roberts* v. *Louisiana
State laws making the death penalty mandatory for first-degree murder are declared unconstitutional by the U.S. Supreme Court. Each case must be decided on an individual basis.

1986
Ford* v. *Wainwright
The Supreme Court rules that the death penalty cannot be applied to insane people.

1989
Fierro* v. *Gomez
U.S. Court of Appeals declares the gas chamber a violation of the Eighth Amendment.

Debates about capital punishment continue to rage, just as they have since the 1960s. Opponents of capital punishment have had limited success using the election pathway. Instead, they have focused their efforts on the court pathway. Supporters of the death penalty, on the other hand, have used the elections and lobbying pathways to push revisions of state capital punishment laws that would satisfy the Supreme Court. Highly publicized cases of innocent people being convicted and later released from death row have helped spur grassroots mobilization and pardons and moratoriums by governors. However, the fear of crime and terrorism attacks may have solidified public support for the death penalty in specific cases, such as convicted terrorists and serial killers.

Essay Questions

1. Many observers expect the Supreme Court to turn its attention to the question of whether it is "cruel and unusual" to execute murderers suffering from mental illnesses. Imagine that you are a lawyer. Choose a side—for or against—and create arguments concerning this issue.

2. Several states are attempting to create more careful processes that will guard against the risk that innocent people will be convicted of murders and sentenced to death. Create three suggestions for ways to reduce the risk of mistakes in murder trials. Explain how your suggestions will improve the process.

2008
Baze* v. *Rees
Supreme Court refuses to ban lethal injection as a means of execution.

1997

2000–02

2005

2007

2008

1997
The American Bar Association passes a resolution requesting all death penalty jurisdictions to place a moratorium on executions until they confirm their systems are not flawed.

2000
New Hampshire state legislature votes to abolish the death penalty but the bill is vetoed by the governor.

2002
Atkins* v. *Virginia
Supreme Court prohibits the execution of mentally retarded individuals.

2000
Governor George Ryan of Illinois places a moratorium on capital punishment when a media investigation discovers more than a dozen men on death row are innocent. Opponents of the death penalty lobby Ryan for the moratorium.

2005
Stanley "Tookie" Williams is put to death by lethal injection in California. Grassroots organizations on both sides of the divide mobilize prior to Williams' death.

2005
Roper* v. *Simmons
Supreme Court rules the execution of murderers who commit crimes while they are under the age of 18 is "cruel and unusual punishment."

2007
New Jersey legislature bans the use of capital punishment.

2008
Advances in DNA testing and reinvestigation of cases since the mid-1970s lead to the release of 129 prisoners who had been wrongly convicted and sentenced to death. (Nine more were released in 2009.)

2008
Kennedy* v. *Louisiana
Supreme Court prohibits the death penalty for the crime of child rape.

Resource Center
• Glossary
• Vocabulary Example
• Connect the Link

■ **Right to Privacy:** A constitutional right created and expanded in U.S. Supreme Court decisions concerning access to contraceptives, abortion, private sexual behavior, and other matters, even though the word *privacy* does not appear in the Constitution.

EXAMPLE: *Although some Americans believe that laws should forbid sexual behavior between same-sex couples (gays and lesbians), the U.S. Supreme Court has declared that consenting adults have a right to privacy that protects their ability to control their own noncommercial sexual activities inside their own homes (Lawrence v. Texas, 2003).*

Privacy

4.6 Explain why the right to privacy is controversial.

(pages 110–113)

The word *privacy* does not appear in the Constitution. The Supreme Court has nevertheless used its interpretive powers to recognize a **right to privacy**■ that protects people from government interference in a number of contexts. The justices first explicitly recognized a right to privacy in 1965. In this case, Connecticut had a statute that made it a crime to sell, possess, use, or counsel the use of contraceptives. After the law was challenged in the court pathway, the Supreme Court struck it down (*Griswold* v. *Connecticut,* 1965). The majority opinion by Justice William O. Douglas concluded that a right to privacy exists as an unstated element of several rights in the Bill of Rights: the First Amendment right to freedom of association, the Third Amendment protection against the government housing troops in private homes, the Fourth Amendment protection against unreasonable searches, and the Fifth Amendment privilege against compelled self-incrimination. Douglas wrote:

> The present case . . . concerns a relationship lying within the zone of privacy created by several fundamental constitutional guarantees. . . . Would we allow the police to search the sacred precincts of marital bedrooms for telltale signs of the use of contraceptives? The very idea is repulsive to the notions of privacy surrounding the marriage relationship.

Critics complained that the Court's decision created a new constitutional right that was not grounded in the Bill of Rights. In the words of Justice Hugo Black's dissenting opinion, "I like my privacy as well as the next [person], but I am nevertheless compelled to admit that government has a right to invade it unless prohibited by some specific constitutional provision." Critics feared from this that a five-member majority on the Supreme Court could invent any new rights that the justices wanted to impose on society. By contrast, defenders of the flexible approach to constitutional interpretation claimed that the Court is obligated to adjust the Constitution's meaning to make sure that it remains consistent with the changing values and needs of American society. In subsequent cases, the Court's flexible approach to constitutional interpretation led to the application of a right to privacy to new situations.

Abortion

In 1969, two young lawyers in Texas, Linda Coffee and Sarah Weddington, met a woman who claimed that she had become pregnant as the result of being raped. Because Texas, like other states, made abortion a crime, the woman could not legally terminate the

Justice William O. Douglas (1898–1980) served on the U.S. Supreme Court for 36 years (1939–1975), a longer period than any other justice in history. His most controversial opinion came in *Griswold* v. *Connecticut* (1965), in which he explained the Supreme Court's recognition of a constitutional right to privacy, even though the word "privacy" does not appear in the Constitution. The Supreme Court still faces privacy issues in the court pathway. —*Should a right of choice concerning abortion be considered as a part of a constitutional right to privacy? Why or why not?*

pregnancy. Although the woman gave birth to the baby, she wanted to use her case to challenge the Texas statute through the court pathway. The lawyers took the case, ***Roe v. Wade*** ■, all the way to the U.S. Supreme Court. ("Jane Roe" was not the woman's real name; it was used in the case to protect her privacy.) Her lawyers argued that the Texas statute violated the woman's right to make choices about abortion. In 1973, after the Supreme Court heard arguments from lawyers on both sides of the issue, the justices voted 7–2 that the Texas statute violated the Constitution. Justice Harry Blackmun wrote the majority opinion:

> The Court has recognized that a right of personal privacy, or a guarantee of certain areas or zones of privacy, does exist under the Constitution. . . . This right of privacy, whether it be founded in the Fourteenth Amendment's concept of personal liberty and restrictions upon state action, as we feel it is, or as the District Court determined, in the Ninth Amendment's reservation of rights to the people, is broad enough to encompass a woman's decision whether or not to terminate her pregnancy.

Several state legislatures and city councils sought to counteract the Court's decision by enacting statutes and ordinances

■ *Roe v. Wade* **(1973):** Controversial U.S. Supreme Court decision that declared women have a constitutional right to choose to terminate a pregnancy in the first six months following conception.

EXAMPLE: *Because the American public is divided on the issue of whether abortion should be illegal, politicians supporting each side of the debate have sought to influence the selection of new Supreme Court justices in the hope of either maintaining or reversing the* Roe *decision. Thus the Supreme Court continues to address cases concerning abortion, and the possibility exists that the original* Roe *decision may eventually be overturned.*

to make obtaining abortions more difficult by specifying expensive medical procedures and other matters during the second trimester. In addition, abortion opponents in Congress fought against the Court's decision by using their authority to limit public funding for abortion. Initially, the Court struck down several of these restrictive state laws. Later, however, as new justices were appointed, the Court became more flexible about accepting regulations. In *Webster* v. *Reproductive Health Services* (1989), for example, a majority of justices upheld Missouri's new abortion regulations.

Abortion became a central consideration in the appointment of newcomers to the Supreme Court. Interest groups on both sides of the abortion issue sought to influence the composition of the Supreme Court by lobbying presidents and senators to either favor or oppose specific judicial nominees. Presidents Ronald Reagan (1981–1989) and George H. W. Bush (1989–1993) vowed to use their appointment powers to put new justices on the Court who would work to overturn the right of choice established in *Roe v. Wade.* Thus the stage seemed set for a reconsideration of *Roe v. Wade* when the case known as *Planned Parenthood* v. *Casey* (1992) reached the Court.

Pennsylvania had enacted statutes requiring that doctors provide women seeking abortions with detailed information about fetal development, mandating a 24-hour waiting period before a woman could proceed with an abortion, and specifying that minors obtain parental consent and that married women notify their spouses before obtaining an abortion. These regulations were challenged as interfering with women's rights to make choices about their own health care. In 1992, only one member of *Roe*'s seven-member majority, Justice Blackmun, remained on the Court to defend that decision. In a ruling that surprised observers, however, three

appointees of Presidents Reagan and Bush joined in writing an opinion that preserved the right of choice originally created by *Roe.*

Justices Sandra Day O'Connor, Anthony Kennedy, and David Souter applied an "undue burden test" that accepts government regulations, as long as they do not pose an undue burden on women's choices about abortion during the first six months of pregnancy. This test, developed by Justice O'Connor in several of her opinions in abortion cases, became influential in determining how the Court examined abortion issues. However, Justices O'Connor, Kennedy, and Souter believed that a decision to overturn *Roe* after nearly 20 years would cause "profound and unnecessary damage to the Court's legitimacy, and to the Nation's commitment to the rule of law" by making it appear as if the right of choice disappeared merely because the Court's composition changed.

Justice Blackmun, an appointee of President Nixon, and Justice John Paul Stevens, an appointee of President Ford, also voted to keep the *Roe* precedent. Thus, by a 5–4 vote, the Court approved most of Pennsylvania's regulations but preserved the essence of the right of choice by declining to overturn *Roe.* The majority supporting the preservation of *Roe* later increased to six justices when President Bill Clinton appointed Ruth Bader Ginsburg upon the retirement of Justice Byron White in 1993. Many observers believe that the *Roe* supporters on the Court were subsequently reduced from six to five, however, when Justice Samuel Alito replaced Justice O'Connor in 2006. It is likely that any justices appointed by President Barack Obama will help to preserve *Roe* v. *Wade,* but it remains to be seen how his first appointees, Justices Sonia Sotomayor and Elena Kagan, appointed in 2009 and 2010, respectively, will decide abortion cases.

Both opponents and supporters of abortion rights use the grassroots mobilization, elections, and lobbying decision makers pathways as well as the court pathway. —*If you chose to become involved in actions to influence the abortion issue, which pathway would you recommend for your allies to use? Why?*

Although some people hope—or fear—that legal abortion will disappear if *Roe* is eliminated, in reality the Court's decision merely tells states what laws they *cannot* create. Although overturning *Roe* would permit states to prohibit or severely restrict abortion, it is likely that abortion would remain legal in certain states, even if it were no longer recognized by the Supreme Court as a constitutional right. Therefore, debates and political battles about abortion may ultimately have direct effects on only two groups of women: those who are too poor or too young to travel to a state where abortion is legal and available (see Figure 4.2).[12]

Private Sexual Conduct

Griswold v. *Connecticut* (1965), the case that produced the Supreme Court's first explicit recognition of a constitutional right to privacy, concerned married couples' personal lives. The public did not generally object to recognizing a right to privacy in this context. By contrast, the private sexual conduct of non-married adults can produce controversy.

In *Bowers* v. *Hardwick* (1986), a young gay man in Georgia was charged with violating the state's sodomy law—which mandated sentences of up to 20 years in prison for sexual conduct other than intercourse between a man and a woman—when a police officer entered his home and found him in a bedroom having sex with another man. The Supreme Court was deeply divided on the question of whether the right to privacy should protect the private sexual behavior of gays and lesbians. The five-member majority of the Court treated the case as if it only concerned, in Justice Byron White's words, "whether the Federal Constitution confers a fundamental right upon homosexuals to engage in sodomy." To that question, the majority answered no. By contrast, the four dissenters, who argued that the law was unconstitutional, viewed the Georgia law as making a general attack on privacy. According to Justice Harry Blackmun's dissenting opinion:

> This case is about "the most comprehensive of rights and the right most valued by civilized men," namely "the right to be let alone." The statute at issue denies individuals the right to decide for themselves whether to engage in particular forms of private, consensual sexual activity.

Seventeen years later, the Supreme Court revisited the issue in **Lawrence v. Texas (2003),** a case challenging the constitutionality of a Texas statute that criminalized sexual conduct between persons of the same gender. This time, however, the majority on the Supreme Court overruled *Bowers* v. *Hardwick* and declared that the right to privacy protects the private, noncommercial sexual conduct of adults, including

FIGURE 4.2 ▪ Data on Abortion

Since the Supreme Court's decision in *Roe* v. *Wade*, changes have occurred with respect to who gets abortions. Most notably, in the aftermath of *Roe*, nearly 28 percent of women who obtained abortions were married. The percentage of married women obtaining abortions declined over time to less than 14 percent in 2008. Similarly, teenagers accounted for nearly one-third of those obtaining abortions in 1974. By 2008, that percentage had been reduced to just under 17 percent. Over time, the percentage of women aged 25 to 34 who obtain abortions has increased. —*What factors may have affected these trends in abortion?*

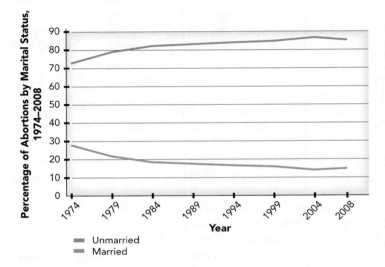

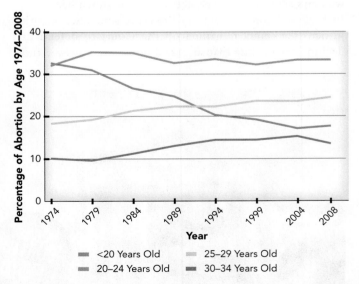

SOURCES: Data from Guttmacher Institute. http://www.guttmacher.org/pubs/2008/09/18/Report_Trends_Women_Obtaining_Abortions.pdf, pp. 10, 11. R.K. Jones, L.B. Finer, and S. Singh. *Characteristics of U.S. Abortion Patients, 2008.* Guttmacher Institute, May 2010, p.6.

gays and lesbians. In the words of Justice Anthony Kennedy's majority opinion:

> The petitioners are entitled to respect for their private lives. The State cannot demean their existence or control their destiny by making their private sexual conduct a crime. Their right to liberty under the Due Process Clause gives them the full right to engage in their conduct without intervention by the government.

Do you believe that the Supreme Court has gone too far in identifying and defining the right to privacy? Some people are concerned that judges will do whatever they want to do in creating new rights and affecting public policy. Because of new technology as well as increased governmental surveillance efforts related to computer crime, Internet child pornography, and antiterrorism efforts, additional privacy issues are likely to emerge concerning government intrusion into e-mail, computer systems, and wireless communications. It remains to be seen whether or how the Court will define privacy protections in these contexts.

Privacy

4.6 **Explain why the right to privacy is controversial.**

PRACTICE QUIZ: UNDERSTAND AND APPLY

1. One source of controversy about the Supreme Court's decisions concerning the right of privacy is
   a. the First Amendment's words that say "privacy is a right for adults, but not for children."
   b. the First Amendment's words that say "no law shall abridge the right to privacy."
   c. the Fourth Amendment's words that say "a right to privacy in one's secure home."
   d. the lack of any mention of the word "privacy" in the Constitution.

2. The Supreme Court majority opinion in *Roe* v. *Wade* (1973)
   a. applied the right to privacy only to federal laws restricting abortion.
   b. based a right of choice on the right to "equal protection" for women who want to make their own health care decisions.
   c. declared that states could decide for themselves whether to make abortion legal.
   d. used the right to privacy to establish women's opportunity to make choices about abortion.

3. The Supreme Court case *Griswold* v. *Connecticut* (1965)
   a. concerned the personal lives of a gay couple.
   b. generated the Court's first explicit recognition of a right to privacy.
   c. was based solely on the First Amendment.
   d. concerned the issue of abortion.

4. If the police find two adult gay men together in a bedroom in a private home
   a. the Fourth Amendment will bar any arrests unless the officer personally observes sexual activity.
   b. the right to privacy will protect any consensual, noncommercial sexual conduct.
   c. officers are obligated to uphold "community standards" for morality by making arrests for any behavior they observe that is "obscene."
   d. officers can take no actions unless they observe behavior that violates federal laws that regulate same-sex relationships.

ANALYZE

1. What would be the consequences for both politics and public policy if the Supreme Court overturned *Roe* v. *Wade*?

2. How do changes in the Supreme Court's membership affect the Court's decisions?

IDENTIFY THE CONCEPT THAT DOESN'T BELONG

a. Abortion
b. Contraception
c. Gays and lesbians
d. Self-incrimination
e. Undue burden test

Conclusion

Civil liberties are an especially important part of the governing system in the United States. They reflect the high value that the U.S. Constitution accords to personal liberty, individualism, and limited government. The Bill of Rights, as well as other provisions in the Constitution and in the state constitutions, describes legal protections for individuals and at the same time imposes limitations on what government can do to individuals. The specific civil liberties enjoyed by individuals are defined and changed through decisions by judges who interpret constitutional provisions.

As you saw with respect to privacy and the death penalty, judges may use flexible approaches to interpretation that enable them to recognize new rights and expand or shrink existing rights. The vagueness of words such as *due process of law* and *cruel and unusual punishment* enabled the U.S. Supreme Court to use its power of interpretation to change the specific civil liberties protections enjoyed by Americans. Debates about the meaning of such constitutional phrases continue to this day, as we saw in the chapter opening example. Lawyers were unsuccessful in having *due process* interpreted to include a right to have DNA tests conducted on biological evidence. Similarly, the words *cruel and unusual punishments* in the Eighth Amendment are vague; judges must give them specific meaning.

Table 4.2 shows how the Supreme Court continues to face new issues concerning the interpretation of the Bill of Rights. The ever-changing world in which we live continually produces conflicts between individuals and government that lead to intense battles in the court pathway. Judges are therefore likely to remain highly influential in determining aspects of public policy related to issues of civil liberties.

Because many civil liberties issues, such as school prayer, abortion, pornography, and the rights of gays and lesbians, are extremely controversial, individuals and groups who are disappointed by judges' decisions often raise questions about the extent of proper judicial authority and whether judges' decisions have "gone too far." These controversies have also made the process of nominating and confirming appointments to federal court positions, especially to the Supreme Court, a matter of high-stakes politics. Americans' lack of agreement about the meaning of the Bill of Rights guarantees that these debates will continue and that presidents will use their appointment powers to try to influence civil liberties cases through the selection of federal judges who share their values and beliefs.

TABLE 4.2	Recent Controversies: Civil Liberties Issues Decided by the Supreme Court in 2010		
AMENDMENT	**RIGHT**	**CASE**	**ISSUES DECIDED BY THE U.S. SUPREME COURT**
First Amendment	Speech	*United States* v. *Stevens*	Does it violate the First Amendment when the federal government prosecutes a man for selling videos of violent dog fights, if the man was not involved in organizing or conducting the dogfights? Yes
First Amendment	Religion–Establishment	*Salazar* v. *Buono*	Does it violate the First Amendment when the federal government transfers an acre of land to the Veterans of Foreign Wars organization, so that a cross erected by the VFW on that federal land in 1934 can remain undisturbed? No
Second Amendment	Bear Arms	*McDonald* v. *Chicago*	Does it violate the Second Amendment for Chicago to have an ordinance that bans private ownership of handguns? Yes
Fifth Amendment	Self-Incrimination	*Florida* v. *Powell*	Does it violate the Fifth Amendment if the police fail to inform an arrested suspect that he has the right to have an attorney present during questioning, even if the police told the suspect that he had the right to talk to an attorney and that one could be appointed to represent him? No
Sixth Amendment	Jury Trial	*Berghuis* v. *Smith*	Did it violate the Sixth Amendment when an African American on trial for murder has an all-white jury because many African American jurors were excused for reasons of childcare, transportation, and work issues, or diverted to trials of minor charges in a city court? No
Eighth Amendment	Cruel and Unusual Punishments	*Sullivan* v. *Florida*	Does it violate the Eighth Amendment to sentence teenagers younger than age 18 to "life without parole" for crimes that did not result in the deaths of any victims? Yes

KEY CONCEPT MAP   How do judicial interpretations of the Constitution limit the power of government?

Praying in Schools

First Amendment—Establishment Clause ?

Engel v. Vitale (1962)
New York developed a nondemoninational prayer for public schoolteachers to use at the start of the school day. Parents sued to challenge the prayer as a violation of the Establishment Clause concept of "separation of church and state." The Supreme Court ruled that public school officials cannot lead or sponsor prayers in the classroom. Such actions involve government in improperly endorsing or advancing religious beliefs.

Why did the Court cite the amendment in deciding this case?

The First Amendment includes a prohibition on the "establishment of religion," which the Supreme Court interprets to limit government involvement in and endorsement of religion.

How did the judicial interpretation of the amendment limit the power of government?...

When the Supreme Court finds an activity in violation of the Establishment Clause, it typically invalidates the law or policy. Thus, many Supreme Court decisions effectively limit what legislative bodies can do in creating laws and policies related to religion.

What does the Court's decision in this case mean for you when it comes to this issue?

Officials cannot require, lead, or endorse prayers in public schools. However, the Supreme Court is less concerned about the risk that such prayers at public colleges and universities will make adult students feel pressured to participate involuntarily in religion.

Critical Thinking Question

Different Supreme Court justices interpret the First Amendment's Establishment Clause in different ways. What if a different set of justices had been serving on the Supreme Court when these issues reached the Court?

Miranda Warnings

Fifth Amendment—Self-Incrimination ?

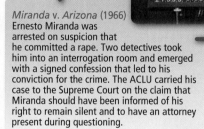

Miranda v. Arizona (1966)
Ernesto Miranda was arrested on suspicion that he committed a rape. Two detectives took him into an interrogation room and emerged with a signed confession that led to his conviction for the crime. The ACLU carried his case to the Supreme Court on the claim that Miranda should have been informed of his right to remain silent and to have an attorney present during questioning.

Why did the Court cite the amendment in deciding this case?

The Fifth Amendment says that "No person… shall be compelled in any criminal case to be a witness against himself." The Supreme Court concluded that police must inform suspects of their rights before questioning them in custody.

How did the judicial interpretation of the amendment limit the power of government?...

The decision requires police to inform suspects of the right to have an attorney present during questioning and the right to remain silent. The decision prevents the police from conducting prolonged, private interrogations of suspects who might wish to have an attorney present or who would remain silent, if they were aware that they possessed that right.

What does the Court's decision in this case mean for you when it comes to this issue?

Arrested suspects receive Miranda warnings before questioning. This means that if you are ever arrested, you should not be forced to answer questions without a defense attorney present.

Critical Thinking Question

Police have adapted their tactics to comply with the formal requirements of Miranda, while still using techniques to obtain confessions. Do Miranda warnings prevent people from feeling pressured to reveal incriminating information about themselves?

In fulfilling its responsibilities for interpreting the Bill of Rights, the Supreme Court often arouses controversy. The Court's decisions may prevent elected officials from carrying out their preferred laws and policies, such as conducting prayers in public schools. These decisions may also provide legal protections for unpopular individuals, including criminal defendants and members of unfamiliar religious minority groups. There are always risks that large segments of the public may believe that the Supreme Court's interpretations grant either too many or too few rights for Americans.—*Are the Supreme Court's interpretations of the Bill of Rights consistent with the purpose of that document? In your view, are there particular rights that have been defined either too broadly or too narrowly?*

Review of Key Objectives

First Amendment Rights: Freedom of Religion

 4.1 Distinguish between the two dimensions of freedom of religion in the First Amendment.

(pages 94–97)

Civil liberties, drawn from the Bill of Rights and judicial decisions, provide legal protections for individuals and limit the authority of government. Freedom of religion in the First Amendment consists of two components: the establishment clause and the free exercise clause. Judicial decisions concerning the establishment clause have forbidden sponsored prayers in public schools and other activities that are judged to provide excessive government support for or entanglement with religion. Congress has sought to protect the free exercise of religion by requiring courts to apply a strict scrutiny or compelling government interest test to such cases. This test forces the government to show a compelling reason for laws and policies that clash with the free exercise of religion.

KEY TERMS

Civil Liberties 94
Due Process Clause 94
Establishment Clause 94
Free Exercise Clause 94
Separationist 94
Accommodationist 94
Lemon **Test** 95
Strict Scrutiny 96

CRITICAL THINKING QUESTIONS

1. How should the Supreme Court decide whether the separationist perspective or the accommodationist perspective is most appropriate for interpreting the First Amendment provision on establishment of religion?
2. Should the government ever be able to interfere with an American's free exercise of religion? If so, when and why?

INTERNET RESOURCES

Examine Web sites of organizations focused on issues of religious liberty: http://www.becketfund.org (Becket Fund for Religious Liberty); http://www.rluipa.com (issues focused on the Religious Land Use and Institutionalized Persons Act), and http://www.aclu.org (American Civil Liberties Union).

ADDITIONAL READING

Levy, Leonard W. *The Establishment Clause: Religion and the First Amendment.* Chapel Hill: University of North Carolina Press, 1994.

Swanson, Wayne R. *The Christ Child Goes to Court.* Philadelphia: Temple University Press, 1992.

First Amendment Rights: Freedom of Speech

4.2 Specify the limits on free speech in the United States.

(pages 98–99)

The actual protections for freedom of speech are less absolute than implied by the words of the First Amendment, because the Supreme Court has accepted time, place, and manner restrictions as well as other limitations that serve society's interests regarding safety, order, and the protection of national security, intellectual property, and personal reputations.

KEY TERMS

Clear and Present Danger Test 98
Political Speech 98
Commercial Speech 98
Symbolic Speech 98
Reasonable Time, Place, and Manner Restrictions 99

CRITICAL THINKING QUESTIONS

1. Because the First Amendment's words seem to prevent any government interference with free speech ("Congress shall make no law . . . abridging the freedom of speech"), is it proper for the Supreme Court to identify situations in which the government can limit speech?
2. Should symbolic actions be protected as "free speech" under the First Amendment?

INTERNET RESOURCES

Many contemporary free speech issues are discussed at the Web site of the First Amendment Center: http://www.firstamendmentcenter.org/

ADDITIONAL READING

Bollinger, Lee, and Geoffrey Stone (eds.). *Eternally Vigilant: Free Speech in the Modern Era.* Chicago: University of Chicago Press, 2003.

Lewis, Anthony. *Freedom for the Thought that We Hate: A Biography of the First Amendment.* New York: Basic Books, 2008.

First Amendment Rights: Freedom of the Press and Obscenity

 4.3 Assess the test for justifying governmental limitations on written words and images.

(pages 100–103)

Courts generally rule against government efforts to impose prior restraints on the press. If individuals' reputations are harmed by inaccurate news articles or other untrue communications, they can seek compensation afterward by suing for defamation based on false written statements (libel) or false spoken statements (slander). However, freedom of the press claims by reporters can clash with other priorities, such as the government's need to gather evidence about witnesses and suspects in criminal cases. The government can also regulate commercial speech in order to protect the public from false or deceptive advertising. The First Amendment does not protect obscenity, but the Supreme Court has struggled to develop a workable definition of what materials are "obscene." As a result, governmental prosecution of obscene material focuses primarily on child pornography, a subject for which a broader consensus about the harm from published materials exists.

KEY TERMS

Prior Restraint 100	**Reporter's Privilege** 101
Defamation 101	**Press Shield Laws** 101
New York Times Company v. United States **(1971)** 101	*Miller* **v.** *California* **(1973)** 102

CRITICAL THINKING QUESTIONS

1. Are press shield laws essential to democracy, or do they harm our ability to investigate criminal cases?
2. How would you define "obscenity" in deciding what kinds of expressions and images could be prohibited by the government?

INTERNET RESOURCES

Examine the Federal Communications Commission's presentation on its duty to prevent obscene and indecent materials over the regulated airwaves on television and radio: http://www.fcc.gov/eb/oip/Welcome.html

ADDITIONAL READING

Epps, Garrett (ed.). *Freedom of the Press.* New York: Prometheus Books, 2008.

Friendly, Fred W. *Minnesota Rag: Corruption, Yellow Journalism, and the Case that Saved Freedom of the Press.* Minneapolis: University of Minnesota Press, 2003.

Civil Liberties and Criminal Justice

4.4 Specify the protections afforded to criminal suspects in the Bill of Rights.

(pages 104–105)

The Fourth Amendment protection against unreasonable searches and seizures requires significant interpretation by courts, especially because so many different situations arise in which the government examines people and their property for evidence of crimes. The Supreme Court has approved a list of situations in which no warrant is required for searches because those searches are regarded as "reasonable." Individuals subjected to unreasonable searches may gain protection from prosecution through the exclusionary rule, but the Supreme Court has created exceptions to this rule that permit the use of improperly obtained evidence in some situations. The Supreme Court's requirement of *Miranda* warnings prior to the questioning of suspects in custody serves as a central component of the Fifth Amendment privilege against compelled self-incrimination.

KEY TERMS

Exclusionary Rule 104
Mapp **v.** *Ohio* **(1961)** 104
Warrant 104
Double Jeopardy 104
Compelled Self-Incrimination 105
Miranda **v.** *Arizona* **(1966)** 105

CRITICAL THINKING QUESTIONS

1. Does the exclusionary rule advance the overall interests of justice even though evidence of a criminal's guilt may be tossed out due to a police officer's error?
2. Why should criminal suspects be protected against incriminating themselves during questioning?

INTERNET RESOURCES

Examine the U.S. Supreme Court's decisions on the exclusionary rule and *Miranda* warnings at http://supreme.justia.com

ADDITIONAL READING

Smith, Christopher E. *Constitutional Rights: Myths and Realities.* Belmont, CA: Thomson-Wadsworth, 2004.

White, Welsh S. *Miranda's Waning Protections.* Ann Arbor: University of Michigan Press, 2003.

Trial Rights and Capital Punishment

4.5 Evaluate the legal protections that ensure only guilty people receive criminal punishment.

(pages 106–107)

The Sixth Amendment contains trial rights, including the right to confrontation, the right to compulsory process, and the right to trial by jury. Without these rights, there would be greater risks of innocent people being convicted of crimes. The right to trial by jury applies only for "serious" charges, and the right to counsel applies only for specific stages of the criminal process.

Capital punishment is a controversial issue that has divided the Supreme Court's justices over questions about whether it is "cruel and unusual" and therefore in violation of the Eighth Amendment. The Supreme Court's decisions have created rules and restrictions that have sought to make death penalty trials produce careful decisions. The Supreme Court's rulings have also limited the categories of people eligible for the death penalty.

KEY TERMS

Speedy and Public Trial 106
Trial by Jury 106
Bench Trials 106
Plea Bargaining 106
Capital Punishment 106

CRITICAL THINKING QUESTIONS

1. Which Sixth Amendment rights are most important for ensuring that criminal defendants receive a fair trial? Why?
2. How would you determine whether capital punishment in general or certain aspects of capital punishment in particular violate the Eighth Amendment prohibition on "cruel and unusual punishments"?

INTERNET RESOURCES

Compare the competing perspectives on capital punishment presented by the Criminal Justice Legal Foundation at http://www.cjlf.org and the Death Penalty Information Center at http://www.deathpenaltyinfo.org

ADDITIONAL READING

Costanzo, Mark. *Just Revenge: Costs and Consequences of the Death Penalty.* New York: St. Martin's Press, 1997.

Smith, Christopher E., Madhavi McCall, and Cynthia Perez McCluskey. *Law and Criminal Justice: Emerging Issues in the Twenty-First Century.* New York: Peter Lang, 2005.

Privacy

4.6 Explain why the right to privacy is controversial.

(pages 110–113)

The Supreme Court used its interpretive powers to identify and develop a right to privacy that has been applied to give individuals rights related to choices about abortion, contraceptives, and private, noncommercial sexual conduct by adults. These are issues about which many Americans vigorously disagree. The identification and expansion of the right to privacy has been especially controversial because the word *privacy* does not appear in the Constitution; the right was produced through interpretive decisions by the Supreme Court.

KEY TERMS

Right to Privacy 110
Roe v. Wade **(1973)** 110
Lawrence v. Texas **(2003)** 112

CRITICAL THINKING QUESTIONS

1. What, if anything, prevents the Supreme Court's justices from defining the right to privacy as broadly or as narrowly as they personally want it to be?
2. Should the government be able to regulate or ban any aspect of the noncommercial (i.e., no money changes hands) sexual behavior of consenting adults in the privacy of their own homes? Why or why not?

INTERNET RESOURCES

Compare the competing perspectives on abortion presented by the National Right to Life Committee at http://www.nrlc.org and NARAL Pro-Choice America at http://www.prochoiceamerica.org

ADDITIONAL READING

Craig, Barbara Hinkson, and David M. O'Brien. *Abortion and American Politics.* Chatham, NJ: Chatham House, 1993.

Hull, N.E.H., and Peter Charles Hoffer. *Roe v. Wade: The Abortion Rights Controversy in American History.* Lawrence: University Press of Kansas, 2001.

Chapter Review   Test Your Knowledge

1. Civil liberties are
   a. privileges that can be suspended by the government.
   b. earned rewards given to citizens based on their good behavior.
   c. freedoms and legal protections that the government cannot take away.
   d. different than the criminal liberties described in the Declaration of Independence.

2. When court decisions define the extent of an individual's civil liberties, those decisions
   a. cannot limit the authority of government officials.
   b. can limit the authority of government officials.
   c. always meet with public approval, because we all share the same ideals.
   d. must be ratified by Congress.

3. If you made a speech advocating a total change in our form of government in today's society,
   a. you could never be prosecuted under any circumstances.
   b. you could not be prosecuted, because the Sixth Amendment's right to confrontation permits you to confront the government.
   c. you could be prosecuted for treason.
   d. you could only be prosecuted if your words created the danger of immediate incitement of imminent lawless action.

4. The Eighth Amendment's prohibition against "cruel and unusual punishments"
   a. has had no impact on imposition of the death penalty.
   b. has helped opponents of the death penalty to limit the forms and applications of capital punishment.
   c. has offered a clear, unchanging standard for death penalty sentences.
   d. only applies to death by torture.

5. The Supreme Court's identification of obscenity that falls outside the protection of the First Amendment relies on the interpretation of the concept of
   a. "religious morality"
   b. "extreme pornography"
   c. "equal expression process"
   d. "community standards"

6. Supreme Court rulings against the government's exercise of prior restraint indicate that
   a. the government generally cannot prevent the expression of nonobscene ideas in publications.
   b. authors and publishers cannot be sued for anything they print.
   c. citizens have free speech, but newspaper reporters are limited in what they can write.
   d. if you let government officials read news articles in advance to check for errors, then you can print them without fear of penalty.

7. The "clear and present danger" test was refined in the 1960s to require that
   a. speech can be limited only when it involves hate speech.
   b. speech can be limited if it produces a dangerous immediate threat.

   c. speech can be limited only if there is symbolic speech involving fire.
   d. police officers must actually observe violence before they can intervene to stop a speech.

8. According to strict separationists, the establishment clause prohibits financial support or endorsement of any religion by government. This means that the government cannot give any aid to parochial schools or permit religious displays on public property.
   a. true   b. false

9. The accommodationist approach to the establishment clause
   a. has the firm support of all Supreme Court justices.
   b. is always supported by the application of the *Lemon* test.
   c. would permit some forms of government support for parochial education.
   d. a, b, and c.

10. The Supreme Court avoids ever interpreting the due process clause because its wording is too vague to be used in defining rights and liberties.
    a. true   b. false

11. The Supreme Court's development of the exclusionary rule as part of the law governing the Fourth Amendment
    a. means that prosecutors cannot exclude evidence from a trial, even if such evidence undermines their case.
    b. means that evidence improperly obtained by law enforcement officials may be used to prosecute an alleged criminal.
    c. can never be used to prevent the imposition of deserved punishment on someone who committed a crime.
    d. can frustrate police and prosecutors, because it may interfere with their preparation of evidence against a defendant.

12. Currently, law enforcement officials
    a. have less flexibility in conducting searches and questioning suspects than they did in the 1970s.
    b. have more flexibility in conducting searches and questioning suspects than they did in the 1970s.
    c. have immunity from the exclusionary rule.
    d. need warrants only for the most politically sensitive searches and seizures.

13. *Miranda* rights
    a. must be administered to suspects who appear voluntarily for questioning.
    b. mean that most guilty criminals go free because the police cannot obtain confessions.
    c. are intended to prevent suspects from feeling compelled to say anything that may incriminate them in court.
    d. are likely to be declared unconstitutional as a violation of due process.

14. Most criminal prosecutions that produce convictions conclude through plea bargaining rather than trials.
    a. true
    b. false

15. With respect to indigent criminal defendants, the Supreme Court
    a. eliminated the Sixth Amendment right to compulsory process.
    b. demonstrated that the Supreme Court shows favoritism to prosecutors.
    c. guaranteed that they would receive enough training to enable them to represent themselves.
    d. established an entitlement to free legal representation whenever they face the possibility of imprisonment.

16. The death penalty (reinstated in 1976) still strikes some observers as unconstitutional, because
    a. death penalty cases involve bifurcated proceedings.
    b. there are debates about whether the legal system can impose the penalty accurately and fairly.
    c. mitigating circumstances, such as the age or mental capacity of the accused, are never taken into consideration by the courts.
    d. the Constitution specifies executions must be carried out by hanging.

17. More than 130 death row inmates have been exonerated as a result of DNA testing or other new sources of evidence.
    a. true
    b. false

18. Controversial Supreme Court decisions such as *Roe* v. *Wade* (1973) reflect a judicial philosophy that
    a. rigidly follows the exact language of the Constitution and ignores modern social problems.
    b. carries out the original intent of the Constitution as written in the eighteenth century.
    c. exercises a flexible approach to constitutional interpretation and adjusts the definition of rights as society changes.
    d. rejects the concept of privacy that has long guided the Supreme Court's decisions.

19. The nomination and confirmation of executive appointments to the federal courts has become highly politicized, because
    a. people enjoy being able to cast their votes to elect federal judges.
    b. political parties do not follow their own rules.
    c. federal judges now control all national policies affecting international relations and homeland security.
    d. federal judges decide controversial issues that deeply divide American society.

20. If the Supreme Court overturns its decision in *Roe* v. *Wade* (1973),
    a. all legal abortions in the United States will cease.
    b. interest groups will no longer be permitted to use the court pathway.
    c. some states will likely still maintain opportunities for women to make choices about abortion.
    d. anyone who travels to Canada to obtain an abortion will be imprisoned upon returning to the United States.

PEARSON
mypoliscilab Exercises

Apply what you learned in this chapter on **MyPoliSciLab.**

Read on mypoliscilab.com

   eText: Chapter 4

✔ **Study** and **Review** on mypoliscilab.com

   Pre-Test
   Post-Test
   Chapter Exam
   Flashcards

Watch on mypoliscilab.com

   Video: Funeral Protesters Push for Limit of Free Speech
   Video: D.C.'s Right to Bear Arms
   Video: Judges and Politics
   Video: Judicial Review
   Video: Selecting Federal Judges

Explore on mypoliscilab.com

   Simulation: You Are a Police Officer
   Simulation: You Are a Supreme Court Justice Deciding a Free Speech Case
   Simulation: Balancing Liberty and Security in a Time of War
   Timeline: Civil Liberties and National Security

Civil Rights

KEY OBJECTIVES

After completing this chapter, you should be prepared to:

5.1 Describe the idea of equality that underlies the governing system of the United States.

5.2 Trace the historical development of civil rights in the United States.

5.3 Analyze how litigation strategies contributed to the dismantling of official racial segregation.

5.4 Differentiate between the various tests used by the Supreme Court when deciding discrimination claims under the equal protection clause.

5.5 Identify the events and factors that influenced the development of the grassroots civil rights movement.

5.6 Compare and contrast the civil rights struggles of women, Latinos, and African Americans.

5.7 Evaluate the continuing debates, lawsuits, and protests over civil rights in the twenty-first century.

"Free the Jena Six! Free the Jena Six!" Thousands of people chanted as they marched through the streets of Jena, Louisiana, carrying signs about justice and racial equality. Among those joining the march in September 2007 were hundreds of college students who arrived on buses from Howard University and other colleges. Several leaders speculated that the participation of impassioned young people could indicate the dawn of a new era of civil rights activism.

> **How far has the United States advanced toward its ideal of equality?**

The marchers were angry that African American high school students had been charged with attempted murder after beating a white student whose injuries were reportedly not severe enough to prevent him from attending a school event later on the day of the incident. The beating stemmed from racial tensions when white students hung nooses from a tree after African American students sat outside at a spot that was normally a gathering place for whites. One of these white students claimed to be unaware of the powerful emotional symbolism of a noose, the tool used for decades to murder and terrorize African Americans. The white students received only brief suspensions from school, a punishment that many African Americans saw as too light. By contrast, the attempted murder charges for the African American students seemed much too severe and were perceived as a sign that racial discrimination still infected the justice system. In the face of international attention and widespread criticism in the United States, local officials entered into plea negotiations with the students that led to convictions for simple battery. Most of them were punished with a small fine and brief period of probation, but one student received a jail sentence.

The United States has a long history of discrimination based not just on race but also on national origin, gender, sexual orientation, and other characteristics. This history clashes with the nation's ideals about equality. Various pathways of policy change—including litigation in courts, mass protests on the streets, and lobbying in legislatures—have been used by people seeking their civil rights—namely, equal political participation, such as the right to vote, and equal opportunities to seek education and employment. In this chapter, we examine the American ideal of equality and political action undertaken to advance the fulfillment of this ideal.

Resource Center
• Glossary
• Vocabulary Example
• Connect the Link

■ **Civil Rights:** Public policies and legal protections concerning equal status and treatment in American society to advance the goals of equal opportunity, fair and open political participation, and equal treatment under the law without regard to race, gender, disability status, and other demographic characteristics.

EXAMPLE: *Lawsuits and protest marches concerning civil rights typically challenge unequal treatment directed at members of specific racial, gender, ethnic, or other groups, such as lawsuits and protests in the 1950s and 1960s against southern states' efforts to prevent African Americans from voting.*

The Ideal of Equality

5.1 Describe the idea of equality that underlies the governing system of the United States.

(pages 124–125)

The concept of **civil rights**■ concerns legal protections for equality and participation in the country's governing processes. As we've discussed in earlier chapters, the founders of the United States wanted to enjoy **political equality,** which would allow them to express their views, own property, and participate in what they called a "republican" governing system. The most famous expression of the founders' emphasis on equality is in the words of the Declaration of Independence: "All men are created equal." The founders believed that political equality was an essential element of the natural world and a fundamental principle of human life, and they considered that principle to be violated when a social system or government granted extra status and power to favored individuals.

The Declaration of Independence focused on equality for *men.* The nation's founders simply took it for granted that women need not participate as important decision makers in political affairs. In addition, many of the founders of the United States were slave owners, and even some who did not own slaves viewed African Americans and Native Americans as less-than-equal beings.

Over the course of American history, several factors have contributed to widespread acceptance of a redefinition of political equality that extends beyond white males. These factors include grassroots mobilization, legislative action, legal cases, and even the bloody Civil War of the 1860s. Political activity and social changes over many decades produced new—and now widely accepted—ideas about equality that embrace women and members of racial and other minority groups (see Table 5.1).

The founders' ideal of equality focused on political participation and civil liberties. By contrast, it is possible to have a governing system that emphasizes equal economic status or **equality of condition**■. Some governing systems use policy decisions rather than constitutional rights as the means to ensure that everyone has access to important goods and services, such as education, medical care, housing, and at least a modest income.

The American system seeks to advance **equality of opportunity**■ or equal opportunities for participation in the economic system and in public life. The American political ideology and our free-enterprise economic system emphasize individual achievement and the acquisition of wealth through hard work. People are expected to be self-reliant and to earn enough money to buy their own goods and services.

TABLE 5.1 | Rights, Pathways, and Results in Advancing Equality of Opportunity

Various groups used specific pathways in order to seek the promise of equality outlined in the Declaration of Independence and the equal protection clause of the Fourteenth Amendment. Multiple pathways were employed, and each group used different strategies.

GROUP	MINORITY RIGHT	PATHWAY	OUTCOME
African Americans	Basic civil rights, prohibit discrimination, voting rights	**Equal access to education:** court pathway **Prohibit discrimination:** grassroots mobilization, elections, and court pathways **Voting rights:** grassroots mobilization pathway	*Brown v. Board of Education* (1954) [school desegregation]; Civil Rights Act of 1964 [no discrimination in employment and public accommodations]; Voting Rights Act of 1965
Women	Voting rights, prohibit discrimination	**Voting rights:** grassroots mobilization and elections pathways **Prohibit discrimination:** elections, court, and cultural change pathways	Nineteenth Amendment (1920) [women's right to vote]; Equal Pay Act of 1963; *Reed v. Reed* (1971) [no discrimination in inheritance laws]
Japanese Americans	Compensation for deprivation of rights during World War II	**Compensation for rights' deprivation:** elections pathways	American Japanese Claims Act of 1948; Civil Liberties Act of 1988
Disabled	Prohibit discrimination	**Prohibit discrimination:** elections and grassroots mobilization pathways	Section 504 of the Rehabilitation Act of 1973 [no discrimination in federally funded programs]; Americans with Disabilities Act of 1990 [no discrimination in employment and public accommodations]

(Continued)

■ **Equality of Condition:** A conception of equality that values equal economic status as well as equal access to housing, health care, education, and government services.

EXAMPLE: *Governments that provide health care and government-financed opportunities to attend universities for all citizens are advancing equality of condition.*

■ **Equality of Opportunity:** A conception of equality that seeks to provide all citizens with opportunities for participation in the economic system and public life but accepts unequal results.

EXAMPLE: *In the United States, there are laws against employment discrimination, but health care is not provided by the government to all citizens.*

TABLE 5.1	Rights, Pathways, and Results in Advancing Equality of Opportunity (Continued)

GROUP	MINORITY RIGHT	PATHWAY	OUTCOME
Older Workers	Prohibit discrimination in employment	**Prohibit discrimination, employment:** elections pathway	Age Discrimination in Employment Act of 1967 [no discrimination against workers age 40 and over]
Latinos	Basic civil rights, prohibit discrimination	**Basic civil rights and prohibit discrimination:** Grassroots mobilization and elections pathways	Agricultural Labor Relations Act of 1975 (California state law) [right of farm workers to unionize]; Voting Rights Act of 1975 [no discrimination against language minority groups]
Gays and Lesbians	Basic civil rights, prohibit discrimination	**Basic civil rights and prohibit discrimination:** court and elections pathways	State court decisions on civil unions and marriage; *Romer v. Evans* (1996) [protection against legislation targeted at gays and lesbians]; state and local antidiscrimination laws
Native Americans	Basic civil rights, prohibit discrimination, economic development	**Basic civil rights, prohibit discrimination, economic development:** elections pathway	Covered by federal antidiscrimination laws concerning race and ethnicity that were primarily spurred by African Americans; economic development, including gambling enterprises, through state laws

The Ideal of Equality

5.1 Describe the idea of equality that underlies the governing system of the United States.

PRACTICE QUIZ: UNDERSTAND AND APPLY

1. Unlike civil liberties, civil rights concern
   a. the individual freedoms that the Bill of Rights protects.
   b. guaranteed education and health care.
   c. equal status and treatment for different groups of people.
   d. social issues addressed exclusively at the federal level.

2. What form of equality is advanced by the American governing system?
   a. equality of condition
   b. equality of opportunity
   c. economic equality
   d. equal access to resources and services

3. What is the source of the inspirational phrase, "all men are created equal"?
   a. Declaration of Independence
   b. Article I, of the U.S. Constitution
   c. The Bible
   d. Articles of Confederation

ANALYZE

1. What would need to be done to achieve political equality for all citizens?

2. Should the United States seek equality of condition instead of equality of opportunity? How would the country be different if we had that goal?

IDENTIFY THE CONCEPT THAT DOESN'T BELONG

   a. Civil rights
   b. Political equality
   c. Equality of opportunity
   d. Self-incrimination
   e. Antidiscrimination laws

Resource Center
• Glossary
• Vocabulary Example
• Connect the Link

Equal Protection of the Law

5.2 Trace the historical development of civil rights in the United States.

(pages 126–129)

From the 1600s, people who were abducted and brought by force from Africa, and their descendants, worked as slaves in North America. Slavery existed in all 13 American colonies, although in the North, it was less extensive and abolished years earlier— within several decades of the American Revolution—than in the South. State laws mandating the gradual emancipation of slaves in New York and Connecticut, for example, meant that there were still small numbers of slaves in those states as late as 1827. Slavery was a brutal life, with dehumanizing effects for the African Americans subjected to violence and oppressive controls, as well as for the whites who absorbed an ideology of racial superiority and animosity to justify their mistreatment of dark-skinned people.[1]

Race-based slavery and the subsequent decades of racial discrimination laid the foundation for today's racial gaps in wealth, education, housing patterns, and employment opportunities.[2] These enduring disadvantages for Americans of African ancestry have often proved extremely difficult to undo or overcome (see Table 5.2).

The descendants of whites could enjoy the benefits of education, business contacts, and employment opportunities through social networks. Yet the visibility of their skin color made African Americans easy to exclude by whites who wished to use discrimination to preserve their superior status and to monopolize educational, political, and business opportunities. To varying degrees, women, Latinos, and members of other minority groups have faced parallel problems of exclusion and discrimination.

Violence, intimidation, and discrimination were used to force African Americans to work and live under harsh conditions for much of American history. In this photo from the 1860s, a family works in a Georgia cotton field. Slavery ended many decades ago, yet its legacy, including the century of harsh racial discrimination that followed, has contributed to continuing inequality in American society. —*What suggestions would you make for reducing the continuing issue of racial inequality?*

TABLE 5.2 | **Educational Attainment and Income by Race, 2008 (percentage of adults)**

Differences in educational attainment and poverty rates are evident among major ethnic groups in the United States. Over time, some of these disparities have become less stark than in the past. However, these issues that affect millions of Americans have not changed easily or swiftly.

ETHNIC GROUP	HIGH SCHOOL OR HIGHER	FOUR OR MORE YEARS OF COLLEGE	MEDIAN HOUSEHOLD INCOME	LIVING IN POVERTY
White, not Hispanic	86.6%	29.8%	$55,530	8.6%
African American	83%	19.6%	$34,218	24.7%
Hispanic	62.3%	13.3%	$37,913	23.2%

SOURCE: Carmen DeNavas-Walt, Bernadette D. Proctor, and Jessica C. Smith, *Income, Poverty, and Health Insurance Coverage in the United States: 2008* (Washington, DC: U.S. Census Bureau, September 2009), pp. 6, 14. U.S. Census Bureau, *2008 American Community Survey*, http://www.census.gov/population/www/socdemo/educ-attn.html

■ **Jim Crow Laws:** Laws enacted by southern state legislatures after the Civil War that mandated rigid racial segregation.

EXAMPLE: *These laws were so thorough that they not only required separate bank teller windows and elevators but also separate Bibles for swearing in African American witnesses in court.*

One central question continues to be debated by individuals and groups who seek to shape American civil rights law and policy: How much should government do to make up for the nation's history of discrimination and its continuing effects? There are significant disagreements about which governmental actions appropriately advance Americans' limited concept of equality of opportunity.

The Fourteenth Amendment and Reconstruction

Immediately after the Civil War, between 1865 and early 1867, President Andrew Johnson—who had succeeded Abraham Lincoln after his assassination—permitted southern whites to determine how the South would reconstruct itself. Not surprisingly, they created laws that sought to maintain white superiority and power.

MYTH EXPOSED Many Americans believe that African Americans were prohibited from voting or running for political office until after passage of the Voting Rights Act of 1965. Because widespread discrimination and mistreatment of African Americans continued for a century after the abolition of slavery, few people recognize that the creation and enforcement of specific laws led to a brief period of true political participation for African American men in the nineteenth century. After passage of the harsh Black Codes in southern state legislatures, northerners in Congress reacted by passing the Reconstruction Act of 1867, which required the southern states to establish new state governments that granted voting rights to African American men.[3] With the southern states still under Union occupation in the years following the Civil War, military commanders repealed many elements of the Black Codes, and African Americans enjoyed their first opportunities to vote—and to run—for political office. African Americans were elected to high political offices, and 18 served as members of Congress.[4] Events in the late 1870s, however, ended this brief period of political participation by African Americans and eventually led to the reintroduction of severe forms of racial discrimination.

Members of Congress from the North also led the effort to create three constitutional amendments after the Civil War to provide important protections for African Americans. The Thirteenth Amendment (1865) abolished slavery. The Fourteenth Amendment (1868) extended to former slaves the rights of full citizenship, including the equal protection of the laws and the right to due process under the law. The Fifteenth Amendment (1870) sought to guarantee that men would not be denied the right to vote because of their race. Women had not yet gained the right to vote and were deliberately excluded from the purview of the Fifteenth Amendment—over the bitter opposition of women's rights crusaders, who had also been abolitionists.

The Fourteenth Amendment, in particular, has had a great impact on the definition of civil rights for all Americans, because it contains the equal protection clause that victims of discrimination rely on when they go to court to seek judicial protection against unequal treatment by state and local government. The amendment says that "no State shall" deprive people of specific rights. According to one historian, "It was the Fourteenth Amendment, approved by Congress in 1866 and ratified two years later, that for the first time enshrined in the Constitution the ideas of birthright citizenship and equal rights for all Americans."[5]

The Rise and Persistence of Racial Oppression

The disputed outcome of the presidential election of 1876 between Republican Rutherford B. Hayes and Democrat Samuel Tilden affected the fates of African Americans. Election returns from several southern states were in dispute, preventing either Hayes or Tilden from claiming an Electoral College victory. After a special commission (consisting of members of Congress and the Supreme Court) awarded Hayes all the disputed electoral votes, Hayes became president—and promptly withdrew the federal occupation troops from the South. Ending federal occupation permitted southern states greater freedom in developing laws and policies.[6]

The absence of federal troops unleashed the Ku Klux Klan and other violent, secret societies that terrorized African Americans—by beatings, house burnings, and murders—to prevent them from voting or otherwise asserting political and social equality. After 1876, in one southern state after another, self-styled "conservative," white-dominated governments came to power and did everything possible to raise legal barriers to black political participation. These laws could not simply say "black people cannot vote," because such wording would clash with the Fifteenth Amendment's prohibition on racial discrimination in voting. Instead, the new laws did such things as impose literacy tests and "government knowledge" tests. Intimidation and violence were also used by police to prevent African Americans from voting. As a result, between the 1870s and the 1890s, the number of African American men who were registered to vote in southern states dropped from tens of thousands to only a handful.

The white-dominated, conservative state governments also began enacting **Jim Crow laws**■, labeled after a minstrel song that ridiculed African Americans. These laws mandated rigid racial segregation throughout southern society. State and local governments required that African Americans attend separate schools and use separate public facilities.

With the rise of state-enforced racial discrimination, life for many African Americans was little better than slavery. They were generally stuck in slavelike positions as poorly

■ *Plessy* v. *Ferguson* **(1896):** A U.S. Supreme Court decision that endorsed the legality of racial segregation laws by permitting "separate but equal" services and facilities for African Americans, even though the services and facilities were actually inferior.

EXAMPLE: *As a result of the U.S. Supreme Court's decision in* Plessy, *school districts throughout the United States were able to require African Americans and whites to attend separate schools, until the Court forbade such forms of racial segregation in* Brown v. Board of Education *(1954).*

From the introduction of slavery through the first five decades of the twentieth century, African Americans were victimized by horrific violence and enjoyed little protection from the legal system. White mobs lynched African Americans—hanged and often mutilated innocent people—based on rumors of criminal acts or even for violating white people's expectations that they show deference and obedience. —*Which pathway had the greatest impact in moving the United States from these gut-wrenching scenes to where we are today—the court pathway, elections pathway, grassroots mobilization pathway, lobbying decision makers pathway, or cultural change pathway?*

paid agricultural workers and other laborers. They were virtually unprotected by the law. If whites committed crimes against African Americans, including such horrific acts as rape and murder, there was little likelihood that any arrest would be made.

In the 1890s, a light-skinned African American man named Homer Plessy worked with lawyers from the North in planning a legal challenge to the rigid segregation of Jim Crow laws. Plessy illegally sat in a "whites only" railroad car and refused to move when asked. Plessy was arrested for violating the law when he disobeyed the racial separation mandated by Louisiana's state law. When the case reached the Supreme Court (*Plessy* v. *Ferguson,* 1896■), Plessy's lawyers argued that racial segregation laws violated the equal protection clause of the Fourteenth Amendment. In 7–1 decision, however, the Supreme Court decided that there was no violation of the constitutional right to equal protection when states had "separate but equal" facilities and services for people of different races. The Court's decision effectively endorsed racial discrimination by government, because the separate facilities provided for African Americans, including railroad cars, public restrooms, and schools, were always inferior to those provided for whites.

In the southern states, rigid segregation and exclusion of African Americans from political participation continued through the 1960s. Black people continued to be intimidated by violence, including lynching, and remained unprotected by the law. Patterns of segregated housing in the North were usually justified by a presumption that African Americans preferred to live together in the poorest section of each city. Many private decision makers, especially real estate agents and mortgage bankers, steered African Americans into ghettos by refusing to show them houses or to finance their attempts to purchase homes in white neighborhoods. In turn, northern school boards used these discriminatory housing patterns as a way to keep African Americans segregated into the worst, most crowded schools in each district.

Other groups also faced discrimination. For example, immigrants from China began to come to the United States before the Civil War, but they were invariably forced into difficult, low-paying jobs with little opportunity for advancement. People of Japanese heritage were victimized by similar treatment in California and other West Coast states where most of them settled. They were also forced from their homes and placed in isolated internment camps during World War II—unjust treatment that was not imposed on German Americans or Italian Americans, even though their ancestral homelands also fought against the United States. In short, unequal treatment and racial discrimination were pervasive aspects of American life throughout the United States for a full century following the Civil War, in spite of the amendments that prohibited slavery and promised "equal protection of the laws."

Equal Protection of the Law

5.2 Trace the historical development of civil rights in the United States.

PRACTICE QUIZ: UNDERSTAND AND APPLY

1. During Reconstruction (1867–1877), the political experience for African Americans in the South can best be described as
   a. identical to that of colonial-era women.
   b. very promising, with some African Americans getting elected to high offices.
   c. without much hope because of the Ku Klux Klan's control over society.
   d. identical to the political experience of illegal immigrants today.

2. The equal protection clause, so important to the civil rights activism in the court pathway, is included in which amendment to the Constitution?
   a. Thirteenth   c. Fifteenth
   b. Fourteenth   d. First

3. The "separate but equal" phrase in *Plessy* v. *Ferguson* had what kind of impact on the country?
   a. It led courts to make sure that private businesses provided equal services for all people.
   b. It led courts to make sure that equal government facilities and services were available to all people.
   c. It permitted cities and states to create unequal facilities and services for whites and African Americans.
   d. It led to a decision in 1896 that abolished racial segregation.

4. The experience of Japanese-Americans was
   a. not so difficult because they succeeded in school, went to college, and were accepted by the white community.
   b. difficult because they initially came to the United States as slaves in the 1840s.
   c. not so difficult because most arrived in the United States in 1960, having already been trained as doctors, engineers, and educated professionals.
   d. difficult because they lost homes and businesses when they were taken from the West Coast and imprisoned in detention camps during World War II.

ANALYZE

1. Why did racial discrimination continue to exist after the Civil War?

2. What is the importance of the U.S. Supreme Court case *Plessy* v. *Ferguson*?

IDENTIFY THE CONCEPT THAT DOESN'T BELONG

a. Sixteenth Amendment
b. Thirteenth Amendment
c. Fourteenth Amendment
d. Fifteenth Amendment
e. Reconstruction Act of 1867

Resource Center
• Glossary
• Vocabulary Example
• Connect the Link

■ *Brown v. Board of Education of Topeka*
(1954): A U.S. Supreme Court decision that overturned *Plessy* v. *Ferguson* (1896) and declared that government-mandated racial segregation in schools and other facilities and programs violates the equal protection clause of the Fourteenth Amendment.

EXAMPLE: *Chief Justice Earl Warren's majority opinion in the* Brown *case declared that "in the field of public education the doctrine of 'separate but equal' has no place. Separate educational facilities are inherently unequal." Thus the Supreme Court highlighted and rejected the* Plessy *case's assumption that separate facilities for African Americans were equal to those of whites.*

Litigation Strategies

5.3 Analyze how litigation strategies contributed to the dismantling of official racial segregation.

(pages 130–131)

The **National Association for the Advancement of Colored People (NAACP),** a civil rights advocacy group founded by African Americans and their white supporters in 1909, sought to use the court pathway to attack the forms of segregation and discrimination endorsed by the Supreme Court's decision in *Plessy* v. *Ferguson* (1896). The group originated during a period that historians regard as one of the worst for African Americans. In the first three decades of the twentieth century, racial attacks on African Americans, often called "race riots," broke out in dozens of northern and southern cities, sometimes over nothing more than an African American crossing an invisible dividing line at a segregated beach. In these riots, whites typically roamed the streets assaulting and murdering African Americans and destroying homes and businesses. Lynchings of African Americans by white mobs continued in the South as well as the North.[7] Thus, the NAACP began its strategic actions at a moment when African Americans faced their greatest hostility from American society.

Instead of directly attacking the "separate but equal" *Plessy* rule, the NAACP's lawyers initiated a series of cases that helped to demonstrate how, in practice, the rule had plenty of "separate" but virtually no "equal." In the 1930s, the organization represented an African American resident of Maryland who was denied admission to the law school at the University of Maryland despite being an outstanding graduate of prestigious Amherst College. Although Maryland sought to defend against the lawsuit by offering to pay for the man to attend an out-of-state school, the state's supreme court recognized in *Murray* v. *Maryland* (1936) that the alternatives offered by Maryland would not be equal for the purposes of someone who planned to practice law in Maryland. Over the years, the NAACP pursued similar lawsuits and eventually won cases in the U.S. Supreme Court that banned specific discriminatory graduate school admissions practices at universities in Missouri, Texas, and Oklahoma.

Having won a series of court victories in cases demonstrating the lack of equality caused by racial segregation in law and graduate schools, the NAACP took the next step: pursuing a similar claim with respect to the public education provided for school-age children. This step was very risky. It was widely—and correctly—assumed that whites would have an easier time accepting the presence of small numbers of college-educated African Americans in graduate schools than they would the prospect of their children attending grade school and high school with students of a race that many of them feared and despised.

In 1953, the Supreme Court heard the case **Brown v. Board of Education of Topeka**■, concerning racial segregation in the public schools of Topeka, Kansas. NAACP attorney Thurgood Marshall, who in 1967 became the first African American appointed to serve as a Supreme Court justice, presented the case and argued that the *Plessy* rule of "separate but equal" was inherently unequal. The Court's new chief justice, former California governor **Earl Warren**■, felt strongly that racial segregation violated the equal protection clause. Using his leadership skills and effective persuasion, he convinced his reluctant colleagues to join a strong opinion condemning racial segregation and overturning the "separate but equal" doctrine of *Plessy* v. *Ferguson*.[8] When the Court announced its highly controversial *Brown* decision in 1954, it became clear that an important branch of government, the federal judiciary, endorsed a new concept of equality that forbade racial segregation by state and local governments, including public school districts.

The *Brown* decision did not immediately end racial segregation. A second Supreme Court decision concerning the *Brown* case (*Brown* v. *Board of Education,* 1955—known as "*Brown* II") left it to individual lower court judges and school districts to design and implement desegregation plans "with all deliberate speed." Ultimately, it took two decades of lawsuits against individual school systems throughout the country, both in the South and in the North, to produce the hundreds of court orders that chipped away at racial segregation. Some observers contend that the Supreme Court has been given too much credit for advancing civil rights, because it was actually the long, slow process of many lawsuits and court decisions after *Brown* II that finally ended official segregation. Still, there is broad agreement that the Supreme Court's first *Brown* ruling was a bold and necessary step in the process of increasing civil rights protections for African Americans by withdrawing the judiciary's earlier endorsement of racial segregation.

Additional lawsuits also challenged racial restrictions imposed by government in other aspects of American life. One of the final breakthroughs occurred in 1967, when the Supreme Court struck down state laws that prohibited people from marrying individuals of a different race (*Loving* v. *Virginia*). Today, many people are surprised to realize that only four decades ago, it was a crime in several American states for people of different races to marry.

The courts barred laws and governmental actions that enforced segregation, but they did not ensure that schools were integrated and/or equal in quality. Eventually, the Supreme Court even limited desegregation by requiring all court orders to only affect students within the boundaries of a single school system (*Milliken* v. *Bradley,* 1974). Today, racial separation results from housing patterns reflecting boundaries of cities and suburbs and the inability of poorer people to afford housing in affluent school districts. Judicial decisions prevent racial segregation created by law, but they do not prevent the sort of racial separation that exists in many metropolitan areas.

■ **Earl Warren (1891–1974):** Chief Justice of the Supreme Court (1953–1969) who led the Court to its unanimous decision in *Brown* v. *Board of Education of Topeka* (1954) and also took a leading role in many decisions expanding civil liberties and promoting civil rights.

EXAMPLE: *Earl Warren played a key role in important civil liberties decisions discussed in Chapter 4, including writing the majority opinion requiring* Miranda *warnings to inform criminal suspects of their rights before questioning in police custody.*

Why did the NAACP use the court pathway instead of other pathways to advance their goals? Official, legal racial segregation was firmly entrenched in the states of the South, where the majority of African Americans lived. Because African Americans were blocked from voting in southern states, they could not elect their own candidates for public office who would seek to eliminate discriminatory laws through the legislative process. Because committee chairmanships in Congress were dominated by seniority-protected southern senators and representatives, these segregationists blocked proposals for federal laws against racial discrimination, which could seldom reach the point of even being considered for a vote.

Presidents and others in the federal executive branch had little authority over the local and state laws that imposed racial segregation and discrimination. Presidents could propose and endorse federal civil rights legislation. However, they could not make sure

that Congress passed such laws, nor could they do anything to change the laws and policies set by state legislatures, city councils, and school districts; state and local laws and policies are not under the control of the federal government. If a federal judge rules against a state or local law, then a president may act to enforce the judge's order, as when President Eisenhower sent troops to oversee the desegregation of Little Rock Central High School in 1957. As a result of the unresponsiveness and lack of effectiveness of elected officials, the NAACP saw courts as the only institutions through which to advance the principles of equal protection.

The preceding discussion does not mean that the court process was the only pathway of action on civil rights. As we shall see later in this chapter, the grassroots mobilization pathway was important, too, as ordinary people sought to expand civil rights through protest marches, voter registration drives, and other forms of citizen activism.

Litigation Strategies

5.3   Analyze how litigation strategies contributed to the dismantling of official racial segregation.

PRACTICE QUIZ: UNDERSTAND AND APPLY

1. The NAACP's initial litigation strategy sought to
   a. prove that racially segregated elementary schools were not equal.
   b. prove that racially segregated law schools and graduate schools were not equal.
   c. immediately end segregation in high schools.
   d. immediately end segregation in the U.S. Army.

2. When the NAACP was formed in the early twentieth century, its first lawsuit sought to end segregation in American elementary schools.
   a. true
   b. false

3. The Supreme Court's decision in *Brown* v. *Board of Education of Topeka* (1954) was so important for the advancement of civil rights in this country because
   a. it signaled the federal judiciary's condemnation of racial discrimination and made state-mandated segregation illegal.
   b. it immediately brought an end to segregation nationwide.
   c. it confirmed that racial segregation could not be examined by courts.
   d. it instantly created racial harmony in both the North and the South.

4. In many areas of this country, public schools still reflect racial separation and unequal conditions, because
   a. the Supreme Court's decision in *Brown* v. *Board of Education* has not been enforced.
   b. subsequent court cases have reversed certain portions of the *Brown* decision.
   c. a disproportionate number of African Americans are still too poor to live in school districts with top-notch facilities and programs.
   d. laws by legislatures in some states have removed their schools from the coverage of the *Brown* decision.

ANALYZE

1. Why did the NAACP focus its attention on the court pathway before the 1960s?

2. What was the racial composition of the student body at your high school? What are the reasons for that racial composition? If someone wanted to create more diversity at your high school, what would need to happen to achieve that goal?

IDENTIFY THE CONCEPT THAT DOESN'T BELONG

a. Earl Warren
b. NAACP
c. Reconstruction
d. *Brown* v. *Board of Education*
e. Thurgood Marshall

Resource Center
• Glossary
• Vocabulary Example
• Connect the Link

CONNECT THE LINK

(Chapter 4, page 96) Members of Congress have pushed the U.S. Supreme Court to apply the strict scrutiny standard in cases alleging violations of the First Amendment right to free exercise of religion.

Clarifying the Coverage of the Equal Protection Clause

5.4 **Differentiate between the various tests used by the Supreme Court when deciding discrimination claims under the equal protection clause.**

(pages 132–133)

The Supreme Court analyzes equal protection cases through three different tests, depending on the nature of the discrimination alleged in the case (see Table 5.3). The three tests are strict scrutiny, intermediate scrutiny, and the rational basis test. In cases alleging discrimination by race or national origin, the Court directs judges to provide the greatest level of protection for individuals. In such cases, the courts apply *strict scrutiny*, a concept mentioned in Chapter 4, page 96, with respect to alleged violations of fundamental rights. For these cases, the courts require the government to show a compelling justification for any laws, policies, or practices that result in racial discrimination (or the denial of fundamental rights).

By contrast, the Supreme Court applies *intermediate scrutiny* to claims of gender discrimination. In such cases, the government need only show a substantial justification, rather than a compelling reason, to explain the different treatment of men and women. For example, the courts accept differential treatment of men and women in military matters, such as the requirement that only men must register with the Selective Service (for draft eligibility) when they reach the age of 18.

The third level of scrutiny, called the *rational basis test*, applies for other kinds of equal protection claims. In these cases, the government can justify different treatment by merely providing a rational reason for using a particular policy or practice that advances legitimate governmental goals. For example, the government can have policies and programs that adversely affect the poor.

TABLE 5.3 | Three Tests for the Equal Protection Clause

TYPES OF RIGHTS AND DISCRIMINATION CLAIMS	TYPES OF TESTS: STRICT SCRUTINY TEST	CONTINUING CONTROVERSIES
Fundamental freedoms: religion, assembly, press, privacy. Discrimination based on race, alienage (foreign citizenship), ethnicity: called "suspect classifications" (i.e., such bases for discrimination are especially suspicious in the eyes of judges)	Does the government have a compelling reason for the law, policy, or program that clashes with a fundamental freedom or treats people differently by "suspect" demographic characteristics (i.e., race, alienage, ethnicity)? If there is a compelling justification for the government's objective, is this the least restrictive way to attain that objective?	*Grutter* v. *Bollinger* (2003). A slim, five-member majority of the Supreme Court approved race-conscious affirmative action programs in admissions decisions at public universities by concluding that the advancement of diversity is a compelling government interest.
	INTERMEDIATE SCRUTINY TEST	
Gender discrimination	Is gender discrimination from a law, policy, or government practice substantially related to the advancement of an important government interest?	*Rostker* v. *Goldberg* (1981). Despite the service of and casualties suffered by female military personnel in the war zone of Iraq, the Supreme Court has said that the government is advancing an important interest in military preparedness by limiting mandatory Selective Service registration to males, because women are theoretically not eligible for combat roles.
	RATIONAL BASIS TEST	
Other bases of discrimination, including age, wealth, and other classifications not covered by strict scrutiny or heightened scrutiny	Is the government's law, policy, or practice a rational way to advance a legitimate government interest?	In *Bush* v. *Gore* (2000), the Supreme Court terminated the Florida vote recount that might have affected the outcome of the contested presidential election by asserting that the recount procedures would violate the equal protection rights of individual voters. The Court decision did not directly answer whether this case signaled the Court's willingness to thereafter look at voters as claimants deserving of higher levels of scrutiny for equal protection claims.

PATHWAYS of action

Challenging a State University for Men Only

In 1990, a female high school student complained to the U.S. Justice Department about the state of Virginia's policy of maintaining the Virginia Military Institute (VMI) as an all-male institution. Because the federal government agreed that Virginia's policy violated the equal protection clause of the Fourteenth Amendment, the Justice Department filed a lawsuit.

Virginia lost in the U.S. Court of Appeals and as a result, it proposed creating a separate undergraduate, military-model education program for women at a private liberal arts college within the state. When the lower federal courts accepted Virginia's proposal, the Justice Department took the case to the U.S. Supreme Court. The nation's highest court applied the intermediate scrutiny test and concluded that Virginia's policy violated the equal protection clause because "Virginia has shown no 'exceedingly persuasive justification' for excluding all women from the citizen soldier training afforded by VMI" (*United States* v. *Virginia,* 1996). Thus, the actions of one high school student in filing a complaint helped to initiate litigation in the court pathway that led to the elimination of gender discrimination in admissions at VMI.

STUDENT profile

In 2004, four students at the College of William & Mary were not permitted to register to vote in Williamsburg, Virginia, where the college is located. The city registrar said that they must register to vote in their parents' home communities because they are claimed as dependents on their parents' income tax forms. As voting-age adults, the students believed that they were entitled to choose their own place of residence. With the assistance of attorneys from the American Civil Liberties Union, they filed lawsuits to challenge the practice of the registrar in turning away college students who sought to register to vote. When a Virginia state court ruled in favor of one student, the registrar permitted all four students to register to vote, and the lawsuits were dismissed.

There are often disputes about voter registration rules and election procedures that affect Americans' civil rights to participate in the democratic governing system. The students at William & Mary refused to be discouraged by the city official's initial actions. They sought the assistance of an interest group with expertise and resources for using the court pathway effectively. They also showed persistence and patience during the many months that it took for their claims to be examined in the court.[9]

Clarifying the Coverage of the Equal Protection Clause

5.4   Differentiate between the various tests used by the Supreme Court when deciding discrimination claims under the equal protection clause.

PRACTICE QUIZ: UNDERSTAND AND APPLY

1. If people claim that a state discriminated against them because they are poor, the Supreme Court would
   a. apply the rational basis test because economic status is not a suspect classification.
   b. apply the preponderance of evidence test to determine which equal protection test to use.
   c. apply the intermediate scrutiny test because poverty can be closely associated with race.
   d. apply the strict scrutiny test because the Fourteenth Amendment was intended to abolish wealth discrimination.

2. Which test employed by judges merely looks to see a plausible reason for a particular policy that advances legitimate governmental goals?
   a. rational basis test
   b. preponderance of evidence test
   c. intermediate scrutiny test
   d. strict scrutiny test

3. In cases involving alleged race discrimination, the Supreme Court uses which test to guide its thinking?
   a. rational basis test
   b. preponderance of evidence test
   c. intermediate scrutiny test
   d. strict scrutiny test

ANALYZE

1. Is it appropriate for the Supreme Court to use the equal protection clause to examine cases of gender discrimination if it was originally designed to combat racial discrimination? Why or why not?

2. Should the strict scrutiny test be applied to all allegations of discrimination? Why or why not?

IDENTIFY THE CONCEPT THAT DOESN'T BELONG

a. Intermediate scrutiny
b. Thirteenth Amendment
c. Fourteenth Amendment
d. Strict scrutiny
e. Rational basis

5.4

Resource Center
- Glossary
- Vocabulary Example
- Connect the Link

■ **Martin Luther King Jr. (1929–1968):**
A civil rights leader who emerged from the
Montgomery bus boycott to become a national
leader of the civil rights movement and a
recipient of the Nobel Peace Prize.

EXAMPLE: *The Reverend Dr. Martin Luther King Jr. was a central
figure in many of the most important events in the civil rights movement,
including the Montgomery bus boycott and the 1963 March on Washington.
When he was assassinated by a sniper in 1968, an outpouring of anger and
grief by people throughout the country led to civil disorder in several cities.*

Grassroots Mobilization and Civil Rights

5.5 Identify the events and factors that influenced the development of the grassroots civil rights movements.

(pages 134–137)

African Americans and Civil Rights

Protest marches and other forms of grassroots mobilization were used by various groups before the civil rights movement of the 1950s. American labor unions, veterans' groups, and other organizations had long attempted to mobilize support for their goals. However, African Americans and their supporters became famous for their courage, their visibility, and their success in changing both laws and societal attitudes.

A major problem for the mobilization of African Americans, especially in the South, was the fact that whites controlled the region's entire criminal justice system, including the police and the prosecutors.[10] Any African American who challenged the status quo by complaining about discrimination and inequality ran the risk of being arrested on phony charges, beaten by the police, or even killed by whites who knew that they would not be convicted for their crimes. Thus, the grassroots mobilization of African Americans required great courage in the face of violence by many whites dedicated to preserving the privileges that a segregated society gave them.

One instance of grassroots mobilization was especially important for drawing national attention to racial discrimination and for helping to develop southern organizations for civil rights activism. In December of 1955, African Americans in Montgomery, Alabama, began a boycott of the city bus system in protest against a Jim Crow ordinance that forced them either to sit in the back of the bus or to stand whenever a white person needed a seat. The local chapter of the NAACP had been thinking about initiating a boycott like the ones that had been attempted in other cities. Around that time, one of the organization's active members, a 43-year-old seamstress named Rosa Parks, refused to surrender her seat to a white man who boarded the bus after she did. The bus driver had her arrested, and she was convicted of violating segregation laws.

In response, the NAACP and ministers of local African American churches organized a boycott.[11] In selecting a leader for the boycott organization, the Montgomery Improvement Association (MIA), the civil rights advocates turned to **Martin Luther King Jr.**■, a 26-year-old minister who had only recently arrived in town to lead a local Baptist church. King proved to be

a thoughtful and charismatic leader whose powerful speeches and advocacy for nonviolent methods of protest carried him to the forefront of the national civil rights movement.

The Montgomery bus boycott lasted 13 months. Eventually, the prosecutor in Montgomery charged King and dozens of other leaders with violating a state law against boycotts. King's trial and conviction brought national news media attention to the boycott, and he was invited to give speeches throughout the country about racial discrimination and civil rights.[12] King's prominence as a civil rights leader enabled him to advocate for the benefits of nonviolent, mass mobilization as a means for policy change.

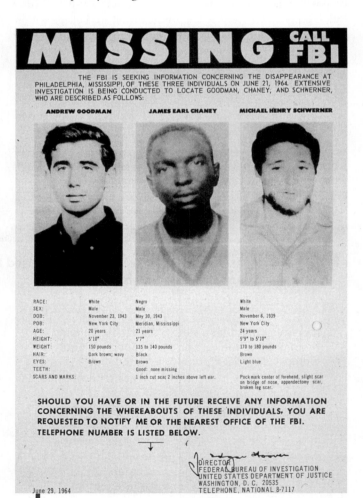

A poster of civil rights workers who were missing for more than a month before Ku Klux Klan informers helped the FBI solve the case and locate their buried bodies. These murders, carried out by local law enforcement officers and members of the Klan, outraged whites in the North and helped to shift public opinion in favor of African Americans' efforts to gain voting rights and political equality. —*How do shifts in public opinion help to change public policy?*

■ **Civil Rights Act of 1964:** A federal statute that prohibited racial discrimination in public accommodations (hotels, restaurants, theaters), employment, and programs receiving federal funding.

EXAMPLE: *The Civil Rights Act of 1964 barred racial discrimination in a number of aspects of American life. It provided a legal basis for prohibiting racial discrimination by one private citizen against another when such discrimination was undertaken by employers in hiring and promotion and by businesses providing services to customers.*

As grassroots protests against racial discrimination continued in many cities, other events contributed to move public opinion as well as the federal government's political power away from acceptance of segregation. For example, the national news media gave great attention to the Little Rock Nine, a group of African American students who attempted to enroll at all-white Little Rock Central High School in Arkansas after a successful court case in 1957. President Dwight D. Eisenhower sent hundreds of troops from the U.S. Army's 101st Airborne Division to escort the students into the school and provide protection for them after they were barred from the school and subjected to harassment, threats, and violence.[13]

The 1963 March on Washington showed a national television audience that tens of thousands of African Americans and whites were working together to advance the cause of civil rights. "The I Have a Dream" speech given by Dr. Martin Luther King Jr. on the steps of the Lincoln Memorial is considered by many observers to be one of the most inspirational moments in American political history. —*How might such memorable events contribute to cultural change?*

Acts of violence against African Americans and white civil rights activists continued to capture headlines and produced gripping television footage. In 1962, whites rioted at the University of Mississippi, leading to two deaths and hundreds of injuries, as they attempted to prevent one man, Air Force veteran James Meredith, from enrolling as the university's first African American student. After dozens of federal marshals were injured, President John F. Kennedy sent soldiers to restore order. In 1963, television showed the vicious use by city police of fire hoses, tear gas, and attack dogs to subdue peaceful protesters in Birmingham, Alabama. The bombing of a Birmingham church that year, which took the lives of four young African American girls attending a Bible study class, shocked the nation. "Revulsion at the church bombing," wrote one historian, "spread swiftly around the world."[14]

In 1964, two young white men from the North, Michael Schwerner and Andrew Goodman, and an African American civil rights worker from Mississippi, James Chaney, were abducted and murdered in Philadelphia, Mississippi, as they sought to register African American voters. The vehemence and violence of white resistance to desegregation helped move national public opinion in favor of the African Americans' cause, and it pushed the federal government to take long-overdue action in support of civil rights.

People came from around the country to participate in the 1963 March on Washington to express support for legislation to combat discrimination and enforce civil rights. The quarter of a million participants included tens of thousands of whites.[15] Among the many leaders who spoke to the crowd from the steps of the Lincoln Memorial was the keynote speaker, Martin Luther King Jr., who delivered what later came to be known as his "I Have a Dream" speech, one of the most famous public addresses in American history (see Figure 5.1). News coverage showed a nationwide television audience the huge throng of people, both African American and white, who peacefully rallied for the cause of civil rights. A few months after President Kennedy was assassinated, the new president, Lyndon Johnson, was able to use public sentiment aroused by the martyred president's death as well as growing concerns about racial discrimination to push the **Civil Rights Act of 1964**■ through Congress.

In 1965, national attention was drawn to Selma, Alabama, where protests focused on registering African American voters. Many locales across the South used rigged literacy tests in which African Americans were flunked by officials no matter how accurate their responses and thus denied the opportunity to vote. A protest march, planned to proceed from Selma to the state capital, Montgomery, was stopped by dozens of Alabama state police, who attacked the peaceful marchers and beat them with clubs. The brutality of the police attack received significant coverage in newspapers and on television.[16] Public reactions to the violence directed at civil rights protesters helped

■ **Voting Rights Act of 1965:** A federal statute that effectively attacked literacy tests and other techniques used to prevent African Americans from voting.

EXAMPLE: *The Voting Rights Act of 1965 gave the U.S. Department of Justice enforcement powers to oversee voter registration and election procedures carried out by state and local governments, and the federal government used these powers to scrutinize closely any racially motivated efforts to change voting districts or use procedures that might interfere with any citizen's right to vote.*

FIGURE 5.1 ■ A Dream Deferred

Although the measures displayed in this figure show progress, this occurred very slowly over the span of two decades, and significant gaps still remain. —*What actions can the government take to speed up the process of attaining equality in these measures? Should the government take such actions?*

 In his memorable "I Have a Dream" speech at the Lincoln Memorial on August 28,1963, Dr. Martin Luther King Jr. looked forward to a time when blacks would live equally with other Americans. While considerable economic progress has been made, blacks still lag well behind. Black Americans own homes at a lower rate than the overall population; a greater percentage live below the poverty line; and a smaller percentage have college degrees.

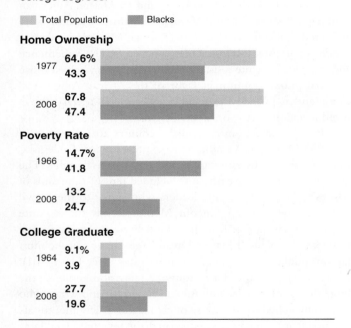

■ Total Population   ■ Blacks

Home Ownership
1977   64.6%   43.3
2008   67.8   47.4

Poverty Rate
1966   14.7%   41.8
2008   13.2   24.7

College Graduate
1964   9.1%   3.9
2008   27.7   19.6

SOURCES: U.S. Census Bureau, Historical Poverty Tables, 2009; "Census Bureau Reports on Residential Vacancies and Home Ownership," *U.S. Census Bureau News*, Feb. 3, 2009; U.S. Census Bureau, *Current Population Survey Supplement, 2009.* January 17, 2005, New York Times Graphics. Copyright © 2005 by the New York Times Co. Reprinted with permission. Updated by permission of the publisher.

push Congress into enacting the **Voting Rights Act of 1965**■, the long-sought federal legislation that finally facilitated the participation of African Americans through voting and campaigning for elective office.

Civil Rights Legislation

As attitudes about racial equality changed, people pressured legislators to create new civil rights laws. Many of these new laws were directed at discrimination practiced by private individuals and businesses—discrimination that was beyond the reach of the equal protection clause. Title II of the Civil Rights Act of 1964, for example, forbids discrimination by race, color, religion, or national origin in "public accommodations," which include hotels, restaurants, gas stations, movie theaters, and sports stadiums.

The Voting Rights Act of 1965 was not the first congressional legislation that sought to prevent the racial discrimination that limited African Americans' access to the ballot—discrimination that the Fifteenth Amendment had sought to outlaw back in 1870. The Civil Rights Acts of 1957, 1960, and 1964 all contained provisions aimed at barriers to voting. However, because they relied on litigation for enforcement, they all proved ineffective, as states frequently found new ways to discriminate.[17] The Voting Rights Act of 1965 (and its subsequent extensions in 1970 and later years) barred the literacy tests that had been used to keep African Americans away from the polls. Table 5.4 shows the impact of the Voting Rights Act in increasing the registration of African American voters. The act was also more powerful and effective because of its "preclearance" provision, which required officials in designated districts, primarily in southern states, to obtain the permission of the attorney general before making any changes in elections and voting procedures. The lawsuits filed under the Voting Rights Act provided the basis for judges to stop efforts in several states to create new voting districts that would dilute the voting power of black voters and thereby reduce the potential for African Americans to be elected to public office or to elect candidates favorable to their interests.

Another result of the civil rights movement was the creation of new government agencies to monitor compliance with and enforcement of antidiscrimination laws. The **U.S. Commission on Civil Rights,** created in 1957, was given the task of investigating and reporting to Congress about discrimination and the deprivation of civil rights. The **U.S. Equal Employment Opportunity Commission,** created in 1964, was charged with investigating complaints about illegal employment discrimination. Subsequently, states and cities created their own agencies to investigate and enforce their own civil rights laws. These agencies are typically called "civil rights commissions" (for example, the Iowa Civil Rights Commission), "human rights commissions" (for example, the San Francisco Human Rights Commission), or "equal opportunity commissions" (for example, the Nebraska Equal Opportunity Commission).

TABLE 5.4 | Percentage of Eligible Citizens Registered to Vote

Voter registration rates for African Americans in southern states increased dramatically after the Voting Rights Act of 1965 helped to eliminate discriminatory barriers.

STATE	MARCH 1965			NOVEMBER 2008		
	AFRICAN AMERICAN	WHITE	GAP	AFRICAN AMERICAN	WHITE	GAP
Alabama	19.3	69.2	49.9	69.9	72.4	2.5
Georgia	27.4	62.6	35.2	70.2	70.5	0.3
Louisiana	31.6	80.5	48.9	75.4	79.7	4.3
Mississippi	6.7	69.9	63.2	81.9	74.6	−7.3
North Carolina	46.8	96.8	50.0	71.0	77.2	6.2
South Carolina	37.3	75.7	38.4	76.1	73.4	−2.7
Virginia	38.3	61.1	22.8	70.5	73.9	3.4

SOURCE: Data from Bernard Grofman, Lisa Handley, and Richard G. Niemi, *Minority Representation and the Quest for Voting Equality* (New York: Cambridge University Press, 1992), pp. 23–24; U.S. Census Bureau, "Voting and Registration in the Election of November 2008" (2009), accessed at http://www.census.gov/hhes/www/socdem/voting/publications/P20/2008/tables.html

Grassroots Mobilization and Civil Rights

5.5 Identify the events and factors that influenced the development of the grassroots civil rights movement.

PRACTICE QUIZ: UNDERSTAND AND APPLY

1. A major problem facing African Americans undertaking grassroots mobilization in the 1950s was that
   a. they were inventing a new form of political action that no other group had ever used before.
   b. no whites in the North were supportive of civil rights and political equality for African Americans.
   c. whites controlled the criminal justice system and could use their authority to arrest and jail African Americans who spoke in favor of civil rights.
   d. no African Americans were willing to become leaders of civil rights organizations.

2. What was an important impact of violence and brutality directed at civil rights activists?
   a. The violence resulted in fewer people participating in civil rights protests.
   b. The violence increased the public opinion support by northern whites for the cause of equality.
   c. The violence led to counterattack violence by African Americans directed against southern whites.
   d. The violence led to a federal takeover of southern cities' police departments.

3. What was the first preliminary effect of the Montgomery bus boycott?
   a. the prosecution of local African Americans
   b. a revision of the city's Jim Crow busing policy, allowing African Americans to sit "in any open seats"
   c. the celebrity of Rosa Parks
   d. the demise of the Montgomery Improvement Association

ANALYZE

1. Why was nonviolence ultimately a successful strategy for African Americans in their struggle for civil rights?

2. Are current laws, such as the Civil Rights Act of 1964, sufficient to prevent all forms of discrimination? If not, what further legislation is needed?

IDENTIFY THE CONCEPT THAT DOESN'T BELONG

a. Martin Luther King Jr.
b. Bus boycott
c. State supreme courts
d. Civil Rights Act of 1964
e. March on Washington

5.5

Resource Center
• Glossary
• Vocabulary Example
• Connect the Link

■ **Universal Suffrage:** The right to vote for all adult citizens.

EXAMPLE: *Women gained the right to vote in various countries at different points in time from 1893 to 2005. Some countries still do not have universal suffrage, however, because women do not yet have the right to vote in those countries.*

Women, Latinos, and Civil Rights

5.6 Compare and contrast the civil rights struggles of women, Latinos, and African Americans.

(pages 138–139)

Women and Civil Rights

Beginning with public meetings and speeches in the first half of the nineteenth century, grassroots mobilization played a crucial role in obtaining the right to vote for women. After the Civil War, the Fifteenth Amendment sought to give African American men the right to vote. Because advocates for women's civil rights were disappointed that the amendment did not help women get the vote, they took action to mobilize supporters in favor of **universal suffrage**■—the right to vote for all adult citizens. One of the most prominent organizations, the National Woman Suffrage Association, was founded in 1869 and led by Susan B. Anthony and Elizabeth Cady Stanton.[18]

Another important strategy involved trying to place the question of women's suffrage on statewide ballots as often as possible. As described by one historian, "From 1870 to 1910, there were 480 campaigns in thirty-three states, just to get the issue submitted to the voters, of which only seventeen resulted in actual referendum votes."[19] In the early twentieth century, the suffrage movement gained momentum after winning successful ballot-issue campaigns in Washington (1910), California (1911), Arizona (1912), Kansas (1912), and Oregon (1912). In 1917, several state legislatures gave women the right to vote for specific elections, such as the presidential election or primary elections.[20] Finally, in 1918, the women's suffrage amendment received sufficient support to pass through Congress and be sent to the states for approval. It was ratified as the Nineteenth Amendment and added to the Constitution in 1920.

Ratification of the Nineteenth Amendment did not ensure that women would enjoy equal rights. Large segments of the public continued to see women as properly destined for subservient roles as wives and housekeepers or in a few "helping professions," such as nursing, teaching, and secretarial services.

Legislatures took little action to initiate laws that would protect women from discrimination until a new grassroots women's movement emerged in the 1960s and 1970s. By then, larger numbers of women were attending college, entering the workforce, participating in campaigns and elections, and challenging traditional expectations about women's subordinate status in society.

Women in New York City march for suffrage in 1913. Advocates of voting rights for women went to great lengths over the course of many decades to educate the public about the need for universal suffrage. The ratification of the Nineteenth Amendment, which established women's right to vote, represented a major change in the American political system. —*Are there still assumptions about politics, government, and women that hinder the possibility of a woman being elected president of the United States?*

Latinos and Civil Rights

Latinos share a Spanish-speaking heritage, but ethnically and racially, they are highly diverse. Also referred to as Hispanics, Latinos' ancestors came from Mexico, Puerto Rico, Cuba, or other places in Latin America. They have long faced discrimination in the United States. Some Americans perceive Latinos to be recent arrivals who may have entered the country without proper permission from immigration authorities. In reality, many Latinos are descended from people who lived in the territory that became the United States even before whites became the numerically dominant group.

For centuries, Latino people lived in parts of what are today California, Texas, New Mexico, and Arizona—all states whose territory originally belonged to Mexico, which the United States annexed in the 1840s after the Mexican War. Latinos from Puerto Rico and Cuba began moving to New York and Florida in the late 1800s. The United States gained control of both islands after the Spanish-American War (1898). Cuba later became an independent country, but Puerto Rico remains under American sovereignty, as an "associated commonwealth." Its people can travel freely to the mainland to live and work.

■ **César Chávez (1927–1993):** Latino civil rights leader who founded the United Farm Workers and used nonviolent, grassroots mobilization to seek civil rights for Latinos and improved working conditions for agricultural workers.

EXAMPLE: *During the 1960s, Chávez led a national boycott of table grapes that led growers to sign a contract with the United Farm Workers union that improved California farm laborers' wages and working conditions and, later, contributed to passage of California's Agricultural Labor Relations Act.*

Prior to the enactment of federal civil rights laws in the 1960s, Latinos in the United States often received less pay than white workers, while being assigned the most difficult and burdensome tasks. Migrant farm workers, who were typically of Mexican or Central American origin, traveled throughout the country harvesting crops, receiving very low pay, and facing difficult living conditions. Latinos suffered discrimination and segregation in housing, employment, public accommodations, and education—and often harsh treatment from police officers and other government officials.[21]

Latinos formed labor unions and civil rights organizations in the early twentieth century at the same time that others in the United States were forming such groups. Other civil rights organizations emerged when Latinos mobilized in conjunction with the highly publicized civil rights movement of African Americans.

The best-known grassroots movement was led by **César Chávez■**, who founded the National Farm Workers Association, later renamed the United Farm Workers (UFW). Chávez led protest marches and organized a national boycott of grapes harvested by nonunion workers during the 1960s. He also went on hunger strikes to protest poor pay and working conditions for farm workers.[22] His efforts contributed to the enactment of new statutes to provide protection for farm workers.

The issue of civil rights and equal treatment for Latinos continues in the twenty-first century, especially because Latinos are now the largest minority group in the United States, surpassing the number of African Americans in 2003 and continuing to grow at a faster rate than most other demographic groups. Latino activists continue to be concerned about such issues as unequal treatment in employment, housing, and the criminal justice system.

Women, Latinos, and Civil Rights

5.6   Compare and contrast the civil rights struggles of women, Latinos, and African Americans.

PRACTICE QUIZ: UNDERSTAND AND APPLY

1. Many observers regard the Supreme Court's decision in *Brown* v. *Board Education* as the first twentieth-century change in national law that set into motion a major move toward civil rights for African Americans. What is the first twentieth-century change in national law that arguably began women's movement toward political equality?
   a. The Supreme Court's decision in *Bradwell* v. *Illinois*
   b. President Woodrow Wilson's executive order that let women fight on the frontlines in World War I
   c. Congressional enactment of the "Women's Civil Rights Act of 1918"
   d. Ratification of the Nineteenth Amendment in 1920

2. Unlike the case of African Americans, who were formally denied equality by law in the late nineteenth century, the fundamental problem for women in that era was that the many laws guaranteeing them equal rights with men were never carried out.
   a. true   b. false

3. Latinos first arrived in the United States during World War II when Americans needed extra workers in factories to make planes, tanks, and jeeps for the war effort.
   a. true   b. false

4. César Chávez brought national attention to the plight of Latinos by
   a. organizing lawsuits that exposed the infringement of Latinos' civil rights.
   b. organizing protests against school segregation.
   c. becoming the first Hispanic to run for public office.
   d. organizing farm workers so that they could jointly try to address discrimination, low pay, and poor working conditions.

ANALYZE

1. What issues of equality do women still confront in the workplace and society? How should these issues be addressed?

2. Should the status of illegal immigrants be considered a civil rights issue? Why or why not?

IDENTIFY THE CONCEPT THAT DOESN'T BELONG

a. Judicial review   d. Nineteenth Amendment
b. Suffrage   e. Susan B. Anthony
c. Agricultural workers

Resource Center
• Glossary
• Vocabulary Example
• Connect the Link

Contemporary Civil Rights Issues

5.7 Evaluate the continuing debates, lawsuits, and protests over civil rights in the twenty-first century.

(pages 140–141)

The visibility and success of litigation and grassroots mobilization strategies by African Americans, women, and Latinos provided examples for plans and action by other individuals and groups who saw themselves as victims of discrimination. Beginning in the 1970s, people with disabilities lobbied legislators and held public demonstrations protesting discrimination in employment and public accommodations. Individuals who use wheelchairs, for example, often found themselves rejected for jobs merely because an employer assumed that they were incapable of working. Similarly, they often could not be served as customers at restaurants, entertainment facilities, and other public accommodations that lacked wheelchair access. In the Rehabilitation Act of 1973, Congress prohibited discrimination against people with disabilities who work in government or who seek services from federally funded programs. The Americans with Disabilities Act, passed in 1990, provided protection against discrimination in employment and public accommodations.

Advocates of civil rights protections for gays and lesbians have used legislative lobbying, litigation, and grassroots mobilization to seek legal protections comparable to those provided for African Americans and women. Gay and lesbian couples used litigation in Iowa, New Jersey, and Massachusetts to gain legal recognition of their committed relationships in civil unions and marriages. Through the lobbying pathway, legislatures in several additional states enacted laws to produce the same result. Although no federal law prevents employment discrimination based on a worker's sexual orientation, some states and cities have enacted statutes and ordinances to prohibit such discrimination in housing and public accommodations. In 2009, Congress enacted a new law making it a federal offense to commit a violent hate crime against someone because of that person's sexual orientation or gender identity. Another important development occurred in 2010, when President Obama's Department of Defense asked Congress to change the rules for military service, so that gays and lesbians would no longer be required to keep their sexual orientation secret in order to have military careers.

Americans are divided over whether new civil rights laws should address discrimination against gays and lesbians. The U.S. Supreme Court has considered two important cases concerning this issue. In *Romer* v. *Evans* (1996), the Court declared that cities such as Aspen, Boulder, and Denver could pass antidiscrimination laws to protect gays and lesbians. The Court relied on the equal protection clause in striking down a statewide referendum approved by Colorado voters that had banned the passage of such antidiscrimination laws. However, in *Boy Scouts of America* v. *Dale* (2000), the Court found that New Jersey's law against sexual orientation discrimination in public accommodations could not be used to require the Boy Scouts to accept a gay man as a troop leader. According to the Court, such an application of the state law would violate the Boy Scouts' First Amendment right of expressive association, which means that a private group cannot be forced to accept a member it does not want.

Although the Court blocked Colorado from creating a law that would single out gays and lesbians for adverse treatment, it has not made any decisions granting specific civil rights for gays and lesbians. As gays and lesbians lobby, litigate, and demonstrate for the right to marry and for legal protections against discrimination, it appears that any success they achieve may initially come on a state-by-state basis. Wider success for these goals will occur only if American society moves closer to a consensus about the need to protect the civil rights of gays and lesbians. For a detailed examination of the political and legal battles over same-sex marriage, see the timeline on pages 142-143.

Issues of equal treatment under the law have long been a matter of concern for Native Americans as well. They have suffered from overt discrimination, nonexistent economic opportunities, and widespread poverty. Because of their relatively small numbers and isolated locations, Native Americans have not enjoyed success through the grassroots mobilization strategies. In recent years, however, they have advanced their cause through the court pathway, especially the case of *Cobell* v. *Kempthorne,* originally filed in 1996 and finally decided in favor of the Native Americans in January 2008. In this case, the federal judge found that over the years, the U.S. Department of Interior's Bureau of Indian Affairs had mismanaged and lost billions of dollars owed to Native Americans for oil and gas revenues and other leases on their lands administered by the federal government. In December 2009, the federal government agreed to settle the claims for $3.4 billion. The slow-moving court process did not instantly solve the problem, but it did set into motion the events that enabled Native Americans to receive compensation. It also put political pressure on members of Congress to provide greater oversight for the Bureau of Indian Affairs.

At the end of the twentieth century, some Native American groups became more capable of exerting pressure through the lobbying pathway. Several Native American groups used their reservations' status as self-governing, sovereign territories as a means to open casinos that would otherwise not have beeen permitted by the states in which the reservations were located. They used revenue from the casinos to increase their efforts to hire lobbyists and make campaign contributions as a means to gain favorable influence and support among members of Congress. These efforts have not gained equality and decent living conditions for all Native Americans. They have, however, influenced decision makers to pay more attention to issues affecting some Native American groups.

PATHWAYS of change from around the world

What would you do if you saw discrimination produced by policies and practices at your college? In December 2006, students carrying signs protested outside of the Sri Lanka Legal Aid Commission offices in Colombo, Sri Lanka, the island nation off the coast of India. The students claimed that Tamils, members of an ethnic and religious minority, experienced discrimination in admissions decisions at the Law College. Reportedly, only one or two Tamil students were admitted to study law even though Tamils comprised nearly 30 percent

of the 10,000 applicants who took the admissions test. The protesters claimed that the admissions committee made numerous errors in translating questions between English and Tamil and that a number of Tamil students were excluded from admission despite obtaining higher scores than admitted students. There were concerns that if such admissions practices continued, eventually there would be no more Tamil-speaking lawyers in the country.

With the nation's recent history of violent conflict between the government and Tamil rebels, who sought to create their own country in the northern portion of the island, international human rights groups have documented abusive actions by police and government soldiers against Tamils. In light of the persistent reports of arbitrary arrests and physical abuses by the police, it took courage for the Tamil students to continue their protest, especially after the police warned them that they would be forcibly removed. Although the protest's impact, if any, can only be judged by the admission of future classes to the country's Law College, the students' efforts to make a nonviolent statement against discrimination in a country that is torn with ethnic conflict demonstrated their recognition that any hope for a peaceful democracy rests, in part, on the development of a legal system that is open to participation from all of the country's people.[23]

Contemporary Civil Rights Issues

5.7 **Evaluate the continuing debates, lawsuits, and protests over civil rights in the twenty-first century.**

PRACTICE QUIZ: UNDERSTAND AND APPLY

1. The Supreme Court has decided a case specifically declaring that private groups, such as the Boy Scouts, are not obligated to accept members who are
   a. disabled
   b. gay
   c. Latino
   d. Presbyterian

2. President Obama's administration has acted on behalf of an emerging group by
   a. opening a new university for Native Americans.
   b. asking Congress to permit gays and lesbians to serve openly in the military.
   c. proposing a constitutional amendment to permit disabled people to own casinos.
   d. proposing a constitutional amendment to make Spanish an official language of the United States.

3. Federal law prohibits employment discrimination based on a worker's sexual orientation.
   a. true
   b. false

4. When the federal government settled some land claims in 2009, it was a result of Native American activists' success in which pathway of action?
   a. elections pathway
   b. grassroots mobilization pathway
   c. cultural change pathway
   d. court pathway

ANALYZE

1. What other civil rights issues are unresolved in today's society? Which pathway(s) of action would be most useful in seeking resolution?

2. Why are gays and lesbians having greater success seeking change state-by-state rather than through national legislation or U.S. Supreme Court decisions?

IDENTIFY THE CONCEPT THAT DOESN'T BELONG

a. Affirmative action
b. Police discretion
c. Gay marriage
d. Native American land lease claims
e. Majority-minority voting districts for women

5.7

The Struggle over Same-Sex Marriage

● COURTS   ● CULTURAL CHANGE   ● ELECTIONS   ● GRASSROOTS MOBILIZATION   ● LOBBYING DECISION-MAKERS

Same-sex marriage is one of the most controversial issues of the twenty-first century. Law and policy have developed through actions and reactions in multiple pathways of change. When same-sex couples first claimed an equal legal right to marry in the 1970s, their claims were quickly rejected. In the 1990s, however, some legislative proposals and court decisions supported the concept, reflecting the first stirrings of cultural change within specific states. Legislatures and voters reacted against these initial events by enacting new legal measures to ban same-sex marriage. In a counter-reaction, supporters of same-sex marriage challenged these legal measures in the courts. By the end of 2009, actions in both the courts and elections pathways led to the legalization of same-sex marriage in several New England states as well as Iowa.

Essay Questions

1. Unlike other law and policy issues that are determined by national institutions, such as Congress or the U.S. Supreme Court, the definition of marriage is determined by each state. How is the development of policy change on a state-by-state basis likely to be different than policy change that is defined by national laws?

2. If we see cultural change moving in a direction that favors the acceptance of same-sex marriage, does that necessarily mean that we will eventually see the legalization of same-sex marriage in all states? Why or why not?

PRO SAME-SEX MARRIAGE

1990
A bill is proposed in the California legislature to permit same-sex marriage; it is supported by several California lawyers' organizations.

1997
Hawaii legislature enacts "domestic partnership" legislation with limited rights for registered, same-sex domestic partners.

1999
In *Baker* v. *State,* the Vermont Supreme Court concludes that same-sex couples "may not be deprived of the statutory benefits and protections afforded persons of the opposite sex who choose to marry."

1970s   **1990**   **1996**   **1997–98**   **1999**

ANTI SAME-SEX MARRIAGE

1970s
Unsuccessful lawsuits in several states seek the right to same-sex marriage.

1997–1998
Anti–same-sex marriage laws are enacted in 12 states.

1996
Congress enacts and President Bill Clinton signs into law the Defense of Marriage Act; it defines marriage as being solely between a man and woman (for federal purposes) and says that states do not have to recognize same-sex marriages that occur in other states.

2004
San Francisco Mayor Gavin Newsome authorizes the issuance of marriage licenses to same-sex couples, and the first same-sex couples also marry in Massachusetts.

2009
Legislatures in New Hampshire and Vermont enact laws approving same-sex marriages.

2009
State supreme courts in Connecticut and Iowa rule that denial of same-sex marriage violates their respective state constitutions.

2005–2007
Legislatures in Connecticut, New Jersey, and New Hampshire enact laws authorizing civil unions for same-sex couples. Oregon and Washington legislatures enact domestic partnership laws to provide rights and entitlements for same-sex couples.

2009
Public opinions polls show that while Americans over age 65 oppose same-sex marriage by more than a 2-to-1 margin, half of Americans age 30 and under support same-sex marriage.

2003
In *Goodridge* v. *Department of Public Health,* the Massachusetts Supreme Judicial Court rules that same-sex couples should be able to marry in the same manner as heterosexual couples.

2010
Lower federal courts strike down laws blocking same-sex marriage. A federal judge in Massachusetts ruled that the Defense of Marriage Act enacted by Congress in the prior decade was unconstitutional. A federal judge in San Francisco invalidated California's 2008 law prohibiting same-sex marriage.

| **2003** | **2004–07** | **2008** | **2009** | **2010** |

2004–2006
Voters in more than 20 states approve constitutional amendments to ban same-sex marriage.

2008
California voters pass constitutional amendment to prohibit same-sex marriage

2005
California legislature enacts law to legalize same-sex marriage, but it is vetoed by Governor Arnold Schwarzenegger.

Conclusion

The United States has a long history of unequal treatment of women and members of various minorities within its society. Although the founders of this country did not advocate for equality for all people, their lofty ideal of equality for most white men provided inspiration for others in American society to share in the benefits of that vision. Hence, there have been efforts throughout American history to gain political equality for women, African Americans, various immigrant groups, and others who were initially excluded from full acceptance and participation in the nation's governing and economic systems.

The court and grassroots mobilization pathways have been especially important for the advancement of civil rights. In the twentieth century, the NAACP's litigation strategy, which gradually succeeded in gaining the Supreme Court's rejection of racial segregation, helped make the Fourteenth Amendment's equal protection clause a viable tool for challenging governmental laws and policies that foster discrimination. Advocates of civil rights for members of other victimized groups could copy the NAACP's strategies in using the court pathway to advance their own causes. Beginning in the 1960s, when Congress and state legislatures began enacting additional civil rights laws, opportunities arose to use the court pathway as a means to gain judicial enforcement of statutes intended to prevent discrimination by employers, landlords, and other private actors. Judicial enforcement of these statutes has facilitated significant changes in American society and created opportunities for upward mobility and respectful treatment that a generation earlier would have been nearly unimaginable to African Americans and women.

Grassroots mobilization is a long-standing method of seeking changes in public policy, going all the way back to the origins of the United States. Over the years, various groups in our society, including labor union organizers and veterans seeking government benefits, have used this pathway. The African American civil rights movement of the 1950s and 1960s had an exceptionally powerful impact on the attitudes of ordinary citizens and eventually convinced the government to create and enforce antidiscrimination laws. Seeing the effectiveness of African Americans' protests, other groups emulated these tactics. For example, women's rights advocates used meetings and protests to educate the public about their struggle to gain the right to vote. Civil rights advocates did not invent grassroots action, but they have employed it in an especially successful manner. As indicated by students' protests in support of the Jena Six, described at the start of this chapter, grassroots action continues to be a useful tool for drawing public attention and spurring governmental action.

Political equality is an important component of democracy. If voting rights are restricted and certain groups are excluded from full participation in society, the governing system will represent only the interests of those who have status and wield power. The efforts to obtain civil rights for excluded groups in the United States constitute an important chapter in this country's history. Without these efforts, the American governing system would fall well short of its professed aspiration to be a democracy that sets an example for other countries around the world.

KEY CONCEPT MAP   **How did the pathways of action shape the civil rights movement?**

1954

Brown v. ***Board of Education***

Supreme Court rules that racial segregation in public schools violates the Fourteenth Amendment.

Courts

The decision ends the legal justification for racial segregation by government and shows that one important government institution supports civil rights.

Critical Thinking Questions

What if a majority of justices had voted to continue "separate but equal" out of fear that supporting civil rights would produce massive disobedience and violence from southern whites?

1955

Montgomery Bus Boycott

African Americans protest racial segregation by refusing to use the Montgomery public transit system.

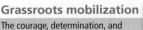

Grassroots mobilization

The courage, determination, and persistence of the boycott participants demonstrate the potential effectiveness of nonviolent grassroots action, which inspires grassroots actions in other cities.

What factors may have prevented whites from ignoring the boycott and simply waiting for African Americans to tire of walking to work and give up?

November 8, 1960

Presidential Election

John F. Kennedy is elected President of the United States.

Elections

The presidential election of 1960 brings to the White House a president who enforces court orders to end segregation at southern state universities and who proposes legislation that eventually becomes the Civil Rights Act of 1964.

To what extent can presidents advance civil rights goals if there is significant opposition from members of Congress and the public? What strategies and powers can a president use to advance such goals?

August 28, 1963

March on Washington

Over 200,000 participants march to the Lincoln Memorial in Washington, D.C., where Rev. Martin Luther King Jr. delivers his *I Have a Dream* speech.

Grassroots mobilization and lobbying decision makers

The peaceful march demonstrates to Congress the growing support for civil rights among whites as well as African Americans. Civil rights legislation passes the following year.

In what ways do the news media affect whether grassroots mobilization is successful?

June 21, 1964

Murders of Three Civil Rights Workers

Three civil rights workers driving at night in Neshoba County, Mississippi, are stopped and killed by law enforcement officers and Ku Klux Klan members.

Cultural change

The murder of white civil rights workers from the North is particularly striking for white Americans, and whites in the northern and western United States increasingly support civil rights for African Americans.

If no white civil rights workers had been injured or killed, would national public opinion have shifted so steadily in favor of civil rights?

1964 and 1965

Civil Rights Act of 1964 and Voting Rights Act of 1965

Congress passes and President Lyndon B. Johnson signs laws that, among other things, outlaw segregation in restaurants and other public-serving businesses as well as discriminatory voting practices.

Lobbying decision makers

When Congress finally enacts meaningful civil rights legislation, it opens the door for African Americans to seek legal remedies for discrimination and to assert themselves in the elections pathway by voting and running for office.

Does it violate Americans' notions of freedom to tell private businesses that they cannot freely choose their own customers? Is there a tension between the constitutional values of individual freedom and equality?

Equality is presented as an important value in the Declaration of Independence and the U.S. Constitution; yet, this American ideal has proven to be extremely difficult to achieve. While developments in politics, society, and law since the mid-twentieth century have moved society closer to the ideal of equality, some Americans still face discrimination and enjoy fewer opportunities for economic success. —*To what extent can the creation of specific laws or the announcement of judicial decisions advance U.S. society closer to its ideal of equality? If there are limits on the ability of lawmakers and judges to advance equality, what other entities or actions can produce change? Do you foresee the attainment of true equality for all Americans in your lifetime? Why or why not?*

Review of Key Objectives

The Ideal of Equality

 5.1 Describe the idea of equality that underlies the governing system of the United States.

(pages 124–125)

"Civil rights" concern issues of equality and involve the development of laws and policies that prevent discrimination, especially forms of discrimination that exclude members of selected groups from full participation in the economic and governing systems. The founders of the United States advocated an ideal of equality for white men that was to become a source of inspiration for women, African Americans, Latinos, and others who sought full inclusion in society. Equality in the United States and laws that advance the American vision of equality focus on equality of opportunity, not on equality of condition.

KEY TERMS

Civil Rights 124
Political Equality 124
Equality of Condition 124
Equality of Opportunity 124

CRITICAL THINKING QUESTIONS

1. How are civil rights different from civil liberties?
2. Why does the United States emphasize equality of opportunity more than equality of condition?

INTERNET RESOURCES

Read about the idea of equality in Sweden, which emphasizes equality of condition, rather than just equality of opportunity, in many aspects of society: http://www.sweden.se/eng/Home/Work/Swedish-model/

ADDITIONAL READING

Ackerman, Bruce. *We the People: Foundations.* Cambridge, MA: Belknap/Harvard, 1991.

Foner, Eric. *The Story of American Freedom.* New York: W. W. Norton, 1998.

Equal Protection of the Law

 5.2 Trace the historical development of civil rights in the United States.

(pages 126–129)

In the United States, a long history of discrimination inspired the development of civil rights action. After the Civil War, three amendments (the Thirteenth, Fourteenth, and Fifteenth Amendments) were added to the Constitution to prohibit slavery and provide legal rights for African Americans.

The racial segregation that existed in the states was produced by formal laws as well as by less formal means. The Supreme Court endorsed formal discrimination in 1896 and thereby helped to facilitate the spread of separate public schools and other public facilities, especially in southern states.

The history of slavery and violent racial oppression in the United States as well as the pervasive discrimination that existed for a century after the abolition of slavery produced lingering inequalities that continue to affect American society today.

KEY TERMS

Jim Crow Laws 127
Plessy **v.** *Ferguson* **(1896)** 128

CRITICAL THINKING QUESTIONS

1. What aspects of the country's history of racial discrimination may have influenced current issues of inequality? How?
2. How might the United States be different today if the Fourteenth Amendment had not been ratified and added to the Constitution?

INTERNET RESOURCES

The Web site of the Public Broadcasting System (PBS) presents maps, photos, and other materials about the post–Civil War Reconstruction period: http://www.pbs.org/wgbh/amex/reconstruction/

ADDITIONAL READING

Litwack, Leon F. *Trouble in Mind: Black Southerners in the Age of Jim Crow.* New York: Knopf, 1998.

Takaki, Ronald. *A Different Mirror: A History of Multicultural America.* Boston: Little, Brown, 1993.

Litigation Strategies

 5.3 Analyze how litigation strategies contributed to the dismantling of official racial segregation.

(pages 130–131)

The U.S. Supreme Court originally endorsed racial segregation in *Plessy* v. *Ferguson* (1896), but the lawyers for the NAACP initiated a litigation strategy in the 1930s to attack the "separate but equal" principle from *Plessy*. They filed lawsuits narrowly focused at unequal, and often nonexistent, facilities for African American college graduates seeking education in state university law schools and graduate programs. After winning several cases over the course of two decades, they filed a similar case against a public school system. As a result, the U.S. Supreme Court became the first major governing institution to firmly reject all segregation laws as violating the equal protection clause (*Brown* v. *Board of Education of Topeka*, 1954).

KEY TERMS

National Association for the Advancement of Colored People (NAACP) 130
***Brown* v. *Board of Education of Topeka* (1954)** 130
Earl Warren 130

CRITICAL THINKING QUESTIONS

1. What factors contributed to the NAACP's success in winning the *Brown* case at the Supreme Court?
2. What would have happened if the NAACP had devoted itself to seeking change through a policy pathway other than litigation?

INTERNET RESOURCES

Examine the Web sites of the NAACP and the NAACP Legal Defense and Educational Fund to see the goals and current activities of these organizations: http://www.naacp.org and http://www.naacpldf.org

ADDITIONAL READING

Kluger, Richard. *Simple Justice: The History of Brown v. Board of Education*. New York: Random House, 1977.

Tushnet, Mark V. *Making Civil Rights Law: Thurgood Marshall and the Supreme Court, 1936–1961*. New York: Oxford University Press, 1994.

Clarifying the Coverage of the Equal Protection Clause

 5.4 Differentiate between the various tests used by the Supreme Court when deciding discrimination claims under the equal protection clause.

(pages 132–133)

The Court uses three tests to address equal protection claims. Claims of racial discrimination are analyzed by judges under the strict scrutiny test, which examines whether the government can present a "compelling" justification for treating racial group members differently. Claims of gender discrimination are analyzed through the moderate or intermediate scrutiny test, which asks whether the government has "important" reasons for treating men and women differently. Nearly all other kinds of discrimination claims filed under the equal protection clause are examined through the rational basis test, which merely asks whether the government has reason to distinguish between people in order to pursue a legitimate government objective. The government almost never wins when there is proof of racial discrimination and the strict scrutiny test is applied. However, the government usually wins when the rational basis test is applied.

CRITICAL THINKING QUESTIONS

1. How would American society be different if the Supreme Court applied strict scrutiny to all situations of alleged discrimination by government?
2. What, if any, forms of discrimination would be rejected by the Supreme Court under an application of the rational basis test?

INTERNET RESOURCES

Examine the Web sites of two organizations focused on women's issues to see how they define and pursue their markedly different goals: National Organization for Women (http://www.now.org) and Eagle Forum (http://www.eagleforum.org).

ADDITIONAL READING

Baer, Judith, and Leslie Friedman Goldstein. *The Constitutional and Legal Rights of Women*. New York: Oxford University Press, 2006.

Hirsch, H. N. *A Theory of Liberty: The Constitution and Minorities*. New York: Routledge, 1992.

Grassroots Mobilization and Civil Rights

5.5 **Identify the events and factors that influenced the development of grassroots civil rights movement.**

(pages 134–137)

A number of significant events in the 1950s and 1960s mobilized African Americans to mount organized, nonviolent protests despite death threats, sniper bullets, and police brutality directed at them. These events included the the Montgomery bus boycott in response to the arrest of Rosa Parks, and the murders of civil rights workers. The violent response of Southern whites to African Americans' nonviolent demonstrations helped dramatize the need for civil rights protections by changing public opinion and spurring the federal government to take action.

The civil rights movement pushed Congress and state legislatures to enact a variety of statutes including the Civil Rights Act of 1964 and the Voting Rights Act of 1965.

KEY TERMS
Martin Luther King Jr. 134
Civil Rights Act of 1964 135
Voting Rights Act of 1965 136
U.S. Commission on Civil Rights 136
U.S. Equal Employment Opportunity Commission 136

CRITICAL THINKING QUESTIONS
1. How does grassroots mobilization make policy change occur?
2. Without the leadership of Martin Luther King Jr. and Lyndon Johnson, would the same changes in society and public policy ultimately have occurred anyway? If so, how?

INTERNET RESOURCES
Read about the Civil Rights Memorial in Montgomery, Alabama, at http://www.splcenter.org/crm/dedication.jsp A monument and a visitors center honor the people who lost their lives during the civil rights movement, either as a result of their political activism or because of the color of their skin. The Web site of the U.S. Commission on Civil Rights describes its work: http://www.usccr.gov/

ADDITIONAL READING
Branch, Taylor. *Parting the Waters: America in the King Years, 1954–1963.* New York: Simon and Schuster, 1988.

———. *Pillar of Fire: America in the King Years, 1963–1965.* New York: Simon and Schuster, 1998.

Women, Latinos, and Civil Rights

5.6 **Compare and contrast the civil rights struggles of women, Latinos, and African Americans.**

(pages 138–139)

Women and Latinos suffered from many decades of discrimination in employment and other aspects of American life. Although they had not experienced the centuries of enslavement and violence directed at African Americans, they still found themselves denied full and equal participation in American government and society. While African Americans relied on a litigation strategy to produce their major civil rights breakthrough in the twentieth century through the Supreme Court decision in *Brown* v. *Board of Education* (1954), women and Latinos focused on grassroots mobilization in order to gain political rights and economic opportunity.

KEY TERMS
Universal Suffrage 138
César Chávez 139

CRITICAL THINKING QUESTIONS
1. What factors may have made women's struggle for universal suffrage different from African Americans' struggle for civil rights, including voting rights?
2. How will American politics and government be affected by the continued growth of the Latino population and its increasing importance as a segment of registered voters in many states?

INTERNET RESOURCES
The Web site of the Susan B. Anthony Center for Women's Leadership at the University of Rochester provides historical information about women's efforts to obtain the right to vote: http://www.rochester.edu/SBA/suffragehistory.html

Learn about contemporary issues affecting farm workers, especially Latino farm workers, at the Web site of the United Farm Workers union, which was founded by César Chávez: http://www.ufw.org/

ADDITIONAL READING
Flexner, Eleanor, and Ellen Fitzpatrick. *Century of Struggle: The Women's Rights Movement in the United States.* Cambridge, MA: Belknap/Harvard, 1996.

Gutierrez, David G. *The Columbia History of Latinos in the United States Since 1960.* New York: Columbia University Press, 2006.

Contemporary Civil Rights Issues

5.7 Evaluate the continuing debates, lawsuits, and protests over civil rights in the twenty-first century.

(pages 140–141)

Additional groups have emerged to seek civil rights protection through the court and grassroots mobilization pathways. These groups include the disabled as well as gays and lesbians. Although disabled people have been successful in pushing for laws to guard against discrimination in employment and public accommodations, gays and lesbians have been successful in only a few states.

CRITICAL THINKING QUESTIONS

1. Could the disabled or Native Americans effectively use the strategies employed by African Americans, women, and Latinos to advance equality and civil rights? Why or why not?

2. Which emerging groups that currently seek civil rights and equality are likely to have the most difficulty advancing their goals? Why?

INTERNET RESOURCES

You can learn about disability rights organizations (http://www.napas.org/) and gay rights organizations (http://www.glaad.org/mission) as you try to understand their role in emerging civil rights issues.

ADDITIONAL READING

Gerstmann, Evan. *Same-Sex Marriage and the Constitution*, 2nd ed. New York: Cambridge University Press, 2008.

Switzer, Jacqueline. *Disabled Rights: American Disability Policy and the Fight for Equality.* Washington, DC: Georgetown University Press, 2003.

Chapter Review   Test Your Knowledge

1. The concept of civil rights concerns
   a. the individual legal protections in the Bill of Rights.
   b. issues about poverty and wealth discrimination.
   c. legal protections for equality and participation in the country's governing processes.
   d. all aspects of law other than those in the criminal justice system.

2. The American system of government promotes equality of opportunity for all citizens, meaning that it
   a. helps guarantee access to essential goods and services to all Americans.
   b. helps ensure individual self-reliance by outlawing *some* discriminatory barriers to education, employment, and public accommodation.
   c. works to reduce economic disadvantages so that all citizens have access to essential goods and services.
   d. assumes that everyone will achieve the American Dream based on their own efforts.

3. The disadvantages of slavery continue to burden African Americans more than a century after emancipation
   a. because descendants of whites, unlike the descendants of slaves, could enjoy the benefits of education, business contacts, job opportunities, and social networks.
   b. because descendants of slaves are barred from certain occupations.
   c. because there have been no leaders to inspire changes in our laws and culture.
   d. because the Supreme Court has refused to make any decisions that might reduce the effects of racial discrimination.

4. The equal protection clause protects citizens from being deprived of their rights if those rights are being infringed upon by
   a. other individuals.
   b. the federal government.
   c. state and local governments and officials employed by such governments.
   d. local clubs or associations.

5. The equal protection clause is contained in the Declaration of Independence.
   a. true
   b. false

6. Why should every student of American civil rights history know about the Supreme Court case *Plessy* v. *Ferguson* (1896)?
   a. It was the first time the Court applied the equal protection clause to individual acts of discrimination.
   b. It started to turn the tide against Jim Crow legislation at the state level.
   c. It changed how interstate railroads conducted business.
   d. It justified legal segregation across the nation, a backward step in civil rights law that would not be remedied until the middle of the twentieth century.

7. What role did presidents play in civil rights legislation during the twentieth century?
   a. no role at all
   b. pushed for passage of antidiscrimination laws in the 1960s

   c. consistently blocked efforts to enact civil rights legislation
   d. never persuaded the public or Congress that civil rights laws were necessary

8. What are the principles of strict scrutiny, intermediate scrutiny, and rational basis?
   a. three levels of citizen participation in national politics, as theorized in *The Federalist Papers*
   b. three tests by which the Supreme Court evaluates cases under the Civil Rights Act of 1964
   c. three tests by which the Supreme Court evaluates cases about the equal protection clause
   d. three levels of discrimination that prosecutors can charge in civil rights cases

9. According to decades of Supreme Court interpretation, the equal protection clause provides general protection for civil rights by always requiring the government to treat all people equally before the law.
   a. true
   b. false

10. Single-sex state universities are permissible if they have military-focused education.
    a. true
    b. false

11. What best explains the relationship between grassroots mobilization and civil rights legislation in the early 1960s?
    a. Grassroots activism helped pave the way for the enactment of progressive legislation.
    b. Dramatic civil rights legislation put an end to all grassroots activism.
    c. Grassroots activists were elected to Congress in large numbers and then easily passed the laws they wanted.
    d. The two activities operated in isolation; neither had much effect on the other.

12. By working to ensure equal access to the ballot box for all voters irrespective of race, the Voting Rights Act of 1965 accomplished what lawmakers had first tried to accomplish with
    a. *Plessy* v. *Ferguson* (1986)
    b. *Marburg* v. *Madison* (1803)
    c. the New Deal legislation during the 1930s.
    d. the Fifteenth Amendment in 1870.

13. The Nineteenth Amendment, granting women the right to vote in national elections,
    a. was accomplished without the assistance of any grassroots mobilization.
    b. catapulted women into positions of authority equal to men.
    c. resulted, in part, from persistent political action in states throughout the country.
    d. was mandated by the Fifteenth Amendment.

14. The political movement to achieve universal suffrage for all adult citizens
    a. was organized by women in the National Woman Suffrage Association.
    b. was led by men in the American Civil Liberties Union.
    c. was led by Cesar Chavez.
    d. has yet to be accomplished in the United States.

15. At the time that the Nineteenth Amendment was ratified and gave women the right to vote,
    a. national action was needed to grant suffrage because women's efforts to gain the vote had failed in every state.
    b. national action on the suffrage issue followed from successful efforts to gain the vote for women in a number of states.
    c. students threatened to shut down every university in the country by boycotting classes if women could not vote.
    d. the Supreme Court had just ruled that preventing women from voting violated the equal protection clause.

16. Civil rights activism on behalf of Latinos will probably continue in the years to come, because
    a. Latinos are now the largest minority group in the country.
    b. television news encourages people to stage protests.
    c. a majority of legislators in Texas and California are now Latinos.
    d. President George W. Bush devoted his presidency to encouraging people to become involved in civil rights issues.

17. Racial segregation in housing existed in the North in the 1960s largely because
    a. all states had laws requiring people of different races to live in different neighborhoods.
    b. African Americans wanted to live around other African Americans and not around whites.
    c. real estate agents and mortgage bankers refused to show houses and grant loans to African Americans who were interested in living in white neighborhoods.
    d. police officers threatened African Americans with arrest if they tried to purchase houses in white neighborhoods.

18. In the United States, laws, by themselves, even if well-written and actively enforced, cannot create complete equality because
    a. people never obey laws with which they disagree.
    b. laws are directed only at specific kinds of discrimination in limited contexts, such as race discrimination in employment.
    c. each individual state has complete control over the antidiscrimination laws that apply within its boundaries.
    d. people are poor due to their own desire to be poor.

19. The Americans with Disabilities Act of 1990 forbids discrimination in employment and public accommodations (e.g., restaurants and other businesses), but it applies only in states with a proven history of discrimination against disabled people.
    a. true   b. false

20. Martin Luther King Jr. and César Chávez are most closely associated with which pathway of action on civil rights issues?
    a. court   c. elections
    b. lobbying   d. grassroots mobilization

mypoliscilab Exercises

Apply what you learned in this chapter on **MyPoliSciLab.**

Read on **mypoliscilab.com**

   eText: Chapter 5

Study and **Review** on **mypoliscilab.com**

   Pre-Test
   Post-Test
   Chapter Exam
   Flashcards

Watch on **mypoliscilab.com**

   Video: Supreme Court: No Race-Based Admissions
   Video: Should Don't Ask Don't Tell Go Away?

Explore on **mypoliscilab.com**

   Simulation: You Are the Mayor and Need to Make Civil Rights Decisions
   Comparative: Comparing Civil Rights
   Timeline: The Civil Rights Movement
   Timeline: The Struggle for Equal Protection
   Timeline: The Mexican-American Civil Rights Movement
   Timeline: Women's Struggle for Equality
   Visual Literacy: Race and the Death Penalty

A PLEDGE TO AMERICA
a new governing agenda built on
THE PRIORITIES OF OUR NATION, THE PRINCIPLES WE STAND FOR & AMERICA'S FOUNDING VALUES
pledge.GOP.gov
A PLEDGE TO AMERICA

Congress

KEY OBJECTIVES

After completing this chapter, you should be prepared to:

6.1 Differentiate between the various ways legislators represent the interests of their constituents.

6.2 Identify the key constitutional provisions that shape the way Congress functions.

6.3 Establish the importance of committees in organizing the legislative process.

6.4 Assess how political parties and leaders manage the legislative process while advancing their own initiatives.

6.5 Show how the rules and norms of behavior help ensure a more orderly, efficient legislative process.

6.6 Outline the process by which a bill becomes a law.

6.7 Determine whether members of Congress mirror America's demographic diversity and why this matters.

6.8 Compare the state of congressional ethics with Americans' perception of the legislative branch.

It took more than a decade for the Democrats to rebound after their stunning defeat in the 1994 midterm election. Led by Newt Gingrich of Georgia, Republicans had run on a platform known as the "Contract with America" in which they promised to enact a series of policy initiatives. In that election some 54 House and 8 Senate seats swung to the Republicans. Even the Democratic Speaker, Tom Foley, lost his seat—an event that had not happened since the Civil War. It was a stunning GOP victory.

Yet, guiding the Republican Party in the House proved difficult, and within a few years Gingrich had resigned his post. It took some time, but through a series of successful elections Democrats were back in charge by 2006. They elected the first female Speaker, Nancy Pelosi of California, and with the election of Barack Obama in 2008, the stage seemed set for the Democrats to affect change.

And affect change they did. In the midst of an increasingly polarized public mood and partisan Congress, and during one of the nation's toughest economic recessions, the Democrats passed an array of new policies, including bills pertaining to economic stimulus,

> **How does the national legislature turn public concerns into public policy?**

health care reform, financial regulatory reform, education reform, and energy policy. While help from Republicans was rare, Democrats claimed to be responding to a mandate from the voters. Or so they thought.

Circumstances can change quickly in American politics, and the 2010 midterm election proved remarkably similar to the 1994 election. Republicans gained a majority in the House, with some 60 seats switching hands. In the Senate, the GOP added 6 seats, just short of the number needed to capture majority control. Voters sent a message that the changes brought by the Democrats were not the changes they had hoped for.

Taking Pelosi's place as Speaker of the House of the 112th Congress would be John Boehner of Ohio. After winning election in 1990, Boehner built a long list of accomplishments. As a novice legislator, he had worked closely with Gingrich to mastermind the "Contract with America," and since then he had become a forceful and steadfast defender of GOP initiatives. It remains to be seen, however, if Boehner will heed the lessons learned in 1994 and steer his colleagues down a different path.

Resource Center
• Glossary
• Vocabulary Example
• Connect the Link

■ **Delegate Model of Representation:** The philosophy that legislators should adhere to the will of their constituents.

SIGNIFICANCE: *This approach places a great deal of emphasis on the perspective of average citizens.*

■ **Trustee Model of Representation:** The philosophy that legislators should consider the will of the people but act in ways they believe best for the long-term interests of the nation.

SIGNIFICANCE: *This model underscores the deliberative powers of the legislator and the long-term interests of the nation.*

The Nature and Style of Representation

6.1 Differentiate between the various ways legislators represent the interests of their constituents.
(pages 154–155)

There are a number of important questions that we can ask about the precise job of members of Congress. Whom do they represent? What do they seek to accomplish? At the core, the job of any representative is to speak and act on behalf of others.

Thomas Paine, the revolutionary propagandist and political thinker, suggested in his famous 1776 pamphlet *Common Sense* that legislators must "act in the same manner as the whole body would act, were they present." This perspective has been called the **delegate model of representation**■ (see Figure 6.1). Here, the legislator does his or her best to discern the will of the people and then acts accordingly.

A very different approach is called the **trustee model of representation**■. This was the outlook favored by most of the delegates at the Constitutional Convention. It holds that the legislator should consider the will of the people but then do what he or she thinks is best for the nation as a whole and in the long term.

There is no right or wrong model, each has held more sway at different points in our history. Although the trustee perspective was dominant in the early years of the Republic, several changes have made the delegate model more popular today. For example, the number of career legislators has shot up in recent decades. To retain their seats, legislators are often eager to appease the public. "Public opinion" is also much easier to discern, given the accuracy and frequency of polls. Two contemporary American political scientists conclude, "The core dictate of this new breed of politician, as we might expect, is to win reelection each year. This means keeping your votes in line with the wishes of those in the district."[2]

Of course, there are middle-ground perspectives, too. The **politico model of representation**■ holds that legislators should feel free to follow their own judgment on matters where the public remains silent. Another perspective is called the **conscience model of representation**■, or what we might call the "pillow test." On most matters, representatives are delegates and heed the wishes of constituents, but if a particular position really disturbs representatives to the point that they can't sleep at night, they turn into trustees and vote the other way.

There is also the issue of whether legislators should spend their time working on broad-based policy initiatives or on

FIGURE 6.1 ■ **Representing the Will of the People**
There are different approaches to representation, as this figure suggests. —*Should legislators act as their constituents would if they were present, or should they work to "enlarge and refine" the public will? Does it depend on the issue at hand? Are there contemporary forces pushing legislators toward one perspective?*

Delegate Model	Politico Model	Conscience Model	Trustee Model
The job of a legislator is to stick to the will of the people	A legislator might follow his or her own sense of what is right until the public becomes involved in the issue, at which point he or she should heed their wishes	A legislator follows the will of the people in most instances until conscience pulls him or her in a different direction	The job of a legislator is to use information and the powers of deliberation to arrive at his or her own assessment; to "enlarge and refine the public's will"
"To say the sovereignty rests in the people, and that they have not a right to instruct and control their representatives, is absurd to the last degree." —**Representative Elbridge Gerry** (1744–1814) of Massachusetts during a debate over the ratification of the First Amendment	"The average legislator early in his career discovers that there are certain interests or prejudices of his constituents which are dangerous to trifle with." —**Senator J. Willian Fulbright** (1905–1995) of Arkansas	Former House member **Sherwood Boehlert** (1936–) of New York called this the "pillow test." He argued that the job of a legislator is to follow the will of constituents until doing so keeps the legislator awake at night.	"Have the people of this country snatched the power of deliberation from this body? Are we a body of agents and not a deliberate one?" —**John C. Calhoun** (1782–1850) of South Carolina, vice president and member of the House and Senate during a debate over a bill fixing compensation for members of Congress

■ **Politico Model of Representation:** Legislators follow their own judgment until the public becomes vocal about a particular matter, at which point they should follow the dictates of constituents.

EXAMPLE: *A legislator who announces "I vote the way I think is best—until the message from folks back home is loud and clear!" would be acting like a politico.*

■ **Conscience Model of Representation:** The philosophy that legislators should follow the will of the people until they truly believe it is in the best interests of the nation to act differently.

EXAMPLE: *A legislator who announces "I usually back what the folks back home want—until that choice keeps me up at night!" would be following this approach.*

Third-grader Sophie Reece asks U.S. Senator Mitch McConnell a question in Maysville, KY in 2009. McConnell was in town to present federal funds for the renovation of a historic building. —*Should legislators always focus on bringing home as much federal aid as possible?*

direct constituency needs. We might call this a question of *representational style*. Some legislators focus on major policy matters, such as health care reform, foreign policy, national defense, international trade, and immigration; others concentrate on helping constituents get their share from the federal government. **Constituent service** (also called *casework*) makes up a great deal of what legislators and their staff do on a daily basis.

Finally, there is the issue of **symbolic representation.** Many analysts have argued that an important facet of the legislators' job is to speak on behalf of the groups they belong to—especially their demographic group. As a prominent scholar of the legislative process recently noted, "When a member of an ethnic or racial group goes to Congress, it is a badge of legitimacy for the entire grouping. . . . Moreover, there can be tangible gains in the quality of representation."[3] More will be said of symbolic representation when we discuss redistricting.

The Nature and Style of Representation

6.1 Differentiate between the various ways legislators represent the interests of their constituents.

PRACTICE QUIZ: UNDERSTAND AND APPLY

1. What is the difference between the delegate model and the trustee model of representation?
   a. Representatives following the delegate model find out the will of their constituents and act on their behalf; representatives following the trustee model simply do what they think is best for the nation.
   b. Representatives following the delegate model delegate their responsibilities to staff members; representatives following the trustee model carry out those responsibilities themselves.
   c. Representatives following the delegate model simply do what they think is best for the nation; representatives following the trustee model find out the will of their constituents and act on their behalf.
   d. Representatives following the delegate model find out the will of their constituents and act on their behalf; representatives following the trustee model consider the will of their constituents but then do what they think is best for the nation in the long run.

2. If a legislator supported a measure letting factories be built on a river in her home district but then reversed her decision when she worried about pollution being sent downstream, what model of representation would she be following?
   a. hypocritical model
   b. politico model
   c. trustee model
   d. conscience model

3. Which of the following would be an example of constituent service performed by a representative?
   a. drafting a bill that would bring federal assistance to the representative's home district
   b. helping parents in the home district find out where their son is stationed overseas
   c. voting to raise veterans' benefits, and announcing that vote to people in the home district
   d. campaigning for reelection by marching in a local parade

ANALYZE

1. A prominent scholar once noted that members of Congress are individually responsive, collectively irresponsible. What do you think this phrase means? Would you agree?

2. What impact do you think "social media" has on the way legislators represent their constituents?

IDENTIFY THE CONCEPT THAT DOESN'T BELONG

a. Survey research
b. Career legislators
c. An indifferent public
d. the Internet
e. Frequent elections

Resource Center
• Glossary
• Vocabulary Example
• Connect the Link

■ **Bicameral Legislature:** A legislature composed of two houses.

EXAMPLE: *Congress is a bicameral legislature because it has two chambers, the House of Representatives and the Senate.*

■ **Seventeenth Amendment:** Change to the U.S. Constitution, ratified in 1913, which provides for the direct election of senators.

SIGNIFICANCE: *Average citizens are now allowed to vote for Senators instead of relying upon state legislators to make the choice.*

Congress and the Constitution

6.2 Identify the key constitutional provisions that shape the way Congress functions.

(pages 156–161)

A Bicameral Legislature

Article I, Section 1, of the Constitution established a two-chamber or **bicameral legislature**■ (see Table 6.1). The House of Representatives, with its legislators directly elected by the people to relatively short terms of office, seemed to stick closely to the spirit of 1776. That is to say, the House reflected the idea that average citizens should select leaders who would follow their wishes rather closely. Yet the other chamber of the legislature, the Senate, allowed state legislatures to pick senators. And by granting senators six-year terms, the Constitution seemed to check the democratic impulses of the day. However, by giving each state equal representation, the Senate also reflects the spirit of 1776. We might say, then, that the battle of the Virginia Plan against the New Jersey Plan in the Philadelphia Convention had involved two conflicting Revolutionary Era visions of representation: sovereign people versus sovereign states.

This balancing act would be revisited throughout much of our history. Before the Civil War, for example, John C. Calhoun, a representative and, later, a senator from South Carolina, as well as vice president under Andrew Jackson, advocated a theory of "nullification." Calhoun's idea was that within their own borders, states had the right to nullify—to declare null and void—acts of Congress. Roughly 100 years later, southern lawmakers again argued that "states' rights" and "state sovereignty" granted them the right to ignore desegregation mandates from the federal courts. More recently, battles over controversial issues such as doctor-assisted suicide, medical marijuana, and same-sex marriage have elicited similar arguments.

Who Can Serve in Congress?

Article I, Section 2, of the Constitution sets the length of terms for House members (two years) and specifies the basic qualifications for service. House members must be 25 years of age, a citizen of the United States for at least seven years, and a resident of the state where they are elected. Notice, however, that the Constitution does *not* say that House members must reside in the district they represent. Throughout our history, on a number of occasions, politicians have been elected to represent districts in which they did not live. Nor does the Constitution put any limit on the number of terms a representative may serve. In the early 1990s, a number of states tried to limit the terms of members of Congress—both in the House and in the Senate. The Supreme Court, however, in *Term Limits, Inc.* v. *Thornton* (1995), found such restrictions unconstitutional. It seems, then, that the only way to limit the number of terms for members of Congress would be a constitutional amendment.

Article I, Section 3, begins with the method of selecting a senator. Originally, the Constitution stated that each state legislature would select its two U.S. senators. This changed with ratification of the **Seventeenth Amendment**■ in 1913,

TABLE 6.1	Key Differences Between the House and the Senate

How do these differences shape the way members of each chamber approach their job of representing the "will of the people"?	
HOUSE OF REPRESENTATIVES	**SENATE**
435 members (apportionment based on state population)	100 members (2 from each state)
2-year terms	6-year terms
Less flexible rules	More flexible rules
Limited debate	Virtually unlimited debate
Policy specialists with an emphasis on taxes and revenues	Policy generalists with an emphasis on foreign policy
Less media coverage	More media coverage
Centralized power (with committee leaders)	Equal distribution of power
More partisan	Somewhat less partisan
High turnover rate	Moderate turnover rate

CONNECT THE LINK (Chapter 7, pages 207-208) How often do presidents veto legislation?

■ **Rotation:** The staggering of senatorial terms such that one-third of the Senate comes up for election every two years.

SIGNIFICANCE: *No more than 34 Senators are up for election in a given year, making it more difficult to dramatically change the composition of the Senate.*

■ **Pocket Veto:** The president's killing of a bill that has been passed by both houses of Congress, simply by not signing it; within 10 days of the bill's passage.

SIGNIFICANCE: *Presidents have used this approach when they wanted to quietly kill a bill, but these days, it is rarely employed.*

and senators are now elected directly by the voters of their state. The next clause deals with the length of senatorial terms (six years) and makes a special provision called **rotation**■. Rather than have all senators come up for election every six years, the Constitution divides the Senate into three "classes," each of which must stand for election every two years. Rotation ensures that the Senate's membership can never be changed all at once just because the public has become outraged over some issue. This gives the Senate greater stability than the House—exactly what the framers intended.

A senator must be 30 years old, a citizen of the United States for at least nine years, and a resident of the state he or she represents. The Constitution, however, does not stipulate *how long* the person has to be a resident of that state before serving in the Senate. Occasionally, politicians are elected to represent a state where they had not previously lived. A good example was the election to the Senate in 2000 of Hillary Rodham Clinton, a native of Illinois and a resident of Arkansas (where her husband had been governor before becoming president), to represent the state of New York.

Aaron Schock was elected to the Peoria, Illinois, school board at the age of 19 and to the state legislature at 23. In this picture, Schock acknowledges applause from supporters after winning—at 27 years of age—the 18th Congressional District Republican primary race in Peoria on February 5, 2008. He went on to win the general election in November. —*Does it make sense to have young Americans in Congress, or should this job be left to seasoned adults?*

Congressional Elections

Article I, Section 4, of the Constitution outlines the congressional election process. Each state can decide the time, place, and manner of elections to the national legislature—so long as Congress remains silent on the matter. For the most part, Congress has left the regulation of congressional elections to the states, but it has stepped in at important and controversial times. Poll taxes, literacy tests, and excessive residency requirements were used, particularly in many southern states, to keep African Americans from voting (in defiance of the Fifteenth Amendment). Congress responded with the Voting Rights Act of 1965. Later, in 1993, hoping to get more Americans to the polls, Congress passed the National Voter Registration Act (also known as the "Motor Voter Law"), which mandates that all states allow citizens to register to vote at certain frequently used public facilities, including motor vehicle offices. More recently, Congress moved to standardize the manner of voting after the recount fiasco in Florida during the 2000 presidential election (the Help America Vote Act of 2002).

Lawmaking

Article I, Section 7, of the Constitution addresses how a bill becomes law and also specifies the checks and balances between the two houses of the legislature and between the other branches of the government. The same piece of legislation must be approved by a majority of each house of the legislature before it goes to the president for signature into law. If the president signs the bill, it becomes law. Should the president fail to act on the bill for 10 days (not counting Sundays), it becomes law anyway—unless Congress has adjourned in the meantime, in which case it is known as a **pocket veto**■. If the president vetoes the bill, however, a two-thirds vote in both houses is necessary to override the veto. (See also Chapter 7, pages 207–208.)

Article I, Section 8, lists the powers of the legislative branch (see Table 6.2). This list was controversial for two reasons: First, although the framers thought it important to define the powers of Congress, there was still widespread public resistance to giving excessive power to the national government. Second, even though the framers were willing to give the national government broad powers, listing them carried a risk of leaving something out—something that might later prove significant. Inclusion of the last clause of Section 8 seemed to provide a solution. This provision, often called the **elastic clause** or the **necessary and proper clause**■, states that Congress has the power to make all laws "necessary and proper" to implement any of the other powers mentioned in the section. This clause suggested that many congressional powers were *implied* rather than spelled out in detail.

By 1819, the Supreme Court had put the argument for implied powers on a stronger foundation. As discussed in Chapter 3, pages 72–77, in his majority opinion in the case of *McCulloch* v. *Maryland,* Chief Justice John Marshall made it

CONNECT THE
LINK
(Chapter 3, pages 72-77)

■ **Elastic Clause/Necessary and Proper Clause:** The Constitution that grants Congress the power to pass all laws "necessary and proper" for carrying out the list of expressed powers.

SIGNIFICANCE: *This clause has been interpreted in ways that grant Congress very broad policymaking powers.*

■ **At-Large Districts:** Districts encompassing an entire state, or large parts of a state, in which House members are elected to represent the entire area.

EXAMPLE: *Because North Dakota is allotted only one House seat, the entire state is an at-large district.*

TABLE 6.2	Powers of Congress under the U.S. Constitution

One of the dangers of listing an organization's powers is that all circumstances may not be covered. The framers of the Constitution understood this and added the final element to deal with unforeseen circumstances. Yet, the "elastic clause" has proved controversial because the Supreme Court has interpreted it in broad terms, thus granting Congress sweeping powers. —**Do you think the national legislature should have these expansive powers?**

CLAUSE	POWER GRANTED IN ARTICLE I, SECTION 8
1	Levy and collect taxes and duties and provide for the common defense
2	Borrow money on credit
3	Regulate commerce with foreign nations and between the states
4	Establish rules on naturalization and bankruptcy
5	Coin money
6	Create punishments for counterfeiting
7	Establish post offices
8	Promote the progress of science and the arts
9	Constitute tribunals below the Supreme Court
10	Punish crimes on the high seas
11	Declare war
12	Raise and support the army
13	Provide and maintain a navy
14	Make rules for the use of armed forces
15	Call out the militia
16	Organize, arm, and discipline the militia
17	Exercise exclusive legislation over the district of the seat of the federal government
18	Make all laws deemed "necessary and proper" for implementing these powers

clear that Congress did, indeed, have "implied powers." The case concerned a branch of the federally chartered Bank of the United States located in the state of Maryland. The Maryland legislature had levied a tax on the Bank of the United States. But could a state government tax an institution created by the national government? And—resurrecting the question that Jefferson and Madison had asked back in 1790—where does the Constitution give Congress the power to create a national bank?

As to the first question, Marshall wrote, "The power to tax involves the power to destroy." That would suggest some sort of supremacy. Yet the Constitution is clear that the national government is supreme, so the tax (which could, if heavy enough, put the national bank out of business) was unconstitutional. As to the broader question—the power to

charter a bank—Marshall used the same argument Hamilton had advanced:

> Let the end be legitimate, let it be within the scope of the constitution, and all means which are appropriate, which are plainly adapted to that end, which are not prohibited, but consistent with the letter and spirit of the constitution, are constitutional.

In one clean sweep, Marshall's ruling greatly expanded the scope of the national government's power.

Redistricting

The Great Compromise had stipulated that Congress be divided into two houses, one with an identical number of

■ **Redistricting:** The process of redrawing legislative district boundaries within a state to reflect population changes.

SIGNIFICANCE: *The exact boundaries of a district can determine the partisan leanings of the electorate, thus aiding particular types of candidates.*

■ **Gerrymandering:** Drawing legislative district boundaries in such a way as to gain political advantage.

SIGNIFICANCE: *The majority party in the state legislature will often try to draw new district lines that give candidates in their party a better chance of victory.*

legislators from each state (the Senate) and the other based on population (the House of Representatives). But how would we know the number of citizens in each state? The Constitution also stipulates that a census be conducted every 10 years and that seats be allocated to each state based on this count. However, if a state gets more than one seat (and most states do), who then is responsible for drawing the boundaries of legislative districts—or should there even *be* legislative districts? The Constitution left these questions to the states to decide, and they have caused considerable controversy ever since.

In the earliest days of the Republic, some states did use **at-large districts**■. If they were granted three seats in the House, they would simply elect three members from the entire state. Those states had no districts. Most states, however, chose to divide their territory into a number of congressional districts equal to the number of seats they were allocated in the House of Representatives. The idea of changing legislative districts in response to population shifts stems from the American idea of **geographic representation.** That is, our representatives should be directly responsible to a group of people living in a specific geographic location. Today, drawing the boundaries for congressional districts has become a tricky and controversial process. In all states except very small ones that have only a single representative, the process must be undertaken every 10 years to reflect changes in the state's overall population relative to the rest of the country, as well as to respond to population shifts within the state. This process of redrawing the boundaries of legislative districts is called **redistricting**■. The Constitution gives state legislatures the redistricting power. Because these bodies have nearly always been partisan (controlled by a majority of members from one party), the process causes a lot of partisan wrangling.

Gerrymandering■ is the drawing of legislative districts for partisan advantage. The word immortalizes one Elbridge Gerry, who as governor of Massachusetts around 1800 persuaded his followers in the state legislature to draw an odd-shaped district, wiggling across the state, designed to elect a political ally. Looking at the map, someone said that the new district looked like a salamander, to which someone else replied that it wasn't a salamander but "a Gerrymander" (see Figure 6.2).[4] The name stuck. Gerrymandering means the creation of oddly shaped districts as a means of shaping the results of future elections in those districts. This has been done in a number of ways, but mostly through either *packing* or *cracking.* Packing is lumping as many opposition voters as possible into one district. For instance, if the state has five districts, the idea is to fill one of these districts overwhelmingly with supporters of the other party. The party in power—the politicians drawing the lines—would give up that one seat, but the other four districts would be shaped to nearly guarantee that candidates of their party would win. Cracking involves splitting up groups of voters thought to favor the opposition so that they do not make up a majority in any district and thus cannot win in any district.

The redistricting process has also been used to minimize the representation of minority groups. Thirty percent of a state's population, for example, might be black, but through cracking, it could be fixed so that these voters would never be able to elect an African American legislator without the help of white voters. Or, through packing, most of the black population might be concentrated in one virtually all-black district, enabling whites to elect representatives from the other districts.

Some states have moved toward using nonpartisan organizations to draw district lines. Iowa has taken this trend furthest, using a complex computer program administered by a nonpartisan commission to draw geographically compact and equal districts. The state legislature then votes these districts up or down, but it cannot amend them. This process has spared Iowa from court challenges and has generally produced competitive congressional races. For example, in the 2006 election, three out of five of Iowa's

FIGURE 6.2 ■ **That's not a salamander, it's a Gerrymander!**

As Governor of Massachusetts in 1812, Elbridge Gerry prompted his fellow Republicans in the state legislature to draw congressional district lines that favored their party. As the story goes, a reporter looked at one of these new districts and commented that it looked like a salamander. Another noted, "That's not a salamander, that's a Gerrymander!" Partisan-based redistricting is an age-old problem. —*Should legislatures allow nonpartisan groups to draw new district lines?*

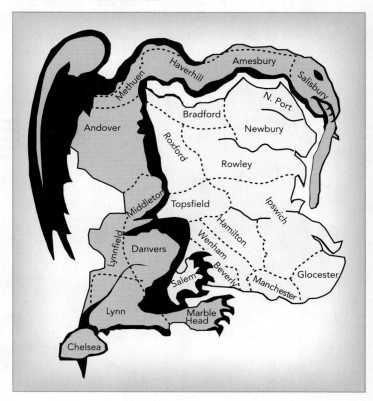

■ *Baker* v. *Carr* (1961): Supreme Court case that set the standard that House districts must contain equal numbers of constituents, thus establishing the principle of "one person, one vote."

SIGNIFICANCE: *Every citizen has the same "weight" in the legislative process. However, in order to get the same number of residents in each district, the boundaries are often oddly shaped, and diverse communities are sometimes lumped together.*

U.S. House races were considered competitive, compared to only 1 out of 10 in the rest of the nation.[5] Several other states are considering similar moves, including New York and Virginia.

For the most part, redistricting has been a tricky issue for the courts. On a number of occasions, the courts refused to get involved in the controversy.[6] However, in more recent decades, the courts have signaled a greater willingness to hear such cases. The complexity of the reapportionment process continues to makes judicial intervention difficult.

POSITIVE GERRYMANDERING Amendments to the Voting Rights Act of 1965, which were passed in 1982, approached the racial gerrymandering issue from an entirely different direction. If the redistricting process has been used in the past to limit minority representation, could it not be used to *increase* minority representation? Perhaps census data could be used to construct districts that would better ensure the election of minority legislators. After the 1990 census, 24 **majority-minority districts**—districts in which a minority group made up a majority of the population—were created in different states. Fifteen of these districts had majorities of African American voters, and nine had a majority of Hispanic voters.

The scheme seemed to work: In each of these districts, the voters chose a minority legislator. Nevertheless, two issues came up. First, the resulting districts were often oddly shaped. In North Carolina's 12th Congressional District, for example, a roughly 100-mile strip of Interstate 85, on which almost no one lived, connected black communities in Durham and Charlotte. Second, the overt consideration of race in drawing highly irregular districts was challenged in the courts as an affront to the equal protection clause of the Fourteenth Amendment. In a series of

decisions in the 1990s, the Court generally supported plans that improved the likelihood of minority representation but seemed reluctant to allow highly irregularly shaped districts (*Shaw* v. *Reno,* 1993) or to approve schemes that use race as the primary criterion for drawing district lines (*Miller* v. *Johnson,* 1995).

NUMBER OF RESIDENTS PER DISTRICT Related to the difficult issue of drawing district lines is the question of the number of residents per district. Oddly enough, the Constitution is silent on this matter, and for most of our history, many states did not ensure that every district had the same number of constituents.

The issue of malapportionment came to a head in the mid-twentieth century when a group of Tennessee residents claimed that the state legislature had denied them equal protection under the law by refusing to draw districts with the same population. In 1961, the Supreme Court decided that the Tennessee districts were so out of proportion that they violated the plaintiffs' constitutional rights. This case, *Baker* v. *Carr* ■, wrote the "one person, one vote" principle into federal law.[7] It also sparked a revolution in the way legislative districts were drawn.

In the post-*Baker* era, geographic concerns took a backseat to ensuring equal population in all districts. These later cases also mandated that redistricting happen every 10 years, even if the size of the state's congressional delegation remained unchanged. This was mandated because population shifts over a decade would mean that old districts would be unlikely to have equal populations. Perhaps most important, *Baker* v. *Carr* inserted the federal courts into the redistricting process, thereby leaving any plan open to a court challenge. Along with the mandate under the Voting Rights Act of 1965 to prevent racial discrimination in voting, *Baker* v. *Carr* has made redistricting a tedious process

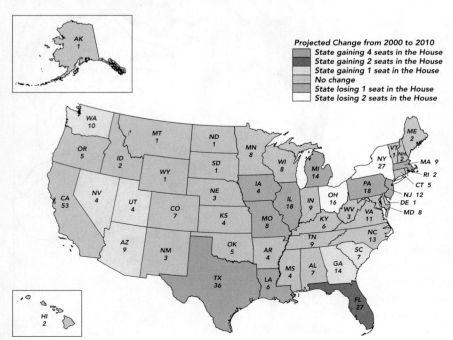

Projected Change from 2000 to 2010
State gaining 4 seats in the House
State gaining 2 seats in the House
State gaining 1 seat in the House
No change
State losing 1 seat in the House
State losing 2 seats in the House

FIGURE 6.3 ■ Projected Distribution of Congressional Power

The framers mandated that a census be taken every 10 years and that the allocation of House seats to each state be reapportioned accordingly. This map shows the projected changes after the 2010 Census. —*What are some of the patterns that emerge? What will be some of the political implications of population changes in the decades to come?*

SOURCE: U.S. Census Burea and http://www.election dataservices.com/NR-Appor2010ESRI-finalwTableMap .pdfs

■ **Reapportionment:** The process by which seats in the House of Representatives are reassigned among the states to reflect population changes following the Census (every 10 years).

SIGNIFICANCE: *Because some states grow in population while others either grow at a slower pace or lose residents, every 10 years each state's allocation of House members is adjusted. Each state is guaranteed at least one House member.*

of moving district lines block by block until the population balance is correct, while constantly facing the threat that a federal court will find the entire scheme unconstitutional.[8]

REAPPORTIONMENT   Finally, the redistricting process is controversial because the allotment of seats per state shifts with each new census (see Figure 6.3). The process of shifting the number of seats allotted to each state is called **reapportionment**■. Originally, the Constitution set the ratio of residents per House member at 1 to 30,000, meaning there were 65 House members in the First Congress. As the nation's population grew, so did the number of representatives in the House. The membership of the House jumped from 141 in 1800 to 240 in 1830. By 1910, the House had grown to 435 members. That seemed large enough, so its membership was capped by Congress. Today, there are roughly 670,000 residents for each House district.

Reapportionment implies that the fastest-growing states gain seats after each census and that seats are taken from the slower-growing states. In recent years, several states—such as Michigan, Rhode Island, Ohio, and North Dakota—have experienced a loss or no growth in population. As a result of the 2010 Census, for example, New York, Pennsylvania, and Ohio are projected to lose House seats. The winners are likely to be southern and southwestern states. For example, it is projected that Florida will gain two seats and Texas will net an additional four seats following the 2010 Census.

Losing seats in the national legislature can be devastating for a state, because much of the federal government's domestic spending is proportionate to a state's population. Having fewer residents means getting fewer federal dollars.

An interesting argument has also emerged over the actual population of each state. Democrats often charge that many citizens are missed in the counting process of the census. They argue that statistical models for estimating populations would actually yield more accurate results than trying to physically count everyone. Republicans, on the other hand, often point out that the Constitution stipulates a full *person-by-person* count; until the Constitution is changed, they say, there is no alternative. The battle over the census counts is partisan, because most analysts agree that the chance of citizens being missed is greatest in the northeastern urban states, which lean Democratic. Arguments made by both sides get louder every 10 years when a new census is conducted, but for now, the Republicans seem to have the courts on their side.

Congress and the Constitution

6.2   **Identify the key constitutional provisions that shape the way Congress functions.**

PRACTICE QUIZ: UNDERSTAND AND APPLY

1. What is the primary difference between the Senate as it was designed by the Constitutional Convention and how it operates today?
   a. Senators were originally limited to two 4-year terms.
   b. Senators could serve an unlimited number of terms, but each was only 2 years long.
   c. Each state was granted a number of senators proportional to its population.
   d. Each state legislature picked its U.S. senators; they were not chosen through popular election.

2. What was the logic behind court decisions mandating that each member of the House represent roughly the same number of constituents?
   a. the notion that each state should receive as much federal money as any other
   b. the democratic principle that all voters are to be granted the same political weight in the House
   c. the idea that no state or district should be paying higher taxes than any other
   d. the recognition that "separate" is never "equal"

3. What provision in the Constitution states that Congress has the power to make all the laws needed to implement the other powers specified in the Constitution?

   a. the sufficient and provisional clause
   b. the necessary and proper clause
   c. the rights and privileges clause
   d. the congressional sovereignty clause

ANALYZE

1. Consider the following paradox: Most Americans agree with the notion of "one person, one vote"; which means there should be the same number of constituents in every House district. However, most Americans also accept the notion of geographic representation that underscores the Senate. Does it make sense for Delaware's residents to have the same say in the Senate as California's residents?

2. Discuss the tactics that have been used to minimize the voting impact of minority groups through legislative redistricting (gerrymandering). Why is it important to know about these tactics as we enter into the redistricting process following the 2010 Census?

IDENTIFY THE CONCEPT THAT DOESN'T BELONG

a. Term limits
b. Regular elections
c. Enumerated powers
d. Elastic clause
e. Redistricting

Resource Center
• Glossary
• Vocabulary Example
• Connect the Link

■ **Subcommittees:**
Specialized groups within standing committees.

EXAMPLE: *The House Subcommittee on Horticulture and Organic Agriculture is relatively new.*

Organizing Congress: Committees

6.3 Establish the importance of committees in organizing the legislative process.

(pages 162–165)

The national legislature is called upon to undertake numerous important functions, which include creating legislation; overseeing federal agencies and departments; creating policies for the collection and appropriation of federal monies; serving constituents (often referred to as *case work*); investigating public issues and matters of growing concern; and providing the president with advice and consent on treaties and appointments to federal offices. Much of this work is defined in the Constitution, but the Constitution says very little about *how* the two legislative chambers should be structured and organized to fulfill these critical governmental functions.

The issues of structure and organization are also important when considering how policy change might be accomplished through the legislative process and how individual citizens might make a difference. Each of the organizing elements discussed in the next three sections gives citizens points of access into the policy development process. We look at the key organizing forces within the legislative process, the nonconstitutional components that help hundreds of individual legislators merge into a lawmaking, appropriating, and oversight body. We begin with the workhorses of the legislature: committees.

Standing Committees

Standing committees are the permanent structures that perform the detailed work of a legislature, such as drafting bills for consideration. There are many advantages to the standing committee system, which was first set up in the House in 1810 and in the Senate shortly thereafter.

First, members of each committee become experts in that policy area so that they can better determine the importance and implications of proposals. To accomplish this, each committee acquires a staff of experts who help legislators make informed decisions. As issues become more and more complex, the "expertise function" becomes even more important.

Second, by dividing the legislature's work between dozens of committees, or "minilegislatures," a vast number of measures can be considered simultaneously. As two leading congressional scholars have noted, "Without committees, a legislative body consisting of 100 senators and 441 House members could not handle roughly 10,000 bills and nearly 100,000 nominations biennially, a national budget over $3 trillion, and a limitless array of controversial issues."[9]

Third, this system enhances the representation process by allowing legislators to sit on committees that deal with issues of interest to their constituents. For example, many legislators from the midwestern Farm Belt might best serve their constituents by sitting on an agriculture committee. Most often, however, constituent interests are varied, making the fit with a particular committee impossible. Even so, many legislators seek committee assignments that allow them to serve their constituents better.

Fourth, committees have taken on a "safety valve" function by becoming the forum for public debate and controversy. They give average citizens a place to vent concerns and frustrations, and they can absorb conflict and resolve the strains of a democratic system. Of course, by blocking action on measures that some citizens and interest groups ardently support, legislative committees can also promote conflict and increase tensions.

Finally, and much related to the pathways of change, committees offer citizens many points of access into the legislative process. It might be too much to expect a citizen or a small group of like-minded citizens to persuade an entire chamber, but shifting the course of committee decisions may be more manageable. Given that very few measures are considered by the full legislature without first being passed at the committee level, and given that committee votes are often won or lost by a few votes, swinging a couple of legislators to your point of view can sometimes change the fate of a piece of legislation. This heightens the power of citizens in the policy process.

The number of standing committees has varied over the years. Different subject areas have been more important in some periods than in others. Today, there are 20 standing committees in the House and 16 in the Senate (see Table 6.3). The size of each committee varies as well, but generally speaking, House committees consist of about 50 members, and Senate standing committees have roughly 20 members. The balance of power between the parties in each chamber is reflected in each committee.

Although standing committees are clearly the most important, there are four other types of legislative committees. Nearly all standing committees have one or more **subcommittees**■ under their jurisdiction. Much the same rationale for apportioning legislative work to committees also applies to subcommittees, whose members and staffers specialize, thus breaking down a broad policy area into more manageable parts. Today, any piece of legislation that comes before a committee usually is quickly referred to the appropriate subcommittee. Most of the day-to-day lawmaking and oversight of Congress occur at the subcommittee level.[10]

Today, both chambers also establish **select committees** to deal with a particular issue or problem. They are temporary, so they disappear either when the problem is resolved or, more likely, when the congressional session ends. They serve primarily in an investigative role and cannot approve legislation or move it forward. Of much more significance is the **conference committee**■. For legislation to become law, both branches of the legislature must first pass exactly the same bill. When each chamber passes similar but not identical legislation, a conference committee is assembled to work out the differences and reach a compromise. Some conference committees are small, consisting of the chairs of corresponding House and Senate

■ **Conference Committee:** A committee of members of the House and Senate that irons out differences in similar measures that have passed both houses to create a single bill.

SIGNIFICANCE: *If the conference committee cannot arrive at one version of a bill, the measure fails.*

TABLE 6.3 | Standing Committees of the 112th Congress

Imagine for a minute that you have been elected to Congress. —*Given your interest, and the concerns of people in your community, which of these committees would you request to serve on? Which committee would make the least sense?*

COMMITTEES OF THE SENATE		COMMITTEES OF THE HOUSE	
Agriculture, Nutrition, and Forestry (21 members)	Homeland Security and Governmental Affairs (17 members)	Agriculture (46 members)	Judiciary (40 members)
Appropriations (30 members)	Judiciary (19 members)	Appropriations (60 members)	Natural Resources (49 members)
Armed Services (26 members)	Rules and Administration (19 members)	Armed Services (62 members)	Oversight and Government Reform (41 members)
Banking, Housing, and Urban Affairs (20 members)	Small Business and Entrepreneurship (19 members)	Budget (39 members)	Rules (13 members)
Budget (23 members)	Veterans' Affairs (15 members)	Education and Labor (49 members)	Science and Technology (44 members)
Commerce, Science, and Transportation (25 members)	SENATE SPECIAL OR SELECT COMMITTEES:	Energy and Commerce (59 members)	Small Business (29 members)
Energy and Natural Resources (23 members)	Aging (21members)	Financial Services (71 members)	Standards of Official Conduct (10 members)
Environment and Public Works (19 members)	Ethics (6 members)	Foreign Affairs (47 members)	Transportation and Infrastructure (75 members)
Finance (23 members)	Intelligence (19 members)	Homeland Security (34 members)	Veterans' Affairs (29 members)
Foreign Relations (19 members)	Indian Affairs (15 members)	House Administration (9 members)	Ways and Means (41 members)
Health, Education, Labor, and Pensions (23 members)			

committees and a few members; others, dealing with higher-profile matters, can have hundreds of members. In some ways, these conference committees actually write legislation—the version that emerges from conference often contains vital details that differ from what either house originally passed and may deal with entirely unrelated matters. So important are conference committees that some have dubbed them the "third house of Congress." Finally, **joint committees** are composed of members selected from each chamber. The work of these committees generally involves investigation, research, and oversight of agencies closely related to Congress. Permanent joint committees, created by statute, are sometimes called **standing joint committees.**

What Committees Do

Committees are critical to the lawmaking process, and it's impossible to imagine a modern legislature functioning without them. But what, exactly, do committees do? Let's take a closer look.

REFERRAL AND JURISDICTION The Legislative Reorganization Act of 1946 stated that every piece of legislation introduced for consideration must first be referred to a committee. This may sound rather mechanical, simply matching the topic of the bill with an appropriate committee. However, the process is much more complex, and at times it can be quite contentious. The job of referral is given to the speaker of the House or, in the Senate, to the majority leader.

During most of our nation's history, bills were referred to just one committee. Sometimes which committee a bill got referred to depended less on jurisdictional fit than on the impact, positive or negative, that the chair of that committee might have on its fate. Referral to one particular committee would often either seal a proposed measure's doom or give it a good chance of enactment. This helped ensure that the committee process was closed and undemocratic. By the early 1970s, the House adopted a process of **multiple referrals.** Now, instead of assigning a new bill to just one committee, it is possible to send the measure to several committees at the same

■ **Hearings:** Committee sessions for taking testimony from witnesses and for collecting information on legislation under consideration or for the development of new legislation.

EXAMPLE: *The House Committee on Oversight and Government Reforms held hearings on steroid use in baseball during the spring of 2008.*

time. It has become customary to designate a "primary committee" that considers a bill but also to assign the bill to other committees as well.

HEARINGS AND INVESTIGATIONS The vast majority of bills that are introduced in the House or Senate, assigned to a committee, and then assigned to a subcommittee wind up being killed (deemed unworthy of consideration). If a measure is not moved out of the committee considering it, that measure dies at the end of the legislative term. Roughly 90 percent of all measures stall in committee.

For measures that have a modest chance of committee approval, **hearings**■ are often the first step. These are fact-finding, informational events that usually take place in a subcommittee. Experts are asked to testify at hearings. These experts can include the sponsor of the bill, state and federal officials, interest group leaders, private officials, and (if arranged for by the bill's sponsor, by its opponents, or by advocacy groups) even ordinary citizens making highly emotional pleas, largely for the benefit of the media. Occasionally, on high-visibility issues, celebrities also get to testify. "Quite candidly, when Hollywood speaks, the world listens," Senator Arlen Specter once commented.[11]

Actress Julia Roberts testifies before a House subcommittee in support of federal funding for Rett Syndrome research. —*Why do you suppose members of Congress seem to pay more attention when famous people testify?*

MARKUP If the measure is still considered important after hearings and investigations have been held, the next step in the process is called **markup.** Here, the actual language of the bill is hammered out. The member responsible for crafting the language is called the *prime sponsor*. Often, but not always, the prime sponsor is the subcommittee chair. The language of the bill must address the concerns of the sponsor, but it also must win the approval of the committee and then the full chamber.

REPORTS For the fraction of measures that win committee approval, the next step is to send the bill to the floor for consideration. At this point, the staff of the committee prepares a report on the legislation. This report summarizes the bill's provisions and the rationale behind them.

THE RULES REPORT There is another step—and a critically important one—before a bill is sent to the floor. Every bill in the House must pass through a Rules Committee. This committee establishes rules regarding the consideration of the legislation, which helps streamline the process and make things fair.

BUREAUCRATIC OVERSIGHT Another critical committee function is **oversight**■, the responsibility of Congress to keep a close eye on the federal bureaucracy's implementation of federal law. The Constitution neither spells out a congressional oversight role, nor prohibits such work. By keeping an eye on the bureaucracy (see Chapter 8, pages 250–251), Congress helps create greater accountability in an otherwise "distant" part of

the federal government. Congress can investigate issues, call agency heads to testify, compel changes in regulations, programs and activities, modify levels of funding (including cut funding altogether), and pass legislation to redirect the agency. Oversight is especially time-consuming and contentious in times of divided government (when the president is of one party and the opposition party controls at least one house of Congress).

THE IMPORTANCE OF COMMITTEE STAFF Given the hectic schedules of members of Congress and the ever-growing complexity of policy alternatives, it should come as no surprise to learn that staffers do most of the committees' work. "Committee staff spend a lot of their time on policymaking activities," the political scientist David Vogler has noted. "They research issues and generate information relevant to administrative oversight; draft bills; prepare speeches, statements, and reports; organize and help run committee hearings; and sometimes engage directly in legislative bargaining."[12] Furthermore, the size of the committee staff—what some observers have termed the "unelected representatives"[13] —grew tremendously in the late twentieth century. In 1967, there were roughly 600 committee staffers at work on Capitol Hill, but by 1994, their number had jumped to more than 3,000.[14]

MYTH EXPOSED Many Americans believe that when a bill is introduced into Congress all legislators have a say in the outcome. Sure, it might be long, uphill battle, but every member in the body will eventually have the chance to vote up or down.

CONNECT THE LINK
(Chapter 8, pages 250–251)

■ **Oversight:** The responsibility of Congress to keep an eye on agencies in the federal bureaucracy to ensure that their behavior conforms to its wishes.

SIGNIFICANCE: *Oversight is a powerful congressional check on the power of the executive branch.*

In reality, a vast majority—upward of 95 percent—of all measures are voted on only in a committee. Some argue that it makes perfect sense to have committees manage the immense workload of the legislature by filtering out most initiatives. Others find it unfortunate, perhaps even undemocratic, that the fate of most bills are decided by a small group legislators—legislators who may or may not represent the views of the entire chamber.

PATHWAYS of action

The Ousting of a Committee Chair

In December 2008, Detroit Congressman John Dingell was the longest serving member in the history of the House, having first been elected in 1955. He was the lead Democrat on the House Energy and Commerce Committee, and when his party took back control of the chamber from Republicans in 2006, Dingell once again became chair of the committee.

But Dingell was not without his critics, especially from the progressive wing of the Democratic Party. Because Dingell was a steadfast supporter of the American automobile industry—he represented Detroit after all—many liberal Democrats were frustrated over his refusal to push for greater governmental control of automobile emissions and climate control legislation. They also fretted that some of President Obama's new initiatives would run into a brick wall with Dingell.

Kicking out a sitting chair, especially a powerful member with decades of seniority, rarely occurs in the House or Senate, and is never done lightly. But progressive Democrats mounted an assault against Dingell. They pushed, and soon the Democratic Steering Policy Committee sanctioned a vote by the full Caucus. Dingell's supporters offered an impassioned plea to keep him on, but opponents spoke eloquently of the need for a change. The room then fell silent as each of the 255 House Democrats cast their ballot. With a vote of 137 to 122, Dingell lost the chairmanship of his committee. According to one account, "Mr. Dingell was surrounded by staff members after the vote, some of them in tears, others furious."[15] Slowly, in a wheelchair, Dingell left the room without a word; it was a powerful, dramatic scene.

Organizing Congress: Committees

6.3 Establish the importance of committees in organizing the legislative process.

PRACTICE QUIZ: UNDERSTAND AND APPLY

1. The structure of standing committees in Congress is spelled out in Article I of the Constitution.
   a. true
   b. false

2. Most of the work of lawmaking and oversight in Congress happens
   a. on the House floor.
   b. at the committee level.
   c. in conference meetings.
   d. in congressional staff meetings.

3. Which of the following takes place when a bill is *first* introduced into the House of Representatives?
   a. The bill is referred to a particular member, who is in charge of overseeing the bill's journey through Congress.
   b. The bill is referred to a standing committee for consideration.
   c. An exact version of the bill is also introduced in the Senate.
   d. All of the above.

ANALYZE

1. We can understand why Congress would use a committee system; there are many advantages to dividing the work of the legislature based on topics. But what are the downsides to this sort of process?

2. Why is congressional oversight so important? How does oversight help "democratize" the federal government?

IDENTIFY THE CONCEPT THAT DOESN'T BELONG

a. Promotes efficiency
b. Limits constituent access
c. Enhances representation
d. Promotes expertise
e. Reduces workload

Resource Center
• Glossary
• Vocabulary Example
• Connect the Link

■ **Voting Cues:** Summaries encapsulating the informed judgment of others in the legislature; members of Congress rely on these to streamline the decision-making process.

SIGNIFICANCE: *Legislators often rely on their party's leadership to provide direction on how they should vote. This becomes a rational short-cut for most busy legislators.*

Organizing Congress: Political Parties and Leadership

6.4 Assess how political parties and leaders manage the legislative process while advancing their own initiatives.

(pages 166–169)

Parties in the Legislatures

Parties in the legislature serve an **orientation function**—the job of familiarizing new members of Congress with the procedures, norms, and customs of the chamber. The job of legislating has always been difficult, but during the past few decades, it has become exceedingly complex. Being a good legislator requires a great deal of time and effort, and few prior positions can prepare anyone for a job as a member of Congress. Both parties conduct extensive orientation sessions for incoming members of Congress. These events often last several days and cover a range of topics. "Beyond the briefings on everything from setting up the office, ethics, legislative customs, and rules," note two scholars of the legislative process, "these orientations help break new representatives into the social fabric of the capital. Scores of receptions and dinners help newcomers feel welcome and at the same time socialize the new representative to the ways of the legislative world."[16]

Second, parties in the legislature set the agenda for the coming session and establish priorities. Each legislator comes to Washington with an agenda, a list of issues that he or she would like to address and in some way resolve. These issues originate with constituents, interest groups, and other elected officials, and they also reflect the convictions of the legislators themselves. Combined, this would make a long, dizzying array of topics. Parties allow rank-and-file members to express their concerns to the leadership, where they are prioritized into an agenda for the session. This process not only narrows the list but also focuses members' efforts on priority items. No longer, for example, are there 200 different members of the same party independently fighting for some type of prescription drug program but rather (or so the party leaders hope) 200 legislators working in a unified, synchronized effort toward a common goal.

Third, parties give their members an important time-saving tool when it comes to committee service and floor voting. Thousands of complex measures are introduced and considered each term. Expecting legislators to be fully informed on all, or even most, of these measures is simply impossible. Parties help legislators cut though the complex maze of initiatives by providing briefs and, more important, **voting cues**■. Party

leaders will often take positions on issues, thereby "suggesting" to other members of their party that they do the same. Members of Congress do not have to follow this cue from leadership, and occasionally, they do not—but quite often they do.

Finally, parties organize the committee appointment process. We noted earlier that legislators try to sit on committees that cover topics of most importance to their constituents. This does not mean, however, that every committee assignment is equally desirable. Some committees, such as those dealing with the raising and distribution of money (Budget, Appropriations, Finance, and Ways and Means), are in more demand than others. There is an important pecking order. Party leaders handle the difficult and sometimes contentious chore of committee appointments—and being a "regular" who goes along with the leadership certainly helps a member get a choice assignment.

THE IMPORTANCE OF MAJORITY STATUS Beyond these organizing functions, another issue to consider is the majority or minority status of political parties. In each branch, there is a majority party and a minority party, determined by the number of legislators in each party. The majority party has many significant advantages. For one, the majority of members on all committees belong to the majority party. The majority party sets the ratio of party representation on each committee, which reflects the size of the majority it enjoys in that chamber, and it names the chair of each committee and subcommittee. And as we have discussed, the majority also manages the critically important Rules Committee in the House, thus controlling the flow of legislation to the floor.

The majority party selects the leaders in each chamber. The House elects a **speaker**■, who has a number of advantages, including the power of referral. These votes to "organize" the House, which are conducted as soon as each session of Congress convenes, are always along party lines, inevitably leading to the victory of someone from the majority party. Similarly, the Senate chooses a **majority leader**■, who has many of the same advantages, although Senate tradition dictates that individual members have more leeway than House members to do what they please. Finally, given the advantages of majority status, external players—interest groups and the media, for example—are much more interested in their interactions with the majority party's members.

LEGISLATIVE PARTIES AND CHANGE There are numerous partisan-based groups in Congress, allowing members in each chamber to come together to promote issues of mutual concern. The term "caucus" can be a verb (working together to accomplish a common goal), and it is also a noun. Congressional caucuses are also sometimes called coalitions, study groups, and task forces. In brief, they are informal, voluntary groups of legislators who have enough in common to meet regularly. The goal is to share information and strategize on policy matters. For example, the Blue Dog Coalition, formed

■ **Speaker:** The presiding officer of the House of Representatives, who is also the leader of the majority party in the House.

EXAMPLE: *The speaker of the 111th Congress was Nancy Pelosi, Democrat from California.*

■ **Majority Leader:** The head of the majority party in the Senate; the second-highest-ranking member of the majority party in the House.

SIGNIFICANCE: *The majority leader in both the House and Senate wields a great deal of power.*

Even when one major party controls both Houses of Congress, it does not mean that policy changes are a snap. Other members of the president's party can hold things up. Pictured here are moderate and conservative Democratic members of Congress who call themselves "Blue Dog Democrats." Much of President Obama's lobbying for health care reform was directed at persuading this group of Democrats. —*Does it make sense that the fate of important bills can often hinge on the actions of a small group of legislators?*

in 1994, is comprised of roughly 20 Democratic House members who are more conservative than average Democrats. This group played a critically important role in shaping health care reform legislation in 2009. On the other side, the Republican Study Committee is comprised of about 100 truly conservative House members. There are racial- and ethnic-based caucuses as well, most notably the Congressional Black Caucus and the Congressional Hispanic Conference. The number varies from session to session, but generally speaking there are at least a dozen such caucuses. There are no formal requirements that a member join a caucus; one might be a conservative Democrat but not belong to the Blue Dogs, for instance. But legislators have realized that there is power in numbers, and these sorts of groups are increasingly popular.

The largest caucus is the *party conference,* which is comprised of all members of a political party in each chamber. If a legislator ran for Congress under one of the two major parties, than he or she is automatically a member of that party's conference. At times, minor party legislators are allowed to join one of the conferences as well. For example, Democratic senators voted to allow Independent senators Joseph Lieberman of Connecticut and Bernard Sanders of Vermont to join the Senate Democratic Conference in 2007. Members of the conference may disagree with their colleagues or the party leadership on any range of topics, but there is one vote deemed critical: Each member of the conference must support a fellow partisan for all

leadership positions. For example, a member of the House Republican Conference would find himself in hot water (likely kicked out of the Conference) if he voted for a Democrat for the position of Speaker.

Legislators vote with their party on most matters—a topic discussed in greater detail in Chapter 15. Party leaders *hope* that all in the conference will "stay the line," but traditionally, elected officials have been able to stray without serious repercussions. Still, the single best predictor of how legislators will vote on any given bill is their party affiliation. One way to assess the extent to which legislators vote with their fellow partisans is through **party unity scores**—measures of party unity based on a gauge of how often members of the same party stick together. Since 1954, there has been a clear pattern of greater unity, echoing what many see as an increasingly polarized Congress.

In fact, many are concerned that record levels of party polarization have made compromise—a mainstay of the legislative process—even more difficult. In the spring of 2010, a series of high-profile retirements from the House and Senate underscored the problem. Two-term Democratic Senator Evan Bayh of Indiana, known for being a moderate, was direct in his rationale for stepping aside: "For some time, I have had a growing conviction that Congress is not operating as it should. There is too much partisanship and not enough progress—too much narrow ideology and not enough practical problem-solving. Even at a time of enormous challenge, the people's business is not being done."[17]

What does this brief discussion of the weight of partisanship say about the pathways of change? On the one hand, all other things being equal, an activist would surely find it more profitable to lobby and work with members of the majority

Senator Evan Bayh, a moderate Democrat, announced in 2010 that he would be retiring from the U.S. Senate. Bayh cited excessive partisanship as the reason. —*Is excessive partisanship a bad thing if legislators from different parties strongly disagree about an issue?*

■ **Whips:** Assistants to House and Senate leaders, responsible for drumming up support for legislation and for keeping count of how members plan to vote on different pieces of legislation.

SIGNIFICANCE: *Whips help party leaders keep track of the preferences of other members and push those members to stick with the party when their vote is needed.*

■ **Minority Leader:** The leading spokesperson and legislative strategist for the minority party in the House or the Senate.

EXAMPLE: *In the 111th Congress, Democrats controlled both the House and the Senate. As such, the minority leaders in both chambers were Republicans.*

party than with members of the minority party. In fact, most seasoned political activists consider it so important that the first step of their lobbying strategy is to focus on elections. But on the other hand, steadfast partisan allegiances in Congress, likely propelled by hardcore partisan activists, seem to have created unprecedented levels of gridlock. Without a willingness to find common ground, little gets done in the legislature—even on matters of national concern. Speaking of the emerging crisis of huge federal deficits, former GOP Senate leader Alan K Simpson of Wyoming noted, "There isn't a single sitting member of Congress—not one—that doesn't know exactly where we're headed. And to use the politics of fear and division and hate on each other—we are at a point right now where it doesn't make a damn whether you're a Democrat or a Republican if you've forgotten you're an American."[18]

Legislative Leadership

The framers of the Constitution believed that giving one legislator, or a group of legislators, more power in the system would upset what should be an enlightened, deliberative process. The Constitution states that each chamber will have "leaders": in the House, a speaker (the title *speaker* was used in the British House of Commons and in the colonial assemblies), and in the Senate, a president. The framers assumed these posts were meant to aid organization; each was to be a mere parliamentarian who structured debate, made sure that rules of order were followed, guaranteed equal access, and so forth. Leaders were to be impartial. And this is precisely what occurred for the first few decades; legislative leaders simply helped create an orderly process. It was rare, in fact, for leaders of either chamber to even cast a vote.

All that changed in the 1820s. First, the election of 1824, leading to the so-called Corrupt Bargain, reinvigorated party spirit in the United States, and partisanship soon intensified in both houses of Congress. Second, Henry Clay of Kentucky had been elected speaker in 1823. An affable, whiskey-drinking, card-playing master of politicking in the Washington boardinghouses where members lived during sessions of Congress, Clay was also aggressive, outspoken, ambitious, and highly partisan. Speaker of the House Clay, in fact, contributed enormously to building what eventually became the Whig Party, and the role of speaker as moderator faded into the history books.[19] In the Senate, the move to aggressive leadership happened more slowly, given the smaller size of the chamber and most senators' insistence on their greater political independence. However, within two decades, the Senate also developed aggressive, partisan leadership.

At the beginning of each legislative term—that is, at each two-year interval—every member of the House casts a vote for a speaker. Since the 1820s, the winner of these internal elections has always been a member of the majority party. It has become customary for the members of each party to decide on their choice for speaker in advance and to expect every member to vote for that person. Because deviations from this party line vote never occur, the majority party's candidate always prevails.

Rather than having one leader, a hierarchy of leadership now exists for both parties in both chambers. In the House, the most powerful person after the speaker is the majority leader, followed by the majority **whip**■—an assistant to the majority leader responsible for garnering support for the party's agenda and for making sure that the party leadership has an accurate count of the votes both for and against different pieces of legislation. In brief, majority leaders and whips work with the speaker to coordinate strategy and to advance the party's policy goals. If members of the party are inclined to vote against a measure deemed important to the leadership, it is the whip's job to help those legislators think otherwise—that is, to "whip" them into line. They also have the added responsibility of passing information along to other members and of working to ensure that members of their party show up for important floor votes.

The Constitution stipulates that the vice president of the United States shall be president of the Senate. Under the Constitution, however, the vice president can vote only to break a tie. The first vice president, John Adams, came into office expecting that even if he did not vote, he would also be able to take a leading role in Senate deliberations—and he was bitterly disappointed and offended when the senators told him that all he could do was preside, in silence. "The most insignificant office that the mind of man ever devised" was Adams's sour verdict on the vice presidency.

When the vice president is not present—which is usually the case except on solemn occasions or when a tie vote is expected—the Senate is formally led by its elected **president pro tempore** (*pro tempore* is a Latin phrase meaning "for the time being" and is usually abbreviated to *pro tem*). Through tradition, this position has become purely ceremonial and is always bestowed on the most senior member of the majority party. The real job of moderating debate in the Senate usually falls to a junior member of the majority party, chosen for that assignment on a rotating basis. The job confers little real power. Much more power in the Senate rests with the majority leader. In some ways similar to the speaker in the House, the majority leader of the Senate is elected and is the head of his or her party. Correspondingly, the Senate **minority leader**■ is the top dog of the minority party. Each has an assistant leader and a whip, charged with much the same responsibilities as those in the House. There are also conference chairs for both parties in the Senate.

LEADERSHIP POWERS What makes legislative leaders powerful? The answer is a mix of formal and informal powers. Speakers of the House refer legislation to committee, preside over floor proceedings, appoint members to conference and other joint committees, and set the rules of how legislation will be debated and how long such debates might last. They establish the floor agenda, meaning that they decide which bills will—and will not—be scheduled for consideration on the floor. These are weighty formal advantages, but they are just the beginning. The speaker can also use the force of personality and prestige to persuade other members of the legislature to go along with his or her wishes. Great speakers have been able to merge their formal and informal powers. The ability of the speaker to attract national press attention has become another powerful tool. Few speakers were more adept at seizing national press coverage, and thus enhancing their power base, than Georgia Republican Newt Gingrich in his first term (1995–1997), and Nancy Pelosi (2007–2011).

Great as the powers of the speaker may be, however, they are not absolute. On a number of occasions, speakers have been humbled by their fellow legislators. Although Newt Gingrich was a powerful speaker at first, many members of his own party conference soon thought him too heavy-handed. He also lost favor with

the public because of his confrontational ways and his advocacy of heavy cuts in popular government programs. When challenged for the post after the 1998 midterm election, in which the Republicans lost seats, Gingrich resigned from the House.

In the Senate, the majority leader's powers are broad but not as extensive as the speaker's. Majority leaders have great influence on committee assignments, on the scheduling of floor debate, on the selection of conference committee members, and in picking their own conference's leaders. Yet majority leaders have less sway in the Senate for several reasons: first, because of that institution's somewhat different internal rules; second, because of the long-standing notion that the Senate is the "upper chamber," filled with more experienced and higher-status politicians; and third, because Senate norms dictate a more egalitarian process. In other words, Senate rules protect each member's right to participate far more than House rules do.

Organizing Congress: Political Parties and Leadership

6.4   Assess how political parties and leaders manage the legislative process while advancing their own initiatives.

PRACTICE QUIZ UNDERSTAND AND APPLY

1. Political parties perform all of the following functions in Congress except
   a. offering judicial nominations for federal judgeships.
   b. setting the agenda for the upcoming legislative session.
   c. conducting orientation sessions for new members.
   d. providing members with briefs and voting cues on important issues.

2. In order to preserve the spirit of bipartisanship, the majority party shares responsibilities for electing committee chairs with the minority party.
   a. true   b. false

3. Garnering support for the party's legislative agenda and keeping an accurate record of votes is the responsibility of the party's
   a. speaker
   b. majority leader
   c. minority leader
   d. whip

ANALYZE

1. An important trend in recent years has been increased party unity in Congress. There are fewer and fewer occasions when members of one party join members of the other party to find a middle ground on controversial legislation. What might be the ramifications of ridged party polarization?

2. What is it about the House that affords legislative leaders more power than legislative leaders in the Senate?

IDENTIFY THE CONCEPT THAT DOESN'T BELONG

a. Orient on legislative process
b. Mandate policy coherence
c. Set policy agenda
d. Provide voting cues
e. Share information

Resource Center
• Glossary
• Vocabulary Example
• Connect the Link

■ **Filibuster:** A process in the U.S. Senate used to block or delay voting on proposed legislation or on an appointment of a judge or other official by talking continuously. Sixty senators must vote to end a filibuster.

SIGNIFICANCE: *This important Senate rule helps promote incremental policy changes.*

Organizing Congress: Rules and Norms

6.5 Show how the rules and norms of behavior help ensure a more orderly, efficient legislative process.

(pages 170–173)

The final organizing elements in any legislative body are its formal and informal rules of behavior. Let's begin with the formal regulations. The Constitution states that each house establishes its own rules. Not surprisingly, given the different sizes of the two chambers, the House has a longer set of rules than the Senate. It is difficult to list all the regulations that structure proceedings in the House, but a few of the most significant deal with how measures proceed from committee to floor consideration and with the actions that might be taken to modify a measure once it reaches the floor. Scheduling refers to floor (full-house) consideration of committee-approved measures. All bills approved at the committee level must be scheduled for consideration on the floor. This might seem a straightforward matter, but many issues come into play with this process,

including when—if ever—the bill will be considered. If a measure finds itself on a floor calendar, the rules regarding amendments become important, as noted earlier.

The Filibuster

The Senate is somewhat less bound by formal rules than the House, but this does not mean that anything goes. Three formal rules stand out as most significant. First, leaders of both parties in the Senate quite often will informally negotiate the terms for debate and amendment of a bill scheduled to be sent to the floor. This is called **unanimous consent,** because all senators must be in agreement. The idea is to try to establish some limits and control in order to expedite floor actions and to impose some predictability. To block legislation or confirmation votes, Senate minorities may resort to use of the **filibuster**■—an unlimited debate in which one senator or a group of senators keeps talking without interruption unless three-fifths of the chamber (60 senators) votes to end the discussion.

Conservative southern Democrats were particularly known for filibustering civil rights bills in the second half of the twentieth century. The longest filibustering speech in American history occurred in 1957, when Senator Strom Thurmond of South Carolina (a Democrat who later became a Republican) held the

The longest speech in the history of the U.S. Senate was made by Strom Thurmond of South Carolina. Thurmond, a Democrat who later became a Republican, spoke for 24 hours and 18 minutes during a filibuster against passage of the Civil Rights Act of 1957. *—Are filibusters undemocratic, or are they an important procedural tool?*

■ **Cloture:** A rule declaring the end of a debate in the Senate.

SIGNIFICANCE: *By requiring 60 senators to vote to end debate on a bill, this promotes compromise and middle-of-the-road legislation.*

■ **Seniority:** Length of time served in a chamber of the legislature. Members with greater seniority have traditionally been granted greater power.

EXAMPLE: *The U.S. senator with the greatest seniority is Daniel Inouye, Democrat from Hawaii. Inouye was first elected to the Senate in 1963.*

floor for more than 24 hours in an effort to block a vote on what became the Civil Rights Act of 1957. More recently, members of both parties have threatened to use this maneuver to stall the approval of controversial legislation and judicial nominations.

To some observers, use of the filibuster is a clear violation of majority rule. However, where you stand on the strategic use of the filibuster is most likely a function of the issue under consideration. When the filibuster was used to block civil rights legislation in the 1950s and 1960s, Democrats argued that it thwarted the majority will. Republicans were outraged by the widespread use of the filibuster during much of George W. Bush's administration, but when Barack Obama took over as president, they seemed quite comfortable with it on a wide range of policy matters and appointments.

Without a unanimous-consent agreement, extended debates can become a problem. A filibuster can be used, but another delay variant is to switch control of floor discussion from one member to another, thereby postponing a vote. The goal is to tie things up until the other side backs down or decides to compromise. The tool used to cut off these debates is called **cloture**■. Here, three-fifths of the senators (60) must vote to end the discussion of a bill—that is, "to invoke cloture." This rule can be used for general floor debate or to end a filibuster. Still another variation, used today, is called a **hold:** A senator signals to the rest of the chamber that it would be pointless to bring a piece of legislation to the floor, because he or she intends to use delaying tactics to stave off a final vote. A hold can be trumped, of course, with 60 votes for cloture.

In 2005, frustrated by what they perceived to be unreasonable delaying tactics by the Democrats in the Senate with respect to the confirmation of court nominees, Republicans responded by threatening the "nuclear option." The plan was for the Senate president to rule that the U.S. Constitution prohibited filibusters against judicial nominations, and then a vote would be held on an appeal. If that happened, only 51 votes would be needed to uphold the ruling. A few years later, as the Democratic Conference hovered around the 60-member mark (the so-called "magic number"), the validity of procedural rules to delay legislation were again called into question. In 2010, as the fate of health care reform and numerous appointments remained uncertain, Vice President Joe Biden suggested a drastic change is needed: "As long as I have served, I've never seen, as my uncle once said, the Constitution stood on its head as they've done. This is the first time every single solitary decision has required 60 senators. No democracy has survived needing a supermajority."[20]

UNWRITTEN RULES You might think that informal rules or legislative norms and customs are less significant than the formal regulations. In fact, informal rules likely do *more* to structure the day-to-day legislative process than any other organizing mechanism. More than 40 years ago, a distinguished political scientist, Donald Matthews, noted the power and importance of "folkways" in the legislature.[21] While the times have changed, much of what Matthews suggested still applies today.

Seniority■ stipulates that the longer a member of either chamber has served, the greater deference and the more power he or she should have. Such senior members usually deserve respect because of their long service and accumulated wisdom, but Senate traditions normally also grant them more power in the chamber. It is no longer a hard-and-fast rule that the longest-serving member of a committee becomes its chair (or, if in the minority party, its ranking minority member), but it still occurs. Senior members are often given a greater share of their appropriation requests than a novice, and they are more likely to have their bills at least considered by a committee. In recent years, junior members perceived to be vulnerable to an election defeat are helped by the party leadership, but generally speaking, seniority still matters.

Along with seniority, there is a powerful **apprenticeship norm.** In the past, novice legislators were expected to work hard, get along, be deferential and polite, keep their mouths shut most of the time, and study the legislative process. They were to be "workhorses" instead of "show horses." This was true even when House members moved to the Senate; junior senators were expected to be seen and not heard. In recent years, this norm, like that of seniority, has been observed less and less. Democratic Senator Al Franken of Minnesota was a particularly outspoken critic of several GOP senators in his very first year in the chamber. In fact, in some instances, party leaders have advised first-term senators to speak up and make a name for themselves.

Civility is another powerful norm in both chambers. Regardless of party, ideology, or position on issues, it is expected that members accord each other respect and a high, even exaggerated level of courtesy. Even when tempers rise, politeness is to remain. "Political disagreements should not influence personal feelings,"[22] suggests Matthews. By tradition, a senator or a representative refers even to his or her bitter political rivals and personal enemies as "the distinguished gentleman [or lady] from" whatever the state might be. When members publicly lapse from this norm of civility, they are expected to apologize, which they very often do. The norm of civility extends to presidents when they formally address Congress. It is taken for granted, for example, that when a president enters the House of Representatives, all members stand and applaud. That is why so many people were shocked on the evening of September 9, 2009, when South Carolina Congressman Joe Wilson shouted "You lie!" at Barack Obama. The president had been giving an address to a joint session of Congress on the subject of health care reform. Later that evening, Wilson issued a formal apology, which President Obama accepted. However, that did not stop

■ **Specialization:** A norm suggesting that members of both chambers have extensive knowledge in a particular policy area.

SIGNIFICANCE: *This norm helps ensure that at least some members of the legislature are well versed in most policy areas. It is an individual action that serves a collective good.*

■ **Reciprocity/Logrolling:** Supporting a legislator's bill in exchange for support of one's own bill.

SIGNIFICANCE: *This norm allows individual legislators to provide specific assistance to constituents.*

South Carolina Congressman Joe Wilson shouts "You lie!" at Barack Obama during an address by the president to a joint session of Congress on September 9, 2009. —*Does the decrease in civility in Congress reflect changes in culture, in politics, or both?*

Wilson's House colleagues from issuing a formal reprimand. As perhaps a sign of changing times, within a matter of days Wilson had raised over $2 million dollars for his reelection.

Specialization■ is a norm that suggests members of both chambers are expected to become well versed in a small number of policy areas. Specialization allows members to defer to their colleagues on some policy matters rather than try to bone up on every issue that might come before the legislature. In this, there is an expectation of **reciprocity**■. That is, members are expected to support each other's initiatives on a "you scratch my back, and I'll scratch yours" basis. According to Matthews, "Every senator, at one time or another, is in the position to help out a colleague. The folkways of the Senate hold that a senator should provide this assistance and that he [or she] be repaid in kind."[23] This is often called **logrolling**, which means that members reciprocally exchange support, often on **earmarks**■, or what is sometimes termed **pork-barrel legislation.** *Pork* is slang for particularized assistance: federal money and programs that largely or wholly benefit just one state or congressional district. Every member wants to "bring home the bacon" to his or her district, and their constituents expect it. One way to get it is through logrolling. For instance, a House member from Tennessee might agree to support a New York City member's appropriation to build a commuter rail station in her district in return for her support for a new stretch of interstate through his part of Tennessee.

PATHWAYS of action

Bridges to Nowhere?

Some of the highest-profile and most controversial earmarks in the past decade have been for the state of Alaska. In 2005, the federal budget included funding for two massive bridges. Longer than the Golden Gate Bridge and higher than the Brooklyn Bridge, the new structure would connect Gravina Island (population 50) with Ketchikan (population 8,002). The price tag for its construction was $400 million. The budget also included several other massive, federally funded construction projects for Alaska. According to Taxpayers for Common Sense, a nonpartisan watchdog group in Washington, D.C., it broke down to $1,150 for every Alaskan—or 25 times what the average American gets for his or her home state. This occurred at a time when most Americans, as well as members of Congress from both parties, had grown increasingly worried about the federal budget deficit. And it also took place at the same time residents of the Gulf Coast were struggling to rebuild after Hurricane Katrina.

So why would federal funds flow to Alaska and not, say, to Louisiana or Mississippi? Why the exceptional treatment for the forty-ninth state? The explanation lies in the clout of the Alaskan congressional delegation. At the time, Alaska's Republican Senator Ted Stevens was the powerful chair of the Appropriations Committee, the committee in charge of overseeing federal spending. And the state's lone member of the House was Republican Don Young, formerly chair of the House Transportation Committee, which oversees all federally funded construction projects across the nation. When Democrats and Republicans in both chambers voiced their opposition to the Alaskan earmarks, Stevens and Young let it be known that they would not take kindly to serious challenges. Few members of Congress wanted to get on the wrong side of these powerful chairs.

But then the national media got wind of the earmark. The conservative Heritage Foundation, for example, circulated a paper saying it was a "national embarrassment." Funding for the

■ **Earmarks Pork-Barrel Legislation:** Legislation that benefits one state or district; also called *particularized legislation*.

EXAMPLE: *In 2009, Senator Carl Levin (D-MI) and Rep. Carolyn Kilpatrick (D-MI) were able to secure $951,500 for downtown Detroit energy-efficient street lamps.*

Even though the "Bridge to Nowhere," slated to be built in Ketchikan, Alaska, was pushed by Republican legislators in 2006, by the 2010 election nearly all GOP and Democratic candidates condemned such pork-barrel projects as wasteful spending. —*Are "state-specific projects" of this sort always wasteful?*

"Bridge to Nowhere" was eventually canceled. Most thought it would fade into the history books, but when John McCain selected Alaska Governor Sarah Palin as his running mate, it was once again a hot topic. While Palin claimed she'd said "thanks—but no thanks" to the project, Democrats dug up evidence suggesting she initially backed the endeavor.

SOURCE: Rebecca Clarren, "A Bridge to Nowhere," August 9, 2005. Accessed at Salon.com, http://www.salon.com/news/feature/2005/08/09/bridges/index_np.html; Heritage Foundation, "The Bridge to Nowhere: A National Embarrassment," Accessed at http://www.heritage.org/Research/Budget/wm889.cfm; October 20, 2005. Accessed at USA Today Online, "Alaska Thanks You," May 17, 2005. Accessed at http://www.usatoday.com/news/opinion/editorials/2005-05-17-alaska-edit_x.htm

Organizing Congress: Rules and Norms

6.5 Show how the rules and norms of behavior help ensure a more orderly, efficient legislative process.

PRACTICE QUIZ: UNDERSTAND AND APPLY

1. Which of the following can be said about official rules and norms of behavior in Congress?
   a. Official rules can have a big impact on the fate of a piece of legislation, but only in the House.
   b. Norms of behavior are an important organizing element in both the House and the Senate.
   c. Filibusters are used more often in the House than in the Senate.
   d. The Senate Rules committee sets clear guidelines on how long a bill can be debated.

2. Floor debate in the Senate and House rarely influences how an individual legislator votes; it is usually conducted for the benefit of the mass media.
   a. true   b. false

3. What is a significant procedural difference between the Senate and the House?
   a. The Senate needs a quorum (an established minimum number of senators present) to conduct the day's business, but the House does not.
   b. Discussion on the floor of the House allows for spontaneous interruption from other representatives, whereas Senate discussion does not.
   c. Discussion on a bill in the House is governed by rules created by a Rules Committee, whereas Senate discussion is not.
   d. Discussion on a bill in the Senate is governed by parliamentary procedure, whereas House discussion is not.

ANALYZE

1. What is your take on the filibuster? Do you agree with Vice President Biden that such rules are turning the Constitution on its head? Or are such rules necessary to make sure that we move slowly with big changes?

2. What is the value of the seniority rule? Does it make sense that more seasoned legislators have more sway in Congress? What if you are from a district with a novice legislator?

IDENTIFY THE CONCEPT THAT DOESN'T BELONG

a. Seniority   d. Politeness
b. Reciprocity   e. Backstabbing
c. Apprenticeship

6.5

Resource Center
• Glossary
• Vocabulary Example
• Connect the Link

■ **Bill Sponsor:** The member of Congress who introduces a bill.

EXAMPLE: *In December 2009, Senate Finance Committee Chairman Max Baucus (D-MT), introduced a health care reform bill that was purported to offer some concessions to moderate Republicans, with the hopes of securing their support.*

How a Bill Becomes a Law

6.6 Outline the process by which a bill becomes a law.

(pages 174–177)

Bills must cross many hurdles in order to become law. Here, we'll walk through this process in greater detail. Please keep in mind that this outline is a theoretical model and that in practice, things are rarely this neat. Also, the process is similar in both chambers, but it is not exactly the same. What follows is a general pattern (see Figure 6.4).

General Steps

Step 1. **Introduction of a Bill.** The idea (and frequently the language) of a bill can originate from many sources. Often, an administrative agency will draw up a bill. Interest groups also often have a hand, both in the broad outlines of a measure and in its exact wording. Yet to begin the actual process of legislating, a member of Congress must always introduce a bill in one chamber of that body. This person becomes the **bill sponsor**■, the official "parent" of the legislation. With the exception of tax bills, which under the Constitution can only be introduced in the House of Representatives, any member of the national legislature can introduce any measure he or she sees fit.

Step 2. **Referral.** Soon after a bill is introduced, it is referred to a committee (occasionally, to two or more committees), and from there, it is usually sent to the appropriate subcommittee.

Step 3. **Committee Consideration.** Most measures go no further than the subcommittee level. As we've seen, hearings are held, the language is sometimes modified (in the markup process), and if a bill is approved at this level, it is reported back to the full committee. Additional changes are sometimes made at the full-committee level, but the committee often will simply accept or reject the measure offered by the subcommittee.

Step 4. **Rules for Floor Action.** Any bill approved by a full committee is sent to the floor for full-chamber consideration. In the House of Representatives, however, a required stop is the Rules Committee. Here, many procedural issues are set, such as the length of time the bill will be debated and the types of amendments, if any, that can be accepted. Once again, the majority party controls the Rules Committee. There is no similar procedure in the Senate.

Step 5. **Floor Consideration.** This is where every member of the chamber has an opportunity to express his or her support (or lack of support) for the bill. Most measures do not entail a lengthy floor debate. The reason for this is that most measures are low-profile, highly technical matters (such as adjustments to complex statutes) that draw little public interest. When the public becomes involved, however, floor debate can be intense.

Step 6. **Conference Committee.** For a bill to become a law, an identical version must be approved in both houses. Measures passed in one house but not the other house are called **one-house bills.** If the other chamber has also passed an identical version of the bill, it goes to the president to be signed—or to face a veto (see step 7). Sometimes a similar (but not identical) bill is passed in the other chamber. To reconcile differences, a conference is created. Three outcomes from conference deliberations are possible. First, one of the versions of the bills might be accepted as the final agreement. When this occurs, the chamber accepting changes has to vote on the measure again (as each chamber must approve exactly the same wording). Second, some sort of compromise position might be crafted, making it necessary for both houses to vote again on the compromise version. Finally, compromise might not be possible (this often happens when Congress is about to adjourn), and each measure remains a one-house bill.

Step 7. **Presidential Action.** When the president is of the same party as the majority in both houses, it is rare that important measures are approved without the president's blessing. (If they are, it is a sure sign that the president is in deep political trouble.) Even when there is a divided government, most bills approved by Congress do wind up winning presidential support. A bill becomes a law when the president signs it. If 10 days pass without the president having signed the bill—a rare occurrence that generally indicates the president does not like the bill but does not want to cause an uproar by vetoing it—the bill becomes law. Or the president can veto the bill, sending it back to the Congress. As we'll discuss in Chapter 7, pages 207–208, vetoes have recently become quite rare, especially compared to the number of measures that win presidential approval. Given a president's grave concern about having his veto overridden, when the president does reject an important bill, it certainly makes news.

Step 8. **Overriding a Presidential Veto.** Presidential vetoes are always accompanied by a written message—a statement to Congress that says why the measure was rejected. The measure can still become a law if two-thirds of each house of Congress votes to override the veto.

CONNECT THE LINK

(Chapter 7, pages 207–208) Are vetoes more common when presidents of one party confront a Congress that is controlled by the other party?

How a Bill Becomes a Law: American Recovery and Reinvestment Act of 2009

Designed to create jobs, promote investment, and encourage customer spending during the recession.

Trigger

Many feel the Economic Stimulus Act of 2008, signed into law by President George W. Bush on February 13, 2008, is insufficient to meet the nation's growing economic challenges. President Barack Obama and the Democrats in Congress believe the additional measures are needed.

Step 1. Introduction

HR 1 introduced on January 5, 2009. The lead sponsor is David Obey (D1-W1) Chair of the House Appropriations Committee.

Senate Majority Leader Harry Reid (D-NV) introduces S1 in the Senate on January 6, 2009.

Step 1. Introduction

Steps 2 and 3: Referral and Committee Action

The Committee on Appropriations considers the House bill and on January 23, 2009, reports the bill to the full chamber for consideration.

The Finance Committee considers the Senate bill, where numerous amendments are made, and on February 7, 2009, reports the bill to the full Senate for consideration.

Step 4. Floor Action

On January 28, 2009, the House passes the bill by a 244-188 vote. All but 11 Democrats vote for the bill, and 176 Republicans vote against it (two Republicans do not vote).

On February 10, 2009, the Senate votes 61-37 to approve the measure (one senator does not vote).

Step 4. Floor Action

Step 5. Resolving Differences Between Bills

Members of both chambers immediately convene to hammer out differeces. A vast number of issues are addressed quickly. On February 11, 2009, the Conference Committee issues its report. The new bill is then sent back to both chambers for approval. The House approves the new measure on February 13, 2009. The vote is 246 to 183 (largely along party lines).

Step 6. Presidential Signature

On February 17, 2009, President Barack Obama signs the $787 billion American Recovery and Reinvestment Act of 2009 into law in Denver, Colorado.

FIGURE 6.4 ▪ How a Bill Becomes a Law

Some would say that the system of checks and balances weeds out unnecessary measures, but others argue that the system is too cumbersome and that it makes change too difficult. —*Does this complex process serve the nation well, or does it inhibit needed change?*

Unorthodox Lawmaking

The steps outlined above explain the process used throughout most of our nation's history for a bill to become law. However, a number of adjustments in recent decades continue to transform the lawmaking process. Many have documented these changes, but at the forefront of this research has been UCLA scholar Barbara Sinclair. In a series of important books and articles, Sinclair documented the routes of "unorthodox lawmaking."[24] She notes, for example, that multiple referrals are increasingly common, and there are occasions when bills will bypass committees altogether. For instance, at the start of the 111th Congress, Democratic House leaders pushed for fast action on several high-profile measures, including the Lilly Ledbetter Fair Pay Act (a bill that made it easier for plaintiffs to sue employers over pay discrimination), and thus bypassed the committee stage.

It is also increasingly common for each chamber to pass generic bills, knowing that the true details of the legislation will be ironed-out in conference committee. In a very real sense, these bills are written and deliberated on in the conference committee, not in the standing committees in both houses. Another approach to reconcile differences, dubbed "ping-ponging," is for each chamber to make amendments back and forth until disagreements are resolved. On occasion, particularly at the end of the legislative session when there is a push to tie up loose ends, bills can "ping-pong" back and forth between the House and Senate on an hourly basis. Omnibus measures, where one bill contains numerous issues and topics, are also no longer rare. Nor are congressional-executive summits, where congressional leadership works with the president and his staff to forge acceptable language—even before any sort of committee deliberations or markup occur.

The traditional route also implies that bills that do not receive approval from a committee are doomed. While this is generally the case, there are a few options available to dislodge a bill, if the committee refuses to report it to the full chamber. One of these methods is a dislodge petition, which is designed to overrule the committee leadership (and often the majority party leadership). Here, a House member must gather 218 signatures from other members (a majority of the members) and then the bill will eventually be sent to the floor for consideration. A second, more controversial, method of dislodging a bill is for the Rules Committee to simply discharge a bill without committee approval, to bypass reluctant committee chairs.

Why have these changes to the traditional lawmaking process occurred? Sinclair and others argue that the increased partisan polarization of Congress has made the traditional legislative process more difficult. There seems to be less and less common ground. Majority party leaders have been granted greater leeway from their members to insert themselves more directly into key stages of the process with the goal of producing results, and there is no question that *both* parties are using unorthodox approaches to advance their initiatives in the contemporary Congress.

Emergency Legislation

The process of passing legislation can be lengthy. Occasionally, however, emergencies arise during which the legislature is called upon to act quickly and to condense the process into a few days.

Such was the case with the Emergency Economic Stabilization Act of 2008, the so-called "Wall Street Bailout Bill." By mid-September of that year, the subprime mortgage crisis had reached a critical stage, with then Secretary of the Treasury Henry Paulson openly concerned about an imminent crisis and the necessity for immediate action. Americans were told this was the most serious economic crisis since the Great Depression.

Paulson, in close consultation with Federal Reserve Chairman Ben Bernanke, proposed a plan under which the U.S. Treasury would acquire up to $700 billion worth of mortgage-backed securities. By doing so, they argued, banks would again start lending money. The plan was backed by President George W. Bush, and negotiations began with leaders in Congress to draft the appropriate legislation. President Bush and Secretary Paulson told the public and members of Congress that a quick agreement was vital; it had to happen within just a few days.

Congress acted quickly, but not as fast as the Bush administration had hoped. On the one hand, many legislators understood that a massive governmental intervention was the only hope to stave off a financial collapse. On the other hand, many also knew that average citizens saw the proposed measure as helping the business elite. In short, the scheme was very unpopular back home.

Early measures passed in the Senate, but the House balked. The election was only weeks away: Every House member would be up for reelection, but only one-third of the Senate would face the voters. The process unfolded precisely as the framers of our system envisioned, with the Senate better able to rise above public opinion and the House seemingly beholden to it. Through a great deal of persuasion, negotiation, compromise, and added "sweeteners" (elements that aided particular districts), the measure passed on October 3, 2008.

A few lessons can be drawn from this issue. First, when emergencies arise, Congress can move quickly, but not nearly as rapidly as the executive branch can. This, too, is what the framers envisioned—immediate action from the executive branch, but greater deliberation in the legislature. Second, members of Congress face particularized constituencies. What is good for the nation might be unpopular in specific districts or states. The president, on the other hand, faces a national constituency. Third, the Senate, with six-year terms and rotation, seems better able than the House to confront important but unpopular measures. Finally, there is no easy answer to the age-old question of whether legislators should be delegates, trustees, or something in between.

Making Laws: A Summary

While the number varies somewhat from year to year, roughly speaking, in the two years that any Congress sits, more than 10,000 measures are introduced. Of these, roughly 400 become law.[25] Sometimes the percentage is even lower. In the 110th Congress, for example, some 14,000 bills were introduced but only 449 (3.2 percent) became law.[26] Most of these are low-profile, technical adjustments to existing laws; only a handful of truly significant measures gets passed each session. "Of the 449 bills that became law in the 110th Congress, 144 of them—32 percent—did nothing more than rename a federal building."[27]

The road from introduction to presidential signature is long and difficult—deliberately so. On the one hand, we might suggest that the difficulty of the process implies a shortcoming in the legislative process: The will of the people should be more easily and more quickly expressed through the national legislature. On the other hand, many people would agree that the process *should* be difficult, and that there *should* be many potholes, roadblocks, and detours along the pathway. They would argue that the federal government must act cautiously when deciding the laws citizens must obey. That, after all, was the intent of the framers of our Constitution.

How a Bill Becomes Law

6.6   Outline the process by which a bill becomes a law.

PRACTICE QUIZ: UNDERSTAND AND APPLY

1. Which of the following is a likely sequence for a bill that becomes law?
   a. It is drafted by a congressional staffer and an interest group, introduced by a member of Congress, signed by the president, amended in the appropriate subcommittee, and approved by a vote on the House floor.
   b. It is drafted by a congressional staffer with input from an interest group, introduced on the House floor by a sponsoring representative, referred to a standing committee, sent to the appropriate subcommittee where hearings about the measure are held and the markup is done, and sent back to the full committee and approved. Rules for its discussion on the House floor are then set by the Rules Committee. It passes by a majority vote in the House. Meanwhile, a nearly identical bill follows a nearly identical path in the Senate. A conference committee realizes there are no real differences between the two bills, and the president signs it into law.
   c. It is drafted in a Senate committee, discussed on the Senate floor, and passed by a majority vote. It is then referred to the House, where it goes into another committee and then to the appropriate subcommittee within that committee. Hearings are held, and language is agreed on. It is sponsored on the House floor, passed by a majority vote there, and then goes into a conference committee, where differences between the House and Senate versions of the bill are ironed out. The president then signs it into law.
   d. It is drafted by a group of staffers in the president's office. A conference committee consisting of powerful senators and members of Congress deliberates over the bill, drafting compromise language. It is then approved in subcommittees in both chambers. Next, the bill is voted for constitutionality by clerks for the Supreme Court and, if necessary, by the justices themselves. It is then signed into law by the president.

2. Which of the following has been increasingly common in a process scholars have dubbed "unorthodox lawmaking"?
   a. the use of omnibus bills
   b. legislative-executive summits
   c. ping-ponging bills from the Conference Committee to the floor
   d. all of the above

3. The framers of the Constitution intended for the passage of bills into laws to be streamlined and fast; they would not approve of the slow pace of modern legislation.
   a. true
   b. false

ANALYZE

1. When we look at the lawmaking process, often the first reaction is, "why did the framers make it so difficult?" But what are the real advantages, especially in a democracy, for slowing down the process of passing laws?

2. Why are presidential vetoes so seldom overridden? Think in terms of both the procedures in Congress as well as politics.

IDENTIFY THE CONCEPT THAT DOESN'T BELONG

a. Conference committee
b. Rules of debate
c. Referral from committee
d. Floor vote
e. Presidential signature

6.6

Resource Center
• Glossary
• Vocabulary Example
• Connect the Link

Who Sits in Congress?

6.7 Determine whether members of Congress mirror America's demographic diversity and why this matters.

(pages 178–181)

As we have emphasized in discussing representative democracy, *representation* means that someone speaks and works on behalf of others. Perhaps this process can be enhanced when the representative understands the issues and concerns that confront a district, and perhaps this is more likely to happen when he or she reflects the demographic makeup of the constituency of the district. Many people feel that, at the very least, a legislative body should look like the nation as a whole. According to this viewpoint, race, ethnicity, gender, sexual orientation, occupation, age, and other demographics matter. This preference for *symbolic* or *descriptive representation* is the logic behind the drive, discussed earlier in this chapter, to create majority-minority districts. In this section, we examine some demographic characteristics of the Americans who have been members of Congress.

Gender

The first woman elected to the House of Representatives was Jeannette Rankin of Montana in 1916. She was elected even before women nationally got the right to vote under the Nineteenth Amendment. A peace activist, Rankin voted against declaring World War I. She was also in the House in 1941, where she cast the only vote against a declaration of war after Pearl Harbor. The first woman to serve in the Senate was Rebecca Felton from Georgia in 1922, who was appointed to fill a vacant seat. There were very few female members of either chamber during the following decades—about a dozen in the House and just two in the Senate. By the 1950s, there were 17 female national legislators in House and Senate combined, and that number actually dipped during the 1960s and 1970s.

Prior to the 2010 midterm election, there had been a steady increase in the number of women serving in Congress since the 1980s, with a big jump that came after the 1992 election (called by journalists the "Year of the Woman" because of the large number of women who ran for office that year). In the 111th Congress, there were 17 women in the U.S. Senate—equal to the total number of women who had served in *all* the years before 1978, as noted in Figure 6.5—and in the House of

FIGURE 6.5 ▪ Occupations, Education, Party Profile, and Gender Composition of the 112th Congress

What conclusions can you draw about the occupations, education and gender of Congress? How can it become more diversified and representative of the average citizen?

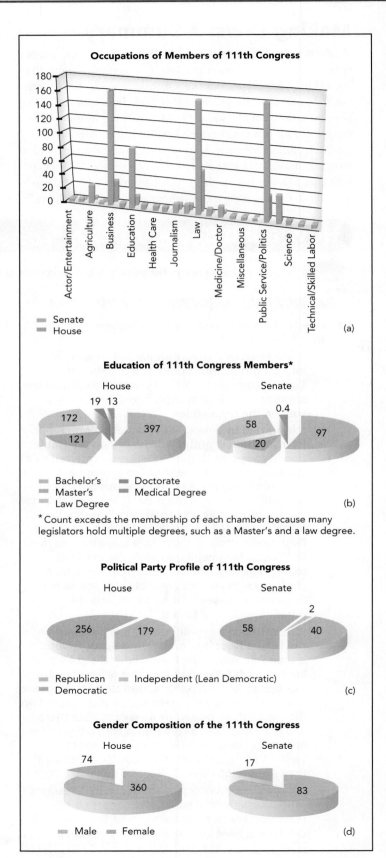

(a)

(b)

* Count exceeds the membership of each chamber because many legislators hold multiple degrees, such as a Master's and a law degree.

(c)

(d)

Representatives, there were 74 women. However, as result of the 2010 midterm election, it is likely that the number of women in Congress will stay the same or drop for the first time since 1979. It would seem that parity between the genders is still a long way off.

Race and Ethnicity

The picture for African Americans in Congress in some ways resembles that for women, and in other ways, it is even more vexing. The first black elected to the House of Representatives was Joseph Hayne Rainey of South Carolina in 1870. Rainey was a slave as a child and was requisitioned for labor by the Confederacy during the Civil War. He escaped on a blockade-runner ship and made his way to Bermuda, a British colony where slavery had been abolished. After the Civil War, he returned to South Carolina and began working with the Republican Party. He was sent to the House after a special election in 1870, where he served for 8 years.[28] The first African American was also elected to the Senate in 1870: Hiram Rhodes Revels, representing Mississippi. Interestingly, he was elected by the "reconstructed" state legislature to complete Jefferson Davis's unfinished term. (Davis had left his place in the U.S. Senate to become president of the Confederacy.) After serving only 1 year, Revels left the Senate to become president of Alcorn State College.[29]

In all, only five African Americans have ever been elected to the Senate. In the House, just over 100 African Americans have served. These are discouraging statistics, but as with women, the numbers have improved since the 1980s. In recent years, about 40 members of the House have been black—roughly 9.5 percent of the chamber. Given that African Americans make up about 13 percent of the national population, we might say that the situation is improving, especially compared to that of women.

Hispanic Americans (Latinos) are the fastest-growing demographic group in America and have recently succeeded African Americans as the nation's largest minority group. It is estimated that by 2012, there will be roughly 54.7 million Hispanic Americans, making up some 17 percent of the population.[30] The U.S. Census Bureau estimates that Hispanics have accounted for 40 percent of the nation's population growth since 1990. Their representation in Congress, however, has lagged far behind. Today, about 25 members of the national legislature, or about 5 percent, are of Hispanic descent.

Why are so few women and minority citizens elected to Congress? One reason is that historically, fewer women and minorities have sought office, likely because of a wide range of factors, including biases in the campaign process, discriminatory voter attitudes, and lags in the number of these groups who entered professions—especially the law—that have typically led to a political career. For whatever reason, some Americans still find it difficult to vote for minority and female candidates. One prominent elections scholar has observed that one way "to achieve fairer and more equal representation for minorities is

Hispanic Americans are the fastest growing demographic group in the nation and will soon make up nearly 20 percent of the population. But only about 5 percent of the members of Congress are of Hispanic descent. —*What explains these low numbers? Do you think things will change in the near future?*

to eliminate the allegiances and attitudes (some consider them biases and prejudices) that favor the majority."[31]

A related explanation lies in the nature of our electoral system and specifically in our reliance on single-member districts. There is no requirement in the Constitution that specific districts be drawn within each state, only (as noted earlier) that states receive an overall number of representatives relative to that state's population. We might consider an at-large system, under which states that have two or more representatives would have no distinct districts: Voters would vote for at-large candidates, and these candidates would get into the House in descending order according to the number of votes they won. Alternatively, large states like California and New York could be divided into a number of large districts, each of which would elect a group of at-large representatives.

Under such a system, if a minority group makes up one-fifth of a state's population, which is often the case, and that state has been allotted 10 seats in the House of Representatives chosen at large, we might expect that more minority candidates—perhaps two—would be elected. When one candidate is selected from a single district, however, that same 20 percent minority group is simply drowned out by the majority. And if attitudes about supporting minority candidates do not change, the prospects for that group gaining a voice in the legislature will be small.

Income and Occupation

When it comes to income and occupation, we find that, once again, the national legislature does not reflect America very well. Members of Congress are far better educated and far wealthier than the average American (Table 6.4). (And that is what the framers of the Constitution—themselves drawn from the elite—expected.) The Senate is often called the "millionaires' club."

TABLE 6.4	Top Twenty Richest Members of Congress in 2009	
RANK	**NAME**	**ESTIMATED NET WORTH**
1	John Kerry (D-MA)	$167,550,000
2	Darrell Issa (R-CA)	$164,700,000
3	Jane Harman (D-CA)	$112,130,000
4	Jay Rockefeller (D-WV)	$ 80,450,000
5	Mark Wagner (D-VA)	$ 72,370,000
6	Jared Polis (D-CO)	$ 71,000,000
7	Vernon Buchanan (R-FL)	$ 49,790,000
8	Frank R. Lautenberg (D-NJ)	$ 48,380,000
9	Dianne Feinstein (D-CA)	$ 42,940,000
10	Harry Teague (D-NM)	$ 40,630,000
11	Michael McCaul (R-TX)	$ 38,080,000
12	Alan Grayson (D-FL)	$ 31,120,000
13	James Risch (R-ID)	$ 19,290,000
14	Rodney Frelinghuysen (R-NJ)	$ 18,150,000
15	Cynthia Lummis (R-WY)	$ 17,120,000
16	Bob Corker (R-TN)	$ 17,090,000
17	Claire McCaskill (D-MO)	$ 16,020,000
18	Edward M. Kennedy (D-MA) (deceased)	$ 15,740,000
19	Nita M. Lowey (D-NY)	$ 14,380,000
20	Carolyn B. Maloney (D-NY)	$ 14,000,000

SOURCE: *Roll Call* analysis of congressional financial disclosure filings, accessed at http://www.rollcall.com/features/Guide-to-Congress_2009/guide/38181-1.html on October 12, 2009.

According to a study conducted by *Roll Call* magazine, at least 50 members of the 110th Congress had a net worth over $5 million.[32] During this same time, the average American household brought in $42,400, and only about 5 percent of Americans earned more than $150,000 per year. Less than 1 percent of Americans are worth a million dollars or more.[33]

And there have always been lawyers in Congress—lots and lots of lawyers. Roughly 40 percent of members of Congress serving at any given time are attorneys. Bankers and business professionals make up about the same percentage, and educators (schoolteachers and professors) account for roughly 15 percent.[34] All other occupational backgrounds, including clergy, farmers, and retired military personnel, have been represented by only 5 percent of the members. Laborers, small farmers, homemakers, service employees, and other blue-collar workers, who make up a vast majority of the American workforce, have never accounted for more than a tiny fraction of the members of Congress (see again Figure 6.5).

Perhaps it makes sense that some occupations are overrepresented in Congress. Lawyers, after all, are trained to understand the nuances of the law; it is natural that they would take the lead in writing laws. We might hope that the best and the brightest would serve in the national legislature—perhaps the same kinds of individuals who have earned advanced degrees and succeeded at their profession (that is, made lots of money). Of course, it is possible that such representatives can understand the concerns of diverse groups of people and work on their behalf. Some of the greatest legislative champions of women's rights have been male legislators, and some of the most aggressive advocates for the poor in Congress have been rich. Many white legislators fought valiant battles against slavery and segregation. Moreover, given that all Americans have the right to vote and that most legislators do everything they can to stay in office, we can imagine that members of Congress would be very attentive to *all* of their constituents—especially to large blocs of voters, many of whom are far from affluent. Yet many of those who are underrepresented in the halls of Congress—women, African Americans, Asian Americans, Hispanics, blue-collar workers, farmers, gays and lesbians, persons with disabilities, and the poor—feel that their concerns would get more attention if more members of their group were players on the field rather than simply spectators from the sidelines or the bleachers.

STUDENT profile

Aaron Schock was elected to the Peoria, Illinois, school board at age 19, the state legislature at age 23, and the U.S. Congress at age 27. Voters in Newark, Delaware put 23-year-old graduate student Kevin Vonck on the city council, and South Dakota voters chose 33-year-old Stephanie Herseth as their sole voice in the U.S. House.

Across the nation, a greater number of younger Americans are running for office than ever before due in large part to a desire to make government service their career. However, this interest in legislative service as a career is rather new. During much of our nation's history, citizens would seek a legislative post as a temporary position, often to advance their "real" career. A lawyer might run for the state legislature to help garner additional clients—as Abraham Lincoln did in the 1840s. Others would serve out of a sense of civic duty, or because a particular issue compelled their involvement. In short, few saw legislative service as a long-term career.

Much of that has changed, and it is best seen in the number of young citizens vying for office. As noted in a *USA Today* article, "An estimated 800 politicians are younger than 35, from city council to Congress. They represent every party and race. Some are second-generation politicians. Others come from families who stayed out of government affairs."

But of course a willingness to serve does not guarantee a legislative career. Derrick Seaver was first elected to the Ohio state legislature as a high school senior at age 18. In 2006, he stepped down to finish his undergraduate college degree, and one year later was convicted of driving under the influence. Ironically, Seaver was prosecuted under laws that he helped create as a state legislator. Only time will tell if Seaver will attempt to get back into political life.

SOURCES: Kathleen Murphy, "Ohio Lawmaker Part of a Kiddy Caucus," Stateline.Org, May 6, 2003, accessed at. http://www.stateline.org/live/ViewPage.action?siteNodeId=136&languageId=1&contentId=15241; Carol Weiser, "Young People Answer the Call to Action, Run for Office," *USA Today*, July 14, 2004. Accessed at http://www.usatoday.com/news/politicselections/nation/2004-07-14-young-pols_x.htm

Who Sits in Congress?

6.7 **Determine whether members of Congress mirror America's demographic diversity and why this matters.**

PRACTICE QUIZ: UNDERSTAND AND APPLY

1. Regarding gender representation in Congress, it's fair to say that
   a. since the 1920s, the number of women in both chambers has steadily increased.
   b. the percentage of women in Congress is finally close to the percentage in the general population.
   c. the number of women in the federal legislature is higher now than in the 1920s, but still not close to reflecting the percentage of women in the general population.
   d. women today make up only about 5 percent of the federal legislature.

2. Joseph Hayne Rainey was the first African American elected to the U.S. House of Representatives. When did that happen?
   a. 1864   c. 1921
   b. 1870   d. 1946

3. Working-class Americans, service employees, small farmers, and ordinary housewives have always constituted a tiny fraction of the members of Congress.
   a. true   b. false

ANALYZE

1. Do you think there is any relationship between gender, race, ethnicity, religion, and economic background and a person's outlook toward public policy? In other words, do you have to be a woman to understand women's issues, or poor to understand the plight of underprivileged Americans?

2. How do you think the close 2008 Democratic primary contest between Barack Obama and Hillary Clinton affected diversity in Congress? Will more women and people of color consider running in the future?

IDENTIFY THE CONCEPT THAT DOESN'T FIT

a. Women
b. Hispanics
c. African Americans
d. Farmers
e. Lawyers

Resource Center
• Glossary
• Vocabulary Example
• Connect the Link

Are Americans Losing Faith in the "People's Branch"?

6.8 Compare the state of congressional ethics with Americans' perception of the legislative branch.

(pages 182–183)

When the Republicans captured control of the House in 1994, Tom DeLay, a Republican from Texas who was first elected in 1984, quickly emerged as a powerful player. By the spring of 2005, however, DeLay's fortunes had taken a dramatic downward turn: A grand jury in Austin, Texas, indicted him on criminal charges of conspiracy to violate election laws. In the spring of 2006, he was forced to relinquish his post as majority leader and by summer, DeLay had withdrawn his name from the November ballot; he had decided to leave the House altogether.

About the same time that DeLay was stepping down from his leadership position, an influential lobbyist named Jack Abramoff, who had been under investigation by federal law enforcement officials for some time, was hit with a string of indictments. Abramoff quickly agreed to cooperate with the prosecutors in exchange for a lighter sentence. A year later, Idaho Senator Larry Craig was arrested for lewd behavior in a men's bathroom at the Minneapolis–St. Paul Airport, and Alaska

Senator Ted Stevens came under investigation by the FBI and the IRS for possible corruption (Stevens was later acquitted of the charges).

Mark Twain's oft-cited line that Congress is the only "distinctly native American criminal class" still seems accurate to many Americans. In one national survey, only 20 percent of Americans rate the ethics of members of Congress as "high" or "very high"[35] (see Figure 6.6).

However, close observers of the legislative branch argue that in the past few decades, members of Congress have actually become more ethical and more upstanding than at any point in our nation's history. According to Fred Harris, a political scientist and former Democratic senator from Oklahoma, members of the national legislature are a good deal cleaner than the average American.[36] Another observer put it this way: "Most observers would suggest that real corruption on the Hill has in fact declined significantly over the past 20 or 30 years, whether the misbehavior is licentiousness or bribery or financial chicanery."[37]

What, then, might explain the gap between perceptions and reality? There are a number of plausible explanations. For one, there is simply much more reporting of ethical transgressions than in the past. Particularly after the Watergate scandal in the early 1970s, when President Richard Nixon resigned from office on the eve of an impeachment trial over his activities in covering up a criminal investigation, aggressive investigative journalism became an omnipresent force in American politics. Finally, members of Congress are subject to tougher rules and procedures and to far more public scrutiny than in the past.

FIGURE 6.6 ▪ Public Opinion Poll on Congressional Ethics

This figure suggests that over the last three decades, Americans have been skeptical about the ethical standards of members of Congress—even though most scholars believe the actual level of corruption has declined. —*Do you think the president has anything to do with the perceptions Americans have of honesty and integrity in Congress? What role might divided government play in public perceptions?*

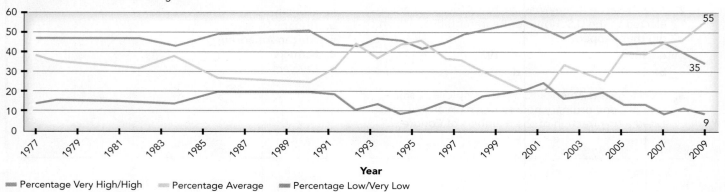

"Please tell me how you would rate the honesty and ethical standards of people in these different fields—very high, high, average, low, or very low? How about … members of Congress?"

Year

▪ Percentage Very High/High   ▪ Percentage Average   ▪ Percentage Low/Very Low

2009 wording split sampled with "Congressmen" (trend wording): combined results shown.

SOURCE: Lydia Saad, "Honesty and Ethics Poll Finds Congress Image Tarnished" Gallup, December 9, 2009. Reprinted by permission of Gallup, Inc.
http://www.gallup.com/poll/124625/honesty-ethics-poll-finds-congress-image-tarnished.aspx#1

In very important ways, however, it is the perception of the public that really matters. Beyond overt corruption, there are signs that the general public may be losing faith in Congress. In a New York Times/CBS poll, taken in February 2010, 75 percent of respondents said they disapproved of the job Congress was doing; just 8 percent said members of Congress deserved re-election.[38] The source of this outrage is likely multifaceted, but surely a large part stems from concerns over partisan-based gridlock. Commenting on the low approval rating, Sinclair notes, "If the problem is lack of legislative productivity, the cause is the combination of partisan polarization and a chamber—the Senate—that requires supermajorities to make almost any decision of consequence."[39]

PATHWAYS of change from around the world

Manure, crackers, and dog food . . . as graft? We might give corrupt American politicians credit for keeping things simple; payoffs are usually in cash, sometimes lots of it, but greenbacks, plain and simple. It seems that corrupt British legislators have somewhat different tastes when it comes to graft. A series of British newspaper accounts in 2009 documented hundreds of outlandish items on the government expense accounts for Members of Parliament (MPs).

One MP charged the government for clearing out a moat around his home, another for a "pet house" for his ducks, another for dog food, and another for paying a nonexistent mortgage. One charged the government for having his trousers pressed and another for the cost of his chauffeur. Several others received reimbursements for renovations on their homes, and still others for their relatives' accommodations. One MP even charged the government for horse manure to fertilize his garden. "Day after day for over three weeks, *The Daily Telegraph* [the lead paper in the inquiry], had mined a trove of legislator expense accounts, stoking its reader's revolution at an aloof ruling class."

Many MPs, even those not caught in the scandal, argued that the amounts were nothing to get upset about. But the public wasn't buying it. And the revelations came at the very time the British government moved to spend billions to bail out banks, and when average citizens were finding it difficult to make ends meet. The fallout was widespread and included the resignation of the Speaker of Parliament; numerous reforms are also in the works.

SOURCE: John F. Burns, "Beneath a British Scandal, Deeper Furies," *New York Times*, May 23, 2009. Accessed at http://www.nytimes.com/2009/05/24/weekinreview/24burns.html? r=1

Are Americans Losing Faith in the "People's Branch"?

6.8 Compater the state of congressional ethics with Americans' perception of the legislative branch.

PRACTICE QUIZ: UNDERSTAND AND APPLY

1. Most political scandals in the United States tend to occur in the executive branch.
   a. true   b. false

2. Recent trends suggest that members of Congress have become *more* ethical than at any other time in our nation's history.
   a. true   b. false

3. Why does the public think there have been more ethical violations in recent times?
   a. The numbers graphically indicate that this is true.
   b. The decline of religious belief among members of Congress contributes to this trend.
   c. Society itself is simply more depraved and licentious.
   d. There is simply much more reporting of ethical transgressions than in the past.

ANALYZE

1. Is there any connection between the strong ties that members of Congress have with special interest groups and problems with congressional ethics? Why or why not?

2. What impact do the "new media" such as cable news programs, blogs, and video-sharing sites have on our perceptions of congressional ethics?

IDENTIFY THE CONCEPT THAT DOESN'T BELONG

a. Tightened rules
b. Greater news coverage
c. Distracted public
d. Greater competition in the news business

Conclusion

Representation is the linchpin of our democracy. It is true that in some tiny communities, all citizens can participate directly in governmental decisions, but direct democracy is rare, is impracticable in all but the smallest settings, and presumes that all citizens *should* be involved in every decision. Our system relies on a small group to speak and act on behalf of the many. Ours is a representative republic, and few Americans would have it any other way.

Congress was established as the "first branch," because the framers believed it would be the part of our government closest to the people. Today, the real issues surrounding Congress have little to do with the value or legitimacy of legislative bodies or whether they should be seen as first among equals. Rather, what we worry about is how to make the system more efficient or more egalitarian. No one could realistically imagine getting rid of standing committees, leadership roles, or party structures, for instance, but at the same time, most people agree that these components do modify the character of the institution. Not every initiative that comes before Congress gets treated the same way, and not every legislator has the same input in the process. In many ways, an open, egalitarian system is sacrificed in the name of efficiency. What's more, for many Americans who are critical of Congress, the *kind* of person who gets to serve in our legislature raises deep questions about the breadth and quality of representation.

What does all this mean for individuals who want to change public policy by lobbying their representative or senator? For one thing, it means that many of Congress' organizational components create points of access for effective citizen action. As noted at the start of this chapter, one way citizens expressed their concern over health care reform was to speak out at the so-called town hall meeting in the summer of 2009. But that was not the only option available for those well versed in the law-making process. Members of the committees dealing with health care were bombarded with emails, letters, phone calls, and visits. Because Senate rules generally require 60 votes to cut off debate, those senators seemingly "on the fence" with health care were inundated with appeals. Of course, this implies that the actors must be well versed in the nuances of legislative procedure—the precise route that measures travel from introduction to law, as well as the numerous pitfalls along the way. Insiders familiar with the complexity of the legislative process and with access to decision makers are in high demand. It is little wonder that former members of Congress are sought—and are very well paid—as lobbyists.

We might revel in the idea of a well-meaning, goodhearted "Mr. Smith" who goes to Washington, learns a few tricks, takes some bruises, and carries the day through grit and faith in the democratic process. (In 1939, the great actor James Stewart played this role in a famous film titled *Mr. Smith Goes to Washington.* You will probably find the film rather naive and simplistic by today's standards.) We now know that Congress is a far more complex place than Mr. Smith could ever imagine. Still, average citizens *can* change the outcome of federal policy by lobbying members of Congress; it is a viable pathway of change today and will remain so in the future. A clear understanding of how legislatures work and where real power resides, however, is critical.

KEY CONCEPT MAP

How does the organization of Congress both enhance and inhibit the legislative process?

The Committee System

Enhances the Legislative Process
Smaller groups of legislative specialists are better able to evaluate complex proposals than a large group of generalists.

Inhibits the Legislative Process
Quite often legislation is killed in committee, which means that most matters are considered only by a small group of representatives.

Critical Thinking Questions
What if membership in Congress were allowed to increase? Or what if the committee system were broadened? Would either of these changes enhance the ability of the legislature to address the numerous complex issues facing the country?

Political Parties

Enhances the Legislative Process
When members of the same political party come together to create and advance a policy agenda, the likelihood of significant change increases.

Inhibits the Legislative Process
The concerns of individual legislators may conflict with the interests of the political party.

Critical Thinking Questions
How do legislators balance the concerns of their constituents with the concerns of their political party when the two are in conflict? Why might some legislators be more inclined to stick with the "party line" than others?

Political Party Leadership

Enhances the Legislative Process
Selecting party leaders in Congress and giving them power leads to a more efficient process.

Inhibits the Legislative Process
The distribution of power in the legislature is unequal; some party leaders have much more say in the outcome than others.

Critical Thinking Questions
What if Congress did not have party leaders and every representative had an equal say in the outcome? What is more important in the modern legislative process, efficiency or internal democracy?

Formal Rules

Enhances the Legislative Process
The formal rules of Congress lend structure and consistency to the legislative process, which creates a fair, open, and more efficient system.

Inhibits the Legislative Process
Sometimes, as with the case of the filibuster in the Senate, the majority will can be thwarted by the skillful use of formal rules.

Critical Thinking Questions
What if Congress could devise its own set of operational rules during each new term? Would this make passing legislation easier or more difficult?

Informal Rules of Behavior

Enhances the Legislative Process
Legislative work can be stressful and contentious, and informal rules of behavior help create a dignified environment for civil debate; they also enable legislators to get things done.

Inhibits the Legislative Process
Some norms of behavior, such as the seniority principle, promote a system whereby certain legislators are afforded more power simply because they have been there longer.

Critical Thinking Questions
Does it make sense that some legislators should be given more deference and more sway in the system simply because they have been there for a long time? Why or why not?

In any legislative body there is an ongoing struggle between legislative autonomy and efficiency. Individual legislators work to advance the interests of constituents, but when they do so, the process can be fractured and slow, making large-scale policy changes difficult. —*How do we balance the need for each representative to play a meaningful role in the legislative process with the necessity of collective action that results in beneficial policies? Should the law-making process be slow and deliberate? Why or why not?*

Review of Key Objectives

The Nature and Style of Representation

 6.1 Differentiate between the various ways legislators represent the interests of their constituents.

(pages 154–155)

There are many approaches to "representation" and many ways a member of Congress might spend his or her time. The trustee approach suggests legislators should consider the wishes of constituents but in the end do what they feel is best for the long-term good of the nation. The delegate model implies legislators should simply reflect the will of the people. There are also middle ground perspectives, including the politico model and the conscience model, but it seems clear that numerous forces are pushing legislators toward the delegate model.

KEY TERMS

Delegate Model of Representation 154
Trustee Model of Representation 154
Politico Model of Representation 154
Conscience Model of Representation 154
Constituent Service 155
Symbolic Representation 155

CRITICAL THINKING QUESTIONS

1. Is it possible for different groups of citizens to have different views about the appropriate model of representation? If so, what types of citizens would prefer each perspective?
2. The late New York Representative Bella Abzug once argued that there should be a constitutional amendment to mandate an equal number of male and female Senators—one of each gender from every state. This would immediately diversify at least one branch of Congress. Does this make sense to you?

INTERNET RESOURCES

To learn more about the history of the U.S. Congress, http://clerk.house.gov/art_history/house_history/index.html

ADDITIONAL READING

Fenno, Richard. *Homestyle: House Members in Their Districts.* Glenview, IL: Scott, Foresman, 1978.

Mayhew, David R. *Congress: The Electoral Connection.* New Haven, CT: Yale University Press, 1974.

Congress and the Constitution

6.2 Identify the key constitutional provisions that shape the way Congress functions.

(pages 156–161)

The framers of our system of government placed a great deal of faith in the legislative branch and provided it with clear, extensive powers. Article I, Section 8, details the numerous powers of the legislative branch, and it also includes a key provision for expanding powers: the elastic clause. Combined, the list of powers and the opportunity to broaden the scope of powers when "necessary and proper," have greatly expanded the reach of congressional action in American society.

KEY TERMS

Bicameral Legislature 156
Seventeenth Amendment 156
Rotation 157
Pocket Veto 157
Elastic Clause (Necessary and Proper Clause) 157
At-Large District 159
Geographic Representation 159
Redistricting 159
Gerrymandering 159
Majority-Minority District 160
Baker v. *Carr* (1961) 160
Reapportionment 161

CRITICAL THINKING QUESTIONS

1. Why would the framers of our system provide the legislative branch with such sweeping powers? How is Congress different from the president or the courts?
2. Given the broad interpretation of the elastic clause, are there any limits to congressional policymaking? What are some of the checks on the legislature?

INTERNET RESOURCES

To read the specifics of Article I and to search for related court cases, see http://caselaw.lp.findlaw.com/data/constitution/article01

To explore the Census Bureau's redistricting data, see http://www.census.gov/rdo

ADDITIONAL READING

Devins, Neal, and Keith E. Whittington, eds., *Congress and the Constitution.* Durham, NC: Duke University Press, 2005.

Organizing Congress: Committees

 6.3 Establish the importance of committees in organizing the legislative process.

(pages 162–165)

Congress is comprised of 535 members, each with their own concerns and unique constituency. The forces promoting self-interest and individual action are great, but collective outcomes happen. One of the main ways collective outcomes happen is through committees, which are the workhorses of the legislature.

KEY TERMS

Subcommittees 162
Select Committees 162
Conference Committee 162
Joint Committees 163
Standing Joint Committees 163
Multiple Referrals 163
Hearings 164
Markup 164
Oversight 164

CRITICAL THINKING QUESTIONS

1. What are some of the disadvantages of relying upon a committee to decide the fate of a piece of legislation? Should a small group be able to "kill" a bill before other legislators get a chance to consider it?
2. If you were elected to Congress, on what sorts of committees would you wish to sit? Should this decision be based on your interests or on the concerns of your constituents?

INTERNET RESOURCES

Learn more about committees, specific pieces of legislation, roll call votes, and much more at http://thomas.loc.gov

ADDITIONAL READING

Davidson, Roger H., Walter J. Oleszek, and Frances E. Lee. *Congress and Its Members,* 12th ed. Washington, DC: CQ Press, 2009.

Deering, Christopher J., and Steven S. Smith. *Committees in Congress,* 3rd ed. Washington, DC: CQ Press, 1997.

Organizing Congress: Political Parties and Leadership

 6.4 Assess how political parties and leaders manage the legislative process while advancing their own initiatives.

(pages 166–169)

Americans often bemoan "partisanship" in Congress, but political parties and their leaders have served key organizing functions for over 200 years. Parties orient new members, set policy agendas, denote leaders, and afford rank-and-file members time-saving voting cues. And for all the talk of "nonpartisan" solutions and "independent-minded" legislators, the role of parties in Congress has actually increased in recent years. Whether or not things have gone too far toward partisan polarization is an open question.

KEY TERMS

Orientation Function 166
Voting Cues 166
Speaker 166
Majority Leader 166
Party Unity Score 167
Whip 168
President Pro Tempore 168
Minority Leader 168

CRITICAL THINKING QUESTIONS

1. Some would suggest that relying upon parties as a "voting cue" is a mistake—that legislators should weigh each issue on its own merits. Others suggest that party voting is a cost-saving, rational process. Who's right?
2. Does relying on powerful legislative leaders drastically limit the egalitarian nature of the national legislature?
3. Do you suppose there are common characteristics among successful legislative leaders? If so, what would those characteristics be?

INTERNET RESOURCES

Learn more about leadership in both chambers as well as party unity scores over time at http://clerk.house.gov/ and http://www.senate.gov/pagelayout/senators/a_three_sections_with_teasers/leadership.htm

ADDITIONAL READING

Davidson, Roger H., Susan Webb Hammond, and Raymond W. Smock, eds. *Masters of the House.* Boulder, CO: Westview Press, 1998.

Organizing Congress: Rules and Norms

6.5 Show how the rules and norms of behavior help ensure a more orderly, efficient legislative process.

(pages 170–173)

While there are important differences between the House and Senate, formal rules and informal norms of behavior help structure the legislative process in both chambers. For example, as a bill moves from a committee to the floor in the House, a set of rules defines how long the bill can be debated, and how many and what type of amendments might be made. A powerful but informal rule in both chambers is specialization, whereby members are expected to become experts in certain policy areas. A norm of civility helps make compromise more likely. Adherence to these modes of behavior streamlines, but limits, the democratic character of the process.

KEY TERMS

Unanimous Consent 170
Filibuster 170
Cloture 171
Hold 171
Seniority 171
Apprenticeship Norm 171
Specialization 172
Reciprocity/Logrolling 172
Earmarks/Pork-Barrel Legislation 172

CRITICAL THINKING QUESTIONS

1. Does it make sense that junior members of Congress should be deferential to more senior legislators? What purpose does seniority play?
2. How do rules like the filibuster sometimes stifle the will of the majority? What is the value of such rules?

INTERNET RESOURCES

For an online directory of members on Congress and details on how to contact them, see http://www.contactingthecongress.org/

ADDITIONAL READING

Lee, Francis *Beyond Ideology: Politics, Principles and Partisanship in the U.S. Senate.* Chicago: University of Chicago Press, 2009.

Matthews, Donald R. *U.S. Senators and Their World.* New York: Vintage Books, 1960.

Schroeder, Pat. *24 Years of House Work ... and the Place Is Still a Mess: My Life in Politics.* Kansas City, MO: McMeel, 1998.

How a Bill Becomes a Law

6.6 Outline the process by which a bill becomes a law.

(pages 174–177)

The process by which a bill becomes a law is complex, with numerous hurdles and pitfalls along the way. In brief, the process moves from specialized subcommittees, where hearings are generally held, to larger standing committees, and then to the full chamber. The Senate version of a bill must be merged with the House version of the same bill through a conference committee. If this challenge is met, the bill is sent to the president for his signature. Some believe the process may be too difficult, but others argue that the bar should be set high and that the framers envisioned a slow, deliberate process, with numerous checks along the way.

KEY TERMS

Bill Sponsor 174
One-House Bill 174

CRITICAL THINKING QUESTIONS

1. Bills often die as a result of the lack of agreement between the House and Senate. Why do you suppose that happens?
2. Are there any changes you would make to allow either easier or more difficult passage of legislation?

INTERNET RESOURCES

For an up-to-date look at what is happening on Capitol Hill, go to http://www.rollcall.com

Believe it or not, many students enjoy seeing "Schoolhouse Rock" from their childhood, an animated cartoon that explains how a bill becomes a law. To see this, visit YouTube at http://www.youtube.com/watch?v=mEJL2Uuv-oQ

ADDITIONAL READING

Hamilton, Lee. *How Congress Works and Why You Should Care.* Bloomington: Indiana University Press, 2004.

Rosenthal, Alan. *Heavy Lifting: The Job of the American Legislature.* Washington, DC: CQ Press, 2004.

Sinclair, Barbara. *Unorthodox Lawmaking: New Legislative Processes in the U.S. Congress,* 3rd ed. Washington, DC: CQ Press, 2007.

Who Sits in Congress

6.7 Determine whether members of Congress mirror America's demographic diversity and why this matters.

(pages 178–181)

It is likely no surprise that the "people's branch" does not exactly look like the rest of America. Congress is comprised of a vastly greater share of men than the rest of society, and a disproportionate number of wealthy whites, Protestants, and lawyers. Some believe this is a problem and that true representation implies not only the reflection of policy preferences, but also the gender, racial, ethnic, and occupational backgrounds of constituents. The trend in both chambers seems to be improving, but there is a long way to go before Congress mirrors the diversity of American society.

CRITICAL THINKING QUESTIONS

1. Some have suggested that America is moving into a period of "post-identity politics," which implies that there is less and less focus on the gender, race, and ethnicity of political leaders. Does it matter to you that Congress is overwhelmingly white and male?
2. Do you suppose the outputs of the legislative process (new laws, appropriations) are shaped by the type of person who sits in Congress? Can you think of any problems that have been neglected by Congress because the white men that control the chamber "just don't get it"?

INTERNET RESOURCES

For an extensive look at the history of women in Congress, see http://womenincongress.house.gov/

For a biographical database of all members of Congress, including your congressperson, go to http://bioguide.congress.gov/biosearch/biosearchasp

ADDITIONAL READING

Bzdek, Vincent. *Woman of the House: The Rise of Nancy Pelosi*. New York: Palgrave Macmillan, 2008.

Are Americans Losing Faith in the "People's Branch"?

6.8 Compare the state of congressional ethics with Americans' perception of the legislative branch.

(pages 182–183)

Long ago, a comedian once joked that our nation has "the best Congress money can buy." Today, many Americans share that sentiment, believing that most legislators are unethical and self-interested; a number of high-profile events have reinforced the perception that the "people's branch" is filled with crooks. However, many scholars suggest that there have been real improvements in the area of ethics due in part to tougher and more robust ethics rules and greater surveillance.

CRITICAL THINKING QUESTIONS

1. If evidence suggests members of Congress are more ethical than in the past, why don't Americans feel better about the institution?
2. Do you think there would be fewer scandals in Congress if more women and minorities were elected?

INTERNET RESOURCES

For a detailed timeline of congressional scandals, go to http://www.foxnews.com/story/0,2933,181733,00.html

ADDITIONAL READING

Hilton, Stanley G., and Ann-Renee Testa. *Glass Houses: Shocking Profiles of Congressional Sex Scandals and Other Unofficial Misconduct*. New York: St. Martin's Press, 1998.

Stone, Peter. *Heist: Superlobbyist Jack Abramoff, His Republican Allies, and the Buying of Washington*. New York: Farrar, Straus and Giroux, 2006.

Chapter Review   Test Your Knowledge

1. In recent years, Congress' mode of representation has shifted from a trustee to a delegate model. This has happened, in part, because
   a. legislators no longer form strong political ideals of their own, so they follow the public's lead.
   b. legislators are not as well educated as they used to be.
   c. the public has become more capable of expressing their agendas to elected officials.
   d. legislators care less about winning reelection and more about addressing the welfare of the public than in previous years.

2. Regarding representational style, members of Congress often decide to focus on either
   a. national policy issues or the needs of their constituents.
   b. the interests of lobbyists or the interests of their constituents.
   c. the agenda of their own political party or a bipartisan agenda.
   d. the dictates of their own conscience or the agenda of their senior colleagues.

3. How did the conflict between the Virginia Plan and the New Jersey Plan during the Constitutional Convention reflect two competing views of representation?
   a. The former held that the states should be sovereign, and the latter held that individuals should be sovereign.
   b. The former held that individuals should be sovereign, and the latter held that the states should be sovereign.
   c. The former required legislators to be trustees of their constituents, and the latter required them to be delegates for their constituents.
   d. The former required legislators to be delegates for their constituents, and the latter required them to be trustees of their constituents.

4. Legislative branch powers include
   a. the power to veto legislation.
   b. the power to declare legislation unconstitutional.
   c. the power to regulate commerce.
   d. the power to invoke executive privilege on behalf of the president.

5. What are majority-minority districts?
   a. districts in which most minorities vote for a majority (usually white) candidate
   b. districts in which most majority voters (usually white) vote for a minority candidate (usually African American or Latino)
   c. districts designated by the Voting Rights Act as likely to produce the majority of the Congress' minority representatives
   d. districts created through redistricting so that the majority of the voters in the district are minorities (African American, Latino, or Asian American, for example).

6. Reapportionment is the process whereby
   a. members of Congress are required to represent more constituents per district because of population growth.
   b. the number of seats granted each state is increased or decreased, depending on that state's population growth.
   c. the total number of seats in the House is changed, depending on the national population growth.
   d. districts within a state shift boundaries, depending on where most of the majority party's voters live.

7. In recent years, the Supreme Court has said that it is unnecessary to have the same number of residents in House districts, so the lines of these districts change every 10 years.
   a. true
   b. false

8. One of the advantages of the standing committee system in Congress is that
   a. in a committee, seniority does not really matter.
   b. committee membership changes frequently, so no small group of representatives possesses entrenched power over that committee.
   c. committee deliberations slow the legislative process, which is what the framers of the Constitution intended.
   d. Several issues can be considered simultaneously, thus improving efficiency.

9. The conference committee has been called
   a. a "mini-legislature."
   b. "the house of executive privilege."
   c. "Congress's Congress."
   d. "the third house of Congress."

10. About 90 percent of all proposed legislation stalls in committee and then dies, never reaching the chamber floor for a full vote.
    a. true
    b. false

11. Markup happens in subcommittees, but what is it exactly?
    a. a bill's sponsor's determination of the cost of enacting the legislature
    b. the prime sponsor's working out of the language of the bill
    c. adding amendments to a bill to make it more likely to pass the House or Senate
    d. deciding which subcommittee considering the legislation will serve as the primary committee

12. Along with policymaking, congressional committees have what other crucial responsibility?
    a. caucusing for partisan decision-making
    b. adjusting a bill's language so that it is consistent with the bill in the other chamber
    c. making sure that legislation gets properly implemented as federal law—that is, exercising congressional oversight
    d. assessing the influence of special-interest groups on the committee's decision-making process

13. To investigate an issue or a matter of serious concern, the Senate or the House
   a. creates a committee for that particular investigation.
   b. uses the existing committee that best suits the circumstances.
   c. creates a joint Senate–House committee specifically for that investigation.
   d. either creates a special committee or uses an existing one that is appropriate for the circumstances.

14. Which of the following is *not* a means for Congress to exert oversight control over executive branch agencies and departments?
   a. modify levels of funding
   b. call agency heads to testify
   c. investigate issues
   d. terminate agency heads (that is, fire them)

15. Congressional committees are the principal decision-making structure of the legislative process
   a. true   **b.** false

16. When members of Congress need to vote on a measure in conference or on the chamber floor but have not had time to study the legislation in much depth,
   a. they invariably vote the way other representatives from their state vote.
   b. they often request a delay in the vote so they can bone up on the details.
   c. they vote the way they are told to vote by a memo from the national chairman of their party.
   d. they often infer and follow voting cues from the positions that senior members in their party have already staked out.

17. Rules in the Senate have the effect of giving individual senators, even when they are in the minority on an issue, much more leverage and freedom to express themselves than House rules grant individual representatives.
   a. true
   b. false

18. What is an example of a significant "folkway" in Congress?
   a. filibuster
   b. floor debate
   c. logrolling
   d. cloture

19. Because women's rights have been championed by male legislators, and white legislators worked tirelessly against slavery and segregation,
   a. we can safely assume that Congress will always gradually move forward on civil rights issues.
   b. we should not automatically assume that the underrepresentation of women and minorities in Congress is a political problem for women and minorities nationwide.
   c. there is no reason for activists to try to improve the representation of women and minorities in Congress.
   d. no real progress is now needed in the area of civil rights.

20. On the whole, Congress is filled with well-to-do, white male lawyers.
   a. true
   b. false

PEARSON mypoliscilab Exercises

Apply what you learned in this chapter on **MyPoliSciLab.**

☐● Read on mypoliscilab.com

   eText: Chapter 6

✓● Study and Review on mypoliscilab.com

   Pre-Test
   Post-Test
   Chapter Exam
   Flashcards

◉● Watch on mypoliscilab.com

   Video: Unknown Wins South Carolina Senate Primary
   Video: Kagan Hearing

⊕● Explore on mypoliscilab.com

   Simulation: You Are a Member of Congress
   Simulation: How a Bill Becomes a Law
   Simulation: You Are Redrawing the Districts in Your State
   Comparative: Comparing Legislatures
   Timeline: The Power of the House
   Visual Literacy: Congressional Redistricting
   Visual Literacy: Why Is It So Hard to Defeat an Incumbent?

The Presidency

KEY OBJECTIVES

After completing this chapter, you should be prepared to:

7.1 Explain the framers' decision to bestow the president with real powers despite their concerns about potential abuses.

7.2 Outline the changes that have led to the expansion of presidential powers.

7.3 Establish how the "power to persuade" expands presidential power beyond the Constitution.

7.4 Identify the duties and functions of modern presidents.

7.5 Evaluate the qualities that contribute to presidential success or failure.

And then there's governing . . . Barack Obama ran one of the most effective political campaigns in American history. As a first-term Senator from Illinois and a relatively unknown national politician, Obama confronted an uphill battle. Most pundits agree that his style and character, a disciplined campaign team, and a message of change that resonated with voters made the difference. Obama went from a long-shot candidacy to residence in the White House.

At the center of Obama's "change" agenda was health care reform. Obama's message during the campaign had been clear: the system was rife with problems and unsustainable in the long-term, and he would make significant reform a top priority. While several other presidents had failed in their quest to reform the health care system, most recently Bill Clinton in the 1990s, Obama would bring a fresh approach and a clear mandate from the public.

But it did not take long for the luster of an exhilarating, inspirational message of change to fade into the grim realities of a nation mired in immense economic and social problems, an ever-partisan legislature, a deeply polarized electorate, and powerful, aggressive lobbyists. Almost immediately after the outlines of the president's reform plan emerged, opposition to "Obamacare" became intense.

During the summer of 2009, members of Congress who supported the broad contours of the plan held "town hall meetings"

> **Have expanded presidential powers transformed the democratic nature of our system?**

in their districts, only to find vitriol and hostility. Many were stunned by the vehemence of the opposition, and polling data suggested shrinking support for reform (even though public support for specific provisions remained popular). In January 2010, when Republican Scott Brown was elected to the Senate in a Massachusetts special election to fill the seat left by the death of long-time Democratic Senator Ted Kennedy, many assumed the drive for health care reform was over.

However, in an effort to build bipartisan support for some changes, President Obama held a televised "health care summit" with leaders of both parties in February 2010 and began calling for an "up or down vote" in Congress. The House would vote on the Senate version, and modest changes dealing with financial elements would be added through a process known as reconciliation—where only 50 votes were needed in the Senate, thus eliminating the risk of a filibuster.

The final vote in the House took place on a bright, sunny day in mid-March. Roughly 40 House members remained on the fence as the hour drew near, and the president made calls to persuade and cajole. The final vote was extremely close: 219 to 212. In the end, President Obama had succeeded where other presidents had failed. Yet, the public remained skeptical about the new law, and opposition to the president grew. It was a victory, but all knew that it would come at a cost.

Resource Center
• Glossary
• Vocabulary Example
• Connect the Link

■ **Prerogative Power:** Extraordinary powers that the president may use under certain conditions.

EXAMPLE: *Lincoln jailed several northern newspaper editors who opposed Union Army efforts during the Civil War.*

CONNECT THE **LINK**
(Chapter 2, page 55) What did the framers of our system of government have in mind for the presidency?

The President and the Constitution

7.1 Explain the framers' decision to bestow the president with real powers despite their concerns about potential abuses.
(pages 194–195)

To put it mildly, the framers were ambivalent about the role of the executive branch under the Constitution. On the one hand, the history of strong executives with whom the framers were familiar was unsettling. From the beginning of history, whenever human beings came together to form governments, the result was either autocracy (rule by one) or oligarchy (rule by a few).[1] Yet governing systems *without* executive power seemed ripe for discord and anarchy. In the end, there were several reasons why the framers were inclined to bestow the president with real powers despite concerns about potential abuses.

A Powerful Executive

The framers were well versed in the philosophies of Hobbes, Montesquieu, and other theorists of the seventeenth and eighteenth centuries who agreed that although we might wish for a political system without a powerful executive, governments that had none had proved ineffectual and short-lived. The English political philosopher John Locke, who was greatly admired by the framers of our Constitution, argued that legislative politics should be at the heart of a limited government—but also that it was necessary to give executives the powers to do "several things of their own free choice, where the law is silent, and sometimes, too, against the direct letter of the law, for the public good."[2] Locke called such action **prerogative power**■.

Moreover, the experience under the Articles of Confederation suggested the need for a strong executive; for, under the Articles, the national government lacked the power and the ability to respond quickly to emergencies. Advocates of an effective executive had an ideal republican leader readily at hand: George Washington, the hero of the Revolution.[3]

Debate at the Convention

At the Philadelphia Constitutional Convention in 1787 (see Chapter 2, page 55), the first scheme for a new government that the delegates discussed, the Virginia Plan (authored principally by James Madison), was vague on the basic questions, including whether one person or a group of people would hold executive power, how long the term of office would be, whether the president could be reelected, and even what the precise powers of the presidency should be. The second scheme to emerge at the convention and gain early support, the New Jersey Plan, was more state-centered, and although many of its provisions were also vague, it envisioned a relatively weak executive office.

However, concerns that the executive branch would be overwhelmed by the power of the legislature, led some of the most prominent and most talented delegates, including James Wilson and Gouverneur Morris of Pennsylvania, to push for a stronger model.[4] Ultimately, on the question of whether the president would have real powers—that is, be an authentic player in the system instead of merely an administrator of what Congress decides—the answer was yes.

There would be no blank checks, wrote one scholar, and nearly all the presidential powers would be shared with Congress, but presidents were meant to be significant players in the system.[5] The principal powers granted by the Constitution to presidents allowed them to influence the judiciary by appointing judges to the bench, to have a modest say in making legislation, to conduct foreign policy, and to be the commander of the nation's armed forces during times of war. As we'll see in this chapter, these formal powers have proved to be merely the foundation of presidential authority.

Article II and Ratification

Previous chapters have noted that many of the fears about the new system of government were calmed by the central role the legislature would play. But if Article I (the legislative branch) calmed citizens' fears, Article II raised their alarm. What was this "presidency," and what sorts of power would its occupants have? How long would this person serve? What would stop this person from gaining too much power and becoming another tyrant? Moreover, the scheme laid out in Article II was unfamiliar. As noted by a leading presidential scholar, "Not only was the presidency the most obvious innovation in the proposed plan of government, but its unitary nature and strong powers roused fears of the most horrifying political specter that most Americans could imagine: a powerful monarchy."[6]

Both proponents and opponents of the Constitution presented their arguments in the form of essays published in newspapers. Several essays in opposition were published under the pseudonym **Cato**■ in the *New York Journal*. (Cato, who lived from 95 B.C. to 45 B.C., was a defender of republican virtues—such as freedoms and liberty—and he was an outspoken opponent of Julius Caesar.) One piece, appearing on September 27, 1787, only 10 days after conclusion of the Constitutional Convention, was a powerful assault on the executive branch:

The deposit of vast trusts in the hands of a single magistrate, enables him in their exercise, to create a numerous train of dependents—this tempts his *ambition,* which in a republican magistrate is also remarked, *to be pernicious* and the duration of his office for any considerable time favors his views, gives

■ **Cato:** The pseudonym for a writer of a series of articles in opposition to the ratification of the Constitution.

SIGNIFICANCE: *This person, who many believe was George Clinton of New York, offered a thoughtful critique on the wisdom of broad executive powers. Many of his arguments resonate today.*

him the means and time to perfect and execute his designs—*he therefore fancies that he may be great and glorious by oppressing his fellow citizens, and raising himself to permanent grandeur on the ruins of his country.* [Emphasis in original.]

Cato worried that the scheme outlined by the framers would allow the president to use his long term of office to take such a firm hold of the reins of power that it would ruin the democratic experiment.

Alexander Hamilton had the difficult chore of countering Cato's argument. He undertook the task of easing fears about the presidency in *Federalist No. 69.* There, Hamilton sought to "place in a strong light the unfairness of such representations" of the proposed executive branch. Repeatedly, Hamilton worked to underscore the differences between a president and a king. He notes that while the president is elected for only four years, a king gains his post through heredity and holds it throughout his life. The president can be impeached for treason, bribery, and other high crimes or misdemeanors, but the king can be subjected to no punishment—he is "sacred and inviolable." A president may be able to veto legislation, but this decision can be overridden by the legislature. In contrast, a king's judgment is absolute.

In the end, however, it was not persuasive arguments that carried the day; rather, it was public sentiment toward one political

This painting by H. Brueckner is called *The Prayer at Valley Forge.* It is not possible to overstate the public's esteem for George Washington. In fact, much of the ambiguity in the Constitution regarding presidential powers springs from the near blind faith the framers had in Washington. —***What was it about Washington that brought him this kind of trust?***

leader. Everyone knew that George Washington would be the first president. He had not abused his authority as the commanding officer of the Continental Army, and many simply could not imagine such a great man amassing power and making himself a king. Faith in Washington allowed citizens to overcome their fears (for the moment) about a powerful executive.

The President and the Constitution

7.1   Explain the framers' decision to bestow the president with real powers despite their concerns about potential abuses.

PRACTICE QUIZ: UNDERSTAND AND APPLY

1. Among the principal powers granted to the president by the Constitution is the power to
   a. conduct foreign policy.
   b. appoint judges.
   c. act as commander in chief of the armed forces.
   d. a, b, and c.

2. During the formation of the Constitution, one strong argument for granting substantial authority to the executive branch was
   a. the geographic breadth of the United States.
   b. the precedent of strong monarchical rule in England.
   c. George Washington's campaign for the position.
   d. George Washington himself.

3. The experience under the Articles of Confederation mattered to the framers' discussion of the presidency because
   a. that experience made it clear the national government needed a decisive commanding figure.
   b. Washington, the acting president during that time, had executed his duties effectively.
   c. that experience demonstrated how ineffective the new state governors were.
   d. Washington, the nominal president during that time, was not an effective president.

ANALYZE

1. The framers of the Constitution intended that the president *share* powers with the other branches of government, especially Congress. Is this true today? If the presidency were more powerful, in what ways would this distort the foundation of our government?

2. "Cato" worried that the president "fancies that he may be great and glorious by oppressing his fellow citizens." Is this a legitimate worry for citizens today? Why or why not?

IDENTIFY THE CONCEPT THAT DOESN'T BELONG

a. Appointing judges
b. Conducting foreign policy
c. Passing legislation
d. Vetoing legislation
e. Overseeing the conduct of wars

CONNECT THE LINK

(Chapter 6, page 156) Why did the framers of our system of government see the legislature as the core of the government?

■ **Whig Model:** A theory of restrained presidential powers; the idea that presidents should use only the powers explicitly granted in the Constitution.

SIGNIFICANCE: *Most nineteenth-century presidents held this view, leading to a legislative-centered government.*

Resource Center
• Glossary
• Vocabulary Example
• Connect the Link

The Evolution of the Presidency

7.2 **Outline the changes that have led to the expansion of presidential powers.**
(pages 196–203)

The fact that the Constitution *allows* for a powerful president does not mean that it *mandates* one. The scope of presidential powers has been a function of the men who have served in the position and used those powers. In addition, the overall evolution of the presidency has been toward ever-greater powers, so much so that today few of us can imagine a time when the president was not at the center of the federal government. But indeed, there have been such times in our history.

Models of Presidential Power

As we saw in Chapter 6, page 156, the framers of our system believed that Congress would be the primary branch of government. And that was precisely what occurred during the first century of our nation's history. Presidents seemed quite willing to follow Congress. There were, of course, strong presidents, such as George Washington, Thomas Jefferson, Andrew Jackson, and Abraham Lincoln. They were exceptions to the rule, however, and their powers sprang from extraordinary circumstances.

There were a number of reasons why it made sense that the presidency was not at the center of nineteenth-century American government: the national economy still centered on agriculture, and supervision and guidance of economic matters was not as important during this time as it would be after industrialization and urbanization; the United States was not a central player in world affairs; and nineteenth-century political campaigning was party centered, with less emphasis on presidential candidates and more attention on party platforms and the entire "ticket." On top of this was the general belief among presidents themselves that they should not be at the center of government. Most nineteenth-century presidents—and a few in the twentieth-century—held closely to the idea that presidents are limited to the powers *explicitly* stated in the Constitution or explicitly granted to the executive branch by Congress in the years since the Constitution was written. This has been dubbed the **Whig model**■ of presidential powers.

Theodore Roosevelt believed that presidents should use their position to articulate values, offer policy alternatives, and challenge accepted wisdom. That is to say, presidents should lead public opinion rather than simply follow it. —*But what if this "bullish" advocacy leads to a divided public? Should presidents be responsible for finding compromises and common ground?*

■ **Stewardship Model:** A theory of robust, broad presidential powers; the idea that the president is only limited by explicit restrictions in the Constitution.

EXAMPLE: *Theodore Roosevelt was a powerful, activist president.*

■ **Modern Presidency:** A political system in which the president is the central figure and participates actively in both foreign and domestic policy.

EXAMPLE: *Franklin D. Roosevelt, with his New Deal Program, ushered in an executive-centered system.*

This view of executive power, however, had begun to erode by the end of the nineteenth century, in part due to changing economic and geopolitical conditions. The nation's economy shifted from farming to industry, and its position in global affairs expanded. Moreover—and perhaps most significant—some of the men who occupied the White House after 1901 transformed the job of the president.

Most historians agree that the first truly assertive president who did not confront extraordinary circumstances was Theodore Roosevelt (1901–1909). Before becoming president, Roosevelt, or TR as the press called him, had been a vigorous, reform-minded governor of New York. There he learned the power of shaping public opinion and using public support to push his reform agenda through the state legislature. As president, he took the same route, transforming the office into a unique opportunity to preach to and inspire a "national congregation." One historian offered this description: "As a master of political theater with an instinctive understanding of how to dramatize himself and the policies he favored, TR was our first modern media president, and a brilliant huckster."[7]

Theodore Roosevelt held firmly to a new view of presidential powers, one with no restrictions on presidential authority except what was strictly *forbidden* in the Constitution. This perspective, often referred to as the **stewardship model**■, reversed the earlier approach. Instead of using only the powers expressly granted, Roosevelt believed that *all* was possible *except* what was prohibited. This was especially true, he argued, when the good of the nation was at stake. Looking back on his presidency, TR boasted, "I did not usurp power, but I did greatly broaden the use of executive power . . . I acted for the common well-being of our people . . . in whatever manner was necessary, unless prevented by direct constitutional or legislative prohibition."[8]

Woodrow Wilson, the twenty-eighth president (1913–1921), also subscribed to the stewardship model. He believed that the president should lead not only in national politics but also in international relations. Following World War I, Wilson set his sights on creating an international body to settle disputes between nations, which he called the League of Nations and which he tried, unsuccessfully, to have the United States join. (The League was the predecessor of the United Nations, which the United States would help form at the end of World War II.) Wilson's efforts have not been lost on historians such as Robert Dallek, who wrote, "No vision in twentieth-century presidential politics has inspired greater hope of human advance or has done more to secure a president's reputation as a great leader than Wilson's peace program of 1918–1919."[9]

Not all of the presidents who came after Wilson shared his activist views of presidential power. For example, his successors Warren G. Harding (1921–1923), Calvin Coolidge (1923–1929), and to a lesser extent, Herbert Hoover (1929–1933) followed the Whig model by deferring to congressional leadership.

President Barack Obama meets with his cabinet in a private room at the White House. The news media can enter the room only for scheduled photo opportunities. *—Should presidents pick only loyal supporters for the cabinet, or should they seek out the very best people regardless of their previous support or partisan leanings?*

However, the election to the presidency in 1932 of Franklin Delano Roosevelt (FDR) ushered in what many historians would describe as the **modern presidency**■. Roosevelt—a distant cousin of TR and, like him, a former governor of New York—ran for the White House at the depths of the Great Depression. He swept into the presidency on a wave of public anger, frustration, and fear. Within a day of being sworn in, FDR took charge of the federal government.

With panicked depositors withdrawing their savings from bank accounts (which at the time were not insured) and thus threatening the country's banking system with collapse, his first move was to declare a national bank holiday—something that most people doubted he had the legal authority to do. Legally or not, Roosevelt ordered every bank in the country temporarily closed until federal inspectors could go through its books and declare it sound, thus reassuring depositors. Then, with equally dubious legality, he banned the buying and selling of gold and halted the practice of linking the value of the dollar to the price of gold. Next, he sent Congress an emergency banking reform bill, which the House passed in 38 minutes and the Senate accepted with very little debate that same night. This was just the beginning of a comprehensive package of measures designed to pull the nation out of the economic crisis. During the Hundred Days, as it was called, Roosevelt submitted to Congress a stream of proposed reform measures, all of which were quickly enacted into law. Roosevelt demanded "action—and action now." The **New Deal,** the name he gave to his series of programs and initiatives that transformed the national

■ **Cabinet:** A group of presidential advisers, primarily the secretaries of federal departments.

EXAMPLE: *As Secretary of State, Hillary Clinton is an important member of Barack Obama's cabinet.*

government, gave birth to the welfare state and shaped the modern presidency.[10]

Today, there no longer seems to be any question about the proactive role of the executive branch. Presidents are expected to lead the nation. They must come up with innovative solutions to our problems, give aid and comfort to American citizens in times of need, maintain a healthy and growing economy, and protect our nation from foreign and domestic threats. In times of peace and prosperity, we congratulate the president (who expects to be rewarded in the polls and at the ballot box), and in bad times, we place the blame squarely on the White House. This transformation has thus presented presidents with a double-edged sword, but there is little question that the stewardship model, first articulated by Theodore Roosevelt, guides the contemporary presidency. Presidents have no choice but to lead—or else stand condemned as failures.

Institutional Changes

Along with the shifting role of the chief executive in the federal government have come changes within the institution of the presidency. We refer here to the cabinet, support staff, and the various offices and agencies designed to help the president succeed, as well as to the changing role of the vice president.

THE CABINET   Since the very beginning, presidents have relied on their staff. The framers of the Constitution rejected the idea of creating any type of council of presidential advisers, but once in office, Washington immediately realized that specific executive departments should handle the responsibilities of the federal government. The people who took charge of these departments became the president's **cabinet**■ (see Table 7.1). The cabinet consists of the secretaries of the major departments of the bureaucracy on whom

TABLE 7.1	Departments of the President's Cabinet

Presidents have always surrounded themselves with policy advisers, especially as the powers and duties of the executive branch broadened with FDR's administration. One source of support comes from the cabinet. Why have the number of cabinet positions increased over time?

DEPARTMENT	CREATED	RESPONSIBILITIES
State	1789	Create foreign policies and treaties
Treasury	1789	Coin money, regulate national banks, and collect income taxes
War, Defense	1789, 1947	Security and defense
Interior	1849	Maintain national parks and natural resources
Agriculture	1862	Protect farmland, nature, and wildlife; provide resources to rural and low-income families; ensure agricultural products are safe for consumers
Justice	1789	Ensure justice and public safety by enforcing the law
Commerce	1903	Promote economic stability, growth, and international trade
Labor	1913	Protect the rights of working citizens and retirees; monitor changes in employment and economic settings
Health and Human Services	1953	Promote research; provide immunizations and health care to low-income families; ensure safety of food and drugs
Housing and Urban Development	1965	Guarantee everyone a right to affordable housing; enhance communities and increase the number of homeowners
Transportation	1966	Provide an efficient and safe transportation system that meets the needs of the American people
Energy	1977	Provide reliable energy and promote science while protecting the environment and national and economic securities
Education	1979	Ensure that all citizens can obtain a quality education
Veterans Affairs	1989	Provide support for the nation's veterans
Homeland Security	2002	Protect the United States from threats

SOURCES: Accessed at http://www.whitehouse.gov; Cabinet Web sites.

■ **Inner Cabinet:** The advisers considered most important to the president—usually the secretaries of the departments of state, defense, treasury, and justice.

EXAMPLE: *As attorney general and brother to the president, Robert Kennedy was a key inner cabinet member in JFK's administration.*

■ **Executive Office of the President (EOP):** A group of presidential staff agencies created in 1939 that provides the president with help and advice.

SIGNIFICANCE: *These various offices provide presidents with massive amounts of information and advice, allowing such staff to remain at the center of domestic and foreign policy.*

the president relies heavily to carry out public policy. These officials are appointed by the president and are confirmed by the Senate. They can be removed at the president's will without the consent of the Senate. Unlike the rules in parliamentary systems, members of the cabinet cannot also be members of Congress: The Constitution dictates that no one can hold more than one post in the federal government at the same time.

In Washington's administration, there were four cabinet members: secretary of state (Thomas Jefferson), to handle foreign affairs; secretary of the treasury (Alexander Hamilton); attorney general (Edmund Randolph); and secretary of war (Henry Knox), in charge of the U.S. Army. In later administrations, a secretary of the navy was added, and after that, secretaries of the interior, commerce, agriculture, labor, and other departments. Some more recent presidents expanded their cabinet by creating new departments. Jimmy Carter pushed Congress to create the Department of Education. Following the terrorist attacks of September 11, 2001, George W. Bush and Congress created the Department of Homeland Security.

Different presidents have used their cabinet in different ways. Some, such as Andrew Jackson, Dwight D. Eisenhower, Gerald Ford, and Jimmy Carter, staffed their cabinets with their closest advisers and allies. Other presidents have kept their cabinet at arm's length, consulting with members only for routine matters or for policy concerns within their particular area. President John F. Kennedy once commented, "Cabinet meetings are simply useless. . . . Why should the Postmaster General sit there and listen to a discussion of the problems of Laos?"[11] Bill Clinton rarely spoke directly with many of his cabinet officers, and Ronald Reagan once mistook his secretary of urban affairs for another official when they were later introduced. Furthermore, most presidents informally establish an "inner" and an "outer" cabinet, with the former being the most important secretaries, usually those representing the departments of state, defense, treasury, and justice. Members of the **inner cabinet**■ have more access to the president and are considered closer advisers. In the Obama administration, several political advisors, like David Axelrod, Valerie Jarrett, and Robert Gibbs, have the president's ear. Rahm Emanuel, the president's chief of staff, is a very close confidant, and in the cabinet, several members, such as Hillary Clinton, Ken Salazar, Tim Geithner, and Robert Gates, regularly offer the president advice. President Obama appears to rely on a broad range of advisors, and these groups shift with different policy questions.

EXECUTIVE OFFICE OF THE PRESIDENT Before Franklin D. Roosevelt, all presidents had a handful of clerks and personal assistants. A few nineteenth-century presidents also relied on informal input from a trusted circle of advisers—for example, the political cronies whom Andrew Jackson named his "kitchen cabinet," who were not part of his official cabinet. As the role of the president in developing and carrying out federal programs expanded, however, so did the number of his personal advisers.

FDR needed lots of experts, a great deal of information, and more staff, and he pushed hard for institutional changes. The greatest single leap in this direction was the creation of the **Executive Office of the President (EOP)**■ in 1939.

An act of Congress established a number of groups of advisers under the broad heading of the EOP, including the White House staff, the Bureau of the Budget, and the Office of Personnel Management. Through the years, new divisions have been created, including the National Security Council, the Council of Economic Advisers, and the Office of Management and Budget. In Barack Obama's administration, the EOP consists of many offices, each with a group of members and a large support staff (see Table 7.2).

Each component of the EOP is important, but some have proved more significant than others. The **National Security Council (NSC)** was established in 1947, and although its membership varies from administration to administration, it always includes the vice president and the secretaries of defense and state. The job of the NSC is to provide the president with information and advice on all matters concerning national security, including foreign and domestic threats. One of the key players of this group is the **national security adviser,** who is appointed by the president without confirmation and is not officially connected with the Department of State or the Department of Defense. As such, he or she is expected to give the president independent, unbiased advice on important national security matters.

The **Office of Management and Budget (OMB)**■ has a number of sweeping responsibilities that include preparing the president's annual national budget proposal, monitoring the performance of federal agencies, and overseeing regulatory proposals. The **Council of Economic Advisers (CEA),** established in 1946, is led by three members—usually

TABLE 7.2	Executive Office of the President in 2010

- Council of Economic Advisers
- Council on Environmental Quality
- Domestic Policy Council
- National Economic Council
- National Security Council
- Office of Administration
- Office of Management and Budget
- Office of National Drug Control Policy
- Office of Science and Technology Policy
- Office of the United States Trade Representative
- President's Intelligence Advisory Board and Intelligence Oversight Board
- White House Military Office
- White House Office

■ **Office of Management and Budget (OMB):** A cabinet-level office that monitors federal agencies and provides the president with expert advice on policy-related topics.

SIGNIFICANCE: *The OMB is one of many offices that have broadened the scope of presidential power in recent decades.*

■ **Social Security:** A federal program started in 1935 that taxes wages and salaries to pay for retirement benefits, disability insurance, and hospital insurance.

SIGNIFICANCE: *This federal "safety net" program, and many others, changed the relationship between citizens and the federal government.*

Pictured here are two of President Barack Obama's closest advisors: Chief of Staff Rahm Emanuel, who until his 2010 resignation, advised Obama on policy, and White House Senior Advisor Valerie Jarrett, an old friend of the president, who is considered a key political strategist. *—In which situations might the interests of policy conflict with those of political advisors?*

eminent economists—who are appointed by the president and confirmed by the Senate. Their duties include assisting the president in preparation of an annual economic report to Congress, gathering timely information concerning economic developments and trends, evaluating the economic impact of various federal programs and activities, developing and recommending policies that boost the nation's economy, and making recommendations on economy-related policies and legislation.

PATHWAYS of action

FDR Takes Charge!

When Franklin D. Roosevelt began his presidency in 1933, voters were looking for bold leadership and dramatic changes. Understanding his mandate, Roosevelt took the lead in redirecting the federal government. In doing so, he forever transformed the nature of the presidency. Many of the ideas for his New Deal programs came from a group of advisers, some of them college professors or other intellectuals, whom he called his "Brain Trust." Roosevelt's advisers and cabinet members did not always agree with one another—sometimes, in fact, their ideas were flatly contradictory—but in the crisis, FDR was willing to try anything that seemed as if it might work. In fact, his leadership style included always listening to advice from different viewpoints, always making the final decision himself, and always keeping his options open to try something else.

A partial list of Roosevelt's policy achievements included the Federal Deposit Insurance Corporation (FDIC), which insured savings deposits to prevent future banking crises; the Securities and Exchange Commission (SEC), which protects investors from fraudulent stock market practices; the Wagner Act of 1935, which strengthened the organizing power of labor unions; and several measures designed to help homeowners finance mortgages and keep their homes. Maximum work hours and minimum wages were also set for certain industries in 1938. The most far-reaching of all the New Deal programs, however, was **Social Security**■, enacted in 1935 and expanded in 1939, which provided benefits for the elderly and widows, unemployment compensation, disability insurance, and welfare programs for mothers with dependent children. (Medicare and Medicaid were added to Social Security in 1964.)

Along with the expansion of presidential responsibilities has come a rapid growth in the president's personal staff. Today, the White House Office is a critical part of the Executive Office of the President. FDR expanded his personal staff significantly, to an average of 47. This number grew to 200 under Harry Truman

CONNECT THE LINK
(Chapter 6, pages 162–165) How does the committee system afford citizens numerous points of access?

■ **Institutional Presidency:** The concept of the presidency as a working collectivity, a massive network of staff, analysts, and advisers with the president as its head.

SIGNIFICANCE: *This term captures the meaning of an important shift in American politics—one where the president is placed at the center of both foreign and domestic politics.*

Riding a wave of popular support, Franklin D. Roosevelt transformed the nature of the presidency and the federal government. His New Deal program ushered in a series of programs and policies designed to pull the nation out of the Great Depression. In doing so, he forever placed the executive branch squarely at the center of American politics. —*What would the framers think about the burgeoning powers of the executive?*

and to 555 under Nixon. When Ronald Reagan left office, some 600 full-time employees had been working for him. These days, the number of White House staffers hovers around 500, scattered through numerous offices. The most important of the president's personal staff assistants is the *chief of staff*. Presidents have used their chiefs of staff differently; some have been granted more control and autonomy than others. Generally speaking, the chief of staff is especially close to the president and oversees all that the president might do on a typical workday, including who is allowed to meet the chief executive, what documents the president reads, and even what issues take up the president's time. Needless to say, this gatekeeping role makes the chief of staff one of the most important figures not only in the executive branch but also in the entire federal government. Barack Obama's chief of staff, Rahm Emanuel, who has garnered the nickname "Rahmbo" (after the 1980s film character, Rambo), is considered tough and shrewd, and he is a key advisor to the president.

RAMIFICATIONS OF STAFFING CHANGES Many observers of the American presidency have noted that the nature of the office has been transformed by the dramatic expansion of the presidential staff. The modern presidency is a massive network of offices, staff, and advisers, requiring a complex organizational chart to keep track of duties and responsibilities. The result is that presidents have become central to the policy process. Scholars now use the term **institutional presidency**■ to describe the burgeoning responsibilities and scope of presidential powers. Some suggest that the massive expansion of support staff has tipped the balance of power between the branches such that the president is now at the center of the federal government and Congress has, in some respects, taken a

back seat. While it is true that over the years congressional staffs have also increased, they have not increased at nearly the pace of those in the executive branch. Others point out that the duties and responsibilities of modern presidents (discussed later in this chapter) have greatly expanded, making all this support necessary.

A second ramification of staffing changes has been growing internal conflict—that is, the balance of power *within* the executive branch seems to be shifting. In the past, cabinet secretaries and other policy experts played a key role in the executive branch. The president could always reject their advice, but it was taken for granted that they would have the president's ear—that they would provide counsel on important issues. However, in recent decades, presidents have surrounded themselves with White House staff, who were essentially *political* experts—with the goal of helping their boss win reelection, boost his poll ratings, and build his historical legacy—and policy advisers have often been pushed to the side. That is to say, the battle for the president's ear has become intense, and most analysts agree that the political experts are winning over the "policy wonks."

Finally, when it comes to shaping the outcome of government, the explosion of executive branch staff has made citizen action a bit more complex. On the one hand, we might say that the number of people to talk to has increased, quite similar to what we saw in Chapter 6, pages 162–165, in the case of Congress. Persuading a staffer close to the president can often be an effective means of shaping public policy. On the other hand, direct access to the president has become difficult. In an effort to protect their boss, White House aides may well be transforming the connection between the president and the people.

It is likely that Delaware Senator Joe Biden, shown here at a political rally, would not have agreed to run as Barack Obama's vice presidential candidate if he had not believed that he would be a "player" in the White House. —*What are some of the changes in our world that compel an expanded role by vice presidents?*

The Transformation of the Vice Presidency

Throughout most of American history, the vice presidency was considered an insignificant office. Benjamin Franklin once quipped that the vice president should be addressed as "your Superfluous Excellency."[12] Thomas Marshall, the vice president under Woodrow Wilson, once told a story of two brothers: "One ran away to sea; the other was elected vice president. And nothing was heard of either of them again."[13] In 1848, Senator Daniel Webster—who as one of his party's most influential figures had long hoped to gain the presidency—declined the vice presidential place on the Whig Party ticket. "I do not propose to be buried until I am dead," he snorted.[14] John Nance Garner, FDR's first vice president and a former speaker of the House, is quoted as saying that the vice presidency is "not worth a pitcher of warm spit."[15]

When Lyndon B. Johnson was asked by John Kennedy to be his running mate, the powerful Texas senator was reluctant to accept. Like Webster, LBJ worried about his political future. The job of vice president was mostly ceremonial—attending the funerals of dignitaries, dedicating bridges and parks, and sitting in the Senate on special occasions—and as majority leader of the Senate, Johnson stood at the hub of the federal government. But he was convinced by friends and colleagues to take the place on the ticket, because he would be a "heartbeat away from the presidency." And as fate would have it, Johnson did become president on November 22, 1963, upon

the assassination of JFK. Indeed, the job of vice president has always been, first and foremost, to stand ready. Nine times in American history, a vice president has assumed the presidency: John Tyler, Millard Fillmore, Andrew Johnson, Chester Arthur, Theodore Roosevelt, Calvin Coolidge, Harry Truman, Lyndon Johnson, and Gerald Ford.

With the advent of the Cold War after 1945 and the proliferation of nuclear weapons, concerns grew about the vice president's readiness to take the helm at a moment's notice, fully abreast of world and military developments.[16] Truman, who became president on FDR's sudden death in April 1945, had been kept in the dark about the American project to build an atomic bomb. He was also not fully apprised of the rapidly mounting tension between the United States and its ally, the Soviet Union, as World War II drew to its close. Truman had to learn everything "on the job"; fortunately for him and for the nation, he was a man of intelligence and strong character.

By the 1950s, in an age of nuclear missiles, many Americans believed that there should be no learning curve for new presidents. Dwight Eisenhower remarked, "Even if Mr. Nixon (his vice president) and I were not good friends, I would still have him in every important conference of government, so that if the Grim Reaper [death] would find it time to remove me from the scene, he is ready to slip in without any interruption."[17] Thus began a move toward bringing vice presidents into the inner circle, and as a result, the job of the vice president changed.

Walter Mondale had full access to President Carter and became a trusted adviser on all important matters. Al Gore, Bill Clinton's vice president for eight years, was given numerous important responsibilities and also had full access to the president, including weekly one-on-one lunch meetings. Gore was very much in the inner circle, "one of three or four people whose advice Clinton sought on virtually every important matter."[18] And Dick Cheney played a very powerful role; some have suggested that he was the most powerful vice president in American history. Although it is still early in Obama's administration, it appears that Joe Biden will continue the trend toward more powerful vice presidents. For example, Biden attends most strategy sessions in the Oval Office, and he was a key player in Obama's push for health care reform. In addition, Biden participated significantly in the discussions about whether or not to expand U.S. forces in Afghanistan. Ultimately, of course, the vice president has only as much power as the president allows him.

STUDENT profile

Have you ever dreamed of working at the White House for the most influential person in the world? Landing such a coveted position is surely out of the question for a college student . . . right?

Actually, 100 college students from across the nation intern at the White House each term. In the fall of 2009 Monique Dorsainvil, a senior at Emory University, was one of those interns. She recalls that during the White House Christmas Press Party she was charged with handing out gift bags to members of the press pool, when the president and the first lady dropped by. Clutching some 15 different bags at the same time, Dorsainvil saw President Obama look over and give her a big smile. "The smile was so endearing because it was a sympathy smile and a 'I've been where you are smile,' " she said.

On a more serious note, Dorsainvil noted, "As an African American lesbian, this opportunity was not only a success for me but for the multiple communities that I am proud to belong to." Christian Peele, also a 2009 intern, commented that "no matter the setting, each day's work required lots of energy, creativity, insight, and help from all those on the team."

It isn't easy to land such a post. Each term there are over 6,000 applicants for the 100 spots, and the competition is fierce. But make no mistake, interns come from all sorts of institutions—Ivy League universities, private liberal arts colleges, and large public community colleges. Strong grades, solid recommendations, demonstrated leadership qualities, and a commitment to public service are important. And who knows, perhaps someday a former intern will return to the White House and be the one doing the smiling!

SOURCE: Matt Vasilogambros, "Obama White House Interns: Bags, Meetings, Unforgettable Experiences," *PoliticsDaily.Com.* Accessed May 4, 2010. http://www.politicsdaily.com/2010/02/18/obama-white-house-interns-bags-meetings-unforgettable-experiences For more information on the White House Internship program, visit http://www.whitehouse.gov/about/Internships

The Evolution of the Presidency

7.2 **Outline the changes that have led to the expansion of presidential powers.**

PRACTICE QUIZ: UNDERSTAND AND APPLY

1. When our government began, most understood that the president should be in charge of advancing significant policy changes.
   a. true   b. false

2. According to the Whig model,
   a. presidential powers are broad and constrained only by the will of the people.
   b. presidential powers are limited to the duties outlined in the Constitution.
   c. only powerful presidents can be successful.
   d. most presidents are bound to fail.

3. The Executive Office of the President was an important part of
   a. the presidencies of Teddy Roosevelt and Woodrow Wilson.
   b. the new limitations on presidential powers.
   c. the expansion of presidential powers.
   d. the shift to presidential control of foreign policy issues.

4. Most would agree that the job of the vice president has remained more or less the same since John Adams held that post.
   a. true
   b. false

ANALYZE

1. Was the expansion of presidential powers throughout our history inevitable? Has the expansion been desirable?

2. What sort of relationship exists between presidential powers and crisis events?

IDENTIFY THE CONCEPT THAT DOESN'T BELONG

a. Presidential personalities
b. Changes to the Constitution
c. Expanded staff
d. Policy experts/advisors
e. Changes in the public's expectations

Resource Center
• Glossary
• Vocabulary Example
• Connect the Link

■ **Going Public:** Appealing directly to the people to garner support for presidential initiatives.

EXAMPLE: *When a president gives a series of speeches to build public support for this budget plan, he is "going public."*

The Informal Powers of the President

7.3 Establish how the "power to persuade" expands presidential power beyond the Constitution.
(pages 204–205)

In 1960, political scientist Richard Neustadt published an important book called *Presidential Power.* It suggested that the formal powers of the presidency, as outlined in the Constitution, were rather minor: They amounted to little more than a clerkship, by which the occupant of the White House is in the position to provide services to others in the federal government.[19] Instead, Neustadt argued, presidential power is the power to persuade.

The Power to Persuade

The real powers of any president are to use a combination of personality and political skills to lobby members of Congress. A president who feels strongly about a program or a policy initiative can tap into the many informal tools that the office makes possible, including the office's prestige, charm, the fear that others have of retribution, the need for special favors, and bargaining skills. Neustadt's book was very much a prescription—a guide for presidents to understand the true breadth of their powers. Both John F. Kennedy and Bill Clinton, for example, were said to have kept *Presidential Power* next to their beds.

President Barack Obama employed a battalion of informal tools, such as invitations to the White House, trips on Air Force One, and telephone calls, to persuade wavering members of Congress to back health care reform in the spring of 2010. Indeed, many attribute the success of the final push for reform to Obama's ability to persuade members of his own party to stay on the ship.

The ability (and necessity) to persuade has more or less always been central to a successful president. As president, Thomas Jefferson was a master of this tactic, holding dinner parties at which matters of state were informally discussed and decided by his cabinet and key members of Congress. New routes to persuasion opened up in the twentieth century, much to the benefit of presidential power. With the successive developments of radio, television, and the Internet, presidents have had widening opportunities to speak directly to the public—a process known as **going public**■. Winning the public's hearts and minds was found to be even more potent than persuading a few members of Congress.

Franklin D. Roosevelt, who broadcast "fireside chats" on the radio, first showed how a president could establish a deep personal bond with the American people. John F. Kennedy used television to build an image that was both glamorous and admired. Ronald Reagan, dubbed "The Great Communicator" by the press, was especially skillful at connecting with the public on television, due in no small measure to his years of training as an actor. As suggested by Figure 7.1, some presidents have been more successful at gathering support than others.

The Political Context

Stephen Skowronek, a Yale University scholar, advances another explanation for the evolution of informal presidential powers.[20] He argues that a president's power is largely determined by broader political forces, what scholars call the political order or context. An approach that works in one era might fall flat in another.

Skowronek identifies four distinct periods. In the first period, stretching from the early years of the nation to the reelection of Andrew Jackson in 1832, presidents garnered power through close, personal interactions with political elites. If the president was able to forge close, personal relations with a small group of decision makers, he was more likely to prevail. Presidential powers during the second period, from 1832 until the end of the eighteenth century, hinged on the ability of presidents to forge agreements with local party bosses. The period from the turn of the nineteenth century until the departure of Richard Nixon in 1973 exemplified pluralist politics. Here, presidential power sprung from the ability to bargain and negotiate agreements among competing interests. Finally, the most recent era has featured plebiscitary politics, in which forging a personal connection with the public is imperative. Central to Skowronek's approach is the suggestion that informal presidential powers are dependent on the political order of the day.

First Ladies

Finally, another critically important source of presidential power has always been first ladies. From Martha Washington to Michelle Obama, these women have provided informal advice, advocated significant policy reform, undertaken a host of symbolic functions, and lobbied lawmakers and foreign dignitaries.

During most of our nation's history, first ladies limited their political work to informal, behind-the-scenes activities. For instance, the profound role played by Abigail Adams in helping her husband John maintain a cool head during his entire political career—and especially his presidency—is well documented. Another critically important first lady was Edith Bolling Galt Wilson. Her husband, Woodrow, suffered a stroke and was left partly paralyzed in 1919. He was incapacitated for several months, during which time Edith spoke and acted on his behalf. Her critics called her the "first lady president."

The activities of first ladies became much more public with Eleanor Roosevelt, the wife of Franklin D. Roosevelt. She traveled extensively and spoke on behalf of her husband's New Deal policies as well as her own concerns (centering mostly on the condition of poor children in America). She also wrote a newspaper column and worked tirelessly for Democratic candidates across the country. After her husband's death, Eleanor Roosevelt became a U.S. delegate to the United Nations, taking a lead on issues related to human rights and world poverty.

FIGURE 7.1 ▪ The Ups and Downs of Presidential Approval Ratings

Presidents may benefit or suffer from the winds of public opinion. But on closer inspection, we see a pattern where most presidents begin their term of office with high approval ratings and end their stay with lagging support. —*Are presidents bound to fail in the eyes of the public? What made Gerald Ford, Ronald Reagan, and Bill Clinton the exceptions?*

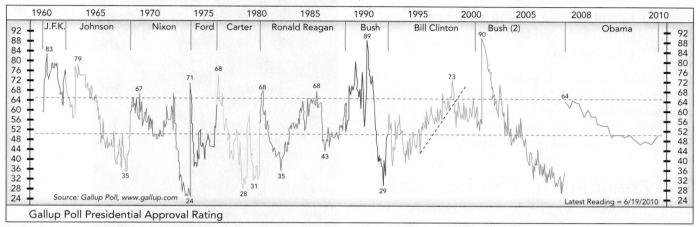

SOURCE: Copyright © 1960–2010 Gallup, Inc. From http://www.usatoday.com/news/washington/presidential-approval-tracker.htm

Perhaps the most dramatic change to the role of first ladies came about with Hillary Rodham Clinton. As a Yale-trained lawyer, Clinton had spearheaded a successful education reform task force while her husband was governor of Arkansas, in the process drawing national media attention. As she and her husband took up residence in the White House, her role as a powerful and public aide to her husband, President Bill Clinton, continued. Upon leaving the White House in 2000, Hillary Clinton was elected U.S. senator of New York and was named Secretary of State in the Obama administration in 2009.

Thus far, Michelle Obama has undertaken the more traditional approach of being a close confidant to her husband but not a key participant in most policy debates. She has taken the lead on issues that are important to her, including support for military families, helping women balance careers and family, and the promotion of national service. She has also brought attention to the problems of obesity and poor eating habits among children in America.

Few people doubt that the role of presidential spouses will evolve in the coming years. As more and more women lead high-profile professional lives, the restricted role of merely providing behind-the-scenes advice and undertaking public ceremonial functions is probably a thing of the past. The real question is, what role will the "first gentleman" perform in the future?

The Informal Powers of the President

7.3   Establish how the "power to persuade" expands presidential power beyond the Constitution.

PRACTICE QUIZ: UNDERSTAND AND APPLY

1. According to political scientist Richard Neustadt, the real power of the president is the power
   a. to manipulate.
   c. to persuade.
   b. to threaten.
   d. to communicate.

2. The idea of "going public" implies
   a. the aggressive use of the media.
   b. the ability to connect with average voters.
   c. going over the heads of legislators to their constituents.
   d. All of the above.

3. According to scholar Stephen Skowronek, the most important aspect of presidential powers is the ability to work with elites—such as party leaders in Congress.
   a. true
   b. false

ANALYZE

1. We understand why modern presidents would look to a "going public" strategy to push their policy agenda, and we also know it often works. But should success or failure hinge on the ability to shape public opinion?

2. What impact, if any, does the Internet have on presidential powers? Will it usher in a new political order?

IDENTIFY THE CONCEPT THAT DOESN'T BELONG

a. Veto power
d. Public appearances
b. Bargaining
e. Working the media
c. Prestige of the office

7.3

Resource Center
• Glossary
• Vocabulary Example
• Connect the Link

The Roles of Modern Presidents

7.4 Identify the duties and functions of modern presidents.

(pages 206–213)

Contemporary presidents are called on to perform a staggering number of duties and to play a dizzying variety of roles. It has been said that no job can prepare you for the presidency, and no job is similar. Still, we can break down a modern president's tasks into several categories or functional roles.

The President as Chief of State

When George Washington took the helm of the federal government in April 1789, his role in ceremonial events was unclear. On the one hand, everyone understood the importance of ritual and formal events. There would be occasions when the nation would need a leader to perform such functions—addressing Congress, greeting foreign dignitaries, speaking on the nation's behalf during times of celebration and grief, or even meeting ordinary citizens. If the president would not perform these functions, who would? In most political systems throughout the world, both then and now, a monarch or dictator undertakes chief-of-state functions.

Washington rejected all titles. Vice President John Adams proposed to the Senate that the president be addressed with a dignified title, such as "His High Mightiness," but neither the senators nor Washington himself accepted such an idea, which would have been hated by most Americans of the time. Nor did Washington wear any sort of robe, crown, or military uniform. It was Washington who established two acceptable titles for all future chief executives: "Mr. President" or "Mr. [last name]." In many ways, presidents would be regular citizens.

Still, all presidents perform ceremonial functions. Washington held formal gatherings, called *levees,* at which citizens would line up and be greeted one by one with a grave presidential bow. That, in the late eighteenth century, was expected, as a way of investing the presidency with dignity. But even that seemed too kingly to many Americans, and beginning with President Jefferson, a more informal tone permeated the presidency. Today, we expect presidents to make a telephone call to the winning Super Bowl team, to throw out a baseball at the start of the World Series, and to pardon the White House turkey on Thanksgiving. We also look to presidents for stability, wisdom, and composure during times of crisis. When the nation was shattered and shaken to its core by the terrorist attacks on September 11, 2001, we all turned to George W. Bush to steady the ship, to bring us together, and to help us move on. And when 29 miners died in West Virginia in the spring of 2010, the worst mining accident in 40 years, it was Barack Obama who gave the eulogy at the memorial service.

At first glance, you might think the ceremonial duties of the president, such as throwing out the first pitch at a baseball game, are rather insignificant. Such events, however, are important in drawing us together as a nation. *—In some constitutional monarchies, such as Great Britain, the king or queen fulfill these functions. Can you think of anyone else who could undertake these important acts, if not the president?*

Some critics look down on the chief-of-state role, suggesting that these sorts of activities are all fluff. But whether we live on a dairy farm in Vermont, in the suburbs of Los Angeles, or on a beach in North Carolina, we are all Americans. Ceremonial dinners and occasions to toss a baseball out at a special game might seem extraneous, but through these and many other events, our diverse nation becomes one.

The President as Chief Legislator

Article I of the Constitution states that Congress will undertake legislative functions—the passing of laws and the collection and distribution of funds. Article II makes the executive branch responsible for implementing the will of the legislative branch. At the same time, in keeping with the design of shared power, presidents are given some legislative authority: the power to veto bills, the ability to recommend measures for consideration, and the duty from time to time to inform Congress as to the "state of the union."

Consistent with the restrained view of presidential powers, occupants of the White House were reluctant to dig deeply into

■ **Veto:** The disapproval of a bill or resolution by the president.

SIGNIFICANCE: *This power allows presidents to play a significant role in shaping the outcome of legislation.*

legislative matters during the first 140 years of our nation's history. Presidents believed it their role to wait for Congress to act. In the eight years of his presidency, George Washington expressed an opinion on only five pieces of legislation.[21] Some presidents during this period—especially Andrew Jackson, Abraham Lincoln, Theodore Roosevelt, and Woodrow Wilson—were deeply immersed in legislative matters, but they were exceptions to the rule. A good estimate is that during this period, only about one-quarter of all significant policy initiatives originated with the executive branch.

This changed in 1933 with the inauguration of Franklin D. Roosevelt. Amid the crisis of the Great Depression, not only did FDR send a stream of measures to Congress for consideration, he and his aides also plunged into the legislative process with gusto, writing bills and twisting congressional arms to make sure that they passed. No one doubted that FDR was in charge of making policy during his first two terms, that he was very much the chief legislator.

All presidents since FDR have sought to lead the policymaking process, but some of them have been better at legislative matters than others. Lyndon Johnson was particularly good at "working the legislature." As a former member of the House, and especially as the Senate's majority leader, Johnson understood how the system worked, including the incentives that might be most effective with a legislative leader or a rank-and-file member. He was aggressive about getting his way, routinely giving reluctant members of Congress the "Johnson treatment." Jimmy Carter's story was altogether different. Having never worked in Washington before moving into the White House, Carter was simply unfamiliar with how things worked in the national legislature. In the

end, Carter got only modest support from Congress, even though his own party (the Democrats) controlled both chambers (see Figure 7.2). President Barack Obama's decision to hire former legislative leader Rahm Emanuel as his Chief of staff and his early legislative successes indicate that he truly understands the process and appreciates the importance of legislative dynamics.

LEGISLATIVE TOOLS: THE VETO Presidents have at their disposal a number of tools and resources to aid their efforts with the legislature. The **veto**■ is critical. Presidents can shape legislation by rejecting measures passed by Congress. Sometimes presidents veto measures on principle, because they strongly disagree with the proposal (for example, when George W. Bush vetoed a measure to increase funding for stem cell research) or think it unconstitutional; at other times, they may consider the goals laudable but the details wrong. There are two types of vetoes. One approach is to simply send the legislation back to Congress with a message as to why the president disapproves—this is called a *veto message*. The legislation can still become law if two-thirds of both houses of Congress vote to override it. Overrides are very rare; only about 3 percent of all vetoes have been overridden because presidents are reluctant to lose face by vetoing bills that are likely to be overridden. If a president fails to act on a piece of legislation within 10 days, it becomes law. If Congress adjourns within those 10 days, however, the president can let the measure die through a *pocket veto*. Here, there is neither a signature nor a veto message. Pocket vetoes are quite rare, especially on major legislation.

Some modern presidents have been more willing than others to veto bills, as Table 7.3 suggests, even when Congress has been controlled by the same party. However, this table is

FIGURE 7.2 ▪ Congressional Support for Presidential Initiatives
This figure charts the percentage of presidential initiatives that are approved by Congress. Clearly, some presidents are more successful with the legislature than others. What makes this figure especially interesting is that presidents can be successful even when the other party controls Congress. —*What force do you suppose leads to greater success with Congress, even when the president faces a "hostile" legislature?*

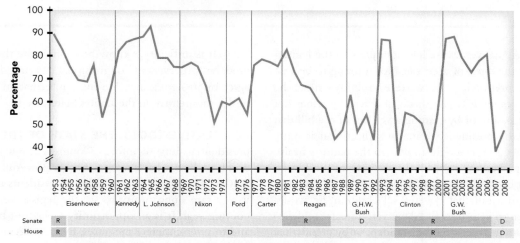

SOURCE: Harold Stanley and Richard Niemi, *Vital Statistics on American Politics, 2009–2010*, pp. 244–245. Reprinted by permission of CQ Press. www.cqpress.com. Data on President Obama was unavailable as of the publication date of this book.

TIMELINE The Battle over Health Care Reform

● COURTS　　● CULTURAL CHANGE　　● ELECTIONS　　● GRASSROOTS MOBILIZATION　　● LOBBYING DECISION-MAKERS

Are democratic governments responsible for the well-being of their citizens? Most would agree that governments should provide military, police, and fire protection, as well as a safety net for those citizens unable to care for themselves. But when it comes to basic medical care for all citizens, not everyone agrees. President Barack Obama's drive for health care reform brought change to our system. While some believe that the reforms are modest compared to what is found in other systems, others suggest that with passage of the Health Care and Education Reconciliation Act of 2010, the nation took a dangerous step toward socialism.

Essay questions:

1. If we have a limited government that is by and for the people, should we expect help with health care costs? If we presume government will provide an education for all citizens, how is health care any different?

2. Why do you suppose so many presidents proposed health care reform, only to see their initiatives stopped in Congress? Is there a difference between the president's constituency and the constituencies of members of Congress? Are members of Congress more responsive to the influence of lobbyists than presidents?

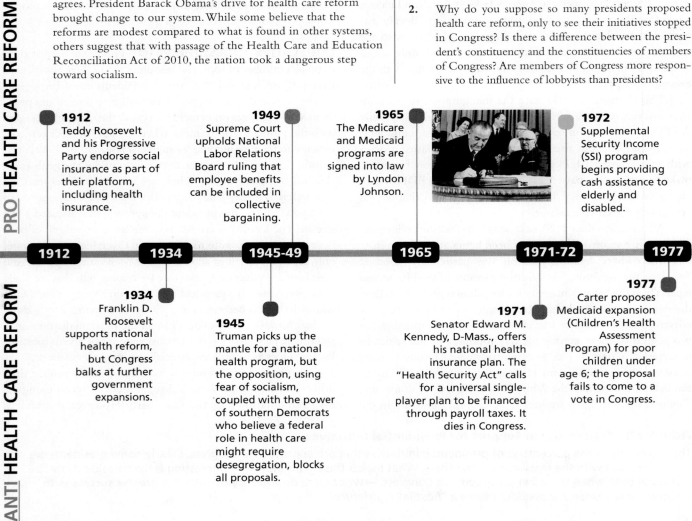

PRO HEALTH CARE REFORM

1912
Teddy Roosevelt and his Progressive Party endorse social insurance as part of their platform, including health insurance.

1949
Supreme Court upholds National Labor Relations Board ruling that employee benefits can be included in collective bargaining.

1965
The Medicare and Medicaid programs are signed into law by Lyndon Johnson.

1972
Supplemental Security Income (SSI) program begins providing cash assistance to elderly and disabled.

1912 — **1934** — **1945-49** — **1965** — **1971-72** — **1977**

ANTI HEALTH CARE REFORM

1934
Franklin D. Roosevelt supports national health reform, but Congress balks at further government expansions.

1945
Truman picks up the mantle for a national health program, but the opposition, using fear of socialism, coupled with the power of southern Democrats who believe a federal role in health care might require desegregation, blocks all proposals.

1971
Senator Edward M. Kennedy, D-Mass., offers his national health insurance plan. The "Health Security Act" calls for a universal single-player plan to be financed through payroll taxes. It dies in Congress.

1977
Carter proposes Medicaid expansion (Children's Health Assessment Program) for poor children under age 6; the proposal fails to come to a vote in Congress.

---

also misleading. Actual vetoes are less significant in the legislative process than the *threat* of their use. Not wanting to be embarrassed by the president or to waste everybody's time, the legislature often responds to the threat of a veto by either not moving on the measure or by crafting a version of the bill that is acceptable to the president. Sometimes the threat is quite public. When Bill Clinton sought to reform the nation's health care system, he picked up a pen during a State of the Union address, waved it back and forth, and declared that if Congress did not send him a bill that covered all children, he would gladly use the pen to veto the bill. Many veto threats are delivered in private, either directly by the president or by presidential aides. It is difficult to know how often the threat of a veto is used, but observers of congressional and presidential dynamics agree on its significance. For more information on the push for health care reform in the Unites States, see the Timeline.

LEGISLATIVE TOOLS: THE STATE OF THE UNION The presidential duty to inform Congress about the state of the union each year has become another powerful legislative tool. Rather than seeing this as a chore, presidents now understand it as a rare opportunity to set the legislative agenda for the coming year. It is an opportunity to lay out broad principles and to offer concrete measures. Even more important, it is an

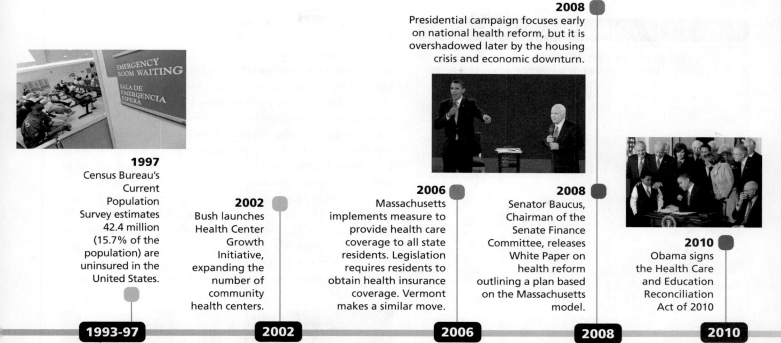

2008
Presidential campaign focuses early on national health reform, but it is overshadowed later by the housing crisis and economic downturn.

1997
Census Bureau's Current Population Survey estimates 42.4 million (15.7% of the population) are uninsured in the United States.

2002
Bush launches Health Center Growth Initiative, expanding the number of community health centers.

2006
Massachusetts implements measure to provide health care coverage to all state residents. Legislation requires residents to obtain health insurance coverage. Vermont makes a similar move.

2008
Senator Baucus, Chairman of the Senate Finance Committee, releases White Paper on health reform outlining a plan based on the Massachusetts model.

2010
Obama signs the Health Care and Education Reconciliation Act of 2010

1993-97 | **2002** | **2006** | **2008** | **2010**

1993
Clinton makes health care reform a priority in his first term. His proposal, named the Health Security Act, is introduced in both houses of Congress but gains little support.

SOURCE: Recreated by authors based on information from "Timeline: History of Health Reform Efforts in the U.S.," The Henry J. Kaiser Family Foundation, 2010. http://healthreform.kff.org/flash/health-reform-new.html. This information was reprinted with permission from the Henry J. Kaiser Family Foundation. The Kaiser Family Foundation is a non-profit private operating foundation, based in Menlo Park, California, dedicated to producing and communicating the best possible analysis and information on health issues.

opportunity to speak directly to the American people. Many Americans watch the State of the Union address, and presidents use this rare occasion to shape public opinion, which of course goes a long way in persuading legislators.

The President as Chief Diplomat

Presidents are in charge of foreign affairs. This is what the framers had in mind, it is strengthened by over 200 years of precedent, and it has been confirmed by several Supreme Court decisions. As stated by the Supreme Court in *United States v. Curtiss-Wright* (1936), the president is the "sole organ" in conducting foreign affairs, and his powers are "exclusive." Indeed, the president enjoys a freedom from congressional restrictions that "would not be admissible where domestic affairs alone are involved."[22]

There are a number of ways in which presidents can conduct foreign policy. Obviously, they can travel around the world, meeting with the leaders of other nations, forging ties and formal alliances. The Constitution states that they can appoint and receive ambassadors. In appointing ambassadors, which the Constitution requires them to do with the advice and consent of the Senate, presidents can choose officials who share their outlook toward a given nation or foreign affairs more generally. Accepting ambassadors might seem a less significant act, but it

■ **Treaty:** A formal agreement between governments.

EXAMPLE: *The North America Free Trade Agreement, signed in 1992, eliminated most tariffs on products traded among the United States, Canada, and Mexico.*

■ **Executive Agreement:** Binding commitments between the United States and other countries agreed to by the president but, unlike treaties, not requiring approval by the Senate.

SIGNIFICANCE: *By not having to secure Senate approval, presidents have often used these "understandings" to craft foreign policy.*

TABLE 7.3	Presidential Vetoes, 1933–2010			
	REGULAR VETOES	**POCKET VETOES**	**TOTAL VETOES**	**VETOES OVERRIDDEN**
F. Roosevelt	372	263	635	9
Truman	180	70	250	12
Eisenhower	73	108	181	2
Kennedy	12	9	21	—
L. Johnson	16	14	30	—
Nixon	26	17	43	7
Ford	48	18	66	12
Carter	13	18	31	2
Reagan	39	39	78	9
G. H. W. Bush	29	17	46	1
Clinton	36	1	37	2
G. W. Bush	8	0	7	1
Obama	0	2	0	0

SOURCES: *Statistical Abstract of the United States,* 1986, p. 235; Senate Library, *Presidential Vetoes* (Washington, DC: Government Printing Office, 1960), p. 199; Thomas Cronin and Michael A. Genovese, *The Paradoxes of the American Presidency* (New York: Oxford University Press, 1998); US Census Bureau, "Congressional Bills Vetoed," 2009. http://www.census.gov/compendia/statab/tables/09s0392.pdf.

can be used as a powerful tool. When presidents "accept" the emissary of another nation, it signifies that the United States recognizes that nation's existence and that its leaders hold power legitimately.

Another critically important foreign policy tool is the **treaty**■, a formal agreement between the United States and one or more other sovereign nations. The intent of the framers was that the Senate would work closely with the executive branch to negotiate and ratify treaties. This approach did not last long, as George Washington became frustrated with both the slow pace of the Senate and the difficulties of arriving at a consensus. From that point onward, presidents have negotiated treaties independently and then asked the Senate to ratify them by the two-thirds margin that the Constitution requires. For example, in April 2010, Barack Obama negotiated a treaty with Russian President Dmitry A. Medvedev to reduce each nation's nuclear warheads and launchers. Given that presidents have usually been of the same party as the majority in the Senate, it should come as no surprise that the Senate has rejected very few treaties. Of the approximately 1,500 that have been sent to the Senate, only 15 have been voted down.

However, a good many, roughly 150, have been withdrawn because they appeared to lack support.

In some ways more important than treaties are less formal **executive agreements**■—also known as "arrangements"—between the United States and other nations. Whereas treaties are generally high-profile matters, attracting a great deal of media attention, executive agreements are often arranged in secret. They do not require Senate approval, which makes them especially appealing to presidents—particularly if they confront a hostile Congress—but the Case Act of 1972 requires the president to inform Congress of executive agreements within 60 days.

Presidents may make executive agreements only in areas where they have the power to act, and they often deal with relatively minor concerns, such as tariffs, customs regulations, or postal matters. Yet some presidents have used executive agreements in very important ways. In 1973, President Nixon used an executive agreement to end the American conflict

The framers of our political system thought presidents would provide information to Congress, at the "state of the union," so that the legislative branch would be better informed. In recent decades, the State of the Union address, held every January, has become an important tool in building support for policy initiatives. Here, Ronald Reagan waves before a State of the Union address in 1984. —*Do average Americans watch these speeches?*

■ **War Powers Resolution:** A measure passed by Congress in 1973 designed to limit presidential deployment of troops unless Congress grants approval for a longer period.

SIGNIFICANCE: *This act seems to compel compliance from Congress for military engagements, but all presidents have said their powers as commander in chief trump congressional control.*

(never a declared war) with North Vietnam and to exchange prisoners of war. Such an agreement was also used by President Reagan in 1981 to form a strategic alliance with Israel. Perhaps not surprisingly, given the growing importance and complexity of world affairs as well as the potential roadblocks to winning Senate approval of treaties, the number of executive agreements made by presidents has increased greatly in the past few decades.

Since the collapse of communism in the Soviet Union and Eastern Europe in 1989, and paralleling the rapid expansion of Asian economies (especially those of China and India), the management of America's trade relationships has been an expanding aspect of presidential foreign policy responsibilities. This change has created unique challenges for presidents. Opening foreign markets for American goods requires lowering or removing trade restrictions and tariffs on goods imported into the United States. Many imported products are cheaper because they are made by low-wage labor. Consumers want low-priced goods, but labor unions and manufacturers protest the importation of low-cost products, which threaten to close American factories and put Americans out of work.

The President as Commander in Chief

Article II, Section 2, of the Constitution appoints the president commander in chief of all American military forces. When they take the oath of office, presidents swear that they will "preserve, protect, and defend" our nation. The framers of our system believed it essential that one person be responsible for decisive action during times of crisis—in the event of an invasion, for example, which was a real threat in the late eighteenth century. As for the oversight of an ongoing conflict or the direction of prolonged military engagements, however, presidents share power with Congress. That is, the president is commander in chief of the armed forces, but Congress is charged with declaring wars (in Article I, Section 8). Also, Congress has the responsibility to raise and support armies (that is, to raise and allocate funds for military matters).

During the first few decades of our nation, the president's decision to go to war was clearly shared with Congress. In 1803, for example, Thomas Jefferson sent the U.S. Navy to fight the Barbary pirates—North African rulers who were seizing American merchant vessels in the Mediterranean Sea and enslaving their crews unless the United States paid them tribute. But Congress had authorized this attack in advance.[23] Presidential war powers took a leap forward during the Civil War. Congress was in recess when the southern states seceded at the end of 1860 and in early 1861, as well as when fighting began at Fort Sumter in April 1861, only a few weeks after Lincoln's inauguration. Without congressional authorization, Lincoln

called up the state militias, suspended the writ of habeas corpus, and slapped a naval blockade on the rebellious southern states. Critics claimed that Lincoln's acts were dictatorial, but he argued that they were necessary to preserve the Union. His defense of his "doctrine of necessity" is rather compelling:

> [My] oath to preserve the Constitution to the best of my ability imposed upon me the duty of preserving, by every indispensable means, that government . . . Was it possible to lose the nation and yet preserve the Constitution? By general law, the limb must be protected, yet often a limb must be amputated to save a life; but a life is never wisely given to save a limb. I felt the measures otherwise unconstitutional might become lawful by becoming indispensable to the preservation of the Constitution through the preservation of the nation.[24]

Essentially, Lincoln acted and left it to Congress either to accept or cancel his action later. Presidents since Lincoln have taken this "presidential prerogative" to heart, arguing that they are uniquely situated to protect the nation and should be given a free hand in all military emergencies.

In 1950, Harry Truman ordered troops to defend South Korea against a North Korean attack without requesting congressional authority (he said that the United States was engaging in a "police action" in support of a United Nations act). In the 1960s and early 1970s, both Lyndon Johnson and Richard Nixon waged the Vietnam War without a formal congressional declaration. Indeed, many observers think that the days of Congress actually declaring war—which last happened right after Japan's 1941 attack on Pearl Harbor—may now be over.

In 1973, after the United States and North Vietnam signed a peace agreement, Congress attempted to rein in presidential war making by passing the **War Powers Resolution**■—and then overriding President Nixon's veto of it. This act requires that the president consult with Congress in "every possible instance" before sending troops to combat, that the president report to Congress in writing within 48 hours after ordering troops into harm's way, and that any military engagement must end within 60 days unless Congress either declares war or otherwise authorizes the use of force (provisions allowed for 90 days under certain circumstances).

Since 1973, every president has claimed that the War Powers Resolution is unconstitutional. Nevertheless, rather than defy the act and test its constitutionality in the federal courts, and also in an effort to build broad public support (a critically important factor in waging successful long-term wars), all presidents who have sent American forces into battle have first sought congressional support for their action. For example, President George W. Bush sought and received a broad congressional authorization before invading Afghanistan in 2001 and Iraq in 2003.

■ **Iran-Contra Affair:** The Reagan administration's unauthorized diversion of funds from the sale of arms to Iran to support the Contras, rebels fighting to overthrow the leftist government of Nicaragua.

SIGNIFICANCE: *While presidents boast commander in chief powers, Congress regulates federal spending—which can be a key factor in military engagements.*

■ **Executive Order:** A regulation made by the president that has the effect of law.

EXAMPLE: *Harry Truman ended segregation of the armed forces though an executive order in 1948.*

Some 58,000 American lives were lost in Vietnam. While public support for our military efforts there was high in the early years, as the atrocities of the war and the number of casualties grew, Americans lost faith in Lyndon Johnson. —*How does Congress have the right (and obligation) to step in and change the course of military engagements after a period of time? At what point should it take such action?*

MYTH EXPOSED Many Americans believe that modern presidents have unlimited foreign policy powers, but this is simply not true. Congress still has the power to allocate or deny funds for military engagements. For example, in 1974, Congress cut off further funding for the war in Vietnam. But what if a situation arises in which the president sees military action as being in our nation's interest but Congress disagrees and fails to appropriate the necessary resources? This issue came to a head in the 1980s in the **Iran-Contra Affair**■, when aides to Ronald Reagan channeled U.S. funds to rebels fighting the leftist government in Nicaragua—even though Congress had passed a measure forbidding it. To many people, this was a clear violation of the law: Congress had spoken, and President Reagan, the executive, had thwarted its will. The Justice Department moved forward and eventually secured a number of felony convictions. The lesson from the Iran-Contra affair is that while presidents see their commander-in-chief authority as sweeping, Congress still has one crucial power—the power of the purse.

The President as Chief Executive

We have discussed several important elements of the president's chief executive function, including the assembling of staff and the cabinet, enforcing laws, and spending the funds that are allocated and appropriated by Congress. The president is in many ways the nation's chief administrator and head bureaucrat. This role might suggest that the president's hands are tied by the will of Congress—that this function

affords little leeway to shape policy—but this is only partially correct. At times, Congress makes its will clear with exact instructions to the executive branch. At other times, only vague outlines are provided, thereby leaving a great deal of ambiguity and leeway. This gives presidents and the federal bureaucracy (see Chapter 8, pages 236–237) a chance to shape public policy.

Second, many authorities believe the very size of the federal bureaucracy has shifted the balance of power toward the executive branch. During the first few decades, our government had only about 1,000 federal employees (most of whom staffed local post offices). Even so, President Jefferson thought that there were too many officials and carried out a severe staff reduction! In recent years, the number of federal employees has climbed to roughly 2.6 million (excluding active-duty members of the military). Although the vast majority of federal employees are civil service workers, the power to appoint certain high officials who lead the massive agencies and set their policies is an important executive function.

On top of this, presidents can issue **executive orders**■, which are essentially rules or regulations that have the effect of law. At times, executive orders are used to clarify existing legislation, but at other times, they have the effect of making new policy. There are three types of executive orders: *proclamations*, which serve the ceremonial purpose of declaring holidays and celebrations, and *national security directives* and *presidential decision directives*, both of which deal with national security and defense matters. Three of the most famous executive orders were used to ease some of the barriers to black men and women caused by generations of racial discrimination. Abraham Lincoln issued the Emancipation Proclamation, freeing the slaves of the South in 1863. Harry Truman issued an executive order in 1948 ending segregation in the armed forces, and Lyndon Johnson issued an executive order in 1966 making affirmative action a federal policy. George W. Bush used an executive order to create the White House Office of Faith-Based and Community Initiatives in 2001, and in 2010, to persuade certain House Democrats to back the health care initiative, Barack Obama issued an executive order affirming that no federal monies would be used for abortions.

Another tool that presidents have at their disposal to shape public policy is what is known as a **signing statement**■—a written proclamation issued when a president signs a bill into law that states how the executive branch will interpret the measure, which is often different from what Congress intended. Controversy has arisen over the constitutionality of signing statements—especially the large number of statements issued by George W. Bush. During his tenure in office, Bush issued nearly 200 signing statements, challenging over 1,200 provisions in various laws.

Finally, presidents can shape public policy by working to secure funding for new or existing programs. While Congress has the ultimate authority to set federal budget policies, each year presidents offer their own budget plans. Developed by an

CONNECT THE **LINK**
(Chapter 8, pages 236–237) How can presidents shape the policy process through appointments to the federal bureaucracy?

■ **Signing Statement:** A written proclamation issued by the president regarding how the executive branch intends to interpret a new law.

SIGNIFICANCE: *Quite often, the president's interpretation differs from the intent of Congress, so signing statements have become quite controversial.*

extensive staff of experts with the Office of Management and Budget (OMB), the president's budget is generally considered the starting point for congressional negotiations. Because the president is "first off the mark" with a budget outline, and because of the expertise of the OMB, savvy presidents often get a great deal of what they want, especially when Congress is controlled by the same party.

The President's Other Roles

While the list of duties and responsibilities outlined above is long, there are many additional roles. For instance, some have suggested that modern presidents must be Economists in Chief. That is, they are expected to keep a close eye on the nation's economy and to take immediate and effective actions when conditions dictate. Presidents are also expected to be moral leaders and to set an ethical tone in both politics and society. Many supported George W. Bush in the 2000 election because they believed he would set a higher moral standard than his predecessor, Bill Clinton. Many also expect presidents to be the heads of their political party, pushing the party's policy agenda and helping other party members raise money during elections.

The Two Presidencies

Scholars have tried to merge these various roles of the president into a neat model. The most successful attempt has been an approach advanced by political scientist Aaron Wildavsky in 1966. He introduced the "two presidency" thesis (sometimes called the duel presidency model).[25] Wildavsky suggested that the numerous roles of the presidency could be broken down into two categories: domestic affairs and defense/foreign policy. Wildavsky argued that presidents are often frustrated when it comes to domestic affairs, given the numerous actors and Congress's ability to check presidential initiatives. Instead, presidents are significantly better equipped to lead in foreign policy and defense matters. Not surprisingly, presidents will often turn to foreign policy matters later on in their tenure, likely due to frustration over the difficulties in advancing domestic policies. Many scholars have offered critiques of the two presidency model, including the idea that the lines between the two areas have blurred in recent years. Yet, the core logic—that presidents confront unique challenges and opportunities in both domestic and foreign policy—is important to bear in mind when considering all that presidents are asked to do.

The Roles of Modern Presidents

7.4 **Identify the duties and functions of modern presidents.**

PRACTICE QUIZ: UNDERSTAND AND APPLY

1. Which of the following is true about the "head of state" functions performed by presidents?
   a. Only certain presidents have undertaken these symbolic functions.
   b. While seemingly inconsequential, head-of-state functions are actually quite important.
   c. Presidents tend to undertake these activities more in their first term than in their second term.
   d. Presidents that are good at these sorts of activities tend to be only modestly effective in other areas.

2. Why are presidential vetoes rarely overridden by Congress?
   a. because senators frequently filibuster to thwart such an action
   b. because presidents rarely exercise a veto that they think will be overridden
   c. because most legislators rarely object to presidential vetoes
   d. because the authority of the executive branch has become nearly overwhelming in the past 80 years

3. The president's status as commander in chief means, in part, that
   a. the president can declare war.
   b. the president is responsible for raising money for military matters.
   c. the president can send U.S. military forces into battle with congressional authorization.
   d. the president can control the size and nature of the country's military forces.

ANALYZE

1. In what way is the "Johnson treatment" an example of Neustadt's power to persuade?

2. Discuss the particulars of the president's role as commander in chief. Is it better to have a decisive leader who acts unilaterally when it comes to military matters, or should Congress play a more direct role?

IDENTIFY THE CONCEPT THAT DOESN'T BELONG

a. Initiating domestic policy changes
b. Conducting foreign affairs
c. Funding military activities
d. Engaging in ceremonial duties
e. Monitoring economic conditions

7.4

Resource Center
• Glossary
• Vocabulary Example
• Connect the Link

■ **Personal Presidency:** The notion that there are greater and greater expectations placed on presidents, due in large measure to the way they run for office. At the same time, presidents are often unable to deliver on the promises they made during campaigns.

SIGNIFICANCE: *Because we now see presidents as being at the center of government, and because they often cannot deliver on what they promise, the public has grown cynical about the responsiveness of our government.*

Presidential Greatness

7.5 Evaluate the qualities that contribute to presidential success or failure.

(pages 214–217)

The term **personal presidency**■ describes the mounting expectations that the public places on the president— "expectations that have grown faster than the capacity of presidential government to meet them."[26] In short, Americans have developed a personal connection, an emotional bond, with their presidents. A number of changes have led to this development, including the growing size and importance of the federal bureaucracy, the expansion of presidential powers, and the heavy use of television advertising during campaigns, which forces candidates to promise things they cannot deliver once in office.

Americans put more and more faith in their presidents to solve their problems and meet all challenges, both foreign and domestic. The problem, however, is that the executive branch is only one piece of the federal government and only one element of the world's economy. "For most Americans the president is the focal point of public life," writes an expert on the presidency. "This person appears to be in charge, [which is] reassuring. But the reality of the presidency rests on a very different truth: Presidents are seldom in command and usually must negotiate with others to achieve their goals."[27] The outcome is dissatisfaction. Presidents often fail to meet our expectations, and we are left feeling disappointed and cynical. Some people would argue that this explains a string of "failed" presidencies.

Harry Truman and Lyndon Johnson—both of them vice presidents who entered the White House upon their predecessors' deaths—were rejected by their own party after leading the nation into controversial military entanglements. Having won reelection in a landslide in 1972, Richard Nixon just two years later resigned in disgrace, facing impeachment and likely conviction, after his criminal misconduct in the Watergate affair was exposed. Jimmy Carter was perceived as bungling the nation's economy and being indecisive during the Iranian hostage crisis (which lasted for more than 12 months between 1979 and 1981), and the voters ejected him from office after just four years. Ronald Reagan faced a congressional inquiry into the Iran-Contra affair and may have escaped impeachment only because he was on the verge of retirement. George H. W. Bush was riding high early in his presidency and drew record high approval ratings after victory was won in the first Gulf War— but one year later, Bill Clinton defeated him, largely because of a downturn in the economy. Clinton served for two full terms but was impeached by the House—on grounds stemming from personal misconduct. And George W. Bush left office with very low approval ratings. One might conclude that modern

Lyndon Johnson was masterful at engineering compromises and pushing through important domestic policies. The war in Vietnam spun out of control during his administration, however, and his popularity plummeted. Modern presidents are powerful, but they are far from omnipotent. *—Do you think presidential greatness can be determined by one event, or one year of a presidency? Or do we need to look at a president's entire time in office to make a determination about greatness?*

executives are destined to fail, that "presidential greatness" is a thing of the past.

But what is presidential greatness? What is it that makes one chief executive better than another? Are there ingredients that can be combined to create a successful, distinguished presidency? Perhaps it is only when our nation confronts adversity that greatness can emerge. The three presidents who top nearly all scholarly lists of great chief executives—Washington, Lincoln, and Franklin D. Roosevelt—each confronted a major national crisis. Washington led the nation in its founding years, when the very success of the federal experiment hung in the balance; Lincoln had to preserve the Union and chose to abolish slavery during a civil war that cost 600,000 lives; and Roosevelt faced the gravest economic crisis in the nation's history and then fought World War II. No other presidents, even those who rank relatively high, had to surmount crises as dangerous as these.

George W. Bush has said that his presidency was shaped by the events of September 11, 2001. Some might conclude that he was a good president because he met the challenge of our new realities. Others will see his tenure in the White House as a failure because of the war in Iraq; they will argue he took the United States into the wrong war at the wrong time and against the wrong enemy.

Perhaps simple luck has much to do with successful or failed presidencies. But bad luck can only explain so much. Herbert Hoover—a man superbly qualified by education and early experience for the presidency—claimed to be the unluckiest president in history, given the stock market's collapse on his watch in 1929. Yet Hoover was crippled by his rigid attempts to apply orthodox economic theories to a situation that required innovative thinking. Lyndon Johnson inherited the unwinnable conflict in Vietnam from his White House predecessors, and despite his noble championing of the civil rights movement and his policies aimed at eradicating poverty, his presidency was plagued by riots and massive antiwar demonstrations on college campuses. In addition, after the glamorous and eloquent Kennedy, LBJ seemed an uncouth, untrustworthy, and ruthless wheeler-dealer who spoke with a widely mocked Texas drawl. Jimmy Carter's hands were tied when the Iranian militants who had seized the U.S. embassy in Tehran threatened to kill the American diplomats whom they had taken hostage. He also faced skyrocketing oil prices and a stagnating economy.

It is worth remembering the words of the man always ranked as one of the greatest presidents, Abraham Lincoln, responding in 1864 to a reporter's question: "I claim not to have controlled events, but confess plainly that events have controlled me." How Lincoln *did* act when confronted with those events, however, is the measure of his greatness.

Circumstances matter. Yet even unlucky events can turn into triumphs of leadership if the president has the necessary character. And what defines great character in a political leader? Scholars and biographers have wrestled with this question for thousands of years, and there is no shortage of lists. The historian and presidential scholar Robert Dallek suggests that five qualities have been constants in the men who have most effectively fulfilled the presidential oath of office:[28]

1. *Vision:* All great presidents have had a clear understanding of where they wanted to lead the nation in its quest for a better future.
2. *Pragmatism:* All great presidents have been realists, leaders who understood that politics is the art of the possible and

that flexible responses to changing conditions at home and abroad are essential.
3. *Consensus building:* All great presidents understood that their success depended on the consent of the governed. Moving government in a new direction, often down a difficult path, requires building a national consensus first.
4. *Charisma:* All great presidents have been able to capture and retain the affection and admiration of average citizens.
5. *Trustworthiness:* All truly successful presidents have had credibility and have earned the faith of their fellow citizens.

Many groups have attempted to measure presidential greatness. The conservative Federalist Society, joining forces with the *Wall Street Journal* in November 2000, undertook one such effort. The study involved 78 randomly selected presidency scholars: historians, political scientists, and law professors. Another, conducted by C-SPAN in 2009, also surveyed scholars, whose responses seem to have been slightly weighted in favor of the more liberal or "progressive" presidents. Table 7.4 shows the results from both polls.

Although we might argue over the precise order of these rankings—whether one president should be ranked higher than another, whether Washington was better than Lincoln, or whether Harding, Buchanan, or Andrew Johnson was the worst of all—nearly all assessments of past presidents suggest similar groupings. Lincoln, Washington, both Roosevelts, and Jefferson were great leaders, and those at the bottom of this list, the presidents whose names seem the most obscure to us, are generally considered failures. The interesting part of this exercise is not the precise order but rather a consideration of the personal qualities and historical events that contributed to the success or failure of a given president. Why are James Madison and John Quincy Adams, who made enormous contributions to this country, not ranked among the greatest presidents? Why was Ulysses S. Grant at best only mediocre, and why did Gerald Ford, fail as a president? Why is James K. Polk listed in the top tier in some rankings? And who *was* James K. Polk, anyway?

As for George W. Bush's place in the rankings, the C-Span survey places him in 36th position. After his first four years in office, some began to speculate he would fall in the "average" range, but during his second term, the economy weakened, budget deficits grew, there were few legislative accomplishments, and the war in Iraq continued. His approval ratings languished in the 30 percent range for the last three years of his presidency. It seems likely that most historians will assess his tenure in office in an unfavorable light. By 2006, one commentator noted, "George W. Bush's presidency appears headed for colossal historical disgrace. Barring a cataclysmic event on the order of the terrorist attacks of September 11th, after which the public might rally around the White House once again, there seems to be little the administration can do to avoid being ranked on the lowest tier of U.S. presidents."[29] Of course, it is

TABLE 7.4	Rankings of American Presidents		
WALL STREET JOURNAL RANKING		**C-SPAN RANKING**	
RANK	**NAME**	**RANK**	**NAME**
1	George Washington	1	Abraham Lincoln
2	Abraham Lincoln	2	George Washington
3	Franklin D. Roosevelt	3	Franklin D. Roosevelt
4	Thomas Jefferson	4	Theodore Roosevelt
5	Theodore Roosevelt	5	Harry S Truman
6	Andrew Jackson	6	John F. Kennedy
7	Harry S Truman	7	Thomas Jefferson
8	Ronald Reagan	8	Dwight D. Eisenhower
9	Dwight D. Eisenhower	9	Woodrow Wilson
10	James K. Polk	10	Ronald Reagan
11	Woodrow Wilson	11	Lyndon B. Johnson
12	Grover Cleveland	12	James K. Polk
13	John Adams	13	Andrew Jackson
14	William McKinley	14	James Monroe
15	James Madison	15	Bill Clinton
16	James Monroe	16	William McKinley
17	Lyndon B. Johnson	17	John Adams
18	John F. Kennedy	18	George H. W. Bush
19	William Howard Taft	19	John Quincy Adams
20	John Quincy Adams	20	James Madison
21	George H. W. Bush	21	Grover Cleveland
22	Rutherford B. Hayes	22	Gerald R. Ford
23	Martin Van Buren	23	Ulysses S. Grant
24	Bill Clinton	24	William Howard Taft
25	Calvin Coolidge	25	Jimmy Carter
26	Chester A. Arthur	26	Calvin Coolidge
27	Benjamin Harrison	27	Richard M. Nixon
28	Gerald R. Ford	28	James A. Garfield
29	Herbert Hoover	29	Zachary Taylor
30	Jimmy Carter	30	Benjamin Harrison
31	Zachary Taylor	31	Martin Van Buren
32	Ulysses S. Grant	32	Chester A. Arthur
33	Richard M. Nixon	33	Rutherford B. Hayes
34	John Tyler	34	Herbert Hoover
35	Millard Fillmore	35	John Tyler
36	Andrew Johnson	36	George W. Bush
37	Franklin Pierce	37	Millard Fillmore
38	Warren G. Harding	38	Warren G. Harding
39	James Buchanan	39	William Henry Harrison
		40	Franklin Pierce
		41	Andrew Johnson
		42	James Buchanan

Note: William Henry Harrison, who died after just 30 days in office, and Garfield, who was mortally wounded 4 months after his inauguration and died 2 months later, are omitted from the *Wall Street Journal* ranking.

President Barack Obama worked with international leaders on an "historic" agreement to combat climate change at the Group of Eight (G8) summit in L' Aquila, in central Italy, on July 9, 2009. Climate change is one of the greatest challenges facing today's leaders. —*Clearly, the world's challenges have become even more complex since the framers described the duties and responsibilities of the executive branch. Do we now expect too much of our presidents?*

too early to tell about Barack Obama, but most would agree that he has taken on a number of big issues. How the public will respond to these changes, especially in the next presidential election, is an open question.

PATHWAYS of change from around the world

Is it possible for a change in leadership to alter the course of a nation? In a country where war has lasted more than a quarter-century, citizens used their right to vote to make a drastic change in leadership. On January 16, 2006, Ellen Johnson Sirleaf took the oath of office as Liberia's first elected female head of state. She was also the first woman to be elected president of an African nation. Having been imprisoned twice by anti-government rebels and narrowly escaping execution during a coup, the American–educated Sirleaf earned the nickname "Iron Lady."

By 2005, Liberia's unemployment rate had rocketed to an astonishing 80 percent. Abject poverty was rampant, and most of the country, including the capital, lacked running water and electricity. The voters were desperate for a change, and Sirleaf offered a new vision for the country.

As soon as she took office, Sirleaf began to rebuild the army, revitalize the farming and fishing industries, balance the government's budget, and bring water and electricity to many of the nation's communities. The country also enacted a new anti-corruption strategy, deemed by many outside observers to be both bold and optimistic. Her efforts to bring peace, security, and economic development to Liberia earned her the U.S. Presidential Medal of Freedom, the U.S. government's highest civilian award, in 2007. In announcing the award, President George W. Bush lauded Sirleaf for her strong spirit and deep desire to enhance democracy and improve the lives of all Liberians.

SOURCES: "Liberian becomes Africa's first female president." January 26, 2006. Associated Press, http://www.msnbc.msn.com/id/10865705/; and "The Government of the Republic of Liberia: The Executive Mansion." 2010, http://www.emansion.gov.lr/index.php

Presidential Greatness

7.5 Evaluate the qualities that contribute to presidential success or failure.

PRACTICE QUIZ: UNDERSTAND AND APPLY

1. Which of the following acts best illustrates the notion of a "personal presidency"?
   a. Ronald Reagan telling the president of the Soviet Union, "Mr. Gorbachev, tear down this wall!"
   b. Bill Clinton telling the American people, "I feel your pain."
   c. John F. Kennedy telling the country in his inaugural address, "Ask not what your country can do for you; ask what you can do for your country."
   d. Abraham Lincoln's Emancipation Proclamation, which outlawed slavery in 1863 by executive order

2. U.S. presidents are less in charge of governmental actions than most Americans assume because
   a. presidents are trained to sound more sure of themselves than they really are.
   b. the president's party in Congress will often balk at White House initiatives.
   c. the legislative branch in the American system is much stronger than the executive branch.
   d. presidents must negotiate with other people to accomplish their goals.

3. Which president stated, "I claim not to have controlled events, but confess plainly that events have controlled me."
   a. Andrew Jackson
   b. Abraham Lincoln
   c. Woodrow Wilson
   d. Franklin D. Roosevelt

4. According to presidential scholar Robert Dallek, what is one of the qualities that effective presidents must possess?
   a. great intelligence
   b. eloquence
   c. charisma
   d. consistency

ANALYZE

1. Consider the concept of the "two presidencies," discussed in the previous section, and apply that logic to our discussion of presidential greatness. Is it possible that much of the "failure" we notice in recent presidencies springs from problems with domestic policy? Explain your answer.

2. What incidents during Obama's presidency thus far might affect his eventual ranking in terms of presidential greatness?

IDENTIFY THE CONCEPT THAT DOESN'T BELONG

a. A clear vision
b. A willingness to compromise
c. Artful use of the media
d. Ability to manipulate public opinion
e. The public's trust

Conclusion

The framers of our system might not have comprehended jet planes, skyscrapers, or suicide bombers. And they surely could not have imagined jets being flown into buildings, killing thousands of innocent people. They also could not have appreciated the speed at which the events of September 11, 2001, could be transmitted around the globe. Ours is a very different world than Franklin, Washington, Adams, Jefferson, and Madison could possibly have imagined.

If anything, however, the events of 9/11 have proved that the framers were visionaries and that they were right about the presidency. They anticipated grievous attacks against the United States and the necessity for an immediate response. They understood that after tragic events, citizens would look to a leader to calm, resolve, and console. They held that the heart of their new republic would be found in the legislature, but they also understood that a strong executive would keep the nation together during times of crisis. It is hard to imagine how our nation would have responded to any of the great challenges without the leadership of the president.

Our first years under the Constitution were uncertain and turbulent, but to some extent, the steady hand and vision of George Washington helped keep the peace and ensure that the Union survived. Congress or state governments did not save the Union in 1861–1865, but the will, intellect, and political skill of Abraham Lincoln helped it to survive and be reborn. Congress and the Hoover White House were paralyzed by the strife and anguish of the Great Depression, so not until Franklin D. Roosevelt took the helm did the federal government respond. From his first inaugural address, FDR calmed the waters by reminding us that "the only thing we have to fear is fear itself," and he rallied a nation horrified by the Japanese attack on December 7, 1941—"a date," he said, "which will live in infamy." After the humiliations of the 1970s, Ronald Reagan made Americans once again feel proud of their nation, and it was through his unwavering mixture of determination and moderation that the Cold War was brought to a peaceful end. The will of the American people is best expressed through representatives, but our resolve, our spirit, and our sense of united purpose rests in the hands of the president. This is especially true during times of crisis.

Much as we may praise the advantages of a single leader, however, endowing this person with too much prerogative distorts the balance of power that the framers so carefully built into the constitutional system. Our nation has grown from fewer than 4 million people in 1790 to more than 300 million today, requiring the federal government to step into all aspects of American life—and the power of the chief executive has mushroomed along with that explosive growth. Facing dramatically different realities from what was envisioned by Madison and his colleagues in Philadelphia in 1787, modern presidents have three main tasks: (1) to develop a legislative program and work to persuade Congress to enact it; (2) to engage in direct policymaking through bureaucratic actions that do not require congressional approval; and (3) to lead a massive network of staff with the singular goal of helping the occupant of the White House succeed in achieving these first two goals.[30]

Presidents do not act in a vacuum. They must constantly respond to public opinion, interest groups, party activists, and the media. Barack Obama's struggle to reform the health care system, outlined at the start of this chapter, speaks volumes about the numerous actors that shape public policy in America. Many pathways of change run through the White House, but presidents also confront immense challenges. Even so, when one person holds so much power in a political system, it is only sensible to wonder about the democratic character of that nation.

KEY CONCEPT MAP   How have presidential powers evolved since the adoption of the Constitution?

1789–1797

George Washington sets the precedent of a powerful but constrained executive.

Other presidents follow Washington's lead, and Congress becomes the focal point of American government.

Critical Thinking Questions

What if Washington had decided to stay in office for life? Why was it so important for him to have stepped down after serving for only two terms?

1861–1865

Abraham Lincoln takes charge during the Civil War.

Lincoln establishes "presidential prerogative." Future presidents recognize that the executive branch should have weighty powers during times of crisis.

While most agree that presidents should have broad powers during times of crisis, what sort of dangers does this type of leeway create for a democracy?

1901–1908

Theodore Roosevelt uses the "bully pulpit" to shape public opinion and push his Progressive Movement reforms through Congress.

Teddy Roosevelt introduces the stewardship model, where presidential powers extend to everything except that which is prohibited by the Constitution.

What if Teddy Roosevelt had not used the bully pulpit to generate public support for his progressive reforms? Would he have been as successful in getting Congress to act?

1933–1945

Franklin D. Roosevelt takes office in the midst of the Great Depression, and his New Deal programs create new federal agencies and institutions, which transform the national government.

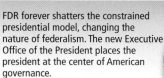

FDR forever shatters the constrained presidential model, changing the nature of federalism. The new Executive Office of the President places the president at the center of American governance.

What if a different president had been elected instead? Were FDR's personality and leadership skills central to the institutional changes that occurred? Or would the changes have occurred regardless of who was in the White House?

1945–1953

Harry S Truman presides over America's rise as a military superpower, in an era of increased global economic interdependence.

The role of presidents in both domestic and foreign affairs is heightened.

What if Truman had not made the decision to use the atomic bomb on Japan to end World War II? What is it about modern warfare that heightens the powers of American presidents?

1981–1989

Ronald Reagan, the "Great Communicator," takes office and makes use of new modes of communication to sell the public on his agenda.

Presidents are able to speak directly to the American public with the aid of television (and later the Internet). By persuading the public, presidents can help shape congressional activities.

Can modern presidents be successful today if they are not great communicators? Has the Internet made this "qualification" more or less important?

1993–2001

Bill Clinton appoints his wife, Hillary Clinton, to lead a task force on health care reform, ushering in an era of expanded influence for running "mates": first ladies and vice presidents.

Vice presidents and first ladies have become important elements of increased presidential powers, especially with the advent of television and the Internet.

Is it also possible for missteps by running "mates" to decrease presidential powers?

The Framers were unsure about executive powers, which helps explain the vagueness of Article II. While they knew that future presidents and events would help fill in the blanks, they likely could not have imagined the steady expansion of executive powers. The irony, of course, is that while presidential powers have greatly expanded, there are growing forces that extend beyond a president's control. —*Would the Framers have accepted the expansion of presidential power as necessary, given the nature of our world? Or would they have balked at the pivotal role that presidents play in nearly every aspect of modern American governance?*

Review of Key Objectives

The President and the Constitution

7.1 Explain the framers' decision to bestow the president with real powers despite their concerns about potential abuses.
(pages 194–195)

Unlike other branches of the new government, the framers of the U.S. Constitution were a bit unsure about the presidency. On the one hand, they wanted to vest the office with real powers—to afford "energy in the executive," as one noted. On the other hand, many worried that giving a president too much power would lead to corruption and perhaps even a new monarchy. In the end, they set aside most of their reservations because they had afforded Congress with an extensive list of powers, and they wanted the presidency to serve as a check on that power. In addition, they knew that George Washington would be the first president and would set the tone of a powerful yet constrained leader.

KEY TERMS

Prerogative Power 194
Cato 194
Alexander Hamilton 195

CRITICAL THINKING QUESTIONS

1. Did it make sense for the framers to allow future presidents to "fill in the blanks" regarding the ambiguity of presidential powers?
2. Do any of the worries of the Anti-Federalists regarding the presidency ring true today?

INTERNET RESOURCES

To explore a range of topics on the presidency, go to the American President: An Online Reference Resource at http://millercenter.org/academic/americanpresident

ADDITIONAL READING

Ellis, Joseph J. *His Excellency: George Washington.* New York: Knopf, 2004.

The Evolution of the Presidency

7.2 Outline the changes that have led to the expansion of presidential powers.
(pages 196–203)

During much of the nineteenth century, most presidents held to the whig model of presidential power, meaning that they were limited to the powers expressly granted in the Constitution. Beginning with Teddy Roosevelt, and continuing with his cousin Franklin D. Roosevelt, the more activist stewardship model of presidential powers took hold. In addition, a host of intuitional changes broadened presidential powers, including the Executive Office of the President, a swathe of additional advisors, and an expanded role for the vice president. Today, there is little question that the presidency is at the very center of our political system.

KEY TERMS

Whig Model 196
Stewardship Model 197
Modern Presidency 197
New Deal 197
Cabinet 198
Inner Cabinet 199
Executive Office of the President (EOP) 199
National Security Council (NSC) 199
National Security Adviser 199
Office of Management and Budget (OMB) 199
Council of Economic Advisers (CEA) 199
Social Security 200
Institutional Presidency 201

CRITICAL THINKING QUESTIONS

1. Other than the personalities of particular presidents, what are some of the forces that seemed to compel expanded presidential powers?
2. How has the system of shared powers/checks and balances been affected by burgeoning presidential powers? Have the scales tipped too far in the president's direction, changing the nature of our democracy? Why or why not?

INTERNET RESOURCES

You can view some 52,000 documents at the American Presidency Project at http://www.presidency.ucsb.edu/index.php

ADDITIONAL READING

Greenstein, Fred I. *The Presidential Difference: Leadership Style from FDR to George W. Bush.* Princeton, NJ: Princeton University Press, 2004.

The Informal Powers of the President

 7.3 Establish how the "power to persuade" expands presidential power beyond the Constitution.

(pages 204–205)

Astute presidents have learned that much of their power comes from their own skills, the trappings of the office, and a steadfast spouse. That is, the powers outlined in the Constitution are just the beginning. Successful presidents have harnessed an array of tools to push their agenda forward and have understood that the most effective tools are those that best match the larger political context of the day.

KEY TERM

Going Public 204

CRITICAL THINKING QUESTIONS

1. If "going public" has become a powerful tool in the arsenal of modern presidents, does that imply style is more important than substance?
2. If scholar Stephen Skowronek is correct in his assertion that informal presidential powers are dependent on broader contextual issues, what might be those forces in the decades to come? What are some of the changes in the years ahead that will impact a president's ability to "persuade?"

INTERNET RESOURCES

Doing a research project on a president or a related topic? Check out the National Archives Web site at http://www.archives.gov/presidential-libraries/research/guide.html and the National First Ladies' Library at http:// www.firstladies.org/

ADDITIONAL READING

Neustadt, Richard E. *Presidential Power: The Politics of Leadership.* New York: Free Press, 1991.

Stephen Skowronek, *The Politics Presidents Make: From John Adams to George Bush,* Cambridge, MA: Harvard University Press, 2008.

The Roles of Modern Presidents

 7.4 Identify the duties and functions of modern presidents.

(pages 206–213)

No job prepares a person for the presidency. Along with expanding powers comes a dizzying array of jobs and responsibilities in both domestic and foreign affairs. The president is a chief of state and must lead the nation in ceremonial events. The president is a chief legislator and must recommend measures to Congress and report to Congress on the "state of the union." The president is a chief diplomat and must appoint and receive ambassadors and represent the United States abroad. The president is commander in chief and must make decisions about when to deploy the armed forces. Finally, the president is chief executive and must carry out the will of Congress: enforcing laws and spending the funds that are allocated and appropriated.

KEY TERMS

Veto 207
Treaty 210
Executive Agreement 210
War Powers Resolution 211
Iran–Contra Affair 212
Executive Order 212
Signing Statement 212

CRITICAL THINKING QUESTIONS

1. Do we expect too much from modern presidents? If so, is there any way to shift some of the responsibilities to others or to other parts of the government? How would that work?
2. This section introduced the concept of the "two presidencies." But isn't it fair to say that the line between domestic and foreign policy has been blurred, if not erased? Haven't things changed since the 1960s, when this idea was advanced?

INTERNET RESOURCES

The American Presidents Web site at http://www.americanpresidents.org contains a complete video archive of the C-SPAN television series *American Presidents: Life Portraits,* plus biographical facts, key events of each presidency, presidential places, and reference materials. You might also take a look at one of the presidential libraries. For links to them, try http://www.archives.gov/presidential-libraries/

ADDITIONAL READING

Schlesinger, Arthur M., Jr. *The Imperial Presidency.* Buena Vista, VA: Mariner Books, 2004 (repr.).

Presidential Greatness

7.5 **Evaluate the qualities that contribute to presidential success or failure.**

(pages 214–217)

While there is no formula for success, there are shared characteristics of great presidents. Truly successful presidents have vision, but they are also pragmatic. They understand the importance of public conscience, and they are trustworthy and charismatic. Perhaps because of growing demands and forces beyond their control, however, it seems that successful presidents are increasingly rare.

KEY TERM

Personal Presidency 226

CRITICAL THINKING QUESTIONS

1. It has been argued that some Americans are increasingly disappointed with their presidents. Why might this be the case? Are there any changes you can think of that might ease some of the disappointment?
2. Of the characteristics of successful presidents, which seems most important? Might a charismatic president who lacks vision succeed? Would a trustworthy leader who lacks charisma get anything done in contemporary politics?

INTERNET RESOURCES

For a wealth of scholarly information on each of the presidents, visit the Miller Center of Public Affairs Web site at http://millercenter.org/academic/americanpresident

The White House Web site at http://www .whitehouse.gov provides a wealth of information about the current presidency.

ADDITIONAL READING

Milkis, Sidney and Marc Landy. *Presidential Greatness*. Lawrence, KS: University of Kansas Press, 2001.

Weisberg, Jacob. *The Bush Tragedy*. New York: Random House, 2008.

Chapter Review   Test Your Knowledge

1. The responsibilities of the executive branch are spelled out in which article of the Constitution?
   a. Article I
   b. Article II
   c. Article III
   d. Article IV

2. One of the central tasks of a modern president is
   a. developing a legislative agenda and persuading Congress to enact it.
   b. declaring wars and ratifying peace treaties with foreign powers.
   c. controlling the revenues and expenditures of the federal government.
   d. interpreting and applying the laws of the land, as described in the Constitution.

3. From the very beginning, all presidents believed that their powers should be extended to all matters except those that were clearly prohibited by the Constitution.
   a. true   b. false

4. Among the informal powers of the presidency are
   a. the power to persuade.
   b. going public.
   c. appointing judges to the federal bench.
   d. a and b.

5. A major component to presidential power in modern times is the personal connection, an emotional bond that Americans form with the president.
   a. true   b. false

6. Over the centuries, the breadth of presidential authority has fluctuated, in part because
   a. many amendments have been added to the Constitution that have widened and narrowed that authority.
   b. some presidents have used the vagueness of the Constitution to maximize their power and some have not.
   c. the American people's attitude toward presidential power has fluctuated as well.
   d. modern society has experienced cultural and technological changes that affect how authority is implemented.

7. As the presidency has evolved, presidential authority has
   a. remained steady.
   b. steadily declined.
   c. steadily increased.
   d. fluctuated between increase and decline.

8. What is the "bully pulpit"?
   a. the president's unique position to shape public opinion on important national issues
   b. the lectern from which Franklin D. Roosevelt delivered his famous fireside chats
   c. a position presidents adopt when they use their own religious convictions to address moral issues in American society
   d. a metaphor for America's military superiority to other countries in the world

9. Which president proudly claimed that he "did not usurp power but . . . acted for the common well-being of our people . . . in whatever manner was necessary, unless prevented by direct constitutional or legislative prohibition"?
   a. Richard Nixon
   b. George Washington
   c. Theodore Roosevelt
   d. Herbert Hoover

10. Scholar Stephen Skowronek suggested that informal presidential powers are
    a. the tenacity of the president.
    b. the president's ability to shape public opinion.
    c. larger contextual issues, such as the nature of party politics.
    d. the quality of presidential advisors.

11. Typically, a president's inner cabinet includes the heads of which departments?
    a. Health, Education, and Labor
    b. Transportation, Interior, and Homeland Security
    c. Energy, Commerce, and Agriculture
    d. Justice, Treasury, and Defense

12. The Executive Office of the President expanded most rapidly under the administration of which president?
    a. Gerald Ford
    b. James Polk
    c. Bill Clinton
    d. Franklin D. Roosevelt

13. The expansion of the president's staff into an enormous network of individuals and offices has meant that
    a. presidents themselves have become politically less significant.
    b. presidents have had to make fewer decisions by themselves.
    c. presidents have been able to play a central role in the policy process.
    d. fewer persons have access to the executive branch.

14. Why have recent presidencies experienced conflict between policy and political advisers within the executive branch?
    a. because presidents now retain advisers whose job is to make sure their boss remains politically popular, even if that means setting aside policy commitments
    b. because presidents have become much more involved with the policy process, making conflict with the political agenda inevitable
    c. because political advisers and policy advisers will inevitably be contentious
    d. because presidents must now respond to the needs of more constituents, some of whom are bound to compete with one another

15. In the 1950s, what changed in the nature of the vice presidency, and why?
    a. Vice presidents no longer attended cabinet meetings because the president's expanded staff could handle those responsibilities.
    b. Vice presidents began to be included in important presidential briefings so that they could quickly and competently assume the president's duties if necessary.

c. Because television gave the office a much higher profile than it had before, vice presidents could take advantage of financial opportunities beyond the office.

d. The vice president presided over the U.S. Senate much more often, because the president really needed an active representative in that forum.

16. What book touting the informal powers of the presidency did Presidents Kennedy and Clinton keep on hand throughout their time in the White House?
   a. *The Imperial Presidency*
   b. *Profiles in Courage*
   c. *Presidential Power*
   d. *Banging the Bully Pulpit*

17. What woman first demonstrated how substantial and public the role of first lady could be?
   a. Edith Bolling Galt Wilson
   b. Abigail Adams
   c. Hillary Rodham Clinton
   d. Eleanor Roosevelt

18. Modern presidents use the State of the Union address to set the legislative agenda for the coming year and try to shape public opinion in support of that agenda.
   a. true
   b. false

19. Despite their expanded authority, modern presidents still cannot initiate the deployment of American forces in foreign lands without the prior approval of Congress.
   a. true
   b. false

20. Given the substantial numbers and authority of bureaucratic decision makers within the executive branch, it is safe to say that
   a. there is not much an outsider can do to affect policy formation in the White House.
   b. a great deal can change in American government without the consent of an elected official.
   c. the president has little control over the policy direction of his own administration.
   d. the executive branch is not a promising pathway for change.

PEARSON mypoliscilab Exercises

Apply what you learned in this chapter on **MyPoliSciLab.**

 **Read** on mypoliscilab.com

   eText: Chapter 7

✓ **Study** and **Review** on mypoliscilab.com

   Pre-Test
   Post-Test
   Chapter Exam
   Flashcards

◉ **Watch** on mypoliscilab.com

   Video: Bush and Congress
   Video: The Government Bails Out Automakers

⊕ **Explore** on mypoliscilab.com

   Simulation: Presidential Leadership: Which Hat Do You Wear?
   Simulation: You Are a President During a Nuclear Power Plant Meltdown
   Comparative: Comparing Chief Executives
   Timeline: The Executive Order over Time
   Visual Literacy: Presidential Success in Polls and Congress

Bureaucracy

KEY OBJECTIVES

After completing this chapter, you should be prepared to:

8.1 Trace the development of specific federal departments and agencies.

8.2 Analyze the debate over whether the heads of federal agencies should be policy experts or loyal political appointees.

8.3 Describe the image people have of the federal bureaucracy, and evaluate the bureaucracy's advantages and disadvantages.

8.4 Assess the mechanisms and processes that influence and oversee the federal bureaucracy.

A deadly explosion on April 20, 2010, aboard the Deepwater Horizon, an offshore oil drilling platform owned by British Petroleum (BP), sent oil gushing into the Gulf of Mexico from the ocean floor. Fifteen oil workers were killed in the blast. During the three months that it took BP to figure out how to successfully cap such a deepwater well, an estimated five million barrels of oil spilled into the ocean. The oil spill devastated the fishing and tourism industries in coastal areas of Louisiana, Alabama, Mississippi, and north Florida. The spill also illustrated the benefits and risks of the operation of federal government agencies.

On the one hand, local public officials pleaded with federal agencies to help stop the leak, contain the damage, and force BP to clean up the oil and compensate people for financial losses. Among the many agencies involved, the U.S. Coast Guard coordinated efforts to contain the oil and the Environmental Protection Agency (EPA) monitored the use of chemicals that BP used to disperse oil slicks on the water. On the other hand, many critics pointed to the Minerals Management Service (MMS)—an agency of the U.S. Department of the Interior—for

> **Is the bureaucracy an essential contributor to the success of government or a barrier to effective government?**

failing to do its job of enforcing safety regulations to prevent such explosions and oil spills from occurring. During the Bush administration, scandals erupted in which MMS employees were caught accepting gifts from oil companies, permitting oil companies to do their own safety inspection reports, and even using drugs and engaging in sexual affairs with oil-company employees. The Obama administration's Secretary of the Interior, Ken Salazar, was criticized for moving too slowly in replacing the leadership within the MMS and forcing the agency to perform its duties properly. Ultimately, the Obama administration abolished the MMS during the oil spill crisis and transferred its duties to other federal agencies.

What does this case show us about government agencies? Clearly, Americans expect government agencies to provide services and respond to crises, including tasks ranging from delivering mail and directing traffic to cleaning up major environmental disasters. Yet, the connections between government officials, interest groups, and politics—as well as other issues, such as limited funding and overwhelming tasks—create risks that agencies will not operate effectively.

Resource Center
• Glossary
• Vocabulary Example
• Connect the Link

■ **Bureaucracy:** An organization with a hierarchical structure and specific responsibilities intended to enhance efficiency and effectiveness. In government, it refers to departments and agencies in the executive branch.

EXAMPLE: *The Internal Revenue Service (IRS) is an agency in the federal bureaucracy that carries out the national tax laws through collection of income taxes and investigation of individuals and businesses that fail to pay the taxes required under the laws enacted by Congress.*

The Federal Bureaucracy

8.1 Trace the development of specific federal departments and agencies.

(pages 228–233)

In this chapter, we'll examine the agencies of the executive branch of the federal government that are collectively known as "the bureaucracy." The word **bureaucracy**■ refers to an organization with a hierarchical structure and specific responsibilities that operates on management principles intended to enhance efficiency and effectiveness. Bureaucracies exist in businesses, universities, and other organizational contexts; however, the general term *bureaucracy* is most frequently used to refer to government agencies. Action or inaction by these agencies determines whether and how policies are implemented and how these policies will affect the lives of Americans.

The departments that comprise the executive branch of the federal government work under the direction of the president to carry out the nation's laws. For example, disaster assistance provided by the Federal Emergency Management Agency (FEMA) is directed by laws enacted by Congress. These laws list the kinds of assistance to be provided by the federal government and authorize the spending of federal funds for disaster relief in specific locations. FEMA and other agencies do not simply decide for themselves when and where they will help. They must act within the guidelines set by Congress and the president. These guidelines typically leave room for agency officials to make specific decisions, but these officials cannot act beyond the scope of their authority as defined by law. For example, FEMA officials may decide that certain disaster-area counties need more money or other specific kinds of assistance than other disaster-affected counties. In essence, Congress and the president write laws to define public policy; the officials who work in federal agencies then act to carry out those laws and policies.

Agency officials can shape public policy through their authority to create rules for administering programs and for enforcing laws enacted by Congress and the president. They are also the source of information and ideas for members of Congress who wish to propose new statutes about various policy issues. The policy preferences of individual agency officials affect the day-to-day actions that these bureaucracies undertake, as do those officials' interactions with representatives from outside interest groups.

Ideally, the officials who work in federal agencies possess knowledge and experience concerning the policy matters that they handle. We want them to be expert professionals who are dedicated to public service for all Americans. We do not want them to be politicians who serve the interests of a particular political party. Despite this idealistic vision of government workers, these officials are not necessarily removed from the

Many Americans may take for granted that their drinking water is safe and clean, yet it is government agencies that set standards and inspections to ensure the safety of our water. —*Do you trust government agencies to make sure that Americans enjoy a healthy, safe environment?*

world of politics. Because the bureaucracy is part of the executive branch—and, thus, under the president's authority—policymaking decisions within government agencies can be affected by partisan political considerations. Moreover, the president's political appointees assume the top positions in each agency. In making their decisions, agency officials may be influenced by lobbying from legislators, state and local officials, and interest groups. Thus the bureaucracy becomes another arena of action for the policy-shaping pathway that relies on the lobbying of decision makers.

PATHWAYS of action

Arsenic Standards for Drinking Water

The Safe Drinking Water Act was passed by Congress in 1974 to protect the quality of drinking water in the United States. The act authorizes the Environmental Protection Agency (EPA) to create regulations that establish purity standards for drinking water systems. Exactly what those purity standards will be, however, can present a thorny issue affecting the safety and welfare of every person in the country. It's a good illustration of the politics of the federal bureaucracy.

A 1999 report by the National Academy of Sciences said that arsenic in drinking water can cause various kinds of cancer. In 2000, an environmentalist interest group, the Natural Resources Defense Council, sued the EPA over arsenic standards, seeking to have the regulations changed to mandate arsenic levels at only 3 parts per billion (ppb) rather than the existing standard of 50 ppb. As a result of the lawsuit, EPA officials in President Bill Clinton's administration proposed a new standard of 5 ppb.

Objections poured in from the mining and wood-preservative industries that use and produce arsenic. Local water systems also raised concerns about the costs of meeting the proposed standard. As a result, the EPA adopted a standard of 10 ppb. This was in the waning days of the Clinton administration—but when President George W. Bush came into office in early 2001, his officials postponed the effective date of the new rule for one year. Critics complained that the Bush administration, which was perceived to be less concerned than the Clinton administration about water pollution and other environmental issues, was sacrificing public health in favor of the interests and profits of the manufacturing and mining industries.

Several months later, at the Bush administration's request, a committee of the National Academy of Sciences produced a new report that reconfirmed the health risks from arsenic in drinking water. So the Bush administration moved forward on the regulation limiting arsenic in drinking water to 10 ppb or less. The new rule angered the National Rural Water Association, an interest group representing small communities. It argued that the new standard would impose excessive costs on small towns that must upgrade their water systems. Nor did the rule satisfy the Natural Resources Defense Council and other environmentalist groups. They awaited new studies with the hope of convincing the EPA to amend the regulation and require an even lower level of arsenic. And there matters rest, with no party truly satisfied with the outcome.

This story is typical of today's regulatory politics. Officials in the bureaucracy make decisions about a policy rule that affects water systems throughout the country—but their rule is shaped by the officials' interactions with and responses to other actors involved with the issue of water quality. Scientists provide influential information for the bureaucracy, and interest groups apply pressure through lobbying and litigation.[2]

Development of the Federal Bureaucracy

The roots of the federal bureaucracy go back to the original U.S. Constitution of 1787. Article I, Section 8, gives Congress the power to enact laws for specified purposes. These include matters such as "lay and collect taxes," "coin Money," "establish Post Offices," and "provide and maintain a Navy." The president, as the head of the executive branch, is responsible for carrying out the nation's laws.

It soon became apparent that agencies must be created to administer specific policies and programs. Post offices, tax agencies, and mints (where money is coined) handle tasks that require specialized personnel and facilities. Indeed, Article I makes reference to congressional authority to "make all laws necessary and proper for carrying into Execution . . . all other Powers vested by this Constitution in the Government of the United States, or in any Department or Officer thereof." Thus the founding document explicitly acknowledged that government agencies, called "departments," would be established to carry out laws and programs.

Article II of the Constitution, which discusses the president and executive power, provides further acknowledgment of the need to create governmental departments that will execute the laws under the president's supervision and control. For example, Article II says that the president "may require the Opinion, in writing, of the principal Officer in each of the executive Departments, upon any subject relating to the Duties of their respective Offices."

Although the Constitution thus clearly anticipated the existence of executive departments, the actual development and organization of those departments over the course of American history were shaped by social developments and the country's response to emerging policy issues and priorities.

THE FIRST DEPARTMENTS   During the nation's first century, the federal government was involved in only a limited range of policy areas. The original departments of the federal government focused on policy matters related to specific powers granted by the Constitution to Congress and the president. Most policy issues came under the authority of state governments. This explains why the federal government after 1789 had only four departments:

Department of State—responsible for diplomacy and foreign affairs

Department of War (in 1947 consolidated, along with the Department of the Navy, a later creation, into the Department of Defense)—responsible for military matters and national defense

Department of Justice—responsible for legal matters under federal law

Department of the Treasury—responsible for tax revenues and government expenditures

Note how many of these agencies focused on matters that had motivated the Constitutional Convention to replace the Articles of Confederation with the new U.S. Constitution.

Under the Articles, the national government had lacked authority to handle taxation and the military. As Congress and the president expanded the scope of federal activities in law and policy, departments were created to operate in new areas. First came the Department of the Navy. Then, in the mid-nineteenth century, Congress created the Department of the Interior to manage federal lands and the Department of Agriculture to assist the nation's most important industry.

During the last decades of the nineteenth century, the United States began to undergo significant changes. Industrialization, urbanization, and immigration shaped a new economy in which people moved to cities to work in factories and service occupations. Congress became increasingly assertive in using its constitutional authority to enact laws regulating interstate commerce to prevent business monopolies, control the exploitation of child labor, improve dangerous working conditions, and deal with other problems created by the new industrial economy. In the first decade of the twentieth century, Congress created the Department of Commerce and the Department of Labor to address these emerging issues.

THE NEW DEAL AND ITS AFTERMATH The Great Depression, which began with the stock market crash of 1929, brought years of record-high unemployment and economic problems. At the depth of the Depression in 1932, Franklin D. Roosevelt was elected to the presidency. He believed that the federal government had to take an active role in the economy

in order to overcome the economic stagnation and correct the underlying causes of the Depression. He called his program the New Deal. The Roosevelt administration (1933–1945) contributed enormously to the growth in the federal bureaucracy by initiating various governmental programs, first in response to the Great Depression and later to wage World War II.

For example, in 1935, Congress created Social Security to provide income for senior citizens and dependents of deceased workers. It later added coverage for disabled workers and their dependents. Other New Deal programs created jobs for the unemployed and regulated economic activity. The size and complexity of the federal government increased tremendously during the Roosevelt administration (see Figure 8.1). By the end of FDR's presidency in 1945, not only had the public accepted the federal government's involvement in a variety of policy issues, many Americans had come to *expect* federal action on important matters, eventually including such areas as education and criminal justice, which had traditionally been the exclusive preserve of state and local governments. Moreover, World War II had demonstrated the necessity of combining the War and Navy departments (as well as the newly created Air Force department) within a single structure, the Department of Defense.

In the 1950s, expanded public expectations of the federal government and the consequently broader range of legislative activity undertaken by Congress led to the creation of the Department of Health, Education and Welfare (HEW). (In the 1970s, HEW was split into two agencies, the Department of

FIGURE 8.1 ▪ Growth in the Size of the Federal Bureaucracy
The Roosevelt administration's programs to address the Depression and World War II dramatically increased the size of the federal bureaucracy. —*After these crises had passed, why didn't the government shrink back to its size in the early years of the twentieth century?*

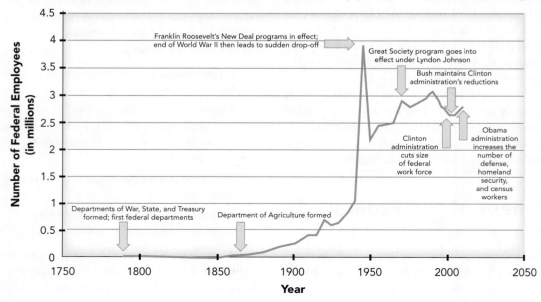

■ **Department:** Any of the 15 major government agencies responsible for specific policy areas whose heads are usually called secretaries and serve in the president's cabinet.

EXAMPLE: *The U.S. Department of State is responsible for managing relationships with foreign governments, issuing passports to U.S. citizens, and providing assistance to Americans traveling in foreign countries. Secretary of State Hillary Clinton, former U.S. senator from New York, was appointed by President Barack Obama in 2009 to be the head of the Department of State.*

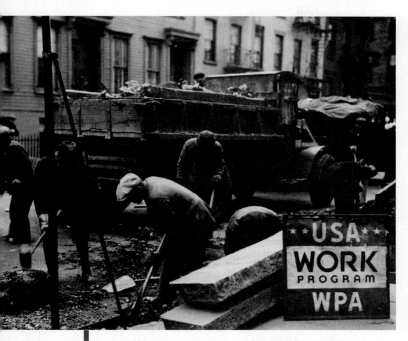

During the Depression, the Roosevelt administration expanded the size of government by creating programs to permit unemployed workers to earn money while repairing roads and undertaking other public service projects. —*In light of recent economic difficulties, should the federal government maintain permanent programs to employ people who cannot find jobs?*

TABLE 8.1	Cabinet Departments and Examples of Other Agencies

Departments	Independent Agencies
Agriculture	Environmental Protection Agency
Commerce	Peace Corps
Defense	Social Security Administration
Education	**Independent Regulatory Commissions**
Energy	
Health and Human Services	
Homeland Security	Federal Communications Commission
Housing and Urban Development	Federal Trade Commission
Interior	Federal Reserve System and Board of Governors
Justice	Nuclear Regulatory Commission
Labor	**Government Corporations**
State	
Transportation	National Railroad Passenger Corporation (Amtrak)
Treasury	Overseas Private Investment Corporation
Veterans Affairs	United States Postal Service

SOURCE: LSU Libraries Federal Agencies Directory, accessed at http://www.lib.lsu.edu/gov/fedgov.html

Education and the Department of Health and Human Services.) The framers of the Constitution never expected the federal government to become increasingly involved in policy areas that were traditionally under the control of states.

Heightened public awareness of urban decay, racial conflict, and poverty during the 1960s produced a new social welfare federal bureaucracy, the Department of Housing and Urban Development (HUD). Similarly, the Department of Transportation, created during the same decade, reflected concerns about urban mass transit as well as a recognition that air travel was expanding.

Organization of the Federal Bureaucracy

Today, the federal bureaucracy consists of four types of organizational entities: departments, independent agencies, independent regulatory commissions, and government corporations (see Table 8.1). **Departments**■ typically are large organizations responsible for a broad policy realm, such as education, national defense, or transportation. **Independent agencies** have narrow

responsibilities for a specific policy issue, such as the environment. They are independent in the sense that they are not subunits of a larger department, but like departments, their leaders are appointed by and under the control of the president.

By contrast, **independent regulatory commissions** are not under the control of the president or a department. They have a focused policy mission governing a specific issue area, but they are run by a body of officials drawn from both political parties and appointed in staggered terms over the course of more than one presidential administration. **Government corporations** have independent boards and are intended to run like private corporations. They handle a specific function, such as the postal system or the passenger railroad, which Congress believes would not be handled effectively by private businesses, either because of the huge scope of the operation or because of issues of profitability.

As you consider the role and operation of each of these components of the federal bureaucracy, ask yourself whether there might be a better way to organize the government. Alternatively, consider whether some of the bureaucracy's functions could be handled effectively and appropriately by private businesses without the expenditure of taxpayers' money.

Changes Since the 1960s

As the nation faced changing political and economic circumstances, Congress reacted to specific issues that it perceived to be the most difficult, immediate challenges by creating new

CONNECT THE **LINK**
(Chapter 7, page 198–199) The members of the president's cabinet are the most visible and publicly recognizable individuals who work in the federal bureaucracy.

departments to address those matters. The creation of a new department represents an opportunity to reorganize the use of governmental resources and apply expertise to address pressing concerns. It also represents a method of showing constituents that Congress is taking action even if members of Congress are unsure about whether the new department will be effective.

DEPARTMENT OF ENERGY   In 1973, the energy crisis struck. That year, the nation's ever-growing thirst for oil, natural gas, and other fossil fuels collided with the determination of the oil-producing countries to increase their profits. Many Americans found themselves waiting in long lines at gas stations and paying skyrocketing prices to fill up their gas-guzzling cars. Responding to the crisis atmosphere, Congress created the Department of Energy to implement new laws and develop policies designed to encourage fuel efficiency, develop new sources of energy, and relieve the nation's dependence on foreign oil producers.

DEPARTMENT OF VETERANS AFFAIRS   At the end of the 1980s, the Veterans Administration (created in 1930) was elevated to the status of a separate department called the Department of Veterans Affairs. By the 1980s, a huge group of World War II veterans had become senior citizens, and they looked to the federal government for health care and other benefits. Korean War veterans and middle-aged Vietnam War veterans followed closely behind, increasingly in need of benefits and services.

When an agency gets the status of an executive department, its head becomes a member of the president's cabinet and is literally "at the table" when the president's top executive appointees discuss policies and budgets. As you saw in Chapter 7 (pages 198–199), the cabinet plays an especially important and influential role in advising the president. Creation of the Department of Veterans Affairs implied a promise that veterans' interests would be taken into account in those discussions. Congress symbolically demonstrated its concern about veterans and simultaneously sought the political benefits of granting increased attention and stature to an important constituency.

DEPARTMENT OF HOMELAND SECURITY   After terrorists attacked the World Trade Center and the Pentagon on September 11, 2001, public shock and congressional demands for action resulted in the creation of the federal government's newest department: the Department of Homeland Security (DHS). Like other departments, the DHS represented a response to a policy issue that had moved to the top of the nation's priorities.

The creation of the DHS involved the development of new agencies, such as the Transportation Safety Administration (TSA), and the consolidation of existing agencies from other departments, to better coordinate government actions related to domestic security issues. Many observers recognized that creating a new department that included agencies from elsewhere in government would inevitably pose a variety of problems. Would agencies

During the 1960s, President Lyndon B. Johnson tried to expand the activity and influence of federal governmental agencies in order to address poverty and racial discrimination. The Department of Housing and Urban Development (HUD) was created during his presidency. —*Has expanded action by the federal government actually helped to solve social problems?*

engage in "turf wars" over who should be in charge of specific tasks? Would employees resist a move to an unfamiliar department with unproven leadership and a still-developing mission?

To give you an idea of the scope of the reorganization, this short list identifies a few of the agencies absorbed into the new department as well as their previous homes within the bureaucracy.

> **Federal Emergency Management Agency (FEMA)—** previously an independent agency

> **Immigration and Naturalization Service (INS)—** previously in the Department of Justice

Coast Guard—previously in the Department of Transportation

Secret Service—previously in the Department of the Treasury

The slow response and general ineffectiveness of FEMA during and after Hurricane Katrina in 2005 led many critics to complain that the DHS was too big. They claimed that individual agencies within the department had lost resources and suffered from diminished focus on their domestic mission in light of the department's broader concerns about preventing attacks by international terrorists.

The Federal Bureaucracy

8.1 Trace the development of specific federal departments and agencies.

PRACTICE QUIZ: UNDERSTAND AND APPLY

1. The first departments of the federal bureaucracy were created as a result of
   a. the requirements of the Declaration of Independence.
   b. the original constitutional design of the federal government.
   c. the Civil War.
   d. President Franklin Roosevelt's New Deal program.

2. President Franklin Roosevelt expanded the federal bureaucracy as a response to
   a. settlers moving westward and taking lands from Native Americans.
   b. the first development of a national railroad system and large corporations.
   c. the Great Depression and World War II.
   d. the development of urban problems and Americans' need for new housing.

3. What department was created in the 1980s in response to growing needs for medical care among a specific segment of the U.S. population?
   a. Department of Disease Control and Prevention
   b. Department of Health and Human Services
   c. Department of Medicinal Arts
   d. Department of Veterans Affairs

4. In response to the terrorist attacks of 9/11 in 2001,
   a. Congress combined existing departments as part of the formation of a new Department of Homeland Security.
   b. the Department of Defense created a Special Liberation Force and immediately launched the invasion of Iran.
   c. Congress reduced the number of departments in the federal government in order to create better coordination.
   d. Congress changed the name of the Department of State and made it the Department of Homeland Security.

ANALYZE

1. Based on the U.S. Constitution and the nature of the early federal government, what kind of bureaucracy did the founders intend to construct?

2. What societal changes and historic events led to the creation of new departments in the federal bureaucracy?

IDENTIFY THE CONCEPT THAT DOESN'T BELONG

a. Article I of the U.S. Constitution
b. Article II of the U.S. Constitution
c. Department of State
d. War of 1812
e. Urban problems of the 1960s

Resource Center
- Glossary
- Vocabulary Example
- Connect the Link

Departments and Independent Agencies

8.2 Analyze the debate over whether the heads of federal agencies should be policy experts or loyal political appointees.

(pages 234–239)

Not all government employees are hidden away in office buildings. Some, like this national park ranger, interact directly with the public every day and provide valuable services, such as preserving natural resources and protecting public land.
—*Which agencies provide services directly to you?*

In order to understand how the bureaucracy operates, you must recognize the policy areas that fall under the authority of the *departments* (governmental units) run by the president's cabinet. By contrast, other kinds of agencies exert more independent influence over certain policy issues, because they are not directly under the supervision of the president and the cabinet.

Departments

During every presidential administration, the president's cabinet consists of the heads of the executive departments. These department heads typically have the title of secretary, such as secretary of defense for the head of the Department of Defense. The head of the Department of Justice, however, is known as the attorney general of the United States. Because new departments have been created over time, the cabinet has grown to include 15 departments as well as the administrators of three agencies within the Executive Office of the President: the Office of Management and Budget (OMB), the Office of National Drug Control Policy, and the Office of the U.S. Trade Representative. The head of one independent agency, the EPA, also has cabinet rank.

At earlier points in American history, the members of the cabinet would advise the president, debate policy options, and develop ideas to determine the president's agenda. In recent administrations, presidents have relied most heavily on their staffs and key cabinet members for advice. Cabinet meetings now serve the function of reporting to the president on the activities of each department. Cabinet members are expected to be loyal to the president to avoid any public indication that they question the president's agenda or actions. Presidents need agency leaders who are willing to support and implement the president's policies. Thus top department and agency leaders are political appointees who serve during one president's administration rather than as permanent employees. However, political appointees sometimes do not have sufficient expertise about the policy issues addressed by their agencies, and their relatively short terms in office can inhibit the effective development and implementation of programs.

The various departments are divided according to areas of policy responsibility. Within each department, various agencies are assigned to implement laws, keep detailed records, and make consistent decisions in accordance with established rules. Table 8.2 lists the 15 cabinet-level departments and some of the agencies housed in each. You'll notice many familiar agency names on the list, but you may be surprised within which department each agency operates. For example, many people don't realize that the National Weather Service is in the Department of Commerce and that the Financial Crimes Enforcement Network belongs to the Department of the Treasury rather than to the primary law enforcement department, the Department of Justice. The location of some agencies is a product of history and politics as much as of topical focus.

Table 8.2 also indicates the number of people employed in each executive department. The Office of Personnel Management reported in 2009 that 2,859,724 civilians were employed in the executive branch of government. Nearly 1.9 million of these worked in the executive departments, and an additional 900,000 were employed in independent agencies that we'll discuss later in this chapter. Although people's perceptions of impersonal, impenetrable bureaucracies often lead them to believe that all federal government agencies are huge, the departments actually vary significantly in size. They range from the Department of Education, which has under 4,200 employees, to the Department of Defense, which has more than 718,000 civilian employees in addition to 1.4 million active-duty military personnel and 1.2 million who serve in various reserve units.

There are also approximately 1,700 people who work directly for the president in the Executive Office of the President and its constituent agencies. Because they come under the direct control of the White House, these employees and agencies are typically considered an arm of the presidency rather than agencies within the federal bureaucracy.

The varying sizes of the bureaucracy's departments depend, in part, on whether they provide services at installations in far-flung locations and employ agents who work in the field or primarily oversee the distribution of federal funds to state and local governments from a central office in Washington, D.C. For example, the Department of Housing

TABLE 8.2	**Departments in the Executive Branch of the Federal Government with Selected Subunits and Total Number of Employees, 2009**

Department of Agriculture (100,125 employees)	**Department of Homeland Security (179,380 employees)**
Agricultural Research Service	Coast Guard
Animal and Plant Health Inspection Service	Customs and Border Protection
Cooperative State Research, Education, and Extension Service	Federal Emergency Management Agency
Economic Research Service	Secret Service
Farm Service Agency	**Department of Housing and Urban Development (9,630 employees)**
Forest Service	Government National Mortgage Association (Ginnie Mae)
Natural Resources Conservation Service	Office of Healthy Homes and Lead Hazard Control
Department of Commerce (118,429 employees)	Public and Indian Housing Agencies
Bureau of the Census	**Department of the Interior (74,362 employees)**
Bureau of Export Administration	Bureau of Indian Affairs
International Trade Administration	Bureau of Land Management
National Institute of Standards and Technology	Fish and Wildlife Service
National Oceanic and Atmospheric Administration	Geological Survey
National Weather Service	National Parks Service
Patent and Trademark Office Database	Office of Surface Mining
Department of Defense (718,802 civilian employees)	**Department of Justice (111,458 employees)**
Air Force	Bureau of Alcohol, Tobacco, Firearms, and Explosives
Army	Drug Enforcement Administration
Defense Contract and Audit Agency	Federal Bureau of Investigation
Defense Intelligence Agency	Federal Bureau of Prisons
Marine Corps	United States Marshals Service
National Guard	**Department of Labor (16,192 employees)**
National Security Agency	Mine Safety and Health Administration
Navy	Occupational Safety and Health Administration
Department of Education (4,100 employees)	**Department of State (36,821 employees)**
Educational Resources and Information Center	**Department of Transportation (56,355 employees)**
National Library of Education	Federal Aviation Administration
Department of Energy (15,601 employees)	**Department of the Treasury (116,647 employees)**
Federal Energy Regulatory Commission	Bureau of Engraving and Printing
Los Alamos Laboratory	Bureau of Public Debt
Southwestern Power Administration	Internal Revenue Service
Department of Health and Human Services (65,680 employees)	Office of the Comptroller of the Currency
Centers for Disease Control and Prevention	United States Mint
Food and Drug Administration	**Department of Veterans Affairs (290,908 employees)**
National Institutes of Health	

SOURCE: Office of Personnel Management, *Federal Civilian Workforce Statistics—Employment and Trends*, accessed at http://www.opm.gov/feddata/

and Urban Development, with only 10,000 employees, oversees the distribution of money, while the Department of Veterans Affairs, which runs veterans' hospitals and maintains other service offices, has 245,000 employees. Obviously, the large size of the Department of Defense is related to the number of bases and other facilities on which American military personnel serve throughout the United States and the world.

The organizational chart for the U.S. Department of Homeland Security in Figure 8.2 illustrates the complexity of departments in the federal government. Within each department, there are various offices responsible for specific aspects of the department's administration and mission. Bear in mind that all of the agencies within the Department of Homeland Security, especially those listed along the bottom row of the organizational chart, each have their own organizational structure with various internal offices that would look similar to that of the overall chart for the department.

FIGURE 8.2 ▪ Organization of the Department of Homeland Security

The Department of Homeland Security contains a variety of governmental agencies that are not necessarily closely connected with each other —*How would you decide if a department of the federal government was too large and therefore needed to be divided into two or more smaller departments?*

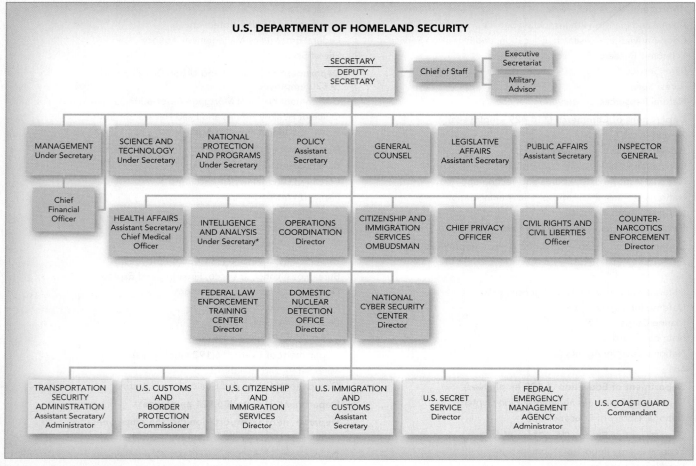

* Under Secretary for Intelligence and Analysis title created by Public Law 110-53, Aug 3, 2007.

SOURCE: Organizational Chart, U.S. Department of Homeland Security. Accessed at http://www.dhs.gov/xlibrary/assets/DHS_OrgChart.pdf on April 11, 2010.

Political Appointees in the Bureaucracy

Presidential appointees who run federal executive departments are expected to be loyal members of the president's team. This means that they will defend the administration's policies and avoid public disagreements with the president. After being appointed by the president, they must be confirmed by the U.S. Senate. These appointees work directly for the president and try to guide and push the bureaucracy to act in accordance with the president's policy preferences.

Secretaries and assistant secretaries who are appointed by the president do not necessarily possess expertise on the policy issues and laws administered by their departments. For example, a former member of Congress or former governor from

the president's political party may be chosen to run an agency, in part as a reward for political loyalty. However, they may also be chosen because the president thinks the person will be an effective spokesperson or good administrator.

Other high-level appointments in the departments, such as assistant secretaries and inspector generals, may go to people with policy experience, but they may also go to party loyalists or to the children of prominent political figures. Critics have cited President George W. Bush's appointment of Michael Brown as the director of FEMA as an example of an appointment based on political connections and loyalty rather than on qualifications and experience. Brown's lack of experience in emergency management received widespread news attention amid the federal government's slow and ineffective response to the destruction, death, and human suffering in New Orleans when Hurricane Katrina struck the city in August 2005. Before gaining a political appointment to a senior leadership position at FEMA in 2001, Brown had previously been a lawyer for the International Arabian Horse Association and had little, if any, training or experience in emergency management.[3]

PATHWAYS of change from around the world

Are there any decisions by government officials in the bureaucracy that could make you angry enough to protest? In December 2005, students at the government dental college in Kozhikode, India, staged a protest against an order from the undersecretary of the government's Department of Health and Family Welfare.[4] In the students' view, the order sought to change the existing procedures for placing dental students in residency programs as part of their training. Although residencies at government dental colleges were supposed to be reserved for students who studied at government colleges, the order sought to place a student from a private dental college in the government institution. Reportedly, the student in question was the daughter of an influential leader of a political organization.

Officials in government bureaucracies control valuable resources, and their decisions help to determine who gains benefits from government programs. Is there a risk that these benefits will be granted based on political connections, especially in a system like that of the United States, in which the heads of many government agencies are political appointees? Think about policy issues of importance to you, such as the environment, education, or other matters. Can you think of decisions by federal officials with which you disagree? If not, do you think the decisions of such officials either have little impact or are not sufficiently visible to the public?

In the confirmation process, senators may expect that the secretaries and other appointed officials in specific departments possess relevant experience and expertise. This is most likely to be true for the departments of State, Defense, and the Treasury, owing to the overriding importance of foreign affairs, national security, and the economy. For other positions, senators look less closely at the nominees' qualifications because they believe that presidents should generally be permitted to choose their own representatives to lead government agencies. Even the president's political opponents in the Senate may vote to confirm nominees simply because they would like other senators to show the same deference for appointments by future presidents from a different political party.

Presidents do not merely reward loyalists in their appointments. They also use the upper-level appointed positions to place above the bureaucracy knowledgeable political figures who will vigorously enforce the laws and regulations with which the president agrees—or alternatively, will fail to enforce, enforce weakly, or attempt to change the laws and regulations with which the president disagrees. These elite actors influence the use of the bureaucracy's power and resources in shaping public policy.

Since the final decades of the twentieth century, presidents have also used their appointment power to demonstrate a commitment to diversity as a means of pleasing their constituencies and attracting more voters. Women and members of minority groups increasingly receive appointments to highly visible positions at the top of executive departments. Presidents also seek geographic diversity so that the cabinet can be regarded as representing the nation. The composition of President Barack Obama's cabinet illustrates this aspiration for diversity. Among the heads of the 15 major executive departments were three former governors and four former members of Congress. There were four women, including former First Lady and New York Senator Hillary Clinton. There were two Hispanic members, most notably former congresswomen Hilda Solis—the first Hispanic woman to be Secretary of Labor—and one African American member, Attorney General Eric Holder. Asian-American men were chosen as the secretaries of the Energy, Veterans Affairs, and Commerce departments. Finally, as past presidents have done, President Obama attempted to demonstrate bipartisanship by appointing two Republicans to his cabinet: Defense Secretary Robert Gates, a holdover from the Bush administration, and former congressman Ray LaHood as Secretary of Transportation.

Only a half-dozen cabinet-level nominees have ever been rejected in the confirmation process by the U.S. Senate. The most recent instance was the Senate's vote against John Tower, President George H. W. Bush's nominee for defense secretary in the late 1980s, after allegations surfaced regarding Tower's excessive drinking and other aspects of his personal life. Generally, senators believe that the president ought to be able to choose the heads of government agencies. However, senators may oppose someone who is viewed as patently unqualified for a specific position or whose political beliefs are viewed as too extreme.

Independent Agencies, Independent Regulatory Commissions, and Government Corporations

The executive branch includes nearly 100 independent agencies, independent regulatory commissions, and government corporations that operate outside the 15 executive departments. Table 8.3 provides examples of some of the independent organizational entities in the federal government.

TABLE 8.3	Examples of Independent Agencies, Independent Regulatory Commissions, and Government Corporations, by Type

Independent Agencies: Facility or Program Administration

General Services Administration

National Archives and Records Administration

National Aeronautics and Space Administration

Peace Corps

Selective Service System

Smithsonian Institution

Social Security Administration

Independent Agencies: Grants of Funds

Harry S Truman Scholarship Foundation

National Endowment for the Arts

National Endowment for the Humanities

National Science Foundation

Independent Regulatory Commissions

Consumer Product Safety Commission (toys, appliances, other products)

Federal Communications Commission (radio, television, cell phones)

Federal Elections Commission (campaign contributions, campaign advertising)

Federal Trade Commission (consumer credit, deceptive advertising)

National Labor Relations Board (labor unions, union voting, unfair practices)

National Transportation Safety Board (collisions involving aircraft, trains, trucks, other vehicles)

Nuclear Regulatory Commission (nuclear materials)

Securities and Exchange Commission (stock market, financial investments)

Government Corporations

Federal Deposit Insurance Corporation

National Railroad Passenger Corporation (Amtrak)

Overseas Private Investment Corporation

Pension Benefit Guaranty Corporation

United States Postal Service

These agencies do not have identical functions. Some provide government grants or administer a specific government facility, such as a museum. Others are regulatory agencies that exert significant influence over public policy, because Congress has delegated to them broad authority to interpret statutes, create regulations, investigate violations of law, and impose sanctions on violators. The regulatory agencies are typically called *commissions* or *boards,* and as such

names imply, they are led by a group of officials. The heads of these agencies often serve staggered terms so that no new president can replace the entire commission or board upon taking office. For example, the members of the Board of Governors of the Federal Reserve Board serve 14-year terms, with one new member appointed to the seven-member board every two years. The Federal Reserve Board acts independently to shape monetary policy by, for example, setting certain interest rates that affect the cost of borrowing money.

For some other commissions, the authorizing legislation requires that the appointees contain a mix of Republicans and Democrats. For example, the Federal Communications Commission (FCC) and the Federal Trade Commission (FTC) each have five members, but the law requires that no more than three members can be from one political party. The FCC regulates television, radio, cell phones, and other aspects of communications. It also investigates and imposes sanctions for violations of law and policy. The FTC enforces consumer protection laws, such as fining companies that do not comply with rules concerning the fair treatment of applicants for credit or loans.

Some independent agencies are government corporations with their own boards of directors. For example, the National Railroad Passenger Corporation manages Amtrak, the nation's national system of passenger trains. These agencies generate their own revenue through the sale of products or services, fees, or insurance premiums. They must convince Congress to provide them with whatever operating funds they need beyond what they can raise from customers. Some members of Congress see Amtrak, the U.S. Postal Service, and similar agencies as providing services that could be handled more efficiently by private businesses. This explains why arguments are sometimes made for cutting off government funding for such enterprises. Defenders of these agencies argue that these essential services must be maintained and that private businesses may cut back or eliminate unprofitable enterprises.

Independent agencies are responsible for government facilities, such as the national museums in Washington, D.C., administered by the Smithsonian Institution, or specific programs, such as the Peace Corps, which sends American volunteers to teach and provide community service around the world. Such facilities and programs are likely to be considered too unique and important to ever be subjected to privatization. Similarly, special agencies, such as the National Aeronautics and Space Administration (NASA), the space exploration agency, may do things that are so expensive and important that private organizations cannot match the federal government's ability to pursue the agency's goals.

Ben Bernanke (left), chairman of the independent Federal Reserve Board, meets with members of the Federal Reserve System's Board of Governors to regulate banks and control the money supply. These officials have significant control over aspects of the nation's economy, and they receive significant attention in the news during times of economic difficulty. —*What advantages, if any, flow from having these powerful decision makers be appointed rather than elected?*

Departments and Independent Agencies

8.2 Analyze the debate over whether the heads of federal agencies should be policy experts or loyal political appointees.

PRACTICE QUIZ: UNDERSTAND AND APPLY

1. Most members of the president's cabinet are heads of what kinds of organizational entities in the bureaucracy?
   a. departments
   b. independent agencies
   c. independent regulatory commissions
   d. government corporations

2. Members of the cabinet are
   a. elected by voters.
   b. appointed by the president and confirmed by Congress.
   c. appointed by the president and confirmed by the Senate.
   d. selected through civil service tests and interviews.

3. What is the advantage of using the current system for selecting cabinet members?
   a. Top leaders within the bureaucracy are usually accountable to the voters.
   b. Top leaders within the bureaucracy are usually policy experts.
   c. Top leaders with the bureaucracy are usually experienced administrators.
   d. Top leaders within the bureaucracy usually seek to carry out the president's policy agenda.

4. What is the disadvantage of using the current system for selecting cabinet members?
   a. Top leaders within the bureaucracy are too eager to satisfy the voters.
   b. Top leaders within the bureaucracy are often not policy experts.
   c. Top leaders with the bureaucracy are never experienced administrators.
   d. Top leaders within the bureaucracy always fight against the president's policy agenda.

ANALYZE

1. What types of people are selected to be members of the president's cabinet? In your view, does this improve or detract from the quality of the executive branch?

2. Would the federal bureaucracy serve the public better if all departments were independent agencies and thereby less influenced by the president?

IDENTIFY THE CONCEPT THAT DOESN'T BELONG

   a. National Aeronautics and Space Administration
   b. Department of Health and Human Services
   c. Peace Corps
   d. National Science Foundation
   e. Social Security Administration

Resource Center
• Glossary
• Vocabulary Example
• Connect the Link

The Nature of Bureaucracy

8.3 Describe the image people have of the federal bureaucracy, and evaluate the bureaucracy's advantages and disadvantages.

(pages 240–245)

Bureaucracies can be public entities, such as a state treasury department that collects taxes and enforces tax laws, or private entities, such as a bank with different departments for mortgages, commercial loans, and checking accounts. As you know very well, colleges and universities are also bureaucracies, with myriad offices responsible for admissions, financial aid, residential life, parking, and security. In a bureaucracy, workers typically have specific tasks and responsibilities, and there are clear lines of authority in the organization's pyramid of supervision and leadership. One person is responsible for leading and supervising the organization, and beneath the leader lie different levels of responsibility and supervisory authority. In a private organization, such as a business corporation, the leader might be called the president or the chief executive officer. In a government agency, the title of the head person may depend on the nature of the agency and the definition of the positions under relevant constitutional provisions or statutes. Departments are generally headed by a secretary, while independent regulatory commissions typically have a chairman.

People wait in line to mail income tax forms on the last day for filing taxes. U.S. post offices always expect long lines as the midnight deadline approaches. *—Have you had positive or negative experiences in dealing with government agencies?*

The Image of Bureaucracy

In the minds of most Americans, the word *bureaucracy* does not conjure up idealistic notions of efficient organizations that carry out specialized responsibilities for the public's benefit. Instead, *bureaucracy* can convey an image of gargantuan organizations filled with employees who push paper around on their desks all day and worry only about collecting their paychecks and earning their pensions. In government service, because these employees have secure jobs, they may be perceived to feel no pressure to work industriously or efficiently.

A poll concerning the performance of five federal agencies conducted by the Pew Research Center for the People and the Press found that "the agencies get generally poor ratings for how well they carry out their administrative tasks." The groups that were polled "criticize the agencies for working too slowly and making their rules and forms too complicated."[5] The negative image of the bureaucracy may be enhanced by Americans' expectations that the government ought to operate for the benefit of the people in accordance with Abraham Lincoln's familiar words describing a "government of the people,

by the people, and for the people." When people's anticipated Social Security checks are late or Medicare benefits are denied, citizens often feel frustrated and resentful about their treatment at the hands of bureaucrats who are paid by taxpayers, yet do not seem responsive and obedient to the public. Frustration can be compounded by the fact that many government employees enjoy job protections that make them very difficult to fire, even if they are rude or incompetent and have been the subject of many complaints by people who come into contact with a particular office of agency. Perhaps you have felt such frustration in dealing with student loan applications, waiting for a tax refund, or otherwise seeking responsiveness from a government agency.

This negative image of bureaucracies obviously includes generalizations about large organizations and the frustrations that individuals may face in dealing with the officials who work there. What is your image of a bureaucracy? When we talk about the bureaucracy in terms of government agencies rather than banks, corporations, and universities, does your image of bureaucracy depend on which government officials come to mind? When a firefighter rushes into a blazing house and saves a child's life, few of us would associate this hero with the negative image of a bureaucracy. Yet the firefighter belongs to a bureaucracy: The fire department is a government agency, hierarchically organized and with specialized responsibilities for each rank, from the chief down through the captain and the individual firefighters.

As this example shows, our perceptions of government agencies may depend on actual experiences. When government officials respond quickly and provide expected services directly to us, there's no reason to associate these officials and their agency with the negative image of a bureaucracy. On the other hand, when responses to our requests are slow and we can't understand why we must fill out complicated forms or meet detailed requirements, the negative images come galloping back.

Because of their size and distance from many citizens, federal agencies may be especially susceptible to generating negative images. When citizens go to their local Social Security Administration office to apply for retirement or disability benefits, the office staff may need to seek approval from other officials back at Social Security headquarters. Meanwhile, they may have to fill out many forms and provide copies of various documents—and then wait weeks for an answer. "Red tape!" they mutter. Direct services from a local firefighter or police officer put a human face on much-appreciated and immediate government services. But federal officials are often distant, faceless decision makers whose contacts with citizens are based on slow and frequently disappointing correspondence in response to questions and requests about important matters such as taxes, Social Security benefits, and medical assistance for veterans.

Unlike the equally faceless customer service representatives for online merchants and credit card companies, who nevertheless seem eager to respond to our phone calls and questions, the government officials with whom we communicate may appear detached and unresponsive—and (it seems) all too often, agents at the IRS, Social Security, or the Veterans Administration either insist that we pay more or tell us that we can't get some benefit. This does not necessarily mean that low-level government officials are coldhearted by nature. They may need to fill out many forms and gain approvals from superiors before they can address our claims and questions in a slow-moving process. Whether or not individual government officials are uncaring, it is easy to understand why the bureaucracy often has a negative image in the minds of Americans.

According to Charles Goodsell, we expect too much from bureaucracies, and we have negative images in part because "we expect bureaucracies not merely to expend maximum possible effort in solving societal problems but to dispose of them entirely, whether solvable or not."[6] Do you agree that government agencies receive blame unfairly for falling short of perfection?

The Advantages of Government Bureaucracy

Officialdom does not exist by accident. Bureaucracies are created and evolve as a means to undertake the purposes and responsibilities of organizations. The German sociologist Max Weber (1864–1920) is known for describing an ideal bureaucracy involving competent, trained personnel with clearly defined job responsibilities under a central authority who keeps detailed records and makes consistent decisions in accordance with established rules. In theory, these are beneficial elements for running an organization efficiently.

If you were in charge of distributing retirement benefits throughout the United States, how would you organize your system of distribution? Would you simply appoint one individual in each state to be the coordinator in charge of the retirees in that state and then send that individual all of the money each month for that state's retirees? This approach appears to eliminate the current centralized bureaucracy of the Social Security Administration, but it also may create many problems. How would you know whether each state coordinator was using the same criteria and rules for determining eligibility for retirement funds? How would you know whether the coordinators were sending out the appropriate amounts of money on time? When agencies are organized in a hierarchical fashion with specialized responsibilities, the federal government can try to diminish the risks from these problems.

MYTH EXPOSED Many Americans believe that bureaucracies always hinder rather than help when action is needed. After waiting in long lines, talking to disinterested and unhelpful officials on the phone, or experiencing long delays in hearing back from a particular office, many people at some point feel dissatisfied with government agencies. However, despite their flaws and problems, bureaucracies provide a number of advantages for implementing laws and public policies.

- **Standardization.** By having a centralized administration and a common set of rules, benefits and services can be provided in a standard fashion that avoids treating similarly situated citizens differently. A retiree in Idaho can receive the same federal benefits and services as a retiree of the same age and employment history in Maine.
- **Expertise and Competence.** When people who work in an agency focus on specific areas of law and policy throughout their careers, they can develop expertise on those issues. This expertise will help them effectively carry out laws and policies and, moreover, permit them to advise Congress and the president on ways to improve law and policy. Presumably, their expertise will make them more competent than people who know little about the subject. Thus people who work for the EPA are typically hired because of their education and interest in environmental issues, and they develop greater expertise on this subject as they spend years working in this area.
- **Accountability.** Congress can authorize a specific budget for particular programs and then monitor results for the targeted policy area. If $50 million are earmarked to combat air pollution, the existence of an agency dedicated to environmental issues—the EPA—permits those funds to be directed

■ **Patronage System (Spoils System):** A system that rewards the supporters of successful political candidates and parties with government jobs while firing supporters of the opposing party.

EXAMPLE: *An aspect of the patronage system continues to exist, as new presidents appoint supporters from their political party to top leadership positions in executive branch agencies. In earlier decades, such political appointments extended to even lower-level government jobs and created risks that government employees would be pressured to support a particular political candidate in order to keep their jobs.*

to the targeted issues and not mixed together with funds destined for education, transportation, and defense, all of which are handled by separate agencies in the bureaucracy. After the money is spent, air pollution can be evaluated, and Congress and the president can assess whether the EPA spent the money effectively and whether their intended policies were carried out correctly.

- **Coordination.** Efforts of different agencies can be more effectively coordinated when each has clearly defined responsibilities and a hierarchical structure. Hierarchy enables the leaders in each agency to direct subordinates to work in cooperation with other agencies. For example, if officials in the Department of Education and the Department of Health and Human Services are instructed to cooperate in implementing an antidrug program or an education program aimed at preventing teen pregnancy, the leaders of the respective agencies can work together to delegate shared responsibilities. When individual officials throughout the country act independently on issues, it is much more difficult to coordinate efforts effectively.

In general, these advantages may be helpful in both government and business organizations.

One additional advantage, a merit-based system for hiring, has special importance for government bureaucracy. Until a little over a century ago, government employees were hired and fired on the basis of their support for particular political parties and candidates for elective office. This was called the **patronage system, or spoils system**■. Political parties rewarded their supporters by giving them government jobs. At the same time, supporters of the opposing party were fired as soon as an election placed new leaders in office. "To the victor belongs the spoils," said a prominent Jacksonian Era politician early in the nineteenth century, giving political patronage its alternative name, the *spoils system*. (By "spoils," he was referring to the practice of an army sacking a conquered city and soldiers carrying off whatever they could grab.)

Of course, the spoils system had many problems. There was an abrupt turnover in many government positions after elections in which a different political party gained power. Unqualified people got government jobs despite lacking the knowledge and interest to carry out their tasks properly. Government workers steered benefits and services to fellow partisans and sought to deprive their political opponents of government services. Officials spent too much time doing things that would help keep their party in power and themselves in their jobs. New roads, government contracts, and other benefits went to citizens who supported the elected officials who had hired the government workers. With self-interest unchecked, there were grave risks of corruption, as government workers and political leaders alike traded bribes for favoritism in distributing government services and benefits.

All these problems came to a head in the early 1880s. During the summer of 1881, a man claiming to be a disappointed office seeker (he was probably insane) shot President James Garfield. Garfield's assassination made him a martyr for the cause of "good government." This event helped push forward previous proposals to reform the employment system within the federal government. Congress and President Chester A. Arthur found themselves under irresistible public pressure to enact legislation establishing a **civil service system**■ based on merit.

In 1883, Congress passed and President Arthur signed the Pendleton Act, creating the first federal civil service system. Under this act, applicants for specified federal government jobs were supposed to be tested, demonstrate their qualifications, and keep their jobs based on competent performance rather than political affiliation. The new system reduced, but did not entirely eliminate, such problems as unqualified employees and bribery. Over time, more federal jobs were brought under civil service rules, and civil service systems eventually developed as well in state and local governments, especially during the Progressive Era in the first decades of the twentieth century.

The civil service system is still the framework for the federal bureaucracy. Today, the president can appoint the top officials who oversee most federal government agencies. In doing so, the president seeks to steer the bureaucracy in policy directions that reflect the voters' presidential choice in the most recent election. However, except for these high officials and the staff in the Executive Office of the President, the vast majority of other federal workers are civil service employees who remain at their jobs as presidential administrations come and go. Standardization, expertise, and competence would all be endangered—indeed, under today's conditions, they would collapse—if federal agencies experienced the kind of massive turnovers in personnel after each election that were typical of America in the mid-nineteenth century.

Civil service rules protect federal employees from being fired for failing to support a specific political party. Federal employees are further protected by the **Hatch Act** of 1939, a law that limits the participation of federal employees in political campaigns (see Table 8.4). They can vote and attend political rallies, but they cannot work on campaigns or endorse candidates. Although this law limits federal workers' political participation, it is intended to prevent them from being pressured by elected officials to donate their money and time to political campaigns. Prior to the implementation of civil service systems, it was very common for government employees to be required to work on political campaigns in order to keep their jobs. The current system spares them from fearing that they will lose promotions, raises, and other benefits for failing to support the party in power.

■ **Civil Service System:** A government employment system in which employees are hired on the basis of their qualifications and cannot be fired merely for belonging to the wrong political party; originated with the federal Pendleton Act in 1883 and expanded at other levels of government in the half-century that followed.

EXAMPLE: *Federal employees in the Internal Revenue Service, National Park Service, Department of Transportation, and other agencies are hired based on their qualifications— education and experience—for a specific job, and they retain their positions over the years as new presidents win election, serve their terms, and are then replaced by new presidents.*

TABLE 8.4 | The Hatch Act of 1939

PERMITTED/PROHIBITED POLITICAL ACTIVITIES FOR FEDERAL EMPLOYEES

Federal employees *may*

- register and vote as they choose.
- assist in voter registration drives.
- express opinions about candidates and issues.
- participate in campaigns where none of the candidates represent a political party.
- contribute money to political organizations or attend political fund raising functions.
- attend political rallies and meetings.
- join political clubs or parties.
- sign nominating petitions.
- campaign for or against referendum questions, constitutional amendments, municipal ordinances.

Federal employees *may not*

- be candidates for public office in partisan elections.
- campaign for or against a candidate or slate of candidates in partisan elections.
- make campaign speeches.
- collect contributions or sell tickets to political fund-raising functions.
- distribute campaign material in partisan elections.
- organize or manage political rallies or meetings.
- hold office in political clubs or parties.
- circulate nominating petitions.
- work to register voters for one party only.
- wear political buttons at work.

SOURCE: U.S. Office of Special Counsel http://www.osc.gov/ha_fed.htm#regulations. Accessed on April 11, 2010.

The Problems of Government Bureaucracy

The advantages of a merit system do not mean, however, that government agencies necessarily fulfill their responsibilities efficiently and satisfy the expectations of citizens, the president, and Congress. Many practical problems tarnish the idealistic vision of civil service bureaucracies as effective, efficient organizations. For example, as organizations grow in size, decision-making layers increase between the employee whom the average citizen encounters and the upper-level managers with final authority. Higher-level decision makers may be far removed from the practical policy problems affecting citizens. When decisions must move through a chain of command, there are obvious risks of delay, including the chance that documents will be misplaced or lost so that new forms must be completed to start a decision-making process all over again.

Civil service protections can make it difficult for top officials to motivate government employees and spur them to take actions, especially when those actions require changing an agency's priorities or operating methods. Almost by nature, large organizations are resistant to change. People who have become accustomed to doing their jobs in a specific way may be reluctant to adopt new priorities and directives. Bureaucracies are not typically associated with innovation and bold ideas. They change slowly, and usually in incremental fashion. When the president or Congress wants law and policy to move in a new direction, getting the bureaucracy to reorder its priorities and operate in different ways can be akin to the familiar image of "turning a battleship at sea"—a slow, gradual, laborious process. If executive agencies are slow to implement new laws, they can hinder or even undermine the achievement of a president's policy goals.

For policy change to be effective, laws and programs must be designed by taking account of the resources, characteristics, experience, and organizational structure of the agencies that must implement those laws and programs. President George W. Bush, for example, touted his No Child Left Behind (NCLB) law, passed in 2002, as the key to improving education throughout the country. The NCLB law required the testing of all students and provided for punishing schools in which students perform poorly. Two years later, however, the federal government found that the law had been poorly implemented, because data about schools and students were not collected consistently and systematically throughout the nation. Implementation problems can be even more significant when, rather than just providing guidance and supervision for state and local governments, an agency bears responsibility for hiring staff, training personnel, and carrying out new tasks. When agencies are large bureaucracies, it can be exceptionally difficult to organize, implement, and monitor programs effectively.

The federal bureaucracy bears responsibility for organizing initiatives nationwide, relying on thousands of individuals spread throughout the country at hundreds of locations. Let's take an example: the Transportation Security Administration (TSA), which was created in November 2001 in the aftermath of the 9/11 terrorist attacks. The TSA is now part of the Department of Homeland Security. Among other responsibilities, the TSA screens passengers and their baggage for weapons and explosives before they board commercial airliners. An airline passenger's unsuccessful attempt to ignite a bomb as his plane approached the Detroit airport from the Netherlands on Christmas Day in 2009, provided a stark reminder of the need for effective, professional security officials conducting screening and searches at all airports.

In its first few years, the TSA was plagued with problems. Eighteen-thousand screeners were hired and initially put to work without required background checks. Among the 1,200 screeners eventually fired after background checks revealed that they had lied on their applications or had criminal records, several with criminal pasts were permitted to remain

■ **Privatization:** The process of turning some responsibilities of government bureaucracy over to private organizations on the assumption that they can administer and deliver services more effectively and inexpensively.

EXAMPLE: *During the wars in Iraq and Afghanistan, the U.S. government hired private companies to handle food services, transportation of supplies, construction of facilities, and even personal protection (i.e., bodyguards) for American officials in Iraq. Problems arose, however, when some companies were accused of overcharging for services, bribing military officials for additional contracts, and violating the standards for behavior that are expected of American personnel.*

Transportation Security Administration (TSA) officers provide an essential service in attempting to protect public safety at airports. —*How can we make sure that we have selected the best candidates to become TSA officers and have provided them with necessary training, equipment, and supervision?*

on the job for weeks or even months before termination.[7] The federal government paid hundreds of thousands of dollars in claims after screeners were caught stealing from passengers' luggage while searching for weapons and explosives. Morale problems also developed as screeners complained of being required to work overtime without adequate compensation and of being assigned to use baggage-scanning equipment without receiving any training.[8] If the TSA had been given more time for planning, more opportunities to screen and train workers, and more resources to ensure adequate personnel and equipment at each airport, the implementation of the policy might have gone more smoothly. The bureaucracy, however, must work in a constrained environment in which limits on time, resources, and expertise often result in implementation problems.

Reform of the Bureaucracy

The gigantic size and nationwide responsibilities of modern federal agencies make it extremely difficult for the bureaucracy to live up to the ideals of efficient performance based on management principles in an organizational hierarchy. Some critics argue that alternative approaches to implementation could reduce the problems of government bureaucracy. One suggestion is to try **decentralization**—a reform in which the federal government could give greater independence to regional offices that would be more closely connected to local issues and client populations. Alternatively, states could be given greater authority to handle their own affairs. For example, state inspection agencies could receive federal funds to enforce national air pollution or workplace safety laws. The argument for decentralization rests

on a belief that smaller agencies, presumably more closely connected to local problems, can be more efficient and effective. There are risks, however, that decentralization would lead to inconsistent standards and treatment for people in different parts of the country. Officials in one state might vigorously enforce pollution laws, while those in another state might turn a blind eye to such problems because of the economic and political power of polluting industries.

Privatization■ has also been suggested as a cure for the problems of government bureaucracy. Critics argue that private businesses working under government contracts could deliver services and benefits to citizens with greater efficiency and less expense than when the bureaucracy handles such matters. All levels of government use private contracts in an effort to save money. Indeed, states have sent convicted offenders to prisons built and operated by private corporations, governments pay private contractors to repair highways and build bridges, and the federal government has hired private contractors to serve as bodyguards for American officials in the war zones of Iraq and Afghanistan.

In theory, businesses and nonprofit agencies are better than the government bureaucracy at finding ways to save money, developing innovations, and responding to feedback from client populations. One way that they save money is through compensation for low-level workers that is less generous than government pay and through flexible personnel policies that allow them to lay off or fire employees whose counterparts in government would have civil service job security protection. Privatization is controversial. In some circumstances, private contractors do not save money and do not deliver services more effectively than government agencies.

In addition, it can be difficult to hold private companies accountable for their actions, because they are not necessarily subject to the same oversight laws that govern public agencies. Moreover, there are risks of favoritism and corruption as private companies use campaign contributions, personal contacts with government officials, and lobbying to encourage expenditures of government funds that add to their profits but do not necessarily address the public's needs.

For example, during the Bush administration, critics questioned the basis for lucrative, no-bid contracts awarded to Halliburton Corporation, an oil-services and construction company. The company had been run by Dick Cheney (prior to his becoming the vice president of President Bush), and it made millions of dollars on projects in Iraq despite prior scandals about poor performance and overbilling on government contracts.

Periodically, efforts are made to reform the bureaucracy in order to improve its effectiveness. For example, in 1978 Congress established the **Senior Executive Service (SES),** a program within the federal executive branch that enables senior administrators with outstanding leadership and management skills to be moved between jobs in different agencies in order to enhance the performance of the bureaucracy. The development of the SES was intended to add flexibility in shifting personnel resources within the federal bureaucracy. Then, during President Clinton's administration (1993–2001), Vice President Al Gore led a task force of senior government officials in an effort known as the National Partnership for Reinventing Government. This effort resulted in several laws to better measure the performance of government agencies, increase cooperation between government and business, and otherwise improve the effectiveness of the bureaucracy.

The Nature of Bureaucracy

8.3   **Describe the image people have of the federal bureaucracy, and evaluate the bureaucracy's advantages and disadvantages.**

PRACTICE QUIZ: UNDERSTAND AND APPLY

1. Which of the following is *not* assumed to be a beneficial aspect of bureaucracy?
   a. employees' expertise on policy issues
   b. citizens' direct access to high-level decision makers
   c. vertical lines of authority for supervision and control
   d. standardization of procedures and equal treatment of citizens

2. Civil service systems were developed in response to
   a. the Great Depression.
   b. Franklin Roosevelt's New Deal programs.
   c. the spoils system.
   d. the creation of independent regulatory commissions.

3. Decentralization of the federal bureaucracy would
   a. give more authority to decision makers in regional and local offices.
   b. eliminate the need for any government officials to work in Washington, D.C.
   c. make the judiciary the most powerful branch of government.
   d. permit the president to issue direct orders to the nation's governors.

4. Proposals for reform of the bureaucracy through privatization assume that
   a. investors want to purchase the U.S. Capitol building.
   b. government agencies should grow larger than they are today.
   c. cabinet officers will be more highly motivated if they receive bonuses.
   d. private businesses operate more efficiently than government agencies.

ANALYZE

1. How can the bureaucracy improve its image?

2. Should the civil service system be changed to make it easier to fire government workers? What would be the risks and benefits?

IDENTIFY THE CONCEPT THAT DOESN'T BELONG

a. Decentralization
b. Standardization
c. Accountability
d. Expertise
e. Coordination

Resource Center
• Glossary
• Vocabulary Example
• Connect the Link

CONNECT THE LINK
(Chapter 6, page 162–165) Congressional committees each have responsibility for specific policy issues, and they interact frequently with officials in their counterpart agencies responsible for the same policy issues in the bureaucracy.

The Lobbying Pathway and Policymaking

8.4 **Assess the mechanisms and processes that influence and oversee the federal bureaucracy.**

(pages 246–251)

From what you've read so far, you can see the bureaucracy's influence over policy through its responsibilities for implementation of laws enacted by Congress. The effectiveness of agencies' implementation efforts can depend on their resources, information, and expertise. However, the bureaucracy can affect policymaking in other ways.

The bureaucracy also influences the formulation of public policy through the decisions and actions of elites—people with political connections, status, or expertise—and through the day-to-day implementation of laws and regulations by lower-level personnel such as FBI agents, forest rangers, postal workers, water-quality inspectors, and others who have direct contact with the public. If an FBI agent does not follow mandated procedures when investigating a case or arresting a suspect, the laws of Congress and the regulations of the Department of Justice have not been implemented properly. Full and proper implementation of many laws and policies can rest in the hands of relatively low-level officials who make discretionary decisions about how they will treat individuals and businesses when conducting investigations or administering the distribution of government services and benefits.

The Bureaucracy and Legislation

The ideal of the bureaucracy envisions employees with competence and expertise who work in a pyramid-shaped organizational structure with clear lines of authority and supervision. The lines of authority in a bureaucracy's organizational chart are meant to indicate that the downward flow of instructions guides the actions of personnel at each level of the agency. In reality, the decisions and actions of personnel within the bureaucracy are more complicated because of the influence of informal networks and relationships with organizations and actors outside the bureaucracy. In prior decades, political scientists often described the influence of these networks and relationships by focusing on the concept of the **iron triangle,** a concept describing the tight relationship and power over policy issues possessed by three entities sharing joint interests concerning specific policy goals: (1) interest groups concerned with a particular policy issue, (2) the key committee members in Congress and their staff with authority over that issue, and (3) the bureaucracy's leaders and

the experts on that particular issue within a given department or subagency. Within their sphere of expertise and interest, these iron triangles could, through discussion, communication, and consensus among members, control the writing of laws and the development of policies.

The linkages and power of the iron triangle were enhanced as interest groups provided campaign contributions to legislators on relevant congressional committees and rallied their own members to support or oppose legislative proposals emanating from the iron triangle. As we saw in Chapter 6 (pages 162–165), the committees in Congress are especially influential in shaping policy. The key committee members could draft legislation, block unwanted bills, and facilitate the passage of desired statutes through the legislative process. The bureaucracy's interested experts could provide needed information, help plan and facilitate implementation, and provide strategic opposition to counterproposals generated by those outside of the iron triangle. The concept of the iron triangle helped encourage recognition of the bureaucracy's role in shaping legislation through informal networks.

Contemporary scholars view the iron triangle concept as limited and outdated. The governing system has changed. Growing numbers of interest groups are active in lobbying, and individual members of Congress today have less absolute power over committee processes. With respect to some policy issues, interest groups use strategies that include advertising campaigns to arouse the public and calling the attention of the news media to issues that previously may have been decided largely behind the closed doors of a congressional committee room.

Realizing the inadequacies of the iron triangle framework for all policy issues, scholars now focus on concepts characterized as either **issue networks** or **policy communities■**. Guy Peters describes these as "involving large numbers of interested parties, each with substantial expertise in the policy area. . . . They may contain competing ideas and types of interests to be served through public policy."[9] Both terms describe ongoing relationships and contacts between individuals interested in specific policy issues and areas. These individuals have expertise and remain in contact over time as their particular public policy concerns rise and fall on the nation's policy agenda. At government conferences presenting research on environmental issues, conference attendees who interact with each other are likely to include a variety of individuals representing different perspectives: scholars who study the environment, officials from the EPA, staff members from relevant congressional committees, representatives from interest groups concerned with such issues, and officials from businesses involved in waste disposal, manufacturing processes, and the cleanup of industrial sites.

Some of these individuals may change jobs over the years and move from universities and businesses into appointed positions in government or from congressional committees to interest groups. In 2004, it was reported that more than 90 former members of Congress were employed as lobbyists by businesses

■ **Issue Networks (Policy Communities):** Interest groups, scholars, and other experts that communicate about, debate, and interact regarding issues of interest and thus influence public policy when the legislature acts on those issues.

EXAMPLE: *The Obama administration's effort to reform the nation's health care system was shaped by input from pharmaceutical companies, insurance companies, health-related interest groups, labor unions, economists, lobbyists for corporate interest groups and senior citizens, doctors, hospitals, and officials in the U.S. Department of Health and Human Services.*

and interest groups, often with an emphasis on issue areas for which they were previously responsible on congressional committees.[10] High officials in the bureaucracy also move in and out of government. As these actors move between jobs, their interests and expertise keep them in contact with each other through conferences and individual communications as they develop working relationships. When bills are formally proposed, individuals from throughout the network are likely to use their contacts in seeking to amend the bill's wording, lobbying for its passage, or attempting to block its progress through the legislative process. The "revolving door" of employees moving between federal government service and interest groups or lobbying firms raises concerns that an agency may be "captured" or controlled by officials who have long alliances with and commitments to specific interest groups.

For example, Gale Norton, the Secretary of the Interior under George W. Bush from 2001 to 2006, had previously worked as an attorney for the Mountain States Legal Foundation, an interest group that challenged environmentalist groups in court by arguing against government restrictions on land use and by advocating for the use of federal lands by ranchers, recreational vehicles, and oil exploration companies. When she left her post in 2006, she became a legal advisor for Royal Dutch Shell, an oil company that obtained lucrative federal land leases for obtaining oil from the Interior Department that Norton had been heading.[11] Such "revolving door" job movements between government agencies and the interest groups and businesses with which they deal create risks of the appearance of impropriety or even corruption. Do these individuals improperly use their government authority to steer agency decisions in favor of specific interests in order to obtain a lucrative job or other benefits for themselves? In Gale Norton's case, the U.S. Department of Justice launched a criminal investigation in late 2009 that sought to determine whether she had violated laws against steering government business to favored companies and discussing employment with a company that has dealings with the government within the area of the government official's authority.[12] News reports stated in 2010 that no charges would be filed against her.

The Bureaucracy and Information

Officials appointed by the president to head executive agencies invariably advocate laws—at least in public—that reflect the president's policy agenda. Occasionally, long-time officials within the bureaucracy with experience and expertise may disagree with laws and policies sought by the president and presidential appointees. They may also disagree with new interpretations of existing laws or with presidential efforts to change current policies. These officials may get in touch with their contacts among personnel who work for congressional committees, thereby alerting sympathetic members of Congress to initiate investigations,

Gale Norton, the first Secretary of the Interior in the Bush administration, shown here with President Bush, was a lawyer with experience as a policy advocate for businesses interested in economic development and energy exploration on federal lands. —*Would the American public have been better served by a Secretary of the Interior who was a scientist specializing in the forestry, wildlife, and water issues that are under the Department's authority?*

publicize the president's actions, and oppose efforts to shape law and policy. They may also leak information to the news media in order to bring public attention to issues of concern to them.

An additional role played by officials in the bureaucracy is to provide information for Congress to use in crafting and approving statutes. They provide this information both formally and informally. Formally, some federal agencies, such as the U.S. Census Bureau, regularly send out a steady stream of information to all kinds of congressional committees that are interested in trends in the nation's population as well as in such demographic issues as home ownership, poverty, and education. Other agencies gather, analyze, and provide information about very specific policy issues, usually working only with those congressional committees that are specifically concerned with these issues. Informal communication between the bureaucracy and Congress occurs when legislative staffers or individual members of Congress contact agency officials with questions about policy issues and government programs. These informal contacts can help build relationships within issue networks that lead to cooperative working relationships as members of Congress rely on agency officials for advice when crafting new legislative proposals.

Congressional reliance on officials in the bureaucracy for information can create problems if presidential appointees use their authority to direct subordinates to withhold or distort information as a means of advancing the president's policy agenda. For example, in 2004, several conservative Republicans threatened to oppose President Bush's Medicare bill if it would

■ **Regulations:** Legal rules created by government agencies based on authority delegated by the legislature.

EXAMPLE: *In order to protect public safety, regulations issued by the U.S. Department of Transportation define how many hours each week truck drivers can be on the road and how many hours of rest they must have between driving shifts.*

cost more than $400 billion, but they had been reassured by the White House that it would not. The chief actuary for the Centers for Medicare and Medicaid Services conducted an analysis that indicated the legislation would cost at least $100 billion more, but his superior, the director of the Medicare office, threatened to fire him if he revealed this to members of Congress. Two months after Congress approved the legislation, the White House budget director revealed that the new law would actually cost more than $530 billion (see Figure 8.3).[13]

This risk of distorted information is one reason that Congress also seeks to gather its own information through legislative committees and through the Congressional Budget Office and Government Accountability Office, an investigative agency that reports to Congress. The range of policy issues is so vast, however, that Congress must inevitably rely on officials in the bureaucracy for important information about many public policies. Even though most employees in the federal bureaucracy are civil servants who are not formally affiliated with a political party, they may face pressure from presidential appointees to take actions that violate their own ideals of

performing their jobs with neutrality and competence. If they disobey superiors, they may be passed over for promotion, transferred to undesirable positions or offices, or threatened with dismissal based on phony charges of incompetence.

Some employees within the bureaucracy stand up against actions by executive branch superiors by providing information about misconduct by government officials. Individuals who are willing to provide such information are known as **whistleblowers,** and they often risk workplace retaliation in the form of dismissal, demotions, and other sanctions intended to punish them for their actions and to deter others from revealing politically damaging information. In 2004, for example, an issue emerged in the presidential campaign when a senior civilian contracting official in the U.S. Army Corps of Engineers claimed that Halliburton Corporation, the business previously chaired by Vice President Dick Cheney, had received preferential treatment in the awarding of lucrative contracts for reconstruction projects in Iraq.[14] Because the disclosure triggered investigative actions in Congress, the official's supporters feared that she would suffer retaliation. Her lawyer asserted that she should be shielded by the **Whistleblower Protection Act of 1989,** a federal law intended to prevent officials in the bureaucracy from being punished for their efforts to protect the country from governmental misconduct.

In theory, this statute should protect whistleblowers, but in individual cases, it may be difficult for affected individuals to refute their superiors' claims that they are being punished for poor performance rather than for providing well-intentioned, revealing information. For example, just as her attorney feared, the civilian whistleblower from the Army Corps of Engineers was removed from her position and demoted, with a reduction in salary, after she testified before a congressional committee.[15]

FIGURE 8.3 ■ The Cost of Medicare Drug Benefits

In seeking to gain congressional approval for its Medicare prescription drug plan, the Bush administration reportedly pressured an expert in the bureaucracy to keep quiet about cost projections that it knew would make the plan unacceptable to many Republican members of Congress. The figures showing significantly higher expected costs were only revealed after the program had been enacted into law. —*Does the president have too much influence over the bureaucracy?*

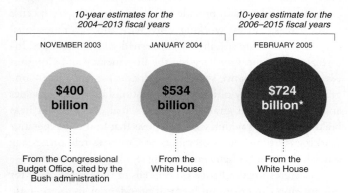

Gauging Medicare Drug Benefit's Cost

New estimates for the cost of the Medicare prescription drug benefit, approved by Congress in 2003, cover a 10-year period different from the one in the original estimates.

10-year estimates for the 2004–2013 fiscal years		10-year estimate for the 2006–2015 fiscal years
NOVEMBER 2003	JANUARY 2004	FEBRUARY 2005
$400 billion	**$534 billion**	**$724 billion***
From the Congressional Budget Office, cited by the Bush administration	From the White House	From the White House

*Reflects the net cost to the government: total payments of $1.2 trillion, minus $468 billion in premiums paid by Medicare beneficiaries, compulsory contributions by states and federal savings in Medicaid.

SOURCE: February 10, 2005, New York Times Graphics. Copyright © 2005 by the New York Times Co. Reprinted with permission.

Regulations

Depending on their responsibilities, federal agencies may receive rule-making authority from the statutes that Congress enacts. The rule-making process gives officials in the bureaucracy power over the development of public policy. In some cases, the legislation creating an agency will use general language to describe its mission. For example, as the political scientist Robert Katzmann concluded from his study of the FTC, "In the absence of clearly defined statutory objectives, the Federal Trade Commission apparently has wide discretion in determining the goal (or goals) that it should pursue."[16]

General statutory language can become the basis for the bureaucracy's development of its own precise rules—agency-created laws called **regulations**■, which govern the topics under a particular agency's jurisdiction. Commentators often describe regulations as filling in the precise details of rules for society based on the broader directives set forth in statutes. In other cases, Congress may enact statutes that specifically delegate to agencies the authority to formulate the precise rules to govern a particular subject.

Statutes written by Congress also specify the procedures that agencies must use in developing regulations. Normally, these procedures include publication of proposed regulations, a period during which the public may comment on the proposals, and a process for hearings about the desirability and potential effects of the proposed regulations. These procedures give interest groups the opportunity to encourage agencies to adopt new proposals, to work for change in proposals that originated with the government or other groups, or to block (if they can) proposed regulations adverse to their interests. For example, in 2010, the Environmental Protection Agency (EPA) used its authority under the Clean Air Act by moving forward with proposed regulations to set standards for greenhouse gas emissions from automobile tailpipes and power plants. Energy companies objected to the regulations and also devoted considerable energy to lobbying Congress for legislation that would block the EPA's action. Environmental groups countered by lobbying members of Congress to withhold support from any new legislation that would stop the EPA regulations.[17]

The rule-making process creates opportunities for influencing the results. Interested individuals' relationships with officials in the bureaucracy come into play through issue networks. Interest groups that give campaign contributions and endorsements to the president's political party can also lobby overtly. Because some regulations are controversial, agencies are often instructed during election campaigns to slow down the processes by which rules are changed and created so that the political party opposing the president cannot use pending regulations as a campaign issue.[18] Clearly, this rule-making process gives officials in the bureaucracy significant influence over the development of regulations affecting a wide range of policy issues, ranging from air pollution rules to workplace safety regulations to the approval of new drugs and medical treatments.

Although judgments about the desirability of specific regulatory changes always depend on the values of a particular observer, it is generally agreed that presidents have opportunities to exploit the rule-making process to advance their own policy agendas. For example, critics accused the Bush administration of using these tactics to lengthen the hours that long-haul truckers could drive in one shift, despite evidence about the risk of car–truck collisions when drivers are tired; approve logging in federal forests without the usual environmental reviews; dilute rules intended to protect coal miners from black lung disease; and relax air pollution regulations for factories and power plants.[19] The Bush administration and its supporters responded to criticisms by claiming that the government hampers business productivity with too many needless regulations. In 2009, the Obama administration used the regulatory process to pursue its own goals, including improved gas mileage standards for motor vehicles, government funding for stem cell research, and federal control over the safety standards for subways and light rail systems.[20]

Quasi-Judicial Processes

The bureaucracy affects policy in some agencies through hearings that look similar to the duties of courts in examining evidence and issuing decisions. In the course of making these decisions, officials in the bureaucracy interpret statutes and regulations and thereby shape policy through their application of the law. Depending on the agency and the purpose of the adjudicative procedures, these processes can be formal or informal. There are also differences in the extent to which these processes are adversarial and thereby permit two sides to argue against each other in front of decision makers within the bureaucracy.

Officials in government agencies may use these processes when investigating whether individuals and corporations are obeying laws and regulations. In 2009, for example, the FCC responded to complaints from members of the public by launching an investigation about swearing and an allegedly obscene gesture by award recipients on NBC's broadcast of the Golden Globe awards.[21] Much like judges in a court, the commissioners make their decisions based on an examination of evidence and an interpretation of the law related to broadcast standards. Moreover, their interpretation of the law and their imposition of strong sanctions help shape policy and provide guidance for other broadcasters about permissible program content.

Judicial processes also exist when citizens are denied requested benefits from the government. For example, if people believe that their physical or mental disabilities prevent them from working and that they qualify for disability payments from the Social Security Administration, they must file an application with their local Social Security office and provide medical evidence about their disability. If their local office deems them ineligible, they can appeal to an **administrative law judge (ALJ)** within the Social Security Administration. The ALJ holds a formal hearing, in which the claimant may be represented by an attorney, and medical evidence is presented to document the claimed disability[22] (see Table 8.5). Similar ALJ hearings and quasi-judicial decisions are made in other agencies concerning matters such as immigration and labor union disputes.

STUDENT profile

In July 2007, two law students at Cornell University, Kristen Echemendia and Heidi Craig, succeeded in persuading the Board of Immigration Appeals that an immigration judge had made mistakes in ordering the deportation of a Guatemalan man. The man had been tortured by military officials in Guatemala and had escaped to the United States, where he lived and worked quietly for 13 years. When he was arrested by American officials for entering the country illegally, he sought to gain asylum—in effect, special permission to stay in the United States—because of the risk that he would be tortured and killed if he was sent back to Guatemala. He had no lawyer

TABLE 8.5 Applying for Social Security Disability Benefits

APPLICANT	DECISION MAKERS
• **Step 1.** *Submit application forms.* Records needed to demonstrate that applicant meets the criteria for (1) enough total years worked contributing money to the social security system to become eligible for consideration; (2) worked at least half the time in years preceding claimed disability; (3) contact information for doctors. If disability claim is denied, then:	*Decision makers:* After officials in Social Security Administration determine if applicant's work history makes the individual qualified for benefits, medical personnel in state agency receive referral from Social Security Administration to obtain medical records and evaluate applicant's capacity to work.
• **Step 2.** *Request reconsideration.* If disability claim is denied, then:	*Decision makers:* Entire file reviewed by officials in Social Security Administration who did not take part in the original decision.
• **Step 3.** *Appeal decision to quasi-judicial process in Social Security Administration.* If disability claim is denied, then:	*Decision makers:* An administrative law judge (ALJ) within Social Security Administration will conduct a hearing at which the applicant and the applicant's attorney (if represented by counsel) can present evidence and witnesses before ALJ decides whether the original denial of benefits was improper.
• **Step 4.** *Appeal decision to the Appeals Council within the Social Security Administration.* If disability claim is denied, then:	*Decision makers:* Members of the Appeals Council within the Social Security Administration will review records and either deny the claim or refer the case back to the ALJ for further review.
• **Step 5.** *File lawsuit in U.S. District Court.*	*Decision makers:* U.S. District Court judge considers evidence and determines whether the denial of benefits by the Social Security Administration was improper.

SOURCE: U.S. Social Security Administration. http://ssa-custhelp.ssa.gov/cgi-bin/ssa.cfg/php/enduser/std_alp.php?p_page=1&p_cv=1.50& p_pv=&p_prods=&p_cats=50 Accessed on April 11, 2010.

to represent him at his original immigration hearing, however, and he spoke little English. The Cornell students reviewed the records of the hearing and argued that he had been denied his constitutional right to a fair trial, because he had not been given adequate opportunity to present evidence about his physical scars and psychiatrists' reports on his depression and other problems resulting from the detention and torture in Guatemala.

As with other judicial-type processes within the bureaucracy, immigration hearings do not receive public attention, and large numbers of cases are processed with relatively little time spent on many of those individual cases. Thus the risks of error may be greater than in a regular criminal or civil court, in which each side is represented by a lawyer in public proceedings.

The Cornell students were able to help the man because they had specialized knowledge and advanced education in law. However, simply by being aware of the nature and importance of Social Security disability processes, immigration hearings, and other matters within the bureaucracy, college students may be able to direct people to helpful resources.

Oversight and Accountability

As you've seen in the various ways by which agency officials shape policy, bureaucrats can have significant influence. Yet their actions typically are not noticed by the public or the news media. Without public attention focused on the decisions of agency officials, it is difficult to know what they are doing and to make sure they do not exceed their authority or otherwise make improper decisions. However, oversight mechanisms do exist.

All three branches of government have the power to subject the bureaucracy to oversight and accountability. The president attempts to oversee, guide, and control the bureaucracy through the supervisory authority of political appointees at the top levels of each agency. These appointees are supposed to monitor the work of subordinates and ensure that officials in each agency, as they produce regulations and implement statutes, are working to advance the president's preferred interpretations of laws. The threat of sanctions exists, because even though it may be difficult to dismiss civil service employees for most of their actions, the superiors in each agency can affect promotions, bonuses, and job assignments through the performance evaluations that they conduct annually on each employee.

There is also legislative oversight. Christopher Foreman describes this as "two interlocking congressional processes: the efforts to *gather information* about what agencies are doing and to *dictate or signal* to agencies regarding the preferred behavior or policy."[23] Oversight by the legislative branch arises when congressional committees summon officials to testify. By pressing these bureaucrats with questions in a public hearing, members of Congress can attempt to discover whether laws are being implemented effectively and justly. If members are unhappy with the performance of officials in specific agencies,

Secretary of the Treasury Timothy Geithner faced tough questioning from members of Congress when summoned to testify about the Obama administration's programs for keeping banks from collapsing and reviving the national economy. —*How does Congress influence the actions of federal agencies?*

they can publicize these problems and thereby cast political blame on the president. This tactic puts pressure on the president and top appointees to ensure that agencies perform properly. Moreover, Congress controls each agency's budget. If agencies disappoint or clash with Congress, they risk losing needed resources. Congressional control over funding therefore creates incentives for cooperation and compliance by officials in the bureaucracy.[24]

Judicial oversight comes into play when individuals and interest groups file lawsuits claiming that agencies are not implementing laws properly or are not following proper procedures in creating regulations. The many quasi-judicial processes within the bureaucracy are also subject to oversight through appeals to the federal courts from adverse judgments by ALJs, agency commissions and boards, and other bureaucratic decision makers.

The Lobbying Pathway and Policymaking

8.4   **Assess the mechanisms and processes that influence and oversee the federal bureaucracy.**

PRACTICE QUIZ: UNDERSTAND AND APPLY

1. The "iron triangle" can be influential over agency decisions because
   a. Congress often requires an ironclad, three-step process for the creation of regulations.
   b. the president, the cabinet secretary, and the Supreme Court must agree on the wording of every regulation.
   c. of relationships and communications between individuals in interest groups, congressional committees, and agencies.
   d. the Constitution divides power between three branches of government.

2. Someone inside the bureaucracy who reveals to Congress that an agency has violated its own rules or misused funds is generally called a
   a. provocateur.   c. administrative law judge.
   b. whistleblower.   d. patron.

3. What term have contemporary scholars used to better illustrate the complexity of the original *iron triangle* concept?
   a. regulatory process   c. issue network
   b. *Federal Register*   d. Senior Executive Service

4. How many branches of the government possess the power to provide oversight and impose accountability on the bureaucracy?
   a. three (Congress, president, judiciary)
   b. two (Congress, president)
   c. one (Congress)
   d. none (the bureaucracy is independent)

ANALYZE

1. Briefly explain what a regulation is and how one is created in the federal bureaucracy.

2. What are quasi-judicial processes of the federal bureaucracy?

IDENTIFY THE CONCEPT THAT DOES NOT BELONG

a. Iron triangle
b. Regulations
c. Federalism
d. Whistleblower
e. Issue networks

8.4

Conclusion

The size of the federal bureaucracy reflects the policy ambitions of the national government. If the government of the United States focused only on national defense, foreign relations, and taxation, as it did in the founding era and for most of the nineteenth century, the federal bureaucracy would be both smaller and narrowly focused on those limited areas. Today, however, Congress writes laws establishing rules and programs covering a host of policy issues, from agriculture to energy to health care. To implement these complex programs, create relevant regulations, and enforce the laws enacted by Congress, the bureaucracy needs sufficient resources and trained personnel.

Despite the negative images the word *bureaucracy* calls to mind, the federal government needs large agencies to gather information, maintain records, educate the public, provide services, and enforce laws. As the national government enters new policy arenas or emphasizes new policy goals, such as homeland security in the aftermath of the terrorist attacks of September 11, 2001, the bureaucracy changes through reorganization and reallocations of money and personnel.

The bureaucracy plays a major role in public policy through a form of the lobbying decision makers pathway. Government agencies influence policy in several ways, none of which are clearly visible to the public or well covered by the media. Personnel in government agencies must implement the laws enacted by Congress and the policy initiatives developed by the president. If officials in the bureaucracy lack resources, knowledge, motivation, or supervision, the impact (or lack thereof) of policies on citizens' lives may differ from the outcomes intended by legislative policymakers and the executive branch. This occurred when MMS officials failed to fulfill their responsibilities for inspecting and supervising offshore oil drilling platforms in the Gulf of Mexico, as discussed at the beginning of this chapter. By becoming too closely tied to the oil companies that they were supposed to oversee, these MMS officials did not enforce laws on safety standards.

Congress and the president rely on the bureaucracy for information and expertise about many policy issues. Officials in the bureaucracy may influence legislation through formal testimony to congressional committees as well as through informal contacts in the issue networks with committee staffers and interest groups. Officials in the bureaucracy also create law and policy through rule-making processes for developing, changing, and eliminating regulations. Modern presidents see the rule-making process as a means to advance their policy agendas without seeking the approval of Congress—and often without announcing to the public the precise implications of the changes that have been made. In light of the bureaucracy's daily involvement in the complete range of policy issues affecting the United States, this component of national government will remain extremely important and influential, despite the fact that the American public does not recognize or understand its actions and impact.

KEY CONCEPT MAP How do elements of the bureaucracy both strengthen and weaken its effectiveness?

Creation of New Departments

PROTECTING THE HOMELAND

Strengths

As the country faces new policy challenges, new departments can be created to increase the federal government's expertise, resources, and capacity to take action.

Weaknesses

The creation of new departments contributes to the size and expense of the bureaucracy; it also enables the federal government to affect policy areas that may be handled better by states and cities.

Critical Thinking Questions

If you had to eliminate an existing federal government department, which department would you eliminate and why? Are there additional federal government departments that should be added to address specific policy issues?

Appointed Political Leaders as Agency Heads

Strengths

Experienced political leaders, such as former governors and members of Congress, are accustomed to dealing with a variety of policy issues and are skilled at dealing with legislators, the news media, and other government officials.

Weaknesses

Political leaders may not have enough issue-specific expertise or be effective at managing complex organizations; they may also have compromising ties to interest groups and political parties.

Critical Thinking Questions

What if all cabinet secretaries had to meet specific educational and experience qualifications to be appointed to their positions? Would departments be run more effectively? Why or why not?

Civil Service Selection Process

Strengths

Civil service employees are hired based on educational qualifications, experience, and expertise. They are protected from being fired for political reasons, which encourages them to make decisions based on expertise, not politics.

Weaknesses

Civil service employees often resist the president's efforts to initiate new policy priorities. They may not be easily fired if they do their jobs poorly or disobey the president.

Critical Thinking Questions

What if all civil service employees could be fired when the president or politically appointed department heads were dissatisfied with their performance? How would that affect government operations?

Privatization

Strengths

The government can give contracts to private businesses that may be able to perform a variety of services and functions in a more efficient and cost-effective manner.

Weaknesses

Private contracts are often steered to friends and political supporters, and the government cannot easily supervise or control how well private contractors do their jobs.

Critical Thinking Questions

Are there specific government functions and services that should never be placed under the control of private contractors? Which functions? Why?

Many Americans have a negative image of the bureaucracy. It can be easy to overlook the role of government agencies in providing the facilities and services that make modern society possible. Without roads, schools, airports, drinking water, sewage systems, and other government services, we would have a very different society. —*If you were running for*

Congress, would you tell voters that the federal government is "too big," "not big enough," or merely "underappreciated" at its current size? What would you do to either change the size of government or to change voters' perceptions about the bureaucracy?

Review of Key Objectives

The Federal Bureaucracy

 8.1 Trace the development of specific federal departments and agencies.

(pages 228–233)

The bureaucracy in the executive branch of the federal government is composed of departments, independent agencies, independent regulatory commissions, and government corporations that have authority over specific topics across the vast array of policy issues facing the United States. The specific departments were created over the course of history as the country encountered policy issues that required the attention of the federal government. The original departments created at the formation of the Constitution, including Treasury and State, reflected recognition of the flaws in the previous Articles of Confederation. Other departments were created later in history as the nation faced new issues such as urbanization, educational reform, and large numbers of aging veterans from World War II and other wars in need of medical care.

KEY TERMS

Bureaucracy 228
Departments 231
Independent Agencies 231
Independent Regulatory Commissions 231
Government Corporations 231

CRITICAL THINKING QUESTIONS

1. Are there any federal departments that are unnecessary because their missions could be handled better by state government or private organizations? How would public policy be different without these agencies?
2. Are there any new departments that should be created in the federal government (e.g., Department of Economic Development) or any agencies that should become cabinet-level departments?

INTERNET RESOURCES

Read about the organization and responsibilities of a federal department, such as the U.S. Department of Transportation at http://www.dot.gov or the U.S. Department of Homeland Security at http://www.dhs.gov

ADDITIONAL READING

Goodsell, Charles T. *The Case for the Bureaucracy,* 4th ed. Washington, DC: CQ Press, 2003.

Departments and Independent Agencies

 8.2 Analyze the debate over whether the heads of federal agencies should be policy experts or loyal political appointees.

(pages 234–239)

The executive branch is organized into departments. The president appoints a secretary to head each department, as well as the attorney general to lead the Department of Justice. These appointees (plus the heads of a few other designated agencies) constitute the president's cabinet. Political appointees may be politicians or individuals with policy expertise who share the president's policy goals. However, most personnel in the bureaucracy are civil service employees who remain on the job as presidents come and go. Although political appointees are typically committed to the president's agenda, the central role of political appointees at the top of government agencies raises questions about whether these individuals have enough knowledge about the issue areas for which they bear responsibility.

CRITICAL THINKING QUESTIONS

1. Should there be minimum qualifications related to education and expertise in order to gain a presidential appointment to lead a department or other agency managed by a political appointee?
2. Is it important for Americans to see diversity in the president's cabinet? Why or why not?

INTERNET RESOURCES

Read about the individual appointees in the president's cabinet and find links to the departments of the executive branch at http://www.whitehouse.gov/government/cabinet.html

Independent agencies have their own Web sites, such as the Federal Communications Commission at http://www.fcc.gov, the Federal Trade Commission at http://www.ftc.gov, and the National Labor Relations Board at http://www.nlrb.gov

ADDITIONAL READING

Katzmann, Robert A. *Regulatory Bureaucracy.* Cambridge, MA: MIT Press, 1979.

Kettl, Donald F., and James W. Fesler. *The Politics of the Administrative Process,* 4th ed. Washington, DC: CQ Press, 2008.

The Nature of Bureaucracy

8.3 Describe the image people have of the federal bureaucracy, and evaluate the bureaucracy's advantages and disadvantages.

(pages 240–245)

The popular image of the bureaucracy is of large, impersonal organizations that are inefficient and unresponsive. The advantages of a bureaucracy stem from providing organizations with clear lines of authority in which each employee has specific responsibilities and expertise. Ideally, bureaucracies are useful for standardization and consistency in providing government services. However, bureaucracies often fall short of their intended performance goals. As a result, critics have suggested that private businesses should assume responsibility for some of the tasks currently handled by government.

KEY TERMS

Patronage System (Spoils Systems) 242
Civil Service System 242
Hatch Act 242
Decentralization 244
Privatization 244
Senior Executive Service (SES) 245

CRITICAL THINKING QUESTIONS

1. Do the advantages of bureaucracy outweigh the disadvantages?
2. What are the advantages and disadvantages of privatization? Can you think of examples of the privatization of government functions that have worked well or worked poorly?

INTERNET RESOURCES

Learn about job opportunities and employment policies in the federal civil service at http://www.usajobs.gov and at the Web site for the U.S. Office of Personnel Management at http://www.opm.gov

Read a report by the Urban Institute on the privatization of government social services at http://www.urban.org/publications/407023.html

ADDITIONAL READING

Meier, Kenneth J., and Laurence J. O'Toole. *Bureaucracy in a Democratic State: A Governance Perspective*. Baltimore: Johns Hopkins University Press, 2006.

Wilson, James Q. *Bureaucracy: What Government Agencies Do and Why They Do It*. New York: Basic Books, 1991.

The Lobbying Pathway and Policymaking

8.4 Assess the mechanisms and processes that influence and oversee the federal bureaucracy.

(pages 246–251)

The bureaucracy implements statutes and creates regulations, but its effectiveness is limited by its resources, information, and expertise.

Whistleblowers in the bureaucracy provide information about misconduct within agencies. They are supposed to be protected from retaliation because they are helping to enhance accountability by calling attention to agencies' failings.

Presidents use the rule-making process to advance policy agendas through regulations and thereby steer the bureaucracy's actions. The rule-making process also provides opportunities for interest groups to influence regulations. Congress uses oversight mechanisms, such as holding hearings that require testimony from agency officials or enacting new legislation to limit actions by government agencies.

KEY TERMS

Iron Triangle 246
Issue Networks (Policy Communities) 246
Whistleblowers 248
Whistleblower Protection Act 248
Regulations 248
Administrative Law Judge (ALJ) 249

CRITICAL THINKING QUESTIONS

1. Do the unelected officials in government agencies possess too much power in the process for creating regulations?
2. Do adequate mechanisms exist to hold bureaucrats accountable for their decisions and actions?

INTERNET RESOURCES

Read published proposed regulations awaiting public comments at http://www.regulations.gov

ADDITIONAL READING

Foreman, Christopher H., Jr. *Signals from the Hill: Congressional Oversight and the Challenge of Social Regulation*. New Haven, CT: Yale University Press, 1988.

Gormley, William T., and Steven J. Balla. *Bureaucracy and Democracy: Accountability and Performance*, 2nd ed. Washington, DC: CQ Press, 2007.

Chapter Review Test Your Knowledge

1. Why do bureaucracies exist?
   a. Individuals naturally seek to pass their authority and power into the hands of groups.
   b. Bureaucracies are intended to prevent politicians from having power over public policy.
   c. Bureaucracies carry out the work of the organizations in an efficient and effective way.
   d. Bureaucracies don't exist; the term refers to a misconception about how government operates.

2. Why is the federal bureaucracy as big as it is?
   a. The size of the federal bureaucracy reflects the policy objectives and commitments of the national government.
   b. Its size is mandated by Article II of the Constitution.
   c. The federal budget deficit has caused 35 cabinet-level departments to be abolished since 2002.
   d. The U.S. Supreme Court instructed Congress to create a specific number of agencies.

3. How does the bureaucracy share public policymaking with other governmental entities?
   a. The president shapes laws that help define public policy; Congress directs bureaucratic agencies to carry out those laws.
   b. Congress and the president create laws to define public policy; officials working in federal agencies carry out those laws and policies.
   c. Experts in bureaucratic agencies enact statutes that are implemented by the president unless Congress vetoes the statutes.
   d. Working upward through a vertical hierarchy of authority, bureaucratic experts inform the president of laws that are necessary to conform to his political views; the president urges Congress to write and pass the appropriate legislation, which the judiciary then signs into law.

4. Which federal agency has the primary responsibility for responding to oil spills in the ocean?
   a. None. It is the responsibility of state and local agencies.
   b. Department of Energy
   c. U.S. Department of Emergency Preparedness
   d. U.S. Coast Guard

5. A successful political candidate or party rewarding supporters with government jobs and firing supporters of the opposing party is known as
   a. gerrymandering.
   b. logrolling.
   c. the merit system.
   d. the spoils system.

6. How many different organizational entities are in the federal bureaucracy?
   a. one (departments)
   b. two (departments and independent agencies)
   c. three (departments, independent agencies, and independent regulatory commissions)
   d. four (departments, independent agencies, independent regulatory commissions, and government corporations)

7. The creation of the Department of Health, Education, and Welfare (HEW) in the 1950s
   a. marked the expansion of the bureaucracy into policy areas that the Constitution did not anticipate.
   b. was a natural extension of the Constitution's original emphasis on federal responsibilities for public education.
   c. required a constitutional amendment, because it radically departed from the policy focus prescribed in the Constitution.
   d. shifted federal authority in policy matters from the legislative to the executive branch.

8. New departments of the federal government have generally been created
   a. because of new amendments added to the Constitution.
   b. because events and changes in American society presented the government with new challenges.
   c. because presidents issued executive orders that created new departments that were of interest to that particular president.
   d. because members of the president's cabinet decided to eliminate existing departments without consulting with Congress.

9. What do the heads of federal executive departments do?
   a. They work within their departments to make sure the officials and employees beneath them are content and well-compensated.
   b. They act as a liaison between the department and the economy.
   c. They work directly for the president in trying to make their department respond in accordance with the president's policy preferences.
   d. They act as a buffer between their own department and foreign governments.

10. Regulatory entities are usually called
   a. councils.
   b. advisory boards.
   c. agencies.
   d. caucuses.

11. The FCC is
   a. a governmental corporation.
   b. an independent agency.
   c. a department.
   d. an independent regulatory commission.

12. "Iron triangles" are required by the Constitution as a means to hold the bureaucracy accountable.
   a. true
   b. false

13. People's negative perceptions of the federal bureaucracy are often unfair
   a. because all federal employees are always working hard and in the best interests of the public at large.
   b. because federal employees do not receive good wages or benefits.
   c. because people often do not realize the difficult challenges of administering government programs.
   d. because "red tape" is an urban myth.

14. Why was the civil service merit system enacted?
    a. so that federal employees would become more courteous on the job
    b. so that federal employees would get and retain their jobs based on their competence, not their political affiliation or personal connections
    c. so that federal employees could be legally bound to carry out their responsibilities effectively
    d. so that federal employees could be held to consistent performance standards and could be fired if their superiors disliked them

15. What is a significant practical problem with the federal bureaucracy?
    a. Standards of competence are so high that it becomes difficult to find and retain suitable employees.
    b. There are few people who want to work for the federal government.
    c. Its size makes it slow to change or respond to policy shifts signaled from the president or Congress.
    d. Workers are fired so frequently at the whim of cabinet members that agencies cannot develop enough expertise to understand the laws that must be carried out.

16. What risks are faced by whistleblowers?
    a. They may be demoted or lose their jobs if protective laws are not applied to them.
    b. They may be arrested for revealing confidential information to members of Congress.
    c. They may be sued by newspaper reporters for defamation.
    d. They face no risks and are most likely to be given awards for service.

17. Why are critics worried about the pattern of officials leaving the federal bureaucracy to join interest groups or lobbying firms in the same field of interest—and even returning to government service in that same field?
    a. because they can often get cynical and burned out
    b. because this pattern prevents a particular issue network from including a diverse group of participants

    c. because such individuals might lack sufficient expertise
    d. because the agencies might in effect become too heavily influenced by alliances in the private sector

18. Why do the Congressional Budget Office and the Government Accountability Office exist?
    a. to gather and communicate to Congress information available only to Washington insiders
    b. to communicate the results of congressional hearings to the public
    c. to gather and provide to Congress information undistorted by the political agendas of the president or bureaucratic agencies
    d. to monitor, in a nonpartisan way, the budgetary and policy actions of the federal courts—especially excise courts

19. When a new president enters the White House, the new administration is likely to
    a. permit Congress to control government agencies until the Supreme Court has confirmed the cabinet's membership.
    b. fire most employees in the federal bureaucracy in order to replace them with political appointees.
    c. seek to issue new regulations that advance the president's policy preferences.
    d. ignore the bureaucracy and let it keep doing its job as it has always done in prior administrations.

20. When government agencies unduly influence the development of new statutes and policy through the "iron triangle" or issue networks, the public
    a. usually finds out about it from the news media.
    b. usually finds out about it from governmental publications.
    c. almost never finds out about it.
    d. really does not need to know about it.

PEARSON mypoliscilab Exercises

Apply what you learned in this chapter on **MyPoliSciLab**.

Read on **mypoliscilab.com**

    eText: Chapter 8

Study and **Review** on **mypoliscilab.com**

    Pre-Test
    Post-Test
    Chapter Exam
    Flashcards

Watch on **mypoliscilab.com**

    Video: The CDC and the Swine Flu
    Video: Internal Problems at the FDA

Explore on **mypoliscilab.com**

Simulation: You Are a Deputy Director of the Census Bureau
Simulation: You Are the Head of the FEMA
Simulation: You Are the President of the MEDICORP
Simulation: You Are a Federal Administrator
Comparative: Comparing Bureaucracies
Timeline: The Evolution of the Federal Bureaucracy
Visual Literacy: The Changing Face of Federal Bureaucracy

The Judiciary

KEY OBJECTIVES

After completing this chapter, you should be prepared to:

9.1 Explain how American court systems are organized.

9.2 Identify the reasons why American judges are powerful actors in the governing system.

9.3 Outline the selection process for federal judges.

9.4 Explain the theories concerning how Supreme Court justices reach their decisions.

9.5 Characterize the litigation strategies used in the court pathway.

9.6 Evaluate the courts' effectiveness in enforcing judicial decisions.

9.7 Describe the debate over whether it is appropriate for judges to shape public policy in a democracy.

How much power should judges have?

The assistant principal at Safford Middle School in Arizona called 13-year-old Savana Redding into his office. He showed her an open planner containing knives and a cigarette. Savana admitted it was her planner but denied owning any of the items. She said that she had loaned the planner to a friend several days earlier. She also denied any knowledge about prescription-strength pain pills in the possession of the assistant principal. A search of Savana's backpack failed to reveal any pills. Because a student claimed that Savana had pills with her, the assistant principal sent her into a room with two female staff members who ordered her to remove her pants and shirt. Savana was told to pull open her underwear and shake it from side to side so that the staff members could see if she had hidden any pills in her underclothing. Afterward, Savana's parents felt that the intrusive and embarrassing search was unjustified and had violated Savana's Fourth Amendment right against unreasonable searches. They filed a lawsuit against school officials and sought financial compensation for the alleged rights violation.

The case made its way to the U.S. Supreme Court, where Savana was represented by an attorney from the American Civil Liberties Union (ACLU), an interest group that uses litigation in the courts to advance its vision of constitutional rights. On June 25, 2009, the Supreme Court announced its decision in the case of *Safford Unified School District* v. *Redding*. By a vote of 8 to 1, the justices concluded that Savana's Fourth Amendment rights had indeed been violated. They referred the case back to the lower courts to determine whether the school district should pay money to the Redding family to remedy the rights violation.

Courts are available as third-party dispute resolvers when individuals, interest groups, or businesses have disputes with each other or with government officials. Some lawsuits filed in courts are also motivated by a desire to use court processes to shape public policy. The case *Safford Unified School District* v. *Redding* illustrates the power of judges to interpret the U.S. Constitution and thereby issue policy directives that tell government officials—in this case, public school staff members—what they can and cannot do.

Resource Center
• Glossary
• Vocabulary Example
• Connect the Link

■ **Adversarial System:** Legal system used by the United States and other countries in which a judge plays a relatively passive role as attorneys battle to protect each side's interests.

EXAMPLE: *As the Supreme Court's justices listened, the attorney from the American Civil Liberties Union argued vigorously on behalf of Savana Redding, while the attorney for the school district tried to defend the actions of school officials.*

Court Structure and Processes

9.1 Explain how American court systems are organized.

(pages 260–265)

American courts use an **adversarial system**■, in which opposing attorneys represent the interests of their clients. By contrast, many other countries use an **inquisitorial system,** in which judges take an active role in investigating cases and questioning witnesses. The U.S. judicial branch is made up of courts that process disputes, determine whether accused individuals have committed crimes, define individuals' rights, and shape public policy. There are two types of courts—trial and appellate—and both types operate in two parallel court systems—state and federal. Dramatic depictions on television and in movies typically show only one type of proceeding (trials) in one type of court (trial courts). They do not adequately convey the idea that most cases in trial courts are settled through plea bargains or negotiated settlements, rather than through trials. Television portrayals also won't educate you about the U.S. Supreme Court and other appellate courts that consider whether errors occurred when a judge or jury decided a case in a trial court.

Trial Courts

The United States has a **dual court system**■. In other words, two court systems, state and federal, exist and operate at the same time in the same geographic areas (see Table 9.1). Sometimes a state court and a federal court are right next door to each other in a downtown district. In small cities and towns, a courthouse may be run by a single judge. In larger cities, a dozen or more judges may hear cases separately in their own courtrooms within a single courthouse. Both court systems handle **criminal prosecutions,** which involve accusations that one or more individuals broke the law and therefore should be punished. In addition, both systems handle **civil lawsuits,** in which people or corporations seek compensation from those whom they accuse of violating contracts or causing personal injuries or property damage. Civil lawsuits can also seek orders from judges requiring the government, corporations, or individuals to take specific actions or refrain from behavior that violates the law.

The existence of two court systems within each state reflects American federalism, under which state governments and the federal government both exercise authority over law and public policy. States are free to design their own court systems and to name the different courts within the state. Thus, in some states, trial courts are called "superior courts," while in others, they are known as "district courts," "circuit courts," or "courts of common pleas."

Federal trial courts are called "U.S. district courts." The country is divided into 94 districts. Each state has at least one district and

one district court, and larger states have multiple districts. Within each district, there may be multiple judges and courthouses. For example, Wisconsin is divided into the Eastern District of Wisconsin, with courthouses at Milwaukee and Green Bay, and the Western District of Wisconsin, with its courthouse located in Madison. These courts handle cases concerning federal law, such as those based on the U.S. Constitution and statutes (laws) enacted by Congress, as well as certain lawsuits between citizens of different states.

Trial courts use specific rules and processes to reach decisions. Lawyers present arguments to a group of citizen jurors in a **jury trial.** In such a trial, the judge acts as a "referee," who makes sure proper rules are followed and the jurors understand the rules of law that will guide their decisions in determining the facts and issuing a verdict in favor of one side. When requested by defendants, cases use bench trials, in which a single judge rather than a jury is the decision maker. Trial courts are courts of **original jurisdiction,** meaning they receive cases first, consider the available evidence, and make the initial decision.

Although the trial is the final possible stage for these lower-level courts, most cases do not get that far. Trial courts actually process most cases through negotiated resolutions, called **settlements** in civil cases and **plea bargains** in criminal cases. Settlements and plea bargains can save time and money for lawyers and courts. They may also benefit the individuals involved by providing a mutually agreed upon outcome and, in criminal cases, a less-than-maximum sentence.

The trial of Saddam Hussein in Iraq for crimes committed against the people of his country included many features that are familiar in American trials, including arguments by attorneys and rulings by a judge. There were also differences in the Iraqi trial, such as the absence of a jury.
—*Why is so much time and money spent on a lengthy trial when everyone agrees that an individual has committed horrible acts?*

■ **Dual Court System:** Separate systems of state and federal courts throughout the United States. Each state court system is responsible for interpreting the laws and constitution of that specific state, while the federal courts are responsible for the U.S. Constitution and laws enacted by Congress.

EXAMPLE: *In 2001, the Georgia Supreme Court used its independent power under the dual court system to rule that use of the electric chair for capital punishment violated the state's constitution, although the U.S. Supreme Court has never formally declared that its use violates the U.S. Constitution.*

TABLE 9.1A   Structure of the American Court System

FEDERAL COURT SYSTEM		STATE COURT SYSTEM
U.S. Supreme Court		**52 State Supreme Courts***
Original jurisdiction in only limited categories of cases that rarely arise: lawsuits between two states and cases involving foreign ambassadors. Appellate jurisdiction in almost all cases that it decides that arrive from U.S. courts of appeals or state supreme courts or Court of Military Appeals.	*Courts of Last Resort*	Appellate jurisdiction for cases concerning state law brought up through their state court systems. There are more than 50 state supreme courts because two states— Texas and Oklahoma—have separate highest courts for civil and criminal cases.
13 U.S. Courts of Appeals		**40 State Courts of Appeals***
No original jurisdiction because no cases are first filed in these courts. These courts handle appeals from cases that were first decided in the U.S. district courts or matters decided by government regulatory commissions.	*Intermediate Appellate Courts*	Appellate jurisdiction over cases from state trial courts. No original jurisdiction. 10 states do not have intermediate appellate courts. Appeals in those states go straight from the trial court to the state supreme court.
94 U.S. District Courts		**State Trial Courts (50 states)**
Original jurisdiction in cases involving: federal criminal and civil law; the federal government; and lawsuits between citizens of different states for amounts over $75,000; bankruptcy; and admiralty (shipping at sea).	*Trial Courts of General Jurisdiction*	Usually called superior courts, district courts, circuit courts, or courts of common pleas. These courts have original jurisdiction and therefore are the first courts to hear cases concerning state law issues for felonies and other serious matters.
(no limited jurisdiction trial court with life-tenured federal judges)		**Lower-level State Trial Courts**
Federal cases begin in the U.S. district courts.	*Trial Courts of Limited Jurisdiction*	Original jurisdiction for minor criminal and civil cases.

TABLE 9.1B   Paths to the U.S. Supreme Court for Criminal and Civil Cases in State and Federal Court Systems

FEDERAL CRIMINAL CASE	FEDERAL CIVIL CASE	STATE CRIMINAL CASE	STATE CIVIL CASE
U.S. Supreme Court	**U.S. Supreme Court**	**U.S. Supreme Court**	**U.S. Supreme Court**
U.S. v. *Stevens* (2010) Decision: Federal law that makes it a crime to sell depictions of animal cruelty (e.g., films of dog fights) violates the right to free expression under the First Amendment (defendant wins)	*United Student Aid Funds* v. *Espinosa* (2010) Decision: A bankruptcy court can discharge a student loan debt even if the student did not claim undue hardship (individual wins)	*Graham* v. *Florida* (2010) Decision: Eighth Amendment violation when a juvenile is sentenced to life without parole for a nonhomicide offense (defendant wins)	*Kelo* v. *New London* (2005) Decision: No constitutional violation when city used its power to force homeowners to sell home so that a private developer could use the property (claimant loses)
U.S. Court of Appeals	**U.S. Court of Appeals**	**Florida Supreme Court**	**Connecticut Supreme Court**
Defendant wins	Individual wins	Defendant loses	Claimant loses
U.S. District Court	**U.S. District Court**	**Florida Appellate Court**	**Connecticut Superior Court**
Defendant loses	Individual loses	Defendant loses	Claimant wins
		Florida Circuit Court	
		Defendant loses	

*States use different names for their courts of last resort (e.g., Court of Appeals in New York and Maryland, Supreme Judicial Court in Maine and Massachusetts).

■ **Majority Opinion:** Appellate court opinion that explains the reasons for the case outcome as determined by a majority of judges.

EXAMPLE: *On behalf of eight of the nine justices, Justice David Souter's majority opinion in Savana Redding's case clarified the legal rule that public school officials cannot strip search students based on an unsupported claim of another student (Safford Unified School District v. Redding, 2009).*

Appellate Courts

Appellate courts have **appellate jurisdiction,** meaning they review specific errors that allegedly occurred in trial court processes or in decisions of appellate courts beneath them in the judicial hierarchy. Most states, as well as the federal court system, have **intermediate appellate courts.** These courts, which are typically called "courts of appeals," hear appeals from judicial decisions and jury verdicts in the trial courts. In the federal system, the U.S. courts of appeals are divided into 11 numbered circuits, and there is also the District of Columbia circuit and a specialized federal circuit for patent and trade cases. The numbered circuits each handle the appeals from districts in specific states (see Figure 9.1). For example, the U.S. Court of Appeals for the Fifth Circuit handles appeals from U.S. district courts in Texas, Louisiana, and Mississippi.[1]

The highest appellate courts in the state and federal systems are **courts of last resort.** In the federal system, the U.S. Supreme Court is the court of last resort. It can also be the court of last resort when issues of federal law, such as questions about civil liberties under the Bill of Rights, arise in cases decided by state supreme courts. State supreme courts are courts of last resort for disputes about the meaning of laws created by a state legislature or about provisions of a state constitution.

There are no juries in appellate courts, and typically three judges hear cases in a state or federal intermediate appellate court. State supreme courts generally have five or seven members, while the U.S. Supreme Court has nine justices. These courts do not make decisions about criminal guilt or issue verdicts in civil cases. Instead, they consider narrow issues concerning alleged errors in the investigation and trial process that were not corrected by the trial judge. Instead of listening to witnesses or examining other evidence, appellate courts consider only elaborate written arguments, called **appellate briefs,** submitted by each side's attorneys, as well as oral arguments.

Appellate judges issue detailed written opinions to explain their decisions. The outcome of the case and any announcements of a legal rule are expressed in the **majority opinion**■. This opinion represents the views of the majority of judges who heard the case. **Concurring opinions** are written by judges who agree with the outcome favored by the majority but wish to present their own reasons for agreeing with the decision. Appellate decisions are not always unanimous, so judges who disagree with the outcome may write **dissenting opinions**■ to express their points of disagreement with the views expressed in the majority opinion.[2] Sometimes concurring and dissenting opinions develop ideas that will take hold in later generations and help shape law after new judges are selected for service on appellate courts.

FIGURE 9.1 ■ Geographic Jurisdiction of Federal Courts

The U.S. Courts of Appeals are divided into regional circuits throughout the country. Each numbered circuit handles appeals from federal cases in a specific set of states. —*In which circuit do you live?*

SOURCE: Map of Federal Court Circuits, Web site of the Administrative Office of the U.S. Courts. Accessed at http://www.uscourts.gov/Federal Courts.aspx on April 11, 2010.

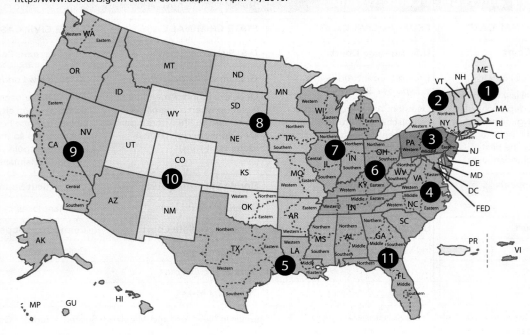

■ **Dissenting Opinion:** Appellate court opinion explaining the views of one or more judges who disagree with the outcome of the case as decided by the majority of judges.

EXAMPLE: *In Savana Redding's case, Justice Clarence Thomas wrote a dissenting opinion that explained his disagreement with the majority opinion and asserted that Savana Redding's Fourth Amendment rights were not violated by the school's strip search to look for illegal pills.*

The U.S. Supreme Court

At the top of the American judicial system stands the U.S. Supreme Court. The Court is an unusual appellate court in that it also has original jurisdiction in limited categories of cases defined in Article III of the U.S. Constitution, usually lawsuits between the governments of two states. The U.S. Supreme Court has authority over federal court cases and any decision by a state court (including those of a state supreme court) that concerns the U.S. Constitution or federal law. In particular, the U.S. Supreme Court is regularly called on to decide whether state statutes violate the U.S. Constitution or whether decisions and actions by state and local officials collide with federal constitutional principles. The U.S. Supreme Court's decisions shape law and public policy for the entire country. Policy advocates often seek favorable decisions from the Court when they have been unsuccessful in persuading other branches of government to advance their goals. Table 9.2 gives the names and backgrounds of the current justices of the Court.

Each case goes through several specific stages in the Supreme Court's decision-making process:

- The justices choose 70 to 80 cases to hear from among more than 7,000 petitions submitted annually by people and corporations.
- Nearly all cases are presented to the Court through a petition for a **writ of certiorari,** a traditional legal order that commands a lower court to send a case forward.

Cases are selected for hearing through the Court's "rule of four," meaning that four justices must vote to hear a specific case in order for it to be scheduled for oral arguments.

- Attorneys in the chosen cases submit detailed written arguments, called *appellate briefs,* for the justices to study before the case is argued.
- At oral arguments, each side's attorney may speak for only 30 minutes, and the justices often interrupt and ask many questions. The justices also sometimes exchange argumentative comments with each other.
- After oral arguments, the nine justices meet privately in their weekly conference to present their views to each other. When all the justices have stated a position, the chief justice announces the preliminary vote based on the viewpoints expressed. The side that gains the support of five or more justices wins.
- The justices prepare and announce the majority opinion that decides the case as well as additional viewpoints expressed in concurring and dissenting opinions. If the chief justice is in the majority, he designates which justice will write the majority opinion for the Court. If the chief justice is in the minority, then the senior justice in the majority assigns the opinion for the Court. Other justices can decide for themselves whether to write a concurring or dissenting opinion. With the assistance of their law clerks, justices draft preliminary opinions as well as comments on other justices'

Supreme Court Justice Sonia Sotomayor is sworn in by Chief Justice John Roberts in 2009. Justice Sotomayor's parents were born in Puerto Rico, and she is considered the first Hispanic justice to serve on the nation's highest court. —*Is it important that the Supreme Court's composition represent the nation's diversity with respect to race, gender, ethnicity, religion, and other demographic factors? Why or why not?*

TABLE 9.2 | Supreme Court Justices

The rate of support for civil rights and liberties claims is typically used to classify justices as "liberal" (frequent support) or "conservative" (infrequent support).

   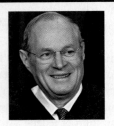

NAME	SONIA SOTOMAYOR	STEPHEN G. BREYER	RUTH BADER GINSBURG	ANTHONY M. KENNEDY
Support for Civil Rights and Liberties Claims, 2009–2010	63%	60%	44%	28%
Nominated by	Barack Obama	Bill Clinton	Bill Clinton	Ronald Reagan
Date Confirmed	August 6, 2009	August 3, 1994	August 10, 1993	February 18, 1988
Confirmation Vote Numbers	68–31	87–9	96–3	97–0
Previous Experience	Federal Judge, Prosecutor	Federal Judge, Law Professor	Federal Judge, Law Professor	Federal Judge, Law Professor

draft opinions. These draft opinions and comments are circulated to all the justices. They help shape the ultimate reasoning of the final opinions issued in the case and can sometimes persuade wavering justices to change sides.

• When the decision of the Court is publicly announced and the opinions for that case are published, the decision becomes final. The legal rule announced in the decision, however, is not necessarily permanent, because the justices can later change their views. If at least five justices agree that the prior decision was wrongly decided, they can use a new case to overrule the Court's earlier opinion and establish a new rule of law on the subject in question. Presidents often focus on this goal when they select new appointees for the Supreme Court, with the hope that the new justices will vote to overrule decisions with which the president disagrees.

JOHN G. ROBERTS, JR.	CLARENCE THOMAS	ANTONIN SCALIA	SAMUEL ANTHONY ALITO, JR.	ELENA KAGAN
20%	16%	12%	16%	N/A
George W. Bush	George H. W. Bush	Ronald Reagan	George W. Bush	Barack Obama
September 29, 2005	October 23, 1991	September 26, 1986	January 31, 2005	August 5, 2010
78–22	52–48	98–0	58–42	63–37
Federal Judge, Government Lawyer	Federal Judge, Government Administrator	Federal Judge, Law Professor	Federal Judge, Government Lawyer	Government Lawyer, Law Professor

Court Structure and Processes

9.1   Explain how American court systems are organized.

PRACTICE QUIZ: UNDERSTAND AND APPLY

1. Legal processes in which the government seeks to prove that an individual is guilty of a crime and deserving of punishment are called
   a. civil lawsuits.
   b. appellate arguments.
   c. criminal prosecutions.
   d. plea bargains.

2. How are most cases in lower-level courts resolved?
   a. jury or bench trial
   b. settlement or plea bargain
   c. criminal prosecution
   d. referral to a higher court

3. The final outcome and explanation for the decision in an appellate court case is expressed by the judges in a written rationale known as
   a. a majority opinion.
   b. a concurring opinion.
   c. a dissenting opinion.
   d. a case brief.

4. Appellate courts do not examine evidence or hear testimony from witnesses. They determine the outcome based solely on written appellate briefs and lawyers' oral arguments.
   a. true
   b. false

ANALYZE

1. Does the adversarial system lead courts to discover the truth, or does the system simply produce victory for whichever side has the best attorney?

2. Does a court system really need appellate courts? Why not just treat the original decision in each case as the final decision?

IDENTIFY THE CONCEPT THAT DOESN'T BELONG

a. Concurring opinion
b. Writ of certiorari
c. Dual court system
d. Veto
e. Appellate briefs

9.1

Resource Center
- Glossary
- Vocabulary Example
- Connect the Link

■ **Statutes:** Laws written by state legislatures and by Congress.

EXAMPLE: *The No Child Left Behind Act of 2002 was a statute enacted by Congress with the hope that students' academic performance would improve as a result of the law's requirements for testing schoolchildren.*

The Power of American Judges

9.2 **Identify the reasons why American judges are powerful actors in the governing system.**

(pages 266–271)

The eighteenth-century authors of the U.S. Constitution did not expect the judicial branch to be as powerful as the executive and legislative branches. Although some of the framers wanted to permit judges to evaluate the constitutionality of statutes, they did not generally believe that the courts would be influential policymaking institutions. In *Federalist No. 78,* Alexander Hamilton called the judiciary the "least dangerous" branch of government because it lacked the power of "purse or sword" that the other branches could use to shape policy and spur people to follow their decisions. Congress could use its "power of the purse" to levy taxes or provide government funds in order to encourage or induce people to comply with government policies. The president, as the nation's commander in chief, could use the "sword" of military action to force people to obey laws. But judges produced only words written on paper and thus appeared to lack the power to enforce their decisions.

Hamilton was not wrong to highlight the inherent weakness of the judiciary's structure and authority. He merely failed to foresee how the Supreme Court and other courts would assert their power and gain acceptance as policymaking institutions.

Despite lacking the constitutional power of the "purse" or "sword," the physical imagery of courts, as well as the dress and language associated with judges, helps convey the message that the judicial branch is powerful and different from other branches of government. Many courts operate in majestic buildings with marble columns, purple velvet curtains, fancy woodwork, and other physical embellishments designed to elicit respect for the importance and seriousness of these institutions. Judges wear black robes and sit on benches elevated above other seats in the courtroom, reinforcing their status and conveying a message that other citizens are subordinate to judicial officers. These elements encourage public acceptance of the courts' legitimate power and help to gain citizens' compliance with judicial decisions.

Perhaps even more important than the physical buildings or the judges' dress and language, however, are the structural elements and traditions in the American judicial system that make judges in the United States powerful actors in the country's governing system. These factors include judges' authority

Alexander Hamilton believed that the judiciary would be the least powerful branch of American government under the U.S. Constitution.
—*Although the judiciary became more powerful than Hamilton predicted, is it more or less powerful than the other branches of government?*

over constitutional and statutory interpretation, the power of judicial review, and in the federal court system, judges' protected tenure in office.

Constitutional and Statutory Interpretation

In the United States, although participants in constitutional conventions write constitutions and elected legislators draft laws referred to as **statutes**■, these forms of law still require judges to interpret them. Inevitably, the wording of constitutions and statutes contain ambiguities. Whenever there are disputes about the meaning of the words and phrases in constitutions and statutes, those disputes come to courts in the form of lawsuits, and judges are asked to provide interpretations that will settle those disputes. Therefore, judges can provide meaning for law produced by other governmental institutions, as well as for law they develop themselves in judicial decisions.

■ **Judicial Review:** The power of American judges to nullify decisions and actions by other branches of government, if the judges decide those actions violate the U.S. Constitution or the relevant state constitution.

EXAMPLE: *In 2010, the U.S. Supreme Court used the power of judicial review to declare aspects of the Bipartisan Campaign Reform Act of 2002 to be unconstitutional for limiting corporations' free speech rights involved in spending money to support or oppose political candidates.*

Legal rules created by judges' decisions are typically referred to as case law.

For example, the Eighth Amendment to the U.S. Constitution forbids the government to impose "cruel and unusual punishments." The provision intends to limit the nature of punishments applied to people who violate criminal laws. The words themselves, however, provide no specific guidance about what kinds of punishments are not allowed. Thus judges have been asked to decide which punishments are "cruel and unusual." Are these words violated when prison officials decline to provide medical care to prisoners? How about when a principal paddles a misbehaving student at a public high school? These are the kinds of cases that judges confront.

Statutes provide similar opportunities for judges to shape the law. Statutes for the entire country are produced by Congress. Each state has its own legislature to write laws that apply only within its borders. Judges, when they interpret statutes, are supposed to advance the underlying purposes of the legislature that made the statutes—but those purposes are not always clear. For example, if workers' compensation statutes provide for payments to workers injured "in the course of employment," does that include coverage for a disability resulting from slipping on an icy sidewalk by the employer's business? Inevitably, judges must answer such questions, because legislatures cannot anticipate every possible situation in which issues about a statute's meaning might arise.

As you will see in the later discussion of methods for selecting judges, political battles in the nomination processes for federal judges largely arise from the interpretive authority that American judges possess. Political parties, interest groups, and politicians seek to secure judgeships for people who share their values and who, they hope, will apply those values in judicial decision-making.

Judicial Review

One of the most significant powers of American judges is that of **judicial review**■—a process that permits judges to invalidate actions by other governmental actors. Judges can strike down statutes enacted by Congress or invalidate actions by the president (or other executive branch officials) by declaring that those statutes or actions violate the Constitution. As indicated in the examples in Table 9.3, federal judges often use their interpretations of the amendments in the Bill of Rights as the

TABLE 9.3	**Judicial Review**			
CASE NAME	**DATE**	**VOTE**	**AFFECTED INSTITUTION**	**OVERVIEW OF CASE**
Granholm, Governor of Michigan v. Heald	May 16, 2005	5–4	State legislatures in Michigan and New York	State laws in Michigan and New York prohibited direct sales of wine to consumers by out-of-state wineries—thus preventing Internet sales and other orders. The U.S. Supreme Court struck down these state laws as violating the Commerce Clause of the U.S. Constitution.
District of Columbia v. Heller	June 26, 2008	5–4	City Council of the District of Columbia	An ordinance enacted by local officials in the District of Columbia barred the ownership and possession of handguns by anyone other than police officers. The U.S. Supreme Court struck down the ordinance by declaring that the prohibition on law-abiding citizens keeping a handgun in their homes for self-protection violated the "right to bear arms" in the Second Amendment.
Hamdi v. Rumsfeld	June 28, 2004	8–1 on the issue in question	President	American citizens detained as terrorism suspects are entitled to appear in court and contest the basis for their detention. The U.S. Supreme Court rejected arguments about the president's power to hold suspects indefinitely without any rights, any contact with attorneys, or any access to the courts.
Citizens United v. Federal Election Commission	January 21, 2010	5–4	Congress	The U.S. Supreme Court invalidated a portion of the Bipartisan Campaign Reform Act of 2002 that sought to prevent corporations from spending funds to support or oppose political candidates. The majority concluded that the statute violated the First Amendment free speech rights of corporations.

■ *Marbury* v. *Madison* (1803): A case in which the U.S. Supreme Court asserted the power of judicial review, despite the fact that the concept is not explicitly mentioned in the U.S. Constitution.

EXAMPLE: *Chief Justice John Marshall and other members of the U.S. Supreme Court first used judicial review in Marbury v. Madison (1803) by declaring that a portion of the Judiciary Act of 1789 was unconstitutional because Congress improperly expanded the kinds of cases that could be filed in the Court.*

basis for judicial review. A leading constitutional law expert describes judicial review as "certainly the most controversial and at the same time the most fascinating role of the courts of the United States."[3]

Article III of the Constitution (reprinted in the Appendix) defines the authority of the judiciary, yet there is no mention of the judiciary's power of judicial review. The framers of the Constitution were aware of the concept, yet they made no mention of it in the founding document. Did this mean that the idea had been considered and rejected by the framers? Apparently not—in *Federalist No. 78,* one of the essays written to advocate for the ratification of the Constitution, Hamilton argued in favor of judicial review, asserting not only that legislative acts violating the Constitution must be invalid but also that federal judges must be the ones who decide whether statutes are unconstitutional. According to Hamilton, limitations on congressional actions "can be preserved in practice no other way than through the medium of the courts of justice, whose duty it must be to declare all acts

contrary to the manifest tenor of the constitution void." Other founders, however, worried that judicial review would elevate the power of the judiciary above that of the other governmental branches.

At the beginning of the nineteenth century, the Supreme Court first asserted its authority to review the actions of other governmental branches in the case of *Marbury* v. *Madison* (1803)■. William Marbury was one of many officials in the administration of Federalist President John Adams who received a last-minute judicial appointment as Adams was leaving office. The appointment of these "midnight judges" was an effort by Adams to place his supporters in positions of judicial influence to counteract the changes in government that would inevitably occur under the administration of the incoming president, Thomas Jefferson. However, in the rush of final activities, the outgoing secretary of state in the Adams administration, John Marshall, never managed to seal and deliver to Marbury his commission as a justice of the peace for the District of Columbia. When Jefferson took office, the

Chief Justice John Marshall's opinion in *Marbury* v. *Madison* helped to establish the concept of judicial review, an important power for American judges. This power was not specifically granted to judges by the U.S. Constitution. —*Do you think it was implied in that document, or did Marshall act improperly in announcing his opinion?*

■ **Impeachment:** Process in Congress for removal of the president, federal judges, and other high officials.

EXAMPLE: *Congress impeached Judge Walter Nixon and removed him from office in 1989 after he was convicted of perjury.*

incoming secretary of state, James Madison, refused to deliver these commissions to Marbury and several other judicial appointees. Marbury sought his commission by filing a legal action. He followed the requirements of the **Judiciary Act of 1789,** the initial act of Congress that designed the federal court system and established its procedures, by seeking a **writ of mandamus** from the U.S. Supreme Court. A writ of mandamus is a traditional legal order through which a court directs a government official to take a specific action required by law.

Marbury's legal action presented the Supreme Court with a difficult dilemma. The Court's new chief justice was John Marshall, also a last-minute Adams appointee—and the very man who had failed to seal and deliver Marbury's commission on time in the first place. If Marshall and the other justices decided that Marbury was entitled to his commission, it seemed very likely that President Jefferson and Secretary Madison would simply disobey the Court. If that were to happen, the Court would have had no practical means to force the president to act, undoubtedly tarnishing its legitimacy. Ultimately, the Supreme Court issued a decision that asserted the power of the judiciary without risking any appearance of weakness.

In a unanimous decision written by Chief Justice Marshall, the Court declared that Marbury was indeed entitled to his commission and that the Court possessed the authority to order President Jefferson to have the commission delivered to him. However, the Court declined to issue such an order to the president because—so it declared—the portion of the Judiciary Act of 1789 that directed litigants to file writs of mandamus directly in the Supreme Court was unconstitutional. Therefore, it ruled, Marbury had relied on an unconstitutional statute in seeking a writ of mandamus from the Supreme Court without first proceeding through the lower courts. According to the Court, statutes, such as the Judiciary Act, cannot define the kinds of cases that may be filed directly in the U.S. Supreme Court without being heard first in the lower courts. Article III of the Constitution specifically lists the kinds of cases in which the Supreme Court has original jurisdiction. Other cases must first be filed in lower courts and reach the Supreme Court through the appeals process. Any effort by Congress to expand that list amounts to an improper effort to alter the Constitution by statute rather than by constitutional amendment.

In general, the Supreme Court has appellate jurisdiction over cases decided in lower courts that are later brought to the highest court through appeals and other posttrial processes. The Constitution specifies that the Supreme Court will make the first or original decision only in cases concerning states and those involving high officials, such as ambassadors. Marbury's action seeking a writ of mandamus did not fit within these narrow categories of cases specified by the Constitution.

Ultimately, Marbury did not pursue his case again in the lower courts, and he never received his commission.

The decision in *Marbury* v. *Madison*—one of the most important Supreme Court decisions in American history—asserted the authority and importance of the Supreme Court without actually testing the Court's power in a confrontation with the president. The Court simply asserted the power of judicial review in striking down a portion of the Judiciary Act without providing any elaborate discussion in its opinion that would raise questions about whether such a power even existed under the Constitution.

The Court did not immediately begin to pass judgment on the appropriateness of executive and legislative actions. Instead, it waited more than 50 years before again asserting its power of judicial review. In 1857, in its highly controversial decision in *Dred Scott* v. *Sandford,* the Court invalidated the Missouri Compromise—a series of decisions by Congress in 1820 and 1821 that had put limits on the spread of slavery into western territories. By 1900, the Court came to use the power of judicial review more frequently, and eventually federal courts struck down hundreds of state statutes and more than 100 acts of Congress. Today judicial review is well entrenched in American governing processes and provides a primary source of judicial power.

Federal Judges' Protected Tenure

Article III of the Constitution specifies that federal judges will serve "during good Behaviour." Effectively, that means lifetime tenure, since these judges typically are removed through **impeachment**■ by Congress only if they commit a crime. The tenure granted to federal judges underscores the emphasis that the Constitution places on ensuring the independence of judicial decision makers. If judges are not afraid of losing their jobs by making unpopular decisions, then presumably they will do the right thing (see Figure 9.2). This protection may be especially important when judges make decisions that protect the rights of minorities. For example, many controversial judicial decisions in the mid-twentieth century advancing the equality of African Americans were vigorously criticized, because of widespread racial prejudice. At other times, unpopular court decisions have protected the interests of corporations and the wealthy. For example, in 2010, the U.S. Supreme Court outraged critics by ruling that corporations possess rights to freedom of speech that prevent Congress from enacting certain laws that seek to limit how much money corporations can spend in their efforts to influence political campaigns and election outcomes (*Citizens United* v. *Federal Election Commission,* 2010).

Because federal judges are exempted from democracy's traditional accountability mechanism—the need to face periodic

■ **Court-Packing Plan:** President Franklin D. Roosevelt's unsuccessful proposal in 1937 to permit the appointment of additional justices to the U.S. Supreme Court.

EXAMPLE: *President Roosevelt hoped to make the Supreme Court more supportive of his New Deal policies by proposing that the president appoint an additional justice whenever a sitting justice reached 70 years of age.*

elections, which often keeps other public officials from making unpopular decisions—judges are better positioned to make decisions that go against society's dominant values and policy preferences (see again Figure 9.2). This lack of accountability also creates the possibility that judges' decisions will go "too far" in shaping law and policy in ways that are unpopular and/or detrimental to society, resulting in a backlash against the courts.

A famous example of backlash against the Supreme Court arose in the late 1930s. In 1937, President Franklin D. Roosevelt was frustrated that the life-tenured justices on the Supreme Court were using their power of judicial review to invalidate New Deal legislation that he believed to be necessary to fight the Great Depression. As a result, he proposed restructuring the Supreme Court to permit the president to appoint an additional justice for each serving justice who reached the age of 70. His **"court-packing plan■,"** as the press and congressional opponents immediately branded it, would have enabled him to select six new justices immediately and thereby alter the Court's dynamics. Political and public opposition blocked Roosevelt's plan, but his actions demonstrated that decisions by life-tenured judges can stir controversy, especially when those decisions clash with policies preferred by the public and their elected representatives in government. The negative reaction against Roosevelt's attempt to pack the Court also demonstrated how much the American public had come to value the judiciary's independence.

FIGURE 9.2 ■ Length of Service of Modern Supreme Court Justices

Some justices have served for several decades and continued to decide cases even after they reached the age of 80. —*What would be a reason not to limit the term in office for Supreme Court justices?*

A Persistence of Vision

Recent Supreme Court justices have tended to remain on the bench longer, and later in life, than their predecessors. Here are the justices whose terms ended after 1940. *

A recent short-timer...

Arthur J. Goldberg
2 years, 9 months, 24 days

... and the record-holder:

William O. Douglas
36 years, 6 months, 25 days

	COURT TENURE	AGE OF JUSTICES
Charles E. Hughes	1910–16, 1930–41	
James C. McReynolds	1914–41	
James F. Byrnes	1941–42	
Owen J. Roberts	1930–45	
Harlan F. Stone	1925–46	
Frank Murphy	1940–49	
Wiley B. Rutledge	1943–49	
Fred M. Vinson	1946–53	
Robert H. Jackson	1941–54	
Sherman Minton	1949–56	
Stanley F. Reed	1938–57	
Harold H. Burton	1945–58	
Felix Frankfurter	1939–62	
Charles E. Whittaker	1957–62	
Arthur J. Goldberg	1962–65	
Thomas C. Clark	1949–67	
Earl Warren	1953–69	
Abe Fortas	1965–69	
Hugo Black	1937–71	
John M. Harlan	1955–71	
William O. Douglas	1939–75	
Potter Stewart	1958–81	
Warren E. Burger	1969–86	
Lewis F. Powell Jr.	1971–87	
William J. Brennan Jr.	1956–90	
Thurgood Marshall	1967–91	
Byron R. White	1962–93	
Harry A. Blackmun	1970–94	
William H. Rehnquist	1971–2005	
Sandra Day O'Connor	1981–2006	
David H. Souter	1990–2009	
John Paul Stevens	1975–2010	
CURRENT JUSTICES:		
Antonin Scalia	1986–	
Anthony M. Kennedy	1988–	
Clarence Thomas	1991–	
Ruth Bader Ginsburg	1993–	
Stephen G. Breyer	1994–	
John G. Roberts, Jr.	2005–	
Samuel A. Alito, Jr.	2006–	
Sonia Sotomayor	2009–	
Elena Kagan	2010–	

AGE OF JUSTICES: 40, 50, 60, 70, 80, 90

COURT TENURE
LIFESPAN

Listed in order of the end of court terms.

The dark shading shows years of Supreme Court service. Justice Black served for 34 years. **Can a judge remain in touch with society's current problems after 30 years on the bench?**

The endpoint of the line shows current or final age. Justice Stevens retired in 2010 at the age of 90. **Should there be an age limit for judges?**

The dark shading begins at age of appointment. Justice Thomas was only 43 when he was appointed. **Does such a young man have enough experience to serve on the Court?**

SOURCE: Photographs: AP Images (left) and George Tames/The New York Times. January 16, 2005, New York Times Graphics. Copyright © 2005 by the New York Times Co. Reprinted with permission. Updated from 2005 Supreme Court to 2009 Supreme Court (as of August, 2009) by permission of the publisher.

The Power of American Judges

9.2   Identify the reasons why American judges are powerful actors in the governing system.

PRACTICE QUIZ: UNDERSTAND AND APPLY

1. As originally conceived by the framers of the Constitution, the judicial branch of the government was supposed to be
   a. as powerful as the other two branches.
   b. more powerful than the legislative branch but less powerful than the executive branch.
   c. more powerful than the executive branch but less powerful than the legislative branch.
   d. less powerful than the other two branches.

2. The power of judicial review is defined in Article III of the U.S. Constitution.
   a. true   b. false

3. Why do judges need to interpret constitutions and statutes?
   a. because the legislators who draft these documents are not trained to do this interpretation themselves
   b. because all judges seize every opportunity to expand their own power
   c. because constitutions and statutes frequently contain ambiguities that need to be resolved
   d. because constitutions and statutes are not considered laws unless judges interpret them

4. Why does judicial review make U.S. judges powerful?
   a. because it grants them the authority to invalidate as unconstitutional statutes enacted by Congress and actions taken by the president
   b. because it comes with the trappings of authority: the black robe, the seat on high
   c. because it means they are appointed for life
   d. because it means they can intervene in any case, ask witnesses and litigants their own questions, and reach verdicts entirely on their own

ANALYZE

1. Does the power of judicial review improperly make the judicial branch more powerful than the executive (President) and legislative (Congress) branches of the federal government?

2. Some commentators suggest that federal judges should serve only limited terms in office. What impact, if any, would limited terms have on the judicial branch and its role in the governing system?

IDENTIFY THE CONCEPT THAT DOESN'T BELONG

a. *Marbury* v. *Madison*
b. Protected tenure
c. Congressional committees
d. Judicial review
e. Constitutional interpretation

Resource Center
• Glossary
• Vocabulary Example
• Connect the Link

■ **Senatorial Courtesy:** Traditional deference by U.S. senators to the wishes of their colleagues concerning the appointment of individuals to federal judgeships in that state.

EXAMPLE: *Democratic senators were angry at their Republican colleagues during Bill Clinton's presidency for blocking judicial appointments and thereby violating the tradition of senatorial courtesy for controlling the selection of federal judges in their home states.*

Judicial Selection

9.3 Outline the selection process for federal judges.

(pages 272–273)

Political parties and interest groups view the judicial selection process as an important means to influence the court pathway. By securing judgeships for individuals who share their political values, these groups can enhance their prospects for success when they subsequently use litigation to shape public policy.

MYTH EXPOSED Many Americans believe that our methods for selecting judges ensure that the most qualified lawyers are chosen. In reality, American lawyers do not become judges because they are the wisest, most experienced, or fairest members of the legal profession. Instead, they are selected through political processes that emphasize their affiliations with political parties, their personal relationships with high-ranking officials, and often their ability to raise money for political campaigns. The fact that judges are selected through political processes does not necessarily mean that they are incapable of making fair decisions. Individuals who are involved in partisan politics may prove quite capable of fulfilling a judge's duty to be neutral and open-minded. On the other hand, the use of openly political processes for selecting state judges inevitably means that some people will be placed in judgeships who are not well-suited to the job.

Judicial Selection in the Federal System

The Constitution specifies that federal judges, like ambassadors and cabinet secretaries, must be appointed by the president and confirmed by a majority vote of the U.S. Senate. Thus, both the White House and one chamber of Congress are intimately involved in judicial selection.

Because there are nearly 850 judgeships in the federal district courts and courts of appeals, the president is never personally knowledgeable about all the pending vacancies. For lower federal court judgeships, the president relies heavily on advice from White House aides, senators, and other officials from his own political party.

Traditionally, senators from the president's political party have effectively controlled the selection of appointees for district court judgeships in their own states. Through a practice known as **senatorial courtesy**■, senators from the president's party have virtual veto power over potential nominees for their home state's district courts. They are also consulted on nominations for the federal court of appeals that covers their state. Because senators are so influential in the selection of federal district court judges, the judges who ultimately get

selected are usually acquainted personally with the senators, active in the political campaigns of the senators and other party members, or accomplished in raising campaign funds for the party.

The process begins with the submission of an appointee's name to the Senate Judiciary Committee. The committee holds hearings on each nomination, including testimony from supporters and opponents. After the Judiciary Committee completes its hearings, its members vote on whether to recommend the nomination to the full Senate. Typically, upon receiving a nomination, the full Senate votes quickly based on the Judiciary Committee's report and vote. But in controversial cases or when asked to confirm appointments to the Supreme Court, the Senate may spend time debating the nomination. A majority of senators must vote for a candidate in order for that person to be sworn in as a federal judge. However, members of the minority political party in the Senate may block a vote through a **filibuster** (see Chapter 6, pages 170–171), keeping discussion going indefinitely unless three-fifths of the Senate's members—60 senators—vote to end it.

Presidents seek to please favored constituencies and to advance their policy preferences in choosing appointees they believe share their values. Interest groups find avenues through which they seek to influence the president's choices as well as the confirmation votes of senators. Judicial selection processes are a primary reason that American courts are political institutions despite their efforts to appear "nonpolitical."

Judicial Selection in the States

Compare the federal judicial selection process with the various processes used to select judges for state court systems. In general, there are four primary methods that states use for judicial selection: partisan elections, nonpartisan elections, **merit selection,** and gubernatorial or legislative appointment. Table 9.4 shows how judges are selected in each state. Although each of these methods seeks to emphasize different values, they are all closely linked to political processes.

Both partisan and nonpartisan elections emphasize the importance of popular accountability in a democratic governing system.

Yet more than 20 states have eliminated judicial elections to reduce the role of politics and give greater attention to candidates' qualifications when selecting judges. These states have adopted various forms of merit selection systems, usually involving a committee reviewing candidates' qualifications and making recommendations to the governor about which individuals to appoint to judgeships. It is presumed that the committee will focus on the individuals' personal qualities and professional qualifications rather than on political party affiliations. In a few states, governors or legislatures possess the authority to directly appoint individuals of their choice to judgeships.

CONNECT THE **LINK**
(Chapter 6, pages 170–171) Can a senator actually
defeat legislation by talking a bill to death?

TABLE 9.4	Methods of Judicial Selection for State Judges					
PARTISAN ELECTION	**NONPARTISAN ELECTION**		**MERIT SELECTION**			**LEGISLATIVE (L) OR GUBERNATORIAL (G) APPOINTMENT**
Alabama	Arkansas	North Carolina	Alaska	Missouri		California (appellate) G
Illinois	Arizona (trial)	North Dakota	Arizona (appellate)	Nebraska		Maine G
Indiana (trial)	California (trial)	Ohio	Colorado	Nevada (trial)		New Hampshire G
Louisiana	Florida (trial)	Oklahoma (trial)	Connecticut	New Mexico		New Jersey G
New York (trial)	Georgia	Oregon	Delaware	New York (appellate)		South Carolina L
Pennsylvania	Idaho	South Dakota (trial)	Florida (appellate)	Oklahoma (appellate)		Virginia L
Tennessee (trial)	Kentucky	Washington	Hawaii	Rhode Island		
Texas	Michigan	Wisconsin	Indiana (appellate)	South Dakota (appellate)		
West Virginia	Minnesota		Iowa	Tennessee (appellate)		
	Mississippi		Kansas	Utah		
	Montana		Maryland	Vermont		
	Nevada (appellate)		Massachusetts	Wyoming		

SOURCE: American Judicature Society, *Judicial Selection in the States: Appellate and General Jurisdiction Courts* (Des Moines, IA: American Judicature Society, 2004), pp. 1–4. Accessed at www.ajs.org

Judicial Selection

9.3 Outline the selection process for federal judges.

PRACTICE QUIZ: UNDERSTAND AND APPLY

1. As dictated by the Constitution, federal judges are appointed by the president and are confirmed by
   a. a majority vote in Congress.
   b. a two-thirds vote in the House of Representatives.
   c. a majority vote in the Senate.
   d. a two-thirds vote in the Senate.

2. What factor do most presidents consider to be especially important in selecting a U.S. Supreme Court nominee?
   a. whether the individual can raise enough money to win reelection to the Supreme Court
   b. whether the individual has ever served in Congress
   c. whether the individual appears to share the president's values
   d. whether the individual has prior experience as a criminal defense attorney

3. Senators play a key role in the selection and confirmation of federal judges.
   a. true   b. false

ANALYZE

1. What is the best way to select judges? Why?

2. How could you design a merit selection system that would truly select the most qualified individuals for judgeships?

IDENTIFY THE CONCEPT THAT DOESN'T BELONG

a. House of Representatives   d. Senatorial courtesy
b. Merit selection   e. Interest groups
c. Presidential appointment

9.3

Resource Center
• Glossary
• Vocabulary Example
• Connect the Link

■ **Case Precedent:** A legal rule established by a judicial decision that guides subsequent decisions. The use of case precedent is drawn from the common law system brought from Great Britain to the United States.

EXAMPLE: *In 2000, the Supreme Court followed its own precedent from Miranda v. Arizona (1966) when it reaffirmed that, prior to questioning, police officers are required to inform detained criminal suspects of their right to remain silent and their right to the presence of an attorney during questioning (Dickerson v. United States, 2000).*

Judicial Decision-Making

9.4 **Explain the theories concerning how Supreme Court justices reach their decisions.**
(pages 274–277)

Many people assume that judges make decisions by following established legal rules—and often this is true. However, the political battles over Supreme Court nominations, as well as over judges at other levels of state and federal court systems, reflect the widespread recognition that judges do not merely "follow the law" in making their decisions. In addition, when judges interpret the U.S. Constitution, state constitutions, and statutes, they rely on their own values and judgments. These values and judgments ultimately have a significant effect on public policy affecting many aspects of American life. Therefore, in appointing federal judges, the president seeks to name men and women with a politically compatible outlook. Similarly, the involvement of political parties and interest groups in supporting or opposing judicial candidates reflects their interests in securing judgeships for those individuals they believe will make decisions that advance their policy preferences.[4]

Although judges can apply their values in making many kinds of decisions, they do not enjoy complete freedom to decide cases as they wish. Lower-court judges in particular must be concerned that their decisions will be overturned on appeal to higher courts, if they make decisions that conflict with the judgments of justices on courts of last resort. What then guides judges to reach conclusions that are not likely to be overturned? First, they determine the facts of the particular case before them. Next, they make their decision by applying the rules established by higher courts for cases with similar fact situations. When judges apply these established rules, we say that they rely on **case precedent**■—the body of prior judicial opinions, especially those from the U.S. Supreme Court and state supreme courts, which establishes the judge-made law developed from interpretations of the U.S. Constitution, state constitutions, and statutes.

Typically, judges will follow the legal principles established by prior cases, no matter what their personal views on the issue. However, if they believe that the precise issue in their case is distinguishable from the issues in prior cases, or if they have new ideas about how such issues should be handled, they can issue an opinion that clashes with established case precedent. Judges make such decisions in the hope that the reasons explained in their opinions will persuade the judges above them to change the prevailing precedent.

For example, when the U.S. Supreme Court decided in 2005 (in *Roper* v. *Simmons*) that the cruel and unusual punishments clause in the Eighth Amendment prohibits the execution of murderers who committed their crimes before the age of 18, it established a new precedent, overturning its previously

established precedent permitting execution as punishment for murders committed at the ages of 16 and 17 (*Stanford* v. *Kentucky*, 1989). In reaching its conclusion, the nation's highest court upheld a decision by the Missouri Supreme Court that advocated a new interpretation of the Eighth Amendment (*State ex. rel. Simmons* v. *Roper*, 2003).

The U.S. Supreme Court often seeks to follow and preserve its precedents in order to maintain stability in the law. However, it is not bound by its own precedents, and no higher court can overturn the Supreme Court's interpretations of the U.S. Constitution. Thus, the justices enjoy significant freedom to shape the law by advancing their own theories of constitutional interpretation and by applying their own attitudes and values concerning appropriate policy outcomes from judicial decisions.[5] State supreme courts enjoy similar freedom when interpreting the constitutions and statutes of their own states. Lower-court judges can also apply their own approaches to constitutional and statutory interpretation, especially when facing issues that have not yet been addressed by any court. Their new approaches may be overturned on appeal, but they may also help establish new law if higher courts agree.

Judicial selection battles in the federal courts, especially those related to the nomination of Supreme Court justices, often focus on the nominee's approach to constitutional interpretation. Among the members of the Supreme Court, Justices Clarence Thomas and Antonin Scalia are known for advocating an original intent approach to constitutional interpretation. These justices and their admirers argue that the Constitution must be interpreted in strict accordance with the original meanings intended by the people who wrote and ratified the document. According to Thomas and Scalia, constitutional interpretation must follow original intent in order to avoid "judicial activism," in which judges allegedly exceed their proper sphere of authority by injecting their own viewpoints into constitutional interpretation.

The accusation of "judicial activism" is frequently directed by political conservatives against judges whose interpretations of the Bill of Rights lead to broad definitions of rights affecting criminal justice, issues of race and gender, and other policy disputes. That is why the followers of the original intent approach call themselves advocates of "judicial restraint," in which judges defer to the policy judgments of elected officials in the legislative and executive branches of government. In reality, judges with conservative political values can also be "judicial activists" by narrowly interpreting or invalidating statutes concerning environmental regulation, employment discrimination, and other policy areas. Thus, despite their claimed use of "judicial restraint," judges who follow original intent still affect public policy with their decisions. They merely disagree with others about which policies should be influenced by judges.

Critics of original intent argue that there is no way to know exactly what the Constitution's authors intended with

■ **Flexible Interpretation:** An approach to interpreting the U.S. Constitution that permits the meaning of the document to change with evolving values, social conditions, and problems.

EXAMPLE: *When the U.S. Supreme Court decided that the Eighth Amendment's prohibition on "cruel and unusual punishments" forbids the application of the death penalty to mentally retarded offenders* (Atkins v. Virginia, *2002), the justices used flexible interpretation rather than just the Constitution's specific words.*

Justice Clarence Thomas is very outspoken about his belief that the Constitution should be interpreted strictly according to "original intent." Would interpretation by original intent reduce the recognition of equal rights for women or members of minority groups? —*If so, should these practical results affect how judges interpret the Constitution?*

to give meaning to those words in light of current values and policy problems. Nearly all of the Supreme Court justices in the past 50 years have used flexible interpretation, including John Paul Stevens, Ruth Bader Ginsburg, and Anthony Kennedy. However, these justices frequently disagree with one another about how much flexibility should apply to various provisions in the Constitution.

As you can see, debates about the proper approach to interpreting the Constitution can be central elements in the political battles over the selection of judges. Presidents try to select judges who they believe share their values and approach to constitutional interpretation, but they cannot accurately predict how a nominee will decide every kind of case, especially because new and unexpected issues emerge each year. Moreover, some Supreme Court justices, as well as judges on lower courts, do change their views over the course of their careers. The views that led the president to select the nominee are not always the views held by nominees at the end of their careers. Justice Harry Blackmun, for example, an appointee of Republican President Richard Nixon, served on the Supreme Court from 1970 to 1994 and became increasingly protective of individuals' rights over the course of his career. Despite the fact that Nixon had envisioned him as a conservative decision maker, he was regarded as one of the Court's most liberal justices at the time of his retirement. It remains to be seen whether President Barack Obama's appointees, Justices Sonia Sotomayor and Elena Kagan, will surprise or disappoint Obama and other interested observers.

respect to each individual word and phrase, or even whether one specific meaning was intended by all of the authors and ratifiers. Moreover, these critics typically argue that the ambiguous nature of many constitutional phrases, such as "cruel and unusual punishments" and "unreasonable searches and seizures," represents one of the document's strengths, because it permits judges to interpret and reinterpret the document in light of the nation's changing social circumstances and technological advances. What would James Madison and the other eighteenth-century founders of the nation have thought about whether the use of wiretaps and other forms of electronic surveillance violate the Fourth Amendment prohibition on "unreasonable searches"? Critics of original intent argue for a **flexible interpretation**■ that enables contemporary judges

Justice Ruth Bader Ginsburg is among the justices who favor a flexible interpretation approach that adapts constitutional principles to contemporary issues and problems. —*What, if anything, prevents Supreme Court justices from going "too far" in using flexible interpretation to say that the Constitution means whatever they want it to mean?*

CONNECT THE **LINK**

(Chapter 4, pages 94–95) The First Amendment's wording requires judges to interpret the meaning of "an establishment of religion" and the "free exercise" of religion.

Elena Kagan, shown here at her Senate confirmation hearings, was nominated by President Obama to replace John Paul Stevens on the U.S. Supreme Court in 2010. Because it was widely believed that Kagan might strengthen the Court's liberal wing, conservative Republican senators opposed her confirmation. —*Is it proper for senators to oppose the nomination of a highly experienced nominee simply because they believe he or she will make decisions with which they will disagree on certain constitutional issues?*

Political Science and Judicial Decision-Making

Supreme Court justices may claim they apply "judicial restraint" or a "flexible interpretation" of the Constitution in making their decisions, and they may honestly believe that these interpretive approaches guide their decisions. Political scientists, however, question whether the justices' decisions can be explained in this way. Through systematic examination of case decisions and close analysis of justices' opinions, researchers have identified patterns and inconsistencies. These examinations of Supreme Court decisions have led to alternative explanations for the primary factors that shape the justices' decisions.

The idea that justices follow specific theories of constitutional interpretation and carefully consider precedents in making decisions is often labeled the **legal model.** Critics argue, however, that the justices regularly ignore, mischaracterize, or change precedents when those case decisions seem to impede the desire of the majority of justices to have a case come out a certain way. As you saw in the discussion of freedom of religion in Chapter 4, pages 94–95, justices seem to decide cases on the separation of church and state according to a specific test of whether government actions advance a particular religion. In particular cases, however, they ignore the test if it leads to a result that they do not desire. For example, the justices permitted the Nebraska state senate to hire a minister to lead prayers at the start of each legislative session (*Marsh* v. *Chambers,* 1984). If they had applied the usual test that asked whether or not a government activity has a religious purpose, however, they would presumably have been required to prohibit this entanglement of church and state. Instead, perhaps seeking to avoid public controversy by ruling out legislative prayers, the majority of justices ignored the established legal test in this case and simply declared that legislative prayers are acceptable as a historical tradition.

An alternative theory of judicial decision-making, known as the **attitudinal model,** states that Supreme Court justices' opinions are driven by their attitudes and values. Advocates of this model see the justices' discussion of interpretive theories and precedent as merely a means to obscure the actual basis for decisions and to persuade the public that the decisions are, in fact, based on law. Researchers who endorse the attitudinal model do systematic analyses of judicial decisions to identify patterns that indicate the attitudes and values possessed and advanced by individual justices. Put more simply, the attitudinal theorists argue that some justices decide cases as they do because they are conservative (e.g., generally supportive of business interests and expanded power for prosecutors and police) and that others decide cases differently because they are liberal (e.g., generally supportive of broad definitions of criminal defendants' rights, environmental regulation, and civil rights).[6]

Other political scientists see judicial decision-making as influenced by a **strategic voting model.**[7] According to this theory, Supreme Court justices vote strategically in order to advance their preferred goals, even if it means voting contrary to their actual attitudes and values in some cases. For example, a chief justice may vote strategically to end up among the majority of justices and thereby retain the authority to decide which justice will write the opinion for the Court. If the chief justice is in the minority after a vote, the senior justice in the majority assigns the opinion. Chief Justice Warren Burger was accused of changing his vote in the controversial abortion decision *Roe* v. *Wade* (1973) when he saw that a majority of his colleagues supported establishing a constitutional right of choice for women. Thus, he was able to assign opinion-writing responsibilities to his long-time friend, Justice Harry Blackmun, whom Burger erroneously believed would write an opinion that established a very weak and limited right of choice.[8]

In recent years, some political scientists have broadened their studies of courts, including judicial decision-making, through what is commonly labeled **new institutionalism**— an approach that emphasizes understanding courts as institutions and seeing the role of courts in the larger political system.[9] The adherents of new institutionalism do not necessarily agree with one another about the causes and implications of judicial action. They do, however, seek to move beyond analyzing judicial decisions solely by looking at the choices of individual Supreme Court justices. Instead, they may focus on the Supreme Court's processes, its reactions to statutes that undercut particular judicial decisions, or its decisions that minimize direct confrontations with other branches of government. Alternatively, the focus could be on judicial inaction, as when the Supreme Court declined to make a decision in a case brought by a U.S. citizen who had been jailed as a suspected terrorist and who had been denied all constitutional rights (*Rumsfeld* v. *Padilla*, 2004). The majority of justices declared that he had originally filed his case in the federal district court of the wrong state. They told him to begin his case again in the

lower courts, likely hoping that by the time the case worked its way through the court system again, Congress and the President would have worked out the details of how to process such terrorism cases.

Political scientists continue to debate which model provides the best explanation for judicial decisions. New models are likely to be developed in the future. For students of American government, these models serve as a reminder that you should not automatically accept government officials' explanations for their decisions and behavior. Systematic examination and close analysis of decisions may reveal influences that the government decision makers themselves do not fully recognize.

Judicial Decision-Making

9.4 Explain the theories concerning how Supreme Court justices reach their decisions.

PRACTICE QUIZ: UNDERSTAND AND APPLY

1. The "legal model" of judicial decision-making presumes that
   a. judges' decisions are based on their attitudes and values.
   b. judges' decisions are based on their rational strategies.
   c. judges' decisions are based on case precedents.
   d. judges' decisions are based on court structure and processes.

2. Critics who oppose interpreting the Constitution according to "original intent"
   a. claim that there is no way to know what the authors of the Constitution intended as the meaning of all the document's ambiguous phrases.
   b. claim that the use of original intent always violates the principle of judicial restraint.
   c. do not believe that Supreme Court justices should interpret the Constitution.
   d. also oppose the flexible interpretation approach to the Constitution.

3. Typically, the decisions of lower-court judges rely on case precedent, even if their personal views on the issue suggest a different decision.
   a. true
   b. false

4. When political scientists view Supreme Court justices' decisions as being shaped by concerns about the courts' role in the larger political system, those political scientists believe in
   a. the legal model of judicial decision-making.
   b. the new institutionalism model of judicial decision-making.
   c. the attitudinal model of judicial decision-making.
   d. the rational choice model of judicial decision-making.

ANALYZE

1. What problems could arise in a system in which all judges freely decide cases according to their own ideas and values without considering existing rules established by case precedents?

2. Is there any way to prevent judges from using their own values and attitudes in making decisions?

IDENTIFY THE CONCEPT THAT DOESN'T BELONG

a. Original intent
b. Judicial activism
c. Attitudinal model
d. Flexible interpretation
e. Inquisitorial system

9.4

Resource Center
• Glossary
• Vocabulary Example
• Connect the Link

Action in the Court Pathway

9.5 Characterize the litigation strategies used in the court pathway.

(pages 278–281)

In theory, any individual can make use of the resources of the judicial branch merely by filing a legal action. Such actions may be directed at small issues, such as suing a landlord to recover a security deposit. They may also be directed at significant national issues, including actions aimed at Congress or the president in battles over major public policy issues.

In reality, filing a lawsuit at any level above small-claims courts (where landlord-tenant cases are typically argued) is expensive and requires professional legal assistance. As a result, the courts are not easily accessible to the average American. Typically, this policy-shaping process is used by legal professionals who have technical expertise and financial resources. Nor will courts accept every kind of claim: Claims must be presented in the form of legal cases that embody disputes about rights and obligations under the law. Thus, organized interests and wealthy individuals are often best positioned to make effective use of court processes.

For an illustration of the court pathway in the Savana Redding case discussed at the beginning of this chapter, see Figure 9.3.

Interest Group Litigation

The court pathway is often attractive to small interest groups because it is possible to succeed with fewer resources than are required for lobbying or mass mobilization. Larger or resource-rich groups also use litigation, but it tends to be just one among several pathways that they use. To be effective in legislatures, for example, groups need lots of money and large numbers of aroused and vocal members. Lobbyists need to spend money by donating to politicians' campaign funds, wining and dining public officials, and mounting public relations campaigns to sway public opinion. By contrast, a small group may be successful using the courts if it has an effective attorney and enough resources to sustain a case through the litigation process. The most important resources for effective litigation are expertise and resources for litigation expenses.[10]

EXPERTISE For effective advocacy in litigation, expertise is essential. This includes thorough knowledge in the areas of law relevant to the case as well as experience in trial preparation or appellate advocacy, depending on which level of the court system is involved in a particular case. Attorneys who

FIGURE 9.3 ■ **Policy-Shaping Litigation on the Savana Redding Case**

Litigation is a long and difficult process. Note how long it took for Savana Redding's case to travel through the courts, from the strip search in 2003 to the Supreme Court's decision in 2009. The final outcome depends on the facts of the case and the persistence, resources, and strategies of the competing sides, as well as the values and interactions of the judges. —*Do you have enough knowledge and resources to pursue policy-shaping litigation?*

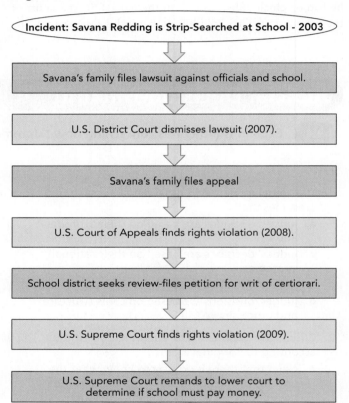

Incident: Savana Redding is Strip-Searched at School - 2003

Savana's family files lawsuit against officials and school.

U.S. District Court dismisses lawsuit (2007).

Savana's family files appeal

U.S. Court of Appeals finds rights violation (2008).

School district seeks review-files petition for writ of certiorari.

U.S. Supreme Court finds rights violation (2009).

U.S. Supreme Court remands to lower court to determine if school must pay money.

have previously dealt with specific issues know the intricate details of relevant prior court decisions and are better able to formulate effective arguments that use those precedents. In addition, attorneys affiliated with large, resource-rich law firms or interest groups have at their disposal teams of attorneys who can handle research and other aspects of investigation and preparation.

LITIGATION RESOURCES Interest groups and individuals who use the court process must have the resources to handle various expenses in addition to the attorneys' fees, which are generally very high unless the lawyers have volunteered to work **pro bono,** which translates from the Latin phrase *pro bono publico* as "for the public good," for little or nothing. It means that attorneys and other professionals are waiving their

■ **Test Case:** A case sponsored or presented by an interest group in the court pathway with the intention of influencing public policy.

EXAMPLE: *The ACLU used the case of a teenage student as a test case to pursue its objective of preventing suspicionless, random urine-drug tests of high school students participating in extracurricular activities, such as choir and band. The ACLU lost the case in* Board of Education *v.* Earls

CONNECT THE LINK
(Chapter 5, pages 130–131) The NAACP's litigation in the court pathway was a key factor leading to increased protection of constitutional rights for African Americans.

Students protested outside the Supreme Court, as the justices were hearing oral arguments in a case that concerned a high school student who was punished for holding up a provocative sign across the street from his school. —*Could such public demonstrations ever influence the justices by informing them of the intensity of people's feelings about an issue? Or do such demonstrations only catch the attention of the news media and the public?*

usual fees to work for a cause in which they believe. Some interest groups rely heavily on securing pro bono professional support.

PATHWAYS of action

The NAACP and Racial Segregation

Beginning in the 1930s, the National Association for the Advancement of Colored People (NAACP), an important civil rights interest group founded in 1910, filed lawsuits to challenge state laws that segregated African Americans into separate, inferior educational institutions. These lawsuits tested the 1896 U.S. Supreme Court decision (*Plessy* v. *Ferguson*) that had ruled no constitutional violation exists when government gives people from different races "separate but equal" facilities and treatment. Unfortunately, many states used that court decision to justify their existing practice of providing separate and grossly inferior schools and services to African Americans. Rigid racial segregation was imposed, especially in the South, after the end of the post–Civil War Reconstruction period, and it was vigorously enforced for decades afterward.

Led by Thurgood Marshall, an attorney who later became the first African American to serve on the U.S. Supreme Court (1967–1991), the NAACP argued that the separate facilities sanctioned by *Plessy* were not equal and therefore violated the equal protection clause of the Constitution's Fourteenth Amendment. As we examined in Chapter 5, pages 130–131, from the 1930s to the 1950s, the NAACP sued such states as Maryland, Missouri, Texas, and Oklahoma for excluding African American students from law schools

and graduate programs at state universities. By 1950, the U.S. Supreme Court had issued several decisions rejecting states' false claims that they provided "separate but equal" facilities for African Americans in colleges and universities. It was at that point that litigation began, backed by the NAACP, which would lead to public school racial segregation being declared unconstitutional.

After Earl Warren, the governor of California, was appointed chief justice in 1953, the nine justices unanimously declared that school segregation laws were unconstitutional because they violated the equal protection clause. That decision, *Brown* v. *Board of Education of Topeka* (1954), was based on a lawsuit filed by the NAACP on behalf of African American parents and schoolchildren in Topeka, Kansas. The *Brown* decision established the foundation for subsequent NAACP lawsuits in the 1960s and 1970s seeking to desegregate public school systems throughout the United States.

Elements of Strategy

All litigants engage in certain types of strategies—for example, presenting evidence and formulating arguments. Interest groups may benefit from additional opportunities to use specific strategies by choosing which case to pursue or by choosing the court in which a case may be filed.

SELECTION OF CASES   Interest groups seek to find an appropriate **test case**■ that will serve as the vehicle to persuade judges to change law and policy. Sometimes they can recruit plaintiffs and then provide legal representation and litigation

■ **Amicus Brief:** A written argument submitted to an appellate court by those who are interested in the issue being examined but are not representing either party in the case; often submitted by interest groups' lawyers to advance a specific policy position.

EXAMPLE: *When Savana Redding's case reached the Supreme Court, the Juvenile Law Center submitted written legal arguments known as amicus briefs to support her position, while the National School Boards Association submitted amicus briefs in support of the Safford school district.*

expenses to carry the case through the court system. In challenging laws that restrict choices about abortion, an interest group would rather bring the case on behalf of a teenage rape victim than pursue the case for a married woman who became pregnant after being careless with birth control. The interest group is likely to believe that the rape victim's case will provide more compelling arguments that may generate sympathy from many judges.

Interest groups cannot always choose precisely which cases would best serve their interests. They may pursue any relevant case available at a given moment, because they cannot afford to wait, especially if other cases working their way through the system may lead to adverse judicial decisions.

CHOICE OF JURISDICTION Another important factor in litigation strategies is the choice of courts in which to pursue a legal action. Because of the country's dual court system, there is often a choice to be made about whether state or federal courts are more likely to produce outcomes favorable to a group's interests. In addition to considering whether state or federal law may be more likely to produce a favorable result, litigators may consider whether a specific federal or state judge would be sympathetic to their values and policy preferences.

FRAMING THE ARGUMENTS Litigants must make strategic decisions about how to frame the legal issues and arguments that they present in court. In some cases, they must decide which legal issues to raise. Lawyers must assess the judges before whom the case will be presented and make strategic decisions about which arguments will appeal to the particular decision makers who will consider the case.

When an interest group is not itself involved in a case, it may still seek permission to present written arguments as *amicus curiae* (Latin for "a friend of the court"). For example, it is very common for multiple interest groups to submit **amicus briefs**■, detailed written arguments that seek to persuade the U.S. Supreme Court to endorse a specific outcome or to adopt reasoning that is favorable to the groups' policy preferences. Amicus briefs can be influential, because justices' opinions sometimes draw from these briefs rather than from the arguments presented by the two parties in the case. Participants in a Supreme Court case typically welcome the submission of amicus briefs on behalf of their side. Indeed, one strategy is to gain the endorsement of as many interest groups as possible to impress the Supreme Court with the broad support that exists for a particular position. Over the course of Supreme Court history, individuals and interest groups have increasingly sought to influence the Court's decisions through amicus briefs. From 1946 through 1955, amicus briefs were filed in only 23 percent of Supreme Court cases, but between 1986 and 1995, they were filed in 85 percent of the cases considered.[11]

PUBLIC RELATIONS AND THE POLITICAL ENVIRONMENT Interest groups have a strong incentive to gain sympathetic coverage from the news media about cases that they pursue through the court pathway. Attorneys often develop relationships with reporters in hopes that sympathetic stories will be written about policy-oriented legal cases. Such stories help educate the public and perhaps shape public opinion about an issue. They may also influence judges, because just like other people, judges read, watch, or listen to the news every day.

STUDENT profile

What would you do if you believed that your rights were being violated by one of your college's policies? Would you have the courage to speak out? Would you have the persistence and determination to find a lawyer to help take your case through the court system? People who seek to use lawsuits to vindicate their rights often learn that the court system involves a very expensive and sometimes lengthy process in which success is not guaranteed.

In 2008, Angela Mensing, Kristen Alonso, and Brian Anderson, editors of *The Inkwell*, the student newspaper at Armstrong Atlantic State University in Georgia, filed a lawsuit against their university alleging a violation of the First Amendment right to freedom of speech and press. They claimed that the university announced significant cuts in the student newspaper's budget because student reporters and editors wrote stories that were critical of the university. For example, they said that a university official attempted to forbid them from publishing an article about expired elevator safety permits in university buildings. Ultimately, the university settled the case, restored the newspaper's budget, and paid the student editors' legal fees.[12]

Action in the Court Pathway

9.5   Characterize the litigation strategies used in the court pathway.

PRACTICE QUIZ: UNDERSTAND AND APPLY

1. One advantage for interest groups in using the court pathway to shape public policy is that
   a. it takes less time than the other pathways.
   b. nearly anyone can do it.
   c. it may require fewer resources than those needed in most other pathways.
   d. it almost always works.

2. When interest groups submit amicus briefs in an appellate case, they are
   a. objecting to the appellate court's decision to accept the case for hearing.
   b. presenting elaborate written arguments on behalf of one side in a case, even though they are not directly involved in the case.
   c. informing the judges that they will provide financial campaign contributions and volunteer workers to help the judges win reelection.
   d. announcing that they will monitor the actions of the legislature and executive.

3. When interest groups look for a test case that will help them with their litigation strategy, they seek
   a. a case that will present the issue in a way that will attract the attention and sympathy of the judges.
   b. the first case that they hear about.
   c. a case involving someone rich, who can pay them a great deal of money.
   d. a case that will be easy to resolve through a negotiated settlement.

4. Interest groups may possess an advantage in litigation dealing with issues of interest to them because
   a. individuals can only be represented by one attorney, but interest groups can be represented by two attorneys.
   b. federal courts only accept lawsuits filed by interest groups; all lawsuits by individuals must go to state courts.
   c. judges are usually active members of interest groups.
   d. interest group attorneys typically possess experience and expertise in their issues of interest.

ANALYZE

1. Why did the NAACP use a litigation strategy instead of lobbying Congress and mobilizing voters to pressure the president to take action against racial segregation?

2. If you wanted to challenge a mandatory drug testing policy imposed by your college, what strategies would you need to use to succeed in the litigation process?

IDENTIFY THE CONCEPT THAT DOESN'T BELONG

a. Expertise
b. Constitutional convention
c. Choice of jurisdiction
d. Test case
e. Pro bono

Resource Center
- Glossary
- Vocabulary Example
- Connect the Link

Implementation and Impact of Court Decisions

9.6 Evaluate the courts' effectiveness in enforcing judicial decisions.
(pages 282–283)

Court decisions are not automatically implemented or obeyed. Judges have the authority to issue important pronouncements that dictate law and policy, especially with respect to the definition and enforcement of constitutional rights. However, they have limited ability to ensure that their orders are carried out. To see their declarations of law translated into actual public policy, judges must typically rely on public obedience and on enforcement by the executive branch of government.

During the Watergate scandal of the 1970s, in which President Richard Nixon conspired to cover up information about a burglary at Democratic Party offices committed by people working for his reelection campaign, the Supreme Court handed down a decision ordering Nixon to provide a special prosecutor with recordings of secretly taped White House conversations. Years later, Supreme Court Justice Lewis Powell observed that had Nixon refused to comply with the Court's order, "there was no way that we could have enforced it. We had [only] 50 police officers [at the Supreme Court], but Nixon had the [U.S. military at his disposal]."[13] Nixon handed over the tapes, however, and shortly thereafter resigned from office, presumably realizing that public support for his impeachment, already strong, would lead to his conviction by the Senate if he disobeyed a unanimous Court decision that citizens and members of Congress viewed as legitimate.

The weakness of courts has been revealed in a number of cases over the course of American history. In the 1830s, the Cherokee Nation successfully litigated a case against laws that ordered the removal of Cherokees from their lands. The state of Georgia supported removal on behalf of whites who invaded Cherokee lands to search for gold. The U.S. Supreme Court, still led by the aged Chief Justice John Marshall, supported the Cherokees' property rights, but President Andrew Jackson and other officials declined to use their power to enforce the ruling ("John Marshall has made his decision," Jackson is supposed to have said, "now let him enforce it."). Thus, despite using the court pathway in an appropriate manner to protect their property rights, the Cherokees were eventually forced off their land. A few years later, they were marched at gunpoint all the way to an Oklahoma reservation, with an estimated 4,000 dying along the way. The Cherokees' infamous Trail of Tears forced march and loss of land demonstrated that courts cannot automatically ensure that their decisions are enforced and obeyed. Unlike the situation in the 1970s, in which President Nixon felt strong public pressure to obey the Supreme Court or face impeachment, the Cherokees and the Supreme Court of the 1830s did not benefit from public acceptance and political support.

In modern times, analysts have questioned the effectiveness of courts in advancing school desegregation. Although the Supreme Court earned praise for declaring racial segregation in public schools unconstitutional in *Brown,* the 1954 decision did not desegregate schools. Racial separation continued in public schools throughout the country for years after the Court's decision. In two highly publicized incidents, military force was necessary to enroll African American students in all-white institutions. In 1957, President Dwight D. Eisenhower sent troops to force Little Rock Central High School to admit a half-dozen black students, and in 1962, President John F. Kennedy dispatched the U.S. Army to the University of Mississippi so that one African American student could enroll. In both situations, there had been violent resistance to court orders, but the presidents effectively backed up the judicial decisions with a show of force. In other cities, desegregation was achieved piecemeal, over the course of two decades, as individual lawsuits in separate courthouses enforced the *Brown* mandate.

According to Professor Gerald Rosenberg, the actual desegregation of public schools came only after the president and Congress acted in the 1960s to push policy change, using financial incentives and the threat of enforcement actions to overcome segregation. In Rosenberg's view, courts receive too much credit for policy changes that actually only occur when other actors become involved. Courts receive this credit, in part, because of the symbolism attached to their publicized pronouncements.[14]

Similar arguments can be made about other policy issues. For example, the Supreme Court's decision recognizing a woman's right to make choices about abortion (*Roe v. Wade,* 1973) does not ensure that doctors and medical facilities will perform such procedures in all locations or that people have the resources to make use of this right.

Other analysts see the courts differently—as important and effective policymaking institutions. They argue that *Brown* and other judicial decisions about segregation were essential elements of social change. Without these judicial decisions initiating, guiding, and providing legitimacy for change, the changes might not have occurred. For example, until the mid-1960s, southern members of Congress who supported segregation were able to block corrective legislation because the seniority system gave them disproportionate power on congressional committees. In the Senate, they also used the filibuster to prevent consideration of civil rights legislation. Thus, they could make sure that proposed bills either died in committee or never came to a vote. In addition, elected officials at all levels of government and in all parts of the country were often too afraid of a backlash from white voters to take strong stands in support of equal protection for African Americans. Analysts point to other court decisions, such as those requiring police officers to inform suspects of their Miranda rights in 1966 and recognizing abortion rights in 1973, to argue that the court pathway has been an important source of policy change.[15] Unelected federal judges were arguably the only actors positioned to push the country into change because they would not lose their jobs as a result of making decisions that were unpopular with some segments of American society.

Implementation and Impact of Court Decisions

9.6 **Evaluate the courts' effectiveness in enforcing judicial decisions.**

PRACTICE QUIZ: UNDERSTAND AND APPLY

1. A court decision is a declaration of law; once it is formulated by a court, it automatically operates as effective public policy.
   a. true
   b. false

2. It's fair to say that the desegregation of public schools in this country moved forward as a result of
   a. the Supreme Court's decision in *Plessy* v. *Ferguson*.
   b. a series of legislative decisions starting with *Brown* v. *Board of Education*.
   c. the Court's reversal of *Plessy* v. *Ferguson*, lower-level courts' complementary decisions, and enforcing actions by President Eisenhower and President Kennedy.
   d. cultural change that inspired most people in segregated school districts to embrace desegregation.

3. Why might it be appropriate in a democracy for federal judges to help formulate public policy?
   a. Federal judges are the elected representatives of the people.
   b. Federal judges can be fired, if their decisions too often run contrary to the sentiments of the majority.
   c. Some democratic principles (such as individual rights) can conflict with majority sentiments. Federal judges, appointed for life and insulated from the pressures of popular sentiment, are well positioned to preserve such principles.
   d. Federal judges are appointed by governmental officials who are themselves elected. The votes that elected officials receive represent a level of citizen trust that transcends the changeable sentiments of a majority, making judges appointed by these officials a purer expression of democracy than elected judges would be.

ANALYZE

1. Are courts powerful or weak? Explain why you believe what you do.

2. How, if at all, could a president be required to enforce a decision of the U.S. Supreme Court?

IDENTIFY THE CONCEPT THAT DOESN'T BELONG

a. Judicial authority
b. Perception of courts
c. Executive enforcement
d. Public obedience
e. Court-ordered mass arrests

Judicial Policymaking and Democracy

9.7 Describe the debate over whether it is appropriate for judges to shape public policy in a democracy.

(pages 284–285)

Notwithstanding the framers' expectation that the judiciary would be the weakest branch of government, American judges possess the power to shape public policy. However, this power often stirs up debates about the role of courts in the constitutional governing system. These controversies are most intense when focused on the actions of appointed, life-tenured, federal judges.[16] In a democratic system, how can unelected, long-serving officials be permitted to make important decisions affecting public policy? This is an important question for our government.

The power of the judicial branch poses significant potential risks for American society. What if life-tenured judges make decisions that create bad public policy? What if they make decisions that nullify popular policy choices made by the people's elected representatives or that force those elected representatives to impose taxes needed to implement those decisions? Because of these risks, some critics call judicial policymaking undemocratic. They argue that judges should limit their activities to narrow decisions that address disputes between two parties in litigation and avoid any cases that might lead judges to supersede the preferences of the voters' accountable, elected representatives in the legislative and executive branches. These critics want to avoid the risk that a small number of judicial elites, such as the nine justices on the U.S. Supreme Court, will be able to impose their policy choices on the nation's millions of citizens.

Although judicial policymaking by unelected federal judges does not fit conceptions of democracy based on citizens' direct control over policy through elections, advocates of judicial policymaking see it as appropriate. According to their view, the design of the governing system in the U.S. Constitution rests on a vision of democracy that requires active participation and policy influence by federal judges. Under this conception of democracy, the U.S. Constitution does not permit the majority of citizens to dictate every policy decision. The Constitution facilitates citizen participation and accountability through elections, but the need to protect the rights of individuals under the Bill of Rights demonstrates that the majority should not necessarily control every decision and policy. In 1954, for example, racial segregation was strongly supported by many whites in the North and the South. Should majority rule have dictated that rigid racial segregation continue? In essence, the American conception of constitutional democracy relies on citizen participation and majority rule plus the protection of rights for individuals, including members of unpopular political, religious, racial, and other minority groups.

The U.S. Supreme Court, shown here in the official 2010 portrait, includes three women for the first time in U.S. history. This small group of unelected officials has significant power to create new law and policy. —*How do you think this has affected the "separation of powers" set forth in the Constitution?*

For example, in the aftermath of the September 11, 2001, terrorist attacks on the World Trade Center and the Pentagon, public opinion polls indicated that a majority of Americans favored requiring Arabs, including those who are U.S. citizens, to undergo special searches and extra security checks before boarding airplanes in the United States.[17] Imagine that Congress responded by enacting a law that imposed these requirements based on ancestry without regard to its detrimental impact on U.S. citizens of Arab descent. Such a policy, if supported by a majority of citizens, would meet many of the requirements for democratic policymaking. However, it would collide with the Fourteenth Amendment's requirement of "equal protection of the laws" for Americans from all races and ethnic groups.

To ensure that majority interests do not trample the rights of minorities, the Constitution positions federal judges as the decision makers to protect constitutional rights. In this position, because they are appointed, life-tenured officials, federal judges are supposed to have the independence and the insulation from politics necessary to make courageous decisions on behalf of minority group members, no matter how unpopular those minorities may be. In practice, federal judges have not always gone against the wishes of the majority, even when the rights of minority group members were threatened or diminished. Such was the case when the Supreme Court endorsed the detention of innocent Japanese Americans in internment camps during World War II (*Korematsu* v. *United States,* 1944). But in other cases, the Supreme Court and other courts have provided a check against the excesses of majority policy preferences.

There is broad agreement that judges must uphold the U.S. Constitution, state constitutions, and laws enacted by legislatures through the use of their power of interpretation. Disagreements exist, however, about whether judges have acted properly in interpreting the law, especially when judicial decisions shape public policy. Was it improper for the Supreme Court to recognize a constitutional right of privacy that grants women the opportunity to make choices about abortion (*Roe* v. *Wade,* 1973)? Should the U.S. Supreme Court have prevented the Florida courts from ordering recounts of votes during the closely contested presidential election of 2000 (*Bush* v. *Gore,* 2000)? These and other questions will continue to be debated for decades to come for three primary reasons. First, courts are authoritative institutions that shape law and policy in ways that cannot be directly controlled by the public and other institutions of government. Second, court decisions often address controversial issues that reflect Americans' most significant disagreements about social values and public policies. And third, elected officials may choose to avoid taking action on controversial issues, thereby leaving the court pathway as the sole avenue for government action.

PATHWAYS of change from around the world

What would you do if the independence of the American judiciary was threatened? What if members of Congress sought to impeach a federal judge simply because they disagreed with his or her decision in a criminal case? Would it matter to you? To the country? Would you even notice? In 2007, law students in Pakistan took to the streets with hundreds of lawyers to protest President Pervez Musharraf's effort to suspend and remove from office the chief justice of Pakistan's Supreme Court, whose judicial opinions had challenged some of the president's decisions and actions. These students felt so strongly about the need for judicial independence that they literally risked their lives as armed soldiers tried to stop the protests. Thankfully, contemporary issues in the United States rarely produce large-scale violence in which soldiers or police use physical force against peaceful protestors. But the question remains—what would you do under similar circumstances? Write a letter? Call your members of Congress? What could you do if an American president sought to ignore orders of the U.S. Supreme Court or otherwise diminish the power of the judiciary?[18]

Judicial Policymaking and Democracy

9.7 Describe the debate over whether it is appropriate for judges to shape public policy in a democracy.

PRACTICE QUIZ: UNDERSTAND AND APPLY

1. The framers of the U.S. Constitution expected that the judiciary would eventually become the most powerful branch of government.
    a. true   b. false

2. Critics of judicial policymaking believe
    a. that judges are not smart enough to make decisions that shape public policy.
    b. that legislators are smarter than judges.
    c. that legislators always know more than judges do about public policy.
    d. that elected officials should be responsible for policy decisions in a democracy.

3. One justification for judicial policymaking in the democratic governing system of the United States relies on
    a. the fact that federal judges are elected by and accountable to the voters.
    b. the provision in Article I of the U.S. Constitution that declares "judges shall have power over public policy."
    c. the need for independent judges to make decisions that protect the constitutional rights of individuals, including members of minority groups.
    d. the United Nations Declaration on Judicial Power in the Modern World.

ANALYZE

1. Are the principles of American democracy violated when judges make decisions that shape public policy?

2. Are there any policy issues that judges should never address?

IDENTIFY THE CONCEPT THAT DOESN'T BELONG

    a. Life-tenured
    b. Unelected
    c. Authority to define and protect constitutional rights
    d. Article II of the U.S. Constitution
    e. Controversial issues

Conclusion

The judicial branch serves important functions under the constitutional governing system of the United States. Judges and juries resolve disputes, determine whether criminal defendants are guilty, impose punishment on those convicted of crimes, and provide individuals with a means to challenge actions by government. These functions are carried out in multilevel court systems, made up of trial courts and appellate courts, which exist in each state as well as in a national system under the federal government. Each system is responsible for its own set of laws, though all must be in accord with the U.S. Constitution, "the supreme law of the land."

The judicial branch provides opportunities for individuals and interest groups to seek to shape law and public policy. Through the litigation process in the court pathway, they can frame arguments to persuade judges as to the best approaches for interpreting the law. Judicial opinions shape many significant public policies for society, including those affecting education, abortion, the environment, and criminal justice. These opinions interpreting constitutions and statutes are written by judges who are selected through political processes, including elections in many states and presidential appointment in the federal system. American judges are exceptionally powerful because of their authority to interpret the U.S. Constitution and their ability to block actions by other branches of government through the power of judicial review. The impact of federal judges on major public policy issues raises difficult questions about the proper role of unelected officials in shaping the course of a democracy.

Think back to the story that opened the chapter, the Supreme Court's decision in the Savana Redding case about the school's authority to conduct student strip searches. In light of what you have learned in this chapter, can you understand why she pursued a litigation strategy instead of just lobbying the school board, the state legislature, or Congress on the issue? Do you agree with the Supreme Court's decision that such school strip searches, based on mere allegations, can be improper as "unreasonable searches" under the Fourth Amendment? Was it appropriate for the Supreme Court to decide this issue? Why or why not?

The courts are not easily accessible to citizens, because their use depends on expensive resources, including the patience to sustain extended litigation and the funds to hire expert attorneys and pay for litigation expenses. Because of their resources and expertise, organized interest groups are often better positioned than individual citizens to use the court pathway in pursuing their own policy objectives or in blocking the policy goals of other interest groups. However, the limited ability of judges to implement their own decisions is one factor that leads some observers to debate whether the court pathway provides processes that can consistently and properly develop public policies that are useful and effective.

KEY CONCEPT MAP

How do politics affect the selection of Supreme Court Justices?

May 1, 2009

Justice David Souter Announces His Retirement
from the U.S. Supreme Court.

Justice Souter presumably wanted his replacement to be named by Democratic President Barack Obama rather than by Republican President George W. Bush because he waited to announce his retirement until after President Obama had been elected and assumed office. This is a standard politics-based decision by judges who hope to be replaced by someone who shares their judicial values.

Critical Thinking Questions

Should Supreme Court justices be able to time their retirements according to who is president at a given moment? Or would it be preferable to have a system in which justices retire at a specific age or after a specific term in office?

May 21, 2009

Republican Senators Warn of Vigorous Opposition
to nominees, including a possible filibuster, if they think that the nominee is too liberal.

Senators from the opposite political party as the president seek to pressure him into selecting a moderate nominee and to reassure and maintain the support of voters from their political party who want to see them oppose the president's agenda.

Should presidents consider the threat of opposition in choosing nominees? Or should they simply choose (and fight for) nominees that they feel will be best for the Supreme Court and country?

May 26, 2009

President Obama Nominates Sonia Sotomayor
An experienced federal judge and former prosecutor—Sotomayor is the first Latino and the third woman nominated for the Supreme Court.

President Obama sought to guard against opposition by choosing someone with sterling academic credentials and impressive experience. In addition, he could enhance his political support from voters in two constituencies of growing importance—Latinos and women.

What if President Obama had nominated a prominent environmentalist attorney who had no prior experience as a judge? What might have been the reaction from Republican senators and the public?

July 13, 2009

Senate Judiciary Committee Hearings Begin
Republican senators pose sharp questions to Judge Sotomayor. Democratic senators ask questions that will enable Judge Sotomayor to explain her perspective in ways that will appeal to the public.

Senators use the televised hearings to affect the image of the nominee and to please the voters from their own political party.

What if a nominee's responses to questions indicated that the nominee had only a weak grasp of constitutional law concerning a particular issue? How might the senators from each political party react to such a situation?

July 28, 2009

Judiciary Committee Votes to Endorse Sotomayor
12 Democrats and 1 Republican vote in favor; 6 Republicans oppose.

Liberal interest groups lobby senators to support Sotomayor's confirmation. Conservative interest groups lobby senators to oppose Sotomayor's nomination.

What if Republicans controlled a majority of seats in the Senate and thus a majority on the judiciary committee?

August 4, 2009

Full Senate Debates the Sotomayor Nomination

Senators' statements during such debates seek to please their own political party and to mobilize public opinion either to favor or oppose the nomination.

Under what circumstances will the American public pay close attention to Supreme Court nominations and the arguments put forward by senators from each party?

August 6, 2009

Senate Votes 68–31 to Approve Sotomayor's Nomination
59 Democrats and 9 Republicans vote in favor; 31 Republicans oppose.

Some Republicans may have wanted to show a willingness to be reasonable and cooperative in order to avoid future Democratic opposition. In addition, most of the Republican senators who voted to confirm Sotomayor came from states that voted Democratic in the 2008 presidential election.

If Republican senators had managed to use a filibuster to block a final vote on the Sotomayor nomination, what political consequences might have followed from such an action?

Many Americans are uncomfortable with the connections between politics and the judicial branch, especially in the partisan battles over the selection of judges and debates about how judges should make decisions. Although people may be attracted to the idea that the Constitution and other laws have clear meanings that are easily identifiable by judges, the reality of vague phrases and unaddressed issues within laws inevitably gives judges power over the meaning of the Constitution and statutes. —*What aspects of the connections between politics and the judicial branch do you see as beneficial? What aspects do you see as undesirable? How could we change the ways that we structure the judicial branch, select judges, or define the powers of judges in order to reduce the undesirable aspects of the connections between politics and the courts?*

Review of Key Objectives

Court Structure and Processes

 9.1 Explain how American court systems are organized.

(pages 260–265)

The United States has a "dual court system," in which each state, as well as the federal government, operates its own multilevel system with trial and appellate courts. The U.S. Supreme Court carefully selects a limited number of cases each year and then decides important issues of law and policy.

KEY TERMS

Adversarial System 260
Inquisitorial System 260
Dual Court System 260
Criminal Prosecutions 260
Civil Lawsuits 260
Jury Trials 260
Original Jurisdiction 260
Settlements 260
Plea Bargains 260
Appellate Jurisdiction 262
Intermediate Appellate Courts 262
Courts of Last Resort 262
Appellate Briefs 262
Majority Opinion 262
Concurring Opinion 262
Dissenting Opinion 262
Writ of Certiorari 263

CRITICAL THINKING QUESTIONS

1. If intermediate appellate courts were eliminated so that American court systems had only two levels—trial courts and courts of last resort, how would that affect the work of the courts and the judicial branch's impact on people in the United States?
2. Is it desirable to permit the U.S. Supreme Court to select which cases it wants to hear? How would the governing system be affected if a constitutional amendment required the Supreme Court to decide at least 200 cases each year?

INTERNET RESOURCES

Explore the federal court system at http://www .uscourts.gov

Explore state court systems at http://www.ncsconline .org/D_kis/info_court_web_sites.html

ADDITIONAL READING

Baum, Lawrence. *American Courts: Process and Policy,* 6th ed. Boston: Wadsworth, 2008.

Smith, Christopher E. *Courts, Politics, and the Judicial Process,* 2nd ed. Chicago: Nelson-Hall, 1997.

The Power of American Judges

 9.2 Identify the reasons why American judges are powerful actors in the governing system.

(pages 266–271)

American judges are powerful because of their authority to interpret constitutions and statutes, their power of judicial review, and in the federal system, their protected tenure in office. They often use their interpretations of rights in the Bill of Rights to invalidate or limit actions by the executive and legislative branches.

KEY TERMS

Statutes 266
Judicial Review 267
Marbury v. *Madison* (1803) 268
Judiciary Act of 1789 269
Writ of Mandamus 269
Impeachment 269
Court-Packing Plan 270

CRITICAL THINKING QUESTIONS

1. How would the American governing system be different if judges did not possess the power of judicial review? Which areas of public policy would be different and how would they be different?
2. Should we make it easier to remove federal judges from office, such as through a decision by the president or a petition signed by 10,000 citizens? How would such changes affect the governing system and public policy?

INTERNET RESOURCES

Read judicial opinions from the U.S. Supreme Court and other courts at http://www.law.cornell.edu, http:// www .oyez.org, and http://supreme.justia.com

ADDITIONAL READING

Burns, James MacGregor. *Packing the Court: The Rise of Judicial Power and the Coming Crisis of the Supreme Court.* New York: Penguin Press, 2009.

O'Brien, David. *Storm Center: The Supreme Court in American Politics,* 8th ed. New York, Norton, 2008.

Judicial Selection

 9.3 Outline the selection process for federal judges.

(pages 272–273)

Federal judges must be appointed by the president and confirmed by the Senate through a political process that involves influence by U.S. senators, predictions about the judges' values and decisions, and activity by political parties and interest groups. States use various methods to select judges, including elections and merit selection.

KEY TERMS

Senatorial Courtesy 272
Filibuster 272
Merit Selection 272

CRITICAL THINKING QUESTIONS

1. Does the process of federal judicial selection ensure that qualified individuals become judges? Why or why not?
2. Former U.S. Supreme Court Justice Sandra Day O'Connor is leading a national effort to eliminate the use of elections as a means of judicial selection. Do you support her efforts? Why or why not?

INTERNET RESOURCES

Examine competing perspectives on judicial selection at http://www.ajs.org (advocates for merit selection of judges) and at http://www.afj.org (advocates for the appointment of politically liberal justices).

ADDITIONAL READING

Goldman, Sheldon. *Picking Federal Judges: Lower Court Selection from Roosevelt Through Reagan*. New Haven, CT: Yale University Press, 1997.

Yalof, David Alistair. *Pursuit of Justices*. Chicago: University of Chicago Press, 2001.

Judicial Decision-Making

 9.4 Explain the theories concerning how Supreme Court justices reach their decisions.

(pages 274–277)

Debates exist about the proper way to interpret the Constitution and statutes, and these debates affect choices about who will be selected to serve as judges. Politicians typically advocate for the selection of judges whom they believe share their preferences concerning public policy. However, scholars recognize that there are several models of judicial decision-making employed by various judges, not all of which simply advance a particular set of policy preferences. While some scholars believe that judges' decisions are guided by personal values, others argue that judges may use case precedents, strategic voting, or concerns about preserving judicial institutions as major influences over decisions.

KEY TERMS

Case Precedent 274
Flexible Interpretation 275
Legal Model 276
Attitudinal Model 276
Strategic Voting Model 276
New Institutionalism 276

CRITICAL THINKING QUESTIONS

1. Which model or models of judicial decision-making may have guided the Supreme Court's decision to recognize a right of choice for women concerning abortion? Explain how the model(s) could lead to that decision.
2. If you were a judge faced with Savana Redding's case about strip searching students in school, what factors would influence your decision?

INTERNET RESOURCES

Examine the contrasting views on judicial decision-making and constitutional interpretation presented on the Web sites of two prominent organizations for lawyers and law students: the Federalist Society for Law and Public Policy Studies (http://www.fed-soc.org) and the American Constitution Society for Law and Policy (http://www.americanconstitutionsociety.org).

ADDITIONAL READING

Baum, Lawrence. *Judges and Their Audiences*. Princeton, NJ: Princeton University Press, 2006.

Epstein, Lee, and Jack Knight. *The Choices Justices Make*. Washington, DC: CQ Press, 1998.

Action in the Court Pathway

 9.5 **Characterize the litigation strategies used in the court pathway.**

(pages 278–281)

Individuals and interest groups use many strategies in the court pathway. Their likelihood of success is enhanced if they have expertise about the specific legal issues in a case, the resources to initiate and sustain litigation, and the patience to follow the court pathway through each of its stages. Interest groups also select test cases that will best present issues to a court in a favorable manner, and they make additional strategic choices about the court in which they will file a case and the way in which they frame their arguments.

KEY TERMS

Pro Bono 278
Test Case 279
Amicus Briefs 280

CRITICAL THINKING QUESTIONS

1. In *Safford Unified School District* v. *Redding*, the competing arguments focused on the extent to which privacy rights exist when school officials feel obligated to protect students from drugs. How would you state the strongest argument for your side if you were Savana Redding's lawyer? What is the opposing argument for the school?
2. How can interest groups use public relations strategies to help their litigation efforts? In what ways might Savana Redding's lawyer have used such techniques to help her case?

INTERNET RESOURCES

Discover interest groups that use the court pathway: Washington Legal Foundation (http://www.wlf.org), Pacific Legal Foundation (http://www.pacificlegal.org), American Civil Liberties Union (http://www.aclu.org), and NAACP Legal Defense Fund (http://www.naacpldf.org).

ADDITIONAL READING

Epstein, Lee, and Joseph F. Kobylka. *The Supreme Court and Legal Change: Abortion and the Death Penalty.* Chapel Hill: University of North California Press, 1992.

Tushnet, Mark V. *Making Civil Rights Law: Thurgood Marshall and the Supreme Court, 1936–1961.* New York: Oxford University Press, 1994.

Implementation and Impact of Court Decisions

 9.6 **Evaluate the courts' effectiveness in enforcing judicial decisions.**

(pages 282–283)

Judges cannot always ensure that their decisions are implemented. They must depend on enforcement actions by the executive branch and compliance by the public. As a result, their ability to shape public policy may vary from issue to issue, depending on whether other governmental actors and public opinion support their decisions.

CRITICAL THINKING QUESTIONS

1. Should judges anticipate implementation problems when making their decisions? If so, how might this affect judicial decision-making?
2. Are judges effective in shaping public policy? What policy issues would you use as examples to answer this question?

INTERNET RESOURCES

Learn about upcoming law and policy controversies that will be addressed by the U.S. Supreme Court at the American Bar Association's Web site: http://www.abanet.org/publiced/preview/briefs/home.html

ADDITIONAL READING

Canon, Bradley C., and Charles A. Johnson. *Judicial Policies: Implementation and Impact,* 2nd ed. Washington, DC: CQ Press, 1999.

Hume, Robert J. *How Courts Impact Federal Administrative Behavior.* New York: Routledge, 2009.

Rosenberg, Gerald N. *The Hollow Hope: Can Courts Bring About Social Change?* 2nd ed. Chicago: University of Chicago Press, 2008.

Judicial Policymaking and Democracy

9.7 Describe the debate over whether it is appropriate for judges to shape public policy in a democracy.

(pages 284–285)

Vigorous debates continue to occur about whether it is appropriate for appointed, life-tenured federal judges to create law and public policy in a democracy. Critics of judicial involvement in policymaking argue that democracy is harmed when unelected judges make decisions that should be the sole responsibility of elected officials in the legislative and executive branches. Supporters of judicial action claim that judges cannot avoid shaping policies when fulfilling their responsibility to protect the constitutional rights of individuals and minority group members.

CRITICAL THINKING QUESTIONS

1. Would judicial policymaking be less controversial if we developed ways to hold federal judges accountable for their decisions? Would this be desirable?
2. If you were a federal judge giving a lecture at a university, how would you respond if a student asked you, "Should judges make decisions that shape public policy?"

INTERNET RESOURCES

Examine information about lawsuits seeking to persuade judges to tell corrections officials how prisons should be run. Consider whether such litigation and resulting judicial policymaking should be viewed as proper under the U.S. constitutional governing system: https://www.prisonlegalnews.org

ADDITIONAL READING

Feeley, Malcolm M., and Edward L. Rubin. *Judicial Policy Making and the Modern State.* New York: Cambridge University Press, 1998.

Sandler, Ross, and David Schoenbrod. *Democracy by Decree: What Happens when Courts Run Government.* New Haven, CT: Yale University Press, 2003.

Chapter Review Test Your Knowledge

1. What happens as a result of politicians' recognition that judges' interpretations of the Constitution and statutes are influenced by values and attitudes and not based solely on established law?
    a. Only the best qualified and most experienced judges receive appointments.
    b. Political parties, interest groups, and elected officials want to see judges selected who share their political values.
    c. Presidents and governors will fire judges whom they believe to be incompetent.
    d. The Senate will only approve judicial nominees who receive top ratings from lawyers' associations.

2. The power of judicial review permits the Supreme Court to invalidate
    a. statutes and executive actions that the Court deems unconstitutional.
    b. the operation of checks and balances between the other two branches.
    c. constitutional amendments that the Court finds to be irrelevant or inconsistent with modern jurisprudence.
    d. constitutional amendments that the Court finds to be inconsistent with trends in public opinion.

3. All of the following statements about the landmark Supreme Court case *Marbury* v. *Madison* are correct EXCEPT:
    a. It asserted the Court's authority without directly ordering the president to take action.
    b. It established judicial review by striking down a section of the Judiciary Act of 1789 without discussing the source of the power.
    c. The power of judicial review established a check on the power of the two elective branches of government.
    d. The power of judicial review has not been used since *Marbury*, but the power makes Congress careful to enact statutes that comply with the Constitution.

4. Lifetime appointments for federal judges are considered essential, because
    a. well-qualified judges are so rare they must be given incentives to serve.
    b. judges must not be pressured to cater to political parties or public opinion.
    c. judges must be discouraged from running for elective office.
    d. judges require years of experience before they can perform their duties effectively.

5. Regarding presidential selection of Supreme Court nominees, which of the following statements is the most accurate?
    a. Justices are selected based upon their reputation for honesty and impartiality.
    b. Only candidates with prior experience as lower-court judges can be nominated.
    c. Candidates are usually selected based on their presumed political values and policy preferences.
    d. All Supreme Court nominees are subject to approval by a majority vote of both chambers of Congress.

6. Most cases heard by the Supreme Court arrive by way of
    a. original jurisdiction.
    b. appellate jurisdiction.
    c. writ of habeas corpus.
    d. writ of certiorari.

7. If you are the chief justice on the U.S. Supreme Court, when do you get to decide which justice writes a majority opinion for the Court?
    a. in all cases.
    b. when you are the most senior (longest-serving) justice in the majority.
    c. when the most senior justice gives you permission to make the assignment.
    d. when you vote with the majority in a case.

8. Which statement accurately describes the Supreme Court's relationship to public policy?
    a. Article III of the Constitution says, "The Supreme Court shall have jurisdiction over all public policy matters."
    b. The Supreme Court uses its powers of constitutional interpretation and statutory interpretation to shape public policy.
    c. The president and Congress recognize that they must always obey and enforce policy-related decisions of the Supreme Court.
    d. Article III of the Constitution says, "The Supreme Court can interpret the Constitution, unless its decisions will affect public policy."

9. All of these statements about Supreme Court procedure are correct EXCEPT:
    a. Each attorney is limited to 2 hours of uninterrupted time to present a case.
    b. Appellate briefs must be submitted prior to oral argument.
    c. Four justices must agree to hear a case before it will be accepted.
    d. The court receives thousands of petitions each year, but very few cases are granted a hearing.

10. A traditional legal order requiring a government official to take a specific action is known as
    a. a writ of habeas corpus.
    b. a writ of certiorari.
    c. a writ of mandamus.
    d. an obiter dictum.

11. President Franklin D. Roosevelt's plan to appoint additional justices to the Supreme Court in order to challenge the Court's hostility to the New Deal was known as
    a. gerrymandering.
    b. court-packing.
    c. court-bashing.
    d. executive privilege.

12. The tactic of using lengthy speeches in the Senate to delay proposed legislation or block the appointment of a federal judge is known as
    a. senatorial privilege.
    b. gerrymandering.
    c. log-rolling.
    d. filibuster.

13. Which of the following is NOT a method of judicial selection used by states?
 a. partisan election.
 b. presidential appointment.
 c. nonpartisan election.
 d. merit selection.

14. Which courts' judges are most likely to feel obligated to decide cases by following rules established in decisions previously made by other judges?
 a. Trial court judges—because they can be overturned on appeal if appellate judges disagree with their decisions.
 b. Court of appeals judges—because they need to demonstrate their knowledge of existing law to gain appointments to the Supreme Court.
 c. Supreme Court justices—because they do not want to appear to be inconsistent.
 d. None—all judges feel completely free to use their best judgment and decide whatever they wish in any case.

15. A legal rule established by a judicial decision that guides subsequent judicial decisions is known as
 a. judicial courtesy.
 b. judicial restraint.
 c. statutory interpretation.
 d. case precedent.

16. Those Supreme Court justices who interpret the Constitution based on the writings and rationales of the founders are following the _____ approach.
 a. flexible interpretation
 b. preferred freedoms
 c. original intent
 d. gradual expansionist

17. The political science model suggesting that justices reach their decisions based upon calculated tactics to achieve their preferred case outcomes is known as
 a. the legal model.   c. the strategic voting model.
 b. the attitudinal model.   d. new institutionalism.

18. Which potential litigants are best positioned to make effective use of the court pathway for policy impact?
 a. indigent petitioners and minorities.
 b. interests groups and wealthy individuals.
 c. ideological conservatives.
 d. ideological liberals.

19. Regarding enforcement of judicial decisions, which of the following statements is the most accurate?
 a. Judges may issue directives but have limited ability to ensure that they are implemented.
 b. Courts are designed to obey executive bureaucracies.
 c. The intent of the legislative branch will always overcome the intent of the judicial branch.
 d. The doctrine of federalism prohibits judges from interpreting the actions of state legislatures.

20. What can be said about federal judges and the protection of rights for members of minority groups?
 a. Interest groups have effectively used litigation to persuade federal judges to make decisions supporting the concept of equal rights.
 b. Interest groups failed in their efforts to persuade federal judges to issue decisions to advance equal rights.
 c. Federal judges decided that Congress is solely responsible for protecting the rights of minority groups.
 d. Federal judges decided that the president is solely responsible for protecting the rights of minority groups.

mypoliscilab Exercises

Apply what you learned in this chapter on **MyPoliSciLab**.

Read on mypoliscilab.com

 eText: Chapter 9

Study and **Review** on mypoliscilab.com

 Pre-Test
 Post-Test
 Chapter Exam
 Flashcards

Watch on mypoliscilab.com

 Video: Court Rules on Hazelton's Immigration Laws
 Video: Prosecuting Corruption
 Video: Most Significant Abortion Ruling in 30 Years
 Video: Prosecuting Cyber Crime

Explore on mypoliscilab.com

 Simulation: You Are a Young Lawyer
 Simulation: You Are the President and Need to Appoint a Supreme Court Justice
 Simulation: You Are a Clerk to Supreme Court Justice Judith Gray
 Comparative: Comparing Judiciaries
 Timeline: Chief Justices of the Supreme Court
 Visual Literacy: Case Overload

Political Socialization and Public Opinion

KEY OBJECTIVES

After completing this chapter, you should be prepared to:

10.1 Explain the relationship between public opinion, public policy, and fundamental values.

10.2 Determine how and why public opinion changes and the factors leading to stability in values and beliefs.

10.3 Differentiate between the dominant political ideologies in the United States, and explain how value structures impact public opinion and political action.

10.4 Illustrate how individuals acquire their political values.

10.5 Assess how membership in various social groups impacts political views and behavior.

10.6 Explain how public opinion is measured.

How do people acquire their political values, and how stable is public opinion?

On January 4, 2010, Amanda Simpson became the first openly transgendered person appointed by a U.S. president. President Barack Obama appointed Ms. Simpson to be a senior technical advisor for the U.S. Commerce Department's Bureau of Industry Security, following a 30-year career in the industry.

Back in 1998 when Tammy Baldwin (a Democrat) became the first woman elected to represent Wisconsin in Congress, she was also the first openly homosexual candidate elected. However, her sexual orientation was generally considered to be irrelevant in the campaign, and she won her first election by 53 percent.

Barney Frank (a Democrat from Massachusetts) was first elected to Congress in 1980 and became the country's first openly gay member of the House in 1987. When Frank publically "came out" (he had begun to tell friends he was homosexual years before), the event received national attention. But his sexuality never became a big issue in his home state of Massachusetts. Frank was so popular in his home district that he was even able to withstand a scandal in 1989 that linked him with a male prostitute who allegedly ran a prostitution ring out of his D.C. apartment.

Do these events signal a change in the public's opinion regarding sexuality? Are people in the United States more accepting of homosexual, transgendered, and transsexual individuals than in the past? Or are these isolated events that do not reflect broad changes in public opinion?

How do people's opinions change regarding issues such as sexuality? By what processes do people acquire values? Although our culture and political values are relatively stable, change does occur—often gradually, but sometimes with dramatic speed. When our culture changes, our government responds. In this chapter, you will examine the power of public opinion and culture to bring about change and influence our world.

Resource Center
• Glossary
• Vocabulary Example
• Connect the Link

■ **Public Opinion:** The attitudes of individuals regarding their political leaders and institutions as well as political and social issues.

EXAMPLE: *Public opinion tends to be grounded in political values and can impact political behavior.*

Public Opinion

10.1 Explain the relationship between public opinion, public policy, and fundamental values.
(pages 296–299)

Our government, Abraham Lincoln reminded us in his Gettysburg Address, is "of the people, by the people, and for the people"—in short, a product and a reflection of the American public. So when you think about public opinion, the concept may at first seem quite straightforward—it is the opinion of the general public. In a society as large and diverse as ours, however, it is no easy job to determine *the* opinion of "the public." It is therefore helpful to think of **public opinion**■ as a mechanism that quantifies the various opinions held by the population or by subgroups of the population at a particular point in time. A complete picture of the opinions of more than 300 million Americans is difficult to estimate but nevertheless insightful.

Public opinion is grounded in political values, but it can be influenced by a number of sources and life experiences. Despite the fact that we are a highly educated society, this advanced level of education has not directly translated into a more politically informed citizenry. Seventy percent of Americans cannot name their senators or their members of Congress. Those who are politically knowledgeable, however, tend to have more stable political opinions. Many experts and political commentators believe that since most people don't base their opinions on specific knowledge, their opinions are neither rational nor reasonable.[1]

Other scholars have argued that a general sense of political understanding is enough to cast an informed ballot and to form reasonable political opinions.[2] Therefore, even though most citizens cannot name the chief justice of the U.S. Supreme Court, they can nevertheless form rational and coherent opinions on issues of public policy and political preferences. It is important to note that research on public opinion most often focuses on the voting population rather than on the general population. This is an important distinction, because the voting population is generally more educated and more politically knowledgeable than the general population.

The Relationship Between Public Opinion and Public Policy

To what extent should public opinion drive public policy? There are many answers to this question, and they reflect assorted takes on the nature of democracy itself. Of central importance is the role of the public in the governing process. How influential should public opinion be? How much attention should our political leaders pay to the public's positions and attitudes? Some authorities believe (though they may not say this openly) that public opinion should have little influence on the behavior and decision making of our leaders. They argue that democracies need to limit the influence of the people, allowing the better-informed and more educated leaders to chart our path. Others argue that the views of the people should be given great weight, as a representative democracy needs to pay attention to the will of the people.

Those who believe that democracies need to limit the ability of the public to influence events argue that information must be controlled and narrowly shared. Leaders should do the thinking and the planning, and the masses should step up occasionally to select their leaders in periodic elections and spend the rest of their time as spectators.[3] Many analysts are concerned that public opinion changes too easily and that people are too busy to pay much attention to politics. People are lacking in interest, not in intelligence. Some researchers have found evidence to support the notion that it might be best for leaders to minimize the impact of public opinion and to allow citizens to influence policymakers primarily through elections.[4] This **elitism**■ was forthrightly expressed in the early days of our republic, but it is not widely acknowledged among political leaders and commentators today.

HISTORICAL VIEWS The founders, on the whole, thought that too much influence was given to the preferences of the people under the Articles of Confederation. As you've seen, the Articles created a system that was responsive to the broad public but not receptive to the elite. In the new constitutional system they created, the founders reacted by diminishing the relationship between the government and public opinion. The new system was designed to impose a sort of waiting period on the masses, reflecting the thought that officials should shape public opinion, not respond to it.

For example, *Federalist No. 63* asserts that a "select and stable" Senate would serve as "an anchor against popular fluctuations," which would protect the people from their "temporary errors." In *Federalist No. 49,* Madison warns of the "danger of disturbing the public tranquility by interesting too strongly the public passions." Hamilton argues in *Federalist No. 68* for the indirect election of the president by a council of wise men (the Electoral College) who must not react too quickly to the passion of the people, and in *Federalist No. 71* he further warns against following the "sudden breeze of passion" or listening to every "transient impulse" of the public.

The founders saw the government as our guardian, protecting us from ourselves. They did believe that long-held views—those that lasted over the presidential term and the staggered Senate elections—should affect the course of government. They were more concerned with curbing *transient* ("here today, gone tomorrow") opinions, which they viewed as "common." Today, as we have become more educated and have adopted a political system with universal adult suffrage, people have come to expect their government to be open and responsive.

CONNECT THE LINK
(Chapter 13, pages 380–381) Do you think the power of interest groups is overestimated by most Americans?

■ **Elitism:** The theory that a select few—better educated, more informed, and more interested—should have more influence than others in our governmental process.

EXAMPLE: *Many believe that the framers of our Constitution were elitists, because they were typically more wealthy and educated than the masses. Elites tend to view the world differently than those who are less advantaged.*

CONTEMPORARY CONSIDERATIONS In direct opposition to this elitist theory—and by far the more commonly held view of contemporary political leaders and political scientists—has been a position based on *pluralism*. Whereas elitists have argued that complex decisions need to be made free from public pressure, pluralists believe that citizens should be informed and should participate in democratic decision making to ensure the health and vitality of the system. They argue that participation by the public gives legitimacy to the political process and governing officials. Pluralists urge officials to pay close attention to the desires of the people in charting their actions, because active participation is an essential part of a healthy democracy. This line of reasoning goes back to the ancient Greek philosopher Aristotle, who believed that collective judgments were more likely to be wise and sound than the judgments of a few.

Political scientist Sidney Verba makes a strong case that public opinion, as measured by polls, should be heeded because polls are a more egalitarian form of political expression than other forms of participation, which tend to benefit the more educated and affluent. Since each citizen has an equal (but small) chance of being selected to participate in a poll, there is a greater chance that the opinion of the broad public will be accurately determined. Some theorists insist that other forms of political expression are better gauges of public opinion, because they require more effort from people. Verba, however, presents a strong argument that economic differences between the affluent and the less affluent make it difficult for the views of the general population to be heard, because the wealthy are better able to articulate and present their points of view. Hence, Verba says, it is a bit utopian to think that the concerns of all demographic groups could be fairly and accurately portrayed without public opinion polls.[5]

The reality of the situation probably lies somewhere between these two theories. There are times when officials respond to the views of the people—especially when the opinion is fairly popular and when an issue is presented that offers a chance to gain a political advantage. If the voting population is interested in an issue and a dominant viewpoint emerges, elected officials will be under great pressure to pay attention to the opinions and act accordingly. Even unelected officials, including judges, are often influenced by public opinion.

At other times, officials pay less attention to the views of the public, including the views of voters. This is likely to happen when the public has focused relatively little attention on an issue. Officials may also choose not to be responsive when their convictions come into conflict with the views of the people. Elected officials may take unpopular positions that they nevertheless believe in, risking their public support for their beliefs. Knowing when to follow public opinion and when to resist it is one of the marks of a truly great political leader.

One example of public opinion *not* swaying government policy is in the area of gun control. Imposing some form of gun control is popular among a large segment of the citizenry (especially in times following a publicized gun tragedy), but significant federal gun control legislation is rare. Passed in 1993, the Brady Bill, which mandated waiting periods when purchasing handguns, was the first major federal gun control law since 1968—and it was allowed to quietly die in 2004 despite its popularity among a large majority of Americans. Many critics cite this example to argue that public opinion is not influential in American politics.

Consider, however, a different example: drug policy. Following the highly publicized deaths of a few famous athletes, and with increased media coverage of drug abuse and the widespread availability of illicit drugs in the mid-1980s, the public became very concerned with drug abuse, citing it as the nation's most important problem. Congress and the White House struggled to catch up with public concern, each quickly presenting initiatives to address the country's "drug crisis." Significant legislation passed, increasing the role of the federal government in a problem that historically had been viewed as primarily the responsibility of state governments. A major public service campaign was launched to persuade Americans to "just say no" to drugs. A federal "drug czar" was appointed, and a "War on Drugs" was declared.[6] Unlike gun control, this example demonstrates the power of the public in influencing government to respond to a problem.

Why did the government respond to public concerns over drugs but fail to respond to the support for additional gun control provisions? Chapter 13, pages 380–381, will offer one explanation: Organized and powerful interest groups vehemently have opposed gun control, whereas no organized interest groups have opposed the War on Drugs. This, however, is the simple answer. The complete answer is far more complex. One reason why officials responded to the concern over drugs but not over guns is that people were more worried about the drug crisis than they were about assault weapons. In social science jargon, the drug crisis was simply more "salient" to the population. Moreover, the media reinforced the concern many felt about drug problems, but they did not focus much attention on concerns over the availability of military-style assault weapons. When public officials discuss issues and keep them in the limelight (as they did with drugs), public opinion can often be influenced.

The Relationship Between Public Opinion and Fundamental Values

Shared support for fundamental values tends to temper disagreements and leads to stability in public opinion. Countries that lack agreement on essential values tend to be far more volatile and to have higher levels of unstable public opinion. Most Americans agree on a number of key political values and are proud to live in the United States. Americans believe in

■ **Equality of Opportunity:** The belief that all should have equal chances for success in education, employment, and political participation.

EXAMPLE: *Public schools were founded to allow all children equal opportunity to become educated and achieve success.*

■ **Equality of Outcome:** An egalitarian belief that government must work to diminish differences between individuals in society so that everyone is equal in status and value.

EXAMPLE: *Equality of outcome has produced calls to end discrimination in pay and was the theory that motivated the Equal Pay Act of 1963.*

First Ladies have for some time taken up projects of particular interest to them. For instance, Lady Bird Johnson was committed to beautification, Rosalynn Carter worked on behalf of mental health, and Laura Bush promoted education. Pictured here is Michelle Obama playing with kids at a free fitness clinic as a component of her campaign to combat childhood obesity and improve the health of children. —*Do you think that the projects of a First Lady should be seen as central to the president's administration? How do you see the role of the First Lady evolving?*

limits on speech? Can the speech of the wealthy drown out the speech of the poor? When we move from the abstract to specific policies, there is often disagreement.

INDIVIDUALISM In addition to freedom, Americans highly value the idea of **individualism,** a belief that goes back to the earliest days of our republic. A reverence for individualism and individual rights is central to our democracy, because the government is expected to protect individuals and design policies that enhance the chances of reaching self-fulfillment. It is also central to our economic system: At the heart of capitalism lies a belief in individualism that in many cases permits individual interests to win out over community interests. (Socialism, by contrast, values community needs over individual wants.) The spirit of individualism also stresses the right of citizens to own property and to control their earnings (hence the conflict over tax policies). Comparing the general sense of individualism in the United States to that in Europe provides a vivid example of how varied opinions can be.

Europeans generally expect their governments to address individual concerns, such as providing health care and alleviating poverty. They believe that such programs are valuable and should be funded. While Americans would like for everyone to have health insurance, for the most part we do not believe it is the government's role to fund universal health insurance programs. The high levels of conflict surrounding health care reform that spread throughout the country in 2009 and 2010 are evidence of this conflict. The root of this markedly different set of attitudes is the difference of opinion between individual and community responsibility.

majority rule, coupled with the need to protect minority rights. We see fair, free, and competitive elections as essential to our democracy. We feel strong national loyalty and patriotism, which together provide solid and crucial support for our governmental system. Even though we see problems, we would rather live here than anywhere else. But while we share many common values, we often disagree over their meaning and differ on specific policies related to these values.

PERSONAL LIBERTY One area of broad agreement is support for personal liberty. Our country was founded on the idea of protecting individual liberties and freedoms. As you saw in Chapters 4 and 5, our Constitution and Bill of Rights were written to protect individual freedoms "from" and "to." We are protected *from* unreasonable searches, *from* cruel and unjust punishments, and (with the Fourteenth Amendment) *from* discrimination. We are protected against infringement on our freedom *to* practice our religion freely, *to* express our minds, and *to* join with others in forming organizations. Most of us cherish these liberties, but the specific meaning of these freedoms can cause disagreement. Should hate groups have no

EQUALITY Americans also strongly support the idea of equality, a complex notion involving both political and social aspects. There is near-universal support for political equality: The notion of one person, one vote is deeply embedded in our culture. But when we speak of equality in our society (meaning economic equality, educational attainment, social status, and power, for example), the issue becomes more complex. Most of us believe in the idea of **equality of opportunity**■ (the belief that everyone should have a chance of success), but many Americans find the idea of **equality of outcome**■ (using the government to ensure equality) more controversial. Examples of policies that grant equal opportunities for success are public schools and public defenders for people accused of crimes who cannot afford their own lawyers. In contrast, the Equal Pay Act of 1963, which required employers to pay men and women equal wages for equal work, was motivated by a belief in equality of outcome. Today, the idea of equal wages for both sexes is not controversial, but other policies to promote equality are.

Affirmative action is an example of a public policy that tries to achieve equality of opportunity and equality of outcome, depending on how the policy is designed. Affirmative action in college admissions and scholarships provides equality of opportunity, as many well-qualified students might not otherwise have a chance to attend college. Affirmative action in granting governmental contracts to minority-owned construction firms, for example, is motivated by the goal of equality of

outcome, ensuring that these firms are treated equally and without bias in business. Current controversies over affirmative action, however, provide a good example of how even though many people agree on the basic notion of equality, disagreement occurs when we put these values into action.

Public Opinion

10.1 Explain the relationship between public opinion, public policy, and fundamental values.

PRACTICE QUIZ: UNDERSTAND AND APPLY

1. Our highly educated society has resulted in a far more politically informed citizenry.
   a. true b. false

2. *The Federalist Papers* warned about granting too much political authority to the unstable opinions of the general public.
   a. true b. false

3. Contemporary political leaders and political scientists view the participation of citizens in governmental decision making
   a. from an intellectually elitist perspective.
   b. as a force that legitimizes our political process.
   c. as a serious problem, given how transient public opinion can be.
   d. b and c.

4. Which of the following are fundamental values in America?
   a. personal liberty c. individualism
   b. economic equality d. a and c

ANALYZE

1. Are there times when political leaders need to oppose public opinion? What are some examples of instances in which leaders may need to act in a manner that is opposed by the majority?

2. What fundamental values do Americans support? Why? How are these shared values reflected in the federal budget?

IDENTIFY THE CONCEPT THAT DOESN'T BELONG

a. Personal liberty
b. Equality of opportunity
c. Equality of outcome
d. Individualism
e. Majority rule and minority rights

10.1

Resource Center
• Glossary
• Vocabulary Example
• Connect the Link

■ **Catalyst-for-Change**
Theory: The assertion that public opinion shapes and alters our political culture, thus allowing change.

EXAMPLE: *As public opinion became more accepting of less traditional roles for women in society, our political culture changed to support these less traditional roles.*

The Stability of Political Beliefs

10.2 Determine how and why public opinion changes and the factors leading to stability in values and beliefs.

(pages 300–303)

Political culture is the set of norms, customs, and beliefs that help citizens understand appropriate ways to act in a political system and provide support for political institutions and practices. It also involves the shared economic and political values about how government should operate. Evidence shows that political culture is relatively stable over time, with party identification being the most stable.[7] Opinions can and do change over a lifetime, but major ways of thinking (partisanship, ideology, and economic and social values) tend to remain stable once a person reaches adulthood. Evidence also exists that adults often adjust their views to adapt to changing political environments and to changing life circumstances.[8]

One source of stability is the broad consensus on the key values we have just discussed. Because our political elites tend to be better educated, they are even more supportive of democratic ideals than are typical individuals. Although we experience conflict, there have been few significant controversies over fundamental issues that have led individuals and groups desiring change to go beyond the established channels to promote their cause. A few exceptions exist: The Civil War is the foremost example of a fundamental conflict, but it ended in the decisive victory of one side, permanently settling the issues of slavery and secession. And a century later, U.S. society faced serious conflicts over the Vietnam War and civil rights. But on the whole, our society has been successful in avoiding violence by using political channels to promote change. Another reason our system is stable is that in the United States, levels of distrust in our institutions of government and our constitutional system (which can be very dangerous and lead to instability) are relatively low. Although trust goes up and down over the years, sufficient levels of trust remain to sustain our system.

Shifts in Public Opinion

There have been periods in our history in which large shifts in opinion have occurred; often these shifts have reflected major transformations in American politics. Perhaps the greatest such shift was in the 1760s and 1770s, when overwhelmingly loyal British-American subjects turned into republican rebels against the Crown.

From the 1950s to the 1970s, there were large increases in support for civil liberties for communists, socialists, and atheists. From the end of World War II through the early 1970s, a national consensus emerged condemning racial segregation. Since the 1960s, opinion has become much more approving of interracial marriage and of equal employment rights for homosexuals. In 1958, only 4 percent of Americans approved of interracial marriages. The number has steadily increased since that time, rising from 20 percent in 1968 to 43 percent in 1983 and reaching 77 percent in 2007.[9] Today, interracial marriage is widely accepted by all racial groups in the United States, with young Americans being the most supportive.[10] Support for equal employment opportunities for homosexuals has also risen steadily: 56 percent of Americans supported equal rights in 1977, 71 percent in 1989, and 89 percent in 2007.[11] In 2010, for the first time in the United States, slightly more than half (52 percent) of Americans stated that gay and lesbian relationships were morally acceptable—up from 40 percent in 2001.[12] However, other dimensions of homosexual rights, including same-sex marriage and the adoption of children by homosexuals, remain hotly debated. One of the biggest shifts in public opinion was the 48-percent increase between 1938 and 1975 in the number of people who agreed that it was appropriate for a married woman to work outside of the home for wages, even if she had a husband who could financially support her.[13]

Most of the significant changes in American public opinion have occurred gradually, over several decades. Rather than sharp changes, we more commonly find very slow changes in Americans' beliefs and life circumstances. Attitudes toward abortion, for example, provide a good illustration of the stability of public opinion (see Figure 10.1). Abortion has been a controversial issue since the 1970s, but overall public opinion has remained consistent over the years. Most gradual change can be explained by **cohort replacement,** which simply means that younger people replace older people; and as each generation has experienced a different world, it is logical that each would have different opinions. It is estimated that 50 percent of the electorate is replaced every 20 years.[14] Demographic changes in society also help to explain gradual change, and so does changing technology. For example, computer usage clearly affects the way in which people become informed.

Sometimes, we do see rather abrupt changes in public opinion, particularly in the area of foreign policy. Political scientists Benjamin Page and Robert Shapiro found that shifts in opinions on foreign policy were three times as rapid as changes in domestic preferences, presumably because the landscape of international politics changed more quickly than that of domestic affairs.[15] Areas that saw abrupt changes were opinions regarding wars (World War II, Korea, Vietnam, the war in Iraq), foreign aid, defense spending, and the Middle East.[16] For example, before the attack on Pearl Harbor, public opinion overwhelmingly favored an isolationist foreign policy; those attitudes shifted with dramatic suddenness after December 7, 1941, the day of the attack on Pearl Harbor and the beginning of U.S. involvement in World War II.

■ **Barometer of Public Attitudes:** The theory that the media reflect popular culture.

EXAMPLE: *Popular culture is reflected by the characters on network sitcoms, because the programs serve as barometers of public attitudes competing for acceptance.*

■ **Interactive theory:** The theory that popular culture both shapes and reflects popular opinion.

EXAMPLE: *When someone or something challenges the dominant views reflected in our popular culture, popular opinion often changes, and so does political culture. Changing views of homosexuality both reflect and lead to changes in political culture.*

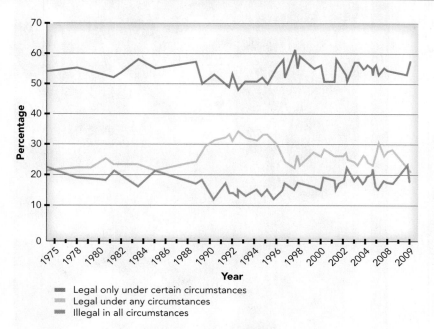

Legend:
- Legal only under certain circumstances
- Legal under any circumstances
- Illegal in all circumstances

FIGURE 10.1 ■ U.S. Public Opinion on Abortion, 1975–2009

As you can see, opinion on this controversial issue has remained fairly stable. In 1976, 54 percent of Americans thought abortion should be legal under certain circumstances; today, that number is stable at 53 percent. Over the past three decades, the percentage in support of the idea that abortion should be legal under certain circumstances has ranged only between 48 and 59 percent.

SOURCE: Reprinted by permission of Gallup, Inc. http://www.gallup.com/poll/1576/abortion.aspx

The Impact of Popular Culture on Political Opinions and Values

Many people believe that our popular culture can influence our political values and culture, and several historical examples demonstrate ways in which popular culture has had a significant effect. One early example occurred during the abolitionist era, an antislavery movement that began in the North during the early 1800s but did not get onto the mainstream agenda until after the publication of Harriet Beecher Stowe's novel *Uncle Tom's Cabin* in 1851. The novel personalized the horror of slavery and mobilized people who had previously been unaware about the depth of the problem. The book sold more than 300,000 copies in the first year, and within 10 years it had sold more than 2 million copies, becoming the all-time American best-seller as a percentage of population. The film *Birth of a Nation* (released in 1916), which glorified the Ku Klux Klan and is arguably one of the most racist movies ever made in the United States, clearly harmed American race relations, especially after it was shown to children in many southern schools as a "history lesson." Finally, Betty Friedan's 1963 book *The Feminine Mystique* invigorated the feminist movement in the 1960s.

Today, politics and entertainment have become increasingly intertwined.[17] Celebrities often make political statements, ranging from open expressions of support for a particular candidate or party to organizing and articulating support for political issues or movements. When discussing the effect of popular culture on political culture, we discover several controversies, most notably focusing on the issue of cause and effect. Does popular culture affect values and beliefs, or do values and beliefs affect popular culture? For example, when in 1997 Ellen DeGeneres "came out" as a gay woman (both personally and as her character, Ellen Morgan, on the then-popular TV show *Ellen*), did she do so because the climate had changed, making it more acceptable to be gay? Or did her coming out lead to changed attitudes toward homosexuality? Was it both? It is difficult to determine what came first.

Several theories have been advanced to explain the relationship between popular culture and political culture. According to the **catalyst-for-change theory**■, popular culture promotes change and shapes the independent attitudes and beliefs of the public. One example of this theory occurred in 1947 when Jackie Robinson became the first black player in Major League Baseball. Watching him display remarkable athletic ability as he played for the Brooklyn Dodgers, and his remarkable control and refusal to respond to the hail of racial slurs from fans that he faced in his first year, caused many people to rethink the common racial stereotypes of the time. In the same way, when Vanessa Williams was crowned the first black Miss America in 1983, many people in society began to think differently about issues of race and beauty.

A second theory sees popular culture as a **barometer of public attitudes**■, not as the shaper of those attitudes. According to this theory, Ellen DeGeneres was able to come out because our culture and beliefs had changed, permitting a more tolerant view of homosexuality. Furthermore, this theory explains the popularity of media stars Perez Hilton and Adam Lambert, and the Academy Award–winning film *Brokeback Mountain*—not because they caused us to see homosexuality differently, but because our attitudes had already begun to change.

Still another explanation, **interactive theory**■, asserts that popular culture both changes *and* reflects social values and beliefs. In a highly interactive process, popular culture serves as both a catalyst and as a barometer. This last theory seems most logical and dynamic.[18]

Pioneers in sports: In 1947 Jackie Robinson broke the color barrier in Major League Baseball, and in 2008 Danica Patrick (right) became the first woman to win an Indy 500 car race when she defeated her competitors in the Indy Japan race. Despite crashing in her NASCAR debut in Daytona Beach, she remains popular with the fans—in part because of her off-track behavior —*Since Patrick's accomplishment came after women were competitive, will it have the impact of Robinson's breakthrough? Do you think that young girls should view Patrick as a positive role model, since she broke key barriers in sports? Or should they be encouraged to find their role models elsewhere because she uses her gender for financial gain?*

FIGURE 10.2 ▪ U.S. Public Opinion on Who Possesses the Most Valued Leadership Traits

The percentage of Americans who believe that women are more likely to possess the most valued leadership traits is substantial (50 percent think that women are more honest than men, while only 20 percent believe that men are more honest than women). However, only 6 percent believe that women make better political leaders than men. —*What do you think is causing this paradox? Are these values changing in our society?*

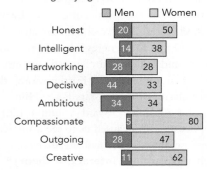

Percentage saying this trait is more true of

	Men	Women
Honest	20	50
Intelligent	14	38
Hardworking	28	28
Decisive	44	33
Ambitious	34	34
Compassionate	5	80
Outgoing	28	47
Creative	11	62

Traits listed in order of the public's ranking of their importance to leadership. "Equally true" and "don't know" responses are not shown.

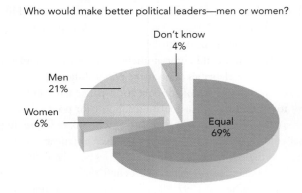

Who would make better political leaders—men or women?

Don't know 4%
Men 21%
Women 6%
Equal 69%

SOURCE: "A Paradox in Public Attitudes. Men or Women: Who's the Better Leader?" (Washington, DC: Pew Research Center, August 25, 2008), pp. 1,3. Reprinted by permission of the Pew Social and Demographic Trends Project http://pewsocialtrends.org/assets/pdf/gender-leadership.pdf

Consider how public opinion has changed regarding the status of women in our society. Because of a concerted effort to improve the position of women, support for women's equality is higher today than ever in our history. Figure 10.2 shows that Americans today believe that women possess many of the traits important for political leadership—in fact, a substantially larger percent of the public rates women as superior to men in the two most important leadership traits, honesty and intelligence.[19]

However, in the same survey, only 6 percent of respondents thought that women made better political leaders than men (21 percent thought that men made better political leaders than women, while the vast majority—69 percent—thought men and women were equally good). This paradox reflects the fact that although women have reached record levels of success in educational attainment and in the workforce, very few have reached the highest levels of political or corporate leadership. Before the rise of the modern women's rights movement in the 1960s, only 46 percent of Americans thought women should be equal with men in business, industry, and government; in 2004, the numbers had risen to 78 percent.[20]

A number of consequences have emerged from this important cultural change. First, women are seeing growth in opportunities, most notably in education and business. Today, there are more female-headed businesses than ever before. Nearly half of incoming business graduate students are women, and more than half of law students are women. Proportionately more women are now earning associate's and bachelor's degrees, and 42 percent of the doctoral degrees in the United States are awarded to women (though women disproportionately major in the lower-paid and less prestigious fields of education and the humanities).

Although women have made progress in many sectors of society, they are still significantly underrepresented in our government: Women make up nearly 17 percent of Congress, 33 percent of statewide elective executive officials, and 24 percent of state legislators.[21] Women run only 3 percent of Fortune 500 companies; however, the number of female CEOs of these companies increased from seven in 2005 to 15 in 2009 (with only 28 women leading Fortune 1000 companies).[22] The Department of Labor examined the "glass ceiling" and found it to be lower than many people thought, often keeping women from top corporate leadership positions.

Recent class action lawsuits against Wal-Mart and Costco alleging sexual discrimination testify to the problem. The Wal-Mart case (*Dukes* v. *Wal-Mart Stores, Inc.*) is the largest civil rights class action ever certified. Both lawsuits charge that the companies discriminated against female employees in decisions involving pay and promotion. In April, 2010, the certification of this class-action suit was upheld. Wal-Mart has pledged to appeal the suit to the Supreme Court. It is doubtful that such lawsuits would ever have been brought in the era before our culture changed to see women as equal participants in our society. Shifts in public opinion can result in tangible cultural change.

The Stability of Political Beliefs

10.2 Determine how and why public opinion changes and the factors leading to stability in values and beliefs.

PRACTICE QUIZ: UNDERSTAND AND APPLY

1. The theory that popular culture shapes the independent attitudes and beliefs of the public is known as
   a. cohort replacement.
   b. catalyst-for-change.
   c. barometer of public attitudes.
   d. elitism.

2. The fact that Americans tend to agree on fundamental values tends to
   a. result in universal support of important public policies.
   b. stabilize our political system.
   c. cause noncompetitive elections.
   d. allow challengers to win more often in elections.

3. What percentage of the electorate is replaced every 20 years?
   a. 10   c. 50
   b. 20   d. 80

4. Public opinion regarding foreign policy changes more rapidly than public opinion toward domestic policy.
   a. true
   b. false

ANALYZE

1. What aspects of society tend to stabilize public opinion?

2. Why do you think that most shifts in public opinion are largely incremental as a result of cohort replacement? What types of issues can result in dramatic and rapid shifts in opinions?

IDENTIFY THE CONCEPT THAT DOESN'T BELONG

a. Incremental change
b. Shared values
c. Gradual change
d. Rapid change
e. Cohort replacement

10.2

Resource Center
• Glossary
• Vocabulary Example
• Connect the Link

■ **Political Ideology:** A consistent set of beliefs that forms a general philosophy regarding the proper goals, purposes, functions, and size of government.

EXAMPLE: *Once people develop their ideology, barring major world events, it is unlikely to change significantly throughout their lifetimes.*

Political Ideology

10.3 Differentiate between the dominant political ideologies in the United States, and explain how value structures impact public opinion and political action.

(pages 304–305)

Political ideology■ is a consistent set of basic beliefs about the proper purpose and scope of government. Americans generally tend to fall into two camps: liberals and conservatives, although at various points in our history, many have been reluctant to identify themselves as either, and some have always identified with other ideologies. In general terms, **liberals**■ tend to support social and cultural change (especially in connection with issues of equality) and want an activist government that encourages change. **Conservatives**■, by contrast, tend to favor traditional views on social, cultural, and economic matters and demand a more limited role for government in most spheres. Although there is some ideological variation within each party, today's Republican Party is, generally speaking, the party of conservatives, whereas most liberals tend to identify with the Democratic Party.

Although not nearly as popular as liberal and conservative ideology, a number of people today identify with populist and libertarian ideology. **Populists** believe that the government can be a positive agent to protect "common people" (which historically included farmers and workers) against the moneyed elite. Populists favor governmental action to promote equality but also support policies to uphold order. **Libertarians** support individual liberty in economic, personal, and social realms over government authority. Libertarians acknowledge that government must have some authority, but they believe that most governmental action must be severely regulated and limited.

MYTH EXPOSED Many Americans believe that liberals prefer more government involvement, while conservatives favor less government involvement. This more-less distinction holds true when looking at economic issues and spending on public goods that benefit many people. For instance, liberals favor government spending on environmental protection, education, public transportation, national parks, and social services. In these areas of public policy, conservatives want smaller governmental budgets and fewer governmental programs. However, when it comes to government involvement with respect to social issues, conservatives generally support more governmental intervention in the form of restrictions on abortion, pornography, and same-sex marriage, while liberals tend to prefer less government intervention in these same areas.

Today, the critical difference between liberals and conservatives concerns not so much the *scope* of governmental activity as the *purpose* of governmental actions. Generally speaking, conservatives approve of using governmental power to promote order, including social order, though there are exceptions to these generalizations. Conservatives typically favor firm police action, swift and severe punishments for criminals, and more laws regulating behavior, such as teen curfews. Such beliefs led many conservatives to support stringent anticommunist domestic and foreign policies in the 1940s and 1950s. Programs to fight domestic terrorism (such as the USA PATRIOT Act, which was initially bipartisan and very popular as an immediate reaction to the September 11, 2001) now gets more conservative than liberal support. Conservatives want to preserve traditional patterns of social relations, including the importance of the domestic role of women in family life and the significance of religion in daily life and school. Conservatives today do not oppose equality, but they tend not to view securing equality as a prime objective of governmental action.

In general, liberals tend to worry more than conservatives do about the civil liberties implications of the USA PATRIOT Act and government surveillance of potential terrorists. Liberals are less likely to approve the use of governmental power to maintain order but are more willing to use governmental power to promote equality. Thus they tend to support laws to ensure that homosexuals receive equal treatment in employment, housing, and education. They favor policies that encourage businesses to hire and promote women and minorities, and they want to raise the minimum wage and provide greater access to health care for all people.

Table 10.1 shows how people have identified with ideology in the United States since 1974. There has been an increase in the

TABLE 10.1	**Percentage of Americans Identifying with a Particular Political Ideology, 1974–2008**

Why do you think the number of liberals declined to a low of 14 percent in 1994 but then returned in 2008 to levels seen in 1974? Why do you think the percentages identified with conservative ideology saw a steady increase from 1974 until 1994 then a large decline? How do the groups of people you come into contact with compare to this distribution?

SELF-CHARACTERIZATION	1974	1984	1994	2008
Extremely liberal, liberal, or slightly liberal	21	18	14	21
Moderate or middle-of-the-road	27	23	26	22
Extremely conservative, conservative, or slightly conservative	26	29	36	27
Don't know, or haven't thought about it	27	30	24	30

SOURCES: Data from "The ANES Guide to Public Opinion and Electoral Behavior: ANES Time Series Cumulative Data File." *American National Election Studies* downloaded from http://www .electionstudies.org/studypages/download/datacenter_all.htm August 13, 2010. Reprinted with permission.

■ **Liberal:** A person who generally supports governmental action to promote equality, favors governmental intervention in the economy, and supports environmental issues.

EXAMPLE: *Liberals believe the promotion of equality is a prime governmental responsibility; they support policies that allow for legal protection for homosexuals.*

■ **Conservative:** A person who believes in limiting government spending, preserving traditional patterns of relationships, and that big government is a threat to personal liberties.

EXAMPLE: *Conservatives argue that government ought to promote morality and traditional values; they oppose same-sex marriages.*

percentage of people who consider themselves conservatives and a slight increase in the percentage of people who label themselves liberal. The growth of both groups has come at the expense of the "undecided" category (reflecting the manner in which society has become more polarized and has been growing more conservative).

STUDENT profile

One is Greater than None (1>0) is an organization started in 2007 by eight Long Island, New York, girls to help free forced child laborers in Ghana, Africa. The eight girls (then only 13 and 14 years old) became interested in the plight of enslaved child laborers following an emotional *Oprah Winfrey Show* (titled "The Little Boy That Oprah Couldn't Forget"), which aired on February 9, 2007 and depicted the horrific working conditions of enslaved children. The girls worked after school selling bracelets, necklaces, and clothes to raise money (as well as social awareness) to free the children. Rather than become discouraged to learn that it would cost approximately $4,300 to free each child, they were determined to do what they could—deciding that saving even one child is more than none (hence the name of the group).

In the first nine months, the girls raised enough money to rescue and care for eight children for two and a half years. To date, they have helped rescue forty-eight children in Ghana. Their work has been profiled on the *Martha Stewart Show*, the *Today Show*, and *The Morning Show*, and they have won awards for their activism from the Encouragement Foundation and at the 2009 Youth Summit. Most recently, they have turned their

FIGURE 10.3 ■ Annual Trends in Political Ideology

"How would you describe your political views—'very conservative,' 'conservative (or) moderate,' 'liberal (or) very liberal'?"

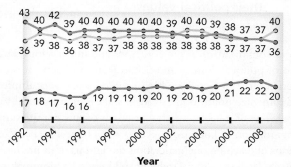

Year

Annual averages 1992–2009 data based on January-September Surveys

▬ Percentage Conservative   ▬ Percentage Moderate
▬ Percentage Liberal

SOURCE: Lydia Saad, "Conservatives Maintain Edge as Top Ideological Group." Gallup, October 26, 2009. Reprinted by permission of Gallup, Inc. http://www.gallup.com/poll/123854/conservatives-maintain-edge-top-ideological-group.aspx

attention to collaborating with Remote Area Medical (RAM) to help raise money to provide desperately needed medical care for rural Americans. For more information, see their Web page (http://www.oneisgreaterthannone.org).

SOURCE: *Teen Vogue*, December/January 2008, p. 68.

Political Ideology

10.3 Differentiate between the dominant political ideologies in the United States, and explain how value structures impact public opinion and political action.

PRACTICE QUIZ: UNDERSTAND AND APPLY

1. According to Table 10.1, today most Americans characterize themselves as
   a. liberal.
   b. moderate.
   c. conservative.
   d. uncertain about their ideology.

2. If you favor using government resources to promote equality you are more
   a. liberal.   c. radical.
   b. conservative.   d. libertarian.

3. One clear distinction between liberals and conservatives in the United States is that the former always favor governmental regulation and the latter never do.
   a. true   b. false

ANALYZE

1. What is political ideology? How do liberals differ from conservatives?

2. How do individuals' core values relate to their partisan ideology? Do you think Americans are more or less ideological than they were in years past? Or are differences between liberals and conservatives being exaggerated?

IDENTIFY THE CONCEPT THAT DOESN'T BELONG

a. Increased spending on social services
b. Capital punishment
c. Same-sex marriage
d. Increased spending on environmental protection
e. Affirmative action programs

Resource Center
• Glossary
• Vocabulary Example
• Connect the Link

■ **Agents of Political Socialization:** Factors that influence how we acquire political facts and knowledge and develop political values.

EXAMPLE: *People who have similar experiences tend to have similar political views. Agents of socialization are especially important for young people and continue to shape political views throughout young adulthood.*

Political Socialization

10.4 **Illustrate how individuals acquire their political values.**

(pages 306–309)

Political socialization is the conscious and unconscious transmission of political culture and values from one generation to another. It is the process by which people learn political information, organize political knowledge, and develop political values. Socialization is not a onetime event; it occurs continuously. The transmission of knowledge as a part of political socialization is a means of teaching one generation the lessons of its predecessors, ideally leading to social stability and better decision making.

Research demonstrates that learning during childhood and adolescence affects adult political behavior;[23] we must therefore examine very carefully the process by which people learn about politics. Factors that influence the acquisition of political facts and the formation of values are called **agents of political socialization**■. Let's examine six such agents: family, school, peers and community, religion, the media, and events.

Family

Children learn a wide range of social, moral, religious, economic, and political values from their families, and what they learn can dramatically shape their opinions. When parents are interested in politics, they tend to influence their children to become more politically interested and informed, because children often try to copy the behavior of loved ones.[24] For this reason, families are a very important agent of socialization, serving as an intermediary between children and society.

Observing how parents react to different situations can affect values that are learned and beliefs that are developed. For example, how parents react to the police can set the stage for how children will view authority. Parents' views of poverty can affect the attitudes of their children about welfare and social services. Parents are often most influential in transmitting party identification to their children, especially when both parents are of the same political party. If children do not adopt their parents' political party, they are more likely to define themselves as independents than to align with the opposite party.[25]

Researchers have shown that parents are especially influential in teaching gender roles and racial attitudes. Children who are raised by mothers who work outside the home for wages, for example, tend to have more progressive views of gender. Girls who are encouraged by a parent to be more assertive tend to be more independent and to have more independent careers.[26] Prejudiced parents are more likely to have prejudiced children. Children learn bigotry directly (from parental attitudes and comments) and indirectly (from watching parental interactions with others). Once children are exposed to different factors in

adolescence, however, the relationship between parental intolerance and children's bigotry diminishes.[27] Parental influence wanes when children mature and other factors increase in importance.

Recent research concerning the influence of the family on political values has been mixed, finding that the actual levels of influence depend on a number of factors. Families with strong relationships and strong mutual ties tend to be the most likely to transmit values. As the nature of the family changes, we will need to continue examining its influence in shaping the development of children's values. Children today are more likely to be home alone and less likely to spend time with their parents, for example, and the number of families eating together has steadily declined. Moreover, the number of children living in single-parent homes has increased. The number of single mothers rose from 3 million in 1970 to 12 million in 2007, and during that same period, the number of single fathers from 393,000 to 2 million.[28] It's not hard to see that these changes in family structure and interaction may affect the role families will play in influencing children in the future.

School

Schools teach political knowledge, the value of political participation, and the acceptance of democratic principles. Their effectiveness in doing so, however, is debated. Schools seem to be more effective in transmitting basic political knowledge than in creating politically engaged citizens.

Elementary schools introduce children to authority figures outside the family, such as the teacher, the principal, and police officers, while also teaching about the hierarchical nature of power. In doing so, the schools prepare children to accept social order, to follow rules, and to learn the importance of obedience. Children learn that good citizens obey the laws (just as good children obey the rules of the schools and of their parents). School elections for student council and mock presidential elections teach students important democratic principles and procedures, such as the notion of campaigning, voting, and majority rule. Most children emerge from elementary school with a strong sense of nationalism and an idealized notion of American government, thus building a general sense of goodwill for the political system that lays the foundation for future learning.[29] As they mature, children start to see their place in the political community and gain a sense of civic responsibility.

High schools continue building "good citizens" through activities and curriculum. Field trips to the state legislature and classes with explicit political content can result in a greater awareness of the political process and the people involved in it. The school curriculum teaches political facts, while the school atmosphere can affect political values. Students with positive experiences in school, who develop trust in school leaders, faith in the system, and a sense of worthiness are more likely to show higher levels of support for the national political system. Students who feel they are treated fairly by school officials tend to have more

■ **Efficacy:** The belief that individuals can influence government. *Internal political efficacy* is the belief that individuals have the knowledge and ability to influence government. *External political efficacy* refers to the belief that governmental officials will respond to individuals.

EXAMPLE: *People with high levels of political efficacy tend to be better educated and politically active.*

Schools are important agents of socialization, teaching children not only political facts but also a sense of patriotism and a belief in democratic practices. Children across the country begin their day by pledging allegiance to the American flag and reciting school rules. These practices help create a strong sense of loyalty and nationalism. —*Do you think that schools focus too much on allegiance, failing to teach students to critically analyze our government, leaders, and policies? When, if at all, should one learn to question authority?*

trust in officials and feel less alienated from their government.[30] Civics classes in high school are a potentially good mechanism for encouraging student engagement in politics. Researchers have found that the simple existence of such classes is not enough to produce civically engaged students; the dynamic of the class is also important. Civics classes that are taught by people who generally like the subject matter and who themselves are politically engaged are far more successful in positively socializing students. On the whole, however, high school seniors are not very well informed about politics, are not very interested in politics, and have only moderate levels of support for democratic practices.[31]

Research consistently demonstrates that a college education has a liberalizing effect when it comes to noneconomic issues. Adults with college experience tend to be more liberal on social issues than adults with less education. Several explanations have been put forward to account for this. College tends to make individuals aware of differences between people and allows them to see the complexity of public policy issues. In classes such as the one you are now in, students are exposed to controversies in our society and learn that the issues are far more complicated than previously thought. Moreover, they learn that intelligent people can disagree. Therefore, they tend to be more supportive of changing opinions and less supportive of the status quo. College students often meet a wider range of people than they had contact with in high school, giving them evidence to reject some social stereotypes and prejudices and to accept more diversity. Also, college faculty are significantly more liberal than their students—and than most people in society. Notwithstanding individual differences among faculty, those in the liberal arts and the sciences tend to be the most liberal.[32] This leads some conservatives to hypothesize that liberal college faculty indoctrinate students, causing them to become more liberal. Whatever the explanation, people with a college education are generally more liberal on social issues than those who haven not been to college.

Peers and Community

Community and peers are also agents of political socialization. Your community consists of the people, of all ages, with whom you come in contact through work, school, or your neighborhood. Peers are friends, classmates, and coworkers who tend to be around the same age as you and who live in your community. Peer influence tends to be weaker than that of school and family, but our companions do affect us. Differences of opinions and preferences between generations are likely due to peer influence (especially regarding tastes in music, entertainment, clothing, hairstyle, and speech). Peers generally serve to reinforce one another, as people tend to socialize with those like themselves. Research shows that in heterogeneous communities, political participation tends to be higher, with more hotly contested and more competitive elections and more political debate, than in homogeneous environments. People are more likely to participate and pay attention to politics if they believe their vote counts, as is the case when there are a variety of views or disagreements and the election is closely contested.[33]

Politically diverse environments are also more likely to provide interesting stimuli and often result in a greater sense that one can have an effect on government.[34] Minorities living in racially diverse environments tend to have higher political **efficacy**■ than minorities living in segregated environments. Researchers found that African Americans living in predominantly black communities generally do not experience political socialization in a manner that encourages political participation and civic engagement.[35] Racial segregation tends to develop a sense of isolation and disinterest in the political system. Areas with high voter turnout, with politically engaged adult role models, and with racial diversity appear to be the best environments to raise politically aware and knowledgeable children who have a sense that their voice can count.

Religion

Religions and religious leaders are important instructors, particularly when it comes to issues of morality, self-sacrifice, and altruism, and they are an important factor in the development of personal identity. Individuals raised in religious households tend to be socialized to contribute to society and to get involved in their communities.[36] Conservative denominations and religions (such as Southern Baptist, traditionalist Catholics, and evangelicals) tend to impart more conservative attitudes (especially regarding abortion and other issues involving personal morality and sexuality) than more liberal churches do.[37] Those raised in religiously diverse communities are more likely to be engaged in politics and have higher levels of political participation.[38]

CONNECT THE **LINK**
Chapter 11, pages 346–347) How important do you think the media are in influencing the values of young people?

Religion can act as a reinforcing mechanism of community and family values on a wide array of moral and political issues.

The Media

We will look more closely at the effect of the media in influencing values, politicians, and society in Chapter 11, pages 346–347. Here, it is appropriate to note that the media are an important agent of political socialization, with varied effects on public opinion. Many authorities believe that the effect of the media on political values and opinions has increased in the past several decades. Today, it is estimated that American children between the ages of 8 and 18 spend more than 53 hours using entertainment media per week (averaging out to nearly 2,800 hours per year).[39] If we add to that the time spent listening to music, reading magazines, and watching movies and music videos, it becomes obvious that entertainment may have a big role in influencing values.

Entertainment media often present behavior at odds with what is approved in the family, schools, and places of worship. Promiscuous sex, drug use, and materialism are common in contemporary programming, with little attention paid to potential consequences. By the time a typical child reaches 18, he or she will have seen 40,000 murders on television.[40] What can result is a competition for influence between media, parents, schools, and religion. Many analysts worry that this focus on negativity can adversely affect political efficacy and trust in government.[41]

However, recent research demonstrates that people do learn valid political information from the media, although great variation exists. A 2008 poll by the Pew Research Center found that 18 percent of the American public could correctly identify the majority party in Congress, the secretary of state, and the prime minister of the U.K. However, differences existed in knowledge levels depending upon the source of media regularly consumed. Regular consumers of the *New Yorker* and *Atlantic*, NPR (national public radio), and *Hardball* were the best informed, while audiences of religious radio programs, the Weather Channel, CBS News, *Access Hollywood*, and the *National Enquirer* had the lowest levels of political knowledge. Interestingly, differences were also found in levels of political knowledge among audiences of late-night television programs. The best informed were fans of *The Colbert Report,* followed by fans of *The Daily Show with Jon Stewart*, with the least politically knowledgeable audiences favoring Letterman and Leno. All of these scores are above the national average, although it should be noted that viewers of the *Colbert Report* and *Daily Show* are more educated and more affluent than most, explaining some of the variation.[42]

PATHWAYS of action

Celebrities and Global Activism

Celebrities possess the unique ability to focus international attention upon world events. Increasingly, we have seen celebrities

Nighttime talk-show hosts often joke about politics, governmental officials, and current affairs. Perhaps the best-known hosts today are Jon Stewart, host of *The Daily Show with Jon Stewart,* and Stephen Colbert, host of *The Colbert Report,* on Comedy Central. On October 30, 2010, the two led the "Rally to Restore Sanity and/or Fear" on the National Mall in Washington D.C. The rally was laced with satirical comedy and watched by millions. Viewers of these programs tend to be better informed than the general public on current affairs. —*Do you think they are better informed because of the programs or because they tend to be better educated? Do you think that either comedian would be a viable candidate for political office? Why or why not?*

use their fame and prominence to raise awareness and money. Preceding the opening ceremonies to the Vancouver 2010 Olympics, the video for *We Are the World—25 for Haiti* made its world premiere. The song brought together more than 70 artists, from a multitude of music genres, to raise money for the victims of the 2010 earthquake in Haiti. In 1985, Michael Jackson and Lionel Richie had assembled 40 artists for the original version, which raised over $60 million for famine relief in Africa.

U2's Bono and Bobby Shriver (who formed DATA—Debt, AIDS, Trade in Africa) created Product Red, a multinational nongovernmental organization working to promote equality and justice in Africa. DATA is dedicated to eliminating the African AIDS epidemic through the promotion of debt relief and fair trade. Save the Children, an international organization to help children in need around the globe, also has a number of celebrity spokespersons, including Gwyneth Paltrow, Jennifer Garner, America Ferrera, Ben Stiller, Chris Daughtry, Gwen Stefani, Hugh Grant, Keira Knightley, Kelly Clarkson, Sacha Baron Cohen, Randy Jackson, Pink, Julianne Moore, Daniel Radcliffe, Stephen Colbert, and Ben Affleck. Examples of these types of activities abound.

Many celebrities are using their fame to alter the public's perception about our definition of community and social responsibility and to promote a sense of shared global citizenship. While some may diminish celebrity efforts as being superficial and self-serving, their actions speak loudly and focus interest on areas in desperate need of attention.

Events

No event of recent decades has had a more dramatic impact on Americans than the terrorist attacks of September 11, 2001. In response to the attacks, the United States embarked upon two, initially popular though increasingly contentious, wars in Afghanistan and Iraq. In the short term, these events altered public opinion in two ways. First, the public has become more aware of the danger of terrorism. Before the terrorist attacks, many Americans did not believe that our country was vulnerable to terrorist threats. Americans often viewed terrorism as a problem that occurred in other countries (with the clear exception of the Oklahoma City bombing in 1995). Following the 9/11 attacks, the number of Americans who expressed confidence that our government could keep us safe declined significantly. The second observed short-term change was a surge in patriotism and a sense of uniting in battle, especially in the years immediately following the attacks. As time has passed, the urgency of terrorism has diminished, as has the popularity of the wars in Iraq and Afghanistan, but a general sense of fear remains high.

Sufficient time has not passed to enable social scientists to assess the long-term consequences of the 9/11 attacks on youth socialization. However, research shows that important events can affect the socialization process, because significant events focus national attention. By examining other events in our nation's past that were of great political importance—the attack on Pearl Harbor, the Vietnam War, the assassination of President Kennedy, and the Watergate scandal are all examples—we can see how shocking events can alter politics.

Political Socialization

10.4 **Illustrate how individuals acquire their political values.**

PRACTICE QUIZ: UNDERSTAND AND APPLY

1. Political socialization refers to
   a. attending important social events involving politicians.
   b. the process whereby political systems become socialist in orientation.
   c. the process whereby each generation develops political consciousness, learns political information, organizes political knowledge, and forms political values.
   d. the process whereby people learn to accept the rules of government—the regulations, laws, and customs of their nation, state, and municipality.

2. Agents of political socialization include
   a. the community and the media.
   b. houses of worship.
   c. peers.
   d. a, b, and c.

3. Heterogeneous environments tend to have higher levels of political participation.
   a. true
   b. false

4. Studies have shown that a college education has the effect of making most people *less* conservative about social issues than they used to be. Why is this so?
   a. Going to college often involves meeting a greater diversity of people, thus encouraging students to become more accepting of cultural differences.
   b. College prompts students to explore the complexities that often lie behind public policy issues.
   c. College education encourages an openness to change, both personally and culturally.
   d. a, b, and c.

ANALYZE

1. Which agents of social change can negatively affect socialization? Which agents are reinforcing?

2. What impact does television have on socialization? How is the effect different among various age groups?

IDENTIFY THE CONCEPT THAT DOESN'T BELONG

a. Elementary schools
b. High schools
c. Parents
d. Organized religion
e. Media

Resource Center
• Glossary
• Vocabulary Example
• Connect the Link

Social Groups and Political Values

10.5 Assess how membership in various social groups impacts political views and behavior.

(pages 310–313)

People with similar backgrounds tend to develop similar political opinions. Dividing Americans along lines of social class, education, religion, race and ethnicity, and gender, these group characteristics also tend to influence public opinion on a variety of domestic and foreign policies.

Before beginning this section, you need to keep in mind several important points. First, we're going to be generalizing about how various factors influence political opinions, but many exceptions exist. Moreover, the effects of specific factors may vary from issue to issue. Rarely do opinions on issues stem from one source—usually, opinions are influenced by many different factors.

We use the term **crosscutting cleavages** to explain how two or more factors work to influence an individual.[43] These cleavages represent splits in the population that seperate people into groups and complicate the work of political scientists, for it is often difficult to say which factors are the most important in shaping particular attitudes. These cleavages can also moderate opinions and lead to stability over time. Take income as an example. There are many issues on which the poor agree; there are also many issues on which they disagree. As you will see, income has an important effect on opinions, but it is not the only factor. Race, gender, region, and religion (to name a few) also affect individuals.

Economic Bases of Partisanship and Public Opinion

Political socialization does not explain the distribution of party loyalties in the United States. Socialization is helpful in describing *how* rather than *why* an individual acquires party loyalty. An important factor that does determine why an individual becomes a Democrat or a Republican is a person's economic standing and that of his or her parents. One principal generalization that you can make about loyalties to the parties in modern times is that they are often based on socioeconomic status.

Traditionally, Democrats have been regarded as the "party of the people" and Republicans as the "party of the rich." This characterization goes back to the 1800s, but it became more pronounced in the 1930s, when Democratic President Franklin D. Roosevelt launched his New Deal programs in the midst of the Great Depression. Labor legislation, Social Security, and minimum wage laws all reinforced the Democratic Party's image as the party of the have-nots. Even African Americans, who had aligned with the Republican Party after the Civil War, partly in loyalty to President Abraham Lincoln, abandoned it in the 1930s for the Democratic Party. Ironically, by aligning with the Democrats, African Americans found themselves in the same party with racist white southerners. Beginning in the late 1960s, southern whites who had opposed or remained lukewarm toward racial integration flocked into the Republican ranks.

However, social class and party loyalties are not as closely linked in the United States as in other Western democracies. Both parties in the United States draw support from upper-, middle-, and lower-status groups. Thus it is difficult for either party to make overt appeals that reflect sharp class differences. When it comes to purely economic issues, the more affluent tend to be more conservative than the less affluent on fiscal issues such as taxation, *assuming that each group is defining its politics strictly on the basis of self-interest.* But when we add education to the equation, liberal views tend to increase along with rising income. In fact, the higher the level of education a person has received, the more liberal that individual tends to be on social and cultural issues. And because education is highly correlated with income, the relationship is complicated. For example, in 2008 the average annual earnings by highest level of education showed clear differences:

$125,618 for individuals holding advanced professional degrees

$60,954 for recipients of bachelor's degrees

$33,618 for high school graduates

$21,491 for adults with less than 9th grade education[44]

Education

As we've discussed, education tends to increase citizens' awareness and understanding of political issues, often having a liberalizing effect when it comes to nonfiscal social issues. For example, a college-educated person will be more likely than a less educated person to choose personal freedom over social order (when they conflict). Thus the more educated groups are more likely to favor gun control and to want limits placed on police authority. There are also differences based on education in issues of foreign policy. The less educated tend to favor isolationist policies that would limit the role of the United States on the world scene, whereas the more educated favor greater U.S. engagement in international affairs.[45]

Table 10.2 illustrates rather significant differences in many areas of public debate. Better-educated people tend to be far more likely than the less educated to support homosexual rights (especially gays' right to adopt children) and far more supportive of abortion rights. Often, however, the more educated (and hence the more affluent) tend to be more fiscally conservative when it comes to economic issues like spending on the poor. The least

TABLE 10.2	Percentage of Americans Favoring Particular Public Policies, by Education, 2008

Do the data presented here surprise you? Considerable differences exist between the more educated and the less educated on issues of reproductive freedom, gun ownership, and homosexual rights. Why do you think this is the case?

PUBLIC POLICY STANCE	LEVEL OF EDUCATION				
	DID NOT COMPLETE HIGH SCHOOL	GRADUATED FROM HIGH SCHOOL	ATTENDED COLLEGE	OBTAINED A COLLEGE DEGREE	OBTAINED AN ADVANCED DEGREE
Favor affirmative action in hiring/promoting	38	24	16	13	19
Favor allowing gays in the military	68	76	79	82	89
Favor allowing gays to adopt	36	49	48	61	62
Favor never allowing abortion	33	15	10	8	8
Favor increased spending on the poor	73	68	61	59	56

SOURCE: Center for Political Studies, *American National Election Studies* Cumulative Data File (Ann Arbor: University of Michigan, 2010). Reprinted with permission.

economically secure people (as measured by income and education) tend to be the most supportive of increasing governmental spending on domestic social services, such as Social Security and the poor.[46] Whereas college-educated people generally favor governmental spending on social services, many of them are hesitant to support increased social spending, because it will result in higher taxes for them (the more affluent). The less educated overwhelmingly favor increased government spending on social programs.

Religion

Religion has always been extremely important in American life. Today, over 83 percent of Americans say that they belong to an organized religion; 70 percent say that religion is important to their lives, and 92 percent say that they believe in God.[47]

Differences in ideology and support of political parties have more effect on voting than do socioeconomic distinctions. When income, education, and occupation are held constant, Catholics and Jews tend to be more liberal and support the Democratic Party, while nonsouthern Protestants tend to be more conservative and support the Republican Party.

In recent decades, these fairly homogeneous alignments have been growing more complicated. Motivated by issues such as abortion and gay rights, "traditional" Roman Catholics today tend to vote Republican, while other Catholics—especially those strongly committed to the reforms of Vatican Council II in the 1960s—have remained in the Democratic column out of concern over social justice and peace issues. Protestants from the

so-called mainline denominations (Episcopalians, most Presbyterians, many Methodists, and some Lutherans, for example) tend to be more split between the political parties.[48] However, white (but not black) evangelicals, who once were mostly either Democrats or nonpolitical, constituted a record 51 percent of the GOP voters in the 2000 presidential election.[49] In 2008, evangelical Protestants were the most supportive of the Republican Party, with 73 percent voting for John McCain. In contrast, only 54 percent of all Protestants voted for John McCain. Barack Obama won 75 percent of the unaffiliated vote, 78 percent of the Jewish vote, and 54 percent of the Catholic vote.[50]

When we examine the differences among religions on public policy issues, important trends emerge. On almost every nonfiscal issue, Jews consistently take the most liberal policy stances, while Protestants take the most conservative. Catholics typically fall in between.

Figure 10.4 illustrates the differences in the distribution of party loyalties based on religion. White Protestants, especially if they describe themselves as evangelicals, are more likely to be Republicans, while black Protestants (who are mostly evangelicals) are far more likely to be Democrats. The more religious Catholics (as measured by the regularity of their church attendance) have become more supportive of the Republican Party, whereas the less observant Catholics vote more heavily Democratic. Jews, on the other hand, have become even more supportive of the Democratic Party than previously. Americans who say that they are not members of organized religions are far more likely to be Democrats than Republicans.

■ **Gender Gap:** Differences in voting and policy preferences between women and men.

SIGNIFICANCE: *The gender gap was coined in the early 1980s to explain the differences between men and women in voting, political party affiliation, and policy preferences. After controlling for other factors, women tend to be more liberal and Democratic than men.*

Race and Ethnicity

At the beginning of the twentieth century, the major ethnic minorities in America were from Ireland, Germany, Scandinavia, Italy, Poland, and other European countries. They came or descended from those who came to the United States in waves from the 1840s to the early 1900s. These immigrants and their offspring concentrated in urban parts of the Northeast and Midwest. The religious backgrounds of these immigrants differed from the predominant Protestantism of those who had settled colonial America. They were politically energized during the Great Depression, becoming an integral component of the great coalition of Democratic voters that Franklin D. Roosevelt forged in the 1930s. For many years, immigrant groups had political preferences that were consistently different from those of "native" Anglo-Saxons. As these groups have assimilated into society and risen in economic standing, however, these differences have been disappearing.

Ever since blacks were brought to North America as slaves, they have been at the bottom of the economic, political, and social totem poles. Their disadvantages still exist despite many important social and legal changes in our society.[51] Before the civil rights movement, black participation in American politics was generally quite limited. But in the generation between about 1930 and 1960, racial politics began slowly to change direction. First, during these years, many blacks moved from the South to northern cities, where they encountered very few obstacles to voting. Second, in the 1950s and 1960s, with the rise of black consciousness and the grassroots civil rights movement led by Martin Luther King Jr. and others, African Americans emerged as a strong, national political force. Civil rights and social policies advanced by the Kennedy and Johnson administrations and the Democratic Congress in the 1960s convinced most blacks that the national Democratic Party was an advocate of racial equality and integration. Ever since, black Americans have identified overwhelmingly with the Democratic Party.

Since the 1960s, whites and blacks have evaluated civil rights issues differently. Whites increasingly believe that "a lot" of positive change has occurred with regard to the life circumstances of African Americans, but fewer blacks feel similarly optimistic. Around 60 percent of African Americans say that black poverty is the result of social factors (discrimination, for example), while a plurality of whites (49 percent) attribute black poverty to its victims' personal characteristics.[52] Although Hispanics make up only about 13 percent of the general population—in southern states, California, the Southwest, and urban areas in northern states—they represent a sizable and a rapidly growing voting bloc. The Hispanic presence in key border states is very large: 25 percent in Arizona, 32 percent in Texas and California, and 42 percent in New Mexico. Although Hispanics are politically strong in some communities, until the last several election cycles, they lagged behind African Americans in organizing across the nation.

African Americans and members of other minority groups display similar political attitudes, for several reasons. First, all racial minorities (excluding second-generation Asians and some Cuban Americans) tend to have low socioeconomic status—a direct result of racism. Substantial differences in earnings continue to exist. Moreover, individuals in all minority groups have been targets of racial prejudice and discrimination. We must be sensitive to issues of race when evaluating many public policies.

Gender

A **gender gap**■ separates American men and women in their patterns of voting behavior, party identification, ways of evaluating presidents, and attitudes toward various public policies. Some political scientists say that the difference in the way men and women vote first emerged in 1920, when newly enfranchised women registered overwhelmingly as Republicans. However, because women did not tend to vote in rates similar to those of men, it

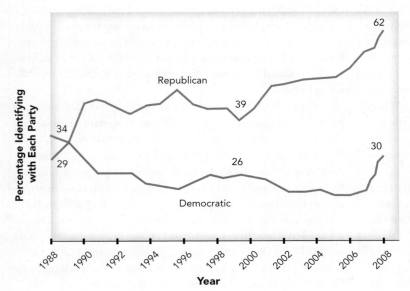

FIGURE 10.4 ■ Party Identification Among White Evangelical Protestants

In 1988, white evangelical Protestants were evenly divided in their party identification between Democrats and Republicans. However, the division has since increased dramatically.
—*What consequences do you think this will have for both parties?*

SOURCE: Scott Keeter, "Will White Evangelicals Desert the GOP?" (Washington, DC: The Pew Research Center for the People and the Press, May 2, 2006). http://pewresearch.org/pubs/22/will-white-evangelicals-desert-the-gop. Reprinted with permission. 2008 updates accessed at http://people-press.org/reports/pdf/445.pdf

was not until the 1980 presidential election that the gender gap attracted much attention.

In that election, when the Republican Ronald Reagan beat the Democratic incumbent Jimmy Carter, he did so with the votes of only 46 percent of the women—but he got the votes of 54 percent of the men. Substantial differences in policy preferences between men and women grew during the 1980s, with women considerably less likely to approve of President Reagan than men were. On many issues, a majority of women embraced the Democratic (or anti-Reagan) position—including a much-publicized movement for declaring a nuclear freeze (a unilateral U.S. cessation in the production and deployment of nuclear weapons), a demand for spending more on social programs, and criticism of the administration's increased defense spending.

According to research from the Center for American Women in Politics at Rutgers University, consistent differences persist between men and women on key issues of public policy.

In foreign affairs, women are more likely to oppose U.S. military intervention abroad and are more apt to favor diplomacy in settling foreign disputes. Domestically, women are more likely than men to support programs that protect health care and meet basic human needs, to support restrictions on the possession and use of firearms, and to favor affirmative action and other governmental efforts to achieve racial equality.[53] On the whole, women tend to be more liberal on all social issues, from capital punishment to gun ownership to gay rights. Perhaps surprisingly, however, men and women tend to have similar views on abortion.

The gender gap, coupled with the fact that more women than men vote, has changed the national agenda and the political landscape. Thus, during the last several presidential and congressional election campaigns, issues of education, health care, prescription drug coverage, and Social Security have dominated the agenda.

Social Groups and Political Values

10.5 Assess how membership in various social groups impacts political views and behavior.

PRACTICE QUIZ: UNDERSTAND AND APPLY

1. What factor tends to increase citizens' understanding of political issues and has a liberalizing affect on non-fiscal social issues?
   - **a.** religion
   - **b.** socioeconomic status
   - **c.** education
   - **d.** ethnicity

2. Studies suggest that within the same socioeconomic group,
   - **a.** Catholics and Jews tend to be more conservative than Protestants.
   - **b.** Catholics tend to be more conservative than Protestants.
   - **c.** Jews tend to be more conservative than Catholics.
   - **d.** Jews and Catholics tend to be more liberal than Protestants.

3. Since gaining true voting rights in the 1960s, most African Americans have voted for Democratic Party candidates.
   - **a.** true
   - **b.** false

4. There is a clear and obvious gender gap in political views in the United States.
   - **a.** true
   - **b.** false

ANALYZE

1. What social factors do you think have an impact on why a gender gap in political views exists in the United States?

2. Why does education tend to have a liberalizing affect on political views?

IDENTIFY THE CONCEPT THAT DOESN'T BELONG

- **a.** Group uniformity
- **b.** Generalizations
- **c.** Group similarities
- **d.** Crosscutting cleavages
- **e.** Group differences

Resource Center
• Glossary
• Vocabulary Example
• Connect the Link

Measuring Public Opinion

10.6 Explain how public opinion is measured.

(pages 314–317)

As a wise individual, often said to be Benjamin Disraeli, once tartly observed, "There are three kinds of lies: lies, damned lies, and statistics." Political scientists and professional pollsters measure public opinion in a variety of ways, but polls are the most accurate tool to objectively measure public opinion.

Use of Polls

Polls represent an opportunity to view a snapshot of public opinion, and they allow officials a quick assessment of public policies. People who value citizen participation in a democracy are more likely to see the virtues of polling. Polls allow people to learn the collective preferences of their fellow citizens, but this has both positive and negative consequences. On the one hand, polls show people that others in their country may have different opinions, thus enabling citizens to grasp the complexity of many political issues. On the other hand, polls can also silence holders of minority opinions by convincing them that most people don't agree with them on a particular issue.

In examining the influence of polls on the public and on our leaders, Elizabeth Noelle-Neumann developed the theory of a "spiral of silence."[54] When the public learns about the dominant view on something or someone, dissenters come under pressure to remain silent and accept the majority viewpoint. One common way in which this phenomenon manifests itself is the "bandwagon" effect—the tendency for individuals to agree with the candidate or opinion that polls show to be attracting the most support or that receives the most media attention.

Many observers of contemporary politics are wary about using polls in our democracy. They argue that polls can be misleading, giving a false sense of the democratic process.[55] They can also be manipulated to advance a political agenda. Thus overreliance on poll data by our officials can be very dangerous.

The political scientist Benjamin Ginsberg thinks that polls weaken the influence of true public opinion.[56] Polls make it easy—perhaps too easy—for people to express their opinions. Often, polls give the impression that opinions are more strongly held than they really are and can create the impression that people actually have opinions on specific topics when in fact they may not. Other forms of political expression require more time and energy; people with deeply held opinions are therefore more likely to turn to them, giving a truer sense of public opinion. Polls rely on a passive form of expression (respondents do not volunteer to participate; they are solicited), hence you cannot be certain that poll results truly reflect the carefully considered opinion of members of the public who are interested in and care about politics.

"Put me down for whoever comes out ahead in your poll."

> We all need to be cautious of public opinion data and to be certain to examine who sponsored the poll, how accurate the poll is, and when it was conducted. —*Why and when do you think that poll data are manipulated?*

Polls may simply capture the fleeting thoughts of a group of people who are approached by the pollsters and agree to respond.

Other critics object that polls tend to measure bluntly what is sometimes a very complex entity—the opinions of the people. Reliance on poll data, say these critics, raises many concerns: Suggested opinions, sampling errors, the wording of questions, and the way poll questions are asked can all skew the responses that are obtained.

One thing is certain though: Public opinion polling is widespread in our society. Each major TV network has paired with a print media organization to conduct polls—CBS News with the *New York Times,* ABC News with the *Washington Post,* and NBC News with the *Wall Street Journal.* And many newsmagazines—*Newsweek, Time,* and *U.S. News and World Report,* for example—routinely commission polls. Research on these three newsmagazines' cover stories between 1995 and 2003 found that 30 percent of the articles cited polling data.[57] Every year, several million people are called on to participate in polls. Our government alone conducts over a million survey interviews every year.[58] To avoid being manipulated, it is very important for individuals to understand how polls are used, constructed, and interpreted.

Modern Polling Techniques

One of the major scientific breakthroughs of the twentieth century was the development of statistical sampling theory, a technique that made possible scientific public opinion polling and survey research. Because opinion poll results are now

■ **Sample:** A subset of the population under study; if selected correctly, it represents the population from which it was drawn with reliable and measurable accuracy.

SIGNIFICANCE: *Since it is nearly impossible to interview all people in a state, a sample is used to allow a large variety of research.*

■ **Probability Sample:** Selection procedure in which each member of the target population has a known or an equal chance of being selected.

EXAMPLE: *Probability samples are the most commonly employed by professional polling companies, because they have better results than other techniques.*

reported so widely in the media, you must be knowledgeable about polling methods in order to make appropriate use of poll results and avoid being misled or manipulated. Moreover, you must avoid relying on a single poll as a definitive measure of public opinion; often, individual polls provide just a limited "snapshot" view of what the public is thinking.

Researchers almost never question every person in a population; that would be prohibitively expensive and time-consuming. Instead, they take a **sample**■—that is, they obtain a portion of the entire population. The goal of sampling is to be able to make generalizations about a group by examining some of its members. Its basic assumption is that individuals can represent the groups out of which they are selected. Because people in similar situations in life are likely to hold similar opinions, it is not necessary to study all of them. On the other hand, because every person is somewhat different, it is necessary to talk to enough people from each major group so that individual uniqueness can be smoothed out and a typical response obtained.

One of the most important elements in a good sample is how *representative* it is of the major social groups that are apt to hold the opinions being researched. Choosing representative samples requires using the correct sampling technique and an appropriate sample size. The sampling technique most widely used today is based on the **probability sample**■, a selection procedure in which all potential respondents enter the sample with an equal or known probability of being selected. Good probability techniques should ensure a representative sample if the sample is sufficiently large. Commercial polling agencies, such as Gallup or Harris, normally use national samples of around 1,200 people.

Survey Research

Once the sample has been drawn, the researcher must turn to the art of developing a good questionnaire that accurately elicits respondents' opinions.

DEVELOPING QUESTIONNAIRES The proper wording and phrasing of the questions are vitally important to producing reliable, objective data. How questions are worded can dramatically affect the responses people give. Several criteria exist to assist in the development of high-quality questions. First, researchers must use language and vocabulary appropriate for the population under study. For example, different vocabulary would be used in surveying new immigrants to the United States than would be used to poll corporate executives. Questions should also be worded to allow socially acceptable responses, thus minimizing the chance of false replies. If people are not given an acceptable way in which to respond to questions, they may lie.

A good example is voting. People are raised to believe that voting is an important right and responsibility and that a good citizen in our society exercises this right. However, not all people vote. So, when asking about whether a respondent has voted, the researcher will obtain more accurate data if the response options include a socially acceptable reason for nonvoting. If the researcher simply asks, "Did you vote in the last election?" a good percentage of nonvoters might lie to avoid looking bad. However, if respondents are asked, "Did you vote in the last election, or because of work or family responsibilities were you too busy?" nonvoters can say that they were too busy without looking bad. Such sensitivity to social acceptance is an important factor in producing superior questions and research.

Also, to get a person's true opinion, questions must be neutrally worded. Let's say you were interested in a respondent's opinion of underage drinking. There are a number of ways in which you could phrase your question. You could ask, "What is your opinion of irresponsible underage people who consume alcohol?" You certainly would get an opinion, but would it be an objective one? Probably not, because you characterize the person as irresponsible and are thus leading the respondent to agree with your characterization. A more objectively worded question would be to simply ask, "What is your opinion of underage people consuming alcohol?" Poll results can vary dramatically depending on the manner in which the questions are worded and the alternative responses provided. Reliable polling agencies will provide a copy of the survey if asked.

Once the sample has been drawn and the questionnaire developed, it's time to administer the survey. Questionnaires can be administered in a variety of ways—professionals typically do so in person, by mail, or by telephone. Each technique has advantages and disadvantages. The researcher must choose the method that is most appropriate for the research and also fits the available budget. When conducting political polls, researchers typically try to include only people who are likely to vote.

INTERPRETING PUBLIC OPINION POLLS Not all polls are released to the general public. Some are conducted to provide politicians with campaign strategies or to determine likely responses to potential stands on an issue. Some groups commission polls but release the results only when they make them appear in a positive light. You must use caution when consuming public opinion data.

Furthermore, it is important that you understand how to interpret the information presented in a poll. Remember that polls rely on a sample of the target population. Even if all the issues identified earlier are accurately addressed, polls may still be inaccurate. This potential for inaccuracy is an unavoidable cost of using a sample rather than interviewing the entire population (which could never be done even if a pollster had access to unlimited resources). Along with the poll results, the pollster should present two measures of accuracy: the margin of error and the confidence level. We'll provide an example and then explain each.

Say that a hypothetical national poll of likely voters shows that 35 percent of respondents have a favorable opinion of an individual who is considering a run for president. How should

■ **Confidence Level:** The probability that the results found in the sample represent the true opinion of the entire public under study.

EXAMPLE: *The traditional standard confidence level is 95 percent, meaning that researchers are 95 percent sure that the sample accurately represents the views of the population under study.*

you interpret this number? Thirty-five percent of the people who responded to the poll have a favorable view. However, we really aren't interested in the opinion of the poll respondents. We want to use the poll findings to figure out the likely feelings of the general population. To do this, we calculate the **margin of error**—a measurement of the accuracy of the results of a survey—to establish a range in which we think that the actual percentage of favorable ratings will fall. The **confidence level**■ is the percentage of confidence that we have that the poll truly represents the feelings of everyone in the population.

Going back to the original example, let's say that the margin of error is plus or minus 3 percentage points and that the confidence level is 95 percent. This means that we are 95 percent sure that the actual percentage of people in the country who have favorable opinions of the potential candidate is between 32 and 38 percent.

Although the mathematics of calculating these numbers are complex (and not something that you need to understand), to be an informed consumer, it is important that you do understand how to interpret and apply both the margin of error and the confidence level. In many close elections, the numbers fall within the margin of error. When this happens, the media will say that the election is "too close to call."

Controversies Surrounding Polling

Call-in and Internet surveys, often called *pseudo-polls*, are controversial, because the results are often falsely presented to the public as scientific and reliable. Only individuals watching a particular program on TV, tuning in to a particular radio talk show, or visiting certain Web sites can participate in the poll. In addition, people who call in (especially if there is a cost in time or money) tend to hold more extreme positions than those who do not bother to participate. These surveys may be interesting, but they are statistically unreliable. The most reliable information is obtained when researchers select the respondents, not vice versa.

Contemporary technology has made many people question how representative samples are. Caller ID, call-block and other similar technologies have made it increasingly difficult for pollsters to reach many people and to select a random sample of the population. Moreover, refusal rates have been rising, with fewer and fewer of the people reached being willing to cooperate with the pollsters. In some surveys, less than 20 percent of calls result in a completed survey, raising the costs of surveys as well as the level of concern about their accuracy. In the 1960s, it was common for two-thirds of contacted people to participate. Today, cooperation rates hover around 38 percent for the national media surveys that take place over a few days, and overnight surveys often have much lower rates.[59]

Concerns have also arisen over the number of people who no longer use home phones but rely exclusively on cell phones. Research indicates that nearly 15 percent of the adult population

in the United States can only be reached by cell phones; however, the same research indicates that that except for age, those who are only available by cell phones are similar to those who can be reached via landline phones (which are more commonly employed by pollsters as this technique is substantially less expensive).[60] This might, however, be a concern if the survey tries to include a large number of college-age individuals, who are more likely to rely exclusively on cell phones and who tend to move a lot.[61]

One area of public opinion polling that has recently come under much scrutiny is the media's reporting of polling data during campaigns and elections—and especially the use on election day of exit polls to predict outcomes before the votes are counted. **Exit polls**■ are taken at selected precincts while voting is in progress, with the pollsters typically asking every tenth voter how he or she has voted and why. In the past, exit polls have been helpful for news organizations as they raced to be the first to predict the winners of elections. But in 1980, having gotten bad news from exit polls in states in the Eastern and Central time zones, President Jimmy Carter conceded defeat to Ronald Reagan 3 hours before polls on the West Coast had closed. Democratic officials criticized Carter and the networks, claiming that prematurely publicizing adverse poll data had caused many western Democrats not to vote, affecting many congressional, state, and local elections. As a consequence, the networks agreed not to predict the presidential winner of a state until all polls in that state had closed.

In the 2000 presidential election, the exit polls conducted by the Voter News Service (made up of the four major networks, CNN, and the Associated Press) were flawed by sampling errors. Faulty exit poll results in Florida—as well as forgetting that the state's western panhandle observes Central rather than Eastern time, so that voting there was still going on—led CBS to predict the incorrect winner not just once but twice. (This was not the only problem in the 2000 presidential elections; we discuss other issues in Chapter 14, pages 408–410). As a consequence, the networks dropped the Voter News Service and, in 2004, used a new service. Exit polls in the 2004 and 2008 presidential elections were also criticized, especially those conducted in states with close elections. In the future, as we see more and more people choosing early voting, the accuracy of exit polls for predicting winners and providing glimpses into the motivations of voters will be even more precarious.

Poll coverage in elections more generally is also troubling. The media often take the easy road and focus on "horse race" coverage (who's ahead in the polls, who's gaining, and so forth), to the detriment of discussing issues and other matters of substance. In 2004, several weeks before Canada's national election, the Canadian Broadcasting Corporation abruptly quit preelection polling, stating that constantly reporting poll results deflected public attention from issues and emphasized the superficial. Many critics have called for the U.S. networks to follow suit.

CONNECT THE LINK
(Chapter 14, pages 408–410) Do you think the
controversies surrounding the 2000 presidential election
have made people more or less interested in politics?

■ **Exit Polls:** Surveys of voters leaving
polling places; used by news media to gauge
how candidates are doing on election day.

SIGNIFICANCE: *Exit polls can be very helpful in
providing immediate insight into who is voting for whom
and why and in projecting the likely winner of an election.*

Given all the concerns about public opinion polling that
have been discussed in this chapter, many critics question the
wisdom of the incessant reporting of polling to reflect public
opinion and desires for social change. Some argue that we must
rely on other forms of political expression to voice the views
of the public; others believe that pollsters can adapt to these
challenges and continue to provide important information
about what the public is thinking.

PATHWAYS of change from around the world

**What do Aflac Cancer Center and Blood Disorders
Service of Children's Healthcare of Atlanta, the Nature
Conservancy, TPRF: Food for People, OCEF (Overseas
China Education Foundation), and the Tibetan Freedom**

Movement have in common? They are the top five causes
listed on Facebook by total dollars donated.[62] Aflac Cancer
Center of Atlanta had 1,072,706 members, raising $1,165,741;
the Tibetan Freedom Movement had 58,214 members raising
$163,798.

There are more than 10 categories of causes on Facebook, from political campaigns (with 17,570 causes listed), to
public advocacy (37,167 causes), to international causes
(27,089). Facebook and other social networking Web sites allow people to interact, raise awareness, and fundraise with
people across the globe in ways unimaginable only a decade
ago. So when some people criticize Facebook as being mind-
less and harmful, you can remind them that it can also be a
powerful tool to change public opinion, increase social awareness, and mobilize people from around the world to fight
injustice and violence.

Measuring Public Opinion

10.6   **Explain how public opinion is measured.**

PRACTICE QUIZ: UNDERSTAND AND APPLY

1. Why are polls sometimes problematic?
   a. When their results are published, they sometimes
      have the effect of silencing members of the public
      who hold minority views.
   b. As another voice of the people, they sometimes
      reflect the effectiveness of an elected official or
      governmental policy.
   c. Increasing numbers of people, especially young
      people, rely exclusively upon cell phones, thereby
      excluding them from telephone samples.
   d. a and c.

2. In the polling process, the goal of sampling is to get
   a. as diverse a set of responses as possible.
   b. as random a set of responses as possible.
   c. as representative a set of responses as possible.
   d. as rapid a set of responses as possible.

3. If proper techniques and protocols are used, polls can
   reliably assess the opinions of the whole nation by
   gathering the responses of as few as 1,200 people.
   a. true   b. false

ANALYZE

1. Can you think of any objections to exit polling? Some
   critics charge that the main advantage of exit polling
   is to help news organizations in their race to be first
   to predict the outcome on election night. Do you
   agree or disagree? Why?

2. What measures can be taken to ensure that polls are
   more accurate and reliable?

IDENTIFY THE CONCEPT THAT DOESN'T BELONG

a. Scientific
b. Sample
c. Error free
d. Probability
e. Representative

Conclusion

Many people lament a fickle American public that they believe is so quick to change its mind. This may be true of some superficial issues; however, on the whole, levels of public opinion are relatively stable. As we saw at the start of the chapter with Amanda Simpson (the first openly transgendered person appointed by a U.S. president), while opinion does change, it is often slow and incremental, especially when it comes to controversial issues such as sexuality.

Political socialization—the complex process by which people learn political information, organize political knowledge and develop political values—provides a consistent mechanism for transmitting political culture from generation to generation. Important agents for socialization include the family, school, peers, community, religion, the media, and events.

Public opinion polling is an important device to gauge public sentiment and influence change in our society, but it can be hard to predict when public opinion will be influential. Politicians often use poll data to build support for policies and to avoid making unpopular decisions. This creates a reciprocal relationship in which public opinion can influence politicians *and* politicians can use public opinion to influence the people.

Today, public opinion polling operations in the White House have become institutionalized. Each modern administration routinely polls the public.[63] Elites often use poll data to claim legitimacy for their positions. When elites disagree, they try to use poll data to claim the high road, thereby minimizing opposition and garnering additional support for their agenda. Polls become strategic tools by which political leaders seek to sell their views and positions to the public.[64] Politicians often act strategically by "rationally anticipating" shifts in public opinion and examining how these changes can affect future elections. In anticipating these changes, leaders can strategically modify their positions. Thus public opinion influences politicians directly, through elections, and also indirectly, because they tend to act rationally in anticipating change.[65]

KEY CONCEPT MAP How has the way people acquire and maintain their political values and beliefs changed?

Family

People Born in 1945

87.7% of children lived with both parents and 9.1% of children lived with only one parent.*

People Born in 1992

69.8% of children lived with both parents and 26.2% of children lived with only one parent.

Critical Thinking Questions ?

What impact has the changing nature of the family structure had on the ability of families to teach positive values and morals to children?

School

Population had far less formal education: only 48% of all people over age 25 finished high school or attended college.

Population had far more formal education: 86.7% of all people over 25 had finished high school or attended college.

How has the nature of society changed with higher levels of formal education? ?

Peers and Community

Nearly all communication with peers occurred in person and via telephone.

Teens were increasingly communicating with peers electronically. In 2008, 84% of 17-year-olds had cell phones.**

Have changes in technology made ties to peers and communities stronger or weaker? ?

Religious Institutions

Only about 5% of this generation's young were unaffiliated with a religion.

About 25% of this generation's young were unaffiliated with a religion.†

Do you think that religion is less powerful in shaping an individual's values and beliefs today than in the past? ?

Media

Most popular TV shows in 1963:

1. *Beverly Hillbillies*
2. *Bonanza*
3. *The Dick Van Dyke Show*
4. *Petticoat Junction*
5. *The Andy Griffith Show*

Most popular TV shows in 2009 (excluding sports and reality TV)††:

1. *NCIS*
2. *The Mentalist*
3. *NCIS: Los Angeles*
4. *CSI*
5. *Desperate Housewives*

How do values portrayed on entertainment shows impact individuals? Are people able to separate reality from fiction? ?

Events

Civil Rights Movement; Women's Rights Movement; President Kennedy assassinated.

9/11; War in Middle East; Barack Obama elected president.

Do you think that the events of the 1960s had a more profound impact on that generation than the events of the 2000s have had on today's generation? ?

* Typical birth year for grandparents of first-year college students. Figures provided for 1963 (when they were 18). Data for 1960s comes from the 1960 Census; annual surveys on families not available until late in the decade. Data from the U.S. Census Bureau, "Families and Living Arrangements," *Current Population Survey Reports.*
** Accessed at http://www.pewinternet.org/Reports/2009/14--Teens-and-Mobile-Phones-Data-Memo/1-Data-Memo/2--Who-has-a-mobile-phone.aspx?r=1
† Accessed at http://pewforum.org/Age/Religion-Among-the-Millennials.aspx
†† Based on results from Nielsen Media Research.

In general, people who share similar life experiences tend to develop similar world views. Among the most influential agents in the development of values are families, schools, peers, communities, religious institutions, and the media. Major world events can also dramatically impact political views and beliefs. Examining how these agents of socialization impact individuals is crucial because political values are unlikely to change dramatically once fully formed. —*Which agents of socialization likely had the greatest impact on individuals born in 1945? In 1992? Why? How do agents of socialization positively and negatively impact our governing system?*

Review of Key Objectives

Public Opinion

10.1 Explain the relationship between public opinion, public policy, and fundamental values.

(pages 296–299)

Public opinion is a far more complex phenomenon than many people appreciate. Grounded in political values, it tends to be very stable, but it can serve as a mechanism to promote cultural change.

Commentators disagree over the role that public opinion should play in influencing public officials. Some believe public opinion ought to have a limited role in American politics, arguing that people are too easily influenced and manipulated. Other political commentators believe that it is healthy in a democracy for public officials to track public opinion and act in accordance with it.

KEY TERMS

Public Opinion 296
Elitism 296
Individualism 298
Equality of Opportunity 298
Equality of Outcome 298

CRITICAL THINKING QUESTIONS

1. How is public opinion formed? How stable is it? What factors tend to stabilize public opinion, and what factors tend to lead to instability?
2. How do the elitist and pluralistic theories differ regarding the importance public officials ought to give public opinion when making decisions? What do you think?

INTERNET RESOURCES

Learn more about an association for public opinion and survey research professionals at American Association for Public Opinion Research (AAPOR): http://www.aapor.org

Pew Research Center for the People and the Press: http://people-press.org

ADDITIONAL READING

Bardes, Barbara, and Robert Oldendick. *Public Opinion: Measuring the American Mind,* 3rd ed. Florence, KY: Wadsworth, 2006.

Erickson, Robert, and Kent Tedin. *American Public Opinion: Its Origins, Content, and Impact,* 8th ed. New York: Longman, 2011.

Clawson, Rosalee, and Zoe Oxley. *Public Opinion: Democratic Ideals, Democratic Practice.* Washington, DC: CQ Press, 2008.

The Stability of Political Beliefs

10.2 Determine how and why public opinion changes and the factors leading to stability in values and beliefs.

(pages 300–303)

Americans largely agree on a number of fundamental values, including liberty, individualism, democratic institutions, basic principles, and equality. Disagreements occur when the government translates these rather abstract ideas into specific public policies.

Public opinion tends to be stable, though we do see substantial shifts during times of crisis or as a reaction to an important event. As we saw with such issues as gay rights, civil rights, and women's rights, gradual changes in public opinion also occur, as a result of cohort replacement, reflecting and shaping our political and popular culture.

KEY TERMS

Political Culture 300
Cohort Replacement 300
Catalyst-for-Change Theory 301
Barometer of Public Attitudes 301
Interactive Theory 301

CRITICAL THINKING QUESTIONS

1. Do you think that Americans truly agree on basic issues? Is it important that we should agree?
2. How, if at all, does popular culture influence political culture?

INTERNET RESOURCES

To explore more about European public opinion visit EUROPA—Public Opinion Analysis of Europe, Eurobarometer Surveys: http://europa.eu.int/comm/public_opinion/index_en.htm

To learn more about human sexual development visit Kinsey Institute for Research on Sex, Gender, and Reproduction, University of Indiana: http://www.indiana.edu/~kinsey/resources/datasets.html

For more information on gay, lesbian, transgendered, transsexual political activism visit National Gay and Lesbian Task Force: http://thetaskforce.org

ADDITIONAL READING

Caplan, Bryan. *The Myth of the Rational Voter: Why Democracies Choose Bad Policies.* Princeton, NJ: Princeton University Press, 2007.

Lippman, Walter. *Public Opinion.* New York: Harcourt, Brace, 1922.

Political Ideology

10.3 Differentiate between the dominant political ideologies in the United States, and explain how value structures impact public opinion and political action.

(pages 304–305)

Political ideology is a consistent set of personal values and beliefs about the proper purpose and scope of government. Once formed, most people's political ideology remains rather stable (barring a critical world or domestic event). The range of political ideologies in the United States is narrower than in other societies; most Americans place themselves fairly close to the center of the political spectrum. Liberals generally believe that government can be a positive actor to advance equality, while conservatives generally support governmental action only to promote order. Political ideology impacts voting behavior, policy preferences, and worldviews.

KEY TERMS

Political Ideology 304
Liberal 304
Conservatives 304
Populists 304
Libertarians 304

CRITICAL THINKING QUESTIONS

1. What is political ideology? What are the principal differences between liberals and conservatives today?
2. What impact do you think political ideology has on our evaluation of governmental officials, policy proposals, and voting behavior?

INTERNET RESOURCES

For more public opinion data visit Polling Report http://www.pollingreport.com/

ADDITIONAL READING

Fiorina, Morris P., Samuel J. Abrams, and Jeremy C. Pope. *Culture War? The Myth of a Polarized America,* 3rd ed. New York: Longman, 2011.

Persily, Nathaniel, Jack Citrin, and Patrick J. Egan. *Public Opinion and Constitutional Controversy.* New York: Oxford University Press, 2008.

Political Socialization

10.4 Illustrate how individuals acquire their political values.

(pages 306–309)

People acquire their political knowledge and beliefs through a process called political socialization. Family, schools, community and peers, religious groups, the media, and events all serve as agents of socialization, introducing individuals into the world of politics and influencing individuals' political values, beliefs, opinions, and ideologies.

KEY TERMS

Political Socialization 306
Agents of Political Socialization 306
Efficacy 307

CRITICAL THINKING QUESTIONS

1. Why is the process of political socialization so important in our society?
2. What factors are the most important in political socialization, and what role do they play in the process?

INTERNET RESOURCES

To learn more about academic polling visit National Opinion Research Center (NORC), University of Chicago: http://www.norc.uchicago.edu

For more on public opinion in the United States visit Kaiser Family Foundation: http://www.kff.org/kaiserpolls/index2.cfm

ADDITIONAL READING

Gimpel, James G., J. Celeste Lay, and Jason E. Schuknecht. *Cultivating Democracy: Civic Environments and Political Socialization in America.* Washington, DC: Brookings Institution Press, 2003.

Jackson, David J. *Entertainment and Politics: The Influence of Pop Culture on Young Adult Political Socialization,* 2nd ed. New York: Lang, 2009.

Social Groups and Political Values

10.5 Assess how membership in various social groups impacts political views and behavior.

(pages 310–313)

People with similar life circumstances and experiences tend to develop similar opinions and values. We see many significant differences between groups based on their income, education, religion, race or ethnicity, and gender. For example, women tend to be more supportive of social programs that benefit the poor and elderly than men. Understanding the socialization process and the way in which demographic factors affect public opinion is important in fully appreciating the diversity of our country.

KEY TERMS

Crosscutting Cleavages 310
Gender Gap 312

CRITICAL THINKING QUESTIONS

1. How does membership in relevant demographic groups affect public opinion?
2. What are some important differences between members of various groups on contemporary issues?

INTERNET RESOURCES

American National Election Studies is regulary conducted to collect academic data on the voting behavior of Americans. For more information visit http://www .electionstudies.org

For extensive archival data in survey data visit Roper Center for Public Opinion Research: http://www .ropercenter.uconn.edu

ADDITIONAL READING

Mattson, Kevin. *Engaging Youth: Combating the Apathy of Young Americans Toward Politics.* New York: Century Foundation Press, 2003.

Price, Melanye. *Dreaming Blackness: Black Nationalism and African American Public Opinion.* New York: New York University Press, 2009.

Measuring Public Opinion

10.6 Explain how public opinion is measured.

(pages 314–317)

Polls are used to measure public opinion on a plethora of issues that are important to Americans; however, poll data can be easily manipulated, and we must be cautious in using poll data to generalize about the population as a whole. Good public opinion polls are useful for gauging public sentiment, but many factors can adversely affect the quality of the data obtained. Such factors include the representativeness of the sample, the wording of the questions posed and the issues explored, and the manner in which questionnaires are administered. Understanding the issues surrounding public opinion polling is an important part of being an informed consumer of political news and information.

KEY TERMS

Sample 315
Probability Sample 315
Margin of Error 316
Confidence Level 316
Exit Polls 316

CRITICAL THINKING QUESTIONS

1. What are the key considerations in determining the reliability of public opinion polls?
2. Why are many political commentators concerned with the contemporary use of public opinion polling? Do you share their concerns?

INTERNET RESOURCES

For more information on public opinion on current controversies, visit: Gallup Organization: http://www .gallup.com

For reports on trends in American public opinion visit: PollingReport.com: http://www.pollingreport.com

ADDITIONAL READING

Asher, Herbert. *Polling and the Public: What Every Citizen Should Know,* 7th ed. Washington, DC: CQ Press, 2007.

Rusk, Jerrold G. *Statistical History of the American Electorate.* Washington, DC: CQ Press, 2001.

Stanley, Harold W., and Richard G. Niemi. *Vital Statistics on American Politics, 2009–2010.* Washington, DC: CQ Press, 2009.

Chapter Review   Test Your Knowledge

1. Truly great political leaders
   a. never feel obliged to act in accordance with the popular opinions of their constituency.
   b. usually act in accordance with the popular opinions of their constituency.
   c. know when—and when *not*—to follow the popular opinions of their constituency.
   d. will appear as if they care about popular opinion even when they really do not.

2. Most Americans believe it is appropriate for the government to ensure that every U.S. citizen has equal opportunities for success, but not to ensure equal outcomes.
   a. true
   b. false

3. Most gradual change in public opinion happens through
   a. cohort replacement.
   b. dramatic events at the national level, such as Pearl Harbor and 9/11.
   c. changes in technology.
   d. a, b, and c.

4. Although public opinion regarding the rights and status of women has become dramatically more favorable in the past 30 years,
   a. women are still in the minority in many graduate and professional schools.
   b. women still hit a "glass ceiling" when trying to gain promotions in the business world.
   c. many women who are discriminated against in the workforce are still reluctant to challenge the discriminatory practices through legal or other means.
   d. a, b, and c.

5. Political scientist Sidney Verba suggested that
   a. economic differences between rich and poor make it difficult for the views of the general population to be heard.
   b. public opinion polls should be heeded, because they are a more egalitarian form of political expression.
   c. education is not as important as social status in terms of public opinion formation.
   d. b and c.

6. The influence of popular culture on our political culture and public opinion has always been a positive feature of our democracy.
   a. true
   b. false

7. In the past 20 years or so, Americans' political ideology has tended to become
   a. more conservative.
   b. more inconsistent.
   c. more polarized.
   d. a and c.

8. International events can become important factors that impact political ideology in the United States.
   a. true
   b. false

9. Some political scientists study the state of American families because
   a. the nature of family life affects the family's role as an agent of socialization.
   b. family life—how parents and children interact, how much money parents make, and other factors—helps us predict what values children will grow up to embrace.
   c. parents' influence over their children becomes increasingly strong throughout adolescence.
   d. a and b.

10. As agents of socialization, elementary schools have the effect of
    a. training children to value their own contributions to the decision-making process.
    b. training children to think creatively.
    c. training children to accept the hierarchical nature of power.
    d. a, b, and c.

11. Having people live in politically and racially diverse communities is good for our democracy, because
    a. such communities cultivate higher political efficacy among individuals than homogeneous or segregated communities do.
    b. such communities are more likely to produce uninformed children than homogeneous or segregated communities are.
    c. living in such communities is the politically correct thing to do.
    d. a and c.

12. Viewing popular electronic media, such as late-night television comedy programs, is a way that people obtain political information.
    a. true
    b. false

13. For most of the twentieth century, what demographic features characterized Republican Party loyalists?
    a. white and well-to-do
    b. ethnic minority and blue-collar
    c. southern
    d. a and c

14. What explains Jewish Americans' loyalty to the Democratic Party?
    a. a concern for social and economic justice in the Jewish tradition
    b. Jews' long-standing focus on international issues
    c. the fact that Jewish-American immigrants benefited from social services instituted by Democratic administrations in the early twentieth century
    d. a and b

15. For much of the twentieth century, the political preferences of immigrant groups in the United States were consistently different from those of Americans of Anglo-Saxon origin.
    a. true
    b. false

16. What is the gender gap?
    a. the inherent differences of ability between men and women
    b. the difference between how women and men have tended to view political issues in this country
    c. the difference between how many men and how few women become elected governmental officials
    d. b and c

17. The media often take the easy road and focus on "horse race" coverage (who is ahead in the polls, who is gaining, and so forth) to the detriment of discussing issues and other matters of substance.
    a. true
    b. false

18. Professional pollsters almost always use some form of probability sampling in their polling because
    a. it is the most convenient and least expensive method.
    b. its use means that all potential respondents have a known or equal probability of being selected.
    c. it produces more accurate results than other sampling techniques.
    d. b and c

19. Anyone eager to influence American society should understand the nature of both public opinion and political socialization because
    a. both mechanisms can bring about social change by influencing elites in our country.
    b. both reinforce conventional thinking—and therefore are worth resisting.
    c. both are forces that politicians routinely ignore once they are in office.
    d. a, b, and c

20. The political ideology of most Americans is relatively moderate compared to those of people from other countries, and it tends not to change much over the course of an individual's lifetime.
    a. true
    b. false

PEARSON mypoliscilab Exercises

Apply what you learned in this chapter on **MyPoliSciLab.**

Read on mypoliscilab.com

eText: Chapter 10

Study and Review on mypoliscilab.com

Pre-Test
Post-Test
Chapter Exam
Flashcards

Watch on mypoliscilab.com

Video: Obama Approval Rating
Video: Opinion Poll on the U.S. Economy

Explore on mypoliscilab.com

Simulation: You Are a Polling Consultant
Comparative: Comparing Governments and Public Opinion
Timeline: War, Peace, and Public Opinion
Visual Literacy: Who Are Liberals and Conservatives? What's the Difference?

The Politics of the Media

CHAPTER 11

KEY OBJECTIVES

After completing this chapter, you should be prepared to:

11.1 Evaluate the roles played by the media in shaping American politics.

11.2 Outline the development of the American media.

11.3 Illustrate the functions of the media in American politics and society.

11.4 Assess how the media can be influential in American politics.

11.5 Establish how the media have an impact on the cultural values and political opinions of the American public.

11.6 Contrast the rights of a free press to the government's authority to restrict content.

O n September 11, 2001, at 8:45 A.M. Eastern Daylight Time, a commercial airplane crashed into one of the World Trade Center towers in New York City, forever changing the world. Eighteen minutes later, a second airliner crashed into the other tower. Soon came the equally shocking news that a third airliner had hit the Pentagon and that a fourth hijacked plane, presumably bound for an attack on Washington, D.C., had gone down in a field in Shanksville, Pennsylvania.

The media's live coverage of the Twin Towers collapsing vividly conveyed the horror of the attack and dramatically altered history. Americans had shown relatively little concern over domestic terrorism before this attack. After the attack, terrorism dominated dinner conversations, news programs, the national consciousness, and the government's agenda.

In 2004, photos broadcast and printed by the media depicted the deplorable treatment of Iraqi prisoners at Abu Ghraib by U.S. military personnel, setting in motion an international debate regarding the definition of torture and the Bush administration's foreign policies. The domestic and international outrage

> **How powerful are the mass media in the United States?**

was immediate, with many fearing that the scandal would further fuel anti-American sentiment through the Middle East.

On November 4, 2008, millions of people across the globe watched the new first family walk on stage in front of some 200,000 screaming supporters. The media showed us the raw emotion displayed on the faces of people across the country and worldwide, as Barack Obama was announced as the first African-American president-elect of the United States. His candidacy forever changed politics in the United States.

Impressions such as these can change the way people think about themselves, their government, and their world, making the media important actors in shaping and reflecting cultural change. As these experiences so powerfully demonstrated, the contemporary media allow us to see the world beyond our everyday lives, providing the opportunity to share experiences and events. This tremendous power of the media, however, comes with great responsibility. One of our aims in this chapter is to look at how important the media are in the cultural change pathway, paying attention not only to the media's potential to impact the political agenda but also to both reflect and shape popular culture.

Resource Center
- Glossary
- Vocabulary Example
- Connect the Link

■ **Marketplace of Ideas:**
The concept that ideas and theories compete for acceptance among the public.

EXAMPLE: *When new issues arise, political parties, candidates, and interest groups will often present their position on the issues. The marketplace of ideas allows the public debate of issues, which ultimately makes voters better informed regarding complex matters.*

Mass Media

11.1 **Evaluate the roles played by the media in shaping American politics.**
(pages 328–329)

The **mass media** refers to the portion of the media—especially television, radio, newspapers, and magazines—that is designed to transmit information to a large audience across a large region. The importance of free media in a democratic society cannot be exaggerated. The success of our democracy depends on our being informed and aware about the policy issues facing our nation as well as the action—or inaction—of our government leaders in response to those issues. Your effective involvement as an actor in the country's democratic governing process, whether as a voter, an interest group member, or a political candidate, depends on your knowledge of current events. It is through the media that you see world events beyond those directly observed in your private life. The media show us the "big picture" worlds of politics, entertainment, sports, culture, and economics, as well as the lives of people living in other countries and other cultures.

The media's behavior receives intensive scrutiny, for it is widely asserted that the media are powerful in socializing citizens' attitudes, beliefs, and behaviors. Furthermore, many people believe that the media shape the actions of government officials; some have even called the media the fourth branch of government. However, as you read this chapter, you should question how influential the mass media actually are. Rather than *shaping* our values and beliefs, do the media simply *reflect* them? Or do they do both—shape as well as reflect our cultural values and struggles?

The media, public opinion, and democracy are linked together in an interactive relationship; each affects the others. All democratic governments must allow for a **marketplace of ideas■**, in which differing opinions and values compete for acceptance among the public. The media make possible, on a mass scale, this vitally important public debate over opposing opinions, ideas, and thoughts. The media also serve as a "communications bridge" between the governed and the governing. This two-way flow of information, from the government to the people and from the people to the government, is fundamental in a representative democracy (and obstructing this two-way information flow is a tactic that dictators use to preserve their power).

Most Americans know that the media are powerful. The media's news coverage can manipulate public opinion, influence policymaking, and affect elections and even the economy, and the entertainment component can also mold our political, social, and economic values. Today, the average American high school senior has spent more time watching TV than attending school. Even what is learned in school is often influenced by the media's portrayal of events. The average American adult spends nearly half of his or her leisure time watching TV, listening to the radio, and reading newspapers or magazines; the single greatest amount of time is spent watching television. Moreover, TV remains the primary source of news and entertainment in the United States, followed closely by the Internet.[1] The Internet is now the third most popular news platform (behind the local and national news); however, an overwhelming number of Americans get their news from multiple sources in a typical day.[2]

The media provide the opportunity for millions to share events and experiences, sometimes—as on September 11, 2001—with a dramatic power to alter the political climate and world events. We do not observe firsthand most of the things that happen in the world, and therefore we rely on the media to be a mirror to the world and to supply us with almost all of our political knowledge.

Walter Cronkite, the CBS news anchor of the 1960s and 1970s, always ended his broadcast with the words "And that's the way it is." The influence of Cronkite, consistently cited as one of the most trusted people in America, was shown dramatically in 1968. During most of the 1960s, Cronkite had expressed support for the war in Vietnam, but that changed after he visited Southeast Asia in early 1968. Upon returning home, he took the unprecedented step of interjecting a personal opinion at the end of his broadcast on February 27: "For it seems more certain now than ever that the bloody experience of Vietnam is to end in a stalemate." President Johnson, after watching Cronkite's broadcast, is quoted as saying, "That's it. If I've lost Cronkite, I've lost Middle America." A month later, Johnson announced his decision not to seek reelection. Cronkite's words summed up the goal of his news program: his attempt to give Americans a glimpse into the larger world in which they lived.

The media's claim to be a mirror to the world raises many questions. Is this mirror an all-inclusive, unbiased, and neutral representation of world events? Or does the mirror reflect selective pictures, ideas, and opinions? Concerns over the objectivity of the media have caused a good deal of disagreement, which we will discuss throughout this chapter.

Given the impact of the media on public opinion and behavior, many people ask who should control the news. Authoritarian regimes assume that the government knows what's best for its citizens and thus seek to control all flows of information, thereby molding what the public thinks about and believes. Authoritarian governments also believe that news and entertainment programs should not question government or its policies and, should instead build support and loyalty. Conversely, democratic societies assume that government officials can and do make mistakes. This assumption is inherent in the American governing structure, with its checks and balances and its

From 1962 to 1981, Walter Cronkite (1916–2009) served as anchor of the *CBS Evening News,* becoming one of the most trusted people in the country. His trademark exit line, "And that's the way it is," perfectly characterized his efforts to present fair, accurate, and reliable news to his viewers. He is best remembered for his coverage of the Cuban Missile Crisis, the assassination of President Kennedy, and the Vietnam War. —*Do you think we will once again trust and admire journalists as the country did Cronkite? Why or why not?*

division of power. Democracies therefore insist that the public needs a free press to keep government in line. The citizens of a democracy need to challenge the officials' policies and, through public debate and discussion, build consensus and develop better policies. While we may be frustrated at times, especially when we don't agree with the media's portrayal of a news event, a free press is essential for democracy.

Mass Media

11.1   **Evaluate the roles played by the media in shaping American politics.**

PRACTICE QUIZ: UNDERSTAND AND APPLY

1. The media influence cultural change by both
   a. impeding and shaping it.
   b. reflecting and impeding it.
   c. reflecting and shaping it.
   d. shaping and minimizing it.

2. The media serve as a "communication bridge" primarily between
   a. the governed and the governing.
   b. the advertisers and the consumers.
   c. the United States and other countries.
   d. the cultural present and the cultural future.

3. A perennial assumption about our political system is that government officials make mistakes and a free press is therefore needed to monitor them.
   a. true   b. false

ANALYZE

1. Why is a free press vital in a democracy? What would be the consequences of allowing government officials to control the media in the United States? Are there any circumstances under which you believe such control might at least temporarily be justified?

2. Do you think the Internet enhances or lessens the impact of the media's influence on our political knowledge? Why?

IDENTIFY THE CONCEPT THAT DOESN'T BELONG

a. Marketplace of ideas
b. Public debate
c. Censorship
d. Open discussion
e. Two-way flow of communication

Resource Center
• Glossary
• Vocabulary Example
• Connect the Link

CONNECT THE LINK
(Chapter 2, pages 54–55) Do you think
that the original intent of the founders
is still a relevant consideration today?

The Growth of Mass Media

11.2 Outline the development of the American media.

(pages 330–335)

Print media were the first form of mass communication. As technology has developed and changed, so too have the mass media. Today, electronic media are rapidly evolving, with more and more people looking to different sources for information and entertainment.

Print Media

Newspapers were the first mass medium intended to communicate information in a timely fashion to a large audience. The early newspapers were almost always targeted at the elite, and they were created and funded to promote specific political and economic causes. Later newspapers, however, were less expensive and included more sensationalistic coverage designed to appeal to ordinary citizens.

NEWSPAPERS FOR THE ELITE   The first newspaper published in what would become the United States was the *Boston News-Letter,* which began appearing in April 1704. The paper was one page long and was published weekly. By 1725, Boston had three newspapers, and Philadelphia and New York City each had one. At the time of the Revolutionary War five decades later, 50 presses were operating in the 13 colonies.[3] The colonial authorities accepted these early newspapers in part because they generally tried to avoid controversial issues. Many of these early papers relied on government printing jobs as a key source to increase their revenue and could not afford to alienate local officials.

The Revolutionary War changed all this: Newspapers became important tools in building public support for resistance to British policies and, by 1776, for independence. The historian Arthur Schlesinger Sr. wrote that the war for independence "could hardly have succeeded without an ever alert and dedicated press."[4] By the late 1770s, most presses were actively promoting independence. This activity continued during the war, reporting Patriot successes (often with exaggeration) while downplaying losses.

Newspapers were also used to promote public support for ratifying the Constitution. Compared to the extreme partisanship of the Revolutionary War, their coverage was more balanced, giving opportunities for opponents to discuss their concerns. The best examples of the persuasive use of the press to advance a political agenda are the series of newspaper essays written (anonymously) by Alexander Hamilton, James Madison, and John Jay, later published as *The Federalist Papers.* As discussed in Chapter 2, pages 54–55, these essays were powerful and persuasive testimonies in support of the Constitution and helped ensure its ratification in the crucial state of New York. To this day, *The Federalist Papers* remain one of the best expressions of the founders' original intent.

Following ratification of the Constitution, political leaders of the time thought it very important to promote newspapers, which informed citizens of major issues facing the new government. Sharing information was vital. Americans worried that the new federal government would prove too powerful and too remote for citizens to control. Using the press to report the actions of the new government kept people informed and eased their fears. The spread of political information through the press, declared the House of Representatives, is "among the surest means of preventing the degeneracy of a free government."[5] In view of the difficulties and expenses of publishing newspapers at the time, the federal government provided protection for newspapers by granting them special treatment—for example, by charging a reduced rate of postage for papers mailed to subscribers.

The number and circulation of newspapers in the early nineteenth century grew dramatically. For example, by the early 1830s, there were 12 daily newspapers published in Philadelphia and six in New York City. The number of newspapers published across the country soared, from around 200 in 1800 to around 1,200 in the mid-1830s.[6] These early newspapers were almost always created and funded to promote specific political and economic beliefs. For example, parties and political leaders normally encouraged and helped finance newspapers in important cities. Called **party presses,** these papers were best seen as arms of competing political factions. Most newspapers became unabashedly partisan, reaping rewards when their preferred party won an election and suffering when it lost. These papers were targeted to the elite, were relatively expensive, and did not have many subscribers. Ordinary citizens, however, often heard newspapers being read aloud and argued about in public gathering places, including taverns, inns, and coffeehouses.

NEWSPAPERS FOR THE ORDINARY CITIZEN   The year 1833 saw an important change in the nature of journalism in the United States: the advent of the **penny press,** so called because these daily newspapers cost a penny, versus about 6 cents for the established newspapers of the day. These penny papers, the first of which was the *New York Sun,* were marketed to the "common man." (In the sexist thinking of the day, politics, like business, was assumed to be a masculine pursuit, something in which women should not participate.) They offered less political and business coverage but a more diverse range of material—crime and human interest stories, scandals, and sports. These newspapers quickly became very popular, changing the face of journalism by making it a true mass medium. Newspaper publishers covered the costs of publication and made a profit by selling advertising. Unlike earlier newspapers, which had relied on officials or travelers for their political and economic news, the penny presses relied more heavily on reporters who would ferret out stories. These presses were less partisan and were more financially independent of politicians, significantly affecting the way in which politics was covered.[7] This change in the nature of journalism encouraged the press to become freer and more vigorous.

By the mid-nineteenth century, newspapers had become somewhat more objective and fact-based. The invention of the telegraph in the 1840s helped this shift. The Associated Press (the world's largest and oldest news agency), created in 1848, inaugurated a new trend in journalism, marked by direct and simple writing designed to appeal to a wide range of readers.

So-called **yellow journalism,** featuring sensationalism, comics, and scandal in a fierce competition to sell papers, became popular at the end of the nineteenth century. (The name came from the yellow-tinted newsprint that some of these papers used.) William Randolph Hearst, one of the earliest practitioners of yellow journalism, forthrightly said, "It is the [*New York*] *Journal*'s policy to engage brains as well as to get news, for the public is even more fond of entertainment than it is of information."[8] As the newspapers' extreme sensation-mongering generated a public backlash, journalists responded by beginning to develop a code of professional ethics. Many newspapers, oriented toward a more "respectable" readership, rejected sensational journalism and still made profits by selling advertising. (The *New York Times* is a prime example.)

In the early twentieth century, the ownership of newspapers became more centralized, the result of competition that forced many papers to close or merge. This trend was well under way by the 1930s, when the Hearst chain (consisting of 26 daily papers in 19 cities) controlled 13 percent of the nation's newspaper circulation. In 1933, six newspaper chains owned 81 daily papers, representing 26 percent of national circulation.[9] This trend has continued, paralleling a drastic shrinkage in the number of newspapers. In 2003, the Tribune Company owned 13 daily newspapers and 26 TV stations in 21 media markets. When it merged with the *Los Angeles Times* in 2000, the Tribune Company reached nearly 80 percent of U.S. households through one or more media outlets.[10] Currently, the Tribune Company is the only multimedia company that owns newspapers and television stations in all three of the largest media markets (New York, Los Angeles, and Chicago). As we'll discuss later in the chapter, many people are concerned with this trend toward concentration of ownership, as well as allegations of the pending "death" of newspapers. Certainly, the environment surrounding the print media is changing, but their longevity is testimony to their adaptability.

Electronic Media

The twentieth century witnessed an explosion in new means of mass communication, starting with radio and continuing with television and the Internet.

RADIO In 1900, a professor of electrical engineering at the University of Pittsburgh named Reginald Fessenden made the first experimental radio transmission. His successful broadcast made radio communication a reality. During World War I, little was done to exploit this technology commercially, but after the war, there was a rush to set up private radio stations. Presidential election returns were broadcast for the first time in 1920. In 1923, the country had 566 radio stations. At first, radio was primarily an activity for hobbyists who built their own sets. By 1924, however, some 2.5 million Americans owned radio receivers, and the era of mass radio had begun.[11]

When preassembled radios began to be sold in stores, a rapid and dramatic growth of radio audiences occurred. In 1930, for example, radio receivers—14 million of them—were in 45 percent of American households. One decade later, despite the Great Depression, 81 percent of households owned a total of 44 million receivers. By the late 1940s, when television started to become popular, 95 percent of households had radios.[12] Radio had become a source of information and entertainment for practically everyone.

The first radio stations were strictly local, but the formation of radio networks with syndicated programming began in the late 1920s. This trend was encouraged when Congress passed the Radio Act of 1927, which regulated the rapidly growing industry. The Radio Act established the airwaves as a public good, subject to governmental oversight. Under the new federal policy, radio stations were privately owned, with the government regulating the technical aspects and issuing licenses to broadcast on specific frequencies. Freedom-of-speech concerns kept regulation from extending to content.

Not all liberal democracies have privately owned broadcast media. In the United Kingdom, for example, the government owns and controls the British Broadcasting Corporation, known as the BBC. Private stations do exist in Britain and are regulated by an independent regulatory agency, which is responsible to Parliament, but the BBC is the largest broadcasting corporation in the world, sending out programming on television, radio, and the Internet.

Mirroring the trend in American newspaper publishing, radio broadcasting consolidated as the twentieth century wore on. In 1934, one-third of all U.S. radio stations were affiliated with a network, and more than 60 percent were by 1940. Today, radio stations that are not affiliated with networks often have weaker signals and face financial problems. Consolidation helps defer costs, but it also concentrates power.

■ **Technology Gap (Digital Divide):** The differences in access to and mastery of information and communication technology between segments of the community (typically for socioeconomic, educational, or geographical reasons).

EXAMPLE: *Because more and more groups, organizations, and news outlets are relying on the Internet to reach their consumers and supporters, there is great concern that the technology gap is limiting the ability of some segments of the population to access important information.*

TELEVISION The arrival of television marked a breakthrough in personalizing communication from officials to the masses, allowing intimate contact in a diverse and large society. Like radio, once television was perfected, it grew at an astounding rate. Television became technically feasible in the late 1930s, but World War II delayed its commercial development. Commercial TV broadcasting began in the late 1940s. In 1950, there were 98 television stations in the United States, with 9 percent of American households having TV sets. Four years later, the number of families owning sets had exploded, from less than 4 million to 28 million. By 1958, some 41 million families had TV sets. Today, more than 1,100 broadcast TV stations are licensed in the United States, 99 percent of households have televisions, and more than a third of all households have four or more sets.[13] When compared with print news and radio, television is unique in two ways—its immediacy (it can show events live) and its visual content, both of which convey a sense of legitimacy to viewers and increase emotional appeal.

Unlike newspapers and radio stations, which first were independently owned and only later consolidated into chains and networks, high costs dictated that almost from the beginning, TV stations were affiliated with networks, thus centralizing ownership. Today, however, the ownership of television broadcasting is becoming more competitive and diverse. In the last 20 or 30 years, network television's audience has changed dramatically. Cable TV, satellite TV, and DVRs (digital video recorders) have changed the nature of watching TV, reducing the audience for network programming. Meanwhile, the development of 24/7 news networks, such as CNN, FOX News, and MSNBC, coupled with their popular Web pages, has altered the face of the broadcast media.

STUDENT profile

In 2004, Brittany and Robbie Bergquist of Norwell, Massachusetts, were appalled to learn that a soldier incurred an $8,000 telephone bill for calling his family from Iraq. Rather than sit back and do nothing, these two young siblings (then 12 and 13 years old) started Cell Phones for Soldiers, a nonprofit organization, with only $21. During the next three years, they collected enough used cell phones to raise over $1 million and donated 400,000 minutes for soldiers deployed oversees to call their families. As of March 2010, Cell Phones for Soldiers had donated more than 62 million minutes of free calling cards to soldiers. It would have been easy for these two youngsters to ignore the problem, but instead they got involved and have helped many of our troops stay in touch with their loved ones.[14]

Years ago, television watching was a family affair, with most families owning only one television set. In 1975, for example, 57 percent of homes had only one television. Today 55 percent have three or more. —*Should we be concerned over the fact that television watching has become less communal and more isolated? Should families make more of an effort to watch television together?*

THE INTERNET The Internet has revolutionized the way we communicate. Developed in the early 1980s, it was originally used to network Department of Defense computers, linking the Pentagon with far-flung military bases and defense contractors. Later, it was expanded to include large research universities; e-mail was its first main use. The growth of the Internet is tied directly to the explosive growth of personal computers and the development of graphics programming. (Early e-mail appeared on a blank screen, with no cute graphics or icons, and users had to rely on function keys to send messages manually.) As the technology rapidly developed, the public responded avidly. By the late 1980s, the Internet was coming into widespread public use. Recognizing the Internet's economic potential, companies introduced Web pages and developed marketing techniques for the new medium. Public officials also acted strategically, establishing Web sites through which citizens could contact them electronically. Today, virtually all elected officials and organizations maintain Web pages to provide information and enable citizens to reach them directly.

MYTH EXPOSED Many Americans believe that everyone has easy access to the Internet and technology. In fact, while the number of people with access to the Internet has increased greatly, there is still a **technology gap**■ (also referred to as the digital divide) in the United States.[15] According to the Census Bureau, approximately 29 percent of households surveyed still did not have access to the Internet (at home or anywhere) in 2007. Class, race, and age all influence a person's access to the Internet. The benefits made possible by the Internet are likely to be achieved by people who have basic computer skills and thus are already interested in and informed about politics—that is, the educated, the more affluent, and younger people.[16] Although most public libraries provide free Internet access, not all people are able to take advantage of this opportunity (for example, if they have no access to transportation, lack basic computer skills, or are not literate).

Table 11.1 gives details on such access. The least likely to have such access are the elderly (who often find it difficult to learn how to use computers or mobile devices like cell phones), African Americans, Hispanics, and the less educated and less affluent.

Furthermore, the very nature of the Internet makes it a potentially dangerous place to get *reliable* information. Anyone with basic computer skills and the interest can create a Web page and a blog—and there is no mechanism to differentiate irrelevant, biased, or intentionally manipulative information from reliable and accurate knowledge. You need to be an informed consumer, aware of the trustworthiness of each online source and careful not to be misled or swayed by imprecise or biased information.

The instantaneous nature of the Internet has dramatically changed news reporting today. For example, Internet users whose service provider offers instantly updated headline news can read the main stories featured in the newspaper many hours before they appear in print. Consequently, the way in which people get their news has changed, with people relying less on local news programs, cable news, nightly network news, newsmagazines, and daily newspaper for information and more on the Internet and news from their service providers (see Table 11.2). In addition to the issues of race and class with respect to access to the Internet, age also affects the manner in which people consume news. Those under 30 are far more likely to get their news online than from the newspaper or television, whereas people over 50 are more likely to rely on television or the newspaper for their news information, but the differences in the patterns of news consumption by age are diminishing.[17] In 2004, 20 percent of people between the ages of 18 and 29 regularly learned something about the campaign from the Internet. Just four years later, that number increased to 42 percent, making the Internet the most common source of campaign information for young people.[18]

In addition to changing patterns of news consumption, growth in the use of blogs and social networking sites (such as Facebook and Twitter) as a source of information on campaigns

TABLE 11.1   Internet Access by Selected Characteristics

The Census Bureau regularly conducts surveys of the American public, partly to provide the government with information but also to gauge the needs and status of the population (which then can influence public policies and resource allocations). In this survey, the government found that access to the Internet is not evenly divided across important demographic groups. People between the ages of 25 and 64 have more access, as do whites and Asians as well as those with higher educational attainment and family income. —*How might the lack of access to the Internet become an issue in the future?*

	INTERNET ACCESS AT HOME
Age of Householder	
15–24 years	56.4%
25–34 years	55.9%
35–44 years	57.8%
45–64 years	51.1%
65 years and older	20.7%
Race	
White, non-Hispanic	55.6%
African American	34.3%
Asian	51.8%
Hispanic (of any race)	29.8%
Educational Attainment (for those 25 and older)	
Less than high school graduate	9.0%
High school graduate/GED	30.8%
Some college or associate's degree	54.3%
Bachelor's degree or higher	73.5%
Family Income (annual)	
Less than $25,000 lowest quartile	25.1%
$25,000–$49,999 2nd quartile	35.8%
$50,000–$74,999 3rd quartile	49.3%
$75,000–$99,999 4th quartile	63.2%
$100,000 or more highest quartile	74.1%

SOURCE: U.S. Census Bureau, *Current Population Survey*, October 2009. Accessed at http://www.census.gov/compendia/statab/2010/tables/10s1120.xls on April 7, 2010.

TABLE 11.2	Where Americans Learn about Candidates and Campaigns

A national survey of over 1,489 adults 18 and over, conducted December 3–7, 2008, revealed that people are changing their pattern of news consumption compared to similar surveys conducted in 2000 and 2004. Adults in 2008 are relying less on local television news, TV newsmagazines, and daily newspapers for their information regarding candidates and campaigns than they did in 2000 and 2004. Today, they are relying substantially more on the Internet for such information. *—Do you think this is a positive or a negative trend? Does it matter where people get their news from? Why or why not?*

REGULARLY LEARN SOMETHING FROM . . .	2000	2004	2008
Local TV news	48%	42%	40%
Cable news networks	34%	38%	38%
Nightly network news	45%	35%	32%
Daily newspaper	40%	31%	31%
TV newsmagazines	29%	25%	22%
Morning TV shows	18%	20%	22%
Cable political talk	14%	14%	15%
Talk radio	15%	17%	16%
National Public Radio	12%	14%	18%
Newsmagazines	15%	10%	11%
Late-night talk shows	9%	9%	9%
Religious radio	7%	5%	9%
Lou Dobbs Tonight	—	—	7%
Internet	9%	13%	40%

SOURCE: "Internet's Broader Role in Campaign 2008" (Washington, DC: The Pew Research Center for the People and the Press, January 1, 2008). Updated. Accessed at http://people-press.org/report/384/internets-broader-role-in-campaign-2008 on June 2, 2010. Reprinted with permission.

TABLE 11.3	Social Networking Sites and the Campaign, by Age

	TOTAL	18–29	30–39	40+
Use social network sites	22%	67%	21%	6%
Get campaign information from sites	7%	27%	4%	1%
Signed up as a "friend" of candidate	3%	8%	3%	<1%

SOURCE: "Internet's Broader Role in Campaign 2008" (Washington, DC: Pew Research Center for the People and the Press, January 1, 2008). Accessed at http://people-press.org/report/384/internets-broader-role-in-campaign-2008 on June 2, 2010. Reprinted with permission.

PATHWAYS of change from around the world

How did technology change the world's view of democratic protesters in Myanmar? In 1988, a pro-democracy uprising in Myanmar was quickly dispelled when the totalitarian government successfully shut the country's borders, expelled foreign journalists and dissidents, and controlled the flow of information. More than 3,000 people were killed in this Asian nation, with little world scrutiny.

The government thought they could squash a similar uprising that began in 2007 by once again controlling the media and shielding themselves from the world (as they had successfully done a number of times in the past). This time, however, they did not anticipate the use of technology and how difficult it would be to control. Despite the fact that the country has one of the most repressed and censored media in the world and less than 1 percent of the country has access to the Internet, technology was used to change the nature of the conflict and the world's reaction.

Cell phones were used to send text messages, digital photos, and videos, enabling the Buddhist monks to reach a global audience with their desperate calls for democracy. Students throughout the country used text messaging to set up demonstrations and track the location of government soldiers. The government tried to shut down Internet access and cell phone use, but they were rather unsuccessful, especially due to the students' use of satellite telephones.

Exiled Myanmar students founded the Democratic Voice of Burma in Norway, which has become a leading voice to support the rebellion and transmit information to the world. The students' and activists' use of technology makes it impossible for the government to isolate itself from global scrutiny. Currently, the protests continue with both sides deeply entrenched—but thanks to technology, transparency is becoming more commonplace.

has occurred in the last few years. A remarkable 67 percent of people from 18 to 29 use social network sites, with 27 percent of them reporting that they get campaign information from these sites. Only 1 percent of people over 40 reported using these networking sites to get campaign information, though these numbers are expected to grow. Given the success of Barack Obama's campaign in using these technologies, we expect them to be regular elements used by all major candidates for the presidency, Congress, and many statewide elected offices during upcoming elections (see Table 11.3).

The use of cell phones has increased, making individuals and social movements less isolated. Buddhist monks were able to use cell phones to reach a global audience to help energize their efforts to promote human rights. —*Are there circumstances where smart phones may be detrimental to social movements? Under what circumstances do you think instant communication can harm groups?*

The Growth of Mass Media

11.2 Outline the development of the American media.

PRACTICE QUIZ: UNDERSTAND AND APPLY

1. From the beginning, the press in colonial America featured scandal and controversy on the front page of newspapers and circulars.
   a. true
   b. false

2. When did owning and listening to radio first become popular in this country?
   a. between 1880 and 1890
   b. between 1900 and 1910
   c. between 1920 and 1930
   d. between 1940 and 1950

3. One disadvantage of the Internet as a site for political news and ideas is that
   a. the information on it is not always reliable.
   b. the news items are not covered in great depth.
   c. only the best-informed individuals can post material on the Web.
   d. most of the people who use the Internet are young and politically disconnected.

4. Virtually all Americans now have easy access to the Internet.
   a. true
   b. false

ANALYZE

1. How did the function of newspapers change when they became widely available to the public?

2. How have television and the Internet changed the reporting of news? Why must you be cautious about using the Internet as a source of political information?

IDENTIFY THE CONCEPT THAT DOESN'T BELONG

a. Public good
b. Government ownership
c. Rapid growth
d. Consolidation
e. Private ownership

Resource Center
• Glossary
• Vocabulary Example
• Connect the Link

Functions of the Media

11.3 Illustrate the functions of the media in American politics and society.
(pages 336–339)

The media perform a multitude of functions in the United States, which can be summarized as entertaining, informing, and persuading the public. The media provide people with shared political experiences, which can in turn bring people together and affect public opinion. The media model appropriate behavior and reinforce cultural norms, but they also portray behavior that challenges cultural norms and expectations. And sometimes, they do both at the same time. Because the media are increasingly national in scope, the presentation of some issues in one region to one group will reinforce cultural norms while the same material challenges cultural norms in another region. Consider same-sex marriage. In some regions, these unions are more accepted as normal expressions of love and commitment, while in other regions, the majority of people consider them immoral. When the media portray such unions in the news or in sitcoms, the perspective they use can serve to frame the issue.

Entertainment

Even as entertainment, the media can affect the image of officials and institutions. Consider late-night television, where being the frequent butt of jokes can undermine a leader's public image. The media's negative portrayal of governmental officials, even as entertainment, can have negative effects on public perception and attitudes. Research on media images of public officials from the mid-1950s through the 1990s has demonstrated that the way they were shown was more likely to be negative than positive. The only occupation with worse images was business. Before 1975, our political system itself was twice as likely to be portrayed positively on television than negatively, but by the 1980s, positive portrayals had become uncommon. This shift, the researchers claimed, reflected changes in public opinion in the aftermath of the Vietnam War and the Watergate scandal.[19]

The distinction between entertainment and news has become increasingly blurred as the news divisions of network media come under pressure to be entertaining in hopes of appealing to a broader audience and generating money for the network. A perfect example of this occurred when during the 2008 election campaign *Saturday Night Live*'s Tina Fey began a remarkably successful parody of Republican vice presidential nominee Sarah Palin. Almost immediately upon Senator John McCain's nomination of Governor Palin for the Republican ticket, Fey put on her "power red suit and wig" and began

From its beginnings in 1975, *Saturday Night Live* has made a name for itself by spoofing famous people and politicians. Shown here, Sarah Palin watches Tina Fey's impersonation of her. —*How relevant do you think comedy programs are in influencing public opinion of celebrities and politicians?*

a notable impersonation of the governor that dramatically escalated the ratings of *SNL*. Many critics of Governor Palin quickly seized on Fey's characterizations, using them as evidence that the governor was unsuitable to be the vice president and, if the need arose, president. The clouding of entertainment and news media is not new, but given the popularity of social media sites like YouTube, it may be the first time that such material was so widely accessible and available.

Surveillance, Interpretation, and Socialization

As noted, the distinctive nature of the news media in communicating makes them a unique and potentially powerful political actor. In addition to entertaining, the news media have many functions in our society, with great political and social consequences. Harold Lasswell, a prominent political scientist who pioneered studying the effects of the media on American politics, identified three important societal functions of the media: surveillance, interpretation, and socialization.[20]

SURVEILLANCE According to Lasswell, the media have a watchdog role as the "eyes and ears to the world." That is, the media report what's news, thus keeping us informed of significant events not only in our communities but also in the nation and around the globe. Their surveillance function draws attention to problems that need addressing. For example, news coverage on conditions at a local veterans' hospital could demonstrate the need for more oversight and better patient care. The story could then expand, looking at the quality of

■ **Investigative Reporting:** A type of journalism in which reporters thoroughly investigate a subject matter (often involving a scandal) to inform the public, correct an injustice, or expose an abuse.

EXAMPLE: *Some of the most important public scandals, such as Watergate, the Iran–Contra Affair, the collapse of Enron, and the torture of prisoners of war at Abu Ghraib have been made public through investigative reporting.*

care in hospitals across the country, perhaps motivating Congress to examine the care our country provides to veterans, enhancing the quality of their lives.

It is important to note, however, that not all surveillance reporting is positive. For example, research has shown that crime is often overreported, making people believe there is more criminal activity in their community than actually exists. Although it can be helpful for the media to probe into scandals and to uncover abuses, emphasizing negativity can also lead to public cynicism. Negative reporting on the economy has drawn much criticism, with some observers asserting that stories that continually report economic downturns can spread fear among investors, causing them to act in ways that actually do worsen the economy.

One aspect of surveillance is **investigative reporting**■, in which reporters seek out stories and probe into various aspects of an issue in search of serious problems. Some of the earliest forms of investigative journalism, popular around 1900, were called **muckraking**—an expression that President Theodore Roosevelt coined in describing journalists who, he thought, tried to rake up too much sensational social filth. From the 1870s until World War I, there was a good deal of public interest in reforming government, politics, and business. To generate support for reform, journalists would investigate areas they believed needed to be changed and then present their findings to the public.

One of the most famous examples is Upton Sinclair's examination of the Chicago stockyards. His resulting novel, *The Jungle,* published in 1906, was a scathing exposé of the meat-packing industry. It created a public outcry for reform during Theodore Roosevelt's administration, leading the federal government to regulate the industry and demand more sanitary conditions to make meat production safer. Muckraking lost public support around 1912, sending investigative journalism into a prolonged lull. The Watergate scandal of the early 1970s not only revived modern investigative journalism but also firmly entrenched it in the contemporary media.

Many Americans welcomed the return of investigative journalism, pointing to the numerous abuses that reporters have uncovered. One excellent example is the *Chicago Tribune's* investigation into the Illinois death penalty in 1999. The *Tribune* exposed serious flaws in the administration of the death penalty in that state. Its findings ultimately led Governor George Ryan to impose a moratorium on all executions in the state and to appoint a panel to recommend improving the public defender system, which provides lawyers for poor persons accused of committing death-penalty offenses. Some critics, however, believe that investigative journalists often go too far, delving into matters that should be treated confidentially and privately—for example, the behavior of public officials' children. Some areas, these critics say, should be considered off-limits out of respect for individuals' privacy.

INTERPRETATION According to Lasswell, the second societal role of the media is to interpret the news, putting events into context and helping people to understand the complexities of the world. One example occurred upon the death of former president Ronald Reagan in 2004. Retrospective stories in the newspapers and on television put his presidency into context by focusing on his economic and social policies while typically ignoring the more controversial issues of his administration. The media drew historical parallels between Reagan and other presidents and compared his funeral to other presidential funerals. In essence, they put his life and death into context for the nation. The ability to set the context, frame the issue, interpret the facts, and potentially, provide legitimacy for people, issues, or groups gives the media enormous power. In framing how a story is told—in short, by creating heroes and villains—the media tell us, subtly or otherwise, who is "good" and who is "bad" in a way that is difficult to refute thereafter.

Take the civil rights movement as an example. Interpretive stories in the media about prominent figures and events in the movement have generally been framed to focus on the victims of racism rather than to show that civil rights activists challenged the status quo and broke laws doing so. In 1955, Rosa Parks intentionally and in full awareness broke the law of Montgomery, Alabama, by refusing to give up her seat on a city bus to a white man. Yes, she believed that the law was unjust, but it *was* the law at the time. Media accounts about her at the time of her death in 2005 portrayed her not as a lawbreaker but as a victim and a hero in the struggle for justice. Conversely, the media tended to portray the feminist activists of the late 1960s and early 1970s as extremist, man-hating, lesbian bra burners when they could have been depicted more sympathetically as women fighting gender oppression and patriarchy.

Interpretive journalism is very much in evidence in reporting on the war in Iraq. When the United States invaded Iraq in 2003, the American media framed the war primarily as a defensive measure, to rid the world of Saddam Hussein's weapons of mass destruction, and secondarily as a war to liberate the oppressed Iraqi people. Framing the invasion in terms of waging the post-9/11 War on Terror, rather than in terms of attacking another nation unprovoked certainly helped generate public support for the initial invasion. However, when neither the alleged stockpiles of weapons of mass destruction nor links between Saddam's Iraq and al-Qaeda were discovered, and as a bitter Iraqi resistance to the American occupation developed along with mounting U.S. military casualties—and as the media repeatedly reported stories of poor planning for the invasion and of postinvasion chaos—the American public's support for the war and for President George W. Bush eroded.

Consider another example in the United States: the images and controversies that emerged following Hurricane Katrina in 2005. Many people complained that the news coverage of the events following the Hurricane and collapse of the levees in

CONNECT THE **LINK**
(Chapter 10, pages 301–303) Do you think the government should set standards for television shows requiring them to portray positive role models?

The manner in which the actions of individuals are characterized by the media can be significant, influencing the views and opinions of the public. The caption used with the picture of the two Caucasians in the aftermath of Hurricane Katrina (2005) characterized the people as "finding bread and soda," while the caption accompanying the image of the African American stated that the man had "looted" a grocery store. —*Do you think these captions indicate that racism is still prevalent in the United States? Why or why not?*

New Orleans was racist and relied on racial stereotypes. For example, on August 30, 2005, two news sources—the Associated Press (AP) and Getty Images via Agence France-Presse (AFP)—published two similar pictures with very different captions. In the AP picture, an African American man was described as having "looted" a local grocery store, while in the AFP picture, two Caucasian people were depicted "finding" bread and soda at a local grocery store. Critics contended that the characterizations were based on racial stereotypes and were biased.[21] Others claimed that the captions simply reflected stylistic differences associated with the two news agencies. As consumers, you need to be conscious of this sort of potential bias and seek numerous sources of news to ensure objectivity.

Many observers of all political stripes are concerned over what they see as bias in news coverage. Some perceive a liberal bias in the news, especially on public radio and television and in such newspapers as the *New York Times;* conservative political commentators such as Glenn Beck and Bill O'Reilly, as well as conservative politicians, make much of this alleged bias. Democrats and liberals counter by asserting that FOX News has a conservative bias, that the mainstream media actually bend over backward to present conservative views, and that a good deal of reporting is, in fact, shaded in a conservative direction.

Research on this volatile issue is mixed. In 1995, the Media Studies Center and the Roper Center for Public Opinion surveyed Washington-based reporters and national newspaper editors. It found that 50 percent of reporters identified themselves as Democrats, compared with 34 percent of the national public. Editors were more like the national public than reporters, with 31 percent claiming to be Democrats. Only 4 percent of reporters, however, said that they were Republicans, compared to 28 percent of the public and 14 percent of editors.[22] The research also probed political ideology, finding that reporters are far more likely to call themselves liberal than the general population. Editors were more conservative, dividing along the lines found in the population at large.

In 2004, the Pew Center interviewed national and local reporters and found that 34 percent of national and 23 percent of local reporters considered themselves liberals (compared with 20 percent of the general public). Only 7 percent of national and 12 percent of local reporters self-identified as conservatives (compared with 33 percent of the public); the vast majority of each (54 percent and 61 percent, respectively) claimed they were moderates (compared with 41 percent of the public).[23] These data provide some evidence to bolster assertions that reporters are more likely to be liberals. Other research shows that historically, newspapers have been far more likely to endorse Republican presidential candidates, but the current trend is for papers to remain uncommitted at election time.[24] Research has failed to find empirical evidence that news reporting is biased in favor of either party.[25] So, even though reporters may be more liberal, their professional stance on the whole remains neutral. It is difficult to assess whether their neutrality is the result of the influence of editors and owners (both of whom are more conservative), of their ethical commitments, or of the competitiveness inherent in the modern journalistic environment.

If we expand the definition of the media to include talk radio, concerns over a liberal bias disappear. Unquestionably, conservative radio personalities and political commentators dominate talk radio, and self-described liberal or left-wing commentators have had difficulty finding a following in this environment. And as for Web sites and blogs, all shades of political opinion seem to have plentiful outlets.

SOCIALIZATION   The third societal function of the media that Lasswell identified is to socialize people. As noted in Chapter 10, pages 301–303, the media are an agent of socialization, teaching us political facts and opinions that help form our political belief structures and our political culture. The media also reinforce economic and social values. Simply looking at MTV and VH1 provides testimony that the belief in capitalism is alive and well in the United States. Shows such as *The Fabu-*

lous Life, Teen Cribs, and *My Super Sweet Sixteen,* which dwell on material acquisitions, reinforce the basic tenets of capitalism—the desire for more drives our economic system.

In winter, young children spend an average of 31 hours a week watching TV. Eighty percent of the programming children watch is intended for adults and generally goes far beyond their life experiences, making the potential for molding their minds greater than that for adults.[26] Therefore, the concern in many areas of society is about programming content and the negative implications of the high levels of violence, sex, and materialism on television. The media can and do promote positive role models for children, celebrating national holidays and heroes, but there is no denying that negative images in the media far outweigh positive illustrations. For adults whose basic ideology and opinions are already formed, the media provide opportunities for reinforcement, especially with so many options available on TV, cable, and the Internet and in the immense variety of print publications. Adults can thus easily find programming to reinforce their ideology and political views; children are more susceptible to what they learn from TV.

Functions of the Media

11.3   **Illustrate the functions of the media in American politics and society.**

PRACTICE QUIZ: UNDERSTAND AND APPLY

1. The media are dual agents of socialization, transmitting values that are both helpful and harmful to our political system.
   a. true
   b. false

2. A series of articles in the *Chicago Tribune* in 1999 about the death penalty in Illinois is an example of investigative journalism that
   a. goes too far, violating the privacy of noncelebrities.
   b. is really more sensationalism than reporting of hard news.
   c. does not go far enough, leaving social problems unaddressed.
   d. discovers abuses in our system and leads to real change.

3. The personalities and political commentators on talk radio make it clear that this medium
   a. is dominated by liberals.
   b. is dominated by conservatives.
   c. has succeeded in remaining politically neutral.
   d. has shifted from a conservative to liberal bias.

4. The entertaining function of the media can significantly impact politicians and the public.
   a. true
   b. false

ANALYZE

1. How do the entertainment media affect politics? How important do you think this effect is?

2. What are the positive and negative aspects of having the media serve as watchdogs? Why is the power of interpretation a significant tool of the media?

IDENTIFY THE CONCEPT THAT DOESN'T BELONG

a. Inform
b. Highlight
c. Reinforce
d. Transform
e. Frame

Resource Center
• Glossary
• Vocabulary Example
• Connect the Link

■ **Agenda Setting:** The process of featuring specific stories in the media to focus attention on particular issues.

EXAMPLE: *When the media cover a story and focus on a new issue, they raise public consciousness about it. The public then puts pressure on governmental authorities to address the issue, thereby setting the political agenda.*

Political Use of the Media

11.4 Assess how the media can be influential in American politics.

(pages 340–345)

Political parties, politicians, interest groups, and individuals use the media to manipulate the public and politics. Political elites have always used communication for political purposes. In 350 B.C., the ancient Greek philosopher Aristotle, in his *Rhetoric,* discussed the role of communication in keeping political communities intact. Today's modern mass media simply make the process easier. As you'll see, political leaders often directly appeal to the public (with a televised speech, for example) or indirectly (in advertisements designed to sway public opinion). It is important to realize that communication has always been used for political purposes, although today's technology has made it more sophisticated. In light of their exclusive focus on communication, the mass media in the United States should be considered an important political institution.

How Politicians Make the News

Politicians try very hard to get **earned media coverage**— positive press coverage free of charge. Many of their actions are designed to increase the likelihood that the media will cover them. This is especially significant for officials who are up for reelection. As you will see, people tend to put more credence in what they learn from news programs than in information presented during paid advertisements. Hence earned media coverage is very important for political officials and political candidates. It raises their visibility and exposes them to the public.

Elected officials and other ambitious leaders use various means of getting attention. One popular tactic is to stage **pseudo-events** (a term coined by the historian Daniel J. Boorstin in 1961 to characterize events whose primary purpose is to generate public interest and news coverage).[27] Although the press does not like to cover these staged events, preferring to capture more realistic news, they will often show them for fear of getting scooped by rivals. One of the most famous pseudo-events in recent years occurred on May 1, 2003, when then-President George W. Bush emerged from a Navy jet in full flight gear on the aircraft carrier Abraham Lincoln. He later spoke in front of a huge banner declaring "Mission Accomplished." In a prime-time speech scheduled for that Thursday evening—expected to garner the largest television audience—he declared that the "major combat operations in Iraq have ended" and discussed the defeat of "an ally of Al Qaeda." While President Bush was able to use this staged media event to garner attention, in the long run his words were used against him and his party as the war waged on.

Politicians try to control the events, but sometimes, they are unsuccessful. President Bush was caught on camera once reading a children's book upside down, provoking much media ridicule. When announcing an elementary school spelling bee, Vice President Dan Quayle once misspelled *potato.* Innumerable jokes about his intelligence dogged him for the rest of his political career. Vice President Joe Biden has made a number of political gaffes. While on the campaign trail in September 2008, during an interview with Katie Couric, Biden remarked "When the stock market crashed, Franklin D. Roosevelt got on the television and didn't just talk about the, you know, the princes of greed. He said, 'Look, here's what happened' "—only experimental TV sets were available in 1929 when the stock market crashed. More recently, in March 2010, after introducing President Obama just hours after the health care reform bill passed Congress, he embraced the president and called the bill's passage a "big f★★★ing deal." Sometimes damaged by these political gaffes, politicians and their aides spend a great deal of time developing mechanisms to counteract them with positive media attention.

There is often an adversarial relationship between public officials and the media. Officials want to control information about themselves and their policies, including the way such information is framed and presented, while the media reject such "spoon-feeding" and try to retain their independence. Government officials want to be seen in a positive light, whereas the media, perpetually seeking to boost ratings or circulation, always find controversies or conflicts more appealing. At the same time, however, reciprocal relationships bind the media, politicians, and the public together.

Politicians need the media to communicate with their constituents and advance their agendas, the media need politicians to provide news and entertainment, and the public needs both to make informed voting decisions. The media influence the public with programming—but because the media are driven by the profit motive, the public (their source of revenue) influences them. Similarly, the public influences government through elections and by supporting or rejecting policies, and the government influences the public by making and enforcing policies.

How Journalists Report the News

Many people believe that the media's ability to select how and what they report is their greatest source of influence. Called **agenda setting**■, it consists of determining which issues will be covered, in what detail, and in what context—and also deciding which stories are not newsworthy and therefore are not going to be covered. Agenda setting figures very prominently in the media's capacity to influence the public and politicians. As a consequence, much concern exists about how and by whom stories are decided to be newsworthy.

■ **Gatekeepers:** A group or individuals who determine which stories will receive attention in the media and from which perspective.

Example: *When editors of major newspapers decide which stories will be covered and from what angle, they serve as gatekeepers of the news.*

In allowing certain stories to get on the public agenda and by sidelining others, the media are said to be acting as **gatekeepers**■. Historically, concern stemmed from the fact that no one could check the media's selection of news: the media controlled access by selecting which stories would be covered and from what angle. This has changed recently with more individuals participating in the creation of news. For example, a growing number of Americans contribute to news stories by posting videos online, commenting about news stories or forwarding news to their friends and acquaintances. However, we should not underestimate the ability of the media to shine the spotlight on issues because of their presumed credibility, access to policy leaders, and resources.[28]

The media set the political agenda, choose how and when political issues get addressed, and decide which stories draw attention to a problem that is important and needs to be fixed. They thus create a political climate that can frame subsequent discussions and shape public opinion. For instance, in June 1998, the media publicized the gruesome death of a black man, James Byrd Jr., by racist murderers who chained him to the back of a pickup truck and dragged him until he was dead, thus focusing public attention on racial tension and bigotry. In doing so, the media illustrated a problem, discussed its roots, and then demonstrated the need for change, helping set the public agenda.

The amount of time, space, or prominence such a story receives can dramatically affect whether it will make it onto the political agenda. These decisions, made by senior media managers, are often deliberative and conscious, leading some analysts to worry about potential media bias. Consumers should be skeptical as many stories that are socially, politically, and economically important are still not covered by the media for a variety of reasons.

COVERING THE PRESIDENT The nature of the interactions and type of relationship with the media differ from president to president. Presidents use the media differently, depending on their personal style. President Clinton averaged 550 public talks each year (many very informal), while President Reagan, dubbed "the Great Communicator," averaged only 320. At the dawn of the television era, President Truman, who is today remembered for his vigorous and colorful ways of expressing himself in public, averaged a mere 88 talks a year.[29] Clinton's ability to communicate and relate to the public earned him a great deal of flexibility, allowing his candidacy and presidency to survive many scandals and even an impeachment trial. The relationship he was able to develop with the people, via the media, increased his popularity, providing some insulation against the serious charges of personal wrongdoing that he eventually faced. President Obama held five full press conferences in his first year in office (one more than President George W. Bush did in his first year), but he held no full news conferences during the last five months of 2009, preferring instead to deliver briefer remarks where he sometimes took questions from the press. President Obama's relatively low number of press conferences in 2009 and the first half of 2010 has generated criticism especially in light of his campaign pledge to increase transparency and access in Washington.

There is an interesting dynamic between politicians and the media. Even if the relationship is uneasy, open warfare is rare. On the one hand, the relationship is by definition

The relationship between the press and public officials is complex. On the one hand each "side" is leery of the other. On the other hand, the press needs information from public officials, and political leaders need the press to communicate with the public. Pictured here is Barack Obama surprising former White House correspondent Helen Thomas with birthday cupcakes (they both share the same birthday, August 4th). —*Do you think that public officials are less dependent on the press because of social networking sites and other technological changes? Is the press becoming obsolete or do they still play an important watchdog role in American politics?*

adversarial, because both sides want to control how information and events are framed. However, as you have seen, both sides need each other, too. Presidents put great effort into creating photo opportunities ("photo ops") and pseudo-events that are visually appealing and releasing to the press information that is favorable to the White House. News media with limited resources will often cooperate, but those with more resources can subject the material to greater scrutiny, often presenting information in a manner contrary to what the White House might prefer.

The office of the White House press secretary supplies the White House press corps and the Washington-based media with daily information about the administration. The president's press secretary customarily holds a daily press conference. In addition, each administration has an office of communications, which may be structured differently from administration to administration but is always used to oversee long-term public relations and presidential image-making.

Communication from the White House takes three general forms: **press releases, news briefings,** and **news conferences.** Press releases and news briefings are the routine ways to release news. Press releases are prepared text in which officials present information to reporters and are worded in hopes that they will be used just as they are, without rewriting. To allow the media to ask direct questions about press releases or current events, the presidential press secretary and other high officials regularly appear for news briefings. News conferences are direct opportunities for the president to speak to the press and the public. Theodore Roosevelt held the first news conference at the White House, but his and all later presidential news conferences until 1961 were conducted in private. In that year, John F. Kennedy was the first

president to allow live, televised coverage. The number of press conferences held each year has been in a decline in the age of investigative reporting; overall, presidents today try to release information in a more cautious, controlled manner (see Figure 11.1).

Doris Graber has identified four major purposes of media coverage of the executive branch.[30] First, the media serve to inform chief executives about current events, highlighting issues that need attention across the nation and the world. Second, the media inform the executive branch about the needs and concerns of the public, by reporting public opinion polls and by publishing letters to the editor and feature stories. Third, the media also allow presidents to express their positions and policy proposals directly to the people and other government officials by means of press conferences, televised speeches, and staged events, which always supply the administration in power with ample opportunity to explain its positions and garner support. Finally, the media keep the president in public view, reporting every scrap of available information about the first family's daily life. This reporting is generally framed from a human interest angle, but it also includes evaluations of presidential performance.

All four of these functions allow the public to stay in touch with the actions and life of the president and allow the president to keep in touch with the American people. Presidents have used this relationship to their advantage, knowing that they can command a great amount of attention and interest in their words and actions. The first media-conscious president was Theodore Roosevelt, who used the White House as a platform to influence public opinion and pursue his political agenda. "I suppose my critics will call that preaching," Theodore Roosevelt said in 1909, "but I have got such a bully pulpit!"

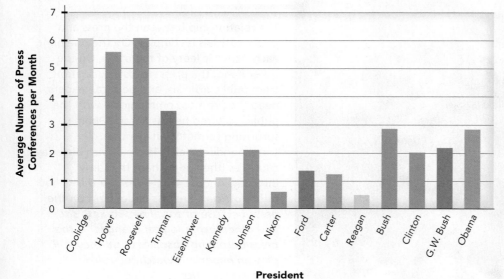

President

FIGURE 11.1 ■ Presidential Press Conferences

Over the last 86 or so years, the average number of presidential press conferences per month has decreased rather dramatically, from Franklin Roosevelt's high of 6 to Ronald Reagan's low of 0.5. —*Why do you think this is the case? Why do you think presidents in the modern era of television are relying on other means to communicate with the country? Do you think this trend isolates the president too much from the press?*

SOURCE: Gerhard Peters, "Presidential News Conferences," in *The American Presidency Project,* ed. John T. Woolley and Gerhard Peters (Santa Barbara: University of California. 1999–2009). Accessed at http://www.presidency.ucsb.edu/news_conferences.php on June 2, 2010.

PATHWAYS of action

The Strategic Use of Leaks

For generations, political actors have utilized leaks to strategically manipulate information. However, new technology allows leaks to be used more purposefully than before. In 2006, The Sunshine Press—an international nonprofit organization funded by such diverse individuals as Chinese dissidents, journalists, mathematicians, and others—launched the Web site WikiLeaks in an effort to expose governmental actions and promote transparency. In just three short years from its debut, much has changed for this whistle-blowing Web site, including a prestigious award from Amnesty International in 2009 for its publication of "Kenya: The Cry of Blood—Extra Judicial Killings and Disappearances." WikiLeaks is most famous for leaking a video of U.S. forces killing Iraqi civilians as well as documents about the wars in Afghanistan and Iraq that were previously unavailable to the public. Wikileaks has also leaked documents regarding accusations stemming from toxic waste disposal, tax evasion, and racism. Once seen as a renegade Web site, the mainstream media is paying much more attention to Wikileaks.

It seems commonplace today to read a news story or watch a news report in which important information is attributed to an unnamed "high-ranking source" or a "police insider." Why aren't these sources named, and what are the implications of relying on information that is leaked?

There are many reasons why public officials leak information to the press. One is to gauge public reaction, sending up a "trial balloon" to see how a potential policy will be received and reported. For example, when Reagan administration officials considered changing the guidelines for food programs for low-income children to allow ketchup to be considered a vegetable, they leaked this idea to the media. Public outcry was fast and negative, the guidelines remained unchanged, and ketchup was ruled out as a vegetable in federal food programs.[31]

Leaks can also be preemptive. Officials can strategically use leaked information to sway public opinion and pressure other officials. Preemptively leaking material can allow officials to change their minds before making a public vote, as it is often easier to pressure officials before they publicly commit to a position. Unflattering or bad news can also be leaked a little at a time to lessen the damage it might cause. It is common knowledge that the best time to leak bad information is on weekends, when many full-time reporters are off and the public is too busy to watch the news. By Monday morning, the initial impact may have faded or been superseded by other news items.

Leaks are also ways to get information from publicity-shy groups or individuals. People involved with the court system or the police are typically reluctant to release sensitive information. Allowing them a chance to release information without being named could often serve as an important prompt for otherwise silent informants who are hesitant to go on record. It is long-established journalistic practice to grant leakers secrecy so that they are more willing to release information—even if it is illegal to do so.

The public should be skeptical, however, when analyzing material that is not attributed to a source, because it is often released for self-serving reasons. Informants often get to influence how the story is told based on the information they provide, which might not be the full story or the objective truth. Since the name and agenda of the informant are withheld, the political dimensions of the story (and its self-serving motivations) are often hidden, with potentially devastating consequences. That is why reporters must exercise diligence in handling leaks.[32]

COVERING CONGRESS For several reasons, the media give far less attention to Congress than to the president. People tend to have more interest in the actions of the president, who is the country's highest-ranking official with a nationwide constituency. No single member of Congress can make that claim or get that recognition. Furthermore, Congress is a much larger institution that requires coalition and consensus building, both of which take time and are not particularly exciting. By contrast, the president is often seen as working alone, so it becomes easier for the press to focus on his actions. Also, as a deliberative body, Congress works slowly, even tediously, and without much drama. Of course, interested people can turn to C-SPAN for gavel-to-gavel congressional coverage—but watching for several hours will reveal just how unexciting such deliberations can be.

The local media often cover the actions and votes of members of Congress, with senators typically getting more attention than representatives, especially in large metropolitan areas that encompass several congressional districts, making it difficult to cover all members of the local congressional delegation in detail. To get mentioned in the local news or local papers, members of Congress often stage pseudo-events and attend local events—even lowly ones like the Watermelon Festival picnic, the Fourth of July parade, or a ribbon-cutting ceremony to celebrate opening a new town library can win visually appealing news coverage.

COVERING THE COURTS Of the three branches of government, the courts tend to get the least amount of coverage. Why? One reason is that federal judges rarely grant interviews lest their impartiality be questioned. Once appointed, judges normally do not receive much specific personal coverage; rather, attention is focused on their rulings and on the specific cases heard in their courts. The courts, moreover, deliberate and reach their decisions in secret, and very rarely do they allow televised or sound-recorded live coverage of cases as they are being argued.

A number of frustrated members of Congress charge up the steps of the Senate building. The women representatives were going to the Senate building to ensure that the charges of sexual harassment brought by Anita Hill against then–Supreme Court nominee Clarence Thomas would be taken seriously and investigated. Many thought the treatment of Hill by the all-white, all-male Senate Judiciary Committee was unfair and disrespectful and may have stimulated some women to run for political office. Moreover, the coverage and analysis of the allegations focused national attention on the matter of sexual harassment, serving to raise awareness of this important issue. *—How powerful do you think role modeling is? Can you think of a time that something you saw in the media stimulated you to take action?*

Another area that receives considerable media attention is controversial confirmation hearings. The Senate must confirm all federal court judges, including Supreme Court justices, after the president has nominated them. Perhaps the most prominent example was the 1991 confirmation hearing for Supreme Court nominee Clarence Thomas. Testifying before the Senate

Judiciary Committee, Anita Hill, a University of Oklahoma law professor, accused Thomas of sexual harassment when she was an employee at the U.S. Department of Education (ED), and the Equal Employment Opportunity Commission (EEOC), on which he served in the 1980s. A sharply divided national audience watched the Judiciary Committee's investigation into the charges. The hearings placed the issue of sexual harassment on the national agenda, resulting in many changes in laws, policies, and opinions. They also prompted many women, outraged by the confrontational manner in which Hill was treated by the all-white, all-male Senate Judiciary Committee, to enter politics and seek elected office.[33]

Under most other circumstances, national judges, including Supreme Court justices, rarely generate stories of a personal nature. However, the press does cover their rulings, especially Supreme Court decisions and controversial federal district and appellate court decisions. Reporting on the Supreme Court is difficult, because the Court tends to release several rulings at once, forcing reporters to cover numerous, often technical and difficult opinions. Typically, the press will select one or two main decisions and discuss them in more detail, while a summary box simply mentions the other Supreme Court decisions released that day. Several key decisions (for example, *Roe v. Wade* [1973], Chapter 4 and *Brown v. Board of Education* [1954],

Supreme Court justices traditionally save their views for their written opinions. However, during President Obama's 2010 State of the Union Address, Supreme Court Justice Samuel Alito mouthed "not true" during President Obama's criticism of a recently issued Supreme Court ruling on campaign finance. *—Do you think that Alito was wrong to break the tradition and publicly disagree with the President? Or should justices be free to express their views like all other citizens? Does this type of behavior make the justices seem political, jeopardizing their role as impartial arbitrators?*

Chapter 5) attracted enormous press coverage at the time they were released as well as retrospective stories on their anniversaries, follow-up analyses of their consequences, and even later revelations about how the decisions were reached. The media have ignored many important cases, however, and in other instances have presented information that had factual errors, largely because of the complexity of case law.[34]

How Groups Use the Media

Interest groups and outsiders use the media to promote their agendas, employing a variety of techniques. One popular technique is to stage events similar to politicians' pseudo-events. A child advocacy group might stage a rally to support a proposal for greater funding of a health insurance program for children, hoping that the news media will report it. Appearing on the news is very important, especially to groups that do not have large budgets, because positive coverage gives them exposure and often credibility.

A second technique used by groups to get media coverage is to issue press releases and bulletins. The National Organization for Women (NOW), for example, routinely issues press releases on matters of importance to its members. Groups often issue video clips directly to news organizations in hopes that the clips will be aired with no editing to show the group in a positive light. So-called video news releases are designed to make it easy for television stations to use the videos. Groups also provide expert interviews and often have members (who do not necessarily identify themselves as members) write letters to the editor or contribute op-ed articles for local and national newspapers.

Finally, groups with sufficient means will often pay for issue advocacy advertising. One example of this is "Pork—the Other White Meat" commercials prompting consumers to consider including pork in a healthy diet. Because the media are such an important means for groups to raise visibility, win support, and influence both the public and officials, interest groups will continue to be creative in developing attention-grabbing tactics.

Political Use of the Media

11.4 Assess how the media can be influential in American politics.

PRACTICE QUIZ: UNDERSTAND AND APPLY

1. Why are public officials and the media frequently adversarial?
   a. Each wants to control political news stories.
   b. Public officials resent how infrequently they get to use the media to reach voters.
   c. Public officials thrive on policy controversies, whereas the media boosts ratings by emphasizing what's right in the world.
   d. The media need politicians to provide news, yet politicians prefer to avoid the media spotlight.

2. Sometimes government officials intentionally leak news before official announcements in order to
   a. confuse the mass media, especially TV reporters.
   b. bypass First Amendment regulations.
   c. measure public reaction to policy changes before they are official.
   d. demonstrate their ideological purity to the public.

3. Why does Congress tend to get less attention from the media than the presidency?
   a. People seem to just be more interested in what the president is doing.
   b. Congress is a much larger institution and requires consensus, which is time-consuming and not very exciting.

   c. The work of Congress is not as important to the legislative process as the work of the president.
   d. a and b

4. Media coverage of the executive is an important tool to keep the public linked with the president and to promote accountability and responsiveness.
   a. true
   b. false

ANALYZE

1. Why do public officials and the media need each other? How do interest groups use the media?

2. What does it mean when we say that the media act as gatekeepers? How powerful is this role? Do you think the Internet is changing the media's role as a gatekeeper? Why or why not?

IDENTIFY THE CONCEPT THAT DOESN'T BELONG

a. Spotlight attention
b. Determine newsworthiness
c. Control public opinion
d. Frame issues
e. Set context for stories

11.4

Resource Center
• Glossary
• Vocabulary Example
• Connect the Link

The Media and the Public in the Political Arena

11.5   Establish how the media have an impact on the cultural values and political opinions of the American public.

(pages 346–349)

The print media—newspapers, magazines, and other periodicals—tend to cater to an upper-class, better-educated segment of society. Print media are effective in translating facts, while TV is better at conveying emotion and feelings. Thus better-educated people are attracted to the print media, and their readers continue to be better informed about events, reinforcing their advantaged position in society.

The fact that the more affluent have greater access to information than the general society gives them more opportunities to influence politics. For example, announcements of city council meetings or school redistricting plans are usually made in local newspapers. Only individuals who routinely read a local paper will know about proposed changes, public meetings, and scheduled forums. Those who habitually do not read the paper remain uninformed about these events, which may have a significant impact on their lives. A cycle exists: Poorer people pay less attention to the print media, because print stories tend to cater to the interests of the more affluent. And because poor people don't subscribe in large numbers, newspapers continue to ignore the needs of the lower class, perpetuating biases in coverage, access to information, and lack of a diverse audience.

Media in Campaigns

It is a long-standing belief that the media are very powerful actors in elections in the United States; some people go so far as to claim that the media actually determine the outcomes of elections. Although this is certainly an overstatement, the media do have a great deal of power, especially in anointing the "front-running candidates" long before an election. Marking one or two candidates as front-runners usually has a snowball effect: The media and the public pay more attention to them, making it easier for them to get on the news and raise money. The more money they raise, the more prominent their campaign becomes, and the bigger the campaign, the more attention it gets from the media and the public.

Front-runner status develops its own cycle of success—though there is certainly some liability in being declared the front-runner, too. (Front-runners get heightened media scrutiny, for example, which can be fatally damaging if they make gaffes or if skeletons lurk in their closets.) Many people are concerned about the power of the media in determining front-runners, because this tends to prematurely narrow the field of candidates, often very early in the nomination cycle. When the media focus on front-runners in polls and stories, lesser-known candidates often encounter many difficulties, especially with fundraising, and are often forced to withdraw early from the race. Moreover, the media often declare winners based not on the absolute vote total but on how well a candidate does compared to what had been expected.

Bill Clinton, at the time governor of Arkansas, serves as a very good example. Massachusetts Senator Paul Tsongas won the most votes in the 1992 New Hampshire primary, but Clinton, simply because he did better than had been expected, was proclaimed "the winner" by the press. This accolade gave him increased media attention and public support. The "winner" designation sent Clinton's candidacy into high gear, and he went on to win the nomination and the election.

During the campaign for the 2008 presidential election, the front-runner status was more difficult to determine for both political parties. For the Republicans, former New York City Mayor Rudy Giuliani held an early lead in the polls, followed closely by Arizona Senator John McCain. Giuliani remained the "front-runner" throughout most of 2007. However, pundits who had all but written off McCain were surprised when Giuliani and McCain were both considered by the media to be front-runners after the second Republican debate in early 2007. The media had an even more difficult time declaring the front-runners for the Democrats. Hillary Clinton, Barack Obama, and John Edwards were all designated with the title at some point during the nomination season.

NEGATIVE COVERAGE   After the 2004 campaign season, a study by the Project for Excellence in Journalism, the Pew Research Center, and the University of Missouri School of Journalism, which analyzed newspaper, broadcast, and cable coverage from late March through early June in 2004, found that negative coverage of the two main presidential candidates was quite prevalent. Stories and images of President Bush were negative by more than a 3-to-1 margin. Media assessment of his Democratic opponent, Massachusetts Senator John F. Kerry, was more likely to be negative by a 5-to-1 margin. Moreover, the study found that the more people read the print media and watch TV coverage, the more they are likely to support the themes being emphasized by the media. The researchers found that the most common public perception about Bush was that "he is stubborn and arrogant," followed by "he lacks credibility." The most common themes reported about Kerry were that "he flip-flops on issues" and "he is very liberal." Both of these negative "definitions" of Kerry echoed the themes of Bush's campaign advertisements and speeches, and vice versa. It is hard to determine whether it was the press or the Bush campaign that influenced the public against Kerry; most likely, it was a combination of two reinforcing messages.[35]

PAID ADVERTISING One key aspect of media usage in campaigns is the need to purchase paid advertising, which is enormously expensive. Paid advertising is essential, however, because research consistently demonstrates that the news media increasingly portray candidates negatively, with fewer and fewer positive stories. Daniel Hallin found that 5 percent of news stories in the 1968 election were positive and 6 percent were negative. By 1988, however, only 1 percent of stories were positive but 16 percent were negative.[36] TV coverage of campaigns has also shrunk, coming to consist chiefly of tiny, frequently repeated visual snippets called **sound bites.** And even the length of the sound bites on network evening news programs shriveled, from an average of 42.3 seconds in 1968 to 7.2 seconds in 1996.[37] Given these circumstances, candidates desiring to get their message and vision out to the people must pay heavily for advertising.

DEBATES Televised debates can also be important in affecting the public's perception of candidates. The most infamous example of this impact occurred in the very first televised presidential debate in 1960. John F. Kennedy's strong visual performance allayed the public's fears that he was too young and inexperienced compared to his well-known opponent, Vice President Richard M. Nixon. This debate underscored the importance of television's visual nature. TV viewers saw the physically attractive, tanned, and seemingly relaxed Kennedy verbally sparring with a sweaty, earnest, and less photogenic Nixon, and a majority of television viewers believed that Kennedy won the debate. Those listening to the debate on the radio, however, believed that Nixon had won on the substance of what was said. This stark contrast changed the way in which subsequent candidates have viewed the power of television and underscored the importance of cultivating visual images. Ronald Reagan's masterful performance in the 1980 and 1984 presidential debates showed that despite his advanced years, he was mentally alert and able. (His professional training as an actor helped him, too.) More recently, George W. Bush exceeded low initial expectations about his abilities when he used his performance in the 2000 debates against Al Gore to persuade many voters that he was sufficiently knowledgeable and capable to serve as president.[38]

The importance of television in campaigns and elections also has a powerful effect on the pool of eligible candidates and the types of people who are perceived to be "electable." Had TV existed in the 1930s, many believe Franklin D. Roosevelt could not have been elected, because having been crippled by polio, he was confined to a wheelchair. Indeed, Roosevelt worried that his disability would make him seem "weak," and newspaper and newsreel photographers of the day were careful not to show him in his chair or on crutches. Television puts charismatic, telegenic candidates at an advantage; hence candidates for high-profile positions usually hire coaches to teach

The media are often criticized for their coverage of elections. —*Do you think they focus too much on the "horse race" and too little on the substance of the campaign? If they focused more attention on issues, do you think people would pay more attention or less?*

them how to behave when appearing on television. For example, public opinion polls might show that a candidate is perceived to be "too stuffy." The campaign will then stage outdoor events to make him or her appear more informal, relaxed, and "ordinary." If a candidate is seen as not intellectual enough, events will be staged at a library or university. These coaches work on body language, speech presentations, clothing, and hairstyle. Although this seems superficial, television has made outward appearance crucial. You might wonder if such past presidents as George Washington and Abraham Lincoln could ever be elected today.

Global Issues

CNN reaches every country in the world and has 85 million subscribers. A Russian edition of the *New York Times* is sold in Moscow. MTV is viewed on five continents, with an audience of 265 million.[39] Such availability of American culture raises concerns for many people, especially in other countries with very different cultures, who fear "McGlobalization." Foreigners worry that our culture and values, many of which they do not share, are "corrupting" citizens in their countries. This concern is especially significant in the Muslim world, where American and Western values are widely perceived as a mortal threat to Islam. Objections to "excessive" American cultural and political influence are heard around the globe, from Canada and France to China. In fact, concerns about American influence led the Chinese government to ban all privately owned satellite dishes. Many historians attribute the fall of communism in the Soviet Union and Eastern Europe in part to exposure to Western thought and values on television. Countries proud of their culture, heritage, and values are greatly troubled by the trend of Americanization made possible by the global media.

■ **News Monopolies:** Single news firms that control all the media in a given market.

Example: *Most locations in the United States are dependent on one print source for their local and national news, creating a news monopoly.*

■ **Competitive News Markets:** Locales with two or more news organizations that can check each other's accuracy and neutrality of reporting.

EXAMPLE: *While most cities have only one major paper, a number—including Boston, Chicago, Dallas/Fort Worth Metroplex, Denver, New York, the Twin Cities, Seattle, and Tampa Bay—have at least two newspapers, which makes for more competitive news markets.*

Narrowcasting

Another area of concern for many is the trend of cable television and the Internet to appeal to narrower audiences. As television and other mass media have become more specialized, the targeting of specific audiences, known as **narrowcasting,** has become far more common. Some observers worry that specialized programming may cause groups to become more fragmented, as the media no longer cater to a mass audience. Consider the changes in print media and in programming for Spanish speakers in the United States. One study found that two-thirds of Hispanic Americans watch Spanish-language programming daily.[40] Telemundo and Univision both have nightly news programs, each with a slightly different focus in their stories than the English-language network news programs. Furthermore, because many Hispanic viewers are not watching national English-language news programs, these "mainstream" networks are less likely to offer programming that appeals to Latinos. As a result, the larger English-speaking audience is not sufficiently exposed to issues of concern primarily to Hispanic viewers. An endless cycle can develop that is troubling to many analysts, who worry that specialized programming with a narrow appeal will further fragment groups within American society.

Citizen Journalism

With the advancements in technology and popularity of social networking sites and blogs, more people are actively involved in the creation of news than ever before. **Citizen journalism** (also known as *street journalism*) is the idea that nonprofessionals are involved in collecting, reporting, commenting, and disseminating news stories. J. D. Lasica classifies different types of citizen journalism including audience participation at mainstream news outlets (bulletin boards, blogs, videos), independent news and information Web sites (consumer reviews such as trip advisor), full-fledged participatory news sites (such as South Korea's OhmyNews), collaborative and contributory media sites (such as Slashdot), and broadcasting sites (such as KenRadio).[41] Some see citizen journalism as a positive mechanism allowing for more variety of content, promoting diversity, and enhancing participatory democracy, while others view it as something that is dangerous for democracy, since there is nearly no regulation of content or quality—in essence anyone can become a "citizen journalist" with no training or qualifications.

Concentration and Centralization of Ownership

Concern also stems from the trend toward more concentrated media ownership, especially of the print media and in radio broadcasting. As media ownership becomes more centralized, a "nationalization" of the news occurs, which tends to promote a sameness of opinion and experience. Concentration has been under way ever since the rise of broadcast networks and of newspaper chains in the 1930s, but today, it is accelerating.

Competition is generally believed to be healthy, because it makes possible a larger variety of opinions and points of view. There is concern today because much of the news comes from national news services and there is minimal or no competition between papers in major cities—especially between two or more morning or evening papers. Examine your local paper to see how many stories in the first section come from centralized news sources, such as the Associated Press, *New York Times,* or *Washington Post.* You will find that it is not uncommon for the entire first page to be from sources outside your community or state. This trend is evident even in college newspapers, where editorials and stories are often picked up from a news source and do not necessarily reflect the concerns of your particular campus community.

It is widely believed that competition results in the best product, an economic and political belief held by most theorists. Observers of the media enthusiastically approve of **competitive news markets**■ and regard **news monopolies**■ as potentially dangerous. Newspaper ownership in recent decades has tended toward monopolies and away from competitive markets.

The changes in broadcasting are less clear. The influence of the networks has diminished thanks to the proliferation of cable and satellite alternatives, although ownership has become more centralized. In 1997, the media critic Ben Bagdikian noted that the number of major media corporations had decreased from

Many areas of the country have newspapers published in a variety of languages to keep the local public informed. *—Do you think that people should be pressured to learn to speak and read English? Or does providing information in a variety of languages show respect for immigrant populations and add to the diversity of the United States?*

more than 50 in the early 1980s to only 10 by the mid–1990s. By 2001, Bagdikian reported, six huge corporations—Time Warner, Disney, Viacom, News Corp., General Electric, and Bertelsmann AG—dominated the mass media.[42] Furthermore, as the media have become deregulated, cross-media ownership is rising, with corporations owning a variety of media outlets, including newspapers, TV and radio stations, newsmagazines, and production companies. In 1995, Capital Cities/ABC owned seven television stations, seven radio networks (with more than 3,000 affiliated stations), 18 radio stations, 75 weekly newspapers, as well as many magazines and trade publications. When it merged with Disney in 1995, this conglomerate grew even larger.[43]

There are many people, however, that believe the advent of citizen journalism, which has resulted in a massive diversification of media—via millions of Web sites, blogs, forums, wikis, and such—counters the negative impact of this concentration of ownership and allows for healthy debate. In addition, the growing diversity of news consumption (with more people consuming news from multiple sources than in the past) may further lessen concerns about concentration of ownership.

The Media and the Public in the Political Arena

11.5 Establish how the media have an impact on the cultural and political opinions of the American public.

PRACTICE QUIZ: UNDERSTAND AND APPLY

1. Why are so many people concerned about the media's ability to help determine the front-runners in a campaign?
   a. because this determination happens so late in the nomination cycle that voters do not have enough time to assess these front-runners before election day
   b. because the media's criteria for declaring favorites in a campaign is often dramatically different from voters' criteria
   c. because the media historically have avoided playing such a political role
   d. because the media declare front-runners so early in the nomination cycle, narrowing the field of candidates prematurely

2. Why has paid political advertising become increasingly important in presidential campaigns?
   a. because voters value and expect it
   b. because it helps overcome negative coverage of candidates in the media
   c. because it is necessary to comply with new FCC regulations
   d. because media coverage is very thorough, and campaigns need to present more simplified images of their candidate

3. What is a potential downside to "narrowcasting"?
   a. It may make mainstream networks less culturally diverse.
   b. It may give minority viewers, such as Latinos, less access to Spanish-speaking shows.
   c. It may create fewer choices for television and Internet users.
   d. It may prevent third-party participation in presidential debates.

4. Why is the centralization of newspaper ownership troubling in a democracy?
   a. because it makes news gathering less efficient
   b. because it makes news gathering more expensive
   c. because it gives readers fewer perspectives from which to see and understand the news
   d. because it makes the newspaper business less profitable

ANALYZE

1. What is meant when we say that the media cater to an upscale audience? What are the consequences of this tendency?

2. Why are many people troubled by the concentration of media ownership and the trend toward media cross-ownership?

IDENTIFY THE CONCEPT THAT DOESN'T BELONG

a. Centralization of ownership
b. Narrowcasting
c. McGlobalization
d. Sound bites
e. Positive coverage

Resource Center
• Glossary
• Vocabulary Example
• Connect the Link

■ **Libel:** The publication of false and malicious material that defames an individual's reputation.

EXAMPLE: *Juries are very sensitive to the issue of libel and often rule in favor of the defendant. Media outlets that appeal to higher courts, however, usually have the lower court decision overturned in favor of the media. Libel suits against public officials are very difficult to win.*

Governmental Regulations

11.6 Contrast the rights of a free press to the government's authority to restrict content.

(pages 350–353)

All societies have laws regulating the media, most commonly stemming from national security concerns. Laws that define and punish treason and sedition are always necessary to ensure national security; the dilemma is how much regulation is needed before it infringes on personal freedoms. There is a tension between the needs of the government to ensure national security and the desire of a people to be free, as guaranteed by the First Amendment to the Constitution. The 9/11 attacks and President George W. Bush's declaration of the War on Terror, which included enacting the USA PATRIOT Act, threw into high relief these concerns about balancing security and liberty.

Media and Government: A Tense Relationship

The media want to be allowed to report what they think is newsworthy, while the government wants to limit disclosure in order to promote protection. This tension is most evident in wartime. Many people in government want to limit the amount of information shared, seeking to enhance national security. Ideally, from the government's perspective, only information it approves for dissemination would be shared with the public. For example, the government successfully structured the sharing of information during the Gulf War of 1991. Information and images passed through a tightly controlled, centralized governmental "feed," which released video to all the media; hence there was little variety in the information available.

With limited information, however, it is difficult to ensure that the public knows how the war is being fought. Abuses occur during times of war, and many people fear that in the absence of media scrutiny, abuse and cruelty could increase. For instance, does the public have the right to know if a presidential administration or high-ranking military officials approve the use of torture against enemy prisoners? The tension between the public's right to know information to hold officials accountable versus the government's need to conduct war with secrecy to promote victory is very real. The revelations of the abuse of Iraqi prisoners at Abu Ghraib, mentioned at the start of the chapter, fanned anti-Americanism throughout the Middle East, putting the lives of American troops in greater danger.

However, most citizens agree that the media should have been allowed to share this information to force reforms mandating the humane treatment of prisoners.

Even nonauthoritarian governments have laws to protect government secrets. For example, in the United States, laws make top-secret documents unavailable for public scrutiny until many years later, after they have been "declassified" (declared no longer secret). Questions of what is and is not "top secret" are often highly controversial. The government has a perspective very different from that of the press, often forcing the courts into the role of arbiter.

The Right to Privacy

Democratic societies also have laws that protect individuals' privacy and society's morals—for example, bans against obscenity. In terms of the right to privacy, two standards apply—those for public figures and those for private individuals. Courts have traditionally allowed a good deal of latitude in publishing personal information about people in the public eye, including celebrities, athletes, and politicians. Public "personalities" are assumed to have lower expectations for privacy and consequently have less protection. Controversy often stems from the right to privacy of *private* citizens, especially as it pertains to the victims of violent crimes.

A 1975 rape and murder case in Georgia (*Cox Broadcasting Corporation* v. *Cohn*) provides a good example. The victim's family wanted her name withheld from news reports to protect her right to privacy, especially given the vicious sexual assault that preceded her murder. When newspapers nevertheless published her name and gave the specific details of her rape and murder, her family sued, claiming violation of the victim's privacy right. The court disagreed. Because her name was a matter of public record, newspapers were held to be within their rights to publish it. Papers often have policies not to publish the names of rape victims, but these rules are a matter of decency, not of law.

One area where the right to privacy is protected is when providing a fair trial is in question. The right to privacy of the accused in order to ensure fair treatment in court is enforced, though less strongly today than in the past. Even in cases involving ordinary citizens—and certainly in cases involving celebrities—media coverage of crimes often reaches a saturation level, impelling some observers to question whether any potential jurors can be impartial. To help ensure a fair trial, gag orders can be issued, ordering all participants to refrain from discussing the case. In extreme circumstances, there can be a change of venue (holding the trial in another city), or the judge might even sequester (put into seclusion) jurors to prevent them from consuming news reports and other media coverage of the trial. In the vast majority of criminal trials, however, these extraordinary measures are neither needed nor employed.

■ **Prior Censorship:** Forbidding publication of material considered objectionable.	**EXAMPLE:** *Excluding times of war, the government has not been very successful in censoring material that is published or aired in the media. During times of war, the courts, in order to promote national security, are more likely to allow prior censorship than during times of peace.*	**CONNECT THE LINK** (Chapter 4, pages 101–102) Should the government be allowed greater flexibility in censoring material that the press is allowed to publish to advance the acceptance of certain societal views?

Rules Regarding Content and Ownership

The media are prohibited from publishing material that they know to be incorrect. **Libel**■ laws are designed to protect the reputations of individuals from negative and false reporting. In *New York Times v. Sullivan* (1964), the Supreme Court ruled that publishing a falsehood about a public official did not constitute libel unless that official could demonstrate "actual malice"—meaning that the media knew the published information was false or acted recklessly. Three years later, the *Sullivan* ruling was extended to cover celebrities and athletes. These rulings made it far more difficult for a public official or celebrity to sue for libel. It is easier for private citizens to sue for libel, because the standards of proof are lower. Therefore, private individuals are much more successful in bringing lawsuits.

The most controversial issues regarding content are concerns about **prior censorship**■—the power of the government to prohibit in advance the publication or broadcast of certain material. Because we believe that a free press is the bedrock of a free society, the American courts are very hesitant to allow prior censorship. Instead, our system of government tends to rely on the threat of punishment after publication in order to keep the press in line. As you saw in Chapter 4, pages 101–102, the courts have ruled that prior censorship is allowed only in the most extreme cases. Table 11.4 shows that while most of the American public believes that the press is too free to publish material it deems appropriate, a large segment of the population also believes that too much governmental regulation currently exists.

TABLE 11.4	Public Opinion on Censorship

A national survey of 1,003 adults aged 18 and older found that a majority of Americans believe the media have just about the right amount of freedom to publish materials. However, a large percentage also thinks that there is too much freedom given to the media. —*What do you think? Is there too much or too little governmental regulation of the media? What factors do you think might change public opinion either way?*

"Overall, do you think the press in America has too much freedom to do what it wants, too little freedom to do what it wants, or is the amount of freedom the press has about right?"	
Too much freedom	34%
Too little freedom	13%
About right	50%
Don't know/refused to answer	4%

SOURCE: Survey by Freedom Forum, *American Journalism Review.* Methodology: Interviewing conducted by New England Survey Research, "State of the first Amendment Survey 2007." Associates, August 16–26, 2007, and based upon 1,003 telephone interviews (sampling error is +/- 3.2%). Accessed at http://www.firstamendmentcenter.org/pdf/SOFA2007results.pdf on June 21, 2010.

Section 315 of the Communications Act of 1934 (and its many subsequent amendments) provides the central rules regarding censorship of the broadcast media. These rules do not apply to print media or the Internet. The act applied only to the broadcast media, because it was believed at the time that these media, perceived to be quasi monopolies, needed more regulation. When the law was written, the print media seemed to be less monopolistic—and hence more open to ordinary people. Although this is no longer true today, the distinction still applies. Furthermore, as noted earlier, in 1934 the airwaves were considered part of the public domain, to be used for the public good—and therefore in need of government regulation. Consequently, the print media do not have to comply with these regulations, whereas the broadcast media do.

Regulation of the broadcast media falls to the Federal Communications Commission (FCC), an independent regulatory agency created by the Communications Act of 1934 to "serve the public interest, convenience, and necessity." The bipartisan FCC consists of five commissioners. Appointed by the president and confirmed by the Senate, each commissioner serves for five years. Many observers want the FCC to be stronger and more independent, but the president and Congress continue to exert a good deal of influence on their decisions.

In addition to privacy and censorship, two other rules exist with respect to television content issues in politics. If a station makes time available to one candidate running for political office, it must make similar time available under similar circumstances to other candidates running for the same office. This is the **equal time rule**■. Thus, if the Democratic candidate is allowed to purchase 30 seconds of prime-time television to run an advertisement, the Republican candidate for the same office must also be allowed to purchase 30 seconds of prime time at the same price. The station can refuse to sell time to any candidates from any political party (including minor parties) for particular offices, but if it sells to one, it must sell to the others.

A related and controversial issue regarding access is participation of minor party candidates in presidential debates. In 2004, the Presidential Commission on Presidential Debates ruled that for candidates to participate in the nationally televised presidential debates, they must be constitutionally eligible to hold the office of president, must be on enough state ballots to give them a mathematical chance of securing a majority vote in the Electoral College, and must have the support of 15 percent of the national electorate as measured by public opinion polls. Given the difficulty of meeting these tests, third-party and independent candidates are generally excluded from the nationally televised debates. The equal time rule does not apply to talk shows and regular newscasts. Thus David Letterman can invite one candidate on his show without inviting the others, and just because one candidate's speech is carried on the evening news does not require the network to carry a rival's speech as well.

■ **Equal Time Rule:** An FCC rule requiring the broadcast media to offer all major candidates competing for a political office equal airtime.

SIGNIFICANCE: *Without the equal time rule, lesser-known or less popular candidates would have a very difficult time communicating with voters, adversely impacting their chance for electoral success.*

A similar concept is the **fairness doctrine,** which was in effect from 1949 to 1985. Much broader than the equal time rule, which applies only to political candidates, the fairness doctrine required the broadcast media to allow "reasonable positions" to be presented on controversial issues of public interest. Therefore, we often see or hear news shows that have one person representing one side of an issue and another person speaking for the other side. Although this is not required any longer (partly at the urging of President Ronald Reagan), it is still a common practice.

In addition to regulating the content, the government also regulates the ownership of the media. Until recently, the federal government, attempting to keep the airwaves diverse, limited the number of TV or radio stations that one owner could possess in a single market. The Telecommunications Act of 1996 deregulated many previous ownership restrictions in an attempt to make broadcast media more competitive and responsive to audience concerns and interests, but this deregulation has been controversial. Opponents fear that the law has eliminated the consumer and diversity protections that were present in the Communications Act of 1934. As a result, we are seeing larger and larger mergers, such as Time Warner's acquisition of Turner Broadcasting Company.[44] Even so, one person or entity is still barred from controlling more than 35 percent of network market share and 30 percent of cable market share.[45]

The Role of Profits

The standards used for reporting news are controversial. Many critics attack the media's reliance on exploitative and sensational stories in an obsessive search for profits. The quest for profits, it is said, makes the media bloodthirsty hounds, exploiting the misfortune of others. The central question then becomes, "Who should control the media?" Some observers argue that they should police themselves, establishing their own

standards of decency and ethics. Others argue that the media simply give us, the public, what we want—if we are displeased with what is being shown, we can use the power of the purse, including boycotts, to influence them.

There are two theories regarding self-imposed control of the media. The **libertarian view** says that the media should show what they think the public wants, with no worry about the consequences. If viewers want violence, give them violence; if they want sex, give them sex. In contrast, the **social responsibility theory** (also called the **public advocate model** of news coverage) states that the media need to balance what viewers want with what is in their best interests. In essence, this theory asserts that the media should promote socially desirable behavior by providing information that advances people's ability to be good citizens, conveying information that allows clear and effective popular decision making.[46]

The need to make money often leads news people, especially those working in TV, to determine newsworthiness from the perspective of audience appeal rather than political, educational, or social significance. Historically, the networks did not expect to generate profits from news programs, which they believed were a public good, but in recent years, the networks have decided that news programs must not only cover their costs but also generate profits. Television is dependent on ratings to gauge how much it can charge advertisers. A mere 1 percent increase in the audience can mean millions of dollars in increased advertising revenue. Advertising rates in newspapers are also based on consumption, measured by paid circulation. Changes in programming that reflect profit-driven demands for audience appeal have prompted much criticism.

News journalists increasingly believe that the quest for profits is harming coverage (see Table 11.5). For example, newspapers have made a variety of changes to increase circulation and profits: They now use more graphics, feature more numerous but shorter

---

| **TABLE 11.5** | **Profits Pressures Hurting Coverage: Effect of Bottom-Line Pressure on News Coverage** |

A survey of 547 national and local media reporters, producers, editors, and executives indicates that journalists believe the pressure to make a profit is harming both national and local news coverage. This trend goes back at least a decade. —*Do you agree with the journalists? And if they feel this way, why do you think they can't resist that pressure?*

	NATIONAL			LOCAL		
	1995	1999	2004	1995	1999	2004
Hurting	41%	49%	66%	33%	46%	57%
Just changing	38%	40%	29%	50%	46%	35%
Other/don't know	21%	11%	5%	17%	8%	8%

SOURCE: "Bottom-Line Pressures Now Hurting Coverage, Say Journalists" Washington, DC: The Pew for the People and the Press, May 23, 2004. Accessed at http://people-press.org/report/214/ on August 4, 2008. Reprinted with permission.

stories, provide more news summaries (for example, bulleted lists of how a story relates directly to readers) and put more emphasis on soft news (such as travel, entertainment, weather, and gossip).[47] Similar changes have occurred on TV news shows, the most notable being the increased use of graphics. For example, to get a competitive edge in coverage of the 2008 presidential election, CNN used holograms as a visual tool to attract a larger share of the audience.

Some commentators on the state of the media believe criticism of these developments is unfair and largely elitist. Critics often assert that the "ideal" citizen *should* want hard news—complex, serious, and socially and politically relevant.

But in fact, most people want soft news with light entertainment. Given the reality of their world of daily work, who can blame people for wanting to escape and relax in their leisure time? Hard stories and hard entertainment don't allow for diversion or reprieve. In a democracy, the antielitist critics argue, people should be free to choose their own entertainment and sources of information without being criticized for being lowbrow or anti-intellectual. Those who do not accept criticism of the media assert that if we want to make news more factual and intellectual, it nevertheless needs to be presented in a way that is appealing and interesting. This, they say, is the true challenge for reformers.

Governmental Regulations

11.6   Contrast the rights of a free press to the government's authority to restrict content.

PRACTICE QUIZ: UNDERSTAND AND APPLY

1. It is common for a newspaper to refuse to publish the name of a rape victim to protect his or her privacy, but it is not illegal.
   a. true
   b. false

2. Sometimes newspapers do not cover a criminal trial in much detail because
   a. few readers are interested in trial coverage.
   b. such coverage violates the First Amendment.
   c. in some cases, gag orders prevent participants from discussing the case.
   d. in some cases, gag orders prohibit journalists from covering a case.

3. The government is rarely given the power to censor materials that the press finds to be newsworthy.
   a. true
   b. false

4. The theory stating that the media need to balance what the public wants with what's good for it is the
   a. libertarian theory.
   b. social responsibility theory.
   c. market forces theory.
   d. ethical freedoms theory.

ANALYZE

1. Why is there tension between governmental regulation of the media and the desire for an independent and rigorous press?

2. How does the right to privacy differ for public officials and private individuals?

IDENTIFY THE CONCEPT THAT DOESN'T BELONG

a. Fairness doctrine
b. Equal time rule
c. Individual right to privacy
d. Limited view on prior censorship
e. Absolute right to free press

Conclusion

The media have the potential to dramatically impact the way that most people view world events. Since we usually do not witness most events live and in person, we rely upon the media to show us a picture of the world that would otherwise be impossible. Witnessing the terrorist attacks on September 11, 2001, on television and online, for example, forever altered the way millions of Americans thought about security.

The role of traditional media is currently changing as more and more people are getting their news from alternative sources. Americans now are consuming news from more diverse sources than in past generations, with viewer loyalty largely a thing of the past. Moreover, in this digital era, news has become far more immediate and instantaneous. Growing reliance on social networks and Internet news sources presents great challenges to professional news organizations. Perhaps the greatest changes are in the growth of citizen journalism accompanied by threats to professional ethics and established standards of behavior. The challenges facing traditional media outlets can prove helpful in forcing them to retool their approach and to demonstrate their continued relevancy in this changing environment.

Although many researchers have examined the power of the media and their impact, the results are mixed. People certainly believe that the media are a powerful force in American politics. So do politicians. And because politicians believe the media are powerful, they may alter their behavior based on how that behavior might be portrayed in the media and received by the public. This belief is potentially a strong check on our leaders' actions. However, it is very hard to measure this potential impact of the media. Moreover, attempting to isolate how the media's portrayal of a candidate specifically influences voters is nearly impossible. Was it the image portrayed by the media or the candidate's qualifications or demeanor that registered in the minds of voters? The same quandary applies to the issues: Do people support an education bill because it was favorably reported in the news, or was it favorably reported because people support it? In light of these questions, establishing causal links is very hard. The complex task of decision-making simply has too many alternative variables. Clearly, the power of the media to influence the political agenda is important, because agenda setting affects what people see, think, and talk about. And the media's powers of agenda setting and issue framing also have great potential to influence public opinion.

KEY CONCEPT MAP How do the media impact our political system?

Report Political Events

The media are our eyes and ears. They show us what we can't otherwise see for ourselves, and they illuminate issues of political importance to people across the country and the world.

Critical Thinking Questions

What if we had no media to report on political events, and we had to rely solely on our own experiences and those of our friends and family to know what was happening in the country and the world? Given all that happens in the world, what factors determine if a story is newsworthy?

Interpret Complex Political Stories

The media take complex political stories and interpret them, identifying the most important aspects, and making it easier for individuals to comprehend how political issues affect them.

Critical Thinking Questions

What if we had no one to explain the ramifications of new laws, and we had to read hundreds of pages of legislation ourselves? Do you think there is a bias in the way the national media report and interpret the news?

Socialize People Regarding Political Values and Opinions

The media portray and in effect promote positive values such as patriotism and negative values such as conspicuous consumerism (extravagant spending on goods and services to show wealth).

Critical Thinking Questions

Overall, are the values promoted by the media more helpful or more harmful for our democracy? What other values do the media portray and promote?

Influence Political Campaigns

By reporting on the "horse race" of who is ahead and who is behind, and by covering the actions (and transgressions) of certain political candidates and not others, the media play a role in determining the frontrunners of political campaigns.

Critical Thinking Questions

In what other ways do the media influence campaigns? What sort of role does advertising play in political campaigns?

The media impact our political system in a number of ways. They link the public with elected officials, exert great influence in reporting political events and interpreting political stories, help shape and convey a wide variety of values to society, and influence campaigns and elections. Given their widespread influence, many are worried about the media's objectivity. —*How much power and influence do the media have in our political system? Should we be concerned about this power and influence? Why or why not?*

Review of Key Objectives

Mass Media

 11.1 Evaluate the roles played by the media in shaping American politics.

(pages 328–329)

The media are a powerful force in American politics, with the ability to influence what issues people think about and their response to them. A free and vigorous press is essential for the marketplace of ideas to develop and for democratic debate to thrive.

The need to balance a free press with government regulations raises many delicate issues. In times of war, we generally side with allowing more government regulations, but even then, tension exists. The intimacy and immediacy of television make it exceptionally influential.

KEY TERMS

Mass Media 328
Marketplace of Ideas 328

CRITICAL THINKING QUESTIONS

1. How powerful do you think the media are? Do they simply tell us what to think about, or are they able to influence and change our opinions?
2. Do you believe that all reasonable ideas have an equal opportunity to compete for acceptance? Or are the views of some groups or individuals given more attention and therefore are more likely to be adopted?

INTERNET RESOURCES

Presidential campaign commercials from 1952 to 2008 can be found through the Museum of the Moving Image—the Living Room Candidate at http://www.livingroomcandidate.org/

A website devoted to focusing attention on diversified news media, "I Want Media," can be found at http://www.iwantmedia.com/organizations/index.html

ADDITIONAL READING

Graber, Doris A. *Mass Media and American Politics,* 8th ed. Washington, DC: CQ Press, 2009.

Leighley, Jan E. *Mass Media and Politics: A Social Science Perspective.* Boston: Wadsworth, 2004.

The Growth of Mass Media

 11.2 Outline the development of the American media.

(pages 330–335)

Newspapers were the first form of mass communication in the United States. When technological improvements allowed newspapers to be produced more cheaply, they became available to the masses, changing the way the news was reported as well as the ways in which governmental officials communicated with the people.

Once introduced, the electronic media quickly spread across the country. Radios were very popular, with ownership growing quickly upon their introduction. The ownership of television sets grew even quicker once technology was developed to allow mass production.

Since the 1980s, the Internet has witnessed remarkable growth. More and more people have access to the Internet, with its usage growing daily. As our world becomes increasingly interdependent, reliance on the mass media for information grows.

KEY TERMS

Party Presses 330
Penny Press 330
Yellow Journalism 331
Technology Gap (Digital Divide) 332

CRITICAL THINKING QUESTIONS

1. Do you think that the media are more important today than in the past?
2. Do you think that printed versions of newspapers will become obsolete? If so, what are some of the potential consequences (good and bad) of this change?

INTERNET RESOURCES

For information about an organization started by two siblings to help soldiers call home visit. Cell Phones for Soldiers at http://www.cellphonesforsoldiers.com/

For more information about early radio and related technologies in the United States from 1897 to 1927 visit Early Radio History at http://earlyradiohistory.us/index.htm/

For collected and preserved historic and contemporary radio and television content, visit Museum of Broadcast Communications at http://www.museum.tv

ADDITIONAL READING

Briggs, Asa, and Peter Burke. *A Social History of the Media: From Gutenberg to the Internet.* Cambridge, MA: Polity Press, 2005.

Starr, Paul. *The Creation of the Media.* New York: Basic Books, 2004.

Functions of the Media

11.3 Illustrate the functions of the media in American politics and society.

(pages 336–339)

The media perform many important social functions, from monitoring the government to interpreting the news to socializing citizens. These functions all come with the potential for a great degree of power and influence—and responsibility.

KEY TERMS

Investigative Reporting 337
Muckraking 337

CRITICAL THINKING QUESTIONS

1. Given the fact that the line between the entertainment and news functions of the media are increasingly being blurred, do you think that people are influenced by the public statements and behavior of celebrities? Do you think that celebrity endorsements of presidential candidates are helpful or simply irrelevant?
2. Under what circumstances should readers be skeptical of investigative reporting? How and why can it be abused?

INTERNET RESOURCES

To compare broadcasting and news from another country visit British Broadcasting Company website at http://www.bbc.co.uk

The Freedom Forum at http://www.freedomforum.org is a nonprofit foundation dedicated to free press and free speech.

Univision at http://www.univision.com is a Spanish-language media company serving residents of the United States.

ADDITIONAL READING

Gillmor, Dan. *We the Media: Grassroots Journalism by the People, for the People.* Cambridge, MA: O'Reilly Press, 2006.

Graber, Doris A., ed. *Media Power in Politics,* 6th ed. Washington, DC: CQ Press, 2010.

Political Use of the Media

11.4 Assess how the media can be influential in American politics.

(pages 340–345)

Since the earliest days of recorded history, individuals have used communication for political purposes. Today, with the advent of technology, mass communication expands the opportunities individuals, leaders, and groups have to advance their political causes. An uneasy relationship between the press and public officials exists. On the one hand, they need each other; on the other, they both want to control the manner in which the news is reported. Officials want to have the news framed supportively, while the media often look for controversy to generate audience interest. Candidates, officials, and groups use many tactics to get positive press coverage, which enhances their legitimacy and visibility and may help garner support.

KEY TERMS

Earned Media Coverage 340	**Press Releases** 342
Pseudo-Events 340	**News Briefings** 342
Agenda Setting 340	**News Conferences** 342
Gatekeepers 341	

CRITICAL THINKING QUESTIONS

1. Given the variety of news outlets today, do you believe that the power of the media in gatekeeping is exaggerated?
2. How has the Internet impacted the power of the media elite to exert influence over political agendas?

INTERNET RESOURCES

To explore a nonprofit, grassroot citizen's watchdog of the news media, go to Accuracy in Media at http://www.aim.org

C-SPAN (Cable-Satellite Public Affairs Network) is owned and operated by the cable industry as a public service: http://www.cspan.org/

Popular cable and news media websites are CNN: http://www.cnn.com; FOX News: http://www.foxnews.com; and the New York Times: http://www.nytimes.com

ADDITIONAL READING

Burns, Lisa M. *First Ladies and the Fourth Estate: Press Framing of Presidential Wives.* Dekalb, IL: Northern Illinois University Press, 2008.

Wayne, Mike, Julian Petley, Craig Murry and Lesley Henderson. *Television News, Politics and Young People: Generation Disconnected?* New York: Palgrave Macmillian, 2010.

The Media and the Public in the Political Arena

11.5 Establish how the media have an impact on the cultural values and political opinions of the American public.

(pages 346–349)

The media both shape and reflect our cultural, political, and economic values by serving as a conduit of information and allowing the two-way flow of information. The media conduct public opinion polls, interview people and cover stories, focus attention on issues, and serve as an important link between political leaders and the general public.

Earned media coverage (obtained free of charge) is especially important, because Americans believe it to be more trustworthy and objective than paid advertisements, which are nevertheless important tools to reach an audience. They allow candidates to repeat controlled messages in attempts to sway public opinion.

KEY TERMS

Sound Bites 347   Competitive News Markets 348
Narrowcasting 348   News Monopolies 348
Citizen Journalism 348

CRITICAL THINKING QUESTIONS

1. Do you feel there is reason to be concerned over the centralization of news coverage? Why or why not?
2. Do you think that the public would tune in to longer advertisements, or are sound bites the best mechanism for politicians to communicate with the public?

INTERNET RESOURCES

Started as a gossip column and now largely seen as a conservative news reporting Web site is the Drudge Report at http://www.drudgereport.com

OhmyNews is a citizen journalism website with the motto "Every Citizen is a Reporter"—is found at http://english.ohmynews.com/

Pew Center for Civic Journalism reports on "experiments" with civic journalism (public journalism) from around the country, found at http://www.pewcenter.org

Slashdot—a technology related "new for nerds" website owned by Geeknet, Inc., is found at http://slashdot.org/

ADDITIONAL READING

Bagdikian, Ben H. *The New Media Monopoly.* Boston: Beacon Press, 2004.

Entman, Robert. *Scandals of Media and Politics.* Cambridge, MA: Polity Press, 2010.

Falk, Erika. *Woman for President: Media Bias in Eight Campaigns.* Urbana: University of Illinois Press, 2007.

Governmental Regulations

11.6 Contrast the rights of a free press to the governments authority to restrict content.

(pages 350–353)

The government exercises some regulation of the content and ownership of the media. There are laws dealing with prior restraint, privacy, and those related to accurate and fair reporting. It is complex to balance the competing desires of the press to be free and vigorous and the need for governmental regulation. Generally, we support the most regulation during times of national conflict (typically involving threats to domestic security). However, many argue that the press needs to be most free during times of war to investigate the government to promote accountability and institutional integrity.

KEY TERMS

Libel 351
Prior Censorship 351
Equal Time Rule 351
Fairness Doctrine 352
Libertarian View 352
Social Responsibility Theory
 (Public Advocate Model) 352

CRITICAL THINKING QUESTIONS

1. Do you think that the media need to be restrained during times of war or should they be free to investigate, criticize, and hold the governmental accountable? Can we have a free and vigorous press and still maintain domestic security?
2. Do you think it should be easier for celebrities, public officials, and others in the public eye to sue for libel? Or is this type of scrutiny the "price of fame"?

INTERNET RESOURCES

Free Press (www.freepress.net) is a national nonpartisan, nonprofit organization that works to reform the media through education and advocacy.

The Free Child Project (www.freechild.org) we as created to advocate, inform, and celebrate social change led by and with young people around the world.

ADDITIONAL READING

Lewis, Anthony. *Freedom for the Thought that We Hate: A Biography of the First Amendment.* New York: Basic Books, 2010.

Rich, Frank. *The Greatest Story Ever Told: The Decline of Truth from 9/11 to Katrina.* New York: Penguin Press, 2006.

Schudson, Michael. *Why Democracies Need an Unlovable Press.* Cambridge, MA: Polity Press, 2008.

Chapter Review   Test Your Knowledge

1. The media are a particularly significant force in which two pathways of political action?
   a. the grassroots mobilization and court pathways
   b. the lobbying decision makers and elections pathways
   c. the court and cultural change pathways
   d. the cultural change and election pathways

2. Free media are crucial for a democratic society because
   a. citizens depend on the publication or broadcasting of polling data to know the majority opinions about policy issues.
   b. free media make possible national public debate on important political issues.
   c. without TV, voters would not know how charismatic their potential political leaders are.
   d. politicians' electoral success depends in part on their savvy use of the media.

3. Which statement best summarizes the functions of the media in the United States?
   a. The media entertain, inform, and persuade the public.
   b. The media divide the public and make reality less vivid.
   c. To reach the widest audience and make as much money as possible, the media strive only to entertain the public.
   d. The media primarily inform the public, with little concern for profit-making.

4. Surveys of national and local media reporters, producers, editors, and executives indicates that journalists believe that the pressure to make a profit is harming both national and local news coverage.
   a. true   b. false

5. In the early decades of the nineteenth century, newspapers in the United States were usually created to support a specific political party or set of economic beliefs.
   a. true   b. false

6. As the American newspaper industry became more centralized, newspaper reporting became much more objective.
   a. true   b. false

7. What makes televised news so powerful?
   a. the fact that it is not censored
   b. the clear distinctions it makes between news and entertainment
   c. its objective, unbiased approach
   d. its intimacy and visual nature

8. The broadcast media in all liberal democracies are privately owned.
   a. true   b. false

9. Late night comedy programs illustrate that the line between the news and entertainment can become blurred.
   a. true   b. false

10. What would be an example of the surveillance function that the media can play in the realm of American politics?
    a. a television exposé about the mistreatment of undocumented workers at a few Wal-Mart stores
    b. television cameramen hiding outside a candidate's house and waiting to document an illicit affair
    c. a radio news program that makes use of secretly recorded phone calls between a criminal suspect and his or her lawyer
    d. a long newspaper article putting a politician's career in historical context after she has died

11. Glenn Beck is an example of
    a. a political liberal whose popularity suggests the left-leaning tendency of the media.
    b. someone who has been censored by the FCC.
    c. an enormously popular conservative commentator who has emphasized the liberal bias of mainstream media.
    d. someone who has moved from public office to broadcast journalism.

12. Only since about 1950 have politicians in this country used the media for political purposes.
    a. true
    b. false

13. What best describes the interrelationship of the public, the government, and the media?
    a. The government influences the media, which influence the public.
    b. The public influences the government, which influences the media.
    c. The media influence the government, which influences the public.
    d. Each of the three influences the others and is influenced by the others.

14. Who was the first president to discern and make effective use of the power of the media?
    a. Abraham Lincoln
    b. William McKinley
    c. Theodore Roosevelt
    d. John Kennedy

15. Why is it wise to regard news stories that are leaked with some skepticism?
    a. because they are usually not true
    b. because the leaker sometimes presents the information in an incomplete and self-serving way
    c. because leaking information is illegal
    d. because most people who leak secrets they are entrusted to keep are not trustworthy

16. Which branch of government gets covered least by the media?
    a. the judicial branch
    b. the legislative branch
    c. the executive branch
    d. All branches are covered about equally.

17. Issue advocacy advertising is an example of
   a. how work in the elections pathway uses the media.
   b. how interest groups use the media.
   c. the fairness doctrine in action.
   d. muckraking.

18. How do newspapers potentially worsen the political disengagement of poor people?
   a. by routinely endorsing candidates whose agendas disadvantage the poor
   b. by circulation policies that exclude poor neighborhoods, keeping poor residents ignorant about national affairs
   c. by using overly sophisticated language that only college-educated readers can easily understand
   d. by not covering many stories involving the poor, simply because most people with lower incomes cannot afford to subscribe to newspapers

19. What is cross-media ownership?
   a. owning one kind of media outlet, such as a radio station; selling it; and then buying another kind of media outlet, such as a newspaper
   b. owning all or nearly all of one kind of media outlet
   c. owning a variety of media outlets simultaneously
   d. the running of a media-owning corporation by a diverse group of individuals

20. Scholarly studies suggest that the effects of the media on American politics are clear and can be described statistically.
   a. true
   b. false

mypoliscilab Exercises

Apply what you learned in this chapter on **MyPoliSciLab.**

Read on mypoliscilab.com

   eText: Chapter 11

Study and **Review** on mypoliscilab.com

   Pre-Test
   Post-Test
   Chapter Exam
   Flashcards

Watch on mypoliscilab.com

   Video: YouTube Politics
   Video: The Pentagon's Media Message

Explore on mypoliscilab.com

   Simulation: You Are the News Editor
   Comparative: Comparing News Media
   Timeline: Three Hundred Years of American Mass Media
   Visual Literacy: Use of the Media by the American Public

Interest Groups and Civic and Political Engagement

KEY OBJECTIVES

After completing this chapter, you should be prepared to:

12.1 Illustrate how beliefs in collective action, self-government, and citizen action laid the foundation for activism and protest in the United States.

12.2 Explain the key factors that facilitate political protest and activism.

12.3 Identify four different types of interest groups, and explain the function of interest groups in a democracy.

12.4 Show how interest groups mobilize their memberships in the face of organizational barriers.

12.5 Describe how interest groups appeal to public officials and the public to gain support for their causes.

12.6 Assess the ways interest groups positively and negatively impact our society.

On President's Day in February 2009, Keli Carender organized a protest—her first—in her hometown of Seattle. Deeply opposed to the $787 billion stimulus bill, and frustrated by the lack of response from her senators and representatives, Carender planned a protest against what she coined "porkulus." This first protest attracted a mere 120 people, but it has grown into a mass populist protest movement that has been coined the "Tea Party Movement."

Carender, now 30, is cited as one of the original Tea Party advocates. Six weeks after her first protest, 1,200 people gathered at the Tax Day Tea Party she organized in Seattle. In January 2010, she was one of 60 Tea Party leaders flown to Washington to receive election activism training by Freedom Works (a conservative advocacy organization led by Dick Armey, a former Republican

> **How do individuals influence our government and our society through organized action?**

leader in the House). When considering her discontent, Carendar states that "I basically thought to myself: 'I have two courses. I can give up, go home, crawl into bed and be really depressed and let it happen. Or I can do something different, and I can find a new avenue to have my voice get out.'"

Whether Ms. Carendar and other leaders of the Tea Party Movement will succeed in seeing their vision of a limited government reach fruition is uncertain, but the movement most definitely helped shape the agenda for the 2010 midterm election, propelling Republican victories in House elections across the nation. Ms. Carendar's decision to "do something" is making a difference and prompting many who previously were apolitical to become involved in local and national politics.

Resource Center
• Glossary
• Vocabulary Example
• Connect the Link

Activism and Protest in the United States

12.1 Illustrate how beliefs in collective action, self-government, and citizen action laid the foundation for activism and protest in the United States.

(pages 364–365)

We claim as our birthright as Americans some of the most profound liberties and freedoms. Our Bill of Rights establishes many cherished liberties including freedom of speech, religion, press, and assembly. As a result, we have the unrivaled ability to influence our government and our fellow citizens. We have the freedom to speak our minds and to express our most controversial and complex thoughts—thoughts that might be unpopular or even unreasonable, but still ideas that can be presented in public and compete for acceptance. Furthermore, we have constitutionally guaranteed liberties that allow us to appeal to our government to address our concerns and issues. Using group action has a distinctive appeal to Americans, for whom the tradition is deeply ingrained in the national political culture. In this chapter, we will examine people and groups working to change our society, our laws, and our culture. Grassroots mobilization is an important pathway to influence our society, our government, and our social structures.

Belief in Collective Action

While traveling throughout the United States in 1831 and 1832 and studying our society, Alexis de Tocqueville, a young Frenchman, noted that group activities were essential for the development and maintenance of democracy. Compared to Europeans of his time, he observed, Americans had a much stronger tendency to join together to solve problems, to articulate collective interests, and to form social relationships. He asserted that people living in democratic nations must join together to preserve their independence and freedoms. Collective action is especially important for people who have little influence individually, as like-minded people can come together and act with greater strength. Tocqueville pointed out that the freedom of association allowed "partisans of an opinion" to unite in the electoral arena. In his words:

> The liberty of association has become a necessary guarantee against the tyranny of the majority. . . . There are no countries in which associations are more needed, to prevent the despotism of faction or the arbitrary power of the prince, than those which are democratically constituted. . . . The most natural privilege of man, next to the right of acting for himself, is that of combining his exertions with those of his

fellow-creatures, and of acting in common with them. I am therefore led to conclude that the right of association is almost as inalienable as the right of personal liberty.[1]

Tocqueville's journey resulted in the book *Democracy in America,* originally published in 1835. Tocqueville was only 25 years old when he came to America to observe our democracy, yet his account of our society is one of the most perceptive ever published.[2]

The right to associate and to be active in public affairs is one of the most fundamental rights on which participatory democracy depends. To live in a free society, citizens must have the right of association to petition their government to address their grievances and concerns. Such an understanding of the functioning of collective action in democracies goes back to the infancy of our country. The importance of citizen participation is even greater today, because our society has grown far more complex, diverse, and technological, with intimate ties to the global community.

DE TOCQUEVILLE.

Alexis Henry de Tocqueville (1805–1859), French writer and commentator, traveled across our country in 1831–1832. His account, *Democracy in America,* is still widely read and cited today. —*Why do you think this 25-year-old was so able to characterize the nature of our democracy? Do you think you have to be an outsider to best understand a country?*

CONNECT THE LINK
(Chapter 2, pages 38–42) Do you think that people still feel connected to their government?

■ **Egalitarianism:** A doctrine of equality that ignores differences in social status, wealth, and privilege.

EXAMPLE: *Egalitarianism has led to laws that promote equality, such as equal pay for equal work for all people.*

Activism is at the root of our "do something" political culture, and forming groups is essential for political action. Throughout our history, groups have emerged to challenge the status quo—and opposition groups have emerged to fight to preserve the status quo. Our main purpose in the following sections is to illustrate the validity of Tocqueville's observations about the importance of group action in the United States to promote change and to enhance liberty, as well as to provide a context for analyzing contemporary group behavior. These activities are fundamentally important in shaping the very nature and definition of our democracy.

Belief in Self-Government

One central idea underlying our political system is a belief in self-government and citizen action. At the end of the seventeenth century, the English philosopher John Locke argued that people have certain God-given, or natural, rights that are inalienable—meaning that they can neither be taken away by nor surrendered to a government (see Chapter 2, pages 38–42). Locke's social contract theory holds that people set up governments for the very specific purpose of protecting natural rights. All legitimate political authority, said Locke, exists to preserve these natural rights and rests on the consent of the governed. When a ruler acts against the purposes for which government exists, the people have the right to resist and remove the offending ruler. Thomas Jefferson relied on Locke's social contract theory of government when writing the Declaration of Independence: The central premise of this document is that people have a right to revolt when they determine that their government has denied them their legitimate rights.

One consequence of the American Revolution was that faith in collective action, as well as in self-rule, became entrenched in the new United States. Rioting and mass mobilization had proved an effective tool to resist oppressive government. The Revolution also helped establish in the United States the sense of **egalitarianism**■—the belief that all people are equal. Our republican form of government, in which power rests in the hands of the people, reinforces this egalitarianism. A faith in the legitimacy of collective action, even violent action, in defense of liberty entered into our political culture.

Activism and Protest in the United States

12.1 **Illustrate how beliefs in collective action, self-government, and citizen action laid the foundation for activism and protest in the United States.**

PRACTICE QUIZ: UNDERSTAND AND APPLY

1. According to Tocqueville, civic engagement serves all of the following purposes except
   a. promoting and transferring shared values and beliefs.
   b. strengthening the ability of isolated individuals and groups to come together for collective action.
   c. allowing like-minded individuals to unite to influence the electoral arena.
   d. allowing tyranny of the majority to develop and thrive.

2. Tocqueville believed that the right to associate is one of the most fundamental rights.
   a. true   b. false

3. On whose theories of governance did Thomas Jefferson rely when writing the Declaration of Independence?
   a. Plato   c. Aristotle
   b. Tocqueville   d. Locke

4. A central premise of the Declaration of Independence is that people have a right to revolt when government denies legitimate rights.
   a. true   b. false

ANALYZE

1. What do you think Jefferson meant when he commented that a little rebellion was necessary from time to time to preserve liberty? Do you think that people still support this concept today or is it too dangerous? Is rebellion necessary today to preserve liberty?

2. Where does our belief in collective action come from? Is it more or less powerful than our belief in self-government? Why?

IDENTIFY THE CONCEPT THAT DOESN'T BELONG

a. Right to privacy   d. Freedom of religion
b. Freedom of speech   e. Freedom of assembly
c. Freedom of press

Resource Center
• Glossary
• Vocabulary Example
• Connect the Link

Influencing Government Through Mobilization and Participation

12.2 Explain the key factors that facilitate political protest and activism.

(pages 366–367)

Grassroots mobilization and interest group activities are essential for a healthy democracy. For democracy to function and to thrive, there must be a collective sense of community: People must feel tied to each other and united with their government, whether or not they agree with its actions. Constitutional guarantees and organized interests facilitate political protest and activism by providing pathways for individuals to influence government.

Constitutional Guarantees

The U.S. Constitution provides substantial guarantees that allow for citizen participation, activism, and mass mobilization. As an example, the Bill of Rights lists liberties that together ensure our right to petition the government. First Amendment freedoms are fundamental in our democracy, because they dramatically determine how we can influence our world, including our fellow citizens and leaders.

In totalitarian systems, lobbying, activism, protest, and other forms of political engagement among citizens are severely limited—indeed, they are usually forbidden and harshly punished. One vivid illustration of this occurred in June 1989, in Beijing, China, when thousands of pro-democracy students gathered in Tiananmen Square to protest political oppression. The world watched in horror as the Chinese government massacred several thousand young pro-democracy protesters on live television. These students were demonstrating their desire for rights that all Americans enjoy but that many fail to appreciate.

How do we allow citizens to pursue their self-interest while protecting society's interest as well? Balancing these often competing desires is difficult. One short example illustrates this dilemma. Imagine that a developer wants to build a large factory just outside your neighborhood. You worry about increased traffic, environmental impacts, and decreased property values. What do you do? You could form an association to address your problem, gathering neighbors who share your concerns and petitioning your city council and zoning commission. The neighborhood is rational in its concerns. Factories do alter traffic patterns, affect the local ecosystem, and lower property values. But factories also employ people who might desperately need the work, and they pay taxes that can benefit the entire community. How does the community

In 1989, pro-democracy and anti-corruption protests erupted in China. Led largely by students and intellectuals, an estimated 100,000 people gathered at Tiananmen Square on the eve of Hu Yaobang's funeral (Hu was an activist fighting to advance change). Thousands of protesters were killed. Following the protests, the government implemented widespread arrests and banned the foreign press. —*How often do you think about the extent of the freedoms we have in the United States? What responsibilities, if any, come with these freedoms?*

navigate between the needs of local homeowners and the needs of the larger community? Who should win—homeowners or unemployed people in need of jobs? It is a difficult question, underscoring a central dilemma of government.

PATHWAYS of change from around the world

Have you ever seen a poor child begging and felt guilty, but thought to yourself that there was nothing you could do? Audrey Cordera found herself in these circumstances, but she acted. As a young child, Audrey realized that she was privileged—a point that became very clear to her when she was nine years old and saw a girl the same age begging for money in her home country of the Philippines. This experience made an impression on young Audrey and convinced her to make a change. She decided that if young people could have money and technical support, they could change their lives.

In 2005, Audrey (then in her mid-twenties) founded YouthWorks, Inc., the first microfinance institution for young people in the Philippines. To start, she borrowed $200 (U.S.) and loaned it to three young people. They repaid the loan (with interest) in 3 months, giving her confidence in expanding her enterprise. To date, YouthWorks has supported more than

CONNECT THE **LINK**
(Chapter 1, pages 8–14) Do you think that Americans believe in organized groups more or less than they did 20 years ago?

20 young people who have made large contributions in their communities. For example, one loan of $100 (U.S.) allowed a group of seven young people (aged 13–16) to start a community organic fertilizer in Manila that has provided short-term employment to almost 1,000 people.

Audrey was selected as one of 20 YouthActionNet Global fellows in 2007. The fellowship was established by Nokia and the International Youth Foundation in 2001 to provide peer-to-peer learning, mentoring, and training to young leaders committed to improving their community around the globe. To learn more about YouthWorks, see their Web page at http://www.youthmicrofinance.com. You can also get information from YouthActionNet at http://www.youthactionnet.org/.

Organized Interests

Organized interests prompt leaders to "do something"—to address pressing problems in society, thus activating the "safety valve" that we discussed in Chapter 1, pages 8–14.

Without organized interests, many issues are likely to be overlooked by governments and to develop into real problems. Race rioting in the 1960s, for example, resulted from the frustration of African Americans at being marginalized and disregarded by white society. Years of discrimination and bigotry yielded to frustration and rage—which had no structured outlet. By ignoring the racism that was evident in the United States, Americans created a situation that at last exploded violently.[3]

Pressure from organized interests serves to hold governing officials accountable by forcing them to pay attention to issues that are important to people. Involvement also fosters the acquisition of attributes important to democracy—tolerance, political efficacy (effectiveness), and political trust. Being civically engaged allows people to develop associations and skills that are essential for healthy democratic communities. Moreover, competing groups can counteract the self-serving tendencies of each, balancing perspectives and increasing the likelihood for broader and more diverse representation.

Influencing Government Through Mobilization and Participation

12.2   **Explain the key factors that facilitate political protest and activism.**

PRACTICE QUIZ: UNDERSTAND AND APPLY

1. All of the following are important constitutional rights that promote political participation except
   a. freedom of speech.
   b. freedom of religion.
   c. right to assemble.
   d. right to privacy.

2. When an individual's self-interest is at odds with society's interest,
   a. the Bill of Rights grants the individual the upper hand.
   b. the interest most effectively lobbied for usually wins out—and should.
   c. society's interest should usually win out, since it represents the greater good.
   d. the conflict typically presents a difficult balancing act for our society and government.

3. For democracy to work, people must always feel united with one another and their government.
   a. true   b. false

ANALYZE

1. What role do Internet blogs play in an individual's ability and willingness to engage in political action?

2. What are the positive and negative aspects of popular participation in our country in modern times?

IDENTIFY THE CONCEPT THAT DOESN'T BELONG

a. Organized groups
b. Collective sense of community
c. Collective accountability
d. Constitutional protection of minorities
e. Individualism

Resource Center
• Glossary
• Vocabulary Example
• Connect the Link

■ **Interest Group:** A group of like-minded individuals who band together to influence public policy, public opinion, or governmental officials.

EXAMPLE: *Common Cause is an interest group that works to promote more effective government and advocates campaign finance reform. As such, it is highly critical of other interest groups that spend excessive amounts of money to influence elections.*

Functions and Types of Interest Groups

12.3 Identify four different types of interest groups, and explain the function of interest groups in a democracy.

(pages 368–371)

Interest groups■ are organizations outside the government that attempt to influence the government's behavior, decision making, and allocation of resources. Interest groups perform many valuable functions in our democracy. Often, there is tension between what is best for the group and its members and what is best for society. This tension can be healthy, however, because it focuses attention on issues that otherwise would not receive much notice and can promote constructive public debate.

Characteristics of Interest Groups

In our diverse society, people join interest groups to find a place to belong, to articulate their point of view, and to promote their common goals. Three primary characteristics define interest groups. First, they are voluntary associations of joiners. Some interest groups are formal, including trade groups, such as the American Medical Association (AMA); others are more informal, such as neighborhood groups that form to fight zoning changes. Second, the members of an interest group share common beliefs. Doctors join groups such as the AMA to promote patient care, to safeguard ethics in the practice of medicine, and to ensure their own economic viability. Hunters join organized groups to uphold their gun ownership rights and to ensure access to public land. Third, interest groups focus on influencing government. People join them because they want government policy to reflect their preferences, and consequently, interest groups spend time, energy, and money trying to influence public officials.

As you will see, interest groups use many different tactics in trying to accomplish their goals, but all interest groups exist for the purpose of influencing others—their own members, other like-minded associations, the general public, and elected and appointed officials. **Single-issue interest groups**■ focus primarily or exclusively on one issue, such as the environment, peace, or abortion. **Multi-issue interest groups**■, by contrast, pursue a broader range of issues grouped around a central theme. One example of a multi-issue group is the National Organization for Women (NOW), which works on a number of issues that members believe advance the rights and status of women—educational equality,

sexual harassment, reproductive freedom, and pay issues. Similarly, the Christian Coalition strives to promote its values by fighting same-sex marriage, attempting to stop abortion, promoting abstinence-only sex education, and in general, trying to give religion a greater role in everyday life. Although these two groups often stand on opposite sides of issues, they have in common many characteristics, ranging from the strength of their members' commitment to the tactics they use in influencing our government and our society.

PATHWAYS of action

LULAC

The League of United Latin American Citizens (LULAC) is one of the oldest and most influential organizations representing Hispanics in the United States. It was founded in 1929 in Corpus Christi, Texas, when three separate Hispanic groups banded together to demand equal rights and opportunities in education, government, law, business, and health care. Today, LULAC has 115,000 members in the United States and Puerto Rico, organized into 700 councils. LULAC provides its members with a number of important services, ranging from conducting citizenship and voter registration drives to pressuring localities into providing more low-income housing. It also strives to help Hispanic youth by providing training programs and educational counseling as well as by offering more than $1 million annually in scholarships. At sixteen regional centers, counseling services are provided yearly to more than 18,000 Hispanic students.

Through its activism, LULAC has won a number of important successes that have advanced the civil rights and liberties of Hispanic Americans. In 1945, the California LULAC Council successfully sued to integrate the Orange County school system, which had justified segregation with the claim that Mexican children were "more poorly clothed and mentally inferior to white children."[4] LULAC also provided financial support and attorneys to challenge the practice of excluding Hispanics from juries (*Hernandez* v. *Texas*); in 1954, the U.S. Supreme Court ruled that such exclusion was unconstitutional. In 1966, LULAC marched with and financially supported the largely Spanish-speaking United Farm Workers union in its struggle for minimum wages. LULAC National Education Service Centers, Inc., created in 1973, today serves more than 20,000 Hispanic students a year. The LULAC Institute was established in 1996 to provide model volunteer programs for Hispanic communities, and since 2004, the LULAC Leadership Initiative has been revitalizing Hispanic neighborhoods by creating grassroots programs in 700 Latino communities.

■ **Single-Issue Interest Group:** A group that is interested primarily in one area of public policy.

EXAMPLE: *The American Association for Affirmative Action (AAAA) was founded in 1974 to promote equal access to educational and economic opportunities.*

■ **Multi-Issue Interest Group:** A group that is interested in pursuing a broad range of public policy issues.

EXAMPLE: *The AARP promotes a wide variety of public policies that impact older Americans—from health care to social security to consumer protection.*

Immigration has become increasingly controversial in the last decade. Many believe we should deport all residents who entered the country illegally and fully secure our boarders. Others believe that amnesty should be granted to those currently living in the country illegally, giving them a means to become legal citizens. On the Statue of Liberty, an iconic symbol of freedom states, "Give me your tired, your poor, Your Huddled masses yearning to breathe free." —*Do you think it is time to reject the spirit of this promise? Or do you think the United States should still be the haven for those seeking freedom and a better life?*

Functions of Interest Groups

Interest groups enable citizens to peacefully express their concerns to government officials—that is, to exercise their First Amendment right to petition their government. In the United States, interest groups serve the five specific functions shown in Figure 12.1. First, interest groups *represent constituents* before the government. Without the organization and strength of interest groups, individual voices might drown in our complex society.

Second, interest groups provide a *means of political participation,* often coupled with other forms of political activity. Volunteering

time, taking part in a group, and contributing money are all important ways in which people can gain a sense of individual and collective power and thus a voice in our society.

A third function of interest groups is to *educate the public.* By sponsoring research, serving as advocates, testifying before congressional committees, conducting public relations campaigns, and engaging in similar activities, members of the public learn about various issues in more detail.

Fourth, interest groups influence policymaking by *building agendas*—that is, simply by bringing an otherwise little-known issue to the forefront. By attempting to educate the public about certain issues or by running public relations campaigns, they focus the attention of both the public and officials on issues that might otherwise be ignored.

Finally, interest groups contribute to the governing process by *serving as government watchdogs.* They monitor government programs, examining their strengths and weaknesses and thereby assessing the effectiveness of programs that are important to their members.

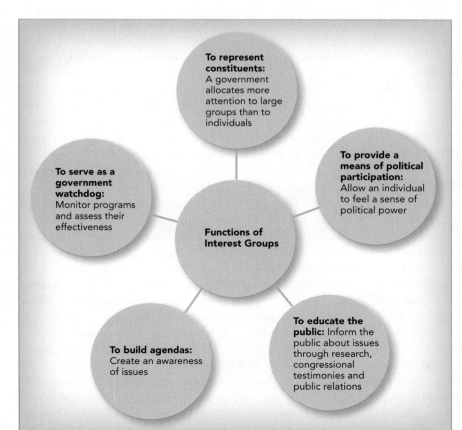

To represent constituents: A government allocates more attention to large groups than to individuals

To provide a means of political participation: Allow an individual to feel a sense of political power

To serve as a government watchdog: Monitor programs and assess their effectiveness

Functions of Interest Groups

To build agendas: Create an awareness of issues

To educate the public: Inform the public about issues through research, congressional testimonies and public relations

FIGURE 12.1 ■ **Five Functions of Interest Groups**

Many are skeptical about the role interest groups play in the United States, largely because people fail to completely understand the variety of positive functions these groups fulfill. —*What would our society be like without interest groups monitoring governmental programs, representing like-minded individuals, promoting political participation, educating the public about complex and controversial issues, and helping raise awareness of issues that would otherwise be ignored?*

■ **Disturbance Theory:** The idea that interest groups form when resources become scarce in order to contest the influence of other interest groups.

EXAMPLE: *NARAL Pro-Choice America (an organization that supports reproductive freedom and choice) was formed in 1969 to work to repeal laws that prohibited abortion. When the Supreme Court decided in* Roe v. Wade *(1973) that prohibiting abortions was unconstitutional, many pro-life groups (such as National Right to Life) were created to fight to reverse the decision.*

Types of Interest Groups

Interest groups span the political spectrum. To make sense of the variety, it is best to divide interest groups into four categories: economic groups, public interest groups, think tanks and universities, and governmental units. Each type of group exists to advance its goals, which may or may not be in the nation's best interest.

ECONOMIC GROUPS Economic groups include trade associations, labor unions, and professional associations. Trade associations are organized commercial groups, ranging from industrial corporations to agricultural producers. One of the most prominent trade associations is the U.S. Chamber of Commerce.

Labor unions are groups of workers who have joined together to negotiate collectively with employers and to inform the government and the public of their needs. **Professional associations** represent people—generally well-paid and highly educated ones—in a specific profession. Two prominent examples are the AMA for physicians and the American Bar Association (ABA) for attorneys.

PUBLIC INTEREST GROUPS Over the past 40 years, there has been a dramatic growth in **public interest groups,** which political scientist Jeffrey Berry defines as groups that form in the pursuit of "a collective good, the achievement of which will not selectively and materially benefit the membership or activists of the organization."[5] One of the earliest modern public interest groups was Common Cause, created in 1970 to advocate for governmental reform. The National Association for the Advancement of Colored People (NAACP), the National Rifle Association (NRA), and the environmentalist Sierra Club are all public interest groups, as are the many right-to-life groups that oppose abortion. The AARP (formerly the American Association of Retired Persons) is a public interest group that represents approximately 38 million Americans over age 50. It speaks for its members' concerns on such issues as health care, grandparents' rights, and Social Security.

THINK TANKS **Think tanks** are nonprofit institutions that conduct research and often engage in advocacy on issues of public interest. Think tanks often advocate a strong ideological viewpoint; examples include the conservative American Enterprise Institute and the Heritage Foundation. Universities also use a variety of techniques to petition the government for resources.

GOVERNMENTAL UNITS Finally, state- and local-level governmental units form interest groups that petition the federal authorities for help and to otherwise voice their concerns. As we saw in Chapter 3, when Congress cuts its financial support to the states and municipalities while at the same time piling more obligations on them, these government entities

have to compete for scarce resources. So, naturally, they form interest groups, too. Two excellent examples of such groups are the National Governors Association (NGA) and the U.S. Conference of Mayors (USCM). The NGA is a bipartisan organization of the nations' governors that helps represent states before the federal government. The USCM is a nonpartisan organization representing cities with populations larger than 300,000. It links national and urban-suburban policy and strengthens federal and city relationships.

The Interest Group Explosion

Between the 1960s and the 1990s, the United States witnessed an explosion in the number and activity level of interest groups. In 1959, there were 5,843 organizations with a national scope. That number almost doubled by 1970, reaching 10,308; a decade later, 14,726 organizations had registered with the federal government. By the mid-1990s, the level of growth had tapered off to slightly over 22,200 national organizations, which is about the number of groups that exist today.[6]

One of the many reasons why interest groups exist in the United States is to unify subgroups of people in our diverse and complex society. As the country grew in size and began to broaden the range of political power exercised by people of different religions, ethnicities, income levels, genders, and racial makeups, differences deepened into social divisions or **cleavages**. Many interest groups strive to gather supporters across social cleavages, serving as a unifying factor in a fragmented society. Other interest groups try to exploit cleavages, often using fear to mobilize their supporters.

The nature of our governmental system itself is a second explanation for why interest groups have existed in our society since its earliest days. The American federal system provides many opportunities to influence government at different levels. Groups can appeal to the federal government, to state governments, to county and municipal governments, and to special jurisdictions, such as school districts.

Our federal system helps explain why a larger percentage of Americans are involved in interest groups compared to citizens of other democracies. People who live in more centralized countries, such as the United Kingdom and France, have fewer opportunities to bring pressure on government. There, a great many issues that would be dealt with locally in the United States are the responsibility of the national legislature. These more unified governments simply do not offer as many points of access as our relatively decentralized system does.

A third explanation of the large growth in interest groups has been put forward by political scientist David Truman. His **disturbance theory**■ states that groups form whenever other interests are perceived as threatening or the status quo is disturbed. Essentially, *social change* causes the growth of interest groups. As society becomes more complex, divisions emerge,

Five weeks after the April 20, 2010 Deepwater Horizon BP oil platform explosion and oil spill in the Gulf of Mexico—the worst in U.S. history—environmental groups used texting and social networks to coordinate members for a "flashmob" protest at a BP gas station in New York. Groups involved included Times Up and Code Pink. —*Do you think flashmobs (in which protesters gather and disperse quickly) are effective in garnering public attention?*

which then become the basis for new groups. Not everyone agrees with this theory, however. Others argue that the development of groups depends crucially on the *quality of leadership* of the group.[7] If we modify the disturbance theory to include the role of leaders in causing social change, we can offer a hybrid explanation: charismatic individuals come forward to lead the new groups that result from social change.

A fourth explanation for the growth of interest groups in the United States can be attributed to the growth of government. As government takes on new responsibilities, interest groups arise to attempt to influence how those responsibilities are carried out and how government resources are allocated.

A final explanation for the rapid proliferation of interest groups lies in the changing social characteristics of the American population. Today, Americans are more educated and have more disposable income, making it easier for interest groups to target and activate them. In addition, groups have also benefited from new technology, which makes it easier to target potential members and contact interested people.

Functions and Types of Interest Groups

12.3 Identify four different types of interest groups, and explain the function of interest groups in a democracy.

PRACTICE QUIZ: UNDERSTAND AND APPLY

1. Which of the following is a multi-issue interest group?
  a. the NRA
  b. LULAC
  c. the Sierra Club
  d. the UFW

2. The Nature Conservancy, an international environmental group, would best be characterized as what?
  a. a think tank
  b. a governmental unit
  c. a public interest group
  d. a political action committee

3. Which of the following is *not* a factor that helps explain the rapid growth of interest groups since the 1960s?
  a. rapid social change
  b. more educated and wealthier citizens
  c. the growth of government itself
  d. voting

ANALYZE

1. How might the influence of interest groups conflict with the interest of the public at large?

2. What are some of the consequences of the increase in the number and type of interest groups?

IDENTIFY THE CONCEPT THAT DOESN'T BELONG

  a. Controlling member behavior
  b. Voluntary associations of joiners
  c. Common belief systems or shared values
  d. Influencing government
  e. Influencing others in the community

Resource Center
• Glossary
• Vocabulary Example
• Connect the Link

■ **Free-Rider Problem:** The fact that public goods can be enjoyed by everyone, including people who do not pay their fair share of the cost for providing those goods.

EXAMPLE: *Public television relies on funding from viewers; however, people can watch programming without contributing. Programs such as* Sesame Street, Barney, Frontline, Eyes on the Prize, *and* The McLaughlin Group *are free to all even if no contributions are made.*

Interest Group Mobilization

12.4 Explain how interest groups mobilize their memberships in the face of organizational barriers.

(pages 372–375)

Before we examine how groups organize, it is important to discuss the barriers that affect organizing—the obstacles that any group must overcome before it can succeed. In this section, we will generalize about the experiences of all groups. It is important to stress, however, that specific subgroups in the American population may face additional barriers and that some barriers may affect certain groups differently than others.

Imagine, for example, that you are troubled by the economic exploitation of Latinos in the construction business in your state and want to organize the workers. However, you learn that the majority of Spanish-speaking construction workers are not citizens or legal immigrants. They would likely be afraid of speaking up or identifying themselves for fear of facing legal repercussions. As another example, imagine that you are a student on a conservative college campus where a number of hate-based crimes have been committed in recent months against homosexual students. You want to form a group composed of homosexual, bisexual, and transgender students and their supporters to pressure the university to protect the students' civil rights. However, students that publicly identify themselves as a member of the group would likely face being ostracized and might even face violence.

In both examples, the pressure would be great to remain silent. Does this mean that neither type of group could be organized? Certainly not, but we must be clear about the barriers that may exist in order to overcome them. Moreover, we must look at barriers that are internalized in individuals and those that reflect the reality of collective action. For example, for you to join a group, you must have confidence in your own abilities to make an important contribution, and you also have to believe that your contribution will make a difference. In smaller, more local organizations, this might be easier to achieve, but in the case of larger groups, it may be more difficult to get a sense that your membership truly matters. As you will see, groups that are successful in recruiting and retaining members are sensitive to each concern and able to overcome these considerations.

Organizational Barriers

The economist Mancur Olson described three key barriers facing people who share concerns and want to create formal problem-resolving organizations.[8] The first barrier is the tendency of individuals to allow others to do work on their behalf. (In essence, why should I spend my time and energy when others will do the work and I will benefit?) This is the **free-rider problem**■. Olson notes that free riding is more likely to occur with groups that provide **public goods or collective goods**■—things of value that cannot be given to one group exclusively but instead benefit society as a whole. Clean air is an example. Although one environmentalist group, or more likely a coalition of such groups, gives their time, money, and energy to pass legislation to mandate cleaner automotive emissions, we all benefit from the clean air that legislation provides—even those of us who did not contribute to the group effort. Olson examined the incentives for joining groups from a rational perspective. A person will join a group when the benefits outweigh the costs, but if you can reap the benefits without incurring any costs, why join? Organized groups must be conscious of the free-rider problem so that they can provide other benefits to members to get them to join.

The second barrier that Olson identified in group formation is cost. This is a chief reason why many people who share common concerns do not organize. For one person to form a viable group that attracts many people and can be influential, money must be spent. It takes money to form and maintain a group, but it also takes a large commitment of time and energy. Some people and groups, of course, are better situated to bear the costs of organizing, most notably the affluent. Less affluent people frequently need to spend their time and energy earning money, including holding second jobs, and they simply cannot volunteer or make large contributions to groups they may support.

The absence of a sense of political efficacy—the belief that one person can make a difference—is the third barrier to interest group formation identified by Olson. Even if you have confidence in your own abilities, you might fall into the pessimistic mind-set of "What can one person do?" Imagine that you are concerned about changing the method of trash collection in your city (going from once to twice a week, for example). "But I'm only one person," you might think. "What can I do by myself?" Such pessimism affects not only people thinking of forming new groups but also those who might join or renew their membership in existing groups. Let's say that you're interested in promoting women's rights. You investigate the National Organization for Women (NOW) and find that it advocates many positions with which you agree. You think about joining but then start to wonder: With 500,000 dues-paying members, what good will my $35 annual dues do? In truth, your dues alone won't do too much for the organization, but you might join once you understand the logic of collective action—that is, when you realize that the dues of 500,000 people come to $17.5 million, a sum that can make a large difference.

■ **Public Goods (Collective Goods):** Goods that are used or consumed by all individuals in society.

EXAMPLE: *Clean water, public roads, public parks, community libraries, and public pools are all forms of public goods that are available.*

Overcoming Organizational Barriers

Any group of people who hope to create and maintain an organization must understand the free-rider problem and other barriers to successful organization and mobilization, so that they can work to overcome them. Groups use many means to make membership attractive so that the benefits of membership outweigh the perceived costs. Organizations must also demonstrate to current and potential members that membership is important and that every member helps advance the collective goal. To overcome these barriers, **selective benefits** may be given to members—benefits that only group members receive, even if the collective good for which they strive remains available to everyone.

SELECTIVE BENEFITS The first type of selective benefits is **material benefits**—tangible benefits that have value, such as magazines, discounts, and paraphernalia such as T-shirts and plaques. One of the first groups to offer material benefits was the American Farm Bureau. Many people, even nonfarmers, joined the organization in order to receive its insurance discounts. Today, the AARP uses a wider variety of material benefits to encourage membership, including discounts (on pharmacy services, airlines, automobiles, computers, vacations, insurance, restaurants, hotels, and cruises), tax information, magazine subscriptions, legal advice, and credit cards.

In addition to material benefits, which are a major incentive for numerous individuals to join, many groups also offer **solidary benefits,** which are primarily social. Solidary benefits focus on providing activities and a sense of belonging—meetings, dinners, dances, and other such social activities that groups provide to give members a sense of belonging with other like-minded people.

Finally, there are **purposive benefits** of group membership—"the intangible rewards that derive from the sense of satisfaction of having contributed to the attainment of a worthwhile cause."[9] Groups that organize blood drives often try to convey a purposive benefit. The sense of "helping people" and "doing good" are important motivators for many who give blood, encouraging them to endure a modest amount of discomfort and inconvenience.

Many organizations rely on purposive benefits, typically in combination with other benefits, to attract members. For example, because the National Rifle Association (NRA) works for a collective good—advances in protecting gun ownership apply to all citizens—the NRA must fight the free-rider and efficacy problems and recruit dues-paying members to defer its maintenance costs. To encourage people to join, the NRA successfully recruits members by providing a variety of selective benefits, including the following:[10]

• **Material benefits:** Insurance, training, and discounts. The group offers $25,000 life insurance policies to police officers who are members, if they are killed in the line of duty. It also offers its members gun loss insurance, accidental death insurance at reduced rates, and discounts for eye care, car rentals, hotels, and airfares. The group sponsors training programs for the Olympics and funds research on violent crimes.

• **Solidary benefits:** Safety and training classes (including award-winning Eddy Eagle child safety classes) and shooting competitions (including special tournaments for women and children). Its grassroots groups, Friends of the NRA, hosts dinners, national and state conventions, and art contests, and it publishes magazines.

• **Purposive benefits:** The feeling that one is doing something to advance one's view of the Second Amendment of the Constitution and to preserve access to shooting and hunting.

REQUIRED MEMBERSHIP Some organizations do not have to encourage membership; they can *demand* it. One prominent example of this is labor unions in many states. In accordance with the National Labor Relations Act of 1935, in some states unions can form agreements with employers that prevent nonunion labor from being hired. In other states, "right to work" laws prohibit such contracts, but in nearly 30 states, people can be required, as a condition of employment, to join a union and pay dues. Unions, however, also provide many selective benefits (for example, insurance and employment security) as well as such solidary benefits as dinners, dances, and holiday parties.[11] Although these benefits are more important to recruit members in right-to-work states, they are still used in states that compel membership in order to make the union more attractive and more popular among workers.

Similarly, some corporations use subtle coercion to encourage "voluntary" donations to PACs from executives and their families. Coercion is also prevalent in some professional associations; for example, 32 states require attorneys to be members of the state bar association in order to practice law.[12]

The efforts of **patrons**—individuals or organizations that give money to groups—also help form and sustain interest groups. Each year, private organizations such as the Rockefeller and Ford foundations give millions of dollars to citizen groups and think tanks for purposes ranging from conducting research to founding new organizations. Corporations also give hundreds of millions of dollars to interest groups every year. The federal government allocates money to interest groups, generally in the form of a government contract for research or the provision of some other service. For example, the federal government might hire an environmentalist group to help determine how many snowmobiles should be allowed into a national park without harming the ecosystem. Of course, snowmobile companies and the tourist industry may fear that the estimate by the environmentalist group might be

César Chávez was a dynamic leader who organized an unlikely group of activists—migrant farm workers (many of whom were not citizens). Shown here are César Chávez (third from the right) and Coretta Scott King (fourth from the right) leading a march in New York City to build support for a lettuce boycott in 1970. Through marches, protests, and organized boycotts, Chávez was able to improve the working conditions and compensation for thousands of hardworking laborers. —*What characteristics do you think are the most important in distinguishing a truly great leader?*

too low and may consequently lobby Congress to commission additional research. Few, if any, organizations can rely exclusively on patron support, but support of this sort is very helpful for some.

The Role of Interest Group Leaders

In addition to using incentives to mobilize support, interest groups use inspirational leadership to build their membership. Charismatic and devoted leaders can entice potential members to join an organization. When people believe in the leaders of an organization, they are more supportive of its goals and more likely to support it financially. Effective leaders "sell" their issues to the public, thus attracting media attention and membership.

CHÁVEZ AND THE UFW   César Chávez provides perhaps the best example of a leader's role in winning success for his organization in what appeared to be hopeless circumstances. Chávez grew up a poor migrant worker farming in states along the U.S.–Mexican border. Because he had to move around with his family to work on farms throughout his childhood, he was able to attend school only sporadically. After serving in the U.S. Navy during World War II, Chávez returned to migratory farm work in Arizona and California. Seeing the desperate circumstances and gross exploitation of farm workers firsthand, Chávez dedicated his life to helping them organize and mobilize to demand fair treatment. In 1962, he organized the National Farm Workers Association, a labor union that later merged with other organizations to form the United Farm Workers of America (UFW).

Chávez's UFW ultimately led a 5-year strike by California grape pickers and inspired a national boycott of California grapes. To draw national attention to the grape pickers' plight, Chávez headed a 340-mile march by farm workers across California in 1966 and went on a much-publicized, 25-day hunger strike in 1968. The UFW later led successful campaigns against lettuce growers and other agribusinesses (large, corporate farm industries), demanding fair treatment of farm workers. Chávez and his union gained crucial support from middle-class consumers who boycotted grapes and lettuce harvested by nonunion labor, ultimately forcing the powerful agribusinesses to capitulate.

What is perhaps most remarkable about the success of the groups that Chávez led is their ability to organize the most unlikely people—extremely poor, uneducated immigrants. By the early 1970s, the UFW had grown to 50,000 dues-paying members and had contracts with 300 growers. It succeeded not only in negotiating collective bargaining agreements but also in forcing the enactment of legislation to change migratory pickers' often deplorable working conditions. Activists and scholars alike agree that the success of the UFW owed much to Chávez's energy, appeal, and dedication to social justice. His charisma enabled Chávez to convince farm workers to unite and work with others—for example, California Governor Jerry Brown—to promote their collective interests. As testimony to his commitment to social justice and nonviolent protest, Chávez was posthumously awarded the Presidential Medal of Freedom in 1994.

The UFW is a good example of a group of low-income people uniting to fight large corporations. By overcoming the barriers to organizing, providing membership benefits, and having solid leadership, groups of all kinds can successfully press for change. The challenges are often large, but the rewards can be profound.

Interest Group Mobilization

12.4 Show how interest groups mobilize their memberships in the face of organizational barriers.

PRACTICE QUIZ: UNDERSTAND AND APPLY

1. One of the strongest barriers to mobilizing potential members in socially vulnerable groups, such as gays or illegal immigrants, is
   a. the free-rider problem.
   b. the dangers to such individuals that might come with making their status public.
   c. the likelihood that government officials will not listen to such individuals.
   d. the fact that their causes are not very strong.

2. Money is essential to the creation and ongoing support of an interest group.
   a. true
   b. false

3. If you are attending your labor union's holiday party, you are enjoying what sort of interest group benefit?
   a. material
   c. solidary
   b. purposive
   d. abstract

4. The unlikely success of the UFW in the early 1970s illustrates
   a. the power of a charismatic leader.
   b. the rising importance of technology in grassroots mobilization.
   c. the effectiveness of large-scale protest demonstrations.
   d. the efficacy of professional lobbyists.

ANALYZE

1. What would motivate a group of citizens to form an interest group? Consider this question from both a historical and a modern perspective.

2. What factors make some groups more successful and powerful than others? What role do leaders play in the formation, maintenance, and success of interest groups?

IDENTIFY THE CONCEPT THAT DOESN'T BELONG

a. National Rifle Association
b. National Organization for Women
c. AARP
d. American Bar Association
e. Sierra Club

Resource Center
• Glossary
• Vocabulary Example
• Connect the Link

■ **Inside Lobbying:** Appealing directly to lawmakers and legislative staff either in meetings, by providing research and information, or by testifying at committee hearings.

EXAMPLE: *Lobbyists often provide research and statistics to lawmakers and their aides during meetings on Capitol Hill in order to present the position of their clients.*

Inside and Outside Lobbying

12.5 Describe how interest groups appeal to public officials and the public to gain support for their causes.
(pages 376–379)

The key to understanding influence in our governmental system is to realize that interest groups and individuals use different pathways, often at the same time, to advance their perspectives and petition their government. One pathway may prove a successful vehicle for a group at one point but fail at another time.

Inside Lobbying

Inside lobbying■, a tool used in the lobbying decision makers pathway, openly appeals to public officials in the legislature and the executive branch, which includes the bureaucracy. Because inside lobbying is a matter of personal contact with policymakers, it involves some form of direct interaction—often called **gaining access**■—between a lobbyist and an agency official, a member of Congress, or a member of the legislator's staff. By having an opportunity to present the group's position directly to lawmakers, staffers, or officials, lobbyists have a greater chance of influencing the decision-making process. To be effective, however, lobbyists must be seen as trustworthy and must develop relationships with individuals who have influence in the relevant policy area.

Another inside lobbying tactic is to testify at congressional committee hearings. Such hearings normally occur when Congress is considering a bill for passage, when committees are investigating a problem or monitoring existing programs, or when a nominee for a high executive or judicial position is testifying before a confirmation vote. Testifying allows an interest group to present its views in public and "on the record," potentially raising its visibility and appealing to political actors.

A great deal of money is spent by organizations to lobby the federal government. Lavish spending, coupled with concerns over corruption, prompted the Lobbying Disclosure Act of 1995. Two components of this legislation regulate direct lobbying. The first component of the law tries to provide "transparency" by requiring lobbyists to register with the federal government and report their activities. Many people believe that having full disclosure will raise public confidence in the system by minimizing the potential for abuse and corruption. The second set of provisions in the law bars certain types of informal lobbying activities that have been used in the past, such as giving expensive gifts, purchasing expensive meals, and paying for trips for members of Congress. Fees (called *honoraria*) for speaking engagements were outlawed in 1992. Even with this legislation, however, many people are concerned with the perception of impropriety and potential for corruption.

This concern proved well founded in 2006 when Jack Abramoff, a top political lobbyist, pled guilty to three felony counts of tax evasion, fraud, and conspiracy to bribe a public official. In a deal that required him to cooperate with a broad investigation into public corruption, Abramoff admitted to corrupting governmental officials and defrauding his clients of $25 million. He spent money lavishly on lawmakers, their staffs, and executive branch officials, paying for luxury trips, expensive meals, entertainment, and tickets to sporting events. Moreover, he hired spouses of officials that he was lobbying in efforts to manipulate their behavior.

Outside Lobbying

Outside lobbying (or grassroots lobbying)■, also known as indirect lobbying, is the attempt to influence decision makers indirectly, by influencing the public. In appealing directly to the public, interest groups are trying to build public sentiment in order to bring pressure to bear on the officials who will actually make the decisions. David Truman, in his classic analysis of interest groups, *The Governmental Process,* noted that organized interests engage in "programs of propaganda, though rarely so labeled, designed to affect opinions concerning interests" in hopes that concerned citizens will then lobby the government on behalf of whatever the group is trying to accomplish.[13]

There are several advantages in appealing to the public. First, an interest group can indirectly use the people through the elections pathway to directly affect the selection of officials. Citizens can also pressure officials to take action. Moreover, pressure from interest groups can influence which issues the government decides to address as well as the policies it adopts, modifies, or abandons. Appealing directly to the people can also be advantageous, because citizens can take direct actions that can be used to further the group's agenda. By lobbying supporters and the general public, interest groups seek to show public officials that the issue is important to the people.

STUDENT profile

In 2010, Tim Tebow was one of the most recognized players in college football. People across the country and world became familiar with him and his athletic accomplishments for the Florida Gators when he became the youngest man to win the Heisman Trophy as a sophomore in 2007. Tebow helped lead the Gators to two national championships and was recognized by ESPN as the best Male College Athlete in 2008 and 2009.

However, Tebow generated enormous attention and controversy in 2010 when he appeared in a pro-life Super Bowl

■ **Gaining Access:** Winning the opportunity to communicate directly with a legislator or a legislative staff member to present one's position on an issue of public policy.

EXAMPLE: *Interest groups often host parties or events to which elected officials and their staffs are invited with the hope that private conversations will occur.*

Tim Tebow, pictured here, is perhaps the most recognized college athlete of his generation. Tebow led the Florida Gators to two national championships and became, in 2007, the first underclassman to ever win the Heisman Trophy. Tebow advocates for Focus on the Family, a conservative Christian organization formed by James Dobson. During his days at Florida, Tebow frequently wore Bible verses on his black eye patches, using his role as a star quarterback to advocate for his Christian faith. —*Do you think that a non-Christian athlete would be allowed to advance his religion with the same level of acceptance as Tebow? Should he or she be allowed to?*

XLIV commercial paid for by the conservative religious interest group Focus on the Family. Born in the Philippines to Christian missionaries in 1987, Tebow has served on mission trips, praises God in nearly all of his public comments, and proudly declares that he is remaining a virgin until marriage. While the Super Bowl ad never specifically mentioned abortion, the pro-life message delivered by Tebow and his mother, Pam, was clear. The controversy that surrounded Tebow's actions was great, but many admired his willingness to stand up for his convictions despite the criticism.

Examining the activities of more than 90 interest group leaders, political scientist Ken Kollman found that 90 percent of interest groups engage in some kind of outside lobbying.[14] In studying the effect of mobilization in the 1994 debate over President Bill Clinton's health care proposals, Kenneth Goldstein found

that citizens in states that were targeted by statewide grassroots campaigns had significantly higher voting rates than citizens in nontargeted states.[15] Moreover, more than one-third of the individuals contacted by organized interest groups communicated with their member of Congress, compared with only 10 percent of those who had not been contacted by a grassroots campaign. Seventy-five percent of those who contacted members of Congress said they did so at the request of an interest group. Proportionately, more Americans than ever before are communicating with members of Congress, but this surge in communication is not spontaneous. Much of it is the direct result of coordinated efforts by organized interests.[16]

In addition to directly appealing to the public, interest groups also lobby other groups and try to form alliances with them to advance common interests on a particular issue. Coalition building—bringing diverse interests together to advance a cause—is frequently successful. Normally, the coalitions that result are temporary, limited to one specific issue. The more groups cooperate, the easier political action often becomes; conversely, conflict and competition tend to diminish success.

GRASSROOTS MOBILIZATION Interest groups increasingly rely on grassroots mobilization as a form of outside lobbying to pressure policymakers. A trade association executive interviewed by Kenneth Goldstein gave a good definition of grassroots mobilization: "The identification, recruitment, and mobilization of constituent-based political strength capable of influencing political decisions."[17]

Grassroots work is difficult to measure, and its success is perhaps even more difficult to assess. Most experts, however, believe that grassroots mobilization is becoming far more common. Goldstein found that most Fortune 500 companies have full-time grassroots coordinators with solid plans to present their point of view by stirring up citizen interest, and he also found that the media cover grassroots lobbying with greater frequency today. The depth of support on certain issues is often rather short-lived and superficial. Some refer to such artificially stimulated public interest as "Astroturf," because it gives the *appearance* of widespread popularity but has no real depth. Kollman, however, finds evidence that grassroots lobbying is an important tool for getting a group's message to officials.[18]

MYTH EXPOSED Many Americans believe that indirect lobbying is a new phenomenon. In actuality, indirect lobbying has been going on in our country since its earliest days, although the tools and tactics have evolved with the emergence of new technology. Consider, for example, how westward expansion was sold to the American people. Entities with vested interests in expansion, such as the nineteenth-century railroad companies, stressed in their appeals to the public the ease of obtaining property, the lure of frontier adventure, and the

■ **Outside Lobbying (Grassroots Lobbying):** Activities directed at the general public to raise awareness and interest and to pressure officials.

EXAMPLE: *E-mail alerts that groups send to members to notify them of political events are examples of ways in which interest groups try to mobilize their supporters and sympathizers.*

chance of finding wealth by moving west. Westward expansion would have occurred without these marketing campaigns, but capitalizing commercially on the existing public interest accelerated the rate of expansion. Would-be settlers in turn urged the government to aid westward migration. Responding to this pressure, Congress in 1862 passed the Transcontinental Railroad Act and the Homestead Act. By making land grants to the companies that built the western railroads as well as by encouraging western settlement, Congress dramatically increased the value of railroad property.

GRASSROOTS LOBBYING TACTICS One of the earliest forms of grassroots mobilization was **direct contact**■, a process that goes back to the days of the antislavery movement and is still used today because it is so effective. Having committed supporters personally contact fellow citizens is a valuable tool for interest groups. Seeing others who care deeply enough to give of their time and energy can stimulate people to become involved with a cause.

Direct mail■ is another way for interest groups to contact potential supporters. Modern technology permits mailings to be personalized in ways that allow a group to frame its message narrowly, so that it appeals to specific types of people. Knowing a good deal about the individuals targeted in its direct-mail campaign helps a well-funded interest group personalize its message and thus make it more efficient. Because modern technology today collects and stores so much personal information, interest groups with substantial financial resources can acquire what they want to know about potential recipients, allowing them to exploit this form of propaganda more effectively.

Many of the events used by interest groups to influence the public and pressure policymakers are designed to provide members with solidary benefits, but they can also raise the organization's image in the community and demonstrate its importance. Labor unions and public interest groups are most likely to engage in this type of behavior, organizing rallies, marches, and mass demonstrations to promote their causes.

Finally, to force the pace of change, interest groups have organized boycotts—the organized refusal of large numbers of people to do business with an opponent as a nonviolent expression of disagreement.

The development in recent decades of more sophisticated means of communication has given interest groups far more options than they once had to motivate supporters, recruit new members, and mobilize the public. To sway public opinion, organized interest groups have aggressively and imaginatively tried to use the media to manipulate what gets reported—and occasionally, they succeed. Pressured by deadlines, some reporters are willing to use in their stories information presented by interest groups.

Well-heeled interest groups advertise in major newspapers and magazines as well as on TV and the Internet to increase their visibility and improve their public image. Many of these ads are noncommercial—they are not trying to sell anything or directly attract members but instead are designed to generate favorable public opinion. Because such ads are frequently designed to resemble editorials, they have sometimes been dubbed **advertorials.**

Some interest groups sponsor television shows to influence the public. Groups also try to have their advocates appear as experts on talk shows. Having someone present the group's position on *Larry King Live,* for example, raises the group's visibility and credibility in important ways—because groups must appear credible and trustworthy, when using the lobbying decision makers pathway to influence public officials.

Over the past two decades, the Internet has offered interest groups some of the best possibilities for new tactics. Organized groups can advance their cause in many ways—from Web pages, e-mail campaigns, and chat rooms to blogs and **social networking sites,** which allow people and groups to post information in order to stimulate interest in particular topics, raise public awareness, and influence public opinion. Consumers must use caution when using information posted on these sites, however, because nearly anyone, regardless of level of expertise or knowledge, can set up and maintain a blog. Social networking sites allow groups to appeal to a wide variety of individuals with minimum cost, attracting interest literally from across the globe. The Web has great potential for mobilizing supporters and raising money, but not everyone has access to it or can readily use it. Younger people who are more affluent and better educated access the Web at far greater rates than older, poorer, and less educated people do.

Cliff Landesman of Idealist.org identifies eight purposes for which interest groups use the Web: publicity, public education, communication, volunteer recruitment, research, advocacy, service provision, and fundraising.[19] Certainly, not all groups pursue all eight of these potential uses; many focus on just one or two. For example, Project Vote Smart exists to inform citizens about candidates running for federal office, presenting issue stances in a clear and concise format.

CAMPAIGN ACTIVITIES Interest groups play an active role in the elections pathway in local, state, and national election campaigns. Organized groups obviously want to influence elections so that individuals who support their cause will get into office. Groups also want to influence the public during elections in order to sway incumbent policymakers. Groups get involved in elections in many different ways, with their central motivation being to advance their own causes.

Most interest groups take part in electoral politics by rating and endorsing candidates. At every point on the political spectrum, special-interest groups rate the candidates to help

| ■ **Direct Contact:** Face-to-face meetings or telephone conversations between individuals. | **EXAMPLE:** *Lobbyists try hard to develop relationships with public officials in order to have opportunities for direct contact in either formal or informal settings.* | ■ **Direct Mail:** Information mailed to a large number of people to advertise, market concepts, or solicit support. | **EXAMPLE:** *Political candidates often send mail to voters to present their issue stances and biographical information in order to persuade them to donate money to their campaign and/or vote for them in the upcoming election.* |

influence their supporters and sympathizers. A typical example is the Christian Coalition, which provides voter guides (distributed in sympathetic churches across the nation) that examine candidates' voting records and note what percentage of the time they vote "correctly" on what the group considers key issues. In the same way, the AFL-CIO rates members of Congress on their votes regarding issues important to organized labor, to give supporters a voting cue. So, too, does the U.S. Chamber of Commerce, from the business perspective.

Today, many people worry about the influence that special-interest groups have on elections—and especially about the impact of interest group money on electoral outcomes and the subsequent actions of elected officials. It is important to note, however, that interest groups are simply associations of like-minded people. In a democracy, citizens *should* affect elections, even if those citizens are acting collectively. So, while we should certainly scrutinize interest groups' contributions to candidates and political parties, interest group involvement does not necessarily pollute the electoral system. Interest groups can serve as a political cue to their members, other interest groups, voters, and the media. When an interest group donates money to a candidate, it is making a public show of support that can be an important cue for others, either for or against that candidate.

Money has always been important in politics; today's requirement for limited campaign contributions and full disclosure makes the system more transparent and honest. In the days when we did not know how much candidates received in contributions, or from whom they received contributions, we might have naively thought that there was less corruption. However, the opposite was probably true. Despite ready access to contributions, greater scrutiny today likely induces most politicians to be more honest.

On January 21, 2010, in *Citizens United* v. *Federal Election Commission,* a divided Supreme Court overruled two important precedents that had previously limited corporate wealth from unfairly influencing elections.[20] In a 5–4 decision, the Court ruled that the federal government cannot ban political spending by corporations in elections as such bans infringe upon the political speech of corporations. Dissenters argued that corporate money would be sufficiently large to drown out the speech of less funded entities (most notably individual citizens) and could serve to corrupt democratic elections. As a consequence of the ruling, a record amount of independent expenditures—over $200 million—was spent to influence the 2010 midterm election. Initial reports show that conservative groups had a two-to-one advantage in expenditures.

Inside and Outside Lobbying

12.5   **Describe how interest groups appeal to public officials and the public to gain support for their causes.**

PRACTICE QUIZ: UNDERSTAND AND APPLY

1. Inside lobbying involves a form of direct interaction to be effective. This may be described as
   a. gaining access.
   b. insider trading.
   c. working within the retired military officers corps.
   d. bureaucratic infighting.

2. To be effective at inside lobbying, lobbyists must
   a. be seen as trustworthy.
   b. develop relationships with influential individuals.
   c. testify before congressional committees.
   d. a, b, and c.

3. The activities involved with outside lobbying deal more directly with elected and appointed officials, while those related to inside lobbying do not.
   a. true
   b. false

4. What other types of events and activities can interest groups use to influence public opinion and pressure policymakers?
   a. organizing rallies and marches   c. boycotts
   b. mass demonstrations   d. all of the above

ANALYZE

1. A lot of money is spent on inside lobbying by interest groups. What impact does this have on our electoral system? What does it tell us about the effectiveness of ordinary citizens?

2. Select one type of event or activity that an interest group can use to directly influence public opinion; discuss its merits and deficiencies.

IDENTIFY THE CONCEPT THAT DOESN'T BELONG

a. Building relationships   d. Direct appeals
b. Personal contact   e. Expert testimony
c. Campaign contributions

Resource Center
• Glossary
• Vocabulary Example
• Connect the Link

The Influence of Interest Groups

12.6 Assess the ways interest groups positively and negatively impact our society.

(pages 380–381)

One of the most troubling aspects for many when they consider interest groups is the perception that such groups corrupt politics and politicians. As we have seen, corruption occurs, but more often, it does not. Interest groups do raise and spend a good deal of money, but organizing a diverse society is expensive. Some interests—corporations and professions, for example—are better able to bear these costs than others, such as ordinary citizens. Despite this, as we have seen, citizen groups have thrived and brought about great change.

Interest Group Money

It is difficult to overemphasize the importance of money in mobilization. A significant amount of money is needed just to launch an organization, and continuous funding is needed to maintain it thereafter. Money is needed to recruit members, hire staff, rent offices, pay overhead, and raise additional funds. If the group plans to use many of the tactics discussed in this chapter, substantially more funds will be needed. Advertising and direct mail campaigns are very expensive, and money is also needed to raise more money. Certainly, not many groups can afford the full range of professional services, but for those with sufficient resources, a variety of services can be purchased.

Political scientists have found, not surprisingly, that groups with large resources have many advantages and are more successful.[21] Well-funded groups can afford to hire the best lobbyists and workers, make large campaign contributions, hire specialized professionals, and retain attorneys for legal battles. Moreover, affluent groups can use many lobbying techniques with greater success, for they can sustain such activity over longer periods.

Money is often the key predictor of who wins and who loses in American politics; however, money alone does not always win. Public support is equally important, which is why interest groups put so much effort into outside lobbying. The women's rights, civil rights, and farm workers movements are perhaps the best examples of less affluent groups exerting great power for change.

Bias in Representation: Who Participates?

At first glance, given the variety of groups, you might think that interest groups represent all Americans equally. They do not. Generally, activists are not typical Americans—most of them are drawn from the elite levels of society. Activists are more politically sophisticated, more knowledgeable, and more involved in their

Organizing groups requires a great deal of time, energy, and resources. From calling supporters, to mobilizing voters, to organizing events, committed individuals must be willing to sacrifice for their cause. —*What challenges do you think cell phones represent to groups trying to organize supporters? What new venues for mobilization have opened up because of cell phones and other mobile devices?*

communities. All Americans have the right to form groups, but the fact is that for many reasons, many Americans do not.[22] Educational attainment, family income, and social class are among the largest factors in predicting participation in organized interest groups—and in politics more generally. However, there are exceptions to this general pattern. The least biased form of political participation is voting; not surprisingly, the most skewed form of participation is making campaign contributions: People with more education and more income predominate. Participating in interest groups falls roughly between these two extremes.[23]

Because all American citizens can potentially participate in politics, many observers are not concerned that some Americans choose to remain politically uninvolved. But others are troubled by these patterns of unequal participation and mobilization when they look at the problem from an overall perspective. There is a profound difference among the races, and within races along gender lines, in the level of political participation in the United States. When looking at politics in the aggregate, it is also clear that the immense economic resources of big business give it a disproportionate level of political influence. However, as political scientist James Q. Wilson has noted, "One cannot assume that the disproportionate possession of certain resources leads to the disproportionate exercise of political power. Everything depends on whether a resource can be converted into power, and at what rate and at what price."[24]

Because potential activists *do* have opportunities to organize in American politics, and because one important counterweight to moneyed interests in politics is the power of united and committed citizens, it's important that those with similar interests be mobilized and organized. But we also want to stress how important it is for our democracy that citizens who have traditionally not participated be encouraged to take part in interest group activity. Individuals who participate in group activity, especially those who participate in a diverse range of groups, more often than not tend to develop political tolerance, trust, and a sense of efficacy—qualities that are essential for maintaining a healthy democracy.[25]

Final Verdict?

Interest groups play a mixed role in our society. On the one hand, they give people opportunities to band together to increase their power and ability to influence fellow citizens and government officials. From an early age, we come to appreciate that there is strength in numbers, thus Americans' solid commitment to collective action. On the other hand, a tension exists: While we believe in collective action as a means for us to influence others, we are often wary of the collective action of groups to which we do not belong or whose views we do not support.

Moreover, it has been asked whether interest groups increase or decrease the influence of individuals: Do interest groups represent ordinary people who would otherwise be powerless? Or do they drown out the voices of ordinary people in favor of special interests?

Participating in groups affects individual citizens in several positive ways. According to some researchers, those who are members of organized interest groups are also more likely to participate in other forms of political activity. Allan Cigler and Mark Joslyn found that people who participated in group activities had higher levels of political tolerance, more trust in elected officials, and a greater sense of political efficacy.[26]

Other research that examined the impact of interest groups on social issues, however, paints a different picture.[27] The growth of interest groups correlates with the growth in distrust in government and fellow citizens, voter cynicism, and lower voting rates. Some hypothesize that when interest groups raise the level of conflict surrounding an issue, they simply alienate the public, thus raising the levels of citizen distrust. However, a different interpretation is also possible—that interest groups form because citizens *do* distrust the government, *are* cynical, and *do* have low participation rates. It could be that people join interest groups in order to organize an otherwise chaotic world.

The Influence of Interest Groups

12.6   **Assess the ways interest groups positively and negatively impact our society.**

PRACTICE QUIZ: UNDERSTAND AND APPLY

1. Growth in the number and perceived influence of interest groups is associated with all of the following except
   a. distrust in government.
   b. voter cynicism.
   c. lower voting rates.
   d. greater political participation.

2. According to recent research, participating in organized interest groups usually makes people
   a. more inclined to participate in other forms of political activity.
   b. less inclined to participate in other forms of political activity.
   c. less inclined to make financial contributions to a political campaign.
   d. more likely to denigrate the political process in this country.

3. Research also suggests that the growth of interest groups in this country correlates with the growth in trust in the government and in fellow citizens.
   a. true
   b. false

ANALYZE

1. Why do interest groups need money? How is technology changing the patterns and tactics of fundraising?

2. How influential are interest groups in the United States? How influential does the public *think* interest groups are? What are some of the consequences of this public perception?

IDENTIFY THE CONCEPT THAT DOESN'T BELONG

   a. Higher levels of confidence in government
   b. Increased levels of negative advertising
   c. Higher levels of distrust
   d. Voter cynicism
   e. Lower political participation

Conclusion

In February 2009, Keli Carender, frustrated with her elected officials, honored two of the most cherished political traditions in the United States—she organized a protest and pushed for collective action. The beliefs in the power of collective action and protest are rooted in our country's history from its earliest days as European colonies.

We have a "how to" element in our government, which is focused on bargaining and compromise and is public-driven. Organized groups are among the most important actors in motivating the public; yet as a society, we have mixed feelings about interest groups.

On the one hand, we acknowledge the need and show our support for organized action. To help influence change, many of us join organized interests and readily form associations that range from parent organizations in schools and neighborhood improvement groups to larger, nationally oriented organizations. In fact, approximately 65 percent of Americans over the age of 18 belong to at least one politically active organization.[28] Even if we don't join organizations, many of us feel that an existing group is representing our interests. For example, many senior citizens are not dues-paying members of the AARP but nevertheless feel that the group represents them.

On the other hand, we also fear organized interests. Polls consistently show that Americans are wary about the influence of "special interests" and believe the "common person" is not adequately represented. One lobbyist described the perception that others have of his profession thusly: "Being a lobbyist has long been synonymous in the minds of many Americans with being a glorified pimp."[29] Much of the public believes that interest groups have a great deal of influence with government officials and that their influence has been increasing. Moreover, fully 83 percent of Americans believe that interest groups have more influence than voters.

While campaigning in 2008, Barack Obama pledged to reduce the influence of lobbyists and special interests in government. However, from the earliest days of his administration, President Obama was unsuccessful in challenging the perception that interest groups play a disproportionately large role in Washington. In the health care debate, groups immediately emerged on both sides of the reform issue—with each side vying to frame the debate, mobilize their supporters, and "win" the fight.

Interest groups, as we have emphasized in this chapter, are associations of like-minded people united for a common cause; however, we must be careful not to paint too rosy a picture. Interest groups are primarily concerned with promoting their self-interest. Even groups that seem to be advancing the best interest of the public may not be. Trade-offs are often inevitable. Consider environmentalist groups. They work to protect the environment so that all of us can benefit, but in the process, they sometimes create difficulties for a community or certain individuals. Forcing a mining company out of business, for example, might be important for the local ecosystem, but it will also throw a large number of people out of work. Therefore, it is debatable whether the behavior of the interest group is in the best interests of the mining community. Such concerns and debates are significant when we examine interest group behavior. To understand fully both the potentially positive and potentially negative impacts of interest group actions, a balanced analysis is essential.

KEY CONCEPT MAP How do interest groups mobilize the masses?

Advertising

PETA (People for the Ethical Treatment of Animals) uses its celebrity ad campaign to change the public's perceptions of vegetarianism and make the organization seem more relevant to the public. Jake Shields is a lifelong vegetarian and a mixed martial arts champion.

Critical Thinking Questions

In what ways can using celebrities in advertisements help interest groups to better connect with members of the public? As technology continues to change, will interest groups need to rethink their ad campaigns. Why or why not?

Expert Testimony Before Legislature

Representatives of four different interest groups (the American Civil Liberties Union, the Arab American Institute, the Rights Working Group, and the Sikh Coalition) testified on Capitol Hill during a January 2010 briefing on the subject of racial profiling at airports and American security. Testimony before Congress increases visibility and public awareness of a group's mission.

Critical Thinking Questions

What if some groups can't afford to pay for experts to travel to Washington to testify before Congress? Which interest groups have been most successful in lobbying to change laws?

E-mail/Text Alerts

NOW (National Organization for Women) used cell phones and the Internet to mobilize a group of supporters from many states in opposition to the closing of a family reproductive health clinic in Charlotte, North Carolina.

Critical Thinking Questions

Are e-mail or text alerts an effective way to get young people involved with events sponsored by interest groups? What other ways can technology be used to encourage grassroots activism?

Voter Education/Registration Drives

LULAC (League of United Latin American Citizens) conducts voter education campaigns (informing first-time voters of their rights) and voter registration drives in many areas with low voter turnout.

Critical Thinking Questions

How important is it that interest groups work to inform voters of their rights? Is it possible that new voters could be exploited by interest groups?

Interest groups tend to be viewed with suspicion by a large percentage of the American public. However, interest groups perform many positive functions in the United States. One important role that interest groups perform is to organize like-minded individuals to become active in politics. Interest groups can promote political involvement both by mobilizing their own memberships and by mobilizing their opposition.
—*On the whole, do you think interest groups are positive vehicles for political participation, or do they tend to have a negative, potentially corrupting, impact on politics? Why?*

Review of Key Objectives

Activism and Protest in the United States

12.1 Illustrate how beliefs in collective action, self-government, and citizen action laid the foundation for activism and protest in the United States.

(pages 364–365)

From the earliest days of our republic, individuals treasured the notion of collective action. Alexis de Tocqueville characterized our country as a "nation of joiners"—a characterization that is still true today. Early successes with collective action and self-government set the stage for today's commitment. Organized interests provide a safety valve, especially in times of great social, economic, political, and cultural upheaval and change. In their absence, more violent forms of expression might be employed.

KEY TERM

Egalitarianism 365

CRITICAL THINKING QUESTIONS

1. Do you think collective action is more important today than in the past? Why or why not?
2. Do you think people still believe that we have a "right to revolt" if we disagree with the government? When, if ever, and under what circumstances do we lose this right?

INTERNET RESOURCES

Democracy Matters, a national student organization with a focus on campaign finance reform, is found at http://www.democracymatters.org

Rock the Vote is a nonprofit, nonpartisan organization designed to mobilize and engage young people to vote and become involved in the political process found at http://www.rockthevote.org

ADDITIONAL READING

Baumgardner, Jennifer, and Amy Richards. *Grassroots: A Field Guide for Feminist Activism.* New York: Farrar, Straus and Giroux, 2005.

Cobb, Daniel. *Native Activism in Cold War America: The Struggle for Sovereignty.* Lawrence: University Press of Kansas, 2008.

Milner, Henry. *Civic Literacy: How Informed Citizens Make Democracy Work.* Hanover, NH: University Press of New England, 2002.

Influencing Government Through Mobilization and Participation

12.2 Explain the key factors that facilitate political protest and activism.

(pages 366–367)

Constitutional protections are very important in allowing citizens to petition their government and pursue collective action. The constitutional guarantees of speech, religion, press, and assembly permit them to unite to petition the government about their concerns. These freedoms allow mass movements to develop, often changing both country and culture. Without these protections, we would have great difficulties working with like-minded individuals and influencing our society.

CRITICAL THINKING QUESTIONS

1. Do you think that constitutional protections should be suspended during times of war or conflict? Which elements of the Bill of Rights do you believe should be most guarded and why?
2. Do you think that in the post–9/11 era most people believe interrogation of criminals (especially suspected terrorists) ought to be limited? Do you think they might change their minds if reliable information suggested that the individual had direct knowledge of a terrorist plot?

INTERNET RESOURCES

A nonprofit organization that works to strengthen civic knowledge and foster civic values among young people, Bill of Rights Institute: can be located at http://billofrightsinstitute.org

Constitution Society is a nonprofit international organization that provides online resources about Constitutional history, law, and governmanet (http://constitution.org)

ADDITIONAL READING

Ackerman, Bruce. *Before the Next Attack: Preserving Civil Liberties in an Age of Terrorism.* New Haven: Yale University Press, 2007.

Snow, Nancy. *Information War: American Propaganda, Free Speech, and Opinion Control Since 9/11.* New York: Seven Stories Press, 2003.

Functions and Types of Interest Groups

12.3 Identify four different types of interest groups, and explain the function of interest groups in a democracy.

(pages 368–371)

Interest groups provide tools for participation, educate the public and governmental officials and influence policymaking and governmental action. Interest groups consist of economic groups (such as the Chamber of Commerce), public interest groups (including AARP), think tanks (such as the conservative Heritage Foundation and the liberal Brookings Institution), and governmental units (such as the U.S. Conference of Mayors).

KEY TERMS

Interest Group 368
Single-Issue Interest Group 368
Multi-Issue Interest Group 368
Professional Association 370
Public Interest Group 370
Think Tank 370
Cleavage 370
Disturbance Theory 370

CRITICAL THINKING QUESTIONS

1. Do organized interest groups represent all people? If they do not, does this matter?
2. Why are there so many interest groups in the United States?

INTERNET RESOURCES

Thousands of interest groups exist in the United States. Here is a brief sample of a variety.

Center for Responsive Politics: http://www.opensecrets.org

Coalition to Stop Gun Violence: http://www.csgv.org

Gun Owners of America: http://www.gunowners.org

National Association for the Advancement of Colored People: http://www.naacp.org

National Conference of State Legislatures: http://www.ncsl.org/

U.S. Chamber of Commerce: http://www.uschamber.com

ADDITIONAL READING

Berry, Jeffrey, and Clyde Wilcox. *Interest Group Society,* 5th ed. New York: Longman, 2009.

Cigler, Allan J., and Burdett A. Loomis (eds.). *Interest Group Politics,* 7th ed. Washington, DC: CQ Press, 2007.

Interest Group Mobilization

12.4 Show how interest groups mobilize their memberships in the face of organizational barriers.

(pages 372–375)

The many costs associated with forming and maintaining organized groups include money, time, and overcoming the free-rider and political efficacy problems. To overcome these barriers, interest groups use a variety of tactics, from offering benefits—material, solidary, and purposive—to providing inducements. Leadership is also often a very important factor in group formation, maintenance, and success.

KEY TERMS

Free-Rider Problem 372
Public Goods (Collective Goods) 372
Selective Benefits 373
Material Benefits 373
Solidary Benefits 373
Purposive Benefits 373
Patrons 373

CRITICAL THINKING QUESTIONS

1. What are the barriers to organizing interest groups? How do interest groups overcome these barriers?
2. Which type of benefit—material, purposive, or solidary—is most attractive to new members? How do groups that cannot provide material incentives promote other benefits of membership to make themselves more attractive to new members?

INTERNET RESOURCES

For more information about regional enforcement of environmental law see Commission for Environmental Cooperation (CEC) at http://cec.org

For more information about an environmental group with an international focus visit Greenpeace at http://www.greenpeace.org/usa/

The most active defender of Second Amendments rights is widely recognized to be the National Rifle Association (NRA). For more information visit: http://nra.org

ADDITIONAL READING

Strolovitch, Dara Z. *Affirmative Advocacy: Race, Class, and Gender in Interest Group Politics.* Chicago: University of Chicago Press, 2007.

Inside and Outside Lobbying

12.5 Describe how interest groups appeal to public officials and the public to gain support for their causes.

(pages 376–379)

Trying to gain access to present their positions, interest groups lobby directly by contacting officials and their staffs, testifying at congressional hearings, and building long-term relationships with policymakers. Outside lobbying involves trying to influence the government by mobilizing public support. Grassroots mobilization is one highly effective tactic of outside lobbying. Groups rely on traditional tactics such as direct contact and mail but are increasingly using newer techniques such as blogs and social networking sites to reach the general public.

KEY TERMS

Inside Lobbying 376
Gaining Access 376
Outside Lobbying (Grassroots Lobbying) 376
Direct Contact 378
Direct Mail 378
Advertorials 378
Social Networking Sites 378

CRITICAL THINKING QUESTIONS

1. Do you think inside lobbying corrupts politics, or does it provide much needed information to governmental officials?
2. What is the difference between outside and inside lobbying? Why and how is each used? To which practices do you think the public most objects? Why?

INTERNET RESOURCES

Students for a Democratic Society is a student-activist movement with roots going back to the early 1960s. http:// www.studentsforademocraticsociety.org/

The Center for Media and Democracy is a non-profit organization dedicated to investigation reporting. http://www.prwatch.org

For assistance searching blogs see Blog Search at http://www.blogsearch.google.com

ADDITIONAL READING

Baumgartner, Frank R., Jeffrey M. Berry, Marie Hojnacki, David C. Kimball, and Beth L. Leech. *Lobbying and Policy Change: Who Wins, Who Loses, and Why.* Chicago: University of Chicago Press, 2009.

DeKieffer, Donald E. *The Citizen's Guide to Lobbying Congress.* Chicago: Review Press, 2007.

Nownes, Anthony J. *Total Lobbying: What Lobbyists Want (and How They Try to Get It).* New York: Cambridge University Press, 2006.

The Influence of Interest Groups

12.6 Assess the ways interest groups positively and negatively impact our society.

(pages 380–381)

Debate exists over the actual influence of interest groups in the United States; however, the consensus among the public is that interest groups are very powerful—perhaps too powerful—relative to the influence of voters and other less organized citizens. The uneven growth pattern, with some groups increasing at much faster rates than others, has led some people to worry about potential bias in the articulation of the needs of some over the desires of individuals and groups with less representation. Despite the negative perceptions associated with interest groups, it is important to remember that they allow for like-minded citizens to join together to participate in politics and to make their voices heard.

CRITICAL THINKING QUESTIONS

1. Do you think that interest groups with a lot of material resources are too influential? Do resources always translate into influence and power?
2. On the whole, do you think that interest groups advance or pervert democracy? Why?

INTERNET RESOURCES

For extensive investigative journalism on current controversies visit Center for Public Integrity at http://www.publicintegrity.org

To register to vote online to find out more information about MTV's efforts to mobilize the youth vote, visit Rock the Vote at http://www.rockthevote.org

ADDITIONAL READING

Barbour, Christine, and Gerald C. Wright, with Matthew J. Steb and Michael R. Wolf. *Keeping the Republic: Power and Citizenship in American Politics,* 4th ed. Washington, DC: CQ Press, 2008.

Levine, Bertram J. *The Art of Lobbying: Building Trust and Selling Policy.* Washington, DC: CQ Press, 2009.

Richan, Willard C. *Lobbying for Social Change,* 3rd ed. Binghamton, NY: Haworth Press, 2006.

Chapter Review Test Your Knowledge

1. A citizen's participation in an organized interest group is good for democracy, because it cultivates
  a. self-discipline, patience, and partisan fervor.
  b. wisdom, patriotism, and generosity.
  c. political connections, historical perspective, and political endurance.
  d. tolerance, political efficacy, and political trust.

2. One effect of the American Revolution was that resorting to mobs and rioting became an expected form of expression in the new nation.
  a. true   **b.** false

2. Grassroots mobilization via the Web is particularly effective with
  a. older people who have limited incomes.
  b. people who are not already sympathetic to that particular cause.
  c. young, affluent, and well-educated people.
  d. migrant workers.

3. What is a major reason that interest groups need money?
  a. to pay congressional representatives to legislate in their favor
  b. to run advertisements that publicize their wealth and power over the government
  c. to raise additional money
  d. to testify before congressional committees

4. Being active in an interest group constitutes
  a. a shortcut around the democratic process.
  b. a legitimate form of political participation.
  c. a type of elite mobilization.
  d. a less hopeful means of participation—voting is better.

5. Interest groups contribute to the governing process by
  a. staffing polling agencies.
  b. monitoring government programs.
  c. representing the concerns of ordinary Americans.
  d. b and c

7. Citizens of France and the United Kingdom—countries with more centralized governments than our own—do not join interest groups as often as Americans, because their governmental structure provides fewer opportunities for citizen-based participation.
  a. true   **b.** false

8. Which kind of interest group is the American Bar Association?
  a. a public interest group
  b. a governmental unit
  c. a think tank
  d. an economic group

9. What are think tanks?
  a. Nonpolitical, unbiased research institutions
  b. public research institutions funded with federal tax dollars

  c. nonprofit public interest groups often operating from a partisan point of view
  d. public interest groups devoted to educational issues

10. Interest groups are inherently self-interested, nondemocratic organizations that tend to pollute the electoral system.
  a. true
  b. false

11. Most leaders of interest groups in this country
  a. come from the ranks of the socioeconomic elite.
  b. are Democrats.
  c. are middle class.
  d. are lawyers.

12. A friend refuses to join your fledgling interest group working to legalize the medical use of marijuana. The friend says, "The War on Drugs mentality is too powerful in this country." What barrier to interest group formation is in evidence here?
  a. the free-rider problem
  b. the easy-rider problem
  c. the cost problem
  d. the absence of a sense of political efficacy

13. When a lobbyist for the American Medical Association (AMA) takes a congressional staff member out to lunch to discusses the limitations of HMOs, that's an example of
  a. outside lobbying.
  b. inside lobbying.
  c. indirect lobbying.
  d. illegal lobbying.

14. TV ads funded by interest groups and designed to sway public opinion are often called
  a. infomercials.
  b. paid political announcements.
  c. advertorials.
  d. public service announcements.

15. Interest groups use the Web to recruit volunteers, raise funds, conduct research, and educate the public.
  a. true
  b. false

16. One way that the Christian Coalition participates in elections is by
  a. distributing information in churches about the voting records of candidates, noting who voted "correctly" and who did not.
  b. sponsoring debates among candidates for Congress.
  c. organizing get-out-the-vote drives on college campuses across the country.
  d. supporting candidates with a pro–labor union voting record.

17. Money is often the key predictor of who wins and loses in American politics.
  a. true
  b. false

18. Of Americans over the age of 18, approximately how many belong to at least one politically active organization?

   a. 15 percent   **c.** 45 percent

   b. 25 percent   **d.** 65 percent

19. In the minds of many Americans, which of the following professions is most analogous to that of the lobbyist?

   a. gambler   **c.** thief

   b. pimp   **d.** forger

20. Gun control advocates in this country

   a. represent a minority viewpoint.

   b. have outspent their political opponents and triumphed legislatively.

   c. represent a majority viewpoint but have spent far less than their opponents.

   d. have no chance of succeeding politically.

PEARSON mypoliscilab Exercises

Apply what you learned in this chapter on **MyPoliSciLab**.

Read on **mypoliscilab.com**

   eText: Chapter 12

Study and **Review** on **mypoliscilab.com**

   Pre-Test
   Post-Test
   Chapter Exam
   Flashcards

Watch on **mypoliscilab.com**

   Video: Chicago Worker Protest
   Video: L. A. Riots: 15 Years Later
   Video: Murtha and the PMA Lobbyists
   Video: American Cancer Society Recommendation

Explore on **mypoliscilab.com**

   Simulation: You Are the Leader of Concerned Citizens for World Justice
   Simulation: You Are a Lobbyist
   Comparative: Comparing Political Landscapes
   Comparative: Comparing Interest Groups
   Timeline: Interest Groups and Campaign Finance

Elections and Political Parties in America

KEY OBJECTIVES

After completing this chapter, you should be prepared to:

13.1 Describe the legal challenges that have broadened the democratic character of elections in America.

13.2 Evaluate electoral engagement in America, particularly as it relates to young citizens.

13.3 Identify the functions served by political parties in a democracy, and explain how they help organize the governmental process.

13.4 Trace the evolution of political parties in the United States.

13.5 Outline the process by which party nominees are chosen to run in the general election.

13.6 Explain the process by which we select the president of the United States.

13.7 Assess the critical role that money plays in the election process.

Special elections for vacant U.S. House and Senate seats rarely change the partisan balance in Washington. But in January 2010, the voters of Massachusetts did just that in a special election to fill the U.S. Senate seat vacated after the death of Democrat Edward Kennedy. The seat represented the all important sixtieth vote for the Democrats, the number needed to end filibusters by Republicans. If the Republicans were able to pickup just one more seat, they could grind the new president's agenda to a halt.

The contest between Democrat Martha Coakley, state attorney general, and Republican Scott Brown, a state senator, drew little national attention at first because most assumed it would be an easy win for Coakley. Massachusetts was surely a "blue" state, having gone to the Democratic candidate in all but four presidential elections since 1928. Barack Obama had won the state a year earlier with a whopping 62 percent, and it was, after all, "Kennedy's seat."

But polling data hinted at voter frustrations with business-as-usual in Washington and with Coakley's candidacy. Probably assuming her victory would be easily won, Coakley did not campaign hard, preferring to use massive television buys and robo telephone calls. She was lackluster on the stump and seemed unable to

> **Do elections express the hopes and concerns of average Americans?**

connect with blue collar voters. And then three days before the election, she committed a cardinal sin in "Red Sox Nation" by calling past Red Sox pitching great Curt Schilling a Yankee fan.

Brown, for his part, was much better on the campaign trail. Traveling from town to town in his old GMC pickup truck, Brown told ever-growing crowds that it was not Ted Kennedy's seat, but rather the people's seat. He campaigned long and hard, often in cold, rotten weather. He tapped into growing populist anger at perceived "Wall Street give-aways" and burgeoning federal deficits. Money from out-of-state conservative groups and Tea Party activists poured in.

As poll numbers indicated a close election, prominent figures from both parties, including President Obama, rushed to the state. All understood what hung in the balance. Democrats could not lose the seat . . . but they did. Brown netted 52 percent of the vote. One special election had shifted the balance of power in the Senate.

After the election, Democrats shook their heads in disbelief. What had happened? Why had they taken the race for granted, and why had they nominated such a lackluster candidate? One final bit of data jolted the Democratic Party. Turnout for those under 30 was a scant 15 percent. The youth vote, so important in Barack Obama's victory one year earlier, had evaporated.

Resource Center
• Glossary
• Vocabulary Example
• Connect the Link

■ **Fourteenth Amendment (1868):** Establishes that each state must guarantee equal protection of the laws to its citizens.

SIGNIFICANCE: *This change helped protect individual liberties from the infringement of states and the national government.*

■ **Fifteenth Amendment (1870):** Guarantees the right to vote shall not be denied to anyone on the basis of race.

SIGNIFICANCE: *This change began the voting enfranchisement of African Americans into the election process.*

Expansion of the Electorate and Other Legal Issues

13.1 Describe the legal challenges that have broadened the democratic character of elections in America.

(pages 392–393)

For elections to be a viable avenue for change, two conditions must be present. First, a citizens must believe that their efforts matter. Second, there must be laws affording all citizens the right to participate and a level playing field for candidates. Our system has taken many steps to broaden the right to vote including constitutional amendments and voting and legislative acts to challenge discriminatory practices.

Constitutional Amendments

The first federal constitutional changes that broadened the scope of the electorate were the Fourteenth and Fifteenth Amendments. The first clause of the **Fourteenth Amendment**■, ratified in 1868, guaranteed citizenship and the rights of citizenship to all persons born or naturalized in the United States. The second clause gave the states an incentive to grant minority citizens the right to vote, essentially basing representation in both Congress and the Electoral College on the percentage of male citizens over age 21 who could vote.[1] In 1870, the **Fifteenth Amendment**■ was adopted, stating (in its entirety) that "the right of citizens of the United States to vote shall not be denied or abridged by the United States or by any State on account of race, color, or previous condition of servitude."

The **Nineteenth Amendment**■ enacted in 1920, which gave the vote to women, was the product of a grassroots movement that began in 1848. Frontier life also helped fuel the movement for women's voting rights; on the frontier, women were considered equal partners in the family's fight for survival. The Nineteenth Amendment initiated the most sweeping enlargement of the American electorate in a single act.

The **Twenty-Fourth Amendment**■ outlawed the poll tax in 1964. A fee imposed on voters, the poll tax had been one of the barriers to African American voting in the South.

The **Twenty-Sixth Amendment**■, giving 18-year-old citizens the right to vote, was the most recent change to extend the franchise. By the late 1960s, a growing proportion of Americans were in their late teens and had proved that they could be effective in promoting change. Images of young men going off to die in the Vietnam War but not being able to vote gave the movement its biting edge. The amendment passed with little objection, and the state legislatures ratified it in only three and a half months.[2]

PATHWAYS of change from around the world

Can elections change the leadership in a corrupt political system? The president of Iran in 2009 was Mahmoud Ahmadinejad, an outspoken critic of western governments, especially the United States. Internally, he was beloved by hardline fundamentalists but scorned by secular reformers. With an election at hand, many of the reformers saw the opportunity to oust Ahmadinejad and move their country in a more modern direction. The reform movement candidate was Mir Hossein Mousavi Khameneh; he had served as prime minister of Iran from 1981 to 1989.

After several months of hard campaigning, including three nationally televised debates and some violence, Iranians went to the polls on June 12, 2009. Turnout was unexpectedly high, and polls were forced to stayed open until midnight. Yet, contrary to numerous last-minute surveys that suggested a very tight race, when the government announced the results Ahmadinejad was declared the clear winner with some 63 percent of the vote. As numerous irregularities came to light many concluded that the election was fixed. Soon people were rallying and protesting in the streets. Riot police with tear gas and live ammunition dispelled the crowds. Hundreds were arrested and dozens killed. Ahmadinejad was sworn into office, but the fissure had widened.

Voting and Legislative Acts

Article I of the Constitution says, in essence, that as long as Congress remains silent, voting regulations and requirements are left to the states. There were many state-level restrictions on voting in the early days of the Republic. Some states imposed religious qualifications, and most states had property ownership and tax-paying requirements.[3]

CHALLENGING DISCRIMINATORY PRACTICES Well into the twentieth century, southern states used their power to regulate elections to keep African Americans from the polls. Imposing a variety of restrictions—literacy tests, poll taxes, complicated registration and residency requirements, and the infamous "grandfather clause," which exempted a voter from all these requirements if his (free white) grandfather had voted before 1860—white-ruled southern states managed to disfranchise most blacks.

A favorite exclusionary tool was the white primary. Southern election laws defined political parties as private organizations, with the right to decide their own membership. Thus, while blacks might enjoy the right to vote in the general election, they could not vote in the only election that really counted, the Democratic primary.[4] This practice remained in effect until the Supreme Court ruled in *Smith* v. *Allwright* (1944) that primaries were part of the electoral system, and therefore the exclusion of blacks violated the Fifteenth Amendment.

SIGNIFICANCE:
*Most college students
may participate in
elections today because
of this change.*

■ **Nineteenth
Amendment (1920):**
Granted women the
right to vote.

SIGNIFICANCE: *This
change shows how the grassroots
mobilization pathway can bring
about change.*

■ **Twenty-Fourth
Amendment (1964):**
Eliminated the poll tax.

SIGNIFICANCE: *Prior
to this change, states could
limit poor people and African
Americans from voting.*

■ **Twenty-Sixth
Amendment (1971):**
Granted 18-year-old
citizens the right to vote.

CIVIL RIGHTS AND THE VOTING RIGHTS ACT The
Civil Rights Act of 1957 created the U.S. Civil Rights
Commission to investigate voting rights violations and to suggest
remedies. The most significant change that directly affected elections, however, came with the **Voting Rights Act of 1965.** This
law provided that for any congressional district in which fewer
than 50 percent of adults went to the polls, a five-year "emergency state" would be triggered. Affected districts could change
their election regulations only with the approval of the civil
rights division of the Justice Department. In addition, the Justice
Department could now send election examiners into the states
to register voters and observe elections. Although the act did not
end discrimination, it became the most important tool in
protecting the right to vote.[5] Election data reflect the act's
importance: Overall, in 11 southern states in 1960, a meager
29.7 percent of adult African Americans were registered to
vote. By the end of the decade, this figure had more than doubled, to 63.4 percent.[6]

RESIDENCY AND REGISTRATION LAWS Reforms
during the Progressive Era were designed to clean up the all-too-
common practice of fraudulent voting in general elections. Party
bosses, for example, might pay people to travel around the city
voting in numerous polling places. Frequently, dead or nonexistent voters were discovered to have cast ballots. **Residency and
registration laws** were the solution. Residency laws stipulate
that a person can vote in a community only if that person has
been a resident for a prescribed period. (The length of time

varies from state to state, but the Voting Rights Act of 1970
established a maximum of 30 days.) In some states, a resident can
register up to and including election day, but in most states, there
is a stipulated, pre-election day cutoff.

The idea behind these laws was to reduce corruption, but
in recent years they have become controversial, and some people have even suggested that they are the main reason why
many Americans do not vote. In their provocatively titled book
*Why Americans Still Don't Vote: And Why Politicians Want It That
Way,* Frances Fox Piven and Richard Cloward argue these laws
have always been about keeping certain types of voters out of
the process.[7] Perhaps trying to find a middle ground, Congress
in 1993 required states to allow citizens to register to vote at
numerous public facilities used by low-income people, such as
state motor vehicle, welfare, and employment offices. This so-
called **motor voter law** also stipulated that states must permit
mail-in registration.

HELP AMERICA VOTE ACT In the wake of the confusion surrounding the 2000 presidential election, in 2002 Congress passed the **Help America Vote Act.** This measure was
designed to create a more uniform voting system, replacing
the haphazard, state-by-state process that had existed for two
centuries. The act set federal standards for all voting systems
throughout the United States, provided $325 million to up-
date voting systems, required states to create registered voter
databases, and called for voter education and poll worker
training.

Expansion of the Electorate and Other Legal Issues

13.1 Describe the legal challenges that have broadened the democratic character of elections in America.

PRACTICE QUIZ: UNDERSTAND AND APPLY

1. The only way the federal government can insert itself
   into the election process is through a constitutional
   amendment.
   a. true   b. false

2. Which of the following have been used by states to
   limit the number of residents, often minority
   residents, from voting?
   a. poll taxes   c. residency requirements
   b. literacy tests   d. all of the above

3. Women were granted the right to vote with passage
   of the
   a. Fifteenth Amendment
   b. Nineteenth Amendment
   c. Twenty-Fourth Amendment
   d. Twenty-Sixth Amendment

ANALYZE

1. Why were the framers willing to give states some deference when it came to regulating the conduct of
   elections?

2. What do you suppose has been the most frequent
   pathway of change for groups seeking to advance
   voting rights? Why?

**IDENTIFY THE CONCEPT THAT
DOESN'T BELONG**

a. Registration requirements
b. Acts of Congress
c. Constitutional amendments
d. Lower voting age requirements
e. High profile court cases

13.1

Resource Center
• Glossary
• Vocabulary Example
• Connect the Link

■ **Electoral Behavior:** Any activity broadly linked to the outcome of a political campaign.

EXAMPLE *Making an online donation to a candidate or attending a rally are forms of electoral behavior.*

Individual Participation in Elections

13.2 Evaluate electoral engagement in America, particularly as it relates to young citizens.

(pages 394–397)

There are many ways for citizens to become involved in campaigns and elections. Many citizens are politically active but do not vote, and for some Americans, not voting is either a statement of contentment or a form of political protest. Simply talking about different candidates with friends and family, for example, or reading news stories or watching television programs about election happenings are also types of electoral participation. Any action that is broadly linked to the conduct or outcome of an election can be considered **electoral behavior**■.

Another way to think about forms of political participation is to consider the difference between individual and collective participation. Individual participation occurs when a citizen engages in activity aimed at changing public policy without interacting with other citizens. Examples include voting, giving money to a candidate or party, watching political news on television or online, or writing to a candidate or an office holder. Collective participation occurs when a citizen takes action in collaboration with other like-minded citizens. Examples would be attending a rally, discussing politics with friends and family, working at a party or candidate's headquarters, blogging about a political topic, or attending the local meeting of a political party (see Figure 13.1). While individual participation clearly occurs more often, many of the most significant changes in public policy, such as worker rights, civil rights, and environmental legislation, stemmed from collective action.

Voter Turnout

In thinking about levels of political participation in any democratic system, we often look at **turnout**■—an easily quantifiable number based on the number of citizens who actually vote on election day divided by the total number of citizens who are legally qualified to vote in that election. If 1 million residents are allowed to vote but only 600,000 do so, turnout is 0.6, or 60 percent.

There was little interest in federal elections during the early days of our republic. Election turnout for presidential elections, measured by the percentage of eligible (male) voters, reached only into the teens until 1800, when it jumped to 31 percent. After what Andrew Jackson called the "corrupt bargain" in the election of 1824, political participation shot up dramatically: In 1828, some 57 percent of eligible voters went to

FIGURE 13.1 ■ **Forms of Electoral Participation**
As this figure suggests, there are many ways individuals can be active in electoral politics. —*What was it about the 2004 and 2008 elections that seemed to bring more Americans into the process?*

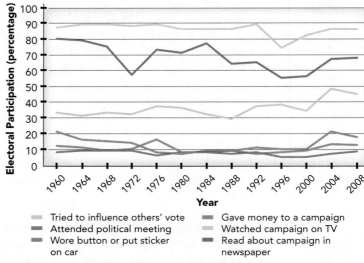

Legend:
- Tried to influence others' vote
- Attended political meeting
- Wore button or put sticker on car
- Gave money to a campaign
- Watched campaign on TV
- Read about campaign in newspaper

SOURCE: American National Election Studies. Graphs 6B and 6D http://www.electionstudies.org/nesguide/gd-index.htm#6. Reprinted with permission.

the polls, and by the 1860s, the voting rate had leveled off hovering around 80 percent for the rest of the nineteenth century.

In the early twentieth century, however, election day turnouts began to slip. There were a number of likely causes. For one, there was a flood of immigration, causing a population boom in urban areas. Although these new citizens would soon be assimilated into the political process, many of them did not immediately vote. Second, registration laws, residency requirements, and other restrictions during the Progressive Era made it harder for people in the lower socioeconomic class to participate in elections. Finally, the Nineteenth Amendment to the Constitution in 1920 granted women the right to vote, but at first, women were slow to exercise that right.

When Vice President Richard M. Nixon and an upstart senator from Massachusetts by the name of John F. Kennedy squared off in the presidential election in 1960, some 61 percent of the electorate turned out to vote (see Figure 13.2). In the decades since, that figure has dropped more or less steadily. From 1980 until 2000, only about half of eligible voters turned out for presidential elections. Even worse is the participation in midterm congressional elections—the elections between presidential contest years: 2002, 2006, 2010, and so forth.

However, in 2008, roughly 62 percent of eligible voters went to the polls. This figure surpassed all presidential turnout levels since the 1960s. The greatest increases in turnout came

■ **Turnout:** The percentage of citizens legally eligible to vote in an election who actually vote in that election. **EXAMPLE** *In the past three presidential elections, turnout was slightly above 50 percent.*

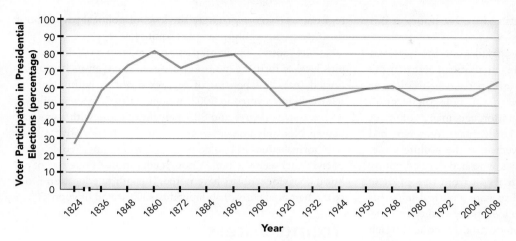

FIGURE 13.2 ■ **Participation in Presidential Elections**

Most Americans believe we are one of the most democratic nations on earth. While that may be true in some respects, our participation in electoral politics is less than stellar. —*What might explain the various fluctuations in turnout? Do you think the 2008 election marked a long-term reversal of the downward trend, or was it simply an exception?*

from less affluent citizens, young voters, African Americans, and Hispanic Americans. Geographically, the largest increases in turnout were seen in the South and Rocky Mountain states. Dramatic candidates, a lengthy primary campaign, crosscutting issues, and massive get-out-the-vote efforts proved to be a "perfect storm" for voter mobilization in 2008.

Explaining Modest Turnout

One of the great questions of our day is the cause—or causes—of modest electoral participation. Why was turnout generally higher 50 years ago, even though more Americans attend college, registration barriers have been all but eliminated, and the civil rights movement opened the door to far greater involvement by African Americans and other previously oppressed groups of citizens? With so many positive changes, why would levels of electoral participation be so modest?

There is no clear answer, but theories abound (see Figure 13.3). One possibility is attitudinal change. Increased cynicism, distrust, and alienation are often identified as the root of the problem. Survey data seem to support the claim that negative attitudes about politics have increased over the decades. For instance, in the mid-1950s, about 75 percent of Americans might have been described as trusting their government to "do what is right all or at least most of the time." This number plummeted to just over 20 percent by the early 1990s. About 22 percent of Americans in the 1950s thought "quite a few" politicians were crooked. That number jumped to 50 percent in the mid-1990s and today stands at about 35 percent. Many other indicators suggest that Americans are less confident about government and politics than in previous times.[8]

Closely related to this perspective is what we might call the lifestyle-change theory. According to this hypothesis, life today is simply busier than in the past and offers more distractions. According to the sociologist Robert Putnam, author of the widely discussed book *Bowling Alone: The*

FIGURE 13.3 ■ **Why People Don't Vote**

One way to read this figure is to consider the reasons for not voting, and explore changes that might help. For instance, if "too busy" explains about 20 percent of why people do not vote, perhaps we should consider making election day a national holiday. Another way to explore the data is with a keen eye toward differences in demographic groups. —*Why would over twice as many respondents with less than a high school degree use "illness and disability" as an excuse for not voting, compared to those with some college? Why are there so many registration problems for Hispanic Americans?*

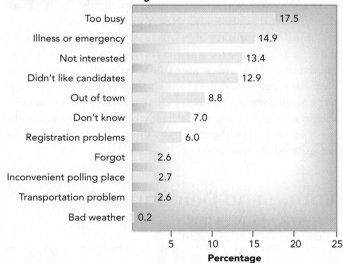

Reasons Given for Not Voting

Too busy	17.5
Illness or emergency	14.9
Not interested	13.4
Didn't like candidates	12.9
Out of town	8.8
Don't know	7.0
Registration problems	6.0
Forgot	2.6
Inconvenient polling place	2.7
Transportation problem	2.6
Bad weather	0.2

Percentage

SOURCE: U.S. Census Bureau Current Population Survey, May 2010.

Collapse and Revival of American Community, "I don't have enough time" and "I'm too busy" are the most often heard excuses for social disengagement.[9] We are more distracted by television, new technologies, and social network sites today then in the past, and we have to spend too many hours commuting long distances or putting in extra hours at our jobs to be heavily involved in politics.

However, although changes in attitudes and lifestyles may account for part of the decline, many analysts suggest that the deepest root lies elsewhere. Local-level party organizations—which historically pushed citizens to the polls on election day—seem to be withering. A generation ago, many volunteer party workers kept track of which known party members had voted and which had not yet showed up at the polling place. By dinner time on election day, those who had delayed voting would get a telephone call or even a visit from one of these workers and be "gently" reminded to vote. Political scientists have tested the relationship between local party vitality and levels of turnout, and the data are convincing: Turnout is much higher in communities that still have strong local parties.[10] But fewer and fewer communities have such organizations.

The nature of campaigns is also cited as a reason for voter alienation. Campaigns, especially for the presidency, have become much longer and more negative, conceivably leading to voter burnout. However, the evidence is not conclusive. Although some studies have found that negative ads do turn voters off, roughly an equal number of other studies have found that turnout actually increases in these negatively charged races.[11] One impressive study suggests that some voters—the less partisan ones—are turned off when the campaign gets nasty but that negative campaigning activates the most partisan voters.[12] Still another line of research suggests that the effects of negative ads depend on the voter's local political culture.[13] A citizen in Provo, Utah, might respond differently to attack ads than, say, a voter in Brooklyn, New York.

Finally, there is the role of the news media. Some social scientists have suggested that the recent turn toward what one scholar has called "attack journalism" or media "feeding frenzies" has repelled voters.[14] In the past, journalists and average citizens alike drew a line between a politician's public and private lives. Probably due to the highly competitive nature of the news business, anything that draws the public's attention seems fair game to the media today.

Voting and Demographic Characteristics

Another closely related question is why certain groups of Americans participate less than others. Here, too, scholarly findings are inconclusive. One perspective centers on "community connectedness." This theory states that the more connected you are to your community, the more likely you are to vote. Demographic data suggest that poor people, for example, move more often than the affluent do, and they are certainly much less likely to own a home. Every time you change your permanent address, of course, you also need to change your voter

registration. Not surprisingly, the level of political participation for these highly mobile people is quite low.

The "costs" of political participation seem to decline as people's level of formal education increases. The Census Bureau reported that 39.4 percent of registered voters without a high school diploma voted in 2008, as opposed to 77 percent of those with a college degree and 82.7 percent of those with a graduate degree. Not only does awareness of the mechanics of voting rise with formal education, so do the benefits of voting. People's sense of civic duty seems to build through education. As one pair of political behavior scholars have noted, "Length of education is one of the best predictors of an individual's likelihood of voting."[15]

Young Voters

Finally, there is the issue of age. Age has always been an excellent predictor of who participates in elections. Simply stated, young Americans have always voted at lower rates than older Americans have. This group has less *completed* education, is less affluent, and has much less likelihood of owning a home—all factors that seem related to participation. Younger citizens are also much more mobile, and they often get tripped up by residency requirements and voter registration issues. Yet survey data also suggest that young Americans are eager to contribute to the betterment of society; their rate of volunteering is comparable to the rates of other age groups, as can be seen in Figure 13.4.

FIGURE 13.4 ▪ Volunteerism by Age Group
Many older Americans believe that youngsters are apathetic, indifferent, and lazy. Yet, as this figure illustrates this is not true. —*Why do you suppose young citizens are so ready to become engaged in numerous community programs and organizations but at the same time refrain from politics? What can be done to convince younger generations to join the political fray?*

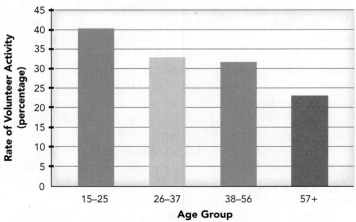

SOURCE: Mark Hugo Lopez, "Volunteering Among Young People," Center for Information and Research on Civic Learning and Engagement. Accessed at http://www.civicyouth.org/PopUps/FactSheets/FS_Volunteering2.pdf, 2004. Reprinted by permission of CIRCLE, School of Public Affairs, University of Maryland.

TABLE 13.1	Percentage of Turnout by Age Groups in 2000, 2004, and 2008 Elections

The dramatic increase in young voter turnout in 2004 and 2008 caught many by surprise. —*What do you think caused this change?*

	18–24	25–44	45–64	65 AND OVER	OVERALL TURNOUT
2000	32.3	49.8	64.1	67.6	51.3
2004	41.9	52.2	66.6	68.9	55.3
2008	48.5	59.9	69.5	70.1	62

SOURCE: U.S. Census Bureau. *Current Population Survey.* November 2008 and earlier reports. Released July 20, 2009.

But, this willingness to become involved does not always spread to political involvement.

Much to the surprise of scholars, pundits, and older Americans, youth voting made a dramatic turnaround in 2004, and 2008 continued the trend. As you can see in Table 13.1, voter turnout in 2004 increased among all Americans by about 4 percent, but the increase was greatest among the youngest voters. In 2008, young voters flocked to the polls; about 49 percent of those under 25 came out to vote for either John McCain or Barack Obama.

Why were so many more young voters flocking to the polls? There are a number of possible explanations. For one thing, the earlier decline in youth participation was so startling that many organizations and programs, such as MTV's Rock the Vote and Generation Engage were initiated to bring young people back to the polls. Several new elections pathway organizations also tried bringing voters to the polls, including Americans Coming Together and MoveOn.org. In addition, the intensity of the campaign and the weight of the issues, such as the state of the economy, climate change, the war in Iraq, gay marriage, the future of Social Security, and health care reform caught young voters' attention.

Unfortunately, there is growing evidence that young voters might once again be tuning out. Those under 30 made up 22 percent of the electorate in New Jersey in 2008—a percentage that dropped to just 8 percent in the 2009 gubernatorial election. In Virginia, it went from 21 percent in 2008, to 10 percent in 2009. As for the Massachusetts special election we noted at the start of the chapter, turnout for those *over* 30 was a healthy 56 percent, but for those *under* 30 it was a mere 15 percent. One columnist, writing for *Newsweek*, put it this way: "[T]here are probably more Yankees fans in Massachusetts than here are young people who voted in the Massachusetts Senate special election."[16] The article went on to note 2010 polling data indicating a 19 percentage point nation-wide drop in the number of young people interested in politics in just one year. Indeed, turnout for those under 30 dropped to just 20 percent in 2010, some three points less than the previous 2006 midterm election.

Individual Participation in Elections

13.2 Evaluate electoral engagement in America, particularly as it relates to young citizens.

PRACTICE QUIZ: UNDERSTAND AND APPLY

1. Attending a rally, discussing politics with friends and family, working at a party or candidate's headquarters, or attending the local meeting of a political party are all examples of
   a. individual participation.
   b. collective participation.
   c. positive campaigning.
   d. cohort campaigning.

2. Voter turnout was much stronger 50 years ago than it has been in modern times.
   a. true   b. false

3. Voter turnout declined in the 2008 election, probably due to the unpopularity of both candidates.
   a. true   b. false

ANALYZE

1. Many young Americans seem attracted to community service but less interested in political action. Can service substitute for politics? Are there problems with a generation removed from politics?

2. Make a case for individual participation being more useful than collective participation, and then argue the opposite case.

IDENTIFY THE CONCEPT THAT DOESN'T BELONG

a. Voting
b. Reading about politics
c. Attending rallies
d. Talking about politics with friends
e. Having faith in the electoral process

Resource Center
• Glossary
• Vocabulary Example
• Connect the Link

■ **Rational Party Model:** The goal is to win offices and to control the distribution of government jobs.

EXAMPLE: *Years ago, many local party "machines" were considered both pragmatic and rational.*

■ **Responsible Party Model:** The goal is to shape public policy.

EXAMPLE: *A local party organization that is dedicated to lowering taxes in its community reflects this model.*

Political Parties in America

13.3 Identify the functions served by political parties in a democracy, and explain how they help organize the governmental process.

(pages 398–401)

One of the great ironies of American politics is that the very forces the framers of our Constitution most feared, political parties, have proved to be the instruments that actually make elections work. One pair of scholars has called them the "institutions Americans love to hate."[17]

Party Functions

No single definition of political parties satisfies everyone. The principal differences focus on the goals of party activity. One definition, often called the **rational party model**■, maintains that parties are organizations that sponsor candidates for political office in hopes of controlling the apparatus of government. A second definition, the **responsible party model**■, holds that parties are organizations that run candidates to shape the outcomes of government—that is, to redirect public policy. Rational parties work to win elections in order to control government, whereas responsible parties work hard during elections in order to shape public policy.

With either approach, three factors distinguish political parties from other political organizations such as interest groups, labor unions, trade associations, and political action committees:[18]

1. Political parties run candidates under their own label; interest groups do not.
2. Political parties have a **platform**■—a broad range of concerns that they support; interest groups limit their efforts to a narrow range of topics.
3. Political parties are subject to numerous state and local laws. They have some characteristics of private institutions, but in other ways they are similar to public organizations. Scholars have thus dubbed them "quasi-public" institutions. Interest groups, on the other hand, are purely private and free of government regulations.

Just as there is disagreement over the precise definition of *party*, people disagree over what parties contribute to a democratic system. Scholars have suggested parties:

1. **Organize the election process:** By organizing primary elections, parties enable voters to narrow the pool of office seekers to party **nominees**■ and establish a platform of issues for their candidates.
2. **Facilitate voter choice:** Given that voters generally do not know everything or even very much about a candidate other than his or her party affiliation, parties help us cast an informed, rational vote. Without party labels, the voter would have to study each candidate's positions in detail.

Party nomination contests have always been contentious "family affairs," where candidates of the same party often slug it out for months, leveling serious assaults on each other's qualifications, character, and issue positions. By the end of the process (the national party nominating convention), the family feud is expected to be over. The convention is a time for the family—the party—to unite and celebrate the victor. (Left) President-elect Obama and Senator Biden appearing at the Democratic national convention with family members. (Right) Senator McCain and Governor Palin appearing at the Republican national convention with family members. —*Do you think the current nomination system is the best way to pick presidential candidates? If not, what changes would you like to see?*

CONNECT THE LINK
(Chapter 6, pages 168–169)
What role do leaders play in organizing the legislative process?

■ **Platform:** The set of issues, principles, and goals that a party supports.

EXAMPLE: *Each of the national party committees created a platform at their conventions in the summer of 2008.*

■ **Nominees:** The individuals selected by a party to run for office under that party's label.

EXAMPLE: *John McCain became the Republican nominee for the presidency.*

3. **Recruit candidates:** To win elections, parties try to recruit good, qualified citizens to run for office and to screen out unqualified or corrupt candidates.

4. **Aid candidates:** Parties help candidates put their best foot forward to voters. In the past, party workers would spread the word about their candidates and work on their behalf leading up to election day. More recently, parties have begun providing many high-technology campaign services, such as polling, computerized targeting, and radio and television productions. Of course, fundraising has also become a huge part of how parties lend a hand.

5. **Organize a complex government:** The complexity of our government was by design, part of the checks and balances envisioned by the framers, but in many ways, this structure makes united action difficult. Parties counteract this effect by helping bring the many pieces of our system into united action.

6. **Educate citizens and promote involvement:** As each party works to build support for its candidates, the by-product is voter education. Not only do the voters learn more about the candidates because of party activities, they also learn more about government policies and the workings of our system. Also, parties work hard to bring citizens into the electoral process as volunteers, donors, and voters. Many studies have found that communities with strong political parties have higher levels of voting and other modes of political participation.[19]

7. **Ensure accountability:** Because our political system is so complex, it is difficult for voters to know who to give credit to when things go well, or who to blame when they go poorly. If most of the government is controlled by members of the same party, and that party has done a good job, its members tend to be voted back into office. If things get worse, voters are more likely to give the other party a chance. Indeed, this accountability process is at the very heart of self-governance.

Party Elements

One of the most confusing aspects of political parties is precisely what the term *party* implies. Some have suggested parties are similar to business firms seeking to attract consumers (voters) by providing good products (candidates). Others have suggested parties should be understood as networks of aligned groups and individuals. For example, while Rush Limbaugh is not a member of the Republican National Committee, he is supportive of Republican issues and candidates; so in some ways, he could be considered a party leader. In this book, we will instead rely upon the most common approach to describe parties. This approach has carried a great deal of weight in scholarly circles since the 1950s when a prominent political scientist named V. O. Key suggested we might best understand

FIGURE 13.5 ▪ The Three Interrelated Elements of American Political Parties
The three core pieces are represented by party-in-government (PIG), party-in-the-electorate (PIE), and party-as-organization (PO). While few would doubt that each exists, some believe that they should be seen as distinct elements rather than linked together. —*When you think of "political party," which element comes to mind?*

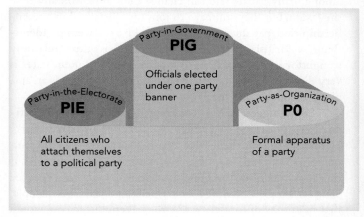

political parties in the United States according to the **tripartite view,** a tripod structure in which political parties have three interrelated elements: party-in-government (PIG), party-in-the-electorate (PIE), and party-as-organization (PO), as illustrated in Figure 13.5.

PARTY-IN-GOVERNMENT Party-in-government refers to the officials who were elected under a party banner. All the Republicans in the House of Representatives, for example, make up one piece of the GOP ("Grand Old Party," which is the nickname for Republicans) party-in-government. They call themselves the Republican Conference, and if they have a majority in the chamber, their leader is the Speaker of the House; if not, he or she is the minority leader (see Chapter 6, pages 168–169). Other segments of the Republican party-in-government include the Republicans in the Senate and any president who is a member of the GOP. There are also sub-branches of the national party-in-government, such as governors, state-level elected officials, municipal officials, and so on. Similarly, the House Democrats call themselves the Democratic Caucus, and all the Democrats in the Buffalo City Council consider themselves part of the same team.

PARTY-IN-THE-ELECTORATE Party-in-the-electorate refers to every citizen who attaches himself or herself to a political party. An average citizen who says "I am a Democrat" or "a Republican" or "a Green" or "a Libertarian" is acknowledging membership in a party-in-the-electorate.[20] Another way of thinking about it is that the party consists of all the voters who consider themselves members of that party.

CONNECT THE **LINK**
(Chapter 11, page 339) What are the most important socialization agents for acquiring party identification?

■ **Party Identification:** A belief that one belongs to a certain party.

SIGNIFICANCE: *One's party identification shapes a great deal of a person's perceptions and behavior during elections. That is, Democrats usually vote for Democrats, and Republicans for Republicans.*

In many other countries, belonging to a political party can be a big deal. In dictatorships such as China, Cuba, and the former Soviet Union, being a member of the Communist Party—the only legal party—means joining the country's ruling class and gaining valuable career opportunities. It also requires proving political reliability and coming under strict discipline. In democratic countries such as Great Britain, citizens can choose among many parties and can change their affiliation any time they want, but they still have to join up officially, sign a membership card, pay dues, and attend local party meetings. Identifying a British party-in-the-electorate is thus relatively straightforward. Belonging to a party in the United States is very different. In this country, party-in-the-electorate is an ambiguous concept and the source of much scholarly debate.

Some suggest that a person's attitude, or **party identification**■, is enough to consider him or her a partisan. Party identification is the belief that a particular party best represents one's interests and outlook toward government and society. It often springs from the childhood socialization process, (see Chapter 11, page 339). If a citizen tells a pollster, for example, that he thinks of himself as a "strong Republican," he would be considered part of the party-in-the-electorate.

As suggested in Figure 13.6, the percentage of Democratic and Republican identifiers has shifted in the past two decades.

In recent years, the number of Democrats seems to be gaining, but so too does the number of nonaligned voters, what we call **independents**■. (There are many independents in the United States but no actual Independent Party.)

A number of factors can lead a citizen to choose an allegiance to one party or the other. Social scientists have noted both short- and long-term factors. Short-term factors include an affinity for a particular candidate or concern about a given issue. Many Americans may have moved to the Democratic Party over concerns about the wars in Iraq and Afghanistan, and some have turned to the Republican Party because of concerns over the growing national debt and President Obama's policy initiatives. Long-term factors, which can be quite powerful, include demographic factors, such as race, level of education, region of the country, and to some extent, even gender.

PARTY-AS-ORGANIZATION   The final piece of the tripod is party-as-organization, which means the formal apparatus of the party, including party headquarters, offices, and leaders. It is the official bureaucracy of the party, and it is found in the form of committees in every state and nearly every community in the nation.

Party organizations exist at each layer of our political system (see Figure 13.7). At the national level are the Democratic National Committee (DNC) and the Republican National Committee (RNC). Each state has both a Republican and a Democratic party, as do most counties and cities across the

FIGURE 13.6 ■ **Trends in Party Identification 1989–2010** —*Why do you think a growing number of Americans are identifying as independents in recent years?*

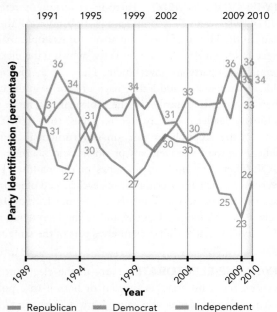

SOURCE: From *Trends in Political Values and Core Attitudes: 1987–2009, Independents Take Center Stage in Obama Era* (Washington, DC: Pew Research Center for the People and the Press, May 21, 2009), p. 12. Accessed at http://people-press.org/reports/pdf/517.pdf. Reprinted with permission. 2010 update from http://people-press.org/reports/questionnaires/645.pdf

FIGURE 13.7 ■ **Layers of the Party System**
While this figure may suggest that the national committee is "above" the state committees, a strong tradition of autonomy in American party politics means that many organizations would balk at the suggestion of a strict hierarchy. —*How has social media changed the ways average citizens can access and influence party structure?*

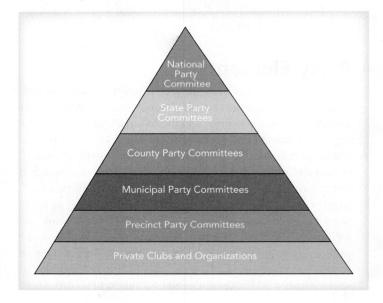

■ **Independent:**
A voter who is not registered or affiliated with any political party.

EXAMPLE: *If a friend implies that he does not belong to any political party, he would be an independent or nonpartisan voter.*

In 1994, Republicans rallied around their leader, Newt Gingrich, and the platform they called the "Contract with America." This platform helped sweep the GOP into office that year. —*Do you think voters appreciate clear party platforms? Do you recognize the legislator standing second from the left? How were the strategies used by Republicans in 2010 similar to the strategies used by Republicans in 1994?*

nation. At the very bottom of the structure, you can still occasionally find ward or precinct organizations. The Chicago Democratic Committee, for example, is made up of a mass of different precinct organizations.

MYTH EXPOSED Many casual observers of party politics believe that a formal hierarchy connects the layers, with the national parties controlling the state parties and the state organizations dictating orders to the county or municipal committees. This is not the case. An unusual aspect of the American parties is that while there is a good bit of interaction between layers of the system, most of it involving the sharing of resources, few commands find their way down to lower-level committees. For the most part, party organizations at all levels of the system operate as semi-independent units.

Political Parties in America

13.3 Identify the functions served by political parties in a democracy, and explain how they help organize the governmental process.

PRACTICE QUIZ: APPLY AND UNDERSTAND

1. Parties perform all of these functions EXCEPT for
   a. focusing on one major issue.
   b. organizing the election process.
   c. facilitating voter choice.
   d. recruiting candidates.

2. Which of the following is true about the impact of party identification on vote choice?
   a. Party identification has little bearing on who a person will vote for.
   b. About 50 percent of partisans vote for members of their party in most elections.
   c. Once a citizen declares a party identification, he or she always votes for candidates of only that party.
   d. One's party identification is not a perfect predictor of vote choice, but it is certainly a powerful factor.

3. For the most part, party organizations at all levels of the system operate as semi-independent units.
   a. true   b. false

ANALYZE

1. It has been said that party identification can create a rational cognitive shortcut for most voters. What does this imply, and do you think it is true?

2. What are the advantages of semi-independent party organizations? Are there advantages to more centralized control of a party's platform? Why or why not?

IDENTIFY THE CONCEPT THAT DOESN'T BELONG

   a. Formal party apparatus
   b. Party-as-organization
   c. Party-in-government
   d. Party-in-the-electorate
   e. Third party

Resource Center
• Glossary
• Vocabulary Example
• Connect the Link

■ **Democratic-Republicans:** The first American political party, formed by believers in states' rights and followers of Thomas Jefferson.

SIGNIFICANCE:
This party challenged the Federalists in the election of 1800, which ushered in the party system.

■ **Federalist Party:** Founded by Alexander Hamilton, its members believed in a strong, centralized government.

SIGNIFICANCE:
This party challenged the Democratic-Republicans in the election of 1800.

Party Eras in American History

13.4 Trace the evolution of political parties in the United States.

(pages 402–403)

Like nearly every other aspect of American government, the nature of the party system has changed over time. From nearly the beginning, political parties have been at the center of the American electoral process, but they must continue to shift and adapt to new conditions.

The Emergence of Parties in America (1790s–1828)

James Madison warned his fellow Americans about the dangers of party-like organizations, which he called "factions," in *Federalist No. 10.* A few years later, George Washington, in his famous Farewell Address, suggested much the same: "Let me . . . warn you in the most solemn manner against the baneful effects of the spirit of party. . . . It is truly [our] worst enemy."

Within a decade after the adoption of the Constitution, however, parties had burst onto the scene. Wishing to fill his cabinet with the best and brightest minds of the day, President Washington selected Thomas Jefferson for secretary of state and Alexander Hamilton for secretary of the treasury. Hamilton and Jefferson passionately disagreed about the future of the nation. Jefferson believed that America's hope lay in small, agriculture-based communities. Hamilton, on the other hand, believed that the future of the nation lay in the development of vibrant cities, and he was convinced that a strong central government was the best mechanism to ensure long-term economic growth.

Partisan animosity got even worse during the presidency of John Adams. Opponents of the administration (led by Jefferson and his "antiparty" friend James Madison) called themselves **Democratic-Republicans**■. Supporters of Adams and Hamilton organized the **Federalist Party**■, a group that was unrelated to the supporters of the Constitution in 1787–1788, who also called themselves Federalists. One prominent historian described this period as the "great consolidation," when parties finally emerged in America.[21]

The dispute over the legitimacy of political parties was mostly settled with the election of 1800. Even James Madison, who had attacked factions in *The Federalist Papers,* had been an ardent Democratic-Republican (he was elected president as Jefferson's successor in 1808) and in his old age embraced the party system.[22] The Federalists, lacking a large base of support outside New England, gradually faded from the scene.

The Heyday of Parties (1828–1900)

An important event occurred early in our nation's history, what most historians refer to as the **Corrupt Bargain of 1824**■. In that year's presidential election, five candidates vied for the office. On election day neither had received a majority of the Electoral College votes, so the issue was sent to the House of Representatives (as per the Constitution). Most assumed that Andrew Jackson of Tennessee, who had come in first, would win in the House. But that did not happen. There is evidence to suggest a deal was made between Speaker of the House Henry Clay (another candidate that year) and John Quincy Adams of Massachusetts (the son of John Adams, and yet another candidate). If Clay would steer his colleagues in the House to Adams' corner, then Adams, once president, would make Clay secretary of state. This appears to be what happened: Adams became president and Clay secretary of state.

Anger and frustration over the alleged bargain was felt across America, which showed itself in two ways. First, the National Republican Party was torn apart, and by the mid-1830s, another major party, the Whig Party, had arisen. Second, what was left of the National Republicans regrouped as the Democratic Party. The leaders of the Democrats were Andrew Jackson and a New York politician named Martin Van Buren. Jackson, on Van Buren's advice, used local party organizations to rally opposition to Adams. These organizations helped Jackson unseat Adams in 1828, to reelect Jackson in 1832, and to elect Van Buren as his successor in 1836. By that time, Van Buren faced the organized opposition of the Whig Party.

This period was a rebirth of party politics at the community level. Party operatives spread the word that unless average citizens became involved, the nation would be ruled through elite deals like the Corrupt Bargain.

Party Decline (1900–1970s)

Responding to public outrage over corrupt politics in the post-Civil War era, a number of important changes were gradually made. To strip political machines of their ability to use the patronage jobs by which they controlled government, the **merit system** (also called the **civil service,** whereby people earned jobs by doing well on exams) was introduced in 1883 and later expanded. To reduce the ability of bosses to control what happened in polling places, the **Australian ballot** (or "secret ballot") was instituted; now voters no longer had to either orally announce their vote or publicly deposit their ballot in the box of one party or the other. And to reduce the chance that bosses would simply handpick nominees who faithfully toed the party line, the direct primary was established. In this system, the rank-and-file would choose the party nominee. These and many other reforms greatly reduced the power of party machines.

The Great Depression dealt another blow to machine politics. The economic crisis of the 1930s tore to shreds the "safety

■ **Corrupt Bargain of 1824:** The alleged secret agreement in the disputed election of 1824 that led the House of Representatives to select John Quincy Adams, who had come in second in the popular vote, as president if he would make Speaker of the House Henry Clay his secretary of state.

SIGNIFICANCE: *This event sparked the birth of popular participation in American elections.*

■ **Candidate-Centered Era:** After 1960, a period when candidates began to portray themselves as independent from party politics, even though they often ran under a party banner.

EXAMPLE: *Candidates who boast about working equally well with both parties often run for office without the aid of either party.*

net" that political machines had provided to help out-of-luck citizens get through tough times. To replace these tattered safety nets, President Franklin D. Roosevelt's New Deal established federal Social Security, unemployment insurance, public works projects, and social welfare programs, all of which undermined ordinary people's dependence on political bosses.

By the 1960s, public attitudes about political parties had grown especially sour, and candidates came to realize that parties were no longer necessary or even desirable. Historically, party workers were needed to bring the candidate's message to the voter, but by the 1960s, television and direct mail could reach more voters in a single day than party operatives could contact in weeks. Moreover, new-style campaign consultants burst on the scene in the 1960s. These professionals could be hired, and their allegiance would be solely to the candidate.

What we might call the post-1960 **Candidate-Centered Era**■ sent repercussions throughout the political system. With candidates pitching themselves as independent, voters saw little reason to hold to any notion of partisanship. As more citizens became independent, voting cues that gave information to citizens about candidates were lost, leading to lower election day turnouts. Once in office, elected officials saw little reason to stick to the party caucus, leading to less policy coherence and a less efficient legislative process.

Organizational Resurgence (1970s–Present)

By the 1970s, many observers came to believe that parties were fading permanently from the scene. Instead of improving their relations with voters, however, the parties chose to expand their services to candidates. Parties became service-oriented, meaning that they broadened their activities to include a host of high-tech services to candidates. They developed, for example, computerized direct-mail operations, in-house television and radio production studios, and sophisticated polling operations.

This change has had significant ramifications. For one thing, sophisticated services require ever-increasing resources. In their efforts to get around campaign finance laws, politicians and their consultants discover new loopholes each year, breeding voter cynicism. At precisely the same time that party organizations are regaining their footing, a growing number of Americans see parties as corrupt. And while the national parties have done well during this period, revitalization has not yet reached the grass roots—that is, local party committees. Finally, while many candidates appreciate the help they receive, the parties know that they can get more mileage out of targeting only a handful of races. In short, the revitalization of the national party *committees* has been significant, but some believe it has also transformed the nature of the party *system*.

Party Eras in American History

13.4   Trace the evolution of political parties in the United States.

PRACTICE QUIZ: UNDERSTAND AND APPLY

1. What best characterizes the disagreement between Thomas Jefferson and Alexander Hamilton that led to the creation of separate political parties?
   a. Hamilton called for the creation of a national bank, and Jefferson abhorred the idea.
   b. Jefferson called for a national investment in a larger army, and Hamilton distrusted raising taxes to support this new army.
   c. Hamilton thought the Constitution should be adjusted to allow more people to vote, but Jefferson disagreed.
   d. Jefferson trusted the average (usually landowning) citizen to dictate policy in the Republic, but Hamilton believed in a more centralized government run by elites.

2. The most significant ramification of the Corrupt Bargain was that it pushed most Americans to the sidelines, leading to a drastic decline in political participation by average citizens.
   a. true
   b. false

3. This quick review of party history in the United States suggests that
   a. once a party is established it never goes away.
   b. dynamic issues and candidates can lead to new political parties.
   c. personalities are more important than issues when it comes to transformations in the party system.
   d. during most of American history parties were shunned by average Americans.

ANALYZE

1. Some people have suggested that regardless of the framers' concerns, parties were inevitable given human nature. Why would that be the case?

2. What are some differences and similarities between the politics of the Gilded Age and the politics of today?

IDENTIFY THE CONCEPT THAT DOESN'T BELONG

a. Resilient
b. Used by candidates
c. Important institutions
d. Key features of politics
e. Candidate-centered

Resource Center
• Glossary
• Vocabulary Example
• Connect the Link

■ **Closed Primary System:** A primary election process in which only registered members of the party are allowed to cast ballots.

EXAMPLE: *In order to vote in a Republican primary in New York, you must be registered as a Republican.*

Parties and the Nomination Process

13.5 Outline the process by which party nominees are chosen to run in the general election.

(pages 404–407)

As you have seen in this chapter, political parties serve many functions. Here, we outline one of the most important: the process of deciding which candidates will appear on the general election ballot under the party's banner—a procedure called *nomination*. For voters, nominations limit their choices on election day, but without party nominations we might find dozens or even hundreds of candidates on each ballot.

In the early years, a handful of party leaders did the choosing. At first, few people objected; if the voters did not like the candidates they chose, they could simply vote for someone else. The nomination process changed during the Progressive Era, when laws were passed mandating that the parties get widespread voter input in selecting nominees. We call this process a **direct primary election.** Today, both major parties choose their candidates by letting rank-and-file members (average citizens) vote.

Different Primary Systems

Not every state uses the same primary system (see Figure 13.8) Roughly half the states have what is called a **closed primary**

system■. In these states, only registered members of the party are allowed to vote in the primary. In some states, the voter must declare his or her party registration in advance of the primary election—often 30 days or so—while in other states, the registration can be done (or changed) on primary day. Either way, the states that rely on this system allow only registered members of the party to vote on prospective nominees. If you are registered as a Democrat or are an independent, you cannot vote in the Republican primary.

Most other states use an **open primary system**■. Under it, voters are allowed to participate in the primary election without declaring membership in a party. On primary day, the voter can choose to vote in the Republican primary or the Democratic primary, and no record is kept. (Of course, one cannot vote in both parties' primaries.) Some people have criticized the open primary system because activists in one party can vote for the *weaker* candidates in the other party's primary election. For example, in the 2010 South Carolina Democratic Senate primary, a virtually unheard of candidate, Alvin Greene—who did not campaign, had essentially no resources, and had recently been arrested for showing pornographic pictures to college students—somehow defeated a well-known, well-funded state official. The outcome left many scratching their heads for an explanation; some believe that the open primary system may have allowed Republican supporters to vote for the weakest Democratic candidates. However, most scholars believe this sort of "strategic primary voting" is rare.

There is also a movement in some states to more or less jettison party-based nominations. In 2004, the voters in the

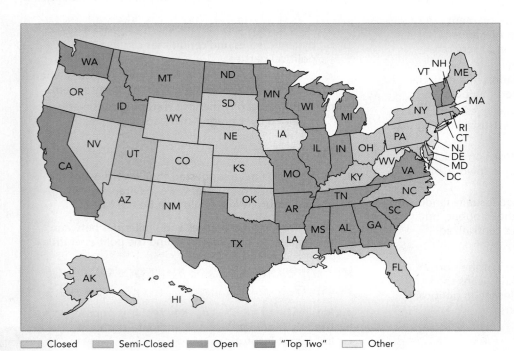

FIGURE 13.8 ■ **Primary Systems in the United States**

As this figure suggests, the split between open and closed primary states is about even. But this does not mean that they are randomly distributed across the United States. —*Can you see any geographic patterns? If so, what might explain the configuration?*

Closed   Semi-Closed   Open   "Top Two"   Other

SOURCE: http://www.csulb.edu

■ **Open Primary System:** A primary election process in which voters are allowed to cast ballots without declaring which party they are voting for.

EXAMPLE: *In South Carolina, a voter can cast a vote in either Democratic or Republican primaries.*

■ **Binding Primaries:** A process established in most states whereby voters in primary elections choose delegates who have pledged their support to a particular presidential candidate. The delegates then vote for this candidate at the nominating convention.

SIGNIFICANCE: *These events have stripped the power of local party bosses in the nomination process.*

state of Washington passed a ballot initiative to create a "top two" nomination process, in which any numbers of candidates are allowed to run in an initial contest, but only the top two are placed on the general election ballot. These two candidates might be of a different party, or they might not. Louisiana has had a similar system for many years. And in the spring of 2010, voters in California made a similar switch to a top-two system. Democratic and Republican party leaders in California were stunned, and they quickly filed a federal lawsuit. The courts will have to decide whether or not the nomination process is an internal party matter that cannot be regulated by state laws.

Presidential Nominations

The framers of the Constitution saw no reason to specify a procedure for nominating presidential candidates. They assumed that the local notables who would gather in each state to cast their Electoral College votes would select the most qualified men. That was how George Washington was unanimously chosen as the first president. When the early party system of Democratic-Republicans and Federalists nevertheless emerged, each party's representatives in Congress named its presidential (and, beginning in 1804, its vice presidential) candidates. The Corrupt Bargain of 1824, however, led to the belief that something less elitist—something that better reflected the will of average voters—should be substituted. The outcome was the **national nominating convention**. The idea was that delegates should be sent from communities across the nation once every four years to discuss the strengths and weaknesses of potential candidates and thus produce the best choice. The convention would also be an opportunity to hammer together a party platform as well as rules for conducting party business. The major parties held their first national conventions in 1832 and have done so every four years since.

One of the sticking points in the convention system was how delegates would be chosen from their communities and what role they might play at the convention. A few states developed mechanisms to allow rank-and-file party members to select delegates, but most simply allowed state and local party bosses to handpick who went to the national convention. Once there, these delegates were obliged to follow the orders of their party leader. This often led to high drama at party conventions. Party bosses used their delegates as negotiating chips, looking to play a key role in nominating the candidate—for what could be better than to be perceived as the party's "kingmaker"?

The strain between party bosses and average party followers came to a head in a fight over the 1968 Democratic presidential nomination. As 1968 began, everyone assumed that President Lyndon B. Johnson would accept his party's renomination. But there arose a groundswell of opposition to Johnson within the Democratic Party over his waging of the Vietnam War. When Johnson failed to win decisively in the March New Hampshire primary, he announced that he was withdrawing from the race.

A sharp division emerged between the party leaders, who backed Vice President Hubert Humphrey, and the "antiwar Democrats," who supported either Minnesota Senator Eugene McCarthy (not to be confused with Senator Joseph McCarthy of Wisconsin, the anticommunist demagogue of the 1950s) and New York Senator Robert F. Kennedy (the late President John F. Kennedy's younger brother and his former attorney general). Kennedy gradually outpaced McCarthy in the primary elections, yet the party bosses continued to back Humphrey, who was staying out of the primaries. Robert Kennedy's assassination in 1968 on the night he won the California primary created a crisis for the antiwar Democrats. Faithful to their bosses, the majority of delegates at the Democratic National Convention in Chicago nominated Humphrey, while thousands of antiwar young people filled the streets in protest outside the convention hall and were beaten and bloodied by police. Humphrey went on to lose the general election to Richard Nixon. The Democratic Party seemed to be in shambles.

After this disastrous election, Democrats implemented a series of changes designed to create a more open, timely, and representative nomination process. Most notably, **binding primaries**■ were established in most states, where voters picked delegates who pledged their support for a particular presidential candidate. The winners in each state were sent to the convention, where they voted to nominate that candidate. Another way to pick delegates, used in about 15 states, is a **nomination caucus.** Here, rank-and-file party members attend a neighborhood meeting, share ideas and concerns about particular candidates, and cast a ballot for pledged delegates to attend a statewide meeting. There, the same process takes place, and the delegates who win at the state level go to the national party convention. The key difference between primaries and caucuses is that the former is an election and the latter a series of "town hall–like" meetings.

The Republican Party was not bound by the new Democratic Party rules, but as the Democrats moved to what was perceived to be a more open system, the older model lost legitimacy, and the Republicans were obliged to make similar changes.

A Better Process?

The nomination reforms of the early 1970s dramatically transformed the way Americans select presidents. It is hard to overstate the importance of the shift from party boss to voter control. While many have applauded the change, critics point to a number of problems:

- The nomination process may *not* reflect the will of the average party member, let alone the average American, because relatively few people participate in the primaries and caucuses—and the ones who do are much more

■ **Invisible Primary:** A process that involves raising money and attracting media attention early in the election process, usually before the primary election year.

SIGNIFICANCE: *The candidate that jumps out quickly in the invisible primary stands a good chance of winning the party's nomination.*

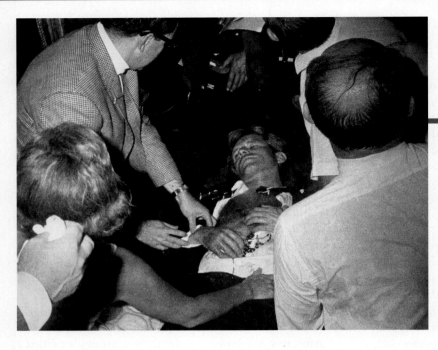

Many agree that 1968 was one of the most turbulent years in American history. Here, Robert Kennedy lies dying after being shot on the evening of the California Democratic presidential primary, which he had won. Hubert Humphrey was later given the nomination, even though many "regulars" in the party wanted a true anti–Vietnam War candidate. Four years later, the party had transformed its nomination rules— leading to binding primaries and caucuses. *—But have these changes made the system truly more democratic?*

ideological, more "extremist," than the typical citizen. Turnout in presidential primaries is generally less than 20 percent of eligible voters, and attendance at caucuses rarely gets beyond 10 percent.

• Because candidates win or lose based on how citizens feel about them, the nomination process has become very expensive, time-consuming, and negative. Candidates who can raise the most money—and raise it the fastest—have every advantage. This money can be used to attack the other candidates, who are all part of the same party. The bitterness of the primaries leaves many Americans distrustful about the electoral process.

• Those candidates who are able to grab media attention before the primary and caucus season do much better, which gives an unfair advantage to the best-known and best-funded candidates. Together, the ability to raise early money and to draw media attention has been called the **invisible primary**■.

• The nomination process puts a premium on winning early primary and caucus contests, which helps raise more money and draw more media hype. Many critics have argued that small and perhaps atypical New Hampshire and Iowa, which hold their events at the very start of the process, exert grossly disproportionate weight in selecting the eventual nominee.

STUDENT profile

In the early 1980s, the Democratic National Committee was anxious to bring their elected officials and prominent figures

into the party fold, so they created a special category of participants at the presidential nomination conventions: superdelegates. Instead of being elected like other delegates, these men and women would be appointed, and they would have the flexibility to vote for whichever candidate they deemed fitting. Yet because they made up less than 20 percent of the overall delegate pool, and because none of the nomination races since the 1980s were protracted, the role of superdelegates in the process drew little attention. Most Americans had never even heard of them until 2008, when all that changed because of the close race between Hillary Clinton and Barack Obama.

A 21-year-old junior at Marquette University in Wisconsin by the name of Jason Rae went from being a U.S. Senate page to the youngest elected representative of the Democratic National Committee. He actually could not vote when he was first elected, because he was 6 months shy of 18. But he wanted to represent what he calls "America's next generation." So he and his friends hand-painted posters with the slogan "A ray of hope for the future." It worked.

Throughout the spring of 2008, Rae was wooed by both sides for his coveted vote. He dined with Hillary Clinton's daughter, Chelsea; had a meeting with Barack Obama; and received dozens of calls from some of the highest-profile politicians from across the country. He also appeared on numerous television programs, including CNN, MSNBC, *Good Morning America,* and *The Early Show* on CBS.

SOURCE: "Young People Who Rock," CNN.com, February 16, 2008. Accessed at http://ypwr.blogs.cnn.com/category/political-activists/ on July 14, 2010.

Parties and the Nomination Process

13.5 Outline the process by which party nominees are chosen to run in the general election.

PRACTICE QUIZ: UNDERSTAND AND APPLY

1. In the first years of our country, a small group of congressional leaders nominated presidential candidates.
   a. true
   b. false

2. When were direct primary elections first instituted?
   a. during the "Era of Good Feelings"
   b. after the Corrupt Bargain of 1824
   c. in the first election after the Civil War
   d. in the Progressive Era (roughly at the turn of the twentieth century)

3. What replaced national conventions as the actual mechanisms for establishing presidential nominees?
   a. binding primaries and nomination caucuses
   b. national primary elections
   c. indirect primaries
   d. national polls

ANALYZE

1. The idea behind binding primaries and caucuses was to make the system more democratic. But given the meager turnout for these contests, would it make sense to go back to a system where party elites make the decisions to save time, resources, and effort?

2. If the primaries tend to determine the party's nominee well in advance of the party convention, why are conventions still held?

IDENTIFY THE CONCEPT THAT DOESN'T BELONG

a. Party bosses
b. Party conventions
c. Members of the media
d. Average party followers
e. Elected officials

Resource Center
• Glossary
• Vocabulary Example
• Connect the Link

■ **Electoral College:** The procedure for selecting the president and vice president of the United States, defined in Article II of the Constitution, whereby the voters in each state choose electors to attend a gathering where the electors make the final decision.

SIGNIFICANCE: *This odd system shapes the way elections are conducted and can also determine the actual winner.*

Presidential Selection

13.6 **Explain the process by which we select the president of the United States.**

(pages 408–411)

In August of 2004, former Vice President Al Gore opened the Democratic National Convention with the following:

> Friends, fellow Democrats, fellow Americans: I'll be candid with you. I had hoped to be back here this week under different circumstances, running for reelection. But you know the old saying: You win some, you lose some. And then there's that little-known third category.
>
> I didn't come here tonight to talk about the past. After all, I don't want you to think I lie awake at night counting and recounting sheep. I prefer to focus on the future because I know from my own experience that America is a land of opportunity, where every little boy and girl has a chance to grow up and win the popular vote.

The joke, of course, was that while Gore had won the popular vote, he did not win the presidency. This breakdown in the election process was caused by the Electoral College—and it was not the first time it happened.

The Electoral College

One of the most innovative and controversial aspects of American elections is outlined in the Constitution: use of the **Electoral College**■ to select the president and vice president. In this process voters in each state choose electors to represent their state at a gathering that chooses the president. Figure 13.9 provides some further details of how the Electoral College works.

It would be hard to overstate the importance of the Electoral College in American politics. Occasionally, it shapes the "winner" of the election but in every election, this awkward procedure shapes the election *process*—from party nominations to the selection of running mates, overall strategy, fundraising activities, candidate events, distributing resources, media coverage, and much else. Depending on which state you live in, citizens will experience presidential campaigns in vastly different ways because of the Electoral College. Many argue that without this institution, elections would be much more democratic. On the other hand, others suggest that given our structure of government, the Electoral College is a necessary, albeit cumbersome, institution.

What Were the Framers Thinking?

The framers believed that only men of the highest caliber and intellect should become president. They worried about politicians with "talents for low intrigue, and the little arts of popularity," as noted by Alexander Hamilton in *Federalist No. 69*. So they worried about giving average citizens a direct voice in selecting the president. Instead, they decided that a group of wise citizens should be assembled for the sole purpose of picking the president. But who, exactly, should make up this group? One proposal, which had significant support at the Constitutional Convention, was to let Congress elect the president. Others suggested that this would blur the important separation between the branches. Also, many were concerned that average citizens should have *some* say in the process. The compromise was to allow each state to select its electors by whatever method that state deemed appropriate.

The Electoral College was also a compromise that helped assuage a concern of delegates from small states. There were no political parties at the time, and it was assumed that each state would advance the candidacy of its "favorite son" meaning that each state's most popular politician would run for the presidency. If the selection of the president was based on popular vote, the largest states (the states with the most voters) would elect their favorite son every time.

So how does the Electoral College solve this problem? The Constitution states that in order to become president, a candidate must receive a majority of Electoral College votes. This does not mean the most votes (a plurality) but rather at least one-half of the overall number of electoral votes cast. When no candidate received at least 50 percent of the votes, the election would be decided in the House of Representatives, where each state, regardless of its size, is given one vote. Because each state would advance a favorite son, and because there were no political parties, most assumed there would be few (if any) elections where a candidate would net a majority of Electoral College votes.

When Things Have Gone Wrong

Originally, each elector was given full independence to name any person he saw fit and would cast two votes, naming two different people. The candidate who got the most votes would become president, and the runner-up would become vice president. During the first decades, only a handful of states allowed voters to pick electors; most were chosen by state legislatures. This method worked smoothly during the first two elections, but it began to unravel as soon as Washington announced that he would not accept a third term.

For one thing, political parties—which the framers had neither foreseen emerging nor wanted—burst onto the scene in the 1790s, which led to partisan electors rather than enlightened statesmen doing the choosing. Also, the original design was to have the top vote getter become president and the second-place finisher become vice president, but this proved completely unworkable as soon as competing political parties arose. In the 1796 election, this arrangement meant that John

■ **Twelfth Amendment (1804):**
Required a separate vote tally in the Electoral College for president and vice president.

SIGNIFICANCE:
Presidential candidates now select their own vice presidential running mates.

■ **Unit Rule:** The practice, employed by 48 states, of awarding all of a state's electoral college votes to the candidate who receives the greatest number of popular votes in that state.

EXAMPLE: *Pennsylvania allots all of its 21 electoral votes to the candidate that receives the most popular votes in the state.*

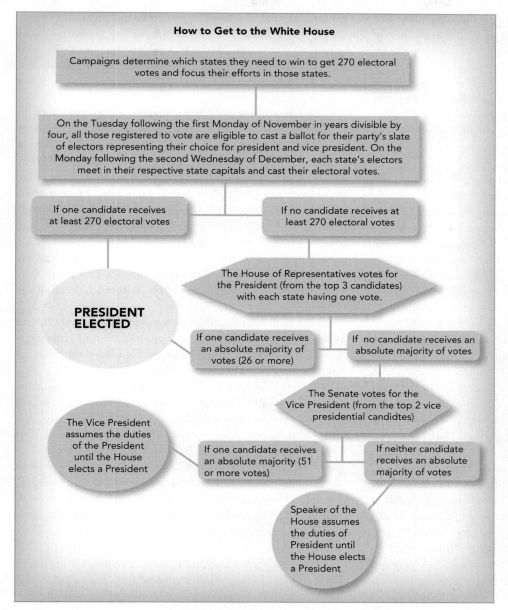

How to Get to the White House

Campaigns determine which states they need to win to get 270 electoral votes and focus their efforts in those states.

On the Tuesday following the first Monday of November in years divisible by four, all those registered to vote are eligible to cast a ballot for their party's slate of electors representing their choice for president and vice president. On the Monday following the second Wednesday of December, each state's electors meet in their respective state capitals and cast their electoral votes.

If one candidate receives at least 270 electoral votes

If no candidate receives at least 270 electoral votes

The House of Representatives votes for the President (from the top 3 candidates) with each state having one vote.

PRESIDENT ELECTED

If one candidate receives an absolute majority of votes (26 or more)

If no candidate receives an absolute majority of votes

The Senate votes for the Vice President (from the top 2 vice presidential candidtes)

The Vice President assumes the duties of the President until the House elects a President

If one candidate receives an absolute majority (51 or more votes)

If neither candidate receives an absolute majority of votes

Speaker of the House assumes the duties of President until the House elects a President

FIGURE 13.9 ■ How to Get to the White House
There are certainly drawbacks to the Electoral College—namely, that candidates that win more popular votes can be denied the presidency. For some, this alone is enough to jettison the scheme. Yet some argue there are problems with a direct election process. —*What were some of the reservations that the framers had about direct elections?*

SOURCE: Daniel M. Shea and Bryan Reece, *2008 Election Preview.* Pearson Prentice Hall, 2008, Figure 4.1 (p. 47). Reprinted by permission of Pearson Education, Inc., Glenview, IL.

Adams got the presidency and his archrival, the leader of the opposing party, Thomas Jefferson, became vice president. For the next four years, each tried to outmaneuver the other.

Finally, the year 1800 brought an electoral rematch between Adams and Jefferson. This time, it seemed that Jefferson had come in first. But, in fact, Jefferson and his running mate, Aaron Burr, were tied: *All* of Jefferson's supporters in the Electoral College had cast their second vote for Burr! The election had to be settled by the House of Representatives. Even though everyone knew that Jefferson was the "top of the ticket," Burr refused to back down, and it took dozens of votes in the House and much wrangling before Jefferson was finally named president and Burr had to settle for the vice presidency.

As a result, the **Twelfth Amendment**■ was adopted, which says that in the Electoral College, the electors must indicate who they are voting for as president and who they are voting for as vice president.

There is yet another controversial part of the process: It is quite possible that the candidate who receives the most popular votes will not receive the most electoral votes. This can happen for two reasons. First, 48 of the 50 states use a winner-takes-all model, also called the **unit rule**■, under which the candidate who receives the most popular votes in that state gets all of that state's electoral votes. Second, the original scheme of allowing electors to use their own independent judgment was quickly replaced by partisan considerations. Today, partisan slates of electors compete against one another, meaning that if a Republican candidate wins that state, a Republican slate of electors are sent to the Electoral College. The same is true for Democratic candidates.

These two changes—the unit rule and partisan slates of electors—makes it *likely* that the most popular candidate (the highest vote getter) will become the president, but it does not *guarantee* it. In fact, the most popular candidate has been denied the presidency four times in American history:

- In 1824, four candidates were in the running. The second-place finisher was John Quincy Adams, who got 38,000 fewer popular votes than the top vote getter, Andrew Jackson. But no candidate won a majority of the Electoral College. Adams was awarded the presidency when the election was thrown to the House of Representatives, which under the Constitution had to choose among the *three* top Electoral College finishers. The fourth-place finisher, Speaker of the House Henry Clay, threw his support to Adams, who later named Clay as secretary of state. Jackson and his supporters howled that a "corrupt bargain" had deprived him of the White House.

- In 1876, nearly unanimous support from small states gave Republican Rutherford B. Hayes a one-vote margin in the Electoral College, despite the fact that he lost the popular vote to Democrat Samuel J. Tilden by 264,000 votes. The election was decided only when a commission of senators, representatives, and a Supreme Court justice declared Hayes the winner.

- In 1888, Republican candidate Benjamin Harrison lost the popular vote by 95,713 votes to the incumbent Democratic president, Grover Cleveland, but Harrison won by an Electoral College margin of 65 votes. In this instance, some say the Electoral College worked the way it is designed to work by preventing a candidate from winning an election based on support from one region of the country. The South overwhelmingly supported Cleveland, and he won by more than 425,000 votes in six southern states. In the rest of the country, however, he lost by more than 300,000 votes.

- In 2000, Vice President Al Gore had over half a million votes more than George W. Bush (50,992,335 votes to Bush's 50,455,156). But after a recount controversy in Florida, and a U.S. Supreme Court ruling in the case of *Bush* v. *Gore* (2000), Bush was awarded the state by 537 popular votes. Thus, Bush became president with 271 electoral votes—the barest possible majority.

Dump the Electoral College?

Given the outcome of the 2000 election, as well as the other problems, many had expected a popular uprising to abolish the Electoral College. There was, indeed, a modest movement after

the election, and it continues to simmer today. But in order to abolish the Electoral College, the Constitution would have to be amended—a complex, difficult process. Surveys suggest that most Americans would like to have a direct vote for the presidency; however, the prospects of passing a constitutional amendment seem limited at this time.

Things are happening at the state level, however. The state of Maryland recently passed a measure that could eventually create a more direct process of choosing the president without amending the Constitution. Specifically, in April 2007, they passed a law that would award the state's electoral votes to the winner of the national popular vote—so long as other states agree to do the same. The Constitution stipulates that each state can select electors as it sees fit. So if every state agrees to appoint electors who would vote for the winner of the national popular vote, no matter who wins their state, the national popular vote would decide the winner. This would be a way to nullify the Electoral College without amending the Constitution.

One of the most significant changes that would result from Maryland's scheme would be the nationalization of presidential campaigns. Candidates would slug it out for votes throughout the nation, not just in particular states.[23]

Other states have considered similar measures, with little success. In 2006, legislation was introduced in Colorado, Illinois, Louisiana, Missouri, New York, and California. California actually passed a bill nearly identical to Maryland's, but it was vetoed by Governor Arnold Schwarzenegger. He argued that the allocation of Electoral College votes was an issue of state's rights, and that the law would make it possible that electors would vote for a candidate rejected by most of their state's residents. In all, some 40 states have had measures introduced to modify the allocation of Electoral College votes.

Not everyone agrees with these schemes. Defenders of the Electoral College argue that it adds to the popular support of winners. In other words, somehow we feel that the victor has more legitimacy if the Electoral College vote is won by a landslide, even if that candidate has won the popular vote by only a few percentage points. The Electoral College also forces candidates to strive for wide geographical appeal rather than concentrating all their efforts in a few large states. As noted by columnist George Will, "The system aims not just for majority rule but rule *by certain kinds of majorities*. It encourages candidates to form coalitions of states with various political interests and cultures."[24] Rural states worry that they would fall by the wayside in the pursuit of the largest national vote. Others worry that campaigns would focus almost exclusively on media and that the grassroots efforts, essential to win particular states, would vanish. Figure 13.10 shows the electoral college vote breakdown in the 2008 election.

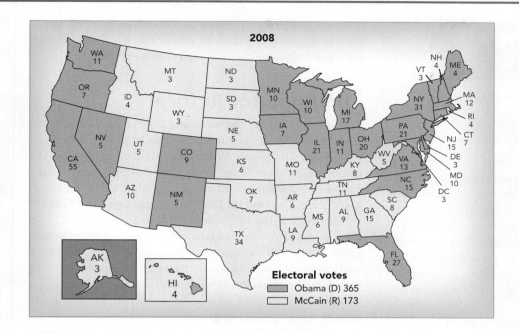

FIGURE 13.10 ▪ Electoral Votes for 2008

Barack Obama's decisive win in the 2008 presidential election sprang from voter shifts that occurred across the country and by flipping several key states, such as Virginia, Ohio, New Mexico, and Nevada. —*Does the Electoral College distort the impact that certain states have on our electoral process? Would that distortion be a valid reason for scrapping the system?*

Presidential Selection

13.6   **Explain the process by which we select the president of the United States.**

PRACTICE QUIZ: UNDERSTAND AND APPLY

1. Why did the framers establish the Electoral College?
   a. They feared ordinary voters would elect a president who was popular rather than qualified.
   b. They wanted smaller states to be more equally represented.
   c. They wanted political parties to play a stronger role in the selection of presidential candidates.
   d. a and b

2. If no candidate receives a majority of the popular vote, who decides who wins the presidency?
   a. The Senate
   b. The House of Representatives
   c. The Supreme Court
   d. A constitutional convention

3. What was so unique about the Electoral College outcome in the 2000 presidential election?
   a. For only the second time in history, the election was decided by the House of Representatives.
   b. The State Election Commission in Florida actually awarded Florida's electoral votes to George W. Bush.

   c. The Supreme Court made a ruling that allowed Florida's electoral votes to be awarded to George W. Bush.
   d. Al Gore never did concede the election.

ANALYZE

1. Why do you suppose the framers were so reluctant to rely upon the wisdom of average citizens to select the chief executive?

2. One argument against eliminating the Electoral College is that a system based on popular vote would push candidates to forgo smaller, more rural areas for the massive population centers. But that's where most people are. What's your take on this issue?

IDENTIFY THE CONCEPT THAT DOESN'T BELONG

a. State legislatures   d. Unit rule
b. Electors   e. Senate
c. House of Representatives

13.6

Resource Center
• Glossary
• Vocabulary Example
• Connect the Link

■ **Federal Election Campaign Act (FECA):** A law designed to limit the amount of money contributed to campaigns for Congress and the presidency and to broaden donation reporting requirements.

SIGNIFICANCE: *This was the first real attempt to limit the flow of big money into elections, but numerous loopholes were found to circumvent parts of the law.*

The Role of Money in Elections

13.7 Assess the critical role that money plays in the election process.

(pages 412–415)

In the early days of the Republic, a common practice was to "treat" voters. George Washington, for example, was said to have purchased a quart of rum, wine, beer, and hard cider for every voter in the district when he ran for the Virginia House of Burgesses in 1751 (there were only 391 voters).[25] A common means of spending campaign money during the nineteenth century was to purchase advertisements in newspapers and, more often, to actually purchase a newspaper completely. As technology changed throughout the twentieth century, so did the cost of elections. By the late 1960s, money had become critical for four main reasons:

1. **Decline of Party Organizations.** Given that party organizations were primarily responsible for connecting with voters, candidates needed new ways of reaching out. Many of these new means were extremely costly.
2. **More Voters Up for Grabs.** In 1790, there were fewer than 4 million Americans, almost a quarter of them slaves. Today, the U.S. population is over 300 million. Reaching such a huge number of voters requires enormous amounts of money.
3. **Television.** In the early 1950s, only a small percentage of homes boasted a television set; by the 1960s, TV was nearly universal. Television changed the way political campaigns were run. And buying advertising time requires huge sums of money.
4. **Campaign Consultants.** Professional campaign consulting burst onto the scene in the 1960s, bringing such sophisticated techniques as direct mail and survey research. These methods proved effective, but they came with a hefty price tag.

In 1952, a presidential election year, *all* campaigns for political office, from president to dogcatcher, added up to approximately $140 million.[26] By 2008, the equivalent figure had swelled to an estimated $5.3 *billion.* In the 1960s, it was common for a successful House candidate to spend less than $100,000, but by 2008, the average cost of winning a seat in the House of Representatives topped $1.4 million. An "expensive" U.S. Senate race in the 1960s was still under half a million dollars; in 2008, the *average* Senate race cost nearly $9 million. With all that money, you might think races would be more competitive than in the past. In fact, in 2008, 94 percent of

House incumbents were reelected, and 83 percent of Senate incumbents were sent back to office. The fundraising figures are staggering, as are the reelection rates (see Figure 13.11).

The Rage for Reform

Efforts to control the flow of money in elections date from the Progressive Era, but these measures were largely symbolic. Real reform came in the early 1970s, when members of Congress began to worry about being thrown out of office by a wealthy candidate—perhaps a political novice—who could simply outspend them. The **Federal Election Campaign Act (FECA)**■ was signed into law by President Richard Nixon in 1971. In brief, the legislation limited how much money candidates could spend, how much an individual or group could give, and how much political parties might contribute. It also established voluntary public financing of presidential elections. Presidential candidates who choose to use this system are limited in the amount they can raise and spend.

Shortly after the amendments took effect, James Buckley, a Conservative Party senator from New York, along with a group of politicians from both ends of the political spectrum, challenged the constitutionality of the law. Buckley argued that spending money was akin to free speech and that limiting it would abridge First Amendment protections. The case of *Buckley* **v.** *Valeo*■ (1976) was the most significant election-centered court decision in American history. For the most part,

FIGURE 13.11 ■ **Campaign Expenditures**

This figure suggests that the cost of elections has grown dramatically, even when inflation is factored in. —*What do you think is at the heart of rising elections costs? Does this suggest a serious flaw in the process or a sign of a robust exchange of ideas?*

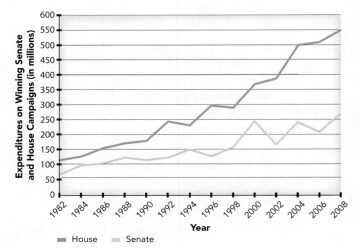

■ ***Buckley v. Valeo* (1976):** The most significant Supreme Court case on campaign finance in American history.

SIGNIFICANCE: *The Court ruled that campaign expenditures are akin to free speech and are therefore protected by the First Amendment.*

■ **Incumbent Advantage:** The various factors that favor officeholders running for reelection over their challengers.

EXAMPLE: *Those in office seem to be able to raise much more money for their reelection campaigns than can their challengers.*

the Supreme Court sided with Buckley by striking down provisions of the law that put limits on overall spending, on spending by the candidates, and on spending by independent groups. However, the justices upheld the public funding of presidential elections, so long as it is voluntary, and surprisingly, the Court allowed limits on how much an individual or a group might *give* to a candidate.

Political Action Committees

Another spinoff of FECA and *Buckley* has been the proliferation of political action committees (PACs). Earlier acts of Congress had barred labor unions and corporations from giving money to federal candidates. The idea of PACs was thought up in the 1940s to get around these restrictions. In PACs, none of the monies used to support a candidate came directly from the union or corporation but instead from these groups' independent political units. The contribution limit for PACs was originally five times higher than for individuals, so the number of groups exploded: In 1974, there were roughly 600 PACs, but by 2008, more than 4,600 were giving out contributions.[27]

Political action committees give money to candidates because the interest group that backs them wants a say in public policy. Businesses, for example, want policies that help them make a profit; environmentalists want policies that help protect the natural world; and labor seeks policies that help working men and women. But do these groups, through their PACs, "buy" policies with their contributions? This is a hotly debated issue. The Center for Responsive Politics is a nonpartisan organization that tracks the flow of money in elections. Its Web site (http://www.opensecrets.org) gives detailed information on who gives and who receives campaign money.[28]

Precisely what PACs buy with their contribution is unclear, but the public perceives a problem. Numerous public opinion polls confirm that regardless of what actually happens between contributors and public officials, average Americans regard the money flowing from PACs to candidates as a threat to the democratic process.

The Incumbent Fundraising Advantage

Candidates vying for office solicit funds from many sources: individuals (friends, spouses, associates, activists), political parties, PACs, and—believe it or not—other candidates. *Incumbents* are candidates already holding the office and up for reelection, *challengers* are those opposing the incumbents, and *open-seat candidates* are running for seats for which no incumbent is seeking reelection. Political action committees hope that their money will somehow produce support for their policies, which means they hope their money will go to the eventual winner. Accordingly, they prefer to send their funds to incumbents, because those already in office have a head start—the so-called **incumbent advantage**■—when it comes to reelection. By sending their money to incumbents, PACs provide an even greater boost to incumbents' chances of reelection.

In some recent elections again, more than 90 percent of incumbent House candidates won (see Figure 13.12), even though many Americans are frustrated with "business-as-usual politics." Incumbents have always had an advantage, but critics point to recent changes that have made matters worse. Yale University scholar David Mayhew was one of the first to draw attention to the problem.[29] In his seminal book *Congress: The Electoral Connection,* Mayhew argues that all legislative activity is now geared toward securing reelection. These efforts fall within three categories: *credit claiming,* which is receiving praise for bringing money and federal projects back to the district; *position taking,* or making sure to be on the popular side of issues; and *advertising,* which implies reaching out to constituents in many ways, especially through mailings. Others have pointed to additional sources of incumbent support, such as ongoing media attention, which challengers rarely get.

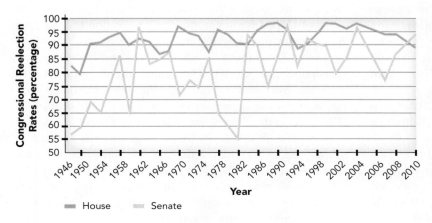

FIGURE 13.12 ■ **Congressional Reelection Rates, 1950–2010**

Reelection rates for the House have hovered around 90 percent for the past few decades. There is more volatility in the Senate, but here, too, the rates have increased over the years.
—*Why do you suppose most members of Congress are returned to office even though many Americans believe that the national legislature is out of touch?*

SOURCES: *Vital Statistics on Congress, 1999–2000* (Washington, DC: AEI Press, 2000); *Vital Statistics on American Politics, 2003–2004* (Washington, DC: CQ Press, 2004); *CQ Weekly,* November 6, 2004; Center for Responsive Politics, 2006 election statistics, http://www.opensecrets.org

■ **Bipartisan Campaign Reform Act (BCRA):** Federal law passed in 2002 that outlawed soft-money contributions to party organizations.

SIGNIFICANCE: *This new law has pushed candidates to raise funds from a greater number of small donors.*

■ **Soft Money:** Funds contributed through a loophole in federal campaign finance regulations that allowed individuals and groups to give unlimited sums of money to political parties.

SIGNIFICANCE: *This massive loophole fueled a public outcry for reform.*

Term Limits

Many reforms have been suggested to reduce the incumbent advantage. One proposal is **term limits**. If we are worried about an unfair advantage given to politicians already in office, why not create more open-seat contests? Limiting legislative terms would guarantee turnover—a stream of new faces, energy, and ideas in the legislature. Representatives should know the concerns of average citizens, and what better way of ensuring that than by forcing entrenched legislators to step aside after a fixed period and make way for fresh blood? Opponents of term limits argue that the legislative process is complex, and it takes time to become familiar with the process. Moreover, term limits deny voters a choice—the chance to reelect a legislator who they think may actually be doing a good job.

By the early 1990s, roughly half the states had adopted term limits for state legislators and candidates for federal office. Many legal scholars, however, wondered whether the states had the constitutional power to limit the terms of U.S. House and Senate members. The issue came to a head in the Supreme Court case of *U.S. Term Limits, Inc. v. Thornton* (1995). In a 5–4 decision, the Court majority stated that "allowing individual States to craft their own qualifications for Congress would . . . erode the structure envisioned by the Framers, a structure that was designed, in the words of the Preamble to our Constitution, to form a 'more perfect Union.' " With that decision, attempts to limit the terms of members of Congress through legislative acts ended; a constitutional amendment remains the only course of action.

Reforming the Reforms: BCRA

While the FECA restrictions limited the amounts individuals and groups could contribute to a candidate, the law put no restrictions on giving money to a political party. By 2000, many Americans had once again come to the conclusion that the campaign finance system was out of whack. One survey found that 75 percent agreed (39 percent "strongly") that "our present system of government is democratic in name only. In fact, special interests run things."[30] Clearly, the reforms of the early 1970s had done little to halt the flow of big money into elections. The public was ripe for change, but reform measures stalled in the legislature. With much effort from Republican Senator John McCain and Democratic Senator Russ Feingold, the **Bipartisan Campaign Reform Act (BCRA)**■ was passed and signed into law by President George W. Bush in February 2002.

The law was sweeping: It outlawed unlimited contributions to the national political organizations and barred group-sponsored advertisements 30 days before primary elections and 60 days before general elections. Yet the law also raised the contribution limits for individuals, and left open the ability for

wealthy individuals to donate **soft money**■, virtually unlimited sums of money, to state and local party organizations. The ban on soft money did not apply to political action committees, which were still free to raise unlimited cash.

In 2003, the law was upheld by the Supreme Court in the case *McConnell v. Federal Election Commission*. In a 5–4 decision, the Court affirmed the law's most important elements. It was, according to a *New York Times* account, a "stunning victory for political reform."[31]

The *Citizens United* Bombshell

The most recent chapter in the story of money in American elections was a decision handed down by the Supreme Court in January 2010. The case was **Citizens United v. Federal Elections Commission**■, and it dealt with a provision of the BCRA that outlawed explicit campaigning by nonpartisan groups within 30 days of a general election and 60 days prior to a primary election. Citizens United, a conservative nonprofit corporation, produced a 90-minute documentary called *Hillary: The Movie*, which was highly critical of the New York Senator. They were anxious to distribute it throughout the fall of 2007 and spring of 2008, even though Clinton was running in a series of primaries and caucuses for the Democratic presidential nomination. Because they were barred from doing so, and because they thought this was a violation of their First Amendment rights, the group took the issue to the federal courts.

The Supreme Court focused its deliberations on the broad issue of the constitutionality of limits on spending by corporations and unions (established a half century before and upheld in several prior cases). In a 5-4 decision, the Court ruled that unions and corporations were entitled to spend money from their general treasuries (without the use of PACs) on federal elections, although they could not give money directly to candidates. The decision reverberated across the political system. One commentator, writing for the *National Review Online*, suggested, "The ruling represents a tremendous victory for free speech . . . The ruling in Citizens United is a straightforward application of basic First Amendment principles."[32] But others feared that the decision would set loose a flood of money and lead to greater corruption. The *New York Times* editorialized, "With a single, disastrous 5-to-4 ruling, the Supreme Court has thrust politics back to the robber-baron era of the 19th century."[33] While accurate figures are somewhat elusive, campaign finance data from the 2010 election suggests a flood of money did, in fact, materialize. Some estimates place the overall spending in the 2010 midterm election at over $3.2 billion, with more than one-half of that coming from outside groups. This is roughly double the amount spent by outside groups in 2008 and in 2006. Republican candidates

■ *Citizens United v. Federal Elections Commission*
(2010): A Supreme Court case that reversed decades of precedent by declaring unconstitutional laws that ban unions and corporations from using general operating funds on elections.

SIGNIFICANCE: *The case will likely lead to more money being spent during elections. Some also believe that corporations and unions might now be able to dominate the election process.*

netted the most from these groups in 2010, but the opposite was true in 2008.[34] Many Americans are troubled by the role played by big money in elections. They believe that it gives some candidates an unfair advantage and spills past the election into the policymaking process. It is one of the many ironies of an open political process: Individuals and interest groups are encouraged to back political candidates vigorously, but in doing so, their efforts distort the playing field. The freedom to participate creates a system with limited participation.

The Role of Money in Elections

13.7   **Assess the critical role that money plays in the election process.**

PRACTICE QUIZ: UNDERSTAND AND APPLY

1. One reason for the steep rise in campaign spending in this country is that
   a. campaigns are now federally subsidized to "even the playing field" for all candidates.
   b. blogs and mass e-mails are enormously expensive.
   c. people are more inclined to vote for a candidate if they know he or she has spent a lot of money campaigning.
   d. there are more potential voters to reach each year, making expensive broadcast advertising a higher priority.

2. These entities give money to candidates because the interest group that backs them wants a say in public policy.
   a. PACs.   c. third parties.
   b. 527 groups.   d. pundits.

3. According to the Supreme Court, in the case of *Citizens United v. FEC*, corporations and unions should have the same constitutional protections as individuals, and

therefore be able to spend money on campaigns from their general treasury.
   a. true   b. false

ANALYZE

1. There are essentially two ways of seeing money in elections: as a corrupting influence or as a form of political speech. What's your opinion on this important issue? Explain your answer.

2. Short of term limits, which the courts have said are unconstitutional for congressional seats, is there anything that can be done to reduce the incumbent advantage?

IDENTIFY THE CONCEPT THAT DOESN'T BELONG

a. Consultants   d. Polling
b. Television   e. Strong political parties
c. Independent voters

13.7

Conclusion

Americans put a great deal of faith in the election process, and over the past two centuries, many changes have opened the system to more involvement. But at the same time, it seems that only a modest number are willing to get involved. What difference does it make if many Americans do not seem interested in politics and that Americans on the whole turn out to vote less often than citizens in other democracies? Is this really something to worry about?

One way to answer such questions is to take a practical point of view. What policy difference would it make if nonvoters got into the act? Would the government head in a different direction if turnout were higher? Early studies suggested that on the whole, the policy preferences of nonvoters essentially paralleled those of voters. There would be little policy change if we had full election turnout. More recent studies suggest, however, that who votes *does* matter. The low turnout in the 1994 election allowed the Republicans to capture control of both houses of Congress and helped bring George W. Bush to the White House in 2000. If more young voters had turned out in the Massachusetts special election in 2010, it is possible that Martha Coakley would have defeated Scott Brown. In each of these cases, and untold more, the outcome of public policy would have been much different with higher voter turnout.

Another way to answer such questions is to examine how you define *democracy*. For example, perhaps precise levels of participation are unimportant; so long as enough citizens are involved to make the process competitive, full participation is inconsequential. The people who refrain from involvement in politics are also likely to be the least well informed. Perhaps we do not want these people involved in the process; is an uninformed vote really preferable to none at all? Along similar lines, some people speculate that less informed citizens (the nonvoters) are more prone to radical policy shifts, so their absence at the polls actually adds a degree of stability to public policy. The conservative columnist George Will, in a piece titled "In Defense of Nonvoting," argues that good government—not the right to vote—is the fundamental human right. He suggests that high voting rates in Germany's Weimar Republic (1919–1933) enabled the Nazis to take power in 1933.[35] Declining turnout in America, Will asserts, is no cause for worry. This perspective is often called the **elite democratic model.** It insists that so long as fairness and political opportunity are guaranteed, the system is healthy.

The **popular democratic model,** by contrast, suggests that the character of any political system is not simply the outcome of public policy but also the process by which it is reached. This model puts a premium on electoral involvement. When this occurs, citizens develop an affinity for the system, because they are convinced that they have a stake in whatever policy results from political decisions. Put a bit differently, this theory says that systems of government designed to reflect the will of the people will do so better, and in the long run will be more prosperous and stable, if average citizens join the electoral process. Echoing this sentiment, the liberal political scientist and journalist E. J. Dionne, in his book *Why Americans Hate Politics,* has written that "a nation that hates politics will not long thrive as a democracy."[36] Which of these well-known commentators, Will or Dionne, in your opinion comes closer to the truth?

416

KEY CONCEPT MAP **How do aspects of the electoral process shape the democratic nature of our political system?**

Political Parties

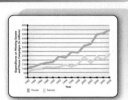

Benefit: Political parties winnow the number of candidates, organize campaign events, and offer voters a convenient way to evaluate candidate policy stands.

Limitation: Many candidates and voters do not fit neatly into the major parties; the nomination process in particular has come under intense scrutiny in recent years.

Critical Thinking Questions

What if political parties somehow vanished? What impact would this have on elections in the United States?

Campaign Spending

Benefit: Campaign money enables candidates to get their message out to voters. Studies have shown that voters know more about candidates when hefty resources are spent in a race.

Limitation: The very strong relationship between candidate spending and the chances of winning an election creates an unlevel playing field; the system loses legitimacy in the eyes of some voters.

Critical Thinking Questions

What if the reason some candidates raise more money than others is simply because they are more popular? How would critics of campaign spending respond to this argument?

Voting Requirements

Benefit: Voting requirements have slowly been eased to broaden the electoral process and the democratic character of our government.

Limitation: Certain barriers to voting, such as residency and registration requirements, remain and limit the involvement of certain groups of voters, including young Americans.

Critical Thinking Questions

What if Congress made same-day voter registration the law in every state? How might this affect voter turnout?

The Media

Benefit: Media coverage aids voters by giving them more information and helping them sort through candidate data.

Limitation: Studies confirm that the media tend to give incumbents (those already in office) more coverage than challengers.

Critical Thinking Questions

How much influence do the media have over the electoral process? Should the media be restricted in any way in their coverage of candidates for public office? Why or why not?

Voter Attitudes

Benefit: Many citizens take elections seriously, study candidate qualifications, and vote in all elections.

Limitation: Overall, voter turnout in the United States is modest, and many mistakenly assume elections are the only option for influencing public policy, and so do nothing else.

Critical Thinking Questions

Can *not voting* be interpreted as a sign of contentment, rather than just a sign of apathy? Why or why not?

The framers of our system of government were ambivalent about popular elections. In the end, most agreed that the democratic character of the system would be enhanced through election of at least some offices. Yet, a host of unforeseen factors have transformed this basic democratic practice. And the elections process is vastly different from what it was twenty years, much less two hundred years, ago.

—Should the federal government take greater control of and responsibility for the elections process? Or are state and local governments best able to ensure the participation of the voting eligible population? Would the elections process benefit from greater limits on the length of campaigns or additional public funding of campaigns? Why or why not?

Review of Key Objectives

Expansion of the Electorate and Other Legal Issues

13.1 Describe the legal challenges that have broadened the democratic character of elections in America.

(pages 392–393)

On one level, elections take place outside the boundaries of government. As noted in Chapter 1, elections are "processes," not institutions. In fact, some have thought it a bit strange that the framers of our system made little mention of how elections might be conducted. Yet there have been numerous constitutional and legal changes that have redefined the nature and practice of elections in America. Nearly all of these changes, such as the Fifteenth, Nineteenth, and Tewnty-sixth Amendments, and the Voting Rights Act of 1965, have broadened the number of citizens legally entitled to participate in the process.

KEY TERMS

Fourteenth Amendment 392
Fifteenth Amendment 392
Nineteenth Amendment 392
Twenty-Fourth Amendment 392
Twenty-Sixth Amendment 392
Voting Rights Act of 1965 393
Residency and Registration Laws 393
Motor Voter Law 393
Help America Vote Act 393

CRITICAL THINKING QUESTIONS

1. What, if any, additional legal changes do you think would enhance the democratic character of elections in America?
2. Some have speculated that younger Americans, perhaps beginning at age 16, should be given the right to vote. One proposal is to give them a partial vote, sort of like a "learner's permit." Does this make sense to you?

INTERNET RESOURCES

For information on a range of campaign-related issues, see the Federal Election Commission Web site at http://www.fec.gov

ADDITIONAL READING

Piven, Frances Fox, and Richard A. Cloward. *Why Americans Still Don't Vote: And Why Politicians Want It That Way.* Boston: Beacon Press, 2000.

Ryden, David K., ed., *The U. S. Supreme Court and the Electoral Process,* Washington, DC: Georgetown University Press, 2000.

Individual Participation in Elections

13.2 Evaluate electoral engagement in America, particularly as it relates to young citizens.

(pages 394–397)

There are many ways that citizens can become involved in the election process—from voting or attending a rally to sending in a check to a candidate or talking about issues and candidates with friends. For many of us, elections are an important part of our civic lives. To others, electoral participation does not seem to be worth their time and effort. This might be especially true for young citizens. There are signs that this generation has discovered the power and potential of political action, but there are countertrends that suggest they may once again retreat to the sidelines.

KEY TERMS

Electoral Behavior 394
Turnout 394

CRITICAL THINKING QUESTIONS

1. Most likely some of your friends and family do not participate in electoral politics. What do you think is at the root of their inactivity and/or indifference?
2. Data presented in this section suggest young Americans are paying greater attention to electoral politics. Why do you suppose this is true? What is different now than a few decades ago? Will it last?

INTERNET RESOURCES

For information on levels of political participation in America, see the Center for the Study of the American Electorate Web page at http://www.american.edu/ia/cdem/csae/

For information on youth political engagement, see the Center for Information and Research on Civic Learning and Engagement (CIRCLE) at http://www.civicyouth.org

ADDITIONAL READING

Patterson, Thomas E. *The Vanishing Voter: Public Involvement in an Age of Uncertainty.* New York: Knopf, 2002.

Shea, Daniel M., and John C. Green. *Fountain of Youth: Strategies and Tactics for Mobilizing America's Young Voters.* Lanham, MD: Rowman and Littlefield, 2007.

Political Parties in America

13.3 Identify the functions served by political parties in a democracy, and explain how they help organize the governmental process.

(pages 398–401)

Political parties serve numerous important functions, not the least of which is helping to organize the election process. They also make vote choices easier, recruit candidates, screen candidates, help candidates during elections, overcome constitutional obstruction, educate citizens, and bring citizens into the political process. The three interrelated elements of American political parties are party-in-government, which refers to the elected officials of the same party; party-in-the-electorate, which refers to all citizens who attach themselves to a political party; and, party-as-organization, which refers to the formal apparatus of a party.

KEY TERMS

Rational Party Model 398
Responsible Party Model 398
Platform 398
Nominees 398
Tripartite View of Parties 399
Party Identification 400
Independent 400

CRITICAL THINKING QUESTIONS

1. Parties aid candidates in many ways, but if paid political consultants can do the same, why are parties necessary in a democracy? What's so special about parties?
2. It has been said that parties and party leaders help structure the legislative process, but at what cost? That is, are legislatures less democratic when party pressures are significant?

ADDITIONAL READING

Aldrich, John. *Why Parties? The Origin and Transformation of Political Parties in America.* Chicago: University of Chicago Press, 1995.

Hershey, Marjorie R. *Party Politics in America*, 14th ed. Upper Saddle River, NJ: Pearson Longman, 2010

Theriault, Sean M. *Party Polarization in Congress.* New York: Cambridge University Press, 2008.

Lewis-Beck, Michael, et al. *The American Voter Revisited.* Ann Arbor, MI: University of Michigan Press, 2008.

White, John K., and Daniel M. Shea. *New Party Politics: From Jefferson and Hamilton to the Information Age,* 2nd ed. Belmont, CA: Wadsworth, 2004.

Party Eras in American History

13.4 Trace the evolution of political parties in the United States.

(pages 402–403)

Even though parties have been with us from nearly the beginning of our nation, their weight in our system of government has fluctuated. Few speculate that they will regain the prominence they had in the second half of the nineteenth century, but there has been a modest resurgence in recent decades. That is, while local organizations seem to be in trouble, state and national parties are gaining strength, due in large measure to increased financial resources.

KEY TERMS

Democratic-Republicans 402
Federalist Party 402
Corrupt Bargain of 1824 402
Merit System (Civil Service) 402
Australian Ballot 402
Candidate-Centered Era 403

CRITICAL THINKING QUESTIONS

1. What external forces likely shape party dynamics? Are parties weaker or stronger when certain things are happening in society?
2. What factors help to explain transformations in party eras?

INTERNET RESOURCES

To explore party history in America, visit NewsVOA .com at http://www.voanews.com/specialenglish/2008-04-23-voa1.cfm

ADDITIONAL READING

Maisel, L. Sandy, and Mark D. Brewer. *Parties and Elections in America: The Electoral Process.* Lanham, MD: Rowman and Littlefield, 2009.

Reichley, A. James. *The Life of the Parties: A History of American Political Parties.* Lanham, MD: Rowman and Littlefield, 2000.

Parties and the Nomination Process

13.5 Outline the process by which party nominees are chosen to run in the general election.

(pages 404–407)

One of the core functions of political parties is to run primary elections that determine the candidates for the general election. Open systems allow any registered citizen to vote in the primary, while closed systems permit only party members to cast ballots. In three states there is also a "top two" system, whereby multicandidate contests lead to two general election candidates, regardless of which party they belong to. The model used to select presidential candidates is evolving and contentious. While some believe the presidential system is broken, due in large measure to the importance of a few early contests, exactly what should replace the current system is a topic of fierce debate.

KEY TERMS

Direct Primary Election 404
Closed Primary System 404
Open Primary System 404
National Nominating Convention 405
Binding Primaries 405
Nomination Caucus 405
Invisible Primary 406

CRITICAL THINKING QUESTIONS

1. Should party nomination contests be limited to only those registered as members of the party (closed primaries), or should all citizens have a say in picking party nominees of either party (open primaries)?
2. Is the current presidential nomination system broken? If so, what reforms would you suggest?

INTERNET RESOURCES

For more information on the presidential nomination process, visit the PBS NewsHour at http://www.pbs.org/newshour/extra/teachers/lessonplans/history/primaries_12-19.html

ADDITIONAL READING

Mayer, William G., and Andrew E. Busch. *The Frontloading Problem in Presidential Nominations.* Washington, DC: Brookings Institution Press, 2003.

Presidential Selection

13.6 Explain the process by which we select the president of the United States.

(pages 408–411)

Many forces shape the conduct of presidential elections, but none is more significant than the Electoral College. This complex, rather odd institution was yet another compromise at the Constitutional Convention, a means to moderate the "passions of the public" and to allow smaller states a greater say in the selection of the president. Today the Electoral College structures how and where campaigns are conducted and, occasionally, as in the 2000 presidential election, who takes up residence at the White House.

KEY TERMS

Electoral College 408
Twelfth Amendment (1804) 409
Unit Rule 409

CRITICAL THINKING QUESTIONS

1. How, exactly, does the Electoral College benefit small states? Was this a fair compromise at the Constitutional Convention? Has the system worked as the framers intended?
2. What are some advantages of the Electoral College? Along similar lines, what would be some downsides to a direct presidential election? How can the Electoral College be made meaningless *without* amending the Constitution?

INTERNET RESOURCES

To learn more about the Electoral College, see the U.S. National Archives and Records Administration at http://www.archives.gov/federal-register/electoral-college/index.html

ADDITIONAL READING

Schumaker, Paul D., and Burdett A. Loomis (eds.). *Choosing a President: The Electoral College and Beyond.* Washington, DC: Congressional Quarterly, 2002.

The Role of Money in Elections

13.7 Assess the critical role that money plays in the election process.

(pages 412–415)

Many Americans believe money distorts the election process. A number of laws have been passed to help level the playing field, most recently the Bipartisan Campaign Reform Act. Others argue that giving and collecting money is a form of political action. An important Supreme Court decision in the case of *Citizens United* v. *Federal Election Commission* seemed to buttress this position; the court found limits on corporate and union campaign spending unconstitutional.

KEY TERMS

Federal Election Campaign Act (FECA) 412
***Buckley* v. *Valeo* (1976)** 412
Incumbent Advantage 413
Term Limits 414
Bipartisan Campaign Reform Act (BCRA) 414
Soft Money 414
Citizens United* v. *Federal Elections Commission 414
Elite Democratic Model 416
Popular Democratic Model 416

CRITICAL THINKING QUESTIONS

1. What is your take on the central issue in *Buckley* v. *Valeo* (1976)? Is money a form of political speech, protected under the First Amendment? If so, would you extend these protections to corporations and labor unions, as the Supreme Court recently did?
2. One way to get around First Amendment protections is to create a voluntary public financing system for all elections. Candidates who chose to take public funds would be barred from additional fundraising. Does this make good sense? Are there downsides to this plan?

INTERNET RESOURCES

For extensive information on campaign finance, see the Center for Responsive Politics at http://www.opensecrets.org

ADDITIONAL READING

Farrar-Myers, Victoria A., and Diana Dwyre. *Limits and Loopholes: The Quest for Money, Free Speech, and Fair Elections.* Washington, DC: Congressional Quarterly, 2007.

Malbin, Michael J. (ed.). *Life after Reform: When the Bipartisan Campaign Reform Act Meets Politics.* Lanham, MD: Rowman and Littlefield, 2003.

Chapter Review   Test Your Knowledge

1. A major reason for the creation of the Electoral College was to ensure that
   a. the will of the majority of voters in each state would be accurately represented in presidential elections.
   b. men of the best character and intellect would be deciding who the next president and vice president would be.
   c. each state in the new Union would have equal representation in the election process.
   d. England would not interfere with the election process.

2. Regarding the role of political parties in elections, the framers of the Constitution
   a. reasoned that electors would rise above partisan preferences and vote for the candidates who would best serve the nation.
   b. assumed that a two-party system would always present the electorate with a clear and fair choice between distinct political philosophies.
   c. worried that partisan politics would compromise the electoral process.
   d. said very little, because they never foresaw the emergence of parties in the first place.

3. According to the Supreme Court case of *Citizens United* v. *Federal Elections Commission*
   a. bans on corporate spending on elections are unconstitutional.
   b. contributing money to a candidate is akin to free speech.
   c. unions should be able to spend money on political campaigns.
   d. All of the above.

4. What federal law was enacted in 2002, following the vote-count chaos in the 2000 presidential election?
   a. the 2002 Voting Rights Act
   b. the Motor Voter Act
   c. the Help America Vote Act
   d. the Butterfly Ballot Abolition Act

5. What prompted popular interest in the motor voter law?
   a. the desire to help democracy and the domestic automobile industry
   b. the desire to confine the pool of registered voters to responsible adults
   c. the desire to counteract state registration laws that may have had the effect of unfairly limiting people's ability to register to vote
   d. the desire to reinforce state registration laws requiring registered voters to be residents of their state and citizens in good legal standing

6. Which of the following is NOT a reason for the massive increase in the cost of political campaigns?
   a. an increased dependence on television advertising
   b. an increase in the number of voters that campaign advertising must reach
   c. campaign consultants
   d. the abolition of poll taxes

7. The unit rule and partisan slates of electors make it *likely* that the most popular candidate (the highest vote getter) will become the president but do not *guarantee* it.
   a. true
   b. false

8. What did the Federal Election Campaign Act and its subsequent amendments prohibit?
   a. limitless campaign spending on the part of candidates, and limitless contributions from individuals, groups, or political parties
   b. warrantless wiretapping
   c. making individual campaign contributions tax deductible
   d. the use of soft money in campaigns

9. One result of the Supreme Court case *Buckley* v. *Valeo* (1976) was to lift most restrictions from the activities of political parties.
   a. true
   b. false

10. The outcome of the 2010 Supreme Court case *Citizens United* v. *Federal Elections Commission* was that
    a. labor unions were allowed to spend money from their general funds to help elect candidates.
    b. corporations were allowed to spend money from their general funds to help elect candidates.
    c. candidates were barred from taking money from citizens groups.
    d. both a and b

11. One explanation for the decline in voter turnout during recent decades is that people's lifestyles have changed.
    a. true   b. false

12. What is so paradoxical about the low turnout of young voters?
    a. The average age of political candidates themselves has steadily declined.
    b. Young people keep up with the news more avidly than older voters do.
    c. Young people are more inclined than ever before to volunteer to help their community.
    d. Surveys indicate that young people are less disenchanted with the government than older people are.

13. Political parties educate voters, aggregate interests, and help turn private citizens into public actors.
    a. true
    b. false

14. What phenomenon seems to be a key reason for the decline of the average citizen's participation in the election process?
    a. how unimportant the issues seem these days
    b. how uninspiring or incompetent most candidates seem these days
    c. the decline in the parties' attempts to communicate with average citizens
    d. the decline of local party organizations

15. A semiformal hierarchy or "chain of command" exists among national, state, and local party committees, in descending order of authority.
   a. true   **b.** false

16. Which political party dominated national politics in the early nineteenth century?
   a. the Federalist Party
   b. the Whig Party
   c. the Democratic-Republican Party
   d. the Liberty Party

17. Which of the following was true during much of the nineteenth century?
   a. Party identification was important to most voters.
   b. Local parties were strong.
   c. Campaigning was generally interpersonal (meaning face-to-face).
   d. Party leaders selected presidential nominees.
   e. All of the above.

18. In recent years, at the same time that party organizations are regaining their footing nationally, a growing number of Americans see parties as corrupt.
   a. true   **b.** false

19. How is an open primary different from a closed primary?
   a. In an open primary, voters from one party can vote in the primary election of the other party.
   b. In an open primary, candidates in one party can run in the primary election of the other party.
   c. In an open primary, voters from either party can cast one vote in *both* parties' primary elections.
   d. In an open primary, a third-party candidate can be on the ballot of either of the two main parties.

20. According to some, one problem with the voter-controlled primary system is that
   a. it has made the nomination a popularity contest.
   b. it has made the nomination process too short.
   c. it grants a disproportionate significance to voters and caucus members in two states with few electoral votes, New Hampshire and Iowa.
   d. it has exaggerated candidates' need to appeal to big-city voters.

mypoliscilab Exercises

Apply what you learned in this chapter on **MyPoliSciLab**.

Read on mypoliscilab.com

eText: Chapter 13

Study and Review on mypoliscilab.com

Pre-Test
Post-Test
Chapter Exam
Flashcards

Watch on mypoliscilab.com

Video: Senator Specter Switches Parties
Video: Dissecting Party Primaries
Video: Oprah Fires Up Obama Campaign
Video: State Primary Race
Video: Who Are the Super Delegates
Video: Money in the 2008 Presidential Race

Explore on mypoliscilab.com

Simulation: You Are an Informed Voter Helping Your Classmates Decide How to Vote
Simulation: You Are a Campaign Manager: Countdown to 270!
Simulation: You Are a Campaign Manager: McCain Navigates Campaign Financing,
Simulation: You Are a Media Consultant to a Political Candidate
Comparative: Comparing Political Parties
Timeline: Television and Presidential Campaigns
Timeline: The Evolution of Political Parties in the United States
Timeline: Nominating Process
Visual Literacy: State Control and National Platforms
Visual Literacy: Iowa Caucuses
Visual Literacy: The Electoral College: Campaign Consequences and Mapping the Results

The Policy Process and Economic Policy

KEY OBJECTIVES

After completing this chapter, you should be prepared to:

14.1 Illustrate how values shape public policy in a democracy.

14.2 Compare and contrast the three main types of public policies.

14.3 Analyze how the policy process is shaped by political influences.

14.4 Identify the key indicators of economic performance used by economists.

14.5 Describe the major actors responsible for creating economic policy.

14.6 Explain the major sources of U.S. government revenue and expenditure.

14.7 Assess the major instruments of monetary policy.

I n February 2009, President Barack Obama made a major speech to Congress. He spoke of the need to foster economic recovery, reform the health care system, and improve the educational system. All of these are policy goals that receive widespread support, but people disagree about the best ways to advance these objectives. Interest groups, political parties, and influential individuals have different ideas about what the government ought to do. Their ideas often flow from their differing assessments of who should bear the costs and receive the benefits of specific policy choices.

During the 2008 election campaign, Barack Obama pledged to reform the nation's health care system so that everyone, including the 45 million Americans without health insurance, would have access to medical care. In his speech to Congress, President Obama, said "I'm bringing together businesses and workers, doctors and health care providers, Democrats and Republicans to begin work on this issue." His statement acknowledged the fact that health care is a policy that affects

Why is public policy political?

many interests in society, including organizations of doctors and insurance companies who have huge financial stakes in the current system.

As Congress held hearings on health care during 2009, Republicans tried to block Democratic proposals; interest groups funded commercials to influence public opinion; and Democrats complained that the president was too willing to compromise. The proposals that emerged posed the choice between accepting compromises that make no one completely happy or failing to produce any policy reform that could receive sufficient support in Congress.

So far, you have learned how a bill becomes a law (in Chapter 6) and how laws are administered (Chapter 8), but public policy is more than passing and enforcing laws. Public policy involves complex interactions among political actors that determine what government does or does not do. The action (or inaction) of government affects people's lives and determines the distribution of benefits and burdens in society.

Resource Center
• Glossary
• Vocabulary Example
• Connect the Link

■ **Policy Process Model:** A way of thinking about how policy is made in terms of steps in a progression.

EXAMPLE: *Most bills passed by Congress go through phases that mirror the early parts of the policy process model.*

Ideas and Values in Public Policy

14.1 Illustrate how values shape public policy in a democracy.
(pages 426–429)

Politicians, members of the media, and average citizens often draw a distinction between politics and policy. This difference rests on the notion that politics is like a game, or even a war, in which strategies are used to gain advantages over opponents and win battles.

Policy is the output of politics and, to some people, not political in itself. You may have heard commentators praising presidential debates as a time for "setting politics aside," forcing the candidates to deal with *policy* issues. But this common notion of an either-or relationship is an artificial way of thinking about these two concepts.

As defined, public policy is what you get after the equal sign in the equation of politics plus government. Elections, social movements, interest group activity, and the actions of political institutions such as Congress or the federal courts all go into the equation *before* this equal sign. Using this metaphor, public policy is inherently political. It reflects the exercise of power in our system of government, our economic system, and our society in general.

Social scientists and other policy specialists often think about public policy as a collection of phases in a process, as though the intricacies of the process were somehow disconnected from the political world. There is a well-worn approach to the study of the process of policy formation, usually called the **policy process model**■, which begins with the identification of a problem and concludes with the analysis of the effectiveness of the solutions applied to that problem.[1] This model forms the core of this chapter, but we will also help you see the pathways that connect politics with public policy and the effect of these variables on the public as well as other segments of our society and political world.

The Steps of Policymaking

The policy process model describes policymaking in five or six steps: (1) identifying the policy problem, (2) setting an agenda, (3) formulating a solution, (4) legitimizing the solution, (5) implementing the solution, and in some versions, (6) evaluating the solution. Taking a different perspective, however, is Deborah Stone, one of several political scientists trying to get us to think beyond the limits of the policy process model. In Stone's view, the policy process model lacks connections to the ways that real people and their governments make decisions about policy:

> The production [process] model fails to capture what I see as the essence of policymaking in political communities: the struggle over ideas. Ideas are a medium of exchange and a mode of influence even more powerful than money and votes and guns. . . . Ideas are at the center of all political conflict. Policymaking, in turn, is a constant struggle over the criteria for classification, the boundaries of categories, and the definition of ideals that guide the way people behave.[2]

For Stone, the heart of policymaking is how people interpret values, such as equity, efficiency, security, and liberty, and how they use these values in the identification of problems and possible solutions. For example, most people would agree that equality is a highly desirable goal for our society. Should we therefore guarantee an equal level of health care for all citizens? Or should the government simply offer the *opportunity* for health care through policies that help businesses hire more workers, who might then receive some health care coverage through their employers? Our answers to such questions reflect our preferences about the role of government in our lives. They also reflect the influence exerted on us by the government, the media, and other organized interests.

Values

Let's look at two terms that are often found at the bull's-eye of debates about public policy: *freedom* versus *equality*. Consider this familiar sentence from the Declaration of Independence: "We hold these truths to be self-evident, that all men are created equal, that they are endowed by their Creator with certain unalienable Rights, that among these are Life, Liberty and the pursuit of Happiness." This often-cited excerpt professes a set of values that, presumably, makes us one people sharing core beliefs in equality and liberty. There is some truth in this statement: Not many people in this country would openly denounce the ideas of freedom or equality. These two values frame many of the policies proposed by our representatives or by those seeking governmental action.

For example, President George W. Bush signed a bill into law that made it harder for people to declare bankruptcy and avoid repaying their debts. He praised the policy as an opportunity for lower-income Americans to get access to loans and other credit, since banks and lenders would approve more loans because of the decreased possibility of failure to repay them. In other words, the president praised the new policy as a way to equalize access to credit for all citizens. Critics of the bill charged that this change in the law would increase profits and reduce risks for the already powerful banks and financial institutions, by decreasing the freedom of the down-on-their-luck defaulters to get out of paying back their debts. *Both* the president and his opponents spoke the language of freedom and equality.

So who is right? How can people on one side see an advancement of equality or freedom when those on the other view the same actions as a retreat from these cherished values? One persuasive answer is that each side defines *freedom* and *equality* in different ways. A number of political thinkers have pondered this solution, and their ideas have much to say about the nature of public policy.

FREEDOM   Many Americans believe that **freedom** simply means the ability of a citizen to live his or her life the way he or she wants, but actually this important concept has many meanings. Is freedom the ability to think, travel, and speak freely and to associate with whomever you want? Or is it a limitation placed on other people to keep them from meddling in your life? The British political theorist Sir Isaiah Berlin called the first version *positive* liberty or freedom, because people tend to express it as the ability to do something. Berlin labeled the second version *negative* liberty or freedom, because the measure of freedom, usually expressed as the freedom from some outside force, is based on how few limits there are on its enjoyment.[3]

These two versions of freedom are connected closely to people's views of the role of government. If freedom is measured and defined by what you can do (positive freedom), then whatever helps you extend this enjoyment of liberty must be a good thing. Students in a public university or college may see that government can create opportunities for a high-quality education that would otherwise not be available to them. Students in both private and public colleges and universities can experience the extension of freedom through federal and state government student loan programs, such as Pell Grants. Without this support, your freedom to learn and gain an advantage in the competition for good jobs and careers would be decreased. From this viewpoint, government creates freedom by expanding opportunity. However, a reasonable person could look at the same example and make the case that to provide a lower-cost, high-quality education to a wider segment of the population at a public college or university, the public must pay higher taxes. This person might view these increased taxes as an intrusion into his or her private life and a limitation on the freedom to use that money as he or she sees fit. If we look at it this way, government activity such as sponsorship of grants, loans, and funding of public colleges and universities causes a loss of personal freedom.

EQUALITY   Like freedom, equality is highly valued by Americans. And like freedom, equality is divisible into two meanings that have powerful effects on public policy. The ideas of Alexis de Tocqueville, the French aristocrat and political thinker who traveled the United States in the 1830s to study our version of democracy, persist today. He argued that Americans often hold conflicting interpretations of equality, especially if it means political equality or something broader, such as social or economic equality.[4] Later political thinkers have elaborated on Tocqueville's insights by asserting that there are two forms of this value, one based on *equality of process* and the other based on *equality of outcomes.*[5]

Deborah Stone illustrates the difference between these two concepts by asking us to do a mental exercise: divide a cake among a group of people. How, she asks, might we go about this task in a way that would ensure equality? One sure way to do this would be to do what happens at most birthday parties: You count the number of people who want cake and then divide the whole cake by that number. What matters here is that the final result is fair, as measured by who gets what. But there's an equally logical way to approach divvying up the cake that reflects another way of thinking about equality. What if the cake were placed in the center of a room and all who wanted some sat in a circle at an equal distance from it? Now everyone has an equal opportunity to get what they want—a messy proposition, especially if you're talking about kids, and if some want more than others. And of course, some may be faster or more ruthless in their pursuit of the cake. It's safe to assume that some party guests will get more cake than others. Stone calls the opportunity-based version of equality the *equality of process.*[6] But is this equality? If it is, it is not the same kind of equality as an equal division based on the number who say that they want cake would be.

The cake example is likely to stick in your mind because of the absurdity of the exercise. We can easily imagine the slapstick results of an all-out, mad dash for cake at a child's birthday party. But what if the desired object is not cake but health care, a well-paying job, or a sound education? Should we strive for equality of outcomes and redistribute those outcomes from the haves to the have-nots? Or should we seek out and support solutions that provide opportunities to equalize competition? The answers to these questions rest on your view of equality.

As with the concept of freedom, this view is closely connected to how you perceive the role of government. If you champion equality of outcomes, you will likely see the need for government action to create equal outcomes, because you see human beings as generally self-interested and unwilling to share their resources. Our nation's founders stated this eloquently in their writings, notably in *Federalist No. 10,* which is reprinted in Appendix 3, pages A-32–A-34. People who believe that equality prevails when the rules of the game are fair and open for participation (equality of process) will view active governmental involvement less favorably: To them, government's role should be limited to setting and enforcing basic standards of fair play and access.

CONNECT THE **LINK**
(Appendix 3, pages A-32–A-34) How do the different types of ideology fit with ideas about economics?

■ **Classical Liberalism:** A political philosophy based on the desire for limited government; the basis for modern conservatism.

SIGNIFICANCE: *Modern conservatives debate whether expansion of government and increased spending violate the true meaning of conservatism.*

Political Ideology

Ideas about freedom and equality are linked to political ideology. Table 14.1 shows that the ideas of someone who holds the *positive* view of equality and the *negative* view of freedom have a strong resemblance to **classical liberalism**■, an ideology of the eighteenth and nineteenth centuries that today we call **conservatism.** In many ways, modern conservatism is a view of politics built on faith in the free market to regulate the economics of a society. Modern conservatives see government's main role as setting basic policies to see that people have equal *opportunities,* but government's activity must stop there so that it does not limit personal liberty. In opposition to this present-day conservative ideology stands **modern liberalism**■, or what is now often called **progressivism.** Liberals or progressives, who tend to favor equal *outcomes* and share faith in the *positive* version of freedom, favor a more activist government. They see government as a powerful force needed to overcome inequality and expand the amount of freedom available to all citizens.[7]

Of course, these are models of pure ideologies, and most Americans have more mixed ideological orientations. Some analysts argue that the pragmatism of America's political culture comes from a mainstream, blended ideology that uses its views of these key values in different ways in different situations. For example, an individual may oppose a government-run health insurance plan on the grounds that such intervention may impinge upon personal freedoms but be highly supportive of the Medicare program, which provides health care coverage to millions of older Americans. In the case of Medicare, the program's popularity often blurs the reality that it is indeed one of the largest and most expensive parts of the federal government.

The underlying beliefs that shape what people want and expect from public policy have clear links to the five pathways of political action. Both liberals and conservatives can and do use the pathways to influence the making of public policy. Elections influence public policy indirectly: We assume, for example, that if we elect different representatives to Congress, they will approach what needs to be done in new ways because of their different skills, talents, and views. Courts can also be a means for citizens and other political actors to influence public policy. As we saw in the landmark 1954 *Brown* v. *Board of Education* case, which declared legally mandated public school segregation unconstitutional, there was a sharp turn along the path of the nation's race relations policies.

The grassroots mobilization and cultural change pathways are other avenues along which citizens can make their mark on government actions. The social movements of the 1960s and 1970s fundamentally changed major policy areas in this country. For example, in the 1970s, the environmentalist movement scored major legislative victories with the passage of laws such as the Clean Air Act and the Clean Water Act (see the Timeline on the Environmental Movement, pages 430-431). This movement also helped mold the mind-set of today's more ecologically aware public, which takes for granted the recycling of glass and plastic bottles and many other formerly discarded items.

The most potent pathway for influencing public policy involves lobbying decision makers. The public often thinks of lobbying as negative, because it implies that a "special interest" is using undue influence to get more than its "fair share." When people agree with or share the goals of those doing the lobbying, however, "special interest" takes on a more positive meaning.

TABLE 14.1	Summarizing Notions of "Freedom" and "Equality"	
	POSITIVE FREEDOM ("FREEDOM TO …")	**NEGATIVE FREEDOM ("FREEDOM FROM …")**
Equality of process	Blended ideology	Conservative ideology
Equality of outcomes	Liberal ideology	Blended ideology

■ **Modern Liberalism (Progressivism):** A political philosophy based on the belief that government is the best actor to solve social, economic, and political problems.

EXAMPLE: *During the Great Depression of the 1930s, the unprecedented expansion of the federal government was welcomed by liberals of the era.*

Ideas and Values in Public Policy

14.1 **Illustrate how values shape public policy in a democracy.**

PRACTICE QUIZ: UNDERSTAND AND APPLY

1. For political scientist Deborah Stone, the key to how public policy is formed is
   a. the sequence that begins with political actors identifying a problem and ends with the implementation and assessment of a solution.
   b. how people interpret principles such as liberty, equality, and efficiency.
   c. who has political power and what their relation to the perceived problem is.
   d. when, in the policy process cycle, political actors converge to address the perceived problem.

2. Negative freedom is accomplished through limits on the activities of government.
   a. true   b. false

3. Recall the two opposing views of publicly funded higher education: that the taxes needed to support it are an unfair intrusion on taxpayers, and that such taxes are worth it because state schools greatly broaden citizens' access to higher education and its rewards. What do these opposing views illustrate?
   a. Democratic and Republican ideology, respectively
   b. the conflict between private and public views of freedom
   c. the conflict between positive and negative views of freedom
   d. the conflict between short-term and long-term views of freedom

ANALYZE

1. How does an active government affect equality of outcomes in American society?

2. Why is lobbying one of the most potent methods of influencing public policy?

3. How do classical liberalism and modern liberalism differ?

IDENTIFY THE CONCEPT THAT DOESN'T BELONG

a. Lobbying
b. Grassroots movements
c. Elections
d. Federalism
e. Public opinion

COURTS **CULTURAL CHANGE** **ELECTIONS** **GRASSROOTS MOBILIZATION** **LOBBYING DECISION-MAKERS**

PRO ENVIRONMENTAL MOVEMENT

1962
Rachel Carson writes *Silent Spring*, a book that alerted the country to the dangers, especially for humans, of pesticides.

1969
National Environmental Policy Act, first major environmental legislation, created the Environmental Protection Agency.

1970
April 22
Earth Day! Millions protest for air and water cleanup and the preservation of nature.

1973
Endangered Species Act passes—a powerful tool in protecting the environment.

1977
Supreme Court upholds the 1973 Endangered Species Act and stops construction of the Tellico Dam (*Tennessee Valley Authority* v. *Hill* et al.). Rules that the extinction of a species is to be prevented no matter the cost.

1979
Three Mile Island nuclear power facility loses coolant and nearly has a meltdown.

1980
Congress passes the "Superfund" legislation (CERCLA: The Comprehensive Environmental Response, Compensation and Liability Act), directing the EPA to clean up abandoned toxic waste dumps.

1962	1969–70	1973	1977–79	1980

ANTI ENVIRONMENTAL MOVEMENT

1973
July 29
Congress approves the Alaska pipeline.

1980
James Watt appointed Secretary of the Interior under President Reagan. Proposes many anti-environmental acts and resolutions.

Joseph Coors organizes the Sagebrush Rebellion and The Heritage Foundation, both anti-environmental groups that attack the rights gained to date by the environmental movement.
1980

As scientific evidence shows increased global warming, a reduction in rain forests, and higher levels of pollution, the international community struggles to cope. Governments today must strike a delicate balance between economic growth and development and environmental protections. If there is too much regulation of business to protect the environment, businesses may relocate to other countries or regions, harming the U.S. economy. If there is too little regulation, the environment suffers, because businesses don't want to risk the higher costs that go along with environmentally friendly practices.

How far should the government go to protect our environment?

Essay Questions

1. Since most regulations to promote clean air and water cost businesses extra money, some believe that they can unduly harm our economy as businesses have less operating funds to expand and invest. Do you think that these concerns are reasonable? Or do you think that environmental protection is worth the costs?

2. Should public opinion influence our environmental policy or should we rely upon the recommendations of the scientific community? How large of a role do you think business leaders ought to play? How should we as a society balance these competing needs?

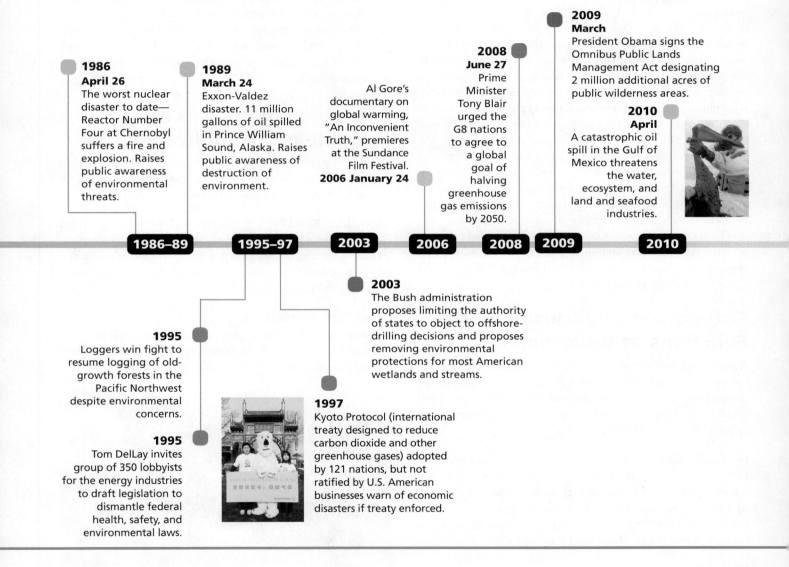

1986
April 26
The worst nuclear disaster to date—Reactor Number Four at Chernobyl suffers a fire and explosion. Raises public awareness of environmental threats.

1989
March 24
Exxon-Valdez disaster. 11 million gallons of oil spilled in Prince William Sound, Alaska. Raises public awareness of destruction of environment.

Al Gore's documentary on global warming, "An Inconvenient Truth," premieres at the Sundance Film Festival.
2006 January 24

2008
June 27
Prime Minister Tony Blair urged the G8 nations to agree to a global goal of halving greenhouse gas emissions by 2050.

2009
March
President Obama signs the Omnibus Public Lands Management Act designating 2 million additional acres of public wilderness areas.

2010
April
A catastrophic oil spill in the Gulf of Mexico threatens the water, ecosystem, and land and seafood industries.

1986–89 **1995–97** **2003** **2006** **2008** **2009** **2010**

2003
The Bush administration proposes limiting the authority of states to object to offshore-drilling decisions and proposes removing environmental protections for most American wetlands and streams.

1995
Loggers win fight to resume logging of old-growth forests in the Pacific Northwest despite environmental concerns.

1995
Tom DelLay invites group of 350 lobbyists for the energy industries to draft legislation to dismantle federal health, safety, and environmental laws.

1997
Kyoto Protocol (international treaty designed to reduce carbon dioxide and other greenhouse gases) adopted by 121 nations, but not ratified by U.S. American businesses warn of economic disasters if treaty enforced.

Resource Center
• Glossary
• Vocabulary Example
• Connect the Link

■ **Policy Categories:** A way of classifying policies by their intended goal and means of carrying out that goal.

EXAMPLE: *Social welfare programs, such as Medicaid, can be categorized as redistributive, because they use tax dollars to provide benefits to a wide segment of the population.*

Types of Public Policy

14.2 Compare and contrast the three main types of public policies.
(pages 432–433)

So far, we've discussed public policy as a process that is influenced by many factors, especially the basic underlying beliefs people hold about politics and government. We've also seen where each of the five pathways can lead in both the substance and the process of public policy. Moving beyond these rather theoretical and somewhat philosophical ideas, how can we study public policy in order to compare one policy choice with another in a meaningful way? How can we find better solutions to ongoing problems?

For answers, we can look at all of the attempts to solve problems in a particular issue area, a broad category, such as the environment. Problems to be solved related to the environment include preserving old-growth forests, managing Yosemite National Park, and addressing climate change. Organizing policies by issue areas helps us make sense of the broad contours of both the problems and their possible solutions, but this approach may not help us understand many of the particular nuances that shape public policies.

Categorizing Policies by Basic Functions of Government

A more sophisticated approach to studying public policy involves creating **policy categories** that classify what policies do and how they do it. To do this, political scientists have identified three basic functions of government: **distribution, regulation,** and **redistribution.**[8]

DISTRIBUTION A government *distributes* a society's resources, such as wealth, services, or other things of value, when it gives benefits to specific groups in that society. When undertaken by a legislature, such distribution is often given the negative label "pork barrel" spending, because it seems designed to bring credit to the legislator who proposed it.

REGULATION *Regulation* takes place when a government uses legislative, military, or judicial power to stop an action by a person, organization, or group or when it mandates other behaviors or actions. For example, because of the actions of environmental organizations and engaged citizens, today's energy producers must meet federal regulations designed to limit air pollution. If an electric plant does not meet these requirements, its owners can be fined or punished in other ways.

REDISTRIBUTION *Redistribution* resembles distribution in many ways, but instead of a specific group benefiting from the actions of government, a much larger segment of society

receives goods or services. Of course, redistributive policies mean that resources are taken from one part of society and given to another. An example of a redistributive policy is taxing workers to fund social welfare programs for the poor. Because redistributive policies usually pit one social class against another, they are generally the most difficult policies to enact and implement.

Because all government policies can be placed in one of these three categories, this approach allows us to see the way governments operate and, with a bit more thought, how each of the pathways of political action can influence each of these government functions.

Categorizing Policies by Tangible or Symbolic Benefits

Categorizing policies by the nature of their benefits is also useful. Policies themselves can produce either tangible benefits for the public or merely symbolic benefits.[9]

TANGIBLE BENEFIT A tangible benefit such as federal assistance for victims of hurricanes and other natural disasters, is something that the recipients will experience in a material way—for instance, receiving truckloads of clean drinking water and dry ice to preserve food.

SYMBOLIC BENEFIT A symbolic benefit does not offer concrete, material results; it provides a theoretical solution to a problem. For example, the independent commission that investigated the intelligence failures leading up to 9/11 could not

Water and ice being distributed in Saucier, Mississippi, following Hurricane Katrina in 2005. —*Do you think such tangible benefits are the responsibility of federal, state, or local government? Why?*

directly change the U.S. government's antiterrorism policy, nor could it restore life to the almost 3,000 people who perished in those attacks. The commission also could not ensure adoption of all of its suggestions. Still, the actions of the commission communicated to the public that the government was working to solve this very difficult problem. The benefit—the feeling of security we may get from knowing that intelligent and dedicated people are trying to make us safer—may not help put food on the table, but it is still a benefit.

PATHWAYS of change from around the world

How much should the government do to help the young individuals of a nation build their futures? In Scotland, the government has embarked on a strategy to help young people avoid or get past some of the more difficult problems that beset young people in any nation, including drug abuse and crime. The programs aimed at addressing these problems are collectively know as "youth work" and have strong support among Scotland's young people. An example of "youth work" in action is the Scottish Government's Youth Health

Panel. The Youth Health panel allows Scots between the ages of 14 and 26 to develop the actual government communications on youth health issues. The youth panelists write health information brochures, produce videos, and create podcasts that are designed to educate young Scots on threats to their health in a relevant and down-to-earth manner.

Some policymakers and educators are pushing to make these programs a part of the curricula for Scotland's schools. However, a number of organizations have been working to keep participation in these youth work programs voluntary. Their argument is that when the programs are compulsory and part of a structured educational setting, those most at-risk—school dropouts—will be left out of the benefits that youth work can offer. The debate over the future of youth work is ongoing, and part of the discussion is generated by young people themselves, who are represented by the Scottish Youth Parliament, an organization supported in part by the Scottish Executive and designed to be a way to have ongoing input about a wide range of policy issues from Scotland's younger citizens.

SOURCE: YouthLink Scotland, The National Agency for Youth Work http://www.youthlinkscotland.org/Index.asp?MainID=7274

Types of Public Policy

14.2 Compare and contrast the three main types of public policies.

PRACTICE QUIZ: UNDERSTAND AND APPLY

1. When the government uses legislative, military, or judicial power to stop an action, or when it mandates other behaviors or actions, it is engaged in
   a. distribution.
   c. redistribution.
   b. regulation.
   d. both a and c

2. Redistribution policies tend to pit one social class against another.
   a. true
   b. false

3. Distribution policies implemented by legislatures often are given the negative label of
   a. logrolling.
   c. bundling.
   b. nest-building.
   d. pork barrel spending.

4. The independent commission that investigated the intelligence failures leading up to the 9/11 terrorist attacks is an example of
   a. a nontaxable benefit.
   c. a symbolic benefit.
   b. a material benefit.
   d. a tangible benefit.

ANALYZE

1. Taxation is one form of redistribution policy; what are some others? What objections would be raised about them?

2. Is military service a tangible benefit, a symbolic benefit, or both? Discuss the reasons for your response.

3. Why are policies that regulate behaviors and actions useful in addressing societal problems such as air pollution?

IDENTIFY THE CONCEPT THAT DOESN'T BELONG

a. Higher education grants
b. Food stamps
c. Medicaid (government provided medical insurance for the poor)
d. Clean air laws
e. Government subsidized day care for poor families

Resource Center
• Glossary
• Vocabulary Example
• Connect the Link

The Public Policy Process

14.3 Analyze how the policy process is shaped by political influences.

(pages 434–437)

Much of what we know about public policy and how it is made can be related to the policy process model, which we mentioned earlier in the chapter. Like all models, it is a generalization—a simplified representation of reality. It must exclude some complexities in order to make a very intricate process easier to understand.

Although scholars in the field of public policy disagree over some details, the major parts of the policy process model are generally thought to consist of the six steps shown in Figure 14.1: (1) identifying the problem, (2) setting an agenda, (3) formulating policy, (4) legitimizing policy, (5) implementing policy, and (6) evaluating policy.

Process implies separate actions that lead to a final goal. However, in many cases, the steps in the process do not directly flow one from the other. What the policy process model does well is to tell us how policy was made—well, poorly, or indifferently. The fact that making public policy is a highly political endeavor helps explain why the model does not always reveal a nice, neat set of predictable steps. Political actors can affect the process at every stage, and sometimes, they cause an unexpected progression of phases or the elimination of phases.

Identifying the Problem

Just how do we know that a problem exists? Perhaps no issue more clearly demonstrates the complexity and importance of problem identification in the formation of policy than global warming, one aspect of climate change. Since the 1980s scientists have warned that the burning of fossil fuels was leading to conditions that trap heat in the atmosphere and thus raise global temperatures.[10] While the projections of scientists caught the attention of government officials both in the United States and abroad, difficulties in establishing the magnitude and timing of climate change have plagued efforts to create policies that address global warming.

Proponents of immediate action to address global warming note existing evidence of climate change—including retreating glaciers, species migration, and some of the hottest years on record—as clear signs that the problem has already been observed and that actions to confront global warming are therefore needed immediately.[11] To these individuals there is no question that the problem exists.

Opponents have consistently held that there is not enough evidence available to firmly establish that humans are altering the planet's climate, and they maintain that any recent warming is the product of natural cycles. Critics contend that climate

FIGURE 14.1 ▪ **The Policymaking Process**

The policy process model presents a picture of policymaking that begins with the identification of a problem and eventually moves to reexamination of the solution or solutions to that problem. Real-world policymaking is not always so orderly. It may begin at some point other than the identification of a problem.

Problem Identification—**Publicize a problem and demand government action.**
Participants: Media • Interest Groups • Citizen Initiatives • Public Opinion

Agenda Setting—**Decide what issues will be resolved and what matters government will address.**
Participants: Elites • President • Congress

Policy Formulation—**Develop policy proposals to resolve issues and ameliorate problems.**
Participants: Think Tanks • Presidents and Executive Office • Congressional Committees • Interest Groups

Policy Legitimation—**Select a proposal, generate political support for it, enact it into law, and rule on its Constitutionality.**
Participants: Interest Groups • President • Congress • Courts

Policy Implementation—**Organize departments and agencies, provide payments or services, and levy taxes.**
Participants: President and White House • Executive Departments and Agencies

Policy Evaluation—**Report outputs of government programs, evaluate policy impact on target and nontarget groups, and propose changes and "reforms."**
Participants: Executive Departments and Agencies • Congressional Oversight Committees • Mass Media • Think Tanks • Interest Groups

change is simply a theory and that costly policies aimed at reducing carbon emissions are unnecessary until the problem can be more firmly established.[12]

Whether an issue is a problem depends, for the most part, on who is advocating each position. Well-organized groups with

CONNECT THE LINK

(Chapter 5, pages 134–138) What is it about social movements that makes them a natural forum for political expression about divisive issues?

■ **Institutional Agenda:** A set of problems that governmental decision makers are actively working to solve.

EXAMPLE: *Bills introduced into Congress are part of the federal government's institutional agenda.*

the resources of money, larger memberships, and connections are more likely to gain access to decision makers to persuade them to see things their way. There is a major debate within the social sciences about this question: To whom do the policymakers listen? Social scientists calling themselves **pluralists** argue that our system of open government, with its multiple points of access to policymakers, allows people without resources like money and connections to still have their voices heard.[13] Others argue that policymaking is really driven by elitism—that only people with power and money will get access to the decision makers.[14]

Without a doubt, some problems simply cry out for action. Terrorism on American soil crystallized in an unforgettable display of violence and brutality on September 11, 2001. Such events, including many of far lower magnitude, are known as **focusing events**—moments that bring a problem to the attention of both the public and policymakers. At least at first, there is no debate about the existence of a problem, and the event serves as a **trigger mechanism,** a means of propelling an established problem on to the next stage of the policy process, setting an agenda.[15]

PATHWAYS of action

FocusDriven

Cell phones have generated a communication revolution around the world, but they have also been the cause of thousands of deaths on America's roadways. Over the past decade, a growing number of Americans have lost their lives to drivers who were distracted by making calls or texting behind the wheel.

In an effort to lower the number of Americans who are killed by cell phone–related causes, a group of individuals who lost loved ones to such accidents banded together in 2010 to create the group FocusDriven, an organization modeled after the very successful Mothers Against Drunk Driving (MADD), which dramatically strengthened laws related to driving under the influence of alcohol or drugs. Through its efforts to increase awareness of cell phone–related driving fatalities, and through direct contacts with legislators both in Washington, D.C., and state capitals, FocusDriven has been behind the growth of laws that ban the use of cell phones and texting while driving throughout the United States.

SOURCE: http://www.focusdriven.org/index.aspx

Setting an Agenda

To make good use of time and provide structure, well-organized meetings are always planned around an *agenda,* a list of issues and ideas up for discussion or actions to be undertaken.

However, the ability to exclude an item from the agenda, for whatever reason, is a powerful way to control what government does.[16]

As an example, in the 1950s and 1960s, one of the Senate's most powerful members, Georgia's Richard Russell, was instrumental in keeping civil rights policy off the nation's agenda by declaring there was no problem with racial segregation, because segregation worked![17]

The process of crafting a solution—even to shockingly obvious problems, such as the racial segregation of the 1950s—cannot begin until formal decision makers, generally those who hold positions of governmental authority, actually place the problem on the nation's formal or **institutional agenda**■.[18] For example, the flood of legislation introduced in Congress after 9/11 gave tangible proof that our national legislators believed the problem of terrorism to be urgent enough to require an immediate solution.

Citizens' actions can also propel problems onto the formal agenda. In Chapter 5, pages 134–138, we traced some of the actions of the people involved in the struggle over civil rights during the 1950s and 1960s. Their efforts forced decision makers to face the problems associated with our racially segregated society.

Like problem identification, agenda setting in the absence of a major crisis is largely determined by the organization and resources of individuals and coordinated interests. People and groups who can best articulate their position or who have what it takes to gain access to policymakers will usually succeed in getting their problem on the agenda.

Once a problem is on the agenda, how do you keep it there? Anthony Downs has created a valuable way of thinking about the nature of agenda items that he calls the **issue-attention cycle.**[19] Downs argues that some issues are more likely to remain on the formal agenda, just as others are doomed to fade away. Even issues that affect small slices of the population, that lack political, economic, or social clout, or that are difficult to address may first grab lots of attention, but they usually fall off the agenda because of the cost and inconvenience associated with solving them or the inability of the affected parties to keep the decision makers' attention.

Formulating and Legitimizing Policy

Once a problem makes it onto the agenda, the political pathways haven't reached their end. In fact, the next phase of the policymaking process, formulation, is as politically driven as agenda setting—if not more so.

FORMULATING POLICY   Formulating policy means crafting solutions to identified problems. Solutions can come in many forms. Clearly, the **laws** passed by legislatures, like those passed

■ **Discretion:** The power to apply policy in ways that fit particular circumstances.

SIGNIFICANCE: *Along with rule-making authority, discretion is one of the major sources of power for the executive branch.*

by Congress, are attempts to solve problems. The legislative process itself, including the introduction of bills, hearings, and floor debates, are all parts of formulating public policy: At each of these stages, the solution can change and evolve. When presidents issue executive orders directing the federal government to do—or to stop doing—various things, they are also engaged in problem solving. The **decisions** made by courts, especially the U.S. Supreme Court, are also policies because other branches of government and the nation's citizens are bound by these decisions as though they were laws passed by Congress.

MYTH EXPOSED Many Americans believe that once Congress creates legislation the agencies and departments of government simply carry out the laws. But in reality the institutions of the federal bureaucracy do far more than carry out legislation; they often make laws. In many cases, Congress delegates its lawmaking authority for specific problem-solving purposes to the departments and agencies of the federal government. Such **rule-making authority** allows a department or an agency to pass rules and regulations that affect our lives, such as imposing standards on the food we eat and the cars we drive. Because thorny problems often require highly skilled and specialized officials to design exceedingly technical solutions—and sometimes, because Congress may simply want to pass off a tough, politically charged problem to someone else—the delegation of rule-making authority has become a fact of modern policymaking life. As long as the federal agencies follow the process for making rules prescribed by Congress, those rules are as powerful as if the laws were made by Congress itself.

In today's federal government, each access point—Congress, the president, the Supreme Court, and the federal bureaucracy—is connected to us by one or more of the pathways of political action. Of the four access points, Congress is the most accessible. Elections can change congressional membership. Lobbying, along with interest group and social movement activism, can influence the nature of solutions. Congress—in particular the House of Representatives, "the people's house"—was designed by the framers to be the most open of the policymaking institutions of the federal government.

THE POWER OF THE PRESIDENCY IN SHAPING POLICY The power of the presidency not only to formulate policy by executive order but also to shape the policymaking by Congress deserves special attention. Routinely, modern presidents have been able to influence policy formulation by exercising a set of informal powers that have grown since the administration of Franklin D. Roosevelt. As we saw in Chapter 7, pages 204–205, the opportunities for going public—meaning to speak directly to the American people and ask them to pressure their own members of Congress—has given presidents of the twentieth and twenty-first centuries the power to

augment the actions of Congress in both agenda setting and policymaking.[20]

LEGITIMIZING POLICY A government's policymaking actions can confer legitimacy on the policies it makes. Legitimacy implies fairness; formal rules and the ability to see the process in action help ensure fairness. When legitimacy is established, people are willing to accept policies—even if they dislike them. Legitimacy is different from **coercion,** which is the threat or actual use of force or punishment to secure compliance with a policy. Massive coercion is necessary to obtain compliance with policies that are widely seen as illegitimate, but policies that are viewed by the public as being fair generally require very little, if any, such action. The fair and open nature of the policymaking process helps ensure that solutions are not favoring one part of society as a payoff or a special favor.

Citizens' ability to affect the formulation of policy is also crucial to the legitimacy and stability of any system of government. Openness and rules may be meaningless if the public does not believe it can influence the solutions that are being crafted to solve problems. Most policymakers take great pains to follow the rules of their institutions and, when practical, make room for public involvement.

Implementing Policy

Once policies have been created, someone actually has to do something with them. As its name implies, the executive branch of government is charged with executing or implementing the policies made by a legislature, the courts, or the executive branch itself. The other two branches, however, also influence how the policies they make are carried out. Add to this the openness of the government to citizen activity, and a picture emerges of implementation as a highly political process.

Many of us, driving above the speed limit, have passed a police officer and yet received no ticket. We clearly broke the law—a policy setting a maximum speed limit. What explains the lack of a ticket in this case is the **discretion**■ given to the individuals who implement policy. Perhaps going a few miles over the speed limit is acceptable for that stretch of road at that time of the day with that level of traffic and that weather. A change in one of these circumstances might mean getting a ticket. Formulating a law for each stretch of highway, while factoring in things such as road conditions and weather, would be nearly impossible, so legislatures often write laws with the presumption that the executive branch will use reasonable discretion in applying them. But, what if a police officer pulled over all drivers sporting a Republican bumper sticker who exceeded the speed limit by *any* amount? Or what if this officer gave speeding tickets only to African Americans? These are dramatic examples of prejudice (which, unfortunately, sometimes occur), but there are other, more subtle ways in which discretion is used that are out of step with the intent of policy and demonstrate the political aspect of implementation. Knowing this, legislators must be especially attuned to the implementation process.

Since all democratic legislatures, including the U.S. Congress, are bodies in which majorities are needed to pass laws, legislation is often written in ways designed to attract wide support among the diverse membership. One way to do this is to write a vaguely worded policy that allows legislators to read their own interests and the interests of their constituents into the proposal.

Because of the need for vaguely worded policy, and the need to rely on the executive branch for expert formulation of the details and implementation, legislators cannot simply walk away from a policy once it is in the implementation phase. Legislatures typically review policy implementation through oversight. Legislative oversight takes two forms, reauthorization and investigation.

REAUTHORIZATION Because Congress controls the government's purse strings, every program must be reauthorized at regular intervals in order for the necessary funds to be appropriated.

Members of Congress use reauthorization hearings to get feedback about how (and how effectively) a policy is being carried out. If the results are unsatisfactory, Congress can influence the executive branch to implement the policy more effectively by threatening to cut off or reduce funding.

INVESTIGATION Another form of oversight is investigation. Congress has the authority to call officials of the executive branch before its committees to answer questions about alleged problems with implementation. Investigations can be launched based on information gleaned during the reauthorization process, from other hearings, from contacts with constituents, from media reports, from court proceedings, or from many other sources. Like reauthorization, investigations can result in measures designed to change the executive branch's implementation of policy.

The courts also exercise a form of oversight. Unlike legislatures, courts do not control the funding of programs directly, but the cases that come before them, either at the trial level or on appeal, can have a major impact on implementation. A decision rendered by a court can direct an agency or department to change its administration of a policy.

The Public Policy Process

14.3 **Analyze how the policy process is shaped by political influences.**

PRACTICE QUIZ: UNDERSTAND AND APPLY

1. The policy process model is
   a. linear.
   c. cyclical.
   b. not always linear.
   d. never cyclical.

2. Which of the following would be the most likely example of a focusing event?
   a. finding illegal immigrants working at a restaurant in California
   b. a 5 percent increase in handgun fatalities in this country in 2007
   c. the federal response to Hurricane Katrina
   d. 100-degree weather on the same day in all 48 states in the continental United States.

3. The courts exercise a form of oversight of policy implementation.
   a. true
   b. false

ANALYZE

1. What sort of focusing events would likely be trigger mechanisms for the general public? What sort would only attract the attention of activist groups?

2. Why does Congress often delegate aspects of its law-making authority to nonelected officials in federal agencies and departments?

IDENTIFY THE CONCEPT THAT DOESN'T BELONG

a. Reauthorization of legislation
b. Judicial rulings on policy implementation
c. Rule-making authority
d. Congressional investigations
e. Appointments of administrative officials

Resource Center
• Glossary
• Vocabulary Example
• Connect the Link

■ **Inflation:** An increase in prices over time.

EXAMPLE: *In the 1970s, inflation emerged as a major concern of federal economic regulators, who prescribed "tight money" policies to try to keep it in check.*

Economic Basics

14.4 Identify the key indicators of economic performance used by economists.
(pages 438–441)

It can be argued that government economic policy has a more profound impact on the quality of our democracy and personal well-being than any other type of government action. There are two primary types of economic policy: (1) *fiscal policy,* which involves the taxing and spending decisions enacted by Congress in cooperation with the president, and (2) *monetary policy,* which concerns the money supply and is managed by the independent Federal Reserve Board ("the Fed"), the nation's central bank. Both fiscal and monetary policy can affect growth, employment, and inflation. Often, the goals of fiscal and monetary policy clash, because the Fed, the president, and Congress do not always share the same objectives.

Indeed, a major divide in our nation concerns different notions of freedom: Some people view most actions by government as a loss of freedom for the citizens, whereas others see government action creating the ability for citizens to enhance their well-being. When government regulates or fails to regulate the mortgage industry, when it drafts legislation to use tax dollars to bail out lenders who made unwise loans, or when it considers using a federal program to help those who are buried in debt because of easy credit, government affects all of us. We are often consumers of or investors in the things that are made and sold, and we are always citizens who pay taxes and live in a nation that has its democracy shaped by the expectations that drive policy decisions.

When economists gauge the economy's performance, they usually focus on five figures: (1) inflation, (2) unemployment, (3) gross domestic product, (4) the balance of trade, and (5) the budget deficit (or surplus). These measures matter to politicians as well. A healthy economy helps incumbents stay in office. Let's examine each of these figures in turn.

Inflation

Inflation■ measures the rate at which prices increase. The classic definition of inflation is "too many dollars chasing too few goods." We all know that inflation is bad, and that high inflation rates can undermine and distort all other aspects of the economy. When inflation is out of control, it can wipe out middle class savings, devalue the dollar, and cause immense social and political unrest. The inflation rate is measured by the **Consumer Price Index (CPI),** a figure computed by the Department of Labor. Calculated at regular intervals, the CPI is based on the changing costs of a specified "market basket" of goods and services.

The Fed must also guard against **deflation**—dropping prices. Although deflation might sound good, falling prices discourage spending. If prices are going down, consumers refuse to spend today in hopes of paying less tomorrow. Consumers who sit on their wallets are not engaging in the kind of economic activity that creates jobs and a vibrant economy.

Unemployment

The **unemployment rate** measures the percentage of Americans who are out of work. It is not a perfect measure, because it accounts only for people who identify themselves as actively seeking work, and sampling techniques are used in calculating it. Those who have given up looking for jobs are not counted, either as employed or unemployed—they are regarded as simply outside the workforce. The several million "undocumented" workers and the people involved in the illegal or "underground" economy are also left out. Unemployment therefore is often understated in particular geographic areas or during periods of great poverty. A "good" unemployment rate is around 5 percent. (One-hundred percent employment would be impossible; a certain number of people are always between jobs or just entering the workforce.) In the 1980s, many economists considered 5 percent to be full employment, only to have unemployment drop below that figure in the late 1990s and again in 2005 and 2006. By the end of 2009, however, the unemployment level had reached 10 percent. More recent employment statistics are noted in Figure 14.2.

Gross Domestic Product

Gross domestic product (GDP)—the value of all the goods and services produced in a nation—measures the size of the American economy. Generally, economic growth is good, but overly rapid economic growth can be harmful because it can feed inflation. This is where the Fed will step in to try to curb runaway growth before inflation can gain a foothold. A good growth target for GDP for the U.S. economy is between 3 and 4 percent. Rapidly developing countries such as China and India have experienced much higher growth rates. The growth rate commonly reported in the media is the "real GDP" rate—GDP adjusted to account for the effects of the CPI, so that actual economic growth does not falsely include the rate of inflation.

Balance of Trade

The **balance of trade** measures the difference between imports and exports. A positive balance means that a nation has a trade surplus—it exports more goods than it imports. A negative balance of trade means a trade deficit—the country

■ **National Debt:** The nation's cumulative deficits.

SIGNIFICANCE: *Our large national debt causes the federal government to borrow vast amounts of money and makes it unlikely that we will soon be able to balance our budget.*

FIGURE 14.2 ▪ Unemployment Rate

This figure charts unemployment levels over the last two decades. What this figure does not show, however, is the level of "underemployment"—the percentage of Americans who are working less than they would prefer, likely due to cutbacks. Most economists put this figure at just under 20 percent. —***What factors best explain the jump in the unemployment rate between 2007 and 2009?***

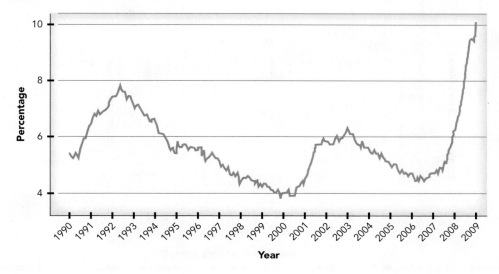

imports more goods than it exports. The United States has been running a significant trade deficit for years. The same American consumers who express their concerns about the outsourcing of American jobs also love to buy cheap imported goods. However, the U.S. trade deficit in goods fell from $840.3 billion in 2008 to $517 billion in 2009. This represents a 38.5 percent reduction and is explained, in part, by a reduction in demand for imports due to the recession.[21]

The Budget Deficit

A major concern for the U.S. economy has been the budget deficit and the rising national debt. The **budget deficit** is the amount by which, in a given year, government spending exceeds government revenue. (The rare circumstance when revenue outstrips expenditures is called a **budget surplus;** see Figure 14.3.) The net sum of the budget deficit minus the surplus is the **national debt▪**, or the amount that the government owes. With the exception of the four years between 1998 and 2001, the United States has run a budget deficit every year since 1970. That has added up to a national debt of about $12.98 trillion by early 2010. The national debt must be financed through money that is borrowed—with interest— both at home and abroad, which makes balancing the budget that much harder with each passing year. The Congressional Budget Office (CBO) estimates that the budget deficit was $1.36 trillion in 2010.[22] According to CBO estimates, the budget deficit will fall to $471 billion in 2015 and rise to $683 billion by 2020.[23]

Status of the Dollar

An important factor in the strength of the American economy is the status of the dollar as the world's most important currency. A stable monetary system is vital for a modern economy. "The history of money is the history of civilization or, more exactly, of some important civilizing values," said former Federal Reserve Board Chairman Alan Greenspan. "Its form at any particular period of history reflects the degree of confidence, or the degree of trust, that market participants have in the institutions that govern every market system, whether centrally planned or free."[24] Throughout the post–World War II era, the long-standing stability of the dollar helped sustain confidence in the American economic system.

However, more recently, the status of the dollar as the world's reserve currency has come under scrutiny. Between 2002 and 2009, the dollar lost about a third of its value against major currencies. This raised concerns about a potential loss of confidence in the American economic system, particularly among major rising economies like China, Brazil, and Russia, which hold significant amounts of dollar assets, most notably in U.S. Treasury debts. In 2009, China alone held 70 percent of its $1.9 trillion foreign currency reserves in dollars. The dollar's devaluation has led countries like China and Russia to suggest that the IMF's Special Drawing Rights—a basket of currencies—should act as the global reserve currency unit.[25] Russia has adjusted its foreign currency holdings so that it is evenly split between the dollar and the Euro.

FIGURE 14.3 ▪ **Federal Deficits and Surpluses**

The federal government has operated with budget deficits for most of the past 20 years. The few years of budget surpluses were caused by a thriving economy in the late 1990s. The return to budget deficits came after 9/11, when the federal government cut taxes and then soon initiated expensive military actions in Afghanistan and Iraq and also experienced rising costs in entitlement programs. —*Does the size of the budget deficits worry you? How would you resolve this problem?*

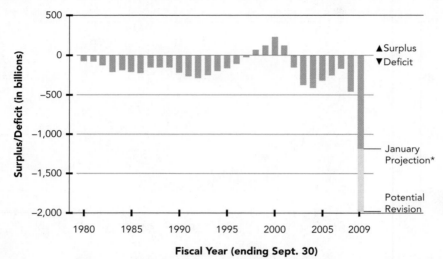

Fiscal Year (ending Sept. 30)

SOURCE: U.S. Office of Management and Budget. *Budget of the United States Government, Historical Tables,* annual. Accessed at http://www.whitehouse.gov/omb/budget/fy2009

STUDENT profile

Daniel Epstein is acutely aware of the challenges facing bright, creative, and energetic young entrepreneurs who want to invest in projects that offer economic, social, and environmental boons. In 2008, as a senior at the University of Colorado, Boulder, Daniel founded the Unreasonable Institute with fellow students Teju Ravilochan, Vladimir Dubovskiy, and Tyler Hartung. The Unreasonable Institute seeks to promote and support social entrepreneurship by young people. The social entrepreneurs get mentoring from experienced professionals and have access to capital, while being given the opportunity to develop appropriate business skills.

The Unreasonable Institute draws its funding primarily from socially conscious investment funds that allow the institute to provide seed capital for socially responsible startup projects. Through a competitive application process, the institute invites young social entrepreneurs with bold ideas from around the world. The institute also attracts experts, innovators, and specialists from areas of social entrepreneurship, investment, business, poverty eradication, engineering, health, and the civil sector to mentor the young social entrepreneurs.

To attend the Summer Institute, participants must raise $6,500 by selling their ideas to would-be patrons and supporters. At the institute, the participants hone their business, marketing, and technological skills under the supervision of mentors. At the end of the 10-week institute, they try to sell their ideas to prospective financiers through an online marketplace. To impress the potential investors, the Unreasonable Institute insists that participants develop their "unreasonable" or bold idea into a sustainable, scalable project that can reach 1 million people. Sustainability requires that the project be able to generate enough revenue to meet its costs without reliance on grants and philanthropy. The institute measures effectiveness of projects in terms of financial viability as well as social and environmental dividends.[26]

Economic Basics

14.4 **Identify the key indicators of economic performance used by economists.**

PRACTICE QUIZ: UNDERSTAND AND APPLY

1. What are the five figures that economists use to measure economic performance?
   a. inflation, interest rate, income tax rate, unemployment, and gross domestic product
   b. gross domestic product, balance of trade, annual percentage rate, federal funds rate, and the budget deficit or surplus
   c. inflation, unemployment, gross domestic product, the balance of trade, and the budget deficit or surplus
   d. prime rate, sales tax rate, inflation, gross domestic product, and unemployment

2. Inflation measures the rate at which prices increase.
   a. true
   b. false

3. In recent years, the status of the dollar as the world's reserve currency has come under scrutiny, in part, because it has lost a third of its value.
   a. true
   b. false

ANALYZE

1. Which of the five economic factors can be influenced by political action? Give some recent examples.

2. Why do countries like China and Russia worry about the value of the U.S. dollar?

IDENTIFY THE CONCEPT THAT DOESN'T BELONG

a. Inflation
b. Unemployment rate
c. Balance of trade
d. Budget deficit
e. Fiscal policy

Resource Center
• Glossary
• Vocabulary Example
• Connect the Link

Fiscal Policy

14.5 Describe the major actors responsible for creating economic policy.

(pages 442–443)

The game of politics is all about deciding who gets what, and part of that involves deciding who pays for what. That is what **fiscal policy**—the politics of taxing and spending—is all about. With the federal budget now at $3.55 trillion, there is a lot of money up for grabs. As you learned in the preceding section, the federal government is currently spending more money than it is collecting in taxes, creating a budget deficit. Collectively, our deficits added up to a national debt of about $12.98 trillion in March 2010. The stage is set for the national debt to become much larger.

Technically, the United States has two budgets. The first is "on budget" and includes general revenue from income tax and corporate taxes, paying for things such as defense, NASA, and poverty prevention programs. The second is "off budget" and includes money from the Social Security and Medicare payroll taxes and trust funds. In reality, this separation is a legalistic fiction. For our purposes, we are going to view the budget as a unified, integrated whole, except when we specifically discuss on-budget and off-budget aspects.

Major Actors

Budgets are created through interactions between Congress and the president, but there are several other major actors in the realm of fiscal policy, the most significant of which is the **Congressional Budget Office (CBO).** A research arm of Congress, the CBO was created by the Budget and Impoundment Act of 1974. The act was for all practical purposes two separate pieces of legislation. The impoundment portion dealt with reining in a power exercised excessively during the administration of President Richard Nixon. If Nixon opposed a program that had been passed and funded by Congress, the president would simply order his secretary of the treasury to "impound" the funds—in other words, to not spend them. By cutting off the money, Nixon could effectively kill a program even if he did not have the votes to have his veto sustained. The 1974 law required House and Senate approval of presidential impoundment; otherwise, the funds would automatically be spent. Since then, impoundment has been rare.

The budget portion of the 1974 act was more significant. It fundamentally changed how the budget of the United States is crafted. Before this, the White House Office of Management and Budget (OMB) had the primary responsibility for drawing up the budget. The president would present the basic document, and Congress would make adjustments. Since 1975, the CBO has created long-term budget outlooks, analyses of the president's proposed budget, and fiscal impact statements for every bill that comes out of a congressional committee. As a result, Congress has become the primary player in creating the budget. The OMB still draws up a budget, but although that budget sometimes has some influence, it is often "dead on arrival" when it gets to Congress.

The OMB provides the president with information and guidance. The power of the veto gives the president an important role in determining the final budget, which is always a compromise. Of course, the OMB carries a little more weight when the presidency and Congress are both controlled by the same party. Since 1946, the president has also had the "help" of the Council of Economic Advisers (CEA). The CEA was created by Congress back when the initial budget document was primarily the chief executive's responsibility in order to help the White House make budget decisions. The CEA's three members are usually leading academic economists and are appointed by the president. Some presidents, notably John F. Kennedy, have relied heavily on the CEA; others, such as Ronald Reagan, have all but ignored it. In 1993, the National Economic Council (NEC) was established to advise the president on economic policy.

Congressional Budget Office (CBO) Director Douglas Elmendorf provides testimony to Congress regarding CBO budgetary projections. Since its creation in 1974, the CBO has played a major role in providing members of Congress with analyses of the budgetary implications of legislative efforts. —*How does the CBO act as a check on the power of the president in terms of budgetary matters?*

CONNECT THE **LINK**

(Chapter 6, pages 162–165) Because it has the constitutional prerogative to start all tax legislation, the House Ways and Means Committee has institutional policymaking advantage over its counterpart in the Senate.

Key Congressional Players

As discussed earlier, committees do the real work of Congress (see Chapter 6, pages 162–165). Although the Constitution requires that all revenue bills originate in the House, the 436 House members sitting together could never write a budget. Instead, appropriations and tax bills are products of committees in the Senate and the House. Each chamber has an appro-

priations committee, which has primary responsibility for deciding where federal money should be spent. The House Ways and Means Committee is responsible for tax bills. The Senate Finance Committee serves as its counterpart. The House and Senate also each have budget committees that review the fiscal process.

Treasury Secretary Timothy Geithner (center) meets with House members Charlie Rangel (D-NY) and Dave Camp (R-MI) as he arrives to testify before the House Ways and Means Committee on "The President's FY2011 Budget" proposals. Like the Senate Finance Committee, Ways and Means is instrumental in shaping the nation's financial policies. Since 2008, Rangel has been the focus of a House Ethics Committee inquiry. Even with the ethics charges hovering over him, Rangel was easily reelected to another term in the House in the 2010 midterm election. —*Does the House or Senate have more power when it comes to the budget process? If the two houses of the legislature are controlled by different parties, what impact is this likely to have on the budget process?*

Fiscal Policy

14.5   Describe the major actors responsible for creating economic policy.

PRACTICE QUIZ: UNDERSTAND AND APPLY

1. Which of the following institutions is primarily responsible for drawing up the budget?
    a. Office of Management and Budget
    b. Council of Economic Advisors
    c. Congress
    d. Congressional Budget Office

2. The House and Senate each have budget committees to review the fiscal process.
    a. true   b. false

3. Members of the president's Council of Economic Advisers are usually
    a. party loyalists.
    b. nationally known leaders of business.
    c. academic economists.
    d. members of the Federal Reserve Board.

ANALYZE

1. In what ways can the president's veto power be a major factor in the budget process?

2. In what ways can Congress affect the budget?

IDENTIFY THE CONCEPT THAT DOESN'T BELONG

a. Congressional Budget Office
b. House Ways and Means Committee
c. Securities and Exchange Commission
d. White House Office of Management and Budget
e. Senate Finance Committee

Resource Center
• Glossary
• Vocabulary Example
• Connect the Link

■ **Progressive Tax:** A tax structured such that higher-income individuals pay a larger percentage of their income in taxes.

EXAMPLE: *The federal income tax is a progressive tax.*

■ **Regressive Tax:** A tax structured such that higher-income individuals pay a lower percentage of their income in taxes.

EXAMPLE: *The Social Security tax is a regressive tax.*

Revenue and Expenditures

14.6 Explain the major sources of U.S. government revenue and expenditure.

(pages 444–449)

The budget of the U.S. federal government can best be understood by thinking about its two primary parts: (1) revenue; and (2) expenditures. Revenue entails all financial resources that the government collects from sources (e.g., taxes and customs duties), while expenditures include all of the funds spent by the government (e.g., salaries for government workers and benefits for Social Security recipients).

Revenue

In 2009, the U.S. government collected about $2.15 trillion in revenue. The largest portion of that total came from taxes on individual income, at $915.3 billion (see Figure 14.4).[27] The tax burden for the majority of Americans comes in the form of income tax and Social Security.

Income tax is levied on wages, rent, interest, and profit, while payroll tax is levied on wage earnings. Income tax is a **progressive tax**■—the more money you make, the higher the percentage you pay in taxes, up to a top rate of 35 percent. The Social Security tax, on the other hand, is a **regressive tax**■. If you make enough money, your Social Security tax burden drops. At first glance, payroll taxes seem flat—everyone pays the same rate. However, this tax is collected only on the first

$90,000 of income; earnings (from salaries and self-employment) above that level are not subject to the Social Security tax. So, the tax burden for higher-income earners is felt more heavily through income taxes, while those with lower incomes are hit harder by payroll taxes.

INCOME TAXES Taxes on income make up just over 7.5 percent of GDP. Currently, there are six different income taxation levels in the United States. As you earn more money in a given year, you move into a higher **marginal tax bracket**—marginal meaning the tax rate you pay on the last dollar you earn that year. In 2009–2010, a family of four paid no taxes, as long as the family's gross income was under $33,075 annually.[28] The tax codes are so complicated and deductions are so difficult to understand that it is almost impossible for many taxpayers to calculate their own taxes. Each year, more and more Americans use tax software programs or hire outside experts or accountants to prepare their tax returns.

PAYROLL TAXES Social Security taxes make up 6.5 percent of GDP. They take the form of a payroll tax, a tax split so that employees pay half and their employers pay the other half. Each pays 6.2 percent into the Social Security Trust Fund and 1.45 percent into the Medicare trust fund. In effect, this tax split obscures the full impact of its burden—half is hidden in your employee benefits. If you are self-employed, however, you carry the full burden: 15.3 percent of the first $90,000 of the net income from your business or profession.

THE TAX BURDEN So, who pays what? Analysis of household income and tax burden by the CBO shows that the top 10 percent of earners pay almost 50 percent of taxes. The bottom 20 percent pay only about 1 percent. Those numbers are a little skewed, however, as they include only the employee's portion of the payroll tax. The top 1 percent of earners pays 21 percent of federal taxes. The bottom line is this: Most American workers pay more per year in payroll taxes than they do in income taxes.

Critics argue that the CBO analysis is flawed because it measures income, not wealth. Capital gains, such as the increase in the value of stock someone owns, are taxed at a lower rate than earned income. Profits from stock and real estate transactions are taxed only when they are sold, so capital gains can accumulate for years without generating any government revenue. As a result, the wealthy—especially the nonworking wealthy—escape taxation on the vast majority of their assets. Critics contend that the poor have little opportunity to accumulate wealth.

CORPORATE TAXES Taxes on corporations generate about 15 percent of the federal government's revenue. The United States has one of the highest effective corporate tax rates in the industrialized world, with a top tax rate of 35 percent. Taking

FIGURE 14.4 ■ **The Federal Revenue Budget**
Federal government revenue comes primarily from individual income tax and payroll taxes for Social Security and Medicare. —*How can an increase in the unemployment rate affect tax revenues?*

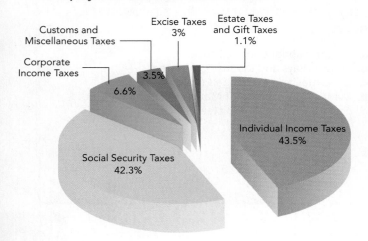

Customs and Miscellaneous Taxes

Excise Taxes 3%

Estate Taxes and Gift Taxes 1.1%

Corporate Income Taxes

3.5%

6.6%

Individual Income Taxes 43.5%

Social Security Taxes 42.3%

into account state corporate taxes as well, the average U.S. corporation has an effective marginal tax rate of almost 40 percent on its net income. At the same time, corporate tax collection amounts to only about 2 percent of GDP, well below the international average of about 3.4 percent. The disparity between the tax rate and the taxes actually collected is explained by the numerous deductions and credits that federal and state laws provide.

The U.S. corporate tax system also has numerous write-offs, often targeted to specific industries that result from successful lobbying, which are intended to elicit certain corporate behavior. In 2010, President Obama announced that small businesses would receive a $5,000 tax credit for each job created during the year. The maximum amount of tax credits received per firm was set at $500,000.[29]

Corporate income tax revenues depend, of course, on whether companies make a profit. During a recession, corporate profits can plummet or even vanish completely. The consensus among most business experts is that worldwide, corporate tax revenues are in a period of decline.

OTHER TAXES   Other taxes include excise taxes, customs duties, inheritance taxes, and miscellaneous receipts. Excise taxes levied on fuel, alcohol, and tobacco are paid by the producer and are folded into the price of the product. Customs duties are taxes on foreign-made goods imported into the United States and, like excise taxes, are part of the consumer's final price. Inheritance taxes are on the asset value of a person's estate. Miscellaneous receipts include income earned by the Federal Reserve in its day-to-day operations.

TAX ANALYSIS   Finding the optimum tax rate is a difficult job for the government to perform. In the mid-1970s, Arthur Laffer, a professor at the University of Southern California, was conversing with a *Wall Street Journal* columnist, when he sketched out an interesting theory on a cocktail napkin. Laffer reasoned that if the tax rate is zero, government revenue is zero. That's pretty obvious—zero times anything is zero. Laffer maintained, however, that government revenue will also be zero if the tax rate is 100 percent. Why? Because if the government takes all their earnings, no one will go to work! Zero times everything is still zero. Laffer sketched out a graph, now known as the **Laffer curve,** to demonstrate that there exists some rate of taxation above which government revenue drops (see Figure 14.5). A sufficiently high tax rate, Laffer concluded, discourages productivity.

An important question that arises when we analyze the tax system is equity. Is it fair? No one likes paying taxes, but the government needs a source of revenue to fund even the most minimal services. Should the wealthy be taxed at a higher rate—a more progressive rate—in order to provide more services for the poor? Critics argue that the current economic

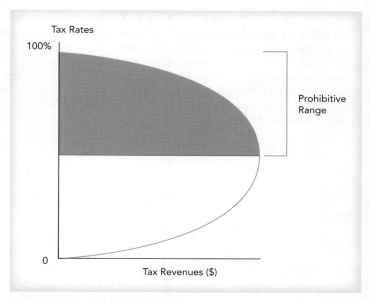

FIGURE 14.5 ▪ The Laffer Curve
The Laffer curve represents an economist's theory about how to design tax rates in a manner that will help the government and the economy. It argues that setting tax rates too high will actually reduce the amount of revenue collected by government. *—Are there any specific assumptions that underlie this theory? Should the theory be proven before it is adopted by government officials?*

system is unfair. They say that the disparity between rich and poor is too wide. Despite significant gains in real GDP (GDP after factoring out inflation), most real-wage increases have gone to the wealthiest Americans. Would a more progressive tax system help reverse that trend? Or would it discourage the wealthy from putting forth the extra effort and productive investments that lead to gains in productivity? A related question: Does fairness matter as much as efficiency? Should the government try to foster an economic system that generates revenue while boosting the overall economy, or is it preferable to sacrifice growth for equity? Many Americans disagree about the answers.

Expenditures

In President Obama's proposed 2011 budget, the U.S. government's largest expenditure was for Social Security benefits and defense, with an estimated outlay of $738 billion for each sector (see Figure 14.6).[30] The Congressional Budget Office estimates the budget deficit for 2010 to be around $1.3 trillion or 9.2 percent of GDP.[31] Government expenditures continually expand, in part because levels of "current services" have become the baseline for most government programs. This means that the starting point for next year's budget is this year's budget, plus increases needed because of increased population and inflation.

FIGURE 14.6 ▪ President Obama's 2011 Proposed Budget (in billions)

In February 2010, President Obama proposed the federal budget. Budgets are an expression of an administration's priorities and of the contemporary needs of the nation at large. It is important to note that this figure does not include mandatory federal expenditures for items such as interest on the national debt and entitlement expenditures for items such as Social Security benefits. These items make up an increasingly large portion of overall federal spending and contribute significantly to federal deficits and the national debt. —*Do you think the allocation of resources to secure the nation's defense compromises our needs in health and education sectors? How do the budget data show us that policy priorities are set by domestic as well as international considerations? Explain your answer.*

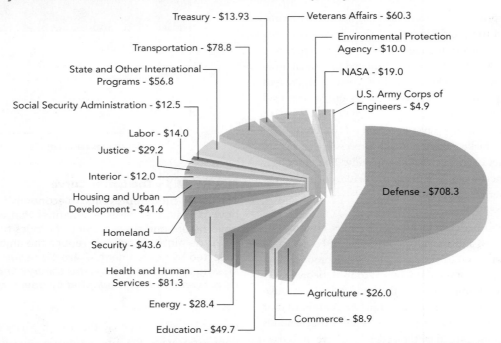

SOURCE: Office of Management and Budget, Department Fact Sheets. Accessed at http://www.whitehouse.gov/omb/budget_factsheets_departments/

When politicians talk about balancing "the budget," they are generally referring to the current services budget.

SOCIAL SECURITY The U.S. government's Social Security program was established in 1935 during the Great Depression. At that time, more than half of the elderly lived in poverty, and the program's goal was to provide a minimal pension for older Americans. In many ways, Social Security was a conservative response to the far more radical demands during the 1930s for guaranteed levels of income and more substantive aid to the poor.

Technically, Social Security is an independent, off-budget program. It was originally intended to be self-financing. As long as there were several workers for each retiree, that concept worked fairly well. In the 1970s, however, Social Security started running a slight deficit. It was evident that the problem would worsen over time. Americans were getting older. There were fewer workers per retiree, and retirees were living longer.

In 1983, a special commission headed by the economist Alan Greenspan generated a number of reform measures that were enacted by Congress. The central purpose of the reforms was to create a surplus, known as the **Social Security Trust Fund,** which would save money over the years to help bridge the gap created as the boomers retired. It did this primarily in two ways. First, the retirement age was raised. Second, the reform significantly increased payroll taxes to the relatively high rate that now prevails. As a result, Social Security immediately began running a surplus, surpassing $50 billion a year by 1989 and $100 billion by 1999. In 2005, the surplus was $173 billion, and was projected to grow through 2015. The recession, however, forced a reestimation of projections. The CBO estimated in 2009 that the surplus would drop to just $3 billion in 2010.[32] Shortly thereafter, the picture will change dramatically: As ever more baby boomers retire, Social Security payments will start to outstrip payroll taxes.

By the time we get to 2018, when Social Security is expected to start paying out more than it is bringing in, the fund will be worth more than $4 trillion. The problem is that the trust fund money is not sitting in a vault somewhere. It has already been spent. One reason the nation has been able to run such large deficits over the past couple of decades is that the

Treasury has borrowed money from the Social Security Trust Fund, depositing an electronic IOU in its place. Although, as we have said, Social Security is supposed to be off-budget, deficit figures subtract the Social Security surplus.

If the $4 trillion has already been spent, does that mean it is gone? Not really. The government owes itself electronic IOUs, which have also accrued interest payments. The strength of the American dollar, and the confidence that it engenders, depends on the United States meeting its financial obligations. However, the long-term consequences of rising Social Security obligations and decreasing surpluses will have significant implications for future U.S. budgets.

DEFENSE   The nation's largest on-budget appropriations are for defense. Roughly $680 billion have been authorized for defense spending in 2010. Since the dawn of history, war and defense have been expensive propositions. Many factors lead to the high costs of maintaining the armed forces. Of course, military personnel need to be paid. Salary and retirement benefits comprise a large portion of the U.S. military budget. In addition, the armed services provide housing and medical care for soldiers and their families, and the military employs a large number of civilian personnel. Throw in administrative costs, base construction and upkeep, training, and logistics, and more than half of the military budget goes for operations and support.

The second large area of defense spending includes the development, testing, and procurement of weapons systems. Weapons development and procurement are always controversial. The Army, for example, has to decide whether it needs more reconnaissance helicopters or whether it should transition to unmanned drones. The Navy has to decide whether to keep all 11 of its massive, nuclear-powered aircraft carriers or build smaller, nonnuclear carriers to allow it to spread its presence over a greater area.

All of these decisions must be made within the context of what is best for national security and for military personnel and within the scope of the overall budget. It also requires military leaders and members of Congress to make certain assumptions about future threat levels that are difficult to predict and that may well change over time. These decisions are also influenced by the lobbying decision makers pathway because companies that supply planes, ships, and other equipment will pressure their members of Congress as well as Department of Defense officials to buy their products.

Many Americans believe that the war on terror and the expenses related to Afghanistan and Iraq have led to increased defense spending, as a percentage of the budget or GDP. However, despite the fact that defense spending, in dollars, is at record levels, it is much lower as a percentage of both GDP and the overall budget than it was during the latter stages of the Cold War—and far below the levels during World War II. In 1944, at the height of World War II, military spending accounted for more than 80 percent of the federal budget and 38 percent of GDP. Today, defense absorbs about 20 percent of the budget and under 5 percent of GDP.[33]

Nevertheless, these percentages could increase depending on international developments. In addition the figures cited above do not take into account the fact that, under the Bush administration, war spending was requested through off-budget measures like emergency supplemental bills. These supplemental bills were not included in the White House deficit projections.

Barack Obama campaigned on a promise to reduce military spending and introduce more transparency in war spending. He was also critical of President Bush's supplemental budget requests to fund wars in Iraq and Afghanistan. President Obama's budgets, however, have exceeded President Bush's combined defense and supplemental budgets, which in 2008 totaled $623.1 billion.[34] President Obama's 2011 defense budget proposal, sent to Congress in February 2010, totals $708 billion. The president also requested another $33 billion to strengthen U.S. force levels in Afghanistan."[35]

A U.S. Air Force C-17 Globemaster III Aircraft airdrops humanitarian aid during earthquake relief efforts in Haiti in January 2010. The cost of this aircraft is over $202 million —*Are such expensive aircraft necessary for our international objectives?*

INCOME SECURITY   The idea behind **income security** is that the government should provide a safety net for the most vulnerable members of society. The largest components of the income security program are the earned-income credit, the child tax credit, supplemental security income, unemployment compensation, and food stamps. Together, these programs comprise almost three-fourths of total federal income security

■ **Entitlements:** Government
expenditures required by law.

EXAMPLE: *Much of the spending on Medicare
and Social Security is required by federal law.*

spending. Unemployment payments tend to rise and fall, depending on the state of the economy. Smaller income security programs include Temporary Assistance to Needy Families (TANF), the Women, Infants, and Children (WIC) program, and federal child support enforcement measures. Even smaller amounts go to foster care and adoption assistance.

GOVERNMENT MEDICAL CARE Health care reform was an important issue in the 2008 presidential election because of skyrocketing costs to both citizens and the federal government. Without significant change, the percentage of health care–related spending by the federal government (for example, for Medicare and Medicaid) is projected to grow dramatically.

Medicare and Medicaid are two separate, often-confused programs with common origins. Both were established in the mid-1960s as part of President Lyndon Johnson's Great Society. Since then, exploding medical costs have been one of the largest contributors to increased government spending. Over the past 40 years, health care costs have outstripped the general rate of inflation. Part of this is due to improvements in treatment procedures, most of which are very expensive. Improvements in the quality of health care lead to longer life expectancy—which means that the average senior citizen spends more years receiving Medicare coverage and that coverage costs far more than it did in the past.

Medicare provides health insurance coverage for retired people (beginning at age 65) as well as for disabled younger people. In 1974, Medicare spending accounted for 0.7 percent of GDP; today, it is over 2.6 percent. By 2050, if no reforms are enacted, Medicare spending alone will account for between 8 and 9 percent of the *total* U.S. economy.

Medicare is for the general over-65 population and for the disabled; the economically disadvantaged receive health services through **Medicaid.** Under this joint program between the federal government and the states, the federal government provides an average of 57 percent of Medicaid's financing. Because some states provide more services than others, matching percentages vary. Most of the 42 million Medicaid enrollees are children and pregnant women, but the overwhelming amount of Medicaid funding goes to the elderly and disabled. Much of that money is spent on nursing homes, home health care, and social services for retired people who have exhausted their life savings.

Five years after it was established in 1965, Medicaid spending comprised 0.3 percent of GDP; today, it accounts for 1.7 percent. If increases continue at current levels, total spending could hit 5 percent of GDP by 2050.

Interest and Other Spending

As government debt rises, interest payments also rise. Interest on the debt for 2011 is estimated at $251 billion. Almost 7 percent of the total budget goes to pay interest on the debt. In the 2010 fiscal year, interest payments on debt are estimated at $207 billion, which constitutes a significant portion of the projected budget deficit of $1.3 trillion.[36]

The size of the debt is only one factor when it comes to interest payments. Because interest rates are set by the open market, the cost of financing the debt can rise or fall independently of the size of the debt. If interest rates were to rise from 4 to 5 percent, debt-financing costs would rise by 25 percent.

Spending for all other programs falls significantly below those that we have discussed in detail. For example, the president's budget requested $49.7 billion for the Department of Education. NASA's share is $19 billion. The Department of Energy, according to the president's proposal, will receive about $28 billion. The Department of Transportation will get approximately $79 billion. The Department of Agriculture budget is slated at $26 billion. The Environmental Protection Agency (EPA) will receive $10 billion. With a proposed $29.2 billion budget, the Department of Justice will run the federal prisons, the Federal Bureau of Investigation (FBI), the Drug Enforcement Agency (DEA), and the Bureau of Alcohol, Tobacco, Firearms, and Explosives (ATF), as well as the U.S. Attorney's Office.[37]

One of the difficulties of creating the budget at the federal level is caused by the pervasiveness of **entitlements**■— mandatory spending required by law that is not subject to the budgetary process. Entitlements account for three out of every five dollars that the federal government spends. Almost all of the spending on Social Security and Medicare is mandatory, as are large percentages of spending on income security and Medicaid. Federal law requires that all who meet certain specifications are entitled to certain benefits. Since discretionary spending (spending that is not mandatory; Congress determines how much funding it will supply each year) accounts for less than half the total budget, congressional hands are somewhat tied as legislators attempt to constrain spending. Of course, since Congress wrote the laws enacting the entitlements in the first place, it can rework legislation to alleviate this complication. As you might suspect, however, that would tend to anger the people benefiting from the current system. All of these spending discussions lead back to one central point: It is still *your* money. The only way you can influence how it is spent is to let federal officials know what you think about their priorities.

Revenue and Expenditures

14.6 Explain the major sources of U.S. government revenue and expenditure.

PRACTICE QUIZ: UNDERSTAND AND APPLY

1. What are progressive income taxes?
   a. Taxation rates get higher and higher each year, usually because the rates are tied to the Consumer Price Index.
   b. Taxation gets progressively lower each year.
   c. Income is taxed at a higher percentage the more income one makes.
   d. Income is taxed at a lower percentage the more income one makes.

2. Arthur Laffer argued that lowering tax rates would ultimately reduce government revenue
   a. true
   b. false

3. Social Security is one of most expensive expenditure items in the federal budget.
   a. true
   b. false

4. What is one reason defense spending involves difficult decisions for the government?
   a. Spending billions on weapons is morally problematic for many people in government.
   b. It is not always clear if national defense is more important to our government than other areas, such as education and the environment.
   c. Specific choices—regarding weapons systems, for instance—are always based on future geopolitical circumstances that are hard to predict.
   d. The public pays attention to such large expenses and will become resentful if they do not perform as advertised.

ANALYZE

1. Do you think that corporations pay their fair share of taxes? What are the consequences of raising corporate taxes?

2. Should the government prioritize defense spending or spending on entitlement programs? Why or why not?

IDENTIFY THE CONCEPT THAT DOESN'T BELONG

a. Social Security
b. Medicare
c. Medicaid
d. Supplemental Nutritional Assistance Program (food stamps)
e. Education

14.6

Resource Center
• Glossary
• Vocabulary Example
• Connect the Link

■ **Prime Rate:** The interest rate that a bank charges its best customers.

EXAMPLE: *As problems rippled from the mortgage crisis of 2007–2008, the fluctuations in the prime rate often had highly negative effects on consumers with adjustable rate mortgages and large amounts of credit-card debt.*

Monetary Policy

14.7 Identify the major instruments of monetary policy.

(pages 450–451)

In the simplest terms, **monetary policy** involves the management of the supply of money in circulation within the United States. It is essential to strike a balance. Too much money coursing through the economy will be inflationary. Too little money will stifle economic growth. Keeping the balance right by managing monetary policy is the job of the Federal Reserve Board of Governors and its Federal Open Market Committee.

The Federal Reserve Board

Created in 1913 by an act of Congress, the **Federal Reserve System (the Fed)** is our nation's independent central bank. Although it is accountable to Congress, the Fed is free from political pressure because of the way it is structured. The seven members of its Board of Governors are appointed by the president of the United States, but they hold staggered, 14-year terms. That makes it difficult for any president or for Congress to exert too much influence over its policies. Moreover, there are 12 regional Federal Reserve banks within the system, each of which selects its own president, subject to approval by the Board of Governors. Although the presidents' terms are 5 years, most are reappointed. This further shields the Fed from political pressure.

The **Federal Open Market Committee (FOMC),** the Fed's policymaking arm, consists of the seven governors, the president of the New York Federal Reserve Board (who has a permanent seat), and four of the remaining 11 regional presidents, who serve on a rotating basis.

Maximizing GDP and employment while minimizing inflation, which has been compared to walking a tightrope while carrying a chainsaw, has been a formal part of the Fed's job description since 1977. When GDP is high and employment is full, the risk of inflation is always present. A tight job market can drive up wages (which sounds good), but that can drive up prices (which is bad). Over the long term, inflation will undercut employment. A stagnant or declining GDP, mounting unemployment, or rapid inflation, whether they occur simultaneously or separately, will all trigger domestic and international demands that the Fed "do something."

The FOMC has five main tools to manipulate monetary policy. The first is **reserve ratios**—the amount of cash that the Fed requires member banks to keep on hand in order to insure against a run on deposits. By raising the reserve ratio—in effect, lowering the amount of money that banks can loan out—the Fed can reduce the money supply.

The second tool is the **federal funds rate**—a market-driven interest rate that banks charge one another for short-term (often overnight) loans. Rates drop when there is excess money in the system; they rise when available loan money is restricted. In fact, interest rates are essentially the "price" of money. Like any other commodity, its price goes up when there is more demand than supply, and its price drops when there is more supply than demand. Because the funds rate is market-driven—member banks negotiate interest rates, with each participant looking for the best deal possible—the Fed has no direct control over this rate. It does, however, greatly influence this rate through the third tool, its **open-market operations,** by which it manipulates the total amount of money available in the market.

Most open-market operations today are carried out electronically, but consider the following simple example. Picture a huge safe with a divider down the middle. On the left side are piles of money. On the right side are piles of treasury bills (T-bills) and savings bonds—the federal government's IOUs. This hypothetical safe belongs to the Fed. Now, suppose that the Fed wants the federal funds rate to rise. Because the Fed cannot set this rate directly, it needs to make money scarcer so that interest rates rise. It takes some of its T-bills and savings bonds from the right side of the safe and sells them on the open market. It takes the cash that it receives from these sales and puts it in the left side of the safe, thus removing those funds from the circulating money supply. With less money available, the federal funds rate will rise. Higher interest rates will put the brakes on the economic engine. Because the member banks immediately pass higher rates on to their customers, businesses and consumers are less likely to borrow, which slows business expansion and spending. If, by contrast, the Fed wants the federal funds rate to fall, it takes money from the left side of the safe and puts it into circulation to buy securities from the open market, thus increasing the supply (and lowering the price) of money.

The fourth way that the Fed can intervene is through the **discount rate**—the interest rate that the Fed charges its member banks for loans. The discount rate is generally about 0.1 percent above the federal funds rate. Although the discount rate does not directly set the **prime rate**■—the rate that banks charge their best customers—there is significant correlation between the two.

Finally, the Fed, using the fifth tool, can buy and sell foreign currencies in an effort to stabilize world financial markets and currency exchange rates. Although this instrument is generally not used to affect the U.S. money supply, it is sometimes used to adjust the value of the dollar relative to other currencies. The most significant of these tools are open-market operations and the discount rate.

The Fed in Action

When Paul Volcker was appointed chairman of the Board of Governors in 1979, the economy was teetering on the edge of disaster. Skyrocketing energy prices, declining productivity, huge budget deficits, and a malignant condition that the media

■ **Stagflation:** The combination of stagnant GDP, rising unemployment, and rapid inflation.

EXAMPLE: *The United States was hit by stagflation in the latter part of the 1970s as energy costs skyrocketed and jobs became scarce.*

dubbed **stagflation**■ (the combination of a stagnant GDP, rising unemployment, and rapid inflation) had thrown the U.S. economy into its worst shape since the Great Depression. Volcker had to make a hard decision. If the Fed cut the money supply, interest rates would rise. That made sense. Less of a commodity drives up the price. But if the money supply went up, interest rates would rise as well. That seemed to violate the rule of supply and demand, but there was another culprit here: inflationary expectations. Inflation erodes the value of money. One dollar today will purchase more than one dollar will buy five years from now, because prices will have increased. Banks and other lending institutions figured out where they thought inflation was headed and only lent at rates high enough to compensate for the devaluing effects of the expected inflation. That particular set of circumstances also violated the **Phillips curve**—an economic model that assumes an inverse relationship between unemployment and inflation.

From Volcker's perspective, the economy's problem was "loose money." The "accommodating" policy that the Fed pursued during the 1970s, along with generous federal spending on domestic and Cold War defense programs, had produced inflationary expectations. As banks forced interest rates up, unemployment rose. Volcker understood that the first order of business was to kill those inflationary expectations—"to wring inflation out of the economy," as it was said at the time. He put a stranglehold on the money supply.

Volcker knew that his prescription would be painful. Tight money drove up interest rates and unemployment, but it killed inflation. After inflation had been brought under control, in the early 1980s, Volcker allowed the money supply to expand, but not fast enough to reignite inflationary expectations. More money in circulation lowered its price, meaning that interest rates fell. With lower interest rates, unemployment rates began to ease. In 1983, President Ronald Reagan appointed Volcker to a second four-year term as chairman, during which he continued to maintain a relatively tight money supply.

Volcker's successor, Alan Greenspan (appointed in 1987), focused more on inflationary risk and interest rates—particularly the discount rate—and less on targeting a certain supply of money. Greenspan's successor, Ben Bernanke (appointed in 2006 and reappointed in 2010), hopes to hit a specific inflation target.

One of the problems the Fed faces in enacting monetary policy is the significant lag time between Fed action and economic results. Efforts to slow the economy and control inflation—such as raising the discount rate—will not affect inflation and unemployment until months later, so the Fed has to be right twice: First, it needs to know where the economy is headed; second, after making the correct initial determination, it needs to conjure up the correct response to the circumstances that it believes are emerging. To make things even more difficult, it has to be right every time, or its actions can make things worse.

Monetary Policy

14.7 **Identify the major instruments of monetary policy.**

PRACTICE QUIZ: UNDERSTAND AND APPLY

1. The most significant tools by which the Fed manipulates the country's money supply are
   a. congressional testimony by the Fed chair and FOMC directives.
   b. open-market operations and the discount rate.
   c. federal treasury directives and the prime lending rate.
   d. closed-market operations and the federal funds rate.

2. The Fed has influence over tax policy.
   a. true
   b. false

3. It is accurate to state that in terms of partisan politics, the Federal Reserve Board's mandate is to be
   a. liberal.
   b. conservative.
   c. independent.
   d. aligned with the sitting president's politics.

ANALYZE

1. Describe some ways in which the Federal Reserve Board can manipulate economic performance using the policies discussed in this chapter.

2. Why is it important for the Federal Reserve Board to remain independent of influence from the executive and legislative branches? Does this independence exist in reality? Why or why not?

IDENTIFY THE CONCEPT THAT DOESN'T BELONG

a. Reserve ratio
b. Federal funds rate
c. Open-market operations
d. Tax hike
e. Discount rate

14.7

Conclusion

Now that you have learned more about public and economic policy, let's go back to the discussion of health care reform at the beginning of the chapter. One might expect that the widespread concerns that Democrats, Republicans, and independents had regarding skyrocketing health care costs and increasing numbers of uninsured Americans would have led to a swift overhaul of the health care system in the United States. But as we have seen both in this chapter and throughout the book, policymaking on a grand scale is rarely easy and almost never swift.

Comprehensive policy change is unusual in the United States for a number of reasons. Our fragmented branches of government, the existence of political parties, the power of interest groups and social movements that are often in competition with one another—these are a few of the main factors that fulfill what James Madison sought in his plan for the Constitution. No single interest or faction, even one comprising a majority of the population, can easily take control of such a system and use it to its own advantage. This plan for society and government often sounds strange to Americans because of our deep belief in the fairness of majority rule. The low popularity of Congress today (and in the past) offers a good example. The negative view of Congress arises, in part, because of the assumption that there is one public good, or one general set of values, that most of us share.

No one disputes the influence of so-called special interests, but congressional policymaking is often a reflection of an increasing diversity of interests in our nation of 300 million people. For many if not most policy issues, there is no one public good but rather a wide range of solutions for the many different people in a single congressional district or state. Even when there is widespread concern about a major aspect of society, as with the U.S. health care system, agreement on the best solution may be difficult to achieve.

Because of the structure of our government and the diversity of our wants and needs, much of our policymaking is best described as incremental in its impact.[38] These small modifications to existing policy make sense in a government as open to the pathways of political action as ours, in which citizens, groups, corporations, the mass media, and other actors have multiple ways to influence outcomes. The pathways can be used to hinder or block the actions of others as well as to open access to the policy process. Large, comprehensive policy changes are often hard to come by unless there is a crisis, or an unusual political change. In their plan for our government and society, the founders sought stability, not flexibility. If the incremental policymaking that we see in the contemporary United States is any indication, they succeeded. Small changes keep political, economic, and social arrangements in relatively the same relationship to one another. People who are happy with the status quo may applaud our incremental policymaking system; others might be willing to trade a degree of stability for a more responsive and responsible policymaking system. How do you feel? In either case, the pathways of political action offer you opportunities to participate in the policymaking process.

KEY CONCEPT MAP   **How can citizens influence the policymaking process?**

Identify the Problem

By collecting evidence that demonstrates a problem exists, citizens can put pressure on government officials to recognize the problem.

In 2010, citizens in northern Pennsylvania gathered samples of well water containing harmful chemicals to demonstrate the health dangers caused by natural gas mining practices.

Critical Thinking Questions

What if the citizens of Pennsylvania had not taken action? Is it likely that the government would have discovered the problem on its own? What types of factors limit citizens' abilities to call attention to problems?

Set the Agenda

By forming groups and using tools such as petitions, marches, and rallies, citizens can persuade government officials to formally consider addressing a problem.

In 2007, Florida residents successfully petitioned their state government to create a law that requires all dogs sold in the state to pass a health examination.

Critical Thinking Questions

Which aspects of the Constitution provide protection for citizens to petition government to address their concerns? Would the Framers have approved of the issues that individuals and organizations petition government about today? Why or why not?

Formulate Policies

Individuals and groups can develop proposals designed to solve problems affecting the public. On many occasions, it is the citizens who are most affected by a problem who have spent the most time thinking about the policies that could be used to solve the problem.

Mothers Against Drunk Driving (MADD), an organization made up of citizens concerned about accidents caused by intoxicated motorists, has proposed numerous pieces of legislation that strengthen the penalties for drunk driving and lower the blood alcohol levels that determine legal intoxication.

Critical Thinking Questions

What if you were part of a student organization that wanted the federal government to increase financial aid to college students? How would you go about developing a proposal? Can citizens without specific academic training play a role in formulating policies for the government to act on?

Legitimize Policies

By contacting elected representatives directly through meetings, letters, e-mails, and phone calls, citizens can make their preferences known to legislators on particular policy votes. Citizens can also express their opinions on Supreme Court cases through submission of *amicus curiae* (friend of the court) briefs.

In 2010, leading up to the votes on health care reform legislation, members of Congress were flooded with letters and calls and confronted by citizens at town hall meetings across the country.

Critical Thinking Questions

Do legislators listen to citizens when it comes to votes on policy issues? Of the various ways that a citizen can contact an elected official, why might a personal visit to an office be the most effective method?

Implement Policies

Citizens have multiple avenues available for influencing the way that policies are implemented. Contact between citizens and government employees (e.g., police officers and teachers) can help ensure that policies are being carried out in a manner consistent with the laws.

Once a school board has changed the curriculum for a school district to include new requirements, students and parents can check to make sure that teachers are following through and actually teaching the new curriculum.

Critical Thinking Questions

What if teachers are not implementing the policies of the school board? What can citizens do to ensure that the policies are implemented correctly?

Evaluate Policies

Once a law or policy is put into place, citizens can play a role in helping government determine its usefulness. By providing examples of policy successes and failures, government officials can judge the effectiveness of laws and regulations.

Citizens living in states bordering Mexico have used video, photos, and other forms of evidence to demonstrate the failures of U.S. border security efforts. By showing the government that the borders remain porous, citizens put pressure on the federal government to adopt policies that tighten border security.

Critical Thinking Questions

Does the fact that citizens have found evidence of policy failures make it more likely that government will act to address a problem than if government officials found the failures themselves? Why or why not?

In a democracy, there should be a direct link between the preferences of citizens and the policies established by government. Because the policy-making process includes numerous steps, citizens have multiple opportunities to influence the ultimate policies that are produced by the institutions of government. —*At what stage in the policy-making process are citizens most likely to be influential? Why? What types of impediments limit the influence that citizens can have on the development of public policy?*

Review of Key Objectives

Ideas and Values in Public Policy

 14.1 **Illustrate how values shape public policy in a democracy.**

(pages 426–429)

Public policy can be thought of as what comes after the "equal sign" in the equation of the structure of government plus the political process. Public policy is both what the government does and does not do.

The nature of public policy rests on the values of the public and of policy decision makers. Freedom and equality are values that are especially important in determining what government ought to do and the way it should go about it. These two concepts are the basis for a model of political ideology that contrasts the liberal and conservative approaches to politics and government.

KEY TERMS

Policy Process Model 426
Freedom 427
Classical Liberalism 428
Conservatism 428
Modern Liberalism 428
Progressivism 428

CRITICAL THINKING QUESTIONS

1. In what ways are classical liberalism and modern conservatism similar?
2. How are positive and negative freedom linked to how a person views the appropriate role for government?

INTERNET RESOURCES

Learn about policy issues from the liberal or progressive viewpoint: http://www.americanprogress.org/

Learn about policy issues from the conservative viewpoint: http://www.heritage.org

ADDITIONAL READING

Stone, Deborah. *Policy Paradox: The Art of Political Decision Making.* New York: Norton, 1997.

Zietlow, Rebecca. *Enforcing Equality: Congress the Constitution, and the Protection of Individual Rights.* New York: NYU Press. 2006.

Types of Public Policy

14.2 **Compare and contrast the three main types of public policies.**

(pages 432–433)

Public policies can be categorized by issue area (such as the environment, education, and agriculture) or by the functions of government necessary to carry out the policy. The three basic types of policy based on the functions of government are distribution, regulation, and redistribution. It is also possible to categorize policy outputs as either tangible or symbolic.

KEY TERMS

Policy Categories 432
Distribution 432
Regulation 432
Redistribution 432

CRITICAL THINKING QUESTIONS

1. Why do redistributive polices cause so much political conflict? Are there distributive and regulatory policies that can cause as much conflict?
2. What criteria are used for placing policies in categories? How easy or difficult is it to place a policy in a specific category?

INTERNET RESOURCES

Learn about the roles of the departments and agencies of the federal government in formulating distributive, regulatory, and redistributive public policies: http://www.firstgov.gov/Agencies/Federal/Executive.shtml

ADDITIONAL READING

Hudson, William. *The Libertarian Illusion: Ideology, Public Policy and the Assault on the Common Good.* Washington, DC: CQ Press, 2007.

Theodoulou, Stella Z., and Chris Kofinis. *The Art of the Game: Understanding American Public Policy Making.* Belmont, CA: Wadsworth, 2004.

The Public Policy Process

 14.3 Analyze how the policy process is shaped by political influences.

(pages 434–437)

The process of making public policy in the United States is tightly tied to many political influences. Interest groups, the media, public opinion, and political parties all exert pressures on policymakers as they identify, formulate and implement public policies. The final design and form of the policies that emerge from the policy process reflect the characteristics of the various political influences.

KEY TERMS

Pluralists 435

Focusing Events 435

Trigger Mechanism 435

Institutional Agenda 435

Issue-Attention Cycle 435

Laws 435

Decisions 436

Rule-Making Authority 436

Coercion 436

Discretion 436

CRITICAL THINKING QUESTIONS

1. The process model of policymaking says a great deal about how the institutions of government function but not much about our role as citizens in any of the phases of the process. At which phases in the process does citizen action have an impact on the final result? Why?

2. Explain how oversight works. Is oversight a necessary part of policymaking? Why or why not?

INTERNET RESOURCES

The House of Representatives is a policymaker with oversight functions. Find out what it is doing in both these areas: http://www.house.gov

The Senate is also a policymaker with oversight functions: http://www.senate.gov

Presidents are powerful policy players. To see what issues President Obama supports, go to http://www.whitehouse .gov

To see what former President George W. Bush supported, go to http://www.gpoaccess.gov/pubpapers/ gwbush.html

Learn about the federal courts and their roles as policymakers: http://www.firstgov.gov/Agencies/Federal/ Judicial.shtml

ADDITIONAL READING

Derthick, Martha A. *Up in Smoke.* Washington, DC: CQ Press, 2002.

Lindblom, Charles E., and Edward J. Woodhouse. *The Policy-Making Process,* 3rd ed. Englewood Cliffs, NJ: Prentice Hall, 1993.

Spitzer, Robert J. *The Politics of Gun Control.* Washington, DC: CQ Press, 2004.

Economic Basics

 14.4 Identify the key indicators of economic performance used by economists.

(pages 438–441)

The most important measures of the health of the U.S. economy are inflation, employment, gross domestic product, the budget deficit or surplus, and the balance of trade.

KEY TERMS

Inflation 438

Consumer Price Index (CPI) 438

Deflation 438

Unemployment Rate 438

Gross Domestic Product (GDP) 438

Balance of Trade 438

Budget Deficit 439

Budget Surplus 439

National Debt 439

CRITICAL THINKING QUESTIONS

1. Is one of the measures of economic performance likely to be a more reliable indicator of economic health than the others? If so, which one? If not, why not?

2. What is the difference between the deficit and the national debt? How is inflation measured?

INTERNET RESOURCES

Read about the Concord Coalition, a nonpartisan group lobbying for sound fiscal policy, at http://www .concordcoalition.org

ADDITIONAL READING

Greenspan, Alan. *The Age of Turbulence: Adventures in a New World.* New York: Penguin Books, 2007.

Skidelsky, Robert. *Keynes: The Return of the Master.* New York: Penguin Books, 2009.

Fiscal Policy

 14.5 Describe the major actors responsible for creating economic policy.

(pages 442–443)

Fiscal policy encompasses the taxing and spending decisions made by the government. The Congressional Budget Office is an important source of budgetary analysis and planning. Congress and its relevant committees shape the budget. The congressional committees make changes to the president's budgetary proposal crafted by Office of Management and Budget.

KEY TERMS

Fiscal Policy 442
Congressional Budget Office (CBO) 442

CRITICAL THINKING QUESTIONS

1. Why is Congress considered the primary player in shaping the budget?
2. What were the major provisions of the Budget and Impoundment Act of 1974?

INTERNET RESOURCES

The Office of Management and Budget (OMB) is a cabinet-level office that prepares the president's budget. For information about the budget, please visit www.whitehouse.gov/omb

The Congressional Budget Office (CBO) is the primary congressional agency that reviews the congressional budget. For a congressional analysis of the president's budget, please visit www.cbo.gov

The United States General Accountability Office (GAO) is the "investigative arm of Congress" and is charged to help improve the performance and accountability of the U.S. federal-government in order to benefit the American people. For more information on GAO activities, please visit www.gao.gov

ADDITIONAL READING

Greider, William. *Secrets of the Temple: How the Federal Reserve Runs the Country.* New York: Touchstone, 1987.

Schick, Allen. *The Federal Budget: Politics, Policy, Process*, 3rd ed. Washington, DC: Brookings Institution, 2007.

Revenue and Expenditures

 14.6 Explain the major sources of U.S. government revenue and expenditure.

(pages 444–449)

The largest source of revenue for the U.S. government is the income tax; the payroll tax is second, and corporate taxes are third. Taxation decisions affect both economic performance and the perception of equity. The largest areas of expenditure for the United States are Social Security and defense, with income security being the third largest. Because of debt and long term commitments for Social Security, medical care, and defense expenditures, the United States faces significant budgetary challenges in the future.

KEY TERMS

Payroll Tax 444
Progressive Tax 444
Regressive Tax 444
Marginal Tax Bracket 444
Laffer Curve 445
Social Security Trust Fund 446
Income Security 447
Medicare 448
Medicaid 448
Entitlements 448

CRITICAL THINKING QUESTIONS

1. What differentiates a progressive tax from a regressive tax? Which tax has the biggest impact on the average American?
2. How have medical care costs affected government spending? What are entitlements, and how are they created?

INTERNET RESOURCES

The National Center for Policy Analysis (NCPA) is a nonpartisan think tank that researches and evaluates public policy areas such as health care and environmental regulation. For more information, visit www.ncpa.org

See Progressive Policy Institute's link to fiscal and economic policy issues at http://www.ppionline.org/ ppi_ka.cfm?knlgAreaID=125

ADDITIONAL READING

Béland, Daniel. *Social Security: History and Politics from the New Deal to the Privatization Debates.* Lawrence: University of Kansas Press, 2007.

Levitt, Steven D. *Freakonomics: A Rogue Economist Explores the Hidden Side of Everything.* New York: William Morrow, 2005.

Monetary Policy

 14.7 Identify the major instruments of monetary policy.

(pages 450–451)

Monetary policy involves managing the nation's money supply in order to stabilize inflation, interest rates, and employment. The Federal Reserve Board's Federal Open Market Committee (FOMC) has primary responsibility for setting monetary policy. The primary instruments of the FOMC are the discount rate and open-market operations. The Fed uses the FOMC to regulate money supply through the buying and selling of Treasury bills. It also uses the discount rate—a rate it charges commercial banks for borrowing its funds—to control the money supply.

KEY TERMS

Monetary Policy 450
Federal Reserve System (the Fed) 450
Federal Open Market Committee 450
Reserve Ratios 450
Federal Funds Rate 450
Open-Market Operations 450
Discount Rate 450
Prime Rate 450
Stagflation 451
Phillips Curve 451

CRITICAL THINKING QUESTIONS

1. What is the Federal Open Market Committee? How can it influence monetary policy?
2. From 1979 to 1987, what actions did Paul Volcker take to get the economy back on track? Did they work? Why or why not?

INTERNET RESOURCES

Information on the Federal Reserve can be found at http://www.federalreserve.gov/

ADDITIONAL READING

Woodward, Bob. *Maestro: Greenspan's Fed and the American Boom.* New York: Simon and Schuster, 2000.

Chapter Review   Test Your Knowledge

1. What is public policy?
   a. another word for the laws that Congress creates and the president signs
   b. laws and policies pertaining to public spaces, such as highways, parks, and public schools
   c. the action or inaction of the government on an issue of concern to the public
   d. governmental decisions that come from public input

2. While policy is the product of political processes, some consider it to be not political in itself.
   a. true
   b. false

3. What political camp would a citizen occupy if he or she defined freedom negatively and believed in an equality of process, not outcome?
   a. progressive
   b. liberal
   c. centrist
   d. conservative

4. What are all the phases, and their chronological order, in the classic policy process model?
   a. a focusing event, setting an agenda, formulating policy, and implementing policy
   b. identifying the problem, setting an agenda, legitimizing policy, formulating policy, and implementing policy
   c. identifying the problem, setting an agenda, formulating policy, legitimizing policy, and implementing policy
   d. a focusing event, setting an agenda, identifying the problem, formulating policy, implementing and assessing policy

5. Why isn't the policy formation process neat?
   a. because policies are always complicated
   b. because of all the different political actors who participate in that process
   c. because the Constitution mandates that policy formation itself be "checked and balanced" by all three branches of the government
   d. because "neat" policy would be much less easy to enforce

6. What is one common reason certain issues on the country's "institutional agenda" fade away and are never acted on?
   a. The issue only serves one geographic segment of the country.
   b. The would-be policy only possesses symbolic value.
   c. The would-be policy excites the emotions of the public, and legislators resist such a coercive context.
   d. The would-be policy would be too costly or inconvenient to enact and enforce.

7. How does public policy acquire legitimacy in this country?
   a. through Americans' traditional faith in political authorities
   b. through the law enforcement authority that often backs up such policy
   c. through a fair and open policymaking process and citizens' input into that process
   d. by the amount of time it is implemented and enforced

8. The step in the policy process that is most influenced by media attention is:
   a. policy implementation.
   b. policy oversight.
   c. agenda setting.
   d. policy legitimization.

9. Why is discretion so essential to the implementation of a law or policy?
   a. Policies are sometimes worded vaguely enough to attract keen interest in Congress, so those doing the actual implementation must decide on the details.
   b. The ambiguous nature of language itself always leaves a lot of room for interpreting policy.
   c. Legislators are often quite proficient in technical matters, but executive agencies or departments that implement policy usually are not. Therefore, laws are written in language that the implementers can understand.
   d. Article II of the Constitution grants those agencies or departments that implement policy the authority to shift the emphasis or focus of any law or policy, provided they do not violate the "spirit of the law."

10. What is congressional oversight?
    a. when high-ranking members of the executive branch monitor the actions of Congress during the policy formation
    b. when Congress monitors what is and is not on its 2-year policy agenda
    c. when Congress makes sure that the policies it helped create are being carried out appropriately
    d. when the House or Senate neglects some segments of legislation the other legislative body has included in a bill

11. What prompts Congress to exercise oversight through the reauthorization process?
    a. the wording in all legislation that includes a reauthorization clause
    b. partisan politics, which usually compels members of the minority party to check up on the policies initiated by their majority colleagues
    c. tradition
    d. the responsibilities that Congress has to tax and spend public funds

12. While Congress does not exercise oversight over policy implementation, the courts do exercise such oversight.
    a. true
    b. false

13. What is one reason that substantial shifts in public policy are rare in the United States?
    a. Politicians tend to feel less passionate about policy in this country than in some others.
    b. Most Americans do not want such policy shifts, even if they would help create a more just and effective government and society.
    c. Powerful interest groups have developed on the opposite sides of many big issues, in effect countering the political influence of each other.
    d. Fewer problems demand policy attention in this country than in some others.

14. What is the difference between fiscal policy and monetary policy?
    a. Fiscal policy concerns the national money supply; monetary policy is focused on taxing and spending decisions.
    b. Monetary policy is focused on deficits and surpluses; fiscal policy is concerned with interest rates and employment rates.
    c. Fiscal policy concerns taxing and spending decisions; monetary policy focuses on the national money supply.
    d. Fiscal policy is economic policy formulated by the Federal Reserve Board; monetary policy is economic policy formulated by the Congress and the president.

15. When measuring the health of the nation's economy, economists usually focus on
    a. the gross domestic product.
    b. the gross domestic product and the budget deficit or surplus.
    c. the gross domestic product, the budget deficit or surplus, and unemployment.
    d. inflation, unemployment, the gross domestic product, the balance of trade, and the budget surplus or deficit.

16. What exactly is the national debt?
    a. how much the U.S. government owes private investors and other countries in a given year
    b. the budget deficit plus the trade deficit in a given year
    c. the net sum of the budget deficit, minus the surplus
    d. the budget deficit plus the trade deficit, minus the Social Security Trust Fund

17. Most American workers pay less per year in payroll taxes than they do in income taxes.
    a. true
    b. false

18. Which of the following is not a leading indicator of economic performance?
    a. unemployment rate
    b. inflation rate
    c. GDP
    d. amount of farm subsidies

19. The primary aim of the Federal Reserve Board is to
    a. make sure the president's economic policy is working well.
    b. make sure congressional economic policy is working well.
    c. regulate the national banking system.
    d. try to control inflation and keep the economy stable and growing.

20. How does the Fed have to be "right twice"?
    a. by creating the correct response to an economic problem, and then knowing when to stop the corrective action
    b. by knowing where the economy is headed, and then by making the correct response to the anticipated circumstances
    c. by knowing when to stop digging one economic hole (the national debt) and when to start digging another (into unemployment)
    d. by knowing where the economy is headed, and then by giving key economic policymakers the right advice about staving off future problems

mypoliscilab Exercises

Apply what you learned in this chapter on **MyPoliSciLab**.

Read on **mypoliscilab.com**

    eText: Chapter 14

Study and **Review** on **mypoliscilab.com**

    Pre-Test
    Post-Test
    Chapter Exam
    Flashcards

Watch on **mypoliscilab.com**

    Video: Health Care Plan
    Video: Raising the Minimum Wage
    Video: Making Environmental Policy
    Video: Recession Hits Indiana
    Video: Economic Policy Debate at the G20
    Video: The Stimulus Breakdown
    Video: America's Aging Population
    Video: Fed Approves Mortgage Crackdown

Explore on **mypoliscilab.com**

Simulation: You Are an Environmental Activist
Simulation: You Are the President and Need to Get a Tax Cut Passed
Simulation: Making Economic Policy
Comparative: Comparing Social Welfare System
Comparative: Comparing Economic Policy
Comparative: Comparing Health Systems
Timeline: The Evolution of Social Welfare Policy
Timeline: Growth of the Budget and Federal Spending
Visual Literacy: Where the Money Goes
Visual Literacy: Evaluating Federal Spending and Economic Policy

Foreign and National Security Policy

KEY OBJECTIVES

After completing this chapter, you should be prepared to:

15.1 Compare and contrast four different approaches to American foreign policy.

15.2 Establish three links between American foreign and domestic policy.

15.3 Assess pathways for citizen participation in foreign policymaking.

15.4 Analyze how political institutions compete for influence in making foreign policy.

15.5 Outline the major foreign policy issues confronting the United States today.

O n October 9, 2009, the world community was shocked to learn that President Barack Obama, less than one year into his first term of office and presiding over wars in Iraq and Afghanistan, had been awarded the Nobel Peace Prize. Obama was "humbled" by the award and called the prize a "call to action." The Norwegian Peace Prize committee stated that they were rewarding Obama's promise of disarmament and diplomacy; however, criticism was sharp and swift.

Approximately eight months earlier, President Obama had pledged to double the number of armed military personnel in Afghanistan (from 17,000 to approximately 34,000) with a larger deployment being considered to "stabilize a deteriorating situation" and to deal with the Taliban resurgence and spread of al-Qaeda. In September, Obama had rejected comparisons between Afghanistan and Vietnam, despite rising unease about the commitment from within his own political party. In addition, a United Nations commission report issued on October 19, 2009 asserted

> **How does U.S. policy reflect its position as the world's leading superpower?**

widespread fraud in the August 2009 Afghanistan elections, putting the administration at odds with Afghan President Hamid Karzai. Beyond the situations in Afghanistan and Iraq, the Obama administration has had conflict with North Korea and Iran over nuclear weapons and has witnessed increasing tensions between Israel and Palestine.

Given these considerations, one must wonder why the Norwegian Nobel Committee selected President Obama. Were his promises of diplomacy and support of nuclear disarmament sufficient to induce the committee to grant this prestigious award to the young (and largely untested) president? Was the award instead a rebuff of the Bush administration by the international community? Perhaps a bit of both? Regardless of the motivations for the award, President Obama leads our country in an increasingly complex world. As his presidency continues, his ability to promote his own foreign policy agenda will be constrained by a host of institutional and ideological constraints.

Resource Center
• Glossary
• Vocabulary Example
• Connect the Link

■ **Neoconservatives:** People who believe that the United States has a special role to play in world politics; they advocate the unilateral use of force and the pursuit of a value-based foreign policy.

SIGNIFICANCE: *Neoconservatives are opposed in their views by neoliberals, people who strongly support international law and organizations and are skeptical about the use of military force, because they attribute many of the world's problems to economic, political, and social conditions.*

Competing Principles for American Foreign Policy

15.1 Compare and contrast four different approaches to American foreign policy.
(pages 462–465)

Today, there are two major approaches to U.S. interaction with the rest of the world. Both perspectives view the United States as a leading power in world politics. They differ, however, on what the United States should try to accomplish from this position of strength. A group we'll call the "transformers" believes that the United States should try to transform the international system in a way that will not just protect American goals and values but allow them to prosper and become universally accepted. According to the second group, the "maintainers," the United States should consolidate its gains as the victor in the Cold War and not try to impose itself or its values on others. Within each perspective, we can identify two major competing camps, for a total of four different stances on American foreign policy (see Table 15.1). After describing the beliefs of these four groups, we will bring them into sharper focus by examining the position of each on the wars in Iraq and Afghanistan.

Transformers

Both the neoconservative and neoliberal transformers are optimists. They view the United States as being in an unchallenged position to bring about fundamental changes in other states that will protect American goals and values and allow them to prosper and become universally accepted.

NEOCONSERVATIVES The **neoconservatives**■ are a group that occupied prominent foreign policy positions in both Bush administrations.[1] Four common themes tend to unite neoconservatives in their views on American foreign policy. First, because the United States is the sole remaining superpower, it plays a fundamentally different role in world politics than other countries do. This means that the United States is in a position to force others to follow rules of proper behavior, but it does not have to abide by those rules itself. Second, the ever-present military power of the United States is the central instrument of American foreign policy, and the United States should not be apologetic or timid about using it. Third, neoconservatives believe that unilateralism is the proper approach for dealing with foreign policy problems. Instead of helping the United States achieve its goals, alliances such as the **North Atlantic Treaty Organization (NATO)**■ and international institutions such as the United Nations more often than not place roadblocks in its way. Rather than be hamstrung by these bodies, neoconservatives insist that America must always be free to act in response to the wishes of American leaders. Fourth, neoconservatives believe that it is in the American national interest to spread democracy around the world.

NEOLIBERALS While neoconservative transformers think about world politics in terms of conflict and struggle, with few opportunities for cooperation, **neoliberals**■ see in much of the world the potential for shared identity and cooperation.[2] Neoliberals do not presume that nations automatically share interests or that cooperation can be easily generated. They do, however, value international institutions and regimes as a way to manage and coordinate expectations among nations and

TABLE 15.1 | Four Perspectives on Foreign Policy

TRANSFORMERS: PERSPECTIVES AND BELIEFS	MAINTAINERS: PERSPECTIVES AND BELIEFS
Neoconservatives • The United States must enforce the rules on other countries (although not necessarily abide by them), because it is the sole unchallenged superpower. • Military power is the most important factor in foreign policy. • The United States must be able to act unilaterally, as its leaders see fit, in dealing with foreign policy problems; international organizations may come between the United States and its best interests. • Spreading democracy to other nations is in the best interests of the United States.	**Conservatives** • The United States must be prepared to use military force. • Global interests may be different from U.S. interests. • Power is an important asset; it must be maintained and used carefully. • Power is more effective if it is viewed as legitimate.
Neoliberals • Spreading democracy is in the American national interest. • Nonmilitary means are preferred over military action. • Support from international organizations and agreements can be important to future endeavors.	**Isolationists** • Military power should be used as a shield to protect U.S. interests. • The United States is minimally accountable to its allies and the international community. • Foreign policy should consist mostly of cultural, commercial, and diplomatic interactions.

■ **North Atlantic Treaty Organization (NATO):** A military alliance set up by the United States and its Western European allies initially for the purpose of containing the expansion of the former Soviet Union.

SIGNIFICANCE: *NATO's military strategic cooperation among member states successfully contained communist expansion during the Cold War.*

■ **Neoliberals:** People who believe that cooperation is possible through the creation and management of international institutions, organizations, and regimes.

SIGNIFICANCE: *Neoliberals stress the value of multinational cooperation to manage complex global interactions.*

COMPETING PRINCIPLES FOR AMERICAN FOREIGN POLICY   **CHAPTER 15**   **463**

other international actors. Neoliberals fear that neoconservative principles will provoke a global backlash that will increase American insecurity and lead to a world less supportive of American values. President Obama, in his short tenure as an international leader, demonstrates many of the characteristics of a neoliberal.

Neoliberal transformers share three common objectives. Similar to neoconservatives, neoliberals seek to spread democracy to further American national interests. However, whereas neoconservatives stress the ability of the United States to come into a society and build democracy, neoliberals maintain that democracy is best built from within, by local political forces. Second, neoliberals tend to stress nonmilitary means for achieving foreign policy ends. They favor foreign aid and economic assistance programs, especially when the aid is made dependent on conditions such as respect for human rights. Neoliberals do not reject the use of military force outright, however. Third, in contrast to the neoconservative embrace of unilateralism, neoliberals stress the importance of international institutions and agreements as ways of accomplishing foreign policy objectives.

Maintainers

Whereas both the neoconservative and neoliberal transformers are optimists, the conservative and isolationist maintainers are pessimists. Maintainers see the international system as a threat to American interests.

CONSERVATIVES   Conservatives believe that an effective American foreign policy must be built around four themes. First is the realization that to protect its interests, the United States must be prepared to act militarily. Diplomacy and economic aid are no substitutes for military power. Second, American national interests are limited and not identical to global interests. When the two are in conflict, national interests must always take precedence. Global crusades, whether to build democracy or defeat terrorism, are dangerous, because they divert the United States from real and more immediate dangers. Third, power—especially military power, as the key measure that countries use to compare one another—must be refreshed constantly and used carefully. It is better to take action through alliances and coalitions than it is to act alone so that the costs and risks of military action can be shared. Fourth, the exercise of American power is most effective when others view it as legitimate.[3]

ISOLATIONISTS   Isolationist maintainers have little doubt about the importance of military power and the need to defend American national interests. Where they part company from the conservative maintainers is in the number and range of events abroad that call for military action by America. For isolationists, the major threats to U.S. security come from an overactive foreign policy and responses that threaten to undermine

core American values.[4] Three themes guide isolationist foreign policy thinking. First, American foreign policy must concentrate on protecting American lives and property, the territory of the United States, and the integrity of the American political system. To do so, American military power must become less a lance to strike out at others and more a shield to defend our homeland. Second, American responsibility to allies and the international community is minimal. Other countries must learn to become responsible for their own defense. Third, the proper way for the United States to be active in the world is through cultural, commercial, and diplomatic interactions. Foreign aid should be reduced and American troops brought home.

Conflicting Evaluations of the Wars in Iraq and Afghanistan

On March 19, 2003, following much public debate in the United States, political maneuvering at the United Nations, and the presentation of a 48-hour ultimatum to Iraq's dictator, Saddam Hussein, the Iraq War began. President George W. Bush had branded Iraq part of an "axis of evil," along with North Korea and Iran, in his 2002 State of the Union address. The Bush administration argued that Iraq's possession of **weapons of mass destruction** required preemptive military action on the part of the United States. (That claim was later recognized as incorrect.) The military operation was a spectacular success. On April 9, Baghdad fell, and on May 1, President Bush declared an end to major combat operations. By December 2003, Saddam Hussein was captured.

The early success in Iraq followed similar successes in Afghanistan. In the aftermath of the 2001 terrorist attacks in the United States, a coalition of nations used military force to bring down the Taliban-led government in Afghanistan and replace it with a democratically elected government led by Hamid Karzai. The early military actions in Afghanistan included relatively few casualties among coalition forces, and there was a general sense that the situation in that nation was under control. However the early appraisals of success in Iraq and Afghanistan would prove to be premature and overly optimistic.

In Iraq violent opposition continued throughout the region, however, and the American occupation of Iraq proved far more difficult than expected. In July 2003, deaths among U.S. combat forces in Iraq reached the level of the 1991 Persian Gulf War. By April 2010, there had been about 4,400 deaths of U.S. combat forces in Iraq. The Iraqi body count had surpassed 100,000.[5]

Political and economic setbacks, unforeseen by the war's planners, were numerous. Iraq's oil production was slow to recover, and U.S. funds aimed at economic recovery had to be diverted to improve security. Amid seemingly endless sectarian and ethnic strife, Iraqi political leaders repeatedly failed to meet reestablished deadlines to lay the foundation for a new democratic political order.

The early successes in Afghanistan were replaced with deteriorating security conditions and a resurgence of the Taliban in many regions of the nation. After becoming president in 2009, Barack Obama spent months evaluating the future of U.S. military intervention in Afghanistan, eventually deciding to increase troop levels in a manner similar to the policies used earlier in Iraq.

We'll now evaluate the Iraq and Afghanistan conflicts from the four foreign policy perspectives we have introduced. We will consider the judgments of each camp in turn, beginning with the neoconservatives, who dominated the Bush administration's decision-making.

NEOCONSERVATIVE EVALUATION   Neoconservatives view the wars in Iraq and Afghanistan as essential to the future security of the United States. The Taliban harbored terrorists in Afghanistan and therefore posed a direct threat to Americans. Removing Saddam Hussein from power was necessary, even if he did not have weapons of mass destruction, because his was a dangerous and aggressive government that once had these weapons and, if permitted, would obtain them again. Removing him from power was also necessary in order to build democracy in Iraq and set the stage for the democratization of the Middle East. In the neoconservative view, the United States cannot leave Iraq until democracy and economic recovery are assured, just as they were in post–World War II West Germany and Japan.

NEOLIBERAL EVALUATION   Neoliberals shed no tears over the downfall of the Taliban and Saddam Hussein, recognizing that both had abysmal records of human rights abuses, and in the case of Hussein a history of foreign incursions. Before the war, however, neoliberals had asserted that nonmilitary means, such as economic sanctions, were a preferable line of action for removing these regimes. They had also cautioned that occupying and reconstructing these nations would be difficult and that democracy could not be imposed from outside. Neoliberals also maintain that if the reconstruction in these nations is to succeed, the United Nations must play a larger role.

CONSERVATIVE EVALUATION   Conservatives make some key distinctions between the wars in Iraq and Afghanistan. First, conservatives favored the broader and more engaged international alliance employed in Afghanistan to the more U.S. centered approach used in Iraq. They believe that such cooperation would reduce the political and economic costs to the United States, both in the actual fighting of the war and during the subsequent occupation. Second, conservatives see the Iraq War as having distracted the United States from pursuing the true enemy: Osama bin Laden and his terrorists. In their view, the Iraq War gave anti-American terrorism new life, as Iraq became

a magnet for international terrorist groups. Related to this is the conservatives' concern that by acting unilaterally, the United States disrupted the balance of global politics, in the end leaving America less secure.

ISOLATIONIST EVALUATION   Finally, the isolationists generally supported the war in Afghanistan, because it was a direct response to the 9/11 terrorist attacks. They saw little value added in the Iraq War, and they regard attempts at building democracy in Iraq and the Middle East as a "fool's errand." Isolationists would prefer to focus on more rigorous efforts to promote homeland security.

Echoes from the Past

Americans have almost always disagreed about the proper ways to interact with the rest of the world. These diverging attitudes have long been shaped by specific historical circumstances, America's strategic interests, and the different foreign policy preferences of American leaders. During the American Revolution, Congress sent diplomats to Europe pleading for crucial military and financial help to defeat the British. Upon leaving office in 1796, President George Washington recommended a foreign policy of isolation and noninvolvement. Succeeding presidents generally kept engagement with other countries close to home in the Western Hemisphere.

Only on the eve of the twentieth century, with the Spanish-American War (1898), did the United States become a major player on the world stage. By defeating Spain, the United States acquired an overseas colony, the Philippines. Under the first twentieth-century presidents—Theodore Roosevelt, William Howard Taft, and Woodrow Wilson—the United States carved out a sphere of influence in Mexico, Central America, and the Caribbean. In 1917, Wilson took the United States into World War I, and American forces contributed significantly to defeating Germany in 1918. Wilson took an active role in negotiating the peace treaty (the Treaty of Versailles) and in creating the League of Nations. But the Senate rejected joining the League of Nations, and American foreign policy in the 1920s was largely confined to bolstering U.S. domination in Latin America. During the 1930s, the United States gave little support to the democratic nations of Britain and France after Adolf Hitler came to power in Germany.

Japan's attack on Pearl Harbor on December 7, 1941, changed forever how Americans saw the outside world. The "Fortress America" strategy of relying on the protection of the oceans no longer seemed realistic. The nation mobilized its military might and achieved victory in Europe and Asia. With World War II over and the onset of the Cold War, the United States had no choice but to play a major and sustained role in world affairs. The United States helped create the United Nations; international economic organizations, such as

A U.S. soldier provides protection for Afghan workers as they construct a road near Bagram, Afghanistan in 2010. Much of the day-to-day work of the U.S. military in Afghanistan involves reconstruction efforts instead of traditional combat missions. —*Is the U.S. military configured in a way that allows it to play a valuable role in rebuilding efforts in countries like Afghanistan?*

the World Bank and the International Monetary Fund; and alliances, such as NATO. The struggle against the Soviet Union and communism became global, especially after communist revolutionaries triumphed in China in 1949. The image of dominoes, standing precariously on edge and tumbling one after the other, was frequently invoked to represent this conflict. No country, in this metaphor, could be allowed to fall to communism, because that would set off a chain reaction in which one country after another would "go communist." The end of the Cold War did not bring the peace dividend many would have hoped for.

The events of September 11, 2001 thrust America into a global "war on terror." Under President Bush's leadership, a multilateral coalition (a coalition made up of several nations) was formed to invade Afghanistan and remove the Taliban from power. NATO presence and European support remain in Afghanistan today, as the country struggles to find stability. With Iraq, however, President Bush and his neoconservative foreign policymakers found it hard to form a broad multilateral coalition. Eventually, the United States and Great Britain led a "coalition of the Willing" that bypassed the UN, to invade Iraq and enforce regime change. Powerful countries like France, Germany, and Russia opposed the invasion of Iraq. The legitimacy of the invasion was called into question from the beginning, and the continued sectarian violence and lack of real stability further alienated the broader global community.

President Obama has imposed a timeline to withdraw troops from Iraq and shift his focus to Afghanistan. His announcement that U.S. combat missions in Iraq will end by August 31, 2010 dovetails with his December 2009 decision to send 30,000 more troops to Afghanistan. In Afghanistan, U.S. troops work within the NATO command structure, rather than acting unilaterally. This fits with President Obama's neoliberal philosophy when it comes to international relations.

Competing Principles for American Foreign Policy

15.1   **Compare and contrast four different approaches to American foreign policy.**

PRACTICE QUIZ: UNDERSTAND AND APPLY

1. Whose foreign policy makes them "transformers" and not "maintainers"?
   a. neoliberals and isloationists
   b. neoconservatives and conservatives
   c. neoliberals and neoconservatives
   d. conservatives and isolationsists

2. Which foreign policy perspective asserts that democracy is best built from within, by local political forces?
   a. isolationists
   b. conservatives
   c. a and b
   d. neoliberals

3. Which foreign policy perspective asserts that American military force should become less like a lance and more like a shield?
   a. isolationists
   b. conservatives
   c. a and b
   d. neoliberals

ANALYZE

1. Compare and contrast the conservative and the neoconservative foreign policy perspectives about the wars in Iraq and Afghanistan.

2. In your view, which of the four foreign policy perspective makes the most sense, given the challenges facing the United States today? Why?

IDENTIFY THE CONCEPT THAT DOESN'T BELONG

a. Warsaw Pact
b. World Bank
c. United Nations
d. NATO
e. International Monetary Fund

15.1

Resource Center
- Glossary
- Vocabulary Example
- Connect the Link

Links Between Foreign and Domestic Policy

15.2 Establish three links between American foreign and domestic policy.

(pages 466–469)

We commonly talk of American foreign policy and domestic policy as two separate areas, but the boundary separating domestic and foreign policy is not, and never has been, watertight. In this section, we will examine three different links between American foreign and domestic policy. First, American foreign policy is often based on ideas and values that guide domestic policy. Second, the U.S. political decision-making process is influenced by the presence and activity of a number of international factors, including lobbyists. Finally, and perhaps most important, U.S. foreign policy can affect the distribution of costs and benefits among different groups in the United States.

Barack Obama speaks at the United Nations Climate Change Conference in Copenhagen, Denmark in 2009. Despite his campaign pledge to improve U.S. efforts to address global warming, President Obama was unable to dramatically alter American climate polices during his first years in office. —*What limits are there on the president's powers to make foreign policy?*

Domestic Policy Values Guide American Foreign Policy

Let's first consider the impact of domestic policy values on American foreign policy by looking at how the United States approaches human rights and environmental issues at the global level.[6] Three guiding principles lie at the heart of our country's human rights foreign policy. First, American policy, both domestic and foreign, emphasizes individual legal rights and civil liberties; it pays less attention to economic and social rights. Second, Washington usually regards hostile, overly strong governments as the primary threat to human rights; rarely does American policy see a need to strengthen foreign governments in order to promote human rights. Third, American foreign policy generally rejects violence as a means for promoting human rights. Attempts to advance workers' rights or civil rights through violence have never been received favorably in the United States; instead, we generally look to legal and electoral means of promoting rights. Because this historical experience is not shared by many other countries, American calls for rejecting violence as a means of change are often met with skepticism.

The influence of American domestic policy values on its foreign policy is also evident in U.S. environmental policy. By and large, international environmental proposals put forward by the United States have not imposed new costs on Americans; they have instead sought to persuade other countries to adopt American standards. For example, the United States was one of the strongest advocates of a 10-year ban on commercial whaling, an area in which the United States has few economic interests but many citizens who worry about the fate of the

world's whale population. But the United States has also vigorously opposed efforts to establish an international register of toxic chemicals, and it has refused to ratify the 1997 **Kyoto Protocol** on reducing greenhouse gases—in both cases citing the costs to American firms and the threat to American living standards. While the Obama administration has made rhetorical commitments about greater U.S. leadership on international environmental accords, the failure of the Copenhagen Climate Summit in 2009 to lead to a new accord, demonstrates that the American government has yet to substantively deliver on the changes that were anticipated by many when Obama took office.

International Factors Influence U.S. Political Activity

Foreign lobbying has become big business in Washington. Between 1998 and 2004, companies with headquarters in 78 foreign nations spent more than $620 million lobbying the U.S. government. These companies employed 550 lobbying firms and a total of 3,800 lobbyists—more than 100 of them former members of Congress. Between July 2007 and December 2008, about 340 foreign interests representing governments, separatist groups, and for-profit corporations, spent about $87 million on lobbying efforts in the United States.[7] These lobbying groups are registered with the U.S. Department of Justice.

In 1990, with his capital city under attack by rebel forces, Liberian President Samuel Doe paid a Washington lobbyist $800,000 to improve his image and increase lukewarm U.S. support. (It didn't help—Doe was later overthrown and executed by the rebels.) In 2008, Liberia spent about $560,000 on U.S. lobbying efforts.[8] In 1990, former South African political

■ **Globalization:** The expansion of economic interactions between countries.

EXAMPLE: *The North American Free Trade Agreement (NAFTA) encourages globalization by lowering or eliminating trade barriers among the United States, Mexico, and Canada.*

Oil company executives are sworn in at a 2010 hearing of the Energy and Environment Subcommittee of the U.S. House of Representatives. The hearing took place as oil continued to spill from British Petroleum's Deepwater Horizon site in the Gulf of Mexico months after an explosion on BP's oil rig initiated the spill. The massive damage to U.S. economic and environmental interests caused by the actions of a British-owned corporation raised concerns about the ability of the government to protect American sovereignty. —*Can the United States limit foreign investments and business operations without damaging international trade and globalized markets?*

prisoner Nelson Mandela traveled to Washington, in part to lobby Congress to keep economic sanctions in place against the white-supremacist government that ruled his country. And in 2003, Bob Livingstone, a former Republican representative from Louisiana and one-time chair of the House Appropriations Committee, helped Turkey defeat an attempt by the Republican-controlled Congress to take away $1 billion worth of foreign aid because of its failure to help the United States in the Iraq War. Countries like Pakistan, Indonesia, and Djibouti, despite their dubious human rights record, have received billions of dollars of additional military aid because of lobbying efforts in the post-911 period. Many of the funds have been disbursed without adequate congressional oversight.[9]

Many foreign governments are deeply concerned about American foreign aid legislation and arms sales. To secure their objectives in these areas, they pursue a two-step lobbying campaign. First, they try to gain leverage by lobbying the executive branch, usually the White House, the State Department, and the Defense Department. Second, as already noted, they also lobby Congress.

The primary concern of foreign firms that operate in the United States is the ability of their affiliates to conduct business profitably and without hindrance. Between 1998 and 2004, for example, 22 foreign companies operating in the United States actively lobbied the Environmental Protection Agency over issues connected with the agency's Superfund cleanup policies. At the state and local levels, taxation, zoning, and education as well as labor laws and policies are all of considerable concern to foreign firms. In one well-known case, Sony threatened to stop planned construction of new plants in California and Florida unless those states repealed portions of their tax codes that would have taxed Sony on its worldwide sales rather than on its sales of items produced in that particular state. After both states changed their tax laws, Sony went ahead and built the new plants. In 2005, Toyota was planning the location of a new automotive plant, in either the United States or Canada. Although several U.S. states offered more lucrative tax packages, both the national government and several provincial governments in Canada offered money for worker training; in addition, the Canadian system of universal health care would allow Toyota to save on the cost of health care benefits. Canada ended up getting the plant.

The scale of foreign political activity in the United States has repeatedly raised two concerns. The first is that the more our representatives listen to foreign lobbyists, the less they will hear from the American public. The second is that foreign interests and American interests are not always compatible. By listening to and responding to foreign voices, policymakers may ignore or, worse, harm American national interests. This concern is reinforced by periodic revelations of foreign attempts at bribery and espionage. For example, in 2002, it was revealed that Taiwan kept a secret $100 million fund to buy influence in this country, and in 2005, two former employees of a pro-Israeli lobbying

firm were indicted for disclosing U.S. defense information. In 2007, two influential scholars—John Mearsheimer and Stephen Walt—published their controversial book *The Israel Lobby and U.S. Foreign Policy.* The authors argue that U.S foreign policy is held hostage to narrowly defined Israeli interests, often represented by the American Israel Public Affairs Committee (AIPAC). As expected, the book received scathing criticism from pro-Israel groups in the American political process.

The ever-increasing pace of **globalization**■—the expansion of economic interactions between countries—has added a third concern. Foreign governments and firms might not stop at seeking to influence American political decisions; they might also seek to influence American economic decisions in ways that harm the United States. In 2005, it was announced that CNOOC Ltd., a Chinese government–controlled oil company, was attempting to buy Unocal Corporation, the third-largest U.S. oil company. When the news broke, many American lawmakers raised economic and security issues and threatened to block the takeover. In their view, China was a major competitor with the United States for global influence and power. Faced with this opposition, CNOOC withdrew its $18.4 billion offer—clearing the way for Chevron, the second-largest American oil company, to acquire Unocal, even though its offer was $700 million less.

In another example of the risks of globalization, a disastrous oil spill in the Gulf of Mexico in 2010 threw British Petroleum (BP), the foreign corporation responsible, under American public scrutiny and led to presidential and congressional criticism. Aside from questions about lack of adequate regulation in off-shore drilling, BP was targeted by politicians and the media for its poor risk-management and damage control strategies. This oil spill raised concerns that private foreign investment and investments by foreign countries in the U.S. economy undermine the sovereignty of the United States.

As countries like China, Russia, and Middle Eastern petro-states create their sovereign wealth funds—country-owned funds that invest globally—questions of sovereignty and influence come to the forefront. Policymakers are concerned about the increased leverage of foreign countries in our domestic political process, as these states ramp up their investments in our economy. At the same time, we need to appreciate that U.S. firms are also investing globally, and many originating U.S. firms are now owned by international bodies of shareholders. As the volume of international trade and investments increases with globalization, Americans need to assess the international and domestic gains and losses from such activities.

International and Domestic Gains and Losses

As we consider the costs and benefits from international trade and investments, we must realize that citizens and governments of other countries are also engaged in their own respective cost-benefit assessments. One of the major stumbling blocks to reaching a new international trade agreement today is the insistence of developing countries on an end to U.S. price support programs for agricultural products. But prospects for ending these subsidies—which today go mainly to agribusinesses and the wealthiest farmers—are very small because of the power of agricultural lobbies in the U.S. Congress. Talks sponsored by the World Trade Organization on trade liberalization have met with many obstacles due to the persistence of European Union and U.S. agricultural subsidies. Developing countries point to "hypocrisy" when the United States insists that they open their markets via deregulation, privatization, and trade liberalization.

Just as globalization of trade and investment has complex economic ramifications for Americans, foreign policy operations can also have economic spillover effects. The fact that we spend vast resources pursuing foreign policy objectives in Iraq and Afghanistan forces us to make sacrifices on the domestic front. As the cost of conducting an interventionist foreign policy increases, requiring that domestic programs be canceled, cut back, or delayed because of economic pressures, support for foreign policy decreases.[10]

The Democratic Party used to be the low-taxes party, going back to its days as an agrarian party based in the South and West. The GOP had always been more protectionist (meaning they believe in protecting domestic producers and workers from foreign competition) because protectionism appealed to manufacturers and (often) workers who feared "cheap foreign competition." Protectionism was widely—and rightly—blamed for intensifying

the Great Depression, however, so in the post–World War II world, U.S. foreign policy favored trade liberalization and the expansion of American exports. Today, the Democrats are becoming increasingly protectionist to appeal to workers threatened with job loss and to environmentalists worried about the environmental impact of industrializing the developing world. And the Republicans have become the party of free trade, because they represent the interests of export-oriented American businesses and emphasize the benefits of international trade to American consumers. Economic downturns heighten concerns about protecting American jobs across the political spectrum. Right-wing and left-wing populists rally against outsourcing and "unfair" foreign economic competition. President Obama has reiterated the need for improving our education and health care systems in order to create a competitive work force in an age of globalization.

Americans also weigh the cost of foreign policy by counting the number of battlefield deaths. This grim equation first contributed to the erosion of the American public's support of the Vietnam War—which ultimately cost the lives of more than 55,000 U.S. troops—in the late 1960s and early 1970s. The conventional wisdom is that the greater the number of American deaths in a foreign war, the less support Americans give to the president who is waging that war. To some extent, this happened to President George W. Bush. In 2006, as casualties mounted and Iraq showed little sign of ending its insurgency and establishing a viable government, Bush's standing in public opinion polls (overall job rating, handling of the war, and honesty) plummeted to record lows. A decline in presidential popularity does not appear to be automatic, however. Even as battlefield deaths mount, solidarity among political elites and a widely accepted military mission may keep a president's standing in the opinion polls high.[11] The U.S. experience in Vietnam, however, suggests that such public support cannot be maintained indefinitely in the absence of visible military success. While President Bush was able to win reelection in 2004, the increasing unpopularity of the Iraq War (coupled with other issues) is partly to blame for the Republican Party's loss of both houses of Congress in 2006 and the White House in 2008.

Public concerns about the benefits and costs of American foreign policy today run high in two areas: international trade policy and protection of civil liberties. In 2005, the Bush administration battled in the House of Representatives for passage of the Central American Free Trade Agreement (CAFTA), which passed by a vote of 217–215. Supporters argued that CAFTA was vital to the overall economic health of the U.S. economy in an era of globalization, because it fostered competition from abroad and provided consumers with more choices at competitive prices. They argued that CAFTA would also help long-impoverished countries develop and diversify their economies. Opponents cited the potential loss of American jobs as firms moved overseas to produce goods and then sell them in the American market. The U.S. sugar lobby also fought

CAFTA because it slightly increased the amount of sugar that Central American countries could export to the United States, cutting into the profits of wealthy American sugar producers.

The second area of public concern is how to safeguard civil liberties while fighting the war against terrorism. Particularly worrisome to some are provisions of the USA PATRIOT Act, which was passed after 9/11 and renewed in 2006. These provisions give law enforcement officials access to an individual's private information without his or her knowledge. New federal laws also curtail the rights of foreigners who are detained on suspicion of being or aiding terrorists. Suspects can be detained for indefinite periods without being charged with a crime or having access to legal representation. Revelations that the Bush administration, on its own authority, approved electronic eavesdropping inside the United States were equally controversial. In February 2010, President Obama signed a one-year extension of provisions of the Patriot Act that includes court-approved roving wiretaps.[12]

PATHWAYS of change from around the World

Can the efforts of young individuals impact a problem as complex and wide-ranging as global climate change? In Australia, one organization aimed at this global issue is built on the dedication and vision of young people. The Australian Youth Climate Coalition (AYCC) was founded in 2006 and is made up of about three dozen environmentally concerned organizations. At the initial meeting, the AYCC drafted the "Australian Youth Declaration on Climate," their manifesto for exploring the linkages between climate science and politics, along with a vision of how to work toward reversing the causes of climate change. They have been intent on creating a young person's social movement rather than simply organizing for traditional political engagement. To this end, they have consciously worked to strengthen the coalition by building connections across groups and by communicating with young people in Australia and around the world to make them aware of the issues and inspire them to participate in the movement.

The Canadian Youth Climate Coalition (CYCC) organized a phone rally in March 2010, where it asked young environmental activists to call on their leaders to provide adequate funding for communities most affected by the climate crisis. The group called attention to the fact that the wealthy countries owe the developing countries a climate debt because the rich are the worst polluters and the poor cannot afford the estimated $100 billion of climate adjustments costs that will be needed by 2020.

SOURCE: AYCC at http://youthclimatecoalition.org/about.php and CYCC at http://www.ourclimate.ca/wordpress/phone-mob-thursday-demand-adequateclimate-financing-on-march25th/

Foreign and Domestic Policy

15.2   **Establish three links between American foreign and domestic policy.**

PRACTICE QUIZ: UNDERSTAND AND APPLY

1. Which of the following is not a way that U.S. foreign and domestic policy is linked?
   a. American foreign policy is often based on ideas and values that guide domestic policy.
   b. U.S. foreign policy always benefits only the United States.
   c. U.S. political decision making is influenced by a number of international factors.
   d. U.S. foreign policy can affect the distribution of costs and benefits among different groups in the United States.

2. Foreign lobbying groups
   a. can influence U.S. foreign policy.
   b. cannot threaten U.S. national security interests.
   c. do not meddle in the domestic political process of the United States.
   d. are all operating illegally in the United States.

3. The BP oil spill raised concerns by some that private foreign investment in the U.S. economy undermines U.S. sovereignty.
   a. true   b. false

ANALYZE

1. To what extent does lobbying for foreign interests pose a threat to U.S. sovereignty? Should our lobbying rules be consistent regardless of which country is doing the lobbying?

2. In what ways do trade issues interact with security issues in crafting useful foreign policy?

IDENTIFY THE CONCEPT THAT DOESN'T BELONG

a. World Trade Organization   d. Agricultural subsidies
b. Trade liberalization   e. Deregulation
c. Privatization

15.2

Resource Center
• Glossary
• Vocabulary Example
• Connect the Link

CONNECT THE LINK
(Chapter 10, pages 314–317) Are the foreign policy options available to presidents limited by the American public's knowledge of international affairs?

The Domestic Context of American Foreign Policymaking

15.3 Assess pathways for citizen participation in foreign policymaking.

(pages 470–473)

Perhaps more than any other aspect of policy in the United States, the making and carrying out of foreign policy seems distant and remote to most Americans. It can be argued that Americans' reluctance to find pathways for expression of their views on American foreign policy, whether supportive or critical, is a major weakness. After all, successful foreign policy must combine a well-crafted response to international challenges and opportunities with public support. Others argue that the public should leave foreign policy to the experts. The question then becomes, who are the experts? The president and his advisers? Professional military and diplomatic officials? Congress? The seemingly knowledgeable journalists and academics who voice their support for or criticism of American foreign policy?

To answer these questions, we will examine public opinion, elections, interest group activity, and political protest in search of pathways for citizen participation in the making of American foreign policy. We will then turn to the national-level political institutions that deal with foreign policy.[13]

Keep in mind that some individuals are better positioned than others to influence public policy. They come from varied backgrounds, but what sets them apart is the knowledge they possess and, even more important, the access they have to policymakers. Some are former government officials now at a think tank or university. Others are major contributors to a political party or leaders in organizations on whose support political parties depend to win elections. Still others are opinion leaders who provide commentaries in the news.

Public Opinion

Public opinion provides a first pathway for most citizens to express their views about American foreign policy. Although they may claim not to be influenced by opinion polls in their decision making, every president since Richard Nixon has employed pollsters to find out what the public thinks (see Chapter 10, pp. 314–317).

The influence of public opinion on American foreign policy can be seen in two ways. First, public opinion can serve as a source of public policy innovation, as when it pressured the Bush administration to create the Department of Homeland Security and the position of director of national intelligence

after the 9/11 terrorist attacks. Alternatively, public opinion can restrain innovation or serve as a policymaking resource to preserve the status quo.

One of the major obstacles President Franklin D. Roosevelt faced in the 1930s, despite being well aware of the growing danger of Nazi Germany, was the American public's strongly isolationist mood. In fact, FDR's efforts to aid Great Britain and the Soviet Union in their resistance to German aggression in the years leading up to World War II were severely constrained by domestic isolationism; only the attack on Pearl Harbor removed this obstacle. American policymakers in the 1970s and 1980s worried about the so-called **Vietnam syndrome**■, the belief that the public was no longer willing to support a prolonged military presence abroad that caused appreciable losses of American soldier's lives if it looked like it might become an unwinnable "quagmire." Concern about the Vietnam syndrome compelled President Reagan to withdraw American forces from Lebanon in 1983 and President Clinton to beat a hasty retreat from Somalia 10 years later—in both cases, these actions were taken after it became apparent that American military casualties were rising.

Policymakers tend to regard public opinion as a resource to be mobilized in international conflicts. They want to show foreign leaders that the American public is united behind the president. This happens almost reflexively when crises erupt that are perceived as threatening American security or when American troops are sent into combat. This **"rally 'round the flag" effect** was very noticeable at the start of the Iraq War. President George W. Bush's rating in the polls jumped 13 points the moment the war began. He had experienced an even bigger leap—39 percentage points—right after the 9/11 attacks.

What conditions are necessary for policymakers to hear the public's voice? Research seems to confirm that at least 50 percent of the American public must be in agreement on a foreign policy issue before their opinion has any influence.[14] Public opinion is likely to be heard most clearly in the agenda-building and ratification stages of foreign policy decision making. Between those two stages, the institutional forces in the executive branch and Congress are the focus of attention.

Elections

The winning candidate in modern presidential elections claims that the results provide a mandate for that candidate's program, and foreign policy is no exception. Do elections really serve as a pathway for influencing foreign policy decisions? The evidence is mixed at best. Both major-party candidates tend to be on the same side of the issue. In 1980, both incumbent President Jimmy Carter and challenger Ronald Reagan favored increasing U.S. military capabilities. In 2008, both presidential contenders Barack Obama and John McCain stood firm in their commitments to defeat terrorism, but they diverged when

■ **Vietnam Syndrome:** The belief, attributed to the American experience in Vietnam, that the public will not support the use of military force if it results in significant American casualties.

SIGNIFICANCE: *While the comparatively lower casualty rate for the Afghan war has made direct comparisons with the Vietnam War difficult, public support for the mission in Afghanistan remains lukewarm as U.S. involvement there drags on amidst concerns of Afghan state failure, widespread corruption, and the rising influence of the Taliban.*

it came to the U.S. presence in Iraq. Obama committed to withdrawing from Iraq within a defined timeline, while McCain promised to remain in Iraq until the mission was completed. Often, presidential elections turn out to be less a debate over foreign policy and more a contest about whom the public trusts to achieve those goals.

Part of the problem is that the American public tends not to be well informed about foreign policy issues. In 1964, at the height of the Cold War, only 38 percent of Americans knew that the Soviet Union was not a member of NATO. In 1979, only 23 percent knew which two countries were participating in the **Strategic Arms Limitation Talks (SALT)** (it was the United States and the Soviet Union, who were negotiating limits on the size of their respective nuclear forces). In 1993, fully 43 percent of Americans could not identify the continent on which Somalia was located, where American peacekeeping forces were facing significant local opposition. And in 2003, an amazing 68 percent of Americans believed—incorrectly—that Iraq had played a major role in the 9/11 terrorist attacks. Some members of Congress believe that the low level of their constituents' information makes incumbents dangerously vulnerable. Challengers can win—and have won—elections by taking foreign policy and

national defense votes out of context and misrepresenting them in a negative light.

There is one way in which presidential elections clearly have influenced American foreign policy. Foreign governments rarely try to do serious business with the United States during presidential elections. Foreign policy measures initiated at that time have always run the risk of failure. During the Cold War, every political candidate dreaded being attacked as "soft on communism"; fear of that accusation was one factor that pulled Lyndon Johnson into the Vietnam War and kept him from cutting his losses. In anticipation of an upcoming election, a president often tries to tie up the loose ends of major foreign policy initiatives—such as trade agreements, treaties, and military activity—in order to keep them from becoming electoral issues.[15]

Similarly, in a post–9/11 era American presidents and their challengers in elections have had to demonstrate that they will be vigilant in protecting the nation from terrorist threats. This is particularly true for Democrats like John Kerry and Barack Obama who were targeted in their campaigns for being too concerned about the legal rights of those accused of terrorist acts and therefore not as steadfast as they should be in protecting the safety of American citizens.

Interest Groups

The third avenue down which the public can travel to express its outlook on foreign policy issues is interest group activity. A wide variety of groups use this pathway to influence American foreign policy. A representative list of interest groups active in trying to influence U.S. policy toward China, for example, would include the AFL-CIO, Amnesty International, the Christian Coalition, the Committee of 100 for Tibet, the Emergency Committee for American Trade, the Family Research Council, and the National Endowment for Democracy.

Among the most influential interest groups are ethnic-identity groups. Most observers view the American–Israeli Public Affairs Committee (AIPAC) and the Cuban–American National Foundation (CANF) as the two most successful such groups, as evidenced by America's pro-Israel and anti-Castro foreign policies, regardless of who is in power. African-American groups have had a mixed record. They were active in opposing **apartheid** (legal segregation) in South Africa and in pressing for humanitarian intervention in Haiti, but they were slow to speak out against the genocide in Rwanda. Hispanic Americans have also been slow to find their foreign policy voice. Although most Latinos take a deep interest in immigration issues, they are more likely to focus on issues related to their countries of origin. When it comes to American foreign policy, Mexican Americans, Cuban Americans, and people from the various countries in Central America and the Caribbean all

During the 2008 presidential campaign, Senators John McCain and Barack Obama disagreed on setting a timetable for the removal of U.S. troops from Iraq, with Obama preferring the establishment of a deadline for the troops to be withdrawn and McCain holding the position that such a deadline damages the chances of success in leaving Iraq in a stable condition. *—What role do presidential elections play in determining the foreign policies of the U.S. government?*

have their own country-specific priorities and interests, and sometimes, these lead to antagonisms among them.

Today, religion-based interest groups are becoming increasingly active on foreign policy issues. Among the most prominent are those on the "religious right." Primarily identified as supporting the Republican Party, these groups were firm opponents of communism during the later part of the Cold War. Today, they actively lobby on family planning and population control policies and in support of Christians persecuted abroad, particularly in China, Russia, and Sudan. By no means, however, does the religious right have a monopoly on religiously motivated interest group activity. During the period leading up to the Iraq War, religious groups were active both for and against. Evangelicals tended to support the war, while the Catholic Church, the Religious Society of Friends (Quakers), the World Council of Churches, and the Muslim Peace Fellowship all spoke out against it.

PATHWAYS of action

Bono and ONE

In the post–9/11 age, national security concerns have been more intricately linked with questions of global poverty and inequity. Increased attention is being paid to the gulf between the "haves" and "have-nots" both within and across countries. Economic stagnation, conflict, extreme poverty, high debt burden and corruption are all inter-related phenomena, and can pose national and international security threats. Nowhere are these problems more obvious than in sub-Saharan Africa. As the world's richest states contemplate ways of aiding Africa, nongovernmental initiatives have mobilized grass-root organizations and activists in an effort to help stabilize the continent.

One such organization is exemplified by "ONE," co-founded by rock icon Bono, lead singer of the Irish rock band U2. ONE's origins date back to 2002, when Bono, along with fellow musician Bob Geldof (of Live Aid fame), Bobby Shriver, and Jamie Drummond joined forces with Bill and Melinda Gates to form DATA (debt, AIDS, trade, Africa), which attempted to induce African states into promoting democracy, accountability, and transparency in return for debt forgiveness, Western help in the fight against AIDS, and the promise of more open and "fair" Western economies as export markets.[*] In 2004, DATA, along with ten other leading antipoverty organizations joined forces to create ONE—a nonpartisan campaign aimed at mobilizing Americans in the fight against extreme poverty and preventable global disease. It is no surprise that a lot of the organization's activity is focused on Africa.

The organization's campaign to raise awareness and funds, and to bring policy shifts was matched by its drive to secure membership. Within a year of its formation, over 2 million grassroots activists joined its ranks. These activists contact members of Congress about pressing global development needs and mobilize new and old constituencies across communities and campuses in the United States.

ONE's activities against poverty and human misery are directly linked to security issues. As the organization points out in its Web page, there are 50 percent more infant deaths in sub-Saharan African countries that are embroiled in conflict, in comparison to those that are not. The conflict ridden countries account for 15 percent more undernourished people, and 20 percent more adult illiteracy than countries at peace. The same source cites that sub-Saharan Africa loses about $148 billion a year to corruption. This amounts to about a quarter of the region's GDP. The average cost of armed conflict in 23 sub-Saharan countries between 1990 and 2005 was about $18 billion a year or 15 percent of these states' GDP. These lost funds and resources not only impoverish the people, but also sustain these conflicts and push the states toward failure. This threatens not only national and regional stability, but also global stability. ONE activists are engaged in work that links humanitarian, development, sustainability, and security issues related to our existence. To find out more about ONE, visit: http://www.one.org/us/

U2's lead singer Bono has been a major force in the formation of ONE, an organization that has worked to have the debt of developing nations either reduced or forgiven as a means of helping nations to grow out of poverty. —*Why would the presence of a celebrity increase the likelihood that a government would pay attention to the requests of an organization?*

---

[*]"Bono, Gates unveil "DATA" agenda for Africa." Accessed at http://archives.cnn.com/2002/TECH/industry/02/02/gates.bono.africa/

Political Protest

Globalization has aroused much debate among Americans, particularly on college campuses. Images in the media of protesters clashing with police in Seattle in December 1999 at a meeting of the World Trade Organization (WTO) brought back for many vivid memories of political protests against the war in Vietnam—a prominent feature on the American political landscape in the late 1960s and early 1970s. Globalization as a political issue has succeeded in mobilizing protesters largely because it taps into two important contemporary issues: quality of life as well as civil rights and liberties.

Images of demonstrators in the streets are an important reminder that the public voice is expressed through both officially sanctioned and unofficial pathways. Not unexpectedly, administrations tend to dismiss protest activity as unimportant, but political protests on the scale of the peace movement and the antiglobalization movement can alter the political agenda, forcing policymakers to confront issues they otherwise would ignore. Protests can also bring new voices into the political process and reenergize long-established political forces, such as labor unions.

The Domestic Context of American Foreign Policymaking

15.3 Assess pathways for citizens participation in foreign policymaking.

PRACTICE QUIZ: UNDERSTAND AND APPLY

1. The American–Israeli Public Affairs Committee (AIPAC) and the Cuban–American National Foundation (CANF) are examples of
   a. interest groups that include American citizens that are focused on influencing U.S. foreign policy.
   b. interest groups that are banned from contributing finances to candidates for public office.
   c. interest groups that have failed to have an impact on U.S. foreign policies.
   d. groups that have been ruled illegal by the U.S. Supreme Court.

2. How effective are elections as a pathway for public input about foreign policy?
   a. Extremely effective: Presidents often claim foreign policy mandates after they win elections.
   b. Effective: Presidential candidates can count on voters to be well informed about foreign affairs and so respect the foreign policy implications of their voting.
   c. Not very effective: Often, the candidates' positions on most foreign policy issues are the same.
   d. Completely ineffective: Foreign policy is the domain of well-qualified elites, and the popularity of their decisions with voters is politically irrelevant.

3. Research seems to confirm that at least 50 percent of the American public must be in agreement on a foreign policy issue before their opinion has any influence.
   a. true
   b. false

ANALYZE

1. Think about major U.S. foreign policy events over the last few years. To what extent do the two major political parties differ on foreign policy? To what extent are they similar?

2. How does the "Vietnam syndrome" still influence foreign policy decision making?

IDENTIFY THE CONCEPT THAT DOESN'T BELONG

a. Vietnam War
b. 9/11 terrorist attacks
c. WTO protests in Seattle
d. Creation of the Department of Homeland Security
e. The American–Israeli Public Affairs Committee (AIPAC)

Resource Center
- Glossary
- Vocabulary Example
- Connect the Link

CONNECT THE LINK
(Chapter 7, pages 211–212) How does the lack of specificity in the Constitution lead to conflicts Congress and the president in terms of the use of the nation's armed forces.

Political Institutions and Foreign Policymaking

15.4 Analyze how political institutions compete for influence in making foreign policy.

(pages 474–481)

As in other policy areas, the Constitution allocates political power among the president, Congress, and the courts in the formation of foreign policy. Three constitutionally defined powers are controversial. The first is treaty-making power. The Constitution states that the president, by and with the consent of the Senate, has the power to make treaties. Confirmation by two-thirds of the Senate is required for ratification of a treaty. Presidents can get around this requirement by signing an executive agreement with another country, which does not require any congressional action.

The second constitutionally defined power is appointment. Presidents nominate ambassadors and other key foreign policy officials to their posts, who must then be confirmed by the Senate. Once again, a president may get around Congress by using personal representatives to conduct negotiations or by making recess appointments—nominations that are automatically approved because Congress is not in session. (Recess appointees do not hold office with the same permanent tenure as confirmed appointees, however, so this is used as a stopgap measure.)

Finally, there are the war powers. The Constitution gives to Congress the power to declare war and the power to raise and maintain military forces. The president is constitutionally designated as commander in chief. A major issue here is that since World War II, no American war has been formally declared by Congress. (For more discussion of this thorny issue, see Chapter 7, pages 211–212.)

The Executive Branch

In today's public eye, the president makes American foreign policy. It is the president who announces decisions on war and peace; meets foreign leaders at the White House, at international summit conferences, or in foreign capitals; and signs treaties and international agreements. Presidents do not make foreign policy decisions in isolation, however. We have already noted that through public opinion polling, they are kept well aware of the domestic political consequences of their foreign policy decisions.

CHIEF OF STAFF The White House Chief of Staff plays an increasing role in foreign policy matters.[16] Rahm Emmanuel,

Barack Obama's former chief of staff, was a key player on foreign policy issues during the first years of the Obama administration, which included a strong role in shaping the White House's opposition to Israeli settlement expansion. Howard Baker Jr., formerly an influential Republican senator, served as chief of staff in the last years of President Ronald Reagan's administration. During that time, he played an important part in controlling the backlash from Reagan's possible involvement in the Iran-Contra scandal, and influenced Reagan to hold frequent summit conferences with Soviet leader Mikhail Gorbachev with the goal of ending the Cold War.

THE VICE PRESIDENCY A relatively new foreign policy voice from within the White House comes from the vice president.[17] Dick Cheney, George W. Bush's vice president, once served as chief of staff to President Gerald Ford and as secretary of defense to President George H. W. Bush. Within George W. Bush's administration, Cheney was a powerful advocate of the Iraq War, and some observers considered him the architect of the president's foreign policy, at least during Bush's first term. Although Cheney's role in foreign policy far exceeded that of many vice presidents, Dan Quayle, the vice president under George H. W. Bush, had been active in designing Latin American policy, and Al Gore, Bill Clinton's vice president, established himself as an expert on Russia.

When Joe Biden joined Barack Obama's presidential campaign, he immediately added foreign policy expertise. Biden, the former chair of the Senate Foreign Relations Committee, was known and respected around the world. Once in office, Biden quickly distinguished himself as influential in articulating and shaping the administration's foreign policy (especially in Afghanistan). Despite their recent prominence in foreign policy matters, vice presidents have only as much influence and authority as presidents accord them.

NATIONAL SECURITY COUNCIL A modern president's most important source of advice about foreign policy problems inside the White House is the National Security Council (NSC).[18] The NSC was created in 1947, at the beginning of the Cold War. At the same time, the Central Intelligence Agency (CIA) was established, and the old War and Navy Departments were consolidated to form the Department of Defense. These changes represented a wide-ranging reorganization of the foreign affairs bureaucracy under the 1947 National Security Act. The term *foreign affairs bureaucracy* is used to describe those bureaucratic units most deeply involved in shaping foreign policy, which commonly include the State Department, the Defense Department, and the CIA. One of the major lessons learned from the attack on Pearl Harbor and World War II was that to protect the United States, much greater coordination and communication were needed among the foreign affairs and domestic bureaucracies.

At a meeting discussing the situation in Pakistan, President Barack Obama listens to his foreign policy advisors. Pictured (from left to right) is Admiral Michael Mullen (chairman of the Joint Chiefs of Staff), Defense Secretary Robert Gates, Vice President Joe Biden, the President, National Security Advisor General James Jones, Secretary of State Hillary Clinton, Director of National Intelligence Admiral Dennis Blair, and CIA Director Leon Panetta. —*Because presidents select advisors who serve at the president's discretion, what are the risks that advisors will simply tell the president what he wants to hear?*

The NSC has evolved over time. Since its inception, the NSC has grown from a small presidential staff of 10 people to a bureaucratic body that at times has employed more than 200, including 100 professional national security analysts. Finding the NSC too large and unmanageable in times of crisis, presidents have routinely relied for advice on smaller groups, such as Lyndon Johnson's "Tuesday Lunch Group" during the Vietnam War and Jimmy Carter's "Friday Breakfast Group" during the Soviet Union's 1979 invasion of Afghanistan and the Iranian hostage crisis. Similarly, George W. Bush established the "War Cabinet" to help with the planning and conduct of the Afghanistan and Iraq wars.

The NSC staff is charged with making policy recommendations and overseeing the implementation of foreign policy decisions. The president sets up the organizational structure for the NSC. Barack Obama significantly expanded the NSC structure to add the attorney general, the secretaries of the treasury and of homeland security, the U.S. ambassador to the United Nations, and the chief of staff to the council. President Obama also sought to increase coordination between national security agencies through the creation of Interagency Policy Committees (IPCs). These committees are tasked with managing development and implementation of national security policies when multiple agencies (such as the CIA and Homeland Security) are involved.

Presidents have turned to the NSC staff for advice out of frustration with the advice they have received from the State Department, the Defense Department, and the CIA. Too often, presidents have felt that these foreign policy bureaucracies have not been sensitive enough to presidential perspectives in making foreign policy. The big issue is time frame. Foreign policy professionals are sensitive to how foreign governments will respond over the long term. Presidents, on the other hand, think in terms of four-year electoral cycles and are of course vitally concerned with how the American public will judge their immediate response to events.

NATIONAL SECURITY ADVISER   The national security adviser was initially intended to be a kind of neutral referee, managing the NSC and reporting to the president. This changed during the Kennedy and Johnson administrations, when national security advisers began openly to advocate policy solutions and paid less attention to their managerial role. Henry Kissinger (under Nixon), Zbigniew Brzezinski (under Carter), Colin Powell (under Reagan), and Condoleezza Rice (under George W. Bush) are among the most visible and most powerful recent national security advisers. President Obama's national security adviser, retired Marine Corps General James L. Jones, plays a central role in formulating American foreign policy, but that role is frequently challenged by other high officials, most notably the secretary of state and the secretary of defense.

STATE DEPARTMENT   According to historical tradition, the president looks first to the State Department in making foreign policy. The State Department is the formal channel of information between the United States and foreign governments and serves as a resource for senior policymakers. Each year, the State Department represents the United States at meetings of more than 50 major international organizations and at more than 800 international conferences. From day to day, the State Department also plays a central role in managing American foreign policy through U.S. embassies abroad, where the ambassador serves as chief of mission and heads the "country team," which is made up of all U.S. personnel assigned to an embassy. CIA officials (who often operate covertly) are left out of the official accounting. Complicating the difficulty of asserting control over such a diverse set of government agencies is the fact that ambassadors frequently are not career foreign service officers. Many—especially in glamorous European capital cities—are political appointees who were made ambassadors as a reward for campaign contributions or as consolation after an election loss or retirement. For example the highly prestigious post of

■ **Powell Doctrine:** A view that cautions against the use of military force, especially where public support is limited, but states that once the decision to use force has been made, military power should be applied quickly and decisively.

EXAMPLE: *Critics of the Iraq War contend that this doctrine was violated by the Bush administration, because they had only limited support for the war, did not bring sufficient force into play to maintain gains on the battlefield, and lacked a reasonable exit strategy.*

On January 21, 2009, Hillary Clinton became the third woman to serve as Secretary of State (Madeleine Albright served from January 23, 1997 until January 20, 2001 and Condoleezza Rice served from January 26, 2005 until January 20, 2009). Clinton is internationally recognized and has already made her presence in this office known across the globe. Many find her straightforward approach to diplomacy refreshing, while others are confounded by her bold moves. *—Do you believe that Clinton's elected experience as a senator from New York and as a former first lady has helped or hindered her success in negotiating with foreign powers?*

Ambassador to the United Kingdom was given to Louis Sussman, a lawyer and banker who raised over $200,000 for the Obama campaign in 2008. He replaced Robert Tuttle, a car dealer and art collector who made large contributions to the campaigns of George W. Bush. The examples of Sussman and Tuttle demonstrate that expertise in foreign relations is by no means a requirement to serve in high ranking positions in the diplomatic core.

DEPARTMENT OF DEFENSE For most of its history, the military security of the United States was provided by forces under the direction of the War Department and the Department of the Navy. These two departments coordinated the activity of the armed forces under the sole direction of the president. This changed dramatically with the passage of the National Security Act in 1947, which established the offices of the secretary of defense and chairman of the Joint Chiefs of Staff and created the National Military Establishment. In 1949, the National Military Establishment was renamed the Department of Defense.

Secretaries of defense have generally adopted one of two approaches. Generalists will defer to military know-how and see themselves as the military's representatives in policy deliberations with the president and other foreign affairs bureaucracies. Secretaries who see themselves as experts in defense matters seek to shape and control the Defense Department in accordance with their views. Donald Rumsfeld, George W. Bush's former secretary of defense, quickly established himself as a controversial military authority whose ideas about how to fight the war on terror, drive Saddam Hussein from power, and occupy Iraq after the war often clashed with those of the professional military officers. These disagreements became public in 2006, when six retired generals, some with combat

commands in Iraq, voiced their opposition to Rumsfeld and called for his resignation. He stepped down in December of that year. Robert M. Gates, director of the CIA in the administration of George H. W. Bush from 1991 until the start of 1993, was President George W. Bush's choice to succeed Rumsfeld in 2006. As a past head of the Central Intelligence Agency, Gates brought a unique background to the job—one that was hailed by some observers and objected to by others. Despite some criticisms at his appointment, Gates was kept on as Secretary of Defense under President Obama, indicating that his more consensual and less controversial approach to managing the Department of Defense had won him bipartisan support.

A major point of debate among civilian and military officials in the Pentagon is the future size and shape of the military. How much emphasis should be given to information technologies in planning for and fighting future wars? For what type of conflicts should the military be trained? The type of military operation that defeated the Iraqi army in 2003 is very different from counterinsurgency operations against terrorists or humanitarian interventions to halt genocide. One consequence of an increased emphasis on technology is a reduction in the size of the military, both at home and abroad. This means reliance on National Guard units for combat missions and the closure of many military bases—both of which can be very disruptive to and unpopular with local communities in the United States.

Another longstanding issue involves the conditions under which American military forces should be sent into combat. There are two poles in this debate: the Powell Doctrine and the McNamara Doctrine. The **Powell Doctrine**■, named for Colin Powell, calls for the decisive use of American military only when there is clear public support for the use of force and an exit strategy is in place. According to the **McNamara Doctrine,** named for Robert McNamara, the secretary of defense during much of the Vietnam War, limited and graduated use of military

This photograph of Army Specialist Zachary Boyd, 19, of Fort Worth, Texas, was seen throughout the world prompting Defense Secretary Robert Gates to state, "Any soldier who goes into battle against the Taliban in pink boxers and flip-flops has a special kind of courage." —*Why do you think the picture was so popular? How important do you think it is for the American public to be reminded of the individual costs of war?*

force is permissible when there is a recognized problem demanding a military response, with or without public support. The professional military tends to favor the Powell Doctrine, and Defense Department civilians are more likely to advocate a position in line with the McNamara Doctrine.

Regardless of the prevailing view concerning the use of military force, the military does not have the final say. Under the Constitution, the president is commander in chief, and in the United States, the military has traditionally deferred to civilian authority.

CENTRAL INTELLIGENCE AGENCY   We often associate the Central Intelligence Agency with **covert action,** but one of the agency's primary functions is the gathering of **intelligence**—information that has been *evaluated* and is not simply news snippets or rumors. Ideally, intelligence should provide policymakers with enough warning and insight to allow them to act in the face of a challenge to American security interests. This is not easy, because surprise is a constant element of global politics.[19]

The CIA's ability to undermine surprise, or at least reduce its negative consequences, is determined largely by two factors. The first is the relationship between the CIA and the president. The second is the relationship between the CIA and the other intelligence agencies.

There are several points of friction in the relationship between the CIA and the president. First, the logic of intelligence clashes with the logic of policymaking. Good intelligence limits policy options by clarifying the assumptions behind and consequences of various policy options, but good policymaking often requires keeping as many options open for as long as possible.

Second, how close should intelligence be to policy? The traditional answer is that intelligence and policy must be kept separate so that the intelligence is not infected by policy considerations and can provide neutral information. Intelligence that is kept separate from policy is likely to be useless, however, because intelligence cannot inform policymaking if it is not aware of policy. Third, there is often a difference between the type of information the president wants to receive and the type of information the CIA is inclined to collect. Policymakers are most eager to obtain information that will help them convince Congress and the American public about the merits of their favored policy. They are frustrated by intelligence that is impossible to use because it is tentative, secretive, or not easily understood. Finally, the CIA is not the president's only source of intelligence. It is in competition for the president's attention with interest groups, lobbyists, the media, and well-placed individuals.

The CIA has a unique relationship with other members of what is known as the "intelligence community." Besides the CIA, the most prominent members of that community are the intelligence units of each branch of the military, the State Department, the Federal Bureau of Investigation (FBI), the National Security Agency (in charge of protecting America's secret communication codes as well as breaking the codes of others), the Defense Intelligence Agency (whose director is the primary adviser to the secretary of defense on military intelligence matters), and the National Reconnaissance Office (charged with developing American information-gathering technology).

Turf wars between these organizations are not uncommon as each seeks to protect its mission from being encroached on by others. Today, one of the most serious disputes is between the CIA, the State Department, and the Pentagon over covert (secret) action. Covert action has traditionally been carried out by the CIA. Since 9/11, however, the military has played an increasing role, and it does not need the approval of the ambassador to a country to carry out such operations.

The various members of the intelligence community often have different approaches to foreign policy problems. Consider the issue of spies. The FBI takes a law enforcement perspective, indicating that people suspected of engaging in espionage for foreign governments should be arrested and prosecuted for breaking the law. The CIA prefers to let spies continue to operate so that it can watch them, discover their contacts, and feed them misinformation. Nor does the CIA want its own operations revealed in a public trial.

Until 2006, when the position of director of national intelligence (DNI) was created, the head of the CIA and the head of the rest of the intelligence community were one and the same, an individual who held the title of director of central intelligence (DCI). Today, these positions are held by two different officials. During the time that the CIA and the intelligence community were both led by the DCI, the DCI had budget authority only over the CIA, so an estimated 80 to 90 percent of the intelligence community's budget was beyond the DCI's control, falling instead under the control of the Pentagon. In the federal government, budget control gives powerful bureaucratic leverage. One of the many unresolved problems facing the director of national intelligence today is that the position lacks effective budget control over all members of the intelligence community.

Concerns about the ability of the CIA to coordinate and share its intelligence information with other agencies continue years after the attacks of 9/11. In December 2009, an attempt to blow up a jet bound for Detroit, Michigan, demonstrated that CIA procedures had problems that had not been resolved through post 9/11 reforms. In particular, the agency had collected information about the attempted bomber, Umar Farouk Abdulmutallab, but had not shared it with the Transportation Safety Administration (TSA), which is responsible for maintaining the federal government's no-fly list. This incident prompted a change in CIA policies, which requires that the agency formally disseminate information on suspected extremists and terrorists within 48 hours and expand name traces on possible extremists and terrorists.[20]

DEPARTMENT OF HOMELAND SECURITY The Department of Homeland Security (DHS) is the newest part of the intelligence community. More than any other government unit, the DHS occupies a gray area between the domestic and foreign policy bureaucracies.[21] The DHS came into existence in November 2002 in response to the terrorist attacks of September 11, 2001. Its creation was the largest bureaucratic transformation in American history, affecting 170,000 employees and combining 22 different agencies from eight different departments. The DHS swallowed up the Federal Emergency Management Agency (FEMA), the Coast Guard, the Secret Service, the Customs

Service, the Immigration and Naturalization Service (INS), and the recently created Transportation Security Administration. Formation of the DHS did not affect the FBI and the CIA directly, but the new DHS does have an intelligence and threat analysis unit that makes it a challenger to these traditional intelligence-gathering agencies in the policymaking process.

The newness of the DHS makes it difficult to judge the role it will play in foreign policy decision making. Its first major venture into policymaking, devising a color-coded nationwide terrorist threat alert system, was not well received. Tom Ridge, its first secretary, left office amid criticism for failing to navigate the shoals of bureaucratic warfare. His successor, Michael Chertoff, quickly proposed a wide range of organizational reforms intended to improve the glaring inadequacies of its organizational performance, which became apparent in the government's response to Hurricane Katrina in September 2005. These proposed reforms include faster funding for first responders, tighter security in American ports, and improved cooperation with intelligence agencies.

Under the Obama administration, the DHS has taken a greater interest in the threats from "domestic terrorists." Domestic terrorists can come in the form of American-born individuals who go abroad to receive training on the use of terrorist techniques or in the form of Americans who plot and train for terrorist strikes within the borders of the nation. In April 2009, the DHS issued a report that warned of the rise of Christian militias, right-wing extremists, and domestic terrorists. These warnings proved to be well founded with the 2010 arrest of nine heavily armed Christian militia members that were plotting to kill law enforcement officers and then attack the funeral procession as part of their fight against the government.[22]

Congress

If you go by newspaper and television accounts, it would seem that the president and Congress are always in conflict over the conduct of American foreign policy. This is not the case. Viewed over time, presidential-congressional relations in foreign policy have alternated between long stretches of presidential dominance and moments when Congress emerged as an important force, fully capable of frustrating presidential initiatives. These swings depend on two factors: the level of congressional *activity* and the level of congressional *assertiveness*.[23] In turn, these two factors are influenced by many other considerations, including the party in control of the White House and of the Congress; the size of the majority one party has in the House, the Senate, or in both houses of Congress; the timing of presidential and congressional elections; the popularity of the president and the Congress with the American public; the impact of interest groups and movements on political actors; the goals and skills of the president and the leadership of the Congress; and a host of other political forces.

CONNECT THE LINK
(Chapter 7, page 211) Even with the passage of the War Powers Act is Congress at a disadvantage in terms of its relationship with the president on matters of military force?

■ **Containment:** A Cold War strategy that sought to control and encircle the Soviet Union rather than defeat it militarily.

EXAMPLE: *President Harry Truman's decision to provide military and economic aid to Turkey and Greece in the late 1940s was an effort to limit Soviet influence in the area.*

SUPPORTIVE CONGRESS A supportive Congress is actively engaged in foreign policy issues but does not try to assert control over them. From the onset of the Cold War around 1947 until the late 1950s, Congress was largely supportive. Relations between the president and Congress were positive. These were the years of "bipartisan" foreign policy, when "politics stopped at the water's edge," meaning that differences between Republicans and Democrats hardly surfaced in foreign policy decision making. A broad consensus existed that the Soviet Union and communism were the enemy and that **containment**—a Cold War strategy that sought to control and encircle the Soviet Union rather than defeat it militarily—was the proper strategy for meeting the threat. Congress saw its role as supporting the president and providing him with the means to carry out his foreign policy. Exceptions to this rule involved a good dose of domestic politics. One such case was the McCarthy hearings, primarily conducted by Republicans, into charges that communists had infiltrated the State Department (controlled by Democrats) and the Defense Department and were responsible for such key foreign policy setbacks as the triumph of communism in China, described at the time as the "loss of China."

STRATEGIC CONGRESS From roughly 1958 through 1968, a "strategic" Congress emerged, mostly encountering presidents from the same Democratic Party that also controlled Congress. This meant that Congress was not particularly active but was willing to be assertive on selected issues. Resolutions of support for presidential foreign policy initiatives were still the rule. Notable examples occurred in 1961, after the failed Bay of Pigs invasion of Cuba to remove Fidel Castro from power; during the 1962 Cuban Missile Crisis, when the world reached the brink of a Soviet–American nuclear confrontation; and in 1964, when Congress passed almost unanimously and with little debate the Gulf of Tonkin Resolution, which gave President Lyndon Johnson a virtual free hand to confront North Vietnam militarily. Key members of Congress, however, such as Senator J. William Fulbright, who chaired the Senate Foreign Relations Committee, clashed with President Johnson as the Vietnam War escalated with little evidence of success. The second issue on which Congress was active during this period was military strength. The biggest military issue of the time was the "missile gap"—the idea that the Soviet Union was ahead of the United States in missile production, and that the president had not done enough to protect American national security. In the 1960 presidential campaign, which pitted Democratic candidate John F. Kennedy against Republican Richard Nixon, the Democrats used the "missile gap" very effectively. Once in office, however, Kennedy discovered that no such gap existed.

COMPETITIVE CONGRESS From 1969 into the mid-1980s, a time that featured divided government and a Congress that was reacting to the excessive use of presidential power by Lyndon Johnson and Richard Nixon, Congress was *competitive*—both active and assertive. During that time, Congress challenged presidents on both the content and the conduct of American foreign policy. For example, in 1974, the Jackson–Vanik Amendment, which made improved economic relations with the Soviet Union contingent on allowing persecuted Jews to emigrate more freely, openly challenged President Richard Nixon's policies toward the Soviet Union. Since better economic relations were a key aspect of Nixon's foreign policy of **détente,** which was designed to improve relations with the Soviets and lessen international tensions, this amendment became a major problem in Nixon's negotiations with the Kremlin. At the end of the 1970s, President Jimmy Carter faced a congressional challenge over the Panama Canal Treaty, which restored the canal to Panamanian control, removing a key irritant from U.S.–Latin American relations. Carter managed to get the treaty approved by the Senate, but only after making concessions to senators who had raised strong objections. In the 1980s, congressional-presidential struggles focused largely on President Reagan's policy of staunch support for the Contra rebels in Nicaragua despite congressional prohibitions on funding rebel activity. A complex arms sales program to Iran was engineered behind the scenes to help accomplish the fall of the Sandinista government in Nicaragua as well as the release of Americans held captive in Lebanon; when revealed, it became known as the Iran-Contra scandal.

WAR POWERS RESOLUTION The most important challenge to the president's ability to conduct foreign policy has been the War Powers Resolution, which Congress passed over President Nixon's veto in 1973 (see Chapter 7, page 211). This law sought to limit the president's ability to use military force by requiring that Congress receive formal notification of troop deployment abroad into combat situations and issue its approval. If congressional approval is not granted, the forces must be withdrawn within 60 days. Although all presidents since 1973 have objected to this law on the grounds that it is unconstitutional, they have all observed it when committing American forces abroad. President George H. W. Bush was careful to obtain a supportive congressional vote before launching the Gulf War in 1991, and Bill Clinton did likewise before he committed American forces to the brief war that NATO waged against Serbia over Kosovo in 1999. So far, Congress has never exercised its power to withdraw military forces.

REEMERGENCE OF THE STRATEGIC CONGRESS A strategic Congress slowly began to reemerge in the mid-1980s, a pattern that was the norm until September 11, 2001. During this period, Congress pulled back from broad-based challenges to the president's conduct of foreign policy and concentrated on a smaller set of highly visible issues. Foremost among these was the annual vote granting China "most favored nation" status; the Comprehensive Nuclear Test Ban Treaty (rejected in 1999); and the North American Free Trade Agreement (passed in 1993).

DISENGAGED CONGRESS The 9/11 terrorist attacks brought back a disengaged Congress. In the immediate aftermath of 9/11, Congress ceded much of its authority and initiative in making crucial foreign policy decisions to the president, including mobilization of resources for the War on Terror. Public opinion poll numbers rose into the 90-percent range for the president, and Congress also benefited from renewed support from the public during this time of national crisis. With both houses of Congress in the hands of the Republican Party and the party's leader in the White House, there was little incentive for either the House or the Senate to challenge President Bush. However, after the 2006 elections returned the Democrats to power in the Congress, the president and his executive branch were treated to a strong dose of congressional oversight as committees reasserted their role of watchdog over the actions of the administration. Members of both parties voiced concern over the Bush administration's postwar policies in Iraq, the use of torture on suspected terrorists in American custody, and the claim of inherent presidential authority to order electronic wiretaps on Americans in order to prosecute the War on Terror. The centerpiece of President Bush's post–9/11 national security legislation, the USA PATRIOT Act, was renewed in 2006 after strongly debated changes were made, and then again in 2010 under the Obama administration.

When Barack Obama took office in 2009 with Democrats controlling both the Senate and House, it was reasonable to expect that his foreign policy initiatives would gain strong backing from Democratic members of Congress. But on the most significant foreign policy decision of Obama's first year in the White House, increasing troop levels by 30,000 in Afghanistan, the president received his greatest opposition from members of his own party and solid support from Republican lawmakers.

This situation demonstrates how members of Congress and presidents view foreign policy in strikingly different ways.

LEGISLATION, FUNDING, AND OVERSIGHT Congress most frequently uses three tools to influence foreign policy: legislation, funding, and oversight. Congress often seeks to assert its influence by attaching amendments to foreign policy legislation that place conditions on the president's actions. It may also target foreign aid and military assistance money for certain countries, as it has done repeatedly for Israel and Egypt. It may make foreign aid conditional on annual reports that give passing grades on such matters as human rights, antidrug and antiterrorism efforts, and nuclear weapons control. Presidents can ignore these limitations, however, by certifying that assistance is in the "national interests" of the United States. Presidents have used this power to continue foreign aid to Mexico and Panama despite those countries' poor records in the War on Drugs and to Pakistan after 9/11 in spite of its questionable record in opposing terrorism and enforcing nuclear nonproliferation.

Congressional budgetary powers are equally blunt and hard to use with finesse, in part because of the committee structure within Congress. In 2003, the Bush administration asked Congress for funds to help rebuild Iraq, yet delays resulting from the insurgency and bureaucratic battles prevented much of this money from being spent. Perhaps the biggest obstacle to using its budgetary powers to control American foreign policy is that whereas programs require funding, presidential policy announcements do not. Congress often finds itself reluctant to undercut a president once the White House has publicly committed the United States to a course of action with important international implications. In the case of Iraq, the notion of simply defunding the ongoing troop deployment

General Stanley A. McChrystal, shown aboard a C-130 aircraft over Afghanistan in 2010, was removed from his post as commander of U.S. operations in Afghanistan by President Obama after his complaints about the president and his staff were published in *Rolling Stone* magazine. —*Why is civilian control of military personnel such an important role in the area of U.S. foreign policy? Is it right for the president to have the final say on military matters if the president and military leaders disagree?*

in Iraq was derided by Republican opponents as "selling out the troops"—something the Democratic leaders in Congress could hardly see as an appealing perception about their party.

Several factors limit the impact of congressional oversight. One is the small political payoff for a great investment of time. Constituent work and shaping of domestic legislation are much more valuable for reelection purposes. A second limiting factor is organization: More than 80 committees have some kind of jurisdiction over the sprawling Department of Homeland Security. Third, most congressional oversight of foreign policy tends to be after the fact. For example, the 9/11 hearings were highly visible undertakings, fraught with emotion and geared toward establishing blame. Routine oversight of foreign policy programs involves far less effort and minimal media attention.

Presidents and critics of Congress tend to see the legislature as an obstacle course that must be run in order to formulate and carry out a coherent foreign policy. Defenders see congressional input as vital to keeping the government in touch with the national mood and ensuring long-term public support for American foreign policy.

The Supreme Court

The Supreme Court seldom voices an opinion regarding American foreign policy. Over the course of its history, however, the Court has produced three types of rulings dealing with foreign policy. First, when there is a conflict between state laws and treaties on a subject involving American foreign policy, the Court has ruled consistently that treaties take precedence over state laws. Second, the Court has consistently supported the president in conflicts with Congress. For example, it has ruled that executive agreements, which do not require congressional approval, have the same validity as treaties, which do require such approval. Finally, the Supreme Court has been reluctant to grant the government broad powers that may restrict American civil liberties and constitutionally guaranteed freedoms. With its more recent decisions in cases dealing with the treatment of accused terrorists and surveillance conducted without the use of a warrant in the United States, the Court has shown a willingness to moderately curtail the powers of the executive branch.

Political Institutions and Foreign Policymaking

15.4 Analyze how political institutions compete for influence in making foreign policy.

PRACTICE QUIZ: UNDERSTAND AND APPLY

1. One significant reason that presidents have turned to the National Security Council for advice on foreign policy is
   a. the quality of their personnel in comparison to other federal agencies.
   b. out of frustration with the advice they have received from the State Department, the Defense Department, and the Central Intelligence Agency.
   c. it has a much larger budget—and therefore more resources.
   d. it relies on universities and think tanks for information instead of on less reliable organizations.

2. The Supreme Court has been very aggressive in limiting the powers of the president in foreign affairs.
   a. true   b. false

3. The decline of the State Department's influence is most obvious in the realm of
   a. military strategy.
   b. diplomatic relations with NATO countries.
   c. economic policy.
   d. relationships with the developing world.

ANALYZE

1. Identify the roles that various intelligence agencies, including the CIA, play in the making of foreign policy? What problems can arise from their input?

2. In what ways has the Department of State's role in foreign policy been affected by political considerations?

IDENTIFY THE CONCEPT THAT DOESN'T BELONG

a. Secretary of State
b. Director of Central Intelligence
c. Chief Justice of the Supreme Court
d. Secretary of Homeland Security
e. National Security Advisor

Resource Center
• Glossary
• Vocabulary Example
• Connect the Link

Foreign Policy and National Security Issues

15.5 Outline the major foreign policy issues confronting the United States today.

(pages 482–487)

The United States faces many current foreign policy problems and challenges. We will examine three categories of foreign policy problems: military security, economic, and human welfare. Although we will discuss them separately, in many cases these problems are intimately connected.

For instance, because there is no cure, it is tempting to treat acquired immunodeficiency syndrome (AIDS) as a health problem, which would put it in the human welfare category. Consider, however, that according to the World Bank, the spread of the human immunodeficiency virus (HIV) and AIDS is in part responsible for the decreased economic growth rate in sub-Saharan African countries. In Africa, the HIV/AIDS pandemic also raises complex military security issues: The presence of large numbers of infected people can be seen as a threat that needs to be contained by neighboring countries, and the presence of a large number of infected individuals within a country's armed forces can drastically reduce its ability to carry out military missions or defend itself from foreign invasion. Furthermore, the lack of ability to resolve this public health issue, along with a myriad of economic and social crises, can push a sub-Saharan state to the brink of failure. Failed states pose a threat to regional and global security.

Military Security Issues

Combating terrorism and stopping the proliferation of weapons of mass destruction (nuclear, chemical, and biological weapons, as well as ballistic missile delivery systems) top everyone's list of pressing military security issues. Responding to them is a challenge not only because of the elevated level of danger but also because the nature of the problem changes constantly.

TERRORISM In the early 1990s, the intelligence community's dominant view was that Middle Eastern terrorists were controlled, or at least heavily influenced, by hostile regional powers, such as Iran, Syria, and Libya. When President Clinton signed an executive order imposing sanctions on 12 Middle Eastern terrorist groups in 1995, al-Qaeda was not even on the list. The United States was aware of Osama bin Laden but regarded him as a financier of international terrorism, not as a terrorist himself. Our understanding of terrorism changed slowly during the 1990s, and portions of the intelligence community began to speak of a new breed of radical Islamic terrorism that operated independently of government control. Gradually, bin Laden's activities came under closer watch, and in 1996, the CIA Counterterrorist Center set up a special office to deal with him alone. Still, few experts in either the Clinton or the George W. Bush administrations placed this new terrorist threat above all others, despite strong evidence of al-Qaeda's complicity in the 1998 bombings of American embassies in Kenya and Tanzania and the attack on the *U.S.S. Cole* in Aden in 2000.

After 9/11, the United States moved quickly to destroy al-Qaeda's sanctuary in Afghanistan, and to a large extent, it succeeded. The March 2004 train bombing in Madrid and the July 2005 attacks on the London mass transit system, however,

It took time for the United States to recognize that Osama bin Laden and his associates posed a serious threat. Now it is well understood that independent terrorist groups around the world are capable of inflicting great harm if given the opportunity. However, it is difficult to identify and stop small cells of terrorists who operate independently. *—If the United States captures or kills bin Laden, will Americans be safer than they are now?*

■ **Preemption:** A military strategy based on striking first in self-defense.

EXAMPLE: *The U.S. invasion of Iraq was a preemptive military action. The Bush administration maintained that Iraq harbored weapons of mass destruction—falsely as it turned out—and that the United States needed to destroy them before they were used against us.*

made it painfully clear that terrorism on Western soil had not been brought to an end. Most experts now argue that we are seeing the emergence of yet another form of terrorism.[24] Instead of being highly centralized and directed by a single leader, such as bin Laden, or a single source, such as al-Qaeda, terrorist groups now operate as independent **jihadist** (Islamic holy war) agents, linked by an anti-Western ideology and the Internet. The number of jihadist-related Web sites has grown from dozens in 2001 to thousands today; these sites provide training information and even manuals on how to build and deploy biological and chemical weapons.

In December 2009, a Nigerian citizen managed to board a Northwest Airlines flight with high powered explosives in his underwear. In May 2010, a Pakistani-born naturalized U.S. citizen attempted to detonate a car bomb in Times Square in New York City. While these attempts failed, jihadists have been successful in killing many in Iraq and Afghanistan. It is clear that the terrorist threat from homegrown and foreign extremists remains a very serious concern.

WEAPONS OF MASS DESTRUCTION A fundamental reality of the nuclear age is that the knowledge needed to build nuclear, chemical, and biological weapons is readily available. Of even greater concern is that security at many facilities in the former Soviet Union where weapons of mass destruction were once built or stored still leaves much to be desired. Until recently, the U.S. position was that the spread of weapons of mass destruction needed to be stopped because they were dangerous weapons in their own right. The Bush administration's position was that it is not so much the proliferation of such weapons as the identity of the recipients. American policymakers therefore do not view Israeli or Indian nuclear weapons in the same light as Iranian and North Korean nuclear weapons projects. The ultimate nightmare scenario involves theft and use of one of these weapons of mass destruction by a terrorist group. President Obama has been more forceful on issues of nuclear proliferation. In his Nobel Peace prize acceptance speech, he spoke of the need for nuclear disarmament and the peaceful use of nuclear energy. In March 2010, he agreed to a nuclear arms reduction treaty with Russian president Dmitry Medvedev, limiting each side to 1,550 warheads. The treaty reduces the nuclear warhead limit by 30 percent.[25]

PREEMPTION AND DETERRENCE In its *2002 National Security Strategy for the United States,* the Bush administration advanced a new strategic doctrine of **preemption**■—a means of dealing with terrorism and the proliferation of weapons of mass destruction by striking first in self-defense. The Iraq War is an example of preemption in action. The Bush administration argued that preemption is necessary because the strategies that were used successfully during the Cold War, do not work against these shadowy and often stateless enemies. **Deterrence** threatens a state-based enemy with swift and overwhelming retaliation for actions such as nuclear attacks or acts of aggression.

Preemption is controversial for several reasons. First, containment and deterrence may be effective against some enemies. If this is true, then preemption might be a policy of last resort rather than the first choice. Second, preemption cannot be carried out very often. The human and economic costs of invading Iraq have shown that it would be difficult to respond effectively to threatening activity by North Korea or Iran. Also, if the United States justifies preemption, other countries might adopt the same policy. This would be especially troubling in the event of an escalation in the conflicts that now simmer between India and Pakistan, China and Taiwan, and Israel and its Arab neighbors. A third concern is morality. Going first in self-defense is an age-old principle of world politics, but the price for being wrong is also very high, including being seen as the aggressor and becoming the object of global condemnation and a potential target for retaliation.

Another element of the Bush administration's strategy for countering terrorist threats was to build a national ballistic missile defense system. It would function as a shield protecting the United States from weapons of mass destruction delivered by intercontinental ballistic missiles.[26] The idea for such a system, which goes back to the 1950s, was actively pursued in the 1980s by the Reagan administration. One of the major roadblocks, then as now, is the technological challenge of building and operating such a system. The system would have to work flawlessly the first time and every time—yet simulating all threat conditions would be almost impossible.

The expense of the system was also a concern because of the fact that terrorists could strike devastatingly at the United States without using ballistic missiles. Only against a "rogue state," such as Iran or North Korea—a potential threat that President Obama may face—might a missile shield offer any potential protection. Russia objected vehemently to the Bush administration's plan to install a tracking radar in Poland and 20 interceptors in the Czech Republic, primarily to ward off a possible Iranian threat, when Iran did not as yet possess medium range missiles. The Obama administration's decision to cancel the Bush plan was hailed by Russia. However, tensions rose again as the Obama administration, in 2010, announced plans to install medium rage interceptors in Romania. Russia felt that it would threaten their long-range nuclear missile force.[27] These interceptor missiles will be operational in 2015.

Economic and Foreign Trade Issues

The most fundamental economic issue in American foreign policy is how to respond to the growing pace of globalization. Goods, people, ideas, and money now move across national borders more frequently and with greater speed than ever before.

Consider that from about 1996 to 2004, Europeans invested more capital in the state of Texas than Americans invested in the entire nation of Japan, and that large American technology firms, such as Microsoft, earn about half of their total revenues from their European operations. Although there are tremendous economic benefits from this heightened economic activity (including many relatively cheap imported consumer goods), there are also significant costs. Jobs are lost to foreign countries, and national policies in areas such as workers' rights and environmental regulation must give way to international standards.

For example, the Byrd Amendment was enacted by Congress in 2000 to provide the aging American steel industry with $710 million worth of financial aid to offset losses suffered as a result of steel imports from Europe, Canada, South Korea, and Japan. The World Trade Organization (WTO)—the international organization that oversees international trade—ruled in 2003 that the Byrd Amendment constitutes an unfair trading practice and must end. The WTO ruling also gave other countries the right to impose penalties on U.S. exports until the United States complies with the ruling, which as of 2010, it had not done. President Obama initially planned to include a "buy American" clause in his stimulus package, whereby most of the government's infrastructure and pubic works spending would go to American suppliers. While popular with the Democrats and unions, many worried that such a clause violated WTO regulations that limit discrimination in government spending, which could bring retaliation from the E.U. and sanctions from the WTO.[28] In February 2009, President Obama backed down from the "Buy American" clause in the face of strong international opposition, stating that he did not want to start a trade war.[29] In the face of opposition from trading partners, the 'buy American" clause was not included in the stimulus package.

GLOBAL ECONOMIC POWERS   How should the United States respond to the growing economic power of other nations? As of 2010, China remains the world's largest recipient of foreign direct investment. It is one of the world's third-largest traders, and it is the largest trading partner for Japan, the second-largest for Europe and Russia, and the fourth-largest for the United States. China also holds the world's second-largest currency reserves. Because many technologies being traded globally today can be used for both commercial and military applications, the stronger China grows economically, the more powerful it is likely to become militarily. As it grows economically and militarily, the political influence of this communist country will increase in Asia and around the world. In addition, China's industrial growth is placing an immense strain on the global environment, with grave implications for climate change and fossil fuel depletion. Yet globalization makes it expensive, if not impossible, to isolate China and curb its growth without causing serious harm to the American economy and to the competitive position of U.S. firms abroad. The United States is

Wal-Mart has 180 stores in China. Like other American corporations, the retail giant has sought to expand its profits by becoming deeply involved in overseas markets. American businesses such as Wal-Mart are keenly interested in foreign policy and the development of good relationships with countries around the world. —*What is the impact of such global economic activities on workers and consumers in the United States?*

politically reliant on China in matters related to Iran and North Korea. China's increasing presence and influence in Africa is elevating its geopolitical influence globally. At the same time, the United States and China lock heads over China's currency manipulation in ways that exacerbate the U.S. trade deficit and Chinese surplus. A devalued Chinese currency makes Chinese exports to the United States appear cheaper, while making U.S. exports to China more expensive.

FOREIGN AID   A second, related question deals with the future of foreign aid. How much aid should be given? For what purposes should aid be rendered?[30]

MYTH EXPOSED   Many Americans believe that large amounts of American money are being sent overseas as foreign aid, which is why it is usually the first item to go in budget battles. Public opinion polls have shown that Americans believe that 20 percent of the federal budget goes to foreign aid.[31] In truth, foreign aid usually makes up a very small percentage of the entire U.S. budget. A breakdown of Barack Obama's fiscal year 2011 budget request shows that less than 1 percent was targeted for foreign aid, compared to about 20 percent for national defense, and over 20 percent for Social Security.[32] When one examines foreign aid comparatively, we can see that while the United States contributes the most foreign aid in absolute dollars of any other advanced industrial country, our contribution, relative to our Gross National Income (GNI), is the lowest of the group (see Table 15.2).

U.S. foreign aid amounts to 0.18 percent of gross national income, which is a far below the figure of 0.98 percent for Sweden or 0.88 percent for Norway. American foreign aid funds are not evenly distributed around the world but are concentrated in a few countries. When food aid is excluded, the six largest recipients of American military and economic aid in 2002, in order, were Israel, Egypt, Pakistan, Colombia, Afghanistan, and Jordan. After 2003, Iraq became a major

TABLE 15.2 | Foreign Aid Spending, 2009

Though the United States contributes the most foreign aid by far in terms of dollars, it is at the bottom of the pack of developed nations in terms of the portion of GNI spent in aid. The United Nations agreed on a target goal of 0.7 percent of GNI. Most nations fall short of this goal. —*Do you think the United States has a moral obligation to be more generous, or is our substantially larger contribution sufficient?*

NATION	TOTAL SPENDING (IN BILLIONS OF U.S. DOLLARS)	PERCENTAGE OF GROSS NATIONAL INCOME (GNI)
Sweden	$4.73	0.98%
Norway	$3.97	0.88%
Denmark	$2.80	0.82%
Netherlands	$6.99	0.80%
Spain	$6.67	0.43%
United Kingdom	$11.41	0.43%
Switzerland	$2.02	0.41%
France	$10.96	0.39%
Germany	$13.91	0.38%
Canada	$4.73	0.32%
Italy	$4.44	0.20%
Japan	$9.36	0.18%
United States	$26.01	0.18%

SOURCE: Organization for Economic Co-operation and Development (2009). Accessed at http://www.oecd.org/dataoecd/48/34/42459170.pdf. Based on Table 1: Net Official Development Assistance in 2008, from "Development Aid at its Highest Level Ever in 2008," Press Release OECD 2009, www.oecd.org/dac/stats

recipient. By 2008, Iraq was the largest recipient of U.S. foreign aid. All play vital roles in American foreign policy, either in the War on Terror or the War on Drugs. At the same time, humanitarian and development aid in Africa was increased from $1.4 billion a year in 2001 to $8 billion a year in 2008. During his presidential campaign, President Obama pledged to double U.S. foreign aid to $50 billion per year by 2010.[33] His 2010 budget included a $50.7 billion foreign aid budget.[34]

One reason why the American public looks suspiciously on foreign aid is our frustration over the failure of such aid to produce meaningful economic results. No contemporary economic development program has duplicated the success of the **Marshall Plan,** which in the late 1940s spurred Western Europe's economic recovery from the devastation of World War II. The difference is that Marshall Plan aid went to rebuild war-ravaged industrial economies, not to modernize traditional, low-income societies. The most important foreign aid initiative under way today is the **Millennium Challenge Account.** Announced by President George W. Bush in 2002, this narrowly focused, foreign aid program, which supports economic growth and reduction of poverty, is directed at low-income countries that have demonstrated a commitment to democracy and good government. Because results often take years of effort, the success of the Millennium Challenge Account has yet to be seen. In spite of the fact that Congress has approved a 26 percent increase in the Millennium Challenge Account's funding from 2009 to 2010, many of the states targeted for the money are incapable of effectively dealing with issues of good governance and corruption due to weak institutions and lack of resources.[35]

Human Welfare Issues

Human welfare issues focus on improving the lives of people around the world. For some Americans, addressing such challenges is an act of unselfishness and a statement about the shared humanity of people around the world. Those who take a more pragmatic approach believe that human rights abuses are a prime contributor to the domestic and international tensions that threaten U.S. interests.

GENOCIDE   Defined by the United Nations as "the intent to destroy, in whole or in part, a national ethnic, racial, or religious group," **genocide** is the most extreme category of human rights violation. The number of victims of genocide in the twentieth century is staggering. Six million Jews, as well as millions more Gypsies (Roma) and various other European minorities, perished in the most notorious instance of modern genocide, the Nazi Holocaust. More than a million Armenians in the Ottoman Empire were killed in genocidal attacks, and in the wars in Southeast Asia in 1975, well over a million Cambodians were massacred by communist guerrillas in the Cambodian "killing fields." Large-scale genocide also occurred in the 1990s in the central African country of Rwanda as well as in Bosnia and other parts of the former Yugoslavia in Eastern Europe. Between 1992 and 1995, about 200,000 predominantly Muslim Bosnians were killed by Serbs and Croats. An estimated 800,000 Rwandans were slaughtered in just a few months during 1994.

Most recently, genocide has raged in Sudan, a vast country in northeastern Africa with mixed Arab and black populations. From early July 2003 through 2004, an estimated 50,000 people were killed in Sudan, and another 2 million, desperately short of medicine and food, were driven into the desert region called Darfur.[36] By 2010, it was estimated that up to 300,000 people had died and 2.5 million more had been displaced.[37] The African Union/United Nations Hybrid Operations had almost 22,000 uniformed personnel (troops and police) deployed in Darfur under UN Security Council Resolution 1881.[38] This is the largest deployment of UN troops.

In spite of these horrific numbers, no clear-cut policy toward genocide has been enunciated in the United States, the United Nations, or anywhere else in the world. The genocide in Rwanda and the former Yugoslavia brought only tepid reactions from the Western powers. Two dilemmas face any attempt to formulate policies against genocide. The first is that the pace of killing sometimes is much faster than the ability of countries to respond. In Rwanda, at least half of the 500,000 Tutsi victims were killed by their Hutu neighbors in three weeks. In 1995, Bosnian Serbs murdered 7,000 Muslims in one day in the town of Srebenica. Second, there is what is known as the "moral hazard": Knowing that the United States and others will respond to genocide may actually encourage some to provoke violence against their people in hopes of involving outside forces.

LAND MINES   One of the greatest tragedies of modern warfare is that the killing and maiming of people often continues after the fighting ends. The culprit? Land mines. It is estimated that about 120 million land mines are still concealed in more than 80 countries today. Annually, they kill or seriously injure 26,000 people—an average of one person every 26 minutes. Each year, some 100,000 land mines are deactivated, but another 2 million are placed in the ground. The United States has played an ambiguous role in the land mine issue. It was a leader in the initial global effort to do away with them and actively funds and supports demining efforts around the world. On the other hand, the United States has refused to sign the 1997 Ottawa Treaty banning the use of land mines in war, maintaining that continued research and development efforts are necessary to preserve military capabilities in potential combat zones such as the Korean peninsula. In place of the Ottawa Treaty, the United States proposes a worldwide ban on land mines that do not deactivate themselves after a given period of time. The Obama administration continues to "review its policy on land mines" while refusing to sign a comprehensive treaty to ban them.[39]

HUMAN TRAFFICKING   It is important to keep in mind that human welfare issues are not solely a result of civil wars or international conflicts. Consider the plight of women and children who are transported across borders as sex workers. The global trafficking of people is now a $12 billion-a-year industry, involving 500,000 to 2,000,000 individuals.[40] Human trafficking is now the third-largest illegal business on earth, following drug and weapons trafficking. The United States is not immune from this problem. It is estimated that 14,500 to 17,500 people are transported into the United States each year for the sex trade or other forms of economic exploitation, and as many as a million people may have been illegally smuggled into the United States since 2000.[41] Since the passage of the little-noticed Trafficking Victims Protection Act by Congress in 2000, the United States is required to cut off most nonhumanitarian foreign aid to countries not making an effort to eliminate this problem.

Land mines continue to cause thousands of deaths and injuries each year around the world, even after military conflict in a specific country has ended. Here a soldier from Thailand uses a trained dog to identify the location of land mines as part of the effort to safely remove these dangerous explosives. The United States has failed to reach an agreement with other countries about whether land mines should be completely banned under international law. —*What position do you think that the United States should adopt on this issue?*

While global enforcement efforts have increased in the last decade, only about 4,000 individuals were convicted of human trafficking violations in 2009.[42]

CLIMATE CHANGE   It is increasingly obvious that environmental issues are a major national security issue for the United States. The relationship between environmental degradation and emerging security risks has become more apparent as the scale and intensity of environmental problems have evolved. In particular, the issue of climate change has been identified as one of the most important threats to long-term international stability. Climate change has been linked to increasing sea levels, more intense storms, and prolonged droughts. These factors have devastating impacts on living conditions throughout the planet and most notably in developing nations.

Under stress from global warming–induced environmental damage, developing countries are more prone to political, economic, and social unrest that can in turn create greater instability at the international level. The U.S. Defense Department has listed climate change among the security threats identified in the 2010 Quadrennial Defense Review, the report that updates Pentagon priorities every four years. And in 2009, the CIA created a new Center on Climate Change and National Security, demonstrating that the federal government's defense and intelligence organizations acknowledge the threats that climate change poses to the nation.[43]

OTHER ISSUES   This short account hardly does justice to the full range of human welfare issues that the United States must face. If you, like many people, are concerned about high gasoline prices, perhaps you consider the price of oil and America's dependence on foreign oil the most important foreign policy issue. Or your primary focus may be the issue of religious freedom; many nations around the world do not permit individuals to practice their religious beliefs freely or to convert from one religion to another. Other important issues include child labor, the status of women, poverty, and access to health care. Almost 3 billion people—nearly half the world's population—live on less than $2 a day. There are 400 million children in the world who have no access to safe water, and 270 million have no access to health services.

STUDENT profile

At 23 years of age, Jonathan Greenacre has seen the results of what must be some of the most horrific actions that humans can bring about against each other. In 2003, while visiting Cambodia as an observer at a land mine aid center, Jonathan

witnessed firsthand the devastation that land mines can inflict on people. He was nearly killed when he started to venture off a road and into a place where mines had been placed. Later, he visited an aid station where he saw maimed bodies of people—often children—who had innocently happened to step in the wrong place. These experiences so affected him that when Jonathan returned to his native Australia, he met a set of youth organizations and started International Network of Youth Against Land Mines (INYA) and, more recently, Safe Step. As the president of Safe Step, Jonathan works to organize people to help support international bans on land mines and to help those injured by land mines.

SOURCE: Accessed at http://www.acs-england.co.uk/iyf/winners.htm; http://64.233.167.104/search?q=cache:WgxCn8D129sJ:www.un.org/esa/socdev/unyin/documents/flashmay05.pdf+Jonathan+Greenacre&hl=en&ct=clnk&cd=1&gl=us&client=firefox-a; http://www.stepsafe.org.au/information.html on August 12, 2008.

Foreign Policy and National Security Issues

15.5   Outline the major foreign policy issues confronting the United States today.

PRACTICE QUIZ: UNDERSTAND AND APPLY

1. Which of the following is currently a top military security concern for the U.S. government?
   a. the threat of totalitarian regimes to global stability
   b. the spread of communism
   c. the proliferation of nuclear weapons
   d. AIDS

2. Which of the following statements is not true of human trafficking?
   a. Human trafficking involves selling children and women as sex workers.
   b. The United States has not yet passed legislation to prevent human trafficking.
   c. The number of human trafficking cases has increased in the past decade.
   d. Smuggling of individuals into the United States is considered part of human trafficking.

3. Prior to the attacks of 9/11, top administration officials viewed al-Qaeda as one of the top national security threats to the United States.
   a. true   b. false

ANALYZE

1. How would you resolve a foreign policy situation that pitted U.S. military security issues against economic interests and human rights concerns?

2. Why do many Americans believe that the United States gives greater amounts of foreign aid than it actually does?

IDENTIFY THE CONCEPT THAT DOESN'T BELONG

a. Terrorism   d. Deterrence
b. Weapons of mass destruction e. Human trafficking
c. Preemption

Conclusion

The decision of President Barack Obama to increase the number of American military personnel in Afghanistan that was discussed at the beginning of this chapter provides an excellent example of the complexities of U.S. foreign policy. As a world superpower, the United States maintains a combination of economic and military power that is unmatched. With this unique position every one of its foreign policy decisions sends ripples throughout the world and often determines the life and death of both Americans and non-Americans in every corner of the globe.

In this chapter, we have looked at the broad outlines of that debate as they are framed by neoconservatives, neoliberals, conservatives, and isolationists. These competing ideas draw on and bring together long-established ways of thinking about American foreign policy, dating back to the founding of the United States.

The making of American foreign policy is the product of the interaction between people and institutions. The American public expresses its voice through public opinion, elections, interest group activity, and political protest. Policymakers often have difficulty understanding what they hear from the public. They also have a desire to use the American public to help achieve their goals, which often reduces their willingness to listen. Presidents face a similar dilemma in reaching out for advice, whether to their White House staff or to the foreign policy bureaucracy. They want and need information but often hear unwelcome news. Competition among offices in the White House and within the foreign affairs bureaucracy provides the president with many choices of information sources and sets the stage for controversy. This controversy is often played out in public, especially when it involves conflict between the president and Congress.

One must also consider the current economic climate that raises questions about the domestic costs and economic burden of projecting and promoting U.S. foreign policy objectives globally. U.S. operations in Iraq and Afghanistan require a tremendous amount of resources that U.S. taxpayers and the government needs to provide. Many would argue that these resources are desperately needed at home. It may be argued that investments in U.S. infrastructure, research and development, education, and health care systems are needed to enhance our economic competitiveness and to protect manufacturing jobs. National-security and foreign-policy concerns compete with pocketbook concerns and this competition is amplified during election season. Given the high unemployment rate slower than desired pace of economic recovery, the Obama administration will be hard pressed by political opponents and many supporters to justify the costs of U.S. engagement in Iraq, Afghanistan, and elsewhere. As a global superpower, our international leadership role in an increasingly uncertain global environment is critical. At the same time, isolationists will challenge the costs of global engagement, especially during times of domestic economic hardship.

Finally, it is important to remember that terrorism is not the only foreign policy issue facing the United States today. A wide range of military security, economic, and human welfare issues are on the national agenda. Failure to address them adequately today may hold dire consequences for the future.

KEY CONCEPT MAP   How are U.S. foreign policy and domestic policy linked?

Instability in Foreign Countries

The political turmoil in Afghanistan is a threat to global security. U.S. engagement there requires political and economic resources that create stress on domestic politics.

Critical Thinking Questions

What if the money and resources that are being allocated to maintaining security and rebuilding in Afghanistan were being devoted instead to social and infrastructure development programs in the United States? Are we neglecting other unstable regions, where our troops are stretched too thin?

Foreign Economic Competition

Cheaper goods from China and other nations often flood American markets. The United States has championed the ideas of free markets and free trade for decades, but high unemployment in the United States has made many question the impact of free trade on U.S. jobs and the U.S. economy as a whole.

Critical Thinking Questions

What if we were to implement higher tariffs on goods imported from foreign countries and sold in the United States? How do economic conditions impact public opinion about free markets and economic competition?

Foreign Aid

As a global superpower, the United States gives strategic, economic, and humanitarian aid to countries around the world. It uses foreign aid as leverage to promote U.S. interests overseas.

Critical Thinking Questions

If you were the current secretary of state, how would you convince detractors that a larger foreign aid budget would be good for American domestic politics? Should the U.S. government give more in foreign aid to countries that are in need? Why or why not?

Presidential Elections

Because candidates are often afraid of looking weak during presidential elections, they will take positions on foreign policy matters that demonstrate strength. These positions often become policies once the election is over.

Critical Thinking Questions

Why are presidential candidates afraid of appearing to be "weak" when it comes to foreign policy? In what ways might U.S. presidential elections impact the foreign policies of other nations?

Interest Groups

Interest groups such as the American Israel Public Affairs Committee (AIPAC) and the Cuban American National Foundation (CANF) have played major roles in influencing U.S. policy toward Israel and Cuba.

Critical Thinking Questions

If you were a member of Congress, you would be regularly contacted by interest groups regarding U.S. foreign policy. What factors would make you want to address the requests of interest groups on foreign affairs matters? How would you balance the demands of interest groups with the demands of your constituents and your own judgment on the right course of action?

Public Opinion

It is difficult to maintain a foreign policy once public support is lost. The prime example of this was the loss of public support for the Vietnam War after it became obvious that the United States was not winning.

Critical Thinking Questions

If the American public had been more supportive of the Vietnam War, would U.S. policy have been any different? Would the outcome of the war have been different? Have changes in public opinion about the wars in Iraq and Afghanistan led to changes in U.S. foreign policy?

The relationship between American foreign policy and public policies focused on domestic issues is tighter than one might expect. Decisions made by the United States regarding relationships with foreign nations can have ramifications for the types of jobs that Americans work in, the types of goods they purchase, and even the subjects they study in school. —*What types of foreign policy issues are most likely to impact domestic policy? How does the standing of the United States as a global superpower directly affect the financial resources available to address domestic problems in areas such as transportation, education and environmental protection?*

Review of Key Objectives

Competing Principles for American Foreign Policy

15.1 Compare and contrast four different approaches to American foreign policy.

(pages 462–465)

Four different schools of thought have existed throughout American history and continue to influence today's thinking on foreign policy. Two groups of "transformers" (neoliberals and neoconservatives) and two groups of "maintainers" (conservatives and isolationists) differ in their view of the proper content and conduct of American foreign policy. Neoliberals look to international organizations and agreements as ways for the United States to engage in foreign policy, while neoconservatives are more supportive of unilateral actions by the United States, if those actions help to preserve the nation's interests and standing in the world. Conservatives believe that the United States should not have to bear the burden for foreign policies that provide benefits to countries other than the United States, and isolationists seek to minimize U.S. entanglements with matters in other parts of the world.

KEY TERMS

Neoconservatives 462
North Atlantic Treaty Organization (NATO) 462
Neoliberals 462
Weapons of Mass Destruction 463

CRITICAL THINKING QUESTIONS

1. What are the most important differences among the views of the neoliberals, neoconservatives, conservatives and isolationists regarding the wars in Iraq and Afghanistan?
2. In what ways did American foreign policy undergo fundamental changes after on Pearl Harbor?

INTERNET RESOURCES

Learn more about Woodrow Wilson and the League of Nations at http://www.indiana.edu/~league/

ADDITIONAL READING

Bacevich, Andrew. *The Limits of Power: The End of American Exceptionalism.* New York: Metropolitan/Holt, 2009.

Links Between Foreign and Domestic Policy

15.2 Establish three links between American foreign and domestic policy.

(pages 466–469)

Three types of linkages exist between American foreign policy and domestic policy. First, American foreign policy is often influenced by some of the same values that guide domestic policy. Second, the U.S. political decision-making process is influenced by the efforts of lobbyists that represent foreign nations, groups, and businesses. Finally, U.S. foreign policy affects the distribution of costs and benefits among individuals and groups in the United States.

KEY TERMS

Kyoto Protocol 466
Globalization 467

CRITICAL THINKING QUESTIONS

1. How does American domestic policy influence American foreign policy, and does American foreign policy affect participation in politics here at home?
2. In what ways does American foreign policy create winners and losers in domestic politics?

INTERNET RESOURCES

For more information on globalization, see the United Nations Environmental Program Web page at http://www.unep.org/

ADDITIONAL READING

Zakaria, Fareed. *The Post American World.* New York: Norton, 2008.

The Domestic Context of American Foreign Policymaking

15.3 Assess pathways for citizen participation in foreign policymaking.

(pages 470–473)

Public opinion, elections, interest group activity, and political protest are four different means by which the public can use pathways to influence foreign policy decisions. Many of the same factors that affect the making of domestic policy also play a role in shaping American foreign policy, but additional factors include lobbyists for foreign nations and other groups that exert influence on the adoption of U.S. policy toward other countries.

KEY TERMS

Vietnam Syndrome 470
"Rally 'Round the Flag" Effect 470
Strategic Arms Limitation Talks (SALT) 471
Apartheid 471

CRITICAL THINKING QUESTIONS

1. Why are some political institutions more open to the influence of the public?
2. While many foreign policy issues have become part of the institutional agenda for governmental decision makers, many have not. Are there certain characteristics that make some issues more likely to grab the attention of decision makers?

INTERNET RESOURCES

World Public Opinion.org, offers comprehensive information on public opinion around the world on international issues at http://www.worldpublicopinion.org

ADDITIONAL READING

Kohut, Andrew, and Bruce Stokes. *America Against the World*. New York: Times Books, 2006.

Sobel, Richard. *The Impact of Public Opinion on U.S. Foreign Policy Since Vietnam*. New York: Oxford University Press, 2001.

Political Institutions and Foreign Policymaking

15.4 Analyze how political institutions compete for influence in making foreign policy.

(pages 474–481)

The president does not make foreign policy decisions alone but relies heavily on advisers and staff within the White House. The relationship between the president and Congress is dynamic and varies from strategic to competitive. Regardless of how they interact, Congress has a fixed number of tools at its disposal to influence foreign policy. The Supreme Court intervenes only rarely in foreign policy matters, but occasionally it reviews a case important to national security and foreign policy issues.

KEY TERMS

Powell Doctrine 476
McNamara Doctrine 476
Covert Action 477
Intelligence 477
Containment 479
Détente 479

CRITICAL THINKING QUESTIONS

1. Which institutions are most involved in making foreign and national security policy?
2. What choices does a president have in seeking advice on foreign policy decisions, and in what ways might the advice from various sources differ?

INTERNET RESOURCES

The Central Intelligence Agency provides information on the global infectious disease threat and its implications for the United States at http://www.fas.org/irp/threat/nie99-17d.htm

Foreign Service dispatches and periodic reports on U.S. foreign policy can be found at http://www.unc.edu/depts/diplomat

Information on the national security strategy of the United States is available at http://www.whitehouse.gov/nsc/nss.html

ADDITIONAL READING

Mearsheimer, John J., and Stephen M. Walt. *The Israel Lobby and U.S. Foreign Policy*. New York: Farrar, Straus and Giroux, 2007.

Ikenberry, G. John. *American Foreign Policy: Theoretical Essays,* 5th ed. Upper Saddle River, NJ: Prentice Hall, 2005.

Foreign Policy and National Security Issues

 15.5 **Outline the major foreign policy issues confronting the United States today.**

(pages 482–487)

A complex set of military security, economic, and human welfare issues confront the United States today. While terrorist threats capture much of the public's attention, other issues such as trade, human trafficking, and environmental degradation increasingly affect the security of the nation.

KEY TERMS

Jihadists 483
Preemption 483
Deterrence 483
Marshall Plan 485
Millennium Challenge Account 485
Genocide 485

CRITICAL THINKING QUESTIONS

1. What is the impact of globalization on American foreign policy?
2. What do you think are the three most pressing human welfare issues facing American foreign policy today?

INTERNET RESOURCES

Information on the International Campaign to Ban Landmines can be found at http://www.icbl.org/

Examine the 9-11 Commission's report online at http://www.9-11commission.gov/

ADDITIONAL READING

Bales, Kevin, and Ron Soodalter. *The Slave Next Door: Human Trafficking and Slavery in America Today.* Berkeley, CA: University of California Press, 2009.

Woodward, Bob. *Plan of Attack.* New York: Simon and Schuster, 2004.

Chapter Review   Test Your Knowledge

1. The U.S. war in Afghanistan reignited three central and long-standing questions about American foreign policy, now considered in the age of terrorism. One of those questions is
   a. Should the United States return to an isolationist approach or try to be "policeman" to the world?
   b. What should be the proper relationship between U.S. foreign policy and domestic policy?
   c. Should the United States maintain its considerable military superiority in the world or scale back that budgetary commitment in the face of other pressing needs?
   d. Should the United States acknowledge the limitations of diplomacy and curtail the authority of the State Department?

2. Which of the following approaches dominated the foreign policy of George W. Bush's administration?
   a. neoliberal
   b. isolationist
   c. conservative
   d. neoconservative

3. Although there are important differences between neoliberal and neoconservative approaches to foreign policy, one belief they share is that
   a. the United States should never hesitate to use its military force to achieve foreign policy ends.
   b. the United States should routinely solicit the support of coalition governments and international institutions, such as the United Nations, to help achieve its foreign policy ends.
   c. the United States should include in its foreign policy objectives the spreading of democracy throughout the world.
   d. world politics is a realm defined by conflict and struggle.

4. Neoliberals probably would have handled Saddam Hussein and the regime change in Iraq
   a. by extending the economic sanctions against Iraq and, if fighting broke out, by trying to enable Iraqis to create a democratic government from within.
   b. by defeating Hussein militarily and installing an interim, U.S.-controlled Iraqi government.
   c. by not doing anything—such regime change would not be a foreign policy priority.
   d. by extending the economic sanctions against Iraq and, if that did not work, by bombing all the Iraqi locations where weapons of mass destruction were thought to exist.

5. The world's response to genocide
   a. has been to use military force to fight it whenever and wherever it takes place.
   b. has been to treat it as a problem that can only be resolved by the governments of the nations where it is taking place.
   c. has been mixed over time; sometimes genocide is stopped by the actions of other nations and sometimes left to continue.
   d. has ensured that genocide will take place in the future.

6. In terms of the nation's foreign policy, the Supreme Court
   a. has a longstanding practice of taking an active role in trying to direct the nation's interactions with other countries.
   b. cannot hear cases in this policy area because the Constitution prohibits them from doing so.
   c. must first get written approval from the U.S. Senate before they can hear a case dealing with a treaty.
   d. has largely refrained from taking cases that involve this policy area.

7. Which of the following best describes U.S. aid to foreign countries?
   a. The United States gives only military aid to other nations.
   b. The United States directs a very large portion of its overall budget to foreign aid.
   c. The United States gives billions in foreign aid, but the total is only a small portion of the overall budget.
   d. The United States has dramatically increased its level of foreign aid in recent years.

8. American policy—both domestic and foreign—pays much more attention to individual legal rights and civil liberties than it does to economic and social rights.
   a. true   b. false

9. What best characterizes current U.S. global environmental policy?
   a. more environmentally progressive than almost any other country
   b. not environmentally progressive at all
   c. environmentally progressive when such progress does not come at the expense of American economic interests
   d. forward thinking about global climate change but not in some other areas

10. What is CAFTA, and who was one of its opponents?
    a. a trade agreement ratified during the Clinton administration; H. Ross Perot strongly opposed it, citing the loss of U.S. jobs as its result
    b. a trade agreement ratified during the George W. Bush administration; wealthy U.S. sugar producers opposed it because it would cut into their profits
    c. a trade agreement ratified during the Reagan administration; the airline industry opposed it because it would tighten competition for them
    d. an organization within the United Nations, created during the Carter administration; American libertarians opposed it because it required funding from industrialized countries, such as the U.S. taxpayers' money

11. How well informed is the American public regarding foreign affairs?
    a. Usually quite well informed: For example, at the height of the Cold War, in 1964, 90 percent of Americans knew that the Soviet Union was not part of NATO.
    b. Not very: For example, in 1979, only 23 percent of Americans knew that the United States and the Soviet Union were the two countries involved in the Strategic Arms Limitation Talks.

c. Moderately well informed: For example, in 1993, only 13 percent of Americans could not identify the continent on which Somalia is located.

d. Very well indeed: For example, in 2003, 94 percent of Americans knew that Iraq did not play a major role in 9/11.

12. Religious groups that try to influence U.S. foreign policy are almost always from the "religious right."
a. true   b. false

13. Of the following powers, which does the Constitution deny the president?
a. the making of treaties
b. the appointment of ambassadors
c. the commanding of the armed forces
d. the declaring of war

14. The Constitution grants the vice president significant responsibilities in the formation of foreign policy.
a. true   b. false

15. Which institution is the formal channel through which the United States and foreign countries pass information?
a. the State Department
b. the National Security Council
c. the Central Intelligence Agency
d. the Department of Defense

16. In the early 1960s, what responsibility did Congress shift from the State Department to a newly created office in the White House?
a. treaty negotiations
b. arms negotiation
c. trade policy and negotiation
d. global environmental policy and negotiation

17. Who has the final say regarding the use of U.S. military force overseas?
a. Congress   c. the American people
b. the Joint Chiefs of Staff   d. the president

18. The Powell Doctrine asserts that military force should be used overseas
a. provided that such a force can be of minimal size and maximum speed and maneuverability and that it enjoys a technological advantage over the adversary.
b. provided that the American public clearly supports the cause, overwhelming force can be brought to bear in the conflict, and a clear exit strategy is in place.
c. provided that an expansion of democracy is a predictable result of the conflict and that America's economic interests are not compromised.
d. provided that such intervention has the support of the international community: the UN, NATO, and the so-called "court of public opinion."

19. In attempting to have their intelligence influence U.S. foreign policy, the CIA is now competing with what other intelligence office?
a. the Pentagon's
b. Homeland Security's
c. the ambassador to the UN's
d. the FBI's

20. During the 1970s, the relationship between Congress and the president could best be described as
a. strategic.
b. competitive.
c. supportive and disengaged.
d. supportive and engaged.

mypoliscilab Exercises

Apply what you learned in this chapter on **MyPoliSciLab.**

Read on mypoliscilab.com

eText: Chapter 15

Study and **Review** on mypoliscilab.com

Pre-Test
Post-Test
Chapter Exam
Flashcards

Watch on mypoliscilab.com

Video: Sanctions on Iran
Video: NYC's Subway Surveillance System
Video: Three Vivid Years—But Progress?

Explore on mypoliscilab.com

Simulation: You Are President John F. Kennedy
Simulation: You Are the Newly Appointed Ambassador to the Country of Dalmatia
Simulation: You Are the President of the United States
Comparative: Comparing Foreign and Security Policy
Timeline: The Evolution of Foreign Policy
Visual Literacy: Evaluating Defense Spending

California: Historical Perspective

KEY OBJECTIVES

After completing this chapter, you should be prepared to:

16.1 Determine the impact of California's geography and climate on its early settlement.

16.2 Outline the historical developments and political transformations that led to the U.S. annexation of California.

16.3 Describe how the construction of the transcontinental railroad shaped the politics and economy of California.

16.4 Summarize the major political and economic developments in California during the twentieth century.

16.5 Identify the major challenges facing California in the current period.

Historically, the relationship between the state government of California and the federal government has been in perpetual flux. During California's early years of statehood in the 1850s, the Southern Democrats dominated Washington, DC. In league with California Democrats, they embraced a states' rights approach that limited the federal presence in the state. Beginning in the mid-1860s, however, the Republicans dominated federal government. They favored federal supremacy and supported policies that were not necessarily popular in California, such as the development of an overland telegraph, transcontinental rail service and slightly better relations with Native Californians. The authoritarian side of federal authority in California was acutely felt during the Civil War when southern sympathizers were imprisoned on Alcatraz Island after the right to writ of habeas corpus was suspended.[1]

From the 1900s onward, both the California state and federal governments once again welcomed a conservative approach to governance. California-based industries received a boost as major suppliers of materials during World War I. During the

> **How much of California's past can be found in its present?**

1920s, the U.S. Navy made Los Angeles and Long Beach the home ports of the Pacific fleet, a decision that resulted in a major infusion of federal dollars into the economies of both these cities. In the mid-1930s, federal funds trickled into California, amounting to $191 million in 1930 out of a $3 billion federal budget.[2] Gradually, depression-era relief, coupled with the material demands of World War II pushed that figure up to $728 million in 1940 and $8.5 billion for 1945.[3] Federal expenditures to California stayed high until the late 1980s when the demise of the Cold War caused major cuts to defense spending.

Even before Governor Arnold Schwarzenegger released his cost-cutting 2010–2011 budget plan, the state Legislative Analyst's Office recommended that government officials "aggressively seek new federal assistance."[4] State officials have also been particularly vocal about the perceived inequity in the amount of revenue Californians send to Washington compared to what the federal government receives in taxes from Californians—about 79 cents on the dollar. Having already received billions in federal stimulus dollars, however, many Californians are now hopeful that the Obama administration will extend a bit more help.

Resource Center
• Glossary
• Vocabulary Example
• Connect the Link

■ **California Gold Rush:** The rapid influx of settlers sparked by the discovery of gold at Sutter's Mill on January 24, 1848.

SIGNIFICANCE: *The gold fields were a rough-and-tumble world of individual initiative where the miners promulgated their own law, often in a swift and harsh manner, unregulated by any territorial or federal government.*

Natural Characteristics and Native Californians

16.1 Determine the impact of California's geography and climate on its early settlement.

(pages 498–501)

California's climate and geography have played a central role in the state's remarkable development. Although Californians have now moved into a postindustrial age increasingly shaped by the forces of technology, the state's physical environment continues to shape the state's social and economic development. It influences government and business policies on energy, water supply, and agriculture. Images of California's balmy weather, bountiful land, and mineral wealth continue to lure generations of immigrants from around the globe who are seeking a better life on the shores of the Pacific Ocean.

A Lure and a Challenge: California's Land and Climate

From the days of the earliest settlers, many of the state's greatest attractions could be found along the coastline. In 1769, during his overland expedition, Gaspar de Portolá first sighted San Francisco Bay, still considered one of the world's greatest natural harbors. Besides its scenic beauty, the Northern California coast offered a moderate climate and a wide variety of edible fish and shellfish. Venturing inland, settlers found coastal valleys with ample water, fertile soil, and plentiful stands of timber. The redwood, one of the world's tallest trees, would supply new arrivals with some of the toughest and most durable wood on the continent. With adequate water, the soil of these coastal valleys could support almost any type of agricultural production. Most of California enjoys a Mediterranean climate with only two distinct seasons: a cool, wet winter and a mild, dry summer.

An even greater lure than climate for most immigrants to California was the mineral wealth soon discovered in the state's valleys and mountains. The most famous find was, of course, the gold strike at Sutter's Mill on the American River in 1848 that inspired the historic **California Gold Rush**■. Many other discoveries followed, and by the twentieth century, California's reserves of oil, chromium, mercury, platinum, and tungsten were proving even more lucrative for their owners than veins of gold.

Mineral resources created unimaginable personal wealth for a few and thriving communities for many. Developers and promoters fostered dreams of the good life in California. Their words would embolden immigrants with visions of flourishing cities. For some of these pioneers, the dream would fade among the mountains that guarded the state's western approaches. The

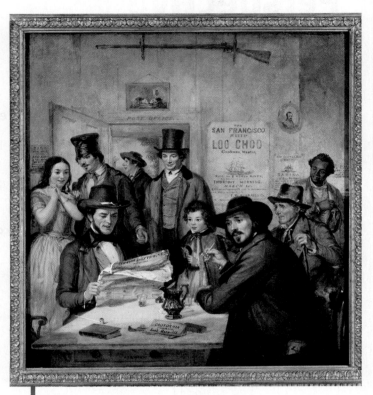

Men and women avidly read news of the California Gold Rush in the painting *California News* by William Sidney Mount. —*What are most likely to be the topics discussed among these men and women?*

jagged granite peaks of the **Sierra Nevada**■, the inland mountain range that covers almost half of the state's total land area, served as a daunting natural barrier.

The Sierra Nevada range is littered with the grave sites of pioneers consumed by starvation or trapped by winter storms. The legendary ordeals of the Bidwell and Donner parties attest to the difficulties early settlers faced in reaching California by crossing this mountain range. Jedediah Smith, the famous explorer and fur trapper considered by many to be the first American to enter California, suffered starvation, a broiling sun, and thirst during his many journeys. It has been said that he found the Mojave Desert one of the most desolate places he had seen on earth.

Mountains and deserts make overland access to California hazardous; ocean access is equally difficult. Although the coastline extends over 1,200 miles, it has only three natural harbors. The Pacific Ocean breeds violent storms, and a strong westward current has always made sailing north along the California coast extremely dangerous. As late as the nineteenth century, sailing ships had less than a 50 percent chance of surviving a voyage of any significant distance northward.[5]

California is a state of diverse subregions. Even those settlers and adventurers fortunate enough to arrive safely in California found it difficult to survive if they settled in one of the state's

■ **Sierra Nevada:** The inland mountain range that makes up almost half of California's total land area.

SIGNIFICANCE: *This mountain range forms a natural barrier that limited migration to California and is littered with the grave sites of pioneers consumed by starvation or trapped by winter storms.*

many inhospitable areas. Without the complex system of irrigation that exists today, large sections of California would still be uninhabited. It is no mystery why most Spanish missions were built along the California coast. Practically all the lowlands of Southern California and the eastern slope of the Sierra Nevada range are either desert or semidesert. Although average yearly rainfall varies from 100 inches on the north coast to 10 inches along the Mexican border, virtually no rain falls in the state during the growing season between May and September.

The earliest Native American inhabitants succeeded in adapting to this severe environment. Estimates vary, but archaeological evidence suggests that these Native Californians have occupied the state for over 6,000 years, fashioning their lifestyles and traditions around the natural landscape and altering few features of their surroundings.[6]

Native American Settlement

Historians and anthropologists estimate that before the first European settlers arrived, as many as 300,000 Native Americans lived in California, accounting for approximately one-sixth of the population of continental North America. When the Spanish navigator Sebastián Vizcaino landed at Monterey on December 16, 1602, after a seven-month voyage from Acapulco, he recorded his impressions of the local population in his diary: "The land is thickly populated with numberless Indians, of whom a great many came several times to our camp. They appear to be a gentle and peaceable people. They said by signs that inland there are many settlements. The food which these Indians most commonly eat, besides fish and crustaceans, consists of acorns and another nut larger than a chestnut."[7]

During Vizcaino's time, native Californians led peaceful, simple lives in almost every region of the state. They spoke some 135 different languages and dialects. Some of the larger tribes were the Shasta, Yurok, Maidu, and Pomo in the north; the Miwok, Modoc, Costanoan, Ohlone, and Yokuts in central California; and the Shoshone, Chumash, Cahulla, Mojave, and Yuma in the south. Native Californians rarely lived in groups larger than 1,000 persons; more often than not, these groups were based on extended families or clans rather than on tribal association. Native communities adapted their cultural and social habits to their surroundings. River and lake communities tended to practice fishing, boat building, and agriculture, while woodland communities relied on hunting and acorn gathering. Indians in the desert were especially resourceful, harvesting at least 60 distinct desert plants for food and 28 other plants for narcotics, stimulants, or medicines. Although isolated from the most advanced world civilizations, the California Indians were not as primitive as pioneers often portrayed them. Their cultural progress is clearly illustrated by their use of currency, their complex social traits, and their artistry in pottery and basket making.

STUDENT profile

In 2006, Pamela Ames, an 18-year-old Native American student from the Yurok tribe, was awarded the nationally recognized Gates Millennium Scholarship sponsored by the Bill and Melinda Gates Foundation. Pamela is from the Hoopa Valley Reservation in Humboldt County, a reservation located in the northwest region of California. Home to the Yurok, Hoopa, and Karuk tribes, the picturesque valley of rivers running through spectacular forests belies the struggles of these Native Californians that began with the onslaught of the U.S. Army, miners, and loggers during the nineteenth century.

In addition to high rates of poverty, 27 percent unemployment, low high school graduation rates, and widespread substance abuse, the Hoopa Valley Reservation must also contend with severe environmental issues. Despite a century and a half of hardship, Yuroks tribal members such as Pamela Ames have persevered. As a student at Hoopa Valley High School, Pamela was on the President's Honor Roll, maintained a 4.14 GPA, served as student body treasurer, played three sports, and worked part-time. She is now planning to major in civil engineering at Sacramento State and use her degree to give back to her community by going back to help rebuild historic old buildings in rural areas. The Native Californians of the Hoopa Valley Reservation will need educated well-equipped individuals such as Pamela to address the ongoing issues and social ills of the reservation.

SOURCE: *Sacramento State Bulletin*, published by the State University of California at Sacramento, April 10, 2006, vol. 12, no. 28; "Pamela Ames," *Tribal Voice Newsletter*, vol. 2, no. 5, California Tribal TANF Partnership; Stephen Magagnini, "Humble Library is Life-Changing for the Hoopa Indian Reservation," *Sacramento Bee*, January 14, 2008, http://www.sacbee.com/101/v-print/story/631843.html

Spanish Exploration and Settlement

In 1519, Hernán Cortés landed near what is now Vera Cruz, Mexico, and claimed the region for Spain. For the next 300 years, beginning with Juan Rodriguez Cabrillo's discovery of San Diego in 1542 (see Table 16.1), the Spanish gradually expanded the boundaries of "New Spain" northward, into the region they would name Alta ("Upper") California.

Gaspar de Portolá, the Spanish governor of Baja ("Lower") California, and the Franciscan missionary Father Junipero Serra established the first Spanish colony and Franciscan mission at San Diego in 1769. Extending their exploration northward later that year, Portolá and his party discovered San Francisco Bay. Not satisfied with the terrain around the bay, Portolá founded the settlement of Monterey in 1770, designating it the administrative

■ **Pueblos:** Centers of trade and Spanish civilization during the period of Spanish colonial rule of California.

SIGNIFICANCE: *In 1781, a small group of multiracial Spanish settlers formally established El Pueblo de Nuestra Señora Reina de Los Angeles del Río de Porciúncula (the Town of Our Lady Queen of the Angels of the River Porciúncula), known over 227 years later as the City of Los Angeles.*

TABLE 16.1 | Important Events in California History

6,000 years ago	Chumash tribe settles along the Southern California coast.
1542	Juan Rodriguez Cabrillo discovers San Diego; he is the first European to land in California, only 50 years after Columbus landed in the Americas.
1577	Sir Francis Drake explores the California coast and claims the region for Great Britain.
1769	Father Junipero Serra founds in San Diego the first of 21 California missions.
1812	Russian traders establish Fort Ross near Bodega Bay; according to legend, the Russians acquired the area for three blankets, three pairs of breeches, two axes, three hoes, and some beads.
1821	Mexico gains its independence from Spain.
1827	Jedediah Smith crosses the Sierra Nevada range, making him the first American to enter California.
1848	James Marshall finds gold at Sutter's Mill.
1848	The Treaty of Guadalupe Hidalgo officially ends the Mexican–American War, resulting in the transfer of Mexican territories, including California, to U.S. control.
1850	California is admitted to the Union as the 31st state.
1851	The Mariposa Indian War ends, with huge numbers of Native Americans killed in gold country.
1869	Transcontinental railroad is completed.
1871	Anti-Chinese riots occur in San Francisco.
1906	Earthquake and fire destroy much of San Francisco, causing over 3,000 deaths and rendering approximately 300,000 people homeless.
1911	First motion picture is made in Hollywood.
1937	Golden Gate Bridge is completed.
1938	Ten thousand people are arriving each month via U.S. Highway 66, mostly from the Dust Bowl states.
1942	Japanese Americans and Japanese immigrants are relocated inland.
1955	Disneyland opens in Anaheim, to be visited by 50 million people during its first 10 years.
1962	California becomes the most populous state.
1965	Major riots take place in African American sections of Los Angeles.
1968	Robert Kennedy wins the California presidential primary but is mortally wounded within minutes of his victory speech.
1971	American Indian protesters occupy Alcatraz Island in San Francisco Bay.
1977	Apple personal computers, developed in "Silicon Valley," are introduced.
1989	The Loma Prieta earthquake, magnitude 7.1, strikes the San Francisco Bay Area, causing almost $3 billion in damage to San Francisco.
2000	The high-tech industry, primarily located in California, suffers a major decline, and over 128,000 workers lose their jobs.
2007	Stockton, California, leads the nation in the number of foreclosures due to the faulty mortgage lending practices, depressed real estates prices, and the global financial crisis.

SOURCE: ClassBrain.com, *Timeline of California History*, www.classbrain.com; *Historical Timeline*, Bancroft Library, University of California, Berkeley, accessed at www.berkeley.edu; SHG Resources, California Timeline of State History, www.sghresources.com; Kevin Starr, *California: A History* (New York: Modern Library Edition, 2005); www.Justdisney.com

■ **Presidios:** Military outposts during the period of Spanish colonial rule of California.

EXAMPLE: *The Santa Barbara Royal Presidio was founded in 1782 and became the last of four military fortresses built by the Spanish at strategic routes along the coast. These presidios rivaled California missions in both architecture and asectic value.*

capital for Spanish settlements in New Spain. Father Serra was so impressed by the nearby countryside that he declared this site the center of his California mission system.[8]

The Mission System

The official colonial policy of Spain dictated the establishment of three distinct organizations at each settlement: *missions* to provide religious activities for the Indians and convert them to Christianity, **pueblos**■ as centers of trade and civilization, and **presidios**■ as military outposts. Although conflicts often arose between the Franciscan friars and the military commanders of the presidios, the three systems of authority generally complemented one another.

Between 1780 and 1821, agriculture production and the raising and handling of livestock in the Spanish settlements became increasingly profitable. The export of animal hides to Europe and the newly independent United States was especially lucrative. The mission system founded by Father Serra grew to include 21 sites along the coast, from San Diego in the south to Solano in the north. Much of the success of the mission system is attributed to the employment—or, as some suggest, the exploitation—of Native Californian labor. The number of

Mission Basilica San Diego de Alcala, built in 1769, was the first of California's Spanish missions. —*This mission would present what advantage as well as disadvantage as the first of California's Spanish missions?*

Spanish settlers and administrators was never greater than a few thousand, but they nevertheless had a profoundly negative effect on the Native Californians' freedom of movement, land use, and health. The Spanish presence clearly marked the beginning of the end for a vibrant Native American culture and community.

Natural Characteristics and Native Californians

16.1 Determine the impact of California's geography and climate on its early settlement.

PRACTICE QUIZ: UNDERSTAND AND APPLY

1. The Sierra Nevada
   a. is a mountain range that makes up almost half of California's total land area.
   b. is a popular California wine.
   c. was the first Spanish mission.
   d. is a lake in Northern California that has become an important source of water.

2. Native Californians have occupied the state for approximately
   a. 1 million years.   c. 6,000 years.
   b. 500 years.   d. 150 years.

3. Native Californians' most significant contribution to the Mission System was their
   a. conversion to   c. labor.
      Christianity.
   b. culture.   d. freedom of movement.

ANALYZE

1. What features of California's geography drew American pioneers to the state? What features kept these pioneers away?

2. How did California's physical environment impact its early settlement by Native Americans and the Spanish colonists?

IDENTIFY THE CONCEPT THAT DOESN'T BELONG

a. Settlement
b. Exploitation
c. Conversion
d. Deregulation
e. Administration

Resource Center
• Glossary
• Vocabulary Example
• Connect the Link

■ **Californios:**
Mexican settlers of
California.

EXAMPLE: *Pío de Jesus Pico IV (1801–1894) was the last Mexican
Governor of Alta California. A Californio of African, Native American,
and Spanish ancestry, Pico became a prominent Los Angeles businessman.*

Mexican Control Yields to U.S. Annexation

16.2 Outline the historical developments and
political transformations that led to the
U.S. annexation of California.

(pages 502–505)

Spanish government in California would come to an end due
to various weaknesses in its colonial administration and, especially, Spain's preoccupation with European politics and its
overstretched colonial empire. The Spanish monarchy could
not withstand the successive military and political challenges
of the American and French revolutions and the rise of
Napoleonic Europe to its position as a world power. Spanish
preoccupation with European challenges and inattention to its
colonies abroad provided the impetus for Mexican independence in 1822. The new, independent Mexican nation, however,
was not much more successful in governing California than the
Spanish had been. Over the next 40 years, the Mexican government was overwhelmed by military coups, political intrigue,
and conspiracy. Political instability made it practically impossible for Mexican governors to control a territory extending as
far north as present-day Colorado. The small number of Spanish and Mexican settlers who occupied land in California were
largely left to fend for themselves.

Two factors would strengthen the position of these
Californios■, as the Mexican settlers were known, while
making their long-term control over the region much more
vulnerable to foreign interests. First was the development of
trade with other countries, which increased the number of
foreigners traveling to California. Many of the newcomers
would remain, bringing an element of self-sufficiency to local
settlements and weakening any dependence they once had on
the Mexican government. Second was the decision by the
Mexican government in 1833 to enact a general secularization
law, confiscating mission lands and redistributing them to
Californios.

Major portions of California territory had been administered by Franciscan priests, in cooperation and sometimes in
competition with local government agencies. The newly independent Mexican government favored a secular society based
more on nationalist sentiments than on religious doctrine.
Many *Californios* felt that the mission system, which allowed the
Catholic Church to control vast amounts of land and native labor, stifled the growth of an independent economy.[9]

The secularization of church land succeeded in redistributing land to the Californios and recent arrivals from Mexico,
but secularization created resentment and division among these
groups as well. The missions, along with the old colonial

administration and the Catholic Church, had kept order
throughout the state. The disappearance of their authority created a power vacuum. The Californios attempted to fill this
vacuum with their own local institutions and private organizations, thereby encouraging home rule and greater independence from Mexico. The Mexican government strongly resisted
any proposal for more independence by the Californios but
nevertheless encouraged foreign settlers, particularly American
fur trappers and maritime traders who sought a closer economic relationship with the Californios. A local movement for
American annexation of California soon emerged.[10]

The poorly trained and ill-supplied troops of the small
Mexican army often encountered conflicts with the Californios. Many Californios and American settlers considered annexation by the United States inevitable. Confidential
discussions had even taken place between the Californios and
Thomas Oliver Larkin, the U.S. consul in California, regarding
annexation. Influential figures within the U.S. government
were becoming more vocal about the right of America to satisfy its destiny as a world power of continental proportions.

One exponent of this **Manifest Destiny**■, Senator
Thomas Hart Benton, sought government support for his son-
in-law, John C. Frémont, an explorer who by 1845 had led two
U.S. Army expeditions to the Pacific Northwest. Today, more
than two centuries later, there is still speculation over Frémont's
true intentions for California. On the eve of the Mexican-
American War of 1846, he took steps to bring large areas of
California under American control by mobilizing settlers and
pro-American Californios, articulating plans to annex California, and providing important topographical information and vital intelligence to the American army. The war that began along
the Texas border soon spread to California, where Frémont was
already challenging Mexican control through his leadership of
the famous yet chaotic **Bear Flag Rebellion**■.

By January 1847, a force composed of Frémont's Bear Flag
rebels and recently arrived U.S. naval and army units accepted
the surrender of Mexican and loyal Californio military units. A
year later, the Treaty of Guadalupe Hidalgo officially ended the
Mexican-American War. This agreement (quite similar to an
offer rejected earlier by the Mexican government) transferred
about 40 percent of Mexico's territory, including California, to
the United States in return for a $15 million payment to Mex-
ico. California had become an official territory of the United
States, but the region's political and economic future would depend on a number of decisions still to be made.[11]

MYTH EXPOSED Many Californians believe that the Mexican-
American War of 1846 was a conflict over the future of the then Texas Republic. Although the bulk of the
fighting between American and Mexican forces would start in
Texas and move south into Mexico, this war would have consequences for the nation well beyond Texas territory. The

■ **Manifest Destiny:**
The belief that the United
States had a divinely inspired
mission to span the
continent of North America.

SIGNIFICANCE: *The
notion of Manifest Destiny
eventually spread to the Pacific,
with the annexation of Hawaii
and the Philippine Islands.*

■ **Bear Flag Rebellion:** A revolt
led by John C. Frémont against
Mexican control of California in 1846.

SIGNIFICANCE: *The initial revolt was a
confused episode of competing alliances motivated by
aspirations of California independence, American
nationalism, and narrow commercial interests.*

A mural by Anton Refregier depicts the Bear Flag of the California Republic being
raised in Sonoma, June 1846. —*How does Anton Refregier attempt to depict
California history in this mural? Does the mural take a realistic approach to this
history or is he trying to convey ideas or perpetuate certain myths?*

Mexican-American War remains for many a controversial event
in American history, lending itself to a variety of interpretations,
but having momentous effects on the shape and design of the
American West. People point to three different causes of the
Mexican-American War: (1) the U.S. military response to
aggression by the Mexican government against the independent
republic of Texas, (2) U.S. annexation of the independent
Republic of Texas in 1845 over Mexico's objections, and
(3) long-term U.S. plans to annex Northern Mexico—California
in particular—regardless of Mexican sovereignty and official
boundaries. In actuality, the war was likely fought because of a
combination of all three reasons.

The Gold Rush and Statehood for California

One of the pivotal events shaping California's development occurred on January 24, 1848, when James W. Marshall discovered
gold while constructing a mill on the American River. Marshall
was actually working for John Sutter, who had built a fort in
the Sacramento Valley that had become a popular trading post.
Although Sutter attempted to keep the discovery secret, by the
end of 1849 over 100,000 people had thronged to the American River and other parts of California in search of easy wealth.

Although the Gold Rush brought riches to some lucky
prospectors and profits to many merchants and outfitters,
it also brought serious social problems with unfortunate

consequences for the original settlers of California. The Gold
Rush miners overran most Native Californian settlements,
committing murder and abuse. A large number of Californios
and former Mexican settlers either lost their property outright or were forced into lengthy disputes over land rights.
Most American settlers made very little profit from the discovery of gold; even Sutter and Marshall ended their lives in
poverty, unable to cope with the onslaught of gold seekers.
The insatiable greed of many gold miners and merchants
stained the pages of California history with racism, price
gouging, and lawlessness.

Although actual dates vary, the California Gold Rush
gradually came to an end during the 1860s. The discovery of
silver at the Comstock Lode in Nevada lured miners with a yen
for easy riches out of California. Historical data on the California Gold Rush suggest that most of the thousands of "Forty-
Niners" never made enough profit to justify their mining
operations; very few made real fortunes. The miners did, however, cause serious ecological problems that are still evident today, such as the degradation of rivers and foothills.

Legacies of the Gold Rush

The chief legacy of the Gold Rush would not be riches but
rather thousands of new residents, increased commerce, and
closer attention from the federal government. It is doubtful so
many people would have risked the perilous journey to California and the hardships they found on arrival were it not for

■ **Proslavery and Antislavery Factions:** The legislative representatives of these groups in Congress were eventually able to compromise and pass a bill that allowed California to become a state quickly.

SIGNIFICANCE: *Within 10 years, the compromise worked out between these two groups would eventually break down upon the election of Abraham Lincoln, and the country would be embroiled in a catastrophic civil war.*

Early Chinese immigrants, who were banned from mining, opened stores and businesses in Chinatown districts. —*What does this picture imply about the plight of early Chinese immigrants and how well they survived after being prohibited from gold mining?*

the lure of gold. The mass migration to the gold fields included settlers from around the world, particularly China and South America, thus laying the foundation for California's emerging diversity. The Gold Rush also produced many lucrative and long-lasting commercial opportunities for enterprising migrants. Among the notable examples are Wells Fargo Bank, originally organized by a stage coach express company; the Levi Strauss Company, founded by a traveling salesperson who became a popular clothing manufacturer; and the hundreds of restaurants and retail stores opened by Chinese immigrants who were legally barred from mining. These commercial activities would be financed by Californian investors who acquired their fortunes either directly from the gold mines or from some related business. Most important, however, the Gold Rush hastened the development of governmental institutions in California, fostering the state's unique political heritage.

There was considerable indecision over California's political future after American annexation in 1848. Legally, the new territory was governed by the U.S. Army, but self-governing communities soon sprang up, San Francisco being one of the more independent. Each major political constituency had its own unique vision for future state government—the former Mexican colonial administrators, southern Californios who followed Pablo de la Guerra, northern Californios represented by Mariano Vallejo, early settler communities led by John Sutter, former federal officials and agents such as Thomas Larkin and John C. Frémont, the Mormon and merchant community represented by Sam Brannan, and the growing number of miners. Typically, years of study and preparation are required before a U.S. territory can be admitted into the Union. A stalemate in Congress over a number of controversial issues regarding slavery, including the decision to permit slavery in California, might have caused an even longer delay. Instead, within a year and a half of annexation, California's military governor, General Bennett Riley, had issued a call for a constitutional convention that would pave the way for California being admitted to the union as the thirty-first state.

Hundreds of thousands of people were migrating to the California gold fields, and Congress could not ignore the possibility of losing a large number of its citizens to the newly annexed territory. Unless California became a state, the national government might be unable to take advantage of the Gold Rush. Both the **proslavery and antislavery factions**■ in Congress ultimately accepted a compromise proposed by Kentucky Senator Henry Clay, agreeing to admit California as a free state while strengthening the fugitive slave law and leaving the slavery issue open in the other territories.

While Congress debated the compromise, General Riley took the extraordinary step of organizing the new California territorial government without federal approval. He was uneasy with the power to exercise what amounted to a military dictatorship over such disparate groups, and he was anxious to find a prompt replacement for traditional Mexican governmental institutions. So when Congress was finally ready to consider admission of California in 1850, Californians already had a government in waiting: a state constitution, a state legislature, and a state executive.[12] Even though powerful mining interests succeeded in establishing a state government with very limited formal powers, numerous provisions in this first constitution—a free public school system and property rights for women, among others—began the California tradition of innovative solutions to social issues and problems.[13]

The institutions of the new government were a mixture of traditions held over from the Spanish and Mexican past, political and commercial expediency, and novel ideas about American society. The first California constitution was strongly influenced by the optimism and inexperience of the 48 delegates to the first California constitutional convention, two-thirds of whom were in their twenties and thirties. The convention would rely on the state constitutions of New York and Iowa as models. Six of the delegates represented the Californios, who argued for the preservation of certain Spanish and Mexican customs and institutions. Although most of their suggestions were voted down, they did succeed in getting Spanish adopted as the official second language of the territory, and they were partly responsible for many of the more progressive features of the new constitution. Unfortunately, political inclusion of the Mexican American community in California would not last, hindered by precarious immigration status, cultural differences, and the tacit restrictions on political participation. In many respects, the eventual advance of Mexican Americans into mainstream politics over the years serves as a testimony to the struggles and perseverance of this community since the period of early statehood when the possibilities for full integration would be delayed for another 100 years.

Mexican Control Yields to U.S. Annexation

16.2   **Outline the historical developments and political transformations that led to the U.S. annexation of California.**

PRACTICE QUIZ: UNDERSTAND AND APPLY

1. Mexican settlers living in California were called
   a. Native Americans.
   b. Spaniards.
   c. Mexicanos.
   d. Californios.

2. Leading political figures in the United States believed the country had a divine mission to be a world power of continental proportions. That mission was called
   a. Manifest Destiny.
   b. New World Obligations.
   c. Imperialism.
   d. Continental Conservatism.

3. Which of these groups would be the least likely to see the Gold Rush as a benefit?
   a. Californios
   b. Native Californians
   c. American settlers
   d. South American immigrants

4. The most important factor in the decision of the U.S. government to grant statehood to California was
   a. the defeat of the Mexican government during the Mexican-American War.
   b. the discovery of gold.
   c. the need for land.
   d. the poor administration of Spanish missions in California.

ANALYZE

1. What factors led to the decline of Spanish and then Mexican influence in California?

2. What role did the doctrine of Manifest Destiny play in the American conquest of California? Would Californians today support this doctrine?

IDENTIFY THE CONCEPT THAT DOESN'T BELONG

a. Commercial opportunities
b. Ecological degradation
c. Mass migration
d. Fundraising prowess
e. Insatiable greed

Resource Center
• Glossary
• Vocabulary Example
• Connect the Link

Early Years of Statehood

16.3 Describe how the construction of the transcontinental railroad shaped the politics and economy of California.
(pages 506–509)

With the economic boost of the Gold Rush and successful development of a working government, few doubted the new state of California would make a major contribution to America's growth and power. Before the state's potential could be realized, however, the enormous distance between California and the rest of the nation would have to be conquered. In 1860, there were three basic routes to California: a two-month, overland trip by horse-drawn wagon from Missouri; a six-month voyage by ship around South America; and a six-week passage from the Gulf of Mexico by way of a 100-mile portage across the malaria-infested Isthmus of Panama, followed by another voyage along the Pacific coast. The most practical, but extremely daunting, alternative was a **transcontinental railroad,** which would cut the travel time between New York City and San Francisco down to one week.

The Big Four

Theodore Judah, the early California pioneer and railroad-building engineer who first conceived of the transcontinental route, succeeded in convincing four of Sacramento's leading businessmen to invest in his new enterprise.

Three of the four—Collis P. Huntington, Mark Hopkins, and Charles Crocker—were successful merchants during the Gold Rush; the fourth, Leland Stanford, was a lawyer who later became governor of California. Together they formed the Central Pacific Railroad Company and earned their place in California history as the **Big Four.** Obtaining generous loans, grants, and property rights from county, state, and federal governments, the Big Four succeeded in completing the western half of the transcontinental railroad, which joined the track laid by the Union Pacific Railroad Company from the east at Promontory Point in Utah Territory on May 10, 1869.

The Pacific Railway Act of 1862, passed by Congress and signed into law by President Abraham Lincoln, was especially instrumental in making the transcontinental railroad a reality. The federal government desperately wanted a transcontinental railroad linking the east and west coasts. In addition to federal loans and grants, the act provided land grants that averaged roughly 10 square miles for every mile of track laid. Once completed, the transcontinental railroad gave the Big Four virtual control over most of the state's economy.[14]

The completion of the transcontinental railroad ended California's geographic isolation and opened up the state for tremendous commercial expansion. The Big Four would eventually control all major forms of transportation, the industries that used them, and the political institutions that depended on them. They would succeed in acquiring or controlling other local and regional railroad networks, giving them control over almost 85 percent of rail transport in California. In 1870, amid charges of fraud and monopoly, the Central Pacific and Southern Pacific railroad companies would merge to provide rail service to Southern California and the American West.

Picks and shovels, wheelbarrows and one-horse dump carts, black powder and hand drills were the meager tools and materials with which Central Pacific laborers dug and hacked their way over the towering Sierra Nevada. —*What conclusions can you reach about the early years of statehood from this photograph? Does this photograph present any ideas about how the state would develop in the future?*

The Central Pacific had accumulated a huge amount of debt building the transcontinental railroad, and the Big Four were determined to maximize their profits with little regard to business ethics. Even before their rail monopoly was complete, the Big Four began buying up international and domestic steamship lines. With little or no effective state regulation of commerce, the Central Pacific was able to set its own shipping rates for more than 30 years. Corporations that enjoyed close business relations with the Big Four were given preferential treatment. The Standard Oil Company, for example, paid lower shipping rates for its oil and in turn supplied cheap fuel for Central Pacific trains. By exploiting their monopolistic powers to the fullest, the Big Four kept whole industries on the verge of bankruptcy with excessive freight charges. They also profited from the outright sale of the free land grants they received from the federal government, which amounted to nearly 11.4 percent of the land in California. The sale of this land, encompassing much of the state's lumber, mineral, petroleum, and water reserves, was very controversial, resulting in many lawsuits and at least one gun battle, which was immortalized in Frank Norris's muckraking novel *The Octopus.*[15]

Through their Southern Pacific Political Bureau, the railroads determined the course of California's political development. The historian Walton Bean writes, "Not only did the railroad control the party organizations, but it played them against each other and secretly fostered new factions to keep the old ones in check." The railroad's money "was the power behind almost every political throne and behind almost every insurgent revolt."[16] To avoid being bypassed by the Southern

Pacific route through Southern California, the city of Los Angeles agreed to give the company 22 miles of track, land for a depot, and thousands of dollars in subsidies. By subsidizing major newspapers, the Big Four also controlled public opinion in the state for decades. As the 1870s came to a close, the Big Four's domination of California was just about complete. Economic depression throughout the state, however, gave opponents of the railroad barons the opportunity to galvanize public opinion in the attempt to break the railroad monopoly.

Revolt Against the Railroads: The Second California Constitution

California in the late nineteenth century was the home of a vigorous working class, brawny and rugged enough to meet the challenges of an isolated and as yet economically undeveloped society. Even the most prosperous families of California had started as ambitious entrepreneurs who benefited from the exploitation of the state's natural wealth. The state's working class blamed these tycoons for the bank failures, stock fraud, unemployment, and rampant poverty of the late 1870s. Led by Denis Kearney, an immigrant sailor from Ireland, the **Workingmen's Party** successfully exploited public condemnation of wealthy merchants and the Big Four to win many local elections. Kearney's inflammatory speeches, which combined denunciation of railroad monopolies with virulent attacks on Chinese workers, became especially popular with California's large, working-class population.

This political cartoon, published in 1878 in San Francisco, backed Denis Kearney and his Chinese labor exclusion policy. —*Beside the obvious aversion to Chinese immigrants, what does this cartoon suggest about the attitudes of people living in California during the late 1800s?*

■ **Grange:**
A farmers' political movement founded in 1867.

EXAMPLE: *After a history of over 140 years, 248 Grange New York State chapters continue to advocate for the interests of farmers. Although membership in the New York State Granges has fallen dramatically, organizers of this rural-based organization, in which membership is open to those aged 5 to 105, hope to attract a new generation of members seeking a return to a simpler, family-oriented lifestyle.*

When workers, during the building of the transcontinental railroad, increasingly jumped ship for the silver mines in Nevada, the Central Pacific Railroad chose to recruit workers from China. These Chinese Californians became a readily available scapegoat for Kearney and the Workingmen's Party, who accused them of undermining the wages of white workers and stealing their jobs. Cultural and physical differences between white and Chinese workers further inflamed the bigotry of the largely uneducated working class. The Workingmen's Party portrayed the Chinese as pawns of the Big Four in a conspiracy to oppress white workers. Kearney and other blue-collar agitators channeled popular outrage into political demands for reform of the state's constitution.

On September 5, 1877, Californians voted to authorize the election of delegates to a convention to be held in Sacramento to reconsider and revise the state constitution of 1849. The 152 delegates who attended the constitutional convention of 1879 included an assortment of Workingmen's Party leaders, representatives of the **Grange**■—a nonpartisan farmers' organization—a small contingent from the Republican Party, and various splinter groups. After six months of drafting and debate, they produced a new California constitution more than seven times as long as the Constitution of the United States. This new constitution contained provisions to regulate railroads and corporate influence in the state through regulatory commissions, new corporate tax laws, and restrictions on the power of the state legislature. The greatest accomplishment of the convention may have been the creation of a state railroad commission of three members elected to four-year terms. This commission would have the power to set railroad rates and impose fines for violations of commission regulations.

Other new provisions sought to improve the lives of workers by establishing an eight-hour workday for government employees and encouraging the expansion of public education. A majority of the delegates also agreed to constitutional language that restricted Chinese employment and removed the Spanish language from official documents.[17] The deletion of Spanish as the other official language of the state was yet another major step that marked the gradual erosion of rights granted to Mexicans who remained after the first constitutional convention or would immigrate to the state. For at least the first 100 years of the Mexican American experience in California, assimilation into the state's political institutions was largely blocked by the type of forces that refused to accept a bilingual California.

This new California constitution made an effort to address economic and political inequality in the state, but the attempted reforms were weakened by divergent interests at the convention, the lack of education of most delegates, and manipulation by powerful interests. Differences among the urban Workingmen's Party, the conservative agrarian interests of the Grange, and the state monopolies represented by a few highly qualified lawyers made it almost impossible to truly address political and economic injustice in the state. Few delegates from the Workingmen's Party or the Grange had much more than a grade school education; they were hardly able to comprehend California's economic and political problems, much less solve them.

The popularity of the Workingmen's Party and the Grange generated enough votes to ratify the new constitution by a small majority, but doubt and disillusionment with the new government were widespread. In the long run, the California constitution of 1879 would have little meaningful impact on social and economic inequality or the power of the Big Four.

The constitutional reforms that the Big Four and other corporate interests could not circumvent through legal loopholes or impede in court were nullified through bribery. Over the years, the Southern Pacific Political Bureau developed a knack for influencing the three permanent railroad commissioners charged with regulating and overseeing the railroad. It would be easy to blame the Big Four and the corporations for California's problems, but in fact, these interests could only corrupt what was already corruptible. The "malefactors of great wealth" had simply perfected the techniques of fraud and force practiced against Native Americans, Californios, and Chinese ever since the Gold Rush. The constitutional convention of 1878 did, however, demonstrate that democratic principles could provide the impetus for change if citizens were intellectually and ethically prepared to grasp the reins of government.

Early Years of Statehood

16.3 Describe how the construction of the transcontinental railroad shaped the politics and economy of California.

PRACTICE QUIZ: UNDERSTAND AND APPLY

1. The Big Four were responsible for
   a. the discovery of gold in California and silver in Nevada.
   b. the suppression of Native Californians.
   c. building the western portion of the transcontinental railroad.
   d. building the railroad equipment used in railroad construction.

2. The best reason for the failure of the revised state constitution of 1879 was
   a. anti-Chinese sentiment.
   b. poor educational background of most delegates.
   c. interference from the federal government.
   d. Native Californian protests.

3. What was the one factor or feature of Chinese workers that made scapegoating them possible?
   a. appearance   c. education
   b. wealth   d. personal habits

ANALYZE

1. Why was the transcontinental railroad built? What impact did it have on politics in California?

2. What were the strengths and weaknesses of the Workingmen's Party?

IDENTIFY THE CONCEPT THAT DOESN'T BELONG

a. State railroad commission
b. Eight-hour workday
c. Anticorruption measures
d. Expansion of public education
e. Restrictions on Chinese employment

16.3

Resource Center
- Glossary
- Vocabulary Example
- Connect the Link

■ **Direct Democracy:** Through the leadership of the California Progressives a constitutional amendment was passed by voters that provided for direct participation in government.

EXAMPLE: *In recent years, the recall has been used to unseat a governor; the referendum has been the regular approval mechanism for bond measures; and the initiative process has been responsible for a major property tax reduction.*

The Twentieth Century: The Progressive Era and Rapid Economic Growth

16.4 Summarize the major political and economic developments in California during the twentieth century.

(pages 510–513)

On November 6, 1908, San Francisco's assistant district attorney, Francis J. Heney, was shot and seriously wounded under suspicious circumstances while prosecuting city boss Abraham Ruef for corruption. Heney's replacement, assistant district attorney Hiram Johnson, faced the daunting task of confronting one of the most powerful and corrupt political organizations in the state. Johnson would rise to the challenge, winning the conviction of Boss Ruef and, in doing so, launching a political career that would set higher ethical standards in California politics.

To the end of his long political career, Hiram Johnson would embody in California the national Progressive movement, which sought to rid government of corruption and restore democratic principles across America.[18] Like others of his generation, Johnson had received the benefits of public education, entered a profession, and shared in California's growth. Yet, as a new century began, the middle class aspirations of Johnson and his generation were stymied by political and economic systems that too often rewarded those who engaged in graft and intimidation. Born into an untamed land that fostered rugged individualism and hardiness, but instilled with a greater appreciation for education and professional status, Johnson and many of his generation realized their power to reject the status quo. Progressivism, the nationwide movement to reform government, provided this new generation of Californians with the ideals and ideology to face Southern Pacific, other powerful interests, and corruption in government.[19]

REGULAR PROGRESSIVE NOMINATIONS
For President
THEODORE ROOSEVELT *OF NEW YORK.*
For Vice-President
HIRAM JOHNSON *OF CALIFORNIA.*

A banner from the 1612 election campaign for Theodore Roosevelt and Hiram Johnson as the Progressive ("Bull Moose") party candidates for president and vice president. *—What are the features of this banner that would cause a voter to support these candidates and what features could discourage a voter? Is it an effective campaign banner?*

"Unquestionably incorruptible and courageous," Hiram Johnson led the California Progressives into government as the newly elected governor of California in 1911. Under his leadership, from 1911 until 1916, when he unsuccessfully ran as Theodore Roosevelt's Bull Moose Party running mate, Governor Johnson pushed through a number of important reform measures that would finally break the near-total control of corporate monopolies and corrupt government officials.

One of the most significant measures of this period, first as state legislation and later as a constitutional amendment, was the strengthening of the railroad commission by increasing its size and budget and by requiring that the commissioners be appointed rather than elected. Not content with only busting up railroads monopolies, the Progressives empowered this commission to regulate all public utilities. Almost single-handedly, Governor Johnson also convinced California voters to approve another constitutional amendment that would provide Californians with avenues for **direct democracy**■, specifically consisting of the initiative, recall, and referendum.

During his tenure as governor, Johnson guided his fellow Progressives in the state legislature to adopt laws regulating child labor and workmen's compensation, form an employment bureau, set a minimum wage for government employees, and reform banking laws. The creation of commissions became a very popular approach for Governor Johnson and the state legislature to keep government both honest and democratic. These commissions addressed such issues as conservation, corporations, immigration and housing, irrigation, civil service, and industrial welfare, but the State Board of Control was especially successful in ensuring for the first time that state government was run professionally and prudently, saving California millions of dollars in the first year of its existence.[20]

Although Governor Johnson and the Progressives championed clean and responsive government, their political orientation was anything but radical—or even liberal in the contemporary sense. Beneath the Progressive ideological surface lay a deep respect for free-market capitalism and other middle-class values that were often at odds with the interests of the working class in California. During this period, anti-Asian sentiment once again became popular, this time directed at the Japanese, and the Progressives quickly translated this fervor into the **Alien Land bill**■. Initially, this bill was designed to exclude all Japanese from land ownership, but because it would cause potential treaty violations with Japan and was constitutionally dubious, the Progressives settled for preventing aliens who were not eligible for citizenship from owning land.

By Governor Johnson's second term, the Progressives became less inclined to support the interests of labor over those of business, especially when it came to union organizing. Their efforts to regulate morality with legislation—banning, for example, prize fighting, horse-race betting, and alcohol consumption—were unpopular. Realizing that their social and economic policies put

■ **Alien Land Bill:** A 1913 law that prohibited aliens not eligible for citizenship from owning land.

EXAMPLE: *During World War II, the state legislature enacted laws that made it easier for the state government to seize the land of Japanese aliens. By 1952, the California Supreme Court found the Alien Land Law of 1913 unconstitutional and in 1956, all Alien Land Laws were repealed in California by popular vote.*

them at odds with the public and many fellow party members, the leaders of the Progressives quietly returned to the California Republican Party and its conservative approach. Governor Johnson hurried this defection when he was elected as U.S. senator and went off to Washington, leaving his California Progressives without a strong progressive voice. Like the constitution of 1879, the California Progressive Era has many detractors, who consider it not much more than a middle-class revolt. On close analysis, however, it is clear the Progressives forced state government to be run in a democratic and efficient manner.[21]

Rapid Economic Growth

California's economy made great strides in the early twentieth century. Agricultural production, initially wheat and later fruit and vegetable cultivation, became a multimillion-dollar industry. This growth was made possible by large-scale water projects such as the Owens Valley Aqueduct, the Hoover Dam–Boulder Canyon and Central Valley, and the Hetch Hetchy Valley, which were also responsible for large population surges in Southern California. For many decades, however, California remained geographically isolated from the rest of the nation. In 1900, the population of California was barely a million and a half people, ranking well below at least half of the other American states. Gradually, Americans did come west to participate in the state's rapid economic growth, fueled in part by discoveries of huge oil reserves in Southern California during the 1920s that coincided with the growth of the automobile industry. The motion picture industry, headquartered in Hollywood, became a highly lucrative form of popular entertainment, enhancing the state's aura of glamour. As the Great Depression spread across the country, California became the last hope of economic survival for many Americans, vividly depicted by John Steinbeck in his tale of the Joad family in his novel *The Grapes of Wrath*.

World War II: The Boom Years

As America entered World War II, California became the major staging area and logistics point for waging war against the Japanese in the Pacific. Almost overnight, the state was transformed as the site for the deployment of over 1.5 million military personnel, the construction of more military installations than in any other state, and the expenditure by the war's end of over $35 billion in federal funds. California also became a major location for defense industries, accounting for 11.9 percent of all U.S. government war contracts and 17 percent of all the material produced for the war. More than 1.6 million Americans moved to California during the war, and a large share were employed by Southern Californian companies specializing in aviation, or the Northern Californian shipbuilding industry. Forty-four percent of all aircraft and close to 40 percent of all naval and freight ships used during the war were constructed in

A group of Bainbridge Island Japanese citizens marches under Army escort at a Seattle dock before heading to a Manzanar, California, detainment camp as friends and relatives, soon to be evacuated, bid them farewell. —*Does this photo raise any ethical or moral issues or can the setting and actions of the individuals depicted ever be justified from an ethical or moral point of view?*

California. The defense industries, competing with the wartime draft for labor, were obliged to employ a diverse workforce, including minorities and women, who had formerly been denied semiskilled industrial jobs. Such job opportunities dramatically increased the African American population in California and gave the struggle for women's equality a major boost, immortalized by the image of "Rosie the Riveter."[22]

Although the war brought about an impressive array of economic benefits to some Californians, it sacrificed the livelihood of

Between 1942 and 1964, the Bracero Temporary Worker Program would recruit over 3 million Mexican workers into the United States before being ended because of the influx of illegal workers, the mechanization of farm production, and mounting complaints about the harsh treatment of these workers. —*Could a temporary foreign worker program similar to the Bracero arrangement solve California's undocumented worker problems today?*

■ **Executive Order 9066:** Franklin Roosevelt's 1942 order that resulted in the relocation and internment of Japanese legal aliens and American citizens of Japanese descent.

EXAMPLE: *Japanese citizens and legal residents living in Hawaii were not subject to mass internment during World War II even though they made up a third of the population. Despite their strategic location, the Hawaiian Islands did not experience a single act of sabotage by members of the Japanese community during the entire war.*

others. Within three months of the bombing of Pearl Harbor, President Franklin Roosevelt issued **Executive Order 9066**■, resulting in the relocation and internment of 110,000 Japanese legal aliens and American citizens, most of whom came from California. The Japanese in California lost much of their property and other possessions. By implementing the evacuation order, America, and California in particular, lost an element of its moral credibility. This episode of American history continues to serve as a reminder about the fragility of freedom.[23]

To alleviate agricultural labor shortages due to the war, the U.S. and Mexican governments instituted the **Bracero Program**■ in 1942, which granted Mexicans temporary employment status in the United States to cultivate and harvest crops. Although the program did offer employment opportunities to impoverished Mexican farmers, Bracero labor contracts permitted unfair wages, poor working conditions, and oppressive restrictions.

PATHWAYS of action

"La Raza" Legacy

By the 1960s, it was apparent to many Latinos that both mainstream political parties were determined to limit significant political participation of the Mexican-American electorate through such tactics as the gerrymandering, blocking voter registration, enacting discriminatory laws, and selective intimidation. In response to this predicament, various activists, led by Jose Angel Gutiérrez in Texas and Rodolfo "Corky" Gonzales in Colorado, attempted to build a third or independent political party that pursued political representation and reform based on the ideas of self-determination, political empowerment, and ethnic solidarity among Mexican Americans. The notion of the La Raza Unida Party (LRUP) became the theme or foundation for that political movement.

From the beginning, La Raza had a difficult time attracting most Mexican-American voters, who had long-standing ties to the Democratic Party. Mexican Americans by and large favored the cultural solidarity advocated by the LRUP but found that the separatist and electoral goals of the party were in conflict with the structure of American electoral politics as well as the economic necessity of assimilation. By the late 1970s, the contradictions and internal disagreements associated with the LRUP caused the party to decline in prominence and jettison its electoral and mass organizing strategy. The LRUP did, however, establish a framework for organizing and unifying the Mexican American community.

However short-lived LRUP's electoral expectation proved to be, the thousands of LRUP chapters established throughout California provided the experience and framework for grassroots action, stressing the importance of political efficacy or political self-reliance. Since the founding of the LRUP, literally thousands of Mexican American political and social groups have emerged,

and a large number of the local, legislative, and statewide Latino leaders in California were either political beneficiaries of the LRUP or organizations that mirrored its tactics. By identifying with La Raza, Mexican Americans are today reaffirming unity, respect of cultural values, and a willingness to work for the betterment of the Latino community.

Certain American pundits and political commentators have found the term "La Raza" offensive, suggesting that it implies racial superiority or anti-Americanism. Although the term has been identified with the jargon of Mexican nationalism that mandates the recapture of territory lost to American annexation and the creation of "Aztlan," few Americans, regardless of their ethnic background, take this view very seriously. Many student and community-based organizations have been successful in fostering and articulating many of the original principles of the LRUP, expanding the meaning of "La Raza" with variations such as "Viva la Raza," "La Nueva Raza," and "Mi Raza Primero." These same groups and principles have been instrumental in mobilizing Mexican Americans and other groups around the issue of immigration that culminated on May 1, 2006 with the "A Day Without Immigrants" demonstration when more than 1 million people in cities throughout California and the United States participated in a massive demonstration to denounce laws proposed by Congress that would increase the penalties for illegal immigration and to advocate for the decriminalization of illegal immigration.

That demonstration was clearly a sign that the notion of La Raza is very much alive and a force to be taken seriously. It is doubtful that La Raza will return to the days of third-party activism, but the specter of that identity and the size of the Mexican American community could prove to be a decisive force in California politics.

SOURCE: Susan Ferriss, "1 Million Protest," *Sacramento Bee*, May 2, 2006, p. A1; James Sterngold, "Spanish-Language Radio Spread Word of L.A. Protest," *San Francisco Chronicle*, March 30, 2006, p. A8; Ernesto Chávez, *"Mi Raza Primero!" (My People First): Nationalism, Identity, and Insurgency in the Chicano Movement in Los Angeles, 1966–1978* (Berkeley: University of California Press, 2002); Carlos Munoz, *Youth, Identity, Power: The Chicano Movement* (New York: Verso, 1989).

The Postwar Years: The Boom Continues

In the immediate postwar years, massive federal wartime expenditures, defense industry innovations, the sacrifices of workers and the armed services, and geographic splendor together propelled California to the forefront of the American experience. For the next 50 years, these factors would help California become the epitome of American culture and progress. Such cultural icons as Disneyland, Hollywood, and the surfer scene would set nationwide trends and transform the Golden State

■ **Bracero Program:** A program granting temporary employment status to Mexicans working in the United States beginning with the start of World War II.

SIGNIFICANCE: *During the Depression, tens of thousands of Mexicans and their American-born children were expelled from California. Mexican nationals would again be recruited for work in California and other states when World War II caused major labor shortages.*

into the envy of the world. For World War II defense industries that failed to retool for a peacetime economy, the Cold War created a continued demand for military weapons and technology, applying, for example, the concentration of aviation technology to the development of missile systems. In the spirit of true Progressives, initially under the leadership of Governor Earl Warren, the state government played a substantial role in guiding California through this era of prosperity, spending massive amounts of funds to facilitate this progress. These massive expenditures resulted in some of the finest public colleges and universities, highways, and health and welfare systems in the world. Yet the state would not be without its problems. California served as a microcosm of the nation, taking part in the hunt for un-American activities of the 1950s, developing pockets of urban and rural poverty, contributing to the degradation of the environment, and falling victim to escalating crime. Slowly, these problems gained ground while California's assets declined. And when government appeared incapable of addressing this narrowing gap between progress and problems, Californians, utilizing the electoral tools inherited from the Progressives, would act.

The Late Twentieth Century: Economic Decline

Like most of the world, at the end of the twentieth century California entered a period of resource scarcity. Globalization made a great deal of the state's industrial capacity obsolete. Beginning in the late 1970s, large quantities of industrial production in California, especially in the steel industry, were supplanted by Asian companies that had built newer factories and could offer more competitive pricing. Once producing enough surplus industrial goods to export them to the world, California found its ports crowded with incoming Chinese goods. The economy of the state was also hurt by the end of the Cold War, which rendered many defense-related industries unnecessary. Stock market failures in the mid-1980s and again at the end of the 1990s cost the state both tax revenue and jobs. California maintained its status as a leading exporting state primarily as the result of its booming high-tech sector. However, even the high-tech industry found itself in crisis at the turn of the century with the dot.com bust, which drained much of the venture capital that had funded the growth of this industry.

The Twentieth Century: The Progressive Era and Rapid Economic Growth

16.4 Summarize the major political and economic developments in California during the twentieth century.

PRACTICE QUIZ: UNDERSTAND AND APPLY

1. Large discoveries of oil occurred in what geographic location of California?
   a. Northern California
   b. San Francisco Bay Area
   c. Southern California
   d. Sierra Nevada range

2. Hiram Johnson would embody in California the
   a. national Progressive movement.
   b. principles of the Workingmen's Party.
   c. work ethic of the immigrant population.
   d. desire to get rich quickly.

3. Agricultural growth was made possible in California through
   a. scientific methods of farming.
   b. the removal of the Sierra Nevada mountain range.
   c. large-scale water projects.
   d. environmental conservation due to the Gold Rush.

4. What was one of the major consequences of World War II for California?
   a. Heavy damage was inflicted on Californian cities due to the war.
   b. The war eliminated the racial hostility that had arisen during the construction of the railroads.
   c. The war was responsible for a major increase in industrial production.
   d. California experienced an economic crisis due to a drop in federal spending in the state.

ANALYZE

1. How similar or dissimilar were the Workingmen's Party and the Progressives? What characteristics of these political parties can be found in California party politics today?

2. How did the influx of federal funding influence California's economy throughout the twentieth century?

IDENTIFY THE CONCEPT THAT DOESN'T BELONG

a. Pearl Harbor
b. Executive Order 9066
c. Bracero Program
d. Japanese internment
e. Alien Land Bill

Resource Center
• Glossary
• Vocabulary Example
• Connect the Link

California in the New Millennium

16.5 **Identify the major challenges facing California in the current period.**

(pages 514–517)

In California state history, there have been many ups and downs. Economic decline was averted several times by the Internet and housing bubbles and the rapid growth of business opportunities that generated immense wealth and plenty of jobs. Prosperity was further sustained by the success of other emerging industries, such as biotechnology, health care, and an explosion of retail consumption.

The overall national banking and mortgage lending calamities of 2008–2009, however, and the burst of the state's own housing bubble, led to the large-scale reduction of California-based lending opportunities and major job loss in a host of housing-related industries. This in turn has caused statewide unemployment rates to go well beyond 10 percent, leading to a serious fiscal crisis. By the spring of 2009, state government revenue had plummeted by almost $34 billion.

Revitalizing the California economy will require a combination of forces, including the emergence of industries that can turn a profit and put people back to work, as well as the replenishment of state government revenue and the efficient restoration and management of the state's resources and infrastructure. California also faces a substantial list of long-term challenges that could have profound effects on future generations.

Few Californians need any polls or surveys to understand the importance of water and energy or that both resources will continue to generate major concern for some time. With limited rainfall, Californians live with the fear of a major drought, and as a result, most regions of the state have experienced increasing water costs to better manage this precious resource. Population growth in the state as well as the inevitability of climate change are causing a major rethinking of water conservation. In 2009, the state legislature approved legislation that would begin to address many of the long-standing problems and issues associated with the delivery of water, such as water supply, deteriorating levees, water quality, and ecological impacts. It remains to be seen whether this legislation can address all of these issues without causing major discord between environmentalists who are adamant about the need to tackle ecological degradation, agribusiness and local water districts that want more water, and southern Californians, who over the objections of the other groups, want more water to flow south. The state legislature is, of course, proposing to pay for these improvements through bond measures that must be approved by voters who are growing evermore skeptical of public debt.

For a state dependent on automobile transportation, high energy-consuming industries, and external electricity generation, Californians can be especially hard on government leaders who are perceived to be insensitive to energy concerns. There is little doubt that in 2003, Governor Gray Davis was recalled in large part because of the unfolding energy crisis in the power industry. Although state residents have historically paid some of the highest gas prices in the nation, the focus on energy in California has shifted in recent years from reliability and cost to ecological concerns, particularly as energy production and use runs counter to effects on climate and the development of renewable sources of energy. State government, under the leadership of Governor Schwarzenegger, responded with laws

With limited rainfall and a dry summer season, California has always been especially vulnerable to the outbreak and spread of raging fires. This vulnerability was evident during the summer of 2008, when over 1,700 fires swept throughout the state, causing billions of dollars in property damage and destruction and requiring nearly 20,000 firefighters to contain them. —*What human factors or conditions increase the likelihood of fires in California?*

■ **Proposition 13:** The law that severely cut property taxes in California.

SIGNIFICANCE: *Proposition 13 reduced the property tax rate by 57 percent. School districts lost roughly half their property tax revenue, which was gradually replaced with income and sales taxes.*

that mandate energy conservation and limit carbon emissions. In fact, California became one of the first states to establish a carbon credit scheme in which major carbon emitters could buy and sell the right to emit greenhouse gases. Slowly, however, opposition concentrated in the business community is growing against such efforts on the grounds that these laws are "job-killers" and will encourage major corporations to relocate to other states with less stringent energy policies.

Water and energy are not the only concerns. According to a statewide poll conducted by the Field Research Corporation in 2005, three out of four Californians identified "the well-being of children" as the issue they were most concerned about.[24] More than 20 percent of the children in the state live in poverty. In the 2000–2001 school year, almost 2.8 million, or 47 percent, of all public school students participated in the free or reduced-price meal programs offered in California schools, which in 2010 grew by almost 17 percent (source: U.S. Department of Agriculture). To be eligible for these programs in 2009–2010, a family of four had to earn less than $40,000 a year.[25] Education and schools, closely related to the plight of children, was ranked second among issues of extreme concern.[26] California has the largest school enrollment of any

state, fueled by a juvenile population that is growing faster than the adult population. Since the passage of **Proposition 13**■ in 1978, the traditional source of education funding, property taxes, have been severely cut. Per-pupil spending in public school districts across the state has been well below the national average. Although an attempt was made to restore lost funds through subsequent propositions and legislative acts, large outlays are required to meet the special needs of "English learners," who comprise more than 25 percent of the public school population.[27]

Over the past 20 years, crime and law enforcement has stayed high on the list of extreme concerns expressed by Californians, but whereas 71 percent of respondents were extremely concerned in 1986, the number dropped to 56 percent in 2005. The decreasing importance of crime and law enforcement may be related to the gradual decline in crime since 1984 and the explosion of the California prison population, which increased from 43,328 in 1984 to 150,354 in 2009.[28] Incarceration is a severe drain on state revenue, however, and it raises serious questions regarding the prison system's ability to prevent recidivism (repeat offenders) or rehabilitate the current inmate population.

Protesters march down Market Street in favor of immigration reform on May 1, 2006, in San Francisco. Immigrants and their allies rallied across the nation, taking part in boisterous protests as businesses that depend on their labor shut their doors. —*What would be the logical and symbolic purpose of the American flag in this photograph? What is the relationship of the signs, banners, and other graphic images to the displaying of the flag?*

Since the California Progressives convinced voters to add avenues for direct democracy—the initiative, referendum, and recall—to the electoral process more than a century ago, the initiative process in particular has become a popular method among California voters, interest groups, and government leaders to address critical as well as divisive issues facing the state. By allowing Californians to place measures on the ballot through petition drives, the initiative process has resulted in the enactment of various popular and controversial laws, including property tax reductions, life imprisonment for habitual criminals, and term limits for state legislators. Such power has caused the executive and legislative branches of government to react rather cautiously to the state's problems, to take steps to insulate themselves from public attention, and to avoid awakening the public's wrath. They have not been entirely successful, however. In 2008, the passage of Proposition 11 removed the state legislature's power to protect itself by creating safe legislative districts and placed the responsibility of redrawing state legislative districts in the hands of a nonpartisan commission.

The California legislature has long suffered from a seeming lack of leadership and low approval rating. The executive branch, led primarily by the governor, has encountered even more problems, partly because of the threatened use of direct democracy by an often impatient public and partly because the legislature has become increasingly partisan and hostile to the executive branch. It has not been uncommon for the radical wing of the governor's own party to rebel against executive policies. No matter how much a governor may oppose an initiative, once it has passed, he is bound to execute the law or policy, which may in turn result in diminished popularity. For example, despite his opposition, Governor Jerry Brown was forced to implement Proposition 13, causing a massive reduction in state revenue and forcing him to slash thousands of government jobs and services.

Gray Davis, elected governor in 1998, hoped to avoid the pitfalls of California politics. Choosing education, an issue popular with most Californians, as his major policy objective, Davis proclaimed that education would be his first, second, and third priorities and actually authorized $1.8 billion above required funding levels. Adept at steering clear of controversies, Governor Davis would follow a middle-of-the-road path, which would come back to haunt him during the energy crisis of 2002. By not taking a firm stand either for or against energy deregulation plans and by failing to provide an immediate and concrete solution to the energy crisis that resulted, Governor Davis became vulnerable to charges of indecisiveness from the Republican opposition. These attacks gave the public an identifiable target for its rage over energy price gouging and supply inequities. That rage ultimately fueled a recall campaign that essentially ended the political career of Gray Davis and replaced him with actor Arnold Schwarzenegger.

Governor Schwarzenegger completed his two terms in office in 2010, a tenure that in many ways typified the unforgiving nature of California politics. Schwarzenegger's success in the recall campaign and his popularity in office clearly met the desire of Californians for a strong but extraordinary leader who did not fit the profile of the stereotypical professional politician. Despite huge state government deficits and economic decline throughout California, a 2008 *Los Angeles Times*/CNN/Politico poll found that roughly three in five Californians believed Governor Schwarzenegger was "doing a good job," and one in five thought he was "doing a *very* good job."[29]

However, following the 2008–2009 national and state economic meltdown, the state government and Schwarzenegger,

With plummeting approval ratings, Governor Schwarzenegger picks a Towery Homes construction site to propose the extension of the homebuyers tax credit to include the purchase not only of new homes, but existing homes as well. —*What affect does the economy have on the approval rating of a governor?*

in particular, seemed incapable of anticipating or of solving the problems with a publically acceptable economic recovery plan. The Republican governor promoted a series of ballot measures that would limit spending, temporarily raise taxes, shift special funds to the state budget, and ban pay raises for state officials. However, not only were these measures rejected by the voters, but Schwarzenegger's approval rating in September 2009 dropped to an all-time low of 30 percent.

And so Schwarzenegger fared little better than Gray Davis, the recalled governor he replaced in 2003. If there were any lessons to be learned from the Schwarzenegger years, it may be that when governors in California promise to cut taxes, balance the budget, and preserve essential services, in the end they are expected to fulfill such promises.[30]

California in the New Millennium

16.5   Identify the major challenges facing California in the current period.

PRACTICE QUIZ: UNDERSTAND AND APPLY

1. Which of the following is not an issue or condition unique to California?
   a. hurricanes
   b. drought
   c. energy shortage
   d. direct democracy

2. The California energy crisis in 2001 occurred during the term of which California governor?
   a. Arnold Schwarzenegger
   b. Gray Davis
   c. Jerry Brown
   d. Earl Warren

3. The increasing popularity of the initiative process has caused the California legislative and executive branches to
   a. raise taxes.
   b. become more cooperative.
   c. become less willing to apply for federal grants to solve social problems.
   d. react rather cautiously to the state's problems.

ANALYZE

1. What are the most important challenges facing Californians in the early twenty-first century? How have California's physical environment and political legacy contributed to the current problems and the solutions Californians are seeking to implement?

2. Are there any long-term solutions to what seems to be California's perpetual energy crisis? Does a solution require either greater government intervention or greater reliance on the marketplace, or is there another answer beyond these two options?

IDENTIFY THE CONCEPT THAT DOESN'T BELONG

a. Automobile transportation
b. Energy-consuming industries
c. Referendum
d. External energy generation
e. Renewable sources of energy

Conclusion

Any review of historical events in California presents the opportunity to better understand the contemporary era and reflect on past accomplishments. Such a survey is also a reminder of lessons not completely learned and new questions to answer. Is California's lure fading today as natural and human-generated ecological challenges seem to be increasing? In addition to the variety of natural disturbances that regularly threaten the state—from earthquakes and flooding to drought and fire—Californians are particularly guilty of degrading the environment through seemingly irreversible long-term effects. California, for example, is home to six of the most polluted cities in the United States.[31] The shortlist of environmental damage across the state is well known if not obvious: water contamination, waste disposal, toxic chemical releases, and natural habitat destruction. In addition, California's carbon footprint and its effects on climate change—which is slowly causing the snowcaps on the Sierra Nevada to evaporate more rapidly each year—are especially worrisome to many Californians as well as individuals across the United States and the globe. Although the state government has taken the lead on attempts to reduce the large amount of carbon dioxide produced in the state, few Californians seem willing to make the types of sacrifice that would substantially reduce their carbon footprint.

Clearly, there is reason to celebrate the economic prosperity that many Native Californians have achieved, reversing centuries of hardship and mistreatment. That prosperity, realized through the proliferation of the gambling industry on tribal lands across California, is all too often produced at the expense of others. Will Native Californians, not unlike many of the beneficiaries of their past dislocation and victimization, live to regret the legacy of this newly found prosperity?

Various features of California's Hispanic legacy continue to confound relations between Californians and Mexicans. It seems that so much of that relationship, not so different from the past, suffers from a crisis of identities: old-fashioned Americanism versus Latino culture, governmental services versus tax contributions, Mexican drug cartels versus America's illicit drug consumption, population growth versus assimilation, and of course labor needs versus immigration laws. The severity of immigration issues and the plight of undocumented workers came to a head on May 1, 2006, when more than 1 million people in cities throughout California and the United States participated in a massive demonstration to denounce laws proposed by Congress that would increase the penalties for illegal immigration and to advocate the decriminalization of illegal immigration. The one-day boycott by employees and students was as much a demonstration of Mexican American solidarity as it was a well-coordinated and visible mass protest. On this day, Mexican Americans exhibited their considerable presence and willingness to circumvent the conventional political process to make their demands.

If events in California history are any indication of the ability to overcome adversity, Californians are destined to persevere despite the hardships of the current economic slump. Just as former residents of the state eventually overcame economic decline during the 1870s, monopolistic control, the Great Depression, and the sacrifices of World War II, Californians will inevitably get beyond the current mortgage crisis, high unemployment rates, and cuts in government services. The devil of course is in the details and questions remain: How long will it take for Californians to find the right balance among the conflicting demands of the 38 million residents who will produce the long-term solutions leading to social and economic recovery?

KEY CONCEPT MAP ### How have key events in California's past shaped its politics?

1848
Discovery of Gold at Sutter's Mill

The discovery of gold leads Congress to agree to a compromise forbidding slavery in California while expanding it in other states. This compromise hastens California's admission to the Union as the 31st state.

Critical Thinking Questions

What if Congress had admitted California as a slave state instead of as a free state? What if Congress had not been able to agree to any sort of compromise? How might this have impacted later events such as the Civil War?

1869
Completion of Transcontinental Railroad

After completing construction of the Transcontinental Railroad, the Big Four (Collis P. Huntington, Mark Hopkins, Charles Crocker, and Leland Stanford) control transportation and also dominate state politics. Their power leads to various political movements and results in major changes to state government.

Would California have experienced greater benefits and less political instability if the construction of the Transcontinental Railroad had been orchestrated by the government instead of private businesses?

1879
Constitutional Restrictions on Chinese Employment

TRIUMPH OF LABOR.

The enactment of laws that restrict Chinese employment continues a pattern of discrimination against specific ethnic and racial groups and limits the political, social, and economic development of the Chinese community until the second half of the 20th century.

Would California be any less divided or prone to social problems if discriminatory laws such as these had not been enacted?

1911–1916
Progressive Era Reforms

In reaction to monopolies and government corruption, California Progressives succeed in enacting three avenues for direct democracy—the initiative, referendum, and recall—which allow voters to enact laws or oust elected officials. Today, the initiative results in numerous popular as well as controversial voter-approved laws.

Would state government be more or less efficient if Californians did not have these electoral pathways at their disposal?

1939–1945
World War II

Defense industries locate in California, resulting in lucrative contracts for California-based companies and well-paying jobs for groups tradition-ally denied skilled labor. This industrial boom generates tax revenue, which fuels growth in government infrastructure and services and also leads to progressive social policies.

Was World War II the only route to the state's subsequent period of economic prosperity? Would California have developed similar long-term avenues for economic development and social equity even without the lucrative defense contracts?

The twentieth century literary giant William Faulkner wrote, "The past is never dead. It's not even past."* This quote has special relevance for California. Embedded within the most modern features of the state are traces of the past that continue to influence culture, architecture, geography, demographics, and politics. —*Which of the historical developments in California's history had the most profound impact on California society and politics today? Why? Were any aspects of contemporary California politics inevitable given historical developments? If yes, which ones? If not, why not?*

*William Faulkner, *Requiem for a Nun* (New York: Random House, 1951).

Review of Key Objectives

Natural Characteristics and Native Californians

16.1 Determine the impact of California's geography and climate on its early settlement.

(pages 498–501)

Images of California's balmy weather, bountiful land, and mineral wealth have lured generations of immigrants from around the globe to seek a better life on the shores of the Pacific. In a state of many unique features, the San Francisco Bay is considered one of the world's greatest natural harbors, and the redwood, one of the world's tallest trees, has played an important role in the settlement of California. An even greater lure than climate for most immigrants to California was the mineral wealth discovered in the state's valleys and mountains. The most famous find was, of course, the gold strike that inspired the historic California Gold Rush.

KEY TERMS

California Gold Rush 498
Sierra Nevada 498
Pueblos 501
Presidios 501

CRITICAL THINKING QUESTIONS

1. Could the history of injustices practiced against Native Californians recur against another group of state residents in the future, or have Californians adopted moral or ethical values that would prevent the recurrence of such actions?
2. Rather than withdrawal after Mexican Independence of 1821, could the Spanish colonial experience in California have ended differently? Could the Spanish colonialists have initiated any other actions or policies that might have avoided the Mexican Independence of 1821, while allowing them to maintain a productive presence?

INTERNET RESOURCES

Learn more about the natural history of the Los Angeles County area with the online exhibits at the Natural History Museum of Los Angeles at http://www.nhm.org/site

The California Historical Society presents information on extensive resources on the history of California's peoples and places at http://www.californiahistoricalsociety.org/

ADDITIONAL READING

Fradkin, Philip L. *The Seven States of California: A Human and Natural History.* New York: Holt, 1994.

Houston, James D. *Californians: Searching for the Golden State.* New York: Knopf, 1982.

Mexican Control Yields to U.S. Annexation

16.2 Outline the historical developments and political transformations that led to the U.S. annexation of California.

(pages 502–505)

Political instability made it practically impossible for Mexican governors to control a territory extending as far north as present-day Colorado. The Californios, as the Mexican settlers were known, were largely left to their own to develop trade and take advantage of the decision by the Mexican government in 1833 to enact a general secularization law. As increasing numbers of Americans made their way to California, many considered annexation by the United States inevitable. Such considerations were encouraged by influential figures within the U.S. government who were becoming more vocal about the right of America to satisfy its destiny as a world power of continental proportions. The notion of Manifest Destiny as it pertained to California was advanced by the explorations of John C. Frémont but was ultimately settled by the Mexican–American War of 1846.

KEY TERMS

Californios 502
Manifest Destiny 502
Bear Flag Rebellion 502
Proslavery and Antislavery Factions 504

CRITICAL THINKING QUESTIONS

1. To what degree can the annexation of California be both challenged and justified? What are the strengths and weakness of Manifest Destiny?
2. If you were a Californio delegate planning to attend the first state constitutional convention, what would be your fears about the outcome?

INTERNET RESOURCES

The Women in the Gold Rush Web site contains excerpts from women's diaries describing their adventures and struggles during the California Gold Rush: http://www.goldrush.com/~joann/

The California as I Saw It Web site contains 190 eyewitness accounts documenting the changes in California from the Gold Rush to the beginning of the twentieth century: http://lcweb2.loc.gov/ammem/cbhtml/cbhome.html

ADDITIONAL READING

McWilliams, Carey. *California: The Great Exception.* New York: Current Books, 1949.

Royce, Josiah. *California from the Conquest in 1846 to the Second Vigilance Committee in San Francisco.* New York: Knopf, 1948.

Early Years of Statehood

16.3 Describe how the construction of the transcontinental railroad shaped the politics and economy of California.

(pages 506–509)

With the economic boost of the Gold Rush and the successful development of a working government, few doubted that the new state of California would make a major contribution to America's growth and power. Before the state's potential could be realized, however, the enormous distance between California and the rest of the nation would have to be conquered. The most practical alternative was a transcontinental railroad, which would cut the travel time between New York City and San Francisco down to one week. Three successful merchants and a lawyer formed the Central Pacific Railroad Company and accomplished this feat, earning their place in California history as the Big Four. Once completed, the transcontinental railroad gave the Big Four virtual control over most of the state's economy. The completion of the transcontinental railroad ended California's geographic isolation and opened up the state for tremendous commercial expansion.

KEY TERMS

Transcontinental Railroad 506
Big Four 506
Workingmen's Party 507
Grange 508

CRITICAL THINKING QUESTIONS

1. How would the Big Four justify their monopoly over California? How would a member of the Workingmen's Party refute that justification?
2. What assumptions that members of the Workingmen's Party made about the outcome of the California constitutional convention of 1879 turned out to be false?

INTERNET RESOURCES

The California State Railroad Museum presents descriptions, photographs, and paintings that highlight the significance of railroads to the growth of California and the United States on their Web site at http://www.csrmf.org/

Visit the Oakland Museum of California to see the Gold Rush! exhibit and find information on California's history: http://www.museumca.org

ADDITIONAL READING

Gilmore, N. Ray, and Gladys Gilmore (eds.). *Reading in California History.* New York: Crowell, 1966.

Hale, Dennis, and Jonathan Eisen. *The California Dream.* New York: Collier Books, 1968.

The Twentieth Century: The Progressive Era and Rapid Economic Growth

16.4 Summarize the major political and economic developments in California during the twentieth century.

(pages 510–513)

As America entered World War II, California became the major staging area and logistics point for the war against the Japanese in the Pacific, sparking an economic boom. By relocating and interning most Japanese legal aliens and American citizens in California, however, the state and country as a whole lost an element of its moral credibility. In the immediate postwar years, California became the epitome of American culture and progress. The "can do" attitude so much a part of the war years drove innovations in the state exemplified by such cultural icons as Disneyland and Hollywood.

KEY TERMS

Direct Democracy 510
Alien Land Bill 510
Executive Order 9066 512
Bracero Program 512

CRITICAL THINKING QUESTIONS

1. What were the ethical features of the Progressive movement? Did these ethical features aid or hinder those who opposed this movement?
2. How could the internment of Japanese American citizens and legal residents be logically justified? What were the implications of justifying internment?

INTERNET RESOURCES

The California History Lectures Web site at http://bancroft.berkeley.edu/info/audiolectures.html provides audio of seven 1-hour lectures on California history. The lectures, were recorded live and originally broadcast in 2002 and 2003.

The California State Library Web site at http://www.library.ca.gov/ provides a directory with the contact information for thousands of libraries around California.

ADDITIONAL READING

Didion, Joan. *Slouching Toward Bethlehem.* New York: Farrar, Straus and Giroux, 1967; Delta Edition, 1968.

Gentry, Curt. *The Last Days of the Late, Great State of California.* Sausalito, CA: Comstock Edition, 1968.

California in the New Millennium

16.5 Identify the major challenges facing California in the current period.

(pages 514–517)

California's entry into the new millennium has been beleaguered with a substantial list of challenges that could have profound effects on future generations. The depressed condition of the state's economy leads the list. California has endured the harsh affects of the global financial crisis more than most states, and Californians' traditional sensitivity to social issues is being slowly eroded by limited resources. California's avenues for direct democracy have become somewhat of an enigma to a large number of Californians. They are often confused by the complicated manner in which ballot initiatives are presented and the tendency of this process to be manipulated by special interests groups.

KEY TERM

Proposition 13 515

CRITICAL THINKING QUESTIONS

1. What have been the positive and negative consequences of the diversity among Californians? In the current era, have the positive consequences of this diversity outweighed the negative, or visa versa?

2. Are there any long-term solutions to what seems to be California's perpetual energy crisis? Does a solution require either greater government intervention or greater reliance on the marketplace, or is there another answer beyond these two options?

INTERNET RESOURCES

"Early History of the California Coast" is a National Park Service (NPS) travel itinerary for several dozen historic sites connected to early periods of coastal California's history, available at http://www.cr.nps.gov/nR/travel/ca/. Find maps and links to individual Web sites for locations such as various missions (founded by Spaniards), Angel Island (an immigration holding station for Chinese immigrants to the United States), and the John Muir National Historic Site.

ADDITIONAL READING

Kotkin, Joel, and Paul Grabowicz. *California, Inc.* New York: Rawson, Wade, 1982.

Schrag, Peter. *California America's High-Stakes Experiment.* Berkeley: University of California Press, 2008.

Chapter Review   Test Your Knowledge

1. What most accurately describes the climate and/or geography for most of California?
   a. California is easy accessible from the rest of the country
   b. California enjoys a Mediterranean climate
   c. California lacks mineral wealth
   d. California's physical environment is relatively uniform across the state

2. Native Californian society
   a. was warlike and aggressive.
   b. had a small population.
   c. was well adapted to its surroundings.
   d. was openly hostile to European settlers.

3. Which early explorer failed to find Monterey Bay?
   a. Gaspar de Portolá
   b. Hernán Cortés
   c. Sebastián Vizcaino
   d. Juan Rodriguez Cabrillo

4. Who was the mission system founded by?
   a. Sebastián Vizcaino
   b. Hernán Cortes
   c. Junipero Serra
   d. Gaspar de Portolá

5. Who were the Californios?
   a. Native Americans living in California
   b. Spanish troops sent to occupy California
   c. white American settlers living in California under Mexican rule
   d. Mexican settlers living in California

6. Manifest Destiny embraced the notion that
   a. the United States had a divine mission to be a world power of continental proportions.
   b. the Catholic Church should spread Christianity in the New World.
   c. Mexico should be independent from Spain.
   d. Spain should rule in California.

7. The Treaty of Guadalupe Hidalgo included
   a. making Colorado a U.S. state.
   b. military intervention in Mexico.
   c. payment of $15 million to Mexico.
   d. recognition of Puerto Rico as a state.

8. The delegates to California's first constitutional convention
   a. were all white settlers.
   b. based their work on Mexico's political system.
   c. included six Californios.
   d. created a state government with broad and almost unlimited powers.

9. California's original constitution created
   a. a state government with strong formal powers.
   b. an expansive welfare system.
   c. extensive regulations of private industry.
   d. a state government with limited formal powers.

10. The leader of the Workingmen's Party was
    a. Denis Kearny.   c. Robert Haas.
    b. Leland Stanford.   d. Hiram Johnson.

11. The Progressive movement was most closely associated with
    a. the middle class.   c. the railroad.
    b. farmers.   d. laywers.

12. The leader of the Progressive movement in California was
    a. Denis Kearny.   c. Mark Hopkins.
    b. Hiram Johnson.   d. Earl Warren.

13. Executive Order 9066
    a. ordered the relocation and internment of 110,000 Japanese legal aliens and U.S. citizens.
    b. declared martial law in California for the first two months of the war.
    c. nationalized key industries for defense production.
    d. seized large tracts of land in California for the federal government to use for new military bases.

14. What granted Mexicans temporary employment status to work in agriculture?
    a. the work campaign
    b. the Bracero Program
    c. the special employment visa of 1912
    d. the U.S. Department of Agriculture

15. During the postwar boom, the California state government
    a. spent massive amounts of money on public colleges and universities.
    b. cut spending on health and welfare services.
    c. decided to limit suburban sprawl by scaling back the water projects that made such development possible.
    d. returned to its old, pre–Progressive Era policy of fewer government projects and regulations.

16. In the late twentieth century, California's economy
    a. experienced increased industrial production.
    b. suffered from the effects of globalization.
    c. grew as a result of new agricultural crops.
    d. benefited from high tariffs.

17. According to a 2005 poll, Californians were most concerned about
    a. crime.   c. the environment.
    b. the war in Iraq.   d. the well-being of children.

18. Once an initiative has passed, the
    a. governor may still veto it.
    b. legislature may amend it without another public vote.
    c. governor is legally bound to execute the law or policy.
    d. governor may suspend it for six months.

19. Which California governor was known for a "middle-of-the-road path"?
    a. Arnold Schwarzenegger c. Jerry Brown
    b. Gray Davis   d. Pete Wilson

20. Governor Schwarzenegger's drop in approval ratings in 2009 was due in part to
    a. a rebellion in the ranks of his own Republican party.
    b. his inability to propose a publicly acceptable economic recovery plan.
    c. a corruption scandal engulfing his administration.
    d. a lack of endorsement by President Obama.

mypoliscilab Exercises

Apply what you learned in this chapter on **MyPoliSciLab.**

📖—Read on **mypoliscilab.com**

eText: Chapter 16

✓—Study and **Review** on **mypoliscilab.com**

Pre-Test
Post-Test
Chapter Exam
Flashcards

👁—Watch on **mypoliscilab.com**

Video: Ellis Island West
Video: California Text City

✦—Explore on **mypoliscilab.com**

Visual Literacy: Explaining Differences in State Laws

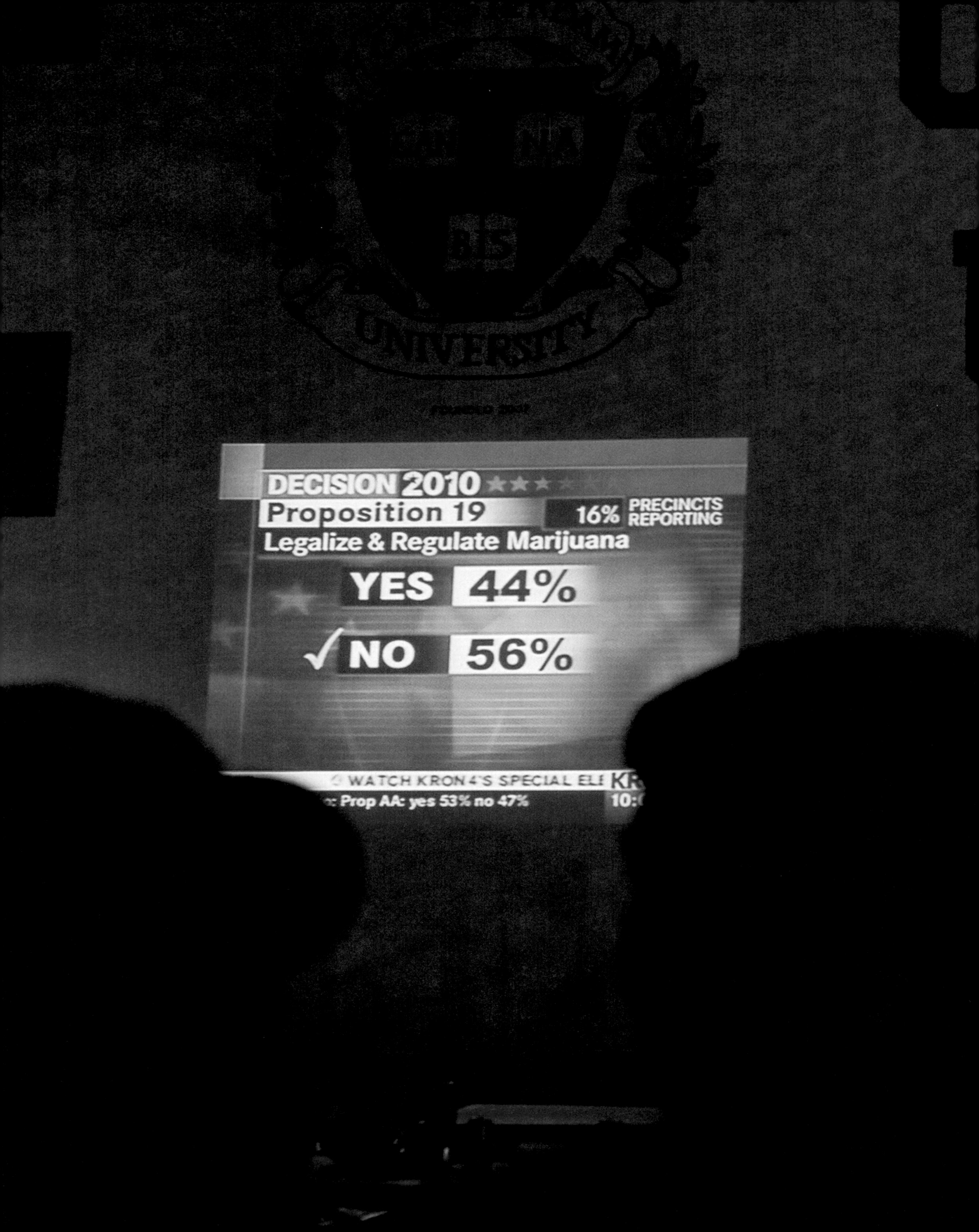
UNIVERSITY
DECISION 2010
Proposition 19
16% PRECINCTS REPORTING
Legalize & Regulate Marijuana
YES 44%
NO 56%
WATCH KRON4'S SPECIAL ELE
Prop AA: yes 53% no 47%

Democracy, California Style

KEY OBJECTIVES

After completing this chapter, you should be prepared to:

17.1 Relate voter participation to the types of elections held in California.

17.2 Evaluate whether the recall, referendum, and initiative have successfully established a more direct democracy in California.

17.3 Explain how campaigns are organized to most effectively influence California voters.

17.4 Identify ways to empower voters.

17.5 Classify the forms of political participation used by Californians.

The California 2010 midterm election is likely to be remembered as an electoral contest that had profound as well as long-term effects on the conduct of state government. In the wake of the anti-Democratic Party tidal wave that swept most of the nation, political analysts were quick to note the rejection of Republican candidates and conservative trends by many California voters.

The gubernatorial victory of Jerry Brown and the reelection of Senator Barbara Boxer epitomized the California Democratic Party's sweep of the state electoral landscape despite major campaign obstacles. Brown overcame the record-smashing $160 million spent by his opponent, Meg Whitman, and Boxer convinced voters to ignore the image promoted by her challenger, Carly Fiorina, of Boxer as an ultra-liberal career politician. Democrats also captured virtually every California state-wide office and picked up seats in the state legislature.

Additionally, state residents voted on a number of landmark ballot measures that are destined to alter the conduct of state government for many years. The California voters approved Proposition 25, which lowered the legislative margin for budget passage from two-thirds to a simple majority. By eliminating the two-thirds

Are average Californians still interested in a democratic system of government?

requirement, the Democratic Party-controlled legislature is much more likely to avoid the almost regular delays in the passage of the annual budget that threatened the solvency of the state's government in the past. However, the fiscal management of state government will face new challenges with the passage of Proposition 22, a constitutional amendment restricting state government's use of funds earmarked for transportation and local governments, and Proposition 26, another constitutional amendment that requires a two-thirds majority to approve fees and taxes.

Finally, with much of the nation closely watching, a majority of California voters declined to approve Proposition 19—the ballot measure that would have legalized marijuana. By garnering 45 percent of the votes cast for this measure, however, it is unlikely that the idea or the supporters of legalizing marijuana will disappear anytime soon.

Whatever satisfaction California Democrats and their supporters may have gained from the 2010 midterm election, it is tempered by the state's poor economic health, among many other problems that the newly elected state government leaders now confront. Failure to adequately address these difficulties could quickly reverse Democratic gains in future elections.

Resource Center
• Glossary
• Vocabulary Example
• Connect the Link

■ **Direct Primary Elections:** Elections in which voters choose the candidates who will compete in a subsequent general election.

SIGNIFICANCE: *Before instituting the direct primary election, Californians voted in the general election for the candidates chosen by party leaders at party conventions.*

Elections in California

17.1 Relate voter participation to the types of elections held in California.

(pages 528–531)

No matter how hard the political parties strive to maintain partisan lines in large portions of the California electoral process, a longing to transcend these lines in selecting candidates remains popular among Californians. A 2010 June primary initiative—Proposition 14: Top Two Open Primary—is the most recent expression of voters. The primary will seek to replace the partisan primaries with an electoral process that lists all candidates on the same ballot. The top two vote-getters for each office, regardless of party affiliation, will advance to the general election.

An earlier attempt to limit partisanship can be traced back to Proposition 198, an initiative approved by voters who in 1996 adopted a blanket primary election that would allow voters to cross party boundaries and select candidates for office regardless of party affiliation. In 1998, California voters used the blanket primary in the state primary election, and most election observers saw very little "raiding" or evidence of a concerted strategy by the parties to influence the outcome of an election by crossing over. Surveys conducted by the California secretary of state found that 77 percent of surveyed voters thought that the blanket primary offered more choice and 80 percent felt that such a primary allowed them to select candidates who more closely reflected voter interests. The blanket primary caused voter turnout to increase by over 1 million voters.

Any opportunity to exercise electoral impartiality or empower the independent and "decline to state" voter were dashed, however, when the U.S. Supreme Court ruled that the blanket primary was unconstitutional. Justice Antonin Scalia wrote that California was "forcing political parties to associate with those who do not share their beliefs."[1] Since that ruling, California has seen a gradual decline in nonpresidential primary election voter turnout. No matter what ultimately happens with Proposition 14, this second shot at less partisan elections will ideally signal to both the federal and state legislative bodies that their current tendency to engage in highly polarized partisan politics is not appreciated by large numbers of their California constituents.

Although political participation is a privilege endowed on us by the development of democratic government, the number of Californians voting in some past elections is not drastically different from that seen among people living under despotic rule. Yet in 2008, the statewide turnout rate of registered voters hit a whopping 80 percent for the presidential election, the most ballots cast in a general election since 1972. Then in May 2009,

voter turn out fell to a record low during a special election. Less than 26 percent of the California electorate turned out to reject the five ballot measures intended to correct the state government's budget deficit. What explains these fluctuations? When do Californians get excited about elections and turn out to vote? California holds several different types of elections, and the participation rates partially reflect a selective interest in high-profile races in general elections. However, not infrequently controversial issues or popular candidates bring Californians to the polls to exercise their democratic privilege.

Voting: Who Can Vote?

Any person who is 18 years old, a citizen of the United States, a resident of California, and a county resident for at least 15 days before the election may register to vote. Registered voters who have recently moved to another county may still be able to vote by absentee ballot or by voting at their former polling place. Recent residents may vote for president of the United States if they apply for a presidential ballot at least seven days before the election. Individuals who have been declared mentally incompetent by a court of law or convicted felons who are either incarcerated or on parole are disqualified from voting. Reregistration is required if the prospective voter has moved, completed an official name change, or changed political party affiliation.

Registering to vote in California and most other states was made significantly more convenient when Congress passed the **National Voter Registration Act,** the so-called "motor voter law" that requires states to allow citizens to register by mail and to accept a universal mail-in voter registration form. It also specifies that voter registration forms be made available at public agencies and requires the department of motor vehicles to incorporate voter registration into the process of applying for or renewing a driver's license or obtaining nondriver identification. An increasing number of Californians are also choosing to vote using an absentee ballot, which has been made much less complicated in recent years. Voters can apply for permanent absentee voter status or request an absentee ballot for a particular election.

In California, voters have the opportunity to participate in three basic types of elections: state primary elections, state general elections, and special elections.

State Primary Elections

Until the turn of the twentieth century, candidates for elected office throughout the United States were nominated or simply chosen at autocratic party conventions, and the average voter had no say in the selection of candidates for general elections. The California Progressives, however, demanded an end to this system and instead promoted **direct primary elections**■. In

■ **Cross-Filing:** A system that allows a candidate to represent multiple parties.

EXAMPLE: *Earl Warren was elected to three terms as governor in part because of the cross-filing provision that enabled his name to be listed on the Democratic are Republican primary ballots.*

■ **Closed Primary System:** An election system that permits registered members of a political party to vote only for their party's candidates.

SIGNIFICANCE: *Many believe that the closed primary is largely responsible for the dominance of the Democratic Party in California today.*

TABLE 17.1	Political Participation by Political Party Membership		
	DEMOCRAT	**REPUBLICAN**	**INDEPENDENT**
Vote regularly	62%	67%	47%
Sign petitions	44%	43%	43%
Attend local meetings	42%	39%	40%
Write to elected officials	32%	35%	30%
Contribute money	23%	34%	16%
Attend rallies	18%	16%	17%
Participate in political party work	10%	8%	4%

SOURCE: S. Karthick Ramakrishnan and Mark Baldassare, *The Ties That Bind: Changing Demographics and Civic Engagement in California* (San Francisco: Public Policy Institute of California, 2004). Reprinted with permission.

1908, California passed a constitutional amendment that made primaries mandatory, less partisan, and more democratic. Although the primary underwent another change when **cross-filing**■, a system that allowed a candidate to represent multiple parties, was abolished in 1959, many Californians remained dissatisfied with the **closed primary system**■, which required registered members of a political party to vote only for their party's candidates.[2]

In 1996, adoption of Proposition 198 transformed the California primary to a **blanket primary**■, in which all registered voters could vote for any candidate, regardless of political affiliation. After its use in the 1998 statewide primary election, the blanket primary was first contested in the courts by the California Democratic Party and later by the Republican, Libertarian, and Peace and Freedom parties as well. The major argument among these parties stemmed from the fear that party supporters would cross over and vote in the primary elections of other parties, acting as "spoilers" by electing the opposing party's least-popular candidates. The spoilers' actions would attempt to guarantee that their party's general election candidate faced the weakest opposition candidate.

In 2000, the U.S. Supreme Court declared California's blanket primary in violation of a political party's First Amendment right of association, forcing the state to adopt a modified closed primary system. Under this system, voters may decline to state their party affiliation in any primary election if this is authorized by the rules of a political party. Otherwise, voters may only receive a ballot for the party for which they are registered.

The state primaries are held on the first Tuesday after the first Monday in June of even-numbered years; this has remained unchanged. The California presidential primaries, however, have undergone considerable modifications over the years,

largely due to the national electoral phenomenon known as *front-loading*. Historically, the California presidential primary took place in June, but as other states moved their primaries earlier, the California primary became increasingly irrelevant. As a result, the presidential primary was moved to March as of the 2000 election year. After some questions and doubts were raised in state government about the practicality of the new date, Governor Arnold Schwarzenegger approved legislation that returned all California primaries to June.

State primaries include not only races for national offices and the state legislature, but also nonpartisan elections at the municipal and county levels. The state constitution specifies that candidates for a nonpartisan office, such as a city council member or district attorney, must receive 50 percent or more of the vote. If no candidate receives a majority, the two candidates with the most votes must face each other in a runoff during the general election. Unfortunately, statewide primaries in nonpresidential years attract low voter turnout. As a result, many Californians miss the opportunity to vote for local elected officials (see Table 17.1).

State General Elections

The state **general election**■ takes place on the first Tuesday after the first Monday in November of even-numbered years. During general elections, voters choose among the nominees chosen during the primaries. Regular or "midterm" general state elections usually have lower voter turnout than presidential elections do. The state's 55 electors for the Electoral College are chosen according to the rules of the two Democratic and Republican state party organizations. The Democratic state party organization permits each member of the California Democratic congressional delegation to

■ **Blanket Primary:** A primary election in which all voters can vote for any candidate, regardless of party affiliation.

EXAMPLE: *California voters vote in one blanket primary during 1998.*

■ **General Election:** An election in which candidates compete directly for election to a given office.

SIGNIFICANCE: *Since the mid-1960s, voter turnout during general elections has gradually been declining.*

choose one elector, and the Republican state party organization selects party officers and elected officials to act as electors.

On rare occasions, a **special election**■ will be held in California to fill vacancies in Congress or the state legislature and to conduct a recall. The governor can call a special election in an attempt to win the approval of one or more initiatives by the voters, but such efforts—including a tax limitation initiative sponsored by Governor Ronald Reagan in 1973, a school voucher initiative in 1993 by Governor Pete Wilson, and the most recent attempt by Governor Arnold Schwarzenegger to get approval for measures that would impose a state spending cap and redirect state funds to balance the state budget—typically are defeated at the polls.

An electoral legacy of the Progressives is the provision for nonpartisan as well as partisan elections. **Partisan elections**■ account for slightly more than 10 percent of the elections in California, and they include congressional representatives, state legislators, and all statewide executive offices, with the exception of the superintendent of education and the insurance commissioner. The election of judges and all local offices are conducted as **nonpartisan elections**■.

Along with nonpartisan elections, Progressive reforms were apparent in attempts to design ballots that minimized the number of offices and items (short ballots) and that listed candidates by office rather than by party (office block ballots). The intent of the Progressives was to create a simple, nonpartisan—or perhaps antiparty—ballot. The short ballot eventually became impractical as the number of offices and ballot measures grew, but the listing of candidates by office remains on the current long ballot. The long ballot has complicated the voting

process by forcing the voter to make important decisions on a long list of candidates and issues without the luxury of voting for a slate of candidates grouped by political party.[3]

PATHWAYS of action

California's Controversial Campaign Finance Reform Law

In 2000, a federal court temporarily halted the implementation of Proposition 208, a campaign finance reform law that the court found was too restrictive in the series of limits it placed on the way candidates raised money. Fearing that either this ruling would soon be overturned or that Proposition 208 would be replaced by an even tougher campaign finance initiative, California state legislators rushed to devise an alternative campaign financing law.

The drafting of Proposition 34 was not only the California legislature's response to campaign finance reform, but it was also that rare occasion when members from both parties worked collaboratively to enact law. These Democrat and Republican members argued that Proposition 34 provided effective limits on campaign contributions and stood the best chance of withstanding any legal challenges. Many members also added that limits set too high on contributions, their subtle criticism of Proposition 208, would benefit candidates who could tap into personal fortunes and restrict the ability of most candidates to communicate with the voters.

Criticized by various civic advocacy groups in 2000 as an ineffective means of limiting the amount of money contributed

Voters cheer on Republican gubernatorial candidate Meg Whitman just before the primary election. —*How do partisan elections enable candidates to rally voters to support their campaign?*

Special Election: An election called to address a specific issue before the next regularly scheduled election.

SIGNIFICANCE: *Special elections tend to attract more white, middle-class, conservative voters, and overall voter turnout is typically low.*

Partisan Elections: Elections in which candidates are identified by party affiliation.

SIGNIFICANCE: *In partisan elections in California, Democrats outnumber Republicans.*

Nonpartisan Elections: Elections in which candidates are not identified by party affiliation.

EXAMPLE: *By the 1950s, more than 60 percent of municipalities nationwide had adopted nonpartisan elections.*

to candidates in the state, Proposition 34 continues to be blamed for soaring campaign expenditures today. Although Proposition 208 set contribution limits from an individual at $250 for assembly and senate candidates and $500 for gubernatorial candidates, Proposition 34 raised those limits to $3,000 and $22,300, respectively. Under Proposition 34, other contributions could come from small contributor committees, political parties, political action committees, and soft money donations. Critics of Proposition 34 were particularly worried about loopholes in the law that would allow for the formation of independent expenditure committees that could raise unlimited amounts of funds to promote a certain candidate as long as they did not coordinate or work directly with the candidate's campaign committee.

Even with the limits imposed on campaign contributions by Proposition 34, California continues to be one of a handful of states that have no limits on the total amount of money that a candidate can raise and spend, and it exceeds every other state in the amount of money contributed to most candidates for legislative and statewide offices. During 2005–2006, California

assembly and state senate candidates raised an average of $385,132 and $495,671, respectively, amounts that tend to insulate legislators from their constituents and favor special interests. In fact, another huge loophole in Proposition 34 allows "bundling"—contributing through third parties when the individual contribution limit to a particular candidate has been reached.

SOURCE: Alex Knott, "California Awash in Campaign Cash, Potentials for Conflict of Interest," Center for Public Integrity, January 25, 2001; Institute on Money in State Politics, "State Elections Overview, 2004"; Bill Ainsworth, "Cash Flow," *California Journal*, February 2002, pp. 54–57; Edwin Garcia, "Campaigns Could Be Publicly Funded," *Contra Costa Times*, January 31, 2006, p. a09; John Wildermuth, "Campaign 2006: Ballot Measures Could Be Pitfalls for Candidates—Governor Hopefuls May Face Backlash for Taking a Stand," *San Francisco Chronicle*, June 28, 2006, p. B4; State Election Overview, 2004, Helena, MT, http://www.followthemoney.org/press/Reports/200601041.pdf

Elections in California

17.1 Relate voter participation to the types of elections held in California.

PRACTICE QUIZ: UNDERSTAND AND APPLY

1. What type of election is held in California in order to address a specific issue before the next regularly scheduled election?
   a. a special election
   b. a general election
   c. a primary election
   d. a presidential election

2. The Progressive movement in California is responsible for the introduction of what type of electoral process?
   a. the special election
   b. the direct primary
   c. the party caucus
   d. the district election

3. In 2000, the U.S. Supreme Court found which of the following electoral contests in California to be a violation of a political party's First Amendment right of association?
   a. the blanket primary
   b. the presidential primary
   c. the closed primary
   d. the party caucus

4. Approximately what percentage of the elections in California are considered partisan?

   a. 50 percent
   b. 1 percent
   c. slightly more than 10 percent
   d. slightly less than 30 percent

ANALYZE

1. What can be done to encourage more Californians to vote?

2. How fair are elections in California?

IDENTIFY THE CONCEPT THAT DOESN'T BELONG

a. Age 18
b. Resident of California
c. County resident for at least 15 days
d. Resident of a legislative district for one year immediately before an election
e. Citizen of the United States

Resource Center
- Glossary
- Vocabulary Example
- Connect the Link

■ **Recall:** A procedure by which voters can remove an elected official from office before the end of the official's term.

EXAMPLE: *Only 15 states have provisions for a recall of state officials, and only North Dakota Governor Lynn J. Frazier in 1921 and California Governor Gray Davis in 2003 have been successfully recalled.*

Direct Democracy: California's Electoral Dilemma

17.2 ■ **Evaluate whether the recall, referendum, and initiative have successfully established a more direct democracy in California.**

(pages 532–539)

Three avenues for direct democracy—the recall, the referendum, and the initiative—have been unique features of the political landscape in California, especially in their broad application and controversial outcomes. In many ways, direct democracy continues to accomplish the goals of the Progressives who enacted these provisions in 1911. The Progressives wanted Californians to have the political power to circumvent an unresponsive state legislature or executive branch. Hiram Johnson proclaimed in 1911 that the avenues for direct democracy "were attempts to bring the government closer to the people," with the hope that "we may yet live in a free republic." The Progressives would probably be surprised and saddened by the influence that wealth, interest groups, and partisanship have over these democratic practices today.

The Recall

The **recall**■ is a constitutional procedure that allows the removal from public office between elections of any person who has proved to be poorly qualified, corrupt, or incompetent. Originally, the Progressives used the recall to target judges who favored corporate interests and corrupt politicians.[4] The recall was one of the most popular constitutional reform proposals in 1911, approved by over 76 percent of the voters.[5]

The two major phases of the recall process are the signature-gathering stage and the election stage. The process begins with a petition that outlines the reasons why an official should be removed from office. A recall petition cannot be circulated against an officeholder during the first six months of his or her term of office. To recall a statewide official, the number of signatures on a recall petition must equal or exceed 12 percent of the total votes cast in the last general election. When attempting to recall a state legislator, judge, member of the Board of Equalization, or countywide officeholder, signatures equal to 20 percent or more of the last vote for the office are required. Sponsors of a recall campaign have 160 days to file signed petitions with the secretary of state. The appropriate office must verify and certify the signatures and petition and then forward them to the governor, who is required to call for a recall election between 60 and 80 days after certification.

During the election stage of the recall process, Californians vote on two separate issues: First, they decide whether to recall

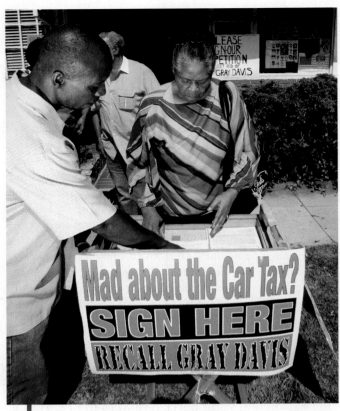

Citizens sign a petition for the recall of California Governor Gray Davis. —*Do the initiative the referendum, and the recall have a positive impact on California democracy?*

the officeholder, and then they select a replacement. Candidates for the office must submit a petition signed by enough registered voters to equal 1 percent or more of the vote cast for that office during the last election and also pay a registration fee. During the election stage, the officeholder is in the difficult position of having to respond to charges in the recall statement as well as campaigning against any replacement candidates.

A simple majority of voters can recall an officeholder, and the replacement candidate who receives the most votes will fill the vacant position. Every vote cast for recall is counted, regardless of whether the voter selects a replacement candidate.

Until recently, the recall process was never used successfully in California against a statewide officeholder. Locally, the recall is a bit more common, being used in recent years to remove an El Dorado County supervisor, Cabrillo Unified School District trustees, Placer County fire protection district board members, Del Norte County school board members, and city council members in Amador, Brisbane, and Grass Valley. Many recall petitions against statewide officials have been circulated over the years, including those seeking to remove Governors Pat Brown

■ **Deregulation:** The removal of government restrictions on businesses or industries.

EXAMPLE: *Enron's manipulation of California's deregulated energy market resulted in vast profits while California suffered huge energy price increases and an energy shortage.*

■ **Initiative:** A process by which voters can directly propose and enact a law or constitutional amendment.

SIGNIFICANCE: *Since the 1960s, initiative measures have appeared on primary, general, and special election ballots.*

and Ronald Reagan, but all were primarily symbolic until 2003 and the recall of Governor Gray Davis.

When taking into account the unsuccessful attempts to recall statewide officials in the past, the reelection of Governor Gray Davis only 11 months earlier, and the dominance of the Democratic Party in California, the recall of Davis appears baffling. On close analysis, however, the unprecedented step of removing Governor Davis was a logical reaction to critical dilemmas facing California in 2002. The statewide energy crisis, probably more than any other factor, caused Californians to become extremely dissatisfied with their state government and seek some remedy to an increasingly intolerable situation.

The **deregulation**■ of energy production and consumption in 1998 resulted in a complicated statewide power-generating system that suffered from out-of-state ownership, dwindling energy resources, lack of oversight, and unscrupulous business tactics. This energy conundrum led to a dramatic rise in energy costs and a rapid drop in supply, punctuated by the infamous "rolling blackouts." Soon thereafter, Internet-based and microcomputer companies headquartered in California, which made substantial tax contributions to the state general fund, began to experience commercial and economic difficulties. Financial losses for that industry as well as the California economy caused an unexpected 20-percent decrease in state tax revenues in 2000, followed by a large state budget deficit equal to about one-quarter of the total state budget. Governor Davis's inability to convince Californians that he could solve these and other mounting problems made him a likely target for public wrath. Under the leadership of Darrell Issa, a wealthy businessman and member of the U.S. House of Representatives, a wide collection of Republican Party elected officials, activists, and supporters formed recall committees and raised millions of dollars to wage sustained attacks on Governor Davis's leadership qualities and channel voter disenchantment toward the recall process.

In the midst of the sudden economic decline, the energy crisis, and the unusual statewide recall campaign, Californians were astonished yet again by the decision of Arnold Schwarzenegger—bodybuilder, film star, and successful businessman without any professional political experience—to run in the recall election to replace Gray Davis as governor. In a field of 135 replacement candidates, including five major and independent party contenders, Schwarzenegger captured 48.6 percent of the vote.[6] Schwarzenegger's campaign, however, stood in stark contrast to the vision of the Progressives whose enactments had made it possible. The campaign demonstrated the effectiveness of a well-funded campaign that employs modern techniques such as television advertisements and professional signature-gathering services. The Schwarzenegger replacement campaign accounted for nearly half of all campaign contributions among all the replacement candidates, with more than $22 million.[7]

Rather than the popular or grassroots efforts the Progressives envisioned would grow out of the avenues for direct

California gubernatorial candidate Arnold Schwarzenegger addresses supporters during a campaign stop in September 2003, at Santa Maria, California. —*Why did citizens support the recall of Governor Davis?*

democracy, all three avenues of direct democracy have in recent years favored interest groups and individuals capable of raising millions of dollars.

The Initiative

In his insightful book *Paradise Lost: California's Experience, America's Future*, award-winning journalist Peter Schrag writes:

> The passage of Proposition 13 serves as a convenient way of dividing the post–World War II era in California between that postwar period of optimism, with its huge investment in public infrastructure and its strong commitment to the development of quality education systems and other public services, and a generation of declining confidence and shrinking public services.[8]

With the passage of Proposition 13 in 1978, California politics underwent a drastic change as the **initiative**■ became a popular avenue for Californians and the interest groups representing them to repudiate the lawmaking authority of representative government and invoke change.

Before the enactment of Proposition 13, the initiative process was used sparingly, although there was a flurry of initiative activity soon after the three avenues for direct democracy gained voter approval in 1911. In the attempt to politically empower Californians and make California politics more democratic, the Progressives led the state to adopt the **direct initiative,** which allows Californians to *directly* propose and enact a law or constitutional amendment. The Progressives could have chosen a process that requires the legislature to pass citizen-proposed laws, a practice still used in nine states, but by implementing the direct initiative instead, the Progressives placed lawmaking power firmly in the hands of any resident who had the wherewithal to place a proposed law on the ballot through a petition circulation process.

Today, that process requires valid signatures of registered voters equal to 5 percent or more of the votes cast in the last gubernatorial election to propose a law and 8 percent or more to propose a constitutional amendment. According to the state constitution, an initiative must be limited to one subject, and it may not name a person to office or grant a duty or power to a private corporation. After the state attorney general's office prepares a title and summary of the proposed law or amendment and forwards a copy to the secretary of state, supporters of the initiative have 150 days to gather signatures. Once the petition process is completed, arguments for and against the initiative are printed in a ballot pamphlet that is mailed to all registered voters, and the initiative is placed on the ballot for the next scheduled election. Approval of an initiative requires a simple majority of those voting on the initiative. Once an initiative is passed, it can be changed or invalidated only by another initiative or a successful legal challenge. It has become a common practice for opponents of an approved initiative to file a lawsuit within days of the election in the hope that a legal technicality or judicial doctrine will prevent the law from going into effect.

Through the power of judicial review, state and federal courts can invalidate a new law enacted by the initiative process if one of those courts determines the initiative violates the U.S. or state constitution or federal law. On very rare instances, state courts have intervened before an initiative election, almost always to enforce the single-subject rule, the constitutional provision that restricts an initiative to one subject. Since 1986, nearly two-thirds of the popular initiatives approved by the voters were challenged in the courts, and half of those were either partially or totally invalidated.[9]

For example, the crowds that gather at Native American reservations across California to gamble would probably be surprised to learn that the California Supreme Court originally struck down Proposition 5, the 1998 initiative allowing Nevada-style casinos on the reservations. Passed by 63 percent of the voters, Proposition 5 permitted gambling on reservations and established regulatory and revenue-sharing guidelines. It caused a dispute between California Indian casino owners and Governor Pete Wilson, on one side, and Nevada casino and California racetracks owners, on the other, over the authority

of the state government to regulate casino gambling. Nearly 6 months after the election, the California Supreme Court ruled 6–1 that the initiative violated the 1984 California State Lottery Act, an initiative constitutional amendment that banned casino-style gambling in the state. The supreme court ruling later became irrelevant, however, when incoming Governor Gray Davis concluded an agreement with California Indian casino owners that permitted gambling on reservations.[10]

Legal challenges to California initiatives are more likely to come from federal courts than from state courts (see Table 17.2). The state constitutional requirement that forces California state court judges and justices to face election after being appointed is one commonly held justification for the reluctance of state courts to invalidate initiatives passed by the very voters they will eventually confront. Federal judges and justices, on the other hand, serve for life and experience no such pressure. Another view finds that federal courts have less appreciation for the "popular" democracy practiced in California, focusing instead on their responsibility to uphold the U.S. Constitution, especially as it pertains to civil liberties and the authority of the federal government. California courts, however, are torn by their responsibility to uphold both constitutions. The invalidation by the U.S. Supreme Court of initiatives granting Californians a blanket primary and establishing limits on campaign contributions are two instances in which the Court found that initiatives approved by California voters were contrary to First Amendment rights.

The passage of Proposition 215 in 1996, which permitted the use of marijuana for medical purposes in California, provides a good example of the delicate legal balance the federal courts must adopt when attempting to enforce federal statutes and constitutional provisions while respecting states' rights. After almost nine years of legal uncertainty regarding the freedom of Californians to ignore federal drug laws and the authority of federal law enforcement agencies to prevent the medical use of marijuana, the U.S. Supreme Court finally addressed this dilemma in *Gonzales* v. *Raich* (2005) when it ruled in a 6–3 decision that the federal government has the constitutional mandate under the commerce clause of the U.S. Constitution to prevent the use, sale, and cultivation of marijuana, thereby effectively allowing agents of the federal government to disregard Proposition 215. The Court did not, however, take the next legal step of finding Proposition 215 to be unconstitutional.[11] Needless to say, a large number of Californians have been displeased with this and various other court rulings that have nullified state initiatives. Some attempt in the future to place checks on the power of judicial review, an almost impossible task against federal courts, could well be the next target of the volatile political tendencies of the California electorate.

Californians have used the initiative to change or influence municipal or county government more often than the state government. At the municipal or county level, the process follows slightly different rules. The signature-gathering period

TABLE 17.2	Propositions Invalidated	
PROPOSITION NUMBER ON BALLOT	**PROPOSITION**	**REASON INVALIDATED**
49	Nonpartisan Offices	U.S. Constitution, First Amendment
68	Legislative Campaign Spending Limits	Conflicting proposition received more votes
105	Disclosures to Consumers, Voters, and Investors	Addressed more than a single subject
164	Term Limits	[never enforced]
198	Open Primaries	U.S. Constitution, First Amendment
208	Campaign Contributions and Spending Limits	U.S. Constitution, First Amendment
225	Congressional Term Limits	U.S. Constitution, Article V
73	Campaign Financing	U.S. Constitution, First Amendment
187	Illegal Aliens, Ineligibility for Public Services	Federal preemption
5	Tribal Gaming	California Constitution Article IV
65	Safe Drinking Water	Some applications preempted by federal law, others not
103	Insurance Rates, Regulation	Insurance rate rollback and required contributions to nonprofits invalid; remainder of initiative valid
115	Criminal Laws	California Proposition 115 was a constitutional amendment known as the Crime Victims Justice Reform Act which made a number of significant and complex changes in California criminal law and in the procedures that judges are required to follow in criminal cases.
132	Marine Resources	Application in some contexts preempted by federal law

SOURCE: David J. Jung and Janis M. Crum, "Ballot Measures and Judicial Review, 1986–2000," PLRI Reports Fall 2000, UC Hastings College of the Law, www.uchastings.edu. Reprinted with permission.

is slightly longer (180 days), and the number of signatures required to place an initiative on the ballot at the county level is based on the number of votes cast in that county during the last gubernatorial election. At the municipal level, the signature-gathering requirement is based on the total number of registered voters in that municipality.

The successful passage of Proposition 13 in 1978 popularized the initiative as a means of attempting to address major issues. Proposition 13 also showed that the chance of winning approval of an initiative depends on access to generous financial support and professional campaign management.

PROPOSITION 13   Proposition 13 grew out of the rapid rise in residential property taxes throughout the 1970s and the highly visible antitax advocacy of Howard Jarvis and Paul Gann,

two representatives of the California real estate industry.[12] In 1978, Jarvis and Gann spearheaded the successful passage of Proposition 13, an initiative that would add a constitutional amendment limiting the total property tax to 1 percent of the assessed value of each parcel or residential home and the annual increase in assessment to 2 percent. The initiative also required that any general tax increases be approved by a majority of voters and that increases in "special taxes" (to fund such things as local transportation) would need to be approved by two-thirds of the voters. Similarly, the state legislature was prohibited from passing any tax increases without a two-thirds vote in each chamber. Proposition 13 benefited Californians who had lived or planned to live in their homes for a long period and those who were able to find moderately priced real estate. As a result of Proposition 13, California residents continue to pay

Supporters wearing stickers that read "Save the American Dream, Vote Yes on 13" celebrate the overwhelming lead taken by Proposition 13 in early returns during the 1978 California primary. —*What impact did Proposition 13 have on California politics? Was it positive or negative?*

property taxes that are considerably lower than elsewhere in the nation, but the result has been a severe reduction in the amount of funds available to state and local governments. California schools were especially affected by the reduction in property taxes, formerly a traditional source of funding for local education.

FORMULA FOR A SUCCESSFUL INITIATIVE The passage of Proposition 13 not only popularized the initiative but also provided the campaign formula that gives proponents of an initiative a better-than-even chance of winning the approval of the voters. The first attribute of this formula is a simple campaign message. In the case of Proposition 13, even though the actual language of the initiative involved complicated tax policy and real estate jargon, the basic campaign message was "If you want lower taxes, vote for Proposition 13." Numerous sources of electoral data and studies of initiative elections suggest that when in doubt or unclear about the intention of an initiative, voters will cast a "no" vote every time (see Table 17.3).

Unfortunately, Proposition 13 and many other successful initiative campaigns achieved that simplicity of message through the distortion or omission of central details.[13] For example, the campaign managers of Proposition 205, another initiative in 1998 to permit casino-style gambling on Native American land in California, omitted most references to "gambling" or "casinos" in their media advertisements.

The second feature of the formula involves the creation of an organizational framework or committee that can stimulate interest, especially among registered voters, and generate endorsements from celebrities and politicians. The more "grassroots" such an entity becomes, the better. Howard Jarvis started his antitax crusade with a group called the United Organizations of Taxpayers, which quickly spun off similar groups to spread the tax-rollback message. Jarvis became personally identified with the tax revolt, publicizing the initiative in frequent speaking engagements and media appearances with a personal style that apparently resonated with prospective voters.

The third feature of the formula entails application of the most advanced campaign techniques available, backed by generous financial support. Both sides of Proposition 13 raised and spent large sums on the campaign, but it was the proponents who most effectively used cutting-edge campaign techniques. Jarvis retained Bill Butcher and Arnold Forde to manage a direct-mail operation that raised thousands of dollars and convinced thousands of targeted registered voters to support Proposition 13 at the polls. Butcher and Forde professionalized the initiative campaign process by employing techniques such as direct-mail petitions and computer-generated letters to property owners.[14] The effectiveness of the Butcher–Forde partnership on the Proposition 13 campaign led to the adoption of even more advanced techniques in subsequent initiative campaigns and the growth of what is now known as the "initiative industrial complex."

During his first two years in office, Governor Schwarzenegger introduced initiatives in two different elections, winning in the first attempt with the approval in 2004 of his California Balanced Budget Act. This constitutional amendment was designed to make state government more fiscally responsible and provide

TABLE 17.3	California Ballot Propositions That Have Passed Since 2006

NOVEMBER 7, 2006

Transportation Funding Protection

Highway Safety/Air Quality/Port Security Bond 2006

Housing/Emergency Shelter Trust Fund 2006

Public Education Facilities Bond 2006

Disaster Preparedness/Flood Prevention Bond 2006

Sex Offenders/Residence Restrictions Monitoring

Water Quality/Flood/Resource Protection/Park Bonds

FEBRUARY 5, 2008

Indian Gaming Compact for Pechanga Band

Indian Gaming Compact for Morongo Band

Indian Gaming Compact for Sycuan Band

Indian Gaming Compact for Agua Caliente Band

JUNE 3, 2008

Eminent Domain. Limits on Government Acquisition

NOVEMBER 4, 2008

Safe, Reliable High-Speed Train Bond Act

Standards for Confining Farm Animals

Children's Hospital Bond Act. Grant Program

Eliminates Right of Same-Sex Couples to Marry

Criminal Justice System. Victims' Rights. Parole.

Redistricting

Veterans' Bond

MAY 19, 2009

State Officer Salary Increases

NOVEMBER 2, 2010

Redistricting of Congressional Districts

Prohibit State from Taking Some Local Funds

Simple Majority Vote to Pass Budget

Two-Thirds Vote for Some State/Local Fees

SOURCE: California Secretary of State—Elections and Voter Information—Initiative Update.

the governor with greater authority on budget matters. The governor's second try at the polls resulted in the defeat of all four initiatives he sponsored in the 2005 special election, which included attempts to restrict teacher employment rights, limit the use of union dues for political purposes, constrain state spending and increase the budget authority of the governor, and strip the state legislature of its redistricting power. The failure of these initiatives is due to the fact that the governor largely disregarded the key features of the initiative formula, choosing instead to rely on his own perceived popularity.

PROBLEMS WITH INITIATIVES In the aftermath of Proposition 13, many campaign consultants and public relations firms that formerly concentrated on electing candidates switched to managing initiative campaigns. Political scientists and journalists have asserted that the growth of these firms is a major reason why the initiative has become such a fixture of California electoral politics. The large sum of money that political consulting firms can earn by managing initiative campaigns creates an incentive for them to encourage an interest group or wealthy individual to sponsor an initiative. For the representatives of interest groups, elected officials, and major corporate interests, attempting to pass an initiative can be easier than achieving a public policy objective through the state legislature, especially when the conditions of the post–Proposition 13 formula converge. The legislative process inevitably involves almost endless lobbying, large campaign contributions to individual legislators, trade-offs, and side deals. With the initiative, by contrast, few concessions need to be made.

Surveys of Californians conducted by the Public Policy Institute of California suggest that the initiative is very popular, but a significant majority "think that the ballot wording for citizens' initiatives is often too complicated and confusing for voters to clearly understand what would happen" if the measure passed.[15] The surveys also reveal that slightly more than half of Californians have more confidence in the initiative process than in the public policy decisions made by the governor and state legislature. Conversely, respondents feel there are too many propositions on the state ballot.[16]

REFORMING THE INITIATIVE PROCESS As more and more initiatives find their way onto the ballot, an increasing number of reports and commissions, such as the *Citizen's Commission on Ballot Initiatives* and the *California Constitution Revisions Commission,* have found problems in the initiative process and recommend implementation of a wide variety of reforms. Critics charge that the initiative process too often fails as an adequate avenue for direct democracy, because so many factors tend to limit popular participation. Such factors include the dominance of special-interest groups, excessive campaign

■ **Referendum:** A process by which voters can demand the review and approval of a particular legislative action by the voters.

EXAMPLE: *The referendum is available in 24 states, but most only allow voters to approve or disapprove laws passed by their state legislatures.*

■ **Petition Referendum:** A procedure that allows voters to request that all or part of a law be submitted to the voters for approval.

EXAMPLE: *One of California's most infamous petition referendums was Proposition 14, which in 1964 repealed the Rumford Fair Housing Act, a law that prohibited discrimination in housing.*

spending, poorly and deceptively written proposals, and a lack of accountability. Various recommended reforms have largely centered on preelection review of initiative proposals, greater disclosure of financial sources and proponents, an increased legislative role, and more stringent qualifying requirements. Any change to initiative provisions would have to be led by the state legislature or passed as a ballot measure requiring a great deal of political capital. And that capital would be needed to convince Californians who have listened to discussion, review, and debate of the initiative process for over a decade and have grown as wary of the motivations of political leaders as they are aware of the difficulties of the initiative process.

The Referendum

The **referendum**■ has been commonly referred to as the least popular avenue of direct democracy. That observation is generally true, but on closer analysis, there is evidence to suggest the two types of referendum in California, *petition* and *compulsory,* have in recent times played a growing and critical role in state politics.

THE PETITION REFERENDUM Of the two types of referendum, the protest or **petition referendum**■ is closer to the spirit of the Progressive movement, because it allows voters to request that all or part of a law be submitted to the voters for approval with the option of preventing a piece of legislation from taking effect. All laws that have been recently passed by the state legislature and signed by the governor, with the exception of urgency statutes, statutes calling elections, or statutes providing for tax levies or appropriations for current expenses of the state, can be subjected to a petition referendum.

Before a petition can be placed on a ballot, supporters must obtain enough signatures of registered voters to equal 5 percent or more of the votes for all candidates in the last gubernatorial election. The petition is considered one of the most difficult direct democracy procedures to implement because of the relatively short time proponents have to gather the hundreds of thousands of signatures required (90 days after enactment of the law). Once the required number of signatures are presented and certified by the secretary of state, the petition will be voted on during the next general election or special statewide election. A simple majority of voters will determine whether the law will be retained or invalidated.

Although the use of the petition has been infrequent, especially in comparison to the initiative, there has been a slight increase over the past 20 years. From 1942 until 1970, only one petition successfully qualified for the ballot, but between 1982 and 2005, the number grew to seven.[17] During the 2000 primary election, insurance regulations became the target of the seldom-used petition, providing a good example of how direct democracy can produce unintended outcomes. The two insurance

claim practices referendums, Propositions 30 and 31, were placed on the 2000 primary election ballot in response to two recently enacted laws that would permit third-party lawsuits. These laws gave accident victims the right to sue insurance companies that denied, delayed, or attempted to "lowball" insurance claims resulting from an automobile accident. Under previous California law, a person who felt an accident settlement was unsatisfactory or unfair could only file a complaint with the Department of Insurance or reject the settlement and sue the individual responsible for causing the accident, but the person could not sue an insurance company for unfair claims practices.[18]

The insurance industry objected to the new laws and had the financial muscle to overcome the difficulties of qualifying two petitions for the ballot. During the campaign phase leading up to the 2000 primary election, the insurance industry spent large sums of money convincing voters that the insurance claims practice laws would cause auto insurance premiums to skyrocket and that the laws would benefit personal injury attorneys, not consumers. Consumer groups argued that the insurance companies regularly deny claims, delay insurance payments, or pay only minimal costs of accident victims. They repeatedly cited the enormous profits insurance companies made in the course of such business practices. In the end, the voters agreed with the insurance companies and rejected Propositions 30 and 31 by 68 and 71 percent, respectively.

THE COMPULSORY REFERENDUM The legislative or **compulsory referendum**■ has generated much more attention and use than the petition referendum, principally because it is an approval device for the state legislature. The compulsory nature of this type of referendum is the consequence of the state constitution, which requires that all debts and liabilities and all constitutional amendments that originate in the state legislature be passed by a two-thirds vote of each house of the legislature and be approved by a majority of the voters during the next scheduled primary or general election. Almost every regularly schedule election since 2000 has included a compulsory referendum that authorizes a bond act.

The issuance of bonds—in most cases **general obligation bonds**■, state debt that is backed by the "full faith and credit of the state"—has become a popular means for the state government to raise revenue without raising taxes. General obligation bonds are typically used to finance major projects or long-term services rather than regular government operating costs. Such bonds place an obligation on future taxpayers and will ultimately cost them far more than the funds received, as a result of the interest that must be paid on the bond. Governor Schwarzenegger's response to California's budget woes in 2004 was to encourage the state legislature to enact the Economic Recovery Bond Act soon after taking office. This $15 billion bond scheme gave the state a much-needed infusion of funds. One year after suffering the defeat of a series of reform-related

■ **Compulsory Referendum:** A requirement that all debts and liabilities over $3 million and constitutional amendments that originate in the state legislature must be passed by a two-thirds vote of each house and approved by a majority of the voters during the next election.

SIGNIFICANCE: *The compulsory referendum was first adopted by the city of Los Angeles at the urging of the Direct Legislation League in 1904.*

■ **General Obligation Bonds:** State debt that is backed by the "full faith and credit of the state."

SIGNIFICANCE: *Most general obligation bonds are paid off within a 30-year period.*

---

initiatives, Schwarzenegger was back in 2006 with a $43 billion "Strategic Growth" bond. Having obtained the blessing of the state legislature, the governor's latest bond was approved by the voters and would be used to restore and expand California's highways, roads and transit systems, as well as schools, housing, parks, levees, and water supply systems.

Constitutional amendments are also often cast as compulsory referendums. Amendments have covered a wide variety of issues and services, including court consolidation, gambling, transportation, election rights, and surplus property. The compulsory referendum method in California is relatively straightforward and can easily be a regular part of the state electoral process. Bruce E. Cain, noted University of California political science professor, has found that the more deliberative methods of constitutional change in the state, involving either a constitutional convention or constitutional revision commissions, have been eclipsed by more direct methods, including legislative constitutional amendments. The result, according to Cain, is that constitutional change in California lacks the "integrated perspective" of constitutional conventions or revision commissions. He

believes that the shift from "revision to amendment may be misshaping California state structure in important and predictable ways."[19] The compulsory referendum has clearly contributed to California's high ranking among states that change their constitutions often.

California residents may also attempt to subject county or municipal laws and ordinances to a referendum, but the process deviates considerably from statewide referendums. The period allowed for gathering signatures in cities and counties is longer (180 days) than the 90 days allowed for a statewide referendum, and all proposals or petitions are submitted to the city or county clerk. Although most local referendums are also approved by a majority vote, local bond measures, with the exception of education bonds, must be passed by a two-thirds majority. Rather than follow the general law for cities and counties, for which election provisions are established by the state legislature, many local governments have adopted charters with prescribed procedures, including the referendum, that are unique to the region and type of government.

Direct Democracy: California's Electoral Dilemma

17.2 Evaluate whether the recall, referendum, and initiative have successfully established a more direct democracy in California.

PRACTICE QUIZ: UNDERSTAND AND APPLY

1. Although surveys suggest the initiative remains very popular with Californians, a significant majority also feels that
   a. the ballot wording for citizens' initiatives is often too complicated and confusing for voters to clearly understand.
   b. the initiative process allows too many unnecessary measures to be placed on the ballot.
   c. the expense of voting on initiatives is costly and should be limited.
   d. special-interest groups should be barred from making large contributions to initiative campaigns.

2. Which of the following has been commonly referred to as the least popular avenue of direct democracy?
   a. recall
   b. referendum
   c. initiative
   d. closed primary

3. The compulsory or legislative referendum requires that all debts and liabilities and all constitutional amendments that originate in the state legislature

must be passed by what margin in each house of the legislature?
   a. simple majority vote
   b. three-fourths vote
   c. a consistent majority vote
   d. two-thirds vote

ANALYZE

1. Do California's avenues for direct democracy continue to reflect the vision or purpose foreseen by the Progressives?

2. Since its enactment, has the initiative process been used to successfully implement a more direct democratic system? In what ways does the initiative process circumvent democratic values? In what ways does it create a more responsive government?

IDENTIFY THE CONCEPT THAT DOESN'T BELONG

a. Signature gathering
b. Joint powers agreements
c. Proposition 13
d. Legal challenges
e. Deceptive wording

17.2

Resource Center
• Glossary
• Vocabulary Example
• Connect the Link

■ **Citizen-Politician:** A candidate who succeeds during a campaign in convincing California voters of his or her political independence and nonpartisanship.

EXAMPLE: *The California Progressives are largely responsible for popularizing this image through the introduction of government reforms and procedures that emphasized nonpartisanship and professionalism in government.*

Campaigning for Votes

17.3 Explain how campaigns are organized to most effectively influence California voters.

(pages 540–545)

Any election—whether for president of the United States, an initiative, or a seat on the city council—is the culmination of a political campaign, and California campaigns reflect the distinctive nature of the politics practiced in this state. If there is any one indication of the importance of each vote, the time, money, and effort spent by political campaigns to win it should be it. Campaigns involve hundreds of millions of dollars, sophisticated technologies and techniques, and the commitment of time and energy by people who are often working as unpaid volunteers. Registered voters are the targets of concerted efforts to determine how they will vote and how to influence their voting decisions. Contemporary campaign techniques, for example, consider carefully which information sources are most persuasive to voters (see Figure 17.1). An individual's vote in California is strongly influenced by a number of factors, including the nonpartisan qualifications of a candidate, where a voter lives, and exposure to mass communications. In addition, voter records and interest groups can have an impact on how campaigns are run and how successful they are. There are, of course, many types of campaigns in

California, distinguished by the office being filled, the number of candidates, and the level of resources and money. However, some general trends can be observed in how these campaigns organize to influence voters.

Nonpartisan Qualification

Because of Progressive Era reforms that made most elective offices nonpartisan, the role of political parties in California is not as significant as it is in other states. Voters are essentially left without a party label as a signal of the candidate's political orientation. The absence of party labels has encouraged a greater sense of independence among California voters as compared to voters in other states. According to the Public Policy Institute of California, "The largest change in the electorate since 1994 is the addition of 1.4 million 'decline to state' or independent voters (1.5 million to 2.9 million), which led to a 7 percentage point increase (11% to 18%) in their share of the electorate."[20] The governorships of Hiram Johnson, Earl Warren, and now Arnold Schwarzenegger are good examples of candidates who succeeded during their campaigns in convincing California voters of their political independence, drawing many voters from the opposite party. Even Ronald Reagan, who began his campaign for governor with very partisan credentials, astutely developed the image of a **citizen-politician**■. Political scientists and California journalists have suggested that nonpartisan elections tend to favor the Republican Party, which is able to compensate for the absence of a party label with well-funded, well-organized campaigns. Another advantage for the Republicans in nonpartisan elections is their traditionally higher voter turnout in elections where overall voter turnout is low.

MYTH EXPOSED Many Californians believe that local government is nonpartisan. Yet behind closed doors and beyond earshot of the general public, partisan politics is very much alive. A survey of state legislators will reveal that at least one-third were former local government officials, recruited and supported for this partisan office based on a previous commitment to their political party. Among the hundreds of delegates chosen to attend either party convention in 2008, a substantial number held local governmental offices. Many local officials are actively involved in the county central committees of their respective parties, partisan organizations that will on occasion indirectly funnel campaign contributions to local candidates. Even the so-called "slate mailer" advertising cards that list partisan candidates typically include local candidates.

FIGURE 17.1 ■ California Initiatives: Effects of Information Sources on Voting

Participants in a poll conducted by the Public Policy Institute of California in 2000 were asked which of these information sources has the biggest effect on voter's decision to vote "yes" or "no" on citizen initiatives. —*What are the qualities of "news stories in the media" that are most likely to make this information source the most popular and what are the qualities of governmental and independent Web sites most likely to make this information source the least popular?*

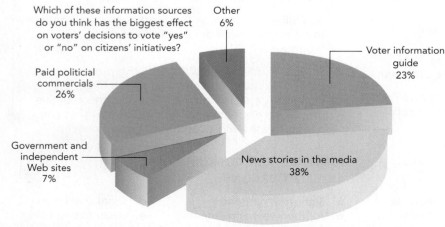

Which of these information sources do you think has the biggest effect on voters' decisions to vote "yes" or "no" on citizens' initiatives?

- Other 6%
- Voter information guide 23%
- Paid political commercials 26%
- News stories in the media 38%
- Government and independent Web sites 7%

SOURCE: J. Fred Silva, "The California Initiative Process," Public Policy Institute of California, Occasional Papers, November 2000, p 26. Reprinted with permission.

■ **Voter Registration Data:** Voter information gathered during the registration process that is available at all county election offices in California.

SIGNIFICANCE: *Today, well-funded campaigns utilize computers with sophisticated programs to create voter profiles and target specific groups of voters based on voter registration data.*

Nonpartisan restrictions undoubtedly limit ideological bias within local government and potential division among office-holders and their constituents. Close examination, however, of the local officeholder's policy preferences regarding such issues as taxation, regulation, and social programs will at a minimum uncover an ideological impulse or at best a party activist.

In California, partisan elections are few in number, consisting of races for congressional representatives, state legislators, and most statewide elective offices, but their importance cannot be overstated. In the current era, with the exception of the governorship, California's majority of Democratic voters tend to produce a majority of Democratic officeholders in partisan contests.

Voter Records

Voter registration information is extremely important in identifying the ideological background and basic personal information about voters that campaigns use to determine their strategies and tactics. State party organizations attempt to register as many potential voters as possible, with the hope that they will vote for that party or a particular candidate. Few of the individuals—or *deputy registrars*, as they are known officially—who actually register prospective voters are volunteers engaged in fulfilling some civic duty. Most are either directly connected to a political party or interest group or hired specifically to register prospective voters in a given area. In California, the Democratic Party has normally been the most active party in conducting voter registration drives, a key factor in its ability to remain the dominant political party. The registration of new Democratic Party voters is, however, often inconsequential, being canceled out by low Democratic Party turnout between general elections and the high number of Democratic voters who are purged from election records either because they failed to vote in the last election or had a change of address.

Political parties often concentrate voter registration drives in areas where their party support is high or where the population is increasing. Both of these factors are significant in California, which tends to have high concentrations of party loyalists and an expanding and mobile population. All the voter information that is gathered during the registration process can be purchased from all county election offices in California. These reports contain data used to build mailing, telephone, precinct canvassing, and poll watcher lists. **Voter registration data**■ also serve to measure trends among registered voters. Using voting records from previous elections, a campaign organization can analyze the voting outcome of one voter precinct or a cluster of precincts for a particular election and attempt to find patterns or make forecasts.

The wide differences in voter registration rates throughout the state frequently present strategic dilemmas for state political party organizations that must decide where to focus its campaign efforts. Does the Democratic Party, for example,

concentrate its financial and human resources in Marin County, where voter registration is regularly above 80 percent, 40 percent vote by absentee ballot, and the Democratic Party is in the majority, or in Imperial County, where registration is below 50 percent, 13 percent vote by absentee ballot, and the majority is also Democratic? The relative affluence of Marin County, with a median household income of about $71,306, is an important source of political contributions in addition to high Democratic Party voter turnout. Yet the ideological principles of the Democratic Party are closer to the working-class population of Imperial County, which has a median household income of approximately $31,870 and the potential to expand the number of registered Democratic voters.[21]

A working-class neighborhood that is predominantly Democratic but voted overwhelmingly to pass a "law and order" proposition could potentially be convinced to vote for another proposition sponsored by conservatives or for a Republican candidate able to downplay his or her party label. The tendency of California voters to lean toward nonpartisanship or switch parties in gubernatorial elections makes the analysis of voter information a necessity.

Interest Groups

Interest groups are formal organizations of people who share a common outlook, social or economic circumstances, or political goals and who band together in the hope of influencing government policy. In California, there are many interest groups and government policies that these groups seek to influence (see Figure 17.2).

The governorship of Arnold Schwarzenegger epitomizes the significance as well as the perils of the relationship

FIGURE 17.2 ■ **Average Dollars Raised During 2006 California Primary and General Elections Campaign for Governor** —*Why do you think the winners were able to raise so much money in comparison to the losers?*

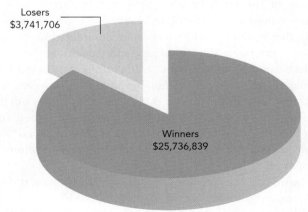

Losers $3,741,706

Winners $25,736,839

SOURCE: www.followthemoney.org/database/StateGlance/state_candidates .phtml?s=CA&y=2006

■ **Political Contributions:** Contributors to campaigns can be found at every level of government in California. Many Californians consider political contributions as nothing more than payoffs, while others feel such contributions are a legitimate form of charitable giving.

SIGNIFICANCE: *After candidate self-financing and party committees, lawyers were the top political contributors in California. At the local level, the real estate development industry typically contributes the most money to campaigns.*

Democratic Assembly Speaker Fabian Nunez tries to squeeze through a hallway in the Capitol filled with California lobbyists. —*How do interest groups seek to gain influence through lobbyists?*

between elected officials or candidates and interest groups. In the 12 months following his election in 2003, Governor Schwarzenegger broke every fundraising record, accumulating approximately $26.6 million—nearly twice the amount raised by Governor Gray Davis during his first year in office.[22] Most of the money was contributed to committees set up by Governor Schwarzenegger to support his ballot measures, thereby avoiding the $21,000 limit on individual contributions to candidates. Much of this money can be traced to interest groups with a stake either in these propositions or in other laws and decisions before the state government. The size and origin of political contributions from interest groups have resulted in constant accusations of influence peddling. In response, the governor and representatives of these interest groups have said that the contributions were merely supporting Schwarzenegger's ideological direction and leadership.[23] Many of the contributors represented industries, such as finance, insurance, automobile, health care, and pharmaceuticals, that evidently did receive some consideration or assistance through the policies and decisions of the Schwarzenegger administration. Other supporters from entertainment, real estate, and technology industries, however, have received intangible returns. Moreover, the return on this money to the governor has been mixed—it helped him get two important propositions passed in 2004 but was irrelevant in 2005, when the voters rejected four propositions he supported.

Although money does not always buy influence, it often determines who will win the election. Figure 17.2 shows how much money is raised by the winning candidates verses the losing candidates in races of the governor's office and seats for the

California House. Winning candidates are strongly dependent on **political contributions**■.

The same dilemmas crop up at each level of electoral politics and are probably most pronounced at the local level, where political contributions and other resources become scarce. The boom in the California real estate market during the early 2000s made local government especially vulnerable to interest groups associated with real estate development. An in-depth report on campaign contributions in the Sacramento metropolitan area in 2002 revealed that the biggest political contributors were developers, land speculators, contractors, and building tradespeople. The report found "regionally, that one campaign dollar out of four came from development and real estate. In slow-growth Yolo County, however, that statistic was one dollar out of six. And in burgeoning Placer County, it was nearly one campaign dollar out of two."[24] Still, the representatives of these real estate industry interest groups denied any wrongdoing, asserting that they were only supporting the best-qualified candidates, that they often made contributions in communities where they have no business interests, and that political donations were only one of many types of charitable giving. This same report also revealed that land development often makes strange bedfellows, bringing the real estate industry and trade unions together to back candidates who are pro-development.[25]

Geography

The geography of California, which encompasses numerous geographic regions within one political entity, is yet another major influence on the outcome of elections. James Q. Wilson, the noted political scientist, observed that the conservative tendencies of Southern California have a lot to do with low-density housing and property ownership. These factors make voters more likely to value individual accomplishment and initiative in political candidates. By contrast, people in dense urban settings, where there is a proliferation of organizations and the individual is more likely to join a group, are more likely to be affected by group affiliations. Wilson goes on to say that the large number of newcomers to Southern California and highly mobile residents "are more likely to vote the way established institutions—newspapers, churches, labor unions, business firms—tell them to vote."[26] Yet the low-density and single-family neighborhoods that have spread across Southern California dilute the influence of established organizations by making the more personal, door-to-door campaigning more difficult. As housing developments multiply in every part of California, aspects of Wilson's thesis on Southern California politics are becoming apparent in other regions as well. The suburban trend in California is causing residents of the state to disconnect from established political traditions and vote more as individuals or independents.

Various generalities regarding the geopolitics of California are vital to understanding who gets elected where, but some

■ **30-Second Advertising Spot:** Commonly used by well-funded political campaigns to feature television political advertisements. The cost of these spots can range from $3,000 to as much as $30,000 depending on the California advertising market.

SIGNIFICANCE: *The campaigns on behalf of Governor Arnold Schwarzenegger's four failed reform initiatives spent over $90 million on television advertisements. The opposing campaigns spent over $63 million on TV ads.*

caution should be exercised because of the many exceptions that mirror California's diverse landscape. Political commentators often suggest that the Republican Party tends to be concentrated in Southern California and that Northern California is the stronghold of the Democrats. The Los Angeles metropolitan area, though in the south, is nevertheless solidly Democratic. The San Francisco Bay Area is one of the most liberal regions in the country, but drive 40 miles to the east, and you could be in Republican country. The major cities along the coast of California tend to be Democratic, again with various exceptions, while the sparsely populated eastern side of the state is much more conservative. In 2004, of the top 10 Democratic Party counties with the highest percentage of party registration, seven were adjacent to the coast, while in the top 10 Republican Party counties with the highest percentage of party registration, nine were inland and five were located in Northern California.[27]

The party orientation of various regions in California will determine not only what type of candidates will be elected but also their campaign strategy. A school board candidate, despite the nonpartisan designation, will be less likely to campaign on the promise of a school bond in a fiscally conservative, Republican-dominated district. Until recently, these geopolitical considerations have in fact become more institutionalized as the state legislature had been inclined to draw boundaries that create safe state legislative districts for both political parties. This trend disturbed both liberal and conservative elected officials and private citizens, from the political advocacy group Common Cause to Governor Schwarzenegger himself, causing an attempt at reforming the redistricting process that culminated in 2008 with the passage of Proposition 11—the Voter FIRST Act. The provisions of this act mandate a Citizen Redistricting Commission composed of 14 members, from whom five members are identified as registered Democrats, four registered as Republicans, and four unaffiliated or decline-to-state members. This commission has the responsibility of creating districts of relatively equal populations for the state legislature and Board of Equalization in response to the results of the decennial census. Whether or not this commission will actually result in a more responsive government remains to be seen, but this reform has made certain elected officials a bit less secure and has caused the political parties to work harder to attract prospective voters. The major point of the geopolitics of California is that where residents of the state live has a lot to do with whether their votes will really make a difference.

Mass Communication

The use of mass communication is vital to political parties and candidates in reaching voters. Of all the major influences on an election, mass communication is probably the most significant. In the past, campaigning was a personal activity. Candidates

were expected to give many speeches, engage in debates, and walk precincts. Today, however, these tactics are fast becoming obsolete except for a small number of local elections. Potential voters now rarely meet with a candidate face to face.

In her book *Phantom Politics: Campaigning in California,* Mary Ellen Leary explores how the mass media have changed the way politics is practiced in California, using the election of Jerry Brown as governor in 1974 for a campaign case study. Quoting a professional campaign manager and media consultant with "15 years of Los Angeles political experience," Leary writes:

> "There are three key factors in a political campaign these days," he said in his staccato manner. "No. 1 is television, No. 2 is television, No. 3 is television. In all our survey work, we ask people why they voted the way they did, and it always comes up television."[28]

And television advertising for any purpose, much less politics, is expensive. During the campaign season leading up to the November 2005 special election, the cost of a **30-second advertising spot**■ in the Los Angeles market started at roughly $3,000. As the election drew closer, that figure shot to $10,000 (see Table 17.4). By the 2010 gubernatorial primary, a 30-second spot during *American Idol* aired in Los Angeles could cost as much as $30,000.[29] Television remains the most widely used media form by politicians, and spending on television advertising continues to rise.

The proliferation of cable and satellite stations has provided a much more affordable, alternative form of television exposure as compared to expensive network television advertising. California government and politics has gotten significantly more visible with the increased programming schedule of the "California Channel," broadcast on many cable networks throughout the state. This C-SPAN-like public broadcast station offers a rare view of the state legislature in action, presenting statewide officials and state legislators that are written about but seldom seen outside Sacramento or their districts. Cable broadcasts are especially appealing to local campaign organizations that attempt to go beyond traditional forms of campaigning but lack the fiscal resources.

News reports on television and radio and in newspapers provide free political publicity, especially for campaigns that can afford to hire media consultants or "spin doctors," who maximize the quality and quantity of a candidate's news media exposure. Of course, getting exposure on **local and regional media outlets**■ presents certain challenges, because there is no guarantee that media coverage will be positive. Media outlets have the additional pressure of covering the election process at a time when their parent companies are more inclined to favor entertainment programming over news. An investigation of local nightly news broadcasts in 11 markets, including Los

■ **Local and Regional Media Outlets:** Media outlets, such as radio, television, and newspapers, have the additional pressure of having to cover the election process at a time when their parent companies are more inclined to favor entertainment programming over news.

SIGNIFICANCE: *Local nightly news broadcasts typically allocate very little coverage to local races.*

| TABLE 17.4 | Nielsen Monitor-Plus Special Industry Spotlight: Political Advertising |

In the 11 markets that make up the state of California, 44,122 political commercials aired between August 1 and October 16, 2005. "Vote No on Proposition 79" had the most activity, with over 18,000 commercials airing, and referendum-related advertising accounted for 43,996, or 99.7 percent, of the spots during this period.

MARKET	SPOT TV-UNITS	SPOT TV-GRP: P18+
Los Angeles	7,796	9,237
San Francisco–Oakland–San Jose	5,660	6,574
San Diego	5,182	8,535
Sacramento–Stockton–Modesto	5,076	10,024
Fresno–Visalia	4,667	8,919
Santa Barbara–Santa Maria–San Luis Obispo	3,119	5,583
Bakersfield	2,967	5,073
Chico–Redding	2,919	5,141
Palm Springs	2,713	4,242
Monterey–Salinas	2,145	3,771
Eureka	1,878	2,821
Total	44,122	69,920

NOTE: The Gross Rating Point (GRP) is a unit of measurement of audience size. It is used to measure the exposure to one or more programs or commercials without regard to multiple exposures of the same advertising to individuals. One GRP equals 1 percent of television households in the total market.
SOURCE: The Nielsen Company. Reprinted with permission.

Angeles, found that a typical half-hour of local news consisted of these segments:

Advertising: 8 minutes, 51 seconds

Sports and weather: 6 minutes, 21 seconds

Elections: 3 minutes, 11 seconds

Presidential coverage: 2 minutes

Noncandidate coverage (initiatives, referendums): 45 seconds

All other races (local, state, and federal): 30 seconds

Crime: 2 minutes, 34 seconds

Local interest: 1 minute, 56 seconds

Teasers, intros, music: 1 minute, 43 seconds

Health: 1 minute, 22 seconds

Other: 1 minute, 12 seconds

Unintentional injury: 55 seconds

Business and economy: 47 seconds

Government (nonelection coverage): 28 seconds

Iraq: 25 seconds

Foreign policy: 13 seconds[30]

In the Los Angeles area, of the four stations included in the investigation, between 1 and 3 percent of all news stories were about local campaigns. As a media outlet for political campaigns, radio is clearly less attractive than television, and it suffers from similar constraints.

To a large extent, mass communication techniques were pioneered in California during the 1934 gubernatorial race, the so-called "Campaign of the Century" between the "socialist" Democratic candidate, Upton Sinclair, and the Republican governor, Frank Merriam. For the first time in California campaign history, an ad agency, Lord & Thomas (later merged into Foote, Cone & Belding), managed a political campaign. With professional assistance of Lord & Thomas, Merriam's political campaign would beat the very popular Upton Sinclair, employing, among many sophisticated marketing techniques, direct mail and the targeting of specific groups.[31] Later, the firm of

■ **Direct-Mail Piece:** Advertising pieces mailed to voters that are created by using sophisticated technologies and techniques that have often been tested through focus groups.

EXAMPLE: *During the infamous gubernatorial campaign of 1934 between Upton Sinclair and Frank Merriam, the Merriam campaign was noted for its colorful direct-mail pieces that regularly carried such headlines as "Sinclair, dynamiter of all churches, will you turn California over to the mercies of Upton Sinclair."*

Gubernatorial candidate Jerry Brown meets with the media as the results of the 2010 Democratic primary election come in. Brown went on to win an unprecedented third term as governor. —*What role do the media play in high profile campaigns?*

Spencer & Roberts would be instrumental in the 1970 election of Ronald Reagan by introducing computer technology to political marketing. The work of the legendary Butcher–Forde political consulting firm on the Proposition 13 campaign, again adopting novel techniques such as designing a solicitation letter to resemble a tax bill, was another milestone in political marketing. Today, for campaigns that lack the funds to acquire media advertisement, direct mail has become the mainstay. Behind each **direct-mail piece**■ are often sophisticated technologies and techniques designed to target various categories of voters using words, colors, and layout styles that have been tested through focus groups and computer simulations.

Campaigning for Votes

17.3 **Explain how campaigns are organized to most effectively influence California voters.**

PRACTICE QUIZ: UNDERSTAND AND APPLY

1. Political parties often concentrate their voter registration drives in areas where
   a. their party support is low, in the hope of attracting new members.
   b. their party support is high.
   c. there are large numbers of unregistered voters.
   d. there are large numbers of independent voters.

2. Why are the active voter registration drives of the Democratic Party often inconsequential?
   a. California voters tend to register in greater numbers with the Republican Party.
   b. Large numbers of Democrats switch to the Republican Party after each election.
   c. Registration drives by the Democrats are cancelled out by low Democratic Party turnout between general elections.
   d. It is very difficult to determine the actual number of voters during each election.

3. Low-density housing and property ownership tend to increase the number of what type of voters?
   a. Republican Party
   b. Democratic Party
   c. Green Party
   d. independent

ANALYZE

1. How do political campaigns use voter records to increase their chances of success?

2. What influence do interest groups and mass communications have on the outcome of elections?

IDENTIFY THE CONCEPT THAT DOESN'T BELONG

a. Resolution
b. Mailing
c. Telephone
d. Precinct
e. Canvassing

Resource Center
• Glossary
• Vocabulary Example
• Connect the Link

■ **Absentee Voting:** In California, absentee voting has been simplified over the years, particularly through temporary mail-in ballot provisions.

SIGNIFICANCE: *There were about 5.3 million permanent absentee ballots mailed to voters in the 2008 election, up from the roughly 4 million in 2006. As of mid-November, the Field poll predicts 55 percent of the ballots in the 2010 midterm election were absentee or mail-in ballots.*

Empowering California Voters

17.4 **Identify ways to empower voters.**

(pages 546–547)

Nonvoters usually harbor misguided notions about why elections are unimportant or their vote would make no difference, but a wealth of evidence bears out the value of the electoral process in a democratic society. The founders of the American Republic viewed elections as vital to establishing a functional democracy, as did the Progressives in California, who provided residents of the state with extraordinary powers to influence government directly.

Many Californians understand the importance of voting but feel intimidated by the process. Many regular voters complain of complicated ballot information, made even more confusing by the large amount of campaign literature, signs, and advertisements. Such intimidation is not surprising considering the lack of education or training that residents receive about the California electoral process. Gallant efforts are being made at the secondary school level through mock elections, model government, and student council elections, but such efforts are ultimately simulations of the process in a very controlled environment. Any contact with the California electoral process will be a fleeting experience for most residents, and in the absence of strong political party organizations in most communities, voters really are on their own. This sense of electoral isolation can be overcome by taking the necessary steps to understand the process and navigate the procedures of voting.

Preparing to Vote

The first step to becoming an empowered voter is to realize that voters do have power. Almost every aspect of life in California—roads, taxes, schools, water, and even the air we breathe—is affected by the electoral process, especially at the local level. Once that fact is realized, the next step is to clearly understand voting procedures. The California Voter Foundation found that "more than half of infrequent voters are not familiar with absentee voting. Fifty percent said they had never voted absentee, and 2 percent said they didn't know whether absentee voting was easy or difficult."[32] **Absentee voting**■ in California has been simplified over the years, particularly through temporary mail-in ballot provisions. In a large number of counties, the voter, after simply downloading forms requesting a mail-in ballot, can complete the registration and voting process by mail within two weeks of an election.

Another example of an electoral procedure often overlooked by prospective voters is the right under California law to take up to two hours off from work without loss of pay to vote on election day. Various organizations and government agencies exist to inform prospective voters of electoral procedures and voters' rights. The League of Women Voters provides assistance to voters, publishes election information, conducts an assortment of voter education programs, and serves as a clearinghouse for similar organizations.

The next major step to becoming an empowered voter is to know what is being voted on. It has often been said that an uninformed voter is worse than a nonvoter, because uninformed voters stand a good chance of voting for candidates or issues that they would oppose if they were better informed. In 1996, Proposition 209 appeared on the ballot as the "California Civil Rights Initiative." The name succeeded in deceiving many uninformed voters, who thought they were voting in favor of civil rights. The initiative that voters actually passed prohibited all race- and gender-based considerations in California public education, contracting, and employment. Voters can avoid or minimize this type of electoral deception by becoming informed.

Newspapers are the first line of defense in combating voter manipulation, providing most of the basic information that is needed to understand the issues of a campaign. Although newspapers do have biases at the journalistic, editorial, or ownership level that affect content, the newspaper is still an important source of information if used comprehensively, which means reading and comparing the features, news stories, editorials, and letters to the editor, which may offer different perspectives on a given issue. The voter ballot guide published by the California secretary of state offers a balanced description of the ballot, but the voter should expect a minimal amount of objectivity in these guides and a lot of partisan arguments. Campaign literature is frequently full of inaccuracies, distortions, and embellishments, but for a voter who is observant or willing to invest a little more time in the information-gathering process, such literature does contain subtle clues that can help determine the worthiness of the candidates. California election law requires that all campaign mailings list the name of the sponsoring organization or individual and reveal the name of the financial backer—though sometimes this is done in tiny, difficult-to-read print. The election slate postcards sent by political party organizations or unions that list all the candidates and propositions being endorsed are sometimes more informative in terms of who and what they do *not* list or endorse.

Voting Electronically

Since 2004, problems with **electronic voting machines**■ in California have occurred. The roots of these difficulties lie in mandates from the federal government encouraging states to modernize the election process.[33] Electronic voting machines are supposed to offer a faster way of voting and tabulation. Yet in 2004, Diebold Election Systems agreed to pay a $2.6 million

■ **Electronic Voting Machines:** With the encouragement of the federal government, California has attempted to modernize the election process with the introduction of electronic voting machines, which in theory would provide faster and more accurate methods of voting and tabulating results.

SIGNIFICANCE: *In 2007, after being severely criticized in 2004 for the performance of its electronic voting machines, California Secretary of State Debra Bowen decertified machines made by Diebold Election Systems.*

settlement to the state of California after Bill Lockyer, the attorney general, found that Diebold representatives misled the secretary of state about the level of security and certification of its electronic voting machines.[34] Before the problems with Diebold electronic voting machines in California, Walden O'Dell, the chief executive officer of Diebold and an active Republican supporter of President George W. Bush, was already viewed with suspicion by many state officials when he promised in a fundraising letter to deliver Ohio's electoral votes for President Bush in 2004.

In 2005, problems again plagued electronic voting machines in California, manufactured this time by Election Systems and Software. Malfunctions occurred with the computerized touch screen and software, resulting in incorrect vote counts. Company spokespersons asserted that the problems were attributable either to operator error or incorrect coding on ballots.[35] The electronic voting machine saga continued as Debra Bowen, the California secretary of state, weighed into the use of these machines in preparation for California's 2008 presidential primary. Bowen, required by law to certify the electronic voting machines used in the state, retained a team of computer science professors and students from the University of California and asked them to attempt to compromise the machines. The team actually found the machines remarkably easy to compromise, initially by picking the physical locks on the machines and later through hacking the

A Sherman Oaks resident uses the electronic voting machines in the 2009 primary elections. —*What steps should California take to ensure votes aren't lost when computer systems fail?*

software defenses meant to block intruders. Bowen eventually decertified many of the machines, banning their use in California while provisionally approving others if the manufacturers agreed to include specified security features.

Empowering California Voters

17.4   **Identify ways to empower voters.**

PRACTICE QUIZ: UNDERSTAND AND APPLY

1. On election day, Californians have the right to
   a. download and mail in a ballot.
   b. take two hours of paid leave to vote.
   c. decide whether or not to use electronic voting machines.
   d. all of the above.

2. A good source of information about voting is available from
   a. the governor's office.
   b. Congress.
   c. the League of Women Voters.
   d. electronic voting machines.

3. The official voter ballot guide is published by
   a. the California secretary of state.
   b. political consultants.
   c. OpenSecrets.org.
   d. the U.S. Post Office.

ANALYZE

1. Can the average Californian be expected to prepare adequately for the electoral process? Does the act of voting require more information and educational resources than are currently available?

2. What are the advantages and disadvantages of utilizing electronic voting machines?

IDENTIFY THE CONCEPT THAT DOESN'T BELONG

a. Regional media outlets
b. Advertising spot
c. Juice bills
d. Cable and satellite stations
e. Direct-mail piece

Resource Center
• Glossary
• Vocabulary Example
• Connect the Link

■ **Political Party Work:** Much of this work is focused on the electoral process and getting fellow party members elected to public office.

SIGNIFICANCE: *"Rank and file" or volunteer work listed on both the Democratic National Party and Republican National Committee Web sites includes posting on a blog, writing letters to the editor, signing a petition, acting as a poll watcher, fundraising, registering people to vote, and organizing and managing events.*

Beyond Voting

17.5 **Classify the forms of political participation used by Californians.**

(pages 548–549)

A number of avenues are open to Californians who want to participate in politics. Some of the more common activities include attending local meetings, writing to elected officials, contributing money, attending rallies, and participating in **political party work**■.

Forms of Political Participation

After voting, attending meetings on community affairs is the most popular form of political participation in California, performed by approximately 35 percent of the state population.

The second most popular form of political participation in California is writing to an elected official, an activity performed by about 20 percent of adult citizens. Letters carry enormous weight in the decisions of government officials.

Monetary contributions to political parties, candidates, and campaigns—as the third most common form of political participation—are made by less than 7 percent of the population. Although only 1 of every 14 California residents makes political contributions, the state's wealth and commercial vitality enables California as a whole to contribute more money to electoral campaigns and other political causes than all the states in the nation.

Less than 10 percent of the state population attends rallies or works for a political party. The physical activity and time required would naturally make these activities the least attractive, especially when compared to the relatively low rates of activity required for the other forms of participation.[36]

California's Tradition of Unconventional Political Participation

Unconventional political participation has long been a fixture in California. The popular soapbox rallies and demonstrations of the Kearneyites and labor unions of the late nineteenth century laid the foundation for a succession of unconventional political movements and actions throughout the decades. Some notable examples include the End Poverty in California campaign of the 1930s, the 1943 "zoot suit" riots in Los Angeles, the **Berkeley free-speech movement**■ and Vietnam protests in the 1960s, and the environmental protests that erupted dramatically in the 1970s.

There are many different ways of engaging in unconventional political action, but in the current era, the peaceful demonstration has become the most popular form. It is regularly used to get the attention of governmental leaders, and each year many groups descend on the state capitol, particularly during periods of budget cutbacks, to visibly demonstrate their concern over a political issue. Some demonstrations are intended to gain media attention in the hope of increasing public support for a concern or cause, usually involving smaller numbers of people.

Demonstrations, like other types of unconventional political activities, generally occur when all conventional avenues for political expression are closed. Throughout the 1930s, the California labor movement supported various major strikes, such as the California farm workers strike in 1933 and the San Francisco Longshoremen strike in 1934 with major nonviolent demonstrations. The Free Speech movement at the University of California, Berkeley, led by Mario Savio, was to some extent a precursor to the continous series of anti-Vietnam War demonstrations that would paralyze many university and college campuses across the state.

The impulse to demonstate public dissatisfaction with the status quo surfaced once again on May 1, 2006 with the "The Great American Boycott" also known as "A Day Without a Mexican" when hundreds of thousands of California residents throughout the state participated in a mass protest of immigration policy. Such relatively peaceful unconventional activities in California often reflect the diversity of the state, but they can also mirror acute social problems that on occasion descend into chaos. On April 22, 1992, Los Angeles was the setting for major civil unrest in the aftermath of the verdict in the Rodney King trial when four white police officers accused of inflicting an appalling beating on King captured on videotape were acquitted by an all-white jury in Simi Valley, a suburb of Los Angeles. The horrific riot that ensued unleashed a wave of violence and destruction that after three days would cause 53 deaths, hundreds of injuries and over $1 billion in damages to the City of Los Angeles. Unfortunately, the socioeconomic conditions that ultimately led to this dramatic eruption of hostility are largely unchanged today.

Violent unrest can of course occur at any time and for a variety of reasons if a sense of anger is mixed with an unruly crowd, as happened in the wake of the controversial killing on New Year's Eve in 2008 by a transit policeman of Oscar Grant, an Oakland resident. A peaceful demonstration on January 8, 2009, would inadvertently explode into a violent confrontation with the police throughout the night and into early morning, as hundreds of protesters smashed windows, set small fires, and threw bottles and rocks at the large contigent of police officers that would assemble. Once again we see how public anger over a perceived injustice often lingers

■ **Berkeley Free-Speech Movement:** A movement sparked by the announcement from the administration of the University of California, Berkeley, that effective September 21, 1964, tables would no longer be permitted at the Bancroft and Telegraph entrance and that political literature and activities about off-campus political issues would be prohibited.

SIGNIFICANCE: *The election of Ronald Reagan as governor in 1966 has been seen by many as partly due to the negative reaction of Californians to the Berkeley free-speech movement.*

on the periphery of conventional state politics and can rapidly descend without much organization into chaos.

The point of unconventional political action runs counter to long-term organization and commitment, usually relying on a dramatic political act or series of acts to force conventional recognition of the issue or cause. For better or worse, California's diversity encompasses an assortment of political differences, many of which are so divergent as to produce groups irredeemably disillusioned with conventional politics. The frustrations of groups in California seeking political solutions to myriad issues—from animal rights and environmental degradation to border security, abortion, and drug laws, to name only a few—present long-term challenges to the political stability of the state. Whether those frustrations will be addressed peaceably through recognition by the conventional political process or remain in the realm of unconventionality will largely depend both on the willingness of these groups to accept the political process as is and on how open the process is to accepting new or unconventional ideas.

STUDENT profile

Students ineligible to vote because of age requirements can still become involved in the electoral process by working as a student poll worker. Most county election offices in California have set up programs for student participation at polling stations, partly to enhance their civic education and partly because of the shortage of people willing to staff voting stations. For students to be eligible for these positions, they must be at least 16 years of age, a U.S. citizen, and maintain at least a 2.5 GPA.

Saad Abu-Dagen, a student at Burlingame High School, is one of thousands of students in California who have made the decision to become a paid student poll worker. As a member of a supervised team managing a polling place on election day, she assisted with the opening and closing of the polls, checking in voters, distributing ballots, and demonstrating how to use the voting machine. Saad said, "Working as a student poll worker was an exhilarating experience. It taught me a lot about the voting process and about people in general. I believe this experience will aid me throughout life and this November when I vote in the presidential election."

SOURCE: Accessed at http://www.shapethefuture.org/democracylive and http://www.sos.ca.gov/elections/pollworker.htm

Beyond Voting

17.5   **Classify the forms of political participation used by Californians.**

PRACTICE QUIZ: UNDERSTAND AND APPLY

1. Compared to the rest of the nation, California contributes more money to electoral campaigns and other causes.
   a. true
   b. false

2. Which of the following is not a reason why people peacefully demonstrate?
   a. to raise funds
   b. to get the attention of elected leaders
   c. to exhibit displeasure
   d. to get media exposure

3. When do unconventional political activities generally occur?
   a. when a very charismatic leader emerges
   b. as people become more educated
   c. when all conventional avenues for political expression are closed
   d. when gridlock occurs in the state legislature and the lawmaking functions come to a halt

ANALYZE

1. Beyond voting, what forms of political participation are popular in California?

2. When can resorting to unconventional political participation be justified?

IDENTIFY THE CONCEPT THAT DOESN'T BELONG

a. Attend meetings
b. Write letters
c. Vote
d. Contribute money
e. Maintain public records

17.5

Conclusion

DECISION 2010 ★ ★ ★ ★
Proposition 19   16% PRECINCTS REPORTING
Legalize & Regulate Marijuana
YES 44%
✓ NO 56%

Despite a difficult economic situation, the democratic process continues to evolve in California as new and at times controversial policies and proposals are introduced. Californians now find it easier to register to vote because of laws passed by Congress, and the recent ruling by the U.S. Supreme Court that overturned major parts of campaign finance law will clearly have an impact in California. The discarding of laws that have been amended and broadened over the last 63 years will present a major challenge to many Californians who are already unhappy with the amount of money spent by campaign organizations in the state. Many California residents seem determined not only to limit campaign contributions but also to advocate for a less partisan electoral process, evidenced by the recent initiative proposals in 2010 for the "Top Two Open Primary" and publicly financed elections.

As Arnold Schwarzenegger nears the end of his second and final term as governor, his exit offers a cautionary tale reminding Californians that however rational the avenues for direct democracy may seem, they are capable of producing negligible if not unwelcome consequences. Although a much more colorful figure than his recalled predecessor, Gray Davis, few would claim that Governor Schwarzenegger succeeded during his almost eight years in office in solving the problems that beset Davis. In fact, Californians could debate whether the recall process or the many initiatives approved by the voters in recent years have on balance resulted in a more prosperous state. How many initiatives—notwithstanding the reduction of property taxes, mandatory life prison sentences, and restrictions on affirmative action

programs—were either successfully implemented or actually improved the quality of life in the state? Yes, the compulsory referendum has bestowed Californians with an element of control over the approval of bond measures, but unfortunately this control has not prevented the huge indebtedness that now consumes state finances. According to most surveys, direct democracy does remain popular in the state, an inclination suggesting that whatever problems there are with these avenues may lie more with their use rather than the process itself.

The high-tech wizardry that candidates use to vie for votes has become increasingly complicated. Although such gadgets will allow them to reach greater numbers of voters, this technology comes with a high price tag for campaign organization budgets that are already strained. For the individual voter, electronic voting machines present the most obvious high-tech advance in California's electoral process. There is the hope among many forward-looking voters that the convenience and reliability of these machines will emerge as the norm, and the issues of insecurity and tampering will become a rarity.

Lurking on the fringes of the democratic process in the state are unconventional forms of political participation—some of them violent or destructive—that threaten to overturn the advances in democracy that have been made for many Californians. Those who choose unconventional participation will of course remain on the fringes if democracy in California continues to encompass greater numbers of voters and to not leave key groups behind.

KEY CONCEPT MAP   **How do the avenues of direct democracy impact California state government?**

Recall

A process that enables voters to remove, between elections, public officials who they believe are incompetent or corrupt. The two major phases of the recall process are the signature-gathering stage and the election stage.

Since 1913, there have been 154 attempts and five successful recalls of state elected officials. The most significant occurred in 2003 when Governor Gray Davis was recalled. The recall process is used much more frequently at the local level.

Critical Thinking Questions

What if an official is the target of a smear campaign by special interests or other entities? How else might the recall process be used illegitimately?

Initiative

A process that permits Californians to propose and enact a law or constitutional amendment by simple majority. A proposed initiative must be limited to one subject and requires a minimum number of valid signatures from registered voters to be placed on the ballot during a regularly scheduled election.

The initiative process has been the source of various laws, including casino gambling, same-sex marriages, and the medical use of marijuana. Passed in 1978, Proposition 13 dramatically reduced property tax rates and is considered to be the state's most controversial initiative to become law.

Critical Thinking Questions

In what ways are California voters politically empowered by the initiative process? Are there downsides to allowing the voters to propose and enact laws without input from the legislature? Is it possible that voters actually relinquish or lose political power as a result of the initiative?

Petition Referendum

A process that allows voters, by a simple majority, to approve or reject all or part of a law recently passed by the state legislature and signed by the governor. The petition is difficult to implement because of the relatively short time proponents have to gather the specified number of signatures to place the petition on the ballot.

Since 1912, 47 of approximately 65 referenda have qualified for the ballot. The use of the petition referendum has been infrequent, but well-financed campaigns typically prevail.

Critical Thinking Questions

Under what circumstances would members of the California state legislature favor a petition referendum? Under what circumstances might they be opposed to this process?

Compulsory Referendum

An approval method for the state legislature, required by the state constitution, which mandates that all debts and liabilities and all constitutional amendments that pass by a two-thirds vote of each house be approved by a majority of the voters during the next scheduled election.

Almost every regularly scheduled election since 2000 has included a compulsory referendum that authorized a bond act. The requirement that all bonds be approved by the voters has become a popular means for the state government to raise revenue without raising taxes.

Critical Thinking Questions

What if the legislature could approve debts and liabilities without a compulsory referendum? Would the legislature be more likely to raise taxes? What types of special or specific considerations are involved in a compulsory referendum?

California uses several methods of direct democracy including the recall, initiative, and referendum. Yet, despite these partici- patory innovations, voter turnout rates in California continue to fluctuate. In some election years, turnout rates are on par with the rest of the nation, and at other times they are unusually low. —*Is it possible that the electoral innovations introduced in California involving direct democracy have served to discourage Californians from becoming civically engaged? Why or why not? What other explanations might account for the wide fluctuations in voter turnout?*

Review of Key Objectives

Elections in California

 17.1 Relate voter participation to the types of elections held in California.

(pages 528–531)

Of the approximately 36 million residents of California, about 22 million are eligible to vote in the various primary, general, and special elections in the state. Voter participation rates vary greatly depending on the type of election held and the issues at stake and the personal appeal of candidates.

KEY TERMS

National Voter Registration Act 528
Direct Primary Elections 528
Cross-Filing 529
Closed Primary System 529
Blanket Primary 529
General Election 529
Special Election 530
Partisan Elections 530
Nonpartisan Elections 530

CRITICAL THINKING QUESTIONS

1. What are the similarities and differences between state primary elections and general elections?
2. Are the requirements for voting too strict or too lenient? What could be done to address either dilemma?

INTERNET RESOURCES

Information about the statewide election process that any California voter would need for an upcoming election, http://www.sos.ca.gov/elections.

The California Voter Foundation is a nonprofit, nonpartisan organization promoting and applying the responsible use of technology to improve the democratic process: http://www.calvoter.org

ADDITIONAL READING

Mitchell, Greg. *The Campaign of the Century*. New York: Random House, 1992.

Rogin, Michael, and John L. Shover. *Political Change in California: Critical Elections and Social Movements, 1890–1966*. Westport, CT: Greenwood Publishing, 1970.

Cain, Bruce E., and Elisabeth Gerber. *Voting at the Political Fault Line: California's Experiment with the Blanket Primary*. Berkeley: University of California Press, 2002.

Mathews, Joe, and Mark Paul. *California Crackup: How Reform Broke the Golden State and How We Can Fix It*. Berkeley: University of California Press, 2010.

Direct Democracy: California's Electoral Dilemma

 17.2 Evaluate whether the recall, referendum, and initiative have successfully established a more direct democracy in California.

(pages 532–539)

Three avenues for direct democracy—the recall, the referendum, and the initiative—have been unique features of the political landscape in California, especially in their broad application and controversial outcomes. In many ways, direct democracy continues to accomplish the goals of the Progressives when they led the state in enacting these provisions in 1911.

KEY TERMS

Recall 532	**Referendum** 538
Deregulation 533	**Petition Referendum** 538
Initiative 533	**Compulsory Referendum** 538
Direct Initiative 534	**General Obligation Bonds** 538

CRITICAL THINKING QUESTIONS

1. What were the events and factors that justified the recall of Governor Gray Davis? Was the recall used appropriately in this case?
2. How would California politics and its electoral process be different without the avenues for direct democracy?

INTERNET RESOURCES

Smart Voter is produced by the League of Women Voters of California Education Fund, a 501(c)(3) organization to help people learn more about elections in California: http://www.smartvoter.org

Easy Voter Guide presents easy-to-use, nonpartisan information for Californians. Sections of the Web site are also available in Spanish, Chinese, and Vietnamese: http://www.easyvoter.org/

ADDITIONAL READING

California Legislative Analyst's Office. "Ballot Initiatives and Constitutional Constraints: Impact on the State Budget and Budgeting Process." Joint Legislative Budget Committee, October 26, 1990.

Aslanian, Talar, et al. "Recapturing Voter Intent: The Nonpartisan Primary in California." Working paper, April 2003. Capstone Seminar Report. Pepperdine School of Public Policy.

Campaigning for Votes

 17.3 Explain how campaigns are organized to influence California voters most effectively.

(pages 540–545)

An individual's vote in California is strongly influenced by a number of factors, including the nonpartisan qualifications of a candidate, where the voter lives, and exposure to mass communications. In addition, voter records and interest groups can have an impact on how campaigns are run and how successful they are. Overall, the amount of money contributed by individuals and interest groups strongly impacts the success of a campaign, allowing the political candidate to reach more potential voters through mass media and other channels.

KEY TERMS

Citizen-Politician 540
Voter Registration Data 541
Political Contribution 542
30-Second Advertising Spot 543
Local and Regional Media Outlets 543
Direct-Mail Piece 545

CRITICAL THINKING QUESTIONS

1. What are the advantages and disadvantages of running for office as a partisan or a nonpartisan candidate? Which qualification has the most benefits?
2. If a candidate for office could only focus on interest groups, geography, or mass communication, which one would provide the greatest benefit?

INTERNET RESOURCES

Cal-Access provides financial information supplied by state candidates, donors, lobbyists, and others: http://cal-access.ss .ca.gov/

The Center for Responsive Politics is a nonpartisan, nonprofit research group based in Washington, D.C., that tracks money in politics and its effect on elections and public policy: http://www.opensecrets.org/

ADDITIONAL READING

Citizen's Commission on Ballot Initiatives. *Report and Recommendations on the Statewide Initiative Process*, Sacramento, January 1994, p. 2.

Lee, Eugene C., and Willis D. Hawley (eds.). *The Challenge of California, with a Concise Introduction to California Government.* Boston: Little, Brown, 1970.

Powell, Adam Clayton, III. "Reinventing Local News: Connecting Communities Through New Technologies." Working paper. USC Annenberg School for Communication.

Public Policy Institute of California. "The Changing Social and Political Landscape of California." *Research Brief.* December 8, 2005, http://www.ppic.org/content/pubs/RB_402MBRB.pdf.

Empowering California Voters

17.4 Identify ways to empower voters.

(pages 546–547)

The state of California has increasingly sought ways to simplify participation in elections through the absentee ballot, laws that provide workers with paid leave to vote, and the rather problematic use of electronic voting machines. Organizations such as the League of Women voters as well as the mass media provide good sources of information to help voters decide which candidates best represent their values.

KEY TERMS

Absentee Voting 546
Electronic Voting Machines 546

CRITICAL THINKING QUESTIONS

1. How have reforms in the mail-in ballots process empowered California voters?
2. When listing reasons for becoming politically active and becoming politically apathetic, which of these reasons tend to outweigh the others?

INTERNET RESOURCES

The Roper Center for Public Opinion Research is one of the world's leading archives of social science data, specializing in information from surveys of public opinion. The data held by the Roper Center range from the 1930s, when survey research was in its infancy, to the present. Most of the data are from the United States, but over 50 nations are represented: http://www.ropercenter.uconn .edu/about_roper.html

The Center for Information and Research on Civic Learning and Engagement (CIRCLE) promotes research on the civic and political engagement of Americans between the ages of 15 and 25: http://www.civicyouth.org/

ADDITIONAL READING

Owens, John R., Edmond Costantini, and Louis F. Weschler. *California Politics and Parties.* New York: Macmillan, 1970.

Ross, Ruth A., and Barbara S. Stone. *California's Political Process.* New York: Random House, 1973.

Gerston, Larry, and Terry Christensen. *Recall: California's Political Earthquake.* Armonk, NY: M. E. Sharpe, 2002.

Beyond Voting

 17.5 **Classify the forms of political participation used by Californians.**

(pages 548–549)

Representative democratic government in the United States almost seems to begin and end with the electoral process, but in reality a number of other avenues are open to Americans who want to participate in politics. Some of the more common activities include attending local meetings, writing to elected officials, contributing money, attending rallies, and participating in political party work. Californians on a per-capita basis attend meetings on community affairs and write letters to government officials at a rate, that is, above the national average, but contribute less money to candidates and attend fewer political rallies and political party meetings.

KEY TERMS

Political Party Work 548
Berkeley Free-Speech Movement 548

CRITICAL THINKING QUESTIONS

1. What forms of political participation are popular with Californians?
2. Why do you think unconventional political participation has become a tradition in California?

INTERNET RESOURCES

The Republican Party was created in the early 1850s by antislavery activists and individuals who believed that government should grant western lands to settlers free of charge: http://www.gop.com/about/

For more than 200 years, the Democratic Party has represented the interests of working families, fighting for equal opportunities and justice for all Americans: http://www.democrats.org/

With over 3.2 million members across United States—from carpenters to work-at-home moms to business leaders—MoveOn.org works to realize the progressive promise of our country: http://www.moveon.org/about.html

ADDITIONAL READING

Hale, Dennis, and Jonathan Eisen (eds.). *The California Dream.* New York: Collier Books, 1968.

Lee, Eugene C., and Willis D. Hawley (eds.). *The Challenge of California, with a Concise Introduction to California Government.* Boston: Little, Brown, 1970.

Chapter Review   Test Your Knowledge

1. Voter turnout in California has
   a. been consistent over the past 20 years.
   b. fluctuates significantly from election to election.
   c. been limited significantly by access to voting stations.
   d. decreased dramatically over the past 10 years.

2. The direct primary system was introduced in California by the
   a. Progressives.
   b. Workingmen's Party.
   c. Big Four.
   d. Democratic Party.

3. Allowing voters to participate in the primaries of either the Republican or Democratic Party takes place in which of the following contests?
   a. primary elections
   b. the blanket primary
   c. partisan and nonpartisan elections
   d. referendums, recalls, and elections

4. Traditionally, California's presidential primary
   a. is held in June.
   b. is one of the first held in the country.
   c. determines who will be the main parties' candidates.
   d. attracts very high voter turnout.

5. Which of the following would run in a partisan election?
   a. county officials
   b. superintendent of education
   c. congressional representatives
   d. mayor

6. All of the following are examples of direct democracy EXCEPT
   a. recall elections.
   b. primary elections.
   c. referendums.
   d. initiatives.

7. The recall process involves a signature-gathering stage and
   a. an election stage.
   b. a petition stage.
   c. a signature-distribution stage.
   d. a withdrawal stage.

8. The initiative process allows Californians to
   a. repeal laws passed by the state legislature.
   b. recall elected officials.
   c. overturn U.S. Supreme Court decisions on constitutional issues.
   d. directly propose and enact a state law or constitutional amendment.

9. Once an initiative has passed, it can only be changed or invalidated by
   a. a two-thirds vote in both chambers of the state legislature.
   b. an act of Congress.
   c. another initiative or a legal challenge.
   d. a governor's veto.

10. The initiative process weakens which branch of government?
    a. the legislature
    b. the executive branch
    c. the judiciary
    d. all of the above

11. The biggest contributors to local political campaigns are
    a. interest groups.
    b. political parties.
    c. individuals.
    d. the political candidates themselves.

12. The majority of the counties with the highest percentage of registered Republicans are
    a. on California's coast.
    b. in the San Francisco Bay Area.
    c. in the inland areas of California.
    d. along the border with Oregon.

13. Because of a federal mandate encouraging states to modernize the electoral process,
    a. nonelectronic equipment was introduced.
    b. voter turnout grew.
    c. there was a miscount in California's 2000 election.
    d. California has been adopting electronic voting machines.

14. After voting, the most popular form of political participation among Californians is
    a. writing to elected officials.
    b. making monetary contributions to candidates.
    c. attending meetings on community affairs.
    d. attending rallies or working for political parties.

15. To recall a statewide official, the number of signatures on a recall petition must
    a. exceed 50 percent of the total votes cast in the last general election.
    b. equal 12 percent of the total votes cast in the last general election.
    c. exceed 10 percent of the total votes cast in the last general election.
    d. equal 50 percent of the total votes cast in the last general election.

16. In the election to recall Governor Gray Davis, what percentage of the vote did Arnold Schwarzenegger capture among the 135 replacement candidates?
    a. 48.6 percent
    b. 20 percent
    c. 65 percent
    d. 10 percent

17. Almost every regularly scheduled election since 2000 has included a compulsory referendum that authorizes
    a. tax increases.
    b. tax cuts.
    c. a bond act.
    d. transportation projects.

18. Much of the $26.6 million Governor Schwarzenegger raised during his first year to support his ballot measures was contributed by
    a. individual citizens from the entire political spectrum.
    b. the Republican Party and other Republica politicians.
    c. interest groups with a stake either in these propositions or in other state legislation.
    d. All these answers are correct.

19. What are formal organizations of people who share a common outlook?
    a. the state legislature
    b. Masonic lodges
    c. interest groups
    d. the California Department of Finance

20. Campaign literature frequently is full of
    a. detailed information about government.
    b. inaccuracies, distortions, and embellishments.
    c. accurate information that downplays the accomplishments of candidates.
    d. ideas from policy specialists.

PEARSON mypoliscilab Exercises

Apply what you learned in this chapter on **MyPoliSciLab.**

Read on **mypoliscilab.com**

   eText: Chapter 17

Study and **Review** on **mypoliscilab.com**

   Pre-Test
   Post-Test
   Chapter Exam
   Flashcards

Watch on **mypoliscilab.com**

   Video: California Teachers Stage Sit-Ins

Explore on **mypoliscilab.com**

   Simulation: You Are Attempting to Revise the California Constitution
   Timeline: Initiatives and Referendums

CHAPTER 18

The California State Legislature

KEY OBJECTIVES

After completing this chapter, you should be prepared to:

18.1 Recount the transformation of the California legislature into a professional body.

18.2 Explain the process of electing California state legislators.

18.3 Identify legislative functions and assess the role of party caucuses in the California state legislature.

18.4 Analyze the roles and responsibilities of the leadership in the California legislature.

18.5 Evaluate the importance of committees in the California legislature.

In 2006, the California state legislature responded to the dangerously high levels of greenhouse gases (GHG) in the state as well as the growing international effort to reduce global warming with the passage of the Global Warming Solutions Act (AB 32 Nunez/Pavley), which was enthusiastically signed into law by Governor Arnold Schwarzenegger. Largely as the result of its large-scale dependence on petroleum-based fuels, California is one of the leading emitters of greenhouse gases in the world. AB 32 essentially committed the state to a 10-percent reduction in greenhouse gas emissions by 2020. Many scientists believe that a warming of the California climate due to greenhouse gases will cause a vital segment of the state water supply in the Sierra Nevada range to drastically decline over the next 50 years. In addition, global climate change is likely to erode sand dunes, warm ocean waters, and present many other challenges.

Almost four years into the passage of AB 32, as key provisions are scheduled to be implemented in 2010, Republican members of the state legislature have launched an attack on the

> **What do Californians really expect from representative democracy?**

GHG reduction law. They charge that California, and its business community in particular, can ill afford the costs of complying with the law at a time when the state economy is suffering from severe recession. Republican Assemblyman Dan Logue led a petition drive that resulted in Proposition 23, an initiative statute that would have suspended most provisions of AB 32 until the unemployment rate falls below 5.5 percent.

The supporters of AB 32 are as determined to sustain the efforts to reduce GHG and fight any campaign to weaken current environmental laws. These supporters believe that the transition away from fossil fuels is not only good for the environment but will also benefit the California economy by improving energy efficiency and generating investments in green technology that will stimulate job creation. Although California continues to remain ahead of many states in the attempt to reduce global warming, that goal remains fraught with policy differences that mirror the contrary approaches within a state government charged with safeguarding of the environment.

Resource Center
• Glossary
• Vocabulary Example
• Connect the Link

■ **Constitutional Revision Commission:** A commission created in 1963 to revise and reform the California constitution.

SIGNIFICANCE: *Three years after its first meeting, the commission presented its first report containing recommendations that addressed almost one-third of the constitution.*

The Role of the California Legislature

18.1 **Recount the transformation of the California legislature into a professional body.**
(pages 560–561)

Known unflatteringly as "the legislature of a thousand drinks" during its early sessions, the California state legislature suffered from a bad reputation as well as constitutional impediments. Embracing the prevailing minimalist notions of government, the original mining and merchant interests that dominated early California created a state government at the first state constitutional convention that was prone to party machine politics and corruption.

State Legislative Origins

The fortunes of the Southern Pacific grew, in part, to the exploitation of the weaknesses in the structure and organization of the state legislature. In fact, the attempt and eventual failure to limit the power of the Southern Pacific through the constitutional convention of 1878–1879 was partly the consequence of the control the Southern Pacific had over state legislators. When the Progressives came to power, rather than reform the state legislature to address corruption and the excessive monopolistic influence on government, they sought to limit the political power of the legislative body, particularly as an instrument for special interests and political parties. Important aspects of the state legislature's power were reduced by Progressive reforms that enlarged the state bureaucracy, empowered the governor, and institutionalized nonpartisanship.

By the early 1920s, as the Progressive Era in California was coming to an end, partisanship and special interests slowly crept back into the state legislature, taking full advantage of its weakened condition. Few individuals in California politics have received more notoriety for their ability to take advantage of these weaknesses than the infamous Art Samish. From the 1920s until 1953, when he was convicted of federal income tax evasion, Samish was the consummate lobbyist, employing his now well-known political tactic of "select and elect." In his own words, "I didn't care whether a man was a Republican or a Democrat or a Prohibitionist. I didn't care whether he voted against free love or for the boll weevil. All I cared about was how he voted on legislation affecting my clients."[1] In his popular book, *The Secret Boss of California,* Samish explained that his success in lobbying the state legislature was based on selecting the individuals he thought would support his clients' interests and on providing the funds to get them elected. He confessed that the $1,200 annual salary for California legislators was a weakness that he readily exploited.

Professionalizing the State Legislature

By the early 1960s, it became clear to the political activists in California that the state government was badly in need of reform, and in 1963, the state legislature authorized the **Constitutional Revision Commission**■. In 1966, the commission issued its final report, recommending the revision of various articles of the California constitution that addressed the three branches of state government and the state bureaucracy; these changes were passed into law by the legislature later that year. The new laws had the overall effect of professionalizing the state legislature by requiring a full-time commitment, establishing compensation that was equivalent to a full-time salary and set by the legislature, instituting conflict-of-interest restrictions, and providing a living expense allowance. This process had already been underway prior to the 1960s. Full-time professionals were added to the legislative staff, including the legislative analyst in 1941 and the legislative auditor in 1955. The legislature has since made funding available to provide support staff for individual members and committees.[2]

By 1971, California was judged to have one of the best legislatures in the country, and it certainly has remained one of the best paid. Until the passage of Proposition 13, allowing Californians to initiate law by collecting a required number of signatures in 1978, this professionalized legislature presided over one of the most grandiose policy agendas in the history of California under the leadership of the Democratic Party. Beginning in the early 1960s, the legislature succeeded in enacting a wide range of laws that addressed water development, civil rights, post–secondary education funding, social welfare, and highway construction—and still managed to maintain a budget surplus. Then, almost out of nowhere, a legislature riding high on a string of achievements ran into a brick wall built on the conservative backlash of California voters.

Public aversion to the state legislature was predicated on a number of factors that began with the election of Ronald Reagan, who defeated the incumbent Democratic governor, Edmund G. "Pat" Brown Sr., and adopted a leadership style that promoted conservative attitudes favoring limited government, elements of which remain popular today. The state legislature has been fighting an uphill battle ever since, due almost as much to its own dysfunction and partisan politics. Major corruption scandals in the 1980s and 1990s that ensnarled state legislators in FBI undercover operations caused tremendous embarrassment for the state legislature. These undercover operations resulted in the conviction of a number of legislators and legislative aides, the humiliation of many other lawmakers, and greater public awareness about the corruptibility of the state legislature by the increasingly sophisticated and well-financed **"third house"**■ of lobbyists and special-interest groups that shower the state legislature with millions of dollars and special

■ **Third House:** Lobbyists and special-interest groups that shower the state legislature with millions of dollars and special privileges.	**SIGNIFICANCE:** *The Fair Political Practices Commission is responsible for overseeing the activities of the "third house" through the maintenance of records on lobbyists and campaign contributions.*	■ **Proposition 140:** A constitutional initiative limiting the terms of office for legislators.	**SIGNIFICANCE:** *In addition to legislative term limits, Proposition 140 also required a 40-percent cut in the legislature's $165 million staffing budget.*

privileges. Amid the accusations of impropriety, the state legislature grew increasingly partisan, in part because of the emergence of divided government upon the successive election of two Republican governors, George Deukmejian and Pete Wilson, who faced a Democratic-controlled legislature. The major economic recession of the early 1990s, coupled with shrinking state government resources, tended to inflame partisan differences. Gridlock became commonplace, most noticeably in the budget process.

In reaction to this dysfunction as well as the contempt many California residents had for the state legislature, voters approved **Proposition 140**■, a constitutional initiative limiting the terms of office for legislators. A quick scan of California history will reveal that negative perceptions among the public about the state legislature are not new and that there have been numerous attempts to reform the structure and procedures of the state legislature and hold that body accountable to the principles of representative democracy. Periodically inspired by a history of charismatic leaders or popular ideas about government, Californians have forced reform and the reconstitution of the state legislature to reflect prevailing attitudes. At times, efforts to make the legislature more responsive have only resulted in a different set of problems for the state.

Enduring the weight of public criticism, the state legislature is nonetheless charged, by the outcome of the electoral process, with developing, funding, and overseeing policies that affect the quality of life in California. The challenges California state legislators face are nothing short of daunting as confirmed by the following passage from the sixth edition of A.G. Block and Claudia Buck's 1990–2000 California Political Almanac:

> Think of the learning curve facing each new legislator, who must master the intricacies associated with every aspect of legislating, from how a bill is introduced and ushered through the legislative process to the solving of constituent problems, from the nuances of budget-making to the complexities inherent in nearly every policy sphere. To cast intelligent votes on a range of issues, a rookie's brain must ricochet among teacher tenure, insurance regulation, renewable energy, welfare reform, public employee pensions, coastal protection, pesticide regulation, auto emission standards, affordable housing, trial-court funding, smog-check programs, highway construction, mass transit, earthquake retrofitting, local tax base, water marketing, agriculture, urban sprawl, state parks, prison overcrowding, death penalty, abortion funding, Medi-Cal eligibility, assault weapons, Internet pornography, class-size reduction, vehicle license fees, workers' compensation, reapportionment, immigration law, border policy, nursing home inspections, child-care centers, electricity deregulation, oil depletion allowances, Indian gaming, tax breaks for filmmakers, election law, fund-raising restrictions, legislative ethics, Proposition 13 overhaul, ATM fees—the list surges across the legislative landscape like a river gone mad.[3]

The Role of the California Legislature

18.1 **Recount the transformation of the California legislature into a professional body.**

PRACTICE QUIZ: UNDERSTAND AND APPLY

1. Which of the following ballot measures limited the terms of office for California state legislators?
   - **a.** Proposition 198
   - **b.** Proposition 140
   - **c.** Proposition 13
   - **d.** Proposition 1A

2. Lobbyists and special-interest representatives are often referred to as
   - **a.** the news media.
   - **b.** the divided house.
   - **c.** the "go-betweens."
   - **d.** the third house.

3. When faced with a dysfunctional legislature, California voters were most likely to
   - **a.** limit the terms of legislators.
   - **b.** increase the terms of legislators.
   - **c.** hold the governor responsible.
   - **d.** convene a constitutional convention.

4. What has typically been the result of any attempt to reform the legislative process?
   - **a.** a much more productive legislative body
   - **b.** economic upheaval
   - **c.** a different set of problems
   - **d.** impeachment of the governor

ANALYZE

1. What steps were taken to transform the California legislature into a professional body?

2. What are the effects of term limits on the ability of the California state legislature to perform its functions and represent the people?

IDENTIFY THE CONCEPT THAT DOESN'T BELONG

- **a.** "Select and elect"
- **b.** "Third house"
- **c.** Lobbyists
- **d.** Clemency power
- **e.** Southern Pacific

18.1

Resource Center
- Glossary
- Vocabulary Example
- Connect the Link

■ **Reapportionment:**
The redistribution of representation in a legislative body.

SIGNIFICANCE: *At the completion of the 2000 census, roughly 425,000 residents were apportioned to each assembly district and about 850,000 residents to each state district. As a new decade approaches, those numbers have increased to almost 500,000 and 1 million residents in the assembly and state senate, respectively.*

The Making of a California State Legislator

18.2   Explain the process of electing California state legislators.

(pages 562–565)

California legislators are confronted by an extremely challenging responsibility that necessitates long working hours, attention to detail, sociability, public scrutiny, management skills, and an in-depth understanding of how government works. The legal qualifications for the state legislature are quite minimal, requiring only that the candidate be a U.S. citizen, 18 years of age or older, a resident of California for three years, and a resident of a legislative district for one year immediately before the election for that office. The actual pathways to a seat in the California legislature are, however, by and large restricted to individuals with experience as locally elected officials or as professional staff members in local or state political party organizations or representative governments. For the state senate, the most obvious stepping-stone is election to the state assembly. Faced with term limits, most state assembly members will attempt to continue their legislative careers by filling the state senate seats being vacated by members of that body who have also been "termed out."

A large number of state assembly members begin their political careers as either city council members or school board trustees, and although most advance gradually—serving, for example, as a county supervisor along the way—it is not unusual for a council member to make the leap directly to the assembly. Local elected office is especially important for gaining name recognition among at least a portion of the voters in a legislative district and building a network of supporters. Candidates running for a seat in the state legislature who have served with distinction as party functionaries or legislative aides normally forgo previous experience in elected office. If they demonstrate the willingness to campaign vigorously and a seat becomes available, the local or state party organization or party leader can be instrumental in generating financial support that will often overcome the lack of name recognition. Other vocations that seem to give candidates an edge in running for an assembly seat are law, journalism, education, and law enforcement, but even individuals with these backgrounds still need substantial financial and political party support.

The two major political parties continue to play an important role in determining which individuals will run and which will stand the best chance of winning. Most members of the legislature maintain a political action committee

(PAC) or an individual campaign contribution fund and will generally contribute this money to fellow party members who get the nod from the state party organization. Moreover, both interest groups and political parties are increasingly using party committees at the county-level to funnel millions of dollars to finance the campaigns of legislators, and in the process circumventing voter-approved contribution limits. Under state campaign finance law, individual donors are limited to $3,300 per candidate during an election year while donors can contribute $27,900 per year to political party organizations, including county central committees. After receiving multiple contributions, the party organizations can in turn contribute an unlimited amount of those funds directly to the candidates.

Possessing the mandatory personal qualities and the support of political organizations, interest groups, and elected officials are really the only prerequisites for advancing to the election stage in becoming a state legislator. Nonetheless, the state legislative campaign and election are fraught with political intrigue, high-stakes strategies, and power plays that will test and very often quash the mettle of California's most experienced and adroit politicians.

Electing the California Legislator

Considering that the reelection rate for California state legislators has been well over 90 percent and that the vast majority of assembly members will successfully make the jump to the state senate, it is safe to assume that the relatively brief tenure of a state legislator is generally a secure job. Candidates for the state legislature must first win the election, a course of action that is often beset by any number of obstacles, not to mention the demands of the campaign process. Even incumbents, who are rarely challenged successfully, are not totally immune to the ambitious politicians in their districts and political party who might gain an edge through funding or popularity. Assembly members may be tempted to sacrifice portions of their three-term limit in the assembly to challenge an incumbent in the state senate from an adjacent legislative district. Completing the three-term limit in the assembly and waiting an additional two years while a popular state senator completes his or her two-term limit may avoid a competitive election—or not. Unexpected maneuverings of legislative electoral politics, such as a rising political personality scandal or controversial issues or policies, can radically alter the fortunes of both challengers and incumbents. In *The Third House: Lobbyists, Money, and Power in Sacramento,* Dan Walters writes:

Allen Hoffenblum, a veteran political consultant, has listed five essential factors in a winning legislative campaign: a

■ **Redistricting:**
Drawing new boundaries for election districts.

SIGNIFICANCE: *In 1990, the Ninth Circuit Court of Appeals upheld a U.S. district court ruling against the Board of Supervisors of the county of Los Angeles that alleged blocks of Hispanic voters in the county had been split among several voting districts. The court ruled this redistricting plan violated the Voting Rights Act and equal protection clause of the Fourteenth Amendment to the Constitution.*

competitive district, one in which the candidate has at least a theoretical chance to win; a candidate that meets at least minimum personal qualifications; a well-organized and experienced campaign team; a realistic campaign strategy; and as the bottom line, enough money to carry out the strategy. And how much is enough? That can vary widely, depending on the district and the circumstances. In a district with a lopsided party registration, where the primary winner is certain to be elected in November and there's little conflict in the primary, as little as $100,000 might do it. But in a highly competitive "swing" district and/or one in which competing factions are battling in the primary— two Latino organizations have been struggling for dominance in Los Angeles, for example—it would not be unusual for an assembly seat campaign to consume a million dollars, and senate seats can easily cost several million.[4]

The legislative incumbent, on the other hand, must try to prevent this type of candidate and campaign from emerging. The electoral defeat of former Republican State Senator Richard Rainey, who represented the Seventh Senate District on the eastern fringe of the San Francisco Bay Area, is an example of the rare occasion when an incumbent can lose. Vulnerable even before the 2000 election year when his district was overtaken by slightly more registered democrats, Rainey was challenged by Assemblyman Tom Torlakson, a moderate Democrat who had good name recognition in his district, got heavy financial support from his party, and by Rainey's own admission, ran an aggressive campaign. Such defeats have become

rare, however, because incumbents in the state legislature have increasingly taken the steps necessary to protect their seats. Both parties have closed ranks, sharing and directing campaign funds and creating safe districts. Furthermore, the accumulation of large campaign funds by individual members of the legislature between elections, which could easily be as much as half a million dollars, is one of the more convincing methods of scaring off would-be challengers.

The real electoral contests for legislative seats usually take place during the state primary campaigns and elections. One consequence of term limits are the open seats that become available every two years, when up to one-third of the state legislators are forced out of office. In the absence of an incumbent, the opportunity for members of political parties in California to win the nomination as the candidate representing his or her party for a seat in the legislature in the general election has dramatically improved. Although most primary candidates for the legislature run campaigns independent of political parties, party involvement can range from outright recruitment of primary candidates to dissuading the candidacy of party members who threaten to siphon votes away from a favored candidate. The extent of political party involvement in a legislative electoral race will largely depend on the strength and depth of local or regional party organizations, which tend to be high in urban areas and low in rural communities. The role of political parties in the primary election process can be complicated, full of intricacies related to personality, demographics, personal relationships, and campaign contributions, but two factors—legislative **reapportionment**■ and **redistricting**■—are a serious influence on the outcome of

Standing on the corner of Mendocino and College avenues, Democratic State Assembly candidate Lee Pierce waves his own campaign signs. —*What advantages do incumbents have over challengers like Lee Pierce?*

CONNECT THE **LINK**

(Chapter 2, pages 46–49) Not unlike the *state-based approach* versus an *individual-based approach* described in Chapter 2, which divided the delegates at the Constitutional Convention of 1787 in Philadelphia, California has been torn by a *county-based approach* versus an *individual-based approach.*

a primary or general election. Reapportionment and redistricting have always been controversial features of the state electoral process, and are seen among many politicians more as a means of "fixing" legislative districts to guarantee the election of party favorites than as a constitutional responsibility of the state legislature.

Reapportionment and Redistricting

Throughout California history, there has been a recurring quandary regarding how Californians as a whole should be represented. The constitutions of the United States and California grant state legislatures the authority to create federal and state legislative districts based on the national census conducted every 10 years. California's bicameral (two-chamber) legislature is one of the smallest in the nation in proportion to the size of its population, which is the largest in the nation. Only 14 states have smaller legislatures, and most have far fewer people.[5] The relatively small size of the California legislature has resulted in some of the largest legislative districts in the country. The average assembly district contains about 450,000 residents, and a state senate district has twice as many.

 From the granting of statehood to the modern era, California has suffered from a dilemma similar to the one the American founders faced when considering representation in Congress, which was ultimately solved through what is known as the Great Compromise (see Chapter 2, pages 46–49). In California, the opposing sides were political leaders from urban and rural regions, each accusing the other of drawing district boundaries to gain political advantage. The "not so great" compromise implemented in 1930 was the Federal Plan, which established a state senate composed of 40 geographic districts that gave no county more than one district and permitted no more than three counties to share a single district. The state senate thus provided equal representation to each county or group of smaller counties. Representation in the 80-seat assembly would remain apportioned on the basis of population.

The Federal Plan's end came in 1964 when the U.S. Supreme Court ruled in *Reynolds* v. *Sims* that the equal protection clause of the U.S. Constitution requires that the seats in both houses of a bicameral state legislature must be apportioned on the basis of population. In reaction to this ruling, the state legislature passed the California Reapportionment Act of 1965, mandating that legislative districts for each house contain relatively equal numbers of people.[6]

The controversy over legislative reapportionment and the redrawing of district boundaries over the past three decades has had less to do with the composition of legislative districts and more about who is doing the reapportioning and redistricting. Since the 1970s, when the Democrats solidified their control over the state legislature, Republican governors, including Ronald Reagan in 1971 and 1973 and Pete Wilson in 1991, vetoed redistricting plans they labeled as attempts to gerrymander districts to favor Democrats running for Congress and the state legislature. Those plans were eventually revised in a less partisan manner by court-appointed, retired appellate judges. Legislative veterans such as Phil Burton—a legendary member of both the state legislature and the U.S. Congress and brother of the former state senate president pro tempore, John Burton—became adept at guaranteeing electoral outcomes by shifting registered voters into one district (a practice known as "packing") while diluting the party base of voters in another district (known as "cracking"). In the 1980s, various initiatives and referendums were introduced in an attempt to strip the state legislature of redistricting power, but they either failed to qualify for the ballot or were rejected by the voters. By 2001, the redistricting and reapportionment process was largely a bipartisan exercise that resulted in the creation of safe legislative districts for both major parties. These districts, according to the veteran political analyst Daniel Weintraub, "were designed to protect the jobs of those then in office, provide opportunities for legislators seeking to move up and freeze the partisan divide as it stood between Democrats and Republicans."[7]

Critics of the redistricting process—which have included a wide range of significant political actors, from Governor Arnold Schwarzenegger to former Governor Gray Davis to Common Cause, a public advocacy group—charge that the legislature has engaged in a gerrymandering of legislative districts that makes a mockery of the electoral process. These groups and individuals joined forces, forming "Voters FIRST," a redistricting reform initiative that was approved by the voters on the November 2008 ballot. Now an amendment to the California constitution, Voters FIRST requires the creation of an independent and open citizen's redistricting commission to draw district boundaries for the state legislature and state Board of Equalization. In an attempt to limit, if not remove, partisanship from the redistricting plan, stringent requirements have been imposed on the selection of commissioners as well as the redistricting process. The backers of Voters FIRST will be anxiously awaiting the first selection of members to the nonpartisan Citizen's Commission and the outcome of the 2010 redistricting process to determine if in fact competitive elections will take place.

The Making of a California State Legislator

18.2   **Explain the process of electing California state legislators.**

PRACTICE QUIZ: UNDERSTAND AND APPLY

1. In 1964, the U.S. Supreme Court ruled in which of the following cases that the equal protection clause of the U.S. Constitution requires that the seats in both houses of a bicameral state legislature must be apportioned based on population?
   a. *Baron* v. *Baltimore*
   b. *Castro* v. *State of California*
   c. *Reich* v. *Gonzales*
   d. *Reynolds* v. *Sims*

2. What profession does not typically give a candidate to the state legislature an advantage?
   a. lawyer
   b. police officer
   c. teacher
   d. actor

3. A member of the Assembly who is "termed out" or cannot run for another term of office in that chamber is likely to
   a. run for a seat in the state senate.
   b. run for governor.
   c. retire from politics.
   d. return to local politics.

ANALYZE

1. Why are incumbents more likely to win an election to the state legislature?

2. How do you think the creation of the Citizen's Redistricting Commission will impact campaign costs? Explain your answer.

IDENTIFY THE CONCEPT THAT DOESN'T BELONG

a. *Reynolds* v. *Sims*
b. "Voting power"
c. State senate districts
d. May revise
e. Population

Resource Center
• Glossary
• Vocabulary Example
• Connect the Link

■ **Standing Rules:** Rules ensuring that the legislature operates in an efficient and civil manner.

SIGNIFICANCE: *Standing rules are referred to more often than any other set of legislative rules, guidelines, or laws. As the basic working plan of the state legislature, these rules establish such matters as meeting times, order of business, and rules of debate.*

The Legislative Universe

18.3 Identify legislative functions and assess the role of party caucuses in the California state legislature.
(pages 566–573)

Every two years, after each general election, the state legislature begins its legislative session starting in December. At the beginning of each session, legislators once again, or for the first time, enter a very exclusive environment composed of a highly select membership with the unparalleled responsibility of making laws for one of the most important states in the country. The organization and functions of the state legislature are based on Article 4 of the California state constitution, which governs **standing rules**■ and **joint rules**■. These laws and rules provide the legislature with self-governing powers, allowing almost total independence from any other public or private authority and control over almost every aspect of the legislature. Most of the standing rules for the state legislature are carried over from one session to the next, but they can be altered, amended, or repealed during each session. The standing rules also ensure that the legislature operates in an efficient and civil manner, covering such areas as meeting times, order of business, number and membership of committees, duties of officers, rules of debate, and votes required on legislative action. The standing rules for the senate and assembly are similar, but there are differences that reflect the structural distinctions between the two chambers. Relations between the two chambers are defined by the joint rules, which establish guidelines for cooperation. The effectiveness of the rules is determined by the way they are applied; they can be used as much to slow, corrupt, or even prevent the completion of legislative functions as they can be used to facilitate legislative responsibilities.

Legislative Functions

Although the state constitution prescribes lawmaking as the main responsibility of the California legislature, this body has taken on many other duties that have become vital to the operation of state government. Although not necessarily prescribed directly by the California constitution, these other functions compel the legislator to adopt qualities of the educator, accountant, personnel director, public relations executive, and law enforcement officer. Understanding these functions will help the constituent better appreciate the workload of California legislators, differentiate between the real and imagined negative perceptions of the state legislature, and participate in the lawmaking process.

LAWMAKING The lawmaking responsibility of the assembly and the state senate focuses largely on drafting, reviewing, and ultimately, voting on bills (proposed laws). Thousands of laws are passed every year that address a broad range of issues. Bills introduced in the state senate or assembly carry the designation SB or AB, a number, and usually the name of the author. The ability to vote on and propose bills is the most important service expected of legislators. California state laws or statutes are divided into 29 different codes—for example, Business and Professions, Fish and Game, and Military and Veterans—that regulate almost all major aspects of life in California. A modification or repeal of a law—or merely one section regulating, say, the alcohol content of wine coolers sold in California, how much concert tickets can be marked up, or whether nurses can work 12-hours shifts—can mean the loss or gain of millions of dollars for a particular industry. Although only members of the state legislature may introduce bills for consideration, lobbyists, state and federal government officials, and private citizens are often able to participate in the drafting of a particular bill or to serve as important sources of information during the drafting process. Once the basic idea of a bill is conceived, it is the job of the Legislative Counsel (the law office of the legislature) to reformat the bill to meet legal technicalities. All laws must be passed by a majority in both chambers and go into effect on the first day of the following calendar year (January 1). Bills approved by the legislature that take effect immediately involve the state budget, calling elections, introducing tax levies, immediate fiscal allocations, and urgency bills, which are intended to address matters of urgency and require a two-thirds majority vote in both chambers.

One of the most important as well as controversial types of proposed laws are known as **"juice bills"**■—bills written to benefit a particular group. The consideration and passage of a juice bill usually results in large campaign contributions and other benefits to the author or sponsor of the bill and to other legislators who have played influential roles in getting the bill passed. There have been many instances of California legislators seeking or actually writing juice bills for their own personal enrichment. One of the most flagrant examples in the history of the California legislature occurred in 1988, when the FBI set up a sting operation using a phony company, Gulf Shrimp Fisheries of Mobile, Alabama, that succeeded in getting a number of Democratic and Republican assembly members to sponsor two bills that would have allowed the Gulf Shrimp Fisheries to sell "tax-exempt" industrial development bonds to finance construction of a food-processing facility in California. The FBI caught many of the assembly members on videotape accepting thousands of dollars for their work on the bills, which easily passed in both chambers but were vetoed by Governor Deukmejian, who had been tipped off by the FBI about the anticorruption sting operation.[8]

■ **Joint Rules:** Guidelines for cooperation between the two chambers of the legislature.

SIGNIFICANCE: *There are roughly 60 to 65 joint rules that govern such relations between the chambers as referral of bills, printing procedures, and conflicts of interests.*

■ **"Juice Bills":** Bills written to benefit a particular group, usually engaged in business.

SIGNIFICANCE: *Many consider the corporate tax law that restricted severance taxes on oil shipped out of the state from 1979 to 1982 to be the result of $2.5 million spent on lobbying efforts by California's oil industry and a clear example of a "juice bill."*

PATHWAYS of action

Lobbying and the Confirmation Process Collide in the California State Senate

Like the U.S. Senate, the California state senate also has the responsibility of confirming appointments made by government's chief executive officer, although this function tends to receive much less attention at the state level. The state senate's confirmation duties did become front page news when Rachelle Chong, a commissioner on the California Public Utility Commission (CPUC), was reappointed in 2009 by Governor Arnold Schwarzenegger.

Commissioner Chong was initially appointed and confirmed in 2006 to fill the vacant seat left by Susan Kennedy, who became chief of staff to the governor. Chong developed a reputation on the commission for having an expertise in telecommunications policy that tended to favor the industry over consumers. Not necessarily the most widely known government agency in California, the CPUC has the immense obligation of regulating the major utilities in the state, including power generation, transportation, and telecommunications. Most of the utility-related consumer protection and public advocacy groups took issue with Commissioner Chong's pro-industry positions, but became particularly dismayed by her sponsorship of an AT&T-backed proposal to deregulate the state's Universal Lifeline program, which requires telephone service providers to offer low-income residents basic low-cost phone service. Advocacy groups became concerned that these consumers, particularly those who were elderly, would be subject to increased costs they could ill afford if the proposal was approved. Consumer protection and public advocacy groups throughout the state thus realized the opportunity presented by Commissioner Chong's reappointment to lobby the state senate to deny her confirmation for another term on the CPUC. That action was naturally opposed by the telecommunications industry, most notably AT&T and Verizon, strong supporters of Commissioner Chong.

Realizing that its major CPUC advocate was in trouble, the telecommunications industry launched a lobby effort of its own. Normally one of the most prolific campaign contributors to the state legislature, the industry, led by AT&T, focused on the state senate rules committee, which is required to hold hearings on confirmations. No senate rules committee confirmation hearings, no reappointment. The telecommunications industry adopted an "Astroturf" strategy—a seemingly "grassroots" effort involving letters from a variety of nonprofit and community-based organizations that touted Commissioner Chong's concern for low-income state residents. Upon closer investigation, it was revealed that most of these organizations took generous donations from telecommunications companies,

in one instance $125,000 from Verizon and $633,000 from AT&T. In contrast, the major consumer and public advocacy utility groups, which included such consumer stalwarts as the Utility Reform Network, Utility Consumers' Action Network and Consumer Federation of California, came together for the first time and initiated an authentic grassroots lobbying campaign based on a broader coalition of low-income, senior citizens, labor, faith-based, and environmental groups. And in addition to many letters that genuinely opposed Chong's reappointment, the coalition was prepared to send a busload of Lifeline customers to testify at confirmation hearings. In the end, favoring the true grassroots effort and possibly fearing the image of numerous angry low-income consumers, State Senate President Pro Tempore Steinberg cancelled rules committee hearings on Commission Chong's reappointment, effectively ending her tenure on the CPUC.

SOURCE: Michael Rothfield, "PUC Member's Bid for Second Term Rejected," *Los Angeles Times*, December 9, 2009; John Howard, "Senate Blocks Confirmation of PUC Member Rachelle Chong"—*Capitol Weekly*, December 10, 2009; Consumer Federation of California, accessed at http://www.consumercal.org/article.php?id=1141

There are very important bills introduced purely for the good of the public, without any direct financial benefit to anyone. Many of these bills are in response to the requests of state governmental agencies regarding the broadening or narrowing of regulatory powers. Bills that arise from the concerns of a partisan official of the executive branch of government may be politically hard for a fellow party member in the legislature to ignore. Bills are often generated from the personal interest of a legislator in solving social problems; at other times, they are a response to media attention on a particular issue. Although for decades the state legislature has passed various laws that have benefited the California Community College System and been very reluctant to cut its budget, this educational community does not have a powerful lobbying group or union to bestow large contributions, nor does it have a constituency that is known to turn out in great numbers at the polls. Most legislators probably have a community college in their district and realize the value of the educational services these colleges provide to their constituents. Chances are that a large number of legislators have even attended a community college at some point in their lives.

The power of the media to pressure legislators to introduce new bills was clearly demonstrated through the crusade of Candace Lightner to bring about tougher drunk driving laws. For years, California lawmakers resisted attempts to lower the legal blood alcohol levels for motorists, in large part because of powerful liquor industry lobbyists. As the mother of a teenage

■ **Resolutions:** Formal statements explaining a decision or expressing an opinion.	**SIGNIFICANCE:** *Typically issued in the form of a formal statement from the California legislature, resolutions cover a wide range of issues and expectations, from support for the construction of an education center near the Vietnam Memorial Wall to honoring the work of the International Council of Thirteen Indigenous Grandmothers.*

daughter who was killed by a drunk driver and who later founded Mothers Against Drunk Driving (MADD), Lightner's compelling personal story attracted news coverage that ignited public interests. This was media attention the legislature simply could not ignore, and it eventually passed a series of bills that lowered the legal blood alcohol levels and increased the penalties for drunk driving.[9]

Many bills that have little or no chance of being approved are introduced solely to advance a legislator's political career. Some of these bills are intended to show a legislator's constituency back home that their concerns are being heard. At times, frivolous bills are deliberate attempts to get media attention. In 2004, Senator John Vasconcellos received plenty of media attention for introducing a bill that proposed lowering the voting age to 14. A bill to require the California Buildings Standards Commission to include feng shui in design principles was another such wasted legislative effort. These exercises in futility unfortunately consume the valuable time of legislators and staff as well as the fiscal resources of state government.

In addition to changes or additions to California statutes, the state legislature may also propose and pass constitutional amendments and resolutions. The depth of the California constitution, nearly 10 times as long as the U.S. Constitution, necessitates regular amending, which the legislature is empowered to perform. Any constitutional amendment proposed by the state legislature, known as an ACA for the assembly or SCA for the senate, must be passed by a two-thirds vote in both chambers and then ratified by a majority of the voters. A number of different types of resolutions are considered and regularly approved by the legislature, consisting of concurrent (ACR or SCR), joint (AJR or SJR), and house (AR or SR), resolutions, most commonly defined as the sentiments or opinions of the legislative body.

Resolutions■ are regularly used by the legislature to recognize the achievements of a particular individual. Concurrent resolutions can originate in either chamber but must be passed in both chambers to go into effect. These resolutions usually authorize the forming of joint temporary committees, request information from the state agencies, adopt joint rules, and establish recess dates. Joint resolutions, which can also originate in either chamber, express the collective positions of the California legislature on matters of public interest. Each chamber may pass a house resolution that pertains directly to its concerns or the conduct of its business; such resolutions normally involve the adoption of rules, selection of committees, allocation of funds, appointment of officers, and hiring of employees.

LAWMAKING AND THE ANNUAL BUDGET PROCESS

The most important aspect of the lawmaking function is passage of the annual state budget, which is essentially treated as a

bill. The annual budget for the state of California reflects the size of the state (see Figure 18.1) and requires detailed consideration and substantial interaction between the legislature and the executive branch. The budget process begins with the governor, who prepares the annual budget and must submit it to both chambers of the legislature by January 10. After its receipt and introduction in both chambers, the annual budget is referred to the Senate Budget and Fiscal Review Committee and the Assembly Budget Committee, which in turn refers sections of the budget to subcommittees by major subject areas, such as education or health and human services. Both the governor and the state legislature are obligated by the state constitution to complete a balanced annual budget that meets other constitutional budgetary mandates, such as the allocation of 40 percent of the general fund to education. After conducting hearings, the subcommittees issues reports with recommendations regarding funding levels and other action in specific areas of the budget and will eventually send the budget back to the

FIGURE 18.1 ■ How Big Is California Government?

Governor Arnold Schwarzenegger proposed state spending of $146 billion in 2007–2008. At that level of spending, California is among the top 30 largest economic entities (national government or corporations) in the world. This graph shows a few sample comparisons.

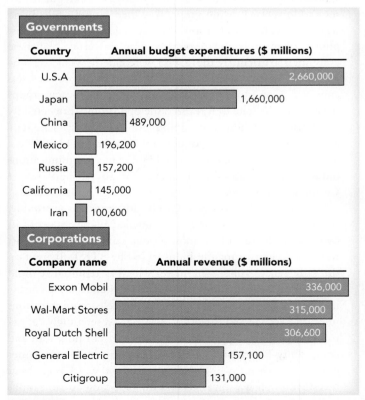

SOURCE: Gregg Miller/*Los Angeles Daily News*, May 22, 2007. Reprinted with permission.

■ **Casework:** The direct assistance legislators offer in response to requests from their constituents.

SIGNIFICANCE: *Casework is usually supervised by a district director and performed by field representatives. District directors commonly start out as field representatives, who either have a degree in political science or a good understanding of California state government.*

Senate Budget and Fiscal Review Committee and the Assembly Budget Committee. These committees review the subcommittee reports, revise the total budget package, and send a completed annual budget to the full body of their respective legislative chambers for debate and vote. Following passage by both chambers, any differences between the assembly and senate versions of the budget are worked out in a conference committee that is comprised of members from both chambers. The compromise budget that emerges from the conference committee is submitted to the full membership of each chamber for a final vote.

Until the passage of Proposition 25 in the aftermath of the 2010 midterm election, the state legislature was constitutionally bound to pass a balanced budget by an extraordinary, or two-thirds majority in both chambers. The constitutional amendment that resulted from Proposition 25 requires only a simple majority for legislative approval of the budget. A supermajority of state legislators must still approve tax hikes, and the amendment also stipulates that the legislature will forfeit salary and benefits if a budget bill is not passed by June 15. While a large portion of the leverage that the minority Republican Party received from the two-thirds rule has been lost, two other propositions passed during the 2010 midterm election will continue to restrict the legislature's fiscal control, especially when it comes to generating revenue. Proposition 22 restricts the legislature in the use of funds earmarked for transportation and local governments, and Proposition 26, prohibits the legislature from raising fees and taxes without a two-thirds majority.

REPRESENTATION The theory of representative or indirect democracy is founded on the principle that voters designate a relatively small number of people to represent their interests; those representatives then meet in a legislative body to make decisions on behalf of the entire citizenry. In the California legislature, representing the interests of Californians through lawmaking and other legislative responsibilities is made especially difficult by the diversity, size, and wide disparity in wealth of the state. Besides fulfilling the democratic ideal, representation can be an important factor in the reelection of state legislators. California legislators have adopted various methods of representation in response to the wide-ranging conditions in California, but the one universal and most basic approach to representation is known as **casework**■—the direct assistance legislators offer in response to requests from their constituents.

Each year, the state legislature allocates a substantial amount of funds for legislators to maintain offices and staff in the state capitol as well as the home districts. The district office staff for state legislators are dedicated to assisting constituents when problems and questions arise. As district director for State Senator Tom Torlakson (D-Seventh Senate District), Craig Cheslog has been on the frontlines of handling the casework generated by Senator Torlakson's constituents. According to

Cheslog, the office staff is incredibly small—only five to seven in number—considering that California state senator districts are about 40 percent larger than congressional districts:[10]

> We have a district director, office manager/scheduler, field representatives and volunteers. We divide our staff by subject area, for example, education and transportation governmental relations. Right now we have about 30 interest areas that we've identified. Interest areas are generally decided by what the legislator is interested in, and then there are issues that are just important to constituents.

For example, Cheslog cited animal rights and education as issues that tend to generate the most constituency interest. Cheslog has found that the most challenging aspect of working in a legislator's district office and handling casework is time management and prioritization. He has also found that constituents can make their voices heard:

> Letters or postcards allow us to show other elected officials or government bureaucrats how constituencies feel on a particular subject. For example, we received 30,000 letters from PTA members in our district in the last 4 months about cuts to education funding. That makes a very tangible and concrete gauge about how people feel about a given subject or issue.

In addition to personal problems, this office also receives requests from local government agencies. "You could have a funding dispute between a local sanitation authority and Caltrans and we have to get involved and figure out what is the path towards solving the issue," Cheslog said. He also believes that attending local events and forming advisory committees are important in helping the legislator maintain contact with constituents and generate ideas for bills. Cheslog considers his office full of middle-persons of sorts, admitting that "we can't really investigate problems on our own. But what we can do is help people navigate government to find the right person or office to resolve that issue or problem."

Representation comes in many different varieties, whether based on the geographic conditions, social or cultural background of constituents, specific policy issues, or personal interests. Legislators will attempt to tailor their legislative agenda, district office organization, committee assignments, and often votes on issues in the legislature to the interests and issues that most affect the majority of their constituents—especially the ones who vote. Representation is undoubtedly very difficult for California legislators, who must spend a significant proportion of their time learning about the legislature as rapidly as possible before being forced into retirement as a result of term limits. The unusually large number of constituents in California districts and the diverse array of special interests inside as well as outside a legislator's district make the representation function

■ **Oversight Function:** The responsibility for supervising the implementation of all laws and the government officials charged with implementing them.

SIGNIFICANCE: *Oversight is carried out by standing committees that exercise jurisdiction over a state agency or an issue of major interest to the state. California statutes empower standing committees to conduct investigations and ultimately propose and adopt laws that correct problems identified during an oversight process.*

even more difficult. Most legislators seem to have resolved this dilemma by focusing on the groups or individuals that will best demonstrate their appreciation for the legislator's efforts. Plenty of evidence supports the notion that money in the form of campaign contributions is a key factor in acquiring representation from legislators on a given issue. Considering the generous benefits correction officers have received over the years and the easing of former prohibitions on gambling in California, it is no surprise that such groups as the California Correctional Peace Officers Association and California Indian casino owners have made substantial campaign contributions to both Democratic and Republican legislators.

OVERSIGHT Although legislators have the primary responsibility of making laws, they are also responsible for overseeing the implementation of all laws as they were originally intended and the government officials who are charged with implementing them. Certain constitutional powers granted to the state legislature, especially passing the annual state budget, conducting public hearings, and the impeachment and removal of elected officials, can be powerful restraints on a wayward or incompetent organization of the executive branch. Former Senator Jim Costa, a Democrat who represented the 16th Senate District, deems the **oversight function**■ as "highly important to making the legislature a coequal branch of government."[11] Senator Costa notes, however, that the California legislature does not typically conduct oversight very well, because "this work is labor intensive and time intensive, and it takes a dedicated legislator to do it properly. We tend to emphasize oversight only when there is a major crisis or a legislator has a deep interest in a particular area."[12] Although not fashionable, Senator Costa has found that "oversight work can be rewarding when you do it well."[13]

Legislative investigations of the California Department of Corrections have been some of the most disheartening but nonetheless important instances of legislative oversight. In 2000, State Senator Richard Polanco, chair of the Joint Legislative Committee on Prison Construction and Operation, along with two other state senators, took the extraordinary step of conducting hearings at Valley State Prison for Women and the Central California Women's Facility at Chowchilla to hear testimony from prisoners, prison advocacy groups, and Department of Corrections staff on "alleged medical abuse and neglect endured by women inside." The testimony heard from more than a dozen prisoners detailed inadequate medical care that resulted in serious illnesses being left untreated for months and misdiagnoses that caused the deaths of at least two inmates who were mistakenly given medication for tuberculosis.[14] Five years later, conditions at both women's prisons remained problematic, prompting State Senator Jackie Speier to take the even more extraordinary action of leading a delegation of state senators from the women's caucus; this delegation spent the night

at Valley State Prison for Women to determine the nature of the conditions there firsthand. Senator Speier, who chaired the Senate Select Committee on Government Oversight, said that the delegation "found conditions that I believe are unacceptable for pregnant inmates, in terms of the quality of attention they receive and the lack of programming in their facilities. Many women had not had a Pap smear or a mammogram in a number of years."[15]

Speier was particularly troubled by the fact that the cost of health care in state prisons for women is 60 percent more expensive than that in institutions for men, yet reports to the Senate Select Committee on Government Oversight and her own observations at Valley State Prison for Women indicated that the quality of health care was substandard. Speier introduced seven bills related to prison reform, addressing a wide range of issues, but such reforms continue to face an uphill battle, primarily against the California Correctional Peace Officers Association, which is very sensitive about any legislative measures that challenge the authority of its members over the California Department of Corrections. In 2006, after receiving numerous complaints regarding substandard health care throughout the entire California prison system, a federal judge placed prison health services for the prison system in receivership. The process of receivership required major improvements in the delivery of health care services, which has resulted in increased spending and improved care.

Patterned after the advice and consent power of the U.S. Senate, the state senate also has the power to confirm or reject many of the appointments made by the governor. These appointments, literally in the hundreds, include the heads of state departments and agencies and various positions on state boards and commissions. Unlike the U.S. Senate, judicial appointments are not reviewed or confirmed by the California state senate.

The state senate confirmation process begins with hearings and background investigations conducted by the Senate Rules Committee, including testimony from individuals who either support or question a nominee's qualifications. This committee issues a recommendation to the entire membership of the state senate about approving or disapproving the nominee. A majority of votes in the full state senate is required to confirm the nomination. Legislators ultimately have to approve someone for vacant government positions, but the confirmation process can still be a very partisan affair, especially with a state government that over the years has often been divided between a Republican governor and a Democratic-controlled legislature. In the instances of divided state government, it is almost inevitable that a number of major appointments will be rejected, although the true intentions of a nomination may have more to do with political payback than a real desire by the governor to nominate the most qualified candidate. Other rejected appointments are clearly the result of ideological differences between the two parties.

■ **Party Caucuses:** Legislators from the same party who meet to establish group goals, policies, and strategies.

SIGNIFICANCE: *As a closed group of legislative political party members, party caucuses in each chamber are controlled by their respective legislative leaders. Although the caucuses allow each member a vote on major decisions, particularly in selecting floor leaders, the influence and legislative power of the presiding officers typically dictate how the members will vote.*

One such rejection occurred when Cindy Tuck, a consultant for the California Council for Environmental and Economic Balance, a coalition of business, labor, and public officials, was nominated by Governor Schwarzenegger to head the California Air Resources Board. Stating in senate hearings that she did not intend to represent business interests and was not clearly affiliated with any political party, Tuck even drew praise from former Democratic senate president pro tempore Don Perata, who conceded she was a "very impressive individual." Public criticism from groups such as the Los Angeles Physicians for Social Responsibility, however, accusing Tuck of being a long-time professional lobbyist for polluting industries that were consistently opposed to California clean air regulations, convinced the state senate to reject her nomination, which it did on a 21–14 vote.[16]

The Partisan Caucus

Much of the action taken in the California legislature is based on the decisions of the legislative **party caucuses**■, which are groups of legislators from the same party who pursue the interests of the party and fellow party members in the legislature. The Democratic and Republican parties have legislative party caucuses in each chamber. The most important tasks of the caucuses are to elect legislative leaders, set policy goals, and support the election of fellow legislators. Party members from each chamber are not legally bound to participate in the activities of their party caucus, but most legislators appreciate the benefits of this interaction—or fear the repercussions of not being actively involved. Assembly Speaker Jesse Unruh began the tradition of having the speaker elected in the Democratic assembly caucus in 1963, despite the constitutional provision that calls for the speaker to be elected by the full membership of the assembly; the gesture was designed to achieve a greater sense of party unity and has been in place ever since.[17] Life for legislators who do not follow the dictates of their respective party caucuses can be rather difficult. When, for example, Assemblyman Joe Canciamilla formed a moderate Democratic caucus known as the Mod Squad in 2004, which opposed many of the policies that came out of the Democratic assembly caucus and cooperated with a number of moderate Republicans, the assembly leadership was quick to strip him of his committee chair.[18] In 2003, Senate Republican Minority Leader Jim Brulte warned, during tense budget negotiations, that he would personally campaign against any member of the Republican caucus who joined the Democrats in voting for a tax increase.

MYTH EXPOSED Many Californians believe that partisan differences are the primary cause of the state legislature's inability to address the problems within the state, but actually a large share of the impediments limiting the legislature's effectiveness can be traced to interparty infighting, partly due to the interest group influence and to factionalism within each party.

Prior to becoming the longest serving Assembly Speaker, Willie Brown developed a reputation for going outside his political party caucus to garner political support. On occasion, the influence of powerful interest groups has trumped the ideological integrity of the caucuses. For example, despite the anti-union orientation of the Republican caucus and the civil libertarian and anti–death penalty positions of the Democratic caucus, both parties have favored generous benefits for the California Corrections Peace Officers Association, a labor union not known for liberal positions. News accounts have regularly cited the large campaign contributions that CCPOA has bestowed on legislative candidates from both parties. Ethnic, gender, and single-issue inclinations by groups of caucus members can at times cause as much internal dissension as interparty conflict. Of late, the sizable numbers of Latino Democratic caucus members wield substantial influence over caucus decisions, especially regarding leadership. The promotion of issues such as bilingual education by this group has occasionally clashed with the broader interests of caucus members, which has included reelection, budgetary matters, and constituency relations. The state legislative party caucuses are powerful influences on the conduct of the legislature, but the various dimensions of the California political landscape may cause legislators to ignore convention in favor of personal political career considerations.

In addition to the party caucuses in both chambers, there are other caucuses, representing ethnic, gender, Internet, and smart growth issues. Most of these caucuses were formed as the result of a perceived lack of attention given to the concerns of these groups by the party caucuses. Recently, there has been some controversy over whether the Latino and Asian Pacific Islander caucuses should admit Latino and Asian Republicans as members. Although the Latino caucus continues to resist the membership of Republican Latinos on the grounds of policy interests, the Asian caucus recently relented and allowed Republicans to join.

Legislative Compensation

Prior to the current fiscal crisis facing state government, California legislators remained the highest-paid legislators in the nation, with an annual base salary of $95,291, which is established by an independent citizens' commission (see Table 18.1). For comparison, the salary of state legislators in New York was $79,500 per year, and members of the Nevada state legislature received $137.90 per day for a maximum of 60 days in the legislative session. In addition to their salaries, California legislators received a per diem of $141 each day their chamber is in session.[19] Additional benefits included an automobile, a cell phone, health insurance, and funds to hire staff and rent office space in their districts. There are of course at least two ways to judge this salary and the benefits. Is this level of compensation

TABLE 18.1	Annual Compensation for California Legislators	
The seven-member California Citizens Compensation Commission was created in June of 1990 as a result of passage of Proposition 112 to determine the salaries and benefits for members of the legislature and other statewide offices. The governor appoints all seven commissioners, who serve for overlapping 6-year terms.*		
California legislators elected after 1990 are not eligible for a pension.		

Assembly and State Senate Salary:
  Assembly speaker, state senate president pro tempore, and minority leader are paid $109,584;
  majority leader and second-ranking minority leader are paid $102,437.
		$95,291

Per Diem Living Expenses:
  Approximate tax-free annual funds provided to each member for each day the legislature is in session.
  This is set by the California Victim Compensation and Government Claims Board, not by the California
  Citizens Compensation Commission.
		$25,420 ($141 per day)

Car Allowance: For purchase of a vehicle on 2-year loan and $350 monthly for a 4-year loan.		$4,920 ($410 per month)
Dental		$1,308 ($109 per month)
Vision		$299 ($25 per month)

Family Health Insurance:
  Monthly cost toward family health insurance, ranging from $332 to $834, depending on the number of covered
  dependents.
		$3,984 ($332 per month)

*The current salaries and benefits of the California state legislature were reduced in 2009 due to the state's fiscal emergency.
SOURCE: California Citizens Compensation Commission: Fact Sheet, www.dpa.ca.gov; Mark Martin and Lyndia Gledhill, "Nation's Highest Paid Legislators Get Raise: First Boost in 7 Years Ups Pay to $110,880 as State Battles Deficit," *San Francisco Chronicle*, May 24, 2005, p.B8.

simply in line with what a corporate executive would expect, especially considering that California is the nation's largest and wealthiest state? Or does this compensation package make it more difficult for legislators to truly appreciate the financial constraints that most of their constituents must face?

STUDENT profile

With limited financial resources, attending a four-year university or college was not an option for Danielle Williams, so the local California community college was her first stop in what would be an arduous yet fulfilling higher educational pathway. Danielle found her calling after taking a series of political science classes that clarified important ideas about life and presented opportunities and vocations that she found exciting. The community college experience, coupled with good grades, facilitated her transfer to the University of California at Berkeley.

Danielle found her courses at Berkeley challenging, and maintaining a high GPA was further complicated by the need to work part-time as a bank teller while pursuing her interest in party politics. After earning a bachelor's degree in political

science from Berkeley, she was ready to take another step: the California Senate Fellows program. Established in 1973, the program is jointly sponsored by the state senate and the Center for California Studies at California State University, Sacramento. By exposing individuals with an interest in government to the legislative process, the Fellows program broadens participants' knowledge of representative democracy and serves as an apprentice opportunity for future legislative professionals. For Danielle, the Fellows program was a natural progression from all the research and writing she had done as an undergraduate as well as a chance to meet and work with people who share her interests.

As one of the 18 individuals selected for the 11-month program, Danielle worked with state senator Roy Ashburn. Her responsibilities included researching and analyzing bills for the senate environmental quality committee and for the select committees on constitutional reform and on autism. Danielle had the distinction of working on a number of legislative bills that were ultimately passed into law. As a fellow, she received a monthly stipend of $1,972 plus full health, vision, and dental benefits. The 12 graduate units she earned as a participant in the program will provide a foundation for graduate school pursuits, but she currently has other more practical plans. Upon completion of the Fellows program, Danielle accepted a position as a project assistant with California Forward, a nonprofit organization dedicated to developing a bipartisan approach to reforming California state government. This will be yet another superb opportunity for Danielle in what is clearly becoming an exciting career in politics and government.

The Legislative Universe

18.3   **Identify legislative functions and assess the role of party caucuses in the California state legislature.**

PRACTICE QUIZ: UNDERSTAND AND APPLY

1. The organization and functions of the state legislature are based on
   a. Article 4 of the state constitution, standing rules, and joint rules.
   b. regulations made by the California Political Fair Practices Commission.
   c. decisions made by the State Senate Rules Committee.
   d. ballot measures approved by California voters.

2. "Juice bills" are
   a. bills written to benefit a particular group.
   b. budgetary bills.
   c. bills governing the manufacture, transportation, and sale of alcohol.
   d. rarely passed due to their controversial nature.

3. Why does the California legislature have difficulty conducting oversight of the California state government?
   a. There is too much ethnic diversity in California and its government.
   b. The task of conducting legislative oversight is labor- and time-intensive and requires dedicated legislators.
   c. California state legislators are not honest enough to be trusted to oversee government.
   d. The system of checks and balances used in California state government makes oversight by the legislature very difficult.

4. Requiring a two-thirds majority in the legislature to approve the state budget has what affect?
   a. It facilitates the approval of the state budget.
   b. It benefits the dominant party in the legislature.
   c. It creates a major hurdle.
   d. None of the above.

ANALYZE

1. What current feature or process of the California state legislature is most in need of change or reform?

2. What are the most important functions of the California state legislature? What are the least important?

IDENTIFY THE CONCEPT THAT DOESN'T BELONG

a. Constituents
b. Casework
c. Juror
d. District office
e. Volunteers

Resource Center
• Glossary
• Vocabulary Example
• Connect the Link

■ **Assembly Speaker:**
The presiding officer of the California state assembly.

SIGNIFICANCE: *There have been slightly more Democratic than Republican speakers, but the Republican Party did dominate this leadership position from the 1880s until the 1930s. Since 1959, the Democratic Party has controlled leadership in the assembly.*

Leadership in the State Legislature

18.4 Analyze the roles and responsibilities of the leadership in the California legislature.
(pages 574–577)

For better or worse, term limits have reduced a substantial amount of the power and stature that characterized leadership positions in past California legislatures. The legislators who held these positions were once prodigious forces in the statewide political arena, competing with governors for dominance over the state government and for media attention. Top legislative leadership positions also were frequent launchpads for election to the state executive office and beyond. Former Speaker of the Assembly Jesse M. Unruh was largely responsible for establishing a model of powerful legislative leadership that lasted more than three decades.

The era of powerful legislative leaders would end with Willie Brown, the longest-serving assembly speaker, who was the epitome of the Unruh-era politician. Known for his fundraising prowess and flamboyance, Speaker Brown frequently demonstrated an astute understanding of legislative politics and was the ultimate deal maker. Today, the formal powers remain intact, but the one term that most legislative leaders serve in this capacity curtails their ability to organize a political agenda, build trust and confidence, and establish relationships in both the legislature and the executive branch.

front-runner, Jenny Oropeza. Amid accusations that he had secretly agreed to back Oropeza, Núñez publicly denied that any deal was made, convincing various factions of the Democratic caucus to support his candidacy. Speaker Nunez relinquished his position due to term limits, but not after leading a failed initiative in 2008 to extend the terms of state legislators. In his place stepped assembly member Karen Bass, the first African American women to lead either house of the state legislature. A 54-year-old nurse turned community activist from Los Angeles, Speaker Bass assumed this position at a time when state residents desperately sought answers to cuts in government services, high home foreclosures, and rising unemployment.[21]

Despite her relatively short reign, Speaker Bass, in league with State Senate President Pro Tempore Darrell Steinberg, accomplished the near impossible: she helped broker a budget deal amid a major decline in revenue. Before relinquishing the assembly speaker position, Karen Bass all but anointed John Perez as the next assembly leader, but not before the plans of other political players were dashed and acrimony spread through the Democratic caucus.

The product of a northeast Los Angeles neighborhood, John Perez was originally a union organizer for the painters' union. But he soon rose to the position of political director for the California Federation of Labor. Perez is the first openly gay state legislative leader, having been a strong advocate for gay rights in addition to an active supporter of environmental issues.[22]

Similar in many respects to the speaker of the U.S. House of Representatives, the position of assembly speaker was made especially powerful by the California constitution and the

Assembly Speaker

The selection of **assembly speaker**■—the presiding officer of the California state assembly—can be a turbulent process, full of political intrigue and backstabbing, and often severely testing the relationships and loyalties among assembly members. The selection of the assembly speaker has for some time been an intraparty contest within the dominant Democratic Party caucus, compelling ambitious assembly members of that party to cultivate factions that will provide the necessary votes when the election for assembly speaker takes place in the party caucus. Jesse Unruh rose to the position of speaker largely because of his tactless manner, chairmanship of the then-powerful Ways and Means Committee, and popularity with lobbyists, all of which allowed him to simply bully his way into the position. Others, such as Bob Moretti, Leo McCarthy, and Willie Brown, were considerably more subtle but no less cunning.[20]

Even with term limits, the struggle for the assembly speakership within the Democratic caucus has been no less malicious, as exemplified by the rise of Fabian Núñez, who ended up beating out four other candidates, including the

California Speaker of the Assembly John Perez gives away rubber duckies during his first day on the job promising not to "duck" difficult questions and challenges. —*What challenges do speakers face?*

standing rules of the assembly. In theory, the assembly speaker is responsible for maintaining order in a neutral or nonpartisan manner. In reality, the partisan nature of legislative politics in California compels the assembly speaker to use the position for very partisan objectives. Considering the range of the assembly speaker's parliamentary authority, it would not be an exaggeration to suggest that this position is probably the second most powerful political office in the state, after the governor. Specific qualities of the assembly speaker's parliamentary powers are derived from the following responsibilities and duties:

- Determines the number and titles of standing committees, special committees, and subcommittees.
- Arranges the schedule for committee meetings.
- Appoints members of the assembly standing committees, special committees, and subcommittees.
- Appoints chairs and vice chairs of all assembly committees.
- Appoints the majority floor leader.
- Appoints three members of the assembly to serve on conference committees.
- Directs the Rules Committee in the referral of bills to specific committees.
- Serves as the ex officio nonvoting member of all assembly committees.
- Presides over the assembly, and can appoint assembly members as temporary replacements as necessary.
- Assigns office space in the capitol to assembly members.

The authority of the assembly speaker is very similar to the role of a judge in a court setting, which includes recognizing the right of members to speak during debates and clarifying parliamentary procedures and rules of the assembly. The one organizational limitation on the speaker's power is the inability to appoint members to the Rules Committee. Because of the partisan nature of the state legislature, the speaker is somewhat indebted as well as accountable to the majority party. For the sake of a successful lawmaking agenda, the presiding officer may be forced to enlist the support of the opposition through compromise. Consequently, the speaker must often walk a very fine line between using the enormous authority of the position to facilitate policymaking and protecting his or her political party.

The supremacy of the speaker does attract the generosity of special-interest groups, which see this position as the most direct and important access point for influencing the lawmaking function. Consequently, the speaker is a main beneficiary of, as well as a fountainhead for, campaign contributions. However difficult it may be for an assembly speaker to accept large sums of money from special-interest groups, that money is vital to the speaker's responsibility of maintaining his or her party's majority in the assembly. Dispensing large sums of campaign contributions or directing generous donors to fellow assembly members and the party is the key to achieving this goal.

Partisan Assembly Leaders

Although the California constitution specifies only the speaker as the presiding officer of the assembly, other leadership positions are derived from the partisan divisions among assembly members.

MAJORITY FLOOR LEADER, ASSISTANT MAJORITY LEADER, WHIP, AND ASSISTANT WHIP Although elected by the majority party caucus, the assembly speaker is largely responsible for selecting the majority floor leader, assistant majority leader, whip, and assistant whip, which serve as the speaker's personal liaison with the majority party. The majority floor leader supervises this team, which represents the speaker on the floor, clarifying assembly proceedings and parliamentary procedures, such as motions and points of order, and promoting unity among the party membership. All of these positions are especially important in coordinating the majority party's efforts to pass legislation and in facilitating a two-way communication flow between the speaker and the assembly membership.

In an environment where assembly members may be reluctant to express personal feelings and positions, the majority floor leader conveys personal opinions to the assembly speaker and gauges the sentiments of the entire assembly membership. The individuals who are selected for these positions generally serve at the discretion of the assembly speaker; hence, they are expected to perform whatever duties will support the position of the assembly speaker and their party, which may include fundraising, policy development, campaign management, and interacting with lobbyists. Thanks to the constant influx of new members with minimal experience, the floor leadership has become increasingly important to the performance of the assembly.

SPEAKER PRO TEMPORE AND ASSISTANT SPEAKER PRO TEMPORE Appointed by the assembly speaker, the speaker pro tempore presides over floor sessions in the absence of the speaker, and the assistant speaker pro tempore presides over floor sessions in the absence of the speaker and the speaker pro tempore.

MINORITY FLOOR LEADER Elected by the minority party caucus, the minority floor leader is generally considered to be the leader of the minority party in the assembly and is responsible for representing that party on the floor of the assembly. The minority floor leader is essentially an assembly speaker in waiting, and there is a considerable amount of pressure on the minority floor leader to assist in the reelection of assembly members from the minority party, which in recent years has been the Republican Party. And when the minority party does lose seats, the party caucus has been quick to replace the minority floor leader, a decision that was made at least four times between 1998 and 2001. In March 2001, for example, Assemblyman Bill Campbell had served only four months as assembly minority leader when assembly Republicans voted unanimously to remove him in favor of Assemblyman Dave Cox.[23]

ASSISTANT MINORITY FLOOR LEADER   The assistant minority floor leader performs roles very similar to those of the assembly majority leadership positions but for a much smaller membership. Rapid turnover in minority floor leaders greatly increases the opportunities for the assistant minority floor leader to rise to the top spot.

PRESIDENT OF THE SENATE   The California constitution designates the lieutenant governor as the president of the senate, similar to the position of the vice president of the United States in the U.S. Senate. And like the vice president, the lieutenant governor's role in the state senate is largely ceremonial, with the exception of the authority to cast a tie-breaking vote. The lieutenant governor may be invited periodically to preside on ceremonial occasions, such as the opening of the legislative session. Serving as lieutenant governor is often seen as a springboard for election as governor, Gray Davis being the most recent example, and any chance to increase name recognition, including appearances in the state senate, is actively sought.

Partisan State Senate Leaders

One of the major differences between leadership in the state senate and in the state assembly is the decentralized nature of senate leadership positions, powers, and responsibilities. In fact, as described in more depth below, this decentralized structure allows the minority party in the senate to exert considerably more influence on the legislative process.

PRESIDENT PRO TEMPORE   The president pro tempore is the actual leader of the state senate and is elected by the members at the beginning of each session. As the presiding officer of the senate, the president pro tem, as the position is commonly known, has much less power than its legislative counterpart, the speaker of the assembly. Not unlike the U.S. Senate, the California state senate was designed to be more "deliberative" as a result of its smaller number of members, decentralized leadership structure, and longer term of office. The committee chairpersons in the state senate oversee critical decisions about bills that pass through their committees, many of which cope with health and safety issues. A "deliberative" senate environment and these critical decisions have resulted in senate committee chair positions that exercise considerable legislative power and autonomy.

Whatever leadership power may exist outside the responsibilities of the committee chairs is exercised by the senate's five-member Rules Committee, which has legislative powers equivalent to those of the assembly speaker. As the chair of that committee, the president pro tem is able to exert substantial control over the legislative agenda and resources of the state senate. The committee is also composed of two senators from each party, who are nominated by their party caucuses and must also receive at least 21 votes from the full senate.

As a result of the senate power to confirm gubernatorial appointments, the president pro tem has the opportunity to interact slightly more with the executive branch of state government than the assembly leader. Not unlike the assembly speaker, there is considerable pressure on the president pro tem to keep current members in office through assistance with fundraising and campaign management.

The departing president pro tem in 2008, Don Perata, was particularly adept at fundraising and distributing campaign funds to the senate candidates that needed it. Elected by the senate Democratic caucus to replace Don Perata in 2008, the current president pro tem, Darrell Steinberg, continues to face a long list of challenges not experienced by a leader of the state legislature in decades. Not expected to term-out until 2014, Steinberg has developed a number of valuable personal and political skills. In addition to fundraising prowess, a quality absolutely vital to leadership aspirations, Steinberg is known for his courteous and affable manner, which engenders even the opposition to embrace civility in legislative affairs.

SENATE MAJORITY LEADER AND MAJORITY WHIP
The senate majority leader and whip are chosen by the majority caucus and serve as the main floor managers for the president pro tempore and the majority party, fulfilling responsibilities that are not very different from those of their counterparts in the assembly.

SENATE MINORITY LEADER   The senate minority leader (also known as the "Republican leader") holds the second most powerful position in the senate. Elected by members of the minority caucus, the senate minority leader speaks for the minority party, maintains party discipline, and interacts with the president pro tempore to set the senate's order of business. As a member of the Rules Committee, the senate minority leader is in a good position to cut deals and take advantage of the decentralized and deliberative nature of the senate. The Republicans have been fortunate to have had a number of strong minority leaders in the past, the most notable being Jim Brulte, who termed out as minority leader in 2006.

MINORITY WHIP   The minority whip is essentially an assistant to the senate minority leader and is elected by the

California Senate President pro tempore Darrell Steinberg meets with members of the Japanese American Citizens League, one of the oldest civil rights groups in Sacramento. —*What responsibilities does the leader of the state senate fulfill both inside and outside the legislature?*

minority caucus to assist in maintaining party discipline and to serve as an informational resource to the caucus.

Nonmember Officers

The important and often critical work carried out in the state legislature cannot be performed without an expert staff well versed in the parliamentary rules and procedures of the California legislature. These critical nonmembers include the chief sergeant-at-arms, chief clerk, and legislative secretary.

CHIEF SERGEANT-AT-ARMS The chief sergeant-at-arms, who is elected by the total membership, is responsible for maintaining order on the senate and assembly floors and in committee meetings.

CHIEF CLERK AND LEGISLATIVE SECRETARY The positions of chief clerk and legislative secretary are nonpartisan and are elected by the majority of the membership at the start of each session. The chief clerk serves as a legislative officer and parliamentarian and the secretary as the primary record keeper.

Leadership in the State Legislature

18.4 Analyze the roles and responsibilities of the leadership in the California legislature.

PRACTICE QUIZ: UNDERSTAND AND APPLY

1. Which of the following legislative leaders was largely responsible for establishing the model of powerful legislative leadership that lasted over 30 years?
   a. Joseph Montoya   c. Jesse Unruh
   b. Jerry Brown   d. Earl Warren

2. Which of the following duties does NOT apply to the speaker?
   a. determines the number and titles of standing committees, special committees, and subcommittees
   b. arranges the schedule for committee meetings
   c. serves as a voting member of all assembly committees
   d. appoints the majority floor leader

3. What are the two likely personal characteristics of a candidate for assembly speaker ?
   a. kindness and courtesy
   b. honesty and reliability
   c. ambition and cunning
   d. modesty and sociability

ANALYZE

1. What is the main role of the majority floor leader in the assembly? How does this position influence the outcome of legislation?

2. What are the major differences between the assembly and state senate leadership positions?

IDENTIFY THE CONCEPT THAT DOESN'T BELONG

a. President pro tempore
b. Voir dire
c. Five-member rules committee
d. Decentralized leadership
e. Deliberative approach

Resource Center
• Glossary
• Vocabulary Example
• Connect the Link

■ **Standing Committees (Policy Committees):** The permanent committees of the legislature.

SIGNIFICANCE: *Each standing committee has basic features that are vital to the operation of that committee. These include specialized committee staff, rules of procedure, specific jurisdiction or area of interest, and meeting place.*

The Legislative Committee System

18.5 **Evaluate the importance of committees in the California legislature.**
(pages 578–581)

With between 5,000 and 6,000 bills introduced each legislative session, the committee system is a logical approach to delegating proposed laws of a specific type to a small group of legislators who have either the expertise or the interest to determine their merits. As in the U.S. Congress, state legislative committees are where most of the work of the legislature takes place, and they are the proving ground for legislators who aspire to higher leadership or are interested in developing a particular expertise. The state legislative committees are vital to the lawmaking process, reflecting the wealth, size, and complexity of California.

Standing Committees

The **standing committees**■ (also known as **policy committees**), are the permanent committees that act as the clearinghouses for bills introduced in the legislature. From time to time, these committees also handle important action required of the state legislature, with executive oversight and confirmations being two of the most obvious. When a legislator is elected, a serious effort is made to appoint that member to several committees that will mirror his or her qualifications and interests. Other factors, such as the legislator's standing in the party and personal idiosyncrasies of the legislative leaders, also influence committee assignments.

The size of standing committees varies, depending on the standing rules adopted for each legislative session; they can have as few as 7 members or as many as 25. The names of committees may also change from session to session and between chambers, but both chambers generally have committees that address similar areas (see Tables 18.2 and 18.3). Probably the most important type of standing committees are the *fiscal committees,* which review the annual state budget and all other bills that create financial obligations for the state. Although each chamber adjusts the number of standing committees at the start of the legislative session, there are usually 23 standing committees in the state senate and 29 in the assembly.

Each committee is managed by a chairperson, who is empowered by the rules of each chamber to maintain order and keep the committee focused. The committee chairs also have a special partisan responsibility to guarantee that the interests of the party in power are supported by each bill. Setting the agenda for committee meetings is one of the most important powers of the committee chairs, thereby focusing attention on certain issues and downplaying or ignoring others. The scope

TABLE 18.2 California Assembly Standing Committees
Aging and Long-Term Care
Agriculture
Appropriations
Arts, Entertainment, Sports, Tourism, and Internet Media
Banking and Finance
Budget
Business, Professions, and Consumer Protection
Education
Elections and Redistricting
Environmental Safety and Toxic Materials
Governmental Organization
Health
Higher Education
Housing and Community Development
Human Services
Insurance
Jobs, Economic Development, and the Economy
Judiciary
Labor and Employment
Local Government
Natural Resources
Public Employees, Retirement, and Social Security
Public Safety
Revenue and Taxation
Rules
Transportation
Utilities and Commerce
Veterans Affairs
Water, Parks, and Wildlife

SOURCE: California Assembly.

of many standing committees is so wide-ranging as to necessitate the creation of subcommittees to address one portion of a broader issue, service, or problem. Members from the parent standing committee serve on the subcommittees.

■ **Select Committees:** Temporary committees formed to conduct investigations of issues or problems that are not specifically related to a standing committee or are of special interest to a legislator.

SIGNIFICANCE: *Each select committee convened by a legislator is usually provided a budget and assigned staff members and can thereby be one way for a legislator to gain additional resources.*

TABLE 18.3	California Senate Standing Committees

Agriculture
Appropriations
Banking, Finance, and Insurance
Budget and Fiscal Review
Business, Professions, and Economic
Development
Education
Elections, Reapportionment, and Constitutional Amendments
Energy, Utilities, and Communications
Environmental Quality
Governmental Organization
Health
Human Services
Judiciary
Labor and Industrial Relations
Local Government
Natural Resources and Water
Public Employment and Retirement
Public Safety
Revenue and Taxation Rules
Transportation and Housing
Veterans Affairs

SOURCE: California State Senate.

The work of the standing committees largely consists of gathering information about a particular bill or issue, correcting perceived problems, or simply preventing the bill from advancing to the full body. The information-gathering process is conducted partly by committee support staff and partly through the hearing process. During the hearing process, a variety of supporters, detractors, and neutral experts will provide testimony. In theory, committee hearings permit the public to participate in the legislative process, providing input about a particular bill or issue. The hearings also place the legislators in the public eye, allowing them the opportunity to appear competent and knowledgeable as well as to increase their standing with the constituents in their home districts. Public awareness regarding hearings may be limited, but legislators must be careful about the exposure they can receive from newspaper reports, the written record of committee meetings, and even the state government cable television coverage of legislative proceedings. To handle "juice bills" that are introduced, legislators have applied a special recognition to committees that attract the attention of generous special-interest groups seeking to influence proposed laws. These "juice committees" are sought after by legislators, who see them as a means of generating the ever-important campaign contributions.

There is a tendency to downplay the role of the legislative staff in conducting the work of the state legislature. Clearly, legislators want to be seen as in control and industrious, and staff members know that their positions are almost entirely dependent on pleasing legislators, regardless of the workload and lack of recognition. In reality, the legislative staff possess an enormous amount of power, especially regarding committee work. Even the more fastidious legislators are often overwhelmed with constituency relations and fundraising and have a limited amount of time to research, draft, or even read proposed laws. After developing an area of expertise, compensation for legislative staff can be attractive, anywhere from between $100,000 to $150,000 for a "special assistant" or "principle consultant." The real payoff for many seasoned staff members is their ability to parlay legislative experience, specific knowledge, and networking for lucrative work in the private sector or governmental executive positions.

Select Committees

Select committees■ are temporary committees formed to investigate issues or problems that are not specifically related to a standing committee or are of special interest to a legislator. These committees do not handle or create legislation; at best, they will generate a report that could be the basis for a bill. In recent years, both chambers have been deluged with select committees, some convened by legislators who are sincerely concerned about a specific problem and others by legislators who use the select committee to grab media attention through high-profile hearings and to enhance their legislative résumé.

Conference Committees

Conference committees■ are based on the constitutional provision that requires a bill to be passed in both legislative bodies before it can become law. The conference committee is charged with reconciling any differences that may arise between two different versions of a bill. Composed of three members from each chamber, the conference committee becomes significant when the two chambers are controlled by different political parties. Otherwise, chances are that any differences between the two versions of a bill will be worked out by the partisan leadership of both chambers long before it reaches the conference committee stage.

■ **Conference Committees:** Committees charged with the task of reconciling any differences that may arise between two different versions of a bill.

SIGNIFICANCE: *If a conference committee has been unable to resolve the differences in a bill, the respective chambers can appoint a new conference committee. No more than three conference committees can be appointed for consideration of one bill, and if there is no resolution after the third committee, the bill is considered dead.*

Joint Committees

There are six **joint committees** in the state legislature that are intended to facilitate the work of the legislature by bringing together equal numbers of legislators from both chambers to address specific issues and policy areas. Joint committees offer a unique forum for both chambers when attempting to reach consensus on an issue of policy while presenting a unified voice to the public. Two of the more noteworthy joint committees are the Joint Legislative Budget Committee and the Joint Rules Committee.

Rules Committees

Each chamber has a **rules committee**■—a group charged with the administration of the legislature and defining its rules of operation. The five-member Rules Committee of the state senate is considered to be the executive committee of the senate, with the authority to assign senators to committees, appoint committee chairs, refer bills, assign office space and support staff, and set the overall policy direction of the senate. The authority of the state senate president pro tempore is derived from his or her position as the chair of this committee.

The Rules Committee of the assembly is chaired by the assembly speaker or the speaker's appointee, and it is responsible for selecting and supervising assembly support staff. Its administrative responsibilities include overseeing the finances of the assembly and proposing changes in house rules.

Legislative Action

After a bill has been introduced into either chamber by its author, it is numbered and referred to a committee. To allow members of the public and the press to become informed about a specific proposal, no committee action may take place until a bill has been in print for 30 days. The members of the committee may recommend approval of a bill and send it to the chamber floor without alteration, may suggest modifications to a bill and recommend that it be passed on the floor as amended, or may allow a bill to die in committee. The great majority of bills that fail to be enacted into law are killed in committee, which demonstrates that the reality of passing a bill is complicated and generally hidden from public view.

The Hidden Side of Lawmaking

Most hearings and legislative offices are open to the public. There are various written records of legislative work and proceedings, not to mention daily newspapers, that most Californians probably assume preserve the free and open ideal of representative democracy. Yet, in the state capitol, all too often the dysfunction and disappointments that many people associate with the legislative process are not necessarily hidden by backroom deals or shadowy figures but rather are shrouded by a legislative process that is often manipulated.

Not many years ago, a bill was proposed in the state legislature that provides a good example of the manipulation of the legislative process and a starting point in understanding what needs to be fixed. The bill that was proposed would allow insurance companies to give discounts to drivers who had no gaps in their automobile coverage. The argument of the bill's backers inside as well as outside the state legislature was that if you stayed with your insurance company for a period of time, you should be entitled to a discount. Consumer advocates, who had supported Proposition 103, the 1988 insurance reform initiative, opposed the attempt to roll-back provisions of the reform initiative

Ralph Nader, consumer advocate, points to a document as he testifies on California's insurance reform Proposition 103. Supported by Nader, Proposition 103 was approved by the voters in 1988. —*How important is the backing of a nationally recognized activist or widely known figure to the success of a ballot initiative?*

■ **Rules Committees:**
Committees charged with administration of the legislature and defining its rules of operation.

SIGNIFICANCE: *After introduction, a bill goes to the rules committee of the chamber, where it is assigned to the appropriate standing committee. It is at this point that a bill is most vulnerable and the rules committee exercises its greatest power. By assigning a bill to a standing committee without the staff and experience to accurately examine it, the rules committee is essentially bringing the life of the bill to an end.*

with this new bill, insisting that prop 103 prohibited companies from discriminating against uninsured motorists who wanted to get coverage. The consumer advocates also found that people in the military and new drivers, through no fault of their own, would have gaps in their auto insurance coverage and would pay what the advocates thought would be an unfair, higher rate.[24] The consumer advocates' view prevailed in the standing committee where the bill was originally sent, which stalled consideration of the bill in the hope that it would die there.

Meanwhile, lobbyists for a large insurance company that had contributed at least $1 million to the politicians in Sacramento—$25,000 of which had gone to the bill's author— were putting pressure on the legislative leaders to intervene. First, using his "fast track" powers, the presiding officer of the legislative body referred the insurance bill ahead of all other bills to a particular committee unrelated to the insurance industry. That unrelated committee, led by the committee chairperson at the direction of the presiding officer, engaged in the "gut and amend" process—a legislative tactic that involves taking out the contents of an unrelated bill, which in this case would have expanded prostate cancer research, and inserting the language of the insurance bill. Any attempt to hold hearings on the bill were subjected to repeated postponements until the last 72 hours of the session. At 8:30 A.M. on a Saturday, the unrelated committee

held an obligatory 15-minute hearing before unanimously voting to pass the bill on to the full chamber. Once on the floor of both chambers, the bill was passed into law.[25]

This concluding account stands in blatant contrast to the description of the Global Warming Solutions Act—(AB 32) and the circumstances surrounding its passage presented at the beginning of this chapter. Regardless of the debate over the validity of the greenhouse gas problem, AB 32 is a good example of the noble intentions that do occur in the state legislature. Such intentions are nonetheless often overshadowed by legislative schemes involving a "third house," notwithstanding the efforts of insurance industry lobbyists who regularly succeed in manipulating the legislative process for less than noble causes. Spending thousands of dollars on the campaign aspirations of California legislators and an in-depth understanding of state legislative procedures has gotten many of these lobbyists almost unlimited access to the legislative process. The influence of "third house," coupled with the ability of legislators to cloak their lawmaking activities within myriad procedures, protend an electoral process that is insufficient to guarantee a balanced approach to lawmaking. Considerably greater public attention to the legislative universe is vital to ensure that the California legislature pursues more laws in the sprit of AB 32 and less that succumb to the "gut-and-amend" maneuver.

The Legislative Committee System

18.5 Evaluate the importance of committees in the California legislature.

PRACTICE QUIZ: UNDERSTAND AND APPLY

1. Roughly how many bills are introduced each legislative session?
   a. between 200 and 300
   b. approximately 1 to 2 million
   c. between 10,000 and 15,000
   d. between 5,000 and 6,000

2. The size of standing committees depends on
   a. the policy agenda of the governor.
   b. how many bills are introduced during each session.
   c. the availability of staff members.
   d. the standing rules adopted for each legislative session.

3. What feature of the legislative process most likely empowers the chairpersons of California legislative committees?
   a. the rules of each chamber
   b. the rules committee
   c. the presiding officers
   d. the prestige of the floor leaders

4. The "executive" functions of the five-member Rules Committee of the state senate consist of
   a. marking up legislation before a full vote in the senate.
   b. overseeing the budgetary process.
   c. setting the overall policy direction of the senate.
   d. facilitating relations between the two chambers.

ANALYZE

1. Why is the conference committee vital to the democratic process in the California state legislature?

2. What are typically the most powerful and least powerful types of committees in the California state legislature?

IDENTIFY THE CONCEPT THAT DOESN'T BELONG

a. Home rule
b. Policy formulation
c. Fiscal matters
d. "Juice bill"
e. Specialized interests

18.5

Conclusion

The California state legislature's statutes on greenhouse gases serve as a good example of an effort by legislators to represent and serve the residents of California in the broadest terms possible. This chapter has revealed how the Global Warming Solutions Act was written and passed with the best of intentions for all Californians. It also shows how, in the normal course of California legislative affairs, such good intentions are clearly not always the primary motivation for legislative action. An influential factor involves the "third house," which has the ability to sway legislative votes with millions of dollars in campaign contributions, steering legislative efforts toward the concerns of generous donors. Because the public is aware at least that money is being traded for special consideration at the state capitol while the basic problems of the state remain unsolved, the approval ratings of the California legislature in recent years have rarely risen above 30 percent. Unfortunately, the state legislature does not give the public much to appreciate as the authorship and approval of most beneficial but intricate laws occurs behind closed doors. In addition, the media regularly cover topics that are much easier to observe and report—for example, as legislators bickering among themselves, with the governor, and sometimes with the public.

Not known to shy away from tinkering with the organization and structure of government through the initiative process, Californians seem increasingly interested in current proposals to reform a select number of governmental processes. The transformation of the legislature into a professional body, the enactment of term limits, the push given to the initiative process by Proposition 13, and the most recent 2008 citizen's redistricting measure are all examples of Californians' willingness to experiment with the legislative process. Some of these efforts are successful, some are unsuccessful, and many simply replace old problems with new ones. The idea that limiting the terms of state legislators would improve the performance and perception of the legislature has not happened. "Voters FIRST," the nonpartisan redistricting process approved by the voters in 2008, may result in many more competitive legislative elections and elected legislators who are less partisan. It may also eliminate safe electoral districts, raising campaign costs and thus increasing candidates' dependence on the "third house."

The Democratic majority in the current legislature has joined forces with California Forward, a so-called bipartisan reform group, and both have agreed to a list of solutions to the state's more problematic features, starting with a constitutional amendment that discards the two-thirds rule for approving the state budget. As elusive as attempts to reform the state legislature have been in the past, the economic recession that has descended on California just might be the impetus to achieve change that actually improves the performance of the lawmaking body and government in general.

KEY CONCEPT MAP **How have historic events in California impacted the professional growth of the state legislature?**

1879

Constitutional Revision

In an attempt to curb corporate influence and corruption in government, the constitution is revised to establish, among other things, restrictions on bribery and lobbying, limits on the size of the legislature and compensation, and the power to regulate utilities.

This revision serves to improve the stature of the state legislature and bring greater structure to the legislative process. It also lays the foundation for subsequent and much more substantial legislative reforms and demonstrates to future legislators the potential power of this government body.

Critical Thinking Questions

Why did Californians want to limit the influence of corporations on the legislature? How would curbing corporate influence have served to improve the stature of the state legislature?

1910

Progressive Era Reforms

In addition to electing Hiram Johnson, a Progressive governor, Californians elect a Progressive Party majority in the state legislature. They enact a series of reforms and innovative public policies, including provisions for direct democracy, women's suffrage, regulation of utilities, fiscal controls, labor law reform, and nonpartisan elections.

Progressive members of the state legislature bring a mixture of activism and astute management skills to lawmaking, which produces effective policies. They also install a long-standing legislative framework emphasizing pragmatism and an activist state government.

What types of Californians would have been most likely to support the legislative agenda of the Progressive Party? What if Progressives had been unable to gain a majority of seats in the state legislature? How would the legislative agenda of this period have differed?

1965

California Reapportionment Act

Until the 1960s, districts in California's rural counties had only a fraction of the population of large urban counties but enjoyed equal representation in the state senate. Federal and state courts ruled that the districts violated the principle of "one person, one vote" and ordered them to be reapportioned by population.

By 1966, the California legislature had completed the process, shifting half of the state senate seats from the rural northern and eastern counties to southern and urban ones. The reapportionment resulted in the largest turnover of state senate seats in the history of the legislature. As a result, representation in the state senate now more closely reflects the demographic orientation of the entire state.

What are the consequences of having a state senate that more closely reflects the demographic orientation of the entire state? Is there a danger that the interests of smaller rural areas will be neglected if the legislature is dominated by senators from larger urban areas? Why or why not?

1966

Proposition 1A: Full-Time Legislature

Voters approve a constitutional amendment authorizing a full-time legislature and establishing provisions for a full-time salary set by the legislature, conflict-of-interest restrictions, a living expense allowance, and full-time professional staff assistance for individual members and committees.

The new law essentially professionalizes the state legislature. By 1971, California is judged to have one of the best (and best paid) legislatures in the country. The newly professionalized legislature presides over one of the most elaborate and far-reaching policy agendas in the history of California.

What if California were to return to being a part-time legislature? How would this impact the legislature's ability to get things done? Would existing legislators be likely to support such a return to part-time status? Why or why not?

1990

Proposition 140: Term Limits

In reaction to a state legislature suffering from gridlock, corruption scandals, and an entrenched leadership, voters approve a constitutional initiative instituting term limits. Legislators may serve a maximum of six years in the assembly and eight years in the senate. Once termed out, a legislator is banned for life from holding a seat in that chamber.

Term limits permit many more residents to serve in the state legislature and in legislative leadership positions. However, the legislature continues to be plagued by issues that existed prior to the imposition of term limits, such as extreme partisanship, special interest influence, and excessive fundraising activities.

Why is it likely that many of the problems that existed in the state legislature prior to the imposition of term limits still exist? Are there any negative consequences to term limits? If so, what are they? If not, why not?

The California legislature has historically suffered from low public approval ratings. However, despite the fact that California voters have the opportunity to elect members to the California legislature every two years, reelection rates for state legislators have typically been around 90 percent. —*Why do you think reelection rates are so high if the public remains* *dissatisfied with the job the California legislature is doing? How much responsibility should Californians accept for the dysfunctional qualities of the California state legislature, such as gridlock and the dominance of special interest groups?*

Review of Key Objectives

The Role of the California Legislature

18.1 Recount the transformation of the California legislature into a professional body.

(pages 560–561)

Beginning in the early 1960s, the legislature succeeded in enacting laws that not only professionalized this body with higher salaries and more experienced staff, but also addressed a wide range of issues—from water development and civil rights to social welfare and highway construction—while still maintaining a budget surplus. By 1971, California was judged to have one of the best legislatures in the country—and certainly one of the best paid. Presiding over one of the most productive policy agendas in the history of California, the Democratic legislature, riding high on a string of achievements, ran into a brick wall built on the conservative backlash of California voters who passed Proposition 13, the major property tax reduction initiative in 1978.

KEY TERMS

Constitutional Revision Commission 560
Third House 560
Proposition 140 561

CRITICAL THINKING QUESTIONS

1. What steps have Californians taken to weaken the legislature since establishing it as a professional body? What are the costs and benefits of these measures?
2. What key issues have tarnished the reputation of the state legislature? What could be done to improve both the function and the reputation of the legislature?

INTERNET RESOURCES

The California State Legislative Portal provides accessible information regarding the California state legislature, including bill information, calendar and schedules, member information, rules and ethics, and leadership and caucuses: http://www.legislature.ca.gov/

ADDITIONAL READING

Samish, Arthur H., and Bob Thomas. *The Secret Boss of California: The Life and High Times of Art Samish.* New York: Crown, 1971.

Ignoffo, Mary Jo. *Gold Rush Politics: California's First Legislature.* Sacramento: California State Senate; California History Center and Foundation, De Anza College, Cupertino, CA, 1999.

The Making of a California State Legislator

18.2 Explain the process of electing California state legislators.

(pages 562–565)

Although the legal qualifications for the state legislature involve only minimal citizenship, age, and residency requirements, the actual pathways to a seat in the legislature are by and large restricted to individuals with experience as locally elected officials or as professional staff members in local or state party organizations. Most legislators maintain political action committees or individual campaign funds that they will contribute to fellow party members who get the nod from the state party organization. Reapportionment and redistricting are other methods of guaranteeing the election of party favorites, but they have been controversial features of the electoral process, perceived by voters more as a means of "fixing" legislative districts.

KEY TERMS

Reapportionment 563
Redistricting 563

CRITICAL THINKING QUESTIONS

1. Why would someone want to become a California state legislator? What does the career path consist of and what can a legislator hope to achieve?
2. What role do political parties play in electing state legislators? Would the election of state legislators be much different if this electoral process were nonpartisan?

INTERNET RESOURCES

Cal-Access provides financial information supplied by state candidates, donors, lobbyists, and others. Select either "Campaign Finance Activity," "Lobbying Activity," or "Cal-Access Resources," on the Web site to get to this information: http://cal-access.ss.ca.gov/

ADDITIONAL READING

Michael, Jay, Dan Walters, and Dan Weintraub. *The Third House: Lobbyists, Money, and Power in Sacramento.* Berkeley: Public Policy Press, Institute of Governmental Studies, University of California, 2002.

The Legislative Universe

18.3 **Identify legislative functions and assess the role of party caucuses in the California state legislature.**

(pages 566–573)

Every two years, after each general election, the state legislature begins a new session, as legislators enter an exclusive environment composed of a select membership with the responsibility of making laws for one of the most important states in the country. The lawmaking responsibility of the assembly and the state senate focuses largely on drafting, reviewing, and ultimately, voting on the thousands of laws that are passed every year to address a broad range of issues. In addition to changes or additions to California statutes, the state legislature may also propose and pass constitutional amendments and resolutions. Although their primary responsibility is to make laws, legislators must also oversee the execution of all laws and the government officials who are charged with implementing them.

KEY TERMS

Standing Rules 566
Joint Rules 566
"Juice Bills" 566
Resolutions 568
Casework 569
Oversight Function 570
Party Caucuses 571

CRITICAL THINKING QUESTIONS

1. What duties does the state legislature fulfill successfully? Which duties does it have more trouble carrying out?
2. What role do the party caucuses serve in the California assembly and the state senate?

INTERNET RESOURCES

The official Web site for California legislative information is maintained by the Legislative Counsel of California at http://www.leginfo.ca.gov

California State Assembly Democrats can be contacted at http://democrats.assembly.ca.gov/

The California State Assembly Republican Caucus can be contacted at http://republican.assembly.ca.gov/

ADDITIONAL READING

Boyarsky, Bill. *Big Daddy: Jesse Unruh and the Art of Power Politics*. Berkeley: University of California Press, 2007.

Jacobs, John. *A Rage for Justice: The Passion and Politics of Phil Burton*. Berkeley: University of California Press, 1995.

Leadership in the State Legislature

18.4 **Analyze the roles and responsibilities of the leadership in the California legislature.**

(pages 574–577)

Today, the formal powers of the speaker remain intact, but the one-term limit that most legislative leaders face curtails their ability to organize a political agenda and build trust. Despite constitutional guidelines that establish the lieutenant governor as the presiding officer of the state senate, the president pro tempore is the actual leader, elected by the assembly members at the beginning of each session but with much less power than its legislative counterpart, the speaker of the assembly. In theory, both positions have the responsibility of maintaining order in a nonpartisan manner. In reality, the partisan nature of legislative politics in California compels legislators to use their power for partisan objectives.

KEY TERM

Assembly Speaker 574

CRITICAL THINKING QUESTIONS

1. How do the assembly speaker and the president pro tempore positions differ? Is there any particular quality of their respective chambers that would cause these leaders to be especially similar or different?
2. What would be the major reasons why a legislator would want to become a leader in the California state legislature?

INTERNET RESOURCES

The Legislative Analyst's Office (LAO) has been providing fiscal and policy advice to the legislature for more than 55 years. It is known for its fiscal and programmatic expertise and nonpartisan analyses of the state's budget: http://www.lao.ca.gov

ADDITIONAL READING

Mathews, Joe, and Mark Paul. *California Cracked Up: How Reform Broke the Golden State and How We Can Fix It*. Berkeley: University of California Press, 2010.

Richardson, James. *Willie Brown*. Berkeley: University of California Press, 1996.

The Legislative Committee System

 18.5 **Evaluate the importance of committees in the California legislature.**

(pages 578–581)

With between 5,000 and 6,000 bills introduced each legislative session, the committee system is a logical approach to delegating proposed laws of a specific type to a small group of legislators who have either the expertise or the interest to determine their merits. As in the U.S. Congress, state legislative committees are where most of the work of the legislature takes place, and they are the proving ground for legislators who aspire to higher leadership or are interested in developing a particular expertise.

KEY TERMS

Standing Committees (Policy Committees) 578
Select Committees 579
Conference Committees 579
Joint Committees 580
Rules Committee 580

CRITICAL THINKING QUESTIONS

1. Why are committees vital to the functioning of the state legislature?
2. If you were elected to the state legislature, what committee would you want to serve on and why? Would the dominant consideration be personal, past experiences, or the needs of your constituents?

INTERNET RESOURCES

The California Channel's mission is to provide an electronic bridge between Californians and their elected officials and to educate a new generation of civic leaders and voting citizens who are knowledgeable about the functions and activities of state government: http://www.calchannel.com/

ADDITIONAL READING

Kenne, Barry. *Making Government Work: California Cases in Policy, Politics and Public Management*, ed. Berkeley: Institute of Government Studies, 2000.

Chapter Review   Test Your Knowledge

1. For much of the nineteenth century, the California state legislature was dominated by
   a. mining interests.
   b. merchant interests.
   c. railroad interests.
   d. agricultural interests.

2. Art Samish was
   a. a celebrated California author.
   b. the richest man in California.
   c. California's consummate lobbyist.
   d. a long-time member of the state legislature.

3. By 1971, California was judged to have
   a. one of the best legislatures in the country.
   b. the largest legislature in the country.
   c. one of the worst legislatures in the country.
   d. the lowest-paid legislature in the country.

4. A campaign for a state senate seat
   a. is often won by the challenger.
   b. never costs more than $100,000.
   c. could cost several million dollars.
   d. always relies on radio ads.

5. In the 1980s and 1990s, the state legislature suffered a tremendous amount of embarrassment when
   a. its members increased the salary and benefits of state legislators.
   b. an FBI undercover sting ensnared state legislators.
   c. most state legislators suffered electoral defeat.
   d. a legislative banking scandal was uncovered.

6. Redistribution of representation in a legislative body is called
   a. realignment.   c. redrawing.
   b. redistricting.   d. reapportionment.

7. Redistricting is the
   a. drawing of new boundaries to election districts.
   b. process by which political parties assign candidates to different legislative districts.
   c. the redrawing of the neighborhood boundaries that determine where one goes to vote.
   d. the redistribution of representation in a legislative body.

8. What is the reelection rate of California legislators?
   a. less than 10 percent
   b. about 50 percent
   c. about 79 percent
   d. over 90 percent

9. California's legislature is
   a. unicameral.
   b. a low-paid legislature.
   c. a full-time legislature.
   d. indirectly elected.

10. Which of the following are guidelines for cooperation between the two chambers of the legislature?
    a. joint rules   c. judicial rules
    b. standing rules   d. cooperation rules

11. Who may introduce bills for consideration in the state legislature?
    a. lobbyists
    b. members of Congress
    c. members of the state legislature
    d. the governor

12. Which of the following would be an example of a "juice bill"?
    a. increased funding for the California Community College System
    b. broadening of an administrative agency's regulatory powers at the agency's request
    c. a bill lowering the voting age to 14
    d. legislation giving a particular corporation a tax break

13. What phenomenon do the efforts of Candace Lightner, the mother of a teenage daughter killed by a drunk driver and who later founded Mothers Against Drunk Driving (MADD), serve to illustrate?
    a. the power of media attention to generate important bills in the state legislature
    b. the ability of the state legislature to avoid passing important bills
    c. the popularity of alcohol consumption in California
    d. the power of the executive branch to generate important bills in the state legislature.

14. A resolution is
    a. another name for a law passed by the legislature.
    b. a budget bill.
    c. a formal statement of decision or expression of opinion by the legislature.
    d. a bill to amend the state constitution.

15. After its receipt and introduction in both chambers, the annual budget is referred to the
    a. Senate Budget and Fiscal Review Committee and the Assembly Budget Committee.
    b. Senate Ways and Means Committee and the Assembly Standing Committee on Taxation.
    c. Senate and Assembly Judiciary Committees.
    d. Senate Transportation Committee and the Assembly Health and Welfare Committee.

16. The annual budget is submitted to the state legislature by
    a. the governor.
    b. the assembly speaker.
    c. the senate president.
    d. the Assembly Budget Committee.

17. In California, passing a budget requires
   a. a two-thirds majority in both houses of the legislature.
   b. the approval of the state supreme court.
   c. a simple majority in both houses of the legislature.
   d. a majority vote by the public.

18. California legislators have adopted various methods of representation in response to the wide-ranging conditions in California, but the one universal and most basic approach to representation is known as
   a. legislative logrolling.
   b. lawmaking.
   c. casework.
   d. vote gathering.

19. Legislative party caucuses
   a. select the party's candidates for elected office.
   b. were banned as part of the Progressives' antipartisan reforms.
   c. are groups of legislators from the same party who establish group goals, policies, and strategies.
   d. are responsible for distributing the party's campaign funds to viable candidates.

20. Which of the following is NOT regarded as a purely partisan leadership position?
   a. majority floor leader
   b. speaker of the assembly
   c. whip
   d. minority floor leader

mypoliscilab Exercises

Apply what you learned in this chapter on **MyPoliSciLab.**

Read on **mypoliscilab.com**

   eText: Chapter 18

Study and **Review** on **mypoliscilab.com**

   Pre-Test
   Post-Test
   Chapter Exam
   Flashcards

Explore on **mypoliscilab.com**

   Simulation: You Are a State Legislator

The California Executive and Bureaucracy

KEY OBJECTIVES

After completing this chapter, you should be prepared to:

19.1 Identify the powers and duties of the California governor.

19.2 Compare and contrast the unique qualities and qualifications of California governors.

19.3 Outline the structure of the plural executive, and identify the functions of the major offices and agencies that make up this branch of California government.

For college students, the accumulation of final grades often serves a gatekeeping function that determines levels of financial aid, shapes a certain career path, and of course determines whether they will graduate from an institution. And while most of us experience the anxiety of "making the grade" at some point in our lives, most California state government agencies and leaders spend billions of taxpayer dollars without ever being subjected to any type of evaluation. Although the state legislature does attempt to oversee these agencies, it has neither the time nor the expertise to post a legitimate grade. In an attempt to institute among state governments the type of evaluation students regularly receive, the Pew Foundation initiated *The Government Performance Project: Grading the States,* which evaluated and graded all 50 state governments on how well they managed their money, employees, infrastructure, and information.[1] In 2005, the project assigned California state government a "C minus" grade based on the

> **Do Californians want an executive with limited responsibilities or one with the resources to resolve the major issues facing the state?**

poor management of state revenues, low credit ratings, an underfunded state pension system, chaotic state purchasing systems, inadequate financial controls and reporting systems, and insufficient revenue sources.

By 2008, California's grade had improved slightly, moving up to a straight "C." The subsequent *Government Performance Project* report for California contained most of the old complaints and expressed particular concerns about the state government's ongoing budget problems. The slightly higher grade was the result of the success California state government had in saving money after establishing a more efficient purchasing process and addressing infrastructure (roads, building maintenance, and waterways) needs that were made possible with funds generated from the 2006 bond referendum passed by the voters. Had more Californians read and acted on the report findings in 2005 and 2008, maybe the state government could have avoided the current financial troubles and other recurring problems.[2]

Resource Center
• Glossary
• Vocabulary Example
• Connect the Link

■ **Governor:** The supreme executive of a state, vested with the power to ensure that the state's laws are carried out.

EXAMPLE: *A member of the "Big Four" group of railroad barons, Leland Stanford was elected as the eighth governor of California in 1862.*

■ **Line-Item Veto Power:** The power to veto individual items in a larger law.

SIGNIFICANCE: *In 2007, Governor Schwarzenegger used his line-item veto power to cut $703 million from a $145 billion state budget proposal.*

Governor: Supreme Executive Authority

19.1 Identify the powers and duties of the California governor.

(pages 592–593)

Unlike many other states, California vests an enormous amount of power in the office of **governor**■, who, according to the California constitution, is vested with "supreme executive power" to ensure that the laws are faithfully executed. The constitution of California identifies the governor as the sole official representative in communication between the state and federal governments and with other states. Over the years, successive California governors have used this authority to further strengthen this position with formal and informal powers that affect all branches of government.

Legislative, Judicial, and Executive Powers

The California governor has considerable legislative powers. The state legislature receives the governor's spending plan for the state, which it treats as a proposed law. Whatever changes are made after passage can be subjected to the governor's use of **line-item veto power**■, allowing the elimination or reduction of all or part of the state budget. The governor also has the power to call the state legislature into special session for a specific purpose. When called into such an **extraordinary session**■, the state legislature cannot take up any legislative matter other than the task specified by the governor. At the beginning of each year and legislative session, the governor is expected to present the State of the State address, informing the legislature about the condition of the state and recommending a course of legislative action. All laws passed by the legislature are subject to approval or veto by the governor. That veto can only be overridden in the state legislature by a two-thirds vote in both legislative chambers. Informally, the governor can threaten or actually use the initiative process to circumvent the lawmaking function or gain the cooperation of the state legislature.

The power of the California chief executive over the state judiciary begins with the authority to appoint judges and state supreme court justices to fill vacancies before they are confirmed during subsequent elections and to fill newly created judgeships. Governors who serves two terms are likely to appoint a fair number of judges and a few justices to the appellate or supreme court. The outcome of any trial in California, with the exception of impeachments, can be altered through the governor's **clemency powers**■—the right to grant pardons, commutation of sentences, and reprieves. In circumstances pertaining to fugitives from justice under the laws of another state, it is the responsibility of the governor to order extradition. Other law enforcement powers allow the governor to offer rewards for information leading to the arrest and conviction of suspects for certain crimes.

As the chief executive officer of the state government, the governor is directly responsible for a vast state bureaucracy and can appoint thousands of people as department and agency heads. The nucleus or control center of the governor's authority is his or her own office, staffed by a wide range of professionals who either facilitate communications and relations with other parts of government or act as advisers on critical matters and policy. Probably one of the most important members in the Office of the Governor is the chief of staff, who is expected to manage day-to-day operations and serve as the governor's closest adviser. In addition to the governor's immediate staff, there are a number of offices, such as the state Office of Emergency Services, Office of Planning and Research, and Military Department, that carry out specific functions, are usually independent of other parts of the California state government, and report directly to the Office of the Governor.

The governor has direct authority over 11 major departments and agencies overseeing food and agriculture; labor and workforce; business, transportation, and housing; education; environmental protection; health and human services; finance; resources; veterans affairs; state and consumer services; and corrections and rehabilitation. These departments implement the policies of the governor through the statutory mandates of the department or agency, and most have between 4 and 13 subareas that are responsible for one aspect of the overall mission of the department or agency. Each of these 11 departments and agencies is headed by a secretary, and these secretaries collectively form the governor's cabinet.

The governor may also choose to reorganize departments and agencies of the state executive branch with the consent of the state legislature. Although the plural executive offices (described later in this chapter) are chosen by election, the governor can fill unexpired terms of such offices upon confirmation by the legislature. Constitutional provisions designate the governor as commander-in-chief of the California National Guard, with the authority to activate the National Guard during periods of state emergency. In the attempt to exert the authority of the office over the state government, the governor also has the prerogative to issue executive orders.

Party Leader and State Spokesperson

The governor is generally assumed by the public to be leader of his or her political party. Running as a partisan candidate during the gubernatorial election, the governor-elect becomes a highly visible and influential officeholder who is expected to advocate for the interests of the political party that supported

■ **Extraordinary Session:** A special session of the state legislature called by the governor for a specific purpose.

SIGNIFICANCE: *Over the years, the governor of California has called extraordinary sessions to address such issues as redistricting, major budget deficits, education, and most recently, comprehensive health care reform.*

■ **Clemency Powers:** The right to pardon or commute the sentence of convicted persons.

SIGNIFICANCE: *After almost 40 years, no California governor since Ronald Reagan, who granted clemency to a brain-damaged death row inmate, has used clemency powers to stop the carrying out of a death sentence.*

his or her campaign. Yet, there is no formal way the governor can control the party organization, and there are always subtle—or not so subtle—disagreements that occur between fellow party members in the state legislature and party. Having the Office of the Governor and the state legislature controlled by the same party does tend to make it easier to carry out the duties of state government. Difficulties that occur in passing a state budget under divided government, for example, rarely arise when the executive and legislature are of the same party.

Elected as the one statewide official representing the entire state government, the governor retains the ceremonial role as head of state. In this role, the governor performs perfunctory duties that might include ribbon-cutting gatherings or appearing at public celebrations. As the one state government figure that most Californians can identify, the governor assumes the role of spokesperson for the state and can be extremely important in maintaining public confidence. However, if the governor has not had a successful policy agenda and is not well received by the public his or her approval ratings will drop.[3]

STUDENT profile

Amid the many California state government departments and agencies, one exclusively employs hundreds of young Californians to perform nature conservation, fire fighting, and emergency services. That agency is the California Conservation Corps (CCC), which for Benson St. Louis and many other corps members has been the source of occupational training and valuable work experience. Originally from Haiti, Benson found life in Los Angeles difficult. "It was about my second month in California that I noticed it was hard to find a job," he explains. "I didn't have any money for school, but I needed to earn a scholarship. I then found the California Conservation Corps, which had much to offer, including the three E's: Education, Experience, and Expertise."

Created by Governor Jerry Brown in 1976, the CCC was modeled on the federal Civilian Conservation Corps dating back to the New Deal programs of the 1930s. Since its founding, the CCC has employed over 95,000 young male and female corps members between the ages of 18 and 25. The arduous work requirements presented a challenge to Benson. "Before the Corps I would quit on anything I tried to do. In the CCC I have learned to develop proper work habits, a positive attitude, and general safety in the job." The strong work ethic and esprit de corps among members has produced such milestones as 6,402 miles of trails and roughly 3.2 million planted trees. Balancing the needs of the CCC with his career goals, Benson said, "I recently completed my HAZWOPER training [which is an oil spill cleanup course], flood training, and a Career Development Course to help me get a job outside of the CCC." And when Corps members such Benson leave the CCC, opportunities for higher-education scholarships are available.

SOURCE: http://www.ccc.ca.gov/DISTRICT/CAMARILO/camarilo.htm and http://www.ccc/ca.gov/

Governor: Supreme Executive Authority

19.1 Identify the powers and duties of the California governor.

PRACTICE QUIZ: UNDERSTAND AND APPLY

1. According to the California constitution, "supreme executive power" is vested with what official office?
   a. state senator
   b. governor
   c. executive manager
   d. speaker of the assembly

2. A veto can be overridden by which of the following?
   a. both legislative chambers
   b. the state senate
   c. the governor
   d. the state controller

3. The outcome of a trial in California can be altered through the governor's power to
   a. appoint judges.   c. grant clemency.
   b. offer rewards.   d. impeach judges.

ANALYZE

1. What are the powers of the governor as chief executive?

2. What powers does the California governor have that check and balance the other two branches of government?

IDENTIFY THE CONCEPT THAT DOESN'T BELONG

a. Appoint assembly members to committees
b. Use line-item veto power
c. Call state legislature into an extraordinary session
d. Use clemency power
e. Appoint judges

19.1

Resource Center
• Glossary
• Vocabulary Example
• Connect the Link

Becoming Governor

19.2 **Compare and contrast the unique qualities and qualifications of California governors.**
(pages 594–597)

The importance and power of the governor of California attract highly qualified candidates to elections that are usually very competitive. Besides the ability to acquire the enormous resources required of most high-stakes campaigns in California, successful gubernatorial candidates have either a known track record of state governmental service or a charismatic personality that appeals to a broad range of Californians.

Formal and Informal Qualifications

Before running for governor, the candidate must meet basic formal qualifications. All candidates must be U.S. citizens, registered voters 18 years of age or older, and residents of California for at least five years immediately preceding the election. The term of office for the governor of California is four years, beginning on the Monday after January 1st following the election, and a governor is limited to two terms.

The election for governor begins with the primary election in June. In recent years, candidates for office have usually had experience in government, either as mayor of a large city or as attorney general or lieutenant governor. It has been very rare for members of the state legislature to win the nomination. The ability to raise large amounts of campaign contributions has been an even more important factor in the race for governor. Since the election of Ronald Reagan in 1966, television has become the main campaign vehicle for this statewide office, offering candidates statewide access to potential voters, although it is very expensive. During the 1998 Democratic gubernatorial primary, corporate executive Al Checchi and Congresswoman Jane Harman together spent more than $50 million, and Gray Davis added roughly $9 million in campaign spending.[4] Six months into his first term in office, Governor Davis had raised over $6.1 million for his reelection campaign, breaking campaign contribution records until the recall election, after which Governor Schwarzenegger accumulated approximately $26.6 million by the end of his first year in office.[5]

Since the election of Hiram Johnson in 1911, more than twice as many Republicans as Democrats have served as governor. In the past half-century, the general election for governor has been quite competitive, with only two exceptions: the election of Ronald Reagan in 1966, who overwhelmingly beat the incumbent, Pat Brown, and Gray Davis's landslide victory in 1998 over Dan Lungren.

Gubernatorial Style

The past governors of California have come from varied personal backgrounds; in fact, only three of the last nine were natives of the state. Since the governorship of Earl Warren, governors have had law degrees and long careers in government service—with the exceptions of Ronald Reagan and Arnold Schwarzenegger. Historically, California voters have used the office of governor as an engine for change, electing inexperienced governors in the case of Reagan and Schwarzenegger and turning out incumbents such as Brown and Davis when the state faced critical issues that the most visible executive of government appeared incapable of solving. Interestingly, the Democratic majority in the state legislature generally survived these critical times, notwithstanding urban riots, college campus unrest in the 1960s, and the energy crisis in 2001. The last nine governors can actually be sorted into two categories: master stewards of government policy and citizen-politicians.

MASTER STEWARDS OF GOVERNMENT POLICY: Although Earl Warren and Goodwin Knight were the last of the Progressive-Era Republican governors who embraced a spirit of bipartisanship, they were nonetheless experienced politicians who served in various government posts and are remembered more for their policies and politics than as public personalities. Governors George Deukmejian and Pete Wilson also fall into the category of master stewards of government policy. They were hardly charismatic leaders, but with the solid backing of the Republican Party, they faced the governance of California with unflinching resolve. When asked why he ran for the office of governor, Deukmejian is said to have replied, "Attorneys general don't appoint judges; governors do." Governor Pete Wilson will be remembered by some for engaging the state legislature in a budget impasse that forced the state to operate without a budget for 61 days in 1962. Disregarding the potential damage in public opinion and the wrath of unpaid state employees and creditors during his first term, Wilson exhibited a toughness during this episode that contributed to his reputation for firm leadership. These governors also demonstrated moderate tendencies, as exemplified by Deukmejian's ability to compromise with a Democrat-controlled legislature led by a flamboyant assembly speaker, Willie Brown. That Gray Davis was a professional politician may in part explain his downfall—becoming only the second governor in U.S. history to be recalled from office. A consummate policy wonk and political strategist and overshadowed throughout most of his political career by more popular politicians, Davis had the ambition, superior knowledge of California politics, and aptitude for fundraising to overcome his incapacity to generate enthusiasm about his campaigns or actions as governor.[6]

CITIZEN-POLITICIANS Californians have at times heralded true leaders of state government based on force of personality and image rather than on track record or managerial competence. Governor Pat Brown, often described as the "backslapping" governor or "amiable owl," was the last of the pre-television politicians. Without the benefits of sophisticated media technology, Governor Brown was able to emanate statesmanship through a seemingly endless series of public appearances and by carefully cultivating affable relationships with key political figures. Many Californians disagreed with his ideological orientation, but few questioned his honesty or sincerity—and these traits won him many votes. Brown had, for example, opposed capital punishment even though most Californians were in favor of it. Unfortunately, he is less well known for the major policy achievements of his administration, most notably in education and racial equality, than for his loss to a challenger after having served two terms in office.

In 1966, Brown became a victim of his own failure to master an emerging media technology that transformed his gracious, statesman-like demeanor into the image of a "stumblebum."[7] In defeating Brown in 1966, Ronald Reagan's media savvy, perfected after years as a Hollywood actor and pitchman for major corporations, was essential in conveying uncomplicated conservative solutions to complex problems and issues at a time when many mainstream Americans were uncomfortable with the rapid pace of social change. Although most California governors probably harbor hopes of being boosted by state politics to the White House, Reagan is the only one who has reached that goal. Reagan's record as governor is open to debate, and historians and journalists see little of his rhetorical affirmations reflected in effective state policies during his administration. His words, projected astutely via

television to millions of Californians, resonated and reassured, persuading many voters to adopt political and social views on the right of the ideological spectrum.

Jerry Brown served as governor from 1974 until 1982 with the force of personality and a message that built on the reputation and notoriety of his father, former Governor Edmund G. (Pat) Brown. He was assumed to be honest because he had gone to divinity school, and his degrees in Latin and Greek established that he was smart. Governor Brown did not just say he wanted to cut taxes and government waste; he lived it by refusing to reside in the grandiose governor's mansion or use the state-owned limousine, choosing instead to rent a modest apartment in Sacramento and drive a state-issued Plymouth—superficial acts to be sure, but nonetheless actions that provided interesting media material about a governor who could otherwise be nondescript. Jerry Brown will be remembered for his social consciousness as governor, making appointments that reflected the diversity of California and signing the first state farm labor law. As the novelty of his personality waned in his second term, however, and passage of Proposition 13, the property tax–cutting measure, reignited a conservative impulse nurtured under the reign of Ronald Reagan, Brown's vision was often at odds with conventional California politics.

In many ways, Arnold Schwarzenegger was a composite of his various citizen-politician and master stewards of government policy predecessors. He initially embraced the backslapping, amiable approach, particularly with members of the state legislature, and sought staged media attention to the point of eschewing public debates during his 2005 campaign in favor of focused media appearances. Unafraid to capitalize on his action movie stardom or employ offbeat remarks, such as his reference to state legislators as "girlie men," Schwarzenegger has used the spotlight to garner maximum media exposure for his various visions of California government and society. In true master steward fashion, the "Governator," more than any other California governor during the twentieth century, has not been afraid to move from conservative to moderate positions when his popularity has been threatened. In a move that would place political strategy over partisan politics, the Governor chose Susan Kennedy, a highly experienced political insider and openly gay life-long Democrat as his chief of staff. In 2009, Schwarzenegger's tendency to do the unexpected became less effective when state residents failed to see how his vision would alleviate the fiscal crisis gripping the state.

Governor Ronald Reagan greets a large crowd of enthusiastic supporters gathered at Leisure World, a retirement community. —*What are the likely reasons for Governor Reagan's popularity among the residents of this retirement community? What is the political importance of this particular group of potential voters?*

PATHWAYS of action

Racial Profiling and the California Highway Patrol

For regular California motorists as well as visitors driving through the state, one of the more visible signs of state government is the

■ **Racial Profiling:** Characterized as an erroneous assumption that any particular individual of one race or ethnicity is more likely to engage in misconduct than an individual of another race or ethnicity.

SIGNIFICANCE: *California is one of about half of the states across the country that have enacted laws prohibiting racial profiling.*

Governor Arnold Schwarzenegger has made frequent appearances on NBC's *The Tonight Show with Jay Leno.* The most noteworthy occurred when he announced his decision to run as a replacement candidate in the recall election of Governor Gray Davis. After a subsequent appearance during Schwarzenegger's second campaign for governor, his challenger, Phil Angelides, accused the governor and NBC of violating the equal-time provision of the Federal Communications Act. —*Has* The Tonight Show *helped Schwarzenegger's political aspirations enough to merit changing these equal-time regulations to include "talk shows"?*

vigilant presence of the black and white California Highway Patrol (CHP) cruiser. Motorists just about anywhere in California are likely at some point in their travels to at least observe, if not interact with, a CHP officer—what may be a love-hate experience that can range from being assisted with a flat tire or mechanical problems to being ticketed for speeding or hauled off to jail on a DUI charge. As constant as the presence of the CHP may be on the highways of the state, the relationship between CHP officers and motorists continues to evolve in response to the unfolding social and legal dimensions occurring within the state. One of the more contentious issues in recent years surrounding the CHP and most police departments for that matter has been the use of **racial profiling**■.

In 1998, after witnessing CHP officers stop a number of Latino drivers, Curtis Rodriguez, a Latino attorney from San Jose, stopped to take photographs of this incident. Upon driving away, Rodriguez was followed and stopped by CHP officers. After Rodriquez refused consent to a search of his car, one of the officers announced "I am in fear for my life" and proceeded to search the vehicle without finding anything of a illegal nature. Angered by what he felt was racial profiling and an illegal search, Rodriguez became a party to the class-action lawsuit *Curtis V. Rodriguez et al.* v. *California Highway Patrol* filed by the American Civil Liberties Union (ACLU) on behalf of Rodriguez and other Latino and African American motorists who felt that they had been unfairly singled out by the CHP.

According to the ACLU attorneys representing Rodriguez, the lawsuit found that within the Coastal and Central CHP divisions in particular, Latinos were three times more likely than whites to be searched without probable cause by the CHP and that African Americans were about twice as likely. "The lawsuit sought to end law enforcement practices and training, associated with the so-called 'war on drugs' that allowed and even encouraged stereotyping of Latino and African American motorists as potential drug dealers and criminals, and resulted in a disproportionate number of them being subjected to prolonged detentions and intrusive and humiliating searches." To the CHP's credit, the agency agreed to settle the lawsuit in 2003, accepting a wide range of reforms, the most significant being a ban on racial profiling that would lead to **consent searches**■. Consent searches are the simplest and most common type of warrantless searches and are based on the consent by an individual to be searched. The CHP actually became the first law enforcement agency in the United States to adopt a ban on consent searches. The lead attorney for the ACLU in this case, Jon Streeter, praised the CHP Commissioner at the time, Spike Helmick, for recognizing that racial profiling was a problem and making a commitment to finding a solution.

SOURCE: *Rodriguez et al.* v. *California Highway Patrol*, 89 F. Supp. 2d 1131 (N.D. Cal. 2000); "In Landmark Racial Profiling Settlement, California Highway Patrol Agrees to Major Reforms," February 27, 2003, http://www.Aclunc.org/news/press_releases/in_landmark_racial_profiling_settlement,_California

■ **Consent Searches:** An individual may consent to a search of his or her person or premises by law enforcement officers who do not have a warrant.

SIGNIFICANCE: *In California, despite the California Highway Patrol's ban on consent searches, CHP officers are still allowed to search any automobile if they have probable cause that the driver has committed a crime.*

Becoming Governor

19.2   Compare and contrast the unique qualities and qualifications of California governors.

PRACTICE QUIZ: UNDERSTAND AND APPLY

1. It has been very rare for what type of government official to win the nomination for the office of governor?
   a. mayor of a large city
   b. attorney general
   c. lieutenant governor
   d. member of the state legislature

2. Who were the last of the Progressive Era Republican governors?
   a. George Deukmejian and Pete Wilson
   b. Willie Brown and Gray Davis
   c. Earl Warren and Goodwin Knight
   d. Edmund G. "Pat" Brown and Ronald Reagan

3. What official act by Governor Pete Wilson caused damage to his public image?
   a. appearing on a late night television program
   b. having a father that was a former governor
   c. driving a state-issued Plymouth
   d. forcing the state to operate without a budget for 61 days

ANALYZE

1. How did former governor Jerry Brown demonstrate leadership by personal example? What type of gubernatorial style did Governor Brown espouse?

2. Uncharismatic governors have at times remained popular among most state residents by adopting what type of attitudes and actions?

IDENTIFY THE CONCEPT THAT DOESN'T BELONG

a. Interact regularly with members of party caucuses
b. Raise enormous amounts of money
c. Have a track record of government service
d. Project a charismatic personality
e. Meet basic qualifications

Resource Center
• Glossary
• Vocabulary Example
• Connect the Link

■ **Plural Executive:** The group of independently elected officials responsible for carrying out the laws of a state.

SIGNIFICANCE: *The plural nature of the executive branch really refers to elected officials. The governor appoints thousands of high government officials who exert considerable control over the California government bureaucracy.*

The California Plural Executive

19.3 Outline the structure of the plural executive, and identify the functions of the major offices and agencies that make up this branch of California government.

(pages 598–605)

California Lieutenant Governor Abel Maldonado meets with students from the Energy and Utility Career Academy in Bakersfield. *—Which of the duties of the lieutenant governor is Maldonado fulfilling here?*

The **plural executive**■—a collection of elected officers who share power with the governor in managing the state bureaucracy—has experienced some changes over the years, but in the main it is very similar to the structure defined by the first California constitution of 1850. In contrast to the federal government but similar to the executive governments in most states, members of the plural executive are elected at the same time as the governor, serve the same four-year term of office, and are limited to two terms. The design of the plural executive has evolved gradually from the original California constitution, which divided the appointment of major executive positions between the governor and the legislature, to an authentic plural executive, in which major statewide offices are elected directly by voters. Later, the California Progressives further developed constitutional provisions to increase the independence of the plural executive branch and strengthen an elaborate system of separation of powers and checks and balances. Constitutional authority over the plural executive does favor the governor, considering the governor's power to develop and control the budgetary process. Ideally, the structure and democratic orientation of the plural executive encourages leaders of the state bureaucracy to speak openly and honestly about the condition of state government.

Lieutenant Governor

The **lieutenant governor**■ is essentially the understudy for the governor, assuming that office in the event of a vacancy and serving as acting governor should the governor be impeached, absent, or temporarily disabled. In the absence of the lieutenant governor, succession to the office of governor goes to the officers of the state legislature and, in their absence, to officers of the plural executive. The lieutenant governor–elect is often paired with an elected governor from another party. This relationship can cause some consternation for the governor, who must entrust the reins of state government to the lieutenant governor when traveling out of state. Mike Curb, the Republican lieutenant governor during the term of Democratic Governor Jerry Brown, had many opportunities to act as interim governor for Brown, who at the time was campaigning for the Democratic presidential nomination. Taking

advantage of Brown's absence, Curb vetoed legislation that Brown would probably have signed and issued executive orders not at all in keeping with the governor's policies. Although many of Curb's actions as interim governor were contested in court, most were upheld, and this established a precedent for the latitude afforded to lieutenant governors when serving as acting governor.

The California constitution also recognizes the lieutenant governor as the president of the state senate, a position with the sole legislative responsibility of casting a vote in the event of a tie in the senate when all 40 members are voting. Otherwise, the lieutenant governor's legislative responsibilities are generally ceremonial—for example, presiding over the state senate during the State of the State address by the governor. Over the years, the lieutenant governor has been given additional duties related to executive departments and agencies, which include ex officio membership on the Board of Regents of the University of California, chair of the state Commission for Economic Development, member of the State Lands Commission and the California Emergency Council, and trustee of the California State University.

Attorney General

As the top legal officer in the state and head of the California Department of Justice, the **attorney general**■, much like the attorney general for the federal government, has many distinct responsibilities at various levels of government that are sometimes at odds. Most of the time, the attorney general is responsible for the enforcement of California law, but in other circumstances, he or she must represent California govern-

■ **Lieutenant Governor:** The official who serves as acting governor when the governor is unable to carry out his or her duties.

SIGNIFICANCE: *Although clearly seen as a stepping-stone to the office of governor, only nine lieutenant governors out of 38 elected governors have reached that higher office.*

■ **Attorney General:** The state's top legal officer.

EXAMPLE: *Ulysses Sigel Webb served the longest of any California attorney general, elected to nine terms from 1902 to 1939 for a total of 37 years in that office.*

ment officials in legal proceedings. Serving as the legal council to all branches of California government, the attorney general is expected to render legal opinions for executive officers and prepare all titles and summarizations for statewide ballot measures.

As the top law enforcement officer of the state, the attorney general is expected to maintain a central registry of law enforcement records and files, supervise state law enforcement training programs, assist local civil and criminal investigations, and investigate and prosecute major civil and criminal misconduct. The attorney general is directly responsible for supervising all district attorneys and sheriff's departments throughout the state. At the direction of the attorney general, the California Department of Justice may intervene in any county that is not considered to be uniformly and adequately enforcing state laws and regulations. Additionally, county grand juries may be convened by the attorney general to investigate allegations or evidence of wrongdoing in government.

After being elected, most attorneys general will concentrate on one or more major law enforcement areas, either as a result of campaign promises or at the request of the governor. As attorney general of California from 1951 to 1959, Pat Brown was asked by Governor Earl Warren to focus on organized crime, and on his own initiative, he launched a major investigation into accusations of brutality at state mental hospitals.[8] During his tenure as attorney general from 1959-1964, Stanley Mosk, before going on to be the longest-serving associate justice of the California supreme court, created new divisions in the California Department of Justice to prosecute antitrust, consumer fraud, and investment fraud cases.

John van de Kamp, who was elected to the position in 1983, took steps to modernize the Department of Justice's scientific and technological resources, pioneering the use of DNA forensic investigations. Although van de Kamp personally opposed the death penalty, he actively enforced the applications of the California death penalty law and sought to limit appeals by condemned prisoners. Elected to the office on a "tough on crime" position in 1991, Dan Lungren was the force behind the "three strikes and you're out" mandatory 25-years-to-life sentencing law as well as the statute that established a database of convicted child molesters. Capital punishment was restarted under his direction after a 25-year interval.

Jerry Brown assumed the office of the attorney general in 2007. His remarkable political odyssey hit yet another major milestone with his election as governor in 2010. Upon assuming office, he will serve his third non-consecutive term as governor (having previously served between 1959 and 1967 and 1975 and 1983.) As of mid-November 2010, the election results for California attorney general between San Francisco District Attorney, Kamala Harris, and Los Angeles District Attorney, Steve Cooley, was still undecided.

Controller

Acting as the state's chief financial officer, the **controller** is responsible for all financial transactions involving the state government and local jurisdictions. The controller oversees the disbursement of state funds and maintenance of all state financial records, adhering to uniform accounting methods. The signature of the controller is readily apparent on the approximately 112,000 warrants (the state equivalent of checks) that are written daily. At the request of the state legislature, the controller may issue periodic reports regarding the fiscal ramifications of state operations and may also release special reports regarding the management of public revenue. The controller is the chief tax collector, monitoring the correct payment of taxes and authorizing court action for the recovery of delinquent tax debt. Regular financial audits of state and local governments can be ordered by the controller to determine if all public funds are being spent in accordance with California law. The controller is also a member of many different boards and commissions, including the Board of Equalization, Franchise Tax Board, State Lands Commission, and State Board of Control.[9]

The role of the controller has not been without controversy. Some observers have argued that there are simply too many agencies responsible for state revenue and expenditure matters, citing the Board of Equalization, Franchise Tax Board, and Department of Finance as only the most important of the fiscally related agencies, and that the controller's job really should be folded into the purview of the governor. Others defend the controller's independence as a means of safeguarding against potential fiscal impropriety, which they suggest is more likely to occur by an official controlled by the governor.

It is not uncommon for a candidate for controller to lack accounting or fiscal management experience. Rather than seek the office out of a desire to channel this experience, the Office of the Controller often attracts candidates who are merely using the position as a springboard to higher elected political office. A controller motivated by politics and higher office may be prone to inattentiveness and actual incompetence or lack the qualifications necessary for the professional demands of the office. Although Kathleen Connell and Steve Westly did have backgrounds in fiscal management, other former controllers, such as Alan Cranston, who later became a U.S. senator, and Gray Davis, a future governor, lacked significant credentials in this area.

State Treasurer

If the controller is the chief accountant of the state, the **state treasurer**■ is the chief banker or financial consultant. The most basic responsibility of the state treasurer is to account for state bank deposits and supervise the receipt of funds by the state as well as the disbursement of state funds authorized by the

■ **State Treasurer:** The chief banker or financial consultant to California state government, principally responsible for an accounting of state government revenue and the state government disbursements.

EXAMPLE: *Elected in 1914, Friend Richardson became the first and, after serving two terms, last Progressive to hold the office of treasurer.*

■ **Help America Vote Act:** A federal law mandating certain measures to modernize voting procedures.

SIGNIFICANCE: *In 2002, Congress passed the Help America Vote Act, authorizing $3.9 billion to modernize as well as improve the election process nationwide. Despite passage of this law, elections in the United States continue to be administered in a decentralized manner, characterized by 50 separate and different election systems.*

controller. A daily report, known as the *daily clearance,* must be filed with the controller, under the direction of the state treasurer, disclosing the amount of money that was disbursed during the preceding day and the source of these funds. As chair of the Pooled Money Investment Board, the state treasurer is responsible for directing the investment of surplus state funds. Moreover, the state treasurer is charged with selling all state bonds. At the request of either chamber of the state legislature and the governor during specified times in the year, the state treasurer is required to present written reports on the fiscal standing of the state.

MYTH EXPOSED Many Californians believe that the state treasurer is a relatively low position with narrow responsibilities, but the treasurer may in fact be subjected to extensive public media attention and be forced to assume conflicting roles—from bearer of bad news to neutral observer to problem solver. For example, in 2009, in an attempt to be more than just the bearer of bad news or impartial accountant, Treasurer Bill Lockyer received significant media attention for a letter he wrote to U.S. Treasury Secretary Timothy Geithner pleading for the inclusion of states and municipalities in Troubled Asset Relief Program (TARP) fund allocation.

Secretary of State

The main functions of the California **secretary of state** are to administer elections and supervise state records and government documents. Serving as the state's chief elections officer, the secretary of state oversees the voter registration process throughout the state, certifies certain nominations and statewide ballot measures, supervises the publishing and printing of ballot pamphlets, compiles reports of statewide voter turnout and election results, and enforces election laws. In recent years, the secretary of state has become increasingly visible as the job of administering elections has been clouded by the vote-counting controversies that arose in several states during the 2000 and 2004 presidential elections and the introduction of electronic voting machines. This responsibility has also been complicated by a number of new federal laws, especially the **Help America Vote Act**■ which require states to certify new electronic voting equipment, supervise the creation of a statewide fraud-resistant voter registration list, and establish voting procedures and facilities that are accessible to disabled and non–English-speaking voters.

These mandates proved to be especially difficult during the terms of Kevin Shelley (2003) and Bruce McPherson (2005), who had to administer such changes in the electoral process throughout a decentralized election system of 58 California county voter registrar offices that independently handle registrations and election procedures. In 2006, Secretary of State McPherson was unable to meet the June deadline for certification of federally mandated electronic voting machines because

Secretary of State Debra Bowen receives the Profile in Courage Awards for her decisions during the 2008 elections. —*What duty was she carrying out and what made her decision so challenging?*

of technical malfunctions and security flaws.[10] As a member of the plural executive, elected on a partisan ballot, McPherson was faced with potential allegations of partisan manipulation of votes through the certification of faulty voting machines.

The electronic voting machine controversy continued in 2008 with Secretary of State Debra Bowen. After a thorough review of newly acquired electronic voting machines that proved vulnerable to hackers and other security breaches, she decertified more than half of the systems that were scheduled to be used during the 2008 presidential primary. As a result of taking this unpopular but necessary action, Bowen received the Profile in Courage award from the John F. Kennedy Library Foundation, which is bestowed on government officials that make difficult decisions without regard to personal or professional consequences. Since decertification of those electronic voting machines, Bowen has pushed for the addition of a paper record within each electronic voting system, but security as well as budgetary issues continue to limit the use of these systems throughout the state.[11]

As the chief custodian of the state's archives and records, the secretary of state assumes less controversial duties. The

■ **Superintendent of Public Instruction:** The elected official responsible for matters of public education in California.

EXAMPLE: *After decades of neglect, the state legislature finally overhauled the education process in California and created the State Department of Education in 1921 along with the director of education and the superintendent of instruction.*

■ **Proposition 98:** A California law requiring that 40 percent of the state general fund be reserved for education.

SIGNIFICANCE: *Under provisions of Proposition 98, the state legislature can suspend the 40 percent requirement if the proposal passes by a two-thirds vote and is approved by the governor.*

California state archives contain more than 100 million permanent government records, 20,000 maps and architectural drawings, 250,000 photographs, 7,500 video and audio recordings, and hundreds of historical artifacts. The secretary of state is also responsible for countless records of official acts, including laws and resolutions, articles of incorporation, and financial transactions. The passage of the Political Reform Act of 1974 made the Office of the Secretary of State the repository for the various registration forms, financial statements, and expenditure reports filed by candidates, elected officials, campaign organizations, political parties, and lobbyists. The secretary of state is expected to maintain this repository in a fair and open manner that will bring greater transparency to the financing of campaigns. As custodian of the Great Seal of California, the secretary of state is also accountable for how and where that seal is affixed.[12]

The resignation of Secretary of State Kevin Shelley in 2005 reveals how the once modest and largely supraclerical Office of the Secretary of State has emerged as a position that can generate significant political influence as well as unwanted public scrutiny and partisan temptations. Shelley's problems apparently began with a report in the *San Francisco Chronicle* that found he had received what appeared to be illegal contributions toward his election campaign.[13] The story eventually led to audits by the controller's office and a grand jury investigation. The investigations resulted in the charge that as secretary of state, Shelley had diverted $1.5 million in federal Help America Vote Act grants to hire Democratic Party workers. Further questions surfaced regarding whether other funds were illegally channeled to political supporters of the secretary of state. Before long, the media had also revealed that staff members in Shelley's office had filed charges of verbal abuse and sexual harassment. The combination of unlawful and embarrassing charges drove Shelley to resign. Ultimately, the Shelley affair demonstrates how overtly partisan acts and bad choices can cause members of the plural executive to stray from constitutional or statutory guidelines and lead to their downfall and disgrace.

Superintendent of Public Instruction

Possessing limited formal political power, the **superintendent of public instruction**■ is generally forced to compete with the policymaking authority of the California Board of Education, budget control of the state legislature, self-governing school districts, and executive authority of the governor. Designated as a nonpartisan office, the influence of the superintendent of public instruction is mainly derived from being the sole publicly elected person responsible for matters of statewide public education. This sense of public accountability gives this office a commanding voice on educational matters and the development of education policy. As secretary and executive

officer of the 11-member Board of Education, the superintendent of public instruction can influence the policies of the board, but it is the Board of Education as a whole that establishes education policy. Exercising the policy decisions of the board as executive officer makes the superintendent of public instruction directly responsible for monitoring public school attendance, distributing funds to school districts, overseeing state educational curricula, and managing federal educational programs.

Although nonpartisan for electoral purposes, the superintendent of public instruction can nonetheless become very political. Three-term Superintendent Bill Honig was forced to resign his office in 1992 after being convicted of conflict-of-interest charges. Honig had been a very vocal advocate of education in California and used his office to force various educational reforms that often drew mixed reactions from government leaders, the education community, and the public. Honig was a major force behind the passage of **Proposition 98**■, which required 40 percent of the state general fund be reserved for education. The measure was an attempt to restore educational funding lost to Proposition 13, but it severely limited the fiscal discretion of the legislature and the governor. The charges against Honig and his subsequent conviction stemmed from an investigation that found the Department of Education, under Honig's direction, had made payments to his wife's education-related firm.[14] At about the same time, the Republican-dominated state Board of Education, mostly appointed by Republican Governor Pete Wilson, launched a legal battle to strip Honig and any subsequent superintendent of public instruction of power over statewide education policy. A California appellate court ruling confirmed the transfer of the superintendent's policymaking power to the Board of Education and local school districts. The Democratic-controlled state legislature introduced legislation that attempted to restore the power of the superintendent, but the bill was subsequently vetoed by Governor Wilson.[15]

State Insurance Commissioner

Established in 1959, the State Insurance Department was headed by a gubernatorial appointee until 1988, when California voters approved **Proposition 103**■, an insurance initiative sponsored by California consumer groups that enhanced the consumer-friendly aspects of insurance industry regulations and created the elected position of **state insurance commissioner**■. Funded by a portion of insurance fees, the state Insurance Department, under the direction of the nonpartisan state insurance commissioner, monitors the financial condition of insurance companies operating in California, licenses companies and insurance professionals, approves workers' compensation insurance rates, publishes annual financial statements of insurance companies in California, and provides

■ **Proposition 103:** A California law imposing the regulation of insurance rates and creating the elected position of state insurance commissioner.

SIGNIFICANCE: *Proposition 103 requires that insurers use motor vehicle records to determine car insurance premiums rather than a driver's ZIP code or address.*

information about insurance rates. Although designated as nonpartisan members of the California plural executive, recent state insurance commissioners have aligned themselves with either the insurance industry or consumer groups. The dilemma for any insurance commissioner has been whether to support policies that result in fair and beneficial insurance services for consumers or to promote a healthy business environment for insurance companies that employ thousands of workers and sustain related industries. Elected as the first nonpartisan state insurance commissioner in 1990, John Garamendi is credited with bringing a pro-consumer perspective to the state Insurance Department, which before Proposition 103 had developed a pro–insurance industry reputation. Although consumers did experience some insurance premium rebates, many of the insurance reforms mandated by Proposition 103 were tied up in court, and insurance consumers lost their chief advocate when Garamendi left office to run for governor in 1994.

In the second election for insurance commissioner, rather than selecting a pro-consumer Democrat similar to John Garamendi, California voters chose Chuck Quackenbush, a Republican closely aligned with the insurance industry. His 1994 successful campaign was largely funded by contributors from this industry who spent over $2.4 million. Two years into his first term, Quackenbush was criticized by the state's auditor general for failing to respond aggressively to complaints about the insurance industry in California.[16] Nevertheless, Quackenbush was elected in 1998 to a second term. Not long thereafter, the insurance commissioner was the target of investigations that alleged he had concluded a settlement highly favorable to insurance companies that deceived victims of the Northridge earthquake. The investigation by the state attorney general's office revealed that Quackenbush had agreed not to fine the companies or to finalize a report on Northridge earthquake claims-handling violations.[17] In return for looking the other way, the investigation charged, insurance companies were convinced to contribute over $4 million to nonprofit foundations Quackenbush had created. As the investigation widened, exposing how the foundations had spent $3 million on political advertising featuring Quackenbush, the commissioner felt obliged to resign.[18]

Workers' compensation benefits emerged as a major issue during the early 2000s, illustrating the tenuous role that government must adopt in resolving conflicts that often arise in the business community over practices that benefit one industry to the disadvantage of another. By 2003, California businesses were paying the highest rates in the nation to cover employees with workers' compensation insurance provided by private insurance companies as required by California law and insurance industry regulations. Threatening to relocate to other states to avoid these high rates, many

California Insurance Commissioner Steve Poizner announces an auto insurance rate cut that will save Californians $34 million. —*What interests do insurance commissioners have to balance when acting on behalf of the people of California?*

companies charged that California's workers' compensation law created an unfavorable business environment in the state. The private insurance companies that provided such coverage contended that they were forced to charge high rates because of the coverage required by insurance regulations. In 2004, pledging to fix the workers' compensation system, Governor Schwarzenegger got the state legislature to enact a law that lowered workers' compensation insurance rates by 37.8 percent for California businesses through limits on coverage for hospital costs, outpatient surgery, and permanent disability claims.[19] Elected in 2006, Republican Steve Poizner was considered by many to be a bit more even-handed than Chuck Quackenbush. Although Poizner has received high marks for pursuing fraud, some consumer advocates have accused him of promoting the deregulation of the insurance industry, which these advocates say will allow insurers to raise insurance premiums.

The travails of the Department of Insurance and the state insurance commissioner over the years demonstrate the difficulty that all plural executive officers face in enforcing California regulations and laws while considering the divergent interests of California residents. Even with certain safeguards, such as the nonpartisan designation of the insurance commissioner, inequities and official abuse persist.

Board of Equalization

The **Board of Equalization**■, created by constitutional amendment in 1879, consists of the state controller, who serves as an ex officio member, and four voting members, who

■ **State Insurance Commissioner:** The official responsible for oversight of the insurance industry and enforcement of insurance regulations in California.

SIGNIFICANCE: *According to various studies of post–Proposition 103 California insurance regulations, state insurance commissioners have administered the most pro-consumer auto insurance regulation in the nation.*

Board of Equalization: A California body that makes rules, based on state laws, governing the collection and payment of certain taxes.

SIGNIFICANCE: *The constitutional revision of 1879 included an elected Board of Equalization to prevent railroad companies from influencing local tax assessments.*

represent Board of Equalization districts. Each board member must reside in his or her respective district for one year preceding election to this partisan office. Although the Board of Equalization has a variety of duties and responsibilities, its most basic task is to adopt guidelines, based on state laws, governing the collection and payment of property, sales, excise, and special taxes. Its property tax responsibilities are focused on setting and evaluating guidelines for the assessment policies of the 58 county tax assessors. These tax assessors subsequently establish property values and corresponding tax liabilities in their respective counties. The Board of Equalization has the authority to directly assess taxes on utilities, insurance companies, items for sale, and the use of certain goods. In addition, the board also acts as a quasi-judicial body, hearing and adjudicating appeals on the decisions of the Franchise Tax Board, which administers the state income tax, bank and corporate taxes, and a variety of other taxes and fees.[20]

Like most segments of the plural executive, the Board of Equalization walks a tightrope of governance, balancing what is necessary for the health of the state against what is fair for residents of the state. During the 1970s, the state government had accumulated a tax surplus as public dissatisfaction over rising property tax bills grew. Some in government at the time assert that had the Board of Equalization foreseen the perceived inequity and sounded the alarm, the resulting backlash of Proposition 13, which brought dramatic property tax reductions and the loss of a large portion of government revenue, might have been avoided. Since the advent of Proposition 13, the "tax burden" has been a major public policy issue, generating a plethora of special-interest and advocacy groups that regularly petition, criticize, and even sue the Board of Equalization. When the board, for example, began considering a new proposal to tax certain prescription drugs, including cosmetic Botox, the Citizens Against Unfair Health Care Taxes was formed, and a campaign was launched branding the proposed tax a "dangerous precedent" and calling on residents of California to write or call their local Board of Equalization members.[21]

On another occasion, the decision by the board to allow a tax credit or refund to companies that manufacture equipment generated public outcry and was severely criticized by California tax advocacy and reform groups—and even one former Board of Equalization member. The criticism focused on the 18 companies that received the tax credit, most of which were technology firms that had not paid any corporate taxes in recent years because of the accumulation of other tax credits. As Senate Appropriations Committee Chair Carole Migden (D–San Francisco), a former chair of the Board of Equalization, pointed out, "These are refunds for taxes not even paid. It is scandalous."[22] In letters to the board, members of the California Tax Reform Association and the Foundation for Taxpayer and Consumer Rights accused the board of "coddling California corporate welfare queens."[23]

California Boards and Commissions

According to the California Performance Review project initiated by Governor Schwarzenegger, an estimated 339 boards and commissions are scattered across the executive branch of California government.[24] Historically, these boards and commissions originated during the late nineteenth century, when the Progressives sought to circumvent the partisan influence of corrupt political "bosses" and "machines" that loaded government departments and agencies with their cronies. The Progressive idea called for the governor, sometimes with the consent of the state legislature, to appoint presumably nonpartisan professionals to boards and commissions who would bring expert knowledge and experience to the management of state government affairs.

Today, the vast majority of these boards and commissions function as appendages of the major departments and agencies, focusing on the narrow features of the overall bureaucratic mission. In most instances, the members of boards and commissions are appointed to fixed terms by the governor and the state legislature and cannot be removed. The Board of Parole Hearing is a subsection of the Department of Corrections and Rehabilitation and is one example of a board with an important mandate under the authority of the governor through the department secretary. The duties and tasks of the state boards and commissions vary considerably, from simply offering guidance on a subject to acting in a quasi-judicial capacity or establishing policy and standards. Many departments and agencies have the authority to create boards and commissions independent of the governor and the state legislature. A number of boards and commissions derive their authority from government statutes and, although their members are appointed by the governor and the state legislature, are designed to be independent of all branches of government. Examples of these include the Fair Political Practices Commission, charged with regulating campaign contributions and spending; the Little Hoover Commission, a state oversight agency that promotes efficient government; and the Public Utilities Commission, responsible for ensuring reasonable and safe utility and transportation services.

In recent years, various advocacy groups and political leaders have complained about what they feel is an excessive number of boards and commissions that very often duplicate efforts, unnecessarily complicate and decentralize decision making, and waste valuable resources and funds. Responding to this criticism in his annual address to the state legislature in 2005, Governor Schwarzenegger portrayed the boards and commissions as expensive, "unnecessary," and filled with unproductive partisan appointees. The governor planned to abolish as many as 88 of them by folding their tasks into other existing departments. A month later, however, Governor Schwarzenegger was forced to drop the proposal after encountering opposition from a wide variety of special-interest groups as well as from Democratic and

Governor Schwarzenegger appoints friends and former colleagues, including Danny DeVito and Clint Eastwood, to the California Film Commission. —*Should this commission have been placed on the cutting block?*

Republican members of the state legislature. One of the most common criticisms of the plan was the secrecy that would envelop the decisions and actions shifted to the state bureaucratic organization under the governor's plan. Boards and commissions, the critics charged, had much more stringent public disclosure policies and avenues for public participation than state agencies had. Without the public meetings and hearings and the representatives from both the private and public sectors normally required of most of boards and commissions, knowledge of state agency action on a given policy would be hidden from public view.

Probably the most damning criticism was the charge that much of the governor's proposal was motivated by politics and did not include those groups with special ties to the governor. Critics cited the governor's decision to keep the New Motor Vehicle Board, a favorite of the California car dealers who have been big Schwarzenegger supporters, and the California Film Commission, composed in part of fellow actor friends of the governor.

Any attempt to streamline state government will inevitably make some influential people or groups unhappy. In response to negative media attention focused on the cost and minimal usefulness of many boards and commissions, the state legislature has during the 2009–2010 session placed the review of these government entities on the legislative agenda. Rather than target the close to 100 boards and commissions that Governor Schwarzenegger slated for elimination, legislative leaders suggest the possible elimination of about a dozen.

The Plural Executive and the Third House

If Californians look closely at the campaign contributions to plural executive officers, they will see the increasing influence of the "third house," the army of lobbyists who represent special-interest groups that seek to shape the decisions of government officials. Like members of the state legislature, the officers of the plural executive must face the question of whether the campaign contributions they accept from special-interest groups and business representatives have any significant influence on their decisions and actions. From a broad, legal point of view, as long as executive officers do not engage in cash-for-deal transactions and comply with the individual donor limits, they are generally free to accept as many contributions as they wish. The reality of accepting this money, however, raises questions regarding the donors' true interests and whether tacit cash-for-deal arrangements have been made.

The campaign experience of Governor Gray Davis during the Democratic gubernatorial primary, in which he faced Al Checchi and Jane Harman, two independently wealthy opponents, reflects why many candidates are preoccupied with raising campaign funds. Had he not taken an aggressive but successful personal fundraising approach or lacked contacts that would net him large contributions in his campaigns for executive office, Davis would not have been able to compete against the personal fortunes of his opponents. (Checchi's spending earned him the nickname "checkbook Checchi" during the primary campaign.) In an examination of Governor Davis's fundraising prowess, Cynthia H. Craft, writer and editor for the formerly published *California Journal*, wrote:

> The spadework is perhaps made all the easier by the power and prestige of the office Davis now holds. But show up he must. "Successful fund-raising is not something you can do without the active involvement of the candidate. People expect…to see the candidate," South testified in trial. "They expect to have some access to the candidate and the process."[25]

This access was implied during the attempt to pass SB 773 in the state legislature, a 2001 consumer privacy bill that would strengthen a 1999 federal law safeguarding financial information that consumers list on loan and credit applications. The bill was set for passage after making its way through the various legislative committees and watered down a bit by way of the amendment process, but it evidently fell into limbo awaiting Governor Davis's decision to either sign or veto the bill. That decision must have been especially difficult for the governor, who during the six-month period leading up to the completion of legislative work on the bill had received at least $500,000 from banking and insurance companies.[26] In the end, Davis did sign the bill, but only after aides from the governor's office and banking and insurance company lobbyists worked together to rewrite it. Another bill in 2000, AB 1963, which would have strengthened credit card company disclosure requirements on billing statements, was not as fortunate. Shelley Curran, a policy analyst with the West Coast Regional Office of the Consumers Union, commented, "It is particularly frustrating that the governor vetoed this measure since it enjoys strong popular support and passed by such a wide margin when it was considered by lawmakers in Sacramento."[27]

The relationship between campaign contributions from lobbyists and the officers of the plural executive is often unclear. How should Californians perceive their attorney general's invitational golf tournament sponsored by the owners of a San Diego County casino? Should Californians believe that the $25,000 paid to the "celebrity sponsor" to attend the tournament had no bearing on former Attorney General Bill Lockyer's constitutional

and statutory responsibility to regulate California's thriving Indian gambling industry?[28] And so, unless campaign finance laws are radically changed, the actual purpose of campaign contributions will continue to be blurred by the two equally justifiable perceptions of these contributions. The one available remedy for the monetary influence of the "third house" is the reduce the need for such contributions. An informed, civically engaged California electorate—immune to the misrepresentation of the facts and the well-financed media blitz—just might be the answer to campaign contributions of questionable purposes.

The California Plural Executive

19.3 Outline the structure of the plural executive, and identify the functions of the major offices and agencies that make up this branch of California government.

PRACTICE QUIZ: UNDERSTAND AND APPLY

1. The attorney general is
   a. elected by the voters
   b. appointed by the governor.
   c. chosen by the state legislature.
   d. appointed by the state supreme court.

2. Acting as the state's chief financial officer, the controller is responsible for
   a. state bank deposits and supervising the receipt of funds.
   b. controlling the borders of the state.
   c. all financial transactions involving the state government and local jurisdictions.
   d. establishing the tax rates for all residents and businesses in the state.

3. As the state's chief banker or financial consultant, the state treasurer is most likely to
   a. account for and supervise state bank deposits and receipt of funds.
   b. audit the boards and commissions that make up the executive branch.
   c. supervise all financial transactions involving the state government and local jurisdictions.
   d. establish the tax rates for all residents and businesses in the state.

4. The influence of the superintendent of public instruction is limited by the existence of what government agency?
   a. Any board or commission that involves education
   b. The state board of education
   c. The board of equalization
   d. The state insurance department

ANALYZE

1. What are the most powerful offices or agencies within the plural executive?

2. What are examples of the partisan nature or qualities of the California plural executive?

IDENTIFY THE CONCEPT THAT DOESN'T BELONG

a. State Insurance Commission
b. Proposition 103
c. Help America Vote Act
d. Workers' compensation benefits
e. Insurance industry regulations

Conclusion

California state government faces a variety of challenges today, many of them illustrated by the poor performance rating the state was given in the "Grading the States" report discussed at the start of this chapter. There are a variety of reasons for the problems cited in this report, many of which are beyond the control of most Californians. But many of these difficulties have been perpetuated by the often unethical manner in which many state residents utilize government services and the way that government leaders and workers provide these services. Although the assumption is that the highest officers of state government should exemplify the highest standards in ethical behavior, this chapter has presented a variety of examples where such standards were not maintained. Clearly, Governor Schwarzenegger's proposal to eliminate 88 boards and commissions while retaining those that included friends and associates lacked a sense of fairness and ultimately hurt his original objective. Too often greed and monetary considerations take precedence over the responsibilities these leaders have to state residents. Such considerations were undoubtedly demonstrated in former Secretary of State Kevin Shelley's diversion of $1.5 million in federal funds, former State Insurance Commissioner Charles "Chuck" Quackenbush's million dollar digressions that led to his resignation, and former Attorney General Bill Lockyer's Invitational golf tournament sponsored by California Indian casino owners. Portrayed both within the state and nationally as a "failed state," at least part of this characterization of California state government is due to the performance of the executive branch. The "C minus" grade that the California state government received from *The Government Performance Project: Grading the States,* referred to at the beginning of this chapter, largely confirms common negative perceptions regarding the conduct of state government affairs. In addition to outlining how California state government operates, focusing on the duties and functions of executive officers, there is of course the hope that this chapter will encourage more Californians to consider alternatives to the current model of state government that could produce improved performance. Such reconsiderations should begin with the various assumptions most Californians hold about the powers and duties of state government officials and institutions. These assumptions, given the current performance of California state government, may not be entirely accurate or always promote the notion of good government. In describing the office of the governor, for example, this chapter outlined an extensive array of powers—from the line-item veto, to clemency, to the control of eleven major departments. Yet, are Californians well-served by the belief that the state should have such a powerful chief executive? There are clearly other state governments that function with weaker governors. On the other hand, maybe this assumption does not go far enough and the governor of California really should be granted more authority over specific aspects of government, such as the state budget.

The California constitution stipulates that most members the plural executive have partisan designations and are elected, but whether these requirements are conductive to a well-functioning executive branch is clearly not a certainty. These requirements have afforded most members of the plural executive a measure of independence at the cost, however, of a highly partisan and divided state government.

California really does have two executive governments; one long list of department heads and other bureaucratic officials appointed by the governor, and another plural executive branch elected by the voters. This dilemma is very apparent with the lieutenant governor who, as an elected member of the plural executive, is largely independent of the governor. The lieutenant governor, is not necessarily predisposed to assist the governor in executive functions, unlike the relationship between the president and vice-president of the United States and the role of the lieutenant governor in other state governments. Questioning the role of the state's fiscal managers could lead some Californians to ask if the state government really does need both a controller and state treasurer in addition to the governor's director of finance among many other financial experts. It is obviously advantageous to have numerous independent officials overseeing an issue as important as the state budget, but the cost of maintaining these separate entities and the inevitable political biases and squabbling between these officials and offices may outweigh the benefits. The questioning of similar assumptions can be subscribed to other members of the plural executive, notwithstanding the non-partisan office of superintendent of public instruction, which has a long history of competing with the governor's vision of public education.

For some time, there has been an on-going concern about the number of California state government commissions and boards, culminating with Governor Schwarzenegger's aborted attempt at reducing these units. Although this chapter outlined the inequity of the governor's plan to abolish as many as 88 of these commissions and boards, the need to reduce the waste and redundancy associated with so many of these organizations remains. Consequently, considering the governor's failed attempt, do most Californians now assume that reducing these commissions and boards in a fair manner is simply not possible, or do most Californians continue to cling to the belief that some equitable method of reduction remains a possibility?

However misguided or wrong some assumptions about California's executive government might be, altering or restructuring this branch would require a near Herculean effort. Attitudes and positions of power are simply too well entrenched. Yet, the notion of the "failed state" and performance reviews conducted by groups such as *The Government Performance Project* presents the impetus for serious consideration of current assumptions about the state government and the start of major reform.

KEY CONCEPT MAP **How do the powers of the governor of California compare with those of the president of the United States?**

Chief Executive Officer

Governor: As the chief executive officer of the state government, has direct authority over 11 major departments and agencies and can appoint the heads of departments and agencies and other influential government posts. Most appointments must be confirmed by the state senate.

President: As the chief executive officer of the U.S. government, has direct authority over the Executive Office of the President and 15 major cabinet departments. Appoints the heads of the cabinet departments; all appointments must be confirmed by the U.S. Senate.

Critical Thinking Questions

What if chief executives abuse their authority? What is the most effective protection or check on their power? Is there a difference in how this protection or check is applied at the state and federal levels?

Legislative Address

Governor: At the beginning of each year and legislative session, presents the State of the State address to inform the legislature about the condition of the state and recommend a course of legislative action.

President: Article II, section 3, of the U.S. Constitution specifies that the president shall "from time to time give to Congress Information of the State of the Union. . . ." The notion of "from time to time" has become an annual duty of the president.

Critical Thinking Questions

Why do both the California state and U.S. constitutions require a report by the chief executive to the legislative body? Is it possible for a poorly presented or substandard speech to affect the governor's or president's ability to govern?

Line-Item Veto

Governor: May reduce or eliminate all or part of the state budget or appropriations. Governor Arnold Schwarzenegger used the line-item veto to eliminate over $500 million from the state budget in 2009.

President: Can only reject (or sign into law) the total budget of the U.S. government. During the Clinton presidency, the Republican-controlled Congress attempted to grant the president line-item veto power; in 1998, the U.S. Supreme Court deemed it unconstitutional because the Constitution gives Congress the power to raise revenue, and the line-item veto would shift that responsibility to the president.

Critical Thinking Questions

What if presidents were allowed to use the line-item veto on appropriations bills? Is there any danger that the legislature's intent could be thwarted? Why do you think California governors have been granted this power but not presidents?

Extraordinary Legislative Sessions

Governor: The governor has the power to call the state legislature into special session for a specific purpose; the state legislature cannot take up any legislative matter other than the task specified by the governor.

President: Article II, section 3, of the U.S. Constitution grants the president authority to call a special session of Congress "on extraordinary Occasions" after it has already adjourned. The president can force Congress to meet but cannot force Congress to act.

Critical Thinking Questions

Why would a president or governor call an extraordinary legislative session? What sorts of issues are so important that they cannot wait for resumption of the normal session? What are the benefits and risks to the president or governor in calling such a session?

Judicial Appointments

Governor: The governor has the power to fill superior court vacancies through appointment; otherwise, these judges are elected to six-year terms by voters on a nonpartisan ballot. Appellate or state supreme court justices are appointed by the governor but must be confirmed by the Commission on Judicial Appointments.

President: Article II, section 2, authorizes the president to appoint "judges of the Supreme Court" for life and the judgeships established later by the Judiciary Act of 1789 and other acts of Congress. The U.S. Senate must confirm these appointments.

Critical Thinking Questions

Why do you think the governor may only make judicial appointments to fill new positions or vacancies? What if federal judges and U.S. Supreme Court Justices had to run for office instead of being appointed by the president? How would this impact their decisions on the bench?

California is typically likened to a nation-state, particularly in the size of its economy and international appeal. In the decades following World War II, California governors led a state known for generous spending on major public projects and services. In recent years, many Californians hold the view that the size, budget, and responsibilities of state government should be reduced regardless of the consequences. This view mirrors the perceptions that many Americans hold about the national government. —*What factors either support or negate the notion that there are an array of issues and problems resulting from California's enormous size and complexity that are simply beyond the powers and authority of the governor and plural executive? Do these same factors apply to the president's powers and authority over the United States? Why or why not?*

Review of Key Objectives

Governor: Supreme Executive Authority

19.1 Identify the powers and duties of the California governor.

(pages 592–593)

In California, the position of governor is a powerful one encompassing legislative, judicial, and executive responsibilities. Unlike many other states, California vests an enormous amount of power in the office of governor, which has the authority to affect the operations of the state government. The constitution of California identifies the governor as the sole official representative in communication between the state and federal governments and with other states. Over the years, successive California governors have used this authority to further strengthen this position with formal and informal powers that affect all branches of government.

KEY TERMS

Governor 592
Line-Item Veto Power 592
Extraordinary Session 592
Clemency Powers 592

CRITICAL THINKING QUESTIONS

1. What official powers does the governor have to direct legislation? What unofficial powers can the governor use to direct the legislature to carry out his or her agenda?
2. What is the nature of the relationship between the governor and the judicial branch of government in California? What short-term and long-term effects can a governor have on the judiciary?

INTERNET RESOURCES

The official Web site of the governor of California can be found at http://gov.ca.gov. It features news reports and events central to the governor's office. Some sections of this site are also available in Spanish.

The California Institute (http://www.calinst.org/) is a charitable 501(c)(3) nonprofit corporation, conceived by the state's bipartisan elected leaders but sustained with the advice and support of the business, labor, and academic communities.

ADDITIONAL READING

Burns, John F., and Richard J. Orsi (eds.). *Taming the Elephant: Politics, Government, and Law in Pioneer California.* Berkeley: University of California Press, 2003.

Cannon, Lou. *Ronnie and Jesse: A Political Odyssey.* New York: Simon and Schuster, 1969.

Sinclair, Upton. *Candidate for Governor: And How I Got Licked.* Berkeley: University of California Press, 1994.

Becoming Governor

19.2 Compare and contrast the unique qualities and qualifications of California governors.

(pages 594–597)

Successful gubernatorial candidates have either a known track record of state governmental service or a charismatic personality that appeals to a broad range of voters. Candidates running for governor must first meet the basic qualifications. They must be U.S. citizens, registered voters 18 years of age or older, and California residents for at least five years immediately preceding the election. The term of office for the governor of California is four years, beginning on the Monday after January 1st following the election, and the governor is limited to two terms. California governors tend to adopt one of two leadership styles: either as experienced politicians who firmly stick to their political strategy and policies or as charismatic citizen-politicians who are more responsive to public opinion.

KEY TERMS

Racial Profiling 596
Consent Search 596

CRITICAL THINKING QUESTIONS

1. What are the personal or leadership qualities shared by California governors since Ronald Reagan? Are these the qualities that Californians expect in future governors?
2. Have the governors of California been representative of California society, or have they been unique in relation to the rest of the population? Have Californians been well served by either quality?

INTERNET RESOURCES

Rough & Tumble: A Daily Snapshot of California Public Policy and Politics (http://www.rtumble.com/) offers an impartial daily roundup of news and commentary on California politics.

KQED, serving Northern California, and KCET, serving Southern California, are PBS stations that deliver multimedia content about California political issues at http://www.kqed.org/ and http://www.kcet.org/

ADDITIONAL READING

Cannon, Lou. *Ronnie to Jesse: A Political Odyssey of Two Political Champions.* Garden City, NY: Doubleday, 1969.

Rapoport, Roger. *California: The Political Odyssey of Pat and Jerry Brown.* Berkeley: Nolo Press, 1982.

Rarick, Ethan. *California Rising: The Life and Times of Pat Brown.* Berkeley: University of California Press, 2004.

The California Plural Executive

19.3 Outline the structure of the plural executive, and identify the functions of the major offices and agencies that make up this branch of California government.

(pages 598–605)

In contrast to the federal government, but not unlike the executive governments in most states, the plural executive in California is a group of elected officers—ranging from the lieutenant governor, attorney general, and controller to various boards and commissions—who share power with the governor in managing the state bureaucracy. Members of the plural executive are elected at the same time as the governor, serve the same four-year term of office, and are limited to two terms. In most instances, the members of boards and commissions are appointed to fixed terms by the governor and the state legislature and cannot be removed.

KEY TERMS

Plural Executive 598
Lieutenant Governor 598
Attorney General 598
Controller 599
State Treasurer 599
Secretary of State 600
Help America Vote Act 600
Superintendent of Public Instruction 601
Proposition 98 601
Proposition 103 601
State Insurance Commissioner 601
Board of Equalization 602

CRITICAL THINKING QUESTIONS

1. Does the plural executive weaken or strengthen the powers of the governor? In what ways can the plural executive facilitate or undermine the governor's agenda?
2. If one plural executive position had to be eliminated, which office should be chosen? Why?

INTERNET RESOURCES

The California Department of Justice (http://ag.ca.gov/ag/) carries out the responsibilities of the attorney general through 10 main divisions.

The California Research Bureau (http://www.library.ca.gov/crb/CRBSearch.aspx) provides nonpartisan research services to the governor and his staff, to both houses of the legislature, and to other state elected officials.

ADDITIONAL READING

Bagley, William T. *California's Golden Years: When Government Worked and Why.* Berkeley: Institute of Government Studies Press, 2009.

Walters, Dan. *The New California: Facing the 21st Century.* Sacramento: California Journal Press, 1992.

Chapter Review   Test Your Knowledge

1. California received what grade in 2005 from *The Government Performance Project: Grading the States?*
   a. B+
   b. A–
   c. C–
   d. F

2. The authority of the governor to appoint and state supreme court justices occurs
   a. before they are confirmed during subsequent elections.
   b. after they are confirmed during subsequent elections.
   c. when the FBI has completed the background examination.
   d. after both chambers of the state legislature have approved the appointment.

3. Line-item veto powers allow the
   a. elimination or reduction of either all or part of the state budget.
   b. elimination or reduction of all of the state budget.
   c. addition of special budget items.
   d. elimination or reduction of special budget items.

4. The lieutenant governor's duties as president of the state senate include
   a. appointing the members of the rules committee.
   b. acting as the senate's speaker and presiding over floor debates.
   c. signing legislation before it is sent to the governor's office.
   d. casting a vote in the event of a tie in the state senate.

5. Because of varied duties, which of the following officials is often seen as second only to the governor in sheer authority and statewide influence?
   a. lieutenant governor
   b. controller
   c. attorney general
   d. insurance commissioner

6. Who is responsible for all financial transactions involving the state government and local jurisdictions?
   a. the controller
   b. the governor
   c. the secretary of state
   d. the attorney general

7. One major drawback of the office of controller is that
   a. it wields too much power over the state budget for an office held by a single individual.
   b. it is a political dead end and therefore attracts few worthy candidates.
   c. it often attracts candidates who do not have an accounting background and are using it as a springboard to higher political office.
   d. it tends to get blamed for the state's financial difficulties.

8. The state's chief banker is the
   a. state treasurer.
   b. controller.
   c. secretary of state.
   d. chair of the Board of Equalization.

9. The superintendent of public instruction is
   a. an appointed position.
   b. a nonpartisan office.
   c. a partisan office.
   d. a civil service position.

10. The passage of Proposition 103 designated which of the following offices?
    a. controller
    b. state treasurer
    c. insurance commissioner
    d. governor

11. California's secretary of state is responsible for
    a. auditing the state's finances.
    b. supervising the sale of state bonds.
    c. administering elections.
    d. supervising public education.

12. The Board of Equalization was created by
    a. constitutional amendment in 1879.
    b. the state legislature in 1945.
    c. executive order in 2005.
    d. voter-approved initiative in 1990.

13. Which political group or party was most responsible for the original creation of California's many boards and commissions?
    a. the Republican Party
    b. the Democratic Party
    c. the Progressives
    d. the Workingmen's Party

14. Which elected official is charged with selling all state bonds?
    a. controller
    b. state treasurer
    c. insurance commissioner
    d. governor

15. The secretary of state has in recent years taken on increasing importance because
    a. the job of administering elections has become clouded by vote counting controversies.
    b. the job of administering elections has become extremely popular among the voters.
    c. the number of candidates for this office has increased.
    d. campaign contributions to candidates in this office have doubled.

16. The term "third house" refers to the
    a. state assembly.
    b. public's legislative role through the proposition system.
    c. news media.
    d. lobbyists who represent special-interest groups.

17. In 2006, Secretary of State Bruce McPherson faced the dilemma of being unable
    a. to verify the voter registration records of 10 counties.
    b. to verify that all the official records of the state were being kept in a safe and environmentally sound location.
    c. to certify federally mandated electronic voting machines that continued to experience serious technical malfunctions and security flaws.
    d. to certify federally mandated voting booths that were regularly subjected to fraudulent voting practices.

18. Which member of the plural executive is accountable for how and where the Great Seal of California is affixed?
   a. governor
   b. controller
   c. superintendent of public instruction
   d. secretary of state

19. The superintendent of public instruction is
   a. nonpartisan.
   b. partisan.
   c. neutral.
   d. extremely political.

20. California's numerous boards and commissions were originally created
   a. as a way for politicians to give government jobs to political allies as a reward for their support.
   b. by the state legislature to increase the influence of lobbyists and interest groups.
   c. to increase partisan control over state departments and agencies.
   d. to circumvent the partisan influence of corrupt political officials.

PEARSON mypoliscilab Exercises

Apply what you learned in this chapter on **MyPoliSciLab.**

Read on **mypoliscilab.com**

   eText: Chapter 19

Study and **Review** on **mypoliscilab.com**

   Pre-Test
   Post-Test
   Chapter Exam
   Flashcards

Watch on **mypoliscilab.com**

   Video: Managing the California Drought
   Video: The 2010 California Governor Candidates Debate Immigration
   Video: Managing the California Drought

Explore on **mypoliscilab.com**

   Simulation: What Are a Governor
   Comparative: Comparing Executive Branches

NEWS RELEASE

Release Number: 26   Release Date: **May 15, 2008**

JUDICIAL COUNCIL OF
CALIFORNIA

ADMINISTRATIVE OFFICE
OF THE COURTS

Public Information Office
455 Golden Gate Avenue
San Francisco, CA 94102-3688
www.courtinfo.ca.gov

415-865-7740

Lynn Holton
Public Information Officer

California Supreme Court
Rules in Marriage Cases

Opinion Available on California Courts Web Site

San Francisco — The California Supreme Court today held that the California legislative and initiative measures limiting marriage to opposite-sex couples violate the state constitutional rights of same-sex couples and may not be used to preclude same-sex couples from marrying. (*In re Marriage Cases*, S147999.)

The court concluded that permitting opposite-sex couples to marry while affording same-sex couples access only to the novel and less-recognized status of domestic partnership improperly infringes a same-sex couple's constitutional rights to marry and to the equal protection of the laws as guaranteed by the California Constitution.

The decision directs state officials who supervise the enforcement of the state's marriage laws to ensure that local officials comply with the court's ruling and permit same-sex couples to marry. The decision becomes final in 30 days unless that period is extended by court order.

The 121-page majority opinion, which sets forth the decision of the court, was authored by Chief Justice Ronald George, and was signed by Justices Joyce Kennard, Kathryn Werdegar, and Carlos Moreno; Justice Kennard also wrote a separate concurring opinion. Justice Marvin Baxter author a concurring and dissenting opinion that was signed by Justice Ming Chin, and Justice Carol Corrigan wrote a separate concurring and dissenting opinion. Both concurring and dissenting opinions disag with the majority's conclusion that the marriage statutes are unconstitutional. All opinions are available online at *http://www.courtinfo.ca.gov/cgi-bin/opinions.cgi* .

Today's ruling resolves several lawsuits that were fi City and County of San Francisco and a number of after the California Supreme Court determined that,

(more)

CHAPTER 20

The California Judiciary

KEY OBJECTIVES

After completing this chapter, you should be prepared to:

20.1 Outline the structure of the California judicial system.

20.2 Evaluate the processes involved in the execution of California civil and criminal law.

20.3 Characterize the role and responsibilities of trial juries and county grand juries in the state of California.

20.4 Identify major trends in the California judicial system.

There are undoubtedly many Californians, including members of the gay and lesbian community, who were surprised by the California Supreme Court ruling in favor of same-sex marriage on May 15, 2008, and many more who were shocked by the passage of Proposition 8, the ban on same-sex marriage, months later, on November 4, 2008. It is hard to know how many people anticipated yet another state supreme court decision on May 26, 2009 to uphold the current ban on same-sex marriage, but many state residents and concerned parties across the nation expect this issue to one day end up in the U.S. Supreme Court. That day moved a bit closer to reality when a U.S. District Court ruled on August 4, 2010 that same-sex couples have a fundamental right to marry the person of their choosing, regardless of gender or sexual orientation. The Chief U.S. District Court Judge in San Francisco, Vaugh Walker, found that Proposition 8 was unconstitutional on the grounds that this successful ballot initiative violated the due process and equal protection clauses of the U.S. Constitution. Rather surprisingly, Theodore Olson, the former U.S. Solicitor General under the Bush administration, agreed to represent the two

> **How successful has the current California judicial system been in preserving the rule of law and order?**

gay couples in this case in partnership with another prominent attorney, David Boies. The conservative background of Olson is peculiar enough, but the involvement of Olson on the Bush legal team and Boies on the Gore legal team during the historic U.S. Supreme Court case that decided the 2000 presidential election conveys an "odd couple" quality to a partnership that will now oppose Chuck Cooper, another nationally recognized attorney.

All three of these lead attorneys have argued cases before the U.S. Supreme Court and have unquestionably prepared their respective arguments in *Perry et al.* v. *Schwarzenegger et al.* for the possibility that one day this case could be appealed to the high court. Chief U.S. District Court Judge Walker, basically implied as much when he said, "This case is only touching down in this court … and this is only a prelude to what's going to happen later." Nevertheless, *Perry et al.* v. *Schwarzenegger et al.* is but one chapter in the same-sex marriage saga that will further define the legality and attitudes surrounding this issue. Regardless of any court ruling, dueling propositions and the battle for the public opinion of Californians is sure to follow.[1]

Resource Center
• Glossary
• Vocabulary Example
• Connect the Link

■ **Superior Courts:** The entry point for the enforcement of California law and the settlement of conflicts or disagreements.

EXAMPLE: *The revised California constitution of 1879 created a new court structure that included a supreme court, district courts of appeal, and superior courts.*

The California Judicial System

20.1 Outline the structure of the California judicial system.

(pages 614–617)

The California court system is the largest in the nation, with more than 2,000 judicial officers and 18,000 court employees who handle approximately 9 million cases each year. The court system is very similar to the pyramid-like structure of the federal court system, with superior or trial courts spread throughout California's 58 counties at the base, six courts of appeal in the middle, and one state supreme court at the top (see Figure 20.1). All California judges and justices are required by the Code of Judicial Ethics to "be faithful to the law regardless of partisan interests, public clamor or fear of criticism."

Superior Courts

The entry point for the enforcement of California law and the settlement of conflicts or disagreements are the California **superior courts**■, which are adjudicated or administered by 1,499 authorized judges and 437 commissioners and referees.[2] In 1998, California voters approved **Proposition 220**■, a constitutional amendment that consolidated superior and municipal

courts into a single superior court with original jurisdiction over all cases that enter the court system, generally consisting of felonies, misdemeanors, and traffic and civil cases. In consolidating these courts, the California judicial system, in cooperation with the state legislature, sought to utilize funding allocations and other resources in a more efficient manner. Of the roughly 9 million cases filed annually, 8.5 million are dealt with by superior courts at over 450 locations. Superior courts also have appellate jurisdiction for small claims cases. During the past 40 years, the superior courts have experienced major increases in caseload, with the greatest growth occurring in criminal cases. Efforts to lessen this caseload have caused courts to increasingly rely on the use of the **plea bargain**■, a formal agreement between the district attorney's office and the defendant to forgo a trial.

Specialty superior courts have been developed to adjudicate specific kinds of cases and more effectively comply with recent initiatives and statutes as well as better coordinate with agencies within the judicial system.[3] California is one of the first states in the nation to initiate the **drug court**—an alternative to the traditional criminal justice process for drug law offenders that offers options other than incarceration. Ideally, these courts would employ California judges and other court professionals who would have the option of diverting drug law offenders to treatment programs and then monitoring their participation. Small claims court is another type of special court where civil disputes involving less than $7,500 are resolved quickly and inexpensively. The parties to a small claims case are not allowed

FIGURE 20.1 ■ California Judicial Branch
The California court system is very similar to the structure of the federal court system.
—*How does the California court system differ from the federal court system?*

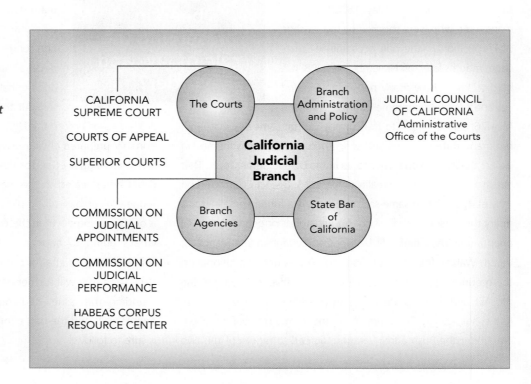

■ **Proposition 220:** A 1998 California constitutional amendment that consolidates superior and municipal courts into a single superior court with original jurisdiction over all cases that enter the court system.

SIGNIFICANCE: *Proposition 220 actually permitted the judges in each county to unify their superior and municipal courts into a single superior court.*

■ **Plea Bargain:** A formal agreement between the district attorney's office and a defendant to forgo a trial in exchange for a guilty plea.

SIGNIFICANCE: *Plea bargains may result in the complete dismissal of all charges.*

to be represented by an attorney in court. The filing fees are relatively inexpensive, and the rules of this court are simple and structured to allow a person without much legal knowledge to present his or her case. In many small claims courts, commissioners take the place of judges and usually inform both parties of the court's ruling by mail.[4]

Court of Appeals

California has six court of appeals, headquartered in San Francisco (First District), Los Angeles (Second District), Sacramento (Third District), San Diego (Fourth District), Fresno (Fifth District), and San Jose (Sixth District), with a total of 105 justices. Each district of the California **court of appeals**■ has three-justice panels that include a presiding justice and associate justices who review approximately 25,000 requests for an appeal each year.[5] Upon completion of a superior court trial, the losing party has the right to appeal the ruling to the California court of appeals with the exception of death penalty cases, which must go straight to the state supreme court. Appeals are usually reviewed in the appellate district where the superior court that originally heard the case was located. The appellate process in the California court of appeals begins with the notice of appeal and written arguments, known as *briefs,* from both sides of the case. Appellate courts do not review new evidence or assess the credibility of witnesses. Required by the California constitution to issue a decision within 90 days of accepting a case, the appellate courts first review the written record of the case to determine if the trial court properly interpreted the law and correctly applied legal procedure. The appellate court justices also read the briefs and hear oral arguments by the parties to the case before issuing a written statement, known as the *opinion,* of the panel's decision. At least two justices on the panel must concur on the final ruling of the court.[6]

The California court of appeals does have original jurisdiction in cases challenging confinement (habeas corpus), ordering government to act (writs of mandamus), requesting review of judicial action (writs of certiorari), and requesting restraint on certain actions. This court also reviews appeals of the decisions made by certain quasi-judicial bodies, such as the Workers' Compensation Appeals Board, Agricultural Labor Relations Board, and Public Employment Relations Board[7] (see Figure 20.2).

Supreme Court

The California **supreme court**■ is the highest court in the state, and its decisions are binding on all other California courts. It is in reality the "court of last resort." There are seven supreme court justices, including the chief justice. The California constitution gives the state supreme court appellate jurisdiction (the power to review decisions) over the California courts of appeals. With the

FIGURE 20.2 ■ **Court of Appeals: Record of Appeal**

Filings in All Districts, Fiscal Years 1996–1997 Through 2005–2006

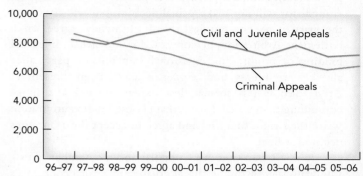

SOURCE: *2007 Court Statistics Report: Statewide Caseload Trends 1996–1997 through 2005–2006* (San Francisco: California Administrative Office of the Courts, 2007), Figure 6 (p. 21). Accessed at www.courtinfo.ca.gov. Reprinted with permission.

exception of death penalty cases, which it must review under the provisions of the California constitution, the supreme court has discretion over what cases it will review, accepting only a small number of the thousands of cases that it receives annually. As the highest state court in California, the supreme court is expected to decide important legal questions and issues and maintain the uniformity or consistency of California law. The supreme court also has original jurisdiction in proceedings for extraordinary relief involving writs of mandamus, writs of certiorari, prohibitions, and habeas corpus. In deciding a case, at least four of the seven supreme court justices must agree on the final decision. The procedure for reviewing cases is very similar to the process in the California court of appeals. In recent years, most criminal cases and about two-thirds of all civil cases that were appealed to either appellate court were affirmed or found to be without legal errors or to have properly followed legal procedures. When a case was reversed or found to have involved errors by the appellate courts, it was almost always sent back to the trial court for retrial.[8]

Alternative Dispute Resolution

In many California counties, especially densely populated ones, it can take up to two years before a civil lawsuit can reach the trial stage. Not only has the criminal and civil caseload grown dramatically, straining the resources of the California court system, but the legal procedures required by civil law cases in particular, such as discovery and taking depositions, can cause major delays in court action and involve costly fees for both the court and attorneys. In response to these judicial impediments, the Judicial Council of California, local courts, and various legal associations are increasingly encouraging the use of **alternative dispute resolution (ADR)**■, a non–court-centered way of expediting the legal process. The two major forms of ADR are mediation and arbitration.

■ **Court of Appeals:** A court that has the power to consider or hear an appeal.

SIGNIFICANCE: *The courts of appeal also receive appeals from decisions of the Workers' Compensation Appeals Board, the Agricultural Labor Relations Board, and the Public Employment Relations Board.*

■ **Supreme Court:** The highest court in the state, the decisions of which are binding on all lower courts.

EXAMPLE: *In 1972, the California supreme court found that the death penalty constituted cruel and unusual punishment under the state constitution.*

When parties to a conflict of some sort opt for mediation, they are basically getting an impartial person to help the parties reach a mutually acceptable resolution of the dispute. A mediator will not make a final decision but will try to get the parties to communicate and ultimately agree on a settlement. Arbitration, by contrast, does involve an impartial binding or nonbinding decision by an outside party after all the arguments and evidence have been presented. Arbitration is less formal, less expensive, and less time-consuming than a trial. Parties that choose binding arbitration waive their right to a trial and agree to accept the arbitrator's decision as final.

As ADR becomes more popular and the number of private firms specializing in this alternative to formal court trials continues to grow, there are concerns that the costs may be as prohibitive as those of the formal legal process for the average Californian.

Judicial Qualifications and Selection

All California court judges and justices must first have been an attorney with the ability to practice law or have served as a judge in California for at least 10 years immediately preceding their election or appointment. The governor fills superior court vacancies through appointment. Otherwise, these judges are elected to six-year terms by voters on a nonpartisan ballot in the county where the superior court is located. Appellate or supreme court justices are appointed by the governor but first must be evaluated by the California State Bar's Commission on Judicial Nominees and confirmed by the Commission on Judicial Appointments which is composed of the chief justice of California, the state attorney general, and a senior presiding justice of the California court of appeals. The Commission on Judicial Appointments reviews the nominee's qualifications, conducts public hearings, and confirms the appointment if it finds the nominee qualified to serve. After the nominee is confirmed and admitted as an appellate or supreme court justice, the appointment must be approved by a majority of voters at the next general election; the term of service is 12 years.

MYTH EXPOSED Many Californians believe that the California judges and justices appointed and subsequently elected are some of the most respected members of the legal profession, if not society at large, but many are regularly accused and often punished for inappropriate behavior and misconduct. Despite their exalted positions, California judges and justices remain susceptible to the frailties of the human condition often leading to personal issues or downright incompetence that may have escaped notice during the judicial selection process or by the voters on election day.

Complaints regarding alleged misconduct by California judges and justices are overseen by the State of California Commission on Judicial Performance. In 2009, of the 1,161 complaints that were filed involving 856 judges, about 31 actually resulted in disciplinary action. The overwhelming majority of complaints came from litigants or defendants or their friends and family while approximately 10 percent were divided between attorneys, court personnel, and non–court-related individuals. When the commission finds evidence of misconduct, disciplinary measures may be imposed. The commission has the power to remove judges, but such action is rare. Disciplinary rulings are usually confidential, but in more serious cases of misconduct, the commission will make the reprimand public. In 2009, the largest number of complaints by judges and justices that resulted in disciplinary action included "demeanor/decorum," which is essentially a behavior problem. The relatively small number of complaints that result in disciplinary action suggest either that a large number California judges are vulnerable to baseless charges or that the commission is less than aggressive in addressing misconduct.

The Judicial Council

The **Judicial Council**■ is the governing body of the California courts and has the responsibility of establishing judicial guidelines, submitting recommendations to the governor and state legislature regarding the judicial system, and adopting and revising the California Rules of Court. The 27-member Judicial Council is chaired by the chief justice of the state supreme court and includes 14 judges appointed by the chief justice, four attorneys appointed by the board of governors of the State Bar Board of California, one member chosen from each house of the legislature, and six advisory members. As the workload of the California judicial system grows and becomes increasingly complex, especially with the advent of new technology, the Judicial Council is expected to continuously review and evaluate methods of meeting these current challenges.[9]

STUDENT profile

Entering the legal profession can be tough. Law school admission is highly competitive, and then there is law school itself—a demanding experience that culminates with the bar examination. Ismael Chinchilla, an English and rhetoric major in college, wanted to find out if the practice of law was really for him and to gain some solid experience. JusticeCorps provided that opportunity to Ismael, as it does for 300 college students each year. Funded through an AmeriCorps grant, JusticeCorps is a collaborative project of the California judicial system, select

■ Alternative Dispute Resolution (ADR): A non–court-centered option for resolving disagreements, such as mediation and arbitration.

SIGNIFICANCE: *According to a report to the California legislature on costs and use of referees, in general civil cases the referee's services ranged from $150 to approximately $92,000, with a median charge of $5,625.*

■ Judicial Council: The body that governs California's courts.

SIGNIFICANCE: *In 1926 California voters overwhelmingly approved a constitutional amendment creating the Judicial Council as the governing body of the California judicial system.*

University of California and California State University campuses, and many community-based organizations. JusticeCorps members receive approximately 30 hours of training and, after completing 300 hours of internship work, receive a $1,000 education award.

The main responsibility of the interns working at JusticeCorps is to help in the process of alleviating the congestion that exists in the Bay Area courts. "I help people correctly fill out their court forms and inform them of the necessary steps to continue their case," Ismael explained. "In small claims cases,

I encourage plaintiffs and defendants to resolve their disputes in out-of-court agreements when possible."

For Ismael, JusticeCorps validated his decision to attend law school. "I feel that being exposed to this as an undergraduate has helped me immensely as a person and will help me even further as an attorney."

SOURCE: Accessed at http://www.courtinfo.ca.gov/programs/justicecorps/jcorps_members.htm and http://career.berkeley.edu/Article/070126a-sd.stm

The California Judicial System

20.1 Outline the structure of the California judicial system.

PRACTICE QUIZ: UNDERSTAND AND APPLY

1. California's superior courts
   a. will normally hear appellate cases.
   b. are the last step for capital punishment cases before they can be appealed to the state supreme court.
   c. hear only civil law cases.
   d. are the entry point for the enforcement of state law and the settlement of conflict and disagreements.

2. California is one of the first states in the nation to initiate
   a. the drug court concept as an alternative to the traditional criminal justice process.
   b. a juvenile justice system that includes corporal punishment after the second conviction of a ward of the court.
   c. mandatory sentences for drunk driving.
   d. armed guards in the courtroom.

3. Why would someone want to have their case heard in a small claims court?
   a. The resolution of their case will be rapid and inexpensive.

   b. The resolution of their case will result in a lower settlement.
   c. They will not have to travel so far to have their case heard.
   d. Judges in these courts tend to be more sympathetic than those in superior courts.

ANALYZE

1. In what ways is the California legal system innovative? How is this innovation achieved?

2. Why would a judge recommend that two parties to a legal problem seek alternative dispute resolution or mediation?

IDENTIFY THE CONCEPT THAT DOESN'T BELONG

a. Proposition 220
b. Plea bargains
c. Civil disputes
d. Municipal advisory councils
e. Judicial Council of California

Resource Center
• Glossary
• Vocabulary Example
• Connect the Link

■ **Proposition 184:** The "three strikes law," which mandates a 25-year-to-life sentence for any third felony conviction for individuals previously convicted of two violent or serious felony offenses.

EXAMPLE: *One of the more highly publicized applications of Proposition 184 was the case of Kevin Weber, who was sentenced to 26 years to life for allegedly stealing four chocolate chip cookies.*

The Elements of California Law

20.2 **Evaluate the processes involved in the execution of California civil and criminal law.**
(pages 618–623)

The work of the California judicial system is largely predicated on interpreting California law, codes, regulations, and ordinances broadly classified as either civil or criminal law. California laws, like most laws in the tradition of American jurisprudence, are "living" articles of California society, evolving gradually in large part but sometimes subject to rapid change. Rapid change to the California legal system is often the result of voters, who can affect the body of California law through the initiative and the referendum. The initiative process in particular regularly generates laws that are more reactions to social attitudes than a result of farsightedness or detailed legal studies.

More than a decade after passage of **Proposition 184**■ —the "three strikes" law, which mandates a 25-years-to-life sentence for any third felony conviction for individuals with two previous violent or serious felony convictions— Californians may be tempted to ask whether they are any safer now than they were before. Some would suggest the slight decrease in crime is a positive sign, while others point to a prison population that has not only become the largest in the nation but also a breeding ground for generations of crime and criminals. The passage of initiatives addressing the insurance industry and tort reform are rare examples of initiative topics that have sought to alter civil law, and such change has been limited in scope.

Although the mission of the California Youth Authority is to educate and rehabilitate offenders sentenced by juvenile courts, state officials and outside experts say it fails in its most basic tasks because of antiquated facilities, undertrained employees, and violence endemic within its walls. Juveniles who cause trouble at the Fred C. Nelles Youth Correctional Facility in Whittier, California, often leave their cells only for instruction or counseling, which they receive in steel-mesh cages. Because federal courts have taken authority over many aspects of prison operations, prison and sentencing reform was a top priority for California politicians in 2007. —*What kinds of guidelines must a juvenile court judge work under when sentencing young offenders?*

■ **Civil Law:** The area of law dealing with relations between private citizens.

EXAMPLE: *In the absence of governmental institutions in the late 1840s, miners in the California goldfields created quasi-legal guidelines to fill the vacuum in legal authority.*

■ **Tort Law:** The area of law dealing with any wrongdoing that results in legal action for damages.

SIGNIFICANCE: *Tort-based rules forbid such things as theft, assault, and murder, and they establish boundaries.*

■ **Probate Law:** The area of law governing cases that pertain to the personal affairs of an individual.

EXAMPLE: *Early California suffrage leaders Marietta L. Stow was denied an inheritance of $200,000 in 1872 by a California court upon her husband's death. In reaction, she campaigned for probate reform in California.*

Civil Law

Civil law■ is intended to help people settle conflicts or disputes that they ordinarily cannot solve themselves. California civil law encompasses a wide variety of topics, including general civil, family, juvenile, landlord-tenant, probate, and small claims law. General civil law, which focuses on contracts, damage to property, and injury, is an extremely broad category. California Civil Code 3342, commonly known as the "dog bite" statute, imposes strict liability on the owner of a dog that bites someone. According to the statute, the dog only has to bite once—even if there was no puncture to the skin—for the dog owner to be liable for the actions of that dog. Although this statute may appear pretty straightforward, harm caused by a dog's barking is not covered by the statute, illustrating the many gradations, exceptions, and difficulties inherent in solving disputes among people in court.

The explosion of litigation in California has been another source of concern regarding general civil law over the past 30 years. This deluge of civil law cases typically pertain to California **tort law**■, defined as any wrongdoing that results in legal action for damages. Detractors of litigation argue that Californians are encouraged by lawyers to take just about all real or imagined disputes to court. Another view considers litigation a just means of resolving disputes that may involve discrimination, product safety, worker rights, and environmental degradation and finds the problem of abuse in the rules and procedures, not in the act of litigation itself. For many years now, California has been the setting for various legal battles between a number of different industries and trial lawyers over the ability to sue and the monetary limits on damages awarded by California courts. Two main advocacy organizations, the California Medical Association and the Consumer Attorneys of California, have clashed repeatedly over limits on malpractice cases and awards. By lobbying the state legislature, spending millions in the process, the California Medical Association has been able to get laws passed that imposed limits on contingency fees, eliminated multiple payment of court awards, qualified the rules for payment of malpractice awards in installments, and placed limits on damages for pain and suffering. The insurance industry has been less successful in containing what has been seen by some as frivolous insurance lawsuits in California. However, the insurance industry and trial lawyers continue to skirmish over workers' compensation and other issues.

Family law tends to take up a great deal of the time and resources of the California courts. These civil law matters usually involve divorce, child support, and child custody. Since the 1980s, the Judicial Council has tried to address the rise in family law cases by introducing a number of special programs and offices, such as the Statewide Office of Family Court Services, child support commissioners, family law facilitators, and the Center for Families, Children, and the Courts.

Probate law■ largely pertains to the personal affairs of an individual and how those personal affairs will be handled in the event of incapacity. Typical probate cases involve wills or trusts, guardianship, name changes, and adoptions, but the field has become increasingly complicated in California with the growing incidence of elder abuse as it relates to the estate or financial assets of the elderly. The state legislature recently added the Elder Abuse and Dependent Adult Civil Protection Act to the Welfare and Institutions Code in reaction to a wave of financially abusive situations affecting California's large aging population. In 2003, most alleged perpetrators of financial elder abuse were adult children or other family members and involved misappropriating income or assets, charging excessive fees, or obtaining money or property by undue influence.[10]

During one of the most publicized criminal trials in American history in which former football star and movie actor O.J. Simpson was accused of murdering his ex-wife, Nicole Brown Simpson, and her friend, Ronald Goldman, in 1994, Johnnie Cochran, defense attorney, and prosecutor, William Hodgman, stand to address Judge Lance Ito. Seated are Simpson and Robert Shapiro, another member of the Simpson defense team.
—*How do high-profile cases influence the public's perception of the judiciary?*

■ **Criminal Law:** The area of law dealing with crime and the legal punishment of criminal offenses.

SIGNIFICANCE: *The first appearance of the defendant in a felony or criminal matter is the arraignment. At this hearing, the defendant will enter a plea. The judge will then set a date for a hearing to determine whether the defendant will be tried and will determine whether the posting of bail will be permitted.*

■ **California Penal Code:** The listing of all crimes defined by statutes.

EXAMPLE: *Although the original California constitution was approved in 1850, it was not until 1872 that a penal code was written and passed by the state legislature.*

Criminal Law

California has established a considerable reputation nationally for crime, in large part because of the long list of highly publicized or infamous crimes that have been tried in California courts. In fact, these cases have been so well publicized and have so frequently involved heinous acts that they have tended to influence state and national standards in criminal justice. During the 1950s, Caryl Chessman's death sentence for a rape conviction based on dubious evidence attracted national media attention and public appeals from celebrities and influential personalities from around the world as well as caused the nation to reflect on capital punishment. The tendency of the state's judicial system to generate high-profile criminal cases would continue, exemplified by the trials of the political activist Angela Davis in the 1960s, Charles Manson and his "Family" during the 1970s, the McMartin preschool child molestation defendants in the 1980s, and of the four police officers in the Rodney King police brutality case, Richard Allen Davis in the Polly Klass case, and O. J. Simpson during the 1990s. One consequence of California's high-profile criminal cases has been to place intense pressure on all levels of the criminal justice system to avoid the perception of coddling criminals while attempting to maintain fairness and professionalism in enforcing **criminal law**■.

Law enforcement begins with the **California Penal Code**■—the listing of all crimes defined by statutes. In the California Penal Code, offenses are divided into two major categories: felonies and misdemeanors. **Felonies**■ are crimes for which a person may be sentenced to imprisonment in the state prison or, in extreme circumstances, executed. **Misdemeanors**■ are lesser crimes that carry a sentence of imprisonment in a county jail, usually for a year or less, and/or fines. **Infractions**■ are classified in California as public offenses; they normally pertain to municipal ordinances or codes and are punishable by fines only. A parking ticket is probably the best example of an infraction. An individual charged with an infraction is not entitled to a trial by jury or public defense.[11]

Every criminal law in California must reflect the notion of **corpus delicti**■, or elements of a crime. Establishing corpus delicti begins with proving that the actions specified in the law really did happen and that there was intent (the accused knowingly planned) to commit the crime outlined in the law. Once the accused is found guilty in a California court, then according to the state penal code, a **determinate sentence**■ will generally be imposed, which means that the judge will have the choice of three punishments, in most cases defined by the number of years in prison—for example, a 6-year, 12-year, or 16-year sentence. If any sentence other than the middle sentence is selected, the judge must explain in writing what aggravating facts justify the lower or higher sentence. California

does have elements of "indeterminate sentencing." The best example is the "three strikes and you're out" law that was enacted by the electorate through passage of Proposition 184. This law imposes an indeterminate, 25-years-to-life imprisonment and other "enhancements" (lengthening of sentences for the commission of felony offenses) for anyone who had been previously convicted of two or more serious or violent felonies. Violation of California criminal law is also punishable by consecutive sentencing, a period of confinement in prison for each separate crime, or concurrent sentencing (one sentence for multiple crimes).[12] In 1984, Peter Chan helped plan the robbery of a jewelry store in Los Angeles, scouting out the location of the robbery, obtaining weapons, and arranging the getaway car, but Chan was never actually present during the crime. In the commission of this crime, however, one Los Angeles police officer was killed, and another was seriously wounded. According to the California criminal statutes, Chan could have been charged for first-degree murder based on the intent and action of the crime. California criminal law stipulates that all principals to a crime are equally guilty, including those who aid and abet other parties to commit a crime, regardless of whether a participant was present during the crime itself. The jury nonetheless found Chan guilty of murder in the second degree, which normally carries a 15-years-to-life sentence with the possibility of parole. By making other criminal violations associated with Chan's case consecutive, the judge chose to essentially impose life imprisonment by sentencing Chan to 38 years to life.[13]

Police Powers

When most Californians hear the term *police,* they tend to visualize the typical police officer, armed and in paramilitary dress. Although the typical municipal police officer has the broadest public authority, literally hundreds of individuals inside and sometimes outside government have police powers. These powers are intended for the enforcement of existing laws as outlined by the Tenth Amendment of the U.S. Constitution and Articles 11 and 12 of the California constitution. The enforcement of these laws, necessitating the granting of police powers, extends to health inspectors, university and community college public safety officers, and even humane society workers, who can be empowered in California to make arrests, carry firearms, use force, and serve warrants. One example of the sometimes vague nature of police powers can be found in one section of a bill proposed not long ago in the California state assembly that granted police powers to homeowners' associations. According to the interpretation of the National Alliance of Homeowners, instead of requiring the use of a "peace officer" to enforce a court order preventing an occupant from gaining physical access to a housing unit, this section of the bill would permit representatives of the homeowners' association to enforce such court orders.[14]

■ **Felonies:** Crimes for which a person may be sentenced to imprisonment in the state prison or execution.

EXAMPLE: *Factors that determine when a crime will be charged as a felony include whether physical injury occurred and prior convictions.*

■ **Misdemeanors:** Crimes for which a person may be imprisoned in a county jail, usually for a year or less, and/or fined.

EXAMPLE: *Most drunk driving arrests are charged as misdemeanors unless the driver was involved in an accident, kills or injures another person, or was arrested for a DUI/DWI charge within 10 years of a previous DUI/DWI conviction.*

It is unfortunate that so many members of California society see a distinction between the duties of an official with police powers and existing law. The controversial aspect of this distinction stems from how far police officers can stray from the law in effectively executing their police powers. One perspective suggests that law enforcement includes many gray areas—unlike laws, which are written to be as specific as possible—and that to see police work in black-and-white hues will only invite lawlessness. Racial profiling is one example of the techniques used in law enforcement that while not codified—and, some people would suggest, while unconstitutional—can be useful in bringing some criminals to justice. Certain California laws, civil libertarians argue, actually encourage the police to violate the law. These civil libertarians point specifically to the Police Safety Officers Procedural Bill of Rights Act, which imposes limits on investigations, internal hearings, and punishment of police officers. California law specifies that most police disciplinary records and citizen complaints against officers be kept secret, unlike at least 30 states that permit partial or complete public access to police personnel records. Despite the merits or failings of either position, the accused or the individual subjected to unlawful action by those with police powers must have his or her day in court, where the legality of such actions ideally will be either affirmed or denied.[15]

The Prosecution

Each California county has a **district attorney (DA)** who is the principal public prosecuting officer. The DA's office is of great importance in the administration of criminal law, responsible for investigating alleged crimes, gathering evidence, submitting formal criminal charges, and representing the state or "the people" in court trials. A DA is under a great deal of social pressure to remove the criminals or lawbreakers from society and, as a result, cannot help but have a certain sensitivity to accusations of being "soft on crime." Regardless of how much investigative work is conducted by police officers and how secure they feel in having captured a perpetrator, it is ultimately the DA's decision to seek punishment. Naturally, the position of DA is made more difficult by the growing number of laws that people in California can violate. Fairly recent additions to the long list of criminal laws include driving under the influence of intoxicating drugs, high-technology crime, gang violence, environmental pollution, and expanded categories for family violence and sexual assault.[16]

Unfortunately, in the pursuit of lawbreakers, California DAs have faced allegations of impropriety. In 2006, the *San Jose Mercury News* reported on a three-year investigation it had conducted of the Santa Clara County criminal justice system and found that "in nearly 100 cases, the prosecution has

engaged in questionable conduct that bolstered its efforts to win convictions. Some Santa Clara County prosecutors withheld evidence that could have helped defendants, some defied judge's orders and some misled juries during closing arguments."[17] Members of the Santa Clara County DA's office, in interviews with *San Jose Mercury News* reporters, conceded some concern about the findings of the investigation while defending other actions as being either proper conduct that was wrongly criticized or "problems that amounted to nothing more than honest mistakes."[18] In response, the report countered that "while many errors were isolated incidents, others fell into patterns that suggested broader problems. And certain prosecutors engaged in questionable behavior in multiple cases, suggesting either sloppiness or a deliberate disregard for ethical rules."[19] It would be unfair to place every DA's office into the same category of problems presented by this article. The truth is that crimes are committed and that the average Californian would much rather have a convicted criminal imprisoned, despite any mistakes in the legal process, than released because of such errors. The *San Jose Mercury News* article does, however, clearly illustrate that mistakes, whether inadvertent or intentional, are made and that perhaps closer scrutiny of the work of county DA offices could help prevent such mistakes and cause Californians to become more sensitive about the responsibilities associated with enforcement of the law.

Punishment in California

The average Californian would like to believe that the conviction of a criminal who has broken the law puts an end to a societal menace and perhaps brings closure for survivors of what may have been a horrible nightmare. What really happens is the shuttling of the convicted criminal from one venue to another to serve the imposed sentence. The convicted are, however, still very much in the system. The "three strikes" law has increased the possibility that criminals convicted of a series of crimes will spend a lifetime in prison, but such criminals and their life sentences will continue to have major repercussions on California society. The three strikes law is but one factor among many that have caused the California prison population to explode over the past 20 years. California has the third-largest penal system in the world, surpassed only by those of China and the United States. The California Department of Corrections has an annual budget of $10 billion, one of the largest single state fiscal liabilities, but continues to suffer from overcrowding, extreme violence, corruption, and substandard services. The philosophy of rehabilitation in state prison was officially discarded more than 25 years ago under Governor Jerry Brown but resurfaced under Governor Schwarzenegger. The rash of recent state prison problems, however, including rapid turnover of corrections heads, prison riots, poor medical

■ **Infractions:**
Public offenses
punishable by a fine.

EXAMPLE: *One recent infraction added to
the California Vehicle Code prohibits a person
to smoke a pipe, cigar, or cigarette in a motor
vehicle any time a minor is present.*

■ **Corpus
Delicti:** The
elements of a
crime.

SIGNIFICANCE:
*Corpus delicti is typically
viewed in California courts as
a procedure that promotes
proper law enforcement
procedures.*

■ **Determinate
Sentence:** The choices
for punishment for a
crime that can be
imposed by a judge.

SIGNIFICANCE: *The
determinate sentence that is imposed
depends on many factors, including
the discretion of the judge and the
criminal history of the defendant.*

Kenneth Marsh hugs Brenda Buell Warter on
the steps of the San Diego Hall of Justice after
his release from prison. —*What consequences
did his case have on the California legal
system?*

services, and federal investigations, has pushed rehabilitation far
down his list of priorities. Nine out of every 10 inmates will be
released eventually, but with the **recidivism rate**■ approaching
80 percent, the chances of the recently released going back to
jail are high.

A major attempt to alleviate prison overcrowding, a
clogged justice system, and many other social problems
associated with illicit drug use and addiction has occurred
through **Proposition 36**■, which essentially mandated state
law to permit the diversion of individuals convicted of drug
law violations to a drug treatment program instead of prison.
Considering that 8 out of 10 felons have substance abuse problems, this program seemed to be a step in a more constructive
direction. After a number of years in use, however, the program
has had mixed results. Although fewer state residents are going
to prison for drug offenses, completion rates for Proposition 36
drug treatment programs have varied widely from county to
county; some county programs registered near 60-percent
completion rates, while many other counties, especially in
major urban areas, had rates in the low 20-percent range.[20]
However, because of the fiscal meltdown in 2009 that caused
across-the-board budget cuts, the completion-rate issue has
become irrelevant for many counties and those eligible for
Proposition 36 programs.

If there is any good news, it is that violent crime—and all
other categories of crime—continued to decline in 2009. More
important, various government and nonprofit agencies have
conducted serious studies of the California Department of
Corrections that contain well-thought recommendations for
prison reform. Reports from the Hoover Commission (a nonpartisan group of state legislators and influential private
citizens) and the state legislative analyst's office recommend,
among many other innovations, expanding community-based
services and residential housing, implementing parole reforms,

improving evaluation measures, and upgrading inadequate
information technology systems. The greatest challenge facing
the corrections system, implied in the aforementioned studies
and well-known assertions by key players, is the capacity to
reduce the California prison population enough to save funds
that can be used for rehabilitation and other programs that will
better prepare inmates and parolees to become productive
citizens.[21]

PATHWAYS of action

Exonerations in California

In 2006, Kenneth Marsh was awarded $756,900, one of the
largest compensation sums for wrongful imprisonment in California history. Under state law, Marsh was entitled to $100 for
every day of the 21 years he was wrongfully incarcerated. For
years, Marsh's wife, Brenda Buell, who was also the mother of
Philip Andrew Buell, the toddler Marsh was convicted of
murdering in the second degree, remained unconvinced of his
guilt. Utilizing the judicial system, the same pathway that sent
Marsh to prison, Buell wrote letters to any legal authority
remotely interested, seeking assistance in getting the case
reopened. After eventually receiving pro bono assistance from
appellate attorney Tracy Emblem and the California Western
School of Law, Buell convinced the San Diego County District
Attorney, Bonnie Dumanis, to review the case. Resolving the
guilt or innocence of Kenneth Marsh involved a complicated
process without the benefit of DNA or recently discovered evidence. District Attorney Dumanis had to decide if Philip really
did die due to head injuries inflicted by Marsh or the fall off a
couch according to Marsh's testimony. Medical evidence in the
case was largely inconclusive in determining guilt. All of
the doctors who provided evidence and information for both

■ **Recidivism Rate:** The percentage of inmates who are convicted of another crime after their release from prison.

SIGNIFICANCE: *Some criminologists suggest that one reason for California's high recidivism rate is that virtually all offenders released from California prisons go on parole supervision.*

■ **Proposition 36:** An initiative that created a diversion program for individuals convicted of offenses.

EXAMPLE: *In the first year of Proposition 30, a total of 469 eligible offenders entered treatment programs; in the second year, 35,947 eligible offenders entered treatment programs.*

---

the original trial and the re-opened case felt that Philip's head injuries were "inconsistent with an accidental fall." There was also the issue of previous injuries suffered by Philip during the period that Buell and her children lived with Marsh. Most of the doctors involved in the case suggested that the previous injuries were common for a toddler and as a result did not necessarily support Marsh's conviction. Brenda Buell added that Philip did have a bleeding disorder that she felt contributed to his death. Twenty-one years earlier, police investigators had informed the San Diego district attorney that there was insufficient evidence of a crime, but for reasons that are still unclear, charges were filed. After reviewing evidence from the original

case and new arguments on Marsh's behalf, District Attorney Dumanis requested dismissal of the case, finding that "although we concede reasonable doubt exists, considerable evidence of the defendant's guilt remains." Any compensation for wrongful imprisonment must be approved by a three-member Victims Compensation Board, which was significantly more definitive than the San Diego District Attorney in ruling that Marsh was not responsible for Philip's death and recommending the standard award of $100 per day for every day he was wrongly imprisoned.

SOURCE: Jim Sanders, "Freedom, Apology," *Sacramento Bee,* January 20, 2006.

The Elements of California Law

20.2 **Evaluate the processes involved in the execution of California civil and criminal law.**

PRACTICE QUIZ: UNDERSTAND AND APPLY

1. What are the two main advocacy organizations that have clashed repeatedly over limits on malpractice cases and awards?
   a. Association of Law Enforcement Officers and the Judge's Union of California
   b. California Association of Physician Groups and the State Bar of California
   c. California Medical Association and the Consumer Attorneys of California
   d. California Correction Officers Association and the California Society of Plastic Surgeons

2. California has established a considerable reputation nationally for crime, in large part because of
   a. the long list of highly publicized or infamous crimes that have been tried in California courts.
   b. the fact that California leads the nation in the number of violent crimes.
   c. the presence of organized crime.
   d. the inability of law enforcement personnel to solve criminal cases and provide the evidence necessary to convict criminals.

3. Which of the following conditions would make for a case that does not meet the requirements of corpus delicti, also known as "the elements of a crime"?
   a. if the defendant committed the transgression unknowingly
   b. if the defendant confessed to the crime

   c. if the judge issued one of three determinate sentences
   d. if the defendant was not present during the crime

ANALYZE

1. How have California initiatives and public concern changed judicial procedures in California? Has this intervention served as a positive or negative force?

2. What pressures are placed on district attorneys that may affect their ability to administer duty in a fair and just manner? What measures can be taken to improve their performance?

IDENTIFY THE CONCEPT THAT DOESN'T BELONG

a. Divorce
b. Child support
c. Penal code
d. Probate law
e. Malpractice

Resource Center
• Glossary
• Vocabulary Example
• Connect the Link

■ **Voir Dire:** The process of selecting a jury (from an Old French expression meaning "speak the truth").

SIGNIFICANCE: *Voir dire usually involves "challenge for cause," which is the reason for excusing a potential juror with some justification, and "peremptory challenges," which require no justification.*

The California Jury System

20.3 Characterize the role and responsibilities of trial juries and county grand juries in the state of California.

(pages 624–625)

In California, as in most states, the jury is a fundamental part of the legal system, ideally guaranteeing fairness in the decision about the guilt or innocence of the accused in a court trial. In California, to serve as a juror, you must be a U.S. citizen, 18 years of age or older, and able to understand the English language. The prospective juror must also live in the county of service, not have served on any jury within the past 12 months, and be free of parole commitments.

For most potential jurors, the jury experience begins and ends with the waiting period before the selection process. Once the court case does start, the jury selection process, known as **voir dire**■, allows the defense and prosecution to interview potential jurors and to ask the judge to excuse certain jurors because of a perceived bias or unsuitability. Throughout the trial, it is the responsibility of the jury to hear the evidence and decide questions of fact, while the judge's concern is to address questions of law. After the facts of a case have been presented, the jury must act on the instructions of the judge, which normally involve the relevant law and the degree of proof required to reach a verdict. In California courts, parties to a civil trial must prove guilt or innocence by a "preponderance of evidence"; in a criminal trial, the jurors must be convinced "beyond a reasonable doubt."

The state of California pays jurors $15 per day, starting on the second day of service, and transportation costs; an exception is government employees, who are entitled to receive full pay and benefits from their employers while on jury duty. The length of jury service in California is based on a "one-day or one-trial jury service" obligation during a 12-month period. Failure to fulfill jury duty, unless this duty has been excused or postponed, could result in a fine of up to $1,500 or time in the county jail.

The role of juries in the California judicial system has been the source of a great deal of criticism in recent decades, stemming in large part from acquittals of the accused in a number of high-profile court cases. The California District Attorneys Association has called on the state legislature to abolish the unanimous verdict and permit juries in California to convict or acquit whenever 10 of 12 jurors agree on a verdict. Anyone who has witnessed a highly publicized trial on television cannot help but wonder what effect the excessive media exposure is having on the outcome of trials and the ability of jurors

to reach a fair verdict. Jurors worry about a decision that will be scrutinized in the media, and there is the possibility of financial rewards from media organizations for jurors willing to report on behind-the-scenes court proceedings.

A far more common problem facing juries in thousands of courtrooms throughout California every day is the lack of participation. In 1996, the Blue Ribbon Commission on Jury Service Improvement convened by the Judicial Council of California concluded that "the jury system is on the brink of collapse."[22] The American Tort Reform Association cited the avoidance of jury service by Californians as a serious problem, in which "barely a quarter of those summoned for jury duty actually serve."[23] The consequence of this reluctance to serve, the association pointed out, is that "the system imposes a disproportionate share of the jury service burden on those willing to serve, which means these good citizens must serve more often."[24] The Judicial Council of California's Blue Ribbon Commission on Jury Service Improvement did make 29 recommendations to remedy problems associated with the jury process, the most significant being the following:

• Use National Change of Address System to update jury source lists to reduce the problem of undeliverable summonses.
• Place a hold on driver's license renewals of persons who fail to respond to jury summonses.
• Create child care programs for jurors who have children in their care.
• Adopt the "one-day, one-trial" system.
• Implement a system requiring prospective jurors to call a standby telephone number the day before their reporting date to learn if they must report as scheduled.
• Increase juror fees to $40 for each day after the first day and to $50 after the 13th day.
• Require employers to pay employees for at least three days of jury service, and provide tax credits to employers who voluntarily pay employees who are absent for more than three days because of jury service.

Since the Blue Ribbon Commission report, a number of the commission's recommendations have been implemented, with most requiring enactment by the state legislature. Of the recommendations listed above, only the National Change of Address System; the "one-day, one-trial" system, and the telephone standby system are now widely used in California courts.

Aside from the regular juries of the California superior courts, the California constitution requires each county to impanel a grand jury every year. Selected by superior court judges, the **county grand jury**■ serves for a term of one year, with the possibility for extensions of service, and it has the responsibility of "inquiring into public offenses committed or triable within the

■ **County Grand Jury:** In California, a jury that investigates public offenses that were committed or are triable within the county.

SIGNIFICANCE: *The grand jury system has been in existence in California since the first state constitution was adopted but was only given the specific task of indictment. Over the years, the state legislature has expanded the duties of the grand jury, including both civil as well as criminal issues.*

county, and may present them to the court by indictment" upon a finding of sufficient evidence. Because of the time and effort required by this process, the grand jury is rarely used to bring an indictment, with most California courts choosing instead to employ preliminary hearings to determine if sufficient evidence exists for a trial. The California grand jury is required, based on provisions of California law, to make an annual examination of the operations, accounts, and records of the county government and special districts within the county and to inquire about the conditions and management of state prisons within the county. The grand jury is also bound to investigate complaints from residents of the county regarding the performance of local government officials or employees. Government agencies that are the target of a grand jury investigation and report are required by law to respond to

specific recommendations by the grand jury. The grand jury has no enforcement power, however, and government agencies are under no legal obligation to implement these recommendations.[25] Over the years, the grand jury has been criticized for being unrepresentative of the community at large, shrouded in secrecy because of the rules governing investigations, and overly influenced by the county district attorney's office.

Each year, hundreds of reports are issued by grand juries in California's 58 counties that contain information vital to improving the performance of local government. In El Dorado County, for example, the grand jury found that the county mental health department failed to spend funds earmarked for a program to help children who have severe emotional problems remain with their families.[26]

The California Jury System

20.3 Characterize the role and responsibilities of trial juries and county grand juries in the state of California.

PRACTICE QUIZ: UNDERSTAND AND APPLY

1. How much does the state of California pay jurors, starting on the second day of service, who are not government employees?
   a. $100 per day
   b. $10 per hour and transportation costs
   c. $15 per day and transportation costs
   d. nothing; jury duty is considered a civic obligation

2. Why would the California District Attorneys Association call on the state legislature to abolish the unanimous verdict and permit juries to convict or acquit whenever 10 of 12 jurors agree?
   a. to lower the cost of convicting the accused
   b. to avoid acquittals due to factors other than the review of evidence
   c. to empower the role of judges to decide guilt or innocence
   d. to begin the process of creating a pool of professional jurors

3. Why would a district attorney not want to use the county grand jury to bring an indictment against someone?
   a. The security measures in the county grand jury chambers are usually not adequate.

   b. The county grand juries tend to attract a lot of media attention.
   c. The process of utilizing a county grand jury requires a good deal of time and effort.
   d. The costs of indictment by grand juries are usually high.

ANALYZE

1. Extensive media exposure of a court trial could have what negative and positive consequences for a juror?

2. What role do county grand juries serve in the judicial system?

IDENTIFY THE CONCEPT THAT DOESN'T BELONG

   a. Voir dire
   b. Selection process
   c. "Triple Flip"
   d. Blue Ribbon Commission
   e. $15-per-day rate

Resource Center
• Glossary
• Vocabulary Example
• Connect the Link

Trends in the California Judicial System

20.4 Identify major trends in the California judicial system.

(pages 626–627)

One of the best ways to appreciate trends in the California judicial system is to focus on the composition and decisions of the California supreme court. More than any one type of court in California, the state's supreme court is in a position to influence not only decisions in lower courts, through the establishment of precedents, but also actions of the legislative and executive branches of government, through the power to interpret California law.

California Supreme Court Chief Justice Ronald George surprised many Californians—particularly among the state's legal professionals—when he announced his retirement, choosing to not seek what most thought would be an almost guaranteed reelection to another 12-year term on the California high court in November, 2010. His retirement ended a 14-year legacy as chief justice marked by hundreds of legal opinions, most noticeably his rulings on same-sex marriages, and the stewardship of major administrative reforms in the state legal system. Chief Justice George was one of many judicial appointments made by Republican governors George Deukmejian and Pete Wilson that guaranteed a conservative majority on the California supreme court that exists to this day. There are currently six registered Republicans and one Democrat on the court. Although almost all owe their positions to appointments by Republicans, the court has exercised a moderate judicial philosophy, taking a pro–"law and order" stance while moving to the center on many social issues. Governor Arnold Schwarzenegger apparently wanted to maintain this moderate direction when he replaced the rather conservative justice Janice Rogers Brown, who became a federal appellate judge, with Carol A. Corrigan, a moderate Republican. Schwarzenegger continued this approach to appointing moderate justices when he selected Tani Cantil-Sakuye, a California court of appeals justice, to replace retiring Chief Justice George. Unanimously approved by the California Commission on Judicial Appointments, which included Chief Justice George, former Attorney General Jerry Brown, and a veteran appeals court justice, Cantil-Sakauye was later overwhelming confirmed by the voters in the 2010 midterm election. She will be the first Filipina-American women to serve on the California high court and will give the seven-member court a majority of four women for the first time in its history.

The current California supreme court has generally taken moderately conservative positions, routinely upholding death penalty convictions even when, for example, the cases involved coerced confessions. In 2008, this court surprised most Californians as well as legal scholars and journalists from across the country when it overturned the ban on gay marriage after invalidating same-sex marriages performed by the city of San Francisco four years earlier. The California supreme court's sweeping 4–3 ruling went well beyond same-sex marriage, banning any law that discriminates on the basis of sexual orientation. In the majority opinion of the court, the normally moderate-conservative Chief Justice George wrote: "An individual's sexual orientation—like a person's race or gender—does not constitute a legitimate basis upon which to deny or withhold legal rights." California became the first state to take such a broad judicial position in favor of same-sex marriages. Yet, when faced with the decision to extend that legal interpretation to Proposition 8, the initiative that placed a state constitutional ban on same-sex marriages, the court returned to its conservative legal roots. In its 6–1 ruling, the California state supreme court found the constitutional amendment valid in restricting the word "marriage" to opposite-sex couples, but suggested that same-sex couples were granted all other rights of married couples through laws that established civil unions.[27] That decision was overturned by a U.S. Federal court ruling that Proposition 8 did indeed violate the due process and equal protection clauses of the U.S. Consitution.

In cases pitting the California business community against employees or consumers, the judicial scorecard suggests that the George court would, in most instances, go with the former. In 1996, the court allowed judges the discretion to waive the third strike when confronted with a third-time offender under the "three strikes" law, and it faced the wrath of California antiabortion advocates after a 4–3 ruling overturned a state law requiring parental consent for abortions performed on minors. The latter ruling was seen by many displeased, prominent Republicans as an extremely broad interpretation of the civil liberty protections provided by the state constitution.[28] The civil libertarian tendencies of the court were on display again in a 2004 case in which the court unanimously overturned the conviction of a 15-year-old student charged with violating the state's criminal threat statute after writing a poem about "dark themes."[29] The court has established a pattern of leaning toward the conservative position in interpreting the California constitution, state law, and lower court cases while refraining from absolute doctrines and leaving some room for more moderate interpretations of similar cases that may surface in the future.[30]

By 2009, the state supreme court seemed to tilt slightly toward a more liberal interpretation of the state constitution and state law. Against considerable anti–drunk driving public sentiment in the state that has supported sobriety checkpoints and harsher sentencing, the high court issued a ruling in 2009 that made challenging DUI breath analyzer tests much easier. In a 2010 case that angered state prosecutors, the court upheld a state law that granted death row inmates access to post-trial evidence from prosecutors who could help their appeals. One of the most widely publicized cases for the supreme court in 2010 involved a California Court of Appeals ruling preventing the California legislature or any other governmental body from passing laws limiting the amount of marijuana that can be grown for medical purposes. Following a trend that has largely affirmed the rights of medical marijuana users, the high court agreed that Proposition 215 did not set such limits and affirmed the lower court decision. However, Californians should not expect the court to stray too far from the moderate Republican ideological views, especially on law-and-order issues.

Although the entire budget for the judicial branch accounts for only about 2 percent of state revenue, Chief Justice George led the Judicial Council in initiating cost-saving measures that included the closure of all courts for one day per month and voluntary pay reductions among roughly 90 percent of judges and justices that were equivalent to pay cuts suffered by furloughed staff.[31]

Members of the Hare Krishna sect parade through Golden Gate Park. —*To what extent are their first amendment rights protected by the state constitution and by court rulings?*

Trends in the California Judicial System

20.4   **Identify major trends in the California judicial system.**

PRACTICE QUIZ: UNDERSTAND AND APPLY

1. More than any one type of court in California, the state's supreme court is in a position to
   a. overrule the legal decisions of the U.S. Supreme Court when they conflict with law.
   b. influence not only decisions in lower courts through the establishment of precedents, but also actions of the state legislature and executive branch of government.
   c. establish legal guidelines for the entire country.
   d. select judges and justices for the California court system.

2. Governor Arnold Schwarzenegger's decision to replace outgoing California Supreme Court Justice Janice Brown with Carol A. Corrigan was motivated by
   a. his desire to maintain the moderate judicial direction of the court.
   b. his desire to maintain the highly conservative orientation of the court.
   c. pressure from the Republican party.
   d. the election of plural executive branch members.

3. What would be the best reason for considering the California Supreme Court, as led by Chief Justice Ronald M. George, to be moderately conservative?
   a. overturning of a ban on gay marriage
   b. overturning of a state law requiring parental support for abortions on minors
   c. preventing a terminally ill patient from being removed from life support
   d. routinely upholding death penalty convictions

ANALYZE

1. Why are California supreme court decisions a harbinger of trends in the state judiciary in general?

2. How and why has decision making in the California supreme court shifted over the past 50 years?

IDENTIFY THE CONCEPT THAT DOESN'T BELONG

a. "One-day, one trial"
b. Alternative dispute resolution
c. Proposition 36
d. Court unification
e. The Brown Act

20.4

Conclusion

nlike most branches of California state government, reform within the judicial system has been underway for a while now and has resulted in mostly positive outcomes. The court unification process (begun in 1998), which eliminated the municipal courts, has not generated many complaints or disparaging press reports, and it has apparently streamlined the California court system. Given the difficult task of implementing Proposition 36, the mandated drug diversion program, the court system does at least have a program up and running to the benefit of numerous offenders. The State Judicial Council's promotion of alternative dispute resolution resources remains popular among segments of the public and has reduced the demands on a congested court system. The "one-day, one-trial" system as well as the slight increase in the fee paid to jurors have been major steps toward improving the jury system and supporting the democratic character of the state's legal process.

Certain problematic aspects of the California judicial system remain despite the best intentions of California judicial officers and administrators. Any reform effort will have difficulty resolving and managing the dramatic increase over the last 20 years in the number of individuals who have entered the criminal side of the state judicial system. This increase has been partly due to the mandatory sentences imposed by Proposition 184—the "three strikes" law, which the California system of criminal justice will at some point either have to administer in a more resourceful manner or become even more insensitive to the negative consequences of this public policy. The high recidivism rate in California has also led to the burgeoning criminal caseload consuming the resources of the judicial system as well as scarce state tax dollars, which must be a major concern of court officials who oversee an almost endless cycle of repeat offenders. "Drug court" is certainly one response to this multi-dimensional dilemma that continues to be a social problem beyond the resources and mission of the judicial system.

The conflicting California Supreme Court decisions regarding the issue of same-sex marriages has illustrated the difficulty the California Supreme Court will face in reconciling initiatives approved by the voters and the interpretation of civil liberty protections in the state and U.S. constitutions. In fact, it is likely that the state high court will be forced to once again address Proposition 8, the ban on same-sex marriage, in yet another form or venue even though this law has reached the federal judicial system. Californians can only hope that the highest judicial body in the state will address same-sex marriages and similar legal issues with judicial wisdom that will be in the best interests of the state over the long term.

KEY CONCEPT MAP   How do the courts enforce California state laws and official guidelines?

California State Constitution

The California constitution establishes and describes the legislative and statewide offices, powers, structure, and function of California government. Amendments can be proposed by the state legislature but must be approved by the voters through a compulsory referendum or enacted by the voters using the initiative process.

In November 2008, California's supreme court ruled that Proposition 8, a ballot initiative and constitutional amendment banning same-sex marriage, and approved by the voters, was constitutionally valid. Currently being reviewed in federal district court, few doubt that this law will one day end up before the U.S. Supreme Court.

Critical Thinking Questions

How should the courts rule on laws that are overwhelmingly approved by voters and appear to be constitutionally valid, but which are based on false assumptions? Is it a judge's duty to uphold the law as it is written or to make decisions based on his or her own analysis of the facts of a case?

Legislative Statutes

The state legislature is generally responsible for enacting laws representing major areas related to the penal, education, and fish and game codes. California voters can also enact laws by using the initiative process.

In *People* v. *Kelly*, the California supreme court ruled that a state law (SB 420) permitting local governments to limit the amount of marijuana an individual can possess for medical use was unconstitutional because it modified aspects of a proposition that was not originally approved by California voters.

Critical Thinking Questions

Are there any circumstances under which a state resident might be justified in disobeying a state law? If so, what are they?

Regulations

The state legislature may delegate quasi-legislative powers to a state agency, allowing that agency to establish certain regulations. For example, the Building Standards Commission is authorized to adopt, approve, and implement California building codes.

In 2006, the U.S. 9th Circuit Court of Appeals issued an injunction that halted executions by the California Department of Corrections (CDC) on the grounds that the CDC's regulations for administering lethal injections could potentially constitute cruel and unusual punishment. Later, when the CDC rewrote the regulations for the lethal injection process in 2010, the California Office of Administrative Law rejected them, citing numerous legal issues and the failure to meet state regulatory standards.

Critical Thinking Questions

What if the state legislature could not delegate quasi-legislative powers to state agencies? How would this impact the way state agencies function? What can legislators and bureaucrats do to avoid the development and adoption of regulations that most residents and the courts would later find undesirable?

Municipal Ordinances

An ordinance is a local law. The California Constitution allows local governments to make and enforce ordinances within their legal jurisdictions as long as the ordinances do not conflict with state or federal laws.

In *O'Connell* v. *Stockton*, the California supreme court ruled that it was illegal for the city of Stockton to seize automobiles from motorists not convicted of any crime. Until 2007, a city ordinance had allowed the police to take possession of an individual's vehicle, if he or she was arrested for soliciting prostitutes or attempting to buy illicit drugs while

Critical Thinking Questions

How might a local government official argue for upholding local ordinances over state regulations and statutes? Are local legislators or state legislators in a better position to write the laws that affect the residents of a city or community? Why?

Court Orders

Court orders are legal decisions made by a court that command or direct something to be done (or not done). Court orders can range from addressing very personal matters, such as a restraining order, to ordering a government agency to perform a function.

In 2001, a class action lawsuit, *Plata* v. *Schwarzenegger*, was brought against the state of California over the quality of medical care in the state's 33 prisons. The state settled the suit but failed to comply with the conditions of the settlement, and the court ordered the California prison system medical facilities to be placed into receivership, an arrangement that strips state government authority and transfers responsibility over to the court-appointed receiver.

Critical Thinking Questions

Under what circumstances should judges be allowed to issue court orders? What if state agencies fail to comply with court orders? Who is charged with enforcing/upholding judges' decisions in those cases?

California has always been torn by conflicting perceptions of the state legal system. Over the years, many attempts to impose "tough on crime" provisions through the initiative process and legislative action have been diluted through legal interpretation. The California supreme court has often enforced constitutional provisions for civil liberties over popular sentiment. —*In what ways does the California legal system mirror the values and beliefs of the average Californian? Does the California court system allow for the incorporation of contemporary attitudes and norms into the judicial process? If so, how? If not, why not?*

Review of Key Objectives

The California Court System

20.1 Outline the structure of the California judicial system.

(pages 614–617)

The California court system is the largest in the nation, with more than 2,000 judicial officers and 18,000 court employees who handle approximately 9 million cases each year. The court system is very similar to the pyramid-like structure of the federal court system, with superior or trial courts spread throughout California's 58 counties at the base, six appellate court districts in the middle, and one state supreme court at the top.

KEY TERMS

Superior Courts 614
Proposition 220 614
Plea Bargain 614
Drug Court 614
Court of Appeals 615
Supreme Court 615
Alternative Dispute
  Resolution (ADR) 615
Judicial Council 616

CRITICAL THINKING QUESTIONS

1. What are the roles and responsibilities of the three levels of the California court system?
2. What has the California Judicial Council done to improve the efficiency of its court system?

INTERNET RESOURCES

The Judicial Council of California website at http://www.courtinfo.ca.gov/ provides court calendars, court opinions, and detailed information on California's supreme court and courts of appeals.

Your Public Law Library (http://www.publiclawlibrary.org/) is compiled by law librarians from various California county law libraries.

Find educational materials and forms for basic legal processes, such as small claims court and buying a house, at the State Bar of California: Public Services Web site at http://www.calbar.ca.gov/state/calbar/calbar_home_generic.jsp?sCategoryPath=/Home/Public%20Services.

ADDITIONAL READING

Abramson, Leslie. *The Defense Is Ready: Life in the Trenches of Criminal Law.* New York: Simon and Schuster, 1997.

Judicial Council of California. *A Visitor's Guide to the California Supreme Court.* San Francisco: Judicial Council of California, 2004.

Rottman, David B. *Trust and Confidence in the California Courts: A Survey of the Public and Attorneys.* Williamsburg, VA: National Center for State Courts, 2005.

The Elements of California Law

20.2 Evaluate the processes involved in the execution of California civil and criminal law.

(pages 618–623)

The work of the California judicial system is largely predicated on interpreting California law, codes, regulations, and ordinances broadly classified as either civil or criminal law. California civil law encompasses a wide variety of topics, including general civil, family, juvenile, landlord-tenant, probate, and small claims law. In the California Penal Code, criminal offenses are divided into two major categories: felonies and misdemeanors. Depending on the seriousness of the crime, a person may be sentenced to execution, imprisonment in the state prison or in a county jail, and/or fined.

KEY TERMS

Proposition 184 618
Civil Law 619
Tort Law 619
Probate Law 619
Criminal Law 620
California Penal
  Code 620
Felonies 620
Misdemeanors 620
Infractions 620
Corpus Delicti 620
Determinate
  Sentence 620
District Attorney 621
Recidivism Rate 622
Proposition 36 622

CRITICAL THINKING QUESTIONS

1. What are the unique qualities of California's laws and how they are administered?
2. If you could change one feature of California law, what would it be? What sort of short- and long-term consequences would this change have?

INTERNET RESOURCES

California Law (http://www.leginfo.ca.gov/calaw.html) presents information on the 29 codes currently in effect.

The California Department of Corrections and Rehabilitation (http://www.cdcr.ca.gov/) presents information about the incarcerated, including trends, history, and how recently sentenced felons and juveniles are evaluated for placement.

ADDITIONAL READING

Payton, George T. *Concepts of California Criminal Law.* San Jose, CA: Criminal Justice Services, 1995.

The California Jury System

20.3 Characterize the role and responsibilities of trial juries and county grand juries in the state of California.

(pages 624–625)

In California, as in most states, the jury is a fundamental part of the legal system, ideally guaranteeing fairness in the decision about the guilt or innocence of the accused in a court trial. Mandated by the California constitution, county grand juries are special legal bodies composed of local residents that are charged with examining public offenses bringing indictments, and investigating the conduct of local government.

KEY TERMS

Voir Dire 624
County Grand Jury 624

CRITICAL THINKING QUESTIONS

1. What are the differences in the role of trial juries and county grand juries in the judicial system?
2. What effect would paid professional jurors have on the legal process in California? What problems would it solve, and what problems would it create? Do you think most Californians would approve of this idea?

INTERNET RESOURCES

The Judicial Council is the policymaking body of the California courts, the largest court system in the nation. Under the leadership of the chief justice and in accordance with the California constitution, the council is responsible for ensuring the consistent, independent, impartial, and accessible administration of justice. Information can be found at http://www.courtinfo.ca.gov/jc/

ADDITIONAL READING

Delsohn, Gary. *The Prosecutors: A Year in the Life of a District Attorney's Office.* New York: Dutton, 2003.
Friedman, Lawrence, and Robert Percival. *Roots of Justice: Crime and Punishment in Alameda County California, 1870–1910.* Chapel Hill: University of North Carolina Press, 1981.
Kelso, J. Clark. "Final Report of the Blue Ribbon Commission on Jury System Improvement." *Hastings Law Journal* (July/August, 1996).

Trends in the California Judicial System

20.4 Identify major trends in the California judicial system.

(pages 626–627)

One of the best ways to appreciate trends in the California judicial system is to focus on the composition and decisions of the California supreme court. More than any one type of court in California, the supreme court is in a position to influence the actions of the legislative and executive branches of government through the power to interpret California law. The court has established a pattern of leaning toward the conservative position in interpreting the California constitution, state law, and lower court cases while refraining from absolute doctrines and leaving some room for more moderate interpretations of similar cases that may surface in the future.

CRITICAL THINKING QUESTIONS

1. What are the most important trends in the California judicial system?
2. What factors encourage and discourage shifts in the ideological perspective of the court system?

INTERNET RESOURCES

Information in the Commission on Judicial Performance can be found at http://cjp.ca.gov/. This independent state agency is responsible for investigating complaints of judicial misconduct and incapacity and for disciplining judges.

The Law and Policy Institutions Guide (http://www.lpig.org/) serves as a comprehensive repository of legal resources, law articles, and legal practice information as well as legislative and judicial resources for U.S. and international legal professionals.

Information on the Supreme Court of California, the state's highest court, can be found at http://www.courtinfo.ca.gov/courts/supreme/. The court conducts regular sessions in San Francisco, Los Angeles, and Sacramento and may also hold special sessions elsewhere.

ADDITIONAL READING

Grodin, Joseph R. *In Pursuit of Justice: Reflections of a State Supreme Court Justice.* Berkeley: University of California Press, 1989.
Sipes, Larry L. *Committed to Justice: The Rise of Judicial Administration in California.* San Francisco: California Administrative Office of the Courts, 2002.
Stolz, Preble. *Judging Judges: The Investigation of Rose Bird and the California Supreme Court.* New York: Free Press, 1981.

Chapter Review   Test Your Knowledge

1. The California Penal Code covers
   a. the rules and regulations for the California prison system.
   b. how police departments must proceed in an arrest.
   c. a long list of crimes that are punishable by state law.
   d. procedures during a court trial.

2. The entry point for the enforcement of California law and the settlement of conflict or disagreements is the
   a. California superior courts.
   b. California municipal courts.
   c. California Federal District courts.
   d. California district courts.

3. Efforts to lessen major increases in the caseload of California courts has caused the use of
   a. habeas corpus procedures.
   b. search and seizure law.
   c. plea bargains.
   d. police powers.

4. The parties to a small claims case are
   a. not allowed to represent themselves.
   b. not allowed representation by an attorney in court.
   c. allowed to conduct lengthy cross examinations.
   d. not allowed to mention their claim in court.

5. Which type of case has become the biggest part of superior courts' civil workload?
   a. family matters
   b. civil liberties cases
   c. environmental cases
   d. contract disputes

6. The middle tier of the California court system is the
   a. six appellate court districts.
   b. superior courts.
   c. Judicial Council of California.
   d. state supreme court.

7. How does the appellate process in the California court of appeals begin?
   a. It begins with a review of the appellate case by the California court of appeals.
   b. It begins with the filing of the notice of appeal and written arguments, known as briefs, from both sides of the case.
   c. It begins with the losing side to a case declaring defeat.
   d. It begins with the filing of a memorandum of understanding between the appellate court and the court of origin.

8. Appeals in death penalty cases in California
   a. are not allowed.
   b. are made in one of the state's six appellate district courts.
   c. go straight to the U.S. Supreme Court.
   d. go straight to the state supreme court.

9. In what types of cases does the state supreme court have original jurisdiction?
   a. cases involving writs of mandamus, writs of certiorari, prohibitions, and habeas corpus
   b. cases involving the federal government
   c. cases where the federal and state courts clash
   d. case involving felonies asand misdemeanors

10. In deciding a case, how many state supreme court justices must agree on the final decision?
    a. at least five of the nine state supreme court justices must agree
    b. at least two of the five state supreme court justices must agree
    c. at least four of the seven state supreme court justices must agree
    d. all decisions must be unanimous

11. How are superior court vacancies filled?
    a. through appointment by the governor or elections
    b. through appointment by the state legislature or referendum
    c. through judicial seniority
    d. by the state's top legal scholars

12. What is the Judicial Council?
    a. the final court of review in California
    b. the governing body of the California courts
    c. the governing body of all courts in the United States
    d. a council of judges, justices, and lawyers that writes case law

13. One reason for the rise of alternative dispute resolution is
    a. people's lack of faith in the courts.
    b. the growing partisanship of judges.
    c. the rising delays and cost of the formal legal process.
    d. a shortage of attorneys to handle cases.

14. What is Proposition 184?
    a. the family leave law
    b. the free-tuition law
    c. the same-sex marriage law
    d. the "three strikes" law

15. Which of the following has been a source of concern regarding California's general civil law over the past 30 years?
    a. the litigation explosion
    b. same-sex marriage
    c. the right of habeas corpus
    d. the cost of a legal defense

16. Rapid change to the California legal system is often the result of
    a. action taken by the state legislature.
    b. decisions made by the Judicial Council.
    c. decrees from the governor's office.
    d. initiatives and propositions passed by the voters.

17. In the California Penal Code, offenses are divided into what two major categories?
    a. probate and family law
    b. felonies and misdemeanors
    c. crimes and nonoffensive laws
    d. search warrants and rulings

18. The length of jury service in California is based on what type of obligation during a 12-month period?
    a. a "one-day or one-trial" jury service
    b. the 12-month on-call provision
    c. a "one week or two-trial" jury service
    d. jury service until trial completion

19. Once a court case begins, the jury selection process known as voir dire allows
   a. a judge to forbid the use of any information that may be of a biased nature
   b. the prosecution to introduce evidence that was not present at the pre-trial hearing.
   c. the defense and prosecution to interview potential jurors and ask the judge to excuse certain jurors.
   d. member of the jury to state why they are interested in serving as a juror.

20. What legal body is required, based on provisions of the California Penal Code, to make an annual examination of the operations, accounts, and records of county government and special districts within a county and to inquire into the conditions and management of state prisons within the county?
   a. the California supreme court
   b. the California grand juries
   c. the California superior courts
   d. the attorney general's office

mypoliscilab Exercises

Apply what you learned in this chapter on **MyPoliSciLab.**

Read on mypoliscilab.com

eText: Chapter 20

Study and **Review** on mypoliscilab.com

Pre-Test
Post-Test
Chapter Exam
Flashcards

Watch on mypoliscilab.com

Video: Pot Possession Now Like Speeding Ticket

Explore on mypoliscilab.com

Comparative: Comparing Judicial Systems

CHAPTER 2

Local Government in California

KEY OBJECTIVES

After completing this chapter, you should be prepared to:

21.1 Trace the historical development of county governments in California.

21.2 Identify the offices and agencies that make up county government in California.

21.3 Characterize the three forms of municipal governments and summarize the procedures adopted by city councils.

21.4 List the standard departments and agencies that make up municipal bureaucracies.

21.5 Identify the purposes of special districts, and explain how they fulfill their goals.

Local governments exist in a precarious position, overshadowed by the larger scope and issues of state and federal governments, but on the frontline during the most challenging situations governments can face. Just about all Californians depend on local governments to provide them with the basic necessities of daily life—especially during national emergencies. Natural disasters such as Hurricane Katrina in 2005 put the functions and failings of local government in the limelight. Matched by the near-total breakdown of federal emergency systems, local governments in the Gulf Region during the hurricane suffered from inadequate emergency resources, insufficient numbers of trained emergency personnel, and technical failures. To their credit, municipal governments surrounding the Gulf provided critical assistance to the victims of this emergency. The devastating effects of Hurricane Katrina should be a reminder of the crucial responsibilities that local governments have in protecting Americans against unexpected disasters.

The residents of California are particularly susceptible to various types of natural disasters, such as floods, wildfires,

> **Will the challenges of the current era cause local governments in California to assume greater civic responsibilities?**

landslides, and of course earthquakes. Since 1976, the Federal Emergency Management Agency (FEMA) has made over 72 major disaster declarations in California, the second-highest number after Texas. All local governments are mandated by state law to have local emergency procedures and agencies prepared to respond in the event of a major emergency. Local governments in California typically have an Office of Emergency Services (OES) as the coordinating agency, which will activate an Emergency Operations Center (EOC) at the time of a major emergency. The EOC directs a local Emergency Medical Service Agency and the Community Emergency Response Team (CERT). Ideally, local residents would be especially concerned about the level of preparedness among these local agencies as well as their ability to withstand a major calamity. In reality, most Californians are just too consumed with their daily routines to worry about unpredictable, catastrophic events. That responsibility unquestionably falls to local government, and Californians can only hope that these institutions are up to the task.[1]

Resource Center
• Glossary
• Vocabulary Example
• Connect the Link

■ **Home Rule:** A county's right to tailor its local charter to its own needs and interests.

SIGNIFICANCE: *Over the years, many of the differences between charter and noncharter cities have disappeared. The state legislature has passed laws amending the general law on cities, granting California municipalities more power, while the power of a charter city has been restricted by court decisions.*

California County Government

21.1 Trace the historical development of county governments in California.

(pages 636–639)

Throughout European history, counties were the principal administrative unit used by those in power to govern wide areas, most noticeably where large cities or towns were spread far apart. This was also true during the American colonial period, when the superiority of the county governing unit prevailed. Most county officials were appointed by the colonial or state governor, and the most important administrative duties for a region were performed by county government. As the nation grew, two models of county government emerged that to some extent remain today. The weaker model of county authority developed in the American Northeast, where cities and towns were more established and closer together, diminishing the need for a strong county government. The larger cities and towns of this region increasingly began to assume duties and services formerly conducted by the county government. In the south and on the western frontier, the strong county model continued to be important in taming expansive wilderness regions where established settlements were sparse. The democratization of the American experience served to empower the strong county model as residents of the county gradually chose to elect county officials, but that model set counties on a collision course with the authority of state government.[2]

Historical Roots of California's Counties

The formation of counties was vital to the growth and administration of early California, which was an unusually large state with a relatively small population and dispersed settlements during its first 50 to 75 years. The importance of county government was demonstrated by the conflicts that arose among county residents over where the county "seat," or government offices, would be located. Without the benefit of modern transportation or roads, the distances between settlements and centers of commerce and these county seats often made the conduct of official business difficult. In the effort to spread government authority and favor other, less scrupulous interests, the early California legislature simplified the process of establishing new counties. The formation of counties was entirely up to the state legislature, which often complied with the requests of wealthy individuals or large groups of settlers without much investigation or scrutiny. Throughout California history, counties

have been viewed in varying degrees by the state government as "legal subdivisions of the state."

Before a number of reform efforts, county government in California was susceptible to corrupting influences, and it was not uncommon for counties to experience periods of virtual lawlessness. Between 1860 and 1890, California historical records are full of major disputes and incidents of crime either involving issues of county governance or necessitating the intervention of county officials. There are reports of gun battles among residents of Lassen and Plumas counties over disputed territory. One San Diego sheriff and his appointed deputies, acting as tax collectors, retained portions of all the taxes collected. The level of corruption became so widespread in Klamath County that the county was abolished in 1875 and its territory divided among four different counties.[3]

Gradually, the state government brought some order to the administration of California counties. Beginning in 1879 with the first major revision of the California constitution and a series of state legislative acts, a framework was created to bring uniformity to all the state's counties. County governments were given police powers and required to designate a grand jury, a superior court, justices of the peace, a superintendent of schools, a board of education, a board of equalization, a treasurer, a recorder, a tax collector, a license collector, an assessor, an auditor, a public administrator, and constables.[4]

The California Progressives built on this reformist trend by advocating for the passage of a state constitutional amendment that gave California counties the option of **home rule**■ charter authority, making California the first state in the nation to grant county residents the authority to tailor their local county charters to the needs and interests of their respective counties. Those counties that did not choose to embrace home rule and write county charters established **general law**■, a basic template for county government that prescribes duties, obligations, and offices, although scholars and government officials have noted few practical differences in government organization between general law and home rule charter counties. After a rash of home rule charter adoptions by California counties (beginning with Los Angeles County), the drafting of these charters in California slowed dramatically and eventually stopped at 13 of the state's 58 counties, including seven of the largest. Home rule charters are particularly useful to highly populated counties that require flexibility and political power in responding to problems or issues that smaller counties do not usually encounter. Initially, many of the home rule charter counties used this flexibility to incorporate the governmental reforms of the Progressive Era into county government, often establishing a civil service system for hiring employees and managing personnel issues. The city and county government of San Francisco would emerge as a unique form of home rule charter that combined the two units into a single, consolidated government with an 11-member board of supervisors.[5]

■ **General Law:** A basic template that lists the duties, obligations, offices, and structure of county government.

SIGNIFICANCE: *The general law for counties is much more restrictive than the general law for cities. Cities have greater revenue-generating authority.*

■ **County Board of Supervisors:** The group responsible for implementing the provisions of a county's charter.

EXAMPLE: *Before the introduction of a board of supervisors, counties were administered by a court of sessions that included a county judge and two justices of the peace.*

County Board of Supervisors

With the exception of the 13 home rule charter counties, the governmental structure of California counties is largely determined by the California constitution and the California Government Code. The execution of these laws is overseen by a **county board of supervisors■**, which is also prescribed by government code. Anyone interested in becoming a member of the board of supervisors must be a registered voter residing in the county district and must run as a nonpartisan candidate for election. The board of supervisors, whose members serve four-year terms of office, exercises both legislative and executive power, and in a number of instances, it also has quasi-judicial authority. Legislative power is based on the ability to pass, by a simple majority of the board, resolutions, board orders, and county ordinances. County ordinances are the equivalent of statutes or laws passed by the state legislature and can be used by the board of supervisors to regulate a wide range of actions and behaviors as long as the ordinances do not conflict with state law. There are different types of ordinances: Urgency ordinances are intended for the immediate protection of the public in matters of health, safety, and civility, and statutory ordinances address procedural or common affairs. This lawmaking power is especially important as the means of proposing revenue-raising sources, such as taxes, assessments, and fees. The board of supervisors can propose these levies, but voters within the county must approve them.

The primary executive responsibility of the board of supervisors is to oversee most county departments and programs. The word *oversee* in this context is almost literal, because the board of supervisors is prohibited from directing or controlling

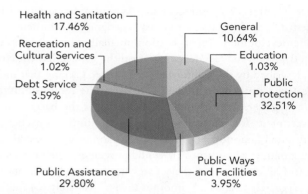

FIGURE 21.1 ▪ Breakdown of California County Expenditures

Counties Annual Report for the fiscal year (FY) ended June 30, 2008.

Health and Sanitation — 17.46%
Recreation and Cultural Services — 1.02%
Debt Service — 3.59%
General — 10.64%
Education — 1.03%
Public Protection — 32.51%
Public Assistance — 29.80%
Public Ways and Facilities — 3.95%

SOURCE: *Counties Annual Report,* 98th edition. Fiscal Year 2007–2008 (Sacramento: California State Controller, August 18, 2009), Figure 16 (p. xii). Reprinted with permission of the California State Controller. http://www .sco.ca.gov/ard_locrep_counties.html

the day-to-day operations of a specific county department. Powers typically used in this oversight function involve requests for regular reports from department heads, approval of county ordinances and orders, development of county priorities, control of all county property, endorsement of the annual budget, and allocation of funds for specific expenditures (see Figure 21.1). Supervision of some elected county officers by the board of supervisors is limited by the dual accountability that these officers have to the board of supervisors and to the members of the statewide executive branch. For example, the county district attorney and sheriff are accountable to the attorney general on law enforcement matters and to the board of supervisors in areas related to the legal obligations of the county. The board does have the authority to establish a joint-powers agreement or joint-powers agency with another public agency or local government. Through joint-powers agreements, county governments provide a service or fulfill a need for one or more local governments. Such agreements often give the board of supervisors some leverage with municipal and other local governments that benefit from the county's economies of scale— for example, the use of the sheriff office's central, countywide dispatcher station by local municipal police departments. Common quasi-judicial powers of the board of supervisors are used to settle claims made against the county and to serve as an appellate body in department-level decisions involving land use and tax issues. A member of the board of supervisors will often facilitate intergovernmental relations by also serving as a member of various government commissions and boards. For example, air-quality management boards for the various regions throughout California usually mandate that counties within these districts be represented by at least one member of the board of supervisors.[6]

Los Angeles County Supervisor Mike Antonovich speaks out against the decision by the Los Angeles County Board of Supervisors to boycott Arizona in response to the new Arizona illegal immigration legislation. Antonovich called the boycott "irresponsible and stupid." —*How would this decision affect the county?*

■ **Municipal Advisory Councils (MACs):** A group formed by the citizens of unincorporated areas to provide representation in matters affecting their communities.

SIGNIFICANCE: *The County Board of Supervisors has the authority to decide whether the five to seven members of a MAC will be elected by the residents of an unincorporated area or appointed by the board.*

Unincorporated Communities and Contract Cities

There are communities within counties that are not incorporated as cities for various reasons—lack of political will or interest, a limited resource or tax base, geographic remoteness, or underdevelopment. Incorporation normally gives cities a certain degree of independence based on the general law for cities as prescribed by the California constitution. Lacking that independence, unincorporated areas become the responsibility of county governments based on state law. As the basic unit of government for unincorporated areas, counties are charged with providing most of the services to an unincorporated area that a municipal government would provide for the municipality. In California, one in every five state residents lives in an unincorporated area, which amounts to approximately 6.4 million people. San Francisco is the only county among the 58 in the state that does not have an unincorporated area. Unincorporated areas can be found in isolated mountain and desert regions, farming areas, suburban housing tracts, and inner-city areas, and they can vary widely in socioeconomic conditions.[7] State regulations mandate that county governments encourage the formation of **municipal advisory councils (MACs)**■, frequently elected by residents of unincorporated areas to furnish representation in matters affecting their communities. MACs have very limited governmental authority, and the residents of an unincorporated area are largely dependent on the county supervisor representing the district where the unincorporated areas are located to serve as an advocate for their interests on the board of supervisors. Administering these areas can be very difficult for county governments, which are already responsible for a variety of services to all residents and local governments within the county.

Many incorporated or independent cities across California are identified as **contract cities**■, which establish contracts with county government for major municipal services, principally in the areas that are normally assumed by municipal governments, such as police and fire protection, animal control, and public works. Since their inception in the 1960s, contract cities have grown dramatically in number. The contracted services provided to cities that may lack a strong tax base and facilities are often instrumental in helping these cities qualify for incorporation. In many instances, county governments welcome the opportunity to maximize their productivity and receive revenue for contract services that might otherwise go to fully independent municipal governments. The arrangements between county governments and contract cities have generated disputes over the costs that counties may charge for contracted services. Criticism of "contract city" arrangements have also come from incorporated municipal governments that do not have the benefit of contracting out services to county governments. Officials from incorporated city governments have objected to contract city agreements as an unfair use of county general tax revenues to subsidize incorporated cities. The state legislature has tried, with mixed results, to resolve such issues through guidelines, but the scramble by a long list of local and state governmental units for increasingly scarce tax revenues guarantees that the concept of contract cities will remain controversial. In the future, depending on political interests and the fortunes of local government, contract cities could develop into a popular idea that eliminates redundancy in the delivery of local services or fall by the wayside because of the fiscal difficulties of county governments.[8]

STUDENT profile

Some California students are gaining valuable work experience as interns and student workers for local governments. Though often not well publicized, such opportunities are available in many places, such as San Diego County, that actively seek students for student worker/internship programs, especially during the summer. While a civil engineering major at California Polytechnic State University, Alex Thornton was hired as a student worker for the Department of Public Works in Wastewater Management in 2005. When Alex began with the department, his knowledge of engineering was limited to the subjects and material from his freshman's academic curriculum. While working under the direct supervision of engineers and project managers, Alex gained experience in AutoCAD drafting as well as construction inspection and design that gave him knowledge beyond what he was learning in college.

The experience of working for the County of San Diego afforded Alex an inside view that students usually do not find in the classroom. "I have also learned that a successful engineering career goes hand-in-hand with excellent communication skills." He said "It is essential for an engineer to have the ability to impart technical information to the general public in a layperson's terms."

The general qualifications for student workers, such as Alex, working for the County of San Diego, are full-time student status and at least a 2.0 grade point average. Although not all internships are paid, the County of San Diego student workers can earn $9 to $12 per hour. The county of San Diego gave Alex the chance to think about his future. "I see myself continuing to work as a student worker for the County, and eventually joining DPW as a member of the full-time engineering staff."

SOURCE: Accessed at http://www.sdcounty.ca.gov/hr/student_worker_program.html; http://www.sdcounty.ca.gov/luegg/internships/testimonials.html

■ **Contract Cities:** Incorporated or independent cities that contract with counties for the provision of major municipal services.

SIGNIFICANCE: *The California Contract Cities Association has over 80 member cities, and although most are centered in Southern California, such as the cities of Compton and Malibu, member cities can be found in most regions of the state, including Elk Grove in the Sacramento area and the cities of Lafayette and Hercules in the San Francisco Bay area.*

California County Government

21.1 Trace the historical development of county governments in California.

PRACTICE QUIZ: UNDERSTAND AND APPLY

1. During the colonial period of American history, county governments
   a. were extremely weak and ineffective administrative units.
   b. performed the most important administrative duties.
   c. were not recognized as administrative units.
   d. were disliked by the colonists.

2. Early county government in California was
   a. relatively inactive.
   b. generally honest and efficient.
   c. nearly as influential as the state government.
   d. plagued by corruption and in some cases violence.

3. The original counties of California were considered to be "legal subdivisions of the state" as a result of their formation by which likely individual or body?
   a. the President of the United States
   b. the state comptroller
   c. the attorney general
   d. the state legislature

4. What would be the most likely reason for not incorporating a city?
   a. a variety of socioeconomic class differences
   b. a limited tax base
   c. the objections of the county sheriff
   d. the overdevelopment of local real estate

ANALYZE

1. Why would a county exercise the option of adopting a "home rule" charter? Why would a county decline to consider such an option?

2. What is the relationship of the county board of supervisors with county departments?

IDENTIFY THE CONCEPT THAT DOESN'T BELONG

   a. Home rule
   b. Board of Supervisors
   c. Unincorporated community
   d. Felonies
   e. Municipal advisory councils

Resource Center
• Glossary
• Vocabulary Example
• Connect the Link

■ **County Administrator:** The official responsible for providing the board of supervisors with reports and information and for managing the day-to-day operations of county government.

SIGNIFICANCE: *The county administrator is a relatively recent addition to executive-level county positions and usually requires an educational and professional background in public management or administration.*

County Bureaucracy

21.2 Identify the offices and agencies that make up county government in California.

(pages 640–643)

County governments are responsible for providing a variety of services to all county residents. Most of these services, performed by the sheriff, district attorney, and tax assessor, are mandated by the California constitution. Other services have been instituted in the absence of other local governmental authorities. According to a report by the County Supervisors Association in 1958, counties performed 22 basic functions in 1850. That number had grown to 167 in larger counties in 1909, and in 1958 counties were performing 900 separate functions.[9] The size and composition of the county bureaucracy varies from county to county, depending on geographic conditions, stages of development, and socioeconomic characteristics. However, a number of county officers and departments are common to nearly all counties because of the vital nature of the services they deliver. Figure 21.2 illustrates the components of the County of Los Angeles.

County Administrator

As far as the board of supervisors is concerned, the most important position in the county bureaucracy is probably the **county administrator**■. Known by various titles, the county administrator has a dual set of responsibilities. Half of these duties involve supplying the board of supervisors with reports and information to make critical decisions and determine policy. The annual county governmental budget is one of the most important items that is prepared by the county administrator and submitted to the board of supervisors for review and approval. This responsibility necessitates close interaction with other county officials who account for aspects of the county's financial health, including the auditor-controller, the treasurer, the tax collector, and the assessor. The other half of the county administrator's duties involve managing the day-to-day operations of county government, normally involving coordination of county department functions and providing administrative guidance. Any major initiative or action by a county department must ordinarily be approved by the county administrator, who needs to determine the countywide ramifications of the measure and its relevance to county policy and fiscal resources.

District Attorney

As a constitutionally mandated, elected county official, the district attorney (DA) is accountable to the state attorney general. The DA is the top law enforcement officer for the county and has wide latitude in deciding which laws will be enforced in the

county. The influence of the DA can be felt in all superior courts adjudicating misdemeanor as well as felony violations, beginning with the investigation, decision to indict, and prosecution. Interaction with the board of supervisors is limited, but the DA can influence the operations of county government as the legal adviser to the county grand jury, which regularly conducts investigations and issues reports regarding the performance of county government. Violations of certain county ordinances are prosecuted by the DA, and this tends to strengthen the authority of the board of supervisors, which passes those ordinances and relies on the force of law to exert authority over the county. The board of supervisors can in turn affect the work of the DA through its control over the county governmental budget and administrative functions.

Sheriff

The **sheriff**■ was one of the first elected county offices created by the first version of the California constitution, and it has undergone numerous alterations in duties and responsibilities. Between 1851 and 1868, for instance, the sheriff was responsible for tax collection in many counties.[10] In most counties today, the sheriff's chief duty is to enforce California state law and county ordinances, usually in areas outside of incorporated cities. In this law enforcement role, the sheriff, like the district attorney, is directly accountable to the state attorney general. The sheriff also works very closely with the county superior court system and supports many of the functions of the county government. In superior courts, the sheriff is considered an officer of the court, and deputy sheriffs provide security and courtroom assistance to judges as bailiffs. In support of local law enforcement agencies and the court system, the sheriffs of most counties operate the county jail, where almost all prisoners within the county are held either during trial or to serve short-term sentences. Interaction between the sheriff's department and the board of supervisors is based first and foremost on county budget allocations, including the salary and benefits of the sheriff. Many of the operations of the sheriff's department are financed by the county budget, and this allocation gives the board a certain amount of leverage. Various departments that are administered by the board of supervisors, such as the Probation Department, are closely associated with the operations of the sheriff's department, providing the board with additional leverage over the sheriff's most counties, the coroner's office is combined with the sheriff's department, supporting criminal investigations as well as attending to unidentified deaths.

Assessor

The **assessor**■ is another constitutionally elected county officer whose principal duty is to determine the value of property within the county. Important aspects of the assessor's obligations are making accurate annual property assessments and maintaining a wide range of records and information

■ **Sheriff:** The county officer whose chief duty is to enforce California state law and county ordinances, usually outside of incorporated cities.

EXAMPLE: *Margaret Queen Adams was the first woman deputy sheriff in the United States, deputized by the Sheriff of Los Angeles County in 1912.*

■ **Assessor:** The county officer whose principal duty is to determine the value of property within the county.

EXAMPLE: *During the early years of statehood, it was not uncommon for the assessor to have a wide variety of duties, often acting as ex officio superintendent of schools.*

FIGURE 21.2 ■ **Organizational Chart for the County of Los Angeles**

Several departments report directly to the Board of Supervisors or are headed by elected officials but work with the Chief Executive Office through the clusters. —*What one issue would cause the supervisors, sheriff, district attorney, assessor, and members of the grand jury to cooperate and what one issue would cause these officials to have difficulty working together?*

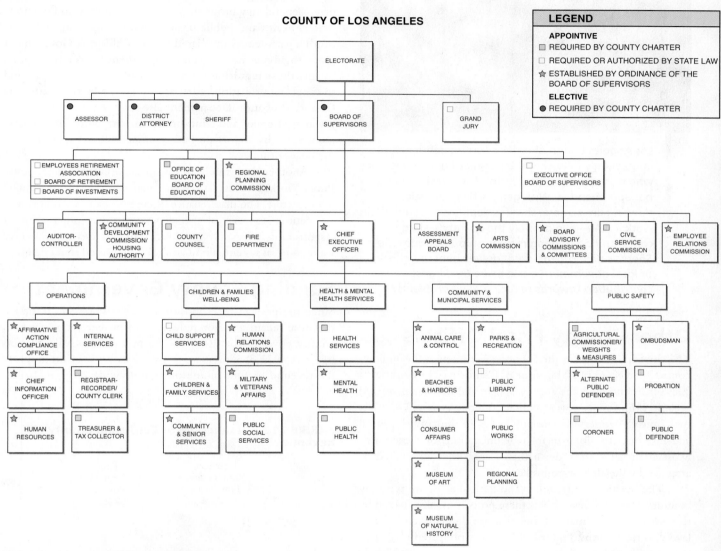

SOURCE: http://lacounty.info/departments.htm

related to property. These records are extremely important in setting property tax rates. Although the board of supervisors oversees the duties of the assessor, the state Board of Equalization has the statutory authority to establish standards for county property assessment and reviews the assessment procedures and records of the county assessor's office.

County Clerk

Except in a few counties where the post is appointed, the **county clerk**■ is an elected official responsible for the public records of the county, including birth and death certificates and marriage licenses. The county clerk is also empowered to perform civil marriage ceremonies. Besides supervising the maintenance of public records, the county clerk acts as the main clerk to the board of supervisors, conducting official clerical duties during board meetings and maintaining all board records. In most counties, the county clerk is responsible for registering voters and maintaining voter records as well as other election information and records.

■ **County Clerk:** The officer responsible for the public records of a county.

SIGNIFICANCE: *Besides overseeing the official records of the county, county clerk offices around the state tend to reflect the organizational requirements of the county rather than fulfilling a specific duty, and they frequently are consolidated with other offices.*

Los Angeles County sheriff's deputies debrief immediately following the pursuit of a gang member who was seen carrying a pistol. The individual was not apprehended. With gang activity statistics showing an increase, sheriff's deputies continue their work in LA's—and possibly the country's—largest concentration of gang membership. —*Besides the Sheriff's department, what department or agency of local government could make the largest contribution towards reducing gang problems?*

Other County Fiscal Officers

The chief accountant for the county government is the auditor-controller, elected in all but four of California's 58 counties.[11] This officer monitors the county budget and disbursements and organizes the county government accounting system. The auditor-controller supervises the processing of the county payroll and monitors the long-term debt obligations of the county. Most audits of county departments are either conducted or arranged by the auditor-controller.

The positions of treasurer and tax collector are typically combined, and whoever holds these posts is usually elected by the voters and has many duties that are determined by state laws and regulations. The tax collector is obligated to generate tax bills and conduct tax collection proceedings. The financial assets of the county and county investments are under the supervision of the treasurer, who also oversees all county bond obligations and is closely involved in county pension boards or systems.

Other Major County Departments

The county counsel is the chief civil legal officer of the county. This appointed officer renders legal services to the board of supervisors and county departments and also represents the county in most civil lawsuits. The County Health Services

Department, led by a director, attends to the health-related issues of the county. This department usually consumes a large part of the county budget, particularly in health care services to low-income residents of the county, but it also administers a wide range of offices and programs, including alcohol- and drug-dependency programs, detention facilities, and environmental health and public health services. The County Probation Department is mandated by the California Government Code to advise the courts on punishment for certain crimes, usually those requiring less than a year in the county jail, and to supervise probation restrictions imposed by the court. The County Probation Department also manages a wide range of juvenile offender and adult probation programs. This department is led by a chief probation officer, who is appointed by the board of supervisors.

Another department of major importance is the County Public Works Department, which manages the county's public infrastructure. The maintenance of county roadways is normally the central concern of this department, but other areas of responsibility, especially in unincorporated areas, can involve waste disposal systems, flood control systems, and street lighting.

Funding County Government

Since the passage of Proposition 13, the statewide initiative that resulted in a major reduction in property tax revenue, county governments have faced a precarious fiscal situation (see Figure 21.3). Counties were especially reliant on property tax revenue to fund numerous countywide services. In the

FIGURE 21.3 ■ **Breakdown of California County Revenues**

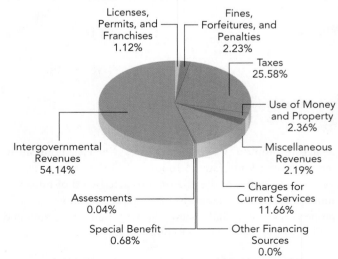

Licenses, Permits, and Franchises 1.12%
Fines, Forfeitures, and Penalties 2.23%
Taxes 25.58%
Use of Money and Property 2.36%
Miscellaneous Revenues 2.19%
Charges for Current Services 11.66%
Other Financing Sources 0.0%
Special Benefit 0.68%
Assessments 0.04%
Intergovernmental Revenues 54.14%

SOURCE: *Counties Annual Report,* 98th edition. Fiscal Year 2007–2008 (Sacramento: California State Controller, August 18, 2009), Figure 4 (p. vi). Reprinted with permission of the California State Controller. http://www.sco.ca.gov/ard_locrep_counties.html

aftermath of Proposition 13, control over the distribution of property tax revenue was transferred from local governments to the state, reducing revenue that remained in the county by approximately 39 percent. Unlike cities, counties have limited taxing power. In response to the property tax shortfall experienced by counties, the California state government directly funds many county health and welfare programs as well as specific categories of county responsibility, particularly in the areas of law enforcement, the courts, and transportation. County funding currently comes from five distinct sources: state government, property tax allocations, the federal government, businesses and corporate taxes, and a variety of other taxes, fees, and interest on deposits and investments.[12]

In 2009, the dramatic decline of the California economy resulted in a major reduction in government revenue and major cuts in funds and services to local government. County revenue was reduced even further, forcing the state government to tap into portions of revenue to local governments. In an attempt to close the state's 2009 $23 billion budget deficit, Governor Schwarzenegger approved a budget bill that borrowed $1.9 billion from local government property tax revenue, $2.05 billion in redevelopment agency property tax funds, and hundreds of millions of dollars in transportation funds.[13]

Along with the 2009 budget bill, the state legislature passed legislation that suspended the provisions of Proposition 1A. Passed in 2004, this proposition was intended to prevent state government from tapping into revenue earmarked for local government except in periods of fiscal emergency. The law does stipulate that only 8 percent of the property tax allocations to local government may be borrowed by state government and that the loan must be repaid within a three-year period, with interest included.[14]

Local governments complained vociferously about the impact of shifting local transportation revenue to the state, which in the case of San Joaquin County would mean a 50 percent reduction in the operating budget for public works. The timing of the decision by the state legislature and governor to borrow from local government was particularly inopportune as counties and cities were already being forced to make budget cuts amidst declining sales and property tax receipts. In response, local governments throughout California joined forces to qualify and pass Proposition 22 in the 2010 midterm elections. Proposition 22 is a constitutional amendment that restricts the legislature from using tax revenue dedicated by law for the funding of local governments. Whether state government will use its unitary powers to circumvent this amendment remains to be seen.[15]

County Bureaucracy

21.2 Identify the offices and agencies that make up county government in California.

PRACTICE QUIZ: UNDERSTAND AND APPLY

1. What elected government body has the statutory authority to establish standards for county property assessment?
   a. state senate
   b. California Bureau of Investigation
   c. state board of education
   d. state board of equalization

2. Many of the operations of the sheriff's department are financed by the county budget.
   a. true
   b. false

3. Which of the following government agencies would most likely have the statutory authority to establish standards for the county assessor?
   a. the office of the attorney general
   b. the county board of supervisors
   c. the county clerk
   d. the board of equalization

ANALYZE

1. What are the key similarities and differences between the county sheriff and the county clerk?

2. What is the most likely complaint a contract city would make against a county government?

IDENTIFY THE CONCEPT THAT DOESN'T BELONG

a. Adjudicating misdemeanors
b. Overseeing the county jail
c. Determining property tax rates
d. Performing civil marriages
e. Redistricting

21.2

Resource Center
• Glossary
• Vocabulary Example
• Connect the Link

■ **Local Agency Formation Commission (LAFCO):** A countywide commission that conducts studies and public hearings to determine the feasibility of establishing a new city.

SIGNIFICANCE: *LAFCO was formed in 1963 in response to the post–World War II boom in housing and commercial development that often produced poorly planned communities.*

The Legal Framework and Formation of Cities

21.3 Characterize the three forms of municipal governments and summarize the procedures adopted by city councils.

(pages 644–647)

For better or for worse, municipal governments are the major influences on the direction that California cities will take. It is the municipal governments, for example, that have the power to enact zoning ordinances and guidelines, provide recreational services, and offer tax breaks to businesses. These units of government are tied to state government in many respects, but unlike county governments, they exercise a considerable amount of independence. For most municipal governments, the dictates from the state government are founded on aspects of the California constitution and the general law on municipal governments, which prescribes the basic obligations that every California city must satisfy. By 1890, cities had gained the right to create home rule charters. Since then, the constitutional and other statutory provisions regarding city charters have evolved, giving chartered cities the opportunity to "make and enforce all laws and regulations in respect to municipal affairs, subject only to the restrictions and limitations provided in their several charters."[16]

In 1896, the state legislature amended the state constitution to subject all cities without home rule charters to a general law that is detailed in the California Government Code. The general law and government code mandates a wide variety of duties that city governments must carry out, necessitating, for example, the formation of planning commissions and the drafting of a general plan. How these duties will be implemented in a specific city is reflected in the municipal ordinances or codes, the laws governing a municipality. In addition to municipal codes, many cities maintain other subcategories of regulations, the most obvious examples being special zoning or building codes. Each city is authorized to enforce these ordinances or codes, the violation of which normally constitutes a misdemeanor or an infraction. Most cities have separate "rules of procedure" for the actual proceedings and actions of a city council as well as rules governing the municipal civil service.

The process of forming a city begins with a resolution by the county board of supervisors or a petition signed by at least 25 percent of the voters living in the area requesting consideration of incorporation. The petition and the accompanying proposal for incorporation are presented to the **local agency formation commission (LAFCO)**■, a countywide commission that in addition to other duties conducts studies and public hearings to determine the feasibility of establishing a city. If the LAFCO approves the proposal to incorporate, the board of supervisors will hold public hearings again. If there are no disputes over the proposal, the board will call an election in which approval by a majority of voters living within the proposed city is needed for incorporation.[17] To date, 480 California cities have incorporated, with 112 of them choosing to write charters and the rest remaining under the general law.[18] If a city decides to disincorporate, which has not been done since 1972, that decision will also be determined by a majority of voters in a special election. California cities do have the right to consolidate with other cities or expand under certain circumstances. State laws and regulations covering annexation allow cities to expand into unincorporated areas as long as the area is contiguous to the city and in the same county. Annexation must be reviewed and approved by the LAFCO, and it follows procedures that are similar to those for incorporation. The consolidation of two cities is a complicated process that requires majority approval of voters in both cities.[19]

The City Council

City councils are the elected bodies that govern California cities. For a number of reasons, these councils are the cornerstone of American democracy and are responsible for making decisions that have immediate as well as long-term consequences on the daily lives of Americans and residents of this nation. If there was ever an example of why each vote counts, it is the city council. In many municipal elections, 200 or 300 votes can make the difference in whether a city elects candidates to the council who are dedicated to the health of the entire city and have the professional qualifications to make informed decisions or candidates who are influenced by special interests and have little understanding of the complex issues that California cities face. Candidates for a nonpartisan city council seat must be registered voters, 18 years of age or older, and live in the city. Voters have the option to circumvent the decisions of the council using the initiative or referendum and to recall a council member via the electoral process.

Once elected, the city council membership, except in the larger California cities, is considered a part-time office with a four-year term. The general law gives cities the option of five-, seven-, or nine-member city councils; the vast majority of California cities have five-member councils. The main responsibilities of a city council are to enact local ordinances (laws), determine municipal policies, approve programs and budgets, and levy local taxes. The city council is the one body that is responsible for overseeing municipal government and it is typically regarded by most city residents as a body of problem solvers. This role can be especially tough on city council

■ **Council-Manager Model:** A model of city government that emphasizes the political leadership and policymaking qualities of the council as a whole while vesting administrative authority in a full-time, professional manager.

SIGNIFICANCE: *One of the biggest drawbacks of the council-manager model is that the mayor is rarely ever chosen because of leadership ability.*

members, who are expected to approach all problems as neither too big nor too small.

The system of governance adopted by city governments is a major factor in the way a city council handles the issues and problems of its city. Governance in California cities is organized around one of three basic of models, although city councils frequently modify these models to reflect the unique qualities of their particular city. Most California cities use the **council-manager model**■, a system that emphasizes the political leadership and policymaking qualities of the council as a whole while vesting administrative authority in a full-time, professional manager. Another legacy of the Progressives, the council-manager model was designed to overcome the drawbacks of a part-time city council and place the day-to-day management of a city under the control of a professional administrator theoretically beyond political pressures. The Progressives hoped this arrangement would prevent council members from becoming too powerful or entrenched. There are provisions for a mayor in the council-manager model, but the post is usually filled either by someone the city council chooses or by the council member who receives the most votes in the city council election. Mayors under this model most often serve only two years and are largely responsible for presiding over city council meetings and conducting ceremonial functions.

The second model is the **weak mayor–council model**■, which has a mayor who uses popular appeal to lead the city government. Although the mayor in the weak mayor–council model does not have much more administrative power than the mayor in the council-manager model, this mayor is directly elected to the position, can in theory count on broader support, and usually serves a four-year term. Of the 478 incorporated cities in California, 147 have directly elected mayors, many of whom serve in city governments that follow a third model, the **strong mayor–council model**■. Again, subject to modifications, this model gives the mayor direct authority over the city government, including the city manager. The mayor's powers are similar to the authority of executive offices such as the governor, and the city council acts as a legislative body, approving or disapproving policies and serving as a check and balance against the executive power of the mayor. This model is generally employed in California's larger cites, where the mayor is a full-time office with broad powers over the municipal government.[20]

There has been much debate in California over which model is the most efficient as well as democratic, and all have received a fair share of criticism. Despite its progressive legacy, the council-manager model has been criticized for empowering and politicizing the municipal bureaucracy, and because of the part-time restrictions on council members, the affairs of local government are often hidden from the public. San Diego is one of the most recent cities to switch from the council-manager model to a semblance of the strong mayor–council

Los Angeles Mayor Antonio Villaraigosa delivers his keynote speech after an inauguration ceremony at City Hall in downtown Los Angeles on, July 1, 2005. As Villaraigosa formally took his oath as the city's forty-first mayor on that day, he became the first Hispanic to hold the office since the nineteenth century. —*Why do large cities adopt the strong mayor-council form of government?*

model after suffering a wave of corruption scandals involving the city bureaucracy and the council.[21] An example of the weak mayor–council model can be found in the city of Sacramento, which various political commentators suggest has worked with a minimum of problems because of the election of mayors who have generally been popular among city residents.[22] The strong mayor–council model is a mainstay of California's larger cities, such as San Francisco, Oakland, and Los Angeles, and it is best suited for cities that face an assortment of difficult issues on a daily basis. This model has attracted such strong personalities and political leaders as former Assembly Speaker Willie Brown, former Governor Jerry Brown, and Antonio Villaraigosa, another former assembly speaker. This model tends to encourage the concentration of political and city resources within the mayor's office and thus is sometimes criticized for encouraging the misuse of power. The demands of the office of the mayor in the strong mayor–council model, especially during elections, can blur the lines between political interests and the needs of the city.

■ **Weak Mayor–Council Model:**
A model of city government that emphasizes the mayor's role as a facilitative leader.

SIGNIFICANCE: *Historically, the city of Los Angeles has had a weak mayor–council system of government, but in reality, the mayor of this city has substantial powers, including the authority to make appointments and propose a municipal budget. The mayor's powers are limited by the approval or confirmation controls of the city council, which may be overcome when the mayor is popular or charismatic.*

A speaker at a community meeting. Dating back to the colonial era when residents directly governed, the "community meeting" is an American tradition that survives today throughout California, providing residents the opportunity for political participation in local affairs. —*As decreasing numbers of residents remain civically engaged, especially among the younger generation, could the "community meeting" become an antiquity of the California political system?*

Democracy in Action: The City Council Meeting

Conducting city council meetings is one of the most important duties of the city council. These meetings provide the public with a rare opportunity to interface with elected leaders on a regular basis, whether to seek the council's guidance or question their capability to tackle a broad range of concerns and problems facing the community. It is true that other elected governments hold regular public meetings, including counties and special districts, but these governments tend to have either a very broad or a very narrow focus that usually precludes the interest of the general public. City council meetings, by contrast, focus on issues close to the concerns of local residents and can be popular affairs for city residents, who often consider them a forum of sorts. However long and tedious or mundane city council meetings may be, they are nevertheless a public setting wherein council members are expected to appear professional, knowledgeable, and in charge. When council members demonstrate these qualities well, the rewards can be reelection, a supportive community, a responsive city bureaucracy, and often, a boost toward higher office, whereas habitually poor performance at city council meetings can lead to defeat in the next election.

For the public, city council meetings can be confusing, largely because of the parliamentary terminology and procedures as well as the bureaucratic jargon. This dilemma no doubt causes many city residents to become disinterested in city governance, but with a minimal understanding of the city council meeting process, residents will gain insight into the workings of their city as well as valuable information that could bring benefits to the neighborhood, personal lifestyle, or commercial interests. This understanding begins with the agenda, the basic

plan of the council meeting and schedule of items to be covered. The Brown Act—a law named after Ralph M. Brown, the former California assemblyman who wrote it—requires that local governments hold their meetings in public except under special circumstances. One important part of this law compels local governments to post the agenda of regular public meetings 72 hours before the meeting takes place, giving the public advance notification of the meeting plan. Items are placed on the agenda at the request of the council or city staff members. The agenda generally follows a specific format and structures the council meeting in the following order:

1. *Study sessions:* The time for the council to publicly review a special issue without taking any formal action. These sessions often take place before the meeting.
2. *Closed sessions:* The time to consider personnel matters or pending litigation that requires confidentiality. These sessions are closed to the general public.
3. *Call to order or roll call:* The start of the official meeting, when the council members in attendance are identified. The roll call will determine if there is a quorum, the minimum number of council members required to be present to make the meeting official and approve any action that necessitates a vote.
4. *Council member reports and remarks:* The time when council members may make brief announcements or informal comments.
5. *Public remarks and comments:* The time when the audience can address the council on issues that are not on the agenda. Most cities impose a 3- to 5-minute time limit on each speaker, and no council action or discussion is conducted during this period.

■ **Strong Mayor–Council Model:** A model of city government that gives the mayor direct authority over the city government, including the city manager.

SIGNIFICANCE: *The ability of the mayor to replace city employees under a strong mayor–council model becomes extremely important when those positions are the city manager, the police chief, or top economic development officials. The power to fire and hire these highly visible and well-paid positions gives the mayor not only an extraordinary amount of leverage over the department head and his or her department but also greater responsibility over the problems or issues associated with these departments.*

6. *The consent calendar:* The time when multiple matters that are considered to be routine or procedural items that require the approval of the council are presented. The council will vote to adopt the entire list of items without separate discussions of the items. Items can be removed from the consent calendar at the request of a member of the council or the public before the vote to adopt.

7. *Approval of minutes:* Another procedural matter that requires a vote of approval by the council. The minutes are the record of the previous meeting and are made official by this vote.

8. *Council reports:* Items on the agenda that supply the staff, commissioners, or council members with the opportunity to present updates about ongoing projects or report on actions by the municipal government.

9. *Public hearing:* The period during the meeting that deals with matters requiring public comment and review by state law. Resolutions and ordinances approved by the council must be subjected to public hearings. Most proposed ordinances require two hearings before being approved by the council, while resolutions need only one public hearing.

10. *Adjournment:* The meeting is officially closed.

The Legal Framework and Formation of Cities

21.3 Characterize the three forms of municipal governments and summarize the procedures adopted by city councils.

PRACTICE QUIZ: UNDERSTAND AND APPLY

1. In comparison to counties, cities
   a. exercise a considerable amount of independence.
   b. exercise less independence.
   c. have about the same amount of independence.
   d. do not have any independence at all.

2. Which of the following is the countywide agency that conducts studies and public hearings to determine the feasibility of establishing another California city?
   a. Local Agency Formation Commission
   b. County Planning Commission
   c. Economic Development Department
   d. County Advisory Council

3. City councils are most often viewed as
   a. authoritarian bodies.
   b. decentralizes groups.
   c. deliberate thinkers.
   d. problem solvers.

4. What unique opportunity is offered by city council meetings?
   a. the opportunity to meet other city residents
   b. the opportunity to interface with elected leaders on a regular basis
   c. the opportunity to meet a member of the state legislature on a regular basis
   d. the chance to meet with celebrities that reside in the city

ANALYZE

1. What is the primary reason that cities adopted the "council-manger" form of governments?

2. What model of city government is most widely adopted by large cities?

IDENTIFY THE CONCEPT THAT DOESN'T BELONG

a. Incorporation
b. Manifest Destiny
c. Council reports
d. Council-manager
e. Nonpartisan

Resource Center
• Glossary
• Vocabulary Example
• Connect the Link

■ **City Manager:** The official responsible for the administration of city services and programs, enforcement of the city's ordinances, and preparation of the annual budget.

EXAMPLE: *Professional management of municipal government in San Diego, as in most California cities, has evolved gradually and continues to change. It was not until 1949 that San Diego got its first city manager.*

The Municipal Bureaucracy

21.4 List the standard departments and agencies that make up municipal bureaucracies.

(pages 648–651)

The needs of modern cities necessitate substantial municipal bureaucracies. Considering that most city council posts are part-time offices, city councils rely on the department heads they select to adhere to municipal policies and honestly report on the process of implementation. In California's larger cities, municipal departments have become enormous institutions that employ thousands of people—often the becoming city's top employer. These bureaucracies also consume hundreds of millions of dollars (see Figure 21.4).

City Manager

Normally appointed by the city council or the mayor, the **city manager**■ is responsible for administration of city services and programs, enforcement of city ordinances, and preparation of the annual budget. The city manager, depending on the model of governance, usually manages the day-to-day operations of city government. It is from the city manager's office that most departments in the municipal government are coordinated. There are many positions within city government that the city manager either directly appoints or recommends to the council for appointment (or termination). Most municipal procedures imply that the city manager basically serves at the pleasure of the city council, which retains the power to part company with the city manager at any time over disagreements or poor job performance.

Cities that adopt the council-manager model of governance are especially dependent on the professionalism and integrity of the city manager. The relationship between the city manager and city council can take many different forms, one of the most basic being similar to employer-employee relationships. This relationship can cause difficulties if the council attempts to micromanage the administration of city government without the necessary time or expertise. The council-manager relationship can also become distorted if the council comes to rely too heavily on the city manager, causing the city manager to dominate the council and initiate or influence actions without consideration of the council's electoral mandate. Ideally, the city manager and the council should have a functional relationship in which both parties work together in an atmosphere of trust and cooperation, each within a specific sphere of responsibility and with all final and highly political decisions being left to the council.

City Attorney

The **city attorney**■ is the legal adviser to the city council and, at the direction of the council, provides legal advice to the city manager and department heads. With the growing number of lawsuits and litigations, the job of city attorney has become especially important in minimizing legal liability for a city and ensuring conformity with legal guidelines. The city attorney also prepares ordinances, contracts, and resolutions that conform to legal requirements.

City Clerk

The **city clerk**■—which in many cities is an elected position—is responsible for the preparation and maintenance of minutes, ordinances, resolutions, agreements, and other legal documents. In addition to compiling material for the city council meeting agenda and administering the records management systems, the city clerk also serves as the local filing officer for the Fair Political Practices Commission. The city clerk assists the county elections department in administering all city elections, and in many cities the clerk prepares and disseminates public information about the city.

City Treasurer and Finance Department

The principal responsibility of the **city treasurer**■ is to audit and supervise all investments made on behalf of the city government. It is not unusual for the city treasurer, sometimes

FIGURE 21.4 ■ Breakdown of California Municipal Revenues. *—If a local municipal government decided to return ten percent of total revenue to as many local taxpayers as reasonably possible, which of these categories of revenue would be the source or sources of an equitable tax cut and why?*

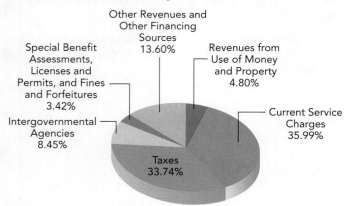

Other Revenues and Other Financing Sources 13.60%

Special Benefit Assessments, Licenses and Permits, and Fines and Forfeitures 3.42%

Revenues from Use of Money and Property 4.80%

Intergovernmental Agencies 8.45%

Current Service Charges 35.99%

Taxes 33.74%

SOURCE: *Cites Annual Report,* 98th edition. Fiscal Year 2007–2008 (Sacramento: California State Controller, April 20, 2010), Figure 2 (p. vii). Reprinted with permission of the California State Controller. http://www.sco.ca.gov/ard_locrep_cities.html

■ **City Attorney:** The legal adviser to the city council.

EXAMPLE: *The office of the city attorney in many California cities is as old as state government.*

■ **City Clerk:** The official responsible for the preparation and maintenance of minutes, ordinances, resolutions, agreements, and other legal documents.

SIGNIFICANCE: *The official responsibilities of the city clerk are dictated in part by two important state laws: the Brown Act and the Fair Political Practices Act.*

referred to as the city auditor, to be elected. The city treasurer reviews and approves quarterly investment reports prepared by staff members for submission to the city council at regularly scheduled meetings. The finance department is primarily responsible for ensuring sound financial management as well as accurate budgeting and accounting methods, collecting revenue, and managing municipal assets. The operations of the finance department are extremely specialized and must adhere to an extensive list of state regulations. These operations are very important to the prosperity of a city, as illustrated by the plethora of near-bankrupt California municipal governments that owe their misfortune to an incompetent or dishonest finance department.

Planning Department

Planning departments have been growing in importance, first because of the explosion of residential development in California and now because of record levels of foreclosures. Residential and other forms of development are closely tied to the work of these departments, involving the development of a general plan and zoning ordinances. These departments must also ensure city compliance with the California Environmental Quality Act and other federal, state, and local environmental regulations. The city's general plan reveals a lot about the present and future characteristics of that city, and many city residents might be a bit surprised by the goals and mapping configurations of this document, especially as they pertain to neighborhoods in which they live. Many city residents and businesspeople rely on planning and zoning information supplied by the planning department. State regulations require that cities have a five-year city capital improvement project (CIP) spending plan, drafted under the direction of the director of the planning department and approved by the city council. These plans, as well as related laws and regulations, lay the groundwork for the construction or improvement of public facilities (generally involving streets and sewer systems) and related laws and regulations.

Housing Department

To the chagrin of many city residents, government-supported housing has become a vital service. With the near collapse of the residential housing market in California, a growing number of Californians are relying on various public housing programs. One of the most popular programs is Section 8 housing, a federally funded program that subsidizes housing costs for lower-income families. Funding is also awarded by the federal government to cities in the form of community development block grants (CDBGs), usually administered by the housing department or housing authority for the elimination and prevention of slums and blight and for the development of housing

California ranks among the top three states in terms of foreclosure rates since 2007, the result of a wide variety of economic difficulties that included the collapse of the nation's financial markets, declining property values, and high energy costs. —*Economic recovery at both the state and national levels will require some government intervention, but at what cost and for whom? Should government go into deep national debt rescuing failed financial institutions or struggling homeowners, or are there fiscal resources available to help both?*

and community projects. The CDBG program is very popular with most municipal governments, involving hundreds of millions of dollars that cities count on, largely because of the relative spending flexibility associated with this type of funding.

Economic Development Department

Cities can no longer afford to take a hands-off approach to local economic development as local business communities and major corporations across the state succumb to the current economic downturn causing major reductions in the local tax base, employment, and many other resources and services. Most county and municipal economic developments are actively engaged in drafting and revising plans for business attraction and retention. The local sales tax revenue generated from local businesses underscores the importance of promoting a strong business climate. These departments endeavor to build close relationships with the members of the business community, including the local Chamber of Commerce, business and industrial associations, and trade unions. Certain tax breaks and financial enticements to lure businesses to the city are usually negotiated by the economic development department, and as the economy becomes even more global these departments will be increasingly involved in marketing local business opportunities abroad.

■ **City Treasurer:** The official whose chief responsibility is to audit and examine all investments made by authorized city personnel.

SIGNIFICANCE: *Recognizing the highly professional nature of the office of the city treasurer, the California Municipal Treasurers Associations was formed in 1959 to address common issues and problems.*

Redevelopment Agency

Redevelopment agencies are growing in popularity while also becoming controversial entities in California. By designating an area within a city as a redevelopment zone, according to state regulations and laws, municipal governments are allowed to retain any increases in property taxes that result from improvements in that zone. In most cases, the city councils function as the redevelopment agency with the power of eminent domain, which is essentially the ability to take ownership of certain properties within the redevelopment zone, ostensibly for the ultimate benefit of the public. Redevelopment zones can also have enterprise zones within them, generating various forms of financial assistance to eligible businesses, including grants, loans, tax credits, and city fee waivers. Many residents in a wide variety of California communities have, however, grown wary of redevelopment zones, because this designation is often used to condemn long-established neighborhoods. Typically, redevelopment plans affect low-income residents of "blighted" neighborhoods who have the misfortune of living in areas that local governments want to upgrade, causing the cost of living in these communities to rise dramatically. It is rare for municipal governments, such as San Francisco and Los Angeles—sites of major redevelopment projects and plans, to have the resources that will accommodate low-income residents displaced, for example, by condominium conversions and the costs of expensive franchise and specialty businesses. Other neighborhoods can be marginal in terms of their "blighted" condition, often an acceptable environment for long-term residents but a major obstacle to officials of local government who want to attract upscale businesses, property developers, and new residents who will pay higher taxes. The U.S. Supreme Court ruling in *Kelo* v. *New London, Connecticut,* which supported a city's right to invoke eminent domain for private development, has alarmed residents and small-business owners in areas that could become prime real estate for developers after being seized by the municipal government.

Frank Finley was evicted from his home in Fresno, California, to make room for a new school. Fresno Unified built ten new schools, eight involved the use of eminent domain to acquire land for the project. —*What restrictions, if any, should be placed on the use of eminent domain by local governments?*

Boards and Commissions

City boards and commissions are important government units outside the municipal bureaucracy that not only support implementation of municipal laws, ordinances, and plans but also offer local residents the opportunity to participate in the governing of the city. State laws and regulations mandate that cities appoint local residents to a **planning commission**■, which is responsible for advising the city council on the adoption and administration of zoning laws and building regulations. Supported by the technical expertise of bureaucrats working for planning departments, planning commissions are regarded as an important body in shaping the appearance of a city, and even though public interest is not always as high as it should be, the participation of local residents on these commissions is a credit to the tradition of American democracy.

Police Department

The primary missions of municipal police departments are to maintain peace and order and to protect property. These departments have felt increasing pressure because of the public's heightened perception of crime and the fact that police departments consume a large portion of the municipal budget. City government maintains a precarious relationship with the police department. Although dependent on vital law enforcement and community protection services, city councils must worry about the perceived independence that most police departments enjoy. The nature of police work tends to generate a considerable number of civil litigation and workers' compensation claims, which can be a serious drain on city revenue.

MYTH EXPOSED Many Californians believe that planning commissions are composed of local residents who are not connected to local government through election or employment and as such are independent sounding boards for their concerns about planning issues. However, such commissions are really much less independent in their relationship to local government. Most planning commissions largely reflect the planning goals and objectives of city councils or county board of supervisors, exercising little independence or authority. These commissioners can be removed at anytime for no apparent reason, and council members and supervisors are under no obligation to accept the findings of the commissioners. Planning commissions are generally dependent on the employees of the city or county planning

■ **Planning Commission:** A group of local residents who have been appointed by the city council to review the adoption and administration of zoning laws and building regulations.

SIGNIFICANCE: *Planning commissions in California are in fact an extension of the city council, which appoints each planning commission member to a fixed term of office.*

department for technical assistance and research support while these employees owe their first allegiance is to the city council or supervisors.

There are planning procedures and regulations that provide commissioners with the opportunity to exert some independence, such as the obligation to hold open regular meetings and conduct hearings on specific issues. Although planning commissions are often unknown to the public, their regular meetings may serve as potential forums that generate public support or criticism for the planning policies being advocated by a city council or board of supervisors. Most importantly, commissioners can gain some leverage by developing a comprehensive understanding of the planning process and being prepared to address land use issues. Ultimately, however, the

independence of any planning commission really is dependent on the amount and nature of attention and support that comes from the community residents who do have real independence when choosing elected leaders.

Other types of commissions commonly formed by city government that reflect the participatory custom are design review boards, human relations boards, parks and recreation boards, and youth commissions. In recent years, there has been some controversy over the role of police commissions. Important as they are in responding to instances of police misconduct and facilitating relations between the community and police departments, some concern exists that these commissions either weaken the crime–fighting ability of the police or have little real authority.

The Municipal Bureaucracy

21.4 List the standard departments and agencies that make up municipal bureaucracies.

PRACTICE QUIZ: UNDERSTAND AND APPLY

1. The city manager is responsible for
   a. providing legal advice to the city council.
   b. the administration of city services and programs.
   c. preparation/maintenance of minutes, ordinances, resolutions, agreements and other legal documents.
   d. conducting audits and examining investments.

2. Which of the following posts is most likely to be an elected position?
   a. city attorney
   b. city clerk
   c. city manager
   d. city treasurer

3. What is the one factor that sometimes causes members of the city council to become dependent on the municipal bureaucracy?
   a. the position of city council member is part-time
   b. the power to hire and fire the city manger
   c. having a city attorney as legal advisor
   d. having a city clerk to compile material for the city council meeting agenda

4. Municipal police departments are primarily responsible for which of the following responsibilities?

   a. preventing the spread of individual and organized crime
   b. maintaining peace and order and protecting property
   c. maintaining moral values and economic vitality
   d. restricting the movement of those individuals accused of crimes

ANALYZE

1. What are the most important positions in a city government? Explain your answer.

2. If one municipal department had to be cut, which one would you cut? Why?

IDENTIFY THE CONCEPT THAT DOESN'T BELONG

a. Audit and supervise all investments made on behalf of city government
b. Administer city service and programs
c. Manage day-to-day operations of city government
d. Recommend the hiring and firing of municipal employees

Resource Center
• Glossary
• Vocabulary Example
• Connect the Link

■ **Special Districts:** Legal districts formed to meet specific needs in an area or community.

SIGNIFICANCE: *The California Special Districts Association suggests that the best way to understand special districts is by considering them as a focused service. Such districts usually provide a single service that the public wants but that transcends county and city boundaries.*

Special Districts

21.5 Identify the purposes of special districts, and explain how they fulfill their goals.
(pages 652–657)

In the late 1800s, farmers in the San Joaquin Valley were faced with an unpredictable water supply, an intransigent local government, and a "water monopoly" that charged fluctuating rates and resisted irrigation expansion. Resolution of this dilemma began with the election to the state legislature of C. C. Wright, a Central Valley schoolteacher and lawyer who campaigned on a platform advocating public water and irrigation. By 1887, he had drafted and ultimately won passage of the Wright Act, giving small regions the right to form local water districts that would act as subdivisions of the state government and to finance these districts with bond sales.[23] Since the passage of the Wright Act, there has been a wave of state laws encouraging the formation of other types of **special districts**■ to meet a specific need in an area or community. These districts now furnish Californians with a wide variety of services in such areas as aviation, cemeteries, drainage, fire protection, health care, irrigation, and transit. Some of them are confined to small communities, while others serve millions of people. Over 85 percent of California's approximately 5,000 special districts provide a single service.

There are two types of districts: independent districts and dependent districts. Independent districts are truly separate from state, county, and local governments, operating with independently elected boards of directors and revenue sources.[24] One prominent example is the massive East Bay Municipal Utility District, which supplies water to various parts of the San Francisco Bay Area. There are about twice as many independent special districts as there are dependent districts. Dependent districts, as the name implies, are subject to local governmental control. A large number of the recreational areas in the Sacramento region, for example, are dependent special districts that have board members appointed by the Sacramento County Board of Supervisors. Special districts also exist in the form of enterprise districts, which offer services for fees, or nonenterprise districts, which make services available to benefit an entire community. Water districts are the most common enterprise districts, which are in fact the most numerous type of special district. Fire protection districts are an example of nonenterprise districts.

The process of forming a special district begins when registered voters put together a proposal that is submitted to the local agency formation commission (LAFCO) for review and possible approval. If the proposal is approved by the LAFCO and passes the public hearing requirements, voters within the proposed district will have the opportunity to approve or

Californians live with the enduring peril of limited rainfall, which can potentially lead to drought conditions and the accompanying upheaval when communities lack water. In recent years, reservoirs such as Camanche Reservoir, pictured here, have suffered from lower-than-normal precipitation and increasing demand for water from a growing population. Many environmental activists and scientists worry that the effects of global warming may present a drain on the state's water supply potentially worse than the 1988 drought, which brought the Camanche Reservoir down to just 10,000 acre-feet of water—out of a capacity of 417,120 acre-feet. —*What should local governments do to address this threat?*

disapprove the proposal. A two-thirds vote in favor of the proposal is required if the new special district plans to levy any new taxes.[25]

The funding of special districts generally comes from service fees, property tax revenues, and bond sales. Charges listed on a typical water bill are probably the best example of a fee paid for the services of a special district. For districts in which it would be difficult or impractical to charge a fee for the service provided, such as fire protection, a property tax is assessed. Annual assessments on homeowners in Northern California for special districts normally include $5 for mosquito and vector control services, $10 for emergency medical services, $77 for street lighting, $191 for sanitation district services, and $3 for the water district.

Special districts will sometimes attempt to raise revenue by placing a bond measure on the ballot, but such electoral exercises have been less popular with the voters in recent years. Bond measures can be initiated by both enterprise and

CONNECT THE **LINK**
(Chapter 22, page 674) What are general obligation bonds?

nonenterprise special districts, but general obligation bonds (see Chapter 22, page 674) require two-thirds majority approval at the polls. The costs to the homeowner for bonds vary widely, from about $9 on the annual property tax bill for a bond to purchase land for a regional park district to $40 for a school district bond. The precarious revenue stream's of local government can have pronounced affects on special districts, as evidenced in 2004 when the state legislature exempted special districts from a deal that would limit future property tax shifts from local governments to the state.[26]

PATHWAYS of action

Toppling the Initiative to Limit Public Power

As California energy producers search out new and innovative forms of energy and its transmission, the Pacific Gas and Electric Company (PG&E)—a major California energy producer—attempted to limit the growth of public power utilities in the state by getting the initiative Proposition 16 placed on the 2010 state primary election ballot. This proposed amendment to the California constitution would require two-thirds voter approval before local governments could spend or borrow public money to establish or expand public power utilities. In reaction to this proposed amendment, a wide variety of consumer and environmental groups and representatives of local government came together in opposition. Many local governments involved in public energy production had a vested interest in defeating Proposition 16, but numerous environmental and consumer groups also opposed the initiative. They were not pleased either with PG&E's past energy rate hikes or with the pace at which the company was converting to renewable energy sources. PG&E was no doubt concerned about a state law passed in 2002 that allowed local governments to buy electricity on behalf of their residents and some suggest that Proposition 16 was one attempt to limit the effect of this law. Supporters of the proposed amendment argued simply that taxpayers should have more control over how public funds are spent on public power initiatives.

As the sole financial sponsor of the measure, PG&E spent more than $45 million in television ads and mailers by election day. For three to four months until the election, primetime television viewers witnessed nightly TV advertisements promoting Proposition 16 and what many charged were "profoundly" misleading accusations. The coalition of consumer and environmental groups, representatives of local government, and the many other residents of the state faced a herculean tasks in attempting to defeat Proposition 16. By election day, this coalition raised only $101,400. Waging a grassroots campaign, however, the coalition effectively utilized any media source willing to report on the proposition. Many residents were

The Sierra Club and other individuals protest against Proposition 16. —*How would Proposition 16 have constricted local authority? What interest groups clashed over this issue and why?*

angered by the possibility that Proposition 16 would not only severely limit the ability of public power utilities to expand into other areas but also hamper the efforts of these utilities to introduce new energy technology and sources. The result was that some Californians grew tired of the endless procession of ads that were an expensive and obvious form of campaigning.

In the end, Proposition 16 was voted down by about a hundred thousand voters about a 2 percent margin over the number of "yes" votes. Although the coalition had won a victory, the state had come perilously close to imposing restrictions on public power, and PG&E has not yet conceded defeat in the war over energy policy.

SOURCE: Cosmo Garvin, "PG&E's Proposition 16 Would Protect the Company from Public-Power Rivals," *Sacramento News and Review,* April 15, 2010, www.newsreview. com/sacramento/content/?old=1404194.
David Baker, "PG&E Measure Requiring Public Power Votes Loses," *San Francisco Chronicle,* June 9, 2010, www.sfgate.com/cgi-bin/article.cgi?f=/c/a/2010/06/10/BAN71DSGNK.DTL.

Fiscal and Political Accountability

One of the major criticisms of special districts revolves around the issue of fiscal accountability. Concern from taxpayer advocacy groups in particular has focused on the large reserves in funds that some special districts maintain while continuing to tax and assess fees at a constant level, particularly in independent special districts. In 2000, the California Taxpayers Association singled out the Water Replenishment District of Southern

California as an obvious culprit, describing how that district "has overcharged water users for nearly a decade, amassed unconscionable reserves, and grew top heavy with highly paid administrators and consultants."[27] Various reports on special districts by the State Auditor's Office, Controller's Office, and Little Hoover Commission suggest that the financial reserves of many districts are hidden, purposely or not, from public view and that certain districts do not include fixed and other kinds of assets when reporting these reserves. This charge implies that machinery or land that could be disposed of for millions of dollars is often omitted from financial statements in some special districts. Another criticism centers on the many enterprise special districts, especially water districts, that have the ability to charge fees for services but also receive property tax assessments. Of course, numerous special districts continue to struggle financially, particularly in the case of nonenterprise districts, such as parks and recreational areas. The broader issue, however, is the level of overall accountability.[28]

Representatives for special districts and their advocacy groups insist that accountability is built into the structure of these types of governments, primarily through the voters who elect the boards of directors that manage the districts. They also refer to oversight by the state government, which requires special districts to submit annual financial reports to the state controller, and to the state laws mandating public hearings, caps on debt obligation, and record keeping. There is also the watchful eye of the LAFCO, regularly conducting special studies that review ways to reorganize and refine the sphere of influence of special districts. Many government leaders and private Californians think otherwise, however, suggesting that most residents of special districts usually know very little about operations in their district; know even less about the board members who run for election; rarely, if ever, attend regular district meetings, let alone hearings; and have difficulty understanding the districts' financial statements. Studies focused on special districts conducted by the Little Hoover Commission in 2000, the California Legislative Analysts Office in 2002, and the California State Senate in 2003 found that many districts fail to even consider many basic steps that could be taken to involve the public and community leaders. These studies also discovered that in its current state, the LAFCO suffered from understaffing, underfunding, and an overall reluctance to challenge the status quo. This report also recommended greater transparency in financial accounting, using financial statement summaries, enhancing the clarity of billing statements, and disclosing to the public full explanations of fiscal reserves, plans, and needs.[29]

School Districts in California

Since the beginning of statehood, education has been a problematic venture for California state government. As Howard De Witt notes in *The California Dream,* "By 1860 many judged public school education a dismal failure in California as less than 25% of the eligible students attended school."[30] One the state's early superintendents of public instruction expressed his disgust with early school allocations, which he claimed amounted to $1 for every $3 spent on prisons. Public schools gradually improved with the imposition of uniform educational standards and funding increases spearheaded by Superintendent John Swett in the mid-1860s, reforms that were later expanded under a Progressive-dominated state government.[31] Slow migration into California kept the state's school-age population low, allowing adequate educational funding levels to be reached by the turn of the twentieth century, although communities of racial minorities were persistently plagued by inferior educational programs and poor school districts. Early school districts were highly autonomous, often consisting of one individual school. Gradually, the state government consolidated elementary, middle, and high schools into unified school districts. In 1932 there were 3,579 school districts, compared to the 1,056 districts that remain today. By the end of World War II, California school districts had again fallen behind as the school-age population exploded, thanks to the arrival of defense industry workers and returning soldiers who quickly began to start families.[32] By 1948, some 27,000 children were forced into part-time attendance in Los Angeles schools because of the shortage of facilities.[33] To the credit of the Earl Warren and Edmund G. "Pat" Brown Sr. gubernatorial administrations, a share of the postwar prosperity was spent on the public school system. And as the state government became increasingly involved in education, local school districts and the school boards that oversaw them gradually relinquished greater portions of control to the state.

Most parents with children in public schools would like to believe that locally elected school boards are accountable for overseeing public education in their communities. Successive governors, state legislatures, and state boards of education, however, have assumed a growing portion of this oversight function through a series of laws and budget allocations, beginning with the State Educational Code, which has grown to five volumes of regulations that influence almost every aspect of the educational process. The California Board of Education, backed by its funding recommendations, now dictates state educational policies for curriculum content, textbook selection, assessment methods, and student standards of performance.

Since the passage of Proposition 13 in 1978, which dramatically cut property taxes—the traditional funding source for local school districts—almost all property taxes have been shifted to the state government. Today, approximately 85 percent of school district funding comes directly from the California state government, as opposed to a 50 percent to 44 percent ratio between state and local funding sources that exists for most for school districts across the country.[34] The funding system in California has caused school districts to lose a great deal of local control over educational plans while remaining frequent targets of angry parents, teachers, and students who blame school boards for policies that regularly require funding or programming cuts. The approval by the voters of Proposition 98 in 1988 was an attempt to respond to funding reductions in education as a result of Proposition 13 by requiring that the state government allocate 40 percent of the general fund to education. This initiative did not, however, restore local revenue sources to the school districts. School districts lose even more control to the categorical programs that the state government creates as a means of earmarking funds for special or specific purposes. Although most categorical programs are designed with the best of intentions, they defy the notion of locally controlled school districts.

The initiative process in California has been commonly associated with education in the state. There have been numerous education-related initiatives over the years, including some that have shown genuine concern for influencing the quality of education and others that have attempted to use education to further other political or policy interests. During the 2005 California special election, two of the eight items on the ballot dealt with education-related issues. One of the most controversial initiatives approved by voters was Proposition 227, which limited the use of bilingual educational programs in California public schools. Both sides of this initiative raised compelling arguments, but many political leaders and residents did not miss the opportunity to express anti-immigrant sentiments or to condemn these viewpoints.

At the school district level, the locally elected school boards, usually consisting of five members, are left with the responsibility of deciding how to spend whatever funds are left after fulfilling mandatory functions. The local allocation process puts the school board face to face with employees and members of the local community, who usually demand costly allocations but nearly always have to settle for less. Contract negotiations between representatives of the school boards and employee unions as well as the decision to cut arts or athletic programs can be very combative. Local or county school bond measures can be one means of generating local revenue outside of state government controls. School district bond measures have become a popular method of raising local revenue but also have been generating growing resistance among local residents, who resent the frequency with which they are proposed. In addition to fiscal matters, the boards of trustees for school districts are actively engaged in an assortment of policy decisions that involve implementation of the state curriculum, managing facilities maintenance and construction plans, hiring a management team, carrying out quasi-judicial functions, and performing ceremonial duties. These kind of obligations are evident on the agenda of a Fresno Unified School District Board meeting:[35]

- Voting on the appointments of an administrator of human resources and assistant superintendent for K–6 school leadership
- Voting on the appointment of two program managers

A high school teacher talks to a Spanish-speaking, Hispanic teenage boy in an ESL class. —*How do the demographics impact the services local governments need to provide?*

- Announcement of the positive evaluation given to the superintendent
- Recognition of a retiring employee after 35 years of service
- Voting on two board resolutions that recognized Week of the School Administrator and the National School Breakfast Program
- Voting on the recommendation of the school board administration to allow seniors who have met academic credit requirements to participate in graduation exercises regardless of whether they took the California High School Exit Examination.

Each school district has a superintendent of schools (or superintendent of education) who functions as the administrator of the day-to-day operations of the school district, similar to the city manager of a municipal government. Responsibilities of the superintendent encompass supervision of financial controls, recruitment and hiring, coordination of curriculum development and student services, completion of state reporting requirements, and many other tasks. The superintendent and the board of trustees form a mutually dependent relationship that is based on clear and effective policy development and decision making by the board and sound management by the superintendent.

Reforming California Schools

Despite California's relative prosperity, the state's public school system has had mixed educational outcomes. The high number of low-income students as well as students with limited proficiency in English present major challenges for school districts. Political leaders and educational advocacy groups have responded to these challenges with a series of proposals for reform. The federal government plays a significant role in the process of education in California, as it does in most states, through the funding of federal education programs, many of which support the reform process in California. Literally

■ **No Child Left Behind Act (NCLB):** A federal law imposing educational reform throughout the country by requiring all schools to adopt student proficiency standards.

SIGNIFICANCE: *The NCLB, signed into law on January 8, 2002, by President George W. Bush is filled with accountability provisions to ensure that states and participating schools understand the new expectations.*

hundreds of educational programs in California are supported by various federal agencies and departments—the U.S. Department of Education in particular—but the **No Child Left Behind Act (NCLB)**■ has by far been one of the most controversial. School district officials and educators alike throughout the county have raised concerns about this national law, which represents a broad effort by the federal government to impose educational reform across the country by requiring that all schools make every attempt to adopt student proficiency standards. Such standards are often imposed at the expense of a well-rounded educational program and curriculum, whereas educational achievement scores take precedence over creative and thought-provoking learning activities. Moreover, many districts lack the fiscal and material resources to meet the standards established by the NCLB.

Now yet another educational challenge from the federal government has emerged with the **Race to the Top** national funding awards. This national competition pits states against each other in the attempt to win hundreds of millions in educational dollars for the most innovative educational-reform plans. After considerable acrimony among the various state educational constituencies and stakeholders regarding the completion of the application, California state government

The Santa Monica Boulevard Community Charter School in Los Angeles is recognized as a California Distinguished School in this ceremony. Many government leaders and educational professionals believe that charter schools have proven to be an effective approach to achieving educational enrichment while, at the same time, ensuring local community control over the educational process.
—*What are the greatest challenges school districts face in California?*

eventually entered the competition, but failed to place in the first round of finalists. Application reviewers for the U.S. Department of Education cited a "contentious relationship" between teacher unions and school districts and "a weak data system for tracking student performance" as the major flaws in California's application. About two-thirds of the Race to the Top funds are available for subsequent rounds of funding and although cash-strapped school districts across California could really use the money, most state government officials and educational professionals do not appear optimistic about the chances of a second application.[36]

Educational reform at the state level has centered on class size reduction, charter schools, vouchers, and "high-stakes" testing and accountability standards. In 1996, the state legislature enacted a law to earmark funding to school districts for class size reduction as well as construction of additional schools. Various studies have indicated that although class sizes were reduced fairly rapidly, such efforts tended to benefit more affluent schools, and overall teacher quality, as measured by experience and credentials, declined. Charter schools have become relatively popular in California; the state was the second in the nation to authorize their use in 1992 and is now fifth among all states in the number of charter schools, which are designed to grant more local control over funding, educational programs, and facilities. Although charter schools remain popular, whether they actually increase academic performance is unclear. The policy to provide vouchers or monetary support to private schools has not taken root in California, and two ballot initiatives to institute vouchers in the state have failed.

Attaching "high stakes" to the outcomes of standardized tests has been very popular among states, and in 1999, the California legislature passed the Public School Accountability Act, largely involving monetary and nonmonetary incentives to schools that meet performance standards on statewide academic assessment tests. Under this act, schools that failed to meet certain academic standards would initially receive assistance but could ultimately face closure if they are unable to demonstrate improvement. Considering that public school students in California have consistently scored lower than the national average on standardized tests, it has been very difficult for the state government to compel all school districts to fully comply with the Public School Accountability Act.[37] Whatever reforms actually occur in California will be severely restricted by the current economic downturn gripping the state economy and reducing state revenue. The 2009–2010 state budget was in fact approved after the mandated 40 percent allocation to education was suspended. This caused mass layoffs and major funding deficits for school districts. Undoubtedly, California school districts will have to do more with less as the student population continues to grow and the public clamors for reform and improvement.

■ **Councils of Government (COGs):**
Regional organizations that bring municipal and county governments together to address common issues and problems.

SIGNIFICANCE: *Founded in 1961 to bring together elected officials from local governments of the San Francisco Bay Area government, the Association of Bay Area Governments (ABAG) was the first council of government formed in California.*

Councils of Government

The federal and state governments have attempted to respond to the needs of local governments by encouraging the formation of, **councils of government (COGs)**■ regional organizations that bring municipal and county governments together to address common issues and problems. Although they generally do not deliver direct services, they have been granted powers by the federal and state governments to allocate funds and monitor compliance with various types of regulations. Through joint-powers agreements, COGs facilitate the pooling of city and county resources and serve as collective planning bodies of governments within one region to exchange ideas and develop regionwide policy. Officially designated as metropolitan planning organizations by the federal government, COGs are required to devise regional plans for transportation, growth management, environmental quality controls, and economic development. In turn, the federal government ties the allocation of federal funds, especially for transportation, to the completion and implementation of these plans. Metropolitan transportation COGs can be found across the state and are one of the few types of COGs that generate long-term, tangible outcomes. Many of California's mass transit systems and policies on highway construction are the direct result of COG collaborations. Most major regions have "associations of government" COGs that provide information and planning services, but the functions of these COGs rarely go beyond the consultative stage. Issues related to growth are among the toughest for COGs to achieve regional agreements and coordination. Cities in particular are still very reluctant to relinquish any authority over local development and often reject COG plans to limit growth in favor of expanding development plans.

Special Districts

21.5 Identify the purposes of special districts, and explain how they fulfill their goals.

PRACTICE QUIZ: UNDERSTAND AND APPLY

1. The Wright Act
   a. requires that local governments hold their meetings in public, except under special circumstances.
   b. mandates that a city have a five-year capital improvement plan.
   c. requires that local residents be appointed to all city commissions.
   d. gives local areas the authority to form local water districts.

2. How many specific services do most of California's special districts provide?
   a. at least three different services
   b. a single service
   c. an unlimited number of services
   d. two distinctly different services

3. The funding of special districts would probably not come from
   a. funds allocated by the federal government.
   b. service fees.
   c. property taxes.
   d. bond sales.

4. What is one of the major criticisms of special districts?
   a. their lack of fiscal accountability
   b. too few members on their governing boards
   c. their lack of strong leadership
   d. their lack of diversity among district employees

ANALYZE

1. What services do special districts provide? Why aren't these services provided by municipal or county governments?

2. Compare and contrast the roles of a school board and the superintendent of schools/education.

IDENTIFY THE CONCEPT THAT DOESN'T BELONG

a. Wright Act
b. Annual assessments
c. Clemency powers
d. LAFCO
e. Enterprise districts

21.5

Conclusion

Local governments are the primary governmental units through which the average citizen can make a real and immediate contribution. The number of Californians who recognize this fact and actually get involved will determine the future success or failure of local governments. How California's local governments are funded is one of the questions that will require the serious attention of all citizens. It is clear now more than ever that the state has never recovered from the Proposition 13 tax cuts, and at some point a reckoning involving either tax increases or service reductions will be required.

Special districts are bound to generate greater attention as the resources they manage—including water, irrigation and sewerage systems, and energy in particular—become less available and more expensive. Ideally, the customers of these districts will utilize the democratic character and framework of most special districts to increase their involvement.

Education in California, representing one of the most important functions of local government, will also merit the close attention of all residents. Regardless of the number of school-age children any Californian may have, he or she will make large tax contributions to an educational system that in general is not working well. Where more money might help, there is no guarantee, especially considering the large number of students who regularly fail to complete their homework and others whose behavioral problems cause disruptions that are costly to the education process. The future of California dictates that all students receive a quality education if the state is to meet workforce requirements and realize a "thinking" public. California cities are growing, but are they becoming better places to live? Have cities outlived their usefulness as the suburban model continues to spread, and are counties in fact better equipped to address the move toward metropolis? But what do Californians lose as they become more suburban? The answers to these questions imply major change could be in store for the communities across the state in the near future.

KEY CONCEPT MAP

How are local government services impacted by budgetary constraints?

Education

Local educational services are primarily the responsibility of unified school districts governed by locally elected school boards and a superintendent. School districts exercise some autonomy, but they must follow certain guidelines to receive state and federal funding.

A considerable amount of education spending in California is provided by the federal government, which has had to cut funding in the face of poor economic conditions. The federal government has instituted a number of programs that mandate certain standards. If such standards are not met, school districts face the loss of funds or personnel.

Critical Thinking Questions

Why do school districts generally operate independently from city governments? What if a local city government assumed responsibility for a local school district? How would this benefit or harm the city government? What would the consequences be for the school district?

Economic Development

Most municipal governments are actively engaged in promoting economic development through their economic development departments. These departments draft and implement plans for business attraction and retention, and build partnerships with members of the business community.

Most municipal economic development departments must promote commercial activity despite reduced allocations from city government. Notwithstanding the crucial importance of stimulating business growth, the funding of vital municipal services typically takes precedence over economic development programs.

Critical Thinking Questions

What if an economic development department and fire department could form a partnership? What types of programs could they conduct that would be mutually beneficial in terms of generating funds?

Water

Water is provided by water districts, which are a form of special districts. Most water districts in California are self-sustaining, largely funded through fees paid by water district customers and the periodic selling of bonds.

As California slowly recovers from years of drought, local water districts must decide whether to relax conservation plans or conserve water through higher rates. Water sources have also been reduced by ecological degradation and pollution. Water districts must convince authorities why residential users should be favored ahead of farm interests and environmental restoration projects.

Critical Thinking Questions

What is the best argument for diverting water from farming interests and putting it toward residential use? Are there other mechanisms by which water districts could raise additional funding other than by raising the fees paid by consumers?

Safety

Local municipal police receive law enforcement support from county sheriff's departments. These departments typically provide services such as detention facilities, 911 central dispatch, search and rescue, and animal control. Most sheriff's departments also provide direct law enforcement services to unincorporated cities.

Economic difficulties have forced county sheriff's departments to cut back on vital services, lay off personnel, and assume the duties of local police departments that have curtailed services or disbanded altogether.

Critical Thinking Questions

What are the consequences for cities and towns when funding for local police and sheriff's departments are reduced? Besides the actual cost, why would a special tax or charge to preserve the personnel and functions of sheriff's departments be unfair?

Transportation

Transportation resources and infrastructure are largely financed and supported through regional transportation organizations that bring municipal and county governments together to devise plans, allocate federal and state funds, and monitor compliance with various regulations.

There is growing pressure to find solutions to California's congested highways, especially amid the trend toward energy conservation and environmental restoration. Regional transportation agencies are often divided between those who favor the expansion of mass transit and those who want highway systems expanded.

Critical Thinking Questions

How would a motorist convince authorities from a regional transportation organization that shifting money to build and maintain highways is the best use of funds? What role might the improvement of alternative energy sources have on the future allocation of transportation funds?

The relationship between state and local governments in California has become increasingly adversarial as portions of revenue earmarked for local government have been shifted to California state government. State legislators acknowledge the importance of funding municipalities, counties, and special districts, but they are under considerably more pressure from special interest groups and political parties to favor state-wide funding obligations. —*What are the best arguments for and against transferring funds and more local government responsibilities to state government? What services normally conducted by state government could be adequately completed by local government if funding were available?*

Review of Key Objectives

California County Government

 21.1 Trace the historical development of county governments in California.

(pages 636–639)

The formation of counties was vital to the growth and administration of early California. The California Progressives led the passage of a state constitutional amendment that gave counties the option of home rule charter authority. A general law was also established for those counties that did not choose to embrace home rule. Today 13 of the state's 58 counties have home rule charters. The governmental structure of California counties is largely determined by the California constitution and the California Government Code.

KEY TERMS

Home Rule 636

General Law 636

County Board of Supervisors 637

Municipal Advisory Councils (MACs) 638

Contract Cities 638

CRITICAL THINKING QUESTIONS

1. Why was the formation of counties in California vital to the growth and administration of the state? Has the importance of counties grown, diminished, or stayed the same?
2. How has the structure of county governments changed over time?

INTERNET RESOURCES

The Web site for the California State Association of Counties (CSAC) can be found at http://www.csac.counties.org/. The CSAC places a strong emphasis on educating the public about the value and need for county programs and services.

ADDITIONAL READING

Richardson, Jesse J., Jr., Meghan Zimmerman, and Robert Puentes. *Is Home Rule the Answer? Clarifying the Influence of Dillon's Rule on Growth Management.* Washington, DC: Brookings Institution Center on Urban and Metropolitan Policy, 2003.

Sonenshein, Raphael J. "The Prospect for County Charter Reform in California." Fullerton, CA: Department of Political Science, California State University, 2001.

Baldassare, Mark. *When Government Fails: The Orange County Bankruptcy.* Berkeley and Los Angeles: University of California Press, 1998.

County Bureaucracy

 21.2 Identify the offices and agencies that make up county government in California.

(pages 640–643)

The size and composition of the county bureaucracy varies from county to county, depending on geographic conditions, stages of development, and socioeconomic characteristics. However, a number of county officers and departments are common to nearly all counties because of the vital nature of the variety of services they deliver to all county residents. Most of the services that are performed by the sheriff, district attorney, and tax assessor are required by the California constitution, and other services have been instituted in the absence of other local governmental authority.

KEY TERMS

County Administrator 640

Sheriff 640

Assessor 640

County Clerk 641

CRITICAL THINKING QUESTIONS

1. What feature of the county bureaucracy is the most difficult for the county board of supervisors to oversee, and which feature would probably be the easiest to manage?
2. Do the various components of the county bureaucracy have one unifying feature, or are they in reality unique or independent organizations?

INTERNET RESOURCES

The California Association of Council of Governments (CALCOG) maintains a Web site at http://www.calcog.org/. Established in 1977, this a statewide association represents 38 regional planning agencies. Most were formed as councils of governments, meaning that they represent joint powers agreements of cities and counties.

ADDITIONAL READING

Lewis, Paul. "Deep Roots: Local Government Structure in California." Public Policy Institute of California, 1998.

Navari, S., et al. (eds.). *Beyond Change: Rethinking California State Government.* Sacramento: Center for California Studies, California State University, 1993.

The Legal Framework and Formation of Cities

21.3 Characterize the three forms of municipal governments and summarize the procedures adopted by city councils.

(pages 644–647)

Governance in California cities is organized around one of three basic of models. Most California cities use the council-manager model, a system that emphasizes the political leadership and policymaking qualities of the council as a whole while vesting administrative authority in a full-time, professional manager. The second model is the weak mayor–council model, which has a mayor who uses popular appeal to lead the city government. Of the 478 incorporated cities in California, 147 have directly elected mayors, many of whom serve in city governments that follow a third model, the strong mayor–council model. The mayor's powers are similar to the authority of executive offices such as the governor, and the city council acts as a legislative body, approving or disapproving policies and serving as a check and balance against the executive power of the mayor.

KEY TERMS

Local Agency Formation Commission (LAFCO) 644

Council-Manager Model 645

Weak Mayor–Council Model 645

Strong Mayor– Council Model 645

CRITICAL THINKING QUESTIONS

1. What problems typically arise in "council-manager" models of city government? How have these problems been addressed?
2. What are the functions of city councils? How do they vary according to the form of government adopted by the municipality?

INTERNET RESOURCES

An extensive variety of resources can be found at the Web site for the Association of Bay Area Governments (ABAG), the official comprehensive planning agency for the San Francisco Bay Area, at http://www.abag.ca.gov/.

ADDITIONAL READING

Gordon, Tracy M. *Local Initiative in California*. San Francisco, CA: Public Policy Institute of California, 2004.

The Municipal Bureaucracy

21.4 List the standard departments and agencies that make up municipal bureaucracies.

(pages 648–651)

In California's larger cities, municipal departments have become enormous institutions that employ thousands of people. The city manager, depending on the model of governance, usually manages the day-to-day operations of city government. It is from the city manager's office that most departments, such as the planning, housing, economic development, and police departments are coordinated. Other offices within the municipal bureaucracy, including the city attorney, clerk, and treasurer, tend to exhibit some independence either because they are directly elected or as a result of the importance of their duties.

KEY TERMS

City Manager 648

City Attorney 648

City Clerk 648

City Treasurer 648

Planning Commission 650

CRITICAL THINKING QUESTIONS

1. What are the similarities and differences between the municipal and county bureaucracies?
2. Of all the municipal departments, which department appears to have grown in importance, and which one seems to have lost importance? What issues, problems, or events have caused this growth and decline?

INTERNET RESOURCES

The California Center for Regional Leadership (http://calregions.urbaninsight.com/) is a statewide, nonprofit organization established to support, facilitate, and promote innovative regional solutions for our major economic, environmental, and societal challenges, to help achieve a more sustainable California. This Web site features the highly informative *Calregions* e-newsletter, a comprehensive roundup of new ideas about local government and society.

ADDITIONAL READING

Horton, John. *The Politics of Diversity: Immigration, Resistance, and Change in Monterey Park, California*. Philadelphia: Temple University Press, 1995.

Rueben, Kim, and Pedro Cerdan. *Fiscal Effects of Voter Approval Requirements on Local Governments*. San Francisco: Public Policy Institute of California, 2003.

Special Districts

21.5 Identify the purposes of special districts, and explain how they fulfill their goals.

(pages 652–657)

In 1887, the Wright Act was passed, giving small regions the right to form local water districts that would act as subdivisions of the state government and financed by bond sales. Since the passage of this act, there has been a wave of state laws encouraging the formation of other types of special districts to meet a specific need in an area or community. These districts now furnish Californians with a wide variety of services in such areas as aviation, cemeteries, drainage, fire protection, health care, irrigation, and transit.

KEY TERMS

Special Districts 652

Race to the Top 656

No Child Left Behind Act (NCLB) 656

Councils of Government (COGS) 657

CRITICAL THINKING QUESTIONS

1. How do special districts raise the funds they need to provide services?
2. What is the future of local government? Which level of local government will become more dominant, and which is likely to decline in influence?

INTERNET RESOURCES

As the designated Metropolitan Planning Organization, the Southern California Association of Governments (http://www.scag.ca.gov/) is mandated by the federal government to research and draw up plans for transportation, growth management, hazardous waste management, and air quality.

For nearly 40 years, the National Association of Regional Councils (http://www.narc.org/) has served as a non-profit, 501(c)(3) organization with unmatched experience in representing proactive, multifunctional, full-service organizations that serve local units of government.

The California Special Districts Association (http://www.csda.net/aboutcsda.htm) is a 501(c)(6), not-for-profit association formed in 1969 to ensure the continued existence of local, independent special districts.

ADDITIONAL READING

Carrol, Stephen J., Cathy Krop, Jeremy Arkes, Peter A. Morrison, and Ann Flanagan. *California's K–12 Public Schools: How Are They Doing?* Santa Monica; CA: Rand Corporation, 2005.

Baldassare, Mark. San Francisco: Public Policy Institute of California, 2000.

Chapter Review   Test Your Knowledge

1. Local governments
   a. may not exercise any power unless granted by the federal government.
   b. may engage only in administrative functions.
   c. have powers not specifically granted to their state government.
   d. have only those powers specially delegated to them by state law.

2. What historical development served to empower the strong county model?
   a. the democratization of the American experience
   b. the Progressive movement
   c. a gradual move toward enfranchisement
   d. the abolition of slavery

3. Counties have always been viewed in varying degrees throughout California history by the state government as
   a. separate entities.
   b. legal subdivisions of the federal government.
   c. legal subdivisions of the state.
   d. legal subdivisions of the state court system.

4. The California Progressives advocated passage of a state constitutional amendment that gave what power to California counties?
   a. the option of home rule charter authority
   b. the ability to impose a homeowner's tax
   c. the option of federal rule charter authority
   d. the power to declare a county emergency

5. Of the 13 counties that adopted home rule charters,
   a. seven were among the state's smallest counties.
   b. seven were among the state's largest counties.
   c. all were among the state's largest counties.
   d. none were among the state's largest counties.

6. Which of the following functions is fulfilled by county governments?
   a. public health   c. police protection
   b. district attorney   d. waste disposal

7. The board of supervisors can propose revenue-raising sources, but
   a. only with the approval of the state legislature.
   b. only with the approval of the state supreme court.
   c. voters within the county must approve these proposals.
   d. mayors of cities within the county must approve these proposals.

8. What is the purpose of joint-powers agreements?
   a. They are usually created to provide a service or fulfill a need that encompasses two or more local governments or is beyond the resources or boundaries of the county government.
   b. They are usually created to provide a service or fulfill a need that encompasses two or more state agencies or is beyond the resources or boundaries of the state legislature.
   c. They are usually created to prevent one county government from assuming the powers of another county government.
   d. They allow the consolidation of two county governments.

9. Unincorporated areas are the responsibility of
   a. the state government.
   b. the nearest city government.
   c. special districts.
   d. the county government.

10. What in particular has caused an enormous strain to be placed on the capacity of county governments?
    a. the explosion of housing developments
    b. the lack of recreational services
    c. the dissolution of city governments
    d. changes in climate

11. The county administrator has dual responsibilities, half of which involve supplying the board of supervisors with reports and information and half of which involve
    a. managing the various offices of the supervisors.
    b. serving as the go-between for county and municipal governments.
    c. organizing the county election office.
    d. managing the day-to-day operations of county government.

12. Which of the following is not a county-provided service or department?
    a. sheriff's department
    b. school district
    c. district attorney's office
    d. assessor's department

13. To whom is the district attorney's first allegiance?
    a. state attorney general
    b. governor
    c. county board of supervisors
    d. chief justice of the California supreme court

14. The biggest source of city revenue is
    a. current service charges.
    b. taxes.
    c. licenses, permits, and fines.
    d. funding from the state and federal governments.

15. In California, most municipal departments are coordinated by the
    a. mayor.
    b. city council.
    c. city clerk.
    d. city manager.

16. Educational reform at the state level has centered on
    a. the behavior of students.
    b. serving nutritious school lunches.
    c. getting parents more involved in their children's education.
    d. class size reduction, charter schools, vouchers, and "high-stakes" testing.

17. The process of forming an incorporated city begins with
    a. a resolution by the county board of supervisors or a petition signed by at least 25 percent of voters living in the unincorporated area requesting consideration of incorporation.
    b. a resolution by the state legislature or a petition signed by at least 25 percent of voters across the state.

c. a resolution by the city council in the city requesting incorporation or a petition signed by at least 25 percent of voters living in the county of the unincorporated area.

d. an official request that is presented to the governor.

18. The vast majority of cities in California have
a. nine-member councils.
b. three-member councils.
c. seven-member councils.
d. five-member councils.

19. The strong mayor–council model is generally found in California's
a. smaller cities
b. older cities.
c. newer cities.
d. larger cities.

20. What percentage of California's special districts provide a single service?
a. 50 percent
b. 20 percent
c. 85 percent
d. 10 percent

mypoliscilab Exercises

Apply what you learned in this chapter on **MyPoliSciLab.**

Read on mypoliscilab.com

e-Text: Chapter 21

Study and Review on mypoliscilab.com

Pre-Test
Post-Test
Chapter Exam
Flashcards

Watch on mypoliscilab.com

Video: L. A. Billboards

Explore on mypoliscilab.com

Simulation: You Are the Mayor and Need to Get a Town Budget Passed
Simulation: You are the Director of Economic Development for the City of Los Angeles, California
Comparative: Comparing States and Local Governments

California Fiscal Policy

KEY OBJECTIVES

After completing this chapter, you should be prepared to:

22.1 Distinguish between a structural budget gap and a budget deficit.

22.2 Identify the sources of state revenue.

22.3 Determine the major state expenditures.

22.4 Outline the state budget process, and assess the effects of direct democracy on the budgetary process.

I n May 2009, in response to the deepening economic downturn, Governor Schwarzenegger proposed to elminate California's work-to-welfare system and more specifically, the California Work Opportunity and Responsibility to Kids (CalWORKs) program, the state's version of the Temporary Assistance to Needy Families Act. The governor's proposal provoked an immediate public outcry. Just one day later, members of the public and county officials gathered before the legislature's Budget Conference Committee calling the governor's proposal reckless.[1] The consequences would be dire, causing 90,000 CalWORKS clients and 14,000 CalWORKS administrators to lose their jobs.[2] With a caseload of about half a million of the state's poorest families with children, the program supports parents toward self-sufficiency allowing them to receive education and training, substance abuse treatment or mental health services, and job search assistance. The parents in the program must devote at least 32 hours a week to work or welfare-to-work programs and face a lifetime limit on aid of 60 months. In addition to cash aid, recipients receive food stamps and county health care services. By most measures, CalWORKs has been a success,

> **How can Californians invoke the state's legacy of innovation to avert fiscal calamity?**

early on reducing the number of families receiving government aid in California by about 50 percent. Today, the program allows single parents to get the training and education they need to earn wages that will support their families. Currently, CalWORKS feeds approximately 1.4 million children in the state.

In response to Governor Schwarzenegger's 2009 proposal, the state government slashed funding to CalWORKS. Then in his 2010 May Revise of Budget Proposal, the governor once again sought to eliminate the program entirely as California's deficit rose above $20 billion. Roughly $2.3 billion is contributed by the state of California to CalWORKS from an approximately $100 billion state government budget. The elimination of the program, however, would actually prevent federal funds from streaming into the state. Funding of CalWORKs consists of an approximately 50/50 matching arrangement between the state and federal governments. Roughly $2.3 billion is contributed by the state of California to CalWORKS from an approximately $100 billion state budget.[3] Hence, by eliminating the program, California would in effect be giving up federal funding for a program that receives only a small portion of the state budget.

Resource Center
• Glossary
• Vocabulary Example
• Connect the Link

■ **Structural Budget Gap:** A long-term excess of state expenditures over state revenues.

SIGNIFICANCE: *The Schwarzenegger administration argued that the statewide health plan will bring down health care costs by encouraging healthy habits, better management of chronic diseases, and electronic record-keeping, all of which would help to reduce costs to the state and contribute to reducing California's structural budget problems.*

A Budget Process in Crisis

22.1 Distinguish between a structural budget gap and a budget deficit.
(pages 668–671)

California is approaching a major economic reckoning. The rapid economic downturn in the housing and mortgage lending industries brought on this difficult fiscal situation, but the state government failed to head off the onslaught of a burgeoning deficit that in 2009 grew to approximately $25 billion, or about 20 percent of the total budget. The crafting of the 2009–2010 state government budget bill, after much political infighting and costly delay, was considered a last ditch effort by the governor and the state legislature to avert the near financial collapse of government and vital services in California.

From the release of the governor's budget in January 2009 to final passage of the state budget bill, a considerable amount of work went into balancing the state budget, culminating with a special election in May. Five, measures were placed on the ballot during this special election that essentially called for raising taxes and shifting money from special funds to the general fund. All of these measures were rejected by the voters, forcing the governor and the legislature to make major budget cuts as well as raid funds earmarked for local government.

The poor condition of the state government's fiscal health was best illustrated by the major funding cuts to the California public school system. Funded at the barest of minimums, allocations to education were cut by $1.6 billion outright and further lowered through reductions in school schedules, purchase suspensions, and other cost-cutting measures. Budget allocations to the California prison system were slated to be reduced by about $1.2 billion, and money for the second-largest state government expenditure, health and human services, was once again reduced. Of the $497 million of the budget vetoed by the governor, $394 million of these funds were from health and human services programs.

The final 2009–2010 budget involved a considerable amount of reshuffling and borrowing, including $1.9 billion from local government property tax revenue, $2.05 billion in redevelopment agency property tax funds, and hundreds of millions of dollars in transportation funds. The decision by the state government to borrow, principally from local government, was made possible by suspending the provisions of Proposition 1A, a ballot measure approved by the voters in 2004 that prevented the state government from tapping into revenue earmarked for local government.

The governor and state legislature also instituted a variety of creative cost-cutting measures that created at least the illusion of saving the state money, including, for example, the mandates that many taxpayers pay a larger share of their state income tax during the first half of the calendar year and that state workers be furloughed three days per month, supposedly saving the state $1.3 billion.

California has roughly one year to determine whether the 2009–2010 budget was a prudent policy decision granting the state a budgetary respite until revenue returns to required levels, or whether deeper and more painful cuts or drastic tax increases are required.[4]

The California Structural Budget Gap

Most governments—and businesses for that matter—endure difficult financial periods. California governors going back as far as Ronald Reagan encountered difficulties in balancing the state budget. California is, however, endowed with a resource-rich economy, and all governors up to Governor Gray Davis, in cooperation with the state legislature, found differing methods of achieving governmental solvency. When Governor Davis took office in 1999, California was prospering economically, and the state government produced a balanced budget. In fact, at the end of his predecessor's term, after a difficult economic period, the state government had about $4 billion in reserve. Under Davis, that money went either to finance tax breaks or to restore cuts in programs that had suffered during lean budgetary years. Still, for the first couple of years of the Davis administration, the state government's financial situation remained stable thanks to the thriving economy, especially in high-tech industries. Any attempt to conserve excess revenue to the state during this period was overridden by the decision to increase spending for a number of governmental services—especially education, a major campaign promise by Davis that was supported by the state legislature. During these boom years, state government took the opportunity to reduce fees, enact special tax breaks, and extend health coverage to uninsured children. Spending for the state government shot up between 25 and 35 percent. Then, in early 2001, the high-tech industry suffered a major decline, and with it went about 15 percent of state tax revenue. Soon after that, California was hit with the energy crisis, forcing the state government to spend $6 billion of its cash reserves to shore up the energy industry. Making the financial situation even worse was a slide in the stock market that delivered yet another major revenue loss to the California state government. By the time Arnold Schwarzenegger took office in 2003, the state was confronted with the realities of a **structural budget gap**■.[5]

The difference between a *structural budget gap* and a *budget problem* or *deficit* is that a gap tends to be either permanent or long-term. In most developing nations, a gap between the

Governor Schwarzenegger announces and explains the California state budget for 2004–2005. —*What fiscal challenges have remained unaddressed since that time?*

money the government accumulates and the cost of government services has existed for decades. Many of these nations carry a perpetual national debt, used to bridge the gap, which even in prosperity could never be paid in full. The California state government is now inching toward a similar situation. California's government revenue problems started with the passage of Proposition 13 in 1978, resulting in a massive property tax cut, and the state government has been trying desperately to make up that loss in revenue ever since. For a while, successive governors have been able to fill the gap with short-term measures, such as shifting funds from one department to another, deferring payments on state debt and other long-term costs, internal borrowing from special funds, and external borrowing. These financial tactics worked well as long as there was the promise of future funds to eventually balance the books, but in recent years, few new revenue sources have materialized.

Upon taking office, Governor Schwarzenegger campaigned for and got approval of a $15 billion bond measure, and two years later, he received voter approval of another $43 billion for

affordable housing, school projects, flood control, and other infrastructure-related projects—essentially borrowing the California state government out of the structural budget gap. In combination with slight increases in revenue during fiscal 2005–2006, this got California over the gap. Clearly, the delay in passing the 2007–2008 budget was largely the consequence of a strategy by state senate Republicans to prevent Attorney General Jerry Brown from filing lawsuits against local governments and industries that refuse to assess and reduce their global warming impacts. Less than a year later, however, the state found itself in yet another budget emergency brought on by a variety of factors, resulting this time in an approximately $17 billion shortfall and another structural budget gap. The question is whether the current economic malaise will have long-term repercussions. The collapse of the housing market, caused by the subprime loan debacle, has had damaging affects throughout lending, construction, and related industries. California quickly became second among all states in the number of foreclosures. These problems, coupled with the nationwide recession, meant much less tax

■ **Legislative Analyst's Office (LAO):** The office responsible for analyzing the California state budget and making recommendations to the state legislature regarding the fiscal efficiency of state government.

SIGNIFICANCE: *Under the leadership of the legislative analyst, this organization must maintain a precarious balance between an accurate analysis of the state budget and related issues and overly angering the governor or state legislators from either political party. Members of both branches will not hesitate to charge partisanship or incompetence if any analysis by the LAO appears to favor a particular group or idea.*

revenue for state government. At the same time, state government spending increased, as it does practically every year. The prevalence of the structural budget gap narrows the options available to a state government struggling to comply with the public's need for services. Ultimately, the answer to bridging the "gap" seems to lie somewhere between reducing wasteful or unnecessary spending and enacting a revenue-raising plan that a broad cross-section of Californians can accept. That answer will undoubtedly necessitate an honest appraisal of the many features of the budget process and encompass large segments of the general public willing to expend the time and energy to understand this process as well as the magnitude of the problem.

The California Budget: Politics and Key Players

There is little doubt in the minds of the elected officers of the executive branch and state legislators that the budget is where reality and ideas part. The annual budget reflects the priorities of the state government, and most Californians would like to believe these priorities correspond to California's best interests. These leaders and legislators owe their positions to political considerations, not prudent economics, and they can be counted on to listen carefully to concerns about the budget from the individuals and groups that have contributed to their political success. As the chief architect of the state budget, the governor is especially susceptible to pressure from a variety of constituencies. Governor Jerry Brown, for example, was adamantly opposed to Proposition 13 and vigorously campaigned against it, but upon passage, he advocated for many of its tax-cutting features.[6] As governor of California, Ronald Reagan was forced to backpedal on his limited government approach and approve tax increases.

The governor is the ringmaster of the California budget circus, but the star performer of that show is clearly the state legislature. Legislators have to overcome the weaknesses they may have in understanding a complicated budget process, the consequences of term limits, and the necessity of having to learn budget details quickly with a large staff of personal aides, committee consultants, and party caucus and research staffs.

The budget drama becomes especially intense for the governor when the state legislature is controlled by the opposing party, which has been the case for four of the last six governors. That legislative body will first and foremost want to craft a budget that caters to members' voting constituents and the special-interest groups that helped them get elected. For the Democrats in the legislature, who tend to represent a wide range of interests, providing for their supporters in the annual budget can be difficult and costly for California taxpayers. The annual state budget is full of tax breaks as well as generous funding for government programs and projects that benefit businesses, unions, and seniors. For years, the Democrat-controlled legislature has given a hefty tax credit to corporations that moved into "enterprise zones" and hired local residents, despite complaints that many businesses were taking advantage of the credit but failing to produce the intended results.[7] Interest groups have a large stake in the budget plan and will not hesitate to use information, campaign contributions, and the initiative process to influence what the budget supports and how it is financed. It is no secret that the oil companies located in California have contributed heavily to the elections of statewide officers and state legislators and receive a number of annual tax breaks. For example, California is one of the few states that do not levy an oil severance tax on the value of each barrel of oil removed from the ground or water in California.

The elected statewide officers of government are another source of political pressure and influence on budgetary matters,

Students rally against Governor Schwarzenegger's education budget cuts.
—*Considering that revenue sources to the state have been dramatically reduced, what would be the most convincing argument these students could make to support the complete funding of education over other major spending areas?*

■ **Proposition 140:** A law that established term limits for both state senators and assembly legislators and cut 60 percent of the budget for the Legislative Analyst's Office.

SIGNIFICANCE: *The cuts to the Legislative Analyst's Office staff due to Proposition 140 would deprive the state legislature of an important resource just as term limits, another product of Proposition 140, was causing the unanticipated retirement of many experienced legislators. Without legislators experienced in budgetary matters and an LAO staff capable of responding to the full state legislative membership, the successive wave of new legislators have had to either avoid detailed budget analysis or increasingly rely on budget experts from special interest groups.*

especially the treasurer and controller, who have direct responsibilities for financial aspects of the government. During 2005, Phil Angelides, the state treasurer, was a vocal critic of the fiscal policies of the Schwarzenegger administration, a position that observers of state capitol politics feel stemmed as much from his roots in Democratic partisan politics and his decision to run for governor as from his duties in the office of the treasurer.

The **Legislative Analyst's Office (LAO)**■ is supposed to be the one governmental entity in the state budget drama not closely associated with any one character or plot. Created in 1941 as the first nonpartisan legislative fiscal office in the country, the LAO is headed by a legislative analyst who is responsible for examining the state budget and making recommendations to the state legislature regarding the fiscal efficiency of state government.[8] Its Web site is full of detailed analyses of the state budget and reports on the performance of specific departments and agencies. Provisions in **Proposition 140**■, however, which mandated term limits for both state senators and assembly legislators also cut 60 percent of the LAO's budget, making certain detailed budget analyses and the former practice of scrutinizing specific fiscal bills nearly impossible.[9]

A number of external but nonetheless important budget-politics players from so-called citizen advocacy groups also specialize in state government fiscal policy. The California Taxpayers Association and the California Tax Reform Association are two of the major statewide organizations that purportedly represent the private citizen's view. Although it is often difficult for these groups to submerge their ideological leanings, they have been important in providing an alternative perspective on budget policy and are often found testifying at state legislative committee hearings.

All of these players—and many others too obscure to mention here—will converge when the time comes to determine the most complete accounting of state government revenue and whether there will be enough to spend on state government expenditures. These decisions are complicated by the various sources of revenue and what appears to be the growing list of government expenses. A reasonably clear understanding of revenue and expenditures is extremely important in forming rational opinions about the state government's financial predicament.

A Budget Process in Crisis

22.1 Distinguish between a structural budget gap and a budget deficit.

PRACTICE QUIZ: UNDERSTAND AND APPLY

1. Which of the following events in early 2001 are largely responsible for a major decline of the California economy?
   a. high unemployment, drought, and political unrest
   b. a troubled high-tech industry, an energy crisis, and a slide in the stock market
   c. the rise in Chinese imports and the recall of Governor Gray Davis
   d. low energy costs, inflation, and the high costs of agricultural production

2. Cuts in income and property taxes (Proposition 13) and the failure of anticipated revenue sources to materialize have resulted in which of the following conditions?
   a. a major decline of high-tech industry
   b. large increases in state spending
   c. a reduction of fees and the enactment of special tax breaks
   d. a structural budget gap

3. The major player in the California budget process is the
   a. treasurer.   c. governor.
   b. controller.   d. speaker of the assembly.

4. The LAO is headed by a legislative analyst who is responsible for
   a. analyzing the state budget and making recommendations.
   b. working under the direction of the governor to formulate the state budget.
   c. analyzing the public policy for local government.
   d. allocating government grants.

ANALYZE

1. What has been the state government's response to the structural budget gap?

2. Who are the key players in the development of the California state budget?

IDENTIFY THE CONCEPT THAT DOESN'T BELONG

a. Budget deficit
b. Financial tactics
c. State debt
d. Casework
e. Proposition 13

Resource Center
• Glossary
• Vocabulary Example
• Connect the Link

■ **General Fund:** The pool of money used to finance the California state government.

EXAMPLE: *From 1945 to 1949, the California general fund actually ended each fiscal year with a surplus of state revenue. However, between 1978 and 1983, California experienced four consecutive years when the state government spent more than it received in revenue.*

Major Sources of State Revenue

22.2 **Identify the sources of state revenue.**
(pages 672–675)

One of the most controversial and misunderstood elements of government, revenue is the fuel that powers the engine of California state government. Ultimately, most of the state revenue will be deposited into the state's **general fund**■, the major pool of money used to finance government (see Figure 22.1). This revenue is largely derived from taxes, although in recent years, borrowing has become much more popular. The question these days among leaders in the executive and legislative branches of California government is not whether to borrow, but how much. There are still many tax dollars flowing to the state, and despite the grumbling of "no new taxes," this extremely important method of raising revenue will probably be around for a while. "Fairness" is one of the fundamental principles of tax policy, and governmental leaders spend long hours trying to devise ways of avoiding criticism for heaping the tax burden onto one particular group. A "fair" tax policy is difficult to achieve simply because of the dilemma in deciding whether to tax everyone equally, regardless of how much fairness is involved, or whether to tax everyone based on level of income. A *progressive tax* is one that takes a greater percentage from individuals with higher incomes than from those with lower incomes. A *regressive tax* imposes a heavier burden on people who are less able to pay the specified tax; applied to income, it is a tax that takes a greater percentage of income from people with low incomes than from those with high incomes.

Personal Income Tax

Adopted in 1935, the state income tax is now the largest source of state revenue, accounting for about 40 percent of the state's general fund (see Figure 22.2). California's income tax is a progressive tax. There are six state income tax rates, beginning at 1.0 percent of total annual income and ending at 9.3 percent, the top rate. The precise numbers can change from year to year, but it is safe to assume that under the current income tax system in California, between 1 and 5 percent of the wealthiest Californians pay at least half of the total income taxes collected.[10] The state legislature has been trying to add a 10-percent bracket for single residents making between $143,000 and $286,000 or married couples earning between $286,843 and $573,686 and an 11-percent bracket for single residents earning over $286,843 and married couples who make over $573,686, but so far, these new rates have been resisted.[11]

Sales Tax

The second-largest number of tax dollars comes from the state sales tax, providing about 28 percent of the general fund. Sales taxes are generally considered to be regressive, because they impose a heavier burden on those who are less able to bear it. Though this condition may not strictly apply to the purchase of a luxury item, it is relevant to the buying of necessities. The statewide sales tax rate until 2009 was set at 7.25 percent of the retail price of purchased goods, but most local governments have exercised their authority to increase the sales tax, with voter approval, to fund various local expenditures. Many cities and counties set the basic sales tax rate at 8.25 percent, while other cities, such as the City and County of San Francisco, have gone as high as 8.50 percent. In 2009, the sales tax was temporarily increased by 1 percent, bringing the additional cost on retail sales close to

FIGURE 22.1 ■ **Total State Revenues, 2008–2009 (in billions)**

General Fund Revenues		Total State Revenues $129.8 Billion	Special Funds Revenues	
Personal Income Tax	$56.5		Motor Vehicle-Related Revenues	$9.5
Sales and Use Tax	29.2		Sales and Use Tax[a]	5.9
Corporation Tax	11.9		Personal Income Tax[b]	1.6
Insurance Tax	2.3		Tobacco-Related Taxes	1.0
All Other	3.0		All Other	9.0
Total	**$102.9**		**Total**	**$26.9**

Details may not total due to rounding.

[a] Includes $3 billion to Local Revenue fund, $1.5 billion redirected to pay defict-financing bonds, and $1.3 billion for transportation-related purposes. Excludes $3 billion allocated to Local Public Safety Fund, which is not included in the governor's budget totals.

[b] For mental services per Proposition 63.

SOURCE: *The 2008–09 Budget: Perspectives and Issues. Report from the Legislative Analyst's Office to the Joint Legislative Budget Committee* (Sacramento, CA: Legislative Analyst's Office), Figure 2, (p. 49). Accessed at http://www.loa.ca.gov/analysis_2008/2008_pandi/pandi_08.pdf

■ **Franchise Tax Board:** The board that sets tax rates for banks and financial institutions in California.

EXAMPLE: *In 1950, California abolished the office of the Franchise Tax Commissioner and created the Franchise Tax Board, whose members are the state controller, the director of finance, and the chair of the state Board of Equalization.*

FIGURE 22.2 ■ The Composition of Revenues Has Changed Over Time

Over the past four decades, personal income tax revenues have increased dramatically—rising from 22 percent to 54 percent of general fund revenues. This growth is the result of growth in real incomes, the state's progressive tax structure, and increased capital gains. The reduced share for the sales tax reflects in part the increase in spending on services, which generally are not taxed. —*Based on the notions of progressive and regressive tax rates, which of these two periods tend to be most fair or equitable in the manner revenue was collected?*

1966–1967

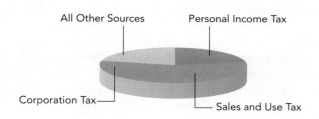

2006–2007

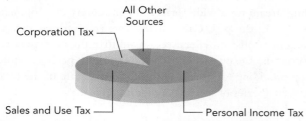

SOURCE: *CAL Facts: California's Economy and Budget in Perspective* (Sacramento, CA: Legislative Analyst's Office), December 2006. Accessed at http://www.lao.ca.gov/2006/cal_facts/calfacts_budget_2006.pdf

10 percent. There have been numerous complaints among Californians over the years about the unevenness with which the sales tax is applied. The charge that certain industries are exempt from the sales tax is usually countered with the argument that the government is merely attempting to restrain its tax policy. For example, according to the Revenue and Taxation Code, a state resident will pay no tax on seeds that produce food for humans but will pay a tax on seeds that produce nonfood plants.

Corporate Taxes

Businesses and corporations that operate in California are subject to what is commonly known as a *franchise tax*, a basic tax rate of 8.84 percent of profits that are earned in the state. For any business transaction that somehow involves selling products or services outside the state or a company outside the state conducting business in California, a corporate tax on profits is levied. The tax rate on banks and financial institutions is determined by the **Franchise**

Even with the national average price for a gallon of regular unleaded gasoline at $4.09 in 2008, Californians were clearly paying the highest prices for gas in the United States, as indicated by this price board at a Shell station in San Bruno, California. As the price of gas rose, Californians, like Americans across the country, debated whether to conserve by driving less or to increase supply by drilling for oil in new locations, such as the Alaskan wilderness or California's own coastal regions. —*How do energy price hikes impact the state economy? What are some good solutions?*

Tax Board■ and will vary from year to year between 10 and 12 percent; the corporate tax rate for the insurance industry in California has been significantly lower. Corporations taxed by the state government generated roughly 10 percent of state revenue.[12]

Excise Tax

Often labeled a "sin tax," the **excise tax**■ is a selective sales tax, imposed only on the sale of specific goods. In California, those specific goods include tobacco, alcoholic beverages, and gasoline. Tobacco is hit hardest by excise taxes, with two separate types of taxes. The first is a surtax on each pack of cigarettes, clearly identified by a stamp, that is paid for by the distributor. The second is a tax levied on all tobacco products, and at least one initiative has been passed over the past decade that puts a special tax on cigarettes to fund smoking prevention, other health-related programs, and youth activities. The construction and maintenance of highways in California have traditionally been financed through a tax on gas and diesel fuel. Taxes on fuel are split between an 18-cent-per-gallon excise tax and a sales tax, but in recent years, the funds generated from these taxes have been shifted to other areas of state expenditures. Excise taxes contribute approximately 4 percent of the general fund and are considered to be regressive. With the introduction of fuel-efficient automobiles, some state legislators as well as transportation and taxation experts suggest that taxing miles driven rather than the gas would be a more equitable way of paying for California's highways and would provide some relief from escalating fuel prices.[13]

MYTH EXPOSED Many Californians believe that corporations are heavily taxed, but actually corporate taxes as a

■ **Excise Tax:** A sales tax imposed only on specific goods. | **SIGNIFICANCE:** *In comparison with other states, California's excise tax ranks about average for beer, slightly lower than most states for distilled spirits, and one of lowest in the country for wine.*

percentage of total state tax revenue have declined from 14.6 percent in 1981 to 10.7 percent in 2010. A number of tax breaks or "loopholes" may be responsible for this. For example, state law allows corporations to choose either the three-factor formula (property, payroll, and sales) or to just pay taxes on a portion of profits that were realized in the state. Now, with sales down in many industries, the latter option may be the best deal. Formerly, corporate tax credits went only to the company actually earning the credit, but now corporations can transfer tax credits to a related or affiliated corporation. There is also a "carry forward," "carry back" provision permitting corporations to claim tax refunds either in past or future tax years. Federal law actually allows corporations that conduct business in multiple states or other countries to avoid the taxation of certain assets in one state by transferring those assets to other locations where taxation is either minimal or nonexistent. Concerned taxpayers throughout the state also charge that the sale of commercial property is often hidden through a variety of legal maneuvers, thus avoiding the reassessment of the property value and potential tax increase.[14]

Bond Debt

Today most politicians are especially sensitive to any consideration of raising taxes and instead are increasingly using bonds to pay for government expenditures that current levels of revenue cannot meet. The use of bonds can be problematic, however, because voter approval is required in most instances. Although bonds are traditionally used for major state-funded construction projects, in 2004 Governor Schwarzenegger succeeded in getting a $15 billion bond plan to address a budgetary shortfall approved by the voters. Basically providing the state government with an opportunity to borrow, bonds come in three basic varieties: (1) general obligation bonds, (2) revenue bonds, and (3) lease-revenue bonds. *General obligation bonds* are backed by the "full faith and credit" of the state government and are a form of long-term financing that is slowly paid back by state revenue, which in most circumstances comes from taxpayers. These so-called "GO bonds" can be used on just about any type of government expenditure at the state level. In 2006, for example, the state legislature and Governor Schwarzenegger also won voter approval of a record-breaking public works bond measure that would furnish funds for roads, schools, ports, mass transit, parks, and levee repair.[15] *Revenue bonds* are used to finance a government facility that will generate funds used to pay back the bond debt.

Many members of the state government as well as private citizens worry about the long-term repercussions of relying on borrowing. Although bonds avoid the need to resort to highly unpopular increases in taxes, they can take between 9 and 14 years to repay and end up costing much more in interest than the amount originally borrowed. California's bond rating has dropped considerably over the years, and there is some doubt about the effect that continued use of bonds will have on that rating in the future. Another type of bond debt, *lease-revenue bonds,* became popular with the California state government in the 1980s. The use of these bonds requires only a simple-majority vote of the state legislature, and they are usually sold to finance the construction and renovation of state facilities. The amount of funds borrowed through lease-revenue bonds is typically small, but the interest rates on these bonds tend to be higher than the rates on GO bonds.[16]

Federal Contributions

The federal government has reduced its spending on a long list of programs that directly benefit Californians in favor of other spending priorities and a mounting national debt. Education, however, is still heavily supported in California by the federal government, particularly vocational, basic adult, preschool, and disadvantaged student programs. Low-income Californians are also the direct beneficiaries of federal spending on child care, food assistance, and housing. Other major federal allocations to California are earmarked for statewide water treatment and a series of block grants to local government. The community development block grant is one of the more noticeable federal grants to local governments in California and is an important funding stream for a wide variety of community development projects.[17] In the past, Californians have received less federal funding per dollar of federal taxes paid than the average state. However, the Obama administration's stimulus package could end up providing California with the largest share of the total package, if a series of special conditions are met.[18]

Other Revenue Sources

In addition to taxes and bonds, the state government receives small amounts of revenue from a number of different sources, supporting the notion that every little bit helps. In 1972, property taxes accounted for about 30 percent of the revenue that went to state and local governments, a large portion of which was earmarked for education.[19] As a result of Proposition 13, that amount is now down to about 13 percent, with the greater part going to state government and small portions going back to local governments. Motor vehicle fees and smaller sources in the revenue mix contribute, on average, about 13 percent of the revenue the state receives.[20] On the heels of his recall election, Governor Schwarzenegger fulfilled a campaign promise to make a temporary reduction in the car tax permanent, resulting in $5 billion less in government revenue, which the state legislature and the governor have been trying to paper over ever since. Other even smaller sources of revenue come from interest earned on state deposits and the lottery. Funds generated from the lottery are specifically earmarked for education, but the amount of this money tends to be unpredictable.

STUDENT profile

Faced with a long list of ecological problems and concerns, many Californians are beginning to dedicate more time and energy to preserving the environment. As an environmental studies major at the University of California at Santa Barbara, (UCSB), Sarah Vitone planned for a career in environmental science. This goal has been supported by the work and training she received at the Cheadle Center for Biodiversity and Eco-logical Restoration (CCBER), a UCSB institution committed to environmental studies, field- and laboratory-based research, and ecological restoration projects. Although Sarah eventually became a paid employee, she was introduced to the CCBER as a restoration intern. "This was a wonderful experience, because it took me out of the classroom and into real restoration proj-ects for the first time," she said. "I was able to learn more about site planning, species identification, and plant material sourcing than any other opportunity I have had here at UCSB. It wasn't all the backbreaking, weed-pulling labor I thought restoration projects were. The CCBER team went out of their way to ensure that, above all, this program would educate and engage students curious about the field of restoration ecology."

Sarah's experience at the CCBER highlights the process and potential benefits of internships. Most importantly, an internship can encompass "hands-on" learning, skill-building, meeting new and interesting people, and a career-related, entry-level, paid position—as Sarah soon discovered. Her work at the center became an extension of her formal academic studies, applying for example the material covered in her class on archiving preservation in a "fun and practical way." This experience also involved more practical tasks, including the gathering and processing of photo information utilizing profes-sional and scientific technology, including Microsoft Excel, Photoshop, different scanning programs, and botany databases. Ultimately, Sarah's work at the CCBER advanced her career in a field that will have long-term benefits for the future of Cali-fornia—and possibly many other parts of the world. Her personal gain was clear: "Interning with CCBER has been a great experience that I will never forget. I am very thankful that CCBER offers these types of opportunities to undergrads looking to apply their knowledge in a fun and useful way."

SOURCE: Accessed at http://ccber.lifesci.ucsb.edu/newsletter / CCBEVolume3/vol003_page_05.php

Major Sources of State Revenue

22.2 **Identify the sources of state revenue.**

PRACTICE QUIZ: UNDERSTAND AND APPLY

1. Which of the following types of taxation is considered a "sin" tax?
   a. income tax
   b. sales tax
   c. corporate tax
   d. excise tax

2. A progressive tax is one that
   a. imposes a heavier burden on those less able to pay the specified tax.
   b. takes a greater percentage of income from those with higher incomes than from those with lower incomes.
   c. is set at one specific percentage.
   d. takes a lower percentage of income from those who work in government than from those who work in the private sector.

3. California's bond rating has
   a. risen sharply over the years.
   b. remained unchanged over the years.
   c. dropped considerably over the years.
   d. been impossible to predict over the years.

4. What has been the level of federal spending in California in recent decades?
   a. less federal funding per dollar of federal taxes paid than the average state
   b. more federal funding per dollar of federal taxes paid than the average state
   c. roughly the same federal funding per dollar of federal taxes paid as the average state
   d. impossible to determine because of the classified nature of the federal expenditures associated with the many military bases in the state

ANALYZE

1. What are the most important sources of state revenue?

2. What type of bond debt is most commonly used by California state government?

IDENTIFY THE CONCEPT THAT DOESN'T BELONG

a. General fund
b. Progressive tax
c. Plea bargains
d. Excise tax
e. Tax rate

Resource Center
- Glossary
- Vocabulary Example
- Connect the Link

Major State Expenditures

22.3 Determine the major state expenditures.
(pages 676–679)

One major concern Californians share is how their hard-earned tax dollars are being spent. Are those dollars being wasted? It would be silly to suggest that no waste occurs in the state government, but the arguments about the squandering of state government revenue are also often misplaced. The state budget for the last five years has been close to $100 billion and a good part of that goes toward providing important basic services for California's residents.

Education

Passed in 1988, Proposition 98 requires the state government to spend a minimum of 40 percent of the general fund on K–12 public school education. Proposition 98 is credited with significantly raising spending per pupil in California after the state fell to forty-seventh in the nation in the aftermath of Proposition 13. Nonetheless, even though significant money goes to education in California, the number of students continues to climb, and overall educational results have been less than stellar. Funding for higher education in California has declined while students at the California state universities and the University of California have experienced steep fee increases. Funding for California's community colleges has suffered major cuts recently after remaining fairly constant over the years, and this share of the budget has been regularly criticized as inadequate considering the large number of students who enroll each year.

Health and Welfare

The bulk of the approximately 28 percent of the general fund allocated for the health and welfare of state residents is consumed by a wide range of health care services that are administered by the counties. These services extend health care coverage to low-income families, low-income elderly, and the disabled through the Medi-Cal program. Surprisingly, the state budget allocation for health care has remained fairly constant in comparison to the skyrocketing costs of private health care providers. Roughly 25 percent of the health and welfare budget goes to Temporary Assistant for Needy Families (TANF) and CalWORKs, the companion program discussed at the opening of this chapter. Other sizable social service programs financed through the general fund are the Supplemental Security Income (SSI) and Supplementary Security Payment (SSP) programs, which help low-income seniors and people with disabilities cover basic living expenses.

Corrections

Alarming growth in the California Department of Corrections is pushing up the price tag for incarcerating a prison population that since the 1980s has grown sevenfold, to 160,000 inmates. The costs have grown to roughly 10 percent of the total state budget, but they are still only barely supporting the costs of maintaining 33 prisons that are at twice their intended capacity and considered to be some of the worst in the nation. There is no shortage of reasons why California prisons are overcrowded, many having to do with high recidivism rates and tough sentencing policies. Barring a major development in crime or criminal justice, the prison population is projected to reach 193,000 inmates by 2011, causing a major increase in the annual cost as well.[21]

A group of California elementary school teachers discuss budget issues in a school library. —*What is likely to be the most important item of a school budget? What is the first item of that budget to be cut?*

CONNECT THE LINK
(Chapter 21, page 638) How do contract cities allow small cities to enjoy the services that major cities enjoy while avoiding the fiscal burden of financing those services directly?

A young girl sits next to a bag of groceries at the Open Door Health Center, which offers free health care to the working poor. The clinic runs with in-kind support from private hospitals, free medicine samples, food donations, and the tireless efforts of staff and volunteers. —*In what ways can California residents work together to help provide services that were previously funded by the state government?*

Other Expenditures

Almost three-fourths of the California state budget is devoted to public education, health and human services for low-income residents, and corrections. The remaining fourth is split among seven major funding categories. These include a wide variety of departments and agencies that have suffered major cutbacks and whose directors can be regularly heard complaining about the lack of funds to complete their mission satisfactorily. Because funds are basically locked into the top three spending areas for statutory, public safety, or public health reasons, there is probably little chance of seeing any increases in the budgets for environmental protection, state government resources, business and housing, consumer services, judicial administration, or workforce development agencies. Transportation would normally be included among these spending areas, but there has recently been serious political pressure to commit highway user taxes and motor vehicle fees and bond measures to transportation improvement.

Financing Local Government

Since the passage of Proposition 13, the amount of revenue generated by county and municipal governments has decreased substantially. California county governments have always had a difficult time financing their operations, and the loss of property tax funds to the state government has made that task even harder. Almost 31 percent of county revenue comes from the state in order to finance state-mandated programs and services that are administered by the county government, the biggest and most expensive being health and welfare services.[22] Administering these services can be problematic for county government, because they are rarely funded at the total or true costs of the services provided. In addition to federal funds for special initiatives usually associated with state-mandated functions, the other revenue sources that go to county government for so-called "general-purpose functions" include property taxes redistributed from the state, special fees, charges for current services, and a variety of smaller forms of revenue. California county governments are experiencing a tight financial situation as residents of local cities remain dependent on them for various services, ranging from voter registration to county jail services, while receiving a diminishing share of state and local revenues. Counties may receive additional revenue by providing services to municipal governments through contract city arrangements, but such contracts have become somewhat controversial, as outlined on Chapter 21, page 638.

City governments do have considerably more flexibility in revenue sources than counties do, but to a large extent, cities are on their own when it comes to raising this revenue. Typical sources of revenue to cities are derived from service charges for utilities, licenses and permits, a portion of state sales taxes, redistribution of property taxes from the state government, and an assortment of smaller forms of revenue. Cities may impose additional percentage points on the standard statewide sales tax rate. This portion of the sale tax revenue to California cities has led municipal governments to promote retail sales establishments, especially the "big box" stores or "megastores" that generate a lot of sales tax revenue. Depending on the city, other revenue sources, such as developer fees and business license and hotel taxes, can provide substantial revenue. Many cities are also increasingly attempting to institute the **Mello-Roos Community Facilities District Act**■, which is a financing tool local governments can use to levy special taxes or assessments for designated community improvements, such as freeway interchanges, library services, or recreation programs.

■ **Mello-Roos Community Facilities District Act:** A financing tool that local governments can use to levy special taxes or assessments for designated community improvements, such as freeway interchanges, library services, or recreation programs.

SIGNIFICANCE: *To form a Mello-Roos Community Facilities District, a written request must be made by two members of the state legislature or a petition must be signed by 50 percent of the voters who reside in the proposed district or by landowners who own 50 percent of property in the district.*

In 1982, two California legislators, State Senator Henry Mello and Assemblyman Mike Roos, led the successful passage of the state law instituting this local revenue-generating process. To institute a Mello-Roos fee, the voters living in the designated community must consent by a two-thirds voting margin.

The fiscal future of counties and cities was improved when voters passed Proposition 1A in 2004, a ballot measure that comes very close to prohibiting the state government from shifting any additional local tax revenues back to the general fund. By 2009, however, the state government revoked provisions of this law by allowing "borrowing" of up to 8 percent of tax allocations to local governments. Proposition 13 and the transfer of most property tax revenues to the state government began a process by the state government of periodically raiding the revenue sources of local governments, most recently the local portion of sales and highway user taxes, to avoid state government budget deficits.[23] The fiscal relationship between local and state governments is getting increasingly complicated as both levels of government search for equitable and creative methods of funding services. The "Triple Flip," instituted in 2004 as a part of Proposition 57, the California Economic Recovery Bond Act was essentially a revenue-swapping procedure. The local government's portion of the sales tax would be shifted to the state. In return, a portion of local property taxes that are normally used for local education would be held by the local governments and used to reimburse the county and city governments for the lost sales tax revenue during January and May of each year. The state government would make up the loss in local educational funding through the minimum-funding guarantee of Proposition 98.[24] However, in 2010, a constitutional amendment (Proposition 22) passed that restricts the legislature from using tax revenue dedicated by law to fund local governments. While this amendment is unlikely to result in more funds, it should offer some budgetary reassurances to cash-strapped local governments.

PATHWAYS of action

Consumer Groups and State Officials Reverse Health Insurance Rate Hike

Health insurance rate hikes in California have been a fairly common occurrence. In early 2010, however, Anthem Blue Cross, California's largest healthcare insurance company, faced highly publicized opposition from consumer groups and state officials when the company informed its approximately 800,000 policyholders that their rates would increase as much as 39 percent. The announcement of this rate increase coincided, to the disadvantage of Anthem Blue Cross, with the national debate over the proposed federal healthcare law, statewide primary election campaigns, and a growing concern over the state's declining economy, all of which served to galvanize opposition. Consumer advocacy groups such as Consumer Watchdog and the Consumer Federation of California were instrumental in focusing widespread media attention on the rate increase, instigating action by the state legislature and the state Department of Insurance, headed by Insurance Commissioner Steve Poizner. Both Poizner, who was a candidate for governor in the Republican primary, and state legislator Dave Jones, the chairperson of the Assembly Health Committee and a candidate for Insurance Commissioner, had to be concerned about the effect media coverage of the rate hike would have on their electoral aspirations.

In his capacity as insurance commissioner, Poizner arranged for an independent audit of the financial records of Anthem Blue Cross. In addition to revealing errors in the methods used by the company to calculate insurance rates, the auditors also found hundreds of violations of state law concerning either the failure to pay medical claims on time or the misrepresentation of policy provisions to customers. Utilizing his position as chairperson of the Assembly Health Committee, Jones convened hearings to investigate the rate hike, subjecting the Anthem Blue Cross President Leslie Margolin, during one session, to an especially harsh series of questions. Margolin attempted to use this hearing as an opportunity to explain the company's side of the rate hike, citing the escalating fees demanded by hospitals and doctors, the high cost of new technologies and pharmaceuticals, and the hidden cost of uninsured individuals who seek medical treatment.

On the heels of the Department of Insurance investigation, Consumer Watchdog filed a class-action lawsuit against Anthem Blue Cross. The lawsuit alleged that the healthcare insurer was actually raising rates in an attempt to encourage policyholders with more expensive health plans to adopt cheaper policies with fewer benefits and higher deductibles. This legal action quickly became unnecessary when Anthem Blue Cross announced in late April 2010 that it was withdrawing the rate increase due to "inadvertent miscalculations" in calculating medical costs.

Unlike home and auto insurance rates, health insurance rates are not subject to prior approval by any state agency. Consequently, Anthem Blue Cross may very well reintroduce the same rate increases sometime in the future. Anthem Blue Cross policyholders can nonetheless, at least for the moment, breathe a sigh of rate-hike relief.

SOURCE: Victoria Colliver, "Anthem Withdraws Rate Increase," *San Francisco Chronicle*, April 30, 2010; Bobby Caina Calvan, "Insurance Rate Hikes Fan Political Firestorm," *Sacramento Bee*, March 2, 2010; Duke Helfand, "Anthem Blue Cross Broke Law More than 700 Times, Official Says," *Los Angeles Times*, February 23, 2010; "CFC supports AB 2578 (Jones) Regulating Insurance Rates," Consumer Federation of California, accessed at www.consumercal.org/article.php?id=943

Major State Expenditures

22.3   **Determine the major state expenditures.**

PRACTICE QUIZ: UNDERSTAND AND APPLY

1. Proposition 98 requires the state government to spend what percentage of the general fund in which area?
   a. a minimum of 40 percent of the general fund on health and welfare
   b. a minimum of 40 percent of the general fund on K–12 public school education
   c. a minimum of 20 percent of the general fund on public safety
   d. a minimum of 50 percent of the general fund on higher education

2. Most of the state's expenditure on health and welfare services is allocated to
   a. the Supplemental Security Income program.
   b. health care services administered by the counties.
   c. CalWORKs.
   d. the Temporary Assistance for Needy Families program.

3. Corrections is what percentage of the state budget?
   a. 7 percent   c. 1 percent
   b. 10 percent   d. 5 percent

4. Which of the following spending categories is funded by large special funding sources outside the general fund?
   a. environmental protection
   b. state government resources
   c. business and housing
   d. transportation

ANALYZE

1. What have been some of the major changes in how state revenue is expended?

2. Why do cities have more flexibility than counties in raising revenue?

IDENTIFY THE CONCEPT THAT DOESN'T BELONG

a. Environmental protection
b. Health and welfare
c. Consumer services
d. Judicial administration
e. Workforce development

Resource Center
• Glossary
• Vocabulary Example
• Connect the Link

■ **Executive Budget Plan:** The spending plan for the state of California that the governor must submit to the state legislature by January 10th each year.

SIGNIFICANCE: *In 1922, the California constitution was amended to include provisions that established the first guidelines for an executive budget plan. This amendment required the governor's budget to be annual (formerly biennial), comprehensive, itemized, and balanced.*

The California Budget Process

22.4 Outline the state budget process, and assess the effects of direct democracy on the budgetary process.
(pages 680–683)

Anyone who is either employed by the state government, heavily taxed, maybe not taxed enough, or has some other vested interest in the budget of the California state government will be focused on the annual budget process that gradually unfolds over the course of the first six—and possibly many more—months of the year. It is tempting to call this process a *cycle*, because it consists of a recurring sequence of specific steps that must follow state laws and legislative procedures. There are, however, certain years when it is difficult to predict what the final budget will look like and whether or not there will be some last-minute "discovery" of a budget surplus or shortfall.

Executive Budget Plan

The governor is required by California law to submit a spending plan, known as the **executive budget plan**■, to the state legislature by January 10th, nearly six months before the fiscal year officially ends on June 30th. In reality, the development of the state budget begins six months *before* the January deadline, when the heads of state departments and agencies first submit their budget requests to the California Department of Finance for review and gradually make budget recommendations to the governor. Because the California state government, like most governments, operates on a pay-as-you-go system and really does not know how much revenue, especially in taxes, it takes in until the end of the fiscal year, the projections made by the Department of Finance regarding future revenue are very important to the governor in devising a new budget plan. Once these projections have been made and the budgets of individual state governmental organizations have been analyzed, the governor is free to authorize the final budget.

State law mandates a balanced budget with equal amounts of revenue and expenditures. The governor can create the illusion of a balanced budget by deferring payments, shifting balances, or even reorganizing government. In addition to submitting the budget plan to the state legislature, this document is first made public in printed form with some fanfare.

The Legislative Budget Approval Process

The system of checks and balances in California's state government is very apparent in the adoption of the state budget. After

January 10th, the state budget is introduced in the legislature and automatically assigned to the Assembly Budget and Senate Budget and Fiscal Review Committees, reviewed for a number of weeks, and then parceled out by subject to the appropriate subcommittees. At about the same time, the Legislative Analyst's Office (LAO) drafts an extensive analysis of the budget, citing the weak and strong points of this financial document. It is not uncommon for the LAO analysis to be critical of the governor's spending and revenue-generating plan, usually attracting significant media attention.

From about late February until the final vote on the budget bill, which according to the California constitution should happen by June 15th, a number of important steps takes place that can influence the numbers in the state budget. Whatever critique of the budget is made by the LAO passes quickly, and the focus shifts to the hearings conducted by the subcommittees of the state legislature. In most instances, the members of the legislative subcommittees know in advance the gist of the testimony to be given by department heads and representatives of particular interest groups, and these hearings remain under the tight control of the committee chairs. However, any real revision of the governor's original spending plan in the state legislature is heavily dependent on political pressures that the state legislature experiences and that can emerge at any moment. Governor Schwarzenegger and the state legislature, for example, had originally planned to cut $7.3 million in state tourism funding from the 2005–2006 budget in response to severe revenue limitations. Before the governor could sign the final budget package, however, the California Lodging Industry Association and other California travel and hospitality industry associations rapidly mobilized lobbyist and industry supporters who lobbied, wrote letters, and called legislators. The result was full restoration of the $7.3 million for the California

Michael Genest, the State Finance Director, sits to the left of Governor Schwarzenegger. During the month of May, when the governor makes major adjustments to his initial annual budget based on revised tax collection projections, Genest as well as other civil servants and private industry economists are regular participants at public meetings involving the state's fiscal matters. —*Why is their role so important in the budgetary process?*

■ **May Revise:** A revised projection of California's financial picture conducted by the head of the state Department of Finance and economists from private industry.

SIGNIFICANCE: *An important source of information and insight for state government in formulating the May revise comes from the UCLA Anderson School of Management, which periodically issues the Anderson Forecast—an analysis of the California economy—and conducts quarterly conferences that are attended by a cross section of business, government, and academic decision makers from across California.*

Travel and Tourism Commission to spend promoting tourism, California's third-largest industry.[25]

The May Revise

Another major step in the budget process is the **May revise**■, a revised projection of the state's financial picture that is conducted by the head of the Department of Finance and economists from private industry. Conducting this review of the financial situation of the state in May has a lot to do with the April 14th tax-filing deadline, offering the state the most accurate accounting of revenue that it receives before the final budget should be voted on in June. During the month of May, the Department of Finance, under the direction of the governor, revises the original budget plan numbers either upward or downward to reflect the current financial picture of the state and the governor's spending priorities and then submits this revision to the budget subcommittees of the state legislature, which are bound by law and procedure to accept it.

The Two-Thirds Requirement and the Conference Committee

California was one of the few states in the Union that required two-thirds of the members in each house of the state legislature to approve the budget. For most of California's legislative history, this constitutional rule was a mere formality, but starting in the 1990s, for various reasons, including term limits and increasing partisanship in the state legislature, this requirement caused passage of the budget to be delayed almost every year. This requirement came to an end with the passage of Proposition 25 in 2010. This constitutional amendment changed the legislative vote requirement for passing the state budget from two-thirds to a simple majority.

A coalition of unions, citizen advocacy groups, and Democratic legislators banded together in qualifying and winning passage of Proposition 25 largely based on the need to approve the budget quickly during this period of economic downturn. Campaign ads for Proposition 25 regularly warned voters that each day that the state budget passage was delayed, it cost the state government $50 million. Although that dollar amount was questionable, the figure underscored the feeling among most Californians that the two-thirds requirement was not worth the regular budget stalemates. The new simple majority requirement removes an important source of legislative leverage that the minority Republican Party has had over the budget process in the past.

Proposition 25 did, however, retain a two-thirds requirement for an increase in taxes. That requirement, along with Proposition 22, a constitutional amendment restricting state government's use of funds earmarked for transportation and local governments, and Proposition 26, a constitutional amendment that requires a two-thirds majority to approve fees and

Fiscal difficulties faced by the California state government, such as an approximately $25 billion dollar deficit and the possibility for a major budget approval stalemate, inevitably leads to major reductions in governmental services and public protests of these cuts. —*Can such protests actually generate any solutions to the state's fiscal problems? Is there anything that these individuals can do beyond protesting to address the state's fiscal difficulties?*

taxes, will present new challenges to the legislature's role in the budget process. Once the budget is finally approved, neither party can realistically disavow the outcome of the spending plan.

Regardless of whatever motivations legislators may have in not approving the budget, the governor must have revenue to carry out the executive duties of the state government, and in 1990 Governor George Deukmejian called together the four party leaders from both chambers to resolve budgetary issues that were preventing passage of the state budget. In effect, the so-called "Big Five" became a sort of court of last resort, with the legislative having a tendency to leave *all* unresolved matters to this highly select group. However, there is good reason to believe that with the passage of Proposition 25, the "Big Five" may have outlived its usefulness.

Final Budget Approval by the Governor

The budget process comes to a close when the governor signs the budget bill. If the typical steps of the budget process are followed, the signing of the budget by the governor is only a formality. The governor of California, unlike the president of the United States, has line-item veto power, the ability to reduce or reject any particular item in the state budget. When a governor decides to "blue-pencil" a specific amount, it is usually for symbolic reasons that all inside players have anticipated, although the governor may not eliminate any budget item that is mandated by law.

The Effect of Direct Democracy on the Budget Process

Commonly known as "ballot-box budgeting," the initiative process in California has had a profound effect on the budget process in a variety of ways. Of all the initiatives passed throughout the history of California, approximately half have had a direct impact on state government fiscal matters, and some 40 to 50 percent of the state budget is locked into certain expenditures as a result of initiative statutes or constitutional amendments based on initiatives. Some initiatives are not necessarily intended to alter fiscal policy but have that effect when implemented. Proposition 184, the "three strikes" initiative, greatly increased the California prison population, causing a dramatic rise in the cost of financing the correctional system.[26]

There are two major opinions regarding the fiscal effect of initiatives and referendums on the budget process, with the first suggesting that initiatives constrain the capacity of elected officials to make decisions regarding fiscal policy. By forcing the state government to commit funding resources to support the goals of ballot measures or replacing revenue that has been decreased by initiatives, elected officials have found it difficult to craft a balanced budget and adjust spending policies to new or emerging problems or societal needs. The paralyzing effect of direct democracy on fiscal policy is further demonstrated, so say the critics of ballot-box budgeting, by the difficulty of altering or removing ballot measures, which in California can be repealed or amended only through the mechanisms of direct democracy.[27]

Other observers of California government have found that rather than the initiative alone, other aspects of the budget process also influence the fiscal policies of the state. Educational costs, some suggest, would probably not be much lower than the amount locked in by Proposition 98, which requires the state government to spend 40 percent of the budget on education. They cite the fact that even with the mandate of this initiative, the expenditure per pupil in California has not risen above the national median. No law or regulation prevents the state legislature from passing tax increases if an initiative has an adverse effect on the fiscal health of the state. The problem is not the initiative, say advocates of direct democracy; the state's recurring budget quandaries are instead the result of poor leadership.[28]

The State Economy: The Foundation of Fiscal Policy

When analyzing the expenditures and revenue of state government, it is often easy to lose sight of the foundation for sound fiscal policies: a healthy economy. The unemployment rate is always a good, albeit incomplete, indicator of economic conditions at the state, local, or national level. In California, the unemployment rate stayed fairly stable, at about 5.4 percent, from 2002 to 2005.[29] By 2010 the unemployment rate climbed to above 12 percent statewide and as high as 25 percent in especially hard-hit regions. There are two very different solutions being debated about how to get the growing number of unemployed Californians working again. One view held by most members of the California Democratic Party—and echoed by the Obama administration—calls for creating public-works projects and other government-funded initiatives to generate jobs and give the state economy a badly needed infusion of cash. Conservative members of the state legislature, backed by the governor and much of the business community, argue for a strategy that will make California businesses more competitive and create a more favorable business climate. They are confident that the state economy will grow and cause the creation of more jobs if the state government relaxes environmental and labor laws, reduces taxes on business, and cuts the government budget.

The real estate market has been especially significant in California, which for many years expanded the housing stock, construction projects and jobs, and a wide variety of services. Costs increased to the point where home ownership for many Californians was out of reach, but relief seemed in sight for first-time home buyers who had the cash to invest, as predictions by economists and real estate analysts of a real estate "bubble burst" actually happened. However, this plunge in home sales and prices also caused substantial declines in job growth and financial markets.

Migration to California has become an intensely debated issue, especially regarding people from abroad. The question as to whether migration is good or bad in the long run depends partly on who is immigrating and what aspects of their presence are most noticeable. Much evidence supports the notion that California would have a labor shortage, especially in select industries, without immigration to the state. The consumption of goods and services by recent arrivals is yet another plus. Migrants can cause social services and infrastructure to become overburdened, however, requiring increased government revenue. Social problems can also result from recent arrivals who for various reasons cannot become integrated into society. The current unemployment rate suggests that migration to California has not created a major labor shortage, but as the population of immigrants becomes more integrated and more educated, competition in all sectors of the state economy could increase dramatically.

Although many California-based businesses complain of a poor business climate, citing housing, energy, and insurance costs as well as government regulations and taxes, the actual number of businesses that have left the state is relatively small. Even with the negative aspects of the California commercial sector, few other markets in the United States can compete with the population size and consumer spending power of California—features that may be more important to a company than the accommodation of its business operations.

The California Budget Process

22.4 Outline the state budget process, and assess the effects of direct democracy on the budgetary process.

PRACTICE QUIZ: UNDERSTAND AND APPLY

1. How can the governor create the illusion of a balanced budget?
   a. by firing the director of the state Department of Finance
   b. by borrowing revenue directly from Wall Street investors
   c. by deferring payments
   d. by preventing the reorganization of government

2. The start of the fiscal year for the California state government is
   a. January 10th
   b. July 1st
   c. December 25th
   d. January 1st

3. The revised projection of the state's financial picture occurs in
   a. December.
   c. May.
   b. January.
   d. July.

ANALYZE

1. What is the most significant obstacle in approving the California state government budget?

2. What are the major indicators of the conditions of the California economy?

IDENTIFY THE CONCEPT THAT DOESN'T BELONG

   a. Petition referendum
   b. Executive budget plan
   c. Legislative analyst
   d. Line-item veto
   e. Two-thirds requirement

Conclusion

Few states suffered more than California from the banking and mortgage crisis, a calamity that could have been avoided had the wide cast of characters, from mortgage lenders to housing developers to home loan borrowers in the state, exercised a bit more personal restraint and regard for the long-term ramifications of their financial decisions. This focus on personal financial gain and accumulation of material goods among state residents has tended to cloud any recognition of such issues as the structural budget gap, which leaves state government in perpetual indebtedness. As this gap continues to grow, Californians must find a rational approach to cutting state government expenditures and instituting sound economic practices.

Yet, could it also be that the fiscal health of the state may revive as a result of a renewed commitment of every Californian, whether in government or the private sector, to strike a balance between their contributions to the fiscal solvency of state government and their utilization of government? Although state government has been burdened with dramatic deficits, California remains a very wealthy state in comparison to the rest of the country. Could a more equitable sharing of the tax burden stem the growth of the budget deficit? More than ever, state government is desperately dependent on individual residents who are willing to contribute to the public good, utilize government services judiciously, become watchdogs of legitimate waste, and introduce cost-saving ideas. The decline in personal income does not necessarily mean that residents cannot make other contributions—for example, exchanging tax dollars for a commitment to volunteerism in areas previously funded by the state government. Hence, the fiscal health of the state may also be dependent in part on the sense of personal responsibility that all California residents are willing to assume.

KEY CONCEPT MAP

How did California's more recent budget and fiscal crises develop?

1978

Proposition 13

Approved by the voters in 1978, Proposition 13 was a tax revolt against what many Californians felt were drastically fluctuating and excessive property tax rates. In the aftermath of Proposition 13, property tax revenue dropped by 57 percent for the fiscal year 1978-1979.

An immediate effect of Proposition 13 was a dramatic decrease in property tax revenue with funding shortfalls among schools, law enforcement, and other government services. The two-thirds vote in the state legislature required by Proposition 13 to raise taxes has made replacing lost property tax revenue virtually impossible.

Critical Thinking Questions

What if Proposition 13 had not passed? Would California still have a budget deficit? Or is it likely that the government would already have raised taxes to make up for the shortfall? Why would a resident of California who did not own a home still favor Proposition 13?

2002

Fiscal Crisis

Until 2002, substantial revenue was generated by the boom in the computer and telecommunications industry. When many of these companies proved unprofitable, the "dot-com bubble" burst, and the state government suffered a major drop in tax revenue. Simultaneously an energy crisis forced state government to subsidize utilities saddling the state with a $36.8 billion budget deficit.

After a record 63-day delay in passing, the 2002 state government budget made slight reductions in expenditures, but largely failed to address a deficit that exceeded $10 billion. The state's budget problems, coupled with the energy crisis, provided the momentum for a successful recall campaign against Governor Gray Davis only a year after he won reelection.

Was there anything that Gray Davis might have done as governor that could have kept him from being recalled? What if the state had not been in a fiscal crisis? Is it likely that the recall would have been successful? How much blame or credit should the governor receive when it comes to the economy?

2003–2006

Housing Bubble

A boom in construction was fueled by low interest rates, lax lending requirements, and the popularity of investing in real estate. As home sales increased, the value of homes in California grew 20 percent annually. Almost 50 percent of the new job market was generated by real estate, construction, mortgage brokering, and other service-related industries.

Despite the housing bubble, which caused moderate increases in revenue, the state government continued to experience a budget shortfall. In addition, restricted by Proposition 13, the state legislature and governor were unable to raise taxes.

What feature of the "housing bubble" had the most positive impact on the lives of average California residents? Is it probable that California will experience another such bubble in the future? Why or why not?

2007

Financial Crisis

By 2007, the California real estate market began to suffer from declining sales and housing prices that sparked the deterioration of the state's financial industry. Hundreds of thousands of California homeowners began to default on their mortgages. And as the real-estate industry declined, employment and other business opportunities slowed as well.

One of the most harmful effects of this crisis was a dramatic reduction in consumer spending, leading to a commercial slowdown and rising unemployment. The state government struggled with shrinking state and income tax revenue and limited lending opportunities. Even the state government's ability to borrow became more difficult as its

Which group is most responsible for the burst of the housing bubble and resulting financial crisis: high-risk borrowers, subprime lending businesses, or local governments that approved an overabundance of housing units? Why? Was California more or less susceptible to the financial crisis than the rest of the nation?

2009

Fiscal Emergency

After the state legislature failed to approve a balanced budget that would eliminate a $24 billion deficit, Governor Arnold Schwarzenegger formally declared a fiscal emergency, an act that required state legislators to meet in a special session to address the budget crisis.

In an effort to prevent the fiscal emergency the governor and legislature placed a package of initiatives on the ballot during a special election, which would have raised taxes and reformed state government fiscal practices. However, all of the ballot measures were rejected by voters.

What if California is unable to make up for continued losses in state government revenue? Which programs will likely be the next to go? Is it more or less likely that voters will approve a tax increase if essential programs are cut? Why or why not?

In recent years, most Californians have been firmly against any type of tax increase. Fearful that any tax proposal might cause a voter backlash, most elected officials have either accepted major state budget shortfalls or sought to borrow funds to cover deficits.—*What aspects of the anti-tax senti-ment in California contributed to the state's most recent budget and fiscal crises? Are there any actions that would reduce the average tax bill of Californians without caus-ing major societal problems? If so, what are they? If not, why not?*

Review of Key Objectives

A Budget Process in Crisis

22.1 Distinguish between a structural budget gap and a budget deficit.

(pages 668–671)

The rapid economic downturn has caused a difficult fiscal situation in the state made even worst by the state government's failure to reduce the burgeoning budget deficit that has approached 20 percent of the total budget in recent years. The difference between a structural budget gap and a budget problem or deficit is that a gap tends to be either permanent or long-term. California is inching toward a permanent gap, which even in prosperity could never be paid in full.

KEY TERMS

Structural Budget Gap 668
Legislative Analyst's Office (LAO) 671
Proposition 671

CRITICAL THINKING QUESTIONS

1. Should California state government leaders reduce spending or raise taxes to solve the structural budget gap? If a spending reduction is the choice, where should the major cuts be made? If a tax increase is the choice, what type of revenue source should be raised?
2. If the collection of key players in the budget process were separated into two teams, how would they be divided and why? Who might serve as a referee?

INTERNET RESOURCES

Information on the the Legislative Analyst's Office (LAO), which has been providing fiscal and policy advice to the state legislature for more than 55 years, can be found at http://www.lao.ca.gov/. LAO is known for its fiscal and programmatic expertise and nonpartisan analyses of the state budget.

ADDITIONAL READING

Fox, Joel, *The Legend of Proposition 13: The Great California Tax Revolt*. Philadelphia: Xlibris, 2003.

Decker, John, *California in the Balance: Why Budgets Matter*. Berkeley: Institute of Government Studies Press, 2009.

Major Sources of State Revenue

22.2 Identify the sources of state revenue.

(pages 672–675)

Ultimately, most state revenue is deposited into the California's general fund, the major pool of money used to finance government. State revenue is largely derived from taxes, although in recent years, borrowing has become much more popular. The state income tax is now the largest source of state revenue, accounting for about 40 percent of the state's general fund, followed by the state sales tax, providing about 28 percent of the general fund. Corporate tax accounts for a decreasing percentage of the state tax revenue, currently at 10.5 percent. In addition, California borrows money through the use of bonds.

KEY TERMS

General Fund 672
Franchise Tax Board 673
Excise Tax 673

CRITICAL THINKING QUESTIONS

1. Why is it so difficult to devise a "fair" tax policy? What features of tax policy are specifically included to provide fairness, and how well do these features succeed in achieving this goal?
2. What are the advantages and disadvantages of issuing bonds?

INTERNET RESOURCES

The California Local Government Finance Almanac provides data, statistics, analyses, and articles on California city and county finance on their Web site at http://www.californiacityfinance.com. Topics include vehicle license fees (VLF), state and local fiscal relationships, legislation, and property taxes. The site also provides links to government and other related sites.

ADDITIONAL READING

Doerr, David R. *California's Tax Machine*. Sacramento: California Taxpayers' Association, 2000.

Decker, John, *California in the Balance: Why Budgets Matter*. Berkeley: Institute of Government Studies Press, 2009.

Major State Expenditures

22.3 Determine the major state expenditures.

(pages 676–679)

Passed in 1988, Proposition 98 requires the state government to spend a minimum of 40 percent of the general fund on K–12 public school education, the largest state government expenditure. The bulk of the approximately 28 percent of the general fund allocated for the health and welfare of state residents is consumed by a wide range of health care services that are administered by the counties. Alarming growth in the prison population in California is now costing the state government roughly 10 percent of the total state budget, The remaining portion of the state budget is split among seven major funding categories that focus on public safety, environmental protection, managing state government resources, business development and housing, consumer services, judicial administration, and workforce development.

KEY TERM

Mello-Roos Community Facilities District Act 677

CRITICAL THINKING QUESTIONS

1. Why is it unlikely that state funding to areas outside of education, health care, and corrections will increase in the near future? What might occur that could change this policy and fiscal direction?

2. If a major state expenditure had to be cut completely, which major spending category would be the most rational choice? What would be the reasons for cutting that expenditure?

INTERNET RESOURCES

Information on the California State Controller, the chief financial officer of California, can be found at http://www.sco.ca.gov/. Elected every four years, the controller makes sure the state's $100 billion budget is spent properly, helps administer more than $300 billion in state pension funds, and serves on 62 state boards and commissions.

ADDITIONAL READING

Gerald C. Lubenow and Bruce E. Cain, eds. *Governing California: Politics, Government and Public Policy in the Golden State.* Berkeley: Institute of Government Studies Press, University of California, 1997.

The California Budget Process

22.4 Outline the state budget process, and assess the effects of direct democracy on the budgetary process.

(pages 680–683)

The governor is required by California law to submit a spending plan to the state legislature by January 10th. The state budget is then introduced in the legislature and automatically assigned to the Assembly Budget and Senate Budget and Fiscal Review Committees. At about the same time, the Legislative Analyst's Office (LAO) drafts an extensive analysis of the budget. Another major step in the budget process is the May revise, an adjusted projection of the state's financial picture that is conducted by the head of the Department of Finance and economists from private industry. Passage of the state government budget in the state legislature requires the mejority to approve in each house. The budget process concludes when the budget bill comes before the governor.

KEY TERMS

Executive Budget Plan 680
May Revise 681

CRITICAL THINKING QUESTIONS

1. Is it likely that passage of Proposition 25 requiring a majority of each house, rather than two-thirds, to pass the budget will result in budgets being passed more quickly? Why or why not?

2. What role does direct democracy play in the budget process?

INTERNET RESOURCES

The California Chamber of Commerce maintains a Web site at http://www.calchamber.com/. This organization has worked to make California a better place to do business by giving private-sector employers a voice in state politics and providing a full range of California-specific products and services.

Information on the California Tax Payers' Association can be found at http://www.caltax.org/. This group closely monitors legislative, tax agency, and local government tax policy deliberations and coordinates with Cal-Tax members and industry representatives to stop unnecessary tax policy changes that would increase its members' cost of doing business in California.

ADDITIONAL READING

Krolack, Richard. *California Budget Dance: Issues and Process,* 2nd ed. Sacramento: California Journal Press, 1994.

Chapter Review Test Your Knowledge

1. A structural budget gap tends to be either
a. short term or solved by the state legislature.
b. permanent or, at best, long-term.
c. permanent or addressed by the voters through the initiative process.
d. solved through tax increases or contributions from public employees.

2. If the governor is the ringmaster of the California budget circus, who are its star performers?
a. the state legislature
b. the mayors of California cities
c. the California voters
d. the members of the plural executive

3. The annual state budget is
a. full of tax increases as well as reduced funding to certain departments that benefit businesses, unions, and seniors.
b. full of generous funding provisions for unions.
c. full of tax breaks as well as generous funding of certain departments that benefit businesses, unions, and seniors.
d. always includes major tax increases for businesses.

4. Which of the following programs consumes the largest part of the state budget?
a. education
b. the Office of Emergency Services
c. "welfare" programs
d. public safety

5. Legislators have balanced the weaknesses they may have on budgetary matters, the consequences of term limits, and the necessity of having to learn budget details quickly with
a. the help of the office of the governor.
b. a large staff of personal aides, committee consultants, party caucus staff, and research staff.
c. a small staff of personal aides, business consultants, union representatives, and University of California political science professors.
d. the assistance of public advocacy and special-interest groups.

6. What is the role of the Legislative Analyst's Office (LAO), headed by the legislative analyst, in the formation of the state budget?
a. The LAO is responsible for assisting the governor in reviewing the budget.
b. The LAO is responsible for reducing specific dollar amounts from the budget.
c. The LAO works very closely with local government in reducing the deficit.
d. The LAO is responsible for analyzing the state budget and making recommendations to the state legislature regarding the fiscal efficiency of state government.

7. Until 2009, the state's basic sales tax rate was
a. 5 percent.
b. 7.25 percent.
c. 8.25 percent.
d. 8.5 percent.

8. The Franchise Tax Board
a. sets the state's sales tax rate.
b. sets the state's income tax rate.
c. sets tax rates for banks and financial institutions.
d. selects which products will be subject to excise taxes.

9. Ultimately, most of the revenue of the state will find its way into
a. the state's general fund, the major pool of money used to finance government.
b. the budgets of local governments.
c. the state's special fund, the main source of funding to the various state government agencies.
d. the pockets of taxpayers when they receive their annual tax rebates.

10. What is the franchise tax rate on the profits of most businesses and corporations that operate in California?
a. 50 percent
b. 8.84 percent
c. 2 percent
d. none; there is no tax on businesses and corporations

11. General obligation bonds are backed by
a. the "full faith and credit" of the federal government.
b. the "necessity and promise" of the state government.
c. the "due process" clause of the Fourteenth Amendment.
d. the "full faith and credit" of the state government.

12. How has Proposition 13 affected the amount of property tax the state will collect?
a. It has reduced property taxes to 13 percent of all revenue collected.
b. It has increased the amount of property tax collected.
c. It has reduced property taxes to 50 percent of all revenue collected.
d. It has not had any noticeable effect on the amount of property taxes collected.

13. How much of the general fund must the state government spend on K–12 school education as a result of Proposition 98?
a. no more than 20 percent
b. a minimum of 40 percent
c. a maximum of 80 percent
d. a minimum of 10 percent

14. A Mello-Roos Community Facilities District is used to fund
a. designated improvements, such as freeway interchanges, library services, and parks.
b. general municipal services, such as police and fire departments.
c. county health care services.
d. regional bodies that oversee transportation spending.

15. Roughly 25 percent of the health and welfare budget line goes to which of the following state government programs?
a. State Highway Patrol and Homeland Security
b. State Legislators Pension System
c. County hospitals
d. Temporary Assistance for Needy Families (TANF) and CalWORKs

16. Each year's state budget starts with a budget plan created by the
   a. assembly.
   c. governor's office.
   b. state senate.
   d. treasurer's office.

17. What are some ways the governor can create the illusion of a balanced budget?
   a. cutting the salaries of teachers and nurses
   b. increasing the amount of money invested by the state
   c. deferring payments, shifting balances, or even reorganizing government
   d. preventing payments, reorganizing balances, and shifting government

18. The line-item veto gives the governor the authority to
   a. increase an appropriation.
   b. transfer funds from special funds to the general fund.
   c. set apart money in the budget for a specific use.
   d. reduce or eliminate any item of appropriation from any bill.

19. What is the May revise?
   a. the deadline for the state legislature to vote on the state budget
   b. a revised projection of the state's financial picture
   c. a revision in the fiscal calendar of the state
   d. another term used for the governor's line-item veto power

20. Who are the Big Five?
   a. the five individuals responsible for the western portion of the transcontinental railroad
   b. the five members of the plural executive who are responsible for the final budget
   c. the governor and the four party leaders from both chambers who usually resolve budgetary issues
   d. the five major California corporations that contribute the greatest amount of revenue to the state

PEARSON mypoliscilab Exercises

Apply what you learned in this chapter on **MyPoliSciLab.**

Read on **mypoliscilab.com**

   eText: Chapter 22

Study and **Review** on **mypoliscilab.com**

   Pre-Test
   Post-Test
   Chapter Exam
   Flashcards

Watch on **mypoliscilab.com**

   Video: California Teacher Layoffs
   Video: California Budget Crisis

Participate and Prepare

CHAPTER 1
American Government: Democracy in Action

> **CAPTURE THE FOCUS: KEY OBJECTIVES**
>
> Review these learning objectives highlighted throughout the introductory chapter:
>
> **1.1** Illustrate how citizens participate in a democracy and why this is important.
>
> **1.2** Relate the themes of this book to American politics today.
>
> **1.3** Outline the various "pathways" of involvement in our political system.
>
> **1.4** Analyze the forces of stability in American politics.

1. Write a brief paragraph in response to each of the learning objectives. Use your responses as a study aid for the chapter.
2. In as few words as possible, describe the main idea in this introductory chapter. Compare your interpretation with the interpretation of a classmate or study group.

Map the Story: Why Political Participation Is Important and How Average Citizens Can Make a Difference

1. List some of the ways that government can affect your life even when you are not paying attention.
2. Discuss levels of political participation in the United States, especially compared to what is found in other nations.
3. Review the various pathways of action available to citizens in a democracy.
4. Explain why diversity continues to be a key aspect of our political system.
5. In two or three sentences, state how the pathways of change help answer the key question of the chapter: Can average citizens play a meaningful role in American politics?

Match the Concepts

Match the statement to the concept with which it is most closely related.

1. "When I was first elected to Congress I thought good ideas would somehow win the day. Boy was I naive!"
2. "You mean to say that I can go to war for my country, but I can't have a beer with my pals because I'm not 21?"
3. "The surest way to change the course of government is to change the personnel of government."
4. "Clearly, it is an important department of government in terms of protecting the individual liberties of the people."
5. "As you dig deeper into the national character of the Americans, you see that they have sought the value of everything in this world only as it relates to the answer to this single question: how much money will it bring in?"
6. "Most realize that if you can win the hearts and minds of average citizens, policy change will follow."
7. "Four score and seven years ago our fathers brought forth, upon this continent, a new nation, conceived in Liberty, and dedicated to the proposition that all men are created equal."
8. "Give me your tired, your poor, your huddled masses yearning to be free."

A. Cultural Change Pathway	**B.** Creation Myth	**C.** Courts Pathway	**D.** American Creed
E. Elections Pathway	**F.** Public Policy	**G.** Politics	**H.** Reverence for Capitalism

Role Play

You are hosting a dinner party for a group of foreign students. After some pleasantries and a few appetizers, one of the guests blurts out a question that stops everyone in their tracks: "Americans like to think that they have the most democratic nation in the world and that the rest of us should follow their lead. But how can that be true when about one-half of voting-age Americans don't even bother to vote?" How would you respond to this question?

What You Can Do

Levels of engagement among young Americans are paradoxical. On the one hand, many studies have found that young people are deeply involved in service projects, such as literacy programs, environmental efforts, senior center volunteer work, and projects to help low-income citizens; they are certainly not disengaged from their communities. On the other hand, many of these same young Americans will refrain from political engagement. They will not vote, read about politics, or even talk to friends and family about political developments. Sit down with a few friends or classmates and discuss this important topic with them. Consider the following questions:

1. Are you active in community projects? If so, why?
2. Do you consider yourself to be politically engaged? If yes, why do you believe political activism is important? And how do you think these efforts can make a difference? If not, why not? Do you think your involvement will be meaningless?
3. What are your foremost concerns about the state of politics today?
4. What changes do you believe could possibly pull more young people into the political process?

CHAPTER 2
Early Governance and the Constitutional Framework

CAPTURE THE FOCUS: KEY OBJECTIVES

Review these learning objectives highlighted throughout the early governance and constitutional framework chapter:

2.1 Identify the difference between government and politics.

2.2 Differentiate between different types of government.

2.3 Describe how forces in Colonial America helped set the stage for the American Revolution.

2.4 Identify the core principles of the American Revolution.

2.5 Determine the reasons for the failure of the Articles of Confederation.

2.6 Assess how compromises at the Constitutional Convention shaped our political system.

2.7 Identify the core principles of the Constitution.

2.8 Analyze how the ratification debate structured the nature of our democracy.

1. Write a brief paragraph in response to each of the learning objectives. Use your responses as a study aid for the chapter.
2. In as few words as possible, describe the main idea in the early governance and constitutional framework chapter. Compare your interpretation with the interpretation of a classmate or study group.

Map the Story: The Drive for Independence

1. List the various factors from the colonial period that contributed to the drive for independence.
2. Identify the key concepts of the Declaration of Independence.
3. Discuss how the colonial period influenced the Articles of Confederation.
4. Chart the overarching elements of the Constitution, and explain how this document was a rather drastic departure from the Articles of Confederation.
5. In two or three sentences, state how the progression from colonial governance to the Constitution aids our understanding of the key question of the chapter: How does our nation's formative period continue to shape contemporary politics?

Match the Concepts

Match the statement to the concept with which it is most closely related.

1. "Look, it's simple: If that guy doesn't vote for the bill, my organization will run him out of office in the next election. He'll get the message."
2. "The court can hand down any decision it likes, but how does it expect to enforce the ruling if the public doesn't agree?"
3. "No taxation without representation!"
4. "Taxes, tariffs, duties! When will Parliament quench its thirst for our blood?"
5. "I say, when a government no longer responds to the concerns of average citizens, it's time to start a new government!"
6. "Given that each state really is equal, it only makes sense that each should have the same say in the national legislature."
7. "Double security arises to the rights of the people. The governments will control each other...."
8. "How can you possibly expect representatives to know what's on the minds of constituents in such a massive country. I'm telling you, democracy is only possible in small nations."

A. New Jersey Plan	**B.** The Great Squeeze	**C.** Anti-Federalists	**D.** Political Power
E. Limited Government	**F.** Direct Democracy	**G.** Social Contract Theory	**H.** Checks and Balances

Role Play

You have found a way to go back in time to attend the Constitutional Convention. As a time-traveler, you can enlighten these men about what the system they are about to create will look like more than 220 years later. There is so much you could say about civil rights, executive powers, federalism, international affairs, nuclear bombs, television, and the Internet! Perhaps you can help them head-off some grievous mistakes, such as slavery and the repression of women and Native Americans. But here's the catch: You only have five minutes. What would you choose to highlight in your five minutes?

What You Can Do

Most students of American government closely examine the U.S. Constitution, but far fewer explore their own state constitution. Most of the laws and regulations that we live under are created by state and local governments, so it is important to understand the basic elements of your state system. Do a quick Web search for your state's constitution, and then answer these questions:

1. Does your state use a system of checks and balances?
2. How do your state's legislative powers compare with those of Congress?
3. How old do you have to be to hold various offices in your state government?
4. Are judges appointed or elected?
5. Does your state's constitution allow for ballot initiatives?
6. How often is your state's constitution amended, and what were some of the most recent changes?

CHAPTER **3**
Federalism

CAPTURE THE FOCUS: KEY OBJECTIVES

Review these learning objectives highlighted throughout the federalism chapter:

3.1 Explain why the framers divided authority between layers of government.

3.2 Characterize dual federalism both before and after the Civil War.

3.3 Compare and contrast cooperative and creative federalism.

3.4 Trace the evolution of federalism in recent decades.

1. Write a brief paragraph in response to each of the learning objectives. Use your responses as a study aid for the chapter.
2. In as few words as possible, describe the main idea in the federalism chapter. Compare your interpretation with the interpretation of a classmate or study group.

Map the Story: Expansion of Federal Government

1. List the ways in which the Constitution limits the federal government and the ways that the federal government was limited during the nineteenth and early twentieth centuries.

2. Identify the key elements that were used to justify the expansion of the federal government in the early twentieth century.
3. Specify the various events that occurred in the 1960s and 1970s that further expanded the scope of the national government.
4. Identify some recent trends in federalism that demonstrate how federal authority has either grown or been curbed.
5. In two or three sentences, state what these changes suggest about the chapter's primary question: How has federalism evolved in the United States?

Match the Concepts

Match the statement to the concept with which it is most closely related.

1. "The power to tax is the power to destroy."
2. "Interactions between the federal government and state governments are marked by tension rather than cooperation."
3. "The Constitution justifies the expansion of Congressional power."
4. "The powers not delegated to the United States by the Constitution, nor prohibited by it to the States, are reserved to the States respectively, or to the people."
5. "State governments have the right to form their own independent governments."
6. "This was the only way to get the economy moving again to end the Great Depression."
7. "The only way to fight poverty and discrimination is to funnel federal money to state and local governments."
8. "The federal government needs to transfer responsibility, including fiscal responsibility, to state governments."

A. Tenth Amendment	**B.** Necessary and Proper Clause	**C.** Dual Federalism	**D.** *McCulloch* v. *Maryland*
E. New Deal	**F.** Devolution	**G.** Doctrine of Succession	**H.** Great Society

Role Play

You have been asked to chair a task force to examine federal, state, and local emergency response plans to natural disasters. You are to determine which level of government should be responsible for making all final decisions—from evacuation orders to plans to ensure public safety. Who do you think should be responsible—the federal government, state government, or local officials? If you decide that state and local officials should be responsible, at what point do you think the federal government has the duty to step in if state and local officials exhibit clear evidence of incompetence or an inability to address the crisis? If you decide the federal government should take the lead, how can you expect the federal government to manage all crises? At what point do we expect too much from our federal government? What is the proper balance between all levels of government in this policy area?

What You Can Do

Invite some of your classmates to discuss the proper role of the federal government in funding state and local projects.

1. Should the federal government be paying for local projects? If so, should it have a say in how the funds are spent and the desired outcomes?
2. What are the benefits of the federal government's role in local policy development? What are the disadvantages?

CHAPTER 4
Civil Liberties

CAPTURE THE FOCUS: KEY OBJECTIVES

Review these learning objectives highlighted throughout the civil liberties chapter:

4.1 Distinguish between the two dimensions of freedom of religion in the First Amendment.

4.2 Specify the limits on free speech in the United States.

4.3 Assess the test for justifying governmental limitations on written words and visual images.

4.4 Specify the protections afforded to criminal suspects under the Bill of Rights.

4.5 Evaluate the legal protections that ensure only guilty people receive criminal punishment.

4.6 Explain why the right to privacy is controversial.

1. Write a brief paragraph in response to each of the learning objectives. Use your responses as a study aid for the chapter.
2. In as few words as possible, describe the main idea in the civil liberties chapter. Compare your interpretation with the interpretation of a classmate or study group.

Map the Story: Capital Punishment

1. List, in order of decision, five cases handled by the Supreme Court concerning capital punishment.
2. Identify the main issue in each case.
3. List two objectives that are illustrated by the Supreme Court decisions concerning capital punishment.

4. In two or three sentences, state what the capital punishment issue shows about the chapter's primary question: Do Americans have too many or too few civil liberties protections?

Match the Concepts

Match the statement to the concept with which it is most closely related.

1. "That word doesn't even appear in the U.S. Constitution, yet the Supreme Court says it is a right that we have and protects our ability to make certain decisions about ourselves and what we want to do."
2. "That's the part of the Constitution that everyone agrees is supposed to mean there cannot be an official national religion, but there are a lot of disagreements about whether it applies in other situations when government comes into contact with religion."
3. "The government wants to tell that newspaper that it cannot run the story about the governor cheating on his wife? Can the government do that?"
4. "When I watched that criminal trial on television, there was no jury—just a judge making all of the decisions. What kind of trial is that?"
5. "The police officers are angry because a judge just decided that they cannot use that evidence in court—even though they found those drugs in the guy's house when they broke down the door last night."
6. "If reporters can't protect their sources, it will be hard for them to find people willing to speak with them and give them the inside scoop."
7. "I can see that they tried to define 'obscenity' with that court decision, but is that really a clear definition?"

A. Establishment Clause	**B.** Exclusionary Rule	**C.** Bench Trial	**D.** Press Sheild Law
E. *Miller v. California*	**F.** Prior Restraint	**G.** Privacy	

Role Play

You are a justice on the U.S. Supreme Court. Your case involves a challenge to the legality of actions taken by several FBI agents. They placed a marble cross in an isolated, mountainous spot of a national park forest at the site where several FBI agents died in a helicopter crash. What part of the Bill of Rights is at issue in the case? State the primary argument supporting the FBI agents' actions and the primary argument opposing the legality of their actions. Which argument is stronger? Why?

What You Can Do

Courtrooms are part of government institutions, and proceedings that take place there are open to the public and the press, except in special situations. Visit a local courthouse to watch preliminary hearings, entry of guilty pleas, or a trial in a criminal case.

1. Briefly describe anything that you observed that shows how, if at all, the rights in the Bill of Rights affected the processing of the case(s).
2. Which right appears to be most important to criminal defendants? Why?

CHAPTER 5
Civil Rights

CAPTURE THE FOCUS: KEY OBJECTIVES

Review these learning objectives highlighted throughout the civil rights chapter:

5.1 Describe the idea of equality that underlies the governing system in the United States.

5.2 Trace the historical development of civil rights in the United States.

5.3 Analyze how litigation strategies contributed to the dismantling of official racial segregation.

5.4 Differentiate between the various tests used by the Supreme Court when deciding discrimination claims under the equal protection clause.

5.5 Identify the events and factors that influenced the development of the grassroots civil rights movement.

5.6 Compare and contrast the civil rights struggles of women, Latinos, and African Americans.

5.7 Evaluate the continuing debates, lawsuits, and protests over civil rights in the twenty-first century.

1. Write a brief paragraph in response to each of the learning objectives. Use your responses as a study aid for the chapter.
2. In as few words as possible, describe the main idea of the civil rights chapter. Compare your interpretation with the interpretation of a classmate or study group.

Map the Story: The Role of the Rev. Dr. Martin Luther King Jr. in the Civil Rights Movement

1. List three events/actions in chronological order that show Dr. King's role in the development of civil rights.
2. Identify two pathways of action in which civil rights developments can be credited to Dr. King.

3. List three objectives that are in some way illustrated by Dr. King's role and actions. Describe in one sentence (for each objective) the ways in which Dr. King's role and actions relate to that objective.
4. In two or three sentences, state how, if at all, Dr. King's role and actions relate to the chapter's primary question: How has the United States advanced toward its ideal of equality, and to what extent does the country still remain short of its ideal?

Match the Concepts

Match the statement to the concept with which it is most closely related.

1. "Government-mandated racial segregation violates the equal protection clause of the Fourteenth Amendment."
2. "Our job as government officials is to make sure that there is no racial discrimination when people apply for jobs. Otherwise we might need to file lawsuits to prevent such violations of the law from occurring."
3. "I supported this law because we should not let one racial group—whites—control every aspect of voting and elections and thereby exclude others from participating in our democracy."
4. "Here in Sweden, our relatively high taxes create benefits for all of society. We try to make sure that we don't have poverty as it exists in other countries, by giving all people financial support, health care, access to education, and the other things needed to live a decent, comfortable life."
5. "The Supreme Court's endorsement of 'separate but equal' facilities for blacks and whites is appropriate for the state of race relations here in the nineteenth century. Blacks should be happy with this progress. After all, not so long ago they were slaves."
6. "The attainment of this goal is finally going to let women fully participate in elections."

A. Equality of Condition	**B.** *Plessy v. Ferguson*	**C.** Universal Suffrage
D. *Brown v. Board of Education of Topeka*	**E.** U.S. Equal Employment Opportunity Commission	**F.** Voting Rights Act of 1965

Role Play

You are an unemployed job-seeker waiting in one of several long lines at a temporary employment agency. You notice that all of the white applicants are told that they will be sent to office jobs, and all of the African American applicants are told that they will be sent to "light industrial" jobs on assembly lines. You hear an African American woman in front of you protest, "But I'm a college graduate—why can't you send me to an office job?" The temp agency official replies, "No. Light industrial assembly work. Take it or leave it!" As you are preparing to leave, you overhear several African American job applicants saying, "That's discrimination. We should do something." If they asked you for advice, what are two actions that you would advise them to pursue?

What You Can Do

Visit the Web site of Anti-Slavery International at http://www.antislavery.org to read about the continuing existence of slavery in various forms around the world. Select "Slavery Today" to read about how they define the various forms of slavery.

1. Would any of the strategies used in the American efforts to advance civil rights be effective in the international effort to end contemporary slavery? Briefly explain why or why not.
2. What role, if any, should the United States play in addressing the issue of continuing forms of slavery around the world? Describe two actions that the United States could take or give two reasons why the United States should not be involved.

CHAPTER 6
Congress

CAPTURE THE FOCUS: KEY OBJECTIVES

Review these learning objectives highlighted throughout the chapter on Congress:

6.1 Differentiate between the various ways legislators represent the interests of their constituents.

6.2 Identify the key constitutional provisions that shape the way Congress functions.

6.3 Establish the importance of committees in organizing the legislative process.

6.4 Assess how political parties and leaders manage the legislative process while advancing their own initiatives.

6.5 Show how the rules and norms of behavior help ensure a more orderly, efficient legislative process.

6.6 Outline the process by which a bill becomes a law.

6.7 Determine whether members of Congress mirror America's demographic diversity and why this matters.

6.8 Compare the state of congressional ethics with Americans' perception of the legislative branch.

1. Write a brief paragraph in response to each of the learning objectives. Use your responses as a study aid for the chapter.
2. In as few words as possible, describe the main idea in the chapter on Congress. Compare your interpretation with the interpretation of a classmate or study group.

Map the Story: Organizing the Legislative Process

1. List the various organizing elements of the legislative process that were designed to make the system more efficient.
2. Identify the core rationale for each of these elements.
3. Discuss how the organizing elements of the legislative process make the system more efficient but at the same time move the process in a less democratic direction.
4. In two or three sentences, state what these organizing elements suggest about the chapter's primary question: How does the national legislature turn public concerns into public policy?

Match the Concepts

Match the statement to the concept with which it is most closely related.

1. "I was sent here to do exactly what my constituents want. How could I serve the people if I did otherwise?"
2. "As a woman, it makes me feel better that more and more women are being elected to Congress."
3. "The power to tax involves the power to destroy."
4. "I don't understand it: About 40 percent of the folks in my state consider themselves Republican, and we send 11 representatives to Congress. But only two are Republican."
5. "The floor? No way! This is where most of the work of the legislature is done."
6. "Federal agencies may think that they can do as they please, but as members of Congress we are in charge. It's our job to keep them in line."
7. "To be honest, it's really tough figuring out how to vote on every single piece of legislation. But like the rest, I rely on a handy shortcut."
8. "Will my dear friend and esteemed colleague from the fine state of Tennessee yield for a question?"

A. Gerrymandering	**B.** Standing Committees	**C.** Delegate Model of Representation	**D.** Bureaucratic Oversight
E. *McCulloch v. Maryland*	**F.** Voting Cues	**G.** Symbolic Representation	**H.** Congressional Norms

Role Play

You are a Whip in your party's caucus. Your job is to round up enough votes in your party to pass important legislation. In the midst of an important policy battle, one member of your caucus comes to you and says that she will likely vote with the opposing party. "Really, what difference should one's party make when it comes to voting," she says. How would you respond? What might you say to convince her of the importance of parties in the legislative process?

What You Can Do

While it is possible to set up an appointment with your member of Congress and have a chat about his or her job, and some legislators will find the time to do this, most are very busy. Why not set up an appointment with one of the staff members from your legislator's local office instead? Likely they will have more time and will enjoy spending 30 minutes with an eager college student. You might ask the staff member the following questions:

1. How did you get your job? What qualifications are most important?
2. Do you like working for a member of Congress?
3. What are the most rewarding aspects of your job? What about the most difficult?
4. What are some of the "realities" of modern legislative politics—places where the textbooks get it wrong?

CHAPTER **7**
Presidency

> ### CAPTURE THE FOCUS: KEY OBJECTIVES
>
> Review these learning objectives highlighted throughout the presidency chapter:
>
> **7.1** Explain the framers' decision to bestow the president with real powers despite their concerns about potential abuses.
>
> **7.2** Outline the changes that have led to the expansion of presidential powers.
>
> **7.3** Establish how the "power to persuade" expands presidential power beyond the Constitution.
>
> **7.4** Identify the duties and functions of modern presidents.
>
> **7.5** Evaluate the qualities that contribute to presidential success or failure.

1. Write a brief paragraph in response to each of the learning objectives. Use your responses as a study aid for the chapter.
2. In as few words as possible, describe the main idea in the presidency chapter. Compare your interpretation with the interpretation of a classmate or study group.

Map the Story: Expansion of Presidential Powers

1. List the various changes to the executive branch that have contributed to the expansion of presidential powers.

2. Identify the rationale for each of these changes.
3. Discuss how each of these changes, while perhaps necessary, may have shifted the balance of power among the three branches of government.
4. In two or three sentences, state what these changes suggest about the chapter's primary question: Have expanded presidential powers transformed the democratic nature of our system?

Match the Concepts

Match the statement to the concept with which it is most closely related.

1. "The White House should be used as a bully pulpit."
2. "There is now an array of offices designed to help the president lead the nation."
3. "Sure, formal powers are one thing, but if you ask me, presidents are successful only when they have good political skills."
4. "Like it or not, when a president speaks, the world listens."
5. "There are two chances a modern president will pay attention to the War Powers Resolution: zero and none."
6. "Local governments and charities are simply not enough during these tough economic times; the federal government must step in to help citizens."
7. "Well, Congress can act through statutory changes, but the president can issue executive orders. Guess which one is faster?"
8. "It's little wonder that presidents seem to focus more on foreign affairs in their second term than during their first four years in office."

A. Two Presidencies Thesis	**B.** President as Chief Diplomat	**C.** Stewardship Model of Presidency	**D.** President as Commander in Chief
E. The Power to Persuade	**F.** Executive Office of the President	**G.** Going Public	**H.** President as Chief Executive

Role Play

You are a close advisor to the president. There is a crisis that the president believes requires immediate action because it poses a national security risk. However, it must be handled in secret. You and some other advisors arrive at the Oval Office to help create the plan, only to learn that a radio talk show host—who has been highly critical of your boss—has learned of the issue and is intending to "go public" with all sorts of information. One of the advisors points to Lincoln's actions during the Civil War and suggests, "Let's arrest the talk show host and keep him in jail until it's done. The nation's security is at risk!" But another advisor says, "National security or not, the president is not above the law. We can't put the talk show host in jail, no matter the risks to innocent lives." What would you advise? Why?

What You Can Do

While certainly imperfect, one way of getting a feel for both a president's style and his policy agenda is to listen to his most important speeches. Visit the Miller Center for Public Affairs Web site at http://millercenter.org/scripps/archive/speeches, and listen to at least two speeches from two former presidents. The Miller Center's audio recordings go back to Franklin D. Roosevelt in 1933.

1. How would you describe each president's oratorical skills?
2. What issues were probably the most important at the time that each speech was given?
3. Who do you think was the intended audience for each of the speeches?
4. Given what you've heard, do you think certain presidents were able to "connect" with average Americans better than others?

CHAPTER 8
Bureaucracy

CAPTURE THE FOCUS: KEY OBJECTIVES

Review these learning objectives highlighted throughout the bureaucracy chapter:

8.1 Trace the development of specific federal departments and agencies.

8.2 Analyze the debate over whether the heads of federal agencies should be policy experts or loyal political appointees.

8.3 Describe the image people have of the federal bureaucracy, and evaluate the bureaucracy's advantages and disadvantages.

8.4 Assess the mechanisms and processes that influence and oversee the federal bureaucracy.

1. Write a brief paragraph in response to each of the learning objectives. Use your responses as a study aid for the chapter.
2. In as few words as possible, describe the main idea of the bureaucracy chapter. Compare your interpretation with the interpretation of a classmate or study group.

Map the Story: Federal Government Departments

1. List the departments represented in the president's cabinet in order of their creation.
2. List the issue or historical development, if any, which led to the creation of each department.

3. List two objectives that are illustrated by examining federal government departments. Describe in one sentence (for each objective) how the topic of federal government departments relates to the objective.
4. In two or three sentences, state what, if anything, this topic shows about the chapter's primary question: Is the bureaucracy an essential contributor to the success of government or a barrier to effective government?

Match the Concepts

Match the statement to the concept with which it is most closely related.

1. "What do you mean I can't work on that political campaign? So what if I'm a government employee? I'm still an American citizen."
2. "Is this the law that protects me if I reveal that my government supervisor has been giving contracts to a company owned by his sister-in-law?"
3. "How can it be a law if it wasn't enacted by a legislature or issued as part of a court decision?"
4. "I'm so glad I won't lose my job in the Department of Education just because a new president comes into office."
5. "Oh yeah, those are the really big organizational entities in government that are headed by a 'Secretary' in the president's cabinet."
6. "I want someone to review this decision by the Social Security Administration that turned down my application for disability benefits."

A. Regulations	**B.** Administration Law Judge	**C.** Departments
D. Hatch Act	**E.** Whistleblower Protection Act	**F.** Civil Service System

Role Play

You are the President of the United States, and you must nominate someone to head the Environmental Protection Agency. The person must interact effectively with legislators, the news media, and various government officials, while overseeing an agency with specific responsibilities. What three specific qualities or qualifications would you seek in your appointee?

What You Can Do

Read about the history of the civil service at the Web site of the U.S. Office of Personnel Management at http://www.opm.gov/biographyofanideal

1. Briefly explain how the bureaucracy would be different today if these reforms had not taken place.
2. Describe one additional change that might improve the bureaucracy.

CHAPTER **9**
Judiciary

CAPTURE THE FOCUS: KEY OBJECTIVES

Review these learning objectives highlighted throughout the judiciary chapter:

9.1 Explain how American court systems are organized.

9.2 Identify the reasons why American judges are powerful actors in the governing system.

9.3 Outline the selection process for federal judges.

9.4 Explain the theories concerning how Supreme Court justices reach their decisions.

9.5 Characterize the litigation strategies used in the court pathway.

9.6 Evaluate the courts' effectiveness in enforcing judicial decisions.

9.7 Describe the debate over whether it is appropriate for judges to shape public policy in a democracy.

1. Write a brief paragraph in response to each of the learning objectives. Use your responses as a study aid for the chapter.
2. In as few words as possible, describe the main idea of the judiciary chapter. Compare your interpretation with the interpretation of a classmate or study group.

Map the Story: The Case of Savana Redding (*Stafford Unified School District* v. *Redding* [2009])

1. List the events of the Savana Redding case in order—from the day in question at school through the U.S. Supreme Court decision.
2. Identify the main issue in the case.
3. List four objectives that are illustrated, at least in part, by Savana Redding's case. Describe in one sentence (for each objective) the ways in which the case relates to the objectives.
4. In two or three sentences, state what, if anything, this case shows about the chapter's primary question: How much power should judges have?

Match the Concepts

Match the statement to the concept with which it is most closely related.

1. "As a Supreme Court justice, I had to vote against accepting that case for hearing. I think it's an important issue, but I'm just afraid that there are not yet five justices who will vote in favor of my position."
2. "I don't want to file a lawsuit yet to challenge that school's policy on strip-searching students—not until they search a young girl rather than one of those high school football players."
3. "We rule that the limits on political campaign spending enacted by Congress violate the Constitution, and therefore the statute is unconstitutional and invalid."
4. "As a Supreme Court justice, I think that the words 'In God We Trust' on U.S. Currency may cause a problem with mixing religion and government in violation of the First Amendment, but I'm not going to vote to accept that issue for hearing for fear that it will cause Congress to initiate a constitutional amendment to limit the Supreme Court's power."
5. "Since we are lawyers for the American Medical Association, why don't we submit some written arguments to the Supreme Court in support of those other lawyers who are arguing in favor of permitting doctors to advise their patients about making their own individual decisions about whether or not to have an abortion?"
6. "I will vote to remove that federal judge from office because I think she took a bribe."
7. "After our panel of three judges makes its decision on this case, the next decision about the case—if there is one—would be issued by the U.S. Supreme Court."

A. Test Case	**B.** Judicial Review	**C.** New Institutionalism	**D.** Amicus Briefs
E. Impeachment	**F.** Intermediate Appellate Courts	**G.** Strategic Voting Model	

Role Play

You are a U.S. Senator. Another senator proposes a constitutional amendment that will limit Supreme Court justices to 18-year terms in office and have Supreme Court justices selected through national elections. What are two arguments you might make against this proposed constitutional amendment?

What You Can Do

Visit the American Judicature Society's Web page on judicial selection in the states at http://www.judicialselection.us/. Select your home state on the national map and read about your state's method for selecting judges. Return to the national map—and read about judicial selection in a state that uses a different method for choosing judges than the one used in your home state.

1. Briefly explain why one state's method is better than the method used by another state.
2. What is the best method for selecting state judges? In two or three sentences, explain why you chose this method as the best approach.

CHAPTER **10**
Political Socialization and Public Opinion

CAPTURE THE FOCUS: KEY OBJECTIVES

Review these learning objectives highlighted throughout the political socialization and public opinion chapter:

10.1 Explain the relationship between public opinion, public policy, and fundamental values.

10.2 Determine how and why public opinion changes and the factors leading to stability in values and beliefs.

10.3 Differentiate between the dominant political ideologies in the United States, and explain how value structures impact public opinion and political action.

10.4 Illustrate how individuals acquire their political values.

10.5 Assess how membership in various social groups impacts political views and behavior.

10.6 Explain how public opinion is measured.

1. Write a brief paragraph in response to each of the learning objectives. Use your responses as a study aid for the chapter.
2. In as few words as possible, describe the main idea in the political socialization and public opinion chapter. Compare your interpretation with the interpretation of a classmate or study group.

Map the Story: The Process of Acquiring Political Ideology

1. List the common values that most Americans share.
2. List the common sources of conflict in the United States.
3. Identify the actors who play key roles in transmitting these shared values and sources of conflict.
4. Chart how each actor has become more influential or less in imparting values to younger generations.
5. In two or three sentences, state what political ideology suggests about the chapter's primary question: How do people acquire their political values, and how stable is public opinion?

Match the Concepts

Match the statement to the concept with which it is most closely related.

1. "Power and influence are centered in the hands of only a select few."
2. "Citizens can and do influence the government through elections, organized interest groups, and collective action."
3. "We might want to blame our media for the content of programming, but they simply reflect our popular culture, giving us what we want."
4. "Popular culture both shapes and reflects public opinion."
5. "Homosexuals should have all the same rights and privileges as heterosexuals."
6. "Society is changing too quickly—government should work to preserve traditional values and behaviors."
7. "I know that I can influence my government."
8. "This reflects the opinion of only a subset of the population."

A. Internal Political Efficacy	**B.** Barometer of Public Attitudes	**C.** Conservatism	**D.** Sample
E. Pluralism	**F.** Liberalism	**G.** Elitism	**H.** Interactive Theory

Role Play

You are meeting with a group of foreign visitors and have been asked to explain the relationship between public opinion and public policy in the United States. They want to know how important public opinion should be in directing the policymaking of Congress. How would you explain the competing theories? The visitors then ask how influential public opinion is in guiding the actions of political actors. How would you respond? They also ask you to provide examples of times when public opinion was highly influential in guiding the government. Finally, they want to know how frequently political leaders ignore public opinion and pursue actions that they believe are best. What examples of each would you provide?

What You Can Do

Explore libertarianism by reviewing policy and issue briefs published by the CATO Institute (http://www.cato.org/). Why do you think libertarianism holds a relatively strong ideological attraction for college students?

CHAPTER **11**
The Politics of the Media

CAPTURE THE FOCUS: KEY OBJECTIVES

Review these learning objectives highlighted throughout the media chapter:

11.1 Evaluate the roles played by the media in shaping American politics.

11.2 Outline the development of the American media.

11.3 Illustrate the functions of the media in American politics and society.

11.4 Assess how the media can be influential in American politics.

11.5 Establish how the media have an impact on the cultural values and political opinions of the American public.

11.6 Contrast the rights of a free press to the government's authority to restrict content.

1. Write a brief paragraph in response to each of the learning objectives. Use your responses as a study aid for the chapter.
2. In as few words as possible, describe the main idea in the politics of the media chapter. Compare your interpretation with the interpretation of a classmate or study group.

Map the Story: Political Uses of the Media

1. List the political uses of the media.
2. Identify the ways in which the three branches of the federal government are covered by the press.
3. Identify the differences between press releases, news briefings, and news conferences. Which form of communication allows politicians greater influence and control over the tone of the news coverage?
4. How do politicians and interest groups try to influence news coverage, and how influential are the media in setting the political agenda?
5. In two or three sentences, state what the political uses of the media suggest about the chapter's primary question: How powerful are the mass media in the United States?

Match the Concepts

Match the statement to the concept with which it is most closely related.

1. "I was the first president to make effective use of the media."
2. "If thoughts and ideas compete for acceptance, the best ideas will win out."
3. "Watch out for this type of story. It is often self-serving and incomplete."
4. "Owning television stations, radio networks, and newspapers is an example of what?"
5. "Anyone can become a journalist—all you need is a computer and an idea."
6. "The more the sensationalism and scandal, the better."
7. "We depend on journalists to dig up serious problems and investigate scandals."
8. "The media have too much power to determine which stories get public attention and which are ignored."

A. Gatekeeping	**B.** Cross-media Ownership	**C.** Muckraking	**D.** Citizen Journalism
E. Yellow Journalism	**F.** Theodore Roosevelt	**G.** News Leaks	**H.** Marketplace of Ideas

Role Play

You have been appointed to a task force by the Society of Professional Journalists to help develop a code of ethics to guide citizen journalists. Professional societies of journalists have established codes of ethical behavior that focus on the principles of truthfulness, impartiality, fairness, and accountability. Should the code you develop be the same code of behavior that is expected of professionals, or should it allow for more flexibility? How would the two codes differ? How would you go about promoting the adherence of citizen journalists to ethical standards? Should the public have lower expectations for citizen journalists? Why or why not?

What You Can Do

Select two news stories, and examine how they are covered by different sources: the newspaper, radio, television network news, cable news, mainstream Internet news source, and a blog.

1. How does the coverage vary by source?
2. How does the medium affect the way the story is told?
3. Are there differences in content, presentation, or both?
4. Do any sources seem biased? If so, how?

CHAPTER 12
Interest Groups and Civic and Political Engagement

CAPTURE THE FOCUS: KEY OBJECTIVES

Review these learning objectives highlighted throughout the interest group and civic and political engagement chapter:

12.1 Illustrate how beliefs in collective action, self-government, and citizen action laid the foundation for activism and protest in the United States.

12.2 Explain the key factors that facilitate political protest and activism.

12.3 Identify four dirrerent types of interest groups, and explain the function of interest groups in a democracy.

12.4 Show how interest groups mobilize their memberships in the face of organizational barriers.

12.5 Describe how interest groups appeal to public officials and the public to gain support for their causes.

12.6 Assess the ways interest groups positively and negatively impact our society.

1. Write a brief paragraph in response to each of the learning objectives. Use your responses as a study aid for the chapter.
2. In as few words as possible, describe the main idea in the interest groups and civic and political engagement chapter. Compare your interpretation with the interpretation of a classmate or study group.

Map the Story: The Power of Interest Groups

1. List the reasons that people join interest groups.
2. Identify the positive functions that interest groups play in democratic societies.
3. Specify concerns that people have over interest group activity.
4. Outline the ways that interest groups influence the political process.
5. In two or three sentences, state what the power of interest groups says about the chapter's primary question: How do interest groups affect decision making and public policy?

Match the Concepts

Match the statement to the concept with which it is most closely related.

1. "Let's get an ad out there to sway public opinion."
2. "Let's get the public behind this so we can show Congress how widely supported our position is."
3. "Let's try one of the earliest tactics used to garner support—get your supporters who care deeply out and about."
4. "We need to develop benefits that go only to our members to increase membership."
5. "Large and active memberships can serve as a counterbalance to this."
6. "Why should I join an environmental group? I'll still get to breathe clean air if I don't."
7. "LULAC is best seen as what kind of interest group?"
8. "Who was a dynamic leader of farm workers that united to form the United Farm Workers of America?"

A. Selective Benefits	**B.** Multi-Issue Interest Group	**C.** César Chávez	**D.** Free-Rider Problem
E. Advertorial	**F.** Grassroots Lobbying	**G.** Gaining Access	**H.** Direct Contact

Role Play

You are deeply concerned about discrimination against gays and lesbians in your state. Attention is focused on a recent rash of suicides by gay youth who were victims of bullying, so you think the time is right for the creation of a new group in your state. Imagine you could recruit any leader for your group. Who would you enlist? Do you think an outsider or someone with political experience would be best? How old should the leader be? Do you think tapping into the fame of a celebrity would be useful, or could that distract from your goals? What characteristics do leaders need to possess to mobilize people for change? Are leaders "born that way," or can leadership be taught?

What You Can Do

Go to the Sierra Club's Web site at http://www.sierraclub.org.

1. What types of solidary, purposive, and material benefits does this organization provide to its members?
2. Which benefits are likely to appeal to whom?
3. Do you think that any of the benefits would appeal to college students?
4. Are the benefits likely to encourage the "typical" environmentalist to join the club?

CHAPTER **13**
Elections and Political Parties in America

CAPTURE THE FOCUS: KEY OBJECTIVES

Review these learning objectives highlighted throughout the elections and political parties in America chapter:

13.1 Describe the legal challenges that have broadened the democratic character of elections in America.

13.2 Evaluate electoral engagement in America, particularly as it relates to young citizens.

13.3 Identify the functions served by political parties in a democracy, and explain how they help organize the governmental process.

13.4 Trace the evolution of political parties in the United States.

13.5 Outline the process by which party nominees are chosen to run in the general election.

13.6 Explain the process by which we select the president of the United States.

13.7 Assess the critical role that money plays in the election process.

1. Write a brief paragraph in response to each of the learning objectives. Use your responses as a study aid for the chapter.
2. In as few words as possible, describe the main idea in the elections and political parties in America chapter. Compare your interpretation with the interpretation of a classmate or study group.

Map the Story: Electing Officials

1. List the various changes to the election process that have transformed the way we elect officials in the United States.
2. Identify the key institutional (legal) changes as well as the rationale for each of these elements.
3. List the most important noninstitutional changes (such as declining voter turnout).
4. Discuss how each of these changes might make the system more or less democratic. That is, how have these changes affected the degree to which elections reflect the concerns of average citizens?
5. In two or three sentences, explain the irony of expanded legal opportunities to vote amidst declining involvement.

Match the Concepts

Match the statement to the concept with which it is most closely related.

1. "I'll be an independent voice for my constituents; my party label really doesn't matter."
2. "Resolved, that the women of this nation in 1876, have greater cause for discontent, rebellion and revolution than the men of 1776."
3. "It only makes sense that if a young man or woman can go off to war for their country, they should be able to help pick the leaders of that country."
4. "Well, I'll give the Republicans a chance this time, but if they can't turn this economy around I'll go back to the Democrats in two years."
5. "Contributing money to a candidate is akin to political speech."
6. "Well, at least soft money, the biggest campaign finance loophole, has been closed by this act."
7. "Corporations and labor unions have a constitutional right to help candidates win elections, just as individuals do."
8. "It just isn't fair that a candidate can win the popular vote but still not win the presidency."

A. *Citizens United* v. FEC	**B.** Twenty-Sixth Amendment	**C.** *Buckley* v. *Valeo*	**D.** Electoral College
E. Accountability Functions	**F.** Nineteenth Amendment	**G.** Candidate-Centered Politics	**H.** Bipartisan Campaign Reform Act (BCRA)

Role Play

You are the leader of a local party organization that has decided to endorse one of two candidates in the coming primary election. The first candidate is very popular, but everyone knows that she will be a "maverick" once in office—meaning that she will probably vote against the party platform on *some* key issues. She is popular, but not ideologically pure. The other candidate is a real partisan. He'll stick with the party on all important issues, but he's not as popular and would have a tougher time winning the general election. The committee has come to you for advice. What would you say to your fellow party activists? Which candidate should they support? Why?

What You Can Do

One of the more central aspects of American elections is that most regulations on how and when people can vote are made at the state level. These rules apply not only for state offices, such as the governor and state legislature, but also for federal elections for Congress and the presidency. It is important to know the rules and regulations of your state. Go to the Web page for your state's secretary of state, and answer the following questions:

1. Does your state allow "same day registration"? If not, how far in advance must a citizen register in order to vote on Election Day?
2. Does your state allow for early voting?
3. Does your state allow for absentee voting?
4. What, if any, are some of the campaign finance rules in your state?
5. What are the age requirements for running for the state legislature?

CHAPTER 14
The Policy Process and Economic Policy

CAPTURE THE FOCUS: KEY OBJECTIVES

Review these learning objectives highlighted throughout the policy process and economic policy chapter:

14.1 Illustrate how values shape public policy in a democracy.

14.2 Compare and contrast the three main types of public policies.

14.3 Analyze how the policy process is shaped by political influences.

14.4 Identify the key indicators of economic performance used by economists.

14.5 Describe the major actors responsible for creating economic policy.

14.6 Explain the major sources of U.S. government revenue and expenditure.

14.7 Assess the major instruments of monetary policy.

1. Write a brief paragraph in response to each of the learning objectives. Use your responses as a study aid for the chapter.
2. In as few words as possible, describe the main idea of the policy process and economic policy chapter. Compare your interpretation with the interpretation of a classmate or study group.

Map the Story: The Policymaking Process

1. List some of the factors that determine if government will recognize an issue as having a place on its agenda.

2. Identify the sources of public policy options that are considered for adoption by government institutions.
3. Identify the key players in the process of policy legitimization at the federal level of government in the United States.
4. Discuss the ways that a government agency can shape how public policies are implemented in a manner that is different from the original intent of Congress.
5. In two or three sentences, state what the public policy process says about the chapter's primary question: Why is public policy political?

Match the Concepts

Match the statement to the concept with which it is most closely related.

1. "Lowering of the tax rate will increase government revenue by stimulating growth and entrepreneurship."
2. "Government should do more to make sure that individuals in the United States do not live in poverty."
3. "Citizens can influence government policies even if they don't have lots of financial resources."
4. "The best tool available to the government for macroeconomic management is controlling the money supply through federal open market operations and tinkering with the interest rate."
5. "The deaths of schoolchildren in the car accident caused by the man who was texting while driving helped get the city council to pass the new law banning the use of cell phones by drivers."
6. "The new tax on yachts helped the state government give aid to the schools in the low income neighborhood."

A. Monetary Policy	**B.** Laffer Curve	**C.** Progressivism
D. Focusing Events	**E.** Redistribution	**F.** Pluralists

Role Play

You are a member of President Obama's Council of Economic Advisers. In the midst of the economic recession, the Fed, fearing inflation, wants to raise taxes and raise interest rates. What are two arguments you might make against the Fed's proposal?

What You Can Do

Visit the Federal Register page at http://www.gpoaccess.gov/fr/. In the quick search box type in the name of a public policy area that you are interested in (e.g., clean air policy or national parks). Choose one of the options, and do the following:

1. Examine the new rules that are being proposed and try to identify what effect those rules will have on the area of policy that you are interested in. Are the rules accessible to individuals who are not policy experts?

2. The Federal Register publishes proposed regulations to allow public involvement in the policymaking process. If you had the chance to comment on the rule that you examined, what would you say?

CHAPTER 15
Foreign and National Security Policy

CAPTURE THE FOCUS: KEY OBJECTIVES

Review these learning objectives highlighted throughout the foreign and national security chapter:

15.1 Compare and contrast four different approaches to American foreign policy.

15.2 Establish three links between American foreign and domestic policy.

15.3 Assess pathways for citizen participation in foreign policymaking.

15.4 Analyze how political institutions compete for influence in making foreign policy.

15.5 Outline the major foreign policy issues confronting the United States today.

1. Write a brief paragraph in response to each of the learning objectives. Use your responses as a study aid for the chapter.
2. In as few words as possible, describe the main idea of the foreign and national security policy chapter. Compare your interpretation with the interpretation of a classmate or study group.

Map the Story: The "One" Organization

1. List the reasons why the organization "One" was founded.
2. Identify the goals of "One."
3. Specify the linkages between poverty, inequality, and security.
4. Do the citizens of wealthy countries have an obligation to mobilize to eradicate poverty in sub-Saharan Africa? Why or why not?
5. In two or three sentences, state how the goals of the organization "One" relate to the chapter's primary question: How does U.S. policy reflect its position as the world's leading superpower?

Match the Concepts

Match the statement to the concept with which it is most closely related.

1. "To prevent terrorists from striking the United States it is necessary to use military force against countries that may be harboring terrorist organizations."
2. "The best way to protect the interests of the United States is for the nation to engage in international organizations like the United Nations and to not act in a unilateral manner."
3. "Before U.S. military forces are put into combat, there should be a clear plan for when their mission will end."
4. "Gradual increases in the use of U.S. military forces are acceptable even if the public does not favor the use of such force."
5. "Because the United States is the only superpower in the world, it does not have to abide by the same rules that apply to other nations."
6. "As the number of Americans killed and wounded in Afghanistan increases, the American people will demand that troops be brought back home."

Role Play

You are a newly appointed neoliberal foreign policy adviser to President Obama. Republicans in Congress are pressuring the president to act unilaterally in Iraq and Afghanistan. What are the two arguments you might make against unilateralism in President Obama's foreign policy plans for Iraq and Afghanistan?

A. Powell Doctrine	**B.** McNamara Doctrine	**C.** Neoliberals
D. Containment	**E.** Vietnam Syndrome	**F.** Preemption

What You Can Do

Visit the State Department's Web page and look at the section devoted to policy issues at http://www.state.gov/policy/.

1. Briefly explain how economic and security issues are represented in the State Department's Web site. Are those sets of issues treated as discrete or interrelated areas of interest?
2. Take a look at the State Department's Muslim Outreach program at http://www.state.gov/s/srmc/index.htm. How would you evaluate the way the department is pursuing this task? What would you suggest to be done differently?

By the early 1770s, relations between Great Britain and 13 colonies in North American had become strained. Actual hostilities broke out in 1775 at Lexington and Concord, marking the beginning of the Revolutionary War. But the "patriot cause" was not universally accepted thoughout the colonies. A second Continental Congress was called, and on May 10, 1775, representatives appointed by state legislatures from all of the colonies except Georgia convened in Philadelphia. A committee consisting of John Adams, Benjamin Franklin, Robert R. Livingston, Roger Sherman, and a slim, quiet delegate from Virginia named Thomas Jefferson (the "Committee of Five") was formed to draft a statement that would justify a war for independence. Adams suggested that Jefferson take the first stab at writing a draft document. With a few minor edits from Adams and Franklin, Jefferson presented his "Declaration" to the Continental Congress on June 28, 1776. Many agree that it is one of the most eloquent political statements ever written.

The Preamble of the Declaration is influenced by Enlightenment philosophy, a seventeenth-century European intellectual movement that held that all questions of math, science, and government could be solved through clear logic and careful experimentation. As such, it rejected superstition and religious "truths."

These words also clearly reflect the writings of English philosopher John Locke (1632–1704), particularly his *Second Treatise on Government*. Jefferson also seemed to be "borrowing" from the Virginia Declaration of Rights, which had been adopted about a month earlier.

Jefferson presents a notion of natural rights. That is, individuals possess certain privileges—certain guarantees by virtue of being human. These rights are *not* granted by government, but instead by God, or what Jefferson calls the "Creator". They cannot be given, nor can they be taken away.

Here Jefferson introduces the social contract theory, drawn in large measure from the writings of John Locke. Humans have the option of living alone in what he called "the state of nature." According to this theory, humans originally lived without government or laws, enjoying complete personal freedom. Yet the state of nature meant "a war of all against all," in which—in the words of another philosopher, Thomas Hobbes—life was "solitary, poor, nasty, brutish, and short." To end this perpetual conflict and insecurity, people created governments, thereby giving up some of their freedoms in order to protect their lives and their property.

Jefferson also agreed with Locke that governments, having been created by the people to protect their rights, are limited; they get their powers from the will of the people and no one else. (In arguing this, Locke was attacking the traditional claim that kings ruled by the will of God.)

When a government fails to respect the will of the people—that is, when it appears no longer to be limited—it becomes the right, indeed the obligation, of citizens to change the government. This passage is Jefferson's call for revolution.

APPENDIX 1

The Declaration of Independence of the Thirteen Colonies

In Congress, July 4, 1776

The Unanimous Declaration of the Thirteen United States of America

When in the Course of human events, it becomes necessary for one people to dissolve the political bands which have connected them with another, and to assume among the powers of the earth, the separate and equal station to which the Laws of Nature and of Nature's God entitle them, a decent respect to the opinions of mankind requires that they should declare the causes which impel them to the separation.

We hold these truths to be self-evident, that all men are created equal, that they are endowed by their Creator with certain unalienable Rights, that among these are Life, Liberty and the pursuit of Happiness. That to secure these rights, Governments are instituted among Men, deriving their just powers from the consent of the governed, that whenever any Form of Government becomes destructive of these ends, it is the Right of the People to alter or to abolish it, and to institute new Government, laying its foundation on such principles and organizing its powers in such form, as to them shall seem most likely to effect their Safety and Happiness.

Prudence, indeed, will dictate that Governments long established should not be changed for light and transient causes; and accordingly all experience hath shewn, that mankind are more disposed to suffer, while evils are sufferable, than to right themselves by abolishing the forms to which they are accustomed. But when a long train of abuses and usurpations, pursuing invariably the same Object evinces a design to reduce them under absolute Despotism, it is their right, it is their duty, to throw off such Government, and to provide new Guards for their future security. —Such has been the patient sufferance of these Colonies; and such is now the necessity which constrains them to alter their former Systems of Government. The history of the present King of Great Britain [George III] is a history of repeated injuries and usurpations, all having in direct object the establishment of an absolute Tyranny over these States. To prove this, let Facts be submitted to a candid world.

> Here Jefferson seems to provide a caution: Governments should be responsive to the will of the people, but just because the public is upset with government does not imply the need for revolution. Yes, governments can be changed, but not for "light and transient causes."
>
> This next section is called the List of Grievances, which is essentially a laundry list of all the bad things that the British Government has done to the colonies. The idea here was to create such a long and powerful list that few would disagree with the need for a change.

He has refused his Assent to Laws, the most wholesome and necessary for the public good. He has forbidden his Governors to pass Laws of immediate and pressing importance, unless suspended in their operation till his Assent should be obtained; and when so suspended, he has utterly neglected to attend to them.

> In all these passages, "He" refers to King George III.

He has refused to pass other Laws for the accommodation of large districts of people, unless those people would relinquish the right of Representation in the Legislature, a right inestimable to them and formidable to tyrants only.

He has called together legislative bodies at places unusual, uncomfortable, and distant from the depository of their public Records, for the sole purpose of fatiguing them into compliance with his measures.

He has dissolved Representative Houses repeatedly, for opposing with manly firmness his invasions on the rights of the people.

> Precisely what defined a "government by the people" was still a bit vague at this time, but many suspected that representative assemblies were a necessary ingredient. So when the King dissolved these legislatures it seemed that he was striking a direct blow against self-rule.

He has refused for a long time, after such dissolutions, to cause others to be elected; whereby the Legislative powers, incapable of Annihilation, have returned to the People at large for their exercise; the State remaining in the mean time exposed to all the dangers of invasion from without, and convulsions within.

An independent judiciary was also an element deemed essential for democratic governance, and the King's control of the courts seems a clear illustration of tyranny.

While most countries keep "standing armies" these days, in the eighteenth-century armies were assembled only when war was at hand. Many colonists saw the King's army as an instrument of aggression and control.

What is interesting about the list of grievances is that many of the items refer to more theoretical matters pertaining to just governance and the rights of citizens. But other items point to pragmatic issues, such as improperly taking money from colonists. Make no mistake, the Revolution was about creating a democratic system of government, a government responsive to "the people," but it was also about creating a system where average citizens could prosper financially.

Many colonists were anxious to pursue independence because they believed in self-rule, but many others were mostly interested in commercial issues (economic gain). So the "open trade" issue was critical for building broad public support for independence.

He has endeavoured to prevent the population of these States; for that purpose obstructing the Laws for Naturalization of Foreigners; refusing to pass others to encourage their migrations hither, and raising the conditions of new Appropriations of Lands.

He has obstructed the Administration of Justice, by refusing his Assent to Laws for establishing Judiciary powers.

He has made Judges dependent on his Will alone, for the tenure of their offices, and the amount and payment of their salaries.

He has erected a multitude of New Offices, and sent hither swarms of Officers to harass our people, and eat out their substance.

He has kept among us, in times of peace, Standing Armies without the consent of our legislatures.

He has affected to render the Military independent of and superior to the Civil power.

He has combined with others to subject us to a jurisdiction foreign to our constitution and unacknowledged by our laws; giving his Assent to their Acts of pretended Legislation:

For Quartering large bodies of armed troops among us:

For protecting them, by a mock Trial, from punishment for any Murders which they should commit on the Inhabitants of these States:

For cutting off our Trade with all parts of the world:

For imposing Taxes on us without our Consent:

For depriving us, in many cases, of the benefits of Trial by Jury:

For transporting us beyond Seas to be tried for pretended offences:

For abolishing the free System of English Laws in a neighbouring Province, establishing therein an Arbitrary government, and enlarging its Boundaries so as to render it at once an example and fit instrument for introducing the same absolute rule into these Colonies:

For taking away our Charters, abolishing our most valuable Laws, and altering fundamentally the Forms of our Governments:

For suspending our own Legislatures, and declaring themselves invested with power to legislate for us in all cases whatsoever.

He has abdicated Government here, by declaring us out of his Protection and waging War against us.

He has plundered our seas, ravaged our Coasts, burnt our towns, and destroyed the lives of our people.

He is at this time transporting large Armies of foreign Mercenaries to compleat the works of death, desolation and tyranny, already begun with circumstances of Cruelty and perfidy scarcely paralleled in the most barbarous ages, and totally unworthy the Head of a civilized nation.

He has constrained our fellow Citizens taken Captive on the high Seas to bear Arms against their Country, to become the executioners of their friends and Brethren, or to fall themselves by their Hands.

He has excited domestic insurrections amongst us, and has endeavoured to bring on the inhabitants of our frontiers, the merciless Indian Savages, whose known rule of warfare, is an undistinguished destruction of all ages, sexes and conditions.

In every stage of these Oppressions We have Petitioned for Redress in the most humble terms: Our repeated Petitions have been answered only by repeated injury. A Prince whose character is thus marked by every act which may define a Tyrant, is unfit to be the ruler of a free people.

Nor have We been wanting in attentions to our British brethren. We have warned them from time to time of attempts by their legislature to extend an unwarrantable jurisdiction over us. We have reminded them of the circumstances of our emigration and settlement here. We have appealed to their native justice and magnanimity, and we have conjured them by the ties of our common kindred to disavow these usurpations, which would inevitably interrupt our connections and correspondence. They too have been deaf to the voice of justice and of consanguinity. We must, therefore, acquiesce in the necessity, which denounces our Separation, and hold them, as we hold the rest of mankind, Enemies in War, in Peace Friends.

Again, many saw colonial assemblies as the foundation of a free society, so the King's suspension of their laws suggested tyrannical rule.

With the French and Indian War only a few years distant, many of the colonists continued to have grave fears about hostilities with Native Americans. So to suggest that the King was inflaming conflict was no small matter.

This was perceived as especially harsh language. To call the King "a Tyrant" was considered an act of treason.

Was the Declaration of Independence effective in rallying support behind the revolutionary cause? We do know that many New Yorkers were so inspired upon hearing these words that they toppled a statue of King George and had it melted down to make 42,000 bullets for war. Still, many balked at joining the Revolution and even enlisted in the British Army. We also know that public support for the Continental Army, headed by George Washington, lagged considerably throughout the Revolution.

All the signers assumed that they were, in effect, signing their own death warrant if indeed the Revolution were to fail. The above paragraph, about absolving allegiances to the British Crown and creating independent states, would surely be interpreted as treason in England. Signing the Declaration was an act of true courage.

On July 19, 1776, Congress ordered a copy be handwritten for the delegates to sign, which most did on August 2, 1776. Two delegates never signed at all. As new delegates joined the Congress, they were also allowed to sign. A total of 56 delegates eventually signed.

The first and most famous signature on the embossed copy was that of John Hancock, President of the Continental Congress.

We, therefore, the Representatives of the united States of America, in General Congress, Assembled, appealing to the Supreme Judge of the world for the rectitude of our intentions, do, in the Name, and by the Authority of the good People of these Colonies, solemnly publish and declare, That these United Colonies are, and of Right ought to be Free and Independent States; that they are Absolved from all Allegiance to the British Crown, and that all political connection between them and the State of Great Britain, is and ought to be totally dissolved; and that as Free and Independent States, they have full Power to levy War, conclude Peace, contract Alliances, establish Commerce, and to do all other Acts and Things which Independent States may of right do. And for the support of this Declaration, with a firm reliance on the protection of divine Providence, we mutually pledge to each other our Lives, our Fortunes and our sacred Honor.

The signers of the Declaration represented the new states as follows:

NEW HAMPSHIRE
Josiah Bartlett, William Whipple, Matthew Thornton

MASSACHUSETTS
John Hancock, Samuel Adams, John Adams, Robert Treat Paine, Elbridge Gerry

RHODE ISLAND
Stephen Hopkins, William Ellery

CONNECTICUT
Roger Sherman, Samuel Huntington, William Williams, Oliver Wolcott

NEW YORK

William Floyd, Philip Livingston, Francis Lewis, Lewis Morris

NEW JERSEY

Richard Stockton, John Witherspoon, Francis Hopkinson, John Hart, Abraham Clark

PENNSYLVANIA

Robert Morris, Benjamin Rush, Benjamin Franklin, John Morton, George Clymer, James Smith, George Taylor, James Wilson, George Ross

> Franklin was the oldest signer, at 70.

DELAWARE

Caesar Rodney, George Read, Thomas McKean

MARYLAND

Samuel Chase, William Paca, Thomas Stone, Charles Carroll of Carrollton

VIRGINIA

George Wythe, Richard Henry Lee, Thomas Jefferson, Benjamin Harrison, Thomas Nelson, Jr., Francis Lightfoot Lee, Carter Braxton

> Two future presidents signed the Declaration —Thomas Jefferson and John Adams.

NORTH CAROLINA

William Hooper, Joseph Hewes, John Penn

SOUTH CAROLINA

Edward Rutledge, Thomas Heyward, Jr., Thomas Lynch, Jr., Arthur Middleton

> Edward Rutledge, at age 26, was the youngest signer of the Declaration.

GEORGIA

Button Gwinnett, Lyman Hall, George Walton

> After its adoption by the Congress, a handwritten draft was then sent a few blocks away to the printing shop of John Dunlap. Through the night between 150 and 200 copies were made, now known as "Dunlap broadsides." One was sent to George Washington on July 6, who had it read to his troops in New York on July 9. The 25 Dunlap broadsides still known to exist are the oldest surviving copies of the document. The original handwritten copy has not survived.
>
> The signed copy of the Declaration of Independence is on display at the National Archives.

"We, the people." Three simple words are of profound importance and contentious origin. Every government in the world at the time of the Constitutional Convention was some type of monarchy, wherein sovereign power was bestowed from the top. The Founders of our new country rejected monarchy as a form of government and proposed instead a republic, which would draw its sovereignty from the people.

It is this very sense of empowerment that allows the "people" to influence our government and shape the world in which we live. We are among the freest people in the world largely because of this document. We are presented with multiple pathways to influence our government and better our lives.

Article I. The very first article in the Constitution established the legislative branch of the new national government. Why did the framers start with the legislative power instead of the executive branch? The framers truly believed it was the most important component of the new government.

It was also something that calmed the anxieties of average citizens. That is, they had experience with "legislative-centered governance" under the Articles and even during the colonial period. It was not perfect, but the legislative process seems to work.

Section 1. Section 1 established a bicameral (two-chamber) legislature, or an upper (Senate) and lower (House of Representatives) organization of the legislative branch.

A bicameral legislature offers more opportunities to influence the policy process, as you can appeal to both your Senators and your representatives through the lobbying decision makers pathway, or indirectly through the elections pathway, the grassroots mobilization pathway, or the cultural change pathway. If you do not like a law passed by Congress, you can appeal to the courts to invalidate it or to change its meaning.

Section 2 Clause 1. This section sets the term of office for House members (2 years) and indicates that those voting for Congress will have the same qualifications as those voting for the state legislatures. Originally, states limited voters to white property owners. Some states even had religious disqualifications, for instance, if citizens were Catholic or Jewish.

There was a great deal of discussion about how long a legislator should sit in office before appealing to constituents for reelection. Short terms of office, such as the 2 years used in the House of Representatives, help force members to pay attention to the needs of their constituents.

Clause 2. This section sets forth the basic qualifications of a representative: at least 25 years of age, a U.S. citizen for at least 7 years, and a resident of the state in which the district is located. Note that the Constitution does not require a person to be a resident of the district he or she represents.

Clause 2 does not specify how many terms a representative can serve in Congress, but some critics support limiting the number of terms members can serve in order to make Congress more in touch with the citizenry—and to overcome some of the advantages incumbents have created to help win elections. Currently the average length of service in the House is 9 years (4.6 terms).

APPENDIX 2

The Constitution of the United States

The Preamble

We, the People of the United States, in Order to form a more perfect Union, establish Justice, insure domestic Tranquility, provide for the common defence, promote the general Welfare, and secure the Blessings of Liberty to ourselves and our Posterity, do ordain and establish this Constitution for the United States of America.

Article I
The Legislative Article

Legislative Power

SECTION 1. All legislative Powers herein granted shall be vested in a Congress of the United States, which shall consist of a Senate and House of Representatives.

House of Representatives: Composition; Qualifications; Apportionment; Impeachment Power

SECTION 2 CLAUSE 1. The House of Representatives shall be composed of Members chosen every second Year by the People of the several States, and the Electors in each State shall have the Qualifications requisite for Electors of the most numerous Branch of the State Legislature.

CLAUSE 2. No Person shall be a Representative who shall not have attained to the Age of twenty five Years, and been seven Years a Citizen of the United States, and who shall not, when elected, be an Inhabitant of that State in which he shall be chosen.

CLAUSE 3. Representatives and direct Taxes[1] shall be apportioned among the several States which may be included within this Union, according to their respective Numbers, which shall be determined by adding to the whole Number of free Persons, including those bound to Service for a Term of Years, and excluding Indians not taxed, three fifths of all other Persons.[2] The actual Enumeration shall be made within three Years after the first Meeting of the Congress of the United States, and within every subsequent Term of ten Years, in such Manner as they shall by Law direct. The Number of Representatives shall not exceed one for every thirty Thousand, but each State shall have at Least one Representative; and until such enumeration shall be made, the State of New Hampshire shall be entitled to chuse three, Massachusetts eight, Rhode-Island and Providence Plantations one, Connecticut five, New-York six, New Jersey four, Pennsylvania eight, Delaware one, Maryland six, Virginia ten, North Carolina five, South Carolina five, and Georgia three.

CLAUSE 4. When vacancies happen in the Representation from any State, the Executive Authority thereof shall issue Writs of Election to fill such Vacancies.

CLAUSE 5. The House of Representatives shall chuse their Speaker and other Officers; and shall have the sole Power of Impeachment.

Senate Composition: Qualifications, Impeachment Trials

SECTION 3 CLAUSE 1. The Senate of the United States shall be composed of two Senators from each State, chosen by the Legislature thereof,[3] for six Years; and each Senator shall have one Vote.

CLAUSE 2. Immediately after they shall be assembled in Consequence of the first Election, they shall be divided as equally as may be into three Classes. The Seats of the Senators of the first Class shall be vacated at the Expiration of the second Year, of the second Class at the Expiration of the fourth Year, and of the third Class at the Expiration of the sixth Year, so that one third may be chosen every second Year; and if Vacancies happen by Resignation, or otherwise, during the Recess of the Legislature of any State, the Executive thereof may make temporary Appointments until the next Meeting of the Legislature, which shall then fill such Vacancies.[4]

CLAUSE 3. No Person shall be a Senator who shall not have attained to the Age of thirty Years, and been nine Years a Citizen of the United States, and who shall not, when elected, be an Inhabitant of that State for which he shall be chosen.

Clause 3. This clause contains the Three-Fifths Compromise, in which American Indians and blacks were only counted as three-fifths of a person for congressional representation purposes. This clause also addresses the question of congressional reapportionment every 10 years, which requires a census. Since the 1911 Reapportionment Act, the size of the House of Representatives has been set at 435. This is the designated size that is reapportioned every 10 years. Based on changes of population, some states gain and some states lose representatives.

While the Constitution never directly addresses the issue of slavery, this clause and others clearly condone its existence. It ultimately took the Civil War (1861–1865) to resolve the issue of slavery.

Clause 4. This clause provides a procedure for replacing a U.S. representative in the case of death, resignation, or expulsion from the House. Essentially, the governor of the representative's state will determine the selection of a successor. Generally, if less than half a term is left, the governor will appoint a successor. If more than half a term is remaining, most states require a special election to fill the vacancy.

Clause 5. Only one officer of the House is specified, the Speaker. The House decides all other officers. This clause also gives the House authority for impeachments—the determination of formal charges—against officials of the executive and judicial branches.

Interestingly, this clause does not stipulate that the Speaker be a member of Congress. The House might choose an outsider to run their chamber, but this has never happened—and will likely not happen in the future.

Section 3 Clause 1. This clause treats each state equally—all have two senators. Originally, state legislators chose senators, but since passage and ratification of the 17th Amendment, they are now elected by popular vote. This clause also establishes the term of a senator—6 years, three times that of a House member.

This clause is very important when thinking about pathways of change. For one, it creates a mechanism by which the minority, through their senators, can thwart the will of the majority. Each state has the same number of senators. A majority of senators, representing states with small populations, have the ability to control the process—or at least stall things. In our system "majority will" does not always prevail.

Also, 6-year terms give senators the chance to worry only periodically about an approaching reelection. Unlike members of the House, who come up for reelection so frequently that their actions may be constantly guided by a concern for pleasing the voters, this extended term in office offers senators some leeway to do what they think is best for their state and the nation, rather than what might be seen as popular.

Clause 2. To prevent a wholesale replacement of senators every 6 years, this clause provides that one-third of the Senate will be elected every 2 years. In other words, in order to remove at least one-half of the Senators from office, two elections are needed.

Senate vacancies are filled in the same way as the House—either appointment by the governor or by special election. Currently the average length of service in the Senate is 11.3 years (slightly less than two terms).

Clause 3. This clause sets forth the qualifications for U.S. senator: at least 30 years old, a U.S. citizen for at least nine years, and a citizen of a state. The equivalent age of 30 today would be 54 years old. The average age of a U.S. senator at present is 59.5 years.

Clause 4. The only constitutional duty of the vice president is specified in this clause—president of the Senate. This official only has a vote if there is a tie vote in the Senate; then the vice president's vote breaks the tie.

The split between Democrats and Republicans in Congress has been tiny in recent years. Not surprisingly, the Vice President has been called upon to cast several deciding votes.

Clause 5. One official office in the U.S. Senate is specified—temporary president, who fills in during the vice president's absence (which is normally the case). All other Senate officers are designated and selected by the Senate.

Clause 6, 7. The Senate acts as a trial court for impeached federal officials. If the accused is the president, the Chief Justice of the U.S. Supreme Court presides. Otherwise, the vice president normally presides. Conviction of the charges requires a two-thirds majority vote of those senators present at the time of the vote. Conviction results in the federal official's removal from office and disqualification to hold any other federal appointed office.

Section 4 Clause 1. Through the years this clause has proven to be a critical aspect of the elections pathway. By allowing states to regulate elections procedures (that is, until Congress acts), the types of citizens able to participate in the process have been limited. First, religious and property qualifications were common, and many southern states used this provision to discriminate against black voters until the 1960s. Many states barred women from voting in elections until the ratification of the 19th Amendment, and still others kept 18-year-olds out until the 25th Amendment.

Lingering issues include residency and registration requirements. In some states citizens can register to vote on Election Day, but in many others they have to take this step 30 days in advance. Indeed, many argue that residency and registration requirements unnecessarily inhibit voting, especially for young people who tend to be more mobile. Others argue that such laws help to reduce voter fraud.

Clause 2. The states determine the place and manner of electing representatives and senators, but Congress has the right to make or change these laws or regulations, except for the election sites. Congress is required to meet annually, and now, by law, annual meetings begin in January.

Section 5 Clause 1. This clause enables each legislative branch to essentially make its own rules. Normally, to take a vote, a quorum is necessary. But if no votes are scheduled, fewer than a quorum can convene a session.

CLAUSE 4. The Vice President of the United States shall be President of the Senate, but shall have no Vote, unless they be equally divided.

CLAUSE 5. The Senate shall chuse their other Officers, and also a President pro tempore, in the Absence of the Vice President, or when he shall exercise the Office of President of the United States.

CLAUSE 6. The Senate shall have the sole Power to try all Impeachments. When sitting for that Purpose, they shall be on Oath or Affirmation. When the President of the United States is tried, the Chief Justice shall preside: And no Person shall be convicted without the Concurrence of two thirds of the Members present.

CLAUSE 7. Judgment in Cases of Impeachment shall not extend further than to removal from Office, and disqualification to hold and enjoy any Office of honor, Trust or Profit under the United States: but the Party convicted shall nevertheless be liable and subject to Indictment, Trial, Judgment and Punishment, according to Law.

Congressional Elections: Times, Places, Manner

SECTION 4 CLAUSE 1. The Times, Places and Manner of holding Elections for Senators and Representatives, shall be prescribed in each State by the Legislature thereof; but the Congress may at any time by Law make or alter such Regulations, except as to the Places of chusing Senators.

CLAUSE 2. The Congress shall assemble at least once in every Year, and such Meeting shall be on the first Monday in December, unless they shall by Law appoint a different Day.[5]

Powers and Duties of the Houses

SECTION 5 CLAUSE 1. Each House shall be the Judge of the Elections, Returns and Qualifications of its own Members, and a Majority of each shall constitute a Quorum to do Business; but a smaller Number may adjourn from day to day, and may be authorized to compel the Attendance of absent Members, in such Manner, and under the Penalties as each House may provide.

CLAUSE 2. Each House may determine the Rules of its Proceedings, punish its Members for disorderly Behaviour, and, with the Concurrence of two thirds, expel a Member.

CLAUSE 3. Each House shall keep a Journal of its Proceedings, and from time to time publish the same, excepting such Parts as may in their Judgment require Secrecy; and the Yeas and Nays of the Members of either House on any question shall, at the Desire of one fifth of those Present, be entered on the Journal.

CLAUSE 4. Neither House, during the Session of Congress, shall, without the Consent of the other, adjourn for more than three days, nor to any other Place than that in which the two Houses shall be sitting.

Rights of Members

SECTION 6 CLAUSE 1. The Senators and Representatives shall receive a Compensation for their Services, to be ascertained by Law, and paid out of the Treasury of the United States. They shall in all Cases, except Treason, Felony and Breach of the Peace, be privileged from Arrest during their Attendance at the Session of their respective Houses, and in going to and returning from the same; and for any Speech or Debate in either House, they shall not be questioned in any other Place.

CLAUSE 2. No Senator or Representative shall, during the Time for which he was elected, be appointed to any civil Office under the Authority of the United States, which shall have been created, or the Emoluments whereof shall have been encreased during such time; and no Person holding any Office under the United States, shall be a Member of either House during his Continuance in Office.

Legislative Powers: Bills and Resolutions

SECTION 7 CLAUSE 1. All Bills for raising Revenue shall originate in the House of Representatives; but the Senate may propose or concur with Amendments as on other Bills.

Clause 2. Essentially, each branch promulgates its own rules and punishes its own members. Knowing exactly how each chamber of the legislature conducts its proceedings is essential for political activists. The lobbying decision makers pathway can be a potent means of shifting public policy, but only when internal rules are well understood. Perhaps this is one of the reasons why former members of Congress make such good lobbyists.

Clause 3. An official record called the Congressional Record, House Journal, etc., is kept for all sessions. It is a daily account of House and Senate floor debates, votes, and members' remarks. However, a record is not printed if a proceeding is closed to the public for security reasons. Many votes are by voice vote, and if at least one-fifth of the members request, a recorded vote of Yeas and Nays will be conducted and documented. This procedure permits analysis of congressional role-call votes.

Clause 4. This clause prevents one house from adjourning for a long period of time or to some other location without the consent of the other house.

Section 6 Clause 1. This section refers to a salary paid to senators and members of the House from the U.S. Treasury. This clearly states that federal legislators work for the entire nation, and not for their respective states.

In 2010, the salary for members of Congress was $174,000; some leadership positions, like Speaker of the House, receive a higher salary. The Speaker receives a salary of $223,500. Members of Congress receive many other benefits: free health care, fully funded retirement system, free round trips to their home state or district, etc. This section also provides immunity from arrest or prosecution for congressional actions on the floor or in travel to and from the Congress. For example, few members of Congress have ever been charged with drunk driving.

Clause 2. This section prevents the U.S. from adopting a parliamentary democracy, since congressional members cannot hold executive offices and members of the executive branch cannot be members of Congress.

Section 7 Clause 1. This clause specifies one of the few powers specific to the U.S. House—revenue bills. Since the House was intended to be more closely tied to the people (since members are elected more frequently and they represent fewer people than the Senate), the founders wanted to grant them the power of the purse.

Given that much of politics centers on the allocation of scarce resources (the distribution of money), this provision is a key piece of information for would-be political activists.

Clause 2. The heart of the checks and balances system is contained in this clause. Both the House and Senate must pass an identical bill and present it to the president. If the president fails to act on the bill within 10 days (not including Sundays), the bill will automatically become law if Congress is in session. If the president signs the bill, it becomes law. If the president vetoes the bill and sends it back to Congress, this body may override the veto by a two-thirds vote in each branch. This vote must be a recorded vote.

The systems of checks and balances, as well as a division of power at the federal level, allow many ways to pursue change by a variety of pathways.

Clause 3. This clause covers every other type of legislative action other than a bill. Essentially, the same procedures apply in most cases. There are a few exceptions. For example, a joint resolution proposing a new congressional amendment is not subject to presidential veto.

Section 8 Clause 1, 2. This power allows the federal government to deficit-spend (which most states are not allowed to do). Thus, when times of economic difficulty arise, individuals and groups can petition government for financial aid and relief with job shortages.

Clause 3. This is one of the most sweeping powers granted Congress, because so much can be linked to interstate "commerce." Since the early twentieth century, the U.S. Supreme Court has defined interstate commerce broadly and thereby enabled Congress to use this power to pass antidiscrimination laws, criminal justice laws, and other statutes.

Clause 4. This provision helps us understand why Congress, rather than state legislatures, has been at the center of the recent immigration reform debate.

CLAUSE 2. Every Bill which shall have passed the House of Representatives and the Senate, shall, before it becomes a Law, be presented to the President of the United States; If he approve he shall sign it, but if not he shall return it, with his Objections to that House in which it shall have originated, who shall enter the Objections at large on their Journal, and proceed to reconsider it. If after such Reconsideration two thirds of that House shall agree to pass the Bill, it shall be sent, together with the Objections, to the other House, by which it shall likewise be reconsidered, and if approved by two thirds of that House, it shall become a Law. But in all such Cases the Votes of both Houses shall be determined by yeas and Nays, and the Names of the Persons voting for and against the Bill shall be entered on the Journal of each House respectively. If any Bill shall not be returned by the President within ten Days (Sundays excepted) after it shall have been presented to him, the Same shall be a Law, in like Manner as if he had signed it, unless the Congress by their Adjournment prevent its Return, in which Case it shall not be a Law.

CLAUSE 3. Every Order, Resolution, or Vote to which the Concurrence of the Senate and House of Representatives may be necessary (except on a question of Adjournment) shall be presented to the President of the United States; and before the Same shall take Effect, shall be approved by him, or being disapproved by him, shall be repassed by two thirds of the Senate and House of Representatives, according to the Rules and Limitations prescribed in the Case of a Bill.

Powers of Congress

SECTION 8 CLAUSE 1. The Congress shall have Power To lay and collect Taxes, Duties, Imposts and Excises, to pay the Debts and provide for the common Defence and general Welfare of the United States; but all Duties, Imposts and Excises shall be uniform throughout the United States.

CLAUSE 2. To borrow Money on the credit of the United States;

CLAUSE 3. To regulate Commerce with foreign Nations, and among the several States, and with the Indian Tribes;

CLAUSE 4. To establish an uniform Rule of Naturalization; and uniform Laws on the subject of Bankruptcies throughout the United States;

CLAUSE 5. To coin Money, regulate the Value thereof, and of foreign Coin, and fix the Standard of Weights and Measures;

CLAUSE 6. To provide for the Punishment of counterfeiting the Securities and current Coin of the United States;

CLAUSE 7. To establish Post Offices and post Roads;

CLAUSE 8. To promote the Progress of Science and useful Arts, by securing for limited Times to Authors and Inventors the exclusive Right to their respective Writings and Discoveries;

CLAUSE 9. To constitute Tribunals inferior to the supreme Court;

CLAUSE 10. To define and punish Piracies and Felonies committed on the high Seas, and Offences against the Law of Nations;

CLAUSE 11. To declare War, grant Letters of Marque and Reprisal, and make Rules concerning Captures on Land and Water;

CLAUSE 12. To raise and support Armies, but no Appropriation of Money to that Use shall be for a longer Term than two Years;

CLAUSE 13. To provide and maintain a Navy;

CLAUSE 14. To make Rules for the Government and Regulation of the land and naval Forces;

CLAUSE 15. To provide for calling forth the Militia to execute the Laws of the Union, suppress Insurrections and repel Invasions;

CLAUSE 16. To provide for organizing, arming, and disciplining, the Militia, and for governing such Part of them as may be employed in the Service of the United States, reserving to the States respectively, the Appointment of the Officers, and the Authority of training the Militia according to the discipline prescribed by Congress;

CLAUSE 17. To exercise exclusive Legislation in all Cases whatsoever, over such District (not exceeding ten Miles square) as may, by Cession of particular States, and the Acceptance of Congress, become the Seat of the Government of the United States, and to exercise like Authority over all Places purchased by the Consent of the Legislature of the State in which the Same shall be, for the Erection of Forts, Magazines, Arsenals, dockYards, and other needful Buildings;

Clause 5, 6, 7. Congressional power over coining money, counterfeiting, and post offices provides the justification for the creation of many criminal laws that are handled by federal law enforcement agencies such as the Federal Bureau of Investigation (FBI) and Secret Service. Because these matters are specified as under federal authority in the Constitution, it is a federal crime—rather than a state crime—to counterfeit money and engage in mail fraud. Most other kinds of crimes, such as murders, robberies, and burglaries victimizing ordinary citizens, are governed by state law.

Clause 9. Congress is responsible for the design of and procedures used in the federal court system. The U.S. Supreme Court is the only court created by the Constitution (see Article III). The lower federal courts are created by—and can be changed by—laws enacted by Congress. When there are changes in the design of the federal court system, such as the creation of a new court, these matters are under the power of Congress rather than under the control of the Supreme Court.

Clause 10, 11. Although Congress possesses the exclusive authority to declare war, presidents use their powers as commander-in-chief (see Article II) to initiate military actions even when there is no formal congressional declaration of war. There have been periodic disputes about whether presidents have exceeded their authority and ignored the Constitution's explicit grant of war-declaring power to Congress.

Clause 11, 12, 13. These three clauses, clauses 11, 12, and 13, ensure that Congress is involved in foreign policy decisions; thus citizens and groups can appeal to Congress if they do not like the president's foreign policy decisions or actions. Giving Congress the power to make appropriations to fund the military is potentially a significant power they have in rivaling the president for influence.

Clause 14, 15, 16. These clauses establish what are known as the "expressed" or "specified" powers of Congress.

Clause 17. This clause establishes the seat of the federal government, which was first located in New York. It eventually was moved to Washington, D.C., when both Maryland and Virginia ceded land to the new national government, which then established the District of Columbia.

Clause 18. This clause, known as the "Elastic Clause," provides the basis for the doctrine of "implied" congressional powers, which was first introduced in the U.S. Supreme Court case of *McCulloch* v. *Maryland* (1819). It greatly expanded the power of Congress to pass legislation and make regulations.

The "necessary and proper" clause increases the powers of Congress, granting the legislature a great deal more authority and influence in our system of government. It has proven essential in creating a stong national government and in placing Congress at the center of the policy process.

Section 9 Clause 1. This clause was part of the Three-Fifths Compromise. Essentially, the new Congress was prohibited from stopping the importation of slaves until 1808, but it could impose a head tax not to exceed $10 for each slave.

Condoning slavery, from today's perspective, clearly clashed with the Declaration of Independence's assertion that all men are created equal. It is hard to understand the hypocrisy of a free society with slaves. Without this provision, however, southern delegates would have left the Constitutional Convention, and southern states would not have voted to ratify the new Constitution.

Clause 2. Habeas Corpus is a judicial order forcing law enforcement authorities to produce a prisoner they are holding, and to justify the prisoner's continued confinement. Congress cannot suspend the writ of habeas corpus except in cases of rebellion or invasion. The writ of habeas corpus permits a judge to inquire about the legality of detention or deprivation of liberty of any citizen. This is one of the few legal protections for individuals enshrined in the Constitution before the Bill of Rights.

Clause 3. This provision prohibits Congress from passing either bills of attainder (an act of legislature declaring a person or group of persons guilty of some crime, and punishing them, without benefit of a trial) or ex post facto laws (retroactive crimes after passage of legislation). Similar restrictions were put in many state constitutions. These protections were among the few specifically provided for individuals in the body of the Constitution before the creation of amendments.

Clause 4. This clause was interpreted to prevent Congress from passing an income tax. When the Supreme Court struck down congressional efforts to impose an income tax, passage of the 16th Amendment in 1913 counteracted the Supreme Court decision and gave Congress this power.

Clause 5. This section establishes free trade within the U.S. That is, one state cannot tax the importation of domestic goods, and the federal government cannot tax state exports.

Clause 6. This clause also applies to free trade within the U.S. The national government cannot show any preference to any state or maritime movements among the states.

Clause 7. This clause prevents any expenditure unless it has been provided for in an appropriations bill enacted by Congress. At the beginning of most fiscal years, Congress has not completed the budget. Technically, the government cannot then spend any money, and would have to shut down. So Congress usually passes a Continuing Resolution Authority providing temporary authority to continue to spend money until the final budget is approved and signed into law.

CLAUSE 18. To make all Laws which shall be necessary and proper for carrying into Execution the foregoing Powers, and all other Powers vested by this Constitution in the Government of the United States, or in any Department or Officer thereof.

Powers Denied to Congress

SECTION 9 CLAUSE 1. The Migration or Importation of such Persons as any of the States now existing shall think proper to admit, shall not be prohibited by the Congress prior to the Year one thousand eight hundred and eight, but a Tax or duty may be imposed on such Importation, not exceeding ten dollars for each Person.

CLAUSE 2. The Privilege of the Writ of Habeas Corpus shall not be suspended, unless when in Cases of Rebellion or Invasion the public Safety may require it.

CLAUSE 3. No Bill of Attainder or ex post facto Law shall be passed.

CLAUSE 4. No Capitation, or other direct, Tax shall be laid, unless in Proportion to the Census or Enumeration herein before directed to be taken.[6]

CLAUSE 5. No Tax or Duty shall be laid on Articles exported from any State.

CLAUSE 6. No Preference shall be given by any Regulation of Commerce or Revenue to the Ports of one State over those of another; nor shall Vessels bound to, or from, one State, be obliged to enter, clear, or pay Duties in another.

CLAUSE 7. No Money shall be drawn from the Treasury, but in Consequence of Appropriations made by Law; and a regular Statement and Account of the Receipts and Expenditures of all public Money shall be published from time to time.

CLAUSE 8. No Title of Nobility shall be granted by the United States: And no Person holding any Office of Profit or Trust under them, shall, without the Consent of Congress, accept of any present, Emolument, Office, or Title, of any kind whatever, from any King, Prince, or foreign State.

Clause 8. Feudalism would not be established in the new country. We would have no nobles. No federal official can accept a title of nobility (even honorary) without permission of Congress.

This section sets out the prohibitions on state actions.

Powers Denied to the States

SECTION 10 CLAUSE 1. No State shall enter into any Treaty, Alliance, or Confederation; grant Letters of Marque and Reprisal; coin Money; emit Bills of Credit; make any Thing but gold and silver; Coin a Tender in Payment of Debts; pass any Bill of Attainder, ex post facto Law, or Law impairing the Obligation of Contracts, or grant any Title of Nobility.

Section 10 Clause 1. This clause is a laundry list of denied powers. These restrictions cannot be waived by Congress. States cannot engage in foreign relations or acts of war. Letters of marque and reprisal were used to provide legal cover for privateers. The federal government's currency monopoly is established. The sanctity of contracts is specified, and similar state prohibitions are specified for bills of attainder, ex post facto, etc.

CLAUSE 2. No State shall, without the Consent of the Congress, lay any Imposts or Duties on Imports or Exports, except what may be absolutely necessary for executing its inspection Laws: and the net Produce of all Duties and Imposts, laid by any State on Imports or Exports, shall be for the Use of the Treasury of the United States; and all such Laws shall be subject to the Revision and Controul of the Congress.

Clause 2. This section establishes the monopoly control of the national government in matters of both national and international trade. The only concession to states is health and safety inspections.

CLAUSE 3. No State shall, without the Consent of Congress, lay any Duty of Tonnage, keep Troops, or Ships of War in time of Peace, enter into any Agreement or Compact with another State, or with a foreign Power, or engage in War, unless actually invaded, or in such imminent Danger as will not admit of delay.

Clause 3. This final section of the Legislative article establishes the war monopoly power of the national government. The only exception to state action is actual invasion or threat of imminent danger.

Article II
The Executive Article

Article II. This article establishes an entirely new concept in government—an elected executive power. This was a touchy topic in 1787. On one hand, there was great worry about executive power—it was seen as the root of tyranny. On the other hand, many believed that a powerful executive was necessary for long-term stability for the new nation. The right balance was a system with a strong executive, where the executive's power could be limited.

Nature and Scope of Presidential Power

SECTION 1 CLAUSE 1. The executive Power shall be vested in a President of the United States of America. He shall hold his Office during the Term of four Years, and, together with the Vice President, chosen for the same Term, be elected as follows:

Section 1 Clause 1. This clause establishes the executive power in the office of the president of the United States of America. It also establishes a second office—vice president. A 4-year term was established, but not a limit on the number of terms. A limit was later established by the 22nd Amendment.

CLAUSE 2. Each State shall appoint, in such Manner as the Legislature thereof may direct, a Number of Electors, equal to the whole Number of Senators and Representatives to which the State may be entitled in the Congress: but no Senator or Representative, or Person holding an Office of Trust or Profit under the United States, shall be appointed an Elector.

Clause 2. This paragraph establishes the Electoral College to choose the president and vice president. Each state can determine how electors will be allotted to different candidates. For instance, today 48 states give the candidate who receives the most votes from citizens all of its electoral votes. This "winner take all" system puts an important twist on presidential election strategy. The trick for the candidates is to amass 270 electoral votes from different combinations of states.

Another implication of this system of choosing an executive is that it is possible for one candidate to receive more votes from citizens than other candidates, but still not become president. This has occurred four times in American history, most recently in 2000, when Al Gore received roughly 500,000 votes more than George W. Bush but fewer Electoral College votes.

Clause 3. This paragraph has been superseded by the 12th Amendment. The original language provided for a House election in the case of no majority vote or a tie vote among the top five candidates. Now the number of candidates is three. The Senate is to select the vice president if a candidate does not have an electoral majority or in the case of a tie vote. The Senate considers only the top two candidates. The amendment also clarifies that the qualifications of the vice president are the same as those for president.

Clause 4. Congress is given the power to establish a uniform day and time for the state selection of electors.

Clause 5. The qualifications for the offices of president and vice president are specified here—at least 35 years old, 14 years' resident in the U.S., and a natural-born citizen. The 14th Amendment clarified who is a citizen of the U.S., a person born or naturalized in the U.S. and subject to its jurisdiction. But the term "natural-born citizen" is unclear and has never been further defined by the judicial branch. Does it mean born in the U.S. or born of U.S. citizens in the U.S. or somewhere else in the world? Unfortunately, there is no definitive answer.

Clause 6. This clause concerns presidential succession and has been modified by the 25th Amendment. Upon the death, resignation, or impeachment conviction of the president, the vice president becomes president. The new president nominates a new vice president, who assumes the office if approved by a majority vote in both congressional branches. The president is also now able to notify the Congress of his or her inability to perform the duties of office.

CLAUSE 3. The Electors shall meet in their respective States, and vote by Ballot for two Persons, of whom one at least shall not be an Inhabitant of the same State with themselves. And they shall make a List of all the Persons voted for, and of the Number of Votes for each; which List they shall sign and certify, and transmit sealed to the Seat of the Government of the United States, directed to the President of the Senate. The President of the Senate shall, in the Presence of the Senate and House of Representatives, open all the Certificates, and the Votes shall then be counted. The Person having the greatest Number of Votes shall be the President, if such Number be a Majority of the whole Number of Electors appointed; and if there be more than one who have such Majority and have an equal Number of Votes, then the House of Representatives shall immediately chuse by Ballot one of them for President; and if no Person have a Majority, then from the five highest on the List the said House shall in like Manner chuse the President. But in chusing the President, the Votes shall be taken by States, the Representation from each State having one Vote; A quorum for this Purpose shall consist of a Member or Members from two thirds of the States, and a Majority of all the States shall be necessary to a Choice. In every Case, after the Choice of the President, the Person having the greatest Number of Votes of the Electors shall be the Vice President. But if there should remain two or more who have equal Votes, the Senate shall chuse from them by Ballot the Vice President.[7]

CLAUSE 4. The Congress may determine the Time of chusing the Electors, and the Day on which they shall give their Votes; which Day shall be the same throughout the United States.

CLAUSE 5. No Person except a natural born Citizen, or a Citizen of the United States, at the time of the Adoption of this Constitution, shall be eligible to the Office of President; neither shall any Person be eligible to that Office who shall not have attained to the Age of thirty five Years, and been fourteen Years a Resident within the United States.

CLAUSE 6. In Case of the Removal of the President from Office, or of his Death, Resignation, or Inability to discharge the Powers and Duties of the said Office, the Same shall devolve on the Vice President, and the Congress may by Law provide for the Case of Removal, Death, Resignation or Inability, both of the

President and Vice President, declaring what Officer shall then act as President, and such Officer shall act accordingly, until the Disability be removed, or a President shall be elected.[8]

CLAUSE 7. The President shall, at stated Times, receive for his Services, a Compensation, which shall neither be encreased nor diminished during the Period for which he shall have been elected, and he shall not receive within that Period any other Emolument from the United States, or any of them.

CLAUSE 8. Before he enter on the Execution of his Office, he shall take the following Oath or Affirmation:—"I do solemnly swear (or affirm) that I will faithfully execute the Office of President of the United States, and will to the best of my Ability, preserve, protect and defend the Constitution of the United States."

Powers and Duties of the President

SECTION 2 CLAUSE 1. The President shall be Commander in Chief of the Army and Navy of the United States, and of the Militia of the several States, when called into the actual Service of the United States; he may require the Opinion, in writing, of the principal Officer in each of the executive Departments, upon any Subject relating to the Duties of their respective Offices, and he shall have Power to grant Reprieves and Pardons for Offences against the United States, except in Cases of Impeachment.

CLAUSE 2. He shall have Power, by and with the Advice and Consent of the Senate, to make Treaties, provided two thirds of the Senators present concur; and he shall nominate, and by and with the Advice and Consent of the Senate, shall appoint Ambassadors, other public Ministers and Consuls, Judges of the supreme Court, and all other Officers of the United States, whose Appointments are not herein otherwise provided for, and which shall be established by Law: but the Congress may by Law vest the Appointment of such inferior Officers, as they think proper, in the President alone, in the Courts of Law, or in the Heads of Departments.

CLAUSE 3. The President shall have Power to fill up all Vacancies that may happen during the Recess of the Senate, by granting Commissions which shall expire at the End of their next Session.

Clause 7. This section covers the compensation of the president, which cannot be increased or decreased during his/her office. The current salary is $400,000/year. The prohibition against decreasing the president's salary was considered an important part of the separation of powers. If Congress were at odds with the president and also able to decrease his pay, then it could drive him from office or punish him by reducing his salary.

Clause 8. This final clause in Section 1 is the oath of office administered to the new president. Interestingly, the phrase "so help me God," is not part of this oath, but has become customary in recent years.

Section 2 Clause 1. This clause establishes the president as commander-in-chief of the U.S. armed forces. George Washington was the only U.S. president to actually lead U.S. armed forces, during the Whiskey Rebellion.

The second provision is the basis for cabinet meetings that are used to hear the opinions of executive department heads. The last provision grants an absolute pardon or reprieve power for the president.

Since the president is commander-in-chief, citizens and groups concerned with U.S. foreign policy (especially armed military conflicts) can hold the president accountable for policy decisions. Litigation, protests, marches, and electoral battles have all been used by citizens dissatisfied with presidential foreign policy decisions.

Clause 2. This clause covers two important presidential powers: treaty making and appointments. The president (through the State Department) can negotiate treaties with other nations, but these do not become official until ratified by a two-thirds vote of the U.S. Senate.

The president is empowered to appoint judges, ambassadors, and other U.S. officials (cabinet officers, military officers, agency heads, etc.) subject to Senate approval.

These powers are important to ensure the division of power between the three branches of our national government as well as the system of checks and balances. Sharing these powers allows for input by the people and organized groups. The Senate approves most treaties and most presidential appointments, especially if it is controlled by members of the same party as the president. But this is not always true; many treaties and appointments have been rejected, often because the Senate was responding to strong public opinion.

Clause 3. This allows recess appointments of the officials listed in Clause 2 above. These commissions automatically expire unless approved by the Senate by the end of the next session. Presidents have used this provision to fill jobs when the nomination process is stalled.

Section 3. This section provides for the annual State of the Union address to a joint session of Congress. Presidents have learned that the ability to reach out to the public can be a source of tremendous power. The State of the Union Address is thus an important opportunity to speak directly to the American public, build support for initiatives, and shape the policy agenda. The president is also authorized to call special meetings of either the House or Senate. If there is disagreement between the House and Senate regarding adjournment, the president may adjourn them. This would be extremely rare. The next-to-last provision, to faithfully execute laws, provides the basis for the whole administrative apparatus of the executive branch.

Section 4. This section provides the constitutional authority for the impeachment and trial of the president, vice president, and all civil officers of the U.S. for treason, bribery, or other high crimes and misdemeanors (the exact meaning of this phrase is unclear and is often more political than judicial). Impeachment proceedings have been undertaken against two presidents in American history: Andrew Johnson, in 1868, and Bill Clinton in 1998. In both cases the Senate failed to convict the president, and both were allowed to stay in office. Richard Nixon would have also confronted impeachment proceedings in 1974 for his involvement in the Watergate scandal, but he resigned from office and avoided the process.

Article III Section 1. This section establishes the judicial branch in very general terms. It only provides for the Supreme Court; Congress must create the court system. It first did so in the Judiciary Act of 1789, when it established 13 district courts (one for each state) and 3 appellate courts. All federal judges hold their offices for life and can only be removed for breaches of good behavior—a very ambiguous term. Federal judges have been removed for drunkenness, accepting bribes, and other misdemeanors. To date, no justice of the U.S. Supreme Court has ever been removed.

The tenure of judges in office, which can be for life, is meant to give judges the ability to make decisions according to their best judgments without facing the prospect of removal from office for issuing an unpopular judgment. While this protected tenure is an undemocratic aspect of the Constitution in the sense that it removes federal judges from direct electoral accountability, it has been an important aspect of the judiciary's ability to enforce civil rights and liberties on behalf of minority groups and unpopular individuals.

This protected tenure is one aspect of government that makes the court pathway especially attractive to individuals, small groups, and others who lack political power. For example, federal judges acted against racial discrimination in the 1950s at a time when most white Americans accepted the existence of such discrimination when applied to African Americans. The salary of federal judges is set by congressional act but can never be reduced.

Section 2 Clause 1, 2, 3. This section establishes the original and appellate jurisdiction of the U.S. Supreme Court. Original jurisdiction cases are essentially limited to disputes between states. The 11th Amendment limited the ability of individuals to sue states. Even in these cases involving states, the Supreme Court now typically appoints a special judge to hear the evidence and make a recommendation to the justices rather than hold an actual trial at the Supreme Court. Since 1925, the Supreme Court no longer hears every case on appeal but can select which cases it will accept, which is now only about 75–85 cases per year. Although this provision mentions trial by jury in all cases, the Supreme Court's interpretations of the jury trial right, also contained in the 6th Amendment, limits the right to criminal cases involving serious crimes with punishments of 6 months or more of imprisonment.

SECTION 3 He shall from time to time give to the Congress Information of the State of the Union, and recommend to their Consideration such Measures as he shall judge necessary and expedient; he may, on extraordinary Occasions, convene both Houses, or either of them, and in Case of Disagreement between them, with Respect to the Time of Adjournment, he may adjourn them to such Time as he shall think proper; he shall receive Ambassadors and other public Ministers; he shall take Care that the Laws be faithfully executed, and shall Commission all the Officers of the United States.

SECTION 4 The President, Vice President and all civil Officers of the United States, shall be removed from Office on Impeachment for, and Conviction of, Treason, Bribery, or other high Crimes and Misdemeanors.

Article III
The Judicial Article

Judicial Power, Courts, Judges

SECTION 1 The judicial Power of the United States, shall be vested in one supreme Court, and in such inferior Courts as the Congress may from time to time ordain and establish. The Judges, both of the supreme and inferior Courts, shall hold their Offices during good Behaviour, and shall, at stated Times, receive for their Services, a Compensation, which shall not be diminished during their Continuance in Office.

Jurisdiction

SECTION 2 CLAUSE 1. The judicial Power shall extend to all Cases, in Law and Equity, arising under this Constitution, the Laws of the United States, and Treaties made, or which shall be made, under their Authority;—to all Cases affecting Ambassadors, other public Ministers and Consuls;—to all Cases of admiralty and maritime Jurisdiction;—to Controversies to which the United States shall be a Party;—to Controversies between two or more States—between a State and Citizens of another State;[9]—between Citizens of different States;—between Citizens of the same State claiming Lands under Grants of different States, and between a State, or the Citizens thereof, and foreign States, Citizens, or Subjects.

CLAUSE 2. In all Cases affecting Ambassadors, other public Ministers and Consuls, and those in which a State shall be Party, the supreme Court shall have original Jurisdiction. In all the other Cases before mentioned, the supreme Court shall have appellate Jurisdiction, both as to Law and Fact, with such Exceptions, and under such Regulations as Congress shall make.

CLAUSE 3. The Trial of all Crimes, except in Cases of Impeachment, shall be by Jury; and such Trial shall be held in the State where the said Crimes shall have been committed; but when not committed within any State, the Trial shall be at such Place or Places as the Congress may by Law have directed.

Treason

SECTION 3 CLAUSE 1. Treason against the United States, shall consist only in levying War against them, or in adhering to their Enemies, giving them Aid and Comfort. No Person shall be convicted of Treason unless on the Testimony of two Witnesses to the same overt Act, or on Confession in open Court.

> **Section 3 Clause 1, 2.** Treason is the only crime defined in the U.S. Constitution. Congress established the penalty of death for treason convictions. Note that two witnesses are required to convict anyone of treason.

CLAUSE 2. The Congress shall have Power to declare the Punishment of Treason, but no Attainder of Treason shall work Corruption of Blood, or Forfeiture except during the Life of the Person attainted.

Article IV
Interstate Relations

> **Article IV Section 1.** This section provides that the official acts and records (for example, marriages and divorces) of one state will be recognized and given credence by other states. It is one of several clauses that were designed to create a strong national government. Concerns about this clause have taken on new importance in recent years, as the gay marriage issue has heated up in most state legislatures.

Full Faith and Credit Clause

SECTION 1 Full Faith and Credit shall be given in each State to the public Acts, Records, and judicial Proceedings of every other State. And the Congress may by general Laws prescribe the Manner in which such Acts, Records and Proceedings shall be proved, and the Effect thereof.

Privileges and Immunities; Interstate Extradition

SECTION 2 CLAUSE 1. The Citizens of each State shall be entitled to all Privileges and Immunities of Citizens in the several States.

> **Section 2 Clause 1.** This clause requires states to treat citizens of other states equally. For example, when driving in another state, a driver's license is recognized.

CLAUSE 2. A person charged in any State with Treason, Felony or other Crime, who shall flee from Justice, and be found in another State, shall on Demand of the executive Authority of the State from which he fled, be delivered up, to be removed to the State having Jurisdiction of the Crime.

> **Clause 2.** A criminal fleeing to another state, if captured, can be returned to the state where the crime was committed. But this is not an absolute (extradition). A state's governor can refuse, for good reason, to extradite someone to another state.

Clause 3. This clause was included to cover runaway slaves. It has been made inoperable by the 13th Amendment, which abolished slavery.

CLAUSE 3. No person held to Service or Labour in one State, under the Laws thereof, escaping into another, shall, in Consequence of any Law or Regulation therein, be discharged from such Service or Labour, but shall be delivered up on Claim of the Party to whom such Service or Labour may be due.[10]

Admission of States

SECTION 3 CLAUSE 1. New States may be admitted by the Congress into this Union; but no new State shall be formed or erected within the Jurisdiction of any other State; nor any State be formed by the Junction of two or more States, or Parts of States, without the Consent of the Legislatures of the States concerned as well as of the Congress.

Section 3 Clause 1, 2. This section concerns the admission of new states to the Union. In theory, no state can be created from part of another state without permission of the state legislature. But West Virginia was formed from Virginia during the Civil War without the permission of Virginia, which was part of the Confederacy. With 50 states now part of the Union, this section has not been used for many decades. The only foreseeable future use may be in the case of Puerto Rico or perhaps Washington, D.C.

CLAUSE 2. The Congress shall have Power to dispose of and make all needful Rules and Regulations respecting the Territory or other Property belonging to the United States; and nothing in this Constitution shall be so construed as to Prejudice any Claims of the United States, or of any particular State.

Republican Form of Government

SECTION 4. The United States shall guarantee to every State in this Union a Republican Form of Government, and shall protect each of them against Invasion; and on Application of the Legislature, or of the Executive (when the Legislature cannot be convened) against domestic Violence.

Section 4. This section commits the federal government to guarantee a republican form of government to each state and to protect the states against foreign invasion or domestic insurrection.

By mandating a republican form of government, the Constitution guarantees that power rests in the hands of the citizens and is exercised by their elected representatives. As such, citizens are able to appeal directly to their governing officials through several pathways, such as through the courts, via elections, or by lobbying.

Article V
The Amending Power

The Congress, whenever two thirds of both Houses shall deem it necessary, shall propose Amendments to this Constitution, or, on the Application of the Legislatures of two thirds of the several States, shall call a Convention for proposing Amendments, which, in either Case, shall be valid to all Intents and Purposes, as Part of this Constitution, when ratified by the Legislatures of three fourths of the several States, or by Conventions in three fourths thereof, as the one or the other Mode of Ratification may be proposed by the Congress; Provided that no Amendment which may be made prior to the Year One thousand eight hundred and eight shall in any Manner affect the first and fourth Clauses in the Ninth Section of the first Article; and that no State, without its Consent, shall be deprived of its equal Suffrage in the Senate.

Article V. Amendments to the U.S. Constitution can be originated by a two-thirds vote in both the U.S. House and Senate or by two-thirds of the state legislatures asking for a convention to propose amendments. Proposed amendments, by either route, must be approved by three-fourths of state legislatures or by three-fourths of conventions convened in the states for purposes of ratification. Only one amendment has been ratified by the convention method—the 21st Amendment, to repeal the 18th Amendment establishing Prohibition.

Thousands of amendments have been proposed; few have been passed by two-thirds vote in each branch of Congress. The Equal Rights Amendment was one such case, but it was not ratified by three-fourths of state legislatures. There have only been 27 successful amendments to the U.S. Constitution.

Since both the federal and state levels of government are involved in amending the Constitution, interested parties have several strategies to pursue to increase the likelihood that a proposed amendment is successful or is defeated.

Article VI
The Supremacy Act

CLAUSE 1.   All Debts contracted and Engagements entered into, before the Adoption of this Constitution, shall be as valid against the United States under this Constitution, as under the Confederation.

> **Clause 1.** This clause made the new national government responsible for all debts incurred during the Revolutionary War. This was very important to banking and commercial interests.

CLAUSE 2.   This Constitution, and the Laws of the United States which shall be made in Pursuance thereof; and all Treaties made, or which shall be made, under the Authority of the United States, shall be the supreme Law of the Land; and the Judges in every State shall be bound thereby, any Thing in the Constitution or Laws of any State to the Contrary notwithstanding.

> **Clause 2.** This is the National Supremacy Clause, which provides the basis for the supremacy of the national government. This seems to be a rather straightforward issue these days, but until the conclusion of the Civil War, "national supremacy" was not a settled concept.

CLAUSE 3.   The Senators and Representatives before mentioned, and the Members of the several State Legislatures, and all executive and judicial Officers, both of the United States and of the several States, shall be bound by Oath or Affirmation, to support this Constitution; but no religious Test shall ever be required as a Qualification to any Office or public Trust under the United States.

> **Clause 3.** This clause requires essentially all federal and state officials to swear or affirm their allegiance to and support of the U.S. Constitution. Note that a religious test was prohibited for federal office. However, some states used religious tests for voting and office qualification until the 1830s.

Article VII
Ratification

> **Article VII.** In the end, all 13 states ratified the Constitution. But it was a close call in several states.

> Realizing the unanimous ratification of the new Constitution by the 13 states might never have occurred, the framers wisely specified that only 9 states would be needed for ratification. Even this proved to be a test of wills between Federalists and Anti-Federalists, leading to publication of the great political work *The Federalist Papers*.

The Ratification of the Conventions of nine States, shall be sufficient for the Establishment of this Constitution between the States so ratifying the Same.

Done in Convention by the Unanimous Consent of the States present the Seventeenth Day of September in the Year of our Lord one thousand seven hundred and Eighty seven and of the Independence of the United States of America the Twelfth. In Witness whereof We have hereunto subscribed our Names.

Amendments

The Bill of Rights

> The first ten amendments were ratified on December 15, 1791, and form what is known as the "Bill of Rights."
>
> The Bill of Rights applied at first only to the federal government and not to state or local governments. Beginning in 1925 in the case of *Gitlow* v. *New York*, the U.S. Supreme Court began to selectively incorporate the Bill of Rights, making its provisions applicable to state and local governments, with some exceptions, which will be discussed at the appropriate amendment.
>
> Until the Supreme Court incorporated the Bill of Rights to include protections from state governments, citizens had to look to state constitutions for protections of civil liberties.

AMENDMENT 1

RELIGION, SPEECH, ASSEMBLY, AND PETITION

Congress shall make no law respecting an establishment of religion, or prohibiting the free exercise thereof; or abridging the freedom of speech, or of the press; or the right of the people peaceably to assemble, and to petition the Government for a redress of grievances.

> **Amendment 1.** This amendment protects five fundamental freedoms: religion, speech, press, assembly, and petition. The press is the only business that is specifically protected by the U.S. Constitution. Freedom of religion and speech are two of the most contentious issues and generate a multitude of Supreme Court cases.
>
> These freedoms are crucial for nearly every pathway of change; without each fundamental right, individuals and groups could not pursue change without fear of reprisal. This amendment is perhaps the most crucial to guarantee a free society.

Amendment 2. Those who favor gun ownership, either for protection, hunting or sport, cite this amendment. This amendment has not been incorporated for state/local governments; that is, state and local governments are free to regulate arms, provided such regulation is not barred by their own state constitutions.

There is controversy as to the meaning of this amendment. Some believe that it specifically refers to citizen militias, which were common at the time of the Constitution but now have been replaced by permanent armed forces (state national guard units), thereby allowing the federal government to regulate gun ownership. Others believe that the amendment refers to individuals directly, therefore guaranteeing private citizens the right to own guns.

Amendment 3. It was the practice of the British government to insist that colonists provide room or board to British troops. This amendment was designed to prohibit this practice. Today, military and naval bases provide the necessary quarters and this issue does not arise. This amendment has not been incorporated and applies only against the federal government.

Amendment 4. This extremely important amendment is designed to prevent the abuse of police powers. Essentially, unreasonable searches or seizures of homes, persons, or property cannot be undertaken without probable cause or a warrant that specifically describes the place to be searched, the person involved, and the suspicious things to be seized.

People who believe that these rights have been violated have successfully used the court-centered pathway for protection, either by seeking to have improperly obtained evidence excluded from use in court or by seeking money damages from police officials to compensate for the invasion of a home or an improper search of an individual's body.

Many people feel that the rights of the accused are often given more precedence than the rights of victims. The Constitution does not contain rights for victims, but a constitutional amendment has been proposed to protect victims' rights. This does not mean that victims are unprotected by the law. States and the federal government have statutes that provide protections and services for crime victims.

Amendment 5. Only a grand jury can indict a person for a federal crime. (This provision does not apply to state/local governments because it has not been incorporated by the Supreme Court.) This amendment also covers double jeopardy, or being tried twice for the same crime in the same jurisdiction. This amendment also covers the prohibition of compelled self-incrimination. The deprivation of life, liberty, or property is prohibited unless due process of law is applied. This provision applies to the federal government, and there is a parallel provision that applies to state and local governments in the 14th Amendment. Finally, private property may not be taken under the doctrine of "eminent domain" unless the government provides just compensation.

AMENDMENT 2

MILITIA AND THE RIGHT TO BEAR ARMS

A well-regulated Militia, being necessary to the security of a free State, the right of the people to keep and bear Arms, shall not be infringed.

AMENDMENT 3

QUARTERING OF SOLDIERS

No Soldier shall, in time of peace be quartered in any house, without the consent of the Owner, nor in time of war, but in manner to be prescribed by law.

AMENDMENT 4

SEARCHES AND SEIZURES

The right of the people to be secure in their persons, houses, papers, and effects, against unreasonable searches and seizures, shall not be violated, and no Warrants shall issue, but upon probable cause, supported by Oath or affirmation, and particularly describing the place to be searched, and the persons or things to be seized.

AMENDMENT 5

GRAND JURIES, SELF-INCRIMINATION,
DOUBLE JEOPARDY, DUE PROCESS,
AND EMINENT DOMAIN

No person shall be held to answer for a capital, or otherwise infamous crime, unless on a presentment or indictment of a Grand jury, except in cases arising in the land or naval forces, or in the Militia, when in actual service in time of War or public danger; nor shall any person be subject for the same offence to be twice put in jeopardy of life or limb; nor shall be compelled in any criminal case to be a witness against himself, nor be deprived of life, liberty, or property, without due process of law; nor shall private property be taken for public use, without just compensation.

AMENDMENT 6

CRIMINAL COURT PROCEDURES

In all criminal prosecutions, the accused shall enjoy the right to a speedy and public trial, by an impartial jury of the State and district wherein the crime shall have been committed, which district shall have been previously ascertained by law, and to be informed of the nature and cause of the accusation; to be confronted with the witnesses against him; to have compulsory process for obtaining witnesses in his favor, and to have the Assistance of Counsel for his defence.

Amendment 6. This amendment requires public trials by jury for criminal prosecutions. However, the Supreme Court only applies the right to trial by jury to serious offenses, not petty offenses. Anyone accused of a crime is guaranteed the rights to be informed of the charges; to confront witnesses; to subpoena witnesses for their defense; and to have a lawyer for their defense. The government must provide a lawyer for a defendant unable to afford one for any case in which the defendant faces the possibility of a jail or prison sentence.

There are serious questions about the adequacy of attorney performance and resources for criminal defense. In some jurisdictions, there are not enough defense attorneys for poor defendants, so that the attorneys spend little time on each case. In addition, the Supreme Court does not have strict standards for attorney performance, so some defendants have been represented by attorneys who know very little about criminal law.

AMENDMENT 7

TRIAL BY JURY IN COMMON LAW CASES

In Suits at common law, where the value in controversy shall exceed twenty dollars, the right of trial by jury shall be preserved, and no fact tried by a jury shall be otherwise reexamined in any Court of the United States, than according to the rules of the common law.

Amendment 7. The right to trial by jury in civil cases will never be incorporated by the Supreme Court for application against state and local governments, because it would impose a huge financial burden (jury trials are very expensive).

AMENDMENT 8

BAIL, CRUEL AND UNUSUAL PUNISHMENT

Excessive bail shall not be required, nor excessive fines imposed, nor cruel and unusual punishments inflicted.

Amendment 8. The Supreme Court has not clearly defined the limits imposed by prohibition of excessive bail or excessive fines. Thus these rights rarely arise in legal cases, and bail amounts in excess of $1 million will periodically be imposed for serious crimes or wealthy defendants. The prohibition on cruel and unusual punishments focuses on criminal punishments, not other contexts (such as the punishment of children in public schools or civil fines against businesses). Cruel and unusual punishments are defined according to current societal values and thus the definition of what is "cruel and unusual" can change over time. This provision bars punishments that are either excessive or torturous.

Capital punishment is covered by this amendment, as well as the treatment of prisoners inside prisons. Court cases challenging the constitutionality of capital punishment cite this amendment's language prohibiting cruel and unusual punishment. For a period of 4 years (1973–1976), the Supreme Court banned capital punishment as it was then being applied by the states. When states modified their statutes to provide a two-part judicial process of guilt determination and punishment, the Supreme Court allowed the reinstitution of capital punishment by the states.

AMENDMENT 9

RIGHTS RETAINED BY THE PEOPLE

The enumeration in the Constitution, of certain rights, shall not be construed to deny or disparage others retained by the people.

Amendment 9. This amendment implies that there may be other rights of the people not specified by the previous amendments, but the wording gives no guidance about what those rights might be. Instead, when the Supreme Court has identified rights not specifically mentioned in the Bill of Rights, it has tended to claim that these rights, such as privacy and the right to travel between states, are connected to the right to "due process" found in the 5th and 14th Amendments.

AMENDMENT 10

RESERVED POWERS OF THE STATES

The powers not delegated to the United States by the Constitution, nor prohibited by it to the States, are reserved to the States respectively, or to the people.

Amendment 10. The 10th Amendment was seen as the reservoir of reserved powers for state governments. But the doctrine of implied national government powers, which was established by the U.S. Supreme Court in *McCulloch* v. *Maryland* (1819), undercut the words and apparent intent of this amendment. With the exception of a few decisions, the Supreme Court has generally deferred to assertions of federal power since the 1930s.

Amendment 11. Article III of the U.S. Constitution originally allowed federal jurisdiction in cases of one state citizen against another state citizen or state. This amendment removes federal jurisdiction in this area. In essence, states may not be sued in federal court by citizens of another state or country.

Amendment 12. This was a necessary amendment to correct a flaw in the Constitution covering operations of the Electoral College. In the election of 1800, Thomas Jefferson and Aaron Burr, both of the same Democratic Republican party, received the same number of electoral votes, 73, for president. Article II of the original Constitution specified that each elector would cast two ballots. It did not specify for whom. This amendment clarifies that the electoral vote must be specific for president and vice president. The original Constitution provided that if no candidate received a majority of electoral votes, the House would decide from the candidates with the top five vote totals. This amendment reduces the candidate field to the top three vote totals. If the House delays in this selection past the fourth day of March, the elected vice president will act as president until the House selects the president. The original Constitution provided that the candidate with the second highest number of electoral votes would become vice president.

This amendment, which requires a separate vote tally for vice president, provides for selection by the U.S. Senate if no vice presidential candidate receives an electoral vote majority.

AMENDMENT 11

SUITS AGAINST THE STATES

[Ratified February 7, 1795]

The Judicial power of the United States shall not be construed to extend to any suit in law or equity, commenced or prosecuted against one of the United States by Citizens of another State, or by Citizens or Subjects of any Foreign State.

AMENDMENT 12

ELECTION OF THE PRESIDENT

[Ratified June 15, 1804]

The Electors shall meet in their respective states, and vote by ballot for President and Vice-President, one of whom, at least, shall not be an inhabitant of the same state with themselves; they shall name in their ballots the person voted for as President, and in distinct ballots the person voted for as Vice-President, and they shall make distinct lists of all persons voted for as President, and of all persons voted for as Vice-President, and of the number of votes for each, which lists they shall sign and certify, and transmit sealed to the seat of the government of the United States, directed to the President of the Senate;—The President of the Senate shall, in the presence of the Senate and House of Representatives, open all the certificates and the votes shall then be counted;—The person having the greatest number of votes for President, shall be the President, if such number be a majority of the whole number of Electors appointed; and if no person have such majority, then from the persons having the highest numbers not exceeding three on the list of those voted for as President, the House of Representatives shall choose immediately, by ballot, the President. But in choosing the President, the votes shall be taken by states, the representation from each state having one vote; a quorum for this purpose shall consist of a member or members from two-thirds of the states, and a majority of all the states shall be necessary to a choice. And if the House of Representatives shall not choose a President whenever the right of choice shall devolve upon them, before the fourth day of March next following, then the Vice-President shall act as President, as in the case of the death or other constitutional disability of the President.[11] The person having the greatest number of votes as Vice-President, shall be the Vice-President, if such a number be a majority of the whole numbers of Electors appointed, and if no person have a majority, then from the two highest numbers on the list, the Senate shall choose the Vice-President; a quorum for the purpose shall consist of two-thirds of the whole number of Senators, and a majority of the whole number shall be necessary to a choice. But no person constitutionally ineligible to the office of President shall be eligible to that of Vice-President of the United States.

AMENDMENT 13

PROHIBITION OF SLAVERY

[Ratified December 6, 1865]

SECTION 1   Neither slavery nor involuntary servitude, except as a punishment for crime whereof the party shall have been duly convicted, shall exist within the United States, or any place subject to their jurisdiction.

SECTION 2   Congress shall have power to enforce this article by appropriate legislation.

AMENDMENT 14

CITIZENSHIP, DUE PROCESS,
AND EQUAL PROTECTION OF THE LAWS

[Ratified July 9, 1868]

SECTION 1   All persons born or naturalized in the United States, and subject to the jurisdiction thereof, are citizens of the United States and of the State wherein they reside. No State shall make or enforce any law which shall abridge the privileges or immunities of citizens of the United States; nor shall any State deprive any person of life, liberty, or property, without due process of law; nor deny to any person within its jurisdiction the equal protection of the laws.

SECTION 2   Representatives shall be apportioned among the several States according to their respective numbers, counting the whole number of persons in each State, excluding Indians not taxed. But when the right to vote at any election for the choice of electors for President and Vice President of the United States, Representatives in Congress, the Executive and Judicial officers of a State, or the members of the Legislature thereof, is denied to any of the male inhabitants of such State, being twenty-one years of age, and citizens of the United States, or in any way abridged, except for participation in rebellion, or other crime, the basis of representation therein shall be reduced in the proportion which the number of such male citizens shall bear to the whole number of male citizens twenty-one years of age in such State.[12]

Amendment 13.   This is the first of the three Civil War amendments. Slavery is prohibited under all circumstances. Involuntary servitude is also prohibited unless it is a punishment for a convicted crime.

Amendment 14 Section 1.   This section defines the meaning of U.S. citizenship and protection of these citizenship rights. It also establishes the Equal Protection Clause, meaning that each state must guarantee fundamental rights and liberties to all of its citizens. It extended the provisions of the 5th Amendment of due process and protection of life, liberty, and property and made these applicable to the states. The due process clause has been especially important for the expansion of civil rights and liberties as the Supreme Court interpreted it in a flexible manner to recognize new rights (e.g., privacy, right of choice for abortion, etc.) and to apply the Bill of Rights against the states.

Section 2.   This section changed the Three-Fifths Clause of the original Constitution. At the time of ratification of this amendment, all male citizens, 21 or older, were used to calculate representation in the House of Representatives. If a state denied the right to vote to any male 21 or older, the number of denied citizens would be deducted from the overall state total to determine representation.

This is the first time that gender was entered into the Constitution. It was not until 50 years later (in 1920 with the 19th Amendment) that women were granted the right to vote.

Section 3. This section disqualifies from federal office or elector for president or vice president anyone who rebelled or participated in an insurrection (that is, the Confederate Army after the Civil War) against the Constitution. This was specifically directed against citizens of Southern states. Congress by a two-thirds vote could override this provision.

Section 4, 5. Section 4 covers the Civil War debts; Section 5 grants to Congress the very specific authority to create legislation that will implement and enforce the provisions of the 14th Amendment.

Unlike the Bill of Rights, which is intended to protect individuals by limiting the power of the federal government, including Congress, Section 5 intends to empower Congress to create laws that will protect individuals from actions by states that violate their rights.

Although the 13th and 14th Amendments were designed to end slavery, and provide citizenship, due process, and equal protection rights for freed slaves and their offspring, they were interpreted very narrowly until the 1960s. Civil rights activists had to use the court-centered, cultural change, and grassroots mobilization pathways to force legal, political, and social change to allow all individuals, regardless of color or race, to enjoy full civil rights.

Amendment 15 Section 1, 2. This final Civil War amendment states that voting rights could not be denied by any states on account of race, color, or previous servitude. It did not mention gender. Accordingly, only male citizens 21 or over were guaranteed the right to vote by this amendment. Some states sought to defeat the intent of the amendment by adopting additional restrictions to voting rights (such as poll taxes, whites-only primaries and literacy tests) in order to block the participation of African-American voters. These restrictions were eliminated in the 1960s as civil rights activists effectively used several pathways for change: court, lobbying decision makers, and grassroots mobilization.

Amendment 16. Article I, Section 9 of the original Constitution prohibited Congress from enacting a direct tax unless in proportion to a census. Congress in 1894 passed an income tax law, levying a 2 percent tax on incomes over $4,000. In 1895, the U.S. Supreme Court in a split decision (5–4) found that the income tax was a direct tax not apportioned among the states and was thus unconstitutional. Thus, Congress proposed an amendment allowing it to enact an income tax. Once this amendment was ratified, the flow of tax money to Washington increased tremendously.

SECTION 3 No person shall be a Senator or Representative in Congress, or elector of President and Vice President, or hold any office, civil or military, under the United States, or under any State, who, having previously taken an oath, as a member of Congress, or as an officer of the United States, or as a member of any State legislature, or as an executive or judicial officer of any State, to support the Constitution of the United States, shall have engaged in insurrection or rebellion against the same, or given aid or comfort to the enemies thereof. But Congress may by a vote of two-thirds of each House, remove such disability.

SECTION 4 The validity of the public debt of the United States, authorized by law, including debts incurred for payment of pensions and bounties for services in suppressing insurrection or rebellion, shall not be questioned. But neither the United States nor any State shall assume or pay any debt or obligation incurred in aid of insurrection or rebellion against the United States, or any claim for the loss or emancipation of any slave; but all such debts, obligations and claims shall be held illegal and void.

SECTION 5 The Congress shall have power to enforce, by appropriate legislation, the provisions of this article.

AMENDMENT 15

THE RIGHT TO VOTE

[Ratified February 3, 1870]

SECTION 1 The right of citizens of the United States to vote shall not be denied or abridged by the United States or by any State on account of race, color, or previous condition of servitude.

SECTION 2 The Congress shall have power to enforce this article by appropriate legislation.

AMENDMENT 16

INCOME TAXES

[Ratified February 3, 1913]

The Congress shall have power to lay and collect taxes on incomes, from whatever source derived, without apportionment among the several States, and without regard to any census or enumeration.

AMENDMENT 17

DIRECT ELECTION OF SENATORS

[Ratified April 8, 1913]

The Senate of the United States shall be composed of two Senators from each State, elected by the people thereof, for six years; and each Senator shall have one vote. The electors in each State shall have the qualifications requisite for electors of the most numerous branch of the State legislatures.

When vacancies happen in the representation of any State in the Senate, the executive authority of such State shall issue writs of election to fill such vacancies: Provided, That the legislature of any State may empower the executive thereof to make temporary appointments until the people fill the vacancies by election as the legislature may direct.

This amendment shall not be so construed as to affect the election or term of any Senator chosen before it becomes valid as part of the Constitution.

Amendment 17.   Before this amendment, U.S. senators were selected by state legislatures. Now U.S. senators would be selected by popular vote in each state. Further, the governor of each state may fill vacancies, subject to state laws.

AMENDMENT 18

PROHIBITION

[Ratified January 16, 1919. Repealed December 5, 1933 by Amendment 21]

SECTION 1   After one year from the ratification of this article the manufacture, sale, or transportation of intoxicating liquors within, the importation thereof into, or the exportation thereof from the United States and all territory subject to the jurisdiction thereof for beverage purposes is hereby prohibited.

SECTION 2   The Congress and the several States shall have concurrent power to enforce this article by appropriate legislation.

SECTION 3   This article shall be inoperative unless it shall have been ratified as an amendment to the Constitution by the legislatures of the several States, as provided in the Constitution, within seven years from the date of the submission hereof to the States by the Congress.[13]

Amendment 18.   This amendment was largely the work of the Women's Christian Temperance Union and essentially banned the manufacture, sale, or transportation of alcoholic beverages. Unintended consequences of this attempt to legislate morality were the brewing of "bathtub gin" and moonshine liquor and the involvement of organized crime in importing liquor from Canada. The 21st Amendment repealed this provision. This is also the first amendment where Congress fixed a period for ratification—7 years.

AMENDMENT 19

FOR WOMEN'S SUFFRAGE

[Ratified August 18, 1920]

The right of the citizens of the United States to vote shall not be denied or abridged by the United States or by any State on account of sex.

Congress shall have power to enforce this article.

Amendment 19.   Women achieved voting parity with men. It took enormous efforts by a large number of women and men to win this right, spanning over 70 years (from the call for the right to vote at the first women's rights convention in Seneca Falls, New York, in 1848). Suffragists protested, sued, marched, lobbied, and were imprisoned in their battle to win equal voting rights for men and women.

Amendment 20. Called the Lame Duck amendment, this amendment fixes the dates for the end of presidential and legislative terms. A new president is elected in November, but the current president remains in office until January 20th of the following year, thus the term "lame duck." Legislative terms begin earlier, on January 3rd.

AMENDMENT 20

THE LAME DUCK AMENDMENT
[Ratified January 23, 1933]

SECTION 1. The terms of the President and Vice President shall end at noon on the 20th day of January, and the terms of the Senators and Representatives at noon on the 3d day of January, of the years in which such terms would have ended if this article had not been ratified; and the terms of their successors shall then begin.

SECTION 2 The Congress shall assemble at least once in every year, and such meeting shall begin at noon on the 3d day of January, unless they shall by law appoint a different day.

SECTION 3 If, at the time fixed for the beginning of the term of the President, the President elect shall have died, the Vice President elect shall become President. If a President shall not have been chosen before the time fixed for the beginning of his term, or if the President elect shall have failed to qualify, then the Vice President elect shall act as President until a President shall have qualified; and the Congress may by law provide for the case wherein neither a President elect nor a Vice President elect shall have qualified, declaring who shall then act as President, or the manner in which one who is to act shall be selected, and such person shall act accordingly until a President or Vice President shall have qualified.

SECTION 4 The Congress may by law provide for the case of the death of any of the persons from whom the House of Representatives may choose a President whenever the right of choice shall have devolved upon them, and for the case of the death of any of the persons from whom the Senate may choose a Vice President whenever the right of choice shall have devolved upon them.

SECTION 5 Sections 1 and 2 shall take effect on the 15th day of October following the ratification of this article.

SECTION 6 This article shall be inoperative unless it shall have been ratified as an amendment to the Constitution by the legislatures of three-fourths of the several States within seven years from the date of its submission.

AMENDMENT 21

REPEAL OF PROHIBITION

[Ratified December 5, 1933]

SECTION 1   The eighteenth article of amendment to the Constitution of the United States is hereby repealed.

SECTION 2   The transportation or importation into any State, Territory, or possession of the United States for delivery or use therein of intoxicating liquors, in violation of the laws thereof, is hereby prohibited.

SECTION 3   This article shall be inoperative unless it shall have been ratified as an amendment to the Constitution by conventions in the several States, as provided in the Constitution, within seven years from the date of the submission hereof to the States by the Congress.

AMENDMENT 22

NUMBER OF PRESIDENTIAL TERMS

[Ratified February 27, 1951]

SECTION 1   No person shall be elected to the office of the President more than twice, and no person who has held the office of President, or acted as President, for more than two years of a term to which some other person was elected President shall be elected to the office of the President more than once. But this article shall not apply to any person holding the office of President when this article was proposed by the Congress, and shall not prevent any person who may be holding the office of President, or acting as President, during the term within which this article becomes operative from holding the office of President or acting as President during the remainder of such term.

SECTION 2   This article shall be inoperative unless it shall have been ratified as an amendment to the Constitution by the legislatures of three-fourths of the several states within seven years from the date of its submission to the states by the Congress.

AMENDMENT 23

PRESIDENTIAL ELECTORS FOR THE
DISTRICT OF COLUMBIA

[Ratified March 29, 1961]

SECTION 1   The District constituting the seat of government of the United States shall appoint in such manner as the Congress may direct:

A number of electors of President and Vice President equal to the whole number of Senators and Representatives in Congress to which the District would

Amendment 21. This unusual amendment nullified the 18th Amendment. The amendment called for the end of Prohibition unless prohibited by state laws.

This is the only instance of one amendment nullifying another. Here, governmental actions reflected the will of the majority. Initially, there was concern that the production and consumption of alcohol was detrimental to society, but as time passed, public opinion shifted. The public became less concerned about consumption and more worried about the illegal manufacture of alcohol and the subsequent growth of illegal markets and urban violence.

Amendment 22. This amendment could be called the Franklin D. Roosevelt amendment. It was FDR who broke the previously unwritten rule, established by George Washington, of serving no more than two terms as president. Democrat Roosevelt won election to an unprecedented four terms as president (although he died before completing his fourth term). When the Republicans took control of the Congress in 1948, they pushed through the 22nd Amendment, limiting the U.S. president to a lifetime of two full 4-year terms of office.

Amendment 23. This amendment gave electoral votes to the residents of Washington, D.C., which is not a state and thus not included in the original scheme of state electoral votes. Currently, Washington, D.C., has 3 electoral votes, bringing the total of presidential electoral votes to 538. Residents of Washington, D.C., do not, however, have voting representation in Congress. Puerto Ricans are citizens of the U.S. but have no electoral votes. Both Washington, D.C., and Puerto Rico are represented in Congress by non-voting delegates.

be entitled if it were a state, but in no event more than the least populous state; they shall be in addition to those appointed by the states, but they shall be considered, for the purposes of the election of President and Vice President, to be electors appointed by a state; and they shall meet in the District and perform such duties as provided by the twelfth article of amendment.

SECTION 2 The Congress shall have power to enforce this article by appropriate legislation.

AMENDMENT 24

THE ANTI–POLL TAX AMENDMENT

[Ratified January 23, 1964]

SECTION 1 The right of citizens of the United States to vote in any primary or other election for President or Vice President, for electors for President or Vice President, or for Senator or Representative in Congress, shall not be denied or abridged by the United States or any state by reason of failure to pay any poll tax or other tax.

SECTION 2 The Congress shall have power to enforce this article by appropriate legislation.

AMENDMENT 25

PRESIDENTIAL DISABILITY,
VICE PRESIDENTIAL VACANCIES

[Ratified February 10, 1967]

SECTION 1 In case of the removal of the President from office or of his death or resignation, the Vice President shall become President.

SECTION 2 Whenever there is a vacancy in the office of the Vice President, the President shall nominate a Vice President who shall take the office upon confirmation by a majority vote of both Houses of Congress.

SECTION 3 Whenever the President transmits to the President pro tempore of the Senate and the Speaker of the House of Representatives his written declaration that he is unable to discharge the powers and duties of his office, and until he transmits to them a written declaration to the contrary, such powers and duties shall be discharged by the Vice President as Acting President.

SECTION 4 Whenever the Vice President and a majority of either the principal officers of the executive departments, or of such other body as Congress may by law provide, transmit to the President pro tempore of the Senate and the Speaker of the House of

---

Amendment 24. The poll tax was a procedure used mostly in southern states to discourage poor white and black voters from registering to vote. Essentially, one would have to pay a tax to register to vote. The tax was around $34/year (sometimes retroactive), which amounted to a great deal of money to the poor, serving to disenfranchise a great proportion of the poor. As part of the fight for universal voting rights for all, the poll tax was abolished. Literacy tests, another device to disqualify voters, were abolished by the Voting Rights Act of 1965.

By banning this tax (coupled with other civil rights reforms), the United States delivered what the civil rights amendments promised—full voting rights for all citizens regardless of race.

Amendment 25. President Woodrow Wilson's final year in office was marked by serious illness. It is rumored that his wife acted as president. There was no constitutional provision to cover an incapacitating illness of a president. This amendment provides a procedure for this eventuality. The president can inform congressional leaders of his/her incapacitation, and the vice president then takes over. When the president recovers, he/she can inform congressional leaders and resume office.

The amendment also recognizes that the president may not be able or wish to indicate this lack of capacity. In this case, the vice president and a majority of cabinet members can inform congressional leaders, and the vice president takes over. When the president informs congressional leadership that he/she is back in form, he/she resumes the presidency unless the vice president and a majority of the cabinet members disagree. Then Congress must decide who is to be president. The likelihood that this procedure will ever be used is relatively small.

The most immediate importance of this amendment concerns the office of vice president. The original Constitution did not address the issue of a vacancy in this office. This amendment was ratified in 1967, only a few years before it was needed. In 1973, the sitting vice president, Spiro Agnew, resigned his office. Under the provisions of this amendment, President Nixon nominated Gerald Ford as vice president. As a former member of the House, Ford was quickly approved by the Congress. But a year later, President Nixon also resigned. Now Vice President Ford became President Ford, and he in turn appointed Nelson Rockefeller as the new vice president. For the first time in our history, neither the president nor the vice president were selected by the Electoral College after a national election.

Representatives their written declaration that the President is unable to discharge the powers and duties of his office, the Vice President shall immediately assume the powers and duties of the office as Acting President.

Thereafter, when the President transmits to the President pro tempore of the Senate and the Speaker of the House of Representatives his written declaration that no inability exists, he shall resume the powers and duties of his office unless the Vice President and a majority of either the principal officers of the executive department, or of such other body as Congress may by law provide, transmit within four days to the President pro tempore of the Senate and the Speaker of the House of Representatives their written declaration that the President is unable to discharge the powers and duties of his office. Thereupon Congress shall decide the issue, assembling within forty-eight hours for that purpose if not in session. If the Congress, within twenty-one days after receipt of the latter written declaration, or, if Congress is not in session, within twenty-one days after Congress is required to assemble, determines by two-thirds vote of both Houses that the President is unable to discharge the powers and duties of his office, the Vice President shall continue to discharge the same as Acting President; otherwise, the President shall resume the powers and duties of his office.

AMENDMENT 26

EIGHTEEN–YEAR–OLD VOTE

[Ratified July 1, 1971]

SECTION 1 The right of citizens of the United States, who are 18 years of age or older, to vote, shall not be denied or abridged by the United States or by any state on account of age.

SECTION 2 The Congress shall have power to enforce this article by appropriate legislation.

AMENDMENT 27

CONGRESSIONAL SALARIES

[Ratified May 7, 1992]

No law varying the compensation for the services of the Senators and Representatives shall take effect until an election of Representatives shall have intervened.

Amendment 26 Section 1, 2. During the Vietnam War, 18-year-olds were being drafted and sent out to possibly die in the service of their country. Yet they did not even have the right to vote. This incongruity led to the 26th Amendment, which lowered the legal voting age from 21 to 18.

Before the passage of this amendment, young people, being denied the ability to express themselves peacefully with the vote, often felt frustrated with their inability to express their concerns and influence public policy. With the passage of this amendment, those citizens over the age of 18 could pursue the election-centered pathway (and others) to instigate change.

Amendment 27. This is a "sleeper" amendment that was part of 12 amendments originally submitted by the first Congress to the states for ratification. The states only ratified 10 of the 12, which collectively became known as the Bill of Rights. But since Congress did not set a time limit for ratification, the other two amendments remained on the table. Much to the shock of the body politic, in 1992, three-fourths of the states ratified original amendment 12 of 12. This reflected the disgust of seeing Congress continuing to increase its salary and benefits. The amendment delays any increase of compensation for at least one election cycle.

---

1 Modified by the 16th Amendment	6 Modified by the 16th Amendment	11 Changed by the 20th Amendment
2 Replaced by Section 2, 14th Amendment	7 Changed by the 12th and 20th Amendments	12 Changed by the 26th Amendment
3 Repealed by the 17th Amendment	8 Modified by the 25th Amendment	13 Repealed by the 21st Amendment
4 Modified by the 17th Amendment	9 Modified by the 11th Amendment	
5 Changed by the 20th Amendment	10 Repealed by the 13th Amendment	

The Federalist, No. 10, James Madison

To the People of the State of New York: Among the numerous advantages promised by a well-constructed union, none deserves to be more accurately developed than its tendency to break and control the violence of faction. The friend of popular governments, never finds himself so much alarmed for their character and fate, as when he contemplates their propensity of this dangerous vice. He will not fail, therefore, to set a due value on any plan which, without violating the principles to which he is attached, provides a proper cure for it. The instability, injustice, and confusion introduced into the public councils, have, in truth, been the mortal diseases under which popular governments have every-where perished; as they continue to be the favorite and fruitful topics from which the adversaries to liberty derive their most specious declamations. The valuable improvements made by the American constitutions on the popular models, both ancient and modern, cannot certainly be too much admired; but it would be an unwarrantable partiality, to contend that they have as effectually obviated the danger on this side, as was wished and expected. Complaints are everywhere heard from our most considerate and virtuous citizens, equally the friends of public and private faith, and of public and personal liberty, that our governments are too unstable; that the public good is disregarded in the conflicts of rival parties; and that measures are too often decided, not according to the rules of justice, and the rights of the minor party, but by the superior force of an interested and overbearing majority. However anxiously we may wish that these complaints had no foundation, the evidence of known facts will not permit us to deny that they are in some degree true. It will be found, indeed, on a candid review of our situation, that some of the distresses under which we labor have been erroneously charged on the operations of our governments; but it will be found, at the same time, that other causes will not alone account for many of our heaviest misfortunes; and, particularly, for that prevailing and increasing distrust of public engagements, and alarm for private rights, which are echoed from one end of the continent to the other. These must be chiefly, if not wholly, effects of the unsteadiness and injustice, with which a factious spirit has tainted our public administrations.

By a faction, I understand a number of citizens, whether amounting to a majority of the whole, who are united and actuated by some common impulse of passion, or of interest, adverse to the rights of other citizens, or to the permanent and aggregate interests of the community.

There are two methods of curing the mischiefs of faction: the one, by removing its causes; the other, by controlling its effects.

There are again two methods of removing the causes of faction: the one, by destroying the liberty which is essential to its existence; the other, by giving to every citizen the same opinions, the same passions, and the same interests.

It could never be more truly said, than of the first remedy, that it was worse than the disease. Liberty is to faction what air is to fire, an aliment without which it instantly expires. But it could not be a less folly to abolish liberty, which is essential to political life, because it nourishes faction, than it would be to wish the annihilation of air, which is essential to animal life, because it imparts to fire its destructive agency.

The second expedient is as impracticable, as the first would be unwise. As long as the reason of man continues fallible, and he is at liberty to exercise it, different opinions will be formed. As long as the connection subsists between his reason and his self-love, his opinions and his passions will have a reciprocal influence on each other; and the former will be objects to which the latter will attach themselves. The diversity in the faculties of men, from which the rights of property originate, is not less an insuperable obstacle to an uniformity of interests. The protection of these faculties is the first object of government. From the protection of different and unequal faculties of acquiring property, the possession of different degrees and kinds of property immediately results; and from the influence of these on the sentiments and views of the respective proprietors, ensues a division of the society into different interests and parties.

The latent causes of faction are thus sown in the nature of man; and we see them everywhere brought into different degrees of activity, according to the different circumstances of civil society. A zeal for different opinions concerning religion, concerning government, and many other points, as well of speculation as of practice; an attachment to different leaders ambitiously contending for preeminence and power; or to persons of other descriptions whose fortunes have been interesting to the human passions, have, in turn, divided mankind into parties, inflamed them with mutual animosity, and rendered them much more disposed to vex and oppress each other, than to cooperate for their common good. So strong is this propensity of mankind, to fall into mutual animosities, that where no substantial occasion presents itself, the most frivolous and fanciful distinctions have been sufficient to kindle their unfriendly passions and excite their most violent conflicts. But the most common and durable source of factions, has been the various and unequal distribution of property. Those who hold, and those who are without property, have ever formed distinct interests in society. Those who are creditors, and those who are debtors, fall under a like discrimination. A landed interest, a manufacturing interest, a mercantile interest, a moneyed interest, with many lesser interests, grow up of necessity in civilized nations, and divide them into different classes, actuated by different sentiments and views. The regulation of these various and interfering interests forms the principal task of modern legislation, and involves the spirit of the party and faction in the necessary and ordinary operations of the government.

No man is allowed to be a judge in his own cause; because his interest will certainly bias his judgment, and, not improbably, corrupt his integrity. With equal, nay, with greater reason, a body of men are unfit to be both judges and parties at the same time; yet what are many of the most important acts of legislation, but so many judicial determinations, not indeed concerning the right of single persons, but concerning the rights of large bodies of citizens? And what are the different classes of legislators, but advocates and parties to the causes which they determine? Is a law proposed concerning private debts? It is a question to which the creditors are parties on one side, and the debtors on the other. Justice ought to hold the balance between them. Yet the parties are, and must be, themselves the judges; and the most numerous party, or, in other words, the most powerful faction, must be expected to prevail. Shall domestic manufacturers be encouraged, and in what degree, by restrictions on foreign manufacturers? Are questions which would be differently decided by the landed and the manufacturing classes; and probably by neither with a sole regard to justice and the public good. The apportionment of taxes, on the various descriptions of property, is an act which seems to require the most exact impartiality; yet there is, perhaps, no legislative act, in which greater opportunity and temptation are given to a predominant party to trample on the rules of justice. Every shilling, with which they overburden the inferior number, is a shilling saved to their own pockets.

It is in vain to say, that enlightened statesmen will be able to adjust these clashing interests, and render them all subservient to the public good. Enlightened statesmen will not always be at the helm, nor, in many cases, can such an adjustment be made at all, without taking into view indirect and remote considerations, which will rarely prevail over the immediate interest which one party may find in disregarding the rights of another, or the good of the whole.

The inference to which we are brought is, that the causes of faction cannot be removed; and that relief is only to be sought in the means of controlling its effects.

If a faction consists of less than a majority, relief is supplied by the republican principle, which enables the majority to defeat its sinister views, by regular vote. It may clog the administration, it may convulse the society; but it will be unable to execute and mask its violence under the forms of the Constitution. When a majority is included in a faction, the form of popular government, on the other hand, enables it to sacrifice to its ruling passion or interest, both the public good and the rights of other citizens. To secure the public good, and private rights, against the danger of such a faction, and at the same time to preserve the spirit and the form of popular government, is then the great object to which our inquiries are directed. Let me add, that it is the great desideratum, by which alone this form of government can be rescued from the opprobrium under which it has so long laboured, and be recommended to the esteem and adoption of mankind.

By what means is this object attainable? Evidently by one of two only. Either the existence of the same passion or interest in a majority, at the same time, must be prevented; or the majority, having such coexistent passion or interest, must be rendered, by their number and local situation, unable to concert and carry into effect schemes of oppression. If the impulse and the opportunity be suffered to coincide, we well know that neither moral nor religious motives can be relied on as an adequate control. They are not found to be such on the injustice and violence of individuals, and lose their efficacy in proportion to the number combined together; that is, in proportion as their efficacy becomes needful.

From this view of the subject, it may be concluded, that a pure democracy, by which I mean a society consisting of a small number of citizens, who assemble and administer the government in person, can admit of no cure for the mischiefs of faction. A common passion or interest will, in almost every case, be felt by a majority of the whole; a communication and concert, results from the form of government itself; and there is nothing to check the inducements to sacrifice the weaker party, or an obnoxious individual. Hence, it is, that such democracies have ever been spectacles of turbulence and contention; have ever been found incompatible with personal security, or the rights of property; and have in general been as short in their lives, as they have been violent in their deaths. Theoretic politicians, who have patronized this species of government, have erroneously supposed, that by reducing mankind to a perfect equality in their political rights, they would, at the same time be perfectly equalized and assimilated in their possessions, their opinions, and their passions.

A republic, by which I mean a government in which the scheme of representation takes place, opens a different prospect, and promises the cure for which we are seeking. Let us examine the points in which it varies from pure democracy, and we shall comprehend both the nature of the cure and the efficacy which it must derive from the union.

The two great points of difference, between a democracy and a republic, are, first, the delegation of the government, in the latter, to a small number of citizens, elected by the rest; secondly, the greater number of citizens, and greater sphere of country, over which the latter may be extended.

The effect of the first difference is, on the one hand, to refine and enlarge the public views, by passing them through the medium of a chosen body of citizens, whose wisdom may best discern the true interest of their country, and whose patriotism and love of justice, will be least likely to sacrifice it to temporary or partial considerations. Under such a regulation, it may well happen, that the public voice, pronounced by the representatives of the people, will be more consonant to the public good, than if pronounced by the people themselves, convened for the purpose. On the other hand the effect may be inverted. Men of factious tempers, of local prejudices, or of sinister designs, may by intrigue, by corruption, or by other means, first obtain the suffrages, and then betray the interest of the people. The question resulting is, whether small or extensive republics are most favourable to the election of proper guardians of the public weal; and it is clearly decided in favour of the latter by two obvious considerations.

In the first place, it is to be remarked that, however small the republic may be, the representatives must be raised to a certain number, in order to guard against the cabals of a few; and that however large it may be, they must be limited to a certain number, in order to guard against the confusion of a multitude. Hence, the number of representatives in the two cases not being in proportion to that of the constituents, and being proportionally greatest in the small republic, it follows, that if the proportion of fit characters be not less in the large than in the small republic, the former will present a greater option, and consequently a greater probability of a fit choice.

In the next place, as each representative will be chosen by a greater number of citizens in the large than in the small republic, it will be more difficult for unworthy candidates to practice with success the vicious arts, by which elections are too often carried; and the suffrages of the people being more free, will be more likely to centre in men who possess the most attractive merit, and the most diffusive and established characters.

It must be confessed, that in this, as in most other cases, there is a mean, on both sides of which inconveniences will be found to lie. By enlarging too much the number of electors, you render the representatives too little acquainted with all their local circumstances and lesser interests; as by reducing it too much, you render him unduly attached to these, and too little fit to comprehend and pursue great and national objects. The federal constitution forms a happy combination in this respect; the great and aggregate interests being referred to the national, the local and particular to the state legislatures.

The other point of difference is, the greater number of citizens, and extent of territory, which may be brought within the compass of republican, than of democratic government; and it is this circumstance principally which renders factious combinations less to be dreaded in the former, than in the latter. The smaller the society, the fewer probably will be the distinct parties and interests composing it; the fewer the distinct parties and interests, the more frequently will a majority be found of the same party; and the smaller the number of individuals composing a majority, and the smaller the compass within which they are placed, the more easily will they concert and execute their plans of oppression. Extend the

sphere, and you take in a greater variety of parties and interests; you make it less probable that a majority of the whole will have a common motive to invade the rights of other citizens; or if such a common motive exists, it will be more difficult for all who feel it to discover their own strength, and to act in unison with each other. Besides other impediments, it may be remarked, that where there is a consciousness of unjust or dishonourable purposes, communication is always checked by distrust, in proportion to the number whose concurrence is necessary.

Hence, it clearly appears, that the same advantage, which a republic has over a democracy, in controlling the effects of faction, is enjoyed by a large over a small republic—is enjoyed by the union over the states composing it. Does this advantage consist in the substitution of representatives, whose enlightened views and virtuous sentiments render them superior to local prejudices, and to schemes of injustice? It will not be denied that the representation of the union will be most likely to possess these requisite endowments. Does it consist in the greater security afforded by a greater variety of parties, against the event of any one party being able to outnumber and oppress the rest? In an equal degree does the increased variety of parties, comprised within the union, increase the security? Does it, in fine, consist in the greater obstacles opposed to the concert and accomplishment of the secret wishes of an unjust and interested majority? Here, again, the extent of the union gives it the most palpable advantage.

The influence of factious leaders may kindle a flame within their particular states, but will be unable to spread a general conflagration through the other states; a religious sect may degenerate into a political faction in a part of the confederacy; but the variety of sects dispersed over the entire face of it, must secure the national councils against any danger from that source: a rage for paper money, for an abolition of debts, for an equal division of property, or for any other improper or wicked project, will be less apt to pervade the whole body of the union than a particular member of it; in the same proportion as such a malady is more likely to taint a particular county or district, than an entire state.

In the extent and proper structure of the union, therefore, we behold a republican remedy for the diseases most incident to republican government. And according to the degree of pleasure and pride we feel in being republicans, ought to be our zeal in cherishing the spirit, and supporting the character of federalists.

The Federalist, No. 51, James Madison

To what expedient, then, shall we finally resort, for maintaining in practice the necessary partition of power among the several departments as laid down in the Constitution? The only answer that can be given is that as all these exterior provisions are found to be inadequate the defect must be supplied, by so contriving the interior structure of the government as that its several constituent parts may, by their mutual relations, be the means of keeping each other in their proper places. Without presuming to undertake a full development of this important idea I will hazard a few general observations which may perhaps place it in a clearer light, and enable us to form a more correct judgment of the principles and structure of the government planned by the convention.

In order to lay a due foundation for that separate and distinct exercise of the different powers of government, which to a certain extent is admitted on all hands to be essential to the preservation of liberty, it is evident that each department should have a will of its own; and consequently should be so constituted that the members of each should have as little agency as possible in the appointment of the members of the others. Were this principle rigorously adhered to, it would require that all the appointments for the supreme executive, legislative, and judiciary magistracies should be drawn from the same fountain of authority, the people, through channels having no communication whatever with one another. Perhaps such a plan of constructing the several departments would be less difficult in practice than it may in contemplation appear. Some difficulties, however, and some additional expense would attend the execution of it. Some deviations, therefore, from the principle must be admitted. In the constitution of the judiciary department in particular, it might be inexpedient to insist rigorously on the principle: first, because peculiar qualifications being essential in the members, the primary consideration ought to be to select that mode of choice which best secures these qualifications; second, because the permanent tenure by which the appointments are held in that department must soon destroy all sense of dependence on the authority conferring them.

It is equally evident that the members of each department should be as little dependent as possible on those of the others for the emoluments annexed to their offices. Were the executive magistrate, or the judges, not independent of the legislature in this particular, their independence in every other would be merely nominal.

But the great security against a gradual concentration of the several powers in the same department consists in giving to those who administer each department the necessary constitutional means and personal motives to resist encroachments of the others. The provision for defense must in this, as in all other cases, be made commensurate to the danger of attack. Ambition must be made to counteract ambition. The interest of the man must be connected with the constitutional rights of the place. It may be a reflection on human nature that such devices should be necessary to control the abuses of government. But what is government itself but the greatest of all reflections on human nature? If men were angels, no government would be necessary. If angels were to govern men, neither external nor internal controls on government would be necessary. In framing a government which is to be administered by men over men, the great difficulty lies in this: you must first enable the government to control the governed; and in the next place oblige it to control itself. A dependence on the people is, no doubt, the primary control on the government; but experience has taught mankind the necessity of auxiliary precautions.

This policy of supplying, by opposite and rival interests, the defect of better motives, might be traced through the whole system of human affairs, private as well as public. We see it particularly displayed in all the subordinate distributions of power, where the constant aim is to divide and arrange the several offices in such a manner as that each may be a check on the other—that the private interest of every individual may be a sentinel over the public rights. These inventions of prudence cannot be less requisite in the distribution of the supreme powers of the State.

But it is not possible to give to each department an equal power of self-defense. In republican government, the legislative authority necessarily predominates. The remedy for this inconveniency is to divide the legislature into different branches; and to render them, by modes of election and different principles of action, as little connected with each other as the nature of their common functions and their common dependence on the society will admit. It may even be necessary to guard against dangerous encroachments by still further precautions. As the weight of the legislative authority requires that it should be thus divided, the weakness of the executive may require, on the other hand, that it should be fortified. An absolute negative on the legislature appears, at first view, to be the natural defense with which the executive magistrate should be armed. But perhaps it would be neither altogether safe nor alone sufficient. On ordinary occasions it might not be exerted with the requisite firmness, and on extraordinary occasions it might be perfidiously abused. May not this defect of an absolute negative be supplied by some qualified connection between this weaker department and the weaker branch of the stronger department, by which the latter may be led to support the constitutional rights of the former, without being too much detached from the rights of its own department?

If the principles on which these observations are founded be just, as I persuade myself they are, and they be applied as a criterion to the several State constitutions, and to the federal Constitution, it will be found that if the latter does not perfectly correspond with them, the former are infinitely less able to bear such a test.

There are, moreover, two considerations particularly applicable to the federal system of America, which place that system in a very interesting point of view.

First. In a single republic, all the power surrendered by the people is submitted to the administration of a single government; and the usurpations are guarded against by a division of the government into distinct and separate departments. In the compound republic of America, the power surrendered by the people is first divided between two distinct governments, and then the portion allotted to each subdivided among distinct and separate departments. Hence a double security arises to the rights of the people. The different governments will control each other, at the same time that each will be controlled by itself.

Second. It is of great importance in a republic not only to guard the society against the oppression of its rulers, but to guard one part of the society against the injustice of the other part. Different interests necessarily exist in different classes of citizens. If a majority be united by a common interest, the rights of the minority will be insecure. There are but two methods of providing against this evil: the one by creating a will in the community independent of the majority—that is, of the society itself; the other, by comprehending in the society so many separate descriptions of citizens as will render an unjust combination of a majority of the whole very improbable, if not impracticable. The first method prevails in all governments possessing an hereditary or self-appointed authority. This, at best, is but a precarious security; because a power independent of the society may as well espouse the unjust views of the major as the rightful interests of the minor party, and may possibly be turned against both parties. The second method will be exemplified in the federal republic of the United States. Whilst all authority in it will be derived from and dependent on the society, the society itself will be broken into so many parts, interests and classes of citizens, that the rights of individuals, or of the minority, will be in little danger from interested combinations of the majority. In a free government the security for civil rights must be the same as that for religious rights. It consists in the one case in the multiplicity of interests, and in the other in the multiplicity of sects. The degree of security in both cases will depend on the number of interests and sects; and this may be presumed to depend on the extent of country and number of people comprehended under the same government. This view of the subject must particularly recommend a proper federal system to all the sincere and considerate friends of republican government, since it shows that in exact proportion as the territory of the Union may be formed into more circumscribed Confederacies, or States, oppressive combinations of a majority will be facilitated; the best security, under the republican forms, for the rights of every class of citizen, will be diminished; and consequently the stability and independence of some member of the government, the only other security, must be proportionally increased. Justice is the end of government. It is the end of civil society. It ever has been and ever will be pursued until it be obtained, or until liberty be lost in the pursuit. In a society under the forms of which the stronger faction can readily unite and oppress the weaker, anarchy may as truly be said to reign as in a state of nature, where the weaker individual is not secured against the violence of the stronger; and as, in the latter state, even the stronger individuals are prompted, by the uncertainty of their condition, to submit to a government which may protect the weak as well as themselves; so, in the former state, will the more powerful factions or parties be gradually induced, by a like motive, to wish for a government which will protect all parties, the weaker as well as the more powerful. It can be little doubted that if the State of Rhode Island was separated from the Confederacy and left to itself, the insecurity of rights under the popular form of government within such narrow limits would be displayed by such reiterated oppressions of factious majorities that some power altogether independent of the people would soon be called for by the voice of the very factions whose misrule had proved the necessity to it. In the extended republic of the United States, and among the great variety of interests, parties, and sects which it embraces, a coalition of a majority of the whole society could seldom take place on any other principles than those of justice and the general good; whilst there being thus less danger to a minor from the will of a major party, there must be less pretext, also, to provide for the security of the former, by introducing into the government a will not dependent on the latter, or, in other words, a will independent of the society itself. It is no less certain that it is important, notwithstanding the contrary opinions which have been entertained that the larger the society, provided it lie within a practicable sphere, the more duly capable it will be of self-government. And happily for the republican cause, the practicable sphere may be carried to a very great extent by a judicious modification and mixture of the federal principle.

Anti-Federalist, Brutus, October 18, 1787

To the Citizens of the State of New York: When the public is called to investigate and decide upon a question in which not only the present members of the community are deeply interested, but upon which the happiness and misery of generations yet unborn is in great measure suspended, the benevolent mind cannot help feeling itself peculiarly interested in the result.

In this situation, I trust the feeble efforts of an individual, to lead the minds of the people to a wise and prudent determination, cannot fail of being acceptable to the candid and dispassionate part of the community. Encouraged by this consideration, I have been induced to offer my thoughts upon the present important crisis of our public affairs.

Perhaps this country never saw so critical a period in their political concerns. We have felt the feebleness of the ties by which these United-States are held together, and the want of sufficient energy in our present confederation, to manage, in some instances, our general concerns. Various expedients have been proposed to remedy these evils, but none have succeeded. At length a Convention of the states has been assembled, they have formed a constitution which will now, probably, be submitted to the people to ratify or reject, who are the fountain of all power, to whom alone it of right belongs to make or unmake constitutions, or forms of government, at their pleasure. The most important question that was ever proposed to your decision, or to the decision of any people under heaven, is before you, and you are to decide upon it by men of your own election, chosen specially for this purpose. If the constitution, offered to your acceptance, be a wise one, calculated to preserve the invaluable blessings of liberty, to secure the inestimable rights of mankind, and promote human happiness, then, if you accept it, you will lay a lasting foundation of happiness for millions yet unborn; generations to come will rise up and call you blessed. You may rejoice in the prospects of this vast extended continent becoming filled with freemen, who will assert the dignity of human nature. You may solace yourselves with the idea, that society, in this favoured land, will fast advance to the highest point of perfection; the human mind will expand in knowledge and virtue, and the golden age be, in some measure, realised. But if, on the other hand, this form of government contains principles that will lead to the subversion of liberty—if it tends to establish a despotism, or, what is worse, a tyrannic aristocracy; then, if you adopt it, this only remaining assylum for liberty will be shut up, and posterity will execrate your memory.

Momentous then is the question you have to determine, and you are called upon by every motive which should influence a noble and virtuous mind, to examine it well, and to make up a wise judgment. It is insisted, indeed, that this constitution must be received, be it ever so imperfect. If it has its defects, it is said, they can be best amended when they are experienced. But remember, when the people once part with power, they can seldom or never resume it again but by force. Many instances can be produced in which the people have voluntarily increased the powers of their rulers; but few, if any, in which rulers have willingly abridged their authority. This is a sufficient reason to induce you to be careful, in the first instance, how you deposit the powers of government.

With these few introductory remarks, I shall proceed to a consideration of this constitution:

The first question that presents itself on the subject is, whether a confederated government be the best for the United States or not? Or in other words, whether the thirteen United States should be reduced to one great republic, governed by one legislature, and under the direction of one executive and judicial; or whether they should continue thirteen confederated republics, under the direction and controul of a supreme federal head for certain defined national purposes only?

This enquiry is important, because, although the government reported by the convention does not go to a perfect and entire consolidation, yet it approaches so near to it, that it must, if executed, certainly and infallibly terminate in it.

This government is to possess absolute and uncontroulable power, legislative, executive and judicial, with respect to every object to which it extends, for by the last clause of section 8th, article 1st, it is declared "that the Congress shall have power to make all laws which shall be necessary and proper for carrying into execution the foregoing powers, and all other powers vested by this constitution, in the government of the United States; or in any department or office thereof." And by the 6th article, it is declared "that this constitution, and the laws of the United States, which shall be made in pursuance thereof, and the treaties made, or which shall be made, under the authority of the United States, shall be the supreme law of the land; and the judges in every state shall be bound thereby, any thing in the constitution, or law of any state to the contrary notwithstanding." It appears from these articles that there is no need of any intervention of the state governments, between the Congress and the people, to execute any one power vested in the general government, and that the constitution and laws of every state are nullified and declared void, so far as they are or shall be inconsistent with this constitution, or the laws made in pursuance of it, or with treaties made under the authority of the United States.—The government then, so far as it extends, is a complete one, and not a confederation. It is as much one complete government as that of New-York or Massachusetts, has as absolute and perfect powers to make and execute all laws, to appoint officers, institute courts, declare offences, and annex penalties, with respect to every object to which it extends, as any other in the world. So far therefore as its powers reach, all ideas of confederation are given up and lost. It is true this government is limited to certain objects, or to speak more properly, some small degree of power is still left to the states, but a little attention to the powers vested in the general government, will convince every candid man, that if it is capable of being executed, all that is reserved for the individual states must very soon be annihilated, except so far as they are barely necessary to the organization of the general government. The powers of the general legislature extend to every case that is of the least importance—there is nothing valuable to human nature, nothing dear to freemen, but what is within its power. It has authority to make laws which will affect the lives, the liberty, and property of every man in the United States; nor can the constitution or laws of any state, in any way prevent or impede the full and complete execution of every power given. The legislative power is competent to lay taxes, duties, imposts, and excises;—there is no limitation to this power, unless it be said that the clause which directs the use to which those taxes, and duties shall be applied, may be said to be a limitation: but this is no restriction of the power at all, for by this clause they are to be applied to pay the debts and provide for the common defence and general welfare of the United States; but the legislature have authority to contract debts at their discretion; they are the sole judges of what is necessary to provide for the common defence, and they only are to determine what is for the general welfare; this power therefore is neither more nor less, than a power to lay and collect taxes, imposts, and excises, at their pleasure; not only [is] the power to lay taxes unlimited, as to the amount they may require, but it is perfect and absolute to raise them in any mode they please. No state legislature, or any power in the state governments, have any more to do in carrying this into effect, than the authority of one state has to do with that of another. In the business therefore of laying and collecting taxes, the idea of confederation is totally lost, and that of one entire republic is embraced. It is proper here to remark, that the authority to lay and collect taxes is the most important of any power that can be granted; it connects with it almost all other powers, or at least will in process of time draw all other after it; it is the great mean of protection, security, and defence, in a good government, and the great engine of oppression and tyranny in a bad one. This cannot fail of being the case, if we consider the contracted limits which are set by this constitution, to the late [state?] governments, on this article of raising money. No state can emit paper money—lay any duties, or imposts, on imports, or exports, but by consent of the Congress; and then the net produce shall be for the benefit of the United States: the only mean therefore left, for any state to support its government and discharge its debts, is by direct taxation; and the United States have also power to lay and collect taxes, in any way they please. Every one who has thought on the subject, must be convinced that but small sums of money can be collected in any country, by direct taxe[s], when the foederal government begins to exercise the right of taxation in all its parts, the legislatures of the several states will find it impossible to raise monies to support their governments. Without money they cannot be supported, and they must dwindle away, and, as before observed, their powers absorbed in that of the general government.

It might be here shewn, that the power in the federal legislative, to raise and support armies at pleasure, as well in peace as in war, and their controul over the militia, tend, not only to a consolidation of the government, but the destruction of liberty.—I shall not, however, dwell upon these, as a few observations upon the judicial power of this government, in addition to the preceding, will fully evince the truth of the position.

The judicial power of the United States is to be vested in a supreme court, and in such inferior courts as Congress may from time to time ordain and establish. The powers of these courts are very extensive; their jurisdiction comprehends all civil causes, except such as arise between citizens of the same state; and it extends to all cases in law and equity arising under the constitution. One inferior court must be established, I presume, in each state, at least, with the necessary executive officers appendant thereto. It is easy to see, that in the common course of things, these courts will eclipse the dignity, and take away from the respectability, of the state courts. These courts will be, in themselves, totally independent of the states, deriving their authority from the United States, and receiving from them fixed salaries; and in the course of human events it is to be expected, that they will swallow up all the powers of the courts in the respective states.

How far the clause in the 8th section of the 1st article may operate to do away all idea of confederated states, and to effect an entire consolidation of the whole into one general government, it is impossible to say. The powers given by this article are very general and comprehensive, and it may receive a construction to justify the passing almost any law. A power to make all laws, which shall be *necessary and proper*, for carrying into execution, all powers vested by the constitution in the government of the United States, or any department or officer thereof, is a power very comprehensive and definite [indefinite?], and may, for ought I know, be exercised in a such manner as entirely to abolish the state legislatures. Suppose the legislature of a state should pass a law to raise money to support their government and pay the state debt, may the Congress repeal this law, because it may prevent the collection of a tax which they may think proper and necessary to lay, to provide for the general welfare of the United States? For all laws made, in pursuance of this constitution, are the supreme lay of the land, and the judges in every state shall be bound thereby, any thing in the constitution or laws of the different states to the contrary notwithstanding.—By such a law, the government of a particular state might be overturned at one stroke, and thereby be deprived of every means of its support.

It is not meant, by stating this case, to insinuate that the constitution would warrant a law of this kind; or unnecessarily to alarm the fears of the people, by suggesting, that the federal legislature would be more likely to pass the limits assigned them by the constitution, than that of an individual state, further than they are less responsible to the people. But what is meant is, that the legislature of the United States are vested with the great and uncontroulable powers, of laying and collecting taxes, duties, imposts, and excises; of regulating trade, raising and supporting armies, organizing, arming, and disciplining the militia, instituting courts, and other general powers. And are by this clause invested with the power of making all laws, *proper and necessary*, for carrying all these into execution; and they may so exercise this power as entirely to annihilate all the state governments, and reduce this country to one single government. And if they may do it, it is pretty certain they will; for it will be found that the power retained by individual states, small as it is, will be a clog upon the wheels of the government of the United States; the latter therefore will be naturally inclined to remove it out of the way. Besides, it is a truth confirmed by the unerring experience of ages, that every man, and every body of men, invested with power, are ever disposed to increase it, and to acquire a superiority over every thing that stands in their way. This disposition, which is implanted in human nature, will operate in the federal legislature to lessen and ultimately to subvert the state authority, and having such advantages, will most certainly succeed, if the federal government succeeds at all. It must be very evident then, that what this constitution wants of being a complete consolidation of the several parts of the union into one complete government, possessed of perfect legislative, judicial, and executive powers, to all intents and purposes, it will necessarily acquire in its exercise and operation.

Let us now proceed to enquire, as I at first proposed, whether it be best the thirteen United States should be reduced to one great republic, or not? It is here taken for granted, that all agree in this, that whatever government we adopt, it ought to be a free one; that it should be so framed as to secure the liberty of the citizens of America, and such an one as to admit of a full, fair, and equal representation of the people. The question then will be, whether a government thus constituted, and founded on such principles, is practicable, and can be exercised over the whole United States, reduced into one state?

If respect is to be paid to the opinion of the greatest and wisest men who have ever thought or wrote on the science of government, we shall be constrained to conclude, that a free republic cannot succeed over a country of such immense extent, containing such a number of inhabitants, and these encreasing in such rapid progression as that of the whole United States. Among the many illustrious authorities which might be produced to this point, I shall content myself with quoting only two. The one is the baron de Montesquieu, spirit of laws, chap. xvi. vol. I [book VIII]. "It is natural to a republic to have only a small territory, otherwise it cannot long subsist. In a large republic there are men of large fortunes, and consequently of less moderation; there are trusts too great to be placed in any single subject; he has interest of his own; he soon begins to think that he may be happy, great and glorious, by oppressing his fellow citizens; and that he may raise himself to grandeur on the ruins of his country. In a large republic, the public good is sacrificed to a thousand views; it is subordinate to exceptions, and depends on accidents. In a small one, the interest of the public is easier perceived, better understood, and more within the reach of every citizen; abuses are of less extent, and of course are less protected." Of the same opinion is the marquis Beccarari.

History furnishes no example of a free republic, any thing like the extent of the United States. The Grecian republics were of small extent; so also was that of the Romans. Both of these, it is true, in process of time, extended their conquests over large territories of country; and the consequence was, that their governments were changed from that of free governments to those of the most tyrannical that ever existed in the world.

Not only the opinion of the greatest men, and the experience of mankind, are against the idea of an extensive republic, but a variety of reasons may be drawn from the reason and nature of things, against it. In every government, the will of the sovereign is the law. In despotic governments, the supreme authority being lodged in one, his will is law, and can be as easily expressed to a large extensive territory as to a small one. In a pure democracy the people are the sovereign, and their will is declared by themselves; for this purpose they must all come together to deliberate, and decide. This kind of government cannot be exercised, therefore, over a country of any considerable extent; it must be confined to a single city, or at least limited to such bounds as that the people can conveniently assemble, be able to debate, understand the subject submitted to them, and declare their opinion concerning it.

In a free republic, although all laws are derived from the consent of the people, yet the people do not declare their consent by themselves in person, but by representatives, chosen by them, who are supposed to know the minds of their constituents, and to be possessed of integrity to declare this mind.

In every free government, the people must give their assent to the laws by which they are governed. This is the true criterion between a free government and an arbitrary one. The former are ruled by the will of the whole, expressed in any manner they may agree upon; the latter by the will of one, or a few. If the people are to give their assent to the laws, by persons chosen and appointed by them, the manner of the choice and the number chosen, must be such, as to possess, be disposed, and consequently qualified to declare the sentiments of the people; for if they do not know, or are not disposed to speak the sentiments of the people, the people do not govern, but the sovereignty is in a few. Now, in a large extended country, it is impossible to have a representation, possessing the sentiments, and of integrity, to declare the minds of the people, without having it so numerous and unwieldly, as to be subject in great measure to the inconveniency of a democratic government.

The territory of the United States is of vast extent; it now contains near three millions of souls, and is capable of containing much more than ten times that number. Is it practicable for a country, so large and so numerous as they will soon become, to elect a representation, that will speak their sentiments, without their becoming so numerous as to be incapable of transacting public business? It certainly is not.

In a republic, the manners, sentiments, and interests of the people should be similar. If this be not the case, there will be a constant clashing of opinions; and the representatives of one part will be continually striving against those of the other. This will retard the operations of government, and prevent such conclusions as will promote the public good. If we apply this remark to the condition of the United States, we shall be convinced that it forbids that we should be one government. The United States includes a variety of climates. The productions of the different parts of the union are very variant, and their interests, of consequence, diverse. Their manners and habits differ as much as their climates and productions; and their sentiments are by no means coincident. The laws and customs of the several states are, in many respects, very diverse, and in some opposite; each would be in favor of its own interests and customs, and, of consequence, a legislature, formed of representatives from the respective parts, would not only be too numerous to act with any care or decision, but would be composed of such heterogenous and discordant principles, as would constantly be contending with each other.

The laws cannot be executed in a republic, of an extent equal to that of the United States, with promptitude.

The magistrates in every government must be supported in the execution of the laws, either by an armed force, maintained at the public expence for that purpose; or by the people turning out to aid the magistrate upon his command, in case of resistance.

In despotic governments, as well as in all the monarchies of Europe, standing armies are kept up to execute the commands of the prince or the magistrate, and are employed for this purpose when occasion requires: But they have always proved the destruction of liberty, and [are] abhorrent to the spirit of a free republic. In England, where they depend upon the parliament for their annual support, they have always been complained of as oppressive and unconstitutional, and are seldom employed in executing of the laws; never except on extraordinary occasions, and then under the direction of a civil magistrate.

A free republic will never keep a standing army to execute its laws. It must depend upon the support of its citizens. But when a government is to receive its support from the aid of the citizens, it must be so constructed as to have the confidence, respect, and affection of the people." Men who, upon the call of the magistrate, offer themselves to execute the laws, are influenced to do it either by affection to the government, or from fear; where a standing army is at hand to punish offenders, every man is actuated by the latter principle, and therefore, when the magistrate calls, will obey: but, where this is not the case, the government must rest for its support upon the confidence and respect which the people have for their government and laws. The body of the people being attached, the government will always be sufficient to support and execute its laws, and to operate upon the fears of any faction which may be opposed to it, not only to prevent an opposition to the execution of the laws themselves, but also to compel the most of them to aid the magistrate; but the people will not be likely to have such confidence in their rulers, in a republic so extensive as the United States, as necessary for these purposes. The confidence which the people have in their rulers, in a free republic, arises from their knowing them, from their being responsible to them for their conduct, and from the power they have of displacing them when they misbehave: but in a republic of the extent of this continent, the people in general would be acquainted with very few of their rulers: the people at large would know little of their proceedings, and it would be extremely difficult to change them. The people in Georgia and New-Hampshire would not know one another's mind, and therefore could not act in concert to enable them to effect a general change of representatives. The different parts of so extensive a country could not possibly be made acquainted with the conduct of their representatives, nor be informed of the reasons upon which measures were founded. The consequence will be, they will have no confidence in their legislature, suspect them of ambitious views, be jealous of every measure they adopt, and will not support the laws they pass. Hence the government will be nerveless and inefficient, and no way will be left to render it otherwise, but by establishing an armed force to execute the laws at the point of the bayonet—a government of all others the most to be dreaded.

In a republic of such vast extent as the United-States, the legislature cannot attend to the various concerns and wants of its different parts. It cannot be sufficiently numerous to be acquainted with the local condition and wants of the different districts, and if it could, it is impossible it should have sufficient time to attend to and provide for all the variety of cases of this nature, that would be continually arising.

In so extensive a republic, the great officers of government would soon become above the controul of the people, and abuse their power to the purpose of aggrandizing themselves, and oppressing them. The trust committed to the executive offices, in a country of the extent of the United-States, must be various and of magnitude. The command of all the troops and navy of the republic, the appointment of officers, the power of pardoning offences, the collecting of all the public revenues, and the power of expending them, with a number of other powers, must be lodged and exercised in every state, in the hands of a few. When these are attended with great honor and emolument, as they always will be in large states, so as greatly to interest men to pursue them, and to be proper objects for ambitious and designing men, such men will be ever restless in their pursuit after them. They will use the power, when they have acquired it, to the purposes of gratifying their own interest and ambition, and it is scarcely possible, in a very large republic, to call them to account for their misconduct, or to prevent their abuse of power.

These are some of the reasons by which it appears, that a free republic cannot long subsist over a country of the great extent of these states. If then this new constitution is calculated to consolidate the thirteen states into one, as it evidently is, it ought not to be adopted.

Though I am of opinion, that it is a sufficient objection to this government, to reject it, that it creates the whole union into one government, under the form of a republic, yet if this objection was obviated, there are exceptions to it, which are so material and fundamental, that they ought to determine every man, who is a friend to the liberty and happiness of mankind, not to adopt it. I beg the candid and dispassionate attention of my countrymen while I state these objections—they are such as have obtruded themselves upon my mind upon a careful attention to the matter, and such as I sincerely believe are well founded. There are many objections, of small moment, of which I shall take no notice—perfection is not to be expected in any thing that is the production of man—and if I did not in my conscience believe that this scheme was defective in the fundamental principles—in the foundation upon which a free and equal government must rest—I would hold my peace.

The Gettysburg Address, Abraham Lincoln

Gettysburg, Pennsylvania
November 19, 1863

Four score and seven years ago our fathers brought forth on this continent, a new nation, conceived in Liberty, and dedicated to the proposition that all men are created equal.

Now we are engaged in a great civil war, testing whether that nation, or any nation so conceived and so dedicated, can long endure. We are met on a great battlefield of that war. We have come to dedicate a portion of that field, as a final resting place for those who here gave their lives that that nation might live. It is altogether fitting and proper that we should do this.

But, in a larger sense, we can not dedicate—we can not consecrate—we can not hallow—this ground. The brave men, living and dead, who struggled here, have consecrated it, far above our poor power to add or detract. The world will little note, nor long remember what we say here, but it can never forget what they did here. It is for us the living, rather, to be dedicated here to the unfinished work which they who fought here have thus far so nobly advanced. It is rather for us to be here dedicated to the great task remaining before us—that from these honored dead we take increased devotion to that cause for which they gave the last full measure of devotion—that we here highly resolve that these dead shall not have died in vain—that this nation, under God, shall have a new birth of freedom—and that government of the people, by the people, for the people, shall not perish from the earth.

SOURCE: *Collected Works of Abraham Lincoln*, edited by Roy P. Basler. The text above is from the so-called "Bliss Copy," one of several versions which Lincoln wrote, and believed to be the final version. For additional versions, you may search *The Collected Works of Abraham Lincoln* through the courtesy of the Abraham Lincoln Association.

Related Links

Battlefield Map (Library of Congress)
Civil War Institute (Gettysburg College)
Gettysburg Address Essay Contest (Lincoln Fellowship of Pennsylvania)
Gettysburg Address Exhibit (Library of Congress)
Gettysburg Address Eyewitness (National Public Radio)
Gettysburg Address News Article (New York Times)
Gettysburg Address Teacher Resource (C-SPAN)
Gettysburg Civil War Photographs (Library of Congress)
Gettysburg Discussion Group (Bob & Dennis Lawrence)
Gettysburg Events (NPS)
Gettysburg National Military Park (NPS)
Letter of Invitation to Lincoln (Library of Congress)
Lincoln at Gettysburg
Lincoln at Gettysburg Photo Tour
Lincoln Fellowship of Pennsylvania
Lincoln's Invitation to Stay Overnight (Library of Congress)
Lincoln's Letter from Edward Everett (Library of Congress)
Photograph of Lincoln at Gettysburg (Library of Congress)
Reading of the Gettysburg Address (NPR)
Recollections of Lincoln at Gettysburg (Bob Cooke)
Response to a Serenade
Seminary Ridge Historic Preservation Foundation
The Gettysburg Powerpoint Presentation (Peter Norvig)
Wills House

Related Books

Graham, Kent. *November: Lincoln's Elegy at Gettysburg.* Indiana University Press, 2001.

Hoch, Bradley R. and Boritt, Gabor S. *The Lincoln Trail in Pennsylvania.* Pennsylvania State University Press, 2001.

Kunhardt, Philip B., Jr. *A New Birth of Freedom—Lincoln at Gettysburg.* Boston: Little, Brown, 1983.

Wills, Garry. *Lincoln at Gettysburg: The Words That Remade America.* Touchstone Books, 1993.

"I Have a Dream," Martin Luther King, Jr.

In 1950s America, the equality of man envisioned by the Declaration of Independence was far from a reality. People of color, blacks, Hispanics, Orientals, were discriminated against in many ways, both overt and covert. The 1950s were a turbulent time in America, when racial barriers began to come down due to Supreme Court decisions, like *Brown* v. *Board of Education*; and due to an increase in the activism of blacks, fighting for equal rights.

Martin Luther King, Jr., a Baptist minister, was a driving force in the push for racial equality in the 1950s and the 1960s. In 1963, King and his staff focused on Birmingham, Alabama. They marched and protested nonviolently, raising the ire of local officials who sicced water cannon and police dogs on the marchers, whose ranks included teenagers and children. The bad publicity and breakdown of business forced the white leaders of Birmingham to concede to some antisegregation demands.

Thrust into the national spotlight in Birmingham, where he was arrested and jailed, King organized a massive march on Washington, D.C., on August 28, 1963. On the steps of the Lincoln Memorial, he evoked the name of Lincoln in his "I Have a Dream" speech, which is credited with mobilizing supporters of desegregation and prompted the 1964 Civil Rights Act. The next year, King was awarded the Nobel Peace Prize.

The following is the exact text of the spoken speech, transcribed from recordings.

I am happy to join with you today in what will go down in history as the greatest demonstration for freedom in the history of our nation.

Five score years ago, a great American, in whose symbolic shadow we stand today, signed the Emancipation Proclamation. This momentous decree came as a great beacon light of hope to millions of Negro slaves who had been seared in the flames of withering injustice. It came as a joyous daybreak to end the long night of their captivity.

But one hundred years later, the Negro still is not free. One hundred years later, the life of the Negro is still sadly crippled by the manacles of segregation and the chains of discrimination. One hundred years later, the Negro lives on a lonely island of poverty in the midst of a vast ocean of material prosperity. One hundred years later, the Negro is still languishing in the corners of American society and finds himself an exile in his own land. So we have come here today to dramatize a shameful condition.

In a sense we have come to our nation's capital to cash a check. When the architects of our republic wrote the magnificent words of the Constitution and the Declaration of Independence, they were signing a promissory note to which every American was to fall heir. This note was a promise that all men, yes, black men as well as white men, would be guaranteed the unalienable rights of life, liberty, and the pursuit of happiness.

It is obvious today that America has defaulted on this promissory note insofar as her citizens of color are concerned. Instead of honoring this sacred obligation, America has given the Negro people a bad check, a check which has come back marked "insufficient funds." But we refuse to believe that the bank of justice is bankrupt. We refuse to believe that there are insufficient funds in the great vaults of opportunity of this nation. So we have come to cash this check—a check that will give us upon demand the riches of freedom and the security of justice. We have also come to this hallowed spot to remind America of the fierce urgency of now. This is no time to engage in the luxury of cooling off or to take the tranquilizing drug of gradualism. Now is the time to make real the promises of democracy. Now is the time to rise from the dark and desolate valley of segregation to the sunlit path of racial justice. Now is the time to lift our nation from the quicksands of racial injustice to the solid rock of brotherhood. Now is the time to make justice a reality for all of God's children.

It would be fatal for the nation to overlook the urgency of the moment. This sweltering summer of the Negro's legitimate discontent will not pass until there is an invigorating autumn of freedom and equality. Nineteen sixty-three is not an end, but a beginning. Those who hope that the Negro needed to blow off steam and will now be content will have a rude awakening if the nation returns to business as usual. There will be neither rest nor tranquility in America until the Negro is granted his citizenship rights. The whirlwinds of revolt will continue to shake the foundations of our nation until the bright day of justice emerges.

But there is something that I must say to my people who stand on the warm threshold which leads into the palace of justice. In the process of gaining our rightful place we must not be guilty of wrongful deeds. Let us not seek to satisfy our thirst for freedom by drinking from the cup of bitterness and hatred.

We must forever conduct our struggle on the high plane of dignity and discipline. We must not allow our creative protest to degenerate into physical violence. Again and again we must rise to the majestic heights of meeting physical force with soul force. The marvelous new militancy which has engulfed the Negro community must not lead us to distrust of all white people, for many of our white brothers, as evidenced by their presence here today, have come to realize that their destiny is tied up with our destiny and their freedom is inextricably bound to our freedom. We cannot walk alone.

As we walk, we must make the pledge that we shall march ahead. We cannot turn back. There are those who are asking the devotees of civil rights, "When will you be satisfied?" We can never be satisfied as long as the Negro is the victim of the unspeakable horrors of police brutality. We can never be satisfied, as long as our bodies, heavy with the fatigue of travel, cannot gain lodging in the motels of the highways and the hotels of the cities. We can never be satisfied as long as a Negro in Mississippi cannot vote and a Negro in New York believes he has nothing for which to vote. No, no, we are not satisfied, and we will not be satisfied until justice rolls down like waters and righteousness like a mighty stream.

I am not unmindful that some of you have come here out of great trials and tribulations. Some of you have come fresh from narrow jail cells. Some of you have come from areas where your quest for freedom left you battered by the storms of persecution and staggered by the winds of police brutality. You have been the veterans of creative suffering. Continue to work with the faith that unearned suffering is redemptive.

Go back to Mississippi, go back to Alabama, go back to South Carolina, go back to Georgia, go back to Louisiana, go back to the slums and ghettos of our northern cities, knowing that somehow this situation can and will be changed. Let us not wallow in the valley of despair.

I say to you today, my friends, even though we face the difficulties of today and tomorrow, I still have a dream. It is a dream deeply rooted in the American dream.

I have a dream that one day this nation will rise up and live out the true meaning of its creed: "We hold these truths to be selfevident: that all men are created equal."

I have a dream that one day on the red hills of Georgia the sons of former slaves and the sons of former slave owners will be able to sit down together at the table of brotherhood.

I have a dream that one day even the state of Mississippi, a state sweltering with the heat of injustice, sweltering with the heat of oppression, will be transformed into an oasis of freedom and justice.

I have a dream that my four little children will one day live in a nation where they will not be judged by the color of their skin but by the content of their character.

I have a dream today.

I have a dream that one day, down in Alabama, with its vicious racists, with its governor having his lips dripping with the words of interposition and nullification; one day right there in Alabama, little black boys and black girls will be able to join hands with little white boys and white girls as sisters and brothers.

I have a dream today.

I have a dream that one day every valley shall be exalted, every hill and mountain shall be made low, the rough places will be made plain, and the crooked places will be made straight, and the glory of the Lord shall be revealed, and all flesh shall see it together.

This is our hope. This is the faith that I go back to the South with. With this faith we will be able to hew out of the mountain of despair a stone of hope. With this faith we will be able to transform the jangling discords of our nation into a beautiful symphony of brotherhood. With this faith we will be able to work together, to pray together, to struggle together, to go to jail together, to stand up for freedom together, knowing that we will be free one day.

This will be the day when all of God's children will be able to sing with a new meaning, "My country, 'tis of thee, sweet land of liberty, of thee I sing. Land where my fathers died, land of the pilgrim's pride, from every mountainside, let freedom ring."

And if America is to be a great nation this must become true. So let freedom ring from the prodigious hilltops of New Hampshire. Let freedom ring from the mighty mountains of New York. Let freedom ring from the heightening Alleghenies of Pennsylvania!

Let freedom ring from the snowcapped Rockies of Colorado!

Let freedom ring from the curvaceous slopes of California!

But not only that; let freedom ring from Stone Mountain of Georgia!

Let freedom ring from Lookout Mountain of Tennessee!

Let freedom ring from every hill and molehill of Mississippi. From every mountainside, let freedom ring.

And when this happens, when we allow freedom to ring, when we let it ring from every village and every hamlet, from every state and every city, we will be able to speed up that day when all of God's children, black men and white men, Jews and Gentiles, Protestants and Catholics, will be able to join hands and sing in the words of the old Negro spiritual, "Free at last! free at last! thank God Almighty, we are free at last!"

SOURCE: Reprinted by arrangement with the Estate of Martin Luther King, Jr., c/o Writer's House as agent for the proprietor, New York, N.Y. © 1963 by Martin Luther King, Jr., copyright renewed 1991 by Coretta Scott King.

Presidents and Congresses, 1789–2010

TERM	PRESIDENT AND VICE PRESIDENT	PARTY OF PRESDIENT	CONGRESS	MAJORITY PARTY	
				HOUSE	SENATE
1789–97	**George Washington** John Adams	None	1st 2d 3d 4th	N/A N/A N/A N/A	N/A N/A N/A N/A
1797–1801	**John Adams** Thomas Jefferson	Fed	5th 6th	N/A Fed	N/A Fed
1801–09	**Thomas Jefferson** Aaron Burr (1801–05) George Clinton (1805–09)	Dem Rep	7th 8th 9th 10th	Dem Rep Dem Rep Dem Rep Dem Rep	Dem Rep Dem Rep Dem Rep Dem Rep
1809–17	**James Madison** George Clinton (1809–12)[1] Elbridge Gerry (1813–14)[1]	Dem Rep	11th 12th 13th 14th	Dem Rep Dem Rep Dem Rep Dem Rep	Dem Rep Dem Rep Dem Rep Dem Rep
1817–25	**James Monroe** Daniel D. Tompkins	Dem Rep	15th 16th 17th 18th	Dem Rep Dem Rep Dem Rep Dem Rep	Dem Rep Dem Rep Dem Rep Dem Rep
1825–29	**John Quincy Adams** John C. Calhoun	Nat'l Rep	19th 20th	Nat'l Rep Dem	Nat'l Rep Dem
1829–37	**Andrew Jackson** John C. Calhoun (1829–32)[2] Martin Van Buren (1833–37)	Dem	21st 22d 23d 24th	Dem Dem Dem Dem	Dem Dem Dem Dem
1837–41	**Martin Van Buren** Richard M. Johnson	Dem	25th 26th	Dem Dem	Dem Dem
1841	**William H. Harrison**[1] John Tyler (1841)	Whig	27th	Whig	Whig
1841–45	**John Tyler** (VP vacant)	Whig	28th	Dem	Whig
1845–49	**James K. Polk** George M. Dallas	Dem	29th 30th	Dem Whig	Dem Dem
1849–50	**Zachary Taylor**[1] Millard Fillmore	Whig	31st	Dem	Dem
1850–53	**Millard Fillmore** (VP vacant)	Whig	32d	Dem	Dem
1853–57	**Franklin Pierce** William R. D. King (1853)[1]	Dem	33d 34th	Dem Rep	Dem Dem
1857–61	**James Buchanan** John C. Breckinridge	Dem	35th 36th	Dem Rep	Dem Dem
1861–65	**Abraham Lincoln**[1] Hannibal Hamlin (1861–65) Andrew Johnson (1865)	Rep	37th 38th	Rep Rep	Rep Rep
1865–69	**Andrew Johnson** (VP vacant)	Rep	39th 40th	Union Rep	Union Rep
1869–77	**Ulysses S. Grant** Schuyler Colfax (1869–73) Henry Wilson (1873–75)[1]	Rep	41st 42d 43d 44th	Rep Rep Rep Dem	Rep Rep Rep Rep
1877–81	**Rutherford B. Hayes** William A. Wheeler	Rep	45th 46th	Dem Dem	Rep Dem
1881	**James A. Garfield**[1] Chester A. Arthur	Rep	47th	Rep	Rep
1881–85	**Chester A. Arthur** (VP vacant)	Rep	48th	Dem	Rep
1885–89	**Grover Cleveland** Thomas A. Hendricks (1885)[1]	Dem	49th 50th	Dem Dem	Rep Rep

[1] Died in office. [2] Resigned from the vice presidency. [3] Resigned from the presidency. [4] Appointed vice president.

TERM	PRESIDENT AND VICE PRESIDENT	PARTY OF PRESDIENT	CONGRESS	MAJORITY PARTY	
				HOUSE	SENATE
1889–93	**Benjamin Harrison** Levi P. Morton	Rep	51st 52d	Rep Dem	Rep Rep
1893–97	**Grover Cleveland** Adlai E. Stevenson	Dem	53d 54th	Dem Rep	Dem Rep
1897–1901	**William McKinley**[1] Garret A. Hobart (1897–99)[1] Theodore Roosevelt (1901)	Rep	55th 56th	Rep Rep	Rep Rep
1901–09	**Theodore Roosevelt** (VP vacant, 1901–05) Charles W. Fairbanks (1905–09)	Rep	57th 58th 59th 60th	Rep Rep Rep Rep	Rep Rep Rep Rep
1909–13	**William Howard Taft** James S. Sherman (1909–12)[1]	Rep	61st 62d	Rep Dem	Rep Rep
1913–21	**Woodrow Wilson** Thomas R. Marshall	Dem	63d 64th 65th 66th	Dem Dem Dem Rep	Dem Dem Dem Rep
1921–23	**Warren G. Harding**[1] Calvin Coolidge	Rep	67th	Rep	Rep
1923–29	**Calvin Coolidge** (VP vacant, 1923–25) Charles G. Dawes (1925–29)	Rep	68th 69th 70th	Rep Rep Rep	Rep Rep Rep
1929–33	**Herbert Hoover** Charles Curtis	Rep	71st 72d	Rep Dem	Rep Rep
1933–45	**Franklin D. Roosevelt**[1] John N. Garner (1933–41) Henry A. Wallace (1941–45) Harry S Truman (1945)	Dem	73d 74th 75th 76th 77th 78th	Dem Dem Dem Dem Dem Dem	Dem Dem Dem Dem Dem Dem
1945–53	**Harry S Truman** (VP vacant, 1945–49) Alben W. Barkley (1949–53)	Dem	79th 80th 81st 82d	Dem Rep Dem Dem	Dem Rep Dem Dem
1953–61	**Dwight D. Eisenhower** Richard M. Nixon	Rep	83d 84th 85th 86th	Rep Dem Dem Dem	Rep Dem Dem Dem
1961–63	**John F. Kennedy**[1] Lyndon B. Johnson (1961–63)	Dem	87th	Dem	Dem
1963–69	**Lyndon B. Johnson** (VP vacant, 1963–65) Hubert H. Humphrey (1965–69)	Dem	88th 89th 90th	Dem Dem Dem	Dem Dem Dem
1969–74	**Richard M. Nixon**[3] Spiro T. Agnew (1969–73)[2] Gerald R. Ford (1973–74)[4]	Rep	91st 92d	Dem Dem	Dem Dem
1974–77	**Gerald R. Ford** Nelson A. Rockefeller[4]	Rep	93d 94th	Dem Dem	Dem Dem
1977–81	**Jimmy Carter** Walter Mondale	Dem	95th 96th	Dem Dem	Dem Dem
1981–89	**Ronald Reagan** George Bush	Rep	97th 98th 99th 100th	Dem Dem Dem Dem	Rep Rep Rep Dem
1989–93	**George Bush** J. Danforth Quayle	Rep	101st 102d	Dem Dem	Dem Dem
1993–2001	**William J. Clinton** Albert Gore, Jr.	Dem	103d 104th 105th 106th	Dem Rep Rep Rep	Dem Rep Rep Rep
2001–2009	**George W. Bush** Richard Cheney	Rep	107th 108th 109th 110th	Rep Rep Rep Dem	Dem Rep Rep Dem
2009–	**Barack H. Obama** Joseph R. Biden, Jr.	Dem	111th 112th	Dem Rep	Dem Dem

[1] Died in office.　　[2] Resigned from the vice presidency.　　[3] Resigned from the presidency.　　[4] Appointed vice president.

Supreme Court Justices

Name[1]	Years on Court	Appointing President	Name[1]	Years on Court	Appointing President
JOHN JAY	1789–1795	Washington	SALMON P. CHASE	1864–1873	Lincoln
James Wilson	1789–1798	Washington	William Strong	1870–1880	Grant
John Rutledge	1790–1791	Washington	Joseph P. Bradley	1870–1892	Grant
William Cushing	1790–1810	Washington	Ward Hunt	1873–1882	Grant
John Blair	1790–1796	Washington	MORRISON R. WAITE	1874–1888	Grant
James Iredell	1790–1799	Washington	John M. Harlan	1877–1911	Hayes
Thomas Johnson	1792–1793	Washington	William B. Woods	1881–1887	Hayes
William Paterson	1793–1806	Washington	Stanley Matthews	1881–1889	Garfield
JOHN RUTLEDGE[2]	1795	Washington	Horace Gray	1882–1902	Arthur
Samuel Chase	1796–1811	Washington	Samuel Blatchford	1882–1893	Arthur
OLIVER ELLSWORTH	1796–1800	Washington	Lucious Q. C. Lamar	1888–1893	Cleveland
Bushrod Washington	1799–1829	J. Adams	MELVILLE W. FULLER	1888–1910	Cleveland
Alfred Moore	1800–1804	J. Adams	David J. Brewer	1890–1910	B. Harrison
JOHN MARSHALL	1801–1835	J. Adams	Henry B. Brown	1891–1906	B. Harrison
William Johnson	1804–1834	Jefferson	George Shiras, Jr.	1892–1903	B. Harrison
Brockholst Livingston	1807–1823	Jefferson	Howel E. Jackson	1893–1895	B. Harrison
Thomas Todd	1807–1826	Jefferson	Edward D. White	1894–1910	Cleveland
Gabriel Duvall	1811–1835	Madison	Rufus W. Peckman	1896–1909	Cleveland
Joseph Story	1812–1845	Madison	Joseph McKenna	1898–1925	McKinley
Smith Thompson	1823–1843	Monroe	Oliver W. Holmes	1902–1932	T. Roosevelt
Robert Trimble	1826–1828	J. Q. Adams	William R. Day	1903–1922	T. Roosevelt
John McLean	1830–1861	Jackson	William H. Moody	1906–1910	T. Roosevelt
Henry Baldwin	1830–1844	Jackson	Horace H. Lurton	1910–1914	Taft
James M. Wayne	1835–1867	Jackson	Charles E. Hughes	1910–1916	Taft
ROGER B. TANEY	1836–1864	Jackson	EDWARD D. WHITE	1910–1921	Taft
Philip P. Barbour	1836–1841	Jackson	Willis Van Devanter	1911–1937	Taft
John Cartron	1837–1865	Van Buren	Joseph R. Lamar	1911–1916	Taft
John McKinley	1838–1852	Van Buren	Mahlon Pitney	1912–1922	Taft
Peter V. Daniel	1842–1860	Van Buren	James C. McReynolds	1914–1941	Wilson
Samuel Nelson	1845–1872	Tyler	Louis D. Brandeis	1916–1939	Wilson
Levi Woodbury	1845–1851	Polk	John H. Clarke	1916–1922	Wilson
Robert C. Grier	1846–1870	Polk	WILLIAM H. TAFT	1921–1930	Harding
Benjamin R. Curtis	1851–1857	Fillmore	George Sutherland	1922–1938	Harding
John A. Campbell	1853–1861	Pierce	Pierce Butler	1923–1939	Harding
Nathan Clifford	1858–1881	Buchanan	Edward T. Sanford	1923–1930	Harding
Noah H. Swayne	1862–1881	Lincoln	Harlan F. Stone	1925–1941	Coolidge
Samuel F. Miller	1862–1890	Lincoln	CHARLES E. HUGHES	1930–1941	Hoover
David Davis	1862–1877	Lincoln	Owen J. Roberts	1930–1945	Hoover
Stephen J. Field	1863–1897	Lincoln	Benjamin N. Cardozo	1932–1938	Hoover

[1]Capital letters designate Chief Justices

[2]Never confirmed by the Senate as Chief Justice

Name[1]	Years on Court	Appointing President
Hugo L. Black	1937–1971	F. Roosevelt
Stanley F. Reed	1938–1957	F. Roosevelt
Felix Frankfurter	1939–1962	F. Roosevelt
William O. Douglas	1939–1975	F. Roosevelt
Frank Murphy	1940–1949	F. Roosevelt
HARLAN F. STONE	1941–1946	F. Roosevelt
James F. Brynes	1941–1942	F. Roosevelt
Robert H. Jackson	1941–1954	F. Roosevelt
Wiley B. Rutledge	1943–1949	F. Roosevelt
Harold H. Burton	1945–1958	Truman
FREDERICK M. VINSON	1946–1953	Truman
Tom C. Clark	1949–1967	Truman
Sherman Minton	1949–1956	Truman
EARL WARREN	1953–1969	Eisenhower
John Marshall Harlan	1955–1971	Eisenhower
William J. Brennan, Jr.	1956–1990	Eisenhower
Charles E. Whittaker	1957–1962	Eisenhower
Potter Stewart	1958–1981	Eisenhower
Byron R. White	1962–1993	Kennedy
Arthur J. Goldberg	1962–1965	Kennedy
Abe Fortas	1965–1970	L. Johnson
Thurgood Marshall	1967–1991	L. Johnson
WARREN E. BURGER	1969–1986	Nixon
Harry A. Blackmun	1970–1994	Nixon
Lewis F. Powell, Jr.	1971–1987	Nixon
William H. Rehnquist	1971–1986	Nixon
John Paul Stevens	1975–	Ford
Sandra Day O'Connor	1981–2006	Reagan
WILLIAM H. REHNQUIST	1986–2005	Reagan
Antonin Scalia	1986–	Reagan
Anthony Kennedy	1988–	Reagan
David Souter	1990	G. H. W. Bush
Clarence Thomas	1991–	G. H. W. Bush
Ruth Bader Ginsburg	1993–	Clinton
Stephen Breyer	1994–	Clinton
JOHN G. ROBERTS, JR.	2005–	G. W. Bush
Samuel A. Alito, Jr.	2006–	G. W. Bush
Sonia Maria Sotomayor	2009–	Obama
Elena Kagan	2009–	Obama

[1]Capital letters designate Chief Justices

[2]Never confirmed by the Senate as Chief Justice

Glossary

A

Absentee Voting In California, absentee voting has been simplified over the years, particularly through temporary mail-in ballot provisions. (Ch. 17)

Accommodationist Interpretive approach to the establishment clause of the First Amendment that would permit the government to provide financial support for certain religious institutions and programs or sponsor specific religious practices, such as prayer in public schools. (Ch. 4)

Acts for Trade A series of moves by Parliament to channel money from the American colonies back to the commercial class in Great Britain during the mid-1700s. (Ch. 2)

Adams, John (1735–1826) One of the founders of the American political system. He served as vice president under George Washington and as president from 1797 to 1801. (Ch. 2)

Administrative Law Judge (ALJ) Official who presides over quasi-judicial proceedings within government agencies and renders decisions about disputes governed by statutes, such as appeals from denials of Social Security disability benefits. (Ch. 8)

Adversarial System Legal system used by the United States and other countries in which a judge plays a relatively passive role as attorneys battle to protect each side's interests. (Ch. 9)

Advertorials Advertisements presented as editorials. (Ch. 12)

Affirmative Action Measures taken in hiring, recruitment, employment, and education to remedy past and present discrimination against members of specific groups. (Ch. 11)

Agenda Setting The process of featuring specific stories in the media to focus attention on particular issues. (Ch. 11)

Agents of Political Socialization Factors that influence how we acquire political facts and knowledge and develop political values. (Ch. 10)

Alien Land Bill A 1913 law that prohibited aliens not eligible for citizenship from owning land. (Ch. 16)

Alternative Dispute Resolution (ADR) A non–court-centered option for resolving disagreements, such as mediation and arbitration. (Ch. 20)

Amicus Brief A written argument submitted to an appellate court by those who are interested in the issue being examined but are not representing either party in the case; often submitted by interest groups' lawyers to advance a specific policy position. (Ch. 9)

Anti-Federalists Opponents of ratification of the U.S. Constitution in 1787 and 1788. (Ch. 2)

Apartheid The system of strict racial segregation and white supremacy in South Africa. (Ch. 15)

Appellate Briefs Written arguments submitted by lawyers in appellate court cases. (Ch. 9)

Appellate Jurisdiction Authority of a court to review lower courts' decisions to determine if the law was correctly interpreted and legal procedures correctly followed. (Ch. 9)

Apprenticeship Norm The norm that new members of Congress are expected to work hard and quietly learn the legislative process. (Ch. 6)

Assembly Speaker The presiding officer of the California state assembly. (Ch. 18)

Assessor The county officer whose principal duty is to determine the value of property within the county (Ch. 21)

At-Large Districts Districts encompassing an entire state, or large parts of a state, in which House members are elected to represent the entire area. (Ch. 6)

Attitudinal Model An approach to analyzing judicial decision making that looks at individual judges' decision patterns to identify the values and attitudes that guide their decisions. (Ch. 9)

Attorney General The state's top legal officer. (Ch. 19)

Australian Ballot The secret ballot, which keeps voters' choices confidential, was first introduced in south Australia in 1856. (Ch. 13)

Authoritarian Regime A system of government in which leaders face few formal or legal restrictions but are checked by noninstitutional forces such as political parties, religious groups, and business leaders. (Ch. 2)

Authority The recognized right of a particular individual, group, or institution to make binding decisions for society. (Ch. 2)

B

Baker v. *Carr* **(1961)** Supreme Court case that set the standard that House districts must contain equal numbers of constituents, thus establishing the principle of "one person, one vote." (Ch. 6)

Balance of Trade The net difference between a nation's imports and its exports. (Ch. 14)

Barometer of Public Attitudes The theory that the media reflect popular culture. (Ch. 10)

Bear Flag Rebellion A revolt led by John C. Frémont against Mexican control of California in 1846. (Ch. 16)

Bench Trials Trials in which a judge presides and makes determinations of fact and law, including decisions about guilt, without a jury. (Ch. 4)

Berkeley Free-Speech Movement A movement sparked by the announcement from the administration of the University of California, Berkeley, that effective September 21, 1964, tables would no longer be permitted at the Bancroft and Telegraph entrance and that political literature and activities about off-campus political issues would be prohibited. (Ch. 17)

Bicameral Legislature A legislature composed of two houses. (Ch. 6)

Big Four The founders of the Central Pacific Railroad Company: Collis P. Huntington, Mark Hopkins, Charles Crocker, and Leland Stanford. (Ch. 16)

Bill of Rights The first 10 amendments to the U.S. Constitution, ratified in 1791, protecting civil liberties. (Ch. 2)

Bill Sponsor The member of Congress who introduces a bill. (Ch. 6)

Binding Primaries A process established in most states whereby voters in primary elections choose delegates who have pledged their support to a particular presidential candidate. The delegates then vote for this candidate at the nominating convention. (Ch. 13)

Bipartisan Campaign Reform Act (BCRA) Federal law passed in 2002 that outlawed soft-money contributions to party organizations. (Ch. 13)

Blanket Primary A primary election in which all voters can vote for any candidate, regardless of party affiliation. (Ch. 17)

Block Grants Funds given to states that allow substantial discretion to spend the money with minimal federal restrictions. (Ch. 3)

Board of Equalization A California body that makes rules, based on state laws, governing the collection and payment of certain taxes. (Ch. 19)

Boycott A coordinated action by many people who agree not to buy a specific product, use a specific service, or shop at a specific store until a policy is changed. (Ch. 2)

Bracero Program A program granting temporary employment status to Mexicans working in the United States beginning with the start of World War II. (Ch. 16)

***Brown v. Board of Education of Topeka* (1954)** A U.S. Supreme Court decision that overturned *Plessy* v. *Ferguson* (1896) and declared that government-mandated racial segregation in schools and other facilities and programs violates the equal protection clause of the Fourteenth Amendment. (Ch. 5)

***Buckley v. Valeo* (1976)** The most significant Supreme Court case on campaign finance in American history. (Ch. 13)

Budget Deficit The amount by which a government's expenditures exceed its revenues. (Ch. 14)

Budget Surplus The amount by which a government's revenues exceed its expenditures. (Ch. 14)

Bureaucracy An organization with a hierarchical structure and specific responsibilities intended to enhance efficiency and effectiveness. In government, it refers to departments and agencies in the executive branch. (Ch. 8)

C

Cabinet A group of presidential advisers, primarily the secretaries of federal departments. (Ch. 7)

California Gold Rush The rapid influx of settlers sparked by the discovery of gold at Sutter's Mill on January 24, 1848. (Ch. 16)

California Penal Code The listing of all crimes defined by statutes. (Ch. 20)

Californios Mexican settlers of California. (Ch. 16)

Candidate-Centered Era After 1960, a period when candidates began to portray themselves as independent from party politics, even though they often ran under a party banner. (Ch. 13)

Capitalism An economic system where business and industry are privately owned and there is little governmental interference. (Ch. 1)

Capital Punishment A criminal punishment, otherwise known as the *death penalty*, in which a person is subject to execution after conviction. Reserved for the most serious offenses. (Ch. 4)

Case Precedent A legal rule established by a judicial decision that guides subsequent decisions. The use of case precedent is drawn from the common law system brought from Great Britain to the United States. (Ch. 9)

Casework The direct assistance legislators offer in response to requests from their constituents. (Ch. 18)

Catalyst-for-Change Theory The assertion that public opinion shapes and alters our political culture, thus allowing change. (Ch. 10)

Categorical Grants Grants of money from the federal government to state or local governments for very specific purposes. These grants often require that funds be matched by the receiving entity. (Ch. 3)

Cato The pseudonym for a writer of a series of articles in opposition to the ratification of the Constitution. (Ch. 7)

Census A precise count of the population. (Ch. 2)

Chávez, César (1927–1993) Latino civil rights leader who founded the United Farm Workers and used nonviolent, grassroots mobilization to seek civil rights for Latinos and improved working conditions for agricultural workers. (Ch. 5)

Checks and Balances A system in our government where each branch (legislative, executive, judicial) has the power to limit the actions of others. (Ch. 1)

Citizen Journalism Nonprofessional members of the public who are involved in the collection, reporting, commenting, and dissemination of new stories; also known as *street journalism*. (Ch. 11)

Citizen-Politician A candidate who succeeds during a campaign in convincing California voters of his or her political independence and nonpartisanship. (Ch. 17)

City Attorney The legal adviser to the city council. (Ch. 21)

City Clerk The official responsible for the preparation and maintenance of minutes, ordinances, resolutions, agreements, and other legal documents. (Ch. 21)

City Manager The official responsible for the administration of city services and programs, enforcement of the city's ordinances, and preparation of the annual budget. (Ch. 21)

City Treasurer The official whose chief responsibility is to audit and examine all investments made by authorized city personnel. (Ch. 21)

***Citizens United v. Federal Elections Commission* (2010)** A Supreme Court case that reversed decades of precedent by declaring unconstitutional laws that ban unions and corporations from using general operating funds on elections. (Ch. 13)

Civil Law A body of law that applies to private rights, such as the ownership of property or the ability to enter into contracts. (Chs. 9, 20)

Civil Liberties Individual freedoms and legal protections guaranteed by the Bill of Rights that cannot be denied or hindered by government. (Ch. 4)

Civil Rights Public policies and legal protections concerning equal status and treatment in American society to advance the goals of equal opportunity, fair and open political participation, and equal treatment under the law without regard to race, gender, disability status, and other demographic characteristics. (Ch. 5)

Civil Rights Act of 1964 A federal statute that prohibited racial discrimination in public accommodations (hotels, restaurants, theaters), employment, and programs receiving federal funding. (Ch. 5)

Civil Service System A government employment system under which public employees are hired and promoted on the basis of their qualifications and abilities and cannot be fired merely for belonging to the wrong political party; originated with the federal Pendleton Act in 1883 and expanded at other levels of government in the half-century that followed. (Chs. 8, 13)

Classical Liberalism A political philosophy based on the desire for limited government; the basis for modern conservatism. (Ch. 14)

Clear and Present Danger Test A test for permissible speech articulated by Justice Oliver Wendell Holmes in *Schenck* v. *United States* (1919) that allows government regulation of some expressions. (Ch. 4)

Cleavage Division among people based on at least one social characteristic, such as educational attainment or race. (Ch. 12)

Clemency Powers The right to pardon or commute the sentence of convicted persons. (Ch. 19)

Closed Primary System A primary election process in which only registered members of the party are allowed to cast ballots. Roughly half the states use this system. (Chs. 13, 17)

Cloture A rule declaring the end of a debate in the Senate. (Ch. 6)

Coercion Using force or punishment to make someone do something the person does not want to do. (Ch. 14)

Coercive Acts/Intolerable Acts A series of laws passed by the British Parliament in 1774 in response to growing unrest in the American colonies. Enforcement of these laws played a major role in precipitating the outbreak of the American Revolutionary War. The colonists called them the **Intolerable Acts.** (Ch. 2)

Cohort Replacement Natural phenomenon of generational replacement due to death. (Ch. 10)

Commercial Speech Texts such as advertising, promoting business ventures. Such speech is subject to government regulation to ensure truthfulness and to protect the public from unsafe products. (Ch. 4)

Compelled Self-Incrimination Being forced through physical abuse or other coercion to provide testimony against oneself in a criminal case, a practice that is prohibited by the Fifth Amendment. (Ch. 4)

Competitive News Markets Locales with two or more news organizations that can check each other's accuracy and neutrality of reporting. (Ch. 11)

Compulsory Referendum A requirement that all debts and liabilities over $3 million and constitutional amendments that originate in the state legislature must be passed by a two-thirds vote of each house and approved by a majority of the voters during the next election. (Ch. 17)

Concurring Opinion Appellate court opinion by judge who endorses the outcome decided by the majority of judges, but wants to express different reasons to justify that outcome. (Ch. 9)

Conference Committee A committee of members of the House and Senate that irons out differences in similar measures that have passed both houses to create a single bill. (Chs. 6, 18)

Confidence Level The probability that the results found in the sample represent the true opinion of the entire public under study. (Ch. 10)

Congressional Budget Office (CBO) The research arm of Congress, a major player in budget creation. (Ch. 14)

Connecticut Compromise See *Great Compromise.* (Ch. 2)

Conscience Model of Representation The philosophy that legislators should follow the will of the people until they truly believe it is in the best interests of the nation to act differently. (Ch. 6)

Consent Search An individual may consent to a search of his or her person or premises by law enforcement officers who do not have a warrant. (Ch. 19)

Conservatism A modern update of classical liberalism. (Ch. 14)

Conservatives People who believe in limiting government spending, preserving traditional patterns of relationships, and that big government is a threat to personal liberties. (Ch. 10)

Constituent Service A legislator's responsiveness to the questions and concerns of the people he or she represents. (Ch. 6)

Constitutional Convention A meeting in Philadelphia in 1787 at which delegates from the colonies drew up a new system of government. The finished product was the Constitution of the United States. (Ch. 2)

Constitutional Government A political system in which leaders are subject to both procedural checks and institutional limits. The United States has a constitutional government. (Ch. 2)

Constitutional Monarchy A political system in which the king or queen performs ceremonial duties but plays little or no role in actually governing the country. (Ch. 2)

Constitutional Revision Commission A commission created in 1963 to revise and reform the California constitution. (Ch. 18)

Consumer Price Index (CPI) Figure representing the cost of a specific set of goods and services tracked at regular intervals by the Department of Labor. (Ch. 14)

Containment A Cold War strategy that sought to control and encircle the Soviet Union rather than defeat it militarily. (Ch. 15)

Contract Cities Incorporated or independent cities that contract with counties for the provision of major municipal services. (Ch. 21)

Controller The state's chief financial officer; responsible for all financial transactions involving the state government and local jurisdictions. (Ch. 19)

Corpus Delicti The elements of a crime. (Ch. 20)

Cooperative Federalism A system in which the powers of the federal and state government are intertwined and shared. Each level of government shares overlapping power, authority, and responsibility. (Ch. 3)

Corrupt Bargain of 1824 The alleged secret agreement in the disputed election of 1824 that led the House of Representatives to select John Quincy Adams, who had come in second in the popular vote, as president if he would make Speaker of the House Henry Clay his secretary of state. (Ch. 13)

Council-Manager Model A model of city government that emphasizes the political leadership and policymaking qualities of the council as a whole while vesting administrative authority in a full-time, professional manager. (Ch. 21)

Council of Economic Advisers (CEA) A group of economists within the Executive Office of the President, appointed by the president to provide advice on economic policy. (Ch. 7)

Councils of Government (COGS) Regional organizations that bring municipal and county governments together to address common issues and problems. (Ch. 21)

County Administrator The official responsible for providing the board of supervisors with reports and information and for managing the day-to-day operations of county government. (Ch. 21)

County Board of Supervisors The group responsible for implementing the provisions of a county's charter. (Ch. 21)

County Clerk The officer responsible for the public records of a county. (Ch. 21)

County Grand Jury In California, a jury that investigates public offenses that were committed or are triable within the county. (Ch. 20)

Court of Appeals A court that has the power to consider or hear an appeal. (Ch. 20)

Court-Packing Plan President Franklin D. Roosevelt's unsuccessful proposal in 1937 to permit the appointment of additional justices to the U.S. Supreme Court. (Chs. 3, 9)

Court of Last Resort The highest courts in each American court system, typically called supreme courts, that hear selected appeals from the lower courts. (Ch. 9)

Covert Action Efforts to secretly influence affairs in another state, which may include propaganda, disinformation campaigns, bribery, fomenting political and economic unrest, and, in the extreme, assassination. (Ch. 15)

Creative Federalism A system in which the role of the federal government is expanded by providing financial incentives for states to follow congressional initiatives. (Ch. 3)

Criminal Law A body of law that applies to violations against rules and regulations defined by the government. (Ch. 20)

Criminal Prosecutions Legal processes in which the government seeks to prove that an individual is guilty of a crime and deserving of punishment for it. (Ch. 9)

Crosscutting Cleavages Divisions in society that separate people into groups. (Ch. 10)

Cross-Filing A system that allows a candidate to represent multiple parties. (Ch. 17)

D

Decentralization Proposed reform for government agencies intended to increase efficiency in administration and create closer contacts with the local public; permits regional and local offices to manage their own performances without close supervision from headquarters. (Ch. 8)

Decisions Court rulings that interpret the meaning of policy. (Ch. 14)

Defamation In law, false, harmful statements either through spoken words (*slander*) or through written words (*libel*). (Ch. 4)

Deflation A decrease in prices over time. (Ch. 14)

Delegate Model of Representation The philosophy that legislators should adhere to the will of their constituents. (Ch. 6)

Democracy A political system in which all citizens have a chance to play a role in shaping government action and are afforded basic rights and liberties. (Chs. 1, 2)

Democratic-Republicans The first American political party, formed by believers in states' rights and followers of Thomas Jefferson. (Ch. 13)

Department Any of the 15 major government agencies responsible for specific policy areas whose heads are usually called secretaries and serve in the president's cabinet. (Ch. 8)

Deregulation The removal of government restrictions on businesses or industries. (Ch. 17)

Détente Reduction of tension or strained relations between previously hostile nations. (Ch. 15)

Determinate Sentence The choices for punishment for a crime that can be imposed by a judge. (Ch. 20)

Deterrence A military strategy associated with the Cold War that sought to prevent an unwanted military action from taking place by raising the prospect of large-scale retaliation. (Ch. 15)

Devolution The transfer of jurisdiction and fiscal responsibility for particular programs from the federal government to state or local governments. (Ch. 3)

Dictator The sole ruler of a political system with the power to control most or all actions of government. (Ch. 2)

Dillon's Rule Iowa state court decision in 1868 that narrowly defined the power of local governments and established the supremacy of state governments when conflict exists with localities. Subsequently upheld by the Supreme Court. (Ch. 3)

Direct Contact Face-to-face meetings or telephone conversations between individuals. (Ch. 12)

Direct Democracy Through the leadership of the California Progressives a constitutional amendment was passed by voters that provided for direct participation in government. (Ch. 16)

Direct Initiative An initiative that allows voters to propose and enact a law or constitutional amendment without the intervention of the state legislature. (Ch. 17)

Direct Mail Information mailed to a large number of people to advertise, market concepts, or solicit support. (Ch. 12)

Direct Primary Election Primary election in which rank-and-file members (average citizens) vote to select their candidates. (Chs. 13, 17)

Discount Rate The rate the Fed charges member banks for shortterm loans. (Ch. 14)

Direct-Mail Piece Advertising pieces mailed to voters that are created by using sophisticated technologies and techniques that have often been tested through focus groups. (Ch. 17)

Discretion The power to apply policy in ways that fit particular circumstances. (Ch. 14)

Dissenting Opinion Appellate court opinion explaining the views of one or more judges who disagree with the outcome of the case as decided by the majority of judges. (Ch. 9)

Distribution Government providing things of value to specific groups. (Ch. 14)

District Attorney Elected official who prosecutes more serious criminal offenses, usually felonies, before state district courts. (Ch. 20)

Disturbance Theory The idea that interest groups form when resources become scarce in order to contest the influence of other interest groups. (Ch. 12)

Doctrine of Nullification Theory that state governments had a right to rule any federal law unconstitutional and therefore null and void in that state. The doctrine was ruled unconstitutional but served as a source of southern rebellion, contributing to the secession of southern states from the Union and ultimately the Civil War. (Ch. 3)

Doctrine of Secession The theory that state governments had a right to declare their independence and create their own form of government. Eleven southern states seceded from the Union in 1860–1861, created their own government (the Confederate States of America), and thereby precipitated the Civil War. (Ch. 3)

Double Jeopardy Being tried twice for the same crime, a practice prohibited by the Fifth Amendment. (Ch. 4)

Drug Court An alternative criminal justice venue for drug law offenders. (Ch. 20)

Dual Court System Separate systems of state and federal courts throughout the United States. Each state court system is responsible for interpreting the laws and constitution of that specific state, while the federal courts are responsible for the U.S. Constitution and laws enacted by Congress. (Ch. 9)

Dual Federalism A theory stating that the powers of the federal and state governments are strictly separate, with interaction often marked by tension rather than cooperation. (Ch. 3)

Due Process Clause A statement of rights in the Fifth Amendment (aimed at the federal government) and the Fourteenth Amendment (aimed at state and local governments) that protects against arbitrary deprivations of life, liberty, or property. The Fourteenth Amendment phrase is also interpreted by the Supreme Court to expand a variety of rights. (Ch. 4)

E

Earmarks/Pork-Barrel Legislation Legislation that benefits one state or district; also called *particularized legislation*. (Ch. 6)

Earned Media Coverage Airtime provided free of charge to candidates for political office. (Ch. 11)

Efficacy The belief that individuals can influence government. *Internal political efficacy* is the belief that individuals have the knowledge and ability to influence government. *External political efficacy* refers to the belief that governmental officials will respond to individuals. (Ch. 10)

Egalitarianism A doctrine of equality that ignores differences in social status, wealth, and privilege. (Ch. 12)

Elastic Clause/Necessary and Proper Clause A statement in Article I, Section 8, of the U.S. Constitution that grants Congress the power to pass all laws "necessary and proper" for carrying out the list of expressed powers. (Ch. 6)

Electoral Behavior Any activity broadly linked to the outcome of a political campaign. (Ch. 13)

Electoral College The procedure for selecting the president and vice president of the United States, defined in Article II of the Constitution, whereby the voters in each state choose electors to attend a gathering where the electors make the final decision. (Ch. 13)

Electronic Voting Machines With the encouragement of the federal government, California has attempted to modernize the election process with the introduction of electronic voting machines, which in theory would provide faster and more accurate methods of voting and tabulating results. (Ch. 17)

Elite Democratic Model The view that a democracy is healthy if people acquire positions of power through competitive elections. The level of involvement by citizens in this process is unimportant so long as elections are fair. (Ch. 13)

Elitism The theory that a select few—better educated, more informed, and more interested—should have more influence than others in our governmental process. (Ch. 10)

Entitlements Government expenditures required by law. (Ch. 14)

Equality of Condition A conception of equality that exists in some countries that value equal economic status as well as equal access to housing, health care, education, and government services. (Ch. 5)

Equality of Opportunity A conception of equality that seeks to provide all citizens with opportunities for participation in the economic system and public life but accepts unequal results in income, political power, and property ownership. (Chs. 5, 10)

Equality of Outcome An egalitarian belief that government must work to diminish differences between individuals in society so that everyone is equal in status and value. (Ch. 10)

Equal Time Rule An FCC rule requiring the broadcast media to offer all major candidates competing for a political office equal airtime. (Ch. 11)

Establishment Clause A clause in the First Amendment guaranteeing freedom from religion by providing a basis for Supreme Court decisions limiting government support for and endorsement of particular religions. (Ch. 4)

Excise Tax A sales tax imposed only on specific goods. (Ch. 22)

Exclusionary Rule A general principle stating that evidence obtained illegally cannot be used against a defendant in a criminal prosecution. The Supreme Court has allowed certain exceptions to the rule in particular circumstances. (Ch. 4)

Executive Agreement Binding commitments between the United States and other countries agreed to by the president but, unlike treaties, not requiring approval by the Senate. (Ch. 7)

Executive Branch Branch of government responsible for carrying out laws. (Ch. 19)

Executive Budget Plan The spending plan for the state of California that the governor must submit to the state legislature by January 10th each year. (Ch. 22)

Executive Office of the President (EOP) A group of presidential staff agencies created in 1939 that provides the president with help and advice. (Ch. 7)

Executive Order A regulation made by the president that has the effect of law. (Ch. 7)

Executive Order 9066 Franklin Roosevelt's 1942 order that resulted in the relocation and internment of Japanese legal aliens and American citizens of Japanese descent. (Ch. 16)

Exit Polls Surveys of voters leaving polling places; used by news media to gauge how candidates are doing on election day. (Ch. 10)

Expressed Powers The powers explicitly granted to the national government in the U.S. Constitution. (Ch. 2)

Extraordinary Session A special session of the state legislature called by the governor for a specific purpose. (Ch. 19)

F

Fairness Doctrine Policy that required television and radio broadcasters to provide time for opposing viewpoints on controversial issues so as to ensure fair and balanced reporting; formally abolished in 1987. (Ch. 11)

Federal Election Campaign Act (FECA) A law designed to limit the amount of money contributed to campaigns for Congress and the presidency and to broaden donation reporting requirements. (Ch. 13)

Federal Funds Rate The interest rate that banks charge each other for overnight loans. (Ch. 14)

The Federalist Papers A series of 85 essays in support of ratification of the U.S. Constitution that were written by James Madison, Alexander Hamilton, and John Jay and published under the byline Publius in New York City newspapers between October 27, 1787, and May 28, 1788. (Ch. 2)

Federalist Party Founded by Alexander Hamilton, its members believed in a strong, centralized government and supported the Washington and Adams administrations. (Ch. 13)

Federalists Supporters of the ratification of the U.S. Constitution. (Ch. 2)

Federal Open Market Committee (FOMC) The policymaking arm of the Federal Reserve Board of Governors. (Ch. 14)

Federal Reserve System (the Fed) The independent central bank of the United States. (Ch.14)

Felonies Crimes for which a person may be sentenced to imprisonment in the state prison or execution. (Ch. 20)

Fifteenth Amendment (1870) A change to the Constitution that guarantees the right to vote shall not be denied to anyone on the basis of race. (Ch. 13)

Filibuster A process in the U.S. Senate used to block or delay voting on proposed legislation or on an appointment of a judge or other official by talking continuously. Sixty senators must vote to end a filibuster. (Chs. 6, 9)

Fiscal Policy Taxation and spending decisions made by the government. (Ch. 14)

Flexible Interpretation An approach to interpreting the U.S. Constitution that permits the meaning of the document to change with evolving values, social conditions, and problems. (Ch. 9)

Focusing Events Moments that capture attention and highlight the existence of a problem. (Ch. 14)

Formula Grants Specific type of categorical grant in which money is allocated and distributed based upon a prescribed formula. (Ch. 3)

Fourteenth Amendment (1868) A change to the Constitution that defines the meaning of U.S. citizenship and establishes that each state must guarantee equal protection of the laws to its citizens. (Ch. 13)

Franchise Tax Board The board that sets tax rates for banks and financial institutions in California. (Ch. 22)

Freedom A core value, usually expressed as either "freedom from" (negative) or "freedom to" (positive). (Ch. 14)

Free Exercise Clause A clause in the First Amendment guaranteeing freedom to practice one's religion without government interference as long as those practices do not harm other individuals or society. (Ch. 4)

Free-Rider Problem The fact that public goods can be enjoyed by everyone, including people who do not pay their fair share of the cost for providing those goods. (Ch. 12)

French and Indian War The nine-year conflict (1754–1763) in North America that pitted Great Britain and its North American colonies against France. France lost, and the British maintained control of much of North America. (Ch. 2)

G

Gaining Access Winning the opportunity to communicate directly with a legislator or a legislative staff member to present one's position on an issue of public policy. (Ch. 12)

Gatekeepers A group or individuals who determine which stories will receive attention in the media and from which perspective. (Ch. 11)

Gender Gap Differences in voting and policy preferences between women and men. (Ch. 10)

General Election An election in which candidates compete directly for election to a given office. (Ch. 17)

General Fund The pool of money used to finance the California state government. (Ch. 22)

General Law A basic template that lists the duties, obligations, offices, and structure of county government. (Ch. 21)

General Obligation Bonds State debt that is backed by the "full faith and credit of the state." (Ch. 17)

Genocide The deliberate and systematic extinction of an ethnic or cultural group. (Ch. 15)

Geographic Representation The idea that a legislator should represent the interests of the people living in a specific geographic location. (Ch. 6)

Gerrymandering Drawing legislative district boundaries in such a way as to gain political advantage. (Ch. 6)

Globalization The expansion of economic interactions between countries. (Ch. 15)

Going Public Appealing directly to the people to garner support for presidential initiatives. (Ch. 7)

Government Corporations Agencies with independent boards and the means to generate revenue through sales of products and services, fees, or insurance premiums, and which are intended to run like private corporations. (Ch. 8)

Governor The supreme executive of a state, vested with the power to ensure that the state's laws are carried out. (Ch. 19)

Grange A farmers' political movement founded in 1867. (Ch. 16)

Grants-in-Aid Funds given from one governmental unit to another governmental unit for specific purposes. (Ch. 3)

Grassroots Lobbying See *Outside Lobbying*. (Ch. 12)

Great Compromise/Connecticut Compromise An agreement at the Constitutional Convention that the new national government would have a House of Representatives, in which the number of members would be based on each state's population, and a Senate, in which each state would have the same number of representatives. (Ch. 2)

Great Squeeze A period prior to the American Revolution when the British Parliament sought to recoup some of the costs associated with the French and Indian War by levying new taxes and fees on colonists. (Ch. 2)

Gross Domestic Product (GDP) The value of all goods and services produced in a nation. (Ch. 14)

H

Hamilton, Alexander (1755–1804) One of the framers of the Constitution and secretary of the treasury in George Washington's administration. (Ch. 7)

Hatch Act (1939) A law that limits the participation of federal employees in political campaigns. (Ch. 8)

Hearings Committee sessions for taking testimony from witnesses and for collecting information on legislation under consideration or for the development of new legislation. (Ch. 6)

Help America Vote Act A measure passed in 2002, designed to create a more uniform voting system throughout the 50 states. (Chs. 13, 19)

Hobbes, Thomas (1588–1679) An English philosopher who argued that humans are selfish by nature and live lives that are "nasty, brutish, and short." For safety, people form governments but give up certain rights. His most influential book was *Leviathan*, published in 1651. (Ch. 2)

Hold Rule that allows a senator to announce the intention to use delaying tactics if a particular piece of legislation moves to a vote. (Ch. 6)

Home Rule The right of a city with a population of more than 5,000 to adopt any form of government the residents choose, provided it does not conflict with the state constitution or statutes. (Chs. 3, 21)

I

Impeachment Process in Congress for removal of the president, federal judges, and other high officials. (Ch. 9)

Income Security The notion that the government should establish programs that provide a safety net for society's poorest members. (Ch. 14)

Incumbent Advantage The various factors that favor officeholders running for reelection over their challengers. (Ch. 13)

Independent A voter who is not registered or affiliated with any political party. (Ch. 13)

Independent Agencies Federal agencies with narrow responsibilities for a specific policy issue, such as the environment, not covered by one of the fifteen departments. (Ch. 8)

Independent Regulatory Commissions Organizational entities in the federal government that are not under the control of the president or a department. (Ch. 8)

Individualism An attitude, rooted in classical liberal theory and reinforced by the frontier tradition, that citizens are capable of taking care of themselves with minimal governmental assistance. (Ch. 10)

Inflation An increase in prices over time. (Ch. 14)

Infractions Public offenses punishable by a fine. (Ch. 20)

Initiative A process by which voters can directly propose and enact a law or constitutional amendment. (Ch. 17)

Inner Cabinet The advisers considered most important to the president—usually the secretaries of the departments of state, defense, treasury, and justice. (Ch. 7)

Inquisitorial System Legal system in most of Europe in which a judge takes an active role in questioning witnesses and seeking to discover the truth. (Ch. 9)

Inside Lobbying Appealing directly to lawmakers and legislative staff either in meetings, by providing research and information, or by testifying at committee hearings. (Ch. 12)

Institutional Agenda A set of problems that governmental decision makers are actively working to solve. (Ch. 14)

Institutional Presidency The concept of the presidency as a working collectivity, a massive network of staff, analysts, and advisers with the president as its head. (Ch. 7)

Intelligence Gathering and analyzing information and communications, often secret, about potential enemies and other national security matters. (Ch. 15)

Interactive Theory The theory that popular culture both shapes and reflects popular opinion. (Ch. 10)

Interest Group A group of likeminded individuals who band together to influence public policy, public opinion, or governmental officials. (Ch. 12)

Intermediate Appellate Courts Courts that examine allegations concerning uncorrected errors that occurred during trials; such courts exist in the federal court system (circuit courts of appeals) and in most state court systems (usually called courts of appeals). (Ch. 9)

Intolerable Acts See *Coercive Acts.* (Ch. 2)

Investigative Reporting A type of journalism in which reporters thoroughly investigate a subject matter (often involving a scandal) to inform the public, correct an injustice, or expose an abuse. (Ch. 11)

Invisible Primary A process that involves raising money and attracting media attention early in the election process, usually before the primary election year. (Ch. 13)

Iran-Contra Affair The Reagan administration's unauthorized diversion of funds from the sale of arms to Iran to support the Contras, rebels fighting to overthrow the leftist government of Nicaragua. (Ch. 7)

Iron Triangle The tight relationships between employees in government agencies, interest groups, and legislators and their staff members, all of whom share an interest in specific policy issues and work together behind the scenes to shape laws and public policy. (Ch. 8)

Issue-Attention Cycle The pattern of problems quickly gathering attention but then failing to remain in the spotlight. (Ch. 14)

Issue Networks (Policy Communities) Interest groups, scholars, and experts that communicate about, debate, and interact regarding issues of interest and thus influence public policy when the legislature acts on those issues. (Ch. 8)

J

Jihadists Participants in a crusade or holy war, especially in defense of Islam. (Ch. 15)

Jim Crow Laws Laws enacted by southern state legislatures after the Civil War that mandated rigid racial segregation. (Ch. 5)

Joint Committees Units that conduct oversight or issue research but do not have legislative power. (Chs. 6, 18)

Joint Rules Guidelines for cooperation between the two chambers of the legislature. (Ch. 18)

Judicial Act of 1789 Early statute in which Congress provided the initial design of the federal court system. (Ch. 9)

Judicial Council The body that governs California's courts. (Ch. 20)

Judicial Review The power of American judges to nullify decisions and actions by other branches of government, if the judges decide those actions violate the U.S. Constitution or the relevant state constitution. (Ch. 7)

"Juice Bills" Bills written to benefit a particular group, usually engaged in business. (Ch. 18)

Jury Trials Trials in which factual determinations, decisions about guilt (criminal cases), and imposition of liability (civil cases) are made by a body of citizens drawn from the community. (Ch. 9)

K

King, Martin Luther, Jr. (1929–1968) A civil rights leader who emerged from the Montgomery bus boycott to become a national leader of the civil rights movement and a recipient of the Nobel Peace Prize. (Ch. 5)

Kyoto Protocol An international agreement to address the problem of global warming. The United States was involved in its negotiation but has refused to ratify the agreement, citing excessive economic costs. (Ch. 15)

L

Labor Union An association of workers formed to promote collective interests, such as fair pay and working conditions. (Ch. 11)

Laffer Curve An economic model that maintains that a higher rate of taxation can result in lower government revenues. (Ch. 14)

***Lawrence* v. *Texas* (2003)** U.S. Supreme Court decision invalidating state laws regulating consenting noncommercial, private sexual conduct between adults as violations of the constitutional right to privacy. Many such laws had been enforced against gays and lesbians. (Ch. 4)

Laws Rules created or recognized by government. (Ch.14)

Legal Model An approach to analyzing judicial decision making that focuses on the analysis of case precedent and theories of interpretation. (Ch. 9)

Legislative Analyst's Office (LAO) The office responsible for analyzing the California state budget and making recommendations to the state legislature regarding the fiscal efficiency of state government. (Ch. 22)

***Lemon* Test** A three-part test for establishment clause violations deriving from the U.S. Supreme Court's decision in *Lemon* v. *Kurtzman* (1971), which examines whether government policies or practices provide support for religion or cause an excessive entanglement between government and religion. (Ch. 4)

Libel The publication of false and malicious material that defames an individual's reputation. (Ch. 11)

Liberal A person who generally supports governmental action to promote equality, favors governmental intervention in the economy, and supports environmental issues. (Ch. 10)

Libertarians People who support individual liberty over government authority in economic, personal, and social realms. (Ch. 10)

Libertarian View The idea that the media should be allowed to publish information that they deem newsworthy or of interest to the public without regard to the social consequences of doing so. (Ch. 11)

Lieutenant Governor The official who serves as acting governor when the governor is unable to carry out his or her duties. (Ch. 19)

Line-Item Veto Power The power to veto individual items in a larger law. (Ch. 19)

Local Agency Formation Commission (LAFCO) A county-wide commission that conducts studies and public hearings to determine the feasibility of establishing a new city. (Ch. 21)

Local and Regional Media Outlets Media outlets, such as radio, television, and newspapers, have the additional pressure of having to cover the election process at a time when their parent companies are more inclined to favor entertainment programming over news. (Ch. 17)

Locke, John (1632–1704) An English political theorist who introduced the notion of a "social contract" under which all just governments derive their powers from the consent of the governed. Locke's writings provided the theoretical framework of Thomas Jefferson's Declaration of Independence and the entire Revolutionary movement in America. (Ch. 2)

Logrolling See *reciprocity*. (Ch. 6)

M

Majority Leader The head of the majority party in the Senate; the second-highest-ranking member of the majority party in the House. (Ch. 6)

Majority-Minority District Voting districts in which members of a minority group make up the majority of the population. (Ch. 6)

Majority Opinion Appellate court opinion that explains the reasons for the case outcome as determined by a majority of judges. (Ch. 9)

Manifest Destiny The belief that the United States had a divinely inspired mission to span the continent of North America. (Ch. 16)

Mapp v. *Ohio* 1961) U.S. Supreme Court decision that applied the exclusionary rule to state criminal justice cases. (Ch. 4)

Marbury v. *Madison* (1803) A case in which the U.S. Supreme Court asserted the power of judicial review, despite the fact that the concept is not explicitly mentioned in the U.S. Constitution. (Ch. 9)

Margin of Error A measurement of the accuracy of the results of a survey to establish a range in which we think that the actual percentage of favorable ratings will fall. (Ch. 10)

Marginal Tax Bracket The tax rate you pay on the last dollar that you earn in a given year. (Ch. 14)

Marketplace of Ideas The concept that ideas and theories compete for acceptance among the public. (Ch. 11)

Markup The section-by-section review and revision of a bill by committee members; the actual writing of a piece of legislation. (Ch. 6)

Marshall Plan The massive post–World War II foreign aid program of the United States that helped speed Western Europe's economic recovery and block the spread of communism. (Ch. 15)

Material Benefits Benefits that have concrete value or worth. (Ch. 12)

Mayflower Compact An agreement made by the male pilgrims aboard the Mayflower in 1620 that provided for the temporary government of the Plymouth Colony. The document created a government that was designed to promote the general good of the colony. (Ch. 2)

May Revise A revised projection of California's financial picture conducted by the head of the state Department of Finance and economists from private industry. (Ch. 22)

McCulloch v. *Maryland* (1819) U.S. Supreme Court decision that defined the respective powers of the state and federal governments. Written by Chief Justice John Marshall, the opinion established that the Constitution grants to Congress implied powers for implementing the Constitution's express powers in order to create a functional national government, and that state action may not impede valid constitutional exercises of power by the Federal government. (Ch. 3)

McNamara Doctrine A view that military power can be applied to situations in controlled and limited amounts that rise over time and that public support should not be a major factor governing its use. (Ch. 15)

Medicaid Health care coverage for the poor. (Ch.14)

Medicare Health care coverage for senior citizens. (Ch. 14)

Mello-Roos Community Facilities District Act A financing tool that local governments can use to levy special taxes or assessments for designated community improvements, such as freeway interchanges, library services, or recreation programs. (Ch. 22)

Merit Selection A proposal under which the governor would appoint state judges from lists compiled by committees of experts. Appointed judges would have to run later in retention elections to keep their seats but would not have opponents on the ballot. (Ch. 9)

Millennium Challenge Account A major U.S. foreign policy initiative that seeks to tie foreign aid to improved government performance in the areas of democratization and economic development. (Ch. 15)

Miller v. *California* (1973) U.S. Supreme Court decision that provided the primary test for obscenity to determine what materials, especially pornography, can be regulated as outside of the protection of the First Amendment. (Ch. 4)

Minority Leader The leading spokesperson and legislative strategist for the minority party in the House or the Senate. (Ch. 6)

Miranda v. *Arizona* (1966) A U.S. Supreme Court decision that requires police officers, before questioning a suspect in custody, to inform that suspect about the right to remain silent and to have a lawyer present during custodial questioning. (Ch. 4)

Misdemeanors Crimes for which a person may be imprisoned in a county jail, usually for a year or less, and/or fined. (Ch. 20)

Modern Liberalism (Progressivism) A political philosophy based on the belief that government is the best actor to solve social, economic, and political problems. (Ch. 14)

Modern Presidency A political system in which the president is the central figure and participates actively in both foreign and domestic policy. (Ch. 7)

Monarchy A system of hereditary rule in which one person, a king or queen, has absolute authority over the government. (Ch. 2)

Monetary Policy Money supply management conducted by the Federal Reserve. (Ch. 14)

Monopolies Exclusive control by companies over most or all of a particular industry. (Ch. 3)

Motor Voter Law A law passed by Congress in 1993 designed to make it easier for Americans to register to vote. (Ch. 13)

Muckraking Investigating and exposing societal ills such as corruption in politics or abuses in business. (Ch. 11)

Multi-Issue Interest Group A group that is interested in pursuing a broad range of public policy issues. (12)

Multiple Referrals The process of assigning a new bill to several committees at the same time. (Ch. 6)

Municipal Advisory Councils (MACs) A group formed by the citizens of unincorporated areas to provide representation in matters affecting their communities. (Ch. 21)

N

Narrowcasting Creating and broadcasting highly specialized programming that is designed to appeal to a specified subgroup rather than to the general population. (Ch. 11)

National Association for the Advancement of Colored People (NAACP) Civil rights advocacy group founded by African Americans and their white supporters in 1909; used the court pathway to fight racial discrimination in the 1930s through the 1950s and later emphasized the election and lobbying pathways. (Ch. 5)

National Debt The nation's cumulative deficits. (Ch. 14)

National Nominating Convention A meeting of delegates from communities across the nation to discuss candidates' qualifications, choose their party's nominee, and adopt a party platform. (Ch. 13)

National Security Adviser The chief adviser to the president on national security matters; a lead member of the National Security Council. (Ch. 7)

National Security Council (NSC) An organization within the Executive Office of the President to advise the president on foreign and domestic military policies related to national security. (Ch. 7)

National Voter Registration Act Law designed to make it easier for voters to register to vote and to maintain their registration. (Ch. 17)

Natural Rights Basic rights that no government can deny. (Ch. 2)

Necessary and Proper Clause See *Elastic Clause.* (Chs. 3, 6)

Neoconservatives People who believe that the United States has a special role to play in world politics; they advocate the unilateral use of force and the pursuit of a value-based foreign policy. (Ch. 15)

Neoliberals People who believe that cooperation is possible through the creation and management of international institutions, organizations, and regimes. (Ch. 15)

New Deal Programs designed by President Franklin D. Roosevelt to bring economic recovery from the Great Depression by expanding the role of the federal government in providing employment opportunities and social services; advanced social reforms to serve the needs of the people, greatly expanding the budget and activity of the federal government. (Chs. 3, 7)

New Institutionalism An approach to understanding judicial decision making that emphasizes the importance of courts' structures and processes as well as courts' roles within the governing system. (Ch. 9)

New Jersey Plan A scheme for government advanced at the Constitutional Convention that was supported by delegates from smaller states. It called for equal representation of states in a unicameral legislature. (Ch. 2)

News Briefings A public appearance by a governmental official for the purpose of releasing information to the press. (Ch. 11)

News Conferences A media event, often staged, where reporters ask questions of politicians or other celebrities. (Ch. 11)

News Monopolies Single news firms that control all the media in a given market. (Ch. 11)

***New York Times Company v. United States* (1971)** U.S. Supreme Court decision prohibiting prior restraint of the Pentagon Papers, thus permitting major newspapers to publish information on the Vietnam War that the government had sought to keep secret. (Ch. 4)

Nineteenth Amendment (1920) A change to the Constitution that granted women the right to vote. (Ch. 13)

No Child Left Behind Act (NCLB) A federal law imposing educational reform throughout the country by requiring all schools to adopt student proficiency standards. (Ch. 21)

Nomination Caucus A meeting of party activists to choose delegates to support candidates at their party's presidential nominating convention. (Ch. 13)

Nominees The individuals selected by a party to run for office under that party's label. (Ch. 13)

Nonpartisan Elections Elections in which candidates are not identified by party affiliation. (Ch. 17)

North Atlantic Treaty Organization (NATO) A military alliance set up by the United States and its Western European allies initially for the purpose of containing the expansion of the former Soviet Union. (Ch. 15)

O

Office of Management and Budget (OMB) A cabinet-level office that monitors federal agencies and provides the president with expert advice on policy-related topics. (Ch. 7)

Oligarchy A government run by a small group of people. (Ch. 2)

One-House Bill A bill that is passed in only one house of Congress. (Ch. 6)

Open-Market Operations The buying and selling of securities by the Federal Reserve Board to manipulate the money supply. (Ch. 14)

Open Primary System A primary election process in which voters are allowed to cast ballots in the primary election without declaring which party they are voting for. (Ch. 13)

Orientation Function The job of familiarizing a new member of Congress with the procedures, norms, and customs of the chamber. (Ch. 6)

Original Jurisdiction The authority of a court to try or resolve a case being heard for the first time. (Ch. 9)

Outside Lobbying (Grassroots Lobbying) Activities directed at the general public to raise awareness and interest and to pressure officials. (Ch. 12)

Oversight The responsibility of Congress to keep an eye on agencies in the federal bureaucracy to ensure that their behavior conforms to its wishes. (Ch. 6)

Oversight Function The responsibility for supervising the implementation of all laws and the government officials charged with implementing them. (Ch. 18)

P

Paine, Thomas (1737–1809) An American revolutionary writer and a democratic philosopher whose pamphlet *Common Sense* (1776) argued for complete independence from Britain. (Ch. 2)

Partisan Elections Elections in which candidates are identified by party affiliation. (Ch. 17)

Party Caucuses Legislators from the same party who meet to establish group goals, policies, and strategies. (Ch. 18)

Party Identification A belief that one belongs to a certain party. (Ch. 13)

Party Presses Newspapers popular in the early nineteenth century that were highly partisan and often influenced by political party machines. (Ch. 11)

Party Unity Score A numerical measure of how often members of the same party vote together on legislation. (Ch. 6)

Pathways of Action The activities of citizens in American politics that affect the creation, alteration, and preservation of laws and policies. (Ch. 1)

Patronage System (Spoils System) A system that rewards the supporters of successful political candidates and parties with government jobs while firing supporters of the opposing party. (Ch. 8)

Patrons Organizations or individuals that contribute money to political leaders or political groups. (Ch. 12)

Payroll Tax A tax on earnings that funds Social Security and Medicare. (Ch. 14)

Penny Press Cheap newspapers containing sensationalized stories sold to members of the working class in the late nineteenth and early twentieth centuries. (Ch. 11)

Personal Presidency The notion that there are greater and greater expectations placed on presidents, due in large measure to the way they run for office. At the same time, presidents are often unable to deliver on the promises they made during campaigns. (Ch. 7)

Petition Referendum A procedure that allows voters to request that all or part of a law be submitted to the voters for approval. (Ch. 17)

Phillips Curve An economic model that assumes an inverse relationship between unemployment and inflation. (Ch. 14)

Pilgrims The name commonly applied to the early settlers of the Plymouth Colony who had left England in 1620 aboard the Mayflower. (Ch. 2)

Planning Commission A group of local residents who have been appointed by the city council to review the adoption and administration of zoning laws and building regulations. (Ch. 21)

Platform The set of issues, principles, and goals that a party supports. (Ch. 13)

Plea Bargaining The process of negotiating a resolution to a criminal case in which the defendant enters a guilty plea in exchange for a less-than-maximum sentence. (Ch. 4)

Plea Bargains Negotiated resolution of a criminal case in which the defendant enters a guilty plea in exchange for a reduction in the nature or number of charges or for a less-than-maximum sentence. (Chs. 9, 20)

***Plessy v. Ferguson* (1896)** A U.S. Supreme Court decision that endorsed the legality of racial segregation laws by permitting "separate but equal" services and facilities for African Americans, even though the services and facilities were actually inferior. (Ch. 5)

Plural Executive The group of independently elected officials responsible for carrying out the laws of a state. (Ch. 19)

Pluralism A system of government in which multiple competing and responsive groups vie for power. (Ch. 2)

Pluralists People who believe that power is widely distributed in a society. (Ch. 14)

Pocket Veto The president's killing of a bill that has been passed by both houses of Congress, simply by not signing it; occurs only if Congress has adjourned within 10 days of the bill's passage. (Ch. 6)

Police Powers The powers reserved to state governments related to the health, safety, and well-being of citizens. (Ch. 2)

Policy Categories A way of classifying policies by their intended goal and means of carrying out that goal. (Ch. 14)

Policy Communities See *Issue Networks*. (Ch. 8)

Policy Process Model A way of thinking about how policy is made in terms of steps in a progression. (Ch. 14)

Political Contribution Contributors to campaigns can be found at every level of government in California. Many Californians consider political contributions as nothing more than payoffs, while others feel such contributions are a legitimate form of charitable giving. (Ch. 17)

Political Culture The norms, customs, and beliefs that help citizens understand appropriate ways to act in a political system; also, the shared attitudes about how government should operate. (Ch. 10)

Political Equality Fundamental value underlying the governing system of the United States that emphasizes all citizens' opportunities to vote, run for public office, own property, and enjoy civil liberties protections under the Constitution. (Ch. 5)

Political Ideology A consistent set of beliefs that forms a general philosophy regarding the proper goals, purposes, functions, and size of government. (Ch. 10)

Political Party Work Much of this work is focused on the electoral process and getting fellow party members elected to public office. (Ch. 17)

Political Socialization The conscious and unconscious transmission of political culture and values from one generation to another. (Ch. 10)

Political Speech Expressions concerning politics, government, public figures, and issues of public concern—the form of expression that contemporary commentators view as most deserving of First Amendment protection. (Ch. 4)

Politico Model of Representation The philosophy that legislators should follow their own judgment (that is, act like a trustee) until the public becomes vocal about a particular matter, at which point they should follow the dictates of constituents. (Ch. 6)

Politics The process by which the actions of government are determined. (Ch. 1)

Popular Democratic Model A view of democracy that stresses the ongoing involvement of average citizens in the political process. (Ch. 13)

Populists People who believe that the government can be a positive agent to protect "common people" against the moneyed elite. (Ch. 10)

Pork-Barrel Legislation See *Earmarks*. (Ch. 6)

Powell Doctrine A view that cautions against the use of military force, especially where public support is limited, but states that once the decision to use force has been made, military power should be applied quickly and decisively. (Ch. 15)

Power The ability to exercise control over others and to get individuals, groups, and institutions to comply. (Ch. 2)

Preemption A military strategy based on striking first in self-defense. (Ch. 15)

Prerogative Power Extraordinary powers that the president may use under certain conditions. (Ch. 7)

President Pro Tempore The chief presiding officer of the Senate in the absence of the vice president. (Ch. 6)

Presidios Military Outposts during the period of Spanish colonial rule of California. (Ch. 16)

Press Releases Written statements that are given to the press to circulate information or an announcement. (Ch. 11)

Press Shield Law A statute enacted by a legislature establishing a reporter's privilege to protect the confidentiality of sources. (Ch. 4)

Prime Rate The interest rate that a bank charges its best customers. (Ch. 14)

Prior Censorship Forbidding publication of material considered objectionable. (Ch. 11)

Prior Restraint Government prohibition or prevention of the publication of information or viewpoints. Since its decision in *Near* v. *Minnesota* (1931), the U.S. Supreme Court has generally forbidden prior restraint as a violation of the First Amendment freedom of the press. (Ch. 4)

Privatization The process of turning some responsibilities of government bureaucracy over to private organizations on the assumption that they can administer and deliver services more effectively and inexpensively. (Ch. 8)

Probability Sample Selection procedure in which each member of the target population has a known or an equal chance of being selected. (Ch. 10)

Probate Law The area of law governing cases that pertain to the personal affairs of an individual. (Ch. 20)

Pro Bono Short for the Latin phrase *pro bono publico,* meaning "for the benefit of the public" and describing lawyers' representing clients without compensation as a service to society. (Ch. 9)

Professional Association Organization that represents individuals, largely educated and affluent, in one particular occupational category. (Ch. 12)

Progressive Tax A tax structured such that higher-income individuals pay a larger percentage of their income in taxes. (Ch. 14)

Progressivism (Modern Liberalism) A political philosophy based on the belief that government is the best actor to solve social, economic, and political problems. (Ch. 14)

Project Grants A type of categorical grant in which a competitive application process is required for a specific project (often scientific or technical research or social services). (Ch. 3)

Proposition 13 The law that severely cut property taxes in California. (Ch. 16)

Proposition 36 An initiative that created a diversion program for individuals convicted of offenses. (Ch. 20)

Proposition 98 A California law requiring that 40 percent of the state general fund be reserved for education. (Ch. 19)

Proposition 103 A California law imposing the regulation of insurance rates and creating the elected position of state insurance commissioner. (Ch. 19)

Proposition 140 A constitutional initiative that established term limits for both state senators and assembly legislators. (Chs. 18, 22)

Proposition 184 The "three strikes law," which mandates a 25-year-to-life sentence for any third felony conviction for individuals previously convicted of two violent or serious felony offenses. (Ch. 20)

Proposition 220 A 1998 California constitutional amendment that consolidates superior and municipal courts into a single superior court with original jurisdiction over all cases that enter the court system. (Ch. 20)

Proslavery and Antislavery Factions The legislative representatives of these groups in Congress were eventually able to compromise and pass a bill that allowed California to become a state quickly. (Ch. 16)

Pseudo-Events Events that appear spontaneous but are in fact staged and scripted by public relations experts to appeal to the news media or the public. (Ch. 11)

Public Goods (Collective Goods) Goods that are used or consumed by all individuals in society. (Ch. 12)

Public Interest Group Citizen organization that advocates issues of public good, such as protection of the environment. (Ch. 12)

Public Opinion The attitudes of individuals regarding their political leaders and institutions as well as political and social issues. (Ch. 10)

Public Policy What government decides to do or not do; government laws, rules, or expenditures. (Ch. 1)

Pueblos Centers of trade and Spanish civilization during the period of Spanish colonial rule of California. (Ch. 16)

Purposive Benefits Intangible rewards people obtain from joining a group they support and working to advance an issue in which they believe. (Ch. 12)

R

Race to the Top A national competition that pits states against each other in the attempt to win hundreds of millions in educational dollars for the most innovative educational-reform plans. (Ch. 21)

Racial Profiling Characterized as an erroneous assumption that any particular individual of one race or ethnicity is more likely to engage in misconduct than an individual of another race or ethnicity. (Ch. 19)

"Rally 'Round the Flag" Effect The expectation that Americans will unite behind the nation's leaders in times of crisis. (Ch. 15)

Rational Party Model A political structure where the goal is to win offices for material gain and to control the distribution of government jobs. (Ch. 13)

Reapportionment The process by which seats in the House of Representatives are reassigned among the states to reflect population changes following the Census (every 10 years). (Chs. 6, 18)

Reasonable Time, Place, and Manner Restrictions Permissible government regulations on freedom of speech that seek to prevent disruptions or threats to public safety in the manner in which expressions are presented. Such regulations cannot be used to control the content of political speech. (Ch. 4)

Recall A procedure by which voters can remove an elected official from office before the end of the official's term. (Ch. 17)

Recidivism Rate The percentage of inmates who are convicted of another crime after their release from prison. (Ch. 20)

Reciprocity/Logrolling Supporting a legislator's bill in exchange for support of one's own bill. (Ch. 6)

Redistribution Government providing a broad segment of the society with something of value. (Ch. 14)

Redistricting The process of redrawing legislative district boundaries within a state to reflect population changes. (Chs. 6, 18)

Referendum A process by which voters can demand the review and approval of a particular legislative action by the voters. (Ch. 17)

Regressive Tax A tax structured such that higher-income individuals pay a lower percentage of their income in taxes; this type of tax imposes a heavier burden on low-income individuals. (Chs. 14)

Regulations Legal rules created by government agencies based on authority delegated by the legislature. (Chs. 8, 14)

Reporter's Privilege The asserted right of news reporters to promise confidentiality to their sources and to keep information obtained from sources, including evidence of criminal activity, secret. The U.S. Supreme Court has held that reporter's privilege does *not* fall within the First Amendment right to freedom of the press. (Ch. 4)

Representative Democracy A republic in which the selection of elected officials is conducted through a free and open process. (Ch. 2)

Republic A system of government in which members of the general public select agents to represent them in political decision-making. (Ch. 2)

Reserve Ratios Minimum percentage of deposits that a financial institution must keep on hand. (Ch. 14)

Residency and Registration Laws State laws that stipulate how long a person must reside in a community before being allowed to vote in that community. (Ch. 13)

Resolutions Formal statements explaining a decision or expressing an opinion. (Ch. 18)

Responsible Party Model A political structure where the goal is to shape public policy. (Ch. 13)

Right to Privacy A constitutional right created and expanded in U.S. Supreme Court decisions concerning access to contraceptives, abortion, private sexual behavior, and other matters, even though the word *privacy* does not appear in the Constitution. (Ch. 4)

Roe v. Wade (1973) Controversial U.S. Supreme Court decision that declared women have a constitutional right to choose to terminate a pregnancy in the first six months following conception. (Ch. 4)

Rotation The staggering of senatorial terms such that one-third of the Senate comes up for election every two years. (Ch. 6)

Rule-Making Authority Lawmaking power delegated to the executive branch agencies or departments. (Ch. 14)

Rules Committee Committees charged with administration of the legislature and defining its rules of operation. (Ch. 18)

S

Sample A subset of the population under study; if selected correctly, it represents the population from which it was drawn with reliable and measurable accuracy. (Ch. 10)

Secretary of State The elected official who administers state election laws, grants charters to corporations, and processes the extradition of prisoners to other states. (Ch. 19)

Select Committees Temporary committees formed to conduct investigations of issues or problems that are not specifically related to a standing committee or are of special interest to a legislator. (Chs. 6, 18)

Selective Benefits Benefits provided only to members of an organization or group. (Ch. 12)

Senatorial Courtesy Traditional deference by U.S. senators to the wishes of their colleagues concerning the appointment of individuals to federal judgeships in that state. (Ch. 9)

Senior Executive Service (SES) Program within the federal executive branch, established by Congress in 1978 to enable senior administrators with outstanding leadership and management skills to be moved between jobs in different agencies to enhance the performance of the bureaucracy. (Ch. 8)

Seniority Length of time served in a chamber of the legislature. Members with greater seniority have traditionally been granted greater power. (Ch. 6)

Separationist Interpretive approach to the establishment clause of the First Amendment that requires the clause saying a "wall of separation" exists between church and state. (Ch. 4)

Settlements Negotiated resolutions of civil lawsuits prior to trial. (Ch. 9)

Seventeenth Amendment Change to the U.S. Constitution, ratified in 1913, which provides for the direct election of senators. (Ch. 6)

Sharing of Powers The U.S. Constitution's granting of specific powers to each branch of government while making each branch also partly dependent on the others for carrying out its duties. (Ch. 2)

Shays's Rebellion An armed uprising in western Massachusetts in 1786 and 1787 by small farmers angered over high debt and tax burdens. (Ch. 2)

Sheriff The county officer whose chief duty is to enforce California state law and county ordinances, usually outside of incorporated cities. (Ch. 21)

Sierra Nevada The inland mountain range that makes up almost half of California's total land area (Ch. 16)

Signing Statement A written proclamation issued by the president regarding how the executive branch intends to interpret a new law. (Ch. 7)

Single-Issue Interest Group A group that is interested primarily in one area of public policy. (Ch. 12)

Single-Subject Rule A ruling that ballot initiatives may contain only one subject of policy (Ch. 20)

Smith, Adam (1723–1790) A Scottish political and economic philosopher whose views on free trade and capitalism were admired in colonial America. (Ch. 2)

Social Contract Theory A political theory that holds individuals give up certain rights in return for securing certain freedoms. If the government breaks the social contract, grounds for revolution exist. This notion was at the core of the Declaration of Independence. (Ch. 2)

Socialism An economic system in which the government owns and controls most factories and much or all of the nation's land. (Ch. 1)

Social Networking Sites Web-based sites that enable people and groups to connect and share information with one another. (Ch. 12)

Social Responsibility Theory (Public Advocate Model) The idea that the media should consider the overall needs of society when making decisions about what stories to cover and in what manner. (Ch. 11)

Social Security A federal program started in 1935 that taxes wages and salaries to pay for retirement benefits, disability insurance, and hospital insurance. (Ch. 7)

Social Security Trust Fund A fund to pay future Social Security benefits, supposedly being built through today's payroll tax. (Ch. 14)

Soft Money Funds contributed through a loophole in federal campaign finance regulations that allowed individuals and groups to give unlimited sums of money to political parties. (Ch. 13)

Solidary Benefits Benefits derived from fellowship and camaraderie with other members. (Ch. 12)

Sound Bites A short outtake from a longer film, speech, or interview. (Ch. 11)

Sovereignty The exclusive right of an independent state to reign supreme and base absolute power over a geographic region and its people. (Ch. 3)

Speaker The presiding officer of the House of Representatives, who is also the leader of the majority party in the House. (Ch. 6)

Special Districts Legal districts formed to meet specific needs in an area or community. (Ch. 21)

Special Election An election called to address a specific issue before the next regularly scheduled election. (Ch. 17)

Special Governments Local governmental units established for very specific purposes, such as the regulation of water and school districts, airports, and transportation services. (Ch. 3)

Specialization A norm suggesting that members of both chambers have extensive knowledge in a particular policy area. (Ch. 6)

Speedy and Public Trial A right contained in the Sixth Amendment to prevent indefinite pretrial detention and secret trials. (Ch. 4)

Spoils System A system of filling public jobs by hiring friends and other politically connected applicants, regardless of their abilities; also known as a patronage system. (Ch. 8)

Stagflation The combination of stagnant GDP, rising unemployment, and rapid inflation. (Ch. 14)

Stamp Act Congress A meeting in October 1765 of delegates from Britain's American colonies to discuss the recently passed Stamp Act. The Congress adopted a declaration of rights and wrote letters to the King and both houses of Parliament. Many historians view this gathering as a precursor of the American Revolution. (Ch. 2)

Standing Committees (Policy Committees) The permanent commitees of the legislature. (Ch. 18)

Standing Joint Committees A congressional committee composed of members from both legislative chambers. Most of its work involves investigation, research, or oversight of agencies that are closely related to Congress. (Ch. 6)

Standing Rules Rules ensuring that the legislature operates in an efficient and civil manner. (Ch. 18)

State Insurance Commissioner The official responsible for oversight of the insurance industry and enforcement of insurance regulations in California. (Ch. 19)

State Treasurer The chief banker or financial consultant to California state government, principally responsible for an accounting of state government revenue and the state government disbursements. (Ch. 19)

Statutes Laws written by state legislatures and by Congress. (Ch. 9)

Stewardship Model A theory of robust, broad presidential powers; the idea that the president is only limited by explicit restrictions in the Constitution. (Ch. 7)

Strategic Arms Limitation Talks (SALT) Negotiations between the United States and Soviet Union during the Cold War that produced two major agreements on limiting the size of each country's nuclear forces. (Ch. 15)

Strategic Voting Model A theory that Supreme Court justices vote in order to advance their preferred goals, even if it means voting contrary to their actual attitudes and values in some cases. (Ch. 9)

Strict Scrutiny An exacting test for violations of fundamental rights by requiring the government to demonstrate a compelling interest when policies and practices clash with certain constitutional rights. (Ch. 4)

Strong Mayor—Council Model A model of city government that gives the mayor direct authority over the city government, including the city manager. (Ch. 21)

Structural Budget Gap A long-term excess of state expenditures over state revenues. (Ch. 22)

Subcommittees Specialized groups within standing committees. (Ch. 6)

Superintendent of Public Instruction The elected official responsible for matters of public education in California. (Ch. 19)

Superior Courts The entry point for the enforcement of California law and the settlement of conflicts or disagreements. (Ch. 20)

Supreme Court The highest court in the state the decisions of which are binding on all lower courts. (Ch. 20)

Symbolic Representation The assumption that a legislator will represent or favor his or her own ethnic group or gender among the constituency, as opposed to the entire population; also known as *descriptive representation*. (Ch. 6)

Symbolic Speech The expression of an idea or viewpoint through an action, such as wearing an armband or burning an object. Symbolic speech can enjoy First Amendment protections. (Ch. 4)

T

Technology Gap (Digital Divide) The differences in access to and mastery of information and communication technology between segments of the community (typically for socioeconomic, educational, or geographical reasons). (Ch. 11)

Term Limits Laws stipulating the maximum number of terms that an elected official may serve in a particular office. (Ch. 13)

Test Case A case sponsored or presented by an interest group in the court pathway with the intention of influencing public policy. (Ch. 9)

Think Tank A group of individuals who conduct research in a particular subject or a particular area of public policy. (Ch. 12)

Third House Lobbyists and special-interest groups that shower the state legislature with millions of dollars and special privileges. (Ch. 18)

30-Second Advertising Spot Commonly used by well-funded political campaigns to feature television political advertisements. (Ch. 17)

Tocqueville, Alexis de A French scholar who traveled throughout the United States in the early 1830s. (Ch. 1)

Tort Law The area of law dealing with any wrongdoing that results in legal action for damages. (Ch. 20)

Totalitarian Regime A system of government in which the ruling elite holds all power and controls all aspects of society. (Chs. 1, 2)

Transcontinental Railroad Railroad completed in 1869 that linked the East and West Coast of North America. (Ch. 16)

Treaty A formal agreement between governments. (Ch. 7)

Trial by Jury A right contained in the Sixth Amendment to have criminal guilt decided by a body of citizens drawn from the community. (Ch. 4)

Trigger Mechanism The means, often tied to focusing events, to push a recognized problem further along in the policy cycle. (Ch. 14)

Tripartite View of Parties A model based on the theory that parties have three related elements: party-in-government, party-in-the-electorate, and party-as-organization. (Ch. 13)

Trustee Model of Representation The philosophy that legislators should consider the will of the people but act in ways they believe best for the long-term interests of the nation. (Ch. 6)

Turnout The percentage of citizens legally eligible to vote in an election who actually vote in that election. (Ch. 13)

Twelfth Amendment (1804) A change to the Constitution that required a separate vote tally in the electoral college for president and vice president. (Ch. 13)

Twenty-Fourth Amendment (1964) A change to the Constitution that eliminated the poll tax. (Ch. 13)

Twenty-Sixth Amendment (1971) A change to the Constitution that granted 18-year-old citizens the right to vote. (Ch. 13)

U

Unanimous Consent Agreement of all senators on the terms of debate, required before a bill goes to the floor. (Ch. 6)

Unemployment Rate The percentage of Americans who are currently not working but are seeking jobs. (Ch. 14)

Unitary System A system of government in which political power and authority are located in one central government that runs the country and that may or may not share power with regional subunits. (Ch. 3)

Unit Rule The practice, employed by 48 states, of awarding all of a state's electoral college votes to the candidate for the presidency who receives the greatest number of popular votes in that state. (Ch. 13)

Universal Suffrage The right to vote for all adult citizens. (Ch. 5)

U.S. Commission on Civil Rights Federal commission created in 1957 to study issues of discrimination and inequality in order for the federal government to consider whether additional laws and policies are needed to address civil rights matters. (Ch. 5)

U.S. Equal Employment Opportunity Commission Federal commission created in 1964 to handle complaints about employment discrimination and file lawsuits on behalf of employment discrimination victims. (Ch. 5)

V

Veto The disapproval of a bill or resolution by the president. (Ch. 7)

Vietnam Syndrome The belief, attributed to the American experience in Vietnam, that the public will not support the use of military force if it results in significant American casualties. (Ch. 15)

Virginia Plan A plan made by delegates to the Constitutional Convention from several of the larger states, calling for a strong national government with a bicameral legislature, a national executive, a national judiciary, and legislative representation based on population. (Ch. 2)

Voir Dire The process of selecting a jury (from an Old French expression meaning "speak the truth"). (Ch. 20)

Voter Registration Data Voter information gathered during the registration process that is available at all county election offices in California. (Ch. 17)

Voting Cues Summaries encapsulating the informed judgment of others in the legislature; members of Congress rely on these to streamline the decision-making process. (Ch. 6)

Voting Rights Act of 1965 A federal statute that outlawed discriminatory voting practices, such as literacy tests, that had been responsible for the widespread disenfranchisement of African Americans. (Chs. 5, 13)

W

War Powers Resolution A measure passed by Congress in 1973 designed to limit presidential deployment of troops unless Congress grants approval for a longer period. (Ch. 7)

Warrant A judicial order authorizing a search or an arrest. Under the Fourth Amendment, police and prosecutors must present sufficient evidence to constitute "probable cause" in order to obtain a warrant from a judge. (Ch. 4)

Warren, Earl (1891–1974) Chief Justice of the Supreme Court (1953–1969) who led the Court to its unanimous decision in *Brown* v. *Board of Education of Topeka* (1954) and also took a leading role in many decisions expanding civil liberties and promoting civil rights. (Ch. 5)

Weak Mayor–Council Model A model of city government that emphasizes the mayor's role as a facilitative leader. (Ch. 21)

Weapons of Mass Destruction Weapons capable of inflicting widespread devastation on civilian populations. (Ch. 15)

Whig Model A theory of restrained presidential powers; the idea that presidents should use only the powers explicitly granted in the Constitution. (Ch. 7)

Whips Assistants to House and Senate leaders, responsible for drumming up support for legislation and for keeping count of how members plan to vote on different pieces of legislation. (Ch. 6)

Whistleblowers An employee who reports or reveals misconduct by government officials or others. (Ch. 8)

Whistleblowers Protection Act (1989) A federal law intended to prevent employees in the bureaucracy from being punished for reporting or revealing governmental misconduct. (Ch. 8)

Workingmen's Party A political party organized by Denis Kearney to combat the political and economic power of wealthy merchants and railroad barons. (Ch. 16)

Writ of Certiorari A legal action that asks a higher court to call up a case from a lower court; the legal action used to ask the U.S. Supreme Court to accept a case for hearing. (Ch. 9)

Writ of Mandamus A legal action that asks a judge to order a government official to take a specific action. (Ch. 9)

Y

Yellow Journalism Sensationalistic stories featured in the daily press around the turn of the twentieth century. (Ch. 11)

Notes

CHAPTER 1

1. Virginia Gray and David Lowery, "Where Do Policy Ideas Come From? A Study of Minnesota Legislators and Staffers," *Journal of Public Administration Research and Theory 10* (2000): 573–595.
2. George F. Cole and Christopher E. Smith, *The American System of Criminal Justice,* 12th ed. (Belmont, CA: Wadsworth, 2008).
3. Quoted in John K. White and Daniel M. Shea, *New Party Politics: From Jefferson and Hamilton to the Information Age,* 2nd ed. (Belmont, CA: Wadsworth, 2004), p. 13.
4. Thomas Dye, *Politics in America,* 8th ed. (New York: Pearson Education, 2009), p. 25.
5. For an interesting discussion of the link between political culture and system stability, see Oliver H. Woshinsky, *Culture and Politics* (Upper Saddle River, NJ: Prentice Hall, 1995).
6. Ibid., pp. 117–118.
7. Gunnar Myrdal, *An American Dilemma: The Negro Problem and Modern Democracy* (New York: Harper, 1944), p. 27.
8. Ibid.
9. Arthur M. Schlesinger Jr., *The Disuniting of America: Reflections on a Multicultural Society* (New York: Norton, 1992), p. 27.
10. Robert A. Dahl, *Who Governs? Democracy and Power in an American City* (New Haven, CT: Yale University Press, 1961), pp. 316–317.

CHAPTER 2

1. Stephen Ambrose, *Undaunted Courage: Meriwether Lewis, Thomas Jefferson and the Opening of the American West* (New York: Simon & Schuster Adult, 1996), p. 316.
2. Max Weber, "Politics as a Vocation" (1918), in *From Max Weber: Essays in Sociology,* ed. H. H. Gerth and C. Wright Mills (New York: Oxford University Press, 1946), p. 128.
3. Theodore J. Lowi and Benjamin Ginsberg, *American Government: Freedom and Power,* 2nd ed. (New York: Norton, 1992), p. 10.
4. Ibid.
5. David McCullough, *John Adams* (New York: Simon and Schuster, 2001), p. 60.
6. McCullough, *John Adams.*
7. Barbara Ehrenreich, "Their George and Ours," *New York Times,* July 4, 2004, sec. 4, p. 9.
8. Ibid.
9. "Thomas Paine: Life in America," Encyclopaedia Britannica Online, http://search.eb.com, 2004.
10. Ray Raphael, *Founding Myths: Stories That Hide Our Patriotic Past* (New York: New Press, 2004), p. 87.
11. Ibid.
12. "Selections from the Diary of Private Joseph Plumb Martin." www.ushistory.org/march/other/Martiandiary.htm, ushistory.org. Accessed July 5, 2008.
13. Ehrenreich, "Their George and Ours."
14. Thomas Jefferson, letter to William Stephens Smith, November 13, 1787.
15. "Articles of Confederation," Encyclopaedia Britannica Online, http://search.eb.com, 2004.
16. Bruce Miroff, Raymond Seidelman, and Todd Swanstrom, *The Democratic Debate: An Introduction to American Politics,* 4th ed. (Boston: Houghton Mifflin, 2007), p. 26.
17. Theodore J. Lowi and Benjamin Ginsberg, *American Government: Freedom and Power* (New York: Norton, 1990), p. 41.
18. Ibid., p. 42.
19. Joseph J. Ellis, *Founding Brothers: The Revolutionary Generation* (New York: Vintage Books, 2002), p. 94.
20. Ibid., p. 91.
21. Alexander Hamilton, James Madison, and John Jay, *Federalist No. 57.*
22. "Essays of Brutus, No. 1," in *The Complete Anti-Federalist,* ed. Herbert Storing (Chicago: University of Chicago Press, 1981).
23. Ibid.
24. Ibid.

CHAPTER 3

1. M. Judd Harmon, *Political Thought: From Plato to the Present* (New York: McGraw-Hill, 1964), p. 289.
2. Jesse J. Richardson, Jr., Meghan Zimmerman Gough, and Robert Puentes "Is Home Rule the Answer?" Brookings Institution. January 2003. Accessed at http://www.brookings.edu/reports/2003/01metropolitanpolicy_richardson.aspx on December 2, 2009.
3. James W. Loewen, *Lies My Teacher Told Me: Everything Your American History Textbook Got Wrong* (New York: Simon and Schuster, 1995), p. 141.
4. See Howard Gillman, *The Constitution Besieged: The Rise and Demise of Lochner Era Police Powers Jurisprudence* (Durham, NC: Duke University Press, 1993).
5. Morton Grozdins, *The American System,* ed. Daniel J. Elazar (Chicago: Rand McNally, 1966).
6. U.S. Office of Management and Budget, 2008, *President's Budget Historical Tables, Table 12.1,* http://www.whitehouse.gov/budget/Historicals/, accessed March 22, 2010.

CHAPTER 4

1. Henry J. Abraham, *Freedom and the Court: Civil Rights and Liberties in the United States,* 5th ed. (New York: Oxford University Press, 1988), p. 131.
2. Linda Greenhouse, "Documents Reveal the Evolution of a Justice," *New York Times,* March 4, 2004, p. A16.
3. Thomas R. Hensley, Christopher E. Smith, and Joyce A. Baugh, *The Changing Supreme Court: Constitutional Rights and Liberties* (St. Paul, MN: West, 1997), p. 329.
4. Joshua Lipton, "Vanessa Leggett: Why She Wouldn't Give Up Her Notes," *Columbia Journalism Review,* March-April 2002. Accessed at http://www.cjr.org/issues/2002/2/qa-leggett.asp on August 23, 2008.
5. Frances Harrison, "'Mass Purges' at Iran Universities," BBC News, December 20, 2006. Accessed at http://news.bbc.co.ut/1/hi/world/middle_east/6196069.stm on August 23, 2008.
6. Frances Harrison, "Student Editor Detained in Tehran," BBC News, May 7, 2007. Accessed at http://news.bbc.co.uk/1/hi/world/middle_east/6631715.stm on August 23, 2008.
7. Christopher E. Smith, *Constitutional Rights: Myths and Realities* (Belmont, CA: Wadsworth, 2004), pp. 115–128.
8. George F. Cole and Christopher E. Smith, *Criminal Justice in America,* 4th ed. (Belmont, CA: Wadsworth, 2004), p. 10.
9. See Lee Epstein and Joseph Kobylka, *The Supreme Court and Legal Change* (Chapel Hill: University of North Carolina Press, 1992).
10. Mark Costanza, *Just Revenge: Costs and Consequences of the Death Penalty* (New York: St. Martin's Press, 1997), pp. 95–111.
11. Stanley Cohen, *The Wrong Men* (New York: Carroll and Graf, 2003), pp. 298–322; Death Penalty Information Center, accessed at http://www.deathpenaltyinfo.org
12. Christopher E. Smith, *Courts and the Poor* (Chicago: Nelson-Hall, 1991), p. 118.

CHAPTER 5

1. For example, see Peter Kolchin, *American Slavery, 1619–1877* (New York: Hill and Wang, 1993); Walter Johnson, *Soul by Soul: Life Inside the Antebellum Slave Market* (Cambridge, MA: Harvard University Press, 1999); Ira Berlin, Marc Favreau, and Steven F. Miller, eds., *Remembering Slavery* (New York: New Press, 1998); John Hope Franklin and Loren Schweninger, *Runaway Slaves: Rebels on the Plantation* (New York: Oxford University Press, 1999).
2. For example, see Andrew Hacker, *Two Nations: Black and White, Separate, Hostile, Unequal* (New York: Scribner, 1992); Tom Wicker, *Tragic Failure: Racial Integration in America* (New York: Morrow, 1996).
3. Kolchin, *American Slavery,* p. 215.
4. Ibid., pp. 220–224.

5. Eric Foner, *The Story of American Freedom* (New York: Norton, 1998), p. 105.

6. William Gillette, *Retreat from Reconstruction, 1869–1879* (Baton Rouge: Louisiana State University Press, 1979), pp. 335–347.

7. Ronald Takaki, *A Different Mirror: A History of Multicultural America* (Boston: Little, Brown, 1993), pp. 191–221.

8. See Richard Kluger, *Simple Justice* (New York: Random House, 1975), pp. 657–747.

9. ACLU of Virginia, "Press Release: William & Mary Students Allowed to Register to Vote; Case Dismissed." October 14, 2004. Accessed at http://www.acluva.org/newsreleases2004/Oct14.html

10. See Gunnar Myrdal, *An American Dilemma: The Negro Problem and Modern Democracy* (New York: Harper, 1944).

11. Taylor Branch, *Parting the Waters: America in the King Years, 1954–1963* (New York: Simon and Schuster, 1988), pp. 128–205.

12. "An Interview with Congressman Charles Diggs," in Juan Williams, *Eyes on the Prize: America's Civil Rights Years* (New York: Viking, 1987), pp. 59–89.

13. Ibid., pp. 99–113.

14. Branch, *Parting the Waters,* pp. 891.

15. Williams, *Eyes on the Prize,* p. 197–200.

16. Ibid., pp. 276–277.

17. Gerald Gunther, *Constitutional Law,* 11th ed. (Mineola, NY: Foundation Press, 1985), p. 932.

18. Eleanor Flexner, *Century of Struggle: The Women's Rights Movement in the United States,* rev. ed. (Cambridge, MA: Harvard University Press, 1975), pp. 154–158.

19. Ibid., p. 228.

20. Ibid., p. 300.

21. Pedro Caban, Jose Carrasco, Barbara Cruz, and Juan Garcia, *The Latino Experience in U.S. History* (Paramus, NJ: Globe Fearon, 1994), pp. 208–220.

22. Ibid., pp. 282–287.

23. "Tamil Law Students Protest Discrimination in Admissions," TamilNet, December 28, 2006. Accessed at http://www.tamilnet.com

Chapter 6

1. Thomas Friedman, "Where Did 'We' Go?" *New York Times,* September 30, 2009. Accessed at http://www.nytimes.com/2009/09/30/opinion/30friedman.html

2. Kelly D. Patterson and Daniel M. Shea, eds., *Contemplating the People's Branch* (Upper Saddle River, NJ: Prentice Hall, 2000), p. 6.

3. Roger H. Davidson and Walter Oleszek, *Congress and Its Members,* 10th ed. (Washington, DC: CQ Press, 2004), p. 122.

4. Gary W. Cox and Jonathan N. Katz, *Elbridge Gerry's Salamander* (Cambridge, England: Cambridge University Press, 2002), p. 3.

5. Adam Clymer, "Why Iowa Has So Many Hot Seats," *New York Times,* October 27, 2002, p. A22.

6. L. Sandy Maisel, *Parties and Elections in America: The Electoral Process,* 3rd ed. (Lanham, MD: Rowman and Littlefield, 1999), p. 207.

7. Cox and Katz, *Elbridge Gerry's Salamander,* pp. 12–13.

8. Ibid., pp. 25–28.

9. Davidson and Oleszek, *Congress and Its Members,* 12th ed., 2009, p. 199.

10. Ibid., p. 205.

11. Opening remarks of Senator Arlen Spector before the Senate Subcommittee on Labor, Health and Human Services, Education, and Related Agencies, Committee on Appropriations, June, 5, 1997.

12. David J. Vogler, *The Politics of Congress* (Madison, WI: Brown and Benchmark, 1993), p. 76.

13. Michael J. Malbin, *Unelected Representatives: Congressional Staff and the Future of Representative Government* (New York: Basic Books, 1979).

14. Charles Peters, *How Washington Really Works* (Reading, MA: Addison-Wesley, 1992), p. 133; Fred Harris, *In Defense of Congress* (New York: St. Martin's Press, 1995), pp. 40–41.

15. John Broder, "Democrats Oust Long-time Leader of House Panel," *New York Times,* November 20, 2008. Accessed at http://www.nytimes.com/2008/11/21/us/politics/21dingell.html

16. Patterson and Shea, *Contemplating the People's Branch,* pp. 133–134.

17. Adam Nagourney, "Democrats Reel As Senator Says No to Third Term," *New York Times,* February 15, 2010, p. A1.

18. Jackie Calmes, "Party Gridlock in Washington Feeds Fears of Debt Crisis," *New York Times,* February 17, 2010, p. A1.

19. Ibid., p. 136.

20. Alexander Burns, "VP: Constitution on Its Head," POLITICO, January 18, 2010, accessed at http://www.politico.com/politico44/perm/0110/biden_slams_filibuster_fe40df44-9045-4c26-a715-51c427035eae.html

21. Donald R. Matthews, *U.S. Senators and Their World* (New York: Vintage Books, 1960).

22. Ibid., p. 97.

23. Ibid., p. 99.

24. Barbara Sinclair, *Unorthodox Lawmaking: New Legislative Processes in the U.S. Congress,* 3rd ed. (Washington DC: Congressional Quarterly, 2007).

25. Davidson and Oleszek, *Congress and Its Members,* p. 234.

26. Paul Singer, "Members Offered Many Bills But Passed Few," *CQ Politics OnLine,* December 1, 2008, accessed at http://www.rollcall.com/issues/54_61/news/30466-1.html

27. ESRI 2007/2012 Demographic Data Trends, WWW.ESRI.COM. Accessed at http://www.esri.com/library/fliers/pdfs/2007-2012-demographic-data-trends.pdf

28. Congressional Black Caucus, http://www.congressionalblackcaucus.net, accessed February 2004.

29. Ibid.

30. http://www.esri.com/library/fliers/pdfs/2007-2012-demographic-data-trends.pdf

31. Stephen J. Wayne, *Is This Any Way to Run a Democratic Election?* 2nd ed. (Boston: Houghton Mifflin, 2003), p. 54.

32. Jennifer Yachnin, Paul Singer and Kristin Coyner. "The 50 Richest Members of Congress: Downturn Hits Even the Wealthiest Lawmakers," Rollcall.com, September 14, 2009, Accessed at http://www.rollcall.com/features/Guide-to-Congress_2009/guide/38181-1.htm on October 8, 2009.

33. U.S. Census Bureau, "Income," accessed at http://www.census.gov/hhes/www/income.html, February 2004.

34. Roger H. Davidson and Walter Oleszek, *Congress and Its Members,* 7th ed. (Washington, DC: CQ Press, 2000), pp. 128–129.

35. Roger H. Davidson and Walter Oleszek, *Congress and Its Members,* 10th ed. (Washington, DC: CQ Press, 2006), p. 479.

36. Harris, *In Defense of Congress,* p. 59.

37. Norman J. Ornstein, "Prosecutors Must Stop Their Big Game Hunt of Politicians," *Roll Call,* April 26, 1993, p. 6.

38. Adam Nagourney and Megan Thee-Brenan, "Poll Finds Edge for Obama Over GOP Among the Public," *New York Times,* February 11, 2010, p. A1.

39. Barbara Sinclair, as cited in, "Hating Congress: A National Occupation," *New York Times On Line,* February 12, 2010, accessed at http://roomfordebate.blogs.nytimes.com/2010/02/12/hating-congress-a-national-occupation/

Chapter 7

1. Theodore J. Lowi and Benjamin Ginsberg, *American Government: Freedom and Power* (New York: Norton, 1990), p. 241.

2. John Locke, *The Second Treatise on Government,* cited in ibid., p. 241.

3. Sidney M. Milkis and Michael Nelson, *The American Presidency: Origins and Development, 1776–1998* (Washington, DC: CQ Press, 1999), p. 26.

4. Milkis and Nelson, *American Presidency, 1776–1998,* p. 28.

5. David Mervin, *The President of the United States* (New York: Harvester Press, 1993), p. 22.

6. Michael Nelson, ed., *The Evolving Presidency,* 2nd ed. (Washington, DC: CQ Press, 2004), p. 10.

7. Robert Dallek, *Hail to the Chief: The Making and Unmaking of American Presidents* (New York: Hyperion, 1996), p. 14.

8. Theodore Roosevelt, "The Stewardship Doctrine," in *Classics of the American Presidency,* ed. Harry Bailey (Oak Park, IL: Moore, 1980), pp. 35–36.

9. Dallek, *Hail to the Chief,* p. 18.

10. Michael A. Genovese, *The Power of the American Presidency, 1789–2000* (New York: Oxford University Press, 2001), p. 132.

11. Ibid, p. 143.

12. Sidney M. Milkis and Michael Nelson, *The American Presidency: Origins and Development, 1776–2002* (Washington, DC: CQ Press, 2003), p. 424.

13. Ibid.

14. Ibid., p. 428.

15. Nathan Miller, *FDR: An Intimate History* (Lanham, MD: Madison Books, 1983), p. 276.

16. Edward S. Greenberg and Benjamin I. Page, *The Struggle for Democracy,* 5th ed. (New York: Longman, 2002), p. 361.

17. Milkis and Nelson, *American Presidency, 1776–2002,* p. 438.

18. Ibid., p. 440.

19. Richard Neustadt, *Presidential Power* (New York: Wiley, 1960), p. 193.

20. Stephen Skowronek, *The Politics Presidents Make: From John Adams to George Bush* (Cambridge, MA: Harvard University Press, 2008).

21. Gary King and Lyn Ragsdale, *The Elusive Executive: Discovering Statistical Patterns in the Presidency* (Washington, DC: CQ Press, 1988), p. 35.

22. The Supreme Court case was *United States* v. *Curtis Wright Corp.,* 299 U.S. 304 (1936).

23. Louis Fisher, "Invitation to Struggle: The President, Congress, and National Security," in James P. Pfiffner and Roger Davidson, eds. *Understanding the Presidency* (New York: Longman, 1996), p. 269.

24. Abraham Lincoln, "A Special Session Message, July 4, 1861," cited in Genovese, *Power of the American Presidency,* p. 81.

25. Aaron Wildavsky, "The Two Presidencies," *Trans-Action.* 4: (1966) 7–14.

26. Theodore J. Lowi, *The Personal President: Power Invested, Promise Unfulfilled* (Ithaca, NY: Cornell University Press, 1985), p. xii.

27. Ibid., p. 1.

28. Dallek, *Hail to the Chief,* p. xx.

29. Sean Wilentz, "The Worst President Ever?" *Rolling Stone,* April 21, 2006.

30. These points are made by political scientist Fred I. Greenstein, "A Change and Continuity in Modern Presidency," in *The New American Political System,* ed. Anthony King (Washington, DC: American Enterprise Institute, 1978), pp. 45–46.

CHAPTER 8

1. Mike Snyder, "After Ike, FEMA Aid Is Hard to Come By," *Houston Chronicle,* October 25, 2008. Accessed at http://www.chron.com/disp/story.mpl/metropolitan/6078556.html on April, 2010.

2. Environmental Protection Agency, "Arsenic in Drinking Water," accessed at http://www.epa.gov/safewater/arsenic/ on July 20, 2008; Alabama Cooperative Extension Service, November 8, 2001, "Bush Administration's Belated Arsenic Decision Doesn't Imply Insensitivity, Expert Says," accessed at http://www.aces.edu/dept/extcomm/newspaper/nov8a01.html on July 20, 2008; "EPA Delays Lower Arsenic Standards for Water," CNN.com, March 21, 2001, accessed at http://archives.cnn.com/2001/HEALTH/03/20/epa.arsenic/index.html on July 20, 2008.

3. Eric Lipton and Scott Shane, "Leader of Federal Effort Feels the Heat," *New York Times,* September 3, 2005, accessed at http://www.nytimes.com/2005/09/03/national/nationalspecial/03fema.html?_r=1&oref=slogin on July 21, 2008. See also Daren Fonda and Rita Healy, "How Reliable Is Brown's Resume?" *Time,* September 8, 2005, accessed at http://www.time.com/time/nation/article/0,8599,1103003,00.html on July 21, 2008.

4. "Dental Students Protest Against 'Illegal' Order," *The Hindu.* December 15, 2005. Accessed at http://www.hindu.com/2005/12/15/stories/2005121507180300.htm on March 20, 2008.

5. Pew Research Center for the People and the Press, "Performance and Purpose: Constituents Rate Government Agencies." Accessed at http://people-press.org/report/41/ on July 21, 2008.

6. Charles T. Goodsell, *The Case for Bureaucracy* (Chatham, NJ: Chatham House, 1983), p. 15.

7. "TSA Takes Heat for Background Check Miscues," *Government Security,* February 11, 2004. Accessed at http://govtsecurity.

securitysolutions.com/ar/security_tsa_takes_heat_index.htm on July 21, 2008.

8. Jeff Johnson, "TSA Screeners Claim They're 'Being Used for Cannon Fodder,'" CNSNews.com. Accessed at www.cnsnews.com/ViewPrint.asp?Page=%5CPolitics%5Carchive%5C200303%5CPOL20030304b.html on March 20, 2008.

9. B. Guy Peters, *American Public Policy: Promise and Performance,* 5th ed. (Chatham, NJ: Chatham House, 1999), p. 33.

10. Elizabeth Gettelman, "The K(a-ching!) Street Congressman," *Mother Jones,* November–December 2004, p. 24.

11. Jim Tankersley and Josh Meyer, "Former Interior Secretary Gale Norton Is Focus of Corruption Probe." *Los Angeles Times,* September 17, 2009. Accessed at http://articles.latimes.com/2009/sep/17/nation/na-norton17 on April 11, 2010.

12. Ibid.

13. Tony Pugh, "Medicare Cost Estimates Concealed, Expert Says," *San Diego Union-Tribune.* Accessed at www.cnsnews.com/ViewPrint.asp?Page=%5CPolitics%5Carchive%5C200303%5CPOL20030304b.html on July 21, 2008.

14. "General: Army Leaned on Whistleblower," CBSNews.com. Accessed at http://www.cbsnews.com/stories/2004/10/28/national/main652183.shtml on July 21, 2008.

15. Neely Tucker, "A Web of Truth," *Washington Post,* October 19, 2005, p. C1.

16. Robert A. Katzmann, *Regulatory Bureaucracy* (Cambridge, MA: MIT Press, 1980), p. 180.

17. Anne C. Mulkern, "As Senate Climate Bill Languishes, Lobbyists Press EPA on Carbon Regs," *New York Times,* January 12, 2010. Accessed at http://www.nytimes.com/gwire/2010/01/12/12greenwire-as-senate-climate-bill-languishes-lobbyists-pr-15488.html on April 11, 2010.

18. Ibid.

19. Joel Brinkley, "Out of Spotlight, Bush Overhauls U.S. Regulations," *New York Times,* August 14, 2004. Accessed at http://www.nytimes.com/2004/08/14/politics/14bush.html?ex=1250136000&en=1bf32d7574b25b2b&ei=5090 on July 21, 2008.

20. Joe Stephens and Lena H. Sun, "Federal Oversight of Subways Proposed," *Washington Post,* November 15, 2009. Accessed at http://www.washingtonpost.com/wpdyn/content/article/2009/11/14/AR2009111402459.html on April 11, 2010.

21. Catherine Elsworth, "Golden Globes Investigated for Breaching Indecency Rules," *London Telegraph,* January 15, 2009. Accessed at http://www.telegraph.co.uk/news/worldnews/northamerica/usa/4249694/Golden-Globes-investigated-for-breaching-indecency-rules.html on April 11, 2010.

22. See Donna Price Cofer, *Judges, Bureaucrats, and the Question of Independence* (Westport, CT: Greenwood Press, 1985).

23. Christopher H. Foreman Jr., *Signals from the Hill: Congressional Oversight and the Challenge of Social Regulation* (New Haven, CT: Yale University Press, 1988), p. 13.

24. See Lawrence C. Dodd and Richard L. Schott, *Congress and the Administrative State* (New York: Wiley, 1979).

CHAPTER 9

1. Christopher E. Smith, *Courts, Politics, and the Judicial Process,* 2nd ed. (Chicago: Nelson-Hall, 1997), p. 37.

2. Stephen L. Wasby, *The Supreme Court in the Federal Judicial System,* 4th ed. (Chicago: Nelson-Hall, 1993), pp. 56–57, 238–244.

3. Henry J. Abraham, *The Judicial Process,* 6th ed. (New York: Oxford University Press, 1993), pp. 96–97.

4. Christopher E. Smith, "Polarization and Change in the Federal Courts: *En Banc* Decisions in the U.S. Courts of Appeals," *Judicature* 74 (1990): 133–137.

5. Lawrence Baum, *Judges and Their Audiences* (Princeton, NJ: Princeton University Press, 2006), pp. 19–24.

6. Jeffrey A. Segal and Harold J. Spaeth, *The Supreme Court and the Attitudinal Model* (New York: Cambridge University Press, 1993), pp. 64–73.

7. Thomas H. Hammond, Chris W. Bonneau, and Reginald S. Sheehan, *Strategic Behavior and Policy Choice on the U.S. Supreme Court* (Palo Alto, CA: Stanford University Press, 2005).

8. David M. O'Brien, *Storm Center: The Supreme Court in American Politics*, 8th ed. (New York: Norton, 2008).

9. Herbert Kritzer, "Martin Shapiro: Anticipating the New Institutionalism," in *The Pioneers of Judicial Behavior*, ed. Nancy Maveety (Ann Arbor: University of Michigan Press, 2003), p. 387.

10. Wasby, *The Supreme Court*, p. 155.

11. Joseph D. Kearney and Thomas W. Merrill, "The Influence of Amicus Curiae Briefs on the Supreme Court," *University of Pennsylvania Law Review* 148 (2000): 753. See also Paul M. Collins Jr., "Lobbyists Before the U.S. Supreme Court," *Political Research Quarterly* 60 (2007): 55–70.

12. Erin Osovets, "Armstrong Atlantic State University, Student Newspaper Settle Lawsuit," Foundation for Individual Rights, November 21, 2008, accessed at www.thefire.org/article/9965.html. See also "2008: Students Sue Georgia School," College Media Advisors, July 3, 2008, accessed at www.collegemedia.org/node/295, on November 15, 2009.

13. Jeff Yates, *Popular Justice: Presidential Prestige and Executive Success in the Supreme Court* (Albany: State University of New York Press, 2002), p. 2.

14. Gerald Rosenberg, *The Hollow Hope: Can Courts Bring About Social Change?* (Chicago: University of Chicago Press, 1991).

15. Bradley C. Canon, "The Supreme Court and Policy Reform: The Hollow Hope Revisited," in *Leveraging the Law: Using the Courts to Achieve Social Change*, ed. David A. Schultz (New York: Lang, 1998), pp. 215–249.

16. See Richard E. Morgan, *Disabling America: The "Rights Industry" in Our Time* (New York: Basic Books, 1984); Jeremy Rabkin, *Judicial Compulsions: How Public Law Distorts Public Policy* (New York: Basic Books, 1989).

17. Gallup Poll, "Civil Liberties," national opinion poll conducted September 14–15, 2001. Accessed at http://www.galluppoll.com

18. Tariq Ali, "Pakistan's People Want an End to the Nightmare," *Guardian Unlimited* (U.K.), August 10, 2007. Accessed at http://www.guardian.co.uk/commentisfree/2007/aug/10/pakistan.comment1 on November 15, 2009

CHAPTER 10

1. For instance, see the seminal work by Angus Campbell, Philip Converse, Warren Miller, and Donald Stokes, *The American Voter* (Chicago: University of Chicago Press, 1960).

2. For instance, see V. O. Key Jr., *The Responsible Electorate* (Cambridge, MA: Belknap Press, 1966); see also Warren E. Miller and J. Merrill Shanks, *The New American Voter* (Cambridge, MA: Harvard University Press, 1996).

3. Walter Lippmann, *Public Opinion* (New York: Macmillan, 1922).

4. Robert Weissberg, *Polling, Policy, and Public Opinion: The Case Against Heeding the "Voice of the People"* (New York: Palgrave-Macmillan, 2002).

5. Sidney Verba, *Participation in America: Political Democracy and Social Equality* (Chicago: University of Chicago Press, 1972).

6. Herbert Asher, *Polling and the Public: What Every Citizen Should Know*, 6th ed. (Washington, DC: CQ Press, 2004), p. 195.

7. Starting with the seminal research of Philip E. Converse, "The Nature of Belief Systems in Mass Publics," in *Ideology and Discontent*, ed. David E. Apter (New York: Free Press, 1964), pp. 206–261.

8. Robert S. Erikson and Kent L. Tedin, *American Public Opinion*, 5th ed. (Boston: Allyn and Bacon, 1995), p. 144.

9. Joseph Carroll, "Most Americans Approve of Interracial Marriages," Gallup Poll. Accessed at http://www.gallup.com/poll/28417/Most-Americans-Approve-Interracial-Marriages.aspx on August 16, 2007.

10. Pew Research Center "A Year After Obama's Election: Blacks Upbeat about Black Progress, Prospects" January 12, 2010. Accessed at http://pewsocialtrends.org/assets/pdf/blacks-upbeat-about-black-progress-prospects.pdf on August 10, 2010.

11. Lydia Saad, "Tolerance for Gay Rights at High-Water Mark," Gallup Poll. Accessed at http://www.gallup.com/poll/27694/Tolerance-Gay-Rights-HighWater-Mark.aspx on May 29, 2007.

12. Lydia Saad, "Americans' Acceptance of Gay Relations Crosses 50% Threshold: Increased acceptance by men driving the change, May 25, 2010. Accessed at http://www.gallup.com/poll/135764/Americans-Acceptance-Gay-Relations-Crosses-Threshold.aspx on August 10, 2010.

13. http://poll.gallup.com/content/default.aspx?ci=1651. Accessed on January 9, 2006.

14. Paul Abramson, *Political Attitudes in America* (San Francisco: Freeman, 1983).

15. Benjamin I. Page and Robert Y. Shapiro, *The Rational Public* (Chicago: University of Chicago Press, 1992), p. 178.

16. Ibid., p. 179.

17. See David J. Jackson, *Entertainment and Politics: The Influence of Pop Culture on Young Adult Political Socialization* (New York: Lang, 2002), ch. 1.

18. See Daniel Shea, "Introduction: Popular Culture—The Trojan Horse of American Politics?" in *Mass Politics: The Politics of Popular Culture*, ed. Daniel Shea (New York: St. Martin's/Worth, 1999).

19. "Men or Women: Who's the Better Leader? A paradox in Public Attitudes," Paul Taylor, Project Director. Accessed at http://pewsocialtrends.org/pubs/708/gender-leadership on January 2, 2010.

20. "The NES Guide to Public Opinion and Electoral Behavior," *American National Election Studies*, graph 4C.1.1. Accessed at http://www.electionstudies.org/nesguide/toptable/tab4c_1.htm on January 8, 2010.

21. "Women in Elective Office, 2009," Center for American Women in Politics. Accessed at http://www.cawp.rutgers.edu/fast_facts/levels_of_office/documents/elective.pdf on October 4, 2009.

22. "Women CEO's." Accessed at http://money.cnn.com/magazines/fortune/fortune500/2009/womenceos/ on January 8, 2010.

23. Jackson, *Entertainment and Politics*, p. 9.

24. M. Kent Jennings and Richard G. Niemi, *Generations and Politics: A Panel Study of Young Adults and Their Parents* (Princeton, NJ: Princeton University Press, 1981).

25. Stuart Oskamp, *Attitudes and Opinions*, 2nd ed. (Englewood Cliffs, NJ: Prentice Hall, 1991), p. 160.

26. Ibid., ch. 15.

27. David Easton, *A Systems Analysis of Political Life* (New York: Wiley, 1965).

28. U.S. Census Bureau, *America's Families and Living Arrangements, 2007* (Washington, DC: Government Printing Office, September 2009).

29. James G. Gimpel, J. Celeste Lay, and Jason E. Schuknecht, *Cultivating Democracy: Civic Environments and Political Socialization in America* (Washington, DC: Brookings Institution Press, 2003), p. 147.

30. Lee Anderson, *The Civics Report Card* (Princeton, NJ: Educational Testing Service, 1990).

31. U.S. Census Bureau, *Educational Attainment in the United States, 2003* (Washington, DC: Government Printing Office, 2003).

32. Ernest Boyer and Mary Jean Whitelaw, *The Condition of the Professorate* (New York: Harper and Row, 1989).

33. Gimpel, Lay, and Schuknecht, *Cultivating Democracy*, p. 63.

34. Ibid.

35. Ibid., p. 92.

36. See, for instance, Penny Edgell Becker and Pawan H. Dhingra, "Religious Involvement and Volunteering: Implications for Civil Society," *Sociology of Religion* 62 (2001): 315–335; Corwin Smidt, "Religion and Civic Engagement: A Comparative Analysis," *Annals of the American Academy of Political and Social Sciences* 565 (1999): 176–192.

37. Gimpel, Lay, and Schuknecht, *Cultivating Democracy*, p. 142.

38. Ibid., p. 143.

39. Kaiser Family Foundation, "Daily Media Use Among Children and Teens up Dramatically from Five Years Ago." Accessed at http://www.kff.org/entmedia/entmedia012010nr.cfm on February 20, 2010.

40. Accessed at http://www.truceteachers.org on July 30, 2008.

41. See, for instance, Gimpel, Lay, and Schuknecht, *Cultivating Democracy*, p. 35.

42. "Who Knows News? What You Read or View Matters, but Not Your Politics." Accessed at http://pewresearch.org/pubs/993/who-knows-news-what-you-read-or-view-matters-but-not-your-politics on February 22, 2010.

43. Paul Lazarfeld, Bernard Berelson, and Hazel Gaudet, *The People's Choice* (New York: Columbia University Press, 1944).

44. U.S. Census Bureau, *Current Population Survey, 2009: Annual Social and Economic Supplement* (Washington, DC: Government Printing Office, 2008). Accessed at http://www.census.gov/hhes/www/cpstables/032009/perinc/new03_001.htm, August 11, 2010.

45. Ibid., p. 183.

46. William H. Flanigan and Nancy H. Zingale, *Political Behavior of the American Electorate,* 11th ed. (Washington, DC: CQ Press, 2006), p. 132.

47. Pew Research Center for the People and the Press, "US Religious Landscape Survey." Accessed at http://religions.pewforum.org/reports on March 1, 2010.

48. Flanigan and Zingale, *Political Behavior,* p. 106.

49. James L. Guth, Lyman A. Delestedt, John C. Green, and Corwin E. Smidt, "A Distant Thunder? Religious Mobilization in the 2000 Elections," in *Interest Group Politics,* 6th ed., ed. Allen J. Cigler and Burdett A. Loomis (Washington, DC: CQ Press, 2002), pp. 161–184.

50. Accessed at http:pewforum.org/docs/?Doc!D=367 on March 2, 2010.

51. Oskamp, *Attitudes and Opinions,* p. 390.

52. Ibid., p. 391.

53. Center for American Women and Politics, *The Gender Gap: Attitudes on Public Policy Issues* (New Brunswick, NJ: Eagleton Institute of Politics, Rutgers University, 1997); Susan J. Carroll and Richard F. Fox, eds., *Gender and Elections* (New York: Cambridge University Press, 2006).

54. Reported in Justin Lewis, *Constructing Public Opinion: How Political Elites Do What They Like and Why We Seem to Go Along with It* (New York: Columbia University Press, 2001), p. 34.

55. Asher, *Polling and the Public,* p. 23.

56. Benjamin Ginsberg, *The Captive Public: How Mass Opinion Promotes State Power* (New York: Basic Books, 1986).

57. Asher, *Polling and the Public,* p. 3.

58. Lewis, *Constructing Public Opinion,* p. 41.

59. Richard Morin, "Don't Ask Me: As Fewer Cooperate on Polls, Criticism and Questions Mount," *Washington Post,* October 25, 2004, p. C1.

60. Scott Keeter, "Research Roundup: Latest Findings on Cell Phones and Polling." Pew Research Center, May 22, 2009. Accessed at http://pewresearch.org/pubs/848/cell-only-methodology on January 2, 2010.

61. Ibid.

62. Accessed on November 19, 2009.

63. Ibid., p. C25.

64. For instance, see Lewis, *Constructing Public Opinion,* p. 37.

65. James A. Stimson, *Public Opinion in America,* 2nd ed. (Boulder, CO: Westview Press, 1999), p. 122.

CHAPTER 11

1. W. Lance Bennett, *News: The Politics of Illusion,* 6th ed. (New York: Longman, 2005), p. 6.

2. Pew Internet and American Life Project, "Understanding the Participatory News Consumer." Accessed at http://www.pewinternet.org/Reports/2010/Online-News.aspx?r=1 on April 4, 2010.

3. Alfred McClung Lee, *The Daily Newspaper in America* (New York: Macmillian, 1937), p. 21.

4. Quoted in Philip Davidson, *Propaganda and the American Revolution, 1763–1783* (Chapel Hill: University of North Carolina Press, 1941), p. 285.

5. *Messages and Papers of the Presidents 1789–1908,* vol. 1 (Washington, DC: Bureau of National Literature and Art, 1909), p. 132.

6. Lee, *Daily Newspaper in America,* pp. 716–717.

7. See Jan E. Leighley, *Mass Media and Politics: A Social Science Perspective* (Boston: Houghton Mifflin, 2004), ch. 1.

8. Quoted in W.W. Swanberg, *Citizen Hurst* (New York: Scribner, 1961), p. 90.

9. Lee, *Daily Newspaper in America,* pp. 215–216.

10. Doris A. Graber, *Mass Media and American Politics,* 8th ed. (Washington, DC: CQ Press, 2006), p. 38.

11. Edwin Emery and Michael Emery, *The Press and America* (Englewood Cliffs, NJ: Prentice Hall, 1984), pp. 372–379.

12. Frank Luther Mott, *American Journalism, A History: 1690–1960* (New York: Macmillian, 1962), p. 679.

13. Richard Mullins, "One-Third of Americans own 4 or more TVs," *Tampa Bay Tribune,* February 25, 2010, Accessed at http://www2.tbo.com/content/2010/feb/25/260045/one-third-americans-own-4-or-more-tvs/ on April 5, 2010.

14. To learn more, see http://www.cellphonesforsoldiers.com

15. See, for instance, Christopher P. Latimer, "The Digital Divide: Understanding and Addressing." Accessed at http://www.nysfirm.org/documents/html/whitepapers/nysfirm_digital_divide.htm on May 15, 2008.

16. See, for instance, Kathy Koch, "The Digital Divide," in *The CQ Researcher Online 10.3* (2000). Published January 28, 2000. Document ID: cqresrre2000012800; Aaron Smith, Kay Lehman Schlozman, Sidney Verba, and Henry Brady, "The Internet and Civic Engagement" September 1, 2009, Pew Internet and American Life Project. Accessed at http://www.pewinternet.org/Reports/2009/15—The-Internet-and-Civic-Engagement.aspx on April 5, 2010.

17. Pew Research Center for the People and the Press, "Key News Audiences Now Blend Online and Traditional Sources," August 17, 2008. Accessed at http://people-press.org/report/444/news-media on April 6, 2010.

18. Pew Research Center for the People and the Press, "Internet's Broader Role in Campaign 2008," January 1, 2008. Accessed at http://www.people-press.org/report/384/internets-broader-role-in-campaign-2008 on August 1, 2008.

19. Robert S. Lichter, Linda S. Lichter, and Daniel Amundson, "Government Goes Down the Tube: Images of Government in TV Entertainment, 1955–1998," *Harvard International Journal of Press/Politics 5* (2000): 96–103.

20. Harold D. Lasswell, "The Structure and Function of Communication in Society," in *Mass Communications,* ed. Wilbur Schramm (Urbana: University of Illinois Press, 1969), p. 103.

21. For a good analysis of the issue of race and media coverage, see Robert M. Entman and Andrew Rojecki, *The Black Image in the White Mind: Media and Race in America* (Chicago: University of Chicago Press, 2001).

22. Reported in Jerry L. Yeric, *Mass Media and the Politics of Change* (Itasca, IL: Peacock Publishers, 2001), ch. 6.

23. "Bottom-Line Pressure Now Hurting Coverage, Say Journalists," Pew Research Center for the People and the Press. Accessed at http://people-press.org/reports/display.php3?PageID=825 on May 23, 2004.

24. Harold W. Stanley and Richard G. Niemi, *Vital Statistics on American Politics, 2003–2004,* 6th ed. (Washington, DC: CQ Press, 2003).

25. See Yeric, *Mass Media and the Politics of Change,* and Graber, *Mass Media and American Politics.*

26. Graber, *Mass Media and American Politics,* p. 198.

27. Daniel J. Boorstin, *The Image: A Guide to Pseudo-Events in America* (New York: Vintage, 1961).

28. Pew Internet and American Life Project, "Understanding the Participatory News Consumer." Accessed at http://www.pewinternet.org/Reports/2010/Online-News.aspx?r=1, on April 7, 2010.

29. Ibid., p. 271.

30. Graber, *Mass Media and American Politics,* p. 185.

31. David L. Protess, Fay Lomax Cook, Jack C. Doppelt, James S. Ettema, Margaret T. Gordon, Donna R. Leff, and Peter Miller, *The Journalism of Outrage: Investigative Reporting and Agenda Setting* (New York: Builford Press, 1991), p. 180.

32. See, for instance, Bennett, *News: The Politics of Illusion.*

33. For a good discussion of the impact the Thomas hearings had in mobilizing women voters and candidates, see Linda Witt, Karen M. Paget, Glenna Matthews, *Running as a Woman: Gender and Power in American Politics* (New York: Free Press, 1994).

34. See, for instance, Graber, *Mass Media and American Politics,* p. 311; see also Vincent James Strickler and Richard Davis, "The Supreme

35. Howard Kurtz, "Paint by Numbers: How Repeated Reportage Colors Perceptions," *Washington Post,* July 12, 2004, p. C1.

36. Daniel C. Hallin, "Sound Bite News: Television Coverage of Elections, 1968–1988," *Journal of Communication 42* (1992): 15.

37. Robert S. Lichter and Richard E. Noyes, "There They Go Again: Media Coverage of Campaign '96," in *Political Parties, Campaigns, and Elections,* ed. Robert E. DeClerico (Upper Saddle River, NJ: Prentice Hall, 2000), p. 98.

38. For a good discussion of debates, see Graber, *Mass Media and American Politics,* ch. 8.

39. Richard Davis, *The Press and American Politics,* 3rd ed. (Upper Saddle River, NJ: Prentice Hall, 2001), p. 93.

40. Ana Vecina-Suarez, *Hispanic Media USA: A Narrative Guide to Print and Electronic Media in the United States* (Washington, DC: Media Institute, 1987).

41. J. D. Lasica, "What Is Participatory Journalism?" *Online Journalism Review,* August 7, 2003. Accessed at http://www.ojr.org/ojr/workplace/1060217106.php on April 4, 2010.

42. Ben H. Bagdikian, *The Media Monopoloy,* 5th ed. (Boston: Beacon Press), p. x.

43. Graber, *Mass Media and American Politics,* p. 41; see also Yeric, *Mass Media and the Politics of Change,* ch. 1.

44. For a good discussion of deregulation, see Leighley, *Mass Media and Politics,* ch. 2.

45. Graber, *Mass Media and American Politics,* p. 49.

46. Ibid., pp. 19–21.

47. Leighley, *Mass Media and Politics,* p. 80.

CHAPTER 12

1. Alexis de Tocqueville, *Democracy in America,* vol. 1, ed. Richard Heffner (New York: New American Library, 1956; originally published 1835, p. 220.

2. His actual charge was to examine our penal system, but his true interest was to examine our democracy so that he could take lessons back to France.

3. For a good discussion of the importance of organized groups in democratic theory, see Jane Mansbridge, "A Deliberative Theory of Interest Representation," in *The Politics of Interests: Interest Groups Transformed,* ed. Mark P. Petracca (Boulder, CO: Westview Press, 1992).

4. League of United Latin American Citizens. Accessed at http://www.lulac.org on June 1, 2008.

5. Jeffrey M. Berry, *Lobbying for the People: The Political Behavior of Public Interest Groups* (Princeton, NJ: Princeton University Press, 1977), p. 7.

6. Frank R. Baumgartner and Beth L. Leech, *Basic Interests: The Importance of Groups in Politics and in Political Science* (Princeton, NJ: Princeton University Press, 1998), p. 103.

7. Robert Salisbury, "An Exchange Theory of Interest Groups," *Midwest Journal of Political Science 13* (February 1969): pp. 1–32.

8. Mancur Olson, *The Logic of Collective Action* (Cambridge, MA: Harvard University Press, 1971).

9. James Q. Wilson, *Political Organizations* (New York: Basic Books, 1974), p. 34.

10. Adapted from National Rifle Association. Accessed at http://www.nra.org

11. Anthony Nownes, *Pressure and Power: Organized Interests in American Politics* (Boston: Houghton Mifflin, 2001), p. 50.

12. Ibid., p. 51.

13. David B. Truman, *The Governmental Process: Political Interests and Public Opinion,* 2nd ed. (New York: Knopf, 1971).

14. Ken Kollman, *Outside Lobbying: Public Opinion and Interest Group Strategies* (Princeton, NJ: Princeton University Press, 1998), p. 58.

15. Kenneth M. Goldstein, *Interest Groups, Lobbying, and Participation in America* (Cambridge, England: Cambridge University Press, 1999), p. 111.

16. Ibid., p. 125; see also Nownes, *Pressure and Power.*

17. Goldstein, *Interests Groups,* p. 3.

18. Kollman, *Outside Lobbying.*

19. Cliff Landesman, "Nonprofits and the World Wide Web," Idealist.org. Accessed at http://www.idealist.org/if/i/en/av/FAQText/319-38 on March 22, 2010.

20. The Supreme Court overturned the precedents established in 1990, *Austin v. Michigan Chamber of Commerce,* and in 2003, *McConnell v. Federal Election Commission*

21. Darrell W. West and Burdett A. Loomis, *The Sound of Money* (New York: Norton, 1998).

22. Truman, *Governmental Process.*

23. Sidney Verba, Kay Lehman Schlozman, and Henry E. Brady, *Voice of Equality: Civic Volunteerism in American Politics* (Cambridge, MA: Harvard University Press, 1995), pp. 150–154.

24. James Q. Wilson, "Democracy and the Corporation," *Does Big Business Rule America?* ed. Ronald Hessen (Washington, DC: Ethics and Public Policy Center, 1981), p. 37.

25. Allan J. Cigler and Mark Joslyn, "Group Involvement and Social Capital Development," in *Interest Group Politics,* 6th ed., ed. Allan J. Cigler and Burdett A. Loomis (Washington, DC: CQ Press, 2002), ch. 2.

26. Ibid.

27. For instance, see Matthew J. Burbank, Ronald J. Hrebenar, and Robert C. Benedict, *Parties, Interest Groups, and Political Campaigns* (Boulder, CO: Paradigm Publishers, 2008).

28. Verba, Schlozman, and Brady, *Voice of Equality,* pp. 81–82.

29. Jeffrey H. Birnbaum, *The Lobbyists* (New York: Times Books, 1992), p. 7.

CHAPTER 13

1. Alan P. Grimes, *Democracy and the Amendments to the Constitution* (Lexington, MA: Lexington Books, 1978), pp. 44–45.

2. Ibid., pp. 131, 142–147.

3. Alexsander Keyssar, *The Right to Vote: The Contested History of Democracy in the United States* (New York: Basic Books, 2000).

4. Ibid., p. 111.

5. Ibid., pp. 264–265.

6. L. Sandy Maisel, *Parties and Elections in America: The Electoral Process,* 3rd ed. (Lanham, MD: Rowman and Littlefield, 1999), p. 97.

7. Frances Fox Piven and Richard A. Cloward, *Why Americans Still Don't Vote: And Why Politicians Want It That Way* (Boston: Beacon Press, 2000).

8. These data, and much else, can be found in the American National Election Study Guide to Public Opinion and Electoral Behavior. Accessed at http://www.electionstudies.org/

9. Robert Putnam, *Bowling Alone: The Collapse and Revival of American Community* (New York: Simon and Schuster, 2000), p. 189.

10. John P. Frendreis, James L. Gibson, and Laura L. Vertz, "Electoral Relevance of Local Party Organizations," *American Political Science Review 84* (1990): 225–235; Stephen Brooks, Rick Farmer, and Kyriakos Pagonis, "The Effects of Grassroots Campaigning on Political Participation." Paper presented at the annual meeting of the Southern Political Science Association, November 8–10, 2001, Atlanta.

11. For details of these studies, see Richard Lau, Lee Sigelman, Caroline Heldman, and Paul Babbit, "The Effects of Negative Political Advertising: A Meta-Analytic Assessment," *American Political Science Review 93* (1999): 851–875.

12. Stephen Ansolabehere and Shanto Lyengar, *Going Negative: How Political Advertisments Shrink and Polarize the Electorate* (New York: Free Press, 1995).

13. Kelly D. Patterson and Daniel M. Shea, "Local Political Context and Negative Campaigns: A Test of Negative Effects Across State Party Systems," *Journal of Political Marketing 3* (2004): 1–20.

14. Larry J. Sabato, *Feeding Frenzy: How Attack Journalism Has Transformed American Politics* (New York: Free Press, 1993).

15. William H. Flanigan and Nancy H. Zingal, *Political Behavior and the American Electorate,* (Washington, DC: CQ Press, 1998), p. 40.

16. Jesse Singal, "Prognosis Negative," *Newsweek,* February 2, 2010. Accessed at http://www.newsweek.com/id/232901/page/1

17. Colin Campbell and Bert A. Rockman, "Introduction," in *The Clinton Presidency: First Appraisals,* ed. Colin Campbell and Bert A. Rockman (Chatham, NJ: Chatham House, 1996), p. 14.

18. John K. White and Daniel M. Shea, *New Party Politics: From Jefferson and Hamilton to the Information Age* (New York: Bedford St. Martin's, 2004), p. 19.

19. See, for example, John P. Frendreis, James L. Gibson, and Laura L. Vertz, "Electoral Relevance of Local Party Organizations," *American Political Science Review 84* (1990): 225–235.

20. White and Shea, *New Party Politics*, p. 20.

21. William Nisbet Chambers, *Political Parties in a New Nation: The American Experience, 1776–1809* (New York: Oxford University Press, 1963).

22. E. E. Schattschneider, *Party Government* (New York: Rinehart, 1942), p. 1.

23. Associate Press, "Maryland Sidesteps Electoral College," MSNBC, April 11, 2007. Accessed at http://www.msnbc.msn.com/id/18053715/ on September 19, 2007.

24. George Will, "From Schwarzenegger, a Veto for Voters' Good," *Washington Post,* October 12, 2006, p. A27.

25. John K. White and Daniel M. Shea, *New Party Politics: From Jefferson and Hamilton to the Information Age* (New York: Bedford St. Martin's, 2000), p. 210.

26. Howard L. Reiter, *Parties and Elections in Corporate America* (New York: St. Martin's Press, 1987), p. 171.

27. White and Shea, *New Party Politics*, p. 220.

28. "Tracking the Payback," Center for Responsive Politics. Accessed at http://www.opensecrets.org/payback/index.asp, April 23, 2003.

29. David Mayhew, *Congress: The Electoral Connection* (New Haven, CT: Yale University Press, 1974).

30. Roper Center for Public Opinion Research, 1994, cited in Center for Responsive Politics, *The Myths About Money in Politics* (Washington, D.C.: Center for Responsive Politics, 1995), p. 19.

31. "A Campaign Finance Triumph" [editorial], *New York Times,* December 11, 2003, p. 42A.

32. Paul Sherman, "Citizens United Decision Means More Free Speech," *National Review* Online, Janary 21, 2010, accessed at http://bench.nationalreview.com/post/?q=MGVlYzczZjZlMTM1YWVlYjJhMzA3NzJjMTVhYmUwZDg=

33. "The Court's Blow to Democracy" [editorial], *New York Times,* January 21, 2010, p. A30.

34. Kenneth Vogel, "Campaign Finance Reform: R.I.P.?" Politico.com, October 13, 2010. Accessed at http://www.politico.com/news/stories/1010/43515.html

35. The Pew Research Center funds the Pew Internet & American Life Project. The Project "produces reports that explore the impact of the Internet on families, communities, work and home, daily life, education, health care, and civic and political life." Reports can be found at http://www.pewinternet.org.

36. Technorati (http://www.technorati.com) is a search engine similar to Google; however, it is exclusively devoted to blogs. They produce a regular industry report (State of the Blogosphere) based on their total indexed blogs.

CHAPTER 14

1. For a well-known example, see Charles E. Lindblom and Edward J. Woodhouse, *The Policy-Making Process,* 3rd ed. (Englewood Cliffs, NJ: Prentice Hall, 1993).

2. Deborah Stone, *Policy Paradox: The Art of Political Decision Making* (New York: Norton, 1997), p. 11.

3. Isaiah Berlin, *Four Essays on Liberty* (Oxford, England: Oxford University Press, 1969).

4. Alexis de Tocqueville, *Democracy in America,* ed. Richard Heffner (New York: American Library, 1956; originally published 1835).

5. Robert Nozick, *Anarchy, State, and Utopia* (New York: Basic Books, 1974).

6. Stone, *Policy Paradox,* p. 53.

7. This is an iteration of Milton Rokeach's "two-value" model of political ideology; see Milton Rokeach, *The Nature of Human Values* (New York: Free Press, 1973).

8. Theodore J. Lowi, "American Business, Public Policy Case Studies, and Political Theory," *World Politics 16* (1965): 677–715.

9. Murray Edelman, *The Symbolic Uses of Politics* (Urbana: University of Illinois Press, 1967), ch. 2.

10. National Aeronautic and Space Administration, *World Book at NASA,* accessed at http://www.nasa.gov/worldbook/global_warming_worldbook.html, on January 20, 2010.

11. Intergovernmental Panel on Climate Change, *Climate Change 2007 Synthesis Report* (Geneva: IPCC, 2007)

12. Keith Johnson, "Climate Emails Stoke Debate," *Wall Street Journal,* November 23, 2009, p. A3.

13. See Robert A. Dahl, *Who Governs? Democracy and Power in an American City* (New Haven, CT: Yale University Press, 1961).

14. See C. Wright Mills, *The Power Elite* (Oxford, England: Oxford University Press, 1956).

15. Roger W. Cobb and Charles D. Elder, *Participation in American Politics: The Dynamics of Agenda Building* (Baltimore: Johns Hopkins University Press, 1983), pp. 82–93.

16. For a fascinating discussion of how power is exercised by controlling the agenda, see Peter Bachrach and Morton S. Baratz, "Two Faces of Power," *American Political Science Review 56* (1962): 947–952.

17. Robert A. Caro, *Master of the Senate: The Years of Lyndon Johnson* (New York: Knopf, 2002), ch. 7.

18. Cobb and Elder, *Participation in American Politics,* p. 86.

19. Anthony Downs, "Up and Down with Ecology: The 'Issue-Attention Cycle,'" *Public Interest* (Summer 1972): 38–50.

20. See Samuel Kernell, *Going Public: New Strategies of Presidential Leadership* (Washington, DC: CQ Press, 1986).

21. US Trade Deficit Falls in 2009, But Larger Share Goes to China. Accessed at www.epi.org/publications/entry/international_picture_20100211/

22. "CBO: Federal Deficit Projected at $13.5T." Accessed at news.yahoo.com/s/ap/20100126/ap_on_bi_ge/us_obama_budget

23. Congressional Budget Office. Accessed at http://www.cbo.gov/ftpdocs/112xx/doc11231/budgetprojections.xls

24. Remarks by Federal Reserve Board Chairman Alan Greenspan at the opening of an American Numismatic Society exhibition, Federal Reserve Bank of New York, New York, January 16, 2002.

25. Andrew Batson, "China Takes Aim at Dollar." Accessed at http://online.wsj.com/article/SB123780272456212885.html on March 24, 2009.

26. Information gathered from www.unreasonableinstitute.org and phone interview with the cofounder of Unreasonable Institute, Daniel Epstein.

27. Accessed at http://www.heritage.org/budgetchartbook/federal-revenue-sources on September 23, 2010.

28. "Income Requirements: 2009–2010 Taxable Income Levels." Accessed at http://www.umbc.edu/upwardbound/?page_id=29

29. "Obama Announces $33B Hiring Tax Credit." January 29, 2010. Accessed at abcnews.go.com/Business/Obama/obama-tax-credit-33-billion-hiring-jobs/story?id=9697334

30. Shan Carter and Amanda Cox, Obama's 2011 Budget Proposal: How It Is Spent. Published February 1, 2010. Accessed at http://www.nytimes.com/interactive/2010/02/01/us/budget.html

31. "Budget and Economy Outlook: Fiscal Years 2010–2020." Testimony Statement of Douglas Elmendorf, Director, CBO before Senate Committee on the Budget. Accessed at www.cbo.gov/ftpdocs/110xx/doc11014/01-28-Testimony_Senate.pdf on May 19, 2010.

32. "President Obama Heads to the Hill to Push the $3.5T Plan." Accessed at http://www.pbs.org/nbr/site/onair/transcripts/obama-capitol-hill-budget-090325/

33. "Defense Spending Remains Below Historical Levels Despite the War on Terror." Accessed at http://www.heritage.org/Research/Features/BudgetChartbook/Defense-Spending-on-the-Decline-Despite-War-on-Terror.aspx

34. Office of Management and Budget, Department of Defense. Accessed at www.whitehouse.gov/omb/rewrite/budget/fy2008/defense.html

35. "DOD Releases Defense Reviews, 2011 Budget Proposal, and 2010 War Funding Supplemental Request — Update." Accessed at www.defense.gov/Releases/Release.aspx?ReleaseID=13281

36. Jackie Calmes, "President Plans Own Panel on Debt." Accessed at www.nytimes.com/2010/01/27/us/politics/27budget.html

37. The Federal Budget 2011. Department Fact Sheets. Accessed at www.whitehouse.gov/omb/budget_factsheets_departments/

38. For a through discussion of the incremental approach, see Charles E. Lindblom, "The Science of Muddling Through," *Public Administration Review 19* (1959): 79–88.

CHAPTER 15

1. Charles Krauthammer, "The Unipolar Moment Revisited," *National Interest* (Winter 2002–2003): pp. 5–18; Max Boot, *The Savage Wars of Peace* (New York: Basic Books, 2002).

2. G. John Ikenberry, *After Victory: Institutions, Strategic Restraint, and the Rebuilding of Order After Major Wars* (Princeton, NJ: Princeton University Press, 2001).

3. Robert Tucker and David Hendrickson, "The Sources of American Legitimacy," *Foreign Affairs 83* (2004): 18–32; Henry Nau, "No Enemies on the Right," *National Interest* (Winter 2004–2005): 19–28.

4. Gary Dempsey, with Roger Fontaine, *Fool's Errands: America's Recent Encounters with Nation Building* (Washington, DC: Cato Press, 2001).

5. Accessed at Iraqi Body Count at http://www.iraqbodycount.org/

6. Glenn Hastedt, ed., *One World, Many Voices* (Englewood Cliffs, NJ: Prentice Hall, 1995), pp. 240–250, 288–300.

7. "Foreign Interests Spend $87 Million Lobbying in U.S." Accessed at http://www.allbusiness.com/government/government-bodies-offices-us-federal-government/13708212-1.html

8. "U.S. Foreign Lobbying, Terrorism Influencing Post-9/11 U.S. Military Aid and Human Rights." Accessed at http://projects.publicintegrity.org/NewsRelease.aspx?=101

9. Ibid.

10. Peter Trubowitz, *Defining the National Interest* (Chicago: University of Chicago Press, 1998).

11. Miroslav Nincic, "Domestic Costs, the U.S. Public and the Isolationist Calculus," *International Studies Quarterly 41* (1997): 593–610; Bruce Jentleson, "The Pretty Prudent Public: Post-Vietnam American Opinion on the Use of Force," *International Studies Quarterly 36* (1990): 49–74.

12. "Obama Signs Patriot Act Extensions." Accessed at http://www.washingtontimes.com/news/2010/feb/27/obama-signs-one-year-extension-patriot-act/

13. For a more extensive discussion, see Glenn Hastedt, *American Foreign Policy: Past, Present, Future,* 6th ed. (Upper Saddle River, NJ: Prentice Hall, 2006).

14. Thomas Graham, "Public Opinion and U.S. Foreign Policy," in *The New Politics of American Foreign Policy,* ed. David Deese (New York: St. Martin's Press, 1994), pp. 190–215.

15. William Quandt, "The Electoral Cycle and the Conduct of American Foreign Policy," *Political Science Quarterly 101* (1986): 825–837.

16. David Cohen, Chris Dolan, and Jerel Rosati, "A Place at the Table," *Congress and the Presidency 29* (2002): 119–149.

17. Paul Kengor, "The Vice President, the Secretary of State, and Foreign Policy," *Political Science Quarterly 115* (2000): 175–190.

18. Amy Zegart, *Flawed by Design: The Evolution of the CIA, JCS, and NSC* (Stanford, CA: Stanford University Press, 2000).

19. Loch Johnson and James Wirtz, eds., *Strategic Intelligence: Windows into a Secret World* (Los Angeles: Roxbury, 2004).

20. Michael Scherer, "The CIA Announces Further Changes to Respond to Intel Failure," *Time Magazine,* January 7, 2010. Accessed at http://swampland.blogs.time.com/2010/01/07/the-cia-announces-further-changes-to-respond-to-intel-failure/

21. Glenn Hastedt, "The Department of Homeland Security: Politics of Creation," in *Contemporary Cases in American Foreign Policy,* ed. Ralph Carter (Washington, DC: CQ Press, 2004).

22. Nick Bunkley, "Militia Charged with Plotting to Murder Officers," *New York Times,* March 29, 2010. Accessed at http://www.nytimes.com/2010/03/30/us/30militia.html

23. James Scott and Ralph Carter, "Acting on the Hill," *Congress and the Presidency 29* (2002): 151–169.

24. Audrey Kurth Cronin and James Ludes, eds., *Attacking Terrorism* (Washington, DC: Georgetown University Press, 2004).

25. British Broadcasting Company, "U.S. and Russia Announce Deal to Cut Nuclear Weapons." Accessed at http://news.bbc.co.uk/2/hi/europe/8589385.stm, March 26, 2010.

26. Ashton Carter, "How to Counter WMD," *Foreign Affairs* (September 2004): 72–85.

27. "US-Russia Treaty Stalls over Obama Missile Defense Plan," *McClatchy Newspapers.* Accessed at http://www.mcclatchydc.com/2010/03/01/89641/us-russia-treaty-stalls-over-obama.html

28. "Obama Risks Flap on 'Buy American'," *Wall Street Journal.* Accessed at http://online.wsj.com/article/SB123370411879745425.html

29. "Obama backs down on 'Buy American' clause." Accessed at http://www.euractiv.com/en/trade/obama-backs-buy-american-clause/article-179157

30. Lael Brainard, "Compassionate Conservatism Confronts Global Poverty," *Washington Quarterly* (Spring 2003): 149–169.

31. Program on International Policy Attitudes, "Americans on Foreign Aid and World Hunger," February 2, 2001. Accessed at http://www.pipa.org/OnlineReports/ForeignAid/ForeignAid_Feb01/ForeignAid_Feb01_quaire.pdf

32. Office of Management and Budget, *Budget of the United States Government, Fiscal Year 2011.* Accessed at http://www.whitehouse.gov/omb/budget/fy2011/assets/tables.pdf

33. "Facts about US Foreign Assistance," Reuters. Accessed at http://www.reuters.com/article/idUSTRE6054DT20100106

34. "OMB: Department of State and Other International Programs." White House. Accessed at http://www.whitehouse.gov/omb/factsheet_department_state/

35. "Facts about US Foreign Assistance." Accessed at http://www.reuters.com/article/idUSTRE6054DT20100106

36. Scott Straus, "Darfur and the Genocide Debate," *Foreign Affairs* (January-February 2005): 123–133.

37. "UNAMID—Background." Accessed at http://unamid.unmissions.org/Default.aspx?tabid=890

38. "UNAMID—Facts and Figures." Accessed at http://www.un.org/en/peacekeeping/missions/unamid/facts.shtml

39. "Review of Land Mine Treaty to 'Take Some Time,' State Dept. Says." Accessed at http://www.nytimes.com/2009/11/26/world/americas/26mines.html

40. United Nations Educational Scientific and Cultural Organization, "Trafficking and HIV/Aids Project Fact Sheet," Accessed at http://www.unescobkk.org/culture/our-projects/cultural-diversity/trafficking-and-hivaids-project/projects/trafficking-statistics-project/data-comparison-sheet/

41. "United States of America Fact Sheet." Accessed at http://www.humantrafficking.org/countries/united_states_of_america

42. U.S. Department of State, *Trafficking in Persons Report 2010.* Accessed at http://www.state.gov/g/tip/rls/tiprpt/2010/

43. John M. Broder "Climate Change as Threat to U.S. Security," *New York Times,* August 8, 2009. Accessed at http://www.nytimes.com/2009/08/09/science/earth/09climate.html

CHAPTER 16

1. Robert J. Chandler, "Crushing Dissent: The Pacific Coast Tests Lincoln's Policy of Suppression, 1862," *Civil War History 30* (September 1984): 235–254.

2. James J. Rawls and Walton Bean, *California: An Interpretive History* (New York: McGraw-Hill, 1998).

3. Ibid.

4. Wyatt Buchanan, "California Leaders Seek Budget Help from D.C.," *SFGate.* Accessed at www.SFGate.com on January 4, 2010.

5. Julian Nava and Bob Barger, *California: Five Centuries of Cultural Contrasts* (Beverly Hills: Glencoe Press, 1976), pp. 10–11.

6. Ibid., p. 28.

7. N. Ray Gilmore and Gladys Gilmore, *Readings in California History* (New York: Crowell, 1966), pp. 9–12.

8. Nava and Barger, *California,* pp. 69–86.

9. Howard A. Dewitt, *The California Dream* (Dubuque, IA: Kendall/Hunt, 1997), pp. 53–68.

10. Ibid., pp. 15–20.

11. Ibid., pp. 76–83.

12. Nava and Barger, *California*, p. 170.
13. Dewitt, *California Dream*, pp. 100–103.
14. Robert G. Cleland, *From Wilderness to Empire: History of California* (New York: Knopf, 1959), pp. 168–174.
15. George E. Mowry, *The California Progressives* (Chicago: Quadrangle Books, 1963), pp. 8–12.
16. Walton Bean, *Boss Ruef's San Francisco* (Berkeley: University of California Press, 1952), p. 5.
17. Nava and Barger, *California*, pp. 259–260.
18. Mowry, *California Progressives*, pp. 18–21.
19. Ibid., p. 36.
20. Ibid., pp. 116–134.
21. Ibid., pp. 135–157.
22. Kevin Starr, *California: A History* (New York: Modern Library, 2005), pp. 235–244.
23. Ibid., pp. 226–227.
24. Field Research Corporation, *Major Issues Facing Californians*, California Opinion Index, San Francisco, Field Research Corporation, March 2005. Accessed at http://www.field.com/Fieldpoilonline/subscribens/C01-05-Mar_CA-Issues.pdf on September 9, 2008.
25. "Who Are California's Students?" *EdSource*, Palo Alto EdSource on-line, June 2002. Accessed at http//www.edsource.org
26. Field Research, *Major Issues.*
27. Ibid.
28. Amanda Bailey and Joseph M. Hayes, "Who's in Prison?" *California Counts—Population Trends and Profiles*, vol. 8, no. 1, 2006, Public Policy Institute of California.
29. "Californians Split on Tax Increases to Balance Budgets," *Los Angeles Times*/CNN/Politico California Survey, January 15, 2008. Accessed at http://www.latimes.com/media/acrobat/2008-01/34771206.pdf on September 9, 2008.
30. Pamela M. Prah, "The Path to California's Fiscal Crisis, Stateline.org, May 15, 2009. Accessed at http://www.stateline.org/live/details/story?contentId=400337
31. Charles W. Schmidt, "Spheres of Influence: California Out in Front," *Environment Health Perspectives*, vol. 115, no. 3 (March 2007), p. A145.

CHAPTER 17

1. California Secretary of State, "Report of Registration." Accessed at http://www.ss.ca.gov/elections/ror_01022004.htm on January 2, 2004.
2. John R. Owens et al., *California Politics and Parties*, (New York: The Macmillan Company, 1970), pp. 103–106.
3. George E. Mowry, *The California Progressives*, (Chicago: Quadrangle Books, 1963), p. 149.
4. Ibid., p. 140.
5. Ibid., p. 149.
6. Margaret Taler, "It's Arnold Schwarzenegger Coast to Victory as Davis Is Ousted in 'Historic Vote," *Sacramento Bee*, October 8, 2003, p. E11.
7. Ibid.
8. Peter Schrag, *Paradise Lost: California's Experience, America's Future* (Berkeley: University of California Press, 2004), p. 10.
9. Charles M. Price, "Shadow Government," in *California Government and Politics Annual, 2001–2002*, ed. A.G. Block and Charles M. Price (Sacramento: State Net, 2001), pp. 72–74.
10. "Tribes Vow to Fight Casino Ruling," *Gambling*, August 26, 1999. Accessed at http://www.gamblingmagazine.com/articles/41/41–216.htm
11. "U.S. Supreme Court Rules on Medical Marijuana," Marijuana Policy Project, December 30, 2005. Accessed at http://www.mpp.org/raich
12. Ronald L. Soble, "Homeowners Get Tax News, Vow to Back Prop. 13," *Los Angeles Times*, May 19, 1978, pp. 1, 20.
13. Jay Matthews, "California Transformed by 'Prop 13,'" *Los Angeles Times*, May 23, 1988, p. A4. See also Robert Fairbanks, "Prop. 13's Super Salesman," *Los Angeles Times*, May 17, 1978, p. 24; Bill Boyarsky, "Grass Roots on Airwaves to Push 13," *Los Angeles Times*, May 28, 1978, p. 18; and Kenneth Reich, "Jarvis Riding Wave of Public Anger," *Los Angeles Times*, June 8, 1978, p. 18.

14. Schrag, *Paradise Lost*, pp. 146–147.
15. Public Policy Institute of California, "The California Initiative Process: How Democratic Is It?" February 2002, pp. 4–5. Accessed at http://www.ppic.org/content/pubs/OP_202XXOP.pdf
16. Ibid., pp. 1–4.
17. J. Allswang, *California Initiatives and Referendums, 1912–1990* (Los Angeles: Edmund G. Brown Institute of Public Affairs, 1991).
18. "Insurers to Seek Referendum to Repeal New 'Bad Faith' Law," California Policy Bulletins, October 18, 1999. Accessed at http://ca.rand.org/statebulls/bulletins/xstatebull218.html
19. Bruce E. Cain, "Constitutional Revision in California: The Triumph of Amendment over Revision" in George Alan Tarr and Robert F. Williams, *State Constitutions for the Twenty-First Century: The Politics of State Constitutioinal Reform* (Albany: SUNY Press, 2005), pp. 201–202.
20. Public Policy Institute of California, "California Voter and Party Profiles," August 2005. Accessed at http://ww.ppic.org/content/pubs/JTF_VoterProfilesJTF.pdf
21. California Secretary of State Election and Voter Information. Accessed at http://www.ss.ca.gov.elections. See also U.S. Census Bureau—America's Factfinder. Accessed at http://www.census.gov/main/www.cen2000.html
22. Christian Berthelsen, "Governor Sets Money-Raising Record," *San Francisco Chronicle*, November 17, 2004, p. A1.
23. Margaret Talev, "Corporate Donations Defended," *Sacramento Bee*, August 27, 2003.
24. Dorothy Korber, "Growth Lobby a Growing Business, Records Show," *Sacramento Bee*, December 8, 2002, p. A1.
25. Ibid.
26. Dennis Hale and Jonathan Eisen, *The California Dream* (New York: Collier, 1968). See also James Q. Wilson, "The Political Culture of Southern California," p. 217.
27. California Secretary of State, "Report of Registration." Accessed at www.ss.ca.gov/elections/ror_01022004.htm
28. Mary Ellen Leary, "Elusive Candidates," in *Phantom Politics: Campaigning in California* (Washington, DC: Public Affairs, 1977), p. 20.
29. Ken McLaughlin, "Meg Whitman's Campaign Shakes the World of Political Advertising," *Mercury News*, March 27, 2010, p. 33; George Rains, "Election 2005: Analysis: Costly TV Ads Doing Little to Sway Voters," *San Francisco Chronicle*, October 29, 2005, p. B2.
30. Martin Kaplan, Ken Goldstein, and Matthew Hale, "Local News Coverage of the 2004 Campaigns: An Analysis of Nightly Broadcasts in 11 Markets" [working paper], Lear Center Local News Archive, Los Angeles, February 15, 2005, p. 12.
31. Greg Mitchell, *The Campaign of the Century* (New York: Random House, 1992), pp. 201–202.
32. California Voter Participation Survey: Overall Findings, California Voter Foundation. Accessed at http://www.calvoter.org/issues/votereng/votpart/keyfindings.html
33. Juliet Williams, "State Election Official Threatens to Block Use of Voting Machines," *Contra Costa Times*, December 24, 2005, p. A11.
34. Greg Lucas, "Settlement in Electronic Voting Lawsuit," *San Francisco Chronicle*, November 11, 2004, p. B3.
35. Juliet Williams, "State Election Official Threatens."
36. Subramanian Karthick Ramakrishnan and Mark Baldassare, *The Ties That Bind: Changing Demographics and Civic Engagement* (San Francisco: Public Policy Institute of California, 2004), pp. 9–18.

CHAPTER 18

1. Arthur H. Samish and Bob Thomas, *The Secret Boss of California: The Life and High Times of Art Samish* (New York: Crown, 1971), p. 35.
2. Ruth A. Ross and Barbara S. Stone, *California's Political Process* (New York: Random House, 1973), pp. 91–92.
3. A. G. Block and Claudia Buck, eds., *California Political Almanac*, 6th ed. (Sacramento: California Journal, 1999), pp. 19, 123–124.
4. Jay Michael, Dan Walters, and Dan Weintraub, *The Third House: Lobbyists, Money, and Power in Sacramento* (Berkeley: Public Policy Press, 2002), p. 75.
5. National Conference of State Legislatures, "Current Number of Legislators, Terms of Office and Next Election Year." Accessed at http://www.ncsl.org/programs/legismgt/about/numoflegis.htm

6. Ibid.

7. Daniel Weintraub, "Governor Should Be Bold, Call for New Lines," *Sacramento Bee,* December 5, 2004, p. E1.

8. Robert B. Gunnison, "Capital Probe: FBI Reportedly Told Deukmejian About Its Sting," *San Francisco Chronicle,* August 30, 1988, p. A1.

9. Michael et al., *Third House,* pp. 95–96.

10. Excerpts from an interview conducted by Milton Clarke with Craig Cheslog, May 20, 2008.

11. Assembly on State Issues Meeting, National Conference of State Legislatures, "Legislative Effectiveness Committee Meeting Summaries." December 2000. Accessed at http://www.ncsl.org on September 13, 2008.

12. Ibid.

13. Ibid.

14. Sabin Russsell, "Female Inmates Beg State Lawmakers for Better Health Care," *San Francisco Chronicle,* October 12, 2000, p. A3.

15. Lisa Katayama, "Reforming California's Prisons: An Interview with Jackie Speier," *Mother Jones,* July 7, 2005. Accessed at http://www.motherjones.com on September 13, 2008.

16. Gary Delsohn, "Rejected Air Board Boss Gets New Post," *Sacramento Bee,* September 29, 2005, p. A3.

17. John R. Owens, Edmond Costantini, and Louis F. Weschler, *California politics and parties,* (New York: Macmillan, 1970) p. 302.

18. Jim Sanders, "Some Moderates Claim Pressure by Nuñez," *Sacramento Bee,* January 9, 2005, p. A3.

19. "Legislator Compensation, 2005," National Conference of State Legislatures. Accessed at http://www.ncsl.org on September 13, 2008.

20. James Richardson, *Willie Brown: A Biography* (Berkeley: University of California Press, 1996), pp. 220–231.

21. Jeff Kearns, "Dems Divided," *Sacramento News and Review,* December 25, 2003. Accessed at http://www.newsreview.com/sacramento/content?oid=26646

22. Marisa Lagos, "New Assembly Leader Faces Enormous Challenges," *San Francisco Chronicle,* December 14, 2009, p. A1.

23. "Assembly GOP Votes for New Minority Leader," *Berkeley Daily Planet,* March 27, 2001. Accessed at http://www.berkeleydailyplanet.com on September 12, 2008.

24. "FTCR Praises Veto of Mercury Insurance Surcharge," Foundation for Taxpayer and Consumer Rights, September 30, 2002. Accessed at http://www.consumerwatchdog.org on September 13, 2008.

25. "Above the Rules: How California Legislators Subvert the Public Interest—and Even the Expressed Will of the Voters," *San Francisco Chronicle,* September 22, 2002, p. D4.

10. John Wildermuth, "State Threatens to Pull Plug on Vote Machine Firm—Company Ordered to Correct Glitches or Lose Certification," *San Francisco Chronicle,* December 24, 2005, p. B2.

11. John Wildermuth, "Secretary of State Doubtful of Electronic Voting's Future," *San Francisco Chronicle,* December 2, 2007, p. C7.

12. "The Secretary of State," Office of the Secretary of State. Accessed at http://www.sos.ca.gov/admin/about-the-agency.htm

13. Lance Williams and Christian Berthelsen, "Shelley's Shock Soul Searching," *San Francisco Chronicle,* February 6, 2005, p. A1.

14. Kirsten Mangold, "The Race for Superintendent of Public Instruction: DiMarco, Easton Tangle for the Job of Schools' Chief," *California Journal,* 1994. Accessed at http://www.calvoter.org/archive/94general/cand/super/journal.htm

15. Ken Chavez, "Wilson Vetoes Bill to Boost Instruction Offices Powers, Would Have Reversed Increase in Education Panel Clout," *Sacramento Bee,* September 9, 1983, p. A6.

16. Peter Schrag, *Paradise Lost: California's Experience, America's Future.* (Berkeley/Los Angeles, CA: University of California Press, 1999), p. 197.

17. Virginia Ellis and Carl Ingram, "Whistle-Blower Emerges in Quackenbush Probe," *Los Angeles Times,* June 23, 2000, p. 1.

18. Emily Bazar, "Quake Insurers Taken to Court," *Sacramento Bee,* November 21, 2000, p. A1.

19. Dan Walters, "Schwarzenegger's Only Big Gain—Workers' Comp—Is at Risk," *Sacramento Bee,* November 20, 2005, p. A3.

20. Block and Buck, *California Political Almanac,* pp. 70–72.

21. Citizens Against Unfair Health Taxes, California Chapter. Accessed at http://www.stophealthcaretaxes.com

22. Evan Halper, "California OK's $80 Million in Tax Refunds to Companies," *Los Angeles Times,* January 26, 2005, p. 31.

23. Ibid.

24. "Evaluating California's Board and Commissions," California Performance Review. Accessed at Project, http://cpr.ca.gov/report/cprrpt/frmfunc/bdscmm.htm

25. Craft, "Gray Davis," p. 12.

26. Robert Salladay, "Consumer Privacy Bill Could Be Weakened, Davis Aides Conferring with Industry Lobbyist," *San Francisco Chronicle,* August 3, 2001, p. A1.

27. "California Governor Vetoes Credit Card Disclosure Bill" [press release], *Consumers Union,* September 29, 2000. Accessed at http://www.consumersunion.org/finance/1963wc900.htm

28. "Campaign Finance Reformers See Gaming Conflict," *Gambling,* 1999. Accessed at http://gambiinQmagazine.com/article/26/26-302.htm

Chapter 19

1. Pew Foundation, *California Performance Review.* Accessed at http://cpr.ca.gov/report

2. "The Government Performance Project: Grading the States, '05," *Government Performance Project.* Accessed at http://results.gpponline.org

3. "Field Poll Trend of Job Performance Ratings of California Governors," Field Research Corp. Accessed at http://field.poll/governors.html on September 16, 2008.

4. A. G. Block and Claudia Buck, eds. *California Political Almanac, 1999–2000,* 6th ed. (Sacramento, CA: California Journal Press/State Net), pp. 36–37.

5. Cynthia H. Craft, "Gray Davis: Show Me the Money," in *California Government and Politics Annual, 2001–2002,* A. G. Block, ed. (Sacramento, CA: California Journal Press), p. 10.

6. "Governors of California." Accessed at http://www.californiagovernors.ca.gov/h/biography/index.html

7. Ethan Rarick, *California Rising: The Life and Times of Pat Brown* (Berkeley: University of California Press, 2006).

8. Ibid., p. 68.

9. "Responsibilities of the Controller's Office," California State Controller's Office. Accessed at http://www.sco.ca.gov/eo/controller/inside/faqs.shtml

Chapter 20

1. Josh Richman, "Federal Judge Fast-tracks Lawsuit Seeking to Overturn Same Sex Marriage Ban," *Contra Costa Times,* July 2, 2009.

2. All details on the superior courts are from Judicial Council of California, *Fact Sheet: California Judicial System: Administrative Office of the Courts* (San Francisco: Judicial Council of California, 2003).

3. Judicial Council of California, *A Visitor's Guide to the California Supreme Court* (San Francisco: Judicial Council of California, 2004).

4. "Small Claims Basics," California Courts, Self-Help Center, 2006. Accessed at http://courtinfo.ca.gov/selfhelp/smallclaims/scbasics.htm

5. Judicial Council, *Fact Sheet.*

6. "Get Ready for Court," California Courts, Self-Help Center, http://www.courtinfo.ca.gov/selfhelp/lowcost/getready.htm

7. Judicial Council, *Fact Sheet.*

8. Ibid.

9. Judicial Council, *Visitor's Guide.*

10. National Center on Elder Abuse, *Abuse of Adults 60+: 2004 Survey of Adult Protective Services* (Washington, DC: National Center on Elder Abuse, 2006).

11. George T. Payton, *Concepts of California Criminal Law* (San Jose, CA: Criminal Justice Services, 1995), pp. 125–131.

12. David Amar Vikram, "An Important Sentencing Ruling from the California Supreme Court," June 24, 2005. Accessed at http://writ.news.findlaw.com/amar/20050624.html

13. Leslie Abramson, with Richard Flaste, *The Defense Is Ready: Life in the Trenches of Criminal Law* (New York: Simon and Schuster, 1997), pp. 183–204.

14. "Assemblywoman Kehoe Pushing for Police Powers for Homeowner Associations," American Homeowners Resource Center, June 21, 2002. Accessed at http://www.ahrc.se/new/index.php/src/news/sub/pressrel/action/ShowMedia/id/148

15. "State Law Protects Officers from Disclosure of Complaints," *San Francisco Chronicle,* February 9, 2006, p. A1.

16. *CDAA Specialized Newsletters,* California District Attorney's Association, 2006. Accessed at http://www.cdaa.org/grantpubs/index.htm

17. Fredric N. Tulsky, "Review of More than 700 Appeals Finds Problems Throughout the Justice System," *San Jose Mercury News,* January 22, 2006. Accessed at the National Association of Criminal Defense Lawyers: http://www.nacdl.org/public.nsf/DefenseUpdates/California011

18. Fredric N. Tulsky, "Tainted Trials, Stolen Justice: A 3-Year Study of Santa Clara County Criminal Trials, *San Jose Mercury News.* Accessed at http://www.mercurynews.com/taintedtrials

19. Fredric N. Tulsky, "Review of More than 700 Appeals.

20. John Howard, "Waiting for Judgment Day," *California Journal,* May 2004; Scott Ehlers and Jason Ziedenberg, "Proposition 36: Five Years Later," Justice Policy Institute, April, 2006. Accessed at http://www.justicepolicy.org/images/upload/06-04_REP_CAProp36FiveYearsLater_DP-AC.pdf

21. Daniel Macallair, "The Death of Prison Reform," *San Diego Union-Tribune,* January 18, 2006. Accessed at http://www.signonsandiego.com/uniontrib/20060118/news_lz1e18macalla.html

22. Daniel Klerman, "American Tort Reform Association: Bringing Greater Fairness, Predictability and Efficiency to the Civil Justice System." Accessed at http://www.atra.org/reports/CA_juries

23. Ibid.

24. Ibid.

25. Accessed at http://www.cgja.org/nss-folder/briefhistoryofgrandjuries/Grdjry.rtf

26. Cathy Lockebee, "Grand Jury Cites Unspent Funds," *Sacramento Bee,* January 12, 2006, p. G1.

27. Maura Dolan, "California Supreme Court Overturns Gay Marriage Ban," *Los Angeles Times,* May 16, 2008. Accessed at http://www.latimes.com/news/local/la-me-gaymarriage16-2008may16,0,6182317story on August 27, 2008.

28. Bob Egelko, "Ronald George," in *California Government and Politics Annual, 2001-2002,* eds. A. G. Block and Charles M. Price. (Sacramento, CA: StateNet, 2001–2002), pp. 22–24.

29. "California Supreme Court Upholds Student's First Amendment Rights: Conviction of 'George T' for Writing Dark Poems Overturned" [press release], American Civil Liberties Union of Northern California, July 22, 2004. Accessed at http://www.aclunc.org

30. Bob Egelko, "Ronald George."

31. State of the Judiciary Address to a Joint Session of the California Legislature by Chief Justice Ronald M. George, February 23, 2010. http://www.courtinfo.ca.gov/reference/soj022310.htm

CHAPTER 21

1. U.S. National Climatic Data Center, California Department of Water Resources, accessed at http://www.publicaffairs.water.ca.gov/dwr50thanniversary/flood/historic.cfm; FEMA, Annual Major Disaster Declarations Totals, accessed at http://www.fema.gov/news/disaster_totals_annual.fema

2. "The History of County Government," National Association of Counties. Accessed at http://www.naco.org/Content/NavigationMenu/About_Counties/History_of_County_Government/Default983.htm

3. Tim I. Purdy, "Lassen's Past*," Lassen County History and Culture: Narrative History.* Accessed at http://www.users.psln.com/pete/lassen_county_history.htm

4. *The Historical Records of County Government in California,* 2nd ed. (Sacramento: California State Archives, 2004), p. 70.

5. Raphael J. Sonenshein, *The Prospect for County Charter Reform in California* (Fullerton: Department of Political Science, California State University, 2001), pp. 14–16.

6. "County Structure," California State Association of Counties. Accessed at http://www.csac.counties.org

7. Alvin D. Sokolow, "Caring for Unincorporated Communities." *San Lorenzo Express,* March–April 2000. Accessed at http://www.sanlorenzoexpress.com

8. "History of Contract Cities," California Contract Cities Association. Accessed at http://www.contracities.org/index.cfm?Page=History

9. *Historical Records,* p. 71.

10. Ibid., p. 63.

11. "County Offices: Auditor-Controller," California State Association of Counties. Accessed at http://www.csac.counties.org/default.asp?id=2274

12. "Lean on Me: California's Local Governments Rely on State Money More Than Those in Rest of Nation" [press release], Public Policy Institute of California, January 27, 2003. Accessed at http://www.ppic.org/main/pressrelease.asp?i=387

13. Stu Woo and Bobby White, "California Cities Irked by Borrowing Plan," *Wall Street Journal,* May 22, 2009. Accessed at http://online.wsj.com/article/SB124294953351345429.html on October 20, 2009.

14. Letter from San Joaquin County Board of Supervisors to State Assembly Member Alyson Huber, "Opposition to Suspension of Proposition 1A and Local Transportation Funding," July 17, 2009. Accessed at http://www.ceaccounties.org/resources/1/Policy%20Areas/Transportation/Resources/HUTA/HUTA_San%20Joaquin%20County_Suspension%20of%20Prop%201A%20and%20Local%20Transp%20Funds.pdf on October 20, 2009.

15. Loretta Kalb, "Balancing the Budget—Million-dollar question: Borrow?—As State Reaches into Local Coffers, Governments Struggle to Cope" *Sacramento Bee,* August 2, 2009 p. B1.

16. Amanda Meeker, "An Overview of the History of Constitutional Provisions Dealing with Local Government," California Constitutional Revision Commission. Accessed at http://digitalarchive.oclc.org/da/ViewObjectMain.jsp?filed=0000020402:000000988712&reqid=349

17. League of Women Voters, "Guide to Government: California State Government," *Smart Voter.* Accessed at http://www.smartvoter.org

18. League of California Cities. "Types of Cities," Accessed at http://www.cacities.org/userfiles/godoc/3242.Types%20of %20Cities.htm

19. League of Women Voters, "Guide to Government."

20. Robert Speer, "Measure A, Nasty Politics, and the Leadership Gap," *Chico News and Review,* March 13, 2006. Accessed at http://www.newsreview.com/chico/Content?oid=4451

21. Kevin F. McCarthy, Fae W. Archibald, and Brian Weatherford, *Facing the Challenge of Implementing Proposition F in San Diego* (Santa Monica: Rand Corporation, 2005).

22. Speer, "Measure A."

23. Modesto Irrigation District, "Dreams Become Reality." Accessed at http://www.mid.org/about/100-year/grnng_of_pvy-03.pdf

24. California Special Districts Association, "About Special Districts," Accessed at http://www.csda.net

25. California Special Districts Association, "Frequently Asked Questions," Accessed at http://www.csda.net/idex.php?option=com_content&task=view&id=188&Itemid=204

26. Howard Fine, "Special Districts Get Stuck with Bigger Tax Losses than Planned," *Los Angeles Business Journal,* December 6, 2004. Accessed at http://goliath.ecnext.com/coms2/gi_0199-3529210/Special-districts-get-stuck-with.html#abstract

27. Marc Titel and Roger Wagner, "Tightening Controls over California's Special Districts: Lessons Learned from the WRD," *Cal-Tax Digest,* July 2000. Accessed at http://www.caltax.org/member/digest/July200/jul00-3.htm

28. Richard R. Terzian, "Special Districts: Relics of the Past or Resources for the Future?" *Cal-Tax Digest,* July 2000. Accessed at http://www.caltax.org/member/digest/July2000/jul00-4.htm

29. Ibid.

30. Howard A. Dewitt, *The California Dream,* 2nd ed. (Dubuque: Kendall/Hunt Publishing Company, 1999), p. 182.

31. Ibid., pp. 182–183.

32. California Department of Education, "District Organization." Accessed at http://www.cde.gov/re/lr/do

33. Carey McWilliams, *California: The Great Exception* (New York: Current Books, 1949), p. 18.

34. "How Do California's School Boards Compare?" Stanford News Service. Accessed at http://news-service.stanford.edu/pr/92/920422Arc2267.html

35. "Board Briefs: News from the School Board Meeting," Fresno Unified School District, February 22, 2006.

36. "Race to the Top Judges Cite Why State Lost Out on Money," *Sacramento Bee - Contra Costa Times,* April 8, 2010, p. A6.

37. Stephen J. Carrol, Cathy Krop, Jeremy Arkes, Peter A. Morrison, and Ann Flanagan, *California's K–12 Public Schools: How Are They Doing?* (Santa Monica: Rand Corporation, 2005).

CHAPTER 22

1. Timm Herdt, "Eliminating CalWORKS 'reckless,' state told," *Ventura County Star,* May 27, 2009. Accessed at http://www.vcstar.com/news/2009/may/27/eliminating-calworks-reckless-state-told/

2. Susan Ferriss, "California Would be Only State Without Welfare-to-Work Program," *Sacramento Bee,* May 15, 2010. Accessed at http://www.sacbee.com/2010/05/15/2752320/california-would-be-only-state.html

3. Richard Wolf, "States' Welfare Caseloads Starting to Rise," *USA Today,* May 4, 2008, accessed at http://www.usatoday.com/news/washington/2008-05-04-welfare_N.htm; Elizabeth G. Hill. "2008–09: Overview of the Governor's Budget," *Legislative Analyst,* September 20, 2008.

4. "Governor Signs Budget Revisions," California Budget Project, revised August 5, 2009. Accessed at www.cbp.org on October 20, 2009.

5. Jeffrey Rabin, "State Spent Its Way into Budget Crisis," *Los Angeles Times,* October 29, 2002, p. A1.

6. Peter Schrag, *Paradise Lost: California's Experience, America's Future* (Berkeley/Los Angeles: University of California Press, 1999), pp. 153–154.

7. Jessica Guynn, "Corporate Tax Break in Jeopardy," *Contra Costa Times,* March 15, 2006, p. C1.

8. "LAO Facts," Legislative Analyst's Office, p. 8. Accessed at http://www.lao.ca.gov/laoapp/LAOMenus/LAOFacts.aspx

9. Max Vanzi, "Liz Hill: Here Today, Here Tomorrow," *California Journal,* July 1999. Accessed at http://www.ca.gov/staff/press_awards/lhill_cal_journal_7-99.html

10. "Annual Report, 2004," California Franchise Tax Board, pp. 1–29. Accessed at http://www.ftb.ca.gov/aboutftb/annrpt/2004/2004ar.pdf

11. "Summary Analysis of Amended Bill (AB 6)," California Franchise Tax Board, amended May 27, 2005, and June 15, 2005.

12. "Annual Report, 2004," pp. 31–51.

13. Tom McClintock, "Highway Robbery," *California Republic.* Accessed at http://www.californiarepublic.org/CROhid/archives/Columns/McClintock/20030709McClintockHwyRob.html on November 17, 2004.

14. "Who Pays Taxes in California?" California Budget Project, accessed at http://www.cbp.org/pdfs/2010/100412_pp_who_pays_taxes.pdf; "To Have and Have Not–Budget Brief," California Budget Project, June 2009, www.cbp.org/pdf/2009/0906_bb_To_Have_and_Have_Not.pdf

15. Don Thompson, "Governor, Others Working to Salvage Bond Measure," *Contra Costa Times,* March 13, 2006, p. A12; "Governor Releases Proposed 2006–07 Budget," California Budget Project, accessed at http://www.cpb.org/pdfs/2006/060110_govbudget.pdf on January 19, 2006.

16. "Budget Background: A Mini-Primer on Bonds," California Budget Project, February 2006. Accessed at http://www.cbp.org/pdfs/2006/060221_bondprimer.pdf

17. "What Would the President's Proposed Budget Mean for California?" California Budget Project. Accessed at http://www.cbp.org/pdfs/2007/02-21federalbudget.pdf on February 2006.

18. "The Facts on California's Tax Climate," Tax Foundation, 2006. Accessed at http://www.taxfoundation.org/research/topic/15.html on September 22, 2008.

19. Schrag, *Paradise Lost,* p. 154.

20. J. Fred Silva and Elisa Barbour, *The State-Local Fiscal Relationship in California: A Changing Balance of Power* (San Francisco: Public Policy Institute of California, 1999).

21. Jenifer Warren, "Jail Population Expected to Rise by Thousands," *Contra Costa Times,* April 23, 2006, p. A4.

22. Silva and Barbour, *State-Local Fiscal Relationship.*

23. Michael Coleman, "A Primer on California City Finance." Accessed at http://www.californiacityfinance.com

24. "Special Notice: How Local Governments Will Be Reimbursed for the Upcoming Reduction in the Local Sales and Use Tax Rate," State Board of Equalization, June 2004.

25. "Tourism Funding Restored," California Lodging Industry Association. Accessed at http://www.clia.org/print.cfm?newsid=181 on August 6, 2005.

26. John G. Matsusaka, "Direct Democracy and Fiscal Gridlock: Have Voter Initiatives Paralyzed the California Budget?" *State Politics and Policy Quarterly,* Fall 2005, pp. 248–264.

27. Ibid.

28. Ibid.

29. Carolyn Said, "A 'Fragile Economy' Ahead," *San Francisco Chronicle,* March 29, 2005, p. C1.

Answers to Practice Quiz and Test Your Knowledge Questions

CHAPTER 1

Practice Quizzes • Page 7: 1-c, 2-b, 3-d. **Page 17:** 1-d, 2-a, 3-a. **Page 19:** 1-b, 2-b, 3-d. **Page 23:** 1-d, 2-d, 3-c, 4-b.

Identify the Concept that Doesn't Belong • Page 7: (d) One of the central points of this section is to impress upon you that government is all around us and that your input can make a difference; public policies are not fixed in stone. "Government" and "politics" are not remote, distant activities, but rather on-going processes that affect our lives every day. **Page 17:** (b) One of the themes of this book is that when it comes to influencing government, citizens have options—various pathways. It is only when no viable avenues for change exist that violence erupts. **Page 19:** (e) While *state* and *federal* laws have been an important part of the story of legalized abortion in the United States, local laws have generally not played a significant role. **Page 23:** (a) We have always had clear notions of what it means to be an "American" and indifference to government and politics has not been part of this list. We assume that being a "good American" implies attentiveness to civic matters and a level of engagement.

Test Your Knowledge • Pages 28-29: 1-d, 2-b, 3-c, 4-d, 5-b, 6-d, 7-d, 8-a, 9-b, 10-b, 11-d, 12-c, 13-a, 14-c, 15-a, 16-d, 17-b, 18-d, 19-b, 20-b.

CHAPTER 2

Practice Quizzes • Page 33: 1-d, 2-d, 3-d. **Page 35:** 1-a, 2-b, 3-b, 4-b. **Page 37:** 1-c, 2-b, 3-b. **Page 43:** 1-b, 2-d, 3-c, 4-b. **Page 45:** 1-d, 2-b, 3-a. **Page 49:** 1-d, 2-d, 3-b, 4-b. **Page 53:** 1-d, 2-a, 3-d, 4-b. **Page 57:** 1-d, 2-d, 3-a, 4-c.

Identify the Concept that Doesn't Belong • Page 33: (b) All of the elements except "negative campaigning" relate to the rules of the game, or what we call government. Candidates and operatives sometimes decide to "go negative" in an effort to win elections, but there are no laws regulating this practice. **Page 35:** (e) All of these terms except for oligarchy (complete control by a small group) can be used to describe our political system. We have a democracy, but leaders have defined limits (constitutional government); we air our concerns to leaders (a republic); groups compete in the policy arena (pluralism); and individuals have defined civil liberties (including liberty). **Page 37:** (c) Many believe that the colonists rebelled against England because new taxes created an unbearable burden. That was not true. While there were new taxes after the French and Indian War, they were modest compared to what other citizens had to pay. The colonists had grown accustomed to minimal taxes, so the new measures seemed to threaten their economic future and infringe on personal liberty. **Page 43:** (a) All of these elements refer to the Declaration of Independence, except "enlightened rules." Jefferson rejected the idea that "enlightened rules" should govern. Instead, he wrote that governments should be limited and spring from the will of the people. **Page 45:** (b) All of these elements except a "strong executive office" refer to the Articles of Confederation. In a very real sense, the Articles represented a rejection of the British model of a strong executive (the King). **Page 49:** (d) All of the elements on this list refer to topics addressed at the Constitutional Convention except for freedom of speech. There is no doubt that many of the delegates worried about individual liberties, but they were not the subject of discussion at the Convention. In fact, the lack of individual protections in the body of the Constitution was widely criticized. **Page 53:** (e) All of these elements touch upon topics related to the delicate balance between the state government and the national government (federalism) except national citizenship. The issue of citizenship was left ambiguous, and actually not really settled until after the Civil War. Were you a "citizen" of your state first or of your nation? Today, most refer to their national citizenship first,

but that was not clear in 1789. **Page 57:** (b) All of these elements refer to the period during the ratification of the Constitution except for violence. Although they were debating critical issues and many had strong opinions, the process was peaceful—through debate, discussion, and logic—and is considered a triumph in our history.

Test Your Knowledge • Pages 64-65: 1-a, 2-d, 3-d, 4-d, 5-c, 6-b, 7-a, 8-d, 9-b, 10-a, 11-b, 12-b, 13-a, 14-d, 15-b, 16-c, 17-d, 18-b, 19-b, 20-d.

CHAPTER 3

Practice Quizzes • Page 71: 1-a, 2-d, 3-d. **Page 77:** 1-d, 2-a, 3-a, 4-b. **Page 81:** 1-d, 2-d, 3-d, **Page 85:** 1-c, 2-b, 3-a, 4-a.

Identify the Concept that Doesn't Belong • Page 71: (b) Federalism does not make governing easier—it makes for a complex system; however, federalism's flexibility helps explain the longevity of our political system and its amazing adaptability throughout time. **Page 77:** (c) All of these elements describe dual federalism except for cooperation and flexibility. Dual federalism is marked by tension, conflict, and a rigid separation of power and authority; neither level of government is superior. **Page 81:** (a) All of the elements except for dual federalism relate to creative federalism. Under a system of dual federalism, each layer of government has distinctive powers and duties. Federalism evolved in the United States to be more cooperative in nature, with various governmental entities combining their efforts to redistribute resources to combat poverty and promote equality. **Page 85:** (b) All of the elements relate to devolution except for unfunded mandates. Devolution was in part a reaction caused by opposition to unfunded mandates.

Test Your Knowledge • Pages 90–91: 1-c, 2-d, 3-a, 4-b, 5-c, 6-c, 7-d, 8-b, 9-b, 10-d, 11-d, 12-b, 13-a, 14-b, 15-c, 16-b, 17-b, 18-b, 19-a, 20-d.

CHAPTER 4

Practice Quizzes •. Page 97: 1-d, 2-b, 3-c, 4-a. **Page 99:** 1-c, 2-d, 3-d. **Page 103:** 1-b, 2-c, 3-b, 4-d. **Page 105:** 1-b, 2-c, 3-d. **Page 107:** 1-d, 2-d, 3-c. **Page 113:** 1-d, 2-d, 3-b, 4-b.

Identify the Concept that Doesn't Belong • Page 97: (c) The concepts concerning First Amendment religious freedom apply only with respect to the *government's* potential involvement or interference with religion. People can send their children to private religious schools where prayers and religious instruction may be required components of education. **Page 99:** (a) All of these elements deal with freedom of speech except for First Amendment free exercise rights, a term used specifically with respect to freedom of religion rather than speech. **Page 103:** (b) First Amendment establishment by government refers to a religion-related clause and not an issue related to freedom of the press. **Page 105:** (a) All of these elements relate to protections afforded to criminal suspects under the Bill of Rights except for *Cupp* v. *Murphy*, a 1973 case that determined immediate warrantless searches were permissible in the case of "exigent circumstances" such as danger to the public or possible loss of evidence. **Page 107:** (c) All of these elements relate to the trial and punishment stages of the justice process except for the Fourth Amendment. The Fourth Amendment concerns search and seizure in the investigation of cases prior to the trial and punishment stages. **Page 113:** (d) All of these elements have been a central focus of Supreme Court decisions defining the right to privacy, except for Self-Incrimination, which concerns a Fifth Amendment criminal justice protection.

Test Your Knowledge • Pages 120-121: 1-c, 2-b, 3-d, 4-b, 5-d, 6-a, 7-b, 8-a, 9-c, 10-b, 11-d, 12-b, 13-c, 14-a, 15-d, 16-b, 17-a, 18-c, 19-d, 20-c.

CHAPTER 5

Practice Quizzes • **Page 125:** 1-c, 2-b, 3-a. **Page 129:** 1-b, 2-b, 3-c, 4-d. **Page 131:** 1-b, 2-b, 3-a, 4-c. **Page 133:** 1-a, 2-a, 3-d. **Page 137:** 1-c, 2-b, 3-a. **Page 139:** 1-d, 2-b, 3-b, 4-d. **Page 141:** 1-b, 2-b, 3-b, 4-b.

Identify the Concept that Doesn't Belong • **Page 125:** (d) The protection against compelled self-incrimination is part of the civil liberties protected by the Bill of Rights and not one of the civil rights issues concerning political equality and equal treatment. **Page 129:** (a) The post–Civil War Amendments (Thirteenth, Fourteenth, and Fifteenth) sought to protect African Americans, and the Reconstruction Act of 1867 required southern states to establish new state governments that granted voting rights to all men. The Sixteenth Amendment was ratified early in the twentieth century and concerned the federal income tax. **Page 131:** (c) All of these elements relate to the litigation strategies used by the NAACP for the advancement of civil rights except for Reconstruction, which refers to the post–Civil War era. **Page 133:** (b) All of these elements relate to the way the Supreme Court decides different kinds of discrimination claims under the equal protection clause (included in the Fourteenth Amendment), except for the Thirteenth Amendment, which prohibits slavery. **Page 137:** (c) All of these elements relate to the grassroots mobilization for civil rights except for state supreme courts; state supreme courts in southern states tended to support the existing system of racial segregation. **Page 139:** (a) The civil rights advancements of women and Latinos are significantly attributable to grassroots action rather than the invalidation of statutes by judicial decisions through the process of judicial review. **Page 141:** (e) All of these elements are contemporary civil rights issues, except for majority-minority voting districts for women. The issue of majority-minority voting districts relates solely to voting districts and housing patterns based on race and ethnicity, not gender.

Test Your Knowledge • **Pages 150–151:** 1-c, 2-b, 3-a, 4-c, 5-b, 6-d, 7-b, 8-c, 9-b, 10-b, 11-a, 12-d, 13-c, 14-a, 15-b, 16-a, 17-c, 18-b, 19-b, 20-d.

CHAPTER 6

Practice Quizzes • **Page 155:** 1-d, 2-d, 3-b. **Page 161:** 1-d, 2-b, 3-b. **Page 165:** 1-b, 2-b, 3-b. **Page 169:** 1-a, 2-b, 3-d. **Page 173:** 1-b, 2-a, 3-c. **Page 177:** 1-b, 2-d, 3-b. **Page 181:** 1-c, 2-b, 3-a. **Page 183:** 1-b, 2-a, 3-d.

Identify the Concept that Doesn't Belong • **Page 155:** (c) All of these elements push legislators toward the delegate model of representation, except for an indifferent public. With the delegate model of representation, legislators stay very close to the wishes of their constituents—the constituents who are paying attention. **Page 161:** (a) All of these elements help define the nature and function of Congress except for term limits. The Constitution does not stipulate any term limits, so members of Congress are free to run for reelection time and again. **Page 165:** (b) All of these elements refer to the value of the congressional committee system except for "limits constituent access." The committee system actually allows average citizens a direct pathway for meaningful involvement. **Page 169:** (b) Political parties provide individual legislators with all of these methods of assistance except for mandating policy coherence. The best predictor of a legislator's vote is his or her party, but our system tolerates a great deal of independence. **Page 173:** (e) All of these elements are informal customs that still apply in the Senate except for backstabbing. Through the centuries legislators have learned that a level of goodwill benefits the system and the nation. **Page 177:** (e) All of these elements refer to the steps that are necessary for a bill to become law except for presidential signature. While most bills become law with a presidential signature, they can also become law when a presidential veto is overridden by a two-thirds vote in both houses or when the bill sits on the president's desk for 10 days without a veto or a signature. **Page 181:** (e) Each of these groups of Americans is underrepresented in Congress, except for lawyers. Some see this as a shortcoming of our system, while others believe it is not a big deal. **Page 183:** (c) All of these elements except for a distracted public have contributed to the *perception* that members of Congress are less ethical than in past generations. While scholars have suggested members of Congress may actually be more ethical than in the past, in politics perceptions matter greatly.

Test Your Knowledge • **Pages 190–191:** 1-c, 2-a, 3-b, 4-c, 5-d, 6-b, 7-b, 8-d, 9-d, 10-a, 11-c, 12-c, 13-d, 14-d, 15-a, 16-d, 17-a, 18-c, 19-b, 20-a.

CHAPTER 7

Practice Quizzes • **Page 195:** 1-d, 2-d, 3-a. **Page 203:** 1-b, 2-b, 3-c, 4-b. **Page 205:** 1-c, 2-d, 3-b. **Page 213:** 1-b, 2-b, 3-c. **Page 217:** 1-b, 2-d, 3-b, 4-c.

Identify the Concept that Doesn't Belong • **Page 195:** (c) All of the elements on this list, with the exception of "passing legislation," are powers of the president outlined in the Constitution. Congress passes legislation, although it has some input from presidents. **Page 203:** (b) All of these items, except for changes to the Constitution, refer to forces that have broadened the scope of presidential power since George Washington's time. **Page 205:** (a) All of the elements on this list except for veto power are considered informal powers and depend on the skills of the president. The veto power is clearly defined in the Constitution. **Page 213:** (c) Presidents are charged with an array of duties and responsibilities, including all of the elements in this list except for funding military activities. The Constitution stipulates that Congress raises funds for the military. **Page 217:** (d) While the idea of "presidential greatness" is subjective, scholars generally agree that all of these elements are necessary except for the ability to manipulate public opinion. Presidents may strive to manipulate the public, but often an approach of this sort fails to work in the long term.

Test Your Knowledge • **Pages 224–225:** 1-b, 2-a, 3-b, 4-d, 5-a, 6-b, 7-c, 8-a, 9-c, 10-c, 11-d, 12-d, 13-c, 14-a, 15-b, 16-c, 17-d, 18-a, 19-b, 20-b.

CHAPTER 8

Practice Quizzes • **Page 233:** 1-b, 2-c, 3-d, 4-a. **Page 239:** 1-a, 2-c, 3-d, 4-b. **Page 245:** 1-b, 2-c, 3-a, 4-d. **Page 251:** 1-c, 2-b, 3-c, 4-a.

Identify the Concept that Doesn't Belong • **Page 233:** (d) All of these elements except for the War of 1812 are associated with the creation by Congress of specific federal departments and agencies and their placement under the control of the president. **Page 239:** (b) All of these are examples of independent agencies that operate outside of the 15 executive departments except for the Department of Health and Human Services. **Page 245:** (a) All of these elements can be considered advantages of bureaucracy except for decentralization. Decentralization is an approach recommended by those who would like to reform the bureaucracy. **Page 251:** (c) All of these elements deal with the creation of regulations by the bureaucracy and the oversight of government agencies in the federal government except for federalism. Federalism refers to the relationship between state and federal government.

Test Your Knowledge • **Pages 256–257:** 1-c, 2-a, 3-b, 4-d, 5-d, 6-d, 7-a, 8-b, 9-c, 10-c, 11-d, 12-b, 13-c, 14-b, 15-c, 16-a, 17-d, 18-c, 19-c, 20-c.

CHAPTER 9

Practice Quizzes • **Page 265:** 1-c, 2-b, 3-a, 4-a. **Page 271:** 1-d, 2-b, 3-c, 4-a. **Page 273:** 1-c, 2-c, 3-a. **Page 277:** 1-c, 2-a, 3-a, 4-b. **Page 281:** 1-c, 2-b, 3-a, 4-d. **Page 283:** 1-b, 2-c, 3-c. **Page 285:** 1-b, 2-d, 3-c.

Identify the Concept that Doesn't Belong • **Page 265:** (d) All of these elements deal with the U.S. court system except for a veto, which is a power exercised by presidents and governors to block laws enacted by legislators. **Page 271:** (c) All of these elements relate to the power of U.S. judges except for Congressional committees. Judges possess the power to interpret statutes enacted by the entire Congress, not individual committees. In addition, because the judiciary is a separate branch of government, congressional committees have no impact on judicial power. **Page 273:** (a) All of these elements relate to the selection of judges except for the House of Representatives. The U.S. Senate—not the House of Representatives—must confirm the nominations of federal judges. **Page 277:** (e) All of these elements relate to judicial decision making except for the "Inquisitorial system," which refers to the judges' role in other countries of investigating cases and questioning witnesses. **Page 281:** (b) All of these elements relate to policy-shaping litigation strategies except for Constitutional conventions, which are used to develop and ratify new constitutions. **Page 283:** (e) All of these elements relate to the implementation and impact of court decisions except for court-ordered mass arrests. The judiciary depends on the executive branch to enforce judicial decisions, and courts do not purport to assert such broad-scale powers, if the public does not comply with a decision. **Page 285:** (d) All of these elements explain why people debate the appropriateness of judges shaping public policy except for Article II of the Constitution. Article II discusses the role and powers of the president.

Test Your Knowledge • Pages 282–293: 1-b, 2-a, 3-d, 4-b, 5-c, 6-d, 7-d, 8-b, 9-a, 10-c, 11-b, 12-d, 13-b, 14-a, 15-d, 16-c, 17-c, 18-b, 19-a, 20-a.

CHAPTER 10

Practice Quizzes • Page 299: 1-b, 2-a, 3-b, 4-d. **Page 303:** 1-b, 2-b, 3-c, 4-a. **Page 305:** 1-c, 2-a, 3-b. **Page 309:** 1-c, 2-d, 3-a, 4-d. **Page 313:** 1-c, 2-d, 3-a, 4-a. **Page 317:** 1-d, 2-c, 3-a.

Identify the Concept that Doesn't Belong • Page 299: (c) All of these represent fundamental values that Americans generally agree upon except equality of outcome. The idea of using government to ensure equality of outcome is highly controversial. **Page 303:** (d) All of these elements describe the stability of public opinion in the United States except for "rapid change." Most change is incremental and gradual, largely by cohort replacement. One large reason that change occurs slowly is that most Americans share common values. **Page 305:** (b) Liberals generally support all of these elements except for capital punishment. They tend to favor life in prison without parole instead. **Page 309:** (e) All of these elements teach and promote values generally considered to be positive to the political system except for the media. The media tend to portray values that can undermine active and "positive" political participation—including glamorizing violence, materialism, promiscuous sexuality, and dishonesty. **Page 313:** (a) All of these elements, except for group uniformity, relate to how membership in different social groups impacts views and behavior. People who experience the world similarly tend to develop similar worldviews, but many exceptions exist. **Page 317:** (c) All of these elements describe modern professional polling except for error free—even the best polls may contain errors.

Test Your Knowledge • Pages 324–325: 1-c, 2-a, 3-a, 4-d, 5-b, 6-b, 7-d, 8-a, 9-d, 10-c, 11-a, 12-a, 13-a, 14-d, 15-a, 16-b, 17-a, 18-d, 19-a, 20-a.

CHAPTER 11

Practice Quizzes • Page 329: 1-c, 2-a, 3-a. **Page 335:** 1-b, 2-c, 3-a, 4-b. **Page 339:** 1-a, 2-d, 3-b, 4-a. **Page 345:** 1-a, 2-c, 3-d, 4-a. **Page 349:** 1-d, 2-b, 3-a, 4-c. **Page 353:** 1-a, 2-c, 3-a, 4-b.

Identify the Concept that Doesn't Belong • Page 329: (c) All of these are elements of free media in a democratic political system except for censorship, which involves the suppression of open discussion and public debate. **Page 335:** (b) All of these elements apply to the mass media in the United States except for government ownership. The U.S. government regulates the airways but does not own the print or electronic media. **Page 339:** (d) Under normal conditions, the media are far more likely to inform the public, reinforce existing cultural attitudes, and frame and highlight issues, rather than transform public opinion. **Page 345:** (c) As part of their ability to set the political agenda, the media can spotlight particular issues, determine which stories are newsworthy, frame the issues, and set the context for stories; however, the media are less successful in controlling public opinion. **Page 349:** (e) All of these elements reflect concerns that people have about the media's impact in the political arena except for positive coverage; in fact, media coverage of campaigns has been trending negative for several decades. **Page 353:** (e) All of these elements, except for an absolute right to free press, are principles of media coverage in the United States. We generally support limiting the press during times of war and to protect national security and privacy rights.

Test Your Knowledge • Pages 360–361: 1-d, 2-b, 3-a, 4-a, 5-a, 6-b, 7-d, 8-b, 9-a, 10-a, 11-c, 12-b, 13-d, 14-c, 15-b, 16-a, 17-b, 18-d, 19-c, 20-b.

CHAPTER 12

Practice Quizzes • Page 365: 1-d, 2-a, 3-d, 4-a. **Page 367:** 1-d, 2-d, 3-b. **Page 371:**, 1-b, 2-c, 3-d. **Page 375:** 1-b, 2-a, 3-c, 4-a. **Page 379:** 1-a, 2-d, 3-b, 4-d. **Page 381:** 1-d, 2-a, 3-b.

Identify the Concept that Doesn't Belong • Page 365: (a) All of these freedoms, except for a right to privacy, facilitate activism and protest by enabling different ideas to compete for acceptance and for Americans to influence government. **Page 367:** (e) All of these elements, except for individualism, allow for mass political engagement including political activism and protest. **Page 371:** (a) Interest groups are associations of like-minded individuals who join together because of shared values or beliefs and a desire to influence their fellow citizens and government. They do not, for the most part, try to control member behavior. **Page 375:** (d) All of these interest groups except for the American Bar Association are likely to suffer from free riders and also to find it difficult to mobilize without providing some sort of solidary or purposive benefits to members. Professional organizations generally have fewer problems with free riders, as they can compel membership. **Page 379:** (c) All of these elements are tools of inside lobbying except for campaign contributions. Lobbyists cannot offer campaign contributions to directly build support for their clients, as this would be unethical and illegal. **Page 381:** (a) All of these elements, except for higher levels of confidence in government, characterize the impact of interest group activity on the population as a whole. While interest groups can and do provide a form of positive political engagement for individuals, their activities tend to have a negative aggregate impact.

Test Your Knowledge • Pages: 388–389 1-d, 2-a, 3-c, 4-c, 5-b, 6-d, 7-a, 8-d, 9-c, 10-b, 11-a, 12-d, 13-b, 14-c, 15-a, 16-a, 17-a, 18-d, 19-b, 20-c.

CHAPTER 13

Practice Quizzes • Page 393: 1-b, 2-d, 3-b. **Page 397:** 1-b, 2-a, 3-b. **Page 401:** 1-a, 2-d, 3-a. **Page 403:** 1-d, 2-b, 3-b. **Page 407:** 1-a, 2-d, 3-a. **Page 411:** 1-d, 2-b, 3-c. **Page 415:** 1-d, 2-b, 3-a.

Identify the Concept that Doesn't Belong • Page 393: (a) Each of these elements, with the exception of registration requirements, has expanded the number of Americans able to participate in elections. Registration requirements keep many citizens from exercising their right to vote. **Page 397:** (e) All of these elements refer to modes of political behavior except for having faith in the electoral process. There are many ways to be "engaged" in politics, but merely having faith does not make someone a player in the electoral system. **Page 401:** (e) All of these are elements of political parties except for Third party, which refers to a type of political party. **Page 403:** (e) All of these descriptions except for candidate-centered, refer to characteristics of parties during each of the phases. The term "candidate-centered" implies the movement away from party politics, which occurred only in the post–World War II period. **Page 407:** (c) At one time or another, each of the actors on this list, with the exception of members of the media, were called upon to pick party nominees. It is true that the media plays an important role in the process, but its input is unofficial. **Page 411:** (a) All of these elements can be part of the contemporary Electoral College process except for state legislatures. In the first few decades of our nation's history, state legislatures selected Electoral College electors, but since the middle of the nineteenth century that process has been given to voters. **Page 415:** (e) All of these elements have contributed to the growing cost of elections except for strong political parties. In fact, as political parties have withered, candidates have used other means to reach voters—most of which require a great deal of money, such as television ads.

Test Your Knowledge • Page 422–423: 1-b, 2-d, 3-d, 4-c, 5-c, 6-d, 7-a, 8-a, 9-a, 10-d, 11-a, 12-c, 13-a, 14-d, 15-b, 16-c, 17-e, 18-a, 19-a, 20-c.

CHAPTER 14

Practice Quizzes • Page 429: 1-b, 2-a, 3-c. **Page 433:** 1-b, 2-a, 3-d, 4-c. **Page 437:** 1-b, 2-c, 3-a. **Page 441:** 1-c, 2-a, 3-a. **Page 443:** 1-c, 2-a, 3-c. **Page 449:** 1-c, 2-b, 3-a, 4-c. **Page 451:** 1-d, 2-b, 3-c.

Identify the Concept that Doesn't Belong • Page 429: (d) All of these elements directly influence the adoption of public policies except for federalism. Federalism creates the structure by which public policies are formed. **Page 433:** (d) All of these are examples of redistributive policies except for clean air laws, which are an example of regulatory policies. **Page 437:** (c) All of these elements deal with policy oversight, except for rule-making authority, which deals with the power of departments and agencies to create policy. **Page 441:** (e) All of these elements are measures of economic performance except for fiscal policy. Fiscal policy refers to the taxing and spending decisions enacted by Congress and the president. **Page 443:** (c) All of these entities are intricately involved with the budget and budgetary process except for the U.S. Securities and Exchange Commission, whose mandate is to protect investors, maintain fair, orderly, and efficient markets, and facilitate capital formation. **Page 449:** (e) All of these elements are considered to be entitlements—that is spending on the programs is mandatory and not subject to the budgetary process—except for education. Spending on education is discretionary, which means that Congress determines how much funding it will supply each year. **Page 451:** (d) All of these are monetary tools except for a tax hike, which is a fiscal policy tool.

Test Your Knowledge • Pages 458–459: 1-c, 2-a, 3-d, 4-c, 5-b, 6-d, 7-c, 8-b, 9-a, 10-c, 11-d, 12-b, 13-c, 14-c, 15-d, 16-c, 17-b, 18-d, 19-d, 20-b.

CHAPTER 15

Practice Quizzes • Page 465: 1-c, 2-d, 3-a. **Page 469:** 1-b, 2-a, 3-a. **Page 473:** 1-a, 2-c, 3-a. **Page 481:** 1-b, 2-b, 3-c. **Page 487:** 1-c, 2-b, 3-b.

Identify the Concept that Doesn't Belong • Page 465: (a) The United States had a hand in creating all of the organizations except the Warsaw Pact. The Soviet Union was behind the creation of the Warsaw Pact. **Page 469:** (d) All of these are concepts associated with free market economic principles except for agricultural subsidies. Agricultural subsidies undermine the notion of free-market economic principles. **Page 473:** (d) All of these elements have exerted external influence on the shape of U.S. foreign policy except for the creation of the Department of Homeland Security, which was an internal action taken by the U.S. government in the wake of the 2001 terrorist attacks. **Page 481:** (c) While all of these offices have some role in foreign policy matters, the Supreme Court and its justices have traditionally avoided involvement in foreign policy matters. **Page 487:** (e) All of these are directly related to military security concerns of the United States except for human trafficking, which is an issue of human welfare.

Test Your Knowledge • Pages 494–495: 1-b, 2-d, 3-c, 4-a, 5-c, 6-d, 7-c, 8-a, 9-c, 10-b, 11-b, 12-b, 13-d, 14-b, 15-a, 16-c, 17-d, 18-b, 19-a, 20-b.

CHAPTER 16

Practice Quizzes • Page 501: 1-a, 2-c, 3-c. **Page 505:** 1-d, 2-a, 3-b, 4-b. **Page 509:** 1-c, 2-b, 3-a. **Page 513:** 1-c, 2-a, 3-c, 4-c. **Page 517:** 1-a, 2-b, 3-d.

Identify the Concept that Doesn't Belong • Page 501: (d) All of these elements were regular features of activities at Spanish Missions, except for deregulation, which is typically an act of government to limit the effect or remove altogether existing laws or regulations. **Page 505:** (d) All of these concepts, except fundraising prowess, were associated with the Gold Rush. **Page 509:** (c) All of these elements were stipulated by the 1879 constitution, except for anticorruption measures. **Page 513:** (e) All of these events are associated with World War II, except for the Alien Land Bill. **Page 517:** (c) All of these concepts, with the exception of the referendum, are issues related to energy consumption in California. The referendum is one of California's major avenues for direct democracy, allowing voters to revise or eliminate California law.

Test Your Knowledge • Page 524: 1-b, 2-c, 3-a, 4-c, 5-d, 6-a, 7-c, 8-c, 9-d, 10-a, 11-a, 12-b, 13-a, 14-b, 15-a, 16-b, 17-d, 18-c, 19-b, 20-b.

CHAPTER 17

Practice Quizzes • Page 531: 1-a, 2-b, 3-a, 4-c. **Page 539:** 1-a, 2-b, 3-d. **Page 545:** 1-b, 2-c, 3-d. **Page 547:** 1-b, 2-c, 3-a. **Page 549:** 1-a, 2-a, 3-c.

Identify the Concept that Doesn't Belong • Page 531: (d) All of these attributes pertain to the requirements for voting in California except for "resident of a legislative district for one year," which is one requirement for candidates to the state legislature. **Page 539:** (b) Each of these characterizations are closely associated with the initiative process, except for joint powers agreements, which usually involve an agreement by county government to provide a service to one or more local governments. **Page 545:** (a) All of these terms are types of lists used during a campaign based on information available at county election offices, except for "Resolution," which is regularly used by the legislature to recognize the achievements of a particular individual, establish new rules or policies, or allocate funds. **Page 547:** (c) All of these entities are a function of mass communication, except for "juice bills," which are proposed laws written to benefit a particular interest group that usually generate large campaign contributions to the legislator that sponsors these bills, **Page 549:** (e) All of these activities deal with conventional political participation except for

"maintain public records," which is the responsibility of the county or municipal clerks who are typically elected to these positions.

Test Your Knowledge • Pages 556–557: 1-b, 2-a, 3-b, 4-a, 5-c, 6-b, 7-a, 8-d, 9-c, 10-d, 11-a, 12-c, 13-d, 14-c, 15-b, 16-a, 17-c, 18-c, 19-c, 20-b.

CHAPTER 18

Practice Quizzes • Page 561: 1-b, 2-d, 3-a, 4-c. **Page 565:** 1-d, 2-d, 3-c. **Page 573:** 1-a, 2-a, 3-b, 4-c. **Page 577:** 1-c, 2-c, 3-c. **Page 581:** 1-d, 2-d, 3-a, 4-c.

Identify the Concept that Doesn't Belong • Page 561: (d) All of these elements are associated with lobbying and influencing the California state legislature, except for "clemency power," which is the right, exercised by the governor, to grant pardons, commutation of sentences, and reprieves. **Page 565:** (d) Each of these elements was an aspect of the Federal Plan in California mandating state senate districts based on geography rather than population, except for the term "May revise," which is a revised projection of the state's financial picture that is conducted during the month of May. **Page 573:** (c) All of these options are related to the representation function of a California state legislator, with the exception of "juror," a U.S. citizen and resident of California who is chosen to serve on a jury. **Page 577:** (b) All of these concepts are important features of the California state senate except for the term "voir dire," a legal procedural that permits attorneys in court to question jurors and request their removal. **Page 581:** (a) All of these elements are associated with the standing committees of the California legislature except for "home rule," which gives local residents some control over shaping the rules and structure of local government.

Test Your Knowledge • Pages 588–589: 1-c, 2-c, 3-a, 4-c, 5-b, 6-d, 7-a, 8-d, 9-c, 10-a, 11-c, 12-d, 13-a, 14-c, 15-a, 16-a, 17-a, 18-c, 19-c, 20-b.

CHAPTER 19

Practice Quizzes • Page 593: 1-b, 2-a, 3-c. **Page 597:** 1-d, 2-c, 3-d. **Page 605:** 1-a, 2-c, 3-a, 4-b.

Identify the Concept that Doesn't Belong • Page 593: (a) All of these options are associated with the powers of the governor with the exception of "appoint assembly members to committees," which is a power delegated to the speaker of the California Assembly. **Page 597:** (a) All of these responsibilities are associated with candidates running for governor except for "interact regularly with members of party caucuses," a responsibility typically fulfilled by members of the state legislature. **Page 605:** (c) All of these items are related to the regulations of the insurance industry in California with the exception of the "Help America Vote Act," which is a federal law that requires states to facilitate and modernize the election process.

Test Your Knowledge • Pages 610–611: 1-c, 2-a, 3-a, 4-d, 5-c, 6-a, 7-c, 8-a, 9-b, 10-c, 11-c, 12-a, 13-c, 14-b, 15-a, 16-d, 17-c, 18-d, 19-a, 20-d.

CHAPTER 20

Practice Quizzes • Page 617: 1-d, 2-a, 3-a. **Page 623:** 1-c, 2-a, 3-a. **Page 625:** 1-c, 2-b, 3-c. **Page 627:** 1-b, 2-a, 3-d.

Identify the Concept that Doesn't Belong • Page 617: (d) All of these options deal with the California court system except for municipal advisory councils, which provide representation to California residents who live in unincorporated areas of the state. **Page 623:** (c) All of these options relate to the practice of civil law except for "penal code," which is a list and description of the laws that define all crimes. **Page 625:** (c) All of these options deal with the California Jury system with the exception of "Triple Flip," which is essentially a revenue-swapping procedure. **Page 627:** (e) All of these options are a part of the attempt to reform the California judicial system except for "The Brown Act," which is a state law that establishes certain guidelines for the conduct of a meeting involving government.

Test Your Knowledge • Pages 632–633: 1-c, 2-a, 3-c, 4-b, 5-a, 6-a, 7-b, 8-d, 9-a, 10-c, 11-a, 12-b, 13-c, 14-d, 15-a, 16-d, 17-b, 18-a, 19-c, 20-b.

CHAPTER 21

Practice Quizzes • Page 639: 1-b, 2-d, 3-d, 4-b. **Page 643:** 1-d, 2-a, 3-d. **Page 647:** 1-a, 2-a, 3-d, 4-b. **Page 651:** 1-b, 2-d, 3-a, 4-b. **Page 657:** 1-d, 2-b, 3-a, 4-a.

Identify the Concept that Doesn't Belong • Page 639: (d) All of these options relate specifically to the leaders, structure and organizations associated with county government with the exception of "felonies," which are crimes for which a person may be sentenced to imprisonment in the state prison. **Page 643:** (e) All of these options are features of the duties performed by county governments, except "redistricting," the task performed by a nonpartisan commission involving the process of redrawing congressional and state legislative district boundaries every 10 years. **Page 647:** (b) All of these elements relate to the power of city councils except for "Manifest Destiny," the belief that America must satisfy its destiny as a world power of continental proportions. **Page 651:** (a) All of these responsibilities are related to the position of city manager except for "audit and supervise all investments made on behalf of city government," a responsibility performed by the city treasurer. **Pages 657:** (c) All of these options are related to the functions of special districts with the exception of "Clemency powers," which is the power to grant pardons, commutation of sentences, and reprieves.

Test Your Knowledge • Pages 664–665: 1-d, 2-a, 3-c, 4-a, 5-b, 6-b, 7-c, 8-a, 9-d, 10-a, 11-d, 12-b, 13-a, 14-a, 15-d, 16-d, 17-a, 18-d, 19-d, 20-c.

CHAPTER 22

Practice Quizzes • Page 671: 1-b, 2-d, 3-c, 4-a. **Page 675:** 1-d, 2-b, 3-c, 4-a. **Page 679:** 1-b, 2-b, 3-b, 4-d. **Page 683:** 1-c, 2-b, 3-c.

Identify the Concept that Doesn't Belong • Page 671: (d) All of these options describe the structural budget gap except for "casework," which in the legislative context, is the process of assisting constituents in a legislator's district with problems and questions. **Page 675:** (c) All of these options are associated with taxation with the exception of "plea bargains," which are formal agreements between the district attorney's office and the defendant to forgo a trial. **Page 679:** (b) All of these options are associated with "other expenditures" of the state government except for health and welfare, one of the three largest state budget expenditures. **Page 683:** (a) All of these options are addressed during the California budget process except for a petition referendum, which allows voters to request that all of part of a law be submitted to the voters for approval or rejection.

Test Your Knowledge • Pages 688–689: 1-b, 2-a, 3-c, 4-a, 5-b, 6-d, 7-b, 8-c, 9-a, 10-b, 11-d, 12-a, 13-b, 14-a, 15-d, 16-c, 17-c, 18-d, 19-b, 20-c.

Credits

COVER: Bill Fredericks

CHAPTER 1: *2* Hulton Archive/Getty Images; *5, top to bottom:* iStockphoto (2); Justin Sullivan/Getty Images; Tom Stewart/Corbis; David Mendelsohn/Masterfile; David Woolley/Getty Images; *7* AP Images/Rich Pedroncelli; *8* Joshua Roberts/Reuters/Landov; *11, top to bottom:* Barrie Fanton/Omni-Photo; Dirck Halstead/Time Life Pictures/Getty Images; Stephen Ferry/Getty Images; Michael Smith/Getty Images; *13* Kevin Dietsch/UPI/Landov; *14, left to right:* Bob Daemmrich; A. Ramey/PhotoEdit Inc. *15, top to bottom:* AP Images/Marcio Jose Sanchez (2); Todd Bigelow/Aurora; *18* Yuri Gripas/UPI/Landov; *21* Joseph Sohm/Visions of America/Corbis; *22* Xinhua/Landov; *23* H. Darr Beiser/USA Today; *25, top to bottom:* AP Images/Elise Amendola; Bettmann/Corbis; AP Images/The Ledger Independent, Terry Prather; AP Images/Seth Perlman; Getty Images

CHAPTER 2: *30* The Granger Collection; *36* Pilgrim Society; *39* The Bridgeman Art Library; *40* Bettmann/Corbis; *41, top to bottom:* The Granger Collection; Cox Newspapers; *45* Bettmann/Corbis; *48* Bettmann/Corbis; *50* The Granger Collection; *51, left to right:* Stan Wakefield/Pearson Education (2); Irene Springer/Pearson Education; *52, top to bottom:* Joseph Sohm, ChromoSohm Media Inc./Photo Researchers, Inc.; Kenneth Garrett/National Geographic Stock; *56* The Granger Collection; *59, top to bottom:* North Wind Picture Archives; Look and Learn/The Bridgeman Art Library; Library of Congress; The Granger Collection; SuperStock; Bettmann/Corbis

CHAPTER 3: *66* Xinhua/Zuma Press; *68* Tim Sloan/AFP/Getty Images; *73* Architect of the Capitol; *74, top to bottom:* Hulton Archive/Getty Images; Bettmann/Corbis; *75* AP Images/Al Grillo; *76* Milwaukee Art Museum; *78* Library of Congress; *83* Gabriel Bouys/AFP/Getty Images; *84* Yuri Dojc/Getty Images; *87, top to bottom:* NOAA; AP Images/Cheryl Gerber; Win Henderson/FEMA; AP Images/David J. Phillip, Pool; Shannon Stapleton/Reuters/Landov; DoD/US Army; Marvin Nauman/FEMA

CHAPTER 4: *92* Louie Psihoyos/Science Faction/Corbis; *95* Keystone Press/Zuma Press; *96* Bettmann/Corbis; *99* AP Images/David J. Phillip; *101* Houston Chronicle; *102* Scott Gries/Getty Images; *104* AP Images/John Marshall Mantel; *108, left to right:* Time & Life Pictures/Getty Images; Bettmann/Corbis; *109, left to right:* John Gress/Reuters/Landov; Jim Wilson/The New York Times/Redux Pictures; *110* Bettmann/Corbis; *111* Alexis C. Glenn/UPI/Landov; *115, top to bottom:* Bettmann/Corbis; Arizona State Library, Archives and Public Records, History and Archives Division, Phoenix, #00-517

CHAPTER 5: *122* AP Images/Matt Rourke; *126* Bettmann/Corbis; *128* Bettmann/Corbis; *134* Getty Images; *135* AP Photo; *138* Bettmann/Corbis; *142* AP Images/Wilfredo Lee; *143, top to bottom:* Liz Mangelsdorf/San Francisco Chronicle/Corbis; Rebecca Cook/Reuters/Corbis; *145, top to bottom:* Bettmann/Corbis; Don Cravens/Time Life Pictures/Getty Images; John F. Kennedy Presidential Library and Museum; AP Images; Getty Images; LBJ Library photo by Cecil Stoughton

CHAPTER 6: *152* Roll Call/Getty Images; *154, left to right:* The Granger Collection; Bettmann/Corbis; AP Images/Kevin Rivoli; Bettmann/Corbis; *155* AP Images/The Ledger Independent, Terry Prather; *157* AP Images/Seth Perlman; *164* Chuck Kennedy/KRT/Newscom; *167, left to right:* Scott J. Farrell/Getty Images; Matt Kryger/Indiana Star/PSG/Newscom; *170* Strom Thurmond Photograph Collection, Special Collections, Clemson University Libraries, Clemson, South Carolina; *172* Chip Somodevilla/Getty Images; *173* Ron Niebrugge/Alamy; *175, top middle:* Chip Somodevilla/Getty Images; *175, bottom middle:* Larry Downing/Reuters/Landov; *179* AP Images/Michael Dwyer; *185, top to bottom:* AP Images/J. Scott Applewhite; Public Domain (2); Alex Wong/Getty Images; Strom Thurmond Photograph Collection, Special Collections, Clemson University Libraries, Clemson, South Carolina; AP Images/Carolyn Kaster

CHAPTER 7: *192* Win McNamee/Getty Images; *195* Library of Congress; *196* Bettmann/Corbis; *197* Official White House Photo by Pete Souza; *200* Official White House Photo by Pete Souza (2); *201* Hulton Archive/Getty Images; *202* Jim Young/Reuters/Landov; *206* AP Images/Lawrence Jackson; *208* AP Images; *209, clockwise from top left:* AP Images/Paul Beaty; Pat Benic/UPI/Landov; Jason Reed/Reuters/Landov; Goddard Claussen Public Affairs; *210* AP Images/Bob Daugherty; *212* AP Images/Pfc. L. Paul Epley; *214* AP Images/Jack Kightlinger; *216* Saul Loeb/AFP/Getty Images; *219, top to bottom:* Public Domain (2); Bettmann/Corbis; Hulton Archive/Getty Images; Public Domain; Library of Congress; AP Images/Doug Mills

CHAPTER 8: *226* U.S. Coast Guard photo by Petty Officer 3rd Class Ann Marie Gorden; *228* TongRo/Beateworks/Corbis; *231* Bettmann/Corbis; *232* Cecil Stoughton/Bettmann/Corbis; *234* AP Images/Jakub Moser; *239* Carol T. Powers/Bloomberg/Getty Images; *240* Mario Tama/Getty Images; *244* Michael Fein/Bloomberg/Getty Images; *247* Luke Frazza/AFP/Getty Images; *251* Joshua Roberts/Bloomberg/Getty Images; *253, top to bottom:* Kevin Lamargue/Reuters/Landov; Susan Gaaghil/Reuters/Landov; AP Images/Gerard Herbert; Patrick Baz/AFP/Getty Images

CHAPTER 9: *258* AP Images/Evan Vucci; *260* Ben Curtis/Pool/Corbis; *263* Jim Young/Reuters/Landov; *264-265* The Collection of the Supreme Court of the United States (9); *266* The Granger Collection; *268* The Boston Athenaeum; *270, left to right:* AP Images; George Tames/The New York Times/Redux Pictures; *275, left to right:* AP Images/J. Pat Carter; AP Images/Madalyn Ruggiero; *376* Chip Somodevilla/Getty Images; *279* Andrea Bruce/Washington Post/Getty Images; *284* The Collection of the Supreme Court of the United States; *287, top to bottom:* Kevin Dietsch/UPI/Landov; Michael Reynolds/ DPA/Corbis; Jason Reed/Reuters/Landov

CHAPTER 10: *294* Getty Images; *298* AP Images/J. Scott Applewhite; *302, left to right:* Time Magazine Inc.; Chad Buchanan/Getty Images; *307* Robyn Beck/AFP/Getty Images; *308* Reuters/Jason Reed/Landov; *314* Joseph Farris/Cartoon Stock; *319, top to bottom:* Jupiter Images/Getty Images; H. Armstrong Roberts/ClassicStock/Corbis; David Young-Wolff/Getty Images; Bettmann/Corbis; AF Archive/Alamy

CHAPTER 11: *326* Angel Chevrest/Zuma Press; *329* Bettmann/Corbis; *332* Owen Franken/Corbis; *335* Raveendran/AFP/ Getty Images; *336* AP Images/APTN; *338, top to bottom:* AP Images/Dave Martin; Chris Graythen/Getty Images; *341* Roger L. Wollenberg/UPI/ Landov; *344, left to right:* Paul Hosefros/The New York Times/Redux Pictures; AP Images/Network Pool; *347* AP Images/Mary Ann Chastain; *348* AP Images/Minnesota Public Radio, Ambar Espinoza; *355, top to bottom:* Angel Chevrest/Zuma Press; Bloomberg via Getty Images; AP Images/David Guttenfelder; Scott Olson/Getty Images

CHAPTER 12: *362* Kevin P. Casey/The New York Times/Redux Pictures; *364* Bettmann/Corbis; *366* AP Images/Jeff Widener; *369* Joshua Lott/The New York Times/Redux Pictures; *371* Splash News and Pictures/Newscom; *374* Hulton Archive/Getty Images; *377* Orlando Sentinel/MCT/Landov; *380* Justin Sullivan/Getty Images; *383, top to bottom:* AP Images/Alex Brandon; Bettmann/Corbis; The Granger Collection; AP Images/The Conroe Carrier, Eric S. Swist

CHAPTER 13: *390* AP Images/Elise Amendola; *398, left to right:* Dennis Brack/Landov; Roger L. Wollenberg/UPI/Landov; *401* Eric Freeland/Corbis; *406* Bettmann/Corbis; *417, top to bottom:* John Moore/Getty Images; Library of Congress; Roger L. Wollenberg/ UPI/Landov; AP Images/David Quinn;

CHAPTER 14: *424* Martin H. Simon/UPI/Pool/Landov; *430, left to right:* Alfred Eisenstaedt/Time & Life Pictures/Getty Images; Bettmann/Corbis; Dan Miller/Time Magazine/Time & Life Pictures/Getty Images; *431, left to right:* Natalie Behring/Greenpeace/Getty Images; U.S. Coast Guard photo by Petty Officer 3rd Class Ann Marie Gorden; *432* AFP/Getty Images; *442* Alex Wong/Getty Images; *443* Jim Young/Reuters/Corbis; *447* DoD Photo by Tech. Sgt. James L. Harper Jr., U.S. Air Force; *453, top to bottom:* Bloomberg via Getty Images; Jim West/Alamy; Dirck Halstead/Time & Life Pictures/Getty Images; Alex Wong/Getty Images; Glow Images/SuperStock; Scott Olson/Getty Images

CHAPTER 15: *460* Thomas Peter/Reuters/Landov; *465* AFP/Getty Images; *466* Larry Downing/Reuters/Landov; *467* Bloomberg via Getty Images; *471* Roger L. Wollenberg/UPI/Landov; *472* Benoit Tessier/Reuters/Landov; *475* Official White House Photo by Pete Souza; *476* Alex Wong/Getty Images; *477* AP Images/David Guttenfelder; *480* AP Images/US Navy/NATO, Navy Petty Officer 1st Class Mark O'Donald; *482* Reuters/Corbis; *484* Adrian Bradshaw/epa/Corbis; *486* Adrees Latif/Reuters/Corbis; *489, top to bottom:* AFP/Getty Images; Adrian Bradshaw/epa/Corbis; Howard Burditt/Corbis; Roger L. Wollenberg/UPI/Landov; AIPAC; Wally McNamee/Corbis

CHAPTER 16: *496* Michael Newman/PhotoEdit Inc.; *498* William Sidney Mount (1807-1868), "California News," 1850. Oil on Canvas. The Long Island Museum of American Art, History and Carriages. Gift of Mr. and Mrs. Ward Melville, 1955.; *501* Darrell Gulin/Getty Images; *503* The Granger Collection; *504* Bettmann/Corbis; *506* The Granger Collection; *507* The Granger Collection; *510* The Granger Collection; *511, top to bottom:* Bettmann/Corbis; National Museum of American History, Smithsonian Institution; *514* Robert Galbraith/Reuters/Landov; *515* AP Images/Marcio Jose Sanchez; *516* The Bakersfield Californian/Zuma Press; *519, top to bottom:* Bettmann/Corbis; The Granger Collection; The Granger Collection; David McNew/Getty Images; Hulton Archive/Getty Images

CHAPTER 17: *526* Bloomberg via Getty Images; *530* Sacramento Bee/Zuma Press; *532* David McNew/Getty Images; *533* AP Images/Michael A. Marian; *536* AP Images/Lennox McLendon; *542* AP Images/Rich Pedroncelli; *545* Sacramento Bee/MCT/Landov; *547* Los Angeles Daily News/Zuma Press; *551 top to bottom:* David McNew/Getty Images; AP Images/M.C.Lendon; AP Images/Damien Dovarganes; David Paul Morris/Getty Images

CHAPTER 18: *558* Max Whittaker/Getty Images; *563* Santa Rosa Press Democrat/Zuma Press; *574* Sacramento Bee/Zuma Press; *577* Sacramento Bee/Zuma Press; *580* AP Images/Doug Mills; *583, top to bottom:* Glen Alllison /Getty Images; The Granger Collection; David Paul Morris/Getty Images, Ric Francis/AP Photo

CHAPTER 19: *590* Hector Amezcua/Sacramento Bee/Zuma Press; *595* Corbis; *596* Paul Drinkwater/NBCU Photo Bank; *598* The Bakersfield Californian/Zuma Press; *600* AP Images/Lisa Poole; *602* AP Images/Nick Ut; *604* Ken James/Reuters/Landov; *607, top to bottom:* Brendan McDemid/EPA/Corbis; AP Images/Rich Pedroncelli; Max Whittaker/Reuters/Landov; Justin Sullivan/Getty Images; Official White House Photo by Pete Souza

CHAPTER 20: *612* Justin Sullivan/Getty Images; *618* Monica Almeida/The New York Times/Redux Pictures; *619* AP Images/Nick Ut; *622* Autumn Cruz/San Diego Union-Tribune/Zuma Press; *627* LPI Photos/Newscom; *629, top to bottom:* Justin Sullivan/Getty Images; Justin Sullivan/Getty Images; William F. Campbell/Timelife Pictures/Getty Images; AP Images/Karen Tam; Monica Almedia/The New York Times/Redux Pictures

CHAPTER 21: *634* David McNew/Getty Images; *637* San Diego Union-Tribune/Zuma Press; *642* Robert Harbison; *645* AP Images/Kevork Djansezian; *646* Spencer Grant/PhotoEdit Inc.; *649* Justin Sullivan/Getty Images; *650* AP Images/Gary Kazanjian; *652* Gina Halferty/Tri-Valley Herald/Zuma Press; *653* AP Images/Eric Risberg; *655* Spencer Grant/PhotoEdit Inc.; *656* Michael Newman/PhotoEdit Inc.; *659, top to bottom:* Spencer Grant/PhotoEdit Inc.; The Bakersfield Californian/Zuma Press; Gina Halferty/Tri-Valley Herald/Zuma Press; Robert Harbison; K.C. Alfred/SDU-T/Zuma Press

CHAPTER 22: *666* Contra Costa Times/Herman Bustamente Jr./Zuma Press; *669* Max Whittaker/Reuters/Landov; *670* Ken James/Corbis; *673* Justin Sullivan/Getty Images; *676* Michael Newman/PhotoEdit Inc.; *677* Ed Kashi/Corbis; *680* J. Emilio Flores/The New York Times/Redux Pictures; *681* Brian Baer/Sacramento Bee/Zuma Press; *685* Top to bottom: Time & Life Pictures/Getty Images; Gregor Schuster/Corbis; Justin Sullivan/Getty Images; Justin Sullivan/Getty Images; Max Whittaker/Reuters/Landov

Index

successful qualities of, 214–216
veto of, 174, 207–208
vice president assuming, 202
Presidential Power (Neustadt), 204
President pro tempore, 168, 576, 577
Presidios, 501
Press conferences, 341–342
Press releases, 342, 345
Press shield laws, 101
Primary elections, 528–529
Primary system, 404–406
Prime rate, 450
Print media, 330–331
Printz v. *United States*, 84
Prior censorship, 351
Prior restraint, 100
Privacy, rights to, 110–113, 350
Privatization, 244
Probability sample, 315
Probate law, 619
Pro bono, 278
Professional associations, 370
Progressive tax, 444, 672
Progressivism, 428, 429
Project grants, 81
Propositions
  8, 613
  11, 543
  13, 515–516, 533, 535–536, 544, 582, 595, 603, 654–655, 658, 669, 676
  14, 528
  16, 653
  15, 527
  19, 527
  22, 527
  34, 530, 531
  36, 622, 623
  57, 678
  98, 601, 655, 676, 682
  103, 580, 601–602
  140, 561, 671
  184, 618, 620, 682
  198, 528
  205, 536
  208, 530
  209, 546
  215, 534
  220, 614, 615
  227, 655
  ballot, 537
  invalidated, 535
Proslavery and antislavery factions, 504
Protests, 7, 8, 13, 473
Pseudo-events, 340
Public
  advocate model, 352
  going, 204
  goods, 372, 373
  interest groups, 370
Public opinion, 296
  on abortion, 301
  on censorship, 351
  changes in, 300
  on civil liberties, 300
  economic bases and, 310
  of foreign policy, 300, 468–470
  fundamental values relationship with, 297–299
  gun control and, 297
  interpreting polls of, 315–316
  on leadership traits, 302

polls measuring, 314–315, 318
popular culture impact on, 301–303
public policy relationship with, 296–297
survey research of, 315–316
value structures impacting, 304–305
Public policy, 4, 5
  bureaucracy and, 252, 284–285
  citizens favoring, 311
  in democracies, 426–428
  education influencing, 306–307
  judges shaping, 284–286
  process of, 434–435
  public opinion relationship with, 296–297
  types of, 432
Public School Accountability Act, 656
Pueblos, 500, 501
Punishment, 621–622
Purposive benefits, 373
Putnam, Robert, 395

Q

al-Qaeda, 337, 340, 461, 482–483
Quackenbush, Chuck, 602, 606
Quasi-judicial processes, 249
Quayle, Dan, 340, 474
Questionnaires, 315

R

Race
  in Congress, 179
  education/income and, 126
  oppression, 127–128
  in political socialization, 312
  segregation of, 279
  social groups ethnicity and, 312
Race to the Top, 656
Radio Act of 1927, 331
Radio stations, 331
Rainey, Joseph Hayne, 179
Rainey, Richard, 563
Rally round the flag effect, 470
RAM. *See* Remote Area Medical
Randolph, Edmund, 46
Rangel, Charlie, 443
Rankin, Jeannette, 178
Rapchik, Jessica, 70
Ratification
  of Constitution, 54–57
  of Nineteenth Amendment, 138
Rational basis test, 132
Rational party model, 398
Ravilochan, Teju, 440
Reagan, Ronald, 82, 86, 111, 199, 201, 214, 218, 544, 560, 564, 594–595
  gender votes of, 313
  as Great Communicator, 204, 341
  Iran-Contra affair and, 212
  media coverage of, 337
  poll results and, 316
  presidential debates by, 347
  State of the Union address of, 210
Reapportionment, 161, 562, 563–564
Reasonable time, place and manner restrictions, 99
Reauthorization, 437
Recall, 532–533
Recidivism rate, 622, 623
Reciprocity, 172
Reconciliation, 193
Reconstruction Act of 1867, 127
Redding, Savana, 259, 278, 286

Redevelopment agency, 650
Redistribution, 432
Redistricting, 158–161, 563–564
Reece, Sophie, 155
Reelection rates, 413
Referendums, 538–539
Reforms
  of bureaucracy, 244–245
  election process, 412–413
  health care, 21, 24, 193, 208–209, 425
  school, 655–656
Refregier, Anton, 503
Regressive tax, 444, 672
Regulations, 432
  legislature creating, 248–249
  media, 350
Rehabilitation Act of 1973, 140
Rehnquist, William, 284
Religion
  discrimination and, 136
  establishment of, 94–95
  under First Amendment, 94–95
  foreign policy and, 472
  freedom of, 95
  interest groups based on, 472
  political socialization influenced by, 307–308
  social groups influenced by, 311
Religious Freedom Restoration Act, 96
Remote Area Medical (RAM), 305
Reporter's privilege, 101
Representation
  conscience model of, 154, 155
  delegate model of, 154
  geographic, 159
  in legislature, 569–570
  politico model of, 154, 155
  style of, 155
  symbolic, 155
  trustee model of, 154
Representative democracy, 12, 34, 178, 296, 328
Representative republicanism, 51
Republic, 34
Republicanism, 51
Republican National Committee (RNC), 400
Republican party
  foreign policy and, 468
  as "party of the rich," 310
Reserve ratio, 450
Residency and registration laws, 393
Resolutions, 568
Responsible party model, 398
Rett Syndrome, 164
Revels, Hiram Rhodes, 179
Revenue bonds, 674
Revenues
  county, 642
  of government, 444–445
  of municipal government, 648
  state sources of, 672–675
Revolutionary War, 42, 55, 330
Reynolds v. *Sims*, 564
Rhetoric (Aristotle), 340
Rice, Condoleezza, 475
Richie, Lionel, 308
Right(s). *See also* Bill of Rights; Civil rights
  to counsel, 106
  natural, 40, 365
  in politics, 6
  to privacy, 110–113, 350
  of sexual conduct, 112–113